Scale 1:250,000
or 3.94 miles to 1 inch

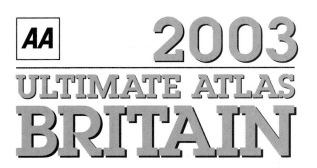

25th edition July 2002

© Automobile Association Developments Limited 2002

Revised version of the atlas formerly known as *Complete Atlas of Britain.*

Original edition printed 1979.

Ordnance Survey® This product includes mapping data licensed from Ordnance Survey® with the permission of the Controller of Her Majesty's Stationery Office. © Crown copyright 2002. All rights reserved. Licence number 399221.

Northern Ireland mapping reproduced by permission of the Director and Chief Executive, Ordnance Survey of Northern Ireland, acting on behalf of the controller of Her Majesty's Stationery Office © Crown copyright 2002. Permit No. 1674.

Republic of Ireland mapping based on Ordnance Survey Ireland by permission of the Government. Permit No. MP001401 © Government of Ireland.

Published by AA Publishing (a trading name of Automobile Association Developments Limited, whose registered office is Millstream, Maidenhead Road, Windsor, Berkshire SL4 5GD. Registered number 1878835).

Mapping produced by the Cartographic Department of The Automobile Association. This atlas has been compiled and produced from the Automaps database utilising electronic and computer technology (A01244).

ISBN 0 7495 3491 5

A CIP catalogue record for this book is available from The British Library.

Printed in Italy by G. Canale & C. S.P.A.

The contents of this atlas are believed to be correct at the time of the latest revision. However, the publishers cannot be held responsible for loss occasioned to any person acting or refraining from action as a result of any material in this atlas, nor for any errors, omissions or changes in such material. The publishers would welcome information to correct any errors or omissions and to keep this atlas up to date. Please write to the Cartographic Editor, Publishing Division, The Automobile Association, Fanum House, Basing View, Basingstoke, Hampshire RG21 4EA.

Information on National Parks provided by the Countryside Agency for England and the Countryside Council for Wales.

Information on National Parks and National Scenic Areas in Scotland provided by Scottish Natural Heritage.

Information on Forest Parks provided by the Forestry Commission.

The RSPB sites shown are a selection chosen by the Royal Society for the Protection of Birds.

National Trust properties shown are a selection of those open to the public as indicated in the handbooks of the National Trust and the National Trust for Scotland.

AA 2003 ULTIMATE ATLAS BRITAIN

Contents

Map pages	inside front cover
AA Risk rating of Britain's roads	II–III
Route planner and mileage chart	IV–IX
Motorways	X–XIII
Restricted junctions X–XI M25 and M60	XII–XIII
Map symbols	XIV–1
Road maps 1:250,000 scale	2–116
The Channel Islands 1:204,080 scale	6–7
Scottish islands 1:918,370 and 1:957,450 scales	111
The Isle of Man 1:250,000 scale	116
Ireland 1:1,000,000 scale	112–115
Town plans	117–129
Key to town plans 117	Central London street index 152–158
Central London 142–151	
District maps	130–141
Birmingham district 130–131	Tyne & Wear district 136–137
Glasgow district 132–133	London district 138–141
Manchester district 134–135	
Index to place names	159–194
County, administrative area map (index opener)	159

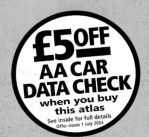

AA risk rating of Britain's motorways and trunk roads

Research led by the AA Foundation for Road Safety Research as part of the European Road Assessment Programme (EuroRAP) shows that the risk of death or serious injury on a single-carriageway road is typically far higher than on a motorway.

This map shows the statistical risk of death or serious injury occurring on Britain's motorways and trunk roads. The risk is calculated by comparing the frequency of death and serious injury on every stretch of road with how much traffic each road is carrying. For example, if there are 20 accidents involving death or serious injury on a stretch of road 5 miles long that carries 10,000 vehicles a day, then the risk is 10 times higher than if the road section has the same number of accidents but carries 100,000 vehicles.

Some of the roads shown have had improvements made to them recently, but during the survey period the risk of a fatal or serious injury accident on the black road sections was more than 10 times higher than on the safest (dark green) roads.

For more information on the statistical background to this research, visit the EuroRAP website at *www.eurorap.org*. For navigation purposes please refer to the road maps in the main section of this atlas.

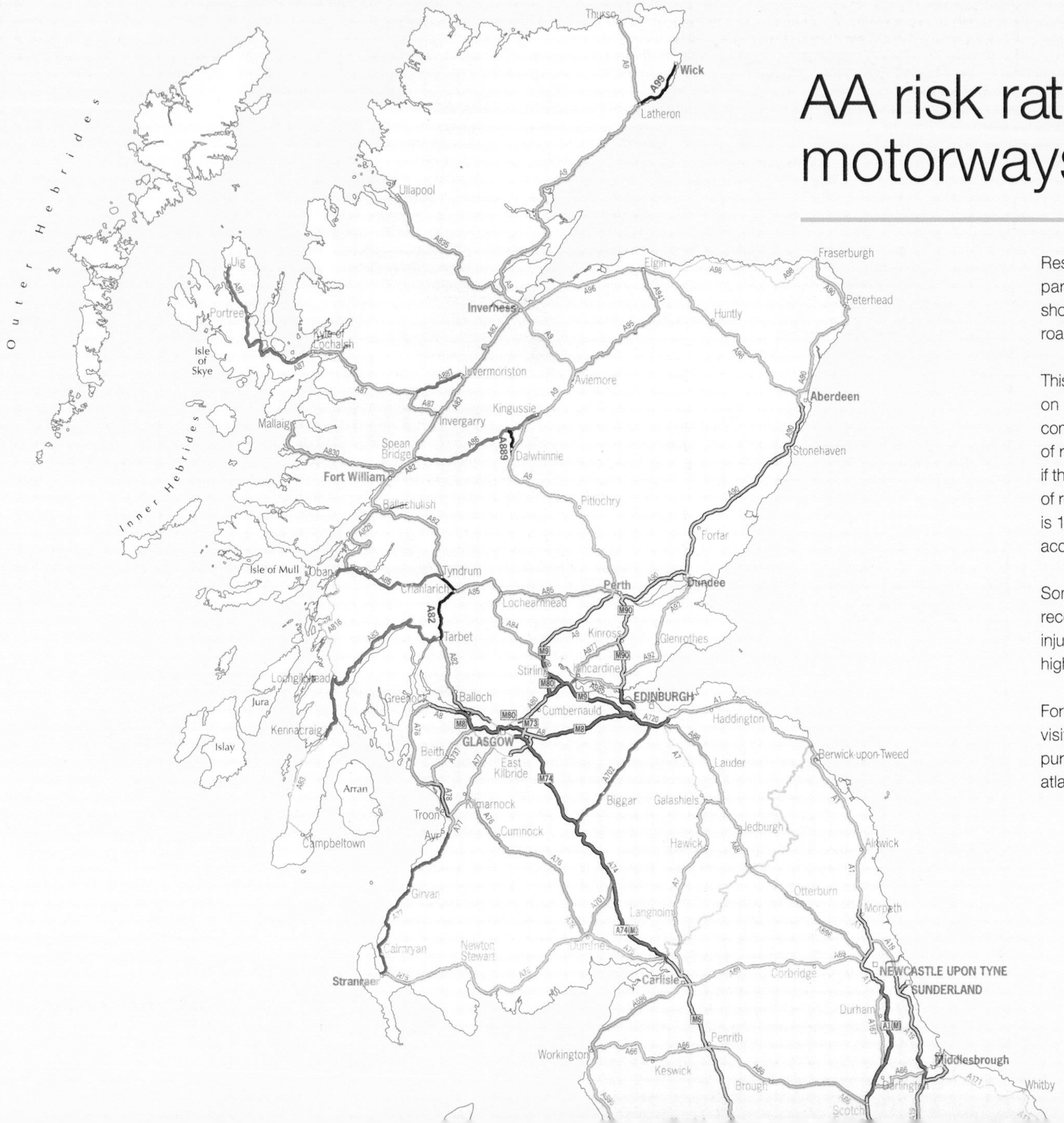

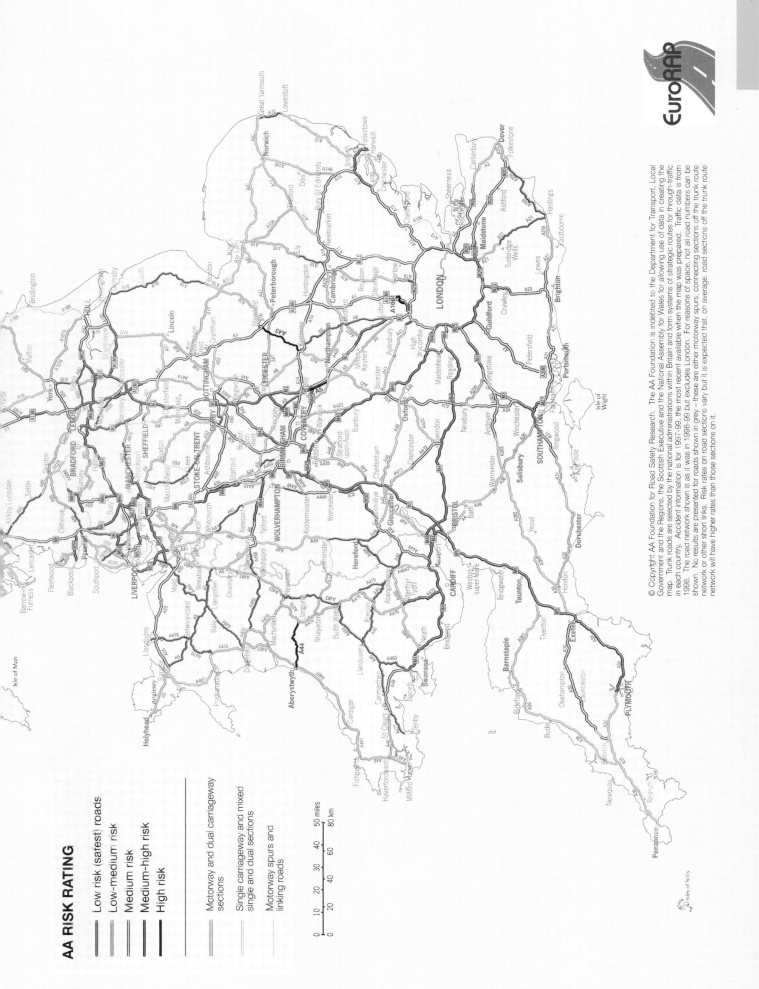
AA RISK RATING
Low risk (safest) roads
Low-medium risk
Medium risk
Medium-high risk
High risk
Motorway and dual carriageway sections
Single carriageway and mixed single and dual sections
Motorway spurs and linking roads
0 10 20 30 40 50 miles
0 20 40 60 80 km
Isle of Man
LONDON
BIRMINGHAM
MANCHESTER
LIVERPOOL
LEEDS
BRADFORD
SHEFFIELD
NOTTINGHAM
LEICESTER
COVENTRY
WOLVERHAMPTON
STOKE-ON-TRENT
DERBY
BRISTOL
CARDIFF
SOUTHAMPTON
PLYMOUTH
HULL
Isle of Wight
Isles of Scilly
EuroRAP

 Trunk roads are selected by the national administrations within Britain and form systems of strategic routes for through-traffic in each country. Accident information is for 1997-99, the most recent available when the map was prepared. Traffic data is from 1998. The road network shown is as it was in 1998-99 but excludes London. For reasons of space, not all road numbers can be shown. No results are presented for roads shown in grey – these are either motorway spurs, connecting sections off the trunk route network or other short links. Risk rates on road sections vary but it is expected that, on average, road sections off the trunk route network will have higher rates than those sections on it.

IV

DUBLIN

Dun Laoghaire

Rosslare
Harbour

Legend

Motorway

Primary route
dual carriageway

Primary route
single carriageway

Other A roads

Bangor — Town with
AA Service Centre

36 — Index to maps in
road map section

0   10   20   30 miles
0   10   20   30   40 kilometres

46

36   Cardigan Bay

24

26

28

38

16

14

6

8

4

2

Holyhead · Anglesey · Llandudno · Colwyn Bay · Rhyl · LIVERPOOL · St Helens · Risley · M60 · Birkenhead · Widnes · Warrington · M56 · Knutsford
Bangor · Conwy · Abergele · Bromborough · Runcorn · M62
Caernarfon · Bethesda · Denbigh · Holywell · Queensferry · Ellesmere Port · Northwich
Betws-y-coed · Mold · Chester · Crewe · Nantwich · Ruthin
Pwllheli · Porthmadog · Bala · Llangollen · Wrexham · Whitchurch · Newcastle-under-Lyme · Market Drayton
Abersoch · Oswestry · Telford · WOLVERHAMPTON
Barmouth · Dolgellau · Welshpool · Shrewsbury · Bridgnorth · Stourbridge
Machynlleth · Newtown · Church Stretton · Kidderminster · Bromsgrove
Aberystwyth · Llangurig · Rhayader · Knighton · Ludlow · Leominster · Worcester
Aberaeron · Tregaron · Llandrindod Wells · Kington · Great Malvern
Cardigan · Lampeter · Builth Wells · Hay-on-Wye · Hereford · Ledbury · Tewkesbury
Newcastle Emlyn · Llandovery · Brecon · Abergavenny · Ross-on-Wye · Gloucester
St David's · Fishguard · Carmarthen · Llandeilo · Merthyr Tydfil · Ebbw Vale · Monmouth · Chepstow
Haverfordwest · St Clears · Llanelli · Neath · Pontypridd · Cwmbran · Newport · Avonmouth · BRISTOL
Milford Haven · Pembroke Dock · Pembroke · Tenby · Swansea · Port Talbot · Bridgend · CARDIFF · Clevedon · Bath
Weston-super-Mare · Cheddar · Frome
Ilfracombe · Lynton · Minehead · Wells · Shepton Mallet
Lundy · Barnstaple · Glastonbury · Wincanton
Bideford · Great Torrington · South Molton · Bridgwater · M5
Bude · Hatherleigh · Tiverton · Taunton · Yeovil · Sherborne · Shaftesbury
Holsworthy · Okehampton · Crediton · Honiton · Ilminster · Chard · Crewkerne · Blandford Forum
Launceston · Exeter · Axminster · Bridport · Dorchester
Wadebridge · Tavistock · Exmouth · Dawlish · Teignmouth · Lyme Regis · Weymouth
Newquay · Bodmin · Liskeard · Saltash · PLYMOUTH · Newton Abbot · Torquay · Paignton · Fortuneswell
Redruth · Truro · Lostwithiel · St Austell · Torpoint · Totnes · Dartmouth · Kingsbridge
Camborne · Penzance · Helston · Falmouth · Land's End · Lizard

CHANNEL ISLANDS

ROSSLARE · CORK · SANTANDER summer only · ROSCOFF · ST MALO winter only

Plymouth (inset)
Plymouth · LISKEARD · TAVISTOCK · DOCKYARD STATION · DEVONPORT STA · PLYMOUTH STA · PLYMOUTH TOWN CENTRE · EXETER · CAR FERRY TERMINAL · Vehicle Ferry to Torpoint · The Sound

Poole (inset)
Poole · DORCHESTER, RINGWOOD · POOLE STATION · Holes Bay · HARBOUR OFFICE · FREIGHT FERRY TERMINAL · BRITTANY FERRIES PASSENGER TERMINAL · Poole Harbour

Route planner

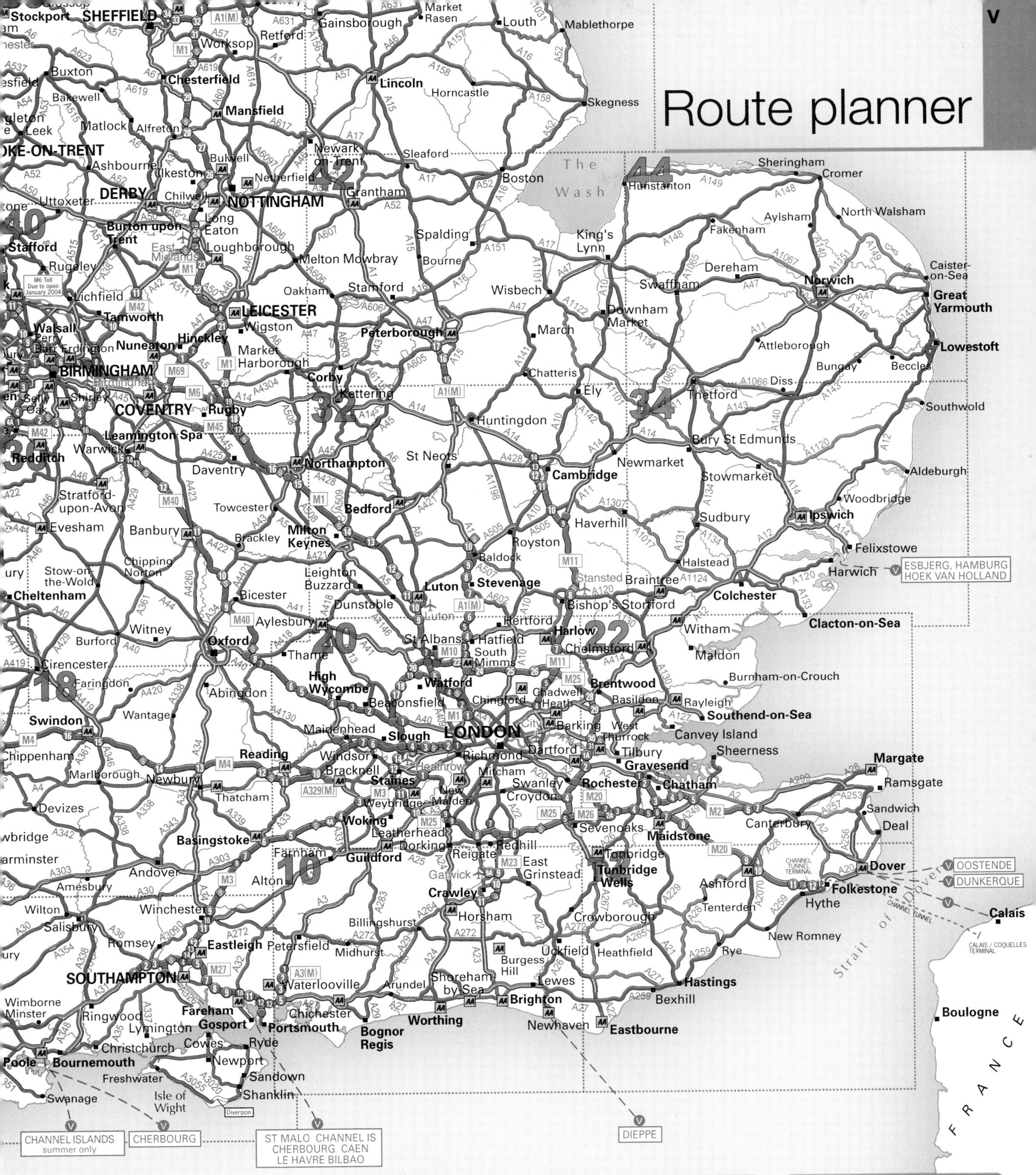

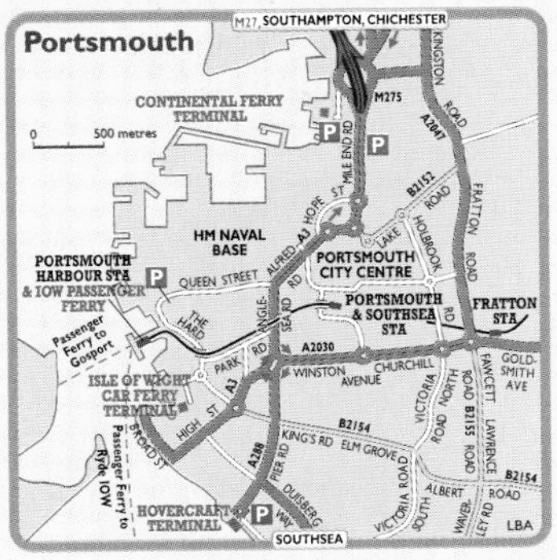

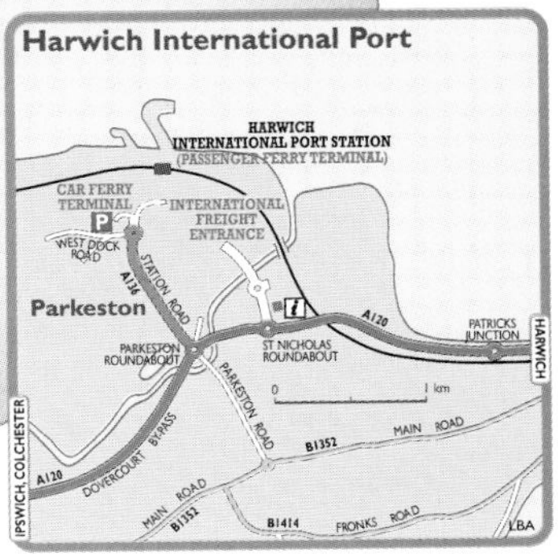

Stockport · SHEFFIELD · Gainsborough · Market Rasen · Louth · Mablethorpe · Buxton · Chesterfield · Retford · Lincoln · Horncastle · Skegness · Bakewell · Matlock · Alfreton · Mansfield · Newark-on-Trent · Sleaford · Boston · The Wash · Sheringham · Cromer · Leek · Ashbourne · Bulwell · Netherfield · Grantham · Spalding · Bourne · Hunstanton · Aylsham · North Walsham · DERBY · NOTTINGHAM · Long Eaton · Loughborough · Melton Mowbray · Stamford · Wisbech · Downham Market · Dereham · Fakenham · Caister-on-Sea · Stafford · Burton upon Trent · Oakham · March · Swaffham · NORWICH · Great Yarmouth · Lichfield · Tamworth · LEICESTER · Wigston · Peterborough · Chatteris · Ely · Thetford · Diss · Attleborough · Bungay · Beccles · Lowestoft · Walsall · Nuneaton · Hinckley · Market Harborough · Corby · Huntingdon · Newmarket · Bury St Edmunds · Southwold · BIRMINGHAM · COVENTRY · Rugby · Kettering · St Neots · Cambridge · Stowmarket · Sudbury · Aldeburgh · Leamington Spa · Northampton · Bedford · Haverhill · Woodbridge · Redditch · Warwick · Daventry · Royston · Halstead · Ipswich · Stratford-upon-Avon · Towcester · Milton Keynes · Baldock · Braintree · Colchester · Felixstowe · Evesham · Banbury · Brackley · Leighton Buzzard · Stevenage · Bishop's Stortford · Witham · Harwich · Cheltenham · Chipping Norton · Bicester · Dunstable · Luton · Hertford · Harlow · Chelmsford · Maldon · Clacton-on-Sea · Stow-on-the-Wold · Witney · Aylesbury · St Albans · Hatfield · Burnham-on-Crouch · Cirencester · Burford · Oxford · Thame · High Wycombe · Watford · Chingford · Brentwood · Basildon · Rayleigh · Swindon · Abingdon · Beaconsfield · Chadwell Heath · Southend-on-Sea · Chippenham · Reading · Maidenhead · Slough · LONDON · Barking · West Thurrock · Canvey Island · Sheerness · Margate · Marlborough · Newbury · Windsor · Heathrow · Richmond · Dartford · Tilbury · Gravesend · Ramsgate · Devizes · Bracknell · Staines · Mitcham · Swanley · Rochester · Chatham · Sandwich · Deal · Thatcham · Weybridge · New Malden · Croydon · Maidstone · Canterbury · Woking · Leatherhead · Sevenoaks · Basingstoke · Dorking · Reigate · Redhill · Tonbridge · Dover · Oostende · Dunkerque · Farnham · Guildford · Gatwick · East Grinstead · Tunbridge Wells · Ashford · Folkestone · Calais · Andover · Alton · Crawley · Crowborough · Hythe · Winchester · Billingshurst · Horsham · Tenterden · New Romney · Amesbury · Wilton · Salisbury · Romsey · Eastleigh · Petersfield · Midhurst · Uckfield · Heathfield · Rye · Hastings · SOUTHAMPTON · Waterlooville · Arundel · Shoreham by Sea · Burgess Hill · Lewes · Bexhill · Boulogne · Wimborne Minster · Ringwood · Fareham · Gosport · Chichester · Worthing · Brighton · Eastbourne · Poole · Bournemouth · Lymington · Portsmouth · Bognor Regis · Newhaven · Christchurch · Cowes · Ryde · Newport · Sandown · FRANCE · Swanage · Freshwater · Shanklin · Isle of Wight · Diversion

M6 Toll Due to open January 2004

CHANNEL ISLANDS summer only · CHERBOURG · ST MALO CHANNEL IS CHERBOURG CAEN LE HAVRE BILBAO · DIEPPE

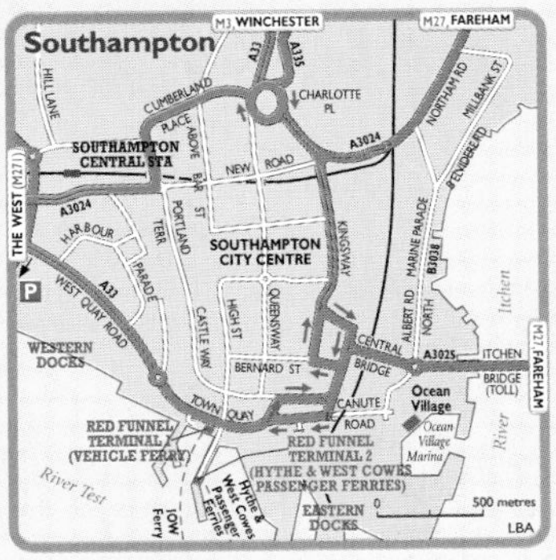

Strait of Dover · CHANNEL TUNNEL · CALAIS / COQUELLES TERMINAL · ESBJERG, HAMBURG HOEK VAN HOLLAND

Southampton
WINCHESTER · FAREHAM · SOUTHAMPTON CENTRAL STA · SOUTHAMPTON CITY CENTRE · WESTERN DOCKS · RED FUNNEL TERMINAL (VEHICLE FERRY) · OCEAN VILLAGE · EASTERN DOCKS · River Test

Portsmouth
SOUTHAMPTON, CHICHESTER · CONTINENTAL FERRY TERMINAL · HM NAVAL BASE · PORTSMOUTH HARBOUR STA & IOW PASSENGER FERRY · PORTSMOUTH CITY CENTRE · FRATTON STA · ISLE OF WIGHT CAR FERRY TERMINAL · HOVERCRAFT TERMINAL · SOUTHSEA

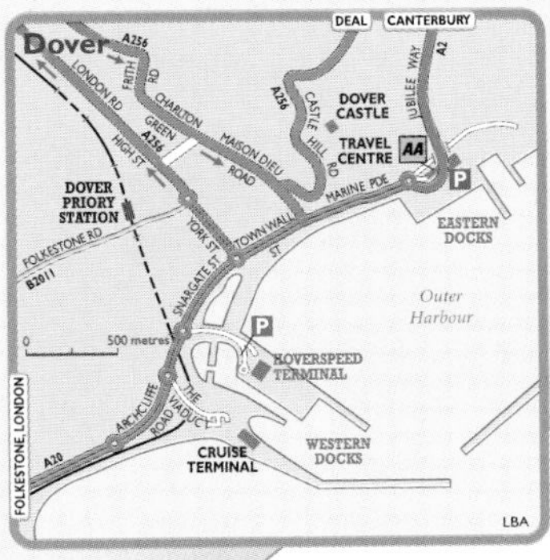

Dover
DEAL · CANTERBURY · DOVER CASTLE · TRAVEL CENTRE · DOVER PRIORY STATION · EASTERN DOCKS · HOVERSPEED TERMINAL · WESTERN DOCKS · CRUISE TERMINAL · Outer Harbour

Harwich International Port
HARWICH INTERNATIONAL PORT STATION (PASSENGER FERRY TERMINAL) · CAR FERRY TERMINAL · INTERNATIONAL FREIGHT ENTRANCE · Parkeston · ST NICHOLAS ROUNDABOUT · PARKESTON ROUNDABOUT · PATRICKS JUNCTION

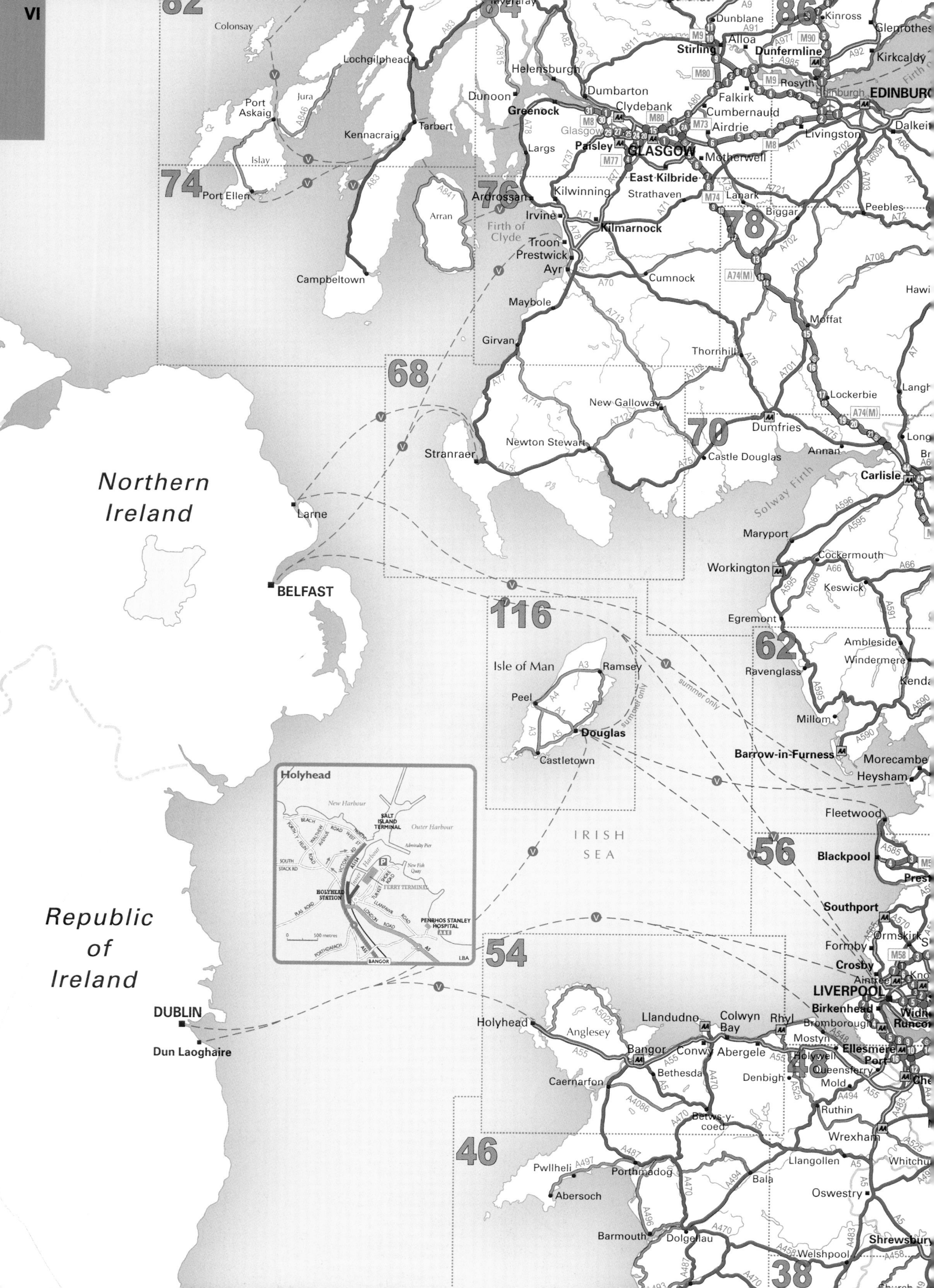
Northern Ireland
Republic of Ireland
IRISH SEA
Isle of Man
Firth of Clyde
Solway Firth
Colonsay
Lochgilphead
Jura
Port Askaig
Islay
Port Ellen
Kennacraig
Tarbert
Arran
Campbeltown
Helensburgh
Dunoon
Greenock
Largs
Ardrossan
Irvine
Troon
Prestwick
Ayr
Maybole
Girvan
Stranraer
Newton Stewart
New Galloway
Castle Douglas
Dumfries
Annan
Thornhill
Moffat
Lockerbie
Cumnock
Kilmarnock
Kilwinning
Strathaven
East Kilbride
Paisley
GLASGOW
Glasgow
Clydebank
Dumbarton
Motherwell
Airdrie
Cumbernauld
Falkirk
Stirling
Dunblane
Alloa
Dunfermline
Kinross
Glenrothes
Kirkcaldy
Rosyth
EDINBURGH
Livingston
Dalkeith
Lanark
Biggar
Peebles
Carlisle
Maryport
Workington
Cockermouth
Keswick
Egremont
Ravenglass
Ambleside
Windermere
Millom
Barrow-in-Furness
Morecambe
Heysham
Fleetwood
Blackpool
Southport
Formby
Ormskirk
Crosby
Aintree
LIVERPOOL
Birkenhead
Bromborough
Ellesmere Port
Runcorn
Widnes
Mostyn
Holywell
Queensferry
Mold
Ruthin
Wrexham
Rhyl
Colwyn Bay
Abergele
Llandudno
Conwy
Denbigh
Bangor
Bethesda
Caernarfon
Anglesey
Holyhead
Betws-y-coed
Llangollen
Bala
Oswestry
Porthmadog
Pwllheli
Abersoch
Barmouth
Dolgellau
Welshpool
Shrewsbury
Whitchurch
Larne
BELFAST
DUBLIN
Dun Laoghaire
Ramsey
Peel
Douglas
Castletown
summer only
Holyhead
New Harbour
Outer Harbour
SALT ISLAND TERMINAL
Admiralty Pier
New Fish Quay
FERRY TERMINAL
HOLYHEAD STATION
PENRHOS STANLEY HOSPITAL
BANGOR
500 metres
74
76
78
86
68
70
116
62
56
54
48
46
38

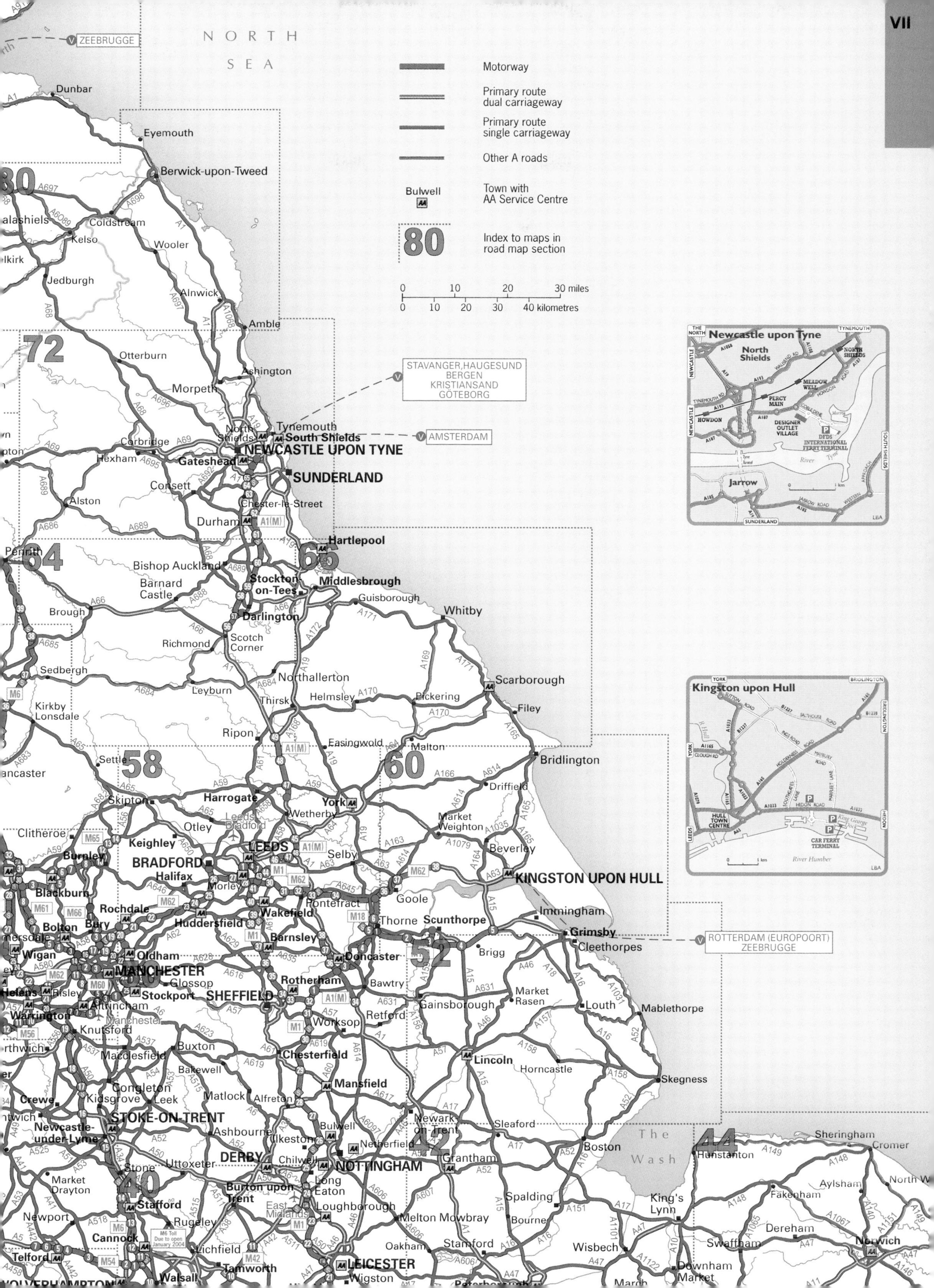

NORTH SEA

Legend

Motorway

Primary route dual carriageway

Primary route single carriageway

Other A roads

Bulwell — Town with AA Service Centre

80 — Index to maps in road map section

0   10   20   30 miles
0 10 20 30 40 kilometres

STAVANGER, HAUGESUND BERGEN KRISTIANSAND GÖTEBORG

AMSTERDAM

ROTTERDAM (EUROPOORT) ZEEBRUGGE

ZEEBRUGGE

Newcastle upon Tyne

North Shields

NORTH SHIELDS

MEADOW WELL

PERCY MAIN

HOWDON

DESIGNER OUTLET VILLAGE

DFDS INTERNATIONAL FERRY TERMINAL

Jarrow

SUNDERLAND

Kingston upon Hull

YORK

BRIDLINGTON

HULL TOWN CENTRE

CAR FERRY TERMINAL

King George Dock

River Humber

LEEDS

Towns and cities:
Dunbar, Eyemouth, Berwick-upon-Tweed, Coldstream, Kelso, Wooler, Jedburgh, Alnwick, Amble, Ashington, Morpeth, Otterburn, Corbridge, Hexham, Consett, Alston, Penrith, Bishop Auckland, Barnard Castle, Brough, Sedbergh, Kirkby Lonsdale, Settle, Richmond, Scotch Corner, Northallerton, Leyburn, Thirsk, Ripon, Skipton, Harrogate, Wetherby, Otley, Keighley, Clitheroe, Burnley, Blackburn, Bolton, Bury, Rochdale, Oldham, MANCHESTER, Stockport, Glossop, Altrincham, SHEFFIELD, Knutsford, Macclesfield, Buxton, Bakewell, Matlock, Congleton, Kidsgrove, Leek, STOKE-ON-TRENT, Newcastle-under-Lyme, Ashbourne, DERBY, Market Drayton, Stone, Uttoxeter, Rugeley, Stafford, Cannock, Telford, Lichfield, Tamworth, Walsall, WOLVERHAMPTON, LEICESTER
NEWCASTLE UPON TYNE, Gateshead, South Shields, Tynemouth, SUNDERLAND, Chester-le-Street, Durham, Hartlepool, Stockton-on-Tees, Middlesbrough, Darlington, Guisborough, Whitby, Scarborough, Filey, Pickering, Helmsley, Easingwold, Malton, Bridlington, Driffield, York, Market Weighton, Beverley, Selby, KINGSTON UPON HULL, Immingham, Grimsby, Cleethorpes, Pontefract, Wakefield, Barnsley, Doncaster, Rotherham, Thorne, Goole, Scunthorpe, Brigg, Worksop, Chesterfield, Bawtry, Retford, Gainsborough, Market Rasen, Louth, Mablethorpe, Mansfield, Alfreton, Lincoln, Horncastle, Skegness, NOTTINGHAM, Newark-on-Trent, Sleaford, Boston, Hunstanton, Sheringham, Cromer, Long Eaton, Loughborough, Grantham, Spalding, King's Lynn, Aylsham, North Walsham, Melton Mowbray, Bourne, Fakenham, Dereham, NORWICH, Oakham, Stamford, Wisbech, Downham Market, Swaffham, Ilkeston, Bulwell, Netherfield, Chilwell, Burton upon Trent

Clitheroe, Blackburn, M65, M61, M66, M62, M60, M56, M6

A1, A697, A698, A1, A68, A696, A69, A686, A685, A66, A684, A19, A1(M), A59, A65, A650, A629, A616, A57, A38, A52, A46, A17, A16, A15, A158, A52, A149, A148, A47, A10, A1101

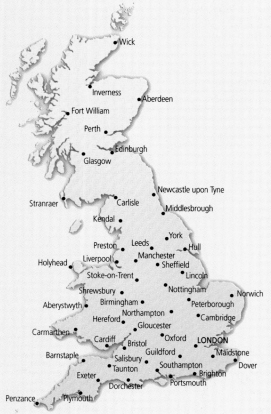

The distances between towns on the mileage chart are given to the nearest mile, and are measured along the normal AA-recommended routes. It should be noted that AA-recommended routes do not necessarily follow the shortest distance between places but are based on the quickest travelling time, making maximum use of motorways and dual carriageways.

	Aberdeen	Aberystwyth	Barnstaple	Birmingham	Brighton	Bristol	Cambridge	Cardiff	Carlisle	Carmarthen	Dorchester	Dover	Edinburgh	Exeter	Fort William	Glasgow	Gloucester	Guildford	Hereford	Holyhead	Hull	Inverness	Kendal	Leeds	Lincoln	Liverpool	Maidstone	Manchester	Middlesbrough	Newcastle	Northampton	Norwich	Nottingham	Oxford	Penzance	Perth	Peterborough	Plymouth	Portsmouth	Preston	Salisbury	Sheffield	Shrewsbury	Southampton	Stoke-on-Trent	Stranraer	Taunton	Wick	York
Aberystwyth	473
Barnstaple	608	214
Birmingham	436	124	177
Brighton	613	288	208	171
Bristol	518	130	100	90	169
Cambridge	463	215	267	97	120	171
Cardiff	536	110	127	108	201	42	202
Carlisle	236	236	371	199	377	281	257	299
Carmarthen	523	48	190	171	264	105	265	67	286
Dorchester	600	206	94	172	119	62	184	119	364	182
Dover	587	326	273	208	82	206	124	238	386	301	200
Edinburgh	126	336	471	299	476	381	333	399	100	381	463	458
Exeter	593	198	44	164	177	84	258	112	356	175	57	248	455
Fort William	156	435	570	398	576	480	456	498	199	485	562	599	137	554
Glasgow	150	332	467	295	473	377	353	396	96	382	459	497	47	451	102
Gloucester	484	112	125	55	155	35	149	61	248	124	117	192	346	110	445	344
Guildford	571	224	175	128	44	106	96	138	335	201	97	97	433	150	532	431	99
Hereford	487	79	144	58	189	54	152	58	250	85	136	225	349	129	448	346	33	132
Holyhead	464	102	339	167	345	249	258	201	228	150	331	369	326	323	425	324	215	302	156
Hull	376	227	320	139	258	230	138	249	170	311	312	262	247	304	367	266	196	239	198	218
Inverness	106	497	632	460	637	542	518	560	261	547	624	661	158	616	66	177	507	595	510	488	431
Kendal	283	190	324	153	330	234	244	253	47	239	316	354	145	309	245	143	200	288	203	181	164	307
Leeds	329	173	302	121	263	212	147	230	122	223	294	272	199	286	320	218	177	221	180	165	60	383	71
Lincoln	388	199	275	98	216	185	95	204	182	267	245	220	258	260	379	278	151	173	154	204	44	442	176	71
Liverpool	362	110	273	101	279	183	192	201	125	167	265	302	224	257	323	222	149	236	151	102	127	386	79	73	139
Maidstone	548	286	233	168	50	166	85	198	341	261	160	41	418	208	539	438	152	57	185	330	223	602	316	231	180	264
Manchester	357	134	261	89	267	171	160	189	120	183	253	291	219	245	318	216	137	224	139	125	97	381	74	44	85	34	251
Middlesbrough	276	244	357	176	318	267	197	285	95	294	349	322	146	341	283	191	232	276	235	235	89	308	84	66	122	145	282	114
Newcastle	235	275	388	207	349	298	229	316	60	325	380	353	106	372	242	153	264	307	266	266	142	267	102	97	154	176	313	145	39
Northampton	485	173	210	55	132	114	54	161	249	224	158	155	347	195	447	345	78	90	111	217	152	509	203	133	93	151	116	139	189	220
Norwich	489	278	329	160	168	233	63	265	282	328	241	172	359	313	480	378	212	160	215	321	148	543	276	172	104	240	133	186	223	254	116
Nottingham	394	161	234	53	195	144	86	163	188	225	226	218	265	218	386	284	110	153	112	178	92	448	148	73	39	112	179	71	129	160	66	120
Oxford	511	159	170	68	109	73	81	106	274	168	115	146	373	154	472	370	48	67	81	242	189	535	228	170	131	176	106	164	226	257	43	144	103
Penzance	702	308	108	273	287	193	367	221	466	284	167	357	564	109	663	562	219	259	238	434	415	726	419	396	370	368	318	356	451	482	304	430	328	264
Perth	87	388	523	351	529	433	378	452	152	438	515	503	42	507	102	64	399	486	401	379	291	115	199	247	303	278	463	273	192	150	400	404	309	426	617
Peterborough	433	204	263	86	158	173	37	192	227	254	204	162	304	248	425	323	139	115	142	223	108	488	221	117	51	157	122	137	168	199	43	78	56	86	357	350
Plymouth	633	239	62	204	218	124	298	152	397	215	98	288	495	44	594	493	150	190	169	365	346	657	350	327	301	299	249	287	382	413	235	361	259	195	78	544	287
Portsmouth	596	243	162	154	52	125	137	157	360	220	73	140	458	131	558	456	118	44	151	328	275	620	314	256	214	262	101	250	312	343	128	204	189	85	241	508	157	172
Preston	326	147	281	110	287	191	201	210	89	196	273	311	188	266	287	185	157	245	160	138	122	350	43	69	134	36	271	33	103	139	158	235	120	184	375	237	180	306	270
Salisbury	550	184	118	122	89	53	144	97	314	160	39	160	412	93	512	410	73	62	106	282	260	574	268	241	201	216	120	204	297	328	113	212	174	70	203	462	164	134	43	224
Sheffield	398	166	272	91	233	182	122	200	161	263	264	247	236	256	359	257	148	191	150	157	66	422	115	35	47	79	207	39	100	131	103	148	44	141	366	309	93	297	227	73	211
Shrewsbury	421	75	220	48	226	130	139	110	185	109	212	250	283	205	383	281	96	184	52	105	162	445	139	122	124	65	210	75	193	224	97	202	86	123	314	333	128	245	209	95	161	90
Southampton	578	225	142	135	66	106	137	139	342	201	53	152	440	111	539	438	100	49	133	309	257	602	295	238	198	244	112	232	294	325	110	204	171	67	221	489	157	152	20	252	23	208	191
Stoke-on-Trent	392	116	220	48	226	130	139	149	156	211	212	250	254	205	353	252	96	184	99	123	129	416	109	93	91	58	210	46	164	195	97	172	54	123	314	303	99	245	209	66	161	51	38	191
Stranraer	235	342	477	305	482	387	363	405	106	392	469	506	132	461	188	86	352	440	355	333	276	262	153	231	288	232	467	227	201	163	354	389	294	380	571	149	333	502	465	195	418	267	290	447	261
Taunton	560	165	50	131	160	51	225	79	323	142	45	224	422	34	521	419	77	126	96	291	272	584	277	253	228	226	185	214	309	340	162	287	186	121	144	471	214	75	114	234	70	224	172	94	172	429
Wick	207	598	733	561	738	643	618	661	362	648	725	762	259	717	166	278	608	696	611	589	532	104	409	487	543	487	723	482	410	368	610	645	550	636	827	216	589	758	721	451	674	523	546	703	517	362	684
York	323	202	314	134	275	224	155	243	117	251	306	280	194	299	314	213	190	233	193	193	38	377	91	24	80	102	240	72	50	89	146	181	86	183	408	239	126	339	269	96	254	58	150	251	121	223	266	478
LONDON	551	239	216	121	59	120	59	152	314	215	128	79	413	200	512	410	102	30	136	282	186	575	268	198	143	216	40	204	254	285	68	118	131	56	310	462	86	241	74	225	88	169	163	80	161	420	167	676	211

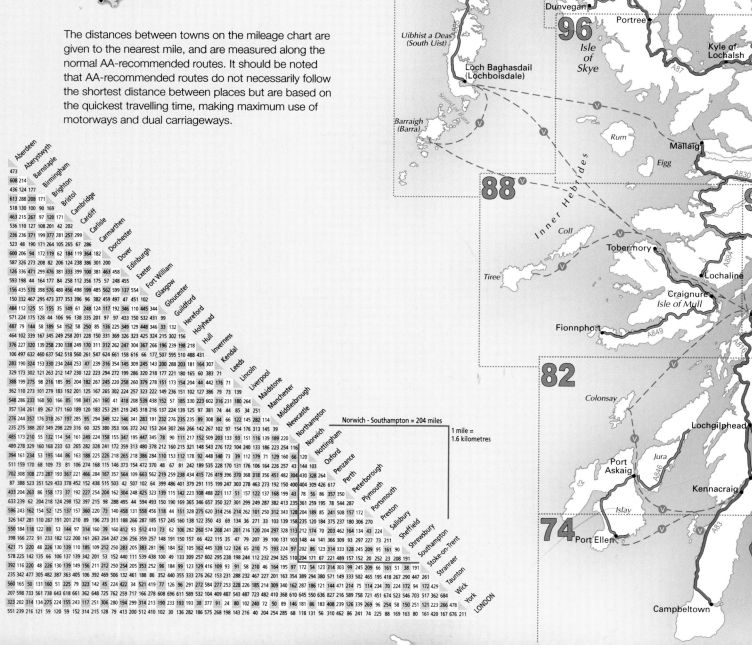

Norwich - Southampton = 204 miles

1 mile = 1.6 kilometres

111

104

96

88

82

74

Port Nis (Port of Ness)
A857
Tolsta Head
Steornabhagh (Stornoway)
The Minch
Isle of Lewis
A859
Taransay
Tairbeart (Tarbert)
Harris
Sound of Harris
Uibhist a Tuath (North Uist)
Loch nam Madadh (Lochmaddy)
Outer Hebrides
Beinn na Faoghla (Benbecula)
Uig
A87
Gairloch
Dunvegan
Portree
Uibhist a Deas (South Uist)
A865
Isle of Skye
Kyle of Lochalsh
Loch Baghasdail (Lochboisdale)
Sound of Barra
Barraigh (Barra)
Rum
Mallaig
Eigg
A830
Inner Hebrides
Coll
Tobermory
Tiree
A884
Lochaline
Craignure
Isle of Mull
Fionnphort
A849
Colonsay
Lochgilphead
Jura
Port Askaig
A846
Kennacraig
Islay
Port Ellen
A83
Campbeltown

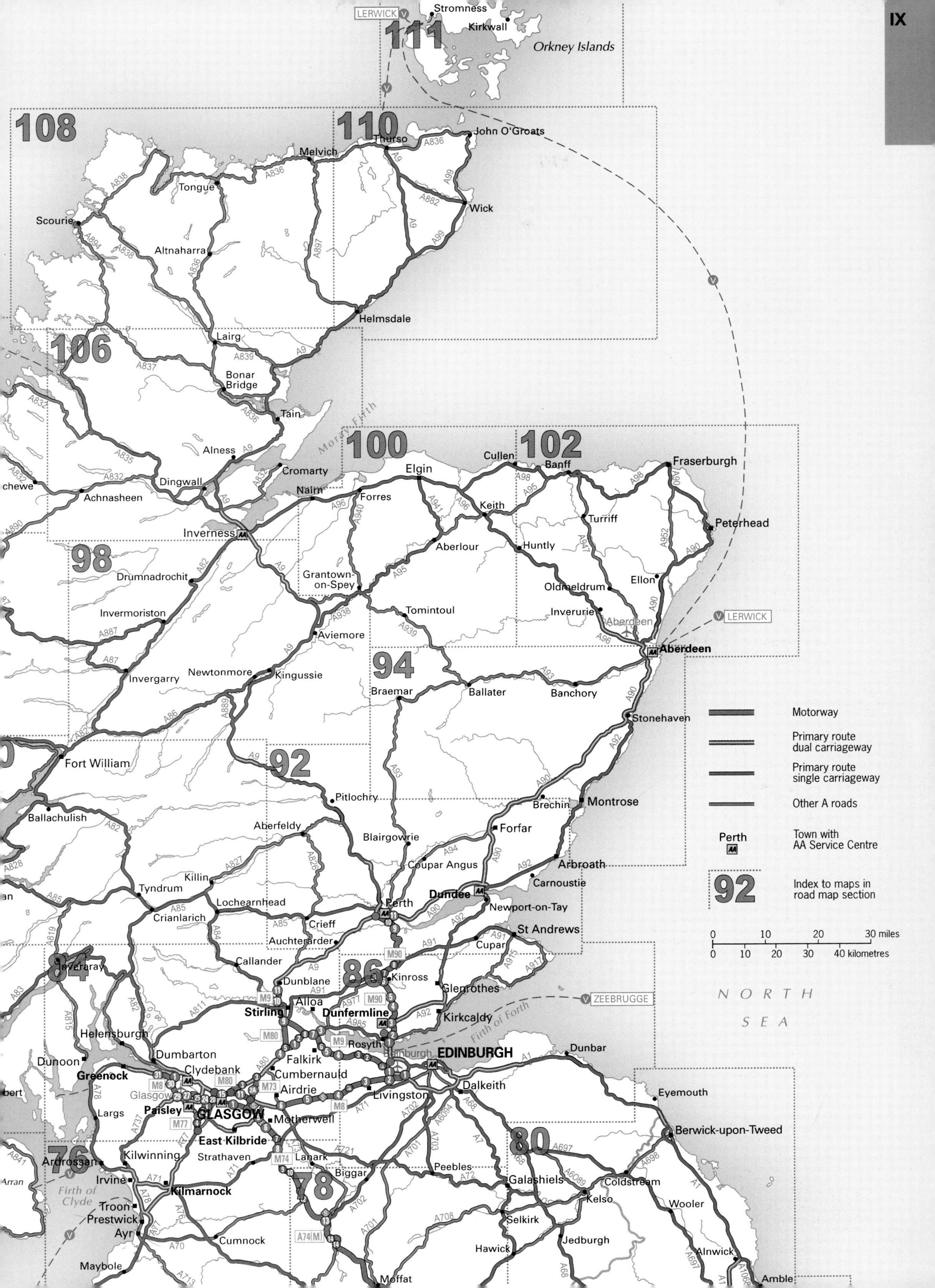

111

110

108

106

100

102

98

94

92

84

86

80

76

78

Orkney Islands

LERWICK

Stromness
Kirkwall
John O'Groats
Thurso
Melvich
Wick
Tongue
Scourie
Altnaharra
Helmsdale
Lairg
Bonar Bridge
Tain
Alness
Cromarty
Dingwall
Achnasheen
chewe
Inverness
Nairn
Elgin
Forres
Cullen
Banff
Fraserburgh
Keith
Turriff
Peterhead
Aberlour
Huntly
Drumnadrochit
Grantown-on-Spey
Tomintoul
Oldmeldrum
Ellon
Invermoriston
Inverurie
Aberdeen
Invergarry
Newtonmore
Kingussie
Aviemore
Aberdeen
Braemar
Ballater
Banchory
Fort William
Stonehaven
Ballachulish
Pitlochry
Aberfeldy
Blairgowrie
Brechin
Montrose
Killin
Tyndrum
Lochearnhead
Coupar Angus
Forfar
Crianlarich
Crieff
Arbroath
Carnoustie
Auchterarder
Perth
Dundee
Newport-on-Tay
Callander
St Andrews
Dunblane
Kinross
Cupar
Inveraray
Glenrothes
Alloa
Stirling
Dunfermline
Kirkcaldy
Helensburgh
Rosyth
ZEEBRUGGE
Dunoon
Dumbarton
Clydebank
Falkirk
Cumbernauld
Airdrie
EDINBURGH
Dunbar
Greenock
Glasgow
Livingston
Dalkeith
Eyemouth
Largs
Paisley
GLASGOW
Motherwell
Kilwinning
East Kilbride
Strathaven
Lanark
Berwick-upon-Tweed
Ardrossan
Biggar
Peebles
Galashiels
Coldstream
Arran
Irvine
Kilmarnock
Selkirk
Kelso
Wooler
Troon
Prestwick
Ayr
Cumnock
Hawick
Jedburgh
Maybole
Moffat
Alnwick
Amble

Morayfirth
Firth of Forth
Firth of Clyde

NORTH SEA

		Motorway
		Primary route dual carriageway
		Primary route single carriageway
		Other A roads

Perth — Town with AA Service Centre

92 — Index to maps in road map section

0   10   20   30 miles
0 10 20 30 40 kilometres

Motorways – restricted junctions

Motorway junctions which have access and exit restrictions,
as shown by ◼3◼ on atlas pages
(Motorways and Service Areas booklet also available tel: **0870 5500 600**)

M1 LONDON–LEEDS

Junction

2 (pg 21)
- Northbound — No exit. Access only from A1 *(northbound)*
- Southbound — No access. Exit only to A1 *(southbound)*

4 (pg 21)
- Northbound — No exit. Access only from A41 *(northbound)*
- Southbound — No access. Exit only to A41 *(southbound)*

6A (pg 20)
- Northbound — No exit. Access only from M25
- Southbound — No access. Exit only to M25

7 (pg 20)
- Northbound — No exit. Access only from M10
- Southbound — No access. Exit only to M10

17 (pg 41)
- Northbound — No access. Exit only to M45
- Southbound — No exit. Access only from M45

19 (pg 41)
- Northbound — Exit only to northbound M6
- Southbound — No access from A14. Access only from M6

21A (pg 41)
- Northbound — No access. Exit only to A46
- Southbound — No exit. Access only from A46

23A (pg 41)
- Northbound — No access. Exit only to A42
- Southbound — No exit. Access only from A42

24A (pg 41)
- Northbound — No exit. Access only from A50
- Southbound — No access. Exit only to A50

34 (pg 51) — Staggered junction; follow signs
- Northbound — No restriction
- Southbound — No restriction

35A (pg 51)
- Northbound — No access. Exit only to A616
- Southbound — No exit. Access only from A616

43 (pg 58)
- Northbound — No access. Exit only to M621
- Southbound — No exit. Access only from M621

48 (pg 60)
- Northbound — No exit. Access only from A1(M)
- Southbound — No access. Exit only to A1(M)

M2 ROCHESTER–FAVERSHAM

Junction

1 (pg 22)
- Westbound — Exit only to A289 *(eastbound)*
- Eastbound — Access only from A289 *(westbound)*

M3 SUNBURY–SOUTHAMPTON

Junction

8 (pg 19)
- Southwestbound — No access. Exit only to A303
- Northeastbound — No exit. Access only from A303

10 (pg 9)
- Southwestbound — No exit. Access only from Winchester & A31
- Northeastbound — No access. Exit only to Winchester & A31

11 (pg 9) — Staggered junction; follow signs
- Southwestbound — No restriction
- Northeastbound — No restriction

13 (pg 9)
- Southwestbound — Access only to M27 *(westbound)* & A33
- Northeastbound — No restriction

14 (pg 9)
- Southwestbound — No access. Exit only to M27 *(eastbound)* & A33
- Northeastbound — No exit. Access only

M4 LONDON–SOUTH WALES

Junction

1 (pg 21)
- Westbound — Access only from A4 *(westbound)*
- Eastbound — Exit only to A4 *(eastbound)*

4A (pg 20)
- Southbound — No exit to A4 *(westbound)*
- Northbound — No restriction

21 (pg 28)
- Westbound — No access. Exit only to M48
- Eastbound — No exit. Access only from M48

23 (pg 28)
- Westbound — No exit. Access only from M48
- Eastbound — No access. Exit only to M48

25 (pg 28)
- Westbound — No access. Exit only to B4596
- Eastbound — No exit. Access only from B4596

25A (pg 28)
- Westbound — No access. Exit only to A4042
- Eastbound — No exit. Access only from A4042

29 (pg 29)
- Westbound — No access. Exit only to A48(M)
- Eastbound — No exit. Access only from A48(M)

38 (pg 26)
- Westbound — No access. Exit only to A48
- Eastbound — No restriction

39 (pg 26)
- Westbound — No exit. Access only from A48
- Eastbound — No access or exit

41 (pg 26) — Staggered junction; follow signs
- Westbound — No restriction
- Eastbound — No restriction

42 (pg 26) — Staggered junction; follow signs
- Westbound — Exit only to A483
- Eastbound — Access only from A483

M5 BIRMINGHAM–EXETER

Junction

10 (pg 29)
- Southwestbound — No access. Exit only to A4019
- Northeastbound — No exit. Access only from A4019

11A (pg 20)
- Southwestbound — Exit only to A417 *(eastbound)*
- Northeastbound — Access only from A417 *(westbound)*

12 (pg 29)
- Southwestbound — No exit. Access only from A38
- Northeastbound — No access. Exit only

18A (pg 28)
- Southwestbound — No exit. Access only from M49
- Northeastbound — Exit only to M49

M6 RUGBY–CARLISLE

Junction

4 (pg 40)
- Northwestbound — No access from M42 *(southbound)*. No exit to M42 *(northbound)*
- Southeastbound — No access from M42 *(southbound)*. No exit to M42

4A (pg 40)
- Northwestbound — No exit. Access only from M42 *(southbound)*
- Southeastbound — No access. Exit only to M42

5 (pg 40)
- Northwestbound — No access. Exit only to A452
- Southeastbound — No exit. Access only from A452

10A (pg 40)
- Northbound — No access. Exit only to M54
- Southbound — No exit. Access only from M54

20A (with M56) (pg 57)
- Northwestbound — No restriction
- Southbound — No access from M56

20 (pg 57)
- Northbound — No exit. Access only from A50
- Southbound — No restriction

24 (pg 57)
- Northbound — No exit. Access only from A58
- Southbound — No access. Exit only to A58

25 (pg 57)
- Northbound — No access. Exit only
- Southbound — No exit. Access only

29 (pg 57)
- Northbound — No direct access, use adjacent slip road to junction 29A
- Southbound — No direct exit, use adjacent slip road from junction 29A

29A (pg 57)
- Northbound — No direct exit, use adjacent slip road from junction 29
- Southbound — No direct access, use adjacent slip road to junction 29

30 (pg 57)
- Northbound — No exit. Access only from M61
- Southbound — No access. Exit only to M61

31A (pg 57)
- Northbound — No access. Exit only
- Southbound — No exit. Access only

M8 EDINBURGH–GLASGOW–BISHOPTON

Junction

3A (pg 86) — Staggered junction; follow signs
- Westbound — No restriction
- Eastbound — No restriction

8 (pg 85)
- Westbound — No access from M73 *(southbound)* or from A8 *(eastbound)* & A89
- Eastbound — No exit to M73 *(northbound)* or to A8 *(westbound)* & A89

9 (pg 85)
- Westbound — No exit. Access only
- Eastbound — No access. Exit only

13 (pg 85)
- Westbound — Access only from M80 *(southbound)*
- Eastbound — Exit only to M80 *(northbound)*

14 (pg 85)
- Westbound — No exit. Access only
- Eastbound — No access. Exit only

16 (pg 85)
- Westbound — No access. Exit only to A804
- Eastbound — No exit. Access only from A879

17 (pg 85)
- Westbound — Exit only to A82
- Eastbound — No restriction

18 (pg 85)
- Westbound — Access only from A82 *(eastbound)*
- Eastbound — No access. Exit only to A814

19 (pg 85)
- Westbound — No access from A814 *(westbound)*
- Eastbound — No access. Exit only to A814 *(westbound)*

20 (pg 85)
- Westbound — No access. Exit only
- Eastbound — No exit. Access only

21 (pg 85)
- Westbound — No exit. Access only
- Eastbound — No access. Exit only to A8

22 (pg 85)
- Westbound — No access. Exit only to M77 *(southbound)*
- Eastbound — No exit. Access only from M77 *(northbound)*

23 (pg 85)
- Westbound — No access. Exit only to B768
- Eastbound — No exit. Access only from B768

25 (pg 85)
- Westbound — No access/exit from/to A8
- Eastbound — No access/exit from/to A8

25A (pg 85)
- Westbound — No access. Exit only
- Eastbound — No exit. Access only

28 (pg 84)
- Westbound — No access. Exit only
- Eastbound — No exit. Access only

28A (pg 84)
- Westbound — Exit only to A737
- Eastbound — No exit. Access only from A737

M9 EDINBURGH–DUNBLANE

Junction

1A (pg 86)
- Northwestbound — No access. Exit only to A8000
- Southeastbound — No exit. Access only from A8000

2 (pg 86)
- Northwestbound — No exit. Access only
- Southeastbound — No access. Exit only

3 (pg 86)
- Northwestbound — No access. Exit only
- Southeastbound — No exit. Access only

6 (pg 85)
- Northwestbound — No exit. Access only from A904
- Southeastbound — No access. Exit only to A905

8 (pg 85)
- Northwestbound — No access. Exit only to M876 *(southwestbound)*
- Southeastbound — No exit. Access only from M876 *(northeastbound)*

M10 ST ALBANS–M1

Junction

with M1 (jct 7) (pg 20)
- Northwestbound — Exit only to M1 *(northbound)*
- Southeastbound — Access only from M1 *(southbound)*

M11 LONDON–CAMBRIDGE

Junction

4 (pg 21)
- Northbound — Access only from A406
- Southbound — Exit only to A406

5 (pg 21)
- Northbound — No access. Exit only to A1168
- Southbound — No exit. Access only from A1168

9 (pg 33)
- Northbound — No access. Exit only to A11
- Southbound — No exit. Access only from A11

13 (pg 33)
- Northbound — No access Exit only to A1303
- Southbound — No exit. Access only from A1303

14 (pg 33)
- Northbound — Exit only to A14 *(eastbound)*
- Southbound — Access only from A14

M20 SWANLEY–FOLKESTONE

Junction

2 (pg 22) — Staggered junction; follow signs
- Southeastbound — No access. Exit only to A227
- Northwestbound — No exit. Access only from A227

3 (pg 22)
- Southeastbound — No exit. Access only from M26 *(eastbound)*
- Northwestbound — No access. Exit only to M26 *(westbound)*

5 (pg 22)
- Southeastbound — For access follow signs. Exit only to A20
- Northwestbound — No exit. Access only from A20

6 (pg 22)
- Southeastbound — For exit follow signs
- Northwestbound — No restriction

11A (pg 13)
- Southeastbound — No access. Exit only
- Northwestbound — No exit. Access only

M23 HOOLEY–CRAWLEY

Junction

7 (pg 21)
- Southbound — Access only from A23 *(southbound)*
- Northbound — Exit only to A23 *(northbound)*

10A (pg 11)
- Southbound — No access. Exit only to B2036
- Northbound — No exit. Access only from B2036

M25 LONDON ORBITAL MOTORWAY
(refer also to atlas pg xii)

Junction

1B (pg 21)
- Clockwise — No access (use slip road via jct 2).Exit only to A225 & A296
- Anticlockwise — No exit (use slip road via jct 2). Access only from A225 & A296

5 (pg 21)
- Clockwise — No exit to M26
- Anticlockwise — No access from M26

9 (pg 21) — Staggered junction; follow signs
- Clockwise — No restriction
- Anticlockwise — No restriction

19 (pg 20)
- Clockwise — No access. Exit only to A41
- Anticlockwise — No exit. Access only from A41

21 (pg 20)
- Clockwise — Access only from M1 *(southbound)*. Exit only to M1 *(northbound)*
- Anticlockwise — Access only from M1 *(southbound)*. Exit only to M1 *(northbound)*

21A (pg 20)
- Clockwise — No link from M1 to A405
- Anticlockwise — No link from M1 to A405

31 (pg 21)
- Clockwise — No exit (use slip road via jct 30)
- Anticlockwise — For access follow signs

M26 SEVENOAKS–WROTHAM

Junction

with M25 (jct 5) (pg 21)
- Eastbound — Access only from anticlockwise M25 *(eastbound)*
- Westbound — Exit only to clockwise M25 *(westbound)*

with M20 (jct 3) (pg 22)
- Eastbound — Exit only to M20 *(southeastbound)*
- Westbound — Access only from M20 *(northwestbound)*

M27 CADNAM–PORTSMOUTH

Junction

4 (pg 9) — Staggered junction; follow signs
- Eastbound — Access only from M3 *(southbound)*. Exit only to M3 *(northbound)*
- Westbound — Access only from M3 *(southbound)*. Exit only to M3 *(northbound)*

10 (pg 9)
- Eastbound — No exit. Access only from A32
- Westbound — No access. Exit only to A32

12 (pg 9) — Staggered junction; follow signs
- Eastbound — Access only from M275 *(northbound)*
- Westbound — Exit only to M275 *(southbound)*

M40 LONDON–BIRMINGHAM

Junction

3 (pg 20)
- Northwestbound — No access. Exit only to A40
- Southeastbound — No exit. Access only from A40

7 (pg 31)
- Northwestbound — No access. Exit only to A329
- Southeastbound — No exit. Access only from A329

Junction	Direction	Restriction
8 (pg 31)	Northwestbound	No access. Exit only to A40
	Southeastbound	No exit. Access only from A40
13 (pg 30)	Northwestbound	No access. Exit only to A452
	Southeastbound	No exit. Access only from A452
14 (pg 30)	Northwestbound	No exit. Access only from A452
	Southeastbound	No access. Exit only to A452
16 (pg 40)	Northwestbound	No exit. Access only from A3400
	Southeastbound	No access. Exit only to A3400

M42 BROMSGROVE–MEASHAM

Junction	Direction	Restriction
1 (pg 40)	Northeastbound	No exit. Access only from A38
	Southwestbound	No access. Exit only to A38
7 (pg 40)	Northeastbound	No access. Exit only to M6 *(northwestbound)*
	Southwestbound	No exit. Access only from M6 *(northwestbound)*
7A (pg 40)	Northeastbound	No access. Exit only to M6 *(southeastbound)*
	Southwestbound	No access or exit
8 (pg 40)	Northeastbound	No exit. Access only from M6 *(southeastbound)*
	Southwestbound	No access. Exit only to M6 *(northwestbound)*

M45 COVENTRY–M1

Junction	Direction	Restriction
unnumbered (Dunchurch) (pg 41)	Eastbound	No access. Exit only to A45 & B4429
	Westbound	No exit. Access only from A45 & B4429
with M1 (jct 17) (pg 41)	Eastbound	Exit only to M1 *(southbound)*
	Westbound	Access only from M1 *(northbound)*

M53 MERSEY TUNNEL–CHESTER

Junction	Direction	Restriction
1 (pg 56)	Southwestbound	No exit. Access only from A554 & A5139
	Northeastbound	No access. Exit only to A554 & A5139
11 (pg 48)	Southeastbound	Access only from M56 *(westbound)*. Exit only to M56 *(eastbound)*
	Northwestbound	Access only from M56 *(westbound)*. Exit only to M56 *(eastbound)*

M54 TELFORD

Junction	Direction	Restriction
with M6 (jct 10A) (pg 40)	Westbound	No exit. Access only from M6 *(northbound)*
	Eastbound	No access. Exit only to M6 *(southbound)*

M56 NORTH CHESHIRE

Junction	Direction	Restriction
1 (pg 57)	Westbound	No exit. Access only from M60 *(westbound)*
	Eastbound	No access. Exit only to M60 *(eastbound)* & A34 *(northbound)*
2 (pg 57)	Westbound	No access. Exit only to A560
	Eastbound	No exit. Access only from A560
3 (pg 57)	Westbound	No exit. Access only from A5103
	Eastbound	No access. Exit only to A5103 & A560
4 (pg 57)	Westbound	No access. Exit only
	Eastbound	No exit. Access only
7 (pg 57)	Staggered junction; follow signs	
	Westbound	No restriction
	Eastbound	No restriction
9 (pg 57)	Westbound	Exit to M6 *(southbound)* via A50 interchange
	Eastbound	Access from M6 *(northbound)* via A50 interchange
15 (pg 48)	Westbound	No access. Exit only to M53
	Eastbound	No exit. Access only from M53

M57 LIVERPOOL OUTER RING ROAD

Junction	Direction	Restriction
3 (pg 56)	Northwestbound	No exit. Access only from A526
	Southeastbound	No access. Exit only to A526
5 (pg 56)	Northwestbound	No exit. Access only from A580 *(westbound)*
	Southeastbound	No access. Exit only to A580

M58 LIVERPOOL–WIGAN

Junction	Direction	Restriction
1 (pg 56)	Eastbound	No exit. Access only
	Westbound	No access. Exit only

M60 MANCHESTER ORBITAL

(refer also to atlas pg xiii)

Junction	Direction	Restriction
2 (pg 57)	Clockwise	No exit. Access only from A560
	Anticlockwise	No access. Exit only to A560
3 (pg 57)	Clockwise	No access from M56
	Anticlockwise	No exit. Access only from A34 *(northbound)*
4 (pg 57)	Clockwise	Access only from A34 *(northbound)*. Exit only to M56
	Anticlockwise	Access only from M56 *(eastbound)*. Exit only to A34 *(southbound)*
5 (pg 57)	Clockwise	Access/exit only from/to A5103 *(northbound)*
	Anticlockwise	Access/exit only from/to A5103 *(southbound)*
7 (pg 57)	Clockwise	No access (use adjacent slip road to junction 8). Exit only to A56
	Anticlockwise	No exit (use adjacent slip road from junction 8). Access only from A56
14 (pg 57)	Clockwise	No exit. Access to M60 from A580 *(eastbound)*. Access to M61 *(westbound)* from A580 *(westbound)*
	Anticlockwise	No access. Exit from M61 *(eastbound)* to A580 *(eastbound)*. No exit from M60
15 (pg 57)	Clockwise	Access only from M61 *(eastbound)*. Exit to M61 *(westbound)*
	Anticlockwise	No access. Exit to M61 *(westbound)* & A580 *(westbound)*
16 (pg 57)	Clockwise	No exit. Access only from A666
	Anticlockwise	No access. Exit only to A666
20 (pg 57)	Clockwise	No access. Exit only to A664
	Anticlockwise	No exit. Access only from A664
22 (pg 57)	Clockwise	No restriction
	Anticlockwise	No access. Exit only to A62
25 (pg 57)	Clockwise	No access. Exit only to A6017
	Anticlockwise	No restriction
26 (pg 57)	Clockwise	No restriction
	Anticlockwise	No access or exit
27 (pg 57)	Clockwise	No exit. Access only from A626
	Anticlockwise	No access. Exit only to A626

M61 GREATER MANCHESTER–PRESTON

Junction	Direction	Restriction
1 (pg 57)	No restriction; follow signs	
2 (pg 57)	No restriction; follow signs	
3 (pg 57)	Northwestbound	No access or exit
	Southeastbound	No access. Exit only to A660
with M6 (jct 30) (pg 57)	Northwestbound	Exit only to M6 *(northbound)*
	Southeastbound	Access only from M6 *(southbound)*

M62 LIVERPOOL–HUMBERSIDE

Junction	Direction	Restriction
23 (pg 58)	Eastbound	No access. Exit only to A640
	Westbound	No exit. Access only from A640

M65 PRESTON–COLNE

Junction	Direction	Restriction
1 (pg 57)	Northeastbound	Access and exit to M6 only
	Southwestbound	Access and exit to M6 only
9 (pg 57)	Northeastbound	No access. Exit only to A679
	Southwestbound	No exit. Access only from A679
11 (pg 57)	Northeastbound	No exit. Access only
	Southwestbound	No access. Exit only

M66 GREATER MANCHESTER

Junction	Direction	Restriction
with A56 (pg 57)	Southbound	Access only from A56 *(southbound)*
	Northbound	Exit only to A56 *(northbound)*
1 (pg 57)	Southbound	No exit. Access only from A56
	Northbound	No access. Exit only to A56

M67 HYDE BYPASS

Junction	Direction	Restriction
1 (pg 50)	Eastbound	No access. Exit only to A6017
	Westbound	No exit. Access only from A6017
2 (pg 50)	Eastbound	No exit. Access only
	Westbound	No access. Exit only to A57
3 (pg 50)	Eastbound	No restriction
	Westbound	No access. Exit only to A627

M69 COVENTRY–LEICESTER

Junction	Direction	Restriction
2 (pg 41)	Northbound	No exit. Access only from B4669
	Southbound	No access. Exit only to B4669

M73 EAST OF GLASGOW

Junction	Direction	Restriction
2 (pg 85)	Northbound	No access from or to A89. No access from M8 *(eastbound)*
	Southbound	No access from or to A89. No exit to M8 *(westbound)*
3 (pg 85)	Northbound	Exit only to A80 *(northeastbound)*
	Southbound	Access only from A80 *(southwestbound)*

M74 GLASGOW–ABINGTON

Junction	Direction	Restriction
2 (pg 85)	Southbound	No exit. Access only from A763
	Northbound	No access. Exit only to A763
3 (pg 85)	Southbound	No access. Exit only
	Northbound	Exit via junction 4. Access only
7 (pg 77)	Southbound	No access. Exit only to A72
	Northbound	No exit. Access only from A72
9 (pg 77)	Southbound	No access. Exit only to B7078
	Northbound	No access or exit
10 (pg 77)	Southbound	No exit. Access only from B7078
	Northbound	No restrictions
11 (pg 77)	Southbound	No access. Exit only to B7078
	Northbound	No exit. Access only from B7078
12 (pg 77)	Southbound	No exit. Access only from A70
	Northbound	No access. Exit only to A70

A74(M) ABINGTON–GRETNA

Junction	Direction	Restriction
14 (pg 77)	Staggered junction; follow signs	
	Southbound	No restriction
	Northbound	No restriction
18 (pg 79)	Southbound	No exit. Access only from B723
	Northbound	No access. Exit only to B723
21 (pg 71)	Southbound	No access. Exit only to B6357
	Northbound	No exit. Access only from B6357
with B7076 (pg 71)	Southbound	No exit. Access only
	Northbound	No access. Exit only
Gretna Green (pg 71)	Southbound	No access. Exit only (use B7076 through Gretna to access A75)
	Northbound	No exit. Access only
with A75 (pg 71)	Southbound	No exit. Access only from A75
	Northbound	No access. Exit only to A75
with A6071 (pg 71)	Southbound	Exit only to A74 *(southbound)*
	Northbound	Access only from A74 *(northbound)*

M77 WEST OF GLASGOW

Junction	Direction	Restriction
with M8 (pg 85)	Southbound	No access from M8 *(eastbound)*
	Northbound	No exit to M8 *(westbound)*
4 (pg 85)	Southbound	No access. Exit only
	Northbound	No exit. Access only
with A77 (pg 85)	Southbound	Exit only to A77 *(southbound)*
	Northbound	Access only from A77 *(northbound)*

M80 STEPPS BYPASS

Junction	Direction	Restriction
3 (pg 85)	Northeastbound	No access. Exit only
	Southwestbound	No exit. Access only

M80 BONNYBRIDGE–STIRLING

Junction	Direction	Restriction
5 (pg 85)	Northbound	No access. Exit only to M876 *(northeastbound)*
	Southbound	No exit. Access only from M876 *(southwestbound)*

M90 FORTH ROAD BRIDGE–PERTH

Junction	Direction	Restriction
2A (pg 86)	Northbound	No access. Exit only to A92 *(eastbound)*
	Southbound	No exit. Access only from A92 *(westbound)*
7 (pg 86)	Northbound	No exit. Access only from A91
	Southbound	No access. Exit only to A911
8 (pg 86)	Northbound	No access. Exit only to A91
	Southbound	No exit. Access only from A91
10 (pg 92)	Northbound	No access from A912. No exit to A912 *(southbound)*
	Southbound	No access from A912 *(northbound)*. No exit to A912

M180 SOUTH HUMBERSIDE

Junction	Direction	Restriction
1 (pg 59)	Eastbound	No access. Exit only to A18
	Westbound	No exit. Access only from A18

M606 BRADFORD SPUR

Junction	Direction	Restriction
2 (pg 58)	Northbound	No access. Exit only
	Southbound	No restriction

M621 LEEDS–M1

Junction	Direction	Restriction
2A (pg 58)	Eastbound	No exit. Access only
	Westbound	No access. Exit only
4 (pg 58)	Southeastbound	No access. Exit only
	Northwestbound	No restriction
5 (pg 58)	Southeastbound	No exit. Access only
	Northwestbound	No access. Exit only
6 (pg 58)	Southeastbound	No access. Exit only
	Northwestbound	No exit. Access only
with M1 (jct 43) (pg 58)	Southbound	Exit only to M1 *(southbound)*
	Northbound	Access only from M1 *(northbound)*

M876 BONNYBRIDGE–KINCARDINE BRIDGE

Junction	Direction	Restriction
with M80 (jct 5) (pg 85)	Northeastbound	Access only from M80 *(northbound)*
	Southwestbound	Exit only to M80 *(southbound)*
2 (pg 85)	Northeastbound	No access. Exit only to A9
	Southwestbound	No exit. Access only from A9
with M9 (jct 8) (pg 85)	Northeastbound	Exit only to M9 *(eastbound)*
	Southwestbound	Access only from M9 (westbound)

A1(M) SOUTH MIMMS–BALDOCK

Junction	Direction	Restriction
2 (pg 21)	Northbound	No access. Exit only to A1001
	Southbound	No exit. Access only from A1001
3 (pg 21)	Northbound	No restriction
	Southbound	No access. Exit only to A414
5 (pg 21)	Northbound	No exit. Access only
	Southbound	No access or exit

A1(M) ALCONBURY–PETERBOROUGH

Junction	Direction	Restriction
14 (pg 32)	Staggered junction; follow signs	
	Northbound	No restriction
	Southbound	No restriction
15 (pg 42)	Staggered junction; follow signs	
	Northbound	No restriction
	Southbound	No restriction

A1(M) EAST OF LEEDS

Junction	Direction	Restriction
44 (pg 59)	Northbound	Access only from M1 *(northbound)*
	Southbound	Exit only to M1 *(southbound)*

A1(M) SCOTCH CORNER–TYNESIDE

Junction	Direction	Restriction
57 (with A66(M)) (pg 65)	Northbound	No access. Exit only to A66(M) *(eastbound)*
	Southbound	No exit. Access only from A66(M) *(westbound)*
65 (with A194(M)) (pg 73)	Northbound	No access. Exit only to A194(M) & A1 *(northbound)*
	Southbound	No exit. Access only from A194(M) *(southbound)*

A3(M) HORNDEAN–HAVANT

Junction	Direction	Restriction
1 (pg 10)	Southbound	No access. Exit only to A3
	Northbound	No exit. Access only from A3
4 (pg 10)	Southbound	No exit. Access only
	Northbound	No access. Exit only

A48(M) CARDIFF SPUR

Junction	Direction	Restriction
29 (with M4) (pg 28)	Westbound	Access only from M4 *(westbound)*
	Eastbound	Exit only to M4 *(eastbound)*
29A (pg 28)	Westbound	Exit only to A48 *(westbound)*
	Eastbound	Access only from A48 *(eastbound)*

A66(M) DARLINGTON SPUR

Junction	Direction	Restriction
with A1(M) (jct 57) (pg 65)	Eastbound	Access only from A1(M) *(northbound)*
	Westbound	Exit only to A1(M) *(southbound)*

A194(M) TYNESIDE

Junction	Direction	Restriction
with A1(M) (jct 65) (pg 73)	Northbound	Access only from A1(M) *(northbound)*
	Southbound	Exit only to A1(M) *(southbound)*

M25 London orbital motorway

Refer also to atlas page 20–21

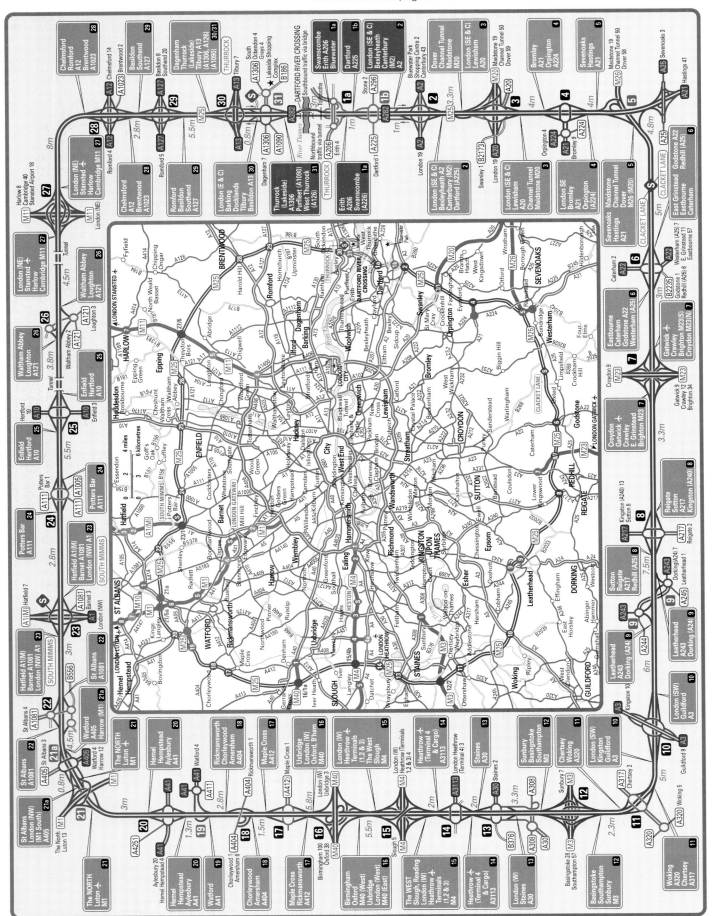

M60 Manchester orbital motorway

Refer also to atlas page 57

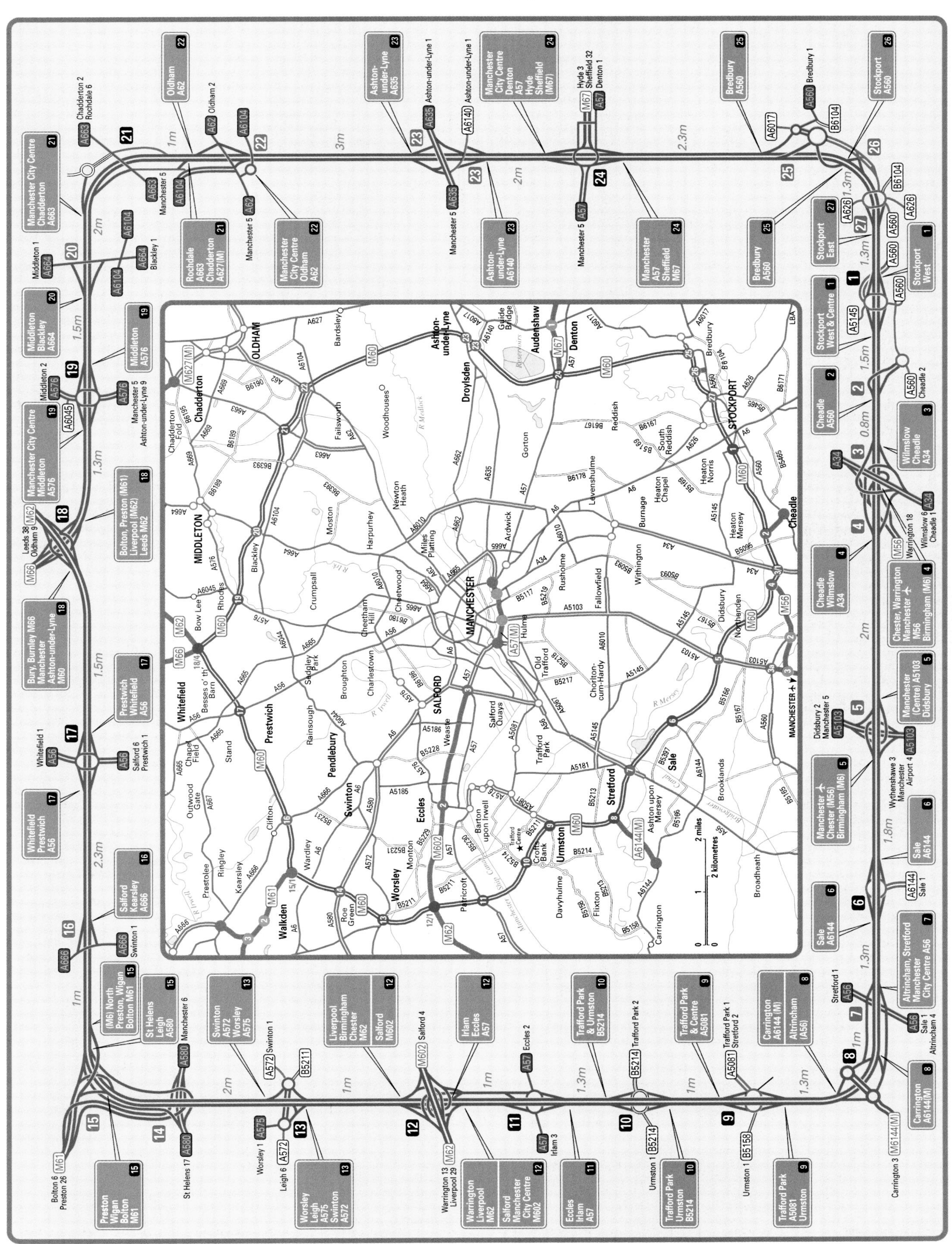

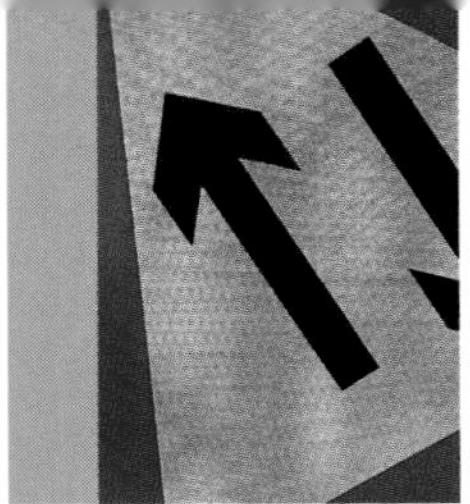

Map symbols

Motoring information

M4	Motorway with number		Unclassified road single/dual carriageway		Railway line/in tunnel		AA telephone
1	Motorway junction with and without number		Roundabout		Railway station and level crossing	AA	AA Service Centre
3	Restricted motorway junctions		Interchange/junction		Tourist railway	628 ▲	Spot height in metres
S Fleet	Motorway service area		Narrow primary/other A/B road with passing places (Scotland)	Ⓐ	Airport	348 Rannoch Moor	Pass
	Motorway and junction under construction		Road under construction	Ⓗ	Heliport		River, canal, lake
A3	Primary route single/dual carriageway	⊨=====⊣	Road tunnel	Ⓕ	International freight terminal		Sandy beach
S Grantham North	Primary route service area		Steep gradient (arrows point downhill)	★	Major shopping centre		National boundary
BATH	Primary route destination	Toll	Road toll	P·R	Park and Ride location (at least 6 days)		County, administrative boundary
A1123	Other A road single/dual carriageway	▼ 5 ▼	Distance in miles between symbols		Urban area and village	23	Page continuation number
B2070	B road single/dual carriageway	V St Malo	Vehicle ferry				

Tourist information

Places of interest are also shown on town plans. See pages 117–129

𝐢	Tourist Information Centre	▼	Agricultural showground		Prehistoric monument		Ski slope – natural
𝐢	Tourist Information Centre (seasonal)		Theme park	✕ 1066	Battle site with year		Ski slope – artificial
𝐕	Visitor or heritage centre		Farm or animal centre		Steam centre (railway)	NT	National Trust property
	Abbey, cathedral or priory		Zoological or wildlife collection	⌒	Cave	NTS	National Trust for Scotland property
	Ruined abbey, cathedral or priory		Bird collection	✹	Windmill	★	Other place of interest
✗	Castle	◄✕	Aquarium	⊥	Monument	☐	Boxed symbols indicate attractions within urban areas
	Historic house or building		Nature reserve	Ⓡ	Golf course		National Park
	Museum or art gallery	RSPB	RSPB site		County cricket ground		National Scenic Area (Scotland)
	Industrial interest	··········	Forest drive	❀	Rugby Union national stadium		Forest Park
�𝗆	Aqueduct or viaduct	– – – – –	National trail		International athletics stadium		Heritage coast
❅	Garden	☼	Viewpoint		Horse racing		Travel Inn
	Arboretum		Picnic site		Show jumping/equestrian circuit		
❖	Vineyard		Hill-fort		Motor-racing circuit		
Y	Country park		Roman antiquity		Air show venue		

Ireland   (see pages 112–115) For tourist information see opposite page

M1 Motorway	N17 National primary route (Republic of Ireland)	A4 Primary route (Northern Ireland)	Road under construction
Motorway junction with and without number	N54 National secondary route (Republic of Ireland)	A21 A road (Northern Ireland)	Distance in miles between symbols
Restricted motorway junctions	R182 Regional road (Republic of Ireland)	B75 B road (Northern Ireland)	International boundary

District maps   (see pages 130–141) For tourist information see opposite page

M60 Motorway	Unclassified road single/dual	Railway station	AA AA Service Centre
Motorway under construction	Road under construction	Inner London Regional Transport (LRT) station	A&E 24-hour Accident & Emergency hospital
Primary route single/dual	Restricted road	Outer London Regional Transport (LRT) station	H Hospital
Other A road single/dual	Railway line/in tunnel	Railway station/LRT interchange	Crem Crematorium
B road single/dual	Tourist railway	Light railway/tramway station	Proposed congestion charge zone (London)

Central London   (see pages 142–151)

Primary route single/dual	Footpath	Ahead only	PO Post Office
Other A road single/dual	Track	Mini-roundabout	POL Police station
B road single/dual	Pedestrian street	Barrier	A&E 24-hour Accident & Emergency hospital
Unclassified road single/dual	Railway line/in tunnel	Railway station	Steps
Unclassified road wide/narrow	One-way street	London Regional Transport (LRT) station	Church
Road under construction	Compulsory turn	Docklands Light Railway (DLR) station	Tourist Information Centre
Road tunnel wide/narrow	Banned turn	P Parking	Tourist Information Centre (seasonal)
Restricted road (access only/private)	Banned turn (restricted periods only)		

Royal Parks (opening and closing times for traffic)
Green Park   Constitution Hill: closed Sundays, 08.00–dusk
Hyde Park   Open 05.00–midnight
Regent's Park   Open 05.00–midnight
St James's Park   The Mall: closed Sundays, 08.00–dusk

Traffic regulations in the City of London include security checkpoints and restrict the number of entry and exit points.

Note: Oxford Street is closed to through-traffic (except buses & taxis) 07.00–19.00, Monday–Saturday. Restricted parts of Frith Street/Old Compton Street are closed to vehicles 12.00–01.00 daily.

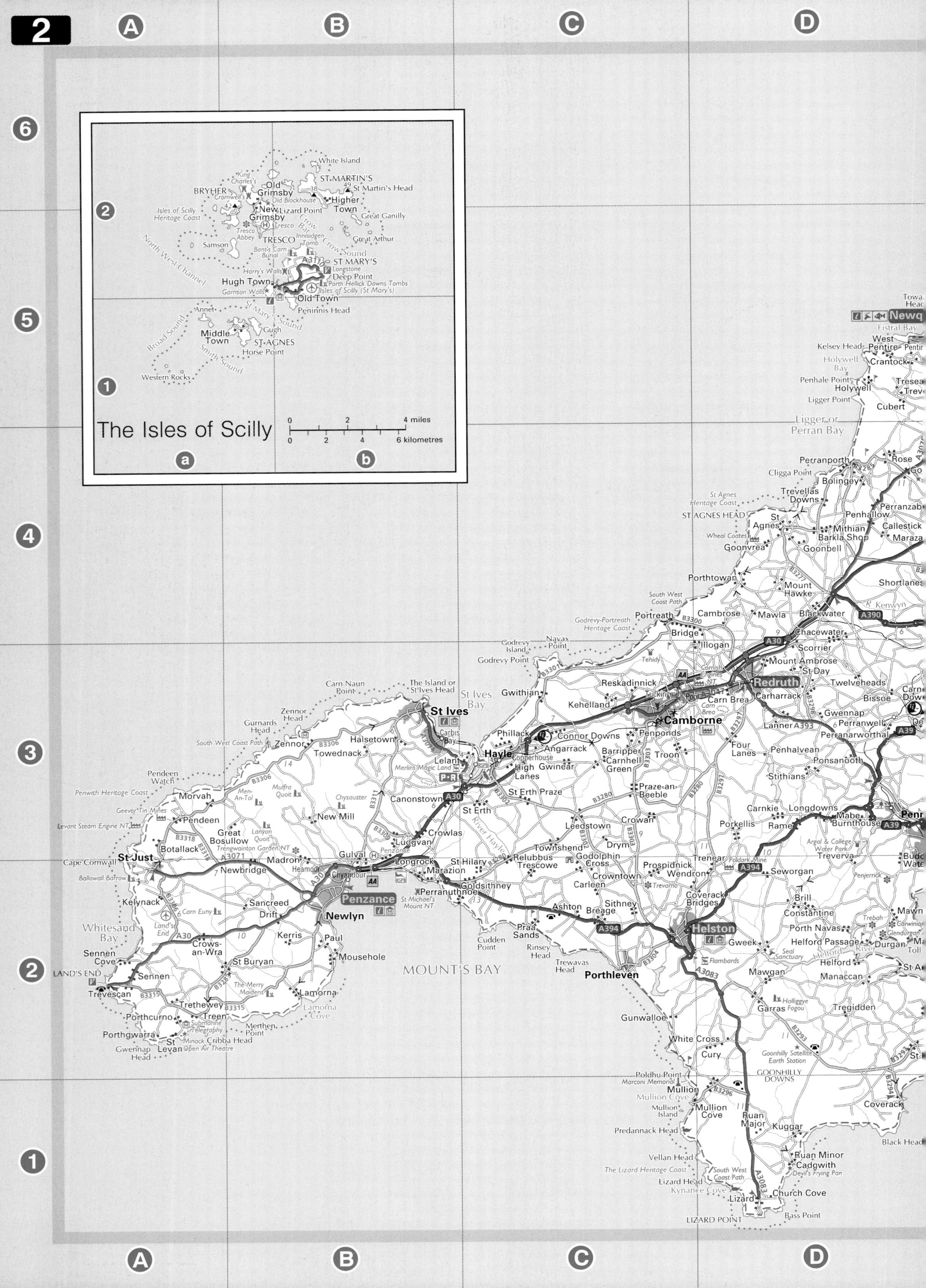

A
B
C
D
6
5
4
3
2
1
The Isles of Scilly
0
2
4 miles
0
2
4
6 kilometres
a
b
White Island
ST MARTIN'S
St Martin's Head
King Charles's
Old Grimsby
BRYHER
Cromwell's
Old Blockhouse
Higher Town
Isles of Scilly Heritage Coast
New Grimsby
Lizard Point
Great Ganilly
Tresco Abbey
Tresco
Crow Bar
Innisidgen Tomb
Great Arthur
Samson
TRESCO
Bant's Carn Burial
Crow Sound
North West Channel
ST MARY'S
Harry's Walls
Longstone
Deep Point
Hugh Town
Porth Hellick Downs Tombs
Garrison Walls
Isles of Scilly (St Mary's)
Old Town
Peninnis Head
Annet
St Mary's Sound
Broad Sound
Gugh
Middle Town
ST AGNES
Horse Point
Smith Sound
Western Rocks
Towan Head
Newquay
Fistral Bay
West Pentire
Kelsey Head
Holywell Bay
Crantock
Penhale Point
Holywell
Treseal
Ligger Point
Cubert
Ligger or Perran Bay
Perranporth
Rose
Cligga Point
Bolingey
St Agnes Heritage Coast
Trevellas Downs
ST AGNES HEAD
Perranzabuloe
Penhallow
St Agnes
Callestick
Mithian
Wheal Coates
Barkla Shop
Goonvrea
Goonbell
Porthtowan
Mount Hawke
Shortlanes
South West Coast Path
Godrevy-Portreath Heritage Coast
Portreath
Cambrose
Mawla
Blackwater
R. Kenwyn
A390
Bridge
Chacewater
Illogan
A30
Scorrier
Godrevy Island
Navax Point
Tehidy
Mount Ambrose
Godrevy Point
St Day
Reskadinnick
Redruth
Twelveheads
Gwithian
Carharrack
Bissoe
Kehelland
Tuckingmill
Pool
Carn Brea
Carnon Downs
The Island or St Ives Head
St Ives Bay
Carn Naun Point
St Ives
Camborne
Gwennap
Zennor Head
Carbis Bay
Perranwell
Gurnards Head
Halsetown
Phillack
Connor Downs
Penponds
Lanner
A393
Perranarworthal
South West Coast Path
Zennor
Towednack
Angarrack
Four Lanes
Lelant
Hayle
Copperhouse
Barripper
Troon
Penhalvean
Ponsanooth
Pendeen Watch
Merlin's Magic Land
Carnhell Green
Penwith Heritage Coast
High Lanes
Gwinear
Stithians
Morvah
Men-An-Tol
Mulfra Quoit
Chysauster
Canonstown
St Erth Praze
Praze-an-Beeble
Geevor Tin Mines
Levant Steam Engine NT
Pendeen
New Mill
St Erth
Carnkie
Longdowns
Mabe Burnthouse
Crowan
Porkellis
Rame
A39
Great Bosullow
Lanyon Quoit
Leedstown
Ludgvan
Crowlas
Drym
River Hayle
Botallack
Trengwainton Garden NT
Townshend
Argal & College Water Park
St Just
A3071
Madron
Gulval
Penzance
Relubbus
Godolphin Cross
Trenear
Treverva
Cape Cornwall
Newbridge
Heamoor
Chyandour
Longrock
St Hilary
Trescowe
Prospidnick
Poldark Mine
A394
Seworgan
Ballowall Barrow
Marazion
Wendron
Penjerrick
Goldsithney
Crowntown
Carleen
Trevarno
Perranuthnoe
Coverack Bridges
Kelynack
Penzance
St Michael's Mount NT
Brill
Carn Euny
Sancreed
Ashton
Sithney
Constantine
Whitesand Bay
Land's End
Drift
Newlyn
Breage
Helston
Trebah
Kerris
Paul
Praa Sands
Porth Navas
Glendurgan
Sennen Cove
Crows-an-Wra
Cudden Point
Rinsey Head
Gweek
Helford Passage
Durgan
Mousehole
Seal Sanctuary
Helford
LAND'S END
St Buryan
MOUNT'S BAY
Trewavas Head
Flambards
Sennen
Porthleven
Mawgan
Manaccan
Trevescan
The Merry Maidens
Lamorna
Trethewey
Treen
Lamorna Cove
Halligye Fogou
Garras
Tregidden
Porthcurno
Submarine Telegraphy
Gunwalloe
Merthen Point
Porthgwarra
St Levan
Minack Open Air Theatre
Cribba Head
White Cross
Goonhilly Satellite Earth Station
Gwennap Head
Cury
GOONHILLY DOWNS
Poldhu Point
Marconi Memorial
Mullion
Mullion Cove
Coverack
Mullion Island
Mullion Cove
Ruan Major
Kuggar
Predannack Head
Black Head
Vellan Head
Ruan Minor
Cadgwith
The Lizard Heritage Coast
South West Coast Path
Devil's Frying Pan
Lizard Head
Kynance Cove
Church Cove
Lizard
LIZARD POINT
Bass Point
A3083
A3083
A30
A30
A394

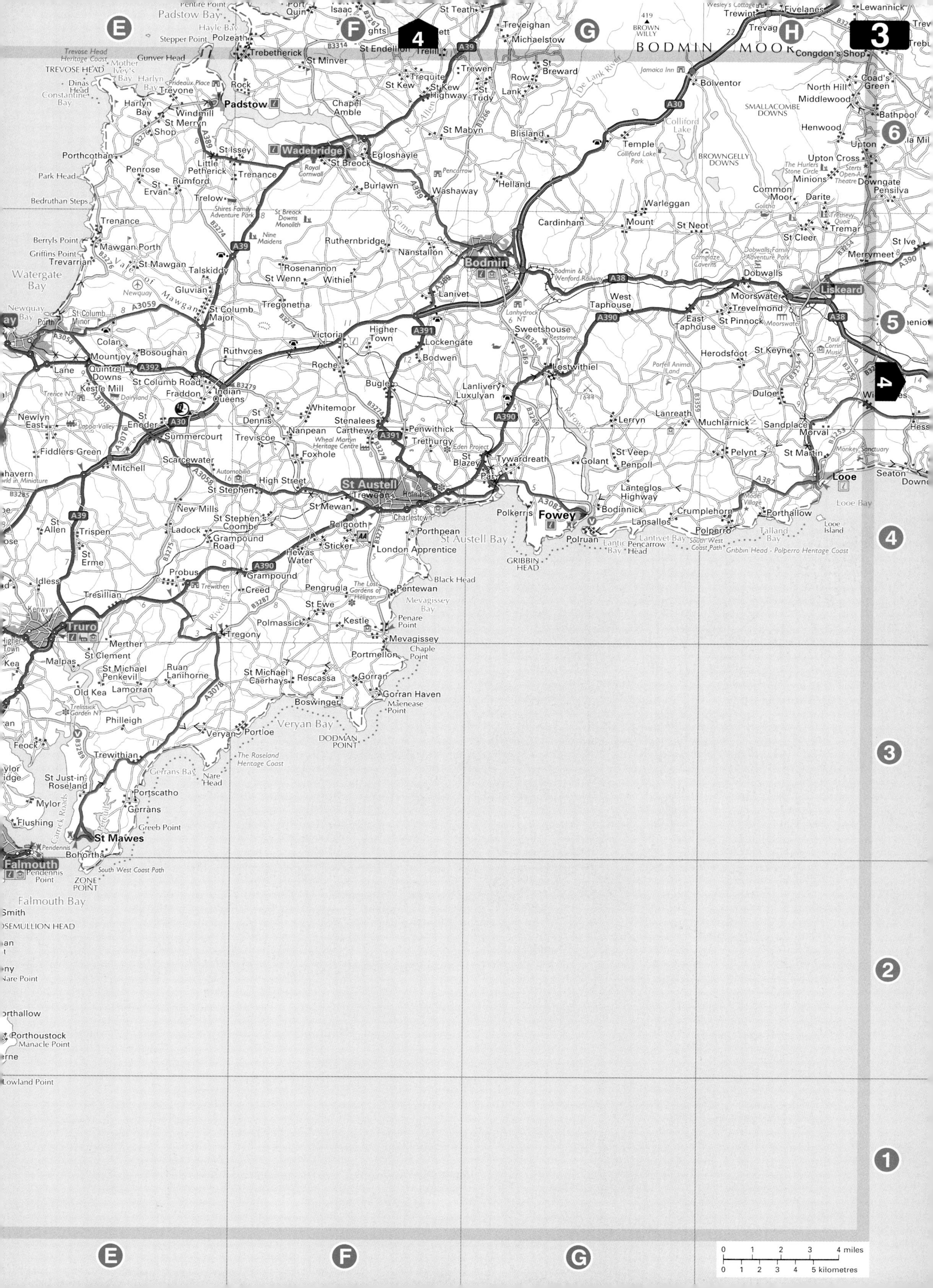

E
F
G
H
4
3
Padstow Bay
Hayle Bay
Stepper Point
Polzeath
Port Quin
Isaac
St Teath
Treveighan
Michaelstow
419
BROWN WILLY
BODMIN MOOR
Trewint
Fivelanes
Lewannick
Trevag
Congdon's Shop
Trevose Head Heritage Coast
TREVOSE HEAD
Mother Ivey's Bay
Gunver Head
Trebetherick
St Minver
St Endellion
Trelill
Trewen
St Breward
Jamaica Inn
Bolventor
Coad's Green
North Hill
Middlewood
Dinas Head
Constantine Bay
Harlyn Bay
Prideaux Place
Trevone
Rock
Trequite
St Kew
St Kew Highway
St Tudy
Row
Lank
De Lank River
A30
SMALLACOMBE DOWNS
Bathpool
Harlyn Bay
Windmill
Padstow
Chapel Amble
St Merryn
Shop
St Mabyn
Blisland
Colliford Lake
Henwood
Upton
St Issey
Wadebridge
Egloshayle
Temple
Colliford Lake Park
BROWNGELLY DOWNS
Upton Cross
Porthcothan
Penrose
Little Petherick
Trenance
Royal Cornwall
St Breock
Pencarrow
Helland
The Hurlers Stone Circle
Minions
Sterts Open-Air Theatre
Downgate
Pensilva
Park Head
St Ervan
Rumford
Burlawn
Washaway
Common Moor
Darite
Bedruthan Steps
Trelow
Shires Family Adventure Park
St Breock Downs Monolith
Warleggan
Golitha
Trethevy Quoit
Trenance
Cardinham
Mount
St Neot
Tremar
Berryls Point
Griffins Point
Mawgan Porth
Trevarrian
Nine Maidens
A39
Ruthernbridge
Nanstallon
St Cleer
St Ive
Vale of Mawgan
St Mawgan
Talskiddy
Bodmin
Dobwalls Family Adventure Park
Merrymeet
A390
Watergate Bay
Newquay
Rosenannon
St Wenn
Withiel
Carnglaze Caverns
Bodmin & Wenford Railway
A38
Dobwalls
Gluvian
Lanivet
West Taphouse
Moorswater
Liskeard
Newquay Bay
St Columb Minor
Porth
A3059
St Columb Major
Tregonetha
Lanhydrock NT
Trevelmond
East Taphouse
St Pinnock
Colan
Higher Town
Victoria
A391
Sweetshouse
Restormel
Mountjoy
Bosoughan
Ruthvoes
Lockengate
Quintrell Downs
Lane
A392
Roche
Bodwen
Porfell Animal Land
Herodsfoot
St Keyne
Paul Corin Music
St Columb Road
Lostwithiel
Kestle Mill
Trerice NT
Fraddon
Indian Queens
Dairyland
Bugle
Lanlivery
Luxulyan
Duloe
Newlyn East
Lappa Valley
St Enoder
St Dennis
Whitemoor
Stenalees
Penwithick
Lerryn
Lanreath
Muchlarnick
Sandplace
Morval
Fiddlers Green
Summercourt
Treviscoe
Nanpean
Carthew
Wheal Martyn Heritage Centre
Trethurgy
Eden Project
St Blazey
Tywardreath
Golant
St Veep
Penpoll
Pelynt
St Martin
Monkey Sanctuary
Mitchell
Scarcewater
Automobilia
Foxhole
Par
Looe
Seaton
Downderry
St Stephen
High Street
St Austell
Trewoon
Holmbush
Lanteglos Highway
Bodinnick
Crumplehorn
Model Village
Porthallow
Looe Bay
New Mills
St Mewan
Charlestown
Polkerris
Fowey
Polruan
Lansallos
Polperro
Talland Bay
Looe Island
St Allen
Trispen
St Stephen's Coombe
Ladock
Grampound Road
Polgooth
Sticker
Porthpean
St Austell Bay
GRIBBIN HEAD
Lantic Bay
Pencarrow Head
Lantivet Bay
South West Coast Path
Gribbin Head - Polperro Heritage Coast
St Erme
Hewas Water
London Apprentice
Black Head
Idless
Probus
Trewithen
Grampound
Creed
Tresillian
Pengrugla
The Lost Gardens of Heligan
Pentewan
Mevagissey Bay
St Ewe
Kenwyn
Truro
River Fal
Polmassick
Kestle
Penare Point
Tregony
Merther
Mevagissey
Chapel Point
Malpas
St Clement
Portmellon
Kea
St Michael Penkevil
Ruan Lanihorne
St Michael Caerhays
Rescassa
Gorran
Gorran Haven
Old Kea
Lamorran
Boswinger
Maenease Point
Trelissick Garden NT
Philleigh
Veryan Bay
Veryan
Portloe
DODMAN POINT
Feock
Trewithian
The Roseland Heritage Coast
Gerrans Bay
Nare Head
St Just-in-Roseland
Portscatho
Mylor
Gerrans
Flushing
Carrick Roads
Greeb Point
St Mawes
Pendennis
Bohortha
Falmouth
Pendennis Point
South West Coast Path
ZONE POINT
Falmouth Bay
Manacle Point
Porthoustock
Lowland Point
1
2
3
4
5
6
0 1 2 3 4 miles
0 1 2 3 4 5 kilometres

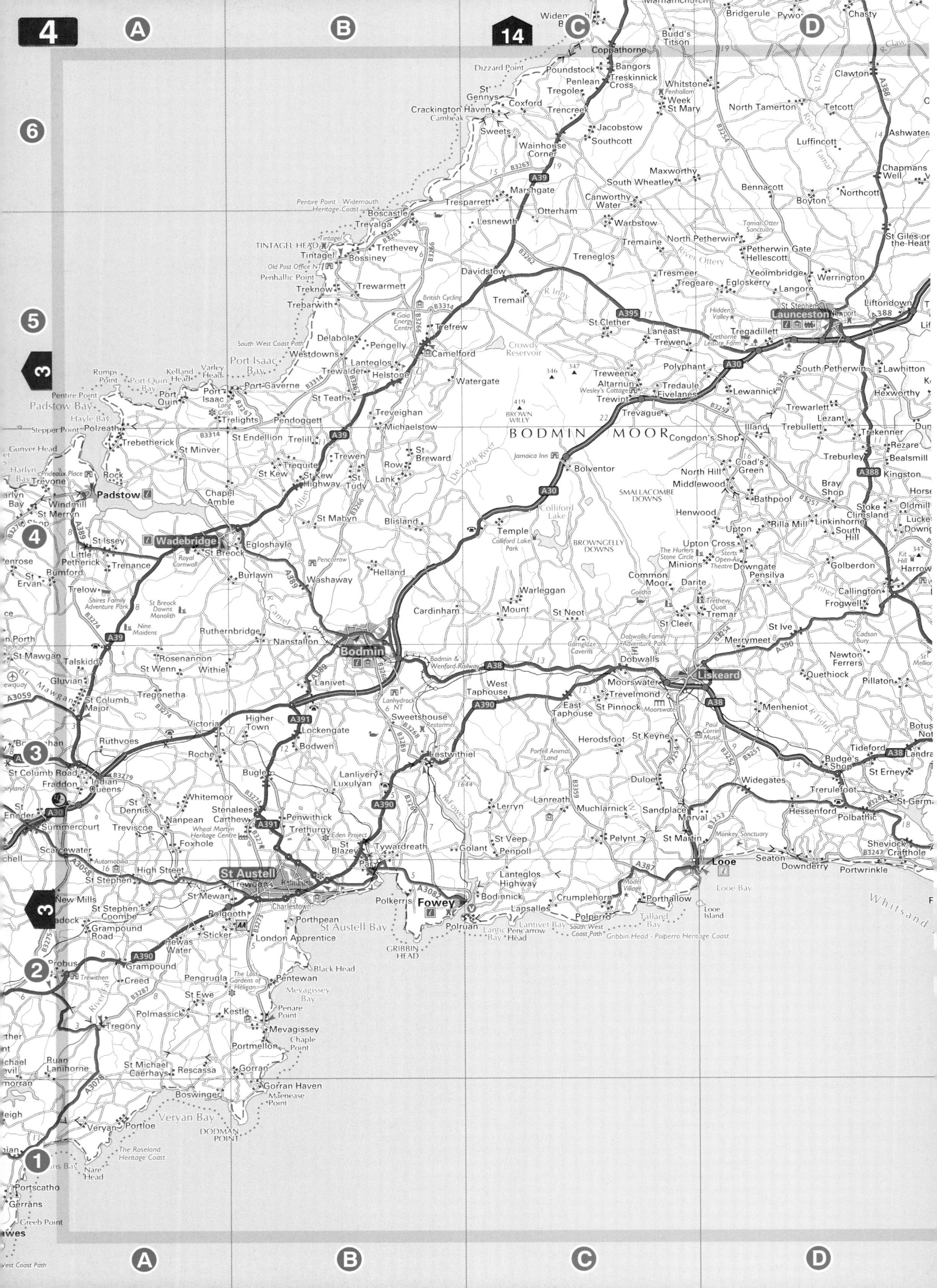

4
A
B
14
C
D
6
5
4
3
2
1
3
3
Widemouth Bay
Marhamchurch
Bridgerule
Pyworthy
Chasty
Budd's Titson
Coppathorne
Dizzard Point
Poundstock
Bangors
Treskinnick Cross
Penlean
Whitstone
Penhallam
Week St Mary
Tregole
St Gennys
Coxford
Trencreek
Crackington Haven
Cambeak
Sweets
Jacobstow
Southcott
Wainhouse Corner
North Tamerton
Tetcott
Clawton
Luffincott
Ashwater
Chapmans Well
Maxworthy
South Wheatley
Bennacott
Boyton
Northcott
Pentire Point - Widemouth Heritage Coast
Tresparrett
Marshgate
Canworthy Water
Otterham
Boscastle
Trevalga
Lesnewth
Warbstow
Tamar Otter Sanctuary
St Giles on the Heath
TINTAGEL HEAD
Tintagel
Trethevey
Bossiney
Old Post Office NT
Tremaine
North Petherwin
Petherwin Gate
Hellescott
River Ottery
Treneglos
Penhallic Point
Davidstow
Yeolmbridge
Werrington
Tresmeer
Tregeare
Egloskerry
Langore
Treknow
Trewarmett
Trebarwith
British Cycling
Tremail
R. Inny
Liftondown
Gaia Energy Centre
Trefrew
St Clether
A395
Hidden Valley
St Stephens
Launceston
Newport
A388
Delabole
Pengelly
Laneast
Trewen
Tregadillett
Trethorne Leisure Farm
South West Coast Path
Westdowns
Camelford
Crowdy Reservoir
Port Isaac Bay
Lanteglos
Trewalder
Helstone
Polyphant
A30
South Petherwin
Lawhitton
Rumps Point
Port Quin Bay
Kelland Head
Varley Head
Watergate
346
347
Treween
Altarnun
Wesley's Cottage
Tredaule
Fivelanes
Lewannick
Hexworthy
Pentire Point
Port Quin
Port Isaac
Port-Gaverne
St Teath
Long Cross
Padstow Bay
Hayle Bay
Trelights
Pendoggett
Treveighan
419
BROWN WILLY
Trewint
Trevague
Trewarlett
Lezant
Stepper Point
Polzeath
Michaelstow
Illand
Trebullett
Trekenner
Trebetherick
St Endellion
Trelill
BODMIN MOOR
Congdon's Shop
Rezare
Gunver Head
St Minver
St Breward
Bealsmill
Harlyn Bay
Prideaux Place
Trewen
Jamaica Inn
Treburley
Trevone
Rock
Trequite
Row
De Lank River
Bolventor
Coad's Green
North Hill
Kingston
St Kew
St Kew Highway
Lank
St Tudy
Middlewood
Padstow
Chapel Amble
Windmill
St Merryn
SMALLACOMBE DOWNS
Bray Shop
Bathpool
Stoke Climsland
Oldmill
St Mabyn
Blisland
Colliford Lake
Henwood
Linkinhorne
Rilla Mill
Upton
South Hill
St Issey
Wadebridge
Egloshayle
Temple
Colliford Lake Park
BROWNGELLY DOWNS
Upton Cross
The Hurlers Stone Circle
Minions
Sterts Open-Air Theatre
Downgate
Little Petherick
St Breock
Royal Cornwall
Trenance
Pencarrow
Helland
Golberdon
Harrowbarrow
Rumford
St Ervan
Burlawn
Washaway
Common Moor
Darite
Pensilva
Callington
Trelow
Shires Family Adventure Park
St Breock Downs Monolith
Warleggan
Golitha
Trethevy Quoit
Frogwell
Nine Maidens
Cardinham
Mount
St Neot
Tremar
R. Camel
Ruthernbridge
A389
A39
St Cleer
St Ive
Nanstallon
Bodmin
Carnglaze Caverns
Dobwalls Family Adventure Park
Merrymeet
A390
Cadson Bury
St Mawgan
Talskiddy
Rosenannon
Bodmin & Wenford Railway
A38
Dobwalls
Newton Ferrers
St Mellion
St Wenn
Withiel
Liskeard
Quethiock
Gluvian
Lanivet
West Taphouse
Moorswater
Pillaton
A3059
St Columb Major
Tregonetha
Lanhydrock NT
Trevelmond
East Taphouse
St Pinnock
Menheniot
Victoria
Higher Town
A391
Lockengate
Sweetshouse
Restormel
Ruthvoes
Bodwen
Herodsfoot
St Keyne
Paul Corin Music
Botus Fleming
Roche
Lostwithiel
Porfell Animal Land
Tideford
St Columb Road
Indian Queens
B3279
Bugle
Lanlivery
Luxulyan
Duloe
Budge's Shop
St Erney
Fraddon
Widegates
Landrake
Whitemoor
St Dennis
1644
Trerulefoot
Stenalees
Carthew
Penwithick
Lerryn
Lanreath
Muchlarnick
Sandplace
Morval
Hessenford
Polbathic
St Germans
St Enoder
Summercourt
Treviscoe
Nanpean
Wheal Martyn Heritage Centre
Trethurgy
Eden Project
St Blazey
Tywardreath
St Veep
Penpoll
Pelynt
St Martin
Monkey Sanctuary
Sheviock
Crafthole
Foxhole
Golant
Scarcewater
Automobilia
A3058
High Street
St Austell
Par
Lanteglos Highway
Looe
Seaton
Downderry
Portwrinkle
St Stephen
Trewoon
Holmbush
Model Village
New Mills
St Mewan
Charlestown
A3082
Polkerris
Fowey
Bodinnick
Crumplehorn
Porthallow
Looe Bay
Whitsand Bay
St Stephen's Coombe
Polgooth
Porthpean
Lansallos
Polperro
Looe Island
Grampound Road
Sticker
St Austell Bay
Polruan
Lantic Bay
Pencarrow Head
Lantivet Bay
Talland Bay
South West Coast Path
Gribbin Head - Polperro Heritage Coast
Hewas Water
London Apprentice
GRIBBIN HEAD
Probus
Trewithen
Grampound
A390
Black Head
Creed
Pengrugla
The Lost Gardens of Heligan
Pentewan
Mevagissey Bay
St Ewe
Penare Point
Polmassick
Kestle
River Fal
Tregony
Mevagissey
Portmellon
Chaple Point
Ruan Lanihorne
St Michael Caerhays
Rescassa
Gorran
A3078
Gorran Haven
Maenease Point
Boswinger
Veryan Bay
Veryan
Portloe
DODMAN POINT
The Roseland Heritage Coast
Nare Head
Portscatho
Gerrans
Greeb Point
West Coast Path

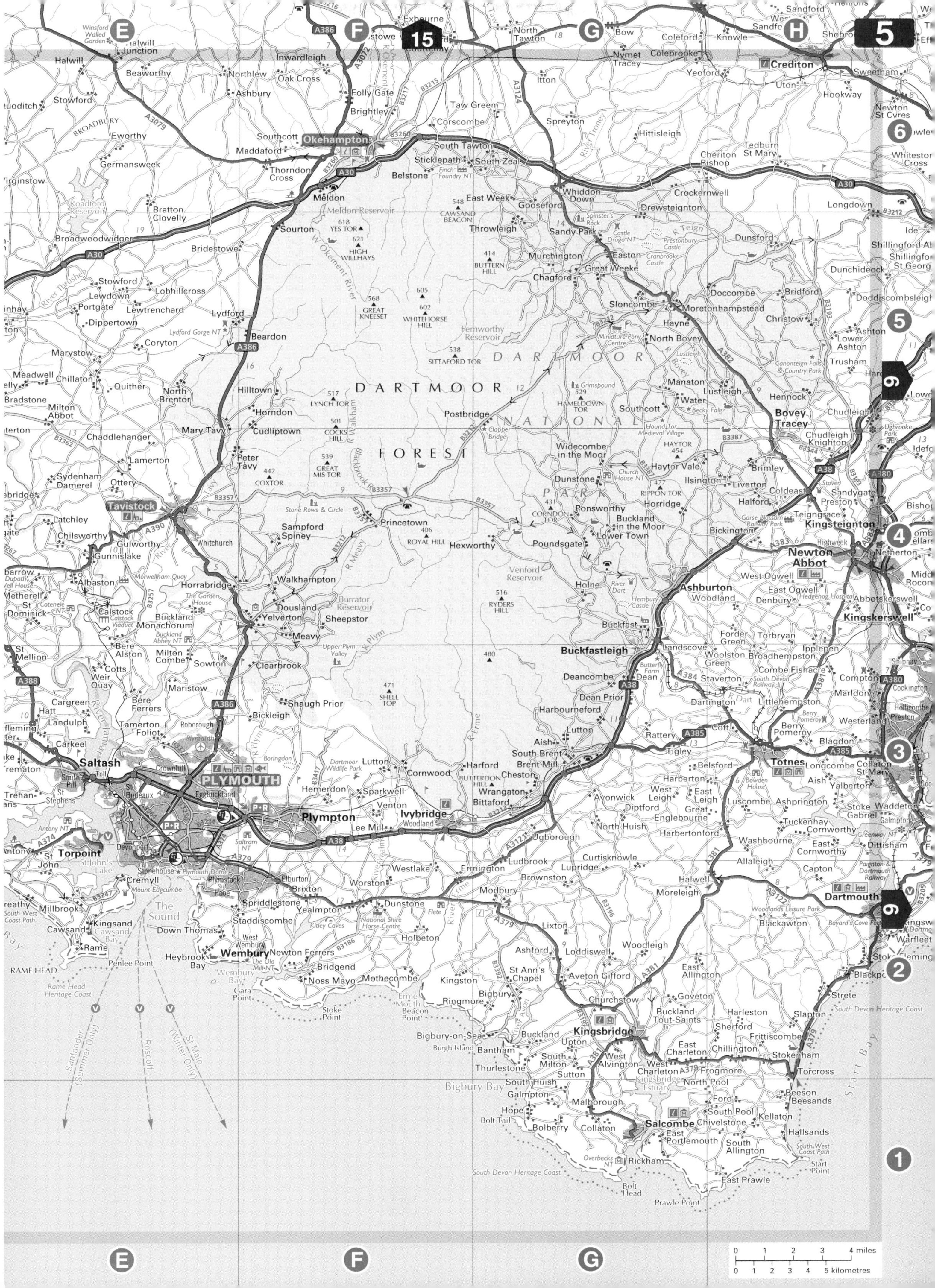

E
F
G
H
15
5
Winsford Walled Garden
Halwill Junction
Halwill
Exbourne
North Tawton
Bow
Sandford
Coleford
Knowle
Shobrooke
Nymet Tracey
Colebrooke
Crediton
Inwardleigh
Beaworthy
Northlew
Oak Cross
Ashbury
Itton
Yeoford
Sweetham
Uton
Hookway
Folly Gate
Brightley
Taw Green
Corscombe
Spreyton
Newton St Cyres
Stowford
Broadbury
Eworthy
Southcott
Okehampton
Hittisleigh
Maddaford
South Tawton
Tedburn St Mary
Cheriton Bishop
Whitestone Cross
Germansweek
Thorndon Cross
Sticklepath
South Zeal
Finch Foundry NT
Belstone
Virginstow
Meldon
Whiddon Down
Crockernwell
Longdown
Roadford Reservoir
Bratton Clovelly
548 East Week
Cawsand Beacon
Gooseford
Drewsteignton
Meldon Reservoir
618 Yes Tor
621 High Willhays
Sourton
Throwleigh
Spinster's Rock
Sandy Park
Castle Drogo NT
Prestonbury Castle
Dunsford
Ide
Broadwoodwidger
Bridestowe
414 Buttern Hill
Murchington
Easton
Cranbrook Castle
Shillingford Abbot
Shillingford St George
Great Weeke
Chagford
Dunchideock
River Thrushel
Stowford
Lewdown
Lobhillcross
Portgate
Lewtrenchard
W Okement River
568 Great Kneeset
605
602 Whitehorse Hill
Sloncombe
Moretonhampstead
Doccombe
Bridford
Doddiscombsleigh
Lydford
Dippertown
Lydford Gorge NT
Beardon
Fernworthy Reservoir
Hayne
Christow
Ashton
Coryton
Miniature Pony Centre
North Bovey
Lower Ashton
Marystow
538 Sittaford Tor
DARTMOOR
Lustleigh
Canonteign Falls & Country Park
Trusham
Meadwell
Chillaton
Quither
Grimspound
Manaton
North Brentor
Hilltown
DARTMOOR NATIONAL FOREST PARK
517 Lynch Tor
529 Hameldown Tor
Lustleigh
Hennock
Bradstone
Milton Abbot
Horndon
Postbridge
Southcott
Water
Becky Falls
Bovey Tracey
Chudleigh
Mary Tavy
Cudliptown
501 Cocks Hill
Clapper Bridge
Hound Tor Medieval Village
Chudleigh Knighton
Ugbrooke Park
Chaddlehanger
Haytor 454
Widecombe in the Moor
Lamerton
Peter Tavy
539 Great Mis Tor
Blackbrook R
Haytor Vale
Brimley
Ideford
Sydenham Damerel
442 Coxtor
Ottery
Dunstone
Church House NT
Ilsington
Liverton
Coldeast
Stover
Sandygate
477 Rippon Tor
Horridge
Halford
Preston
Bishopsteignton
Tavistock
Stone Rows & Circle
Princetown
431 Corndon Tor
Ponsworthy
Buckland in the Moor
Teigngrace
Kingsteignton
Latchley
Sampford Spiney
Lower Town
Gorse Blossom Railway Park
Bickington
Chilsworthy
Gulworthy
Whitchurch
406 Royal Hill
Hexworthy
Poundsgate
Highweek
Combeinteignhead
Gunnislake
Newton Abbot
Netherton
Venford Reservoir
Morwellham Quay
Walkhampton
Holne
River Dart
Albaston
Horrabridge
The Garden House
Burrator Reservoir
Ashburton
West Ogwell
East Ogwell
Denbury
Hedgehog Hospital
Abbotskerswell
Metherell
Cotehele NT
Calstock
Dousland
Sheepstor
516 Ryders Hill
Hembury Castle
Woodland
Kingskerswell
St Dominick
Calstock Viaduct
Buckland Monachorum
Yelverton
Buckfast
Buckland Abbey NT
Meavy
R Plym
Forder Green
Torbryan
Ipplepen
Bere Alston
Upper Plym Valley
Buckfastleigh
Landscove
St Mellion
Milton Combe
Sowton
480
Woolston Green
Broadhempston
Cotts
Clearbrook
Butterfly Farm
Dean
Staverton
South Devon Railway
Combe Fishacre
Weir Quay
Maristow
Deancombe
Compton
Cockington
Cargreen
Bere Ferrers
471 Shell Top
Shaugh Prior
Dean Prior
Marldon
Hatt
Landulph
Tamerton Foliot
Roborough
Bickleigh
Dartington
Littlehempston
Harbourneford
Berry Pomeroy
Westerland
Saltash
Carkeel
Plymouth
Boringdon
Lutton
Aish
Rattery
Tigley
Totnes
Blagdon
Collaton St Mary
Trematon
South Pill
Crownhill
Dartmoor Wildlife Park
Lutton
Cornwood
Harford
South Brent
Brent Mill
Belsford
Longcombe
PLYMOUTH
Eggbuckland
Butterdon Hill
Cheston
Harberton
Aish
Yalberton
Trehan
St Budeaux
St Stephens
Hemerdon
Sparkwell
Wrangaton
Bittaford
West Leigh
East Leigh
Bowden House
Luscombe
Ashprington
Venton
Avonwick
Diptford
Great Englebourne
Stoke Gabriel
Waddeton
Antony NT
Plympton
Ivybridge
Woodland
Lee Mill
Galmpton
Torpoint
Devonport
Saltram NT
Ugborough
North Huish
Harbertonford
Tuckenhay
Cornworthy
Greenway NT
Antony
St John
St John's Lake
Stonehouse
Plymouth Dome
Plymstock
Elburton
Westlake
Ermington
Ludbrook
Curtisknowle
Lupridge
Washbourne
East Cornworthy
Dittisham
Cremyll
Mount Edgcumbe
Hooe
Brixton
Worston
River Yealm
Brownston
Allaleigh
Capton
Paignton & Dartmouth Railway
Halwell
Moreleigh
Dartmouth
Millbrook
Kingsand
South West Coast Path
The Sound
Spriddlestone
Yealmpton
Dunstone
Flete
Modbury
Woodlands Leisure Park
Blackawton
Bayard's Cove Fort
Kingswear
Cawsand
Staddiscombe
Down Thomas
Kitley Caves
National Shire Horse Centre
Lixton
Warfleet
Rame
Heybrook Bay
Wembury
West Wembury
Newton Ferrers
Holbeton
Loddiswell
Woodleigh
Stoke Fleming
Penlee Point
The Old Mill NT
Bridgend
Ashford
Rame Head
Rame Head Heritage Coast
Wembury Bay
Gara Point
Noss Mayo
Mothecombe
Kingston
St Ann's Chapel
Aveton Gifford
East Allington
Blackpool
Erme Mouth
Beacon Point
Ringmore
Bigbury
Churchstow
Goveton
Strete
Stoke Point
Buckland-Tout-Saints
Harleston
Slapton
South Devon Heritage Coast
Santander (Summer Only)
Roscoff
St Malo (Winter Only)
Bigbury-on-Sea
Burgh Island
Buckland
Kingsbridge
Sherford
Frittiscombe
Bantham
Upton
West Alvington
East Charleton
Chillington
Stokenham
Start Bay
Thurlestone
South Milton
West Charleton
Frogmore
Torcross
Sutton
Kingsbridge Estuary
South Huish
North Pool
Bigbury Bay
Galmpton
Malborough
Ford
Beeson
Beesands
Hope
South Pool
Bolt Tail
Bolberry
Collaton
Salcombe
Chivelstone
Kellaton
Hallsands
East Portlemouth
South Allington
South West Coast Path
Start Point
Overbecks NT
Rickham
South Devon Heritage Coast
East Prawle
Bolt Head
Prawle Point
1
2
3
4
5
6
9
0 1 2 3 4 miles
0 1 2 3 4 5 kilometres

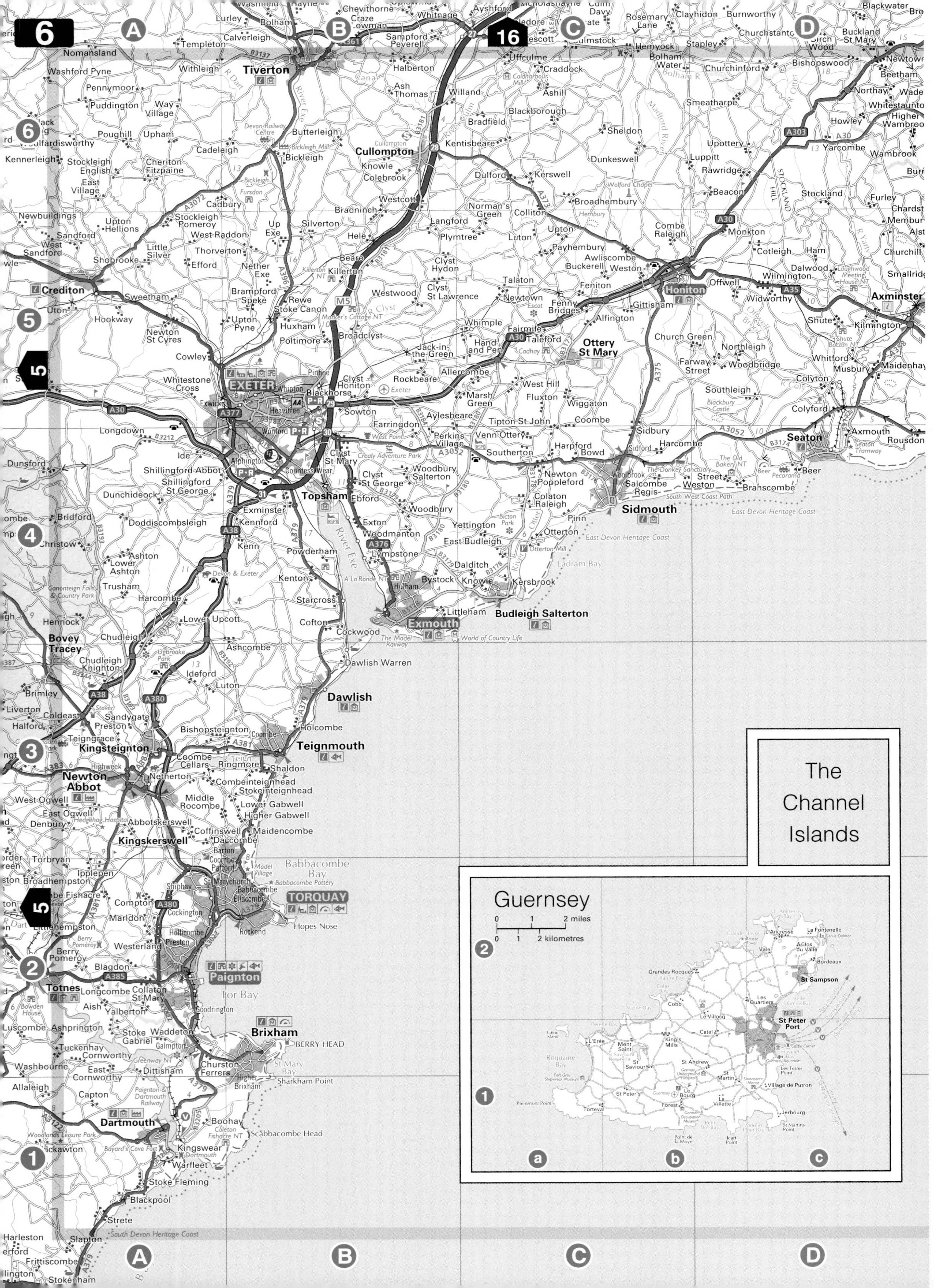

6
A
B
C
D
16
Templeton
Calverleigh
Lurley
Bolham
Chevithorne
Craze Lowman
Sampford Peverell
Whitnage
Ayshford
Uffculme
Culmstock
Hemyock
Clayhidon
Burnworthy
Churchstanton
Rosemary Lane
Stapley
Birch Wood
Buckland St Mary
Blackwater
Nomansland
Washford Pyne
Withleigh
Tiverton
Halberton
Craddock
Bolham Water
Churchinford
Bishopswood
Newtown
Beetham
Pennymoor
Puddington
Way Village
Ash Thomas
Willand
Ashill
Smeatharpe
Northay
Wadeford
Whitestaunton
Poughill
Upham
Woolfardisworthy
Devon Railway Centre
Butterleigh
Bickleigh Mill
Bradfield
Blackborough
Sheldon
Howley
Higher Wambrook
Cadeleigh
Bickleigh
Cullompton
Kentisbeare
Upottery
A30
Yarcombe
Wambrook
Kennerleigh
Stockleigh English
Cheriton Fitzpaine
Knowle
Colebrook
Dunkeswell
Luppitt
Rawridge
East Village
Dulford
Kerswell
Wolford Chapel
Beacon
Stockland
Furley
Chardstock
Cadbury
Westcott
Broadhembury
Newbuildings
Upton Hellions
Stockleigh Pomeroy
West Raddon
Up Exe
Silverton
Bradninch
Norman's Green
Colliton
Langford
Hele
Plymtree
Luton
Upton
Combe Raleigh
Monkton
Membury
Sandford
West Sandford
Little Silver
Thorverton
Efford
Shobrooke
Nether Exe
Beare
Killerton
Clyst Hydon
Payhembury
Awliscombe
Buckerell
Weston
Cotleigh
Ham
Churchill
Dalwood
Wilmington
Smallridge
Crediton
Sweetham
Brampford Speke
Rewe
Stoke Canon
Westwood
Clyst St Lawrence
Talaton
Newtown
Escot
Fenny Bridges
Feniton
Gittisham
Honiton
Offwell
Widworthy
Axminster
Uton
Hookway
Newton St Cyres
Upton Pyne
Huxham
Poltimore
Broadclyst
Whimple
Fairmile
Talaford
Alfington
Ottery St Mary
Church Green
Northleigh
Shute
Kilmington
Cowley
Jack-in-the-Green
Hand and Pen
Cadhay
Farway Street
Woodbridge
Whitford
Musbury
Maidenhayne
Whitestone Cross
EXETER
Pinhoe
Whipton
Clyst Honiton
Blackhorse
Rockbeare
Allercombe
West Hill
Colyton
Southleigh
Exwick
Heavitree
Sowton
Marsh Green
Fluxton
Wiggaton
Colyford
Axmouth
Longdown
Wonford
Farringdon
Aylesbeare
Perkins Village
Tipton St John
Coombe
Venn Ottery
Sidbury
Harcombe
Seaton
Rousdon
Ide
Alphington
Countess Wear
Clyst St Mary
Crealy Adventure Park
Southerton
Harpford
Bowd
Sidford
Beer
Pecorama
Dunsford
Shillingford Abbot
Shillingford St George
Clyst St George
Woodbury Salterton
Newton Poppleford
The Donkey Sanctuary
Salcombe Regis
Street
Weston
Branscombe
Dunchideock
Exminster
Topsham
Ebford
Colaton Raleigh
Sidmouth
South West Coast Path
East Devon Heritage Coast
Bridford
Doddiscombsleigh
Kennford
Woodbury
Yettington
Bicton Park
Pinn
Otterton
Otterton Mill
Christow
Kenn
Exton
Woodmanton
East Budleigh
Powderham
Lympstone
River Exe
Ashton
Lower Ashton
Dalditch
Knowle
Kersbrook
Ladram Bay
Canonteign Falls & Country Park
Trusham
Kenton
A La Ronde NT
Bystock
Harcombe
Starcross
Exmouth
Littleham
Budleigh Salterton
Hennock
Lower Upcott
Cofton
Cockwood
Bovey Tracey
Chudleigh
The Model Railway
World of Country Life
Ashcombe
Ugbrooke Park
Chudleigh Knighton
Ideford
Dawlish Warren
Luton
Brimley
Dawlish
Liverton
Coldeast
Stover
Sandygate
Preston
Halford
Holcombe
Bishopsteignton
Teigngrace
Kingsteignton
Teignmouth
Coombe
Coombe Cellars
Ringmore
Shaldon
Highweek
Newton Abbot
Netherton
Combeinteignhead
Stokeinteignhead
West Ogwell
East Ogwell
Middle Rocombe
Lower Gabwell
Higher Gabwell
Denbury
Hedgehog Hospital
Abbotskerswell
Coffinswell
Maidencombe
Kingskerswell
Daccombe
Barton
Torbryan
Ipplepen
Coombe
Babbacombe Bay
Model Village
Broadhempston
St Marychurch
Babbacombe
Babbacombe Pottery
Shiphay
Fishacre
Compton
Ellacombe
TORQUAY
Marldon
Cockington
Littlehempston
Rockend
Hopes Nose
Berry Pomeroy
Westerland
Livermead
Preston
Blagdon
Paignton
Totnes
Longcombe
Collaton St Mary
Tor Bay
Bowden House
Aish
Yalberton
Goodrington
Luscombe
Ashprington
Stoke Gabriel
Waddeton
Brixham
Galmpton
BERRY HEAD
Tuckenhay
Cornworthy
Greenway NT
Churston Ferrers
St Mary Bay
Washbourne
East Cornworthy
Dittisham
Higher Brixham
Sharkham Point
Allaleigh
Capton
Paignton & Dartmouth Railway
Dartmouth
Boohay
Coleton Fishacre NT
Scabbacombe Head
Woodlands Leisure Park
Blackawton
Boyard's Cove Fort
Kingswear
Dartmouth
Warfleet
Stoke Fleming
Blackpool
Strete
Harleston
Slapton
South Devon Heritage Coast
Frittiscombe
Stokenham
The Channel Islands
Guernsey
0 1 2 miles
0 1 2 kilometres
2
1
a
b
c
L'Ancresse
La Fontenelle
Vale
Clos du Valle
Bordeaux
Grandes Rocques
St Sampson
Cobo
Les Quartiers
Le Villocq
Catel
St Peter Port
L'Erée
Mont Saint
King's Mills
Rocquaine Bay
St Saviour
St Andrew
St Martin
Les Terres Point
St Peter's
Le Bourg
Village de Putron
Pleinmont Point
Torteval
Forest
La Villette
Jerbourg
St Martins Point
Icart Point
Point de la Moye

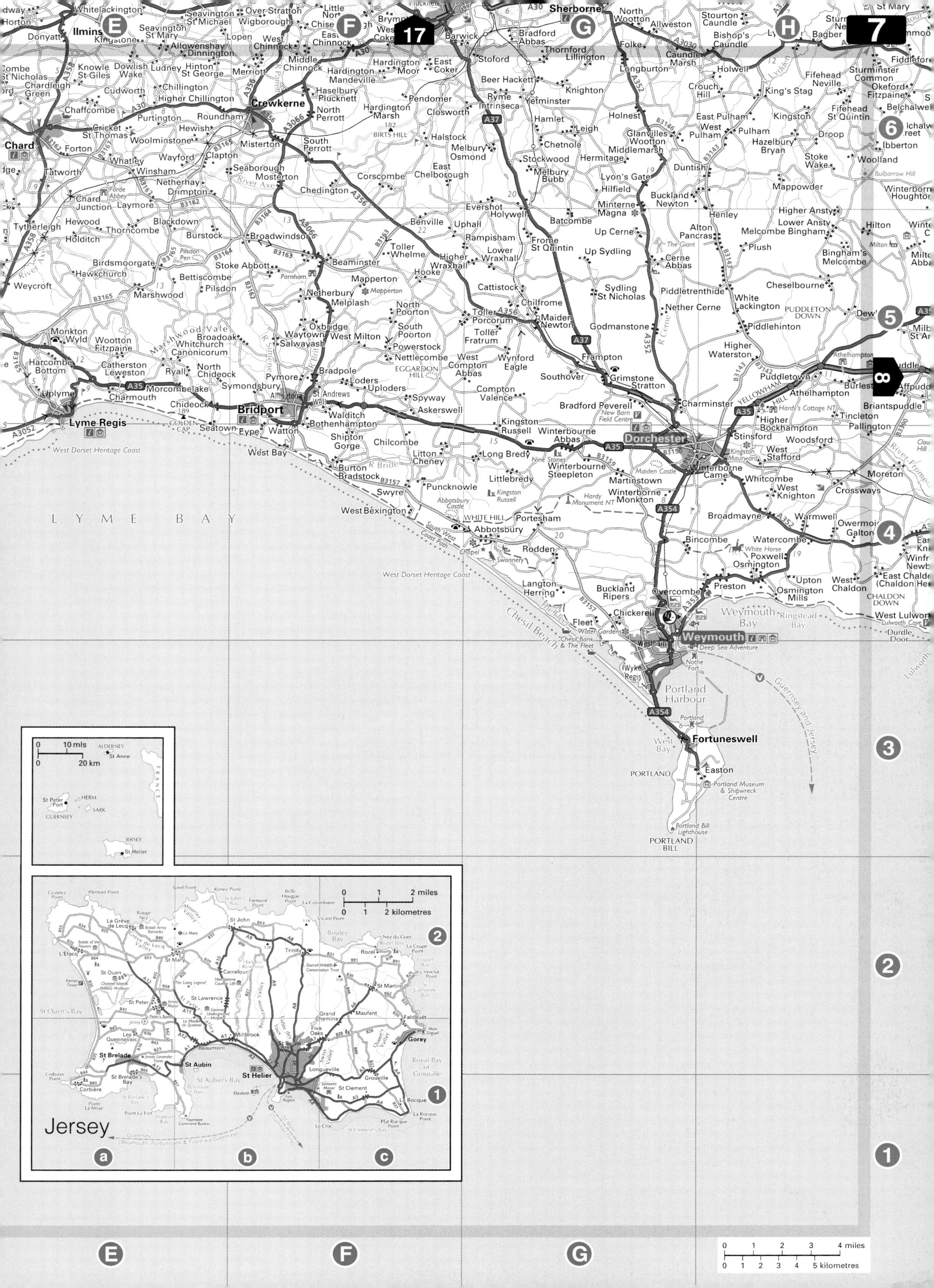

17
7
8
Sherborne
Ilminster
Crewkerne
Chard
Bridport
Lyme Regis
Dorchester
Weymouth
Fortuneswell
Easton
Whitelackington
Seavington St Michael
Over Stratton
Seavington St Mary
Wigborough
Lopen
Allowenshay
Dinnington
West Chinnock
Middle Chinnock
East Chinnock
Hardington Mandeville
Hardington Moor
East Coker
Barwick
Stoford
Bradford Abbas
Thornford
Lillington
North Wootton
Allweston
Stourton Caundle
Bishop's Caundle
Folke
Caundle Marsh
Longburton
Holwell
Fifehead Neville
Sturminster Common
Okeford Fitzpaine
King's Stag
Crouch Hill
Beer Hackett
Knighton
Ryme Intrinseca
Yetminster
Hamlet
Leigh
Holnest
Glanvilles Wootton
Middlemarsh
East Pulham
West Pulham
Pulham
Kingston
Hazelbury Bryan
Droop
Fifehead St Quintin
Ibberton
Woolland
Stoke Wake
Dowlish Wake
Knowle St Giles
Cudworth
Chillington
Higher Chillington
Chaffcombe
Cricket St Thomas
Purtington
Roundham
Hewish
Woolminstone
Misterton
Clapton
Wayford
Forton
Whatley
Winsham
Tatworth
Seaborough
Mosterton
South Perrott
North Perrott
Haselbury Plucknett
Pendomer
Closworth
Halstock
Melbury Osmond
East Chelborough
Corscombe
Chedington
Chetnole
Stockwood
Melbury Bubb
Hermitage
Lyon's Gate
Hilfield
Minterne Magna
Buckland Newton
Duntish
Mappowder
Higher Ansty
Lower Ansty
Melcombe Bingham
Bingham's Melcombe
Henley
Alton Pancras
Plush
Netherhay
Drimpton
Chard Junction
Laymore
Tytherleigh
Holditch
Hewood
Thorncombe
Blackdown
Burstock
Broadwindsor
Evershot
Holywell
Batcombe
Up Cerne
Up Sydling
Cerne Abbas
Benville
Uphall
Rampisham
Frome St Quintin
Toller Whelme
Lower Wraxhall
Higher Wraxhall
Hooke
Beaminster
Birdsmoorgate
Hawkchurch
Stoke Abbott
Bettiscombe
Pilsdon
Weycroft
Marshwood
Mapperton
Netherbury
Melplash
Cattistock
Chilfrome
Sydling St Nicholas
Piddletrenthide
Cheselbourne
White Lackington
Nether Cerne
Piddlehinton
North Poorton
South Poorton
Toller Porcorum
Toller Fratrum
Maiden Newton
Godmanstone
Monkton Wyld
Wootton Fitzpaine
Marshwood Vale
Whitchurch Canonicorum
Broadoak
Oxbridge
Waytown
Salwayash
West Milton
Powerstock
Nettlecombe
West Compton
Compton Abbas
Wynford Eagle
Frampton
Higher Waterston
Harcombe Bottom
Catherston Leweston
Ryall
North Chideock
Pymore
Bradpole
Loders
Uploders
Southover
Grimstone
Stratton
Puddletown
Athelhampton
Burleston
Tolpuddle
Affpuddle
Briantspuddle
Uplyme
Charmouth
Morcombelake
Symondsbury
Chideock
Allington
St Andrews Well
Waldtich
Spyway
Askerswell
Compton Valence
Bradford Peverell
Charminster
Tincleton
Pallington
Seatown
Eype
Watton
Bothenhampton
Shipton Gorge
Chilcombe
Litton Cheney
Long Bredy
Kingston Russell
Winterbourne Abbas
Winterbourne Steepleton
Martinstown
Winterborne Came
Stinsford
Higher Bockhampton
Woodsford
West Stafford
Whitcombe
West Knighton
Moreton
Crossways
West Bay
Burton Bradstock
Swyre
Puncknowle
Littlebredy
Winterborne Monkton
Broadmayne
Warmwell
Owermoigne
Galton
West Bexington
Abbotsbury
Portesham
Rodden
Bincombe
Watercombe
Poxwell
Osmington
Osmington Mills
Preston
Upton
West Chaldon
Langton Herring
Buckland Ripers
Overcombe
Fleet
Chickerell
Westham
Wyke Regis
Weymouth Bay
Portland Harbour
West Bay
PORTLAND
PORTLAND BILL
L Y M E   B A Y
West Dorset Heritage Coast
Chesil Beach
Guernsey and Jersey
Jersey
St Helier
St Aubin
St Brelade
Gorey
St Ouen
St Peter
St Lawrence
St Mary
St John
Trinity
St Martin
St Clement
Grouville
Longueville
La Rocque
Beaumont
Millbrook
Carrefour
L'Etacq
Corbière
St Aubin's Bay
St Ouen's Bay
Royal Bay of Grouville
Bouley Bay
St Anne
St Peter Port
GUERNSEY
HERM
SARK
ALDERNEY
JERSEY
FRANCE
0 10 mls
0 20 km
0 1 2 miles
0 1 2 kilometres
0 1 2 3 4 miles
0 1 2 3 4 5 kilometres

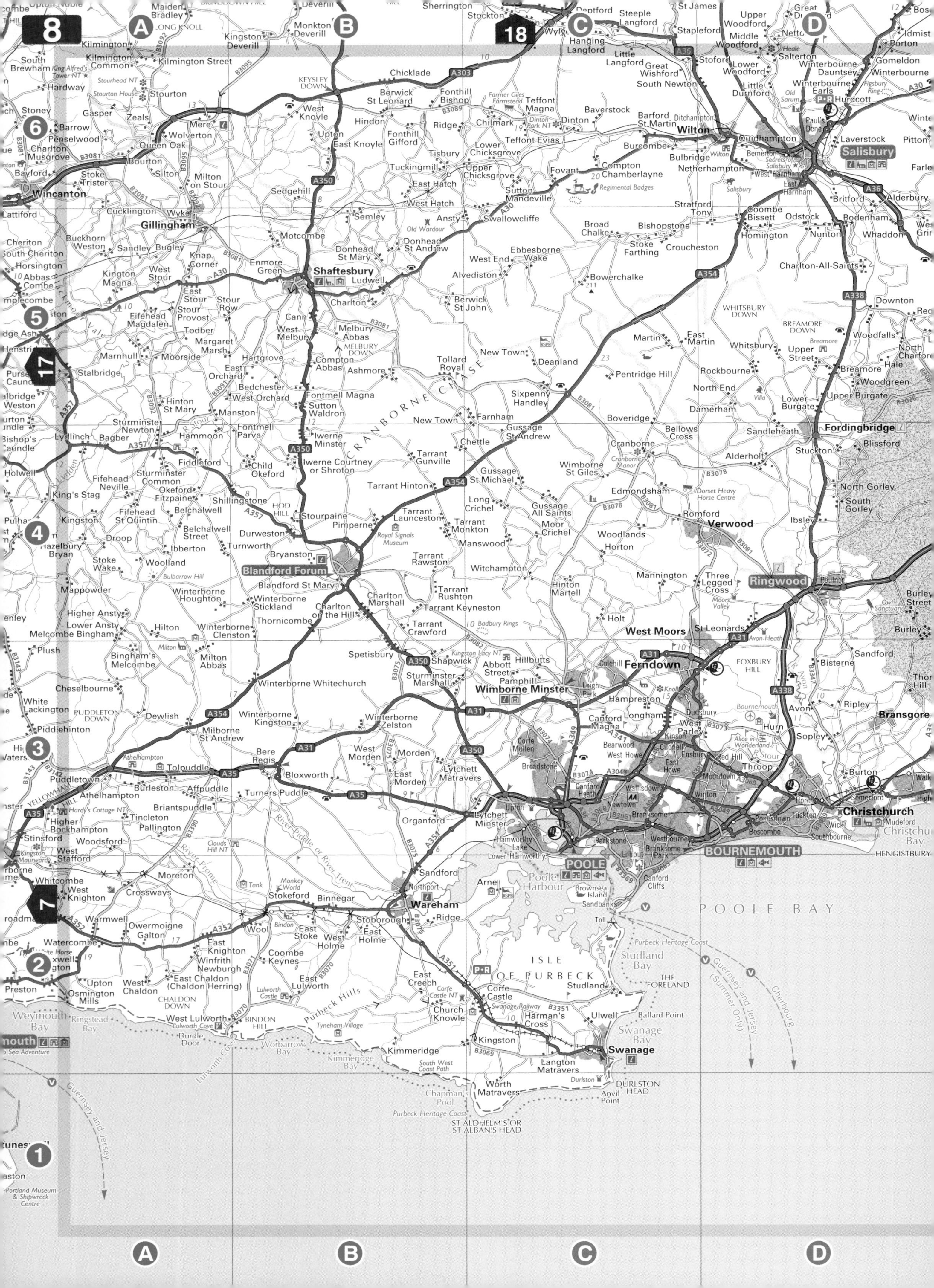

8
A
B
C
D
18
17
7
6
5
4
3
2
1
Maiden Bradley
Long Knoll
Kilmington
Kilmington Common
Kilmington Street
South Brewham
King Alfred's Tower NT
Hardway
Stourhead NT
Stourton House
Stourton
Kingston Deverill
Monkton Deverill
Sherrington
Stockton
Deptford
Wylye
Steeple Langford
Hanging Langford
Little Langford
Great Wishford
South Newton
St James
Stapleford
Upper Woodford
Middle Woodford
Lower Woodford
Little Durnford
Stoford
Heale
Netton
Great Durnford
Salterton
Winterbourne Dauntsey
Winterbourne Earls
Gomeldon
Winterbourne
Porton
Idmiston
Old Sarum
Figsbury Ring
Hurdcott
Chicklade
Keysley Down
Berwick St Leonard
Fonthill Bishop
Farmer Giles Farmstead
Teffont Magna
Stoney Stoke
Barrow
Gasper
Zeals
Mere
Wolverton
West Knoyle
Hindon
Fonthill Gifford
Ridge
Chilmark
Dinton Park NT
Dinton
Baverstock
Barford St Martin
Ditchampton
Wilton
Quidhampton
Bemerton
Penselwood
Charlton Musgrove
Queen Oak
Upton
East Knoyle
Tisbury
Teffont Evias
Lower Chicksgrove
Burcombe
Bulbridge
Netherhampton
Secrets of Salisbury
West Harnham
East Harnham
Paul's Dene
Laverstock
Salisbury
Pitton
Farley
Bayford
Stoke Trister
Bourton
Silton
Milton on Stour
Wincanton
Tuckingmill
Upper Chicksgrove
East Hatch
Fovant
Compton Chamberlayne
Regimental Badges
Sutton Mandeville
Britford
Alderbury
Sedgehill
West Hatch
Semley
Old Wardour
Ansty
Swallowcliffe
Stratford Tony
Coombe Bissett
Odstock
Bodenham
Nunton
Homington
Whaddon
Lattiford
Cucklington
Wyke
Gillingham
Cheriton
South Cheriton
Horsington
Abbas Combe
Templecombe
Buckhorn Weston
Sandley
Bugley
Knap Corner
Motcombe
Donhead St Mary
Donhead St Andrew
Broad Chalke
Bishopstone
Stoke Farthing
Croucheston
Ebbesborne Wake
West End
Charlton-All-Saints
Kington Magna
West Stour
Enmore Green
Shaftesbury
Ludwell
Alvediston
Bowerchalke
East Stour
Stour Row
Stour Provost
Fifehead Magdalen
Cann
Charlton
Berwick St John
Downton
Whitsbury Down
Breamore Down
Woodfalls
Todber
West Melbury
Melbury Abbas
Melbury Down
Margaret Marsh
Hartgrove
East Orchard
Compton Abbas
Ashmore
Tollard Royal
New Town
Deanland
Martin
East Martin
Whitsbury
Upper Street
Breamore
North Charford
Hale
Henstridge
Marnhull
Moorside
Purse Caundle
Stalbridge
Bedchester
West Orchard
Fontmell Magna
Cranborne Chase
Pentridge Hill
Rockbourne
Woodgreen
Stalbridge Weston
Hinton St Mary
Manston
Sutton Waldron
Sixpenny Handley
North End
Damerham
Lower Burgate
Upper Burgate
Sturminster Newton
Fontmell Parva
New Town
Farnham
Boveridge
Bellows Cross
Sandleheath
Fordingbridge
Bishop's Caundle
Lydlinch
Bagber
Hammoon
Iwerne Minster
Gussage St Andrew
Chettle
Cranborne
Cranborne Manor
Blissford
Holwell
Fiddleford
Child Okeford
Iwerne Courtney or Shroton
Tarrant Gunville
Wimborne St Giles
Alderholt
Stuckton
Fifehead Neville
Sturminster Common
Okeford Fitzpaine
Tarrant Hinton
Gussage St Michael
Edmondsham
Dorset Heavy Horse Centre
North Gorley
South Gorley
King's Stag
Shillingstone
Hod Hill
Fifehead St Quintin
Belchalwell
Kingston
Stourpaine
Tarrant Launceston
Long Crichel
Gussage All Saints
Romford
Verwood
Ibsley
Pimperne
Tarrant Monkton
Moor Crichel
Woodlands
Pulham
Droop
Belchalwell Street
Durweston
Royal Signals Museum
Hazelbury Bryan
Ibberton
Turnworth
Manswood
Horton
Bryanston
Stoke Wake
Woolland
Tarrant Rawston
Blandford Forum
Witchampton
Bulbarrow Hill
Mannington
Three Legged Cross
Ringwood
Poulner
Burley Street
Mappowder
Winterborne Houghton
Blandford St Mary
Tarrant Rushton
Hinton Martell
Charlton Marshall
Tarrant Keyneston
Moors Valley
Owl Sanctuary
Higher Ansty
Winterborne Stickland
Charlton on the Hill
Holt
Lower Ansty
Hilton
Thornicombe
Badbury Rings
Tarrant Crawford
West Moors
St Leonards
Burley
Melcombe Bingham
Winterborne Clenston
Milton Abbey
Avon Heath
Plush
Bingham's Melcombe
Milton Abbas
Spetisbury
Kingston Lacy NT
Shapwick
Abbott Street
Hillbutts
Pamphill
Colehill
Ferndown
Foxbury Hill
Bisterne
Sandford
Winterborne Whitechurch
Sturminster Marshall
Wimborne Minster
Leigh Park
Knoll
Hampreston
Cheselbourne
Thorney Hill
White Lackington
Puddleton Down
Dewlish
Winterborne Kingston
Winterborne Zelston
Canford Magna
Longham
Dudsbury
Bournemouth
Ripley
Avon
Bransgore
Piddlehinton
Milborne St Andrew
Corfe Mullen
West Parley
Hurn
Kinson
Alice in Wonderland
Sopley
Bearwood
High Waters
Athelhampton
Bere Regis
West Morden
Morden
Broadstone
West Howe
Ensbury
Red Hill
Throop
Puddletown
Tolpuddle
Bloxworth
Lytchett Matravers
East Howe
Moordown
Burton
Yellowham Hill
Athelhampton
Burleston
Affpuddle
Turners Puddle
East Morden
Canford Heath
Wallisdown
Newtown
Winton
Walkford
Hardy's Cottage NT
Briantspuddle
Upton
Branksome
Pokesdown
Tuckton
Iford
Somerford
Christchurch
Mudeford
Higher Bockhampton
Tincleton
Organford
Lytchett Minster
Hamworthy
Boscombe
Wick
Christchurch Bay
Stinsford
Kingston Maurward
Woodsford
Pallington
River Piddle or River Trent
Clouds Hill NT
Lake
Parkstone
Westbourne
Branksome Park
Southbourne
Hengistbury Head
West Stafford
Lower Hamworthy
Lilliput
Bournemouth
River Frome
Moreton
Tank
Monkey World
Sandford
Poole
Canford Cliffs
Whitcombe
West Knighton
Crossways
Stokeford
Northport
Arne
Poole Harbour
Brownsea Island
Sandbanks
Binnegar
Wareham
Poole Bay
Broadmayne
Warmwell
Owermoigne
Galton
Wool
Bindon
East Stoke
Stoborough
Ridge
Toll
Watercombe
White Horse
Osmington
East Knighton
Winfrith Newburgh
West Holme
East Holme
Purbeck Heritage Coast
Studland Bay
Coombe Keynes
Isle of Purbeck
The Foreland
Guernsey and Jersey (Summer Only)
Cherbourg
Preston
Upton
Osmington Mills
West Chaldon
East Chaldon (Chaldon Herring)
Chaldon Down
East Lulworth
Lulworth Castle
East Creech
Corfe Castle NT
Corfe Castle
Studland
Purbeck Hills
Swanage Railway
Ballard Point
Weymouth Bay
Ringstead Bay
West Lulworth
Lulworth Cove
Bindon Hill
Tyneham Village
Church Knowle
Harman's Cross
Ulwell
Swanage Bay
Weymouth
Sea Adventure
Durdle Door
Worbarrow Bay
Kimmeridge
Kimmeridge Bay
Kingston
Swanage
Lulworth Cove
South West Coast Path
Langton Matravers
Durlston
Durlston Head
Worth Matravers
Chapman's Pool
Anvil Point
Purbeck Heritage Coast
St Aldhelm's or St Alban's Head
Guernsey and Jersey
Fortuneswell
Easton
Portland Museum & Shipwreck Centre
A303
A350
A36
A30
A354
A338
A357
A31
A35
A352
A351
A348
A341
A3049
A3060
B3081
B3089
B3095
B3092
B3078
B3072
B3082
B3075
B3074
B3068
B3065
B3369
B3351
B3069
B3070
B3071
B3390
B3143
B3142
B3073
B3347

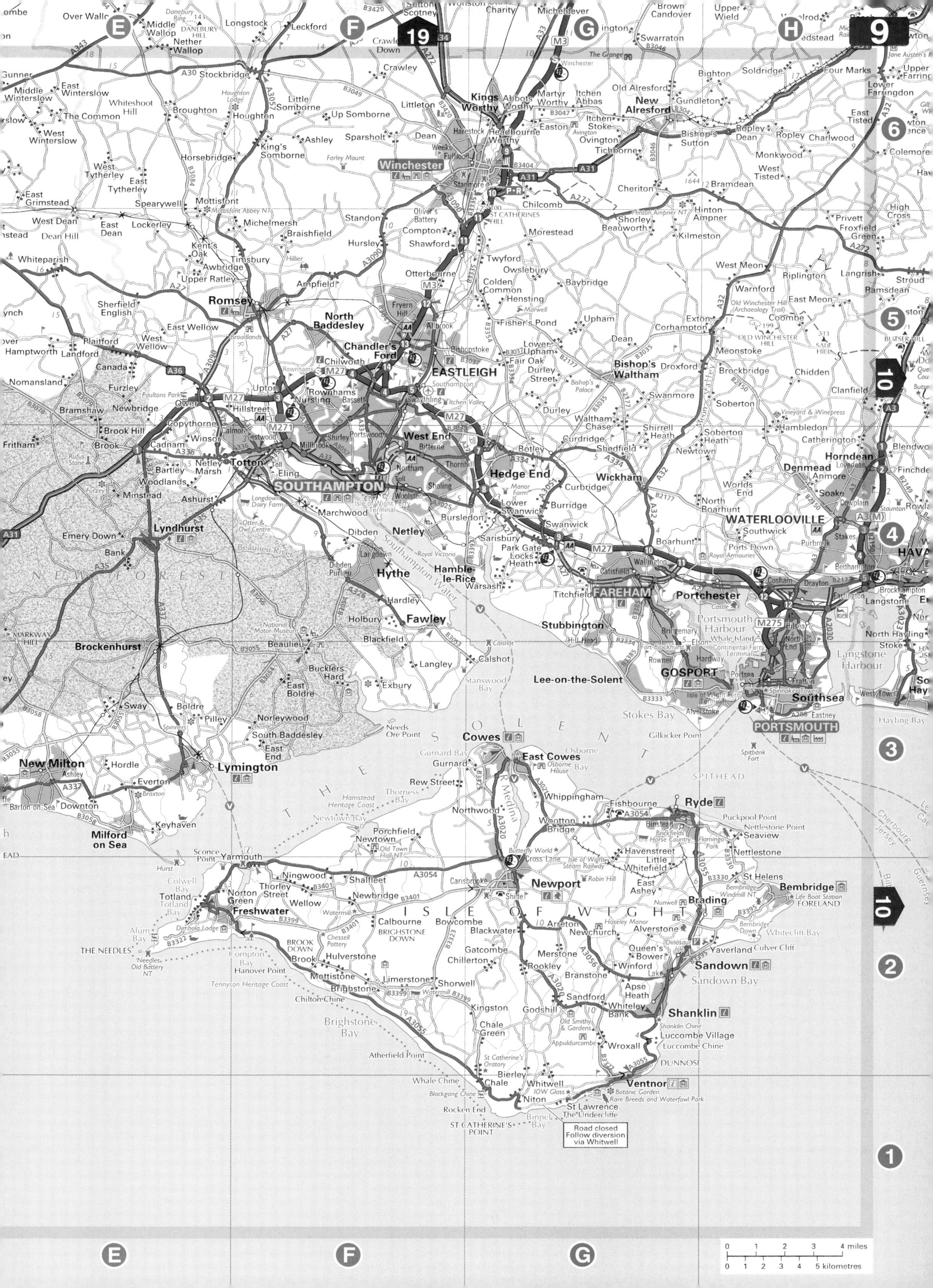

E
F
G
H
19
9
10
6
5
4
3
2
1
Over Wallop
Middle Wallop
Nether Wallop
Longstock
Leckford
Crawley
Stockbridge
Middle Winterslow
East Winterslow
Whiteshoot Hill
Broughton
Houghton
Little Somborne
The Common
West Winterslow
King's Somborne
Up Somborne
Ashley
Sparsholt
Littleton
Kings Worthy
Abbots Worthy
Martyr Worthy
Itchen Abbas
Old Alresford
New Alresford
Bighton
Soldridge
Four Marks
Lower Farringdon
East Tisted
Micheldever
Swarraton
The Grange
Winchester
Harestock
Headbourne Worthy
Weeke
Fulflood
Stanmore
Chilcomb
Easton
Avington
Itchen Stoke
Ovington
Tichborne
Bishop's Sutton
Gundleton
Ropley
Ropley Dean
Charlwood
Monkwood
West Tisted
Colemore
Bramdean
Cheriton
Hinton Ampner
Hinton Ampner NT
Kilmeston
Shorley
Beauworth
High Cross
Privett
Froxfield Green
Horsebridge
West Tytherley
East Tytherley
East Grimstead
Spearywell
Mottisfont
Mottisfont Abbey NT
West Dean
East Dean
Dean Hill
Lockerley
Michelmersh
Braishfield
Standon
Oliver's Battery
Compton
Shawford
Hursley
St Catherines Hill
Morestead
Twyford
Owslebury
Whiteparish
Kent's Oak
Awbridge
Timsbury
Upper Ratley
Ampfield
Otterbourne
Colden Common
Hensting
Marwell
Baybridge
West Meon
Warnford
Riplington
Langrish
Stroud
Ramsdean
East Meon
Old Winchester Hill (Archaeology Trail)
Coombe
Romsey
Sherfield English
East Wellow
West Wellow
Plaitford
Landford
Hamptworth
North Baddesley
Fryern Hill
Allbrook
Chandler's Ford
Chilworth
Bishopstoke
EASTLEIGH
Fisher's Pond
Upham
Lower Upham
Fair Oak
Durley Street
Dean
Exton
Corhampton
Meonstoke
Bishop's Waltham
Droxford
Brockbridge
Chidden
Clanfield
Canada
Furzley
Nomansland
Bramshaw
Newbridge
Paultons Park
Ower
Hillstreet
Upton
Nursling
Rownhams
Bassett
Swaythling
Southampton
Itchen Valley
Durley
Swanmore
Soberton
Hambledon
Brook Hill
Brook
Fritham
Copythorne
Cadnam
Winsor
Calmore
Testwood
Millbrook
Shirley
Portswood
West End
Bitterne
Waltham Chase
Shirrell Heath
Soberton Heath
Catherington
Horndean
Lovedean
Blendworth
Finchdean
Rufus Stone
Bartley
Netley Marsh
Totton
Eling
Woodlands
Minstead
Ashurst
SOUTHAMPTON
Northam
Sholing
Thornhill
Botley
Hedge End
Curdridge
Shedfield
Wickham
Newtown
Denmead
Anmore
Soake
Worlds End
Cowplain
North Boarhunt
WATERLOOVILLE
Southwick
Stakes
Purbrook
Widley
Bedhampton
HAVANT
Rowlands Castle
Longdown Dairy Farm
Otter & Owl Centre
Woolston
Isle of Wight Ferry Terminal
Marchwood
Bursledon
Lower Swanwick
Burridge
Swanwick
Sarisbury
Park Gate
Locks Heath
Manor Farm
Emery Down
Lyndhurst
Bank
Beaulieu River
NEW FOREST
Dibden
Dibden Purlieu
Langdown
Hythe
Netley
Royal Victoria
Hamble-le-Rice
Warsash
Southampton Water
Titchfield
FAREHAM
Catisfield
Wallington
Portchester
Castle
Cosham
Drayton
Farlington
Langstone
Brockhampton
Boarhunt
Ports Down
Royal Armouries
A326
Hardley
Fawley
Holbury
Blackfield
Langley
Calshot
Stanswood Bay
Markway Hill
Brockenhurst
National Motor Museum
Beaulieu
Stubbington
Hill Head
Bridgemary
Elson
Portsmouth Harbour
Whale Island
Continental Ferry Terminal
Hilsea
North End
North Hayling
Stoke
Langstone Harbour
Fort Brockhurst
Rowner
Hardway
GOSPORT
Lee-on-the-Solent
Portsea
Fratton
Southsea
Spinnaker Tower
Eastney
Isle of Wight Ferry Terminal
Alverstoke
Stokes Bay
Gilkicker Point
PORTSMOUTH
Spitbank Fort
West Town
Hayling Bay
Bucklers Hard
East Boldre
Exbury
Sway
Boldre
Pilley
Norleywood
South Baddesley
East End
Needs Ore Point
Spinners
New Milton
Ashley
Hordle
Everton
Lymington
Braxton
Barton on Sea
Downton
Keyhaven
Milford on Sea
Hurst
THE SOLENT
Cowes
East Cowes
Osborne
Osborne House
Osborne Bay
Gurnard Bay
Gurnard
Rew Street
Thorness Bay
Hamstead Heritage Coast
Newtown Bay
Northwood
R Medina
Whippingham
Fishbourne
Ryde
Binstead
Puckpool Point
Nettlestone Point
Seaview
Nettlestone
Brickfields Horse Country
Flamingo Park
Wootton Bridge
Porchfield
Newtown
Old Town Hall NT
Sconce Point
Yarmouth
Colwell Bay
Totland
Totland Bay
Norton Green
Freshwater
Dimbola Lodge
Alum Bay
THE NEEDLES
Needles Old Battery NT
Ningwood
Thorley Street
Shalfleet
Wellow
Newbridge
Watermill
Calbourne
Brighstone Down
Brook Down
Chessell Pottery
Compton Bay
Hanover Point
Tennyson Heritage Coast
Brook
Hulverstone
Mottistone
Brighstone
Chilton Chine
Brighstone Bay
Limerstone
Shorwell
Bowcombe
Carisbrooke
Butterfly World
Cross Lane
Isle of Wight Steam Railway
Robin Hill
Havenstreet
Little Whitefield
Whitefield
East Ashey
Nunwell
Brading
Bembridge Windmill NT
St Helens
Bembridge
Life Boat Station
FORELAND
Bembridge Down
Whitecliff Bay
Culver Cliff
Yaverland
Dinosaur Isle
Sandown
Sandown Bay
Lake
Newport
Shide
ISLE OF WIGHT
Arreton
Haseley Manor
Newchurch
Alverstone
Queen's Bower
Winford
Blackwater
Gatcombe
Chillerton
Merstone
Rookley
Branstone
Apse Heath
Sandford
Godshill
Whiteley Bank
Shanklin
Shanklin Chine
Luccombe Village
Luccombe Chine
Old Smithy & Gardens
Appuldurcombe
Wroxall
DUNNOSE
Kingston
Chale Green
Atherfield Point
St Catherine's Oratory
Bierley
Whale Chine
Blackgang Chine
Chale
Whitwell
IOW Glass
Niton
Rocken End
ST CATHERINE'S POINT
Binnel Bay
St Lawrence
The Undercliff
Ventnor
Botanic Garden
Rare Breeds and Waterfowl Park
Road closed Follow diversion via Whitwell
SPITHEAD
Cherbourg
Jersey
Guernsey
0 1 2 3 4 miles
0 1 2 3 4 5 kilometres

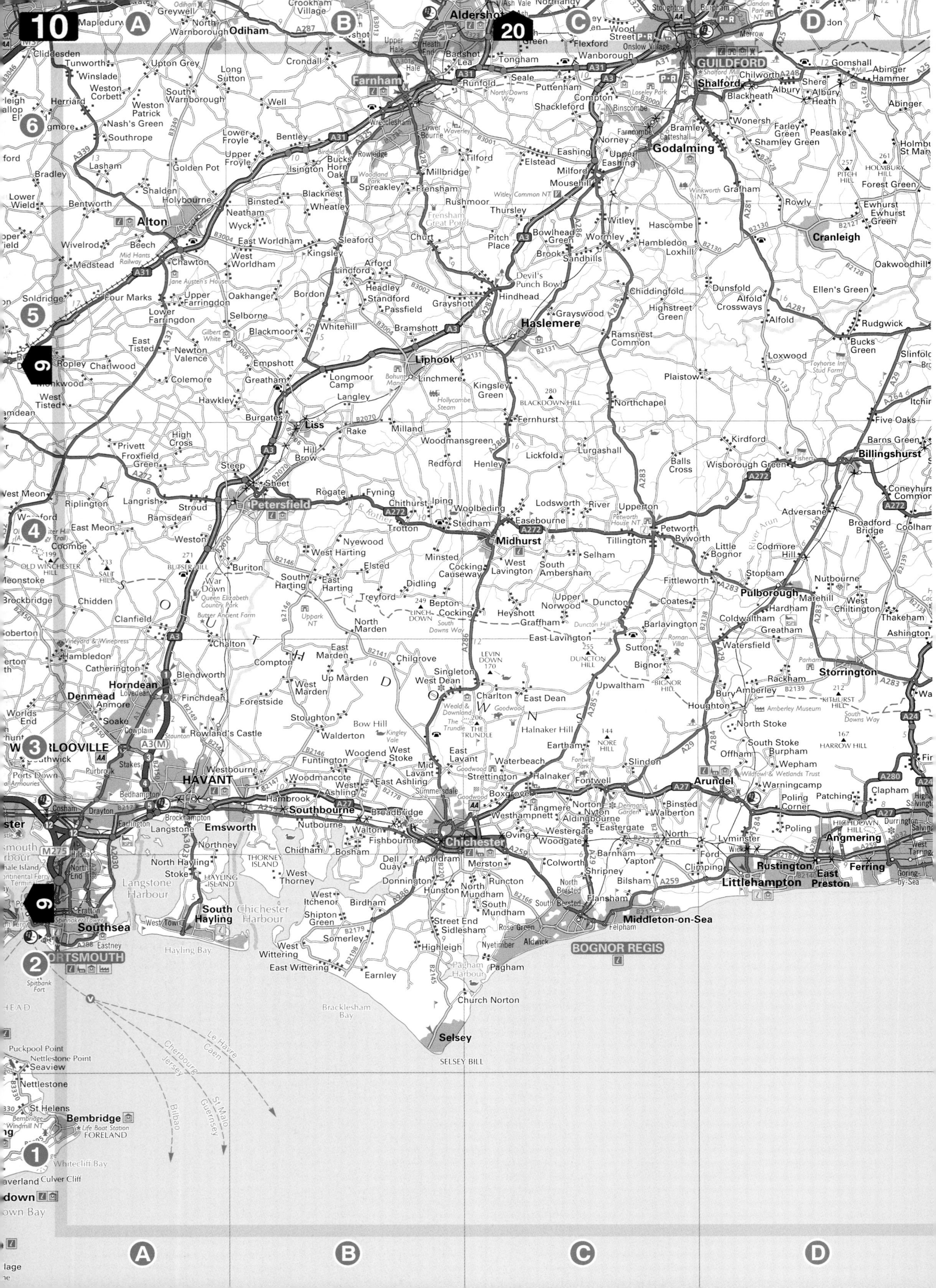

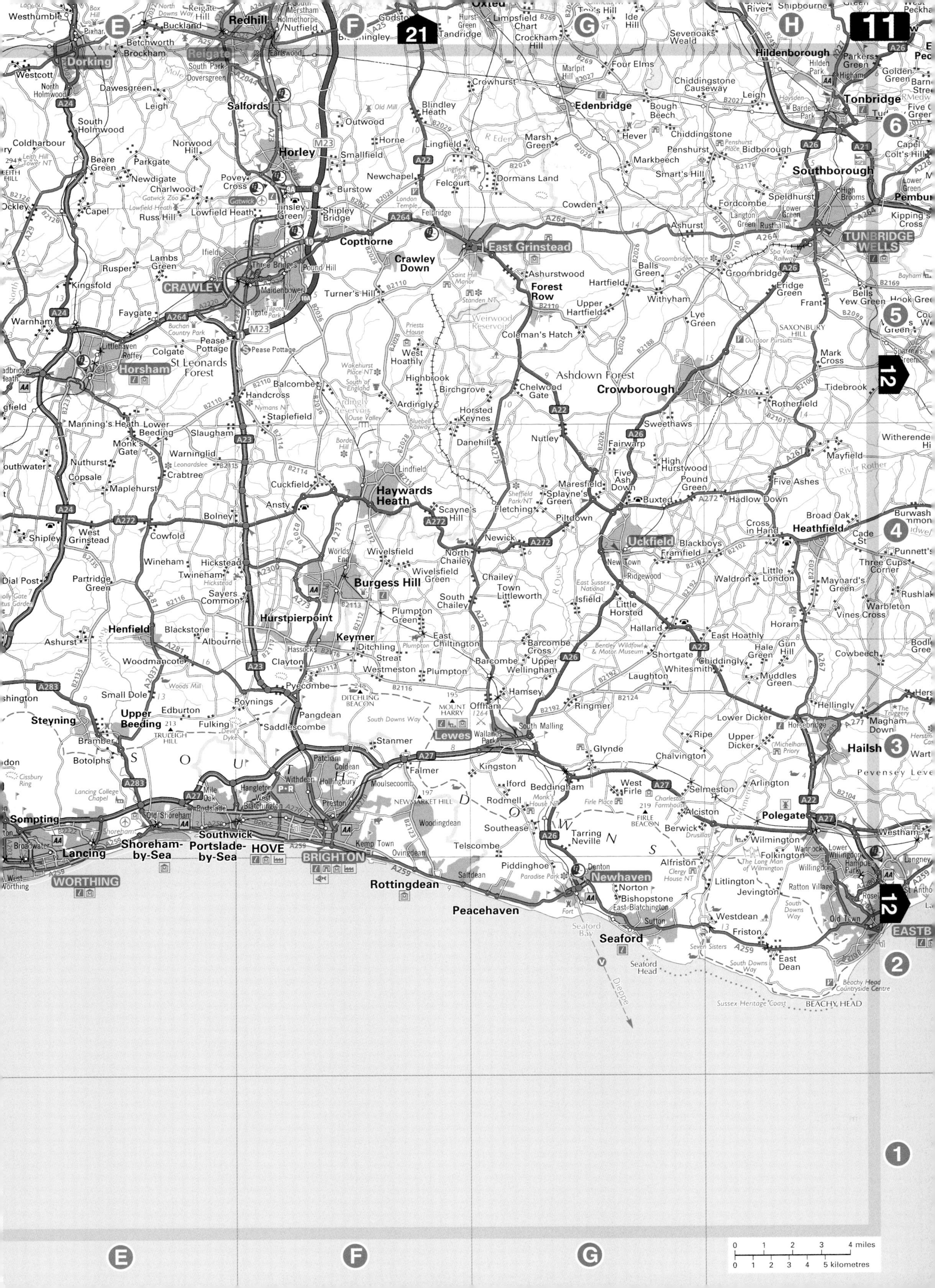

21
11
12
E
F
G
H
1
2
3
4
5
6
Westhumble
Redhill
Reigate
Dorking
Nutfield
Buckland
Betchworth
Brockham
South Park
Doversgreen
Earlswood
Bletchingley
Godstone
Oxted
Tandridge
Limpsfield Chart
Crockham Hill
Toy's Hill
Ide Hill
Sevenoaks Weald
Shipbourne
Hildenborough
Tonbridge
Four Elms
Marlpit Hill
Chiddingstone Causeway
Leigh
Edenbridge
Bough Beech
Hever
Chiddingstone
Penshurst
Bidborough
Southborough
Markbeech
Smart's Hill
Westcott
North Holmwood
Dawesgreen
Leigh
Salfords
Outwood
Blindley Heath
Crowhurst
South Holmwood
Coldharbour
Norwood Hill
Horne
Lingfield
Marsh Green
Horley
Smallfield
Beare Green
Parkgate
Newdigate
Charlwood
Povey Cross
Newchapel
Felcourt
Dormans Land
Burstow
Gatwick
Capel
Russ Hill
Lowfield Heath
Tinsley Green
Shipley Bridge
Felbridge
Copthorne
Crawley Down
East Grinstead
Cowden
Ashurst
Fordcombe
Speldhurst
Rusthall
TUNBRIDGE WELLS
Kipping's Cross
Ifield
Rusper
Lambs Green
Three Bridges
Pound Hill
Kingsfold
CRAWLEY
Maidenbower
Turner's Hill
Ashurstwood
Forest Row
Hartfield
Balls Green
Groombridge
Withyham
Eridge Green
Frant
Bells Yew Green
Warnham
Faygate
Colgate
Pease Pottage
Tilgate
Littlehaven
Roffey
Horsham
St Leonards Forest
Balcombe
Handcross
West Hoathly
Highbrook
Weirwood Reservoir
Coleman's Hatch
Upper Hartfield
Lye Green
Ashdown Forest
Chelwood Gate
Crowborough
Birchgrove
Ardingly
Mark Cross
Tidebrook
Rotherfield
Staplefield
Horsted Keynes
Sweethaws
Manning's Heath
Lower Beeding
Slaugham
Monk's Gate
Warninglid
Danehill
Nutley
Fairwarp
Nuthurst
Copsale
Crabtree
Maplehurst
Cuckfield
Lindfield
Haywards Heath
High Hurstwood
Five Ash Down
Maresfield
Splayne's Green
Pound Green
Buxted
Five Ashes
Mayfield
Hadlow Down
Witherenden
Ansty
Bolney
Scayne's Hill
Fletching
Piltdown
Shipley
West Grinstead
Cowfold
Newick
Uckfield
Blackboys
Framfield
Cross in Hand
Heathfield
Broad Oak
Burwash Common
Cade Street
Punnett's Town
Wineham
Hickstead
Twineham
Worlds End
Wivelsfield
North Chailey
Wivelsfield Green
Chailey
Burgess Hill
Partridge Green
Dial Post
Sayers Common
South Chailey
Town Littleworth
Isfield
New Town
Ridgewood
Little Horsted
Waldron
Little London
Three Cups Corner
Maynard's Green
Warbleton
Rushlake
Vines Cross
Henfield
Blackstone
Hurstpierpoint
Plumpton Green
Keymer
East Chiltington
Halland
East Hoathly
Horam
Ashurst
Albourne
Ditchling
Hassocks
Clayton
Westmeston
Plumpton
Barcombe Cross
Barcombe
Upper Wellingham
Shortgate
Chiddingly
Whitesmith
Laughton
Hale Green
Gun Hill
Muddles Green
Cowbeech
Woodmancote
Small Dole
Pyecombe
Poynings
Hamsey
Ringmer
Hellingly
Steyning
Upper Beeding
Edburton
Fulking
Saddlescombe
Pangdean
Ditchling Beacon
Mount Harry
Offham
Lewes
South Malling
Wallands Park
Lower Dicker
Upper Dicker
Horsebridge
Magham Down
Hailsham
Bramber
Truleigh Hill
Stanmer
Botolphs
Glynde
Chalvington
Ripe
Michelham Priory
Patcham
Coldean
Falmer
Kingston
Iford
Beddingham
West Firle
Selmeston
Arlington
Mile Oak
Hangleton
Withdean
Hollingbury
Moulsecoomb
Portslade
West Blatchington
Preston
Rodmell
Firle Beacon
Alciston
Berwick
Polegate
Sompting
Old Shoreham
Southwick
Woodingdean
Southease
Tarring Neville
Wilmington
Folkington
Lower Willingdon
Westham
Broadwater
Lancing
Shoreham-by-Sea
Portslade-by-Sea
HOVE
BRIGHTON
Kemp Town
Ovingdean
Telscombe
Piddinghoe
Denton
Newhaven
Norton
Bishopstone
East Blatchington
Alfriston
Litlington
Jevington
Willingdon
Ratton Village
Hampden Park
WORTHING
Rottingdean
Saltdean
Peacehaven
Sutton
Seaford
Westdean
Friston
Old Town
EASTBOURNE
Seaford Head
Seven Sisters
East Dean
Beachy Head
Sussex Heritage Coast
South Downs Way
Dieppe
M23
A23
A22
A24
A264
A272
A27
A26
A259
A275
A281
A283
0 1 2 3 4 miles
0 1 2 3 4 5 kilometres

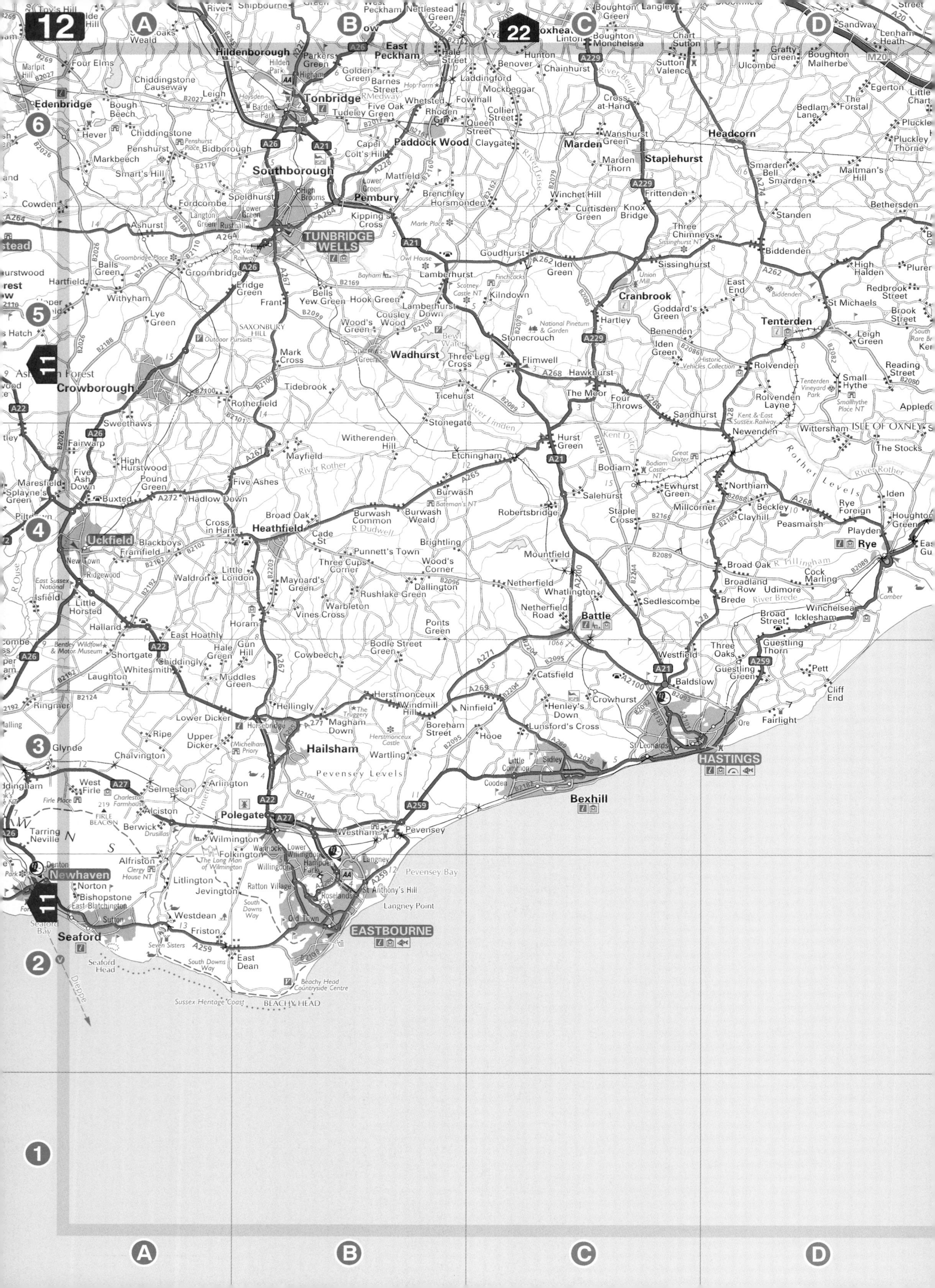
12
22
11
A
B
C
D
1
2
3
4
5
6
Hildenborough
Tonbridge
Edenbridge
Southborough
Paddock Wood
Marden
Staplehurst
Headcorn
Pembury
TUNBRIDGE WELLS
Crowborough
Wadhurst
Cranbrook
Tenterden
Hawkhurst
Rye
Uckfield
Heathfield
Battle
Hailsham
HASTINGS
Bexhill
Polegate
Newhaven
Seaford
EASTBOURNE
Pevensey Bay
Langney Point
BEACHY HEAD
Sussex Heritage Coast
Dieppe

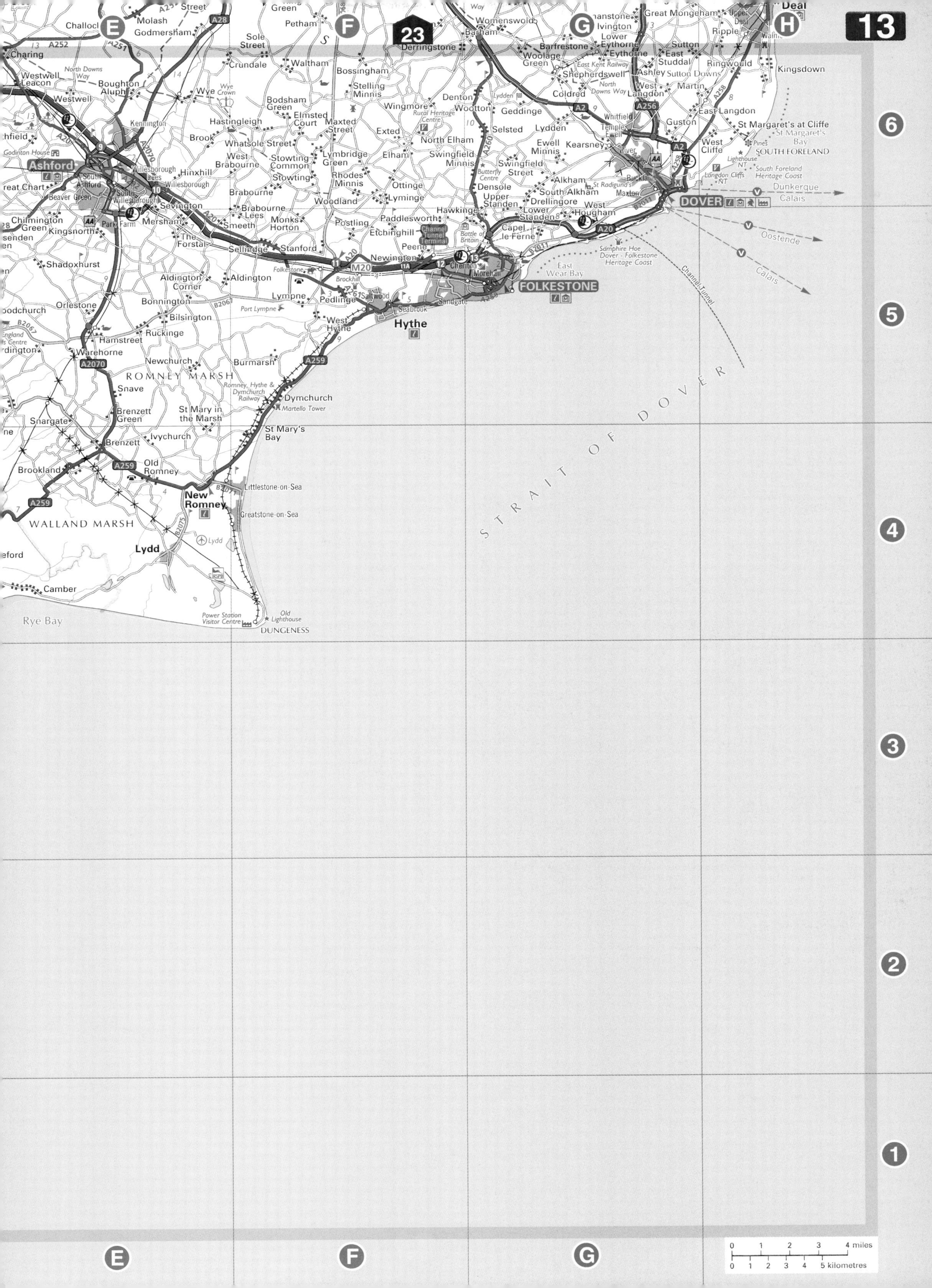

23
E
F
G
H
1
2
3
4
5
6
Ashford
DOVER
FOLKESTONE
Hythe
New Romney
Lydd
Deal
Charing
Challock
Molash
Godmersham
Petham
Womenswold
Barham
Derringstone
Sole Street
Crundale
Waltham
Bossingham
Westwell Leacon
Westwell
Boughton Aluph
Wye
Kennington
Hastingleigh
Brook
Elmsted Court
Bodsham Green
Stelling Minnis
Wingmore
Denton
Wootton
Selsted
Geddinge
Lydden
Coldred
Shepherdswell
Barfrestone
Woolage Green
Eythorne
Ivington
Great Mongeham
Ripple
Sutton
East Studdal
Ringwould
Kingsdown
Ashley
Sutton Downs
West Langdon
Martin
East Langdon
Whitfield
Guston
St Margaret's at Cliffe
West Cliffe
SOUTH FORELAND
Temple Ewell
River
Kearsney
Ewell Minnis
Swingfield Minnis
Swingfield Street
North Elham
Elham
Exted
Maxted Street
Whatsole Street
West Brabourne
Stowting Common
Stowting
Lymbridge Green
Rhodes Minnis
Ottinge
Lyminge
Densole
Upper Standen
Alkham
South Alkham
Drellingore
Hawkinge
Capel-le-Ferne
Lower Standen
West Hougham
Maxton
Buckland
Dunkerque
Calais
Oostende
Channel Tunnel
STRAIT OF DOVER
East Wear Bay
Samphire Hoe Dover - Folkestone Heritage Coast
Cheriton
Morehall
Sandgate
Seabrook
Saltwood
Pedlinge
Lympne
Port Lympne
West Hythe
Newington
Peene
Etchinghill
Paddlesworth
Postling
Woodland
Brabourne
Brabourne Lees
Monks Horton
Smeeth
Sellindge
Stanford
Hinxhill
Willesborough
Willesborough Lees
Sevington
Mersham
The Forstal
Kingsnorth
Chilmington Green
Great Chart
Beaver Green
South Ashford
Park Farm
Shadoxhurst
Aldington
Aldington Corner
Bonnington
Bilsington
Orlestone
Ruckinge
Hamstreet
Warehorne
Newchurch
Burmarsh
ROMNEY MARSH
Snave
Dymchurch
Martello Tower
Brenzett Green
St Mary in the Marsh
St Mary's Bay
Snargate
Brenzett
Ivychurch
Brookland
Old Romney
Littlestone-on-Sea
Greatstone-on-Sea
WALLAND MARSH
Camber
Rye Bay
Power Station Visitor Centre
Old Lighthouse
DUNGENESS
M20
A20
A2
A256
A258
A260
A259
A2070
A28
A252
A251
B2067
B2075
0 1 2 3 4 miles
0 1 2 3 4 5 kilometres

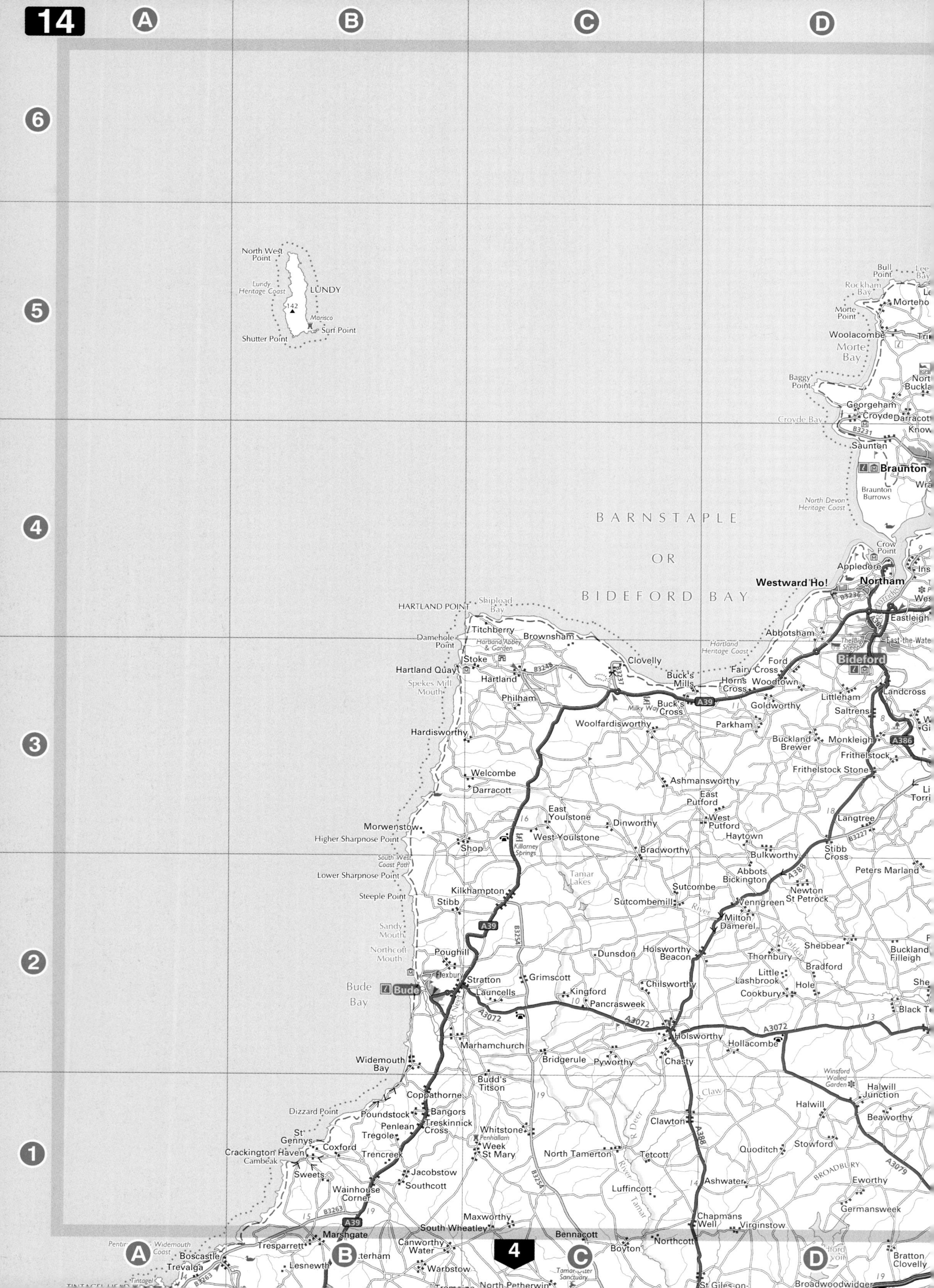
A
B
C
D
6
5
4
3
2
1
North West Point
Lundy Heritage Coast
LUNDY
142
Marisco
Surf Point
Shutter Point
Bull Point
Rockham Bay
Morte Point
Woolacombe
Morte Bay
Baggy Point
Georgeham
Croyde
Croyde Bay
B3231
Saunton
Braunton
Braunton Burrows
North Devon Heritage Coast
BARNSTAPLE
OR
BIDEFORD BAY
Crow Point
Appledore
Westward Ho!
Northam
B3236
Eastleigh
Abbotsham
Bideford
Fairy Cross
Ford
Horns Cross
Woodtown
Littleham
Landcross
HARTLAND POINT
Shipload Bay
Titchberry
Brownsham
Damehole Point
Hartland Abbey & Garden
Hartland Heritage Coast
Clovelly
Buck's Mills
Stoke
Hartland Quay
Hartland
B3248
B3237
Spekes Mill Mouth
Philham
Milky Way
Buck's Cross
A39
Goldworthy
Saltrens
Woolfardisworthy
Parkham
Buckland Brewer
Monkleigh
A386
Hardisworthy
Frithelstock
Frithelstock Stone
Welcombe
Darracott
Ashmansworthy
East Putford
East Youlstone
West Putford
Dinworthy
Langtree
Morwenstow
Higher Sharpnose Point
Shop
West Youlstone
Killarney Springs
Haytown
B3227
Bradworthy
Bulkworthy
Stibb Cross
South West Coast Path
Lower Sharpnose Point
Tamar Lakes
Abbots Bickington
A388
Peters Marland
Kilkhampton
Sutcombe
Newton St Petrock
Steeple Point
Stibb
Sutcombemill
Venngreen
Sandy Mouth
Milton Damerel
A39
B3254
Northcott Mouth
Shebbear
Buckland Filleigh
Poughill
Dunsdon
Holsworthy Beacon
Thornbury
Bradford
Flexbury
Little Lashbrook
Bude Bay
Bude
Stratton
Grimscott
Chilsworthy
Hole
Launcells
Kingford
Cookbury
Pancrasweek
A3072
Holsworthy
A3072
Hollacombe
Marhamchurch
Widemouth Bay
Bridgerule
Pyworthy
Chasty
Budd's Titson
Winsford Walled Garden
Halwill Junction
Coppathorne
Dizzard Point
Poundstock
Bangors
Halwill
Penlean
Treskinnick Cross
Clawton
Beaworthy
St Gennys
Tregole
Whitstone
Penhallam
Week St Mary
Crackington Haven
Coxford
Cambeak
Trencreek
North Tamerton
Tetcott
Quoditch
Stowford
A3079
Sweets
Jacobstow
Southcott
BROADBURY
Wainhouse Corner
Luffincott
Ashwater
Eworthy
B3263
Germansweek
Chapmans Well
Virginstow
Maxworthy
South Wheatley
Trespareatt
Marshgate
Bennacott
Canworthy Water
Boyton
Northcott
Boscastle
Trevalga
Lesnewth
Warbstow
Tamar Otter Sanctuary
Bratton Clovelly
North Petherwin
St Giles-on-
Broadwoodwidger
4

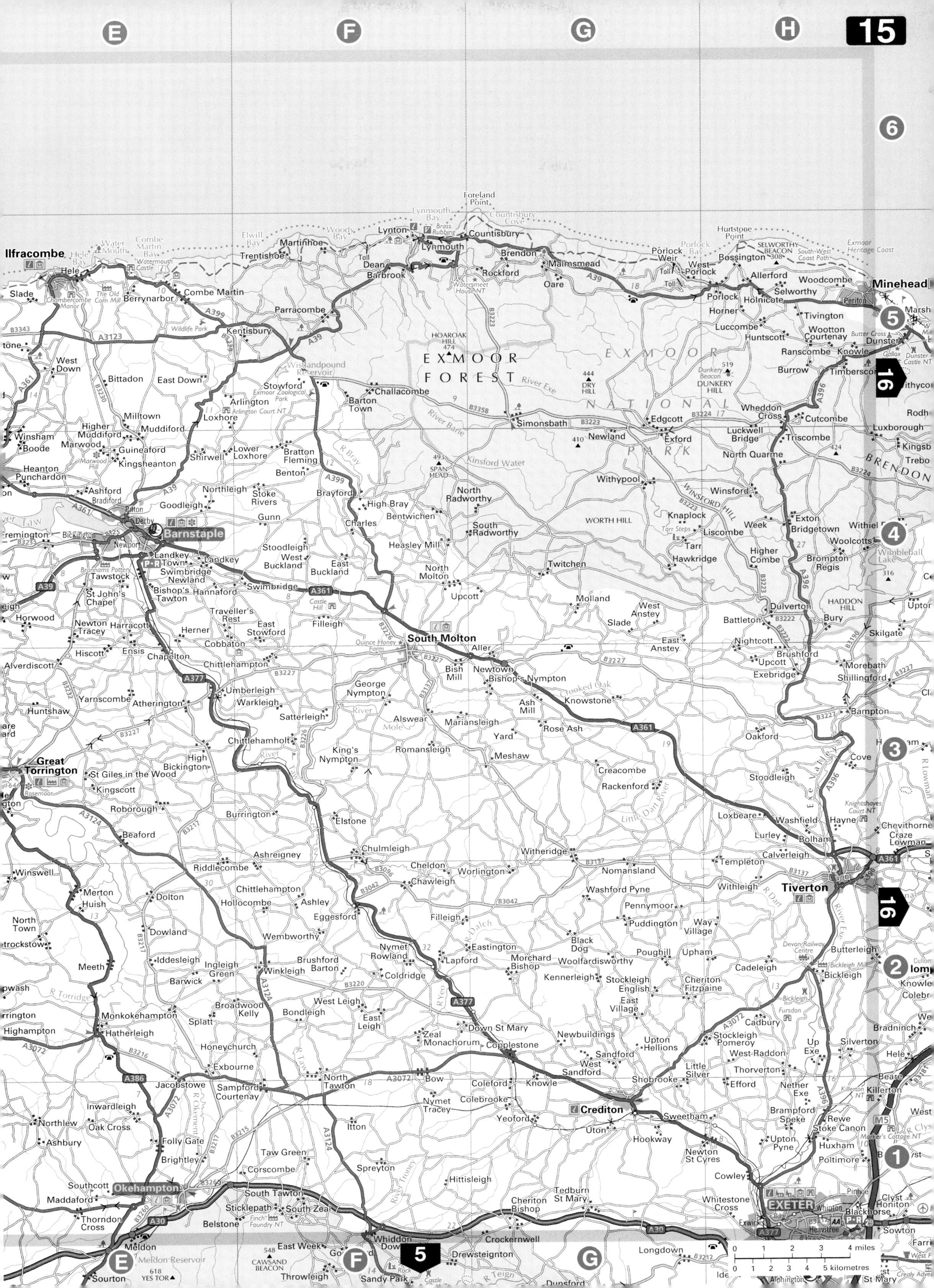
E
F
G
H
6
5
4
3
2
1
16
Foreland Point
Lynmouth Bay
Countisbury Cove
Elwill Bay
Woody Bay
Lynton
Brass Rubbing
Countisbury
Lynmouth
Martinhoe
Trentishoe
Combe Martin Bay
Water Mouth
Hele Bay
Watermouth Castle
Ilfracombe
Hele
Slade
Chambercombe Manor
The Old Corn Mill
Berrynarbor
Combe Martin
Toll
Dean
Barbrook
Brendon
Malmsmead
Rockford
Oare
Watersmeet House NT
Hurtstone Point
Porlock Bay
Porlock Weir
West Porlock
Bossington
SELWORTHY BEACON
South West Coast Path
Exmoor Heritage Coast
Allerford
Porlock
Holnicote
Selworthy
Woodcombe
Minehead
Horner
Marsh
Tivington
Luccombe
Wootton Courtenay
Huntscott
Butter Cross
Dunster
Ranscombe
Knowle
Gallox
Dunster Castle NT
Burrow
Dunkery Beacon
DUNKERY HILL
519
Timberscombe
Parracombe
Wildlife Park
Kentisbury
A3123
A399
A39
A361
B3343
West Down
Bittadon
East Down
Wistlandpound Reservoir
HOAROAK HILL
474
EXMOOR FOREST
EXMOOR NATIONAL PARK
River Exe
444
DRY HILL
Stowford
Exmoor Zoological Park
Challacombe
Arlington
Arlington Court NT
Barton Town
Milltown
Loxhore
Higher Muddiford
Muddiford
Winsham
Boode
Marwood
Marwood Hill
Guineaford
Kingsheanton
Lower Loxhore
Shirwell
Bratton Fleming
Benton
B3358
River Barle
Simonsbath
B3223
B3224
Edgcott
Exford
Newland
410
Wheddon Cross
Cutcombe
Luckwell Bridge
Triscombe
North Quarme
Luxborough
Rodhuish
BRENDON
Heanton Punchardon
Ashford
Bradiford
Pilton
Derby
Barnstaple
Bickington
Fremington
Newport
Northleigh
Goodleigh
Stoke Rivers
Gunn
Brayford
High Bray
Charles
Bentwichen
493
SPAN HEAD
Kinsford Water
North Radworthy
South Radworthy
WORTH HILL
Withypool
Winsford
WINSFORD HILL
Knaplock
Tarr Steps
Liscombe
Tarr
Hawkridge
Week
Exton
Bridgetown
Withiel Florey
Woolcotts
Wimbleball Lake
Higher Combe
Brompton Regis
Landkey
Landkey Town
Brannams Pottery
Tawstock
Swimbridge Newland
Swimbridge
Bishop's Tawton
Hannaford
St John's Chapel
Stoodleigh
West Buckland
East Buckland
Heasley Mill
North Molton
Twitchen
Upcott
A361
Castle Hill
Filleigh
Horwood
Newton Tracey
Harracott
Traveller's Rest
East Stowford
Herner
Cobbaton
Hiscott
Ensis
Chapelton
Chittlehampton
Alverdiscott
Quince Honey Farm
South Molton
Molland
West Anstey
Slade
East Anstey
Dulverton
Battleton
Bury
HADDON HILL
Upton
Skilgate
Nightcott
Brushford
Upcott
Exebridge
Morebath
Shillingford
Aller
Bish Mill
Newtown
Bishop's Nympton
Crooked Oak
Knowstone
George Nympton
Ash Mill
Umberleigh
Warkleigh
Yarnscombe
Atherington
Huntshaw
Satterleigh
River Mole
Alswear
Mariansleigh
Rose Ash
Yard
Bampton
Oakford
Chittlehamholt
King's Nympton
Romansleigh
Meshaw
Great Torrington
Rosemoor
High Bickington
St Giles in the Wood
Kingscott
Roborough
Burrington
Elstone
Creacombe
Rackenford
Little Dart River
Cove
Stoodleigh
Exe Valley
Knightshayes Court NT
Loxbeare
Washfield
Hayne
Chevithorne
Craze Lowman
Lurley
Bolham
Beaford
Chulmleigh
Ashreigney
Riddlecombe
Witheridge
Calverleigh
Templeton
Nomansland
Winswell
Merton
Huish
Dolton
Chittlehampton
Hollocombe
Ashley
Cheldon
Chawleigh
Worlington
Washford Pyne
Withleigh
Tiverton
North Town
Dowland
Eggesford
Filleigh
Pennymoor
Puddington
Way Village
Black Dog
Wembworthy
Nymet Rowland
Eastington
Lapford
Morchard Bishop
Woolfardisworthy
Poughill
Upham
Devon Railway Centre
Butterleigh
Bickleigh Mill
Bickleigh
Cadeleigh
Meeth
Iddesleigh
Ingleigh Green
Winkleigh
Brushford Barton
Coldridge
Kennerleigh
Stockleigh English
Cheriton Fitzpaine
Barwick
River Torridge
Monkokehampton
Hatherleigh
Highampton
Broadwood Kelly
Bondleigh
West Leigh
East Leigh
East Village
Fursdon
Cadbury
Splatt
Honeychurch
Zeal Monachorum
Down St Mary
Copplestone
Newbuildings
Upton Hellions
Stockleigh Pomeroy
Bradninch
Up Exe
Silverton
Exbourne
Jacobstowe
Sampford Courtenay
North Tawton
Bow
Coleford
Knowle
Sandford
West Sandford
Shobrooke
Little Silver
Thorverton
Efford
Nether Exe
Hele
Killerton NT
Killerton
Inwardleigh
Northlew
Oak Cross
Ashbury
Folly Gate
Brightley
Nymet Tracey
Colebrooke
Yeoford
Crediton
Uton
Sweetham
Hookway
Brampford Speke
Rewe
Stoke Canon
Upton Pyne
Huxham
Poltimore
Taw Green
Itton
Spreyton
Newton St Cyres
Cowley
Corscombe
Hittisleigh
Southcott
Okehampton
Maddaford
Thorndon Cross
South Tawton
Sticklepath
Finch Foundry NT
South Zeal
Belstone
Tedburn St Mary
Cheriton Bishop
Whitestone Cross
Exeter
Exwick
Whipton
Pinhoe
Clyst Honiton
Blackhorse
Heavitree
Sowton
A30
A386
A3072
A3124
A377
A396
M5
Meldon
Meldon Reservoir
Whiddon Down
Crockernwell
Drewsteignton
Longdown
East Week
Gidleigh
548 CAWSAND BEACON
618 YES TOR
Sourton
Throwleigh
Sandy Park
Castle Drogo
R Teign
Dunsford
Ide
Alphington
St Mary
0 1 2 3 4 miles
0 1 2 3 4 5 kilometres

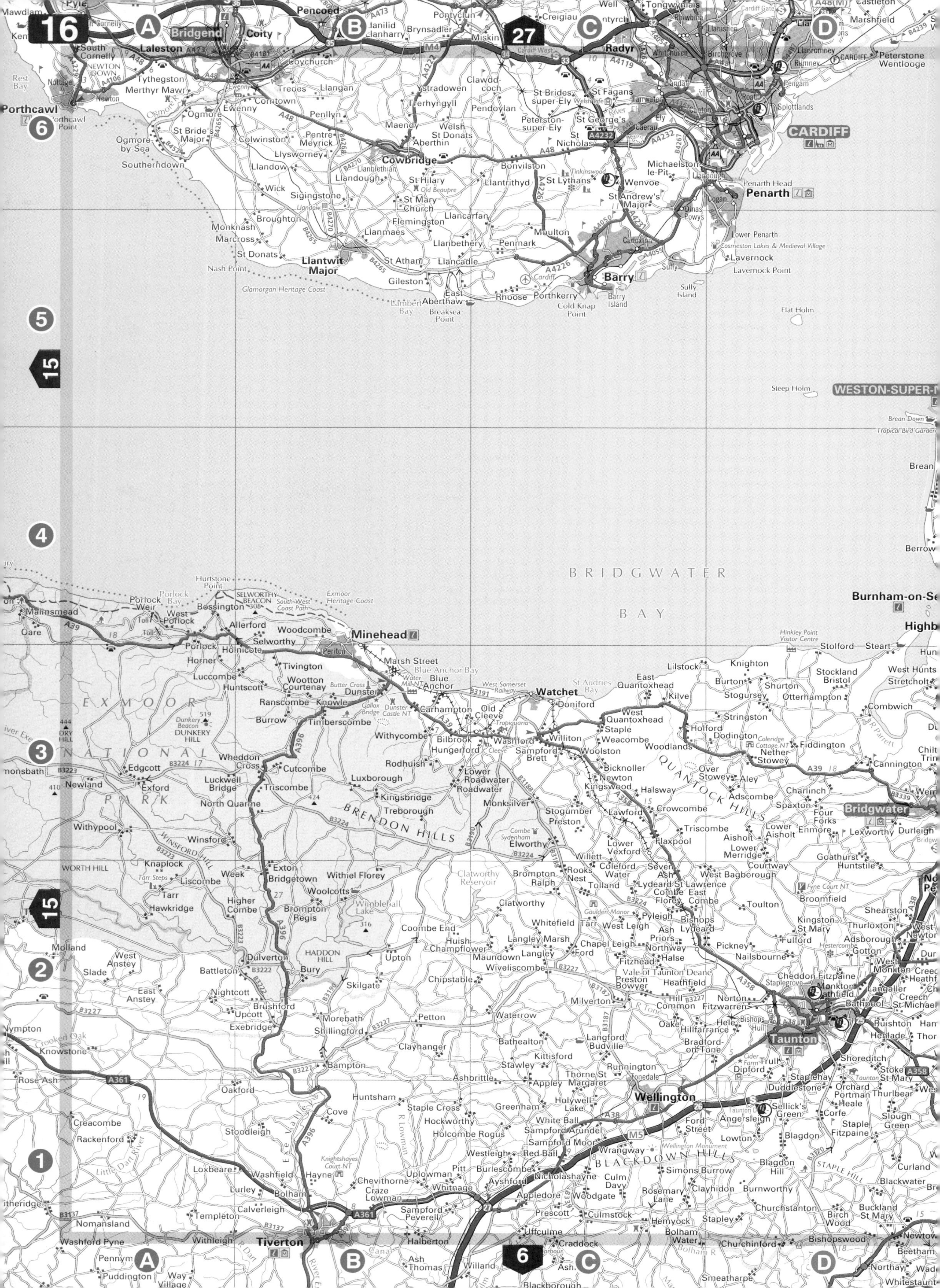

16
A
B
C
D
27
Pyle
Mawdlam
Kenfig
Bridgend
Coity
Pencoed
Llanilid
Llanharry
Brynsadler
Pontyclun
Miskin
Creigiau
Well
Tongwynlais
Pentyrch
Radyr
Whitchurch
Llanishen
Rhiwbina
Birchgrove
Llanrumney
Rumney
Marshfield
Castleton
Peterstone Wentlooge
Cardiff Gate
South Cornelly
Laleston
Newton Down
Nottage
Tythegston
Merthyr Mawr
Rest Bay
Newton
Porthcawl
Porthcawl Point
6
Coychurch
Treoes
Llangan
Ewenny
Corntown
Ogmore
Ogmore by Sea
St Bride's Major
Colwinston
Southerndown
Llysworney
Penllyn
Pentre Meyrick
Ystradowen
Clawdd-coch
Trerhyngyll
Maendy
Aberthin
Welsh St Donats
Pendoylan
St Brides super-Ely
St Fagans
Peterston-super-Ely
St George's
St Nicholas
Fairwater
Caerau
Ely
Canton
Pengam
Splottlands
CARDIFF
Cowbridge
Llanblethian
Llandow
Llandough
Wick
Sigingstone
St Hilary
Old Beaupre
St Mary Church
Llantrithyd
Bonvilston
Tinkinswood
St Lythans
Wenvoe
Michaelston-le-Pit
Llandough
Cogan
Penarth Head
Penarth
Dinas Powys
St Andrew's Major
Broughton
Monknash
Marcross
St Donats
Nash Point
Llantwit Major
Flemingston
Llancarfan
Llanmaes
Llanbethery
Penmark
Moulton
Cadoxton
Lower Penarth
Cosmeston Lakes & Medieval Village
Lavernock
Lavernock Point
Sully
Sully Island
St Athan
Llancadle
Gileston
Barry
Barry Island
Cardiff
Rhoose
Porthkerry
Cold Knap Point
East Aberthaw
Lamberts Bay
Breaksea Point
Glamorgan Heritage Coast
Flat Holm
5
15
Steep Holm
WESTON-SUPER-M
Brean Down
Tropical Bird Garden
Brean
4
Berrow
BRIDGWATER BAY
Burnham-on-Sea
Highbridge
Hurlstone Point
Porlock Bay
Selworthy Beacon
South West Coast Path
Exmoor Heritage Coast
Porlock Weir
West Porlock
Bossington
Allerford
Malmsmead
Oare
Porlock
Holnicote
Selworthy
Woodcombe
Minehead
Periton
Marsh Street
Blue Anchor Bay
Blue Anchor
Horner
Luccombe
Tivington
Wootton Courtenay
Huntscott
Butter Cross
Dunster
Dunster Castle NT
Ranscombe
Knowle
Gallox Bridge
Burrow
Timberscombe
EXMOOR NATIONAL PARK
Dunkery Beacon
DUNKERY HILL
DRY HILL
3
Withycombe
Carhampton
Old Cleeve
West Somerset Railway
Watchet
St Audries Bay
Doniford
Tropiquaria
Washford
Bilbrook
Hungerford
Williton
Sampford Brett
Hinkley Point Visitor Centre
Stolford
Steart
Lilstock
Knighton
East Quantoxhead
Burton
Kilve
West Quantoxhead
Staple
Stogursey
Shurton
Otterhampton
Stockland Bristol
Stringston
Holford
Dodington
Coleridge Cottage NT
Weacombe
Woodlands
Nether Stowey
Fiddington
Combwich
Cannington
Simonsbath
Newland
Edgcott
Exford
Wheddon Cross
Cutcombe
Luckwell Bridge
Rodhuish
Luxborough
Kingsbridge
Treborough
Triscombe
North Quarme
Lower Roadwater
Roadwater
Woolston
Bicknoller
Newton
Kingswood
Halsway
Over Stowey
Aley
Adscombe
Charlinch
Spaxton
QUANTOCK HILLS
BRENDON HILLS
Monksilver
Stogumber
Preston
Lawford
Crowcombe
Triscombe
Lower Aisholt
Aisholt
Four Forks
Enmore
Lexworthy
Durleigh
Bridgwater
Withypool
Winsford
WINSFORD HILL
WORTH HILL
Knaplock
Tarr Steps
Liscombe
Tarr
Hawkridge
Week
Exton
Bridgetown
Withiel Florey
Woolcotts
Wimbleball Lake
Combe Sydenham
Elworthy
Willett
Lower Vexford
Flaxpool
Lower Merridge
Goathurst
Huntstile
Courtway
West Bagborough
Higher Combe
Brompton Regis
Clatworthy Reservoir
Brompton Ralph
Rooks Nest
Coleford Water
Tolland
Seven Ash
Lydeard St Lawrence
Combe Florey
East Combe
Fyne Court NT
Broomfield
Toulton
Clatworthy
Gaulden Manor
Pyleigh
Bishops Lydeard
Kingston St Mary
Thurloxton
Shearston
Whitefield
Tarr
West Leigh
Ash Priors
Coombe End
Huish Champflower
Langley Marsh
Langley
Chapel Leigh
Northway
Halse
Pickney
Adsborough
Fulford
Hestercombe
Gotton
Nailsbourne
Molland
West Anstey
2
Slade
Battleton
Dulverton
HADDON HILL
Upton
Bury
Maundown
Wiveliscombe
Ford
Fitzhead
Vale of Taunton Deane
Cheddon Fitzpaine
Staplegrove
Monkton Heathfield
West Monkton
Creech Heathfield
Creech St Michael
Bathpool
Langaller
East Anstey
Nightcott
Skilgate
Chipstable
Preston Bowyer
Heathfield
Brushford
Upcott
Exebridge
Morebath
Shillingford
Petton
Waterrow
Milverton
Hill Common
Norton Fitzwarren
Bishops Hull
Hele
Oake
Hillfarrance
Taunton
Ruishton
Henlade
Nympton
Crooked Oak
Knowstone
Rose Ash
Clayhanger
Bathealton
Langford Budville
Bradford-on-Tone
Cider Farm
Trull
Dipford
Shoreditch
Stoke St Mary
Kittisford
Stawley
Runnington
Thorne St Margaret
Ashbrittle
Appley
Fonedale
Bampton
Oakford
Huntsham
Cove
Staple Cross
Greenham
Holywell Lake
Wellington
Taunton Deane
Sellick's Green
Staplehay
Duddlestone
Orchard Portman
Thurlbear
Heale
Corfe
Staple Fitzpaine
Slough Green
Creacombe
Rackenford
Stoodleigh
Hockworthy
Holcombe Rogus
White Ball
Sampford Arundel
Sampford Moor
Ford Street
Angersleigh
Lowton
Blagdon
Exe Valley
R Lowman
Knightshayes Court NT
Wellington Monument
BLACKDOWN HILLS
STAPLE HILL
1
Little Dart River
Loxbeare
Washfield
Hayne
Westleigh
Burlescombe
Red Ball
Wrangway
Nicholashayne
Culm Davy
Simons Burrow
Blagdon Hill
Curland
Blackwater
Lurley
Bolham
Chevithorne
Craze Lowman
Pitt
Uplowman
Whitnage
Ayshford
Appledore
Woodgate
Rosemary Lane
Clayhidon
Burnworthy
Witheridge
Calverleigh
Templeton
Nomansland
Tiverton
Sampford Peverell
Prescott
Culmstock
Hemyock
Stapley
Churchstanton
Birch Wood
Buckland St Mary
Washford Pyne
Withleigh
Halberton
Uffculme
Craddock
Bolham Water
Churchinford
Bishopswood
Newtown
Pennymoor
Puddington
Way Village
Ash Thomas
Willand
Ashill
Smeatharpe
Beetham
Northay
Whitestaunton
Blackborough
River Exe
River Dart

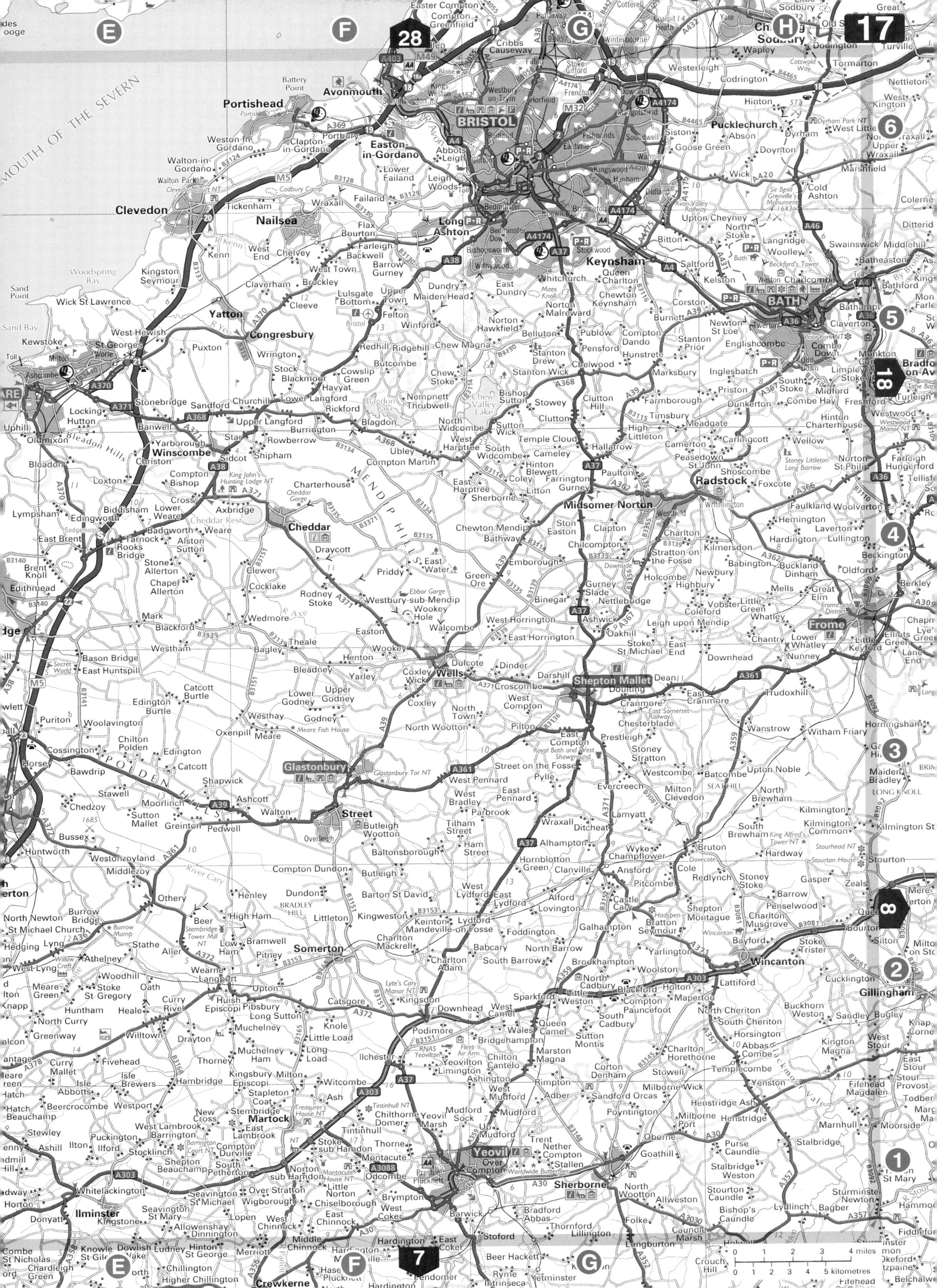

E
F
G
H
28
17
Easter Compton
Compton Greenfield
Cribbs Causeway
Sodbury
Chipping Sodbury
Yate
Wapley
Dodington
Tormarton
Westerleigh
Codrington
MOUTH OF THE SEVERN
Battery Point
Avonmouth
Portishead
Shirehampton
Kings Weston
Westbury on-Trym
Horfield
Stoke Gifford
Frenchay
Downend
Mangotsfield
BRISTOL
M32
M49
M5
Hinton
Pucklechurch
Dyrham
West Kington
Siston
Abson
Goose Green
Doynton
Marshfield
Weston-in-Gordano
Clapton-in-Gordano
Portbury
Easton-in-Gordano
Abbots Leigh
Walton-in-Gordano
Walton Park
Clevedon Court NT
Cadbury Camp
Lower Failand
Leigh Woods
Fishponds
Eastville
Kingswood
Hanham
Wick
Cold Ashton
Clevedon
Tickenham
Wraxall
Failand
Nailsea
Flax Bourton
Long Ashton
Bedminster
Bedminster Down
Bishopsworth
Brislington
Oldland
Upton Cheyney
North Stoke
Langridge
Woolley
Swainswick
Batheaston
Kenn
West End
Chelvey
Farleigh
Backwell
Barrow Gurney
Withywood
Stockwood
Keynsham
Bitton
Saltford
Kelston
Weston
Charlcombe
Bathford
Kingston Seymour
Woodspring Bay
West Town
Brockley
Claverham
Dundry
Maiden Head
East Dundry
Whitchurch
Queen Charlton
Chewton Keynsham
Corston
Newton St Loe
BATH
Claverton
Sand Point
Wick St Lawrence
Cleeve
Lulsgate Bottom
Upper Town
Felton
Winford
Norton Hawkfield
Norton Malreward
Belluton
Publow
Pensford
Compton Dando
Burnett
Stanton Prior
Englishcombe
Combe Down
Monkton Combe
Sand Bay
Yatton
Congresbury
West Hewish
Kewstoke
St Georges
Worle
Milton
Ashcombe
Puxton
Wrington
Redhill
Ridgehill
Chew Magna
Stanton Drew
Chelwood
Hunstrete
Marksbury
Inglesbatch
Priston
Odd Down
Limpley Stoke
South Stoke
Midford
Freshford
Butcombe
Stock
Blackmoor
Cowslip Green
Havyat
Chew Stoke
Stanton Wick
Clutton Hill
Stowey
Farmborough
Dunkerton
Combe Hay
Blagdon Lake
Chew Valley Lake
Nempnett Thrubwell
Bishop Sutton
Clutton
Timsbury
High Littleton
Meadgate
Hinton Charterhouse
Westwood
Locking
Hutton
Stonebridge
Sandford
Churchill
Lower Langford
Upper Langford
Rickford
Blagdon
Burrington
North Widcombe
West Harptree
Sutton Wick
Temple Cloud
Hallatrow
Camerton
Carlingcott
Wellow
Uphill
Oldmixon
Bleadon Hills
Banwell
Winscombe
Yarborough
Star
Rowberrow
Shipham
Sidcot
Christon
Compton Bishop
King John's Hunting Lodge NT
Ubley
Compton Martin
South Widcombe
Cameley
Hinton Blewett
Coley
Litton
Paulton
Peasedown St John
Shoscombe
Norton St Philip
Farleigh Hungerford
Bleadon
Loxton
Charterhouse
Cheddar Gorge
MENDIP HILLS
East Harptree
Sherborne
Farrington Gurney
Radstock
Writhlington
Foxcote
Lympsham
Edingworth
Biddisham
Cross
Lower Weare
Axbridge
Cheddar
Cheddar Resr
Weare
Badgworth
Sedgemoor
Alston Sutton
Tarnock
Rooks Bridge
East Brent
Brent Knoll
Edithmead
Chewton Mendip
Bathway
Ston Easton
Clapton
Chilcompton
Midsomer Norton
Westfield
Charlton
Stratton-on-the-Fosse
Kilmersdon
Faulkland
Woolverton
Hemington
Hardington
Laverton
Lullington
Beckington
Draycott
East Water
Priddy
Green Ore
Emborough
Downside
Holcombe
Babington
Buckland Dinham
Newbury
Highbury
Oldford
Berkley
Stone Allerton
Chapel Allerton
Clewer
Cocklake
Rodney Stoke
Ebbor Gorge
Westbury-sub-Mendip
Wookey Hole
Gurney Slade
Binegar
Nettlebridge
Vobster
Coleford
Little Green
Mells
Great Elm
Whatley
Frome
Mark
Blackford
Wedmore
River Axe
Easton
Walcombe
West Horrington
East Horrington
Ashwick
Oakhill
Leigh upon Mendip
Chantry
Lower Whatley
Westham
Theale
Wookey
Bagley
Stoke St Michael
East End
Downhead
Nunney
Bason Bridge
Secret World
East Huntspill
Bleadney
Henton
Yarley
Dulcote
Dinder
Coxley Wick
Wells
Croscombe
Darshill
Shepton Mallet
Doulting
Dean
Cranmore
East Cranmore
East Somerset Railway
Trudoxhill
Catcott Burtle
Edington Burtle
Lower Godney
Upper Godney
Godney
Coxley
North Town
West Compton
Chesterblade
Puriton
Woolavington
Westhay
Meare
Meare Fish House
Oxenpill
North Wootton
Pilton
East Compton
Royal Bath and West Showground
Prestleigh
Wanstrow
Witham Friary
Horningsham
Cossington
Chilton Polden
Edington
Catcott
POLDEN HILLS
Horsey
Bawdrip
Glastonbury
Glastonbury Tor NT
West Pennard
Street on the Fosse
Pylle
Stoney Stratton
Westcombe
Batcombe
Upton Noble
Evercreech
SEAT HILL
Maiden Bradley
LONG KNOLL
Stawell
Shapwick
Chedzoy
Sutton Mallet
Moorlinch
Ashcott
Greinton
Pedwell
Walton
Street
Overleigh
Butleigh Wootton
West Bradley
East Pennard
Parbrook
Lamyatt
Milton Clevedon
North Brewham
Kilmington
Bussex
Tilham Street
Ham Street
Wraxall
Ditcheat
Alhampton
South Brewham
King Alfred's Tower NT
Stourhead NT
Stourton House
Stourton
Kilmington Common
Huntworth
Westonzoyland
Middlezoy
Baltonsborough
River Cary
Compton Dundon
Butleigh
Hornblotton Green
Clanville
Wyke Champflower
Bruton
Ansford
Cole
Redlynch
Hardway
Stoney Stoke
Gasper
Zeals
Othery
Dundon
Barton St David
BRADLEY HILL
Henley
West Lydford
East Lydford
Alford
Lovington
Castle Cary
Pitcombe
Shepton Montague
Barrow
Penselwood
Charlton Musgrove
Hadspen
North Newton
Burrow Bridge
St Michael Church
Burrow Mump
Beer
Stembridge Tower Mill NT
High Ham
Low Ham
Bramwell
Littleton
Kingweston
Keinton Mandeville
Lydford-on-Fosse
Foddington
Galhampton
Bratton Seymour
Hedging
Lyng
Stathe
Aller
Charlton Mackrell
Pitney
Somerton
Babcary
North Barrow
South Barrow
Charlton Adam
Yarlington
Bayford
Stoke Trister
Wincanton
Cucklington
Gillingham
West Lyng
Athelney
Willow Craft
Woodhill
Stoke St Gregory
Meare Green
Oath
Wearne
Langport
Upton
Lyte's Cary Manor NT
Brookhampton
Woolston
North Cadbury
Blackford
Holton
Lattiford
Curry Rivel
Huish Episcopi
Pibsbury
Long Sutton
Catsgore
Kingsdon
Sparkford
Little Weston
Compton Pauncefoot
Maperton
North Cheriton
Buckhorn Weston
Sandley
Bugley
Huntham
Heale
North Curry
Greenway
Willtown
Muchelney
Knole
Little Load
Long Load
Downhead
West Camel
Podimore
Queen Camel
Wales
South Cadbury
Sutton Montis
South Cheriton
Horsington
Abbas Combe
Kington Magna
West Stour
Curry Mallet
Fivehead
Drayton
Muchelney Ham
Thorney
Ilchester
RNAS Yeovilton
Fleet Air Arm
Yeovilton
Limington
Bridgehampton
Chilton Cantelo
Ashington
Marston Magna
Corton Denham
Charlton Horethorne
Templecombe
Stowell
East Stour
Isle Abbotts
Isle Brewers
Hambridge
Kingsbury Episcopi
Milton
Witcombe
Stapleton
Coat
Ash
West Mudford
Mudford
Rimpton
Adber
Sandford Orcas
Milborne Wick
Yenston
Fifehead Magdalen
Hatch Beauchamp
Beercrocombe
Westport
New Cross
Stembridge
Martock
Treasurer's House NT
Tintinhull NT
Chilthorne Domer
Yeovil Marsh
Mudford Sock
Up Mudford
Poyntington
Henstridge Ash
Henstridge
Milborne Port
Marnhull
Moorside
Stewley
Ashill
Ilton
West Lambrook
East Lambrook
Puckington
Barrington
Ilford
Stocklinch
Barrington Court NT
Compton Durville
Shepton Beauchamp
South Petherton
Stoke sub Hamdon
Tintinhull
Thorne
Montacute
Montacute House NT
Trent
Nether Compton
Over Compton
Stallen
Worldwide Butterflies
Oborne
Goathill
Purse Caundle
Stalbridge
Stalbridge Weston
Yeovil
Preston Plucknett
Norton sub Hamdon
Odcombe
Sherborne
North Wootton
Sturminster Newton
Hinton St Mary
Whitelackington
Seavington St Michael
Over Stratton
Little Norton
Wigborough
Chiselborough
Brympton
West Coker
Bradford Abbas
Allweston
Stourton Caundle
Bishop's Caundle
Lydlinch
Bagber
Ilminster
Seavington St Mary
Kingstone
Donyatt
Allowenshay
Dinnington
Lopen
West Chinnock
East Chinnock
Barwick
Stoford
Thornford
Lillington
Folke
Longburton
Caundle Marsh
Middle Chinnock
Hardington
East Coker
Knowle St Giles
Dowlish
Ludney
Hinton St George
Merriott
Crewkerne
Chillington
Higher Chillington
Chard
Beer Hackett
Ryme Intrinseca
Yetminster
Crouch Hill
Fifehead
Belchalwell
7
8
18
1
2
3
4
5
6
0 1 2 3 4 miles
0 1 2 3 4 5 kilometres

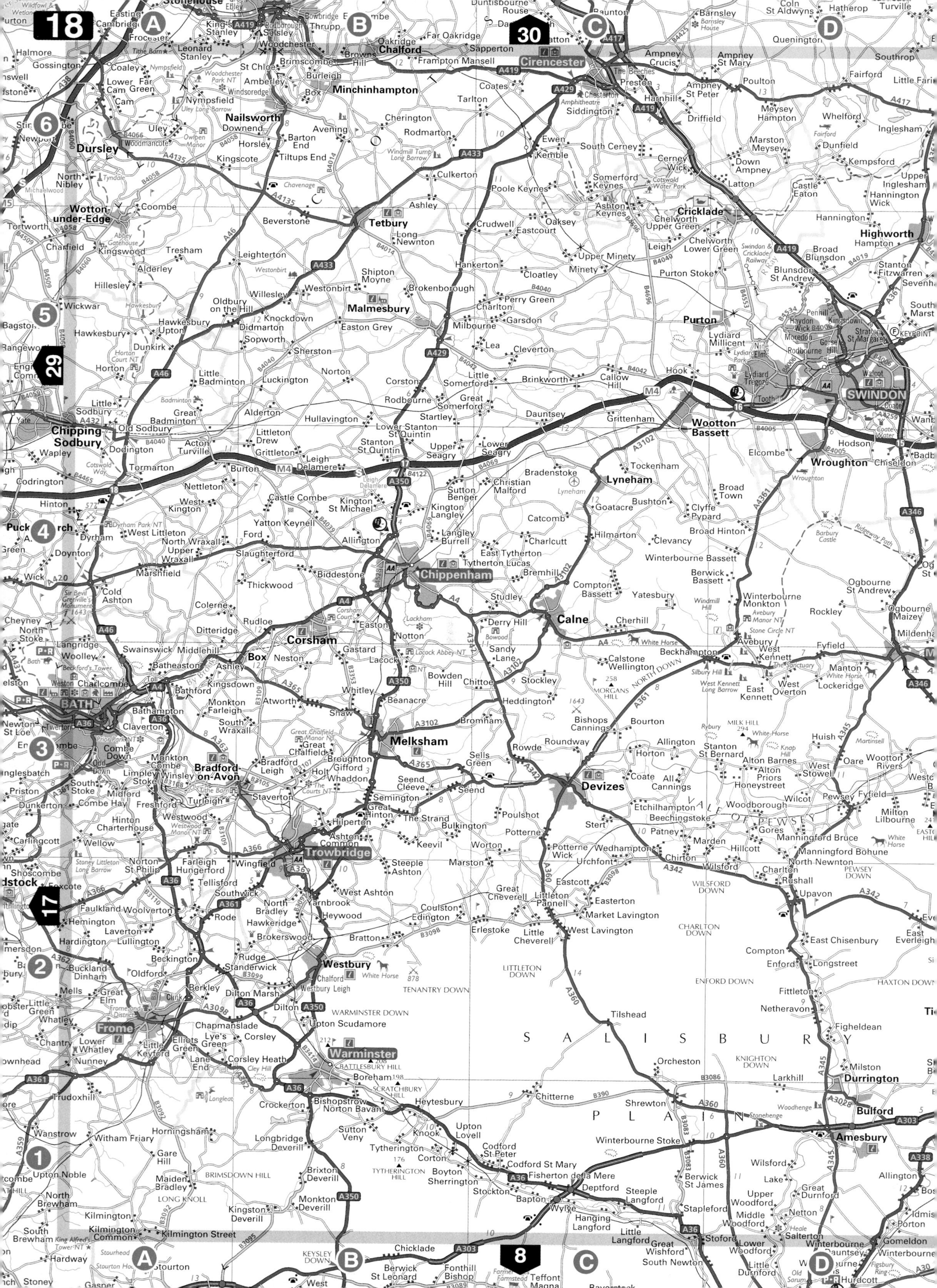

18
30
29
17
8
A
B
C
D
1
2
3
4
5
6
Stonehouse
King's Stanley
Selsley
Woodchester
Frocester
Leonard Stanley
Thrupp
Brimscombe
Chalford
Oakridge
Far Oakridge
Frampton Mansell
Sapperton
Duntisbourne Rouse
Cirencester
Baunton
Coln St Aldwyns
Hatherop
Turville
Barnsley
Quenington
Ampney Crucis
Ampney St Mary
Ampney St Peter
Southrop
Fairford
Little Faringdon
Poulton
Preston
Harnhill
Driffield
Meysey Hampton
Whelford
Inglesham
Marston Meysey
Dunfield
Kempsford
Down Ampney
Halmore
Gossington
Coaley
Lower Cam
Cam
Nympsfield
Uley
Dursley
Amberley
Nailsworth
Minchinhampton
Burleigh
Box
St Chloe
Downend
Horsley
Avening
Barton End
Cherington
Rodmarton
Tarlton
Coates
Siddington
Ewen
Kemble
South Cerney
Cerney Wick
Somerford Keynes
Ashton Keynes
Latton
Castle Eaton
Hannington Wick
Hannington
Highworth
Cricklade
Chelworth Upper Green
Chelworth Lower Green
Leigh
Purton Stoke
Blunsdon St Andrew
Broad Blunsdon
Stanton Fitzwarren
Sevenhampton
Kingscote
Tiltups End
Culkerton
Poole Keynes
North Nibley
Wotton-under-Edge
Coombe
Tortworth
Charfield
Kingswood
Tresham
Beverstone
Tetbury
Long Newnton
Ashley
Crudwell
Eastcourt
Oakley
Upper Minety
Minety
Hankerton
Cloatley
Alderley
Leighterton
Hillesley
Wickwar
Shipton Moyne
Westonbirt
Brokenborough
Perry Green
Charlton
Garsdon
Malmesbury
Willesley
Oldbury on the Hill
Knockdown
Hawkesbury
Hawkesbury Upton
Didmarton
Sopworth
Easton Grey
Milbourne
Lea
Cleverton
Purton
Lydiard Millicent
Haydon Wick
Moredon
Penhill
Stratton St Margaret
Swindon
Lydiard Tregoze
Toothill
Walcot
Coate
Wroughton
Chiseldon
Elcombe
Hodson
Wootton Bassett
Grittenham
Dauntsey
Brinkworth
Callow Hill
Hook
Little Somerford
Great Somerford
Sherston
Dunkirk
Horton
Little Badminton
Luckington
Norton
Corston
Rodbourne
Startley
Yate
Chipping Sodbury
Little Sodbury
Old Sodbury
Great Badminton
Alderton
Hullavington
Lower Stanton St Quintin
Stanton St Quintin
Upper Seagry
Lower Seagry
Littleton Drew
Grittleton
Leigh Delamere
Acton Turville
Dodington
Wapley
Tormarton
Burton
Codrington
Hinton
Pucklechurch
Dyrham
West Littleton
Nettleton
West Kington
Castle Combe
Kington St Michael
Kington Langley
Sutton Benger
Christian Malford
Bradenstoke
Lyneham
Tockenham
Broad Town
Bushton
Clyffe Pypard
Goatacre
Catcomb
Hilmarton
Broad Hinton
Clevancy
Winterbourne Bassett
Berwick Bassett
Yatton Keynell
Ford
Slaughterford
Allington
Langley Burrell
East Tytherton
Tytherton Lucas
Charlcutt
Bremhill
Doynton
North Wraxall
Upper Wraxall
Marshfield
Biddestone
Chippenham
Thickwood
Wick
Cold Ashton
Colerne
Rudloe
Corsham
Ditteridge
Lackham
Studley
Calne
Compton Bassett
Yatesbury
Cherhill
Winterbourne Monkton
Avebury
Ogbourne St Andrew
Ogbourne Maizey
Rockley
Mildenhall
Derry Hill
Sandy Lane
Easton
Notton
Lacock
Gastard
Neston
Box
Middlehill
Swainswick
Batheaston
Ashley
Langridge
Woolley
North Stoke
Cheyney
Weston
Charlcombe
Bath
Bathford
Kingsdown
Bathampton
Claverton
Monkton Farleigh
South Wraxall
Atworth
Shaw
Whitley
Beanacre
Bowden Hill
Chittoe
Stockley
Heddington
Calstone Wellington
Beckhampton
West Kennett
East Kennett
West Overton
Fyfield
Manton
Lockeridge
Bishops Cannings
Bourton
Bromham
Melksham
Rowde
Roundway
Sells Green
Devizes
Allington
Horton
Stanton St Bernard
Alton Barnes
Alton Priors
Honeystreet
Oare
Wootton Rivers
Huish
West Stowell
Pewsey
Milton Lilbourne
Combe Down
Monkton Combe
Winsley
Limpley Stoke
Bradford-on-Avon
Bradford Leigh
Holt
Broughton Gifford
Whaddon
Great Chalfield
Seend Cleeve
Seend
Coate
All Cannings
Etchilhampton
Beechingstoke
Woodborough
Wilcot
Englishcombe
Priston
South Stoke
Midford
Combe Hay
Freshford
Turleigh
Staverton
Semington
Great Hinton
The Strand
Bulkington
Poulshot
Potterne
Stert
Patney
Marden
Gores
Manningford Bruce
Manningford Bohune
North Newnton
Dunkerton
Hinton Charterhouse
Westwood
Hilperton
Trowbridge
Ashton Common
Keevil
Worton
Marston
Potterne Wick
Wedhampton
Urchfont
Chirton
Wilsford
Charlton
Rushall
Upavon
Carlingcott
Wellow
Norton St Philip
Farleigh Hungerford
Wingfield
Steeple Ashton
West Ashton
Tellisford
Southwick
North Bradley
Yarnbrook
Heywood
Great Cheverell
Littleton Pannell
Eastcott
Easterton
Market Lavington
West Lavington
Little Cheverell
Erlestoke
Coulston
Edington
Bratton
Shoscombe
Foxcote
Faulkland
Woolverton
Hemington
Rode
Laverton
Hardington
Lullington
Beckington
Hawkeridge
Brokerswood
Rudge
Standerwick
Westbury
Chalford
Westbury Leigh
Buckland Dinham
Oldford
Berkley
Dilton Marsh
Dilton
Mells
Great Elm
Frome
Whatley
Chantry
Lower Whatley
Little Keyford
Elliots Green
Lye's Green
Chapmanslade
Corsley
Corsley Heath
Lane End
Upton Scudamore
Warminster
Battlesbury Hill
Boreham
Nunney
Trudoxhill
Crockerton
Bishopstrow
Norton Bavant
Heytesbury
Chitterne
Tilshead
Orcheston
Shrewton
Larkhill
Durrington
Bulford
Amesbury
Enford
Longstreet
East Chisenbury
Compton
Fittleton
Netheravon
Fighelden
Milton
Wanstrow
Witham Friary
Horningsham
Longbridge Deverill
Sutton Veny
Tytherington
Knook
Upton Lovell
Codford St Peter
Codford St Mary
Corton
Boyton
Sherrington
Fisherton de la Mere
Deptford
Stockton
Bapton
Wylye
Steeple Langford
Hanging Langford
Little Langford
Winterbourne Stoke
Berwick St James
Stapleford
Great Wishford
South Newton
Stoford
Wilsford
Lake
Upper Woodford
Middle Woodford
Lower Woodford
Great Durnford
Little Durnford
Netton
Salterton
Winterbourne Dauntsey
Winterbourne Earls
Gomeldon
Porton
Allington
Upton Noble
North Brewham
Gare Hill
Maiden Bradley
Brixton Deverill
Monkton Deverill
Kingston Deverill
Kilmington
Kilmington Common
Kilmington Street
South Brewham
Hardway
Stourton
Chicklade
Berwick St Leonard
Fonthill Bishop
Teffont Magna
Hurdcott
Salisbury Plain
Vale of Pewsey
Charlton Down
Wilsford Down
Enford Down
Littleton Down
Tenantry Down
Warminster Down
Knighton Down
Haxton Down
Pewsey Down
Milk Hill
Brimsdown Hill
Long Knoll
Tytherington Hill
Scratchbury Hill
Keysley Down
North Down
Morgans Hill

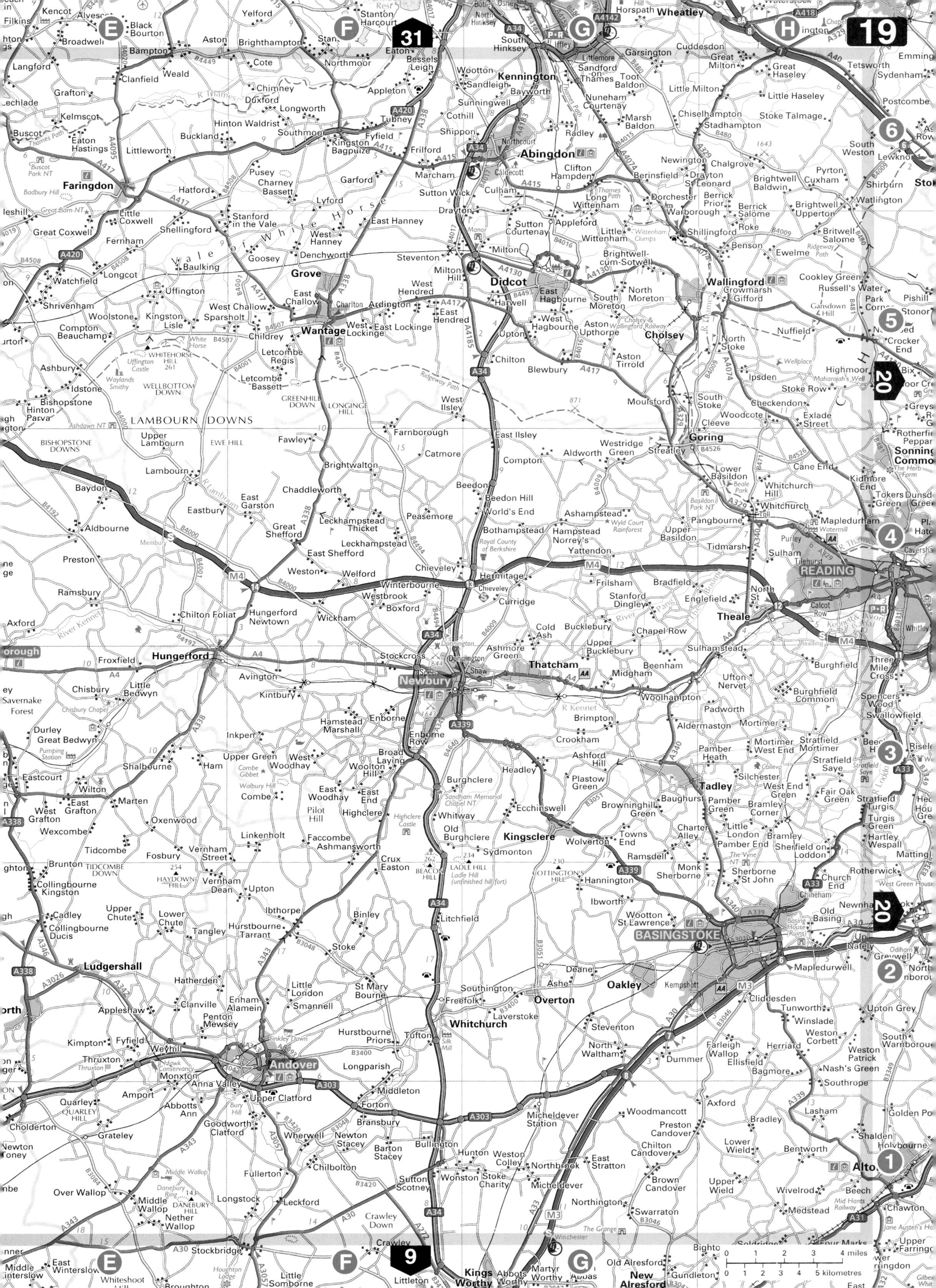
31
20
9
E
F
G
H
Kencot
Alvescot
Black Bourton
Filkins
Broadwell
Bampton
Yelford
Aston
Brighthampton
Stanton Harcourt
Eaton
Bessels Leigh
Botley
North Hinksey
South Hinksey
Iffley
Littlemore
Sandford-on-Thames
Horspath
Wheatley
Garsington
Cuddesdon
Great Milton
Great Haseley
Little Milton
Little Haseley
Tetsworth
Emmington
Sydenham
Postcombe
Langford
Clanfield
Weald
Cote
Northmoor
Chimney
Duxford
Appleton
Wootton
Sandleigh
Kennington
Bayworth
Nuneham Courtenay
Toot Baldon
Marsh Baldon
Chiselhampton
Stadhampton
Stoke Talmage
Lechlade
Grafton
Kelmscot
Hinton Waldrist
Longworth
Buckland
Southmoor
Kingston Bagpuize
Tubney
Fyfield
Sunningwell
Cothill
Shippon
Radley
Northcourt
Buscot
Eaton Hastings
Littleworth
Frilford
Abingdon
Caldecott
Clifton Hampden
Newington
Chalgrove
South Weston
Lewknor
Faringdon
Pusey
Charney Bassett
Garford
Marcham
Culham
Berinsfield
Drayton St Leonard
Brightwell Baldwin
Cuxham
Pyrton
Shirburn
Watlington
Badbury Hill
Hatford
Lyford
Sutton Wick
Long Wittenham
Dorchester
Berrick Prior
Berrick Salome
Brightwell Upperton
Little Coxwell
Stanford in the Vale
Shellingford
Great Coxwell
East Hanney
Drayton
Sutton Courtenay
Appleford
Warborough
Shillingford
Roke
Britwell Salome
Fernham
West Hanney
Denchworth
Milton
Little Wittenham
Benson
Ewelme
Baulking
Goosey
Steventon
Milton Hill
Brightwell-cum-Sotwell
Vale of White Horse
Watchfield
Longcot
Grove
Didcot
Wallingford
Crowmarsh Gifford
Cookley Green
Russell's Water
Pishill
Uffington
West Hendred
North Moreton
South Moreton
Shrivenham
East Challow
Charlton
Ardington
East Hendred
Harwell
East Hagbourne
Park Corner
West Challow
Woolstone
Kingston Lisle
Sparsholt
Compton Beauchamp
Wantage
West Hagbourne
Aston Upthorpe
Childrey
Letcombe Regis
West Lockinge
East Lockinge
Upton
Cholsey
North Stoke
Nuffield
Crocker End
Chilton
Uffington Castle
Whitehorse Hill
Ashbury
Waylands Smithy
Letcombe Bassett
Blewbury
Aston Tirrold
Ipsden
Highmoor
Idstone
Wellbottom Down
Bishopstone
Hinton Parva
Greenhill Down
Longinge Hill
West Ilsley
Moulsford
South Stoke
Stoke Row
Checkendon
Woodcote
Exlade Street
Lambourn Downs
Ashdown NT
Upper Lambourn
Ewe Hill
Fawley
Farnborough
East Ilsley
Cleeve
Goring
Rotherfield Peppard
Bishopstone Downs
Catmore
Compton
Aldworth
Westridge Green
Streatley
Sonning Common
Lambourn
Brightwalton
Lower Basildon
Cane End
Kidmore End
Baydon
Chaddleworth
Beedon
Beedon Hill
Whitchurch Hill
Whitchurch
Tokers Green
East Garston
World's End
Basildon Park NT
Eastbury
Leckhampstead Thicket
Peasemore
Ashampstead
Wyld Court Rainforest
Pangbourne
Mapledurham
Aldbourne
Great Shefford
Bothampstead
Hampstead Norrey's
Upper Basildon
Purley
Leckhampstead
Royal County of Berkshire
Yattendon
Tidmarsh
Sulham
Tilehurst
Caversham
Membury
East Shefford
Preston
Weston
Chieveley
Hermitage
Frilsham
Bradfield
Reading
Welford
Winterbourne
Ramsbury
Westbrook
Curridge
Stanford Dingley
Englefield
North Street
Boxford
Theale
Calcot Row
Axford
Chilton Foliat
Hungerford Newtown
Wickham
Cold Ash
Bucklebury
Chapel Row
Whitley
Upper Bucklebury
Sulhamstead
Donnington
Ashmore Green
Stockcross
Hungerford
Froxfield
Shaw
Thatcham
Beenham
Burghfield
Speen
Midgham
Three Mile Cross
Avington
Newbury
Little Bedwyn
Kintbury
Ufton Nervet
Woolhampton
Burghfield Common
Chisbury
Savernake Forest
Chisbury Chapel
Padworth
Spencers Wood
Swallowfield
Hamstead Marshall
Enborne
Brimpton
Durley
Great Bedwyn
Aldermaston
Mortimer
Enborne Row
Crookham
Inkpen
Pumping Station
Upper Green
West Woodhay
Broad Laying
Woolton Hill
Ashford Hill
Pamber Heath
Mortimer West End
Stratfield Mortimer
Shalbourne
Ham
Headley
Burghclere
Plastow Green
Silchester
Stratfield Saye
Eastcourt
Combe Gibbet
Walbury Hill
Tadley
West End Green
Fair Oak Green
Wilton
East Woodhay
East End
Sandham Memorial Chapel NT
Ecchinswell
Browninghill Green
Baughurst
Pamber Green
Bramley Corner
Stratfield Turgis
Marten
West Grafton
East Grafton
Combe
Pilot Hill
Highclere
Highclere Castle
Whitway
Charter Alley
Little London
Turgis Green
Oxenwood
Wexcombe
Linkenholt
Old Burghclere
Kingsclere
Wolverton
Towns End
Pamber End
Bramley
Hartley Wespall
Faccombe
Ashmansworth
Sydmonton
Sherfield on Loddon
Tidcombe
Fosbury
Vernham Street
Crux Easton
Beacon Hill
Ladle Hill (unfinished hill fort)
Cottington's Hill
Ramsdell
The Vyne NT
Mattingley
Brunton
Tidcombe Down
Haydown Hill
Monk Sherborne
Sherborne St John
Church End
Rotherwick
Collingbourne Kingston
Vernham Dean
Hannington
Chineham
Ibthorpe
Upper Chute
Lower Chute
Binley
Ibworth
Wootton St Lawrence
Old Basing
Basing House (Ruins)
Newnham
Cadley
Collingbourne Ducis
Tangley
Hurstbourne Tarrant
Litchfield
Basingstoke
Nately Scures
Greywell
Odiham
Stoke
North Warnborough
Ludgershall
Hatherden
Little London
St Mary Bourne
Deane
Ashe
Oakley
Kempshott
Mapledurwell
Southington
Freefolk
Overton
Cliddesden
Tunworth
Upton Grey
Appleshaw
Clanville
Enham Alamein
Smannell
Penton Mewsey
Laverstoke
Whitchurch
Steventon
Winslade
Weston Corbett
South Warnborough
Kimpton
Fyfield
Weyhill
Hurstbourne Priors
Tufton
Silk Mill
North Waltham
Farleigh Wallop
Herriard
Weston Patrick
Thruxton
Andover
Longparish
Dummer
Ellisfield
Nash's Green
Monxton
Anna Valley
Amport
Middleton
Bagmore
Southrope
Quarley
Quarley Hill
Abbotts Ann
Upper Clatford
Forton
Micheldever Station
Woodmancott
Axford
Lasham
Golden Pot
Cholderton
Goodworth Clatford
Bransbury
Preston Candover
Bradley
Grateley
Wherwell
Newton Stacey
Barton Stacey
Bullington
Chilton Candover
Shalden
Holybourne
Newton Toney
Hunton
Weston Colley
East Stratton
Lower Wield
Bentworth
Alton
Middle Wallop
Fullerton
Chilbolton
Sutton Scotney
Wonston
Stoke Charity
Northbrook
Micheldever
Brown Candover
Upper Wield
Wivelrod
Beech
Danebury Ring
Danebury Hill
Over Wallop
Longstock
Leckford
Northington
Swarraton
Medstead
Mid Hants Railway
Chawton
Jane Austen's House
Nether Wallop
Crawley Down
The Grange
Four Marks
Upper Farringdon
Stockbridge
Crawley
Winchester
Bighton
Old Alresford
East Winterslow
Middle Winterslow
Whiteshoot
Houghton Lodge
Broughton
Little Somborne
Littleton
Kings Worthy
Abbots Worthy
Martyr Worthy
Itchen Abbas
New Alresford
Gundleton
Lower Farringdon
East Worldham
0 1 2 3 4 miles
0 1 2 3 4 5 kilometres

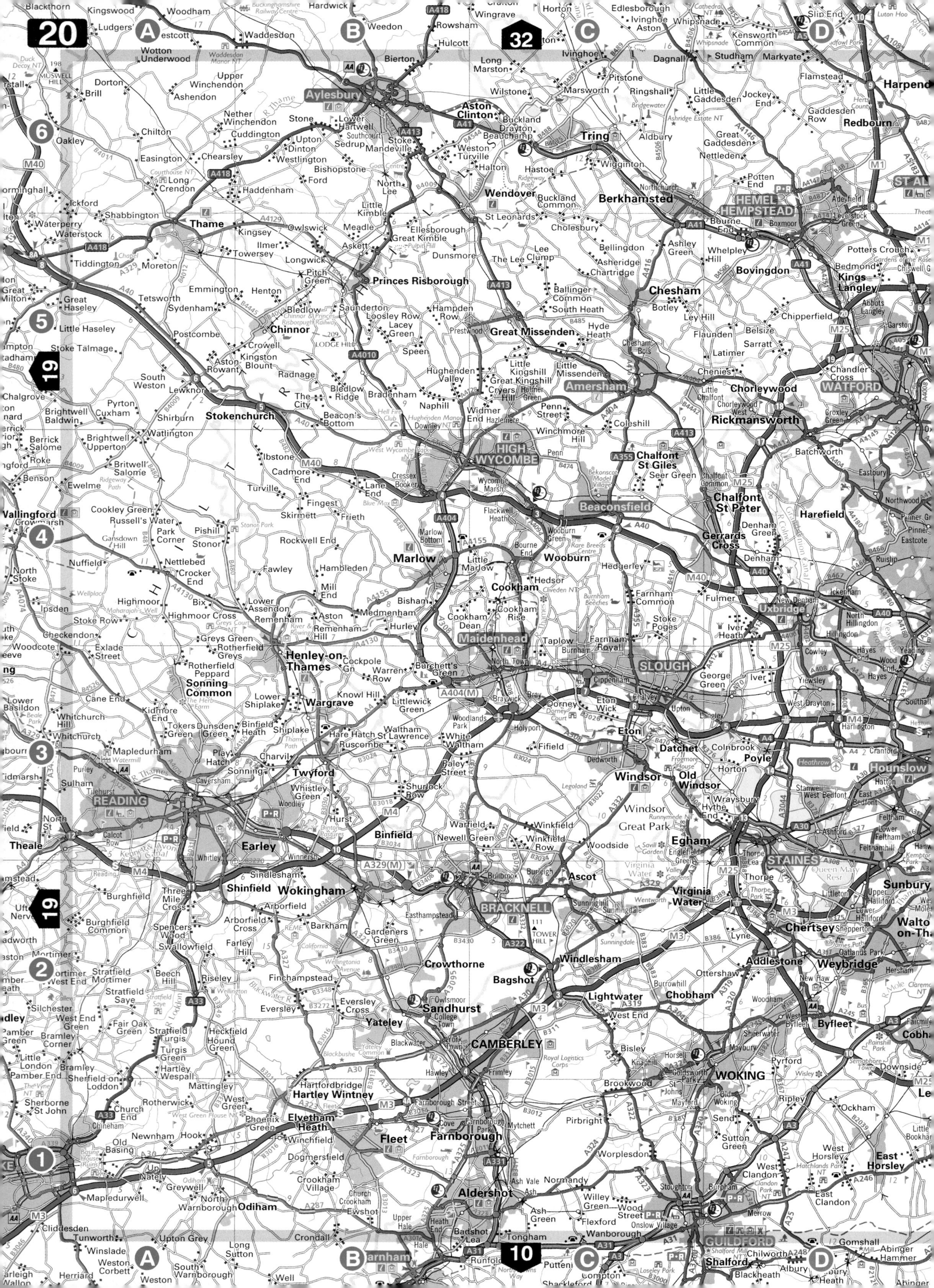

20
32
19
10
A
B
C
D
1
2
3
4
5
6
Aylesbury
Tring
Harpenden
Wendover
Berkhamsted
HEMEL HEMPSTEAD
Thame
Princes Risborough
Chesham
Chinnor
Great Missenden
Amersham
WATFORD
Stokenchurch
Chorleywood
Rickmansworth
HIGH WYCOMBE
Chalfont St Giles
Beaconsfield
Chalfont St Peter
Harefield
Gerrards Cross
Marlow
Wooburn
Cookham
Maidenhead
SLOUGH
Uxbridge
Henley-on-Thames
Sonning Common
Wargrave
Twyford
READING
Earley
Windsor
Eton
Datchet
Hounslow
Egham
STAINES
Ascot
Wokingham
BRACKNELL
Virginia Water
Sunbury
Chertsey
Weybridge
Addlestone
Crowthorne
Bagshot
Windlesham
Sandhurst
Yateley
CAMBERLEY
Chobham
Byfleet
WOKING
Hartley Wintney
Fleet
Farnborough
Aldershot
Odiham
GUILDFORD
Shalford
Vallingford
Theale
Shinfield
Binfield
Lightwater
Elvetham Heath

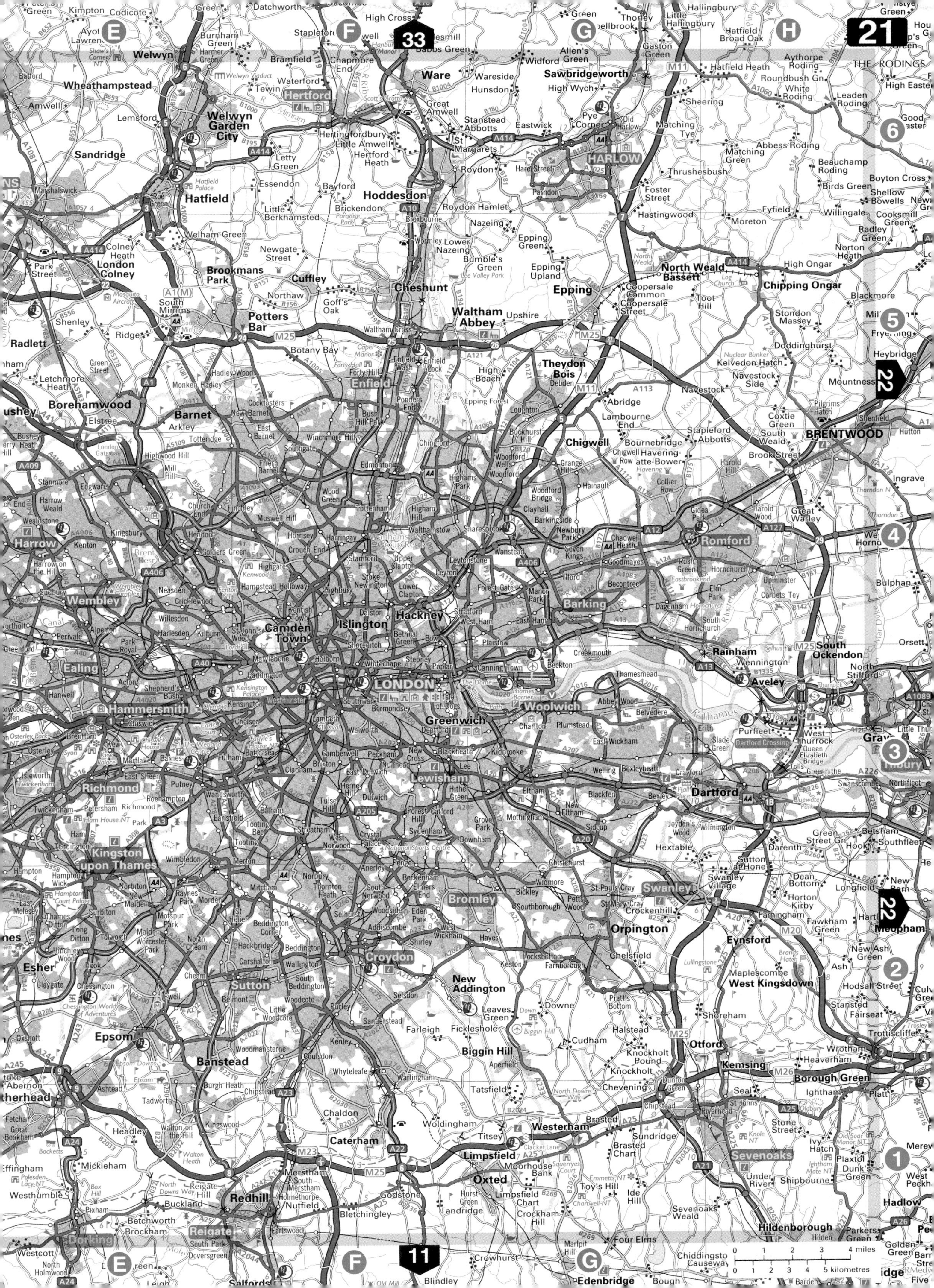

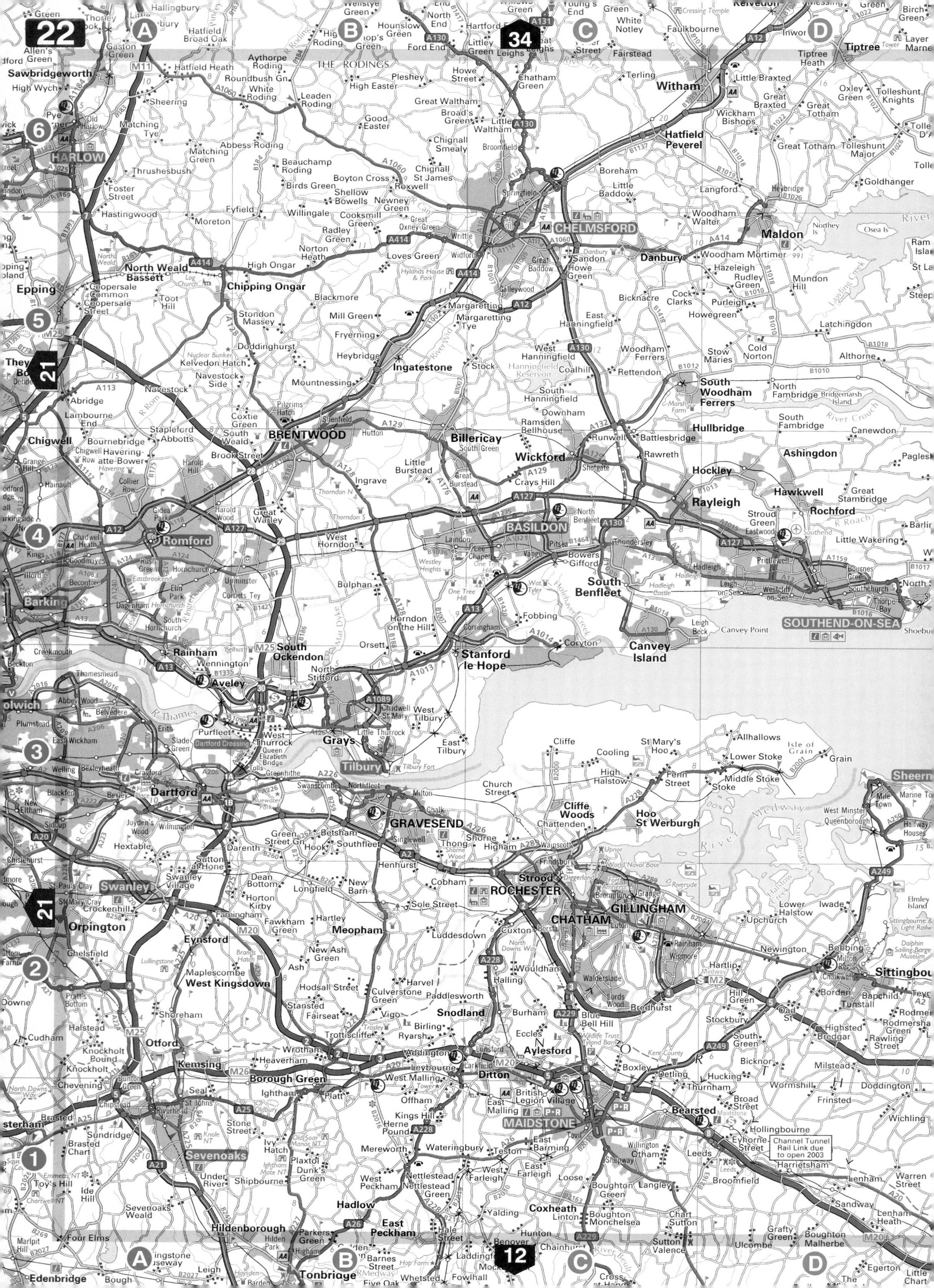
22
A
B
C
D
34
Sawbridgeworth
High Wych
Hatfield Heath
Aythorpe Roding
THE RODINGS
Hatfield Broad Oak
Roundbush Gn.
White Roding
Leaden Roding
High Roding
Pleshey
High Easter
Hounslow Green
Ford End
Littley Green
Howe Street
Great Waltham
Broad's Green
Little Waltham
Chatham Green
Fairstead
Terling
White Notley
Faulkbourne
Cressing Temple
Witham
Little Braxted
Great Braxted
Wickham Bishops
Hatfield Peverel
Tiptree Heath
Tiptree
Inworth
Layer Marney
Oxley Green
Tolleshunt Knights
Great Totham
Tolleshunt Major
Goldhanger
Heybridge
Maldon
Langford
Woodham Walter
Northey Is
Osea Is
Boreham
Little Baddow
Springfield
CHELMSFORD
Danbury
Sandon
Howe Green
Great Baddow
Galleywood
Woodham Mortimer
Hazeleigh
Rudley Green
Purleigh
Cock Clarks
Bicknacre
Mundon Hill
Latchingdon
Howegreen
East Hanningfield
West Hanningfield
Hanningfield Reservoir
Woodham Ferrers
Stow Maries
Cold Norton
Althorne
Rettendon
Coalhill
South Woodham Ferrers
North Fambridge
Bridgemarsh Island
River Crouch
South Fambridge
Canewdon
Hullbridge
Battlesbridge
Runwell
Rawreth
Ashingdon
Paglesham
Hockley
Hawkwell
Great Stambridge
Rayleigh
Rochford
Stroud Green
Eastwood
Little Wakering
Barling
Southend
Prittlewell
Hadleigh
Leigh-on-Sea
Westcliff-on-Sea
Southchurch
Thorpe Bay
Bournes Green
North Shoebury
SOUTHEND-ON-SEA
Shoeburyness
Canvey Point
Leigh Beck
Canvey Island
South Benfleet
Thundersley
Bowers Gifford
Pitsea
Vange
BASILDON
North Benfleet
Wickford
Shotgate
Crays Hill
Billericay
South Green
Great Burstead
Little Burstead
Ramsden Bellhouse
Downham
South Hanningfield
Stock
Ingatestone
Fryerning
Margaretting
Margaretting Tye
Mill Green
Heybridge
Blackmore
Mountnessing
Doddinghurst
Kelvedon Hatch
Nuclear Bunker
Stondon Massey
Chipping Ongar
High Ongar
Norton Heath
Loves Green
Writtle
Widford
Hylands House & Park
Roxwell
Chignall St James
Chignall Smealy
Good Easter
Beauchamp Roding
Abbess Roding
Boyton Cross
Birds Green
Shellow Bowells
Newney Green
Willingale
Cooksmill Green
Radley Green
Great Oxney Green
Fyfield
Moreton
Matching Green
Matching Tye
Sheering
Harlow
Old Harlow
Pye Corner
Thrushesbush
Foster Street
Hastingwood
North Weald Bassett
Epping
Coopersale Common
Coopersale Street
Toot Hill
Theydon Bois
Abridge
Lambourne End
Navestock
Navestock Side
Chigwell
Chigwell Row
Bournebridge
Stapleford Abbotts
Havering-atte-Bower
Coxtie Green
Pilgrims Hatch
South Weald
Brook Street
BRENTWOOD
Shenfield
Hutton
Ingrave
Herongate
Great Warley
Harold Hill
Harold Wood
Gidea Park
Collier Row
Hainault
Romford
Chadwell Heath
Goodmayes
Ilford
Becontree
Rush Green
Hornchurch
Elm Park
Upminster
Cranham
Corbets Tey
Dagenham
South Hornchurch
Barking
Rainham
Wennington
Aveley
South Ockendon
North Stifford
Orsett
Bulphan
West Horndon
Laindon
Lee Chapel
One Tree Hill
Langdon Hills
Horndon on the Hill
Stanford le Hope
Corringham
Fobbing
Coryton
Chadwell St Mary
West Tilbury
East Tilbury
Tilbury
Tilbury Fort
Grays
Little Thurrock
West Thurrock
Purfleet
Dartford Crossing
Thamesmead
Woolwich
Abbey Wood
Belvedere
Erith
Slade Green
Plumstead
East Wickham
Welling
Bexleyheath
Crayford
Dartford
Greenhithe
Stone
Swanscombe
Northfleet
Bexley
Blackfen
New Eltham
Sidcup
Joyden's Wood
Wilmington
Hextable
Darenth
Sutton at Hone
Swanley Village
Swanley
St Pauls Cray
St Mary Cray
Crockenhill
Orpington
Chelsfield
Eynsford
Farningham
Horton Kirby
Fawkham Green
Hartley
Longfield
Green Street Green
Betsham
Southfleet
GRAVESEND
Chalk
Milton
Singlewell
Shorne
Thong
Higham
Henhurst
Cobham
Meopham
Sole Street
Luddesdown
New Ash Green
Ash
Maplescombe
West Kingsdown
Shoreham
Halstead
Cudham
Knockholt Pound
Knockholt
Otford
Kemsing
Chevening
Dunton Green
Chipstead
Riverhead
Seal
Sevenoaks
Brasted
Westerham
Sundridge
Brasted Chart
Toy's Hill
Ide Hill
Emmetts NT
Chartwell NT
Sevenoaks Weald
Underriver
Shipbourne
Hildenborough
Four Elms
Marlpit Hill
Edenbridge
Leigh
Tonbridge
Ightham
Ightham Mote NT
Ivy Hatch
Plaxtol
Dunk's Green
Stone Street
Borough Green
Heaverham
Wrotham
Platt
Trottiscliffe
Stansted
Fairseat
Vigo
Culverstone Green
Harvel
Hodsall Street
Paddlesworth
Snodland
Birling
Ryarsh
Addington
Leybourne
West Malling
Offham
Kings Hill
Herne Pound
Mereworth
Wateringbury
Teston
West Peckham
Nettlestead
Nettlestead Green
West Farleigh
East Farleigh
Hadlow
East Peckham
Yalding
Hale Street
Laddingford
Benover
Coxheath
Linton
Loose
Boughton Monchelsea
Hunton
Chainhurst
12
Ditton
Larkfield
Aylesford
Eccles
Burham
Wouldham
Halling
Cuxton
Borstal
Strood
ROCHESTER
CHATHAM
GILLINGHAM
Brompton
Luton
Rainham
Wigmore
Walderslade
Lords Wood
Bredhurst
Blue Bell Hill
Upchurch
Lower Halstow
Iwade
Newington
Hartlip
Bobbing
Milton Regis
Sittingbourne
Chalkwell
Borden
Bapchild
Tunstall
Rodmersham
Highsted
Bredgar
Oad Street
Stockbury
South Green
Hill Green
Bicknor
Detling
Thurnham
Hucking
Boxley
Bearsted
Broad Street
Hollingbourne
Eyhorne Street
Leeds
Harrietsham
Lenham
Channel Tunnel Rail Link due to open 2003
Wormshill
Milstead
Frinsted
Doddington
Wichling
Warren Street
Sandway
Lenham Heath
Grafty Green
Boughton Malherbe
Ulcombe
Sutton Valence
Chart Sutton
Langley
Boughton Green
Otham
Willington
Shepway
East Barming
MAIDSTONE
British Legion Village
East Malling
Allington
Cliffe
Cooling
St Mary's Hoo
Allhallows
Isle of Grain
Grain
Lower Stoke
Middle Stoke
Stoke
Fenn Street
High Halstow
Church Street
Cliffe Woods
Chattenden
Hoo St Werburgh
Wainscott
Frindsbury
Upnor
River Medway
Sheerness
Queenborough
Halfway Houses
Marine Town
Mile Town
West Minster
Elmley Island
21

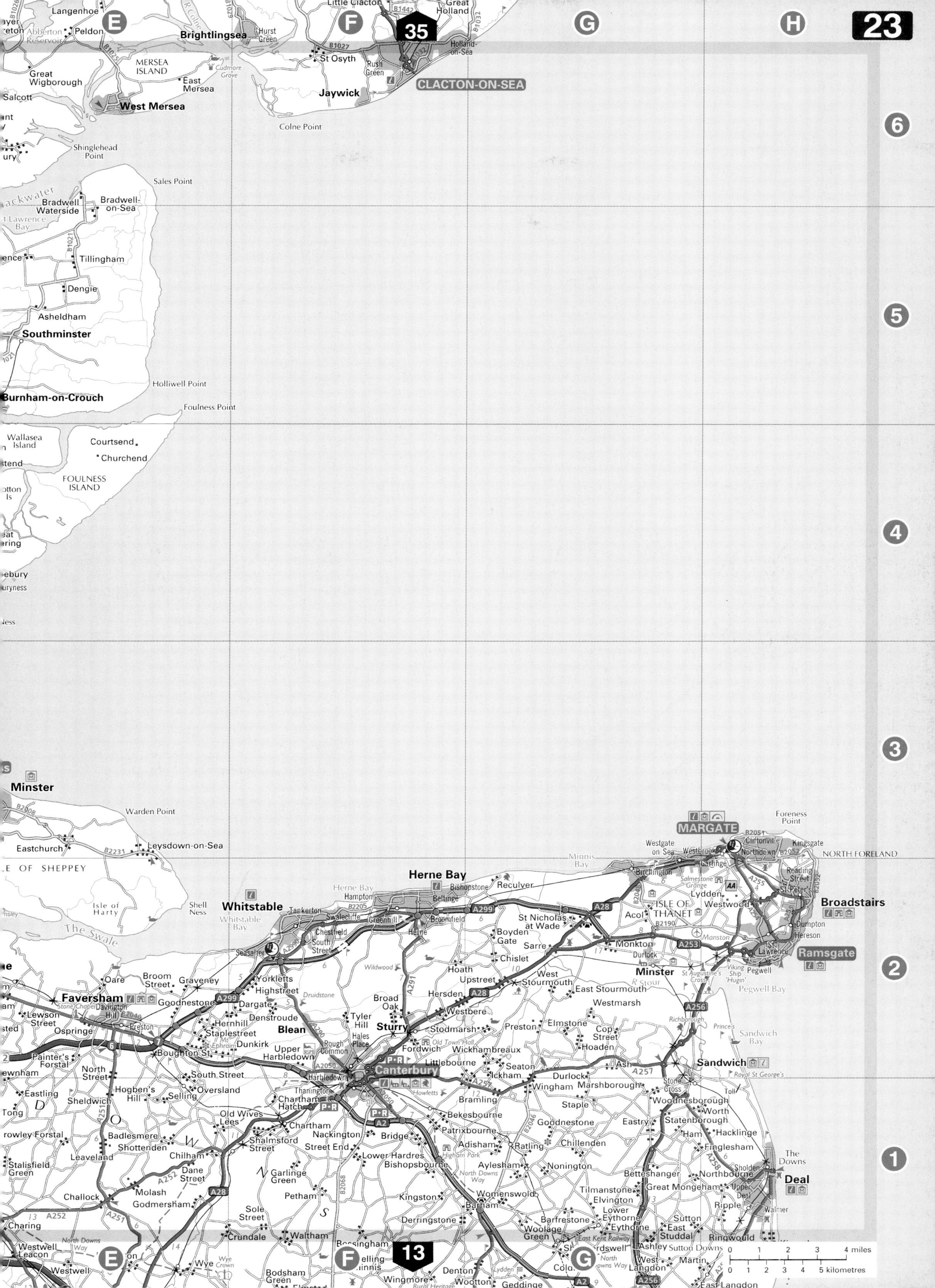
E
F
G
H
35
13
6
5
4
3
2
1
Langenhoe
Peldon
Abberton Reservoir
Brightlingsea
Hurst Green
Little Clacton
Great Holland
Holland-on-Sea
St Osyth
Rush Green
CLACTON-ON-SEA
Jaywick
MERSEA ISLAND
Cudmore Grove
East Mersea
Great Wigborough
Salcott
West Mersea
Colne Point
Shinglehead Point
Sales Point
Bradwell Waterside
Bradwell-on-Sea
St Lawrence Bay
Tillingham
Dengie
Asheldham
Southminster
Holliwell Point
Burnham-on-Crouch
Foulness Point
Wallasea Island
Courtsend
Churchend
FOULNESS ISLAND
Minster
Warden Point
Eastchurch
Leysdown-on-Sea
ISLE OF SHEPPEY
Isle of Harty
Shell Ness
The Swale
Whitstable
Whitstable Bay
Tankerton
Swalecliffe
Chestfield
Herne Bay
Hampton
Greenhill
Beltinge
Bishopstone
Reculver
Herne
Broomfield
Seasalter
South Street
Faversham
Oare
Broom Street
Graveney
Yorkletts
Highstreet
Goodnestone
Dargate
Denstroude
Hernhill
Staplestreet
Dunkirk
Boughton St
Blean
Upper Harbledown
Rough Common
Tyler Hill
Hales Place
Sturry
Broad Oak
Canterbury
Harbledown
Thanington
Chartham Hatch
Chartham
Fordwich
Littlebourne
Stodmarsh
Wickhambreaux
Seaton
Ickham
Hersden
Westbere
Upstreet
Hoath
Chislet
Sarre
Boyden Gate
St Nicholas at Wade
West Stourmouth
East Stourmouth
Westmarsh
Preston
Elmstone
Cop Street
Hoaden
Ash
Durlock
Wingham
Marshborough
Sandwich
Royal St George's
Sandwich Bay
Pegwell Bay
Pegwell
Minster
Monkton
ISLE OF THANET
Acol
Birchington
Westgate on Sea
Westbrook
Garlinge
MARGATE
Cliftonville
Kingsgate
Foreness Point
NORTH FORELAND
Northdown
Reading Street
Broadstairs
St Peter's
Dumpton
Westwood
Lydden
Salmestone Grange
Manston
Ramsgate
St Lawrence
Minnis Bay
Richborough
Stonar Cross
Woodnesborough
Worth
Statenborough
Eastry
Staple
Goodnestone
Chillenden
Nonington
Aylesham
Adisham
Ratling
Bekesbourne
Patrixbourne
Bridge
Bramling
Nackington
Street End
Lower Hardres
Bishopsbourne
Kingston
Barham
Womenswold
Derringstone
Hackllnge
Finglesham
Ham
Sholden
The Downs
Deal
Upper Deal
Walmer
Northbourne
Great Mongeham
Betteshanger
Tilmanstone
Elvington
Lower Eythorne
Eythorne
Barfrestone
Woolage Green
Ripple
Sutton
East Studdal
Ringwould
Ashley
Sutton Downs
West Langdon
Martin
East Langdon
Lewson Street
Ospringe
Painter's Forstal
North Street
Eastling
Sheldwich
Hogben's Hill
Selling
South Street
Oversland
Old Wives Lees
Shalmsford Street
Chilham
Dane Street
Molash
Godmersham
Badlesmere
Shottenden
Leaveland
Challock
Charing
Westwell Leacon
Westwell
Stalisfield Green
Garlinge Green
Petham
Sole Street
Crundale
Waltham
Bossingham
Bodsham Green
Wye
Wingmore
Denton
Wootton
Geddinge
Lydden
Coldred
Shepherdswell
0 1 2 3 4 miles
0 1 2 3 4 5 kilometres

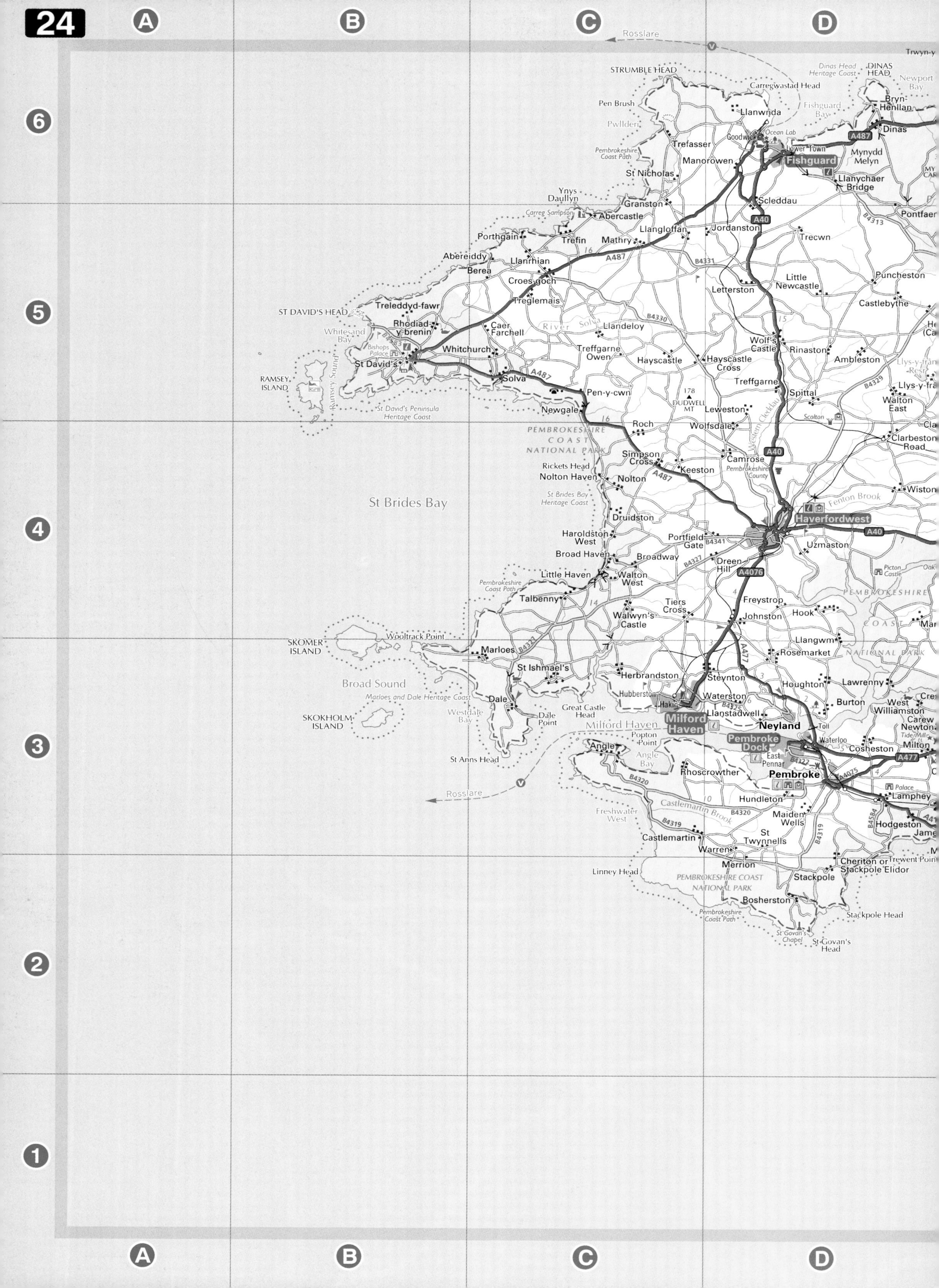
A
B
C
D
6
5
4
3
2
1
Rosslare
STRUMBLE HEAD
Carregwastad Head
Dinas Head Heritage Coast
DINAS HEAD
Newport Bay
Fishguard Bay
Pen Brush
Llanwnda
Bryn-Henllan
Dinas
Pwllderi
Goodwick
Ocean Lab
Trefasser
Lower Town
Fishguard
Mynydd Melyn
Pembrokeshire Coast Path
Manorowen
St Nicholas
Llanychaer Bridge
Ynys Daullyn
Granston
Scleddau
Pontfaen
Carreg Sampson
Abercastle
Porthgain
Llangloffan
Jordanston
Trefin
Mathry
Trecwn
Abereiddy
Llanrhian
Berea
Little Newcastle
Puncheston
Croes-goch
Letterston
Treglemais
Castlebythe
ST DAVID'S HEAD
Treleddyd-fawr
Whitesand Bay
Rhodiad-y-brenin
Caer Farchell
River Solva
Llandeloy
Bishops Palace
Whitchurch
Treffgarne Owen
Hayscastle
Hayscastle Cross
Wolf's Castle
Rinaston
Ambleston
St David's
Solva
Treffgarne
RAMSEY ISLAND
Ramsey Sound
Pen-y-cwn
DUDWELL MT
Spittal
Walton East
Newgale
Leweston
St David's Peninsula Heritage Coast
Scolton
PEMBROKESHIRE COAST NATIONAL PARK
Roch
Wolfsdale
Clarbeston Road
Western Cleddau
Simpson Cross
Camrose
Rickets Head
Keeston
Pembrokeshire County
Nolton Haven
Nolton
Wiston
St Brides Bay
St Brides Bay Heritage Coast
Fenton Brook
Druidston
Haverfordwest
Haroldston West
Portfield Gate
Uzmaston
Broad Haven
Broadway
Dreen Hill
Picton Castle
Little Haven
Walton West
Pembrokeshire Coast Path
Talbenny
Freystrop
Tiers Cross
Walwyn's Castle
Johnston
Hook
SKOMER ISLAND
Wooltrack Point
Marloes
Llangwm
Rosemarket
St Ishmael's
Herbrandston
Steynton
Lawrenny
Broad Sound
Marloes and Dale Heritage Coast
Dale
Hubberston
Hakin
Waterston
Houghton
Burton
Westdale Bay
Dale Point
Great Castle Head
Llanstadwell
West Williamston
SKOKHOLM ISLAND
Milford Haven
Neyland
Carew Newton
Popton Point
Pembroke Dock
Waterloo
Cosheston
Milton
Angle
Angle Bay
East Pennar
St Anns Head
Rhoscrowther
Pembroke
Rosslare
Palace
Lamphey
Hundleton
Freshwater West
Castlemartin Brook
Maiden Wells
Hodgeston
Castlemartin
St Twynnells
Warren
Merrion
Cheriton or Stackpole Elidor
Trewent Point
Linney Head
PEMBROKESHIRE COAST NATIONAL PARK
Stackpole
Bosherston
Stackpole Head
St Govan's Chapel
St Govan's Head
A40
A487
A4076
A477
A4075
B4331
B4330
B4313
B4329
B4341
B4327
B4320
B4319
B4584
B4322

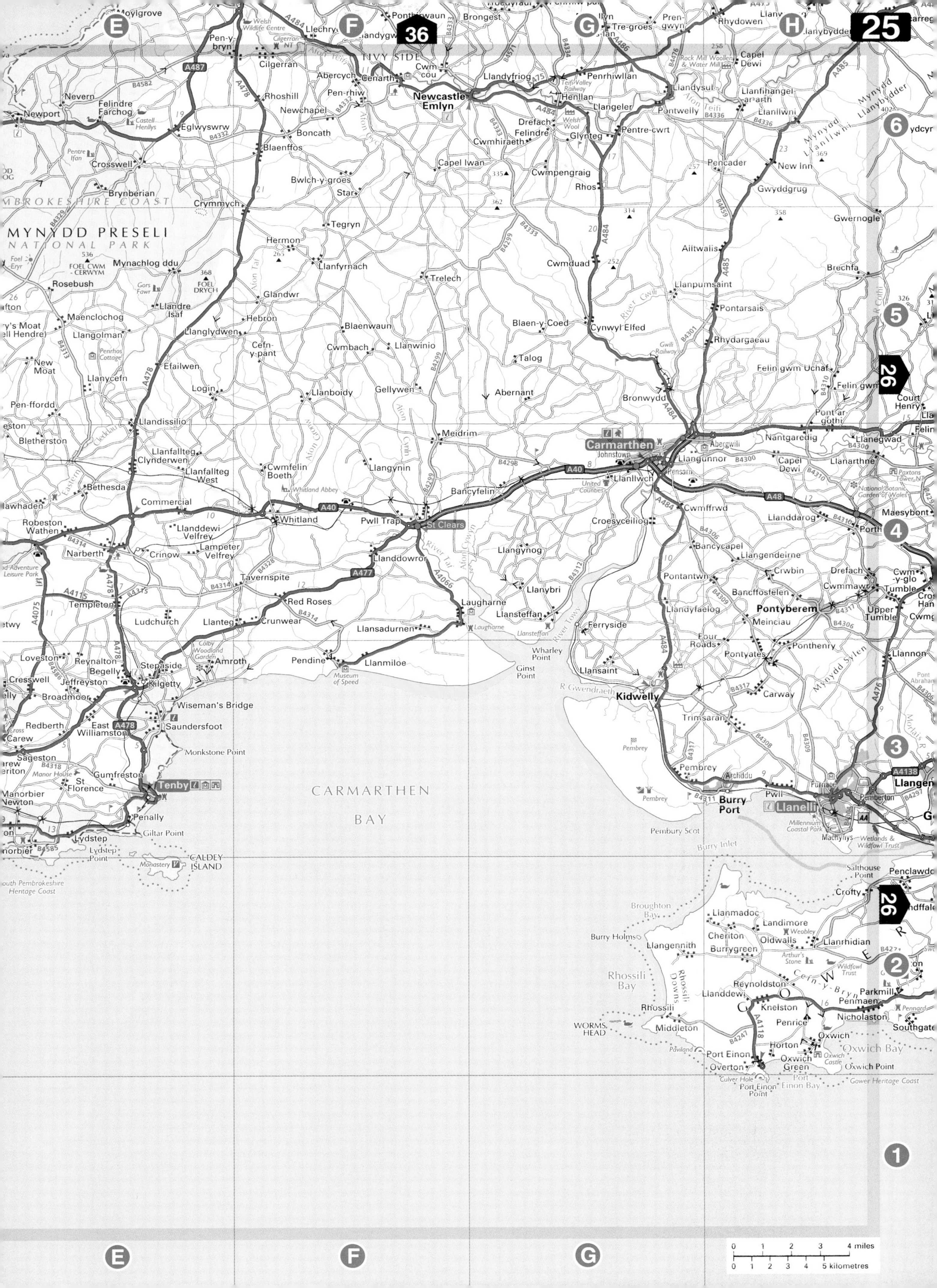

25
36
26
E
F
G
H
1
2
3
4
5
6
Moylgrove
Pen-y-bryn
Cilgerran
Llechryd
Abercych
Cenarth
Newcastle Emlyn
Brongest
Tre-groes
Rhydowen
Llandyfriog
Penrhiwllan
Henllan
Llangeler
Llandysul
Pontwelly
Llanfihangel-ar-arth
Llanllwni
Capel Dewi
Nevern
Felindre Farchog
Newport
Eglwyswrw
Rhoshill
Newchapel
Pen-rhiw
Boncath
Blaenffos
Crosswell
Brynberian
Crymmych
Bwlch-y-groes
Star
Capel Iwan
Cwmhiraeth
Drefach
Felindre
Glynteg
Pentre-cwrt
Cwmpengraig
Rhos
Pencader
New Inn
Gwyddgrug
Gwernogle
MYNYDD PRESELI
NATIONAL PARK
PEMBROKESHIRE COAST
Tegryn
Hermon
Llanfyrnach
Mynachlog ddu
Rosebush
Trelech
Cwmduad
Alltwalis
Brechfa
Llanpumsaint
Glandwr
Llandre Isaf
Hebron
Maenclochog
Llangolman
Llanglydwen
Cefn-y-pant
Blaenwaun
Cwmbach
Llanwinio
Blaen-y-Coed
Cynwyl Elfed
Pontarsais
Rhydargaeau
Talog
New Moat
Llanycefn
Efailwen
Login
Llanboidy
Gellywen
Abernant
Bronwydd
Felin gwm Uchaf
Felin gwm
Court Henry
Pont-ar-gothi
Pen-ffordd
Llandissilio
Bletherston
Llanfallteg
Clynderwen
Llanfallteg West
Cwmfelin Boeth
Meidrim
Llangynin
Carmarthen
Johnstown
Abergwili
Llangunnor
Nantgaredig
Llanegwad
Llanarthne
Capel Dewi
Bethesda
Commercial
Whitland
Pwll Trap
St Clears
Bancyfelin
Llanllwch
Cwmffrwd
Llanddarog
Maesybont
Porth
Robeston Wathen
Narberth
Llanddewi Velfrey
Crinow
Lampeter Velfrey
Croesyceiliog
Llangynog
Bancycapel
Llangendeirne
Crwbin
Drefach
Cwm-y-glo
Cwmmawr
Tumble
Templeton
Taverns pite
Llanddowror
Red Roses
Llanybri
Laugharne
Llansteffan
Pontantwn
Bancffosfelen
Pontyberem
Upper Tumble
Ludchurch
Llanteg
Crunwear
Llansadurnen
Ferryside
Llandyfaelog
Meinciau
Four Roads
Ponthenry
Pontyates
Loveston
Reynalton
Begelly
Stepaside
Amroth
Pendine
Llanmiloe
Wharley Point
Ginst Point
Llansaint
Kidwelly
Carway
Cresswell
Jeffreyston
Kilgetty
Broadmoor
Wiseman's Bridge
Redberth
East Williamston
Saundersfoot
Carew
Trimsaran
Monkstone Point
Sageston
Gumfreston
Manorbier Newton
St Florence
Tenby
Penally
Pembrey
Burry Port
Pwll
Llanelli
Pemberton
Llangennech
Lydstep
Giltar Point
Lydstep Point
CALDEY ISLAND
CARMARTHEN BAY
Burry Inlet
Salthouse Point
Penclawdd
Crofty
Broughton Bay
Llanmadoc
Landimore
Cheriton
Oldwalls
Llanrhidian
Burry Holms
Llangennith
Burrygreen
Rhossili Bay
Rhossili Downs
Reynoldston
Llanddewi
Parkmill
Penmaen
Rhossili
Knelston
Nicholaston
Southgate
WORMS HEAD
Middleton
Penrice
Oxwich
Oxwich Bay
Horton
Port Einon
Oxwich Green
Overton
Oxwich Point
Port Einon Point
Port Einon Bay
Gower Heritage Coast
GOWER
0 1 2 3 4 miles
0 1 2 3 4 5 kilometres

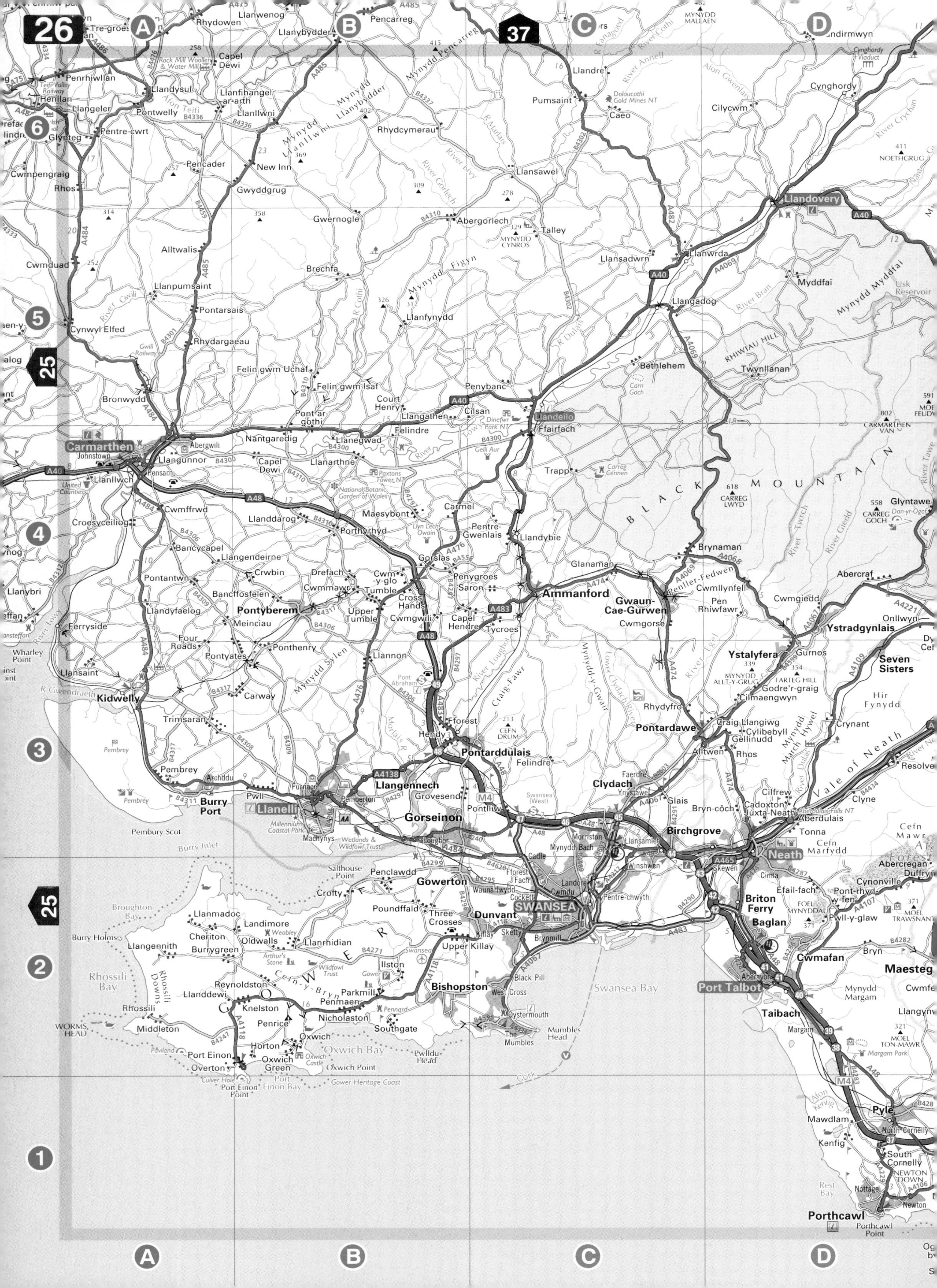
26
37
25
25
A
B
C
D
A
B
C
D
6
5
4
3
2
1
Tre-groes
Rhydowen
Llanwenog
Llanybydder
Pencarreg
Mynydd Pencarreg
Mynydd Mallaen
Llandirmwyn
Cynghordy Viaduct
Penrhiwllan
Rock Mill Woollen & Water Mill
Capel Dewi
Llandysul
Teifi Valley Railway
Henllan
Llangeler
Pontwelly
Llanfihangel-ar-arth
Llanllwni
Afon Teifi
Mynydd Llanybydder
Mynydd Llanllwni
Glynteg
Pentre-cwrt
Cwmpengraig
Pencader
New Inn
Rhos
Gwyddgrug
Rhydcymerau
Llandre
Pumsaint
Dolaucothi Gold Mines NT
Caeo
Cynghordy
Cilycwm
River Cothi
River Annell
Aton Gwenlais
River Crychan
R Marlais
River Gorlech
River Livy
Llansawel
Noethgrug
Llandovery
Alltwalis
Gwernogle
Abergorlech
Talley
Mynydd Cynros
Llansadwrn
Llanwrda
Myddfai
Mynydd Myddfai
Usk Reservoir
Cwmduad
Brechfa
Mynydd Figyn
Llanpumsaint
Pontarsais
Llanfynydd
Llangadog
River Bran
Cynwyl Elfed
River Gwili
Gwili Railway
Rhydargaeau
Rhiwiau Hill
R Dulais
Bethlehem
Twynllanan
Felin gwm Uchaf
Felin gwm Isaf
Carn Goch
Bronwydd
Court Henry
Penybanc
Llangathen
Cilsan
Dinefwr Park NT
Llandeilo
Ffairfach
Pont-ar-gothi
Carmarthen Van
Carmarthen
Johnstown
Abergwili
Nantgaredig
Llanegwad
Felindre
Gelli Aur
Llangunnor
Pensarn
Capel Dewi
Llanarthne
Paxtons Tower NT
National Botanic Garden of Wales
Trapp
Carreg Cennen
Llanllwch
United Counties
Black Mountain
Carreg Lwyd
Carreg Goch
Glyntawe
Dan-yr-Ogof
River Twrch
River Giedd
Cwmffrwd
Llanddarog
Maesybont
Carmel
Croesyceiliog
Porthyrhyd
Llyn Llech Owain
Pentre-Gwenlais
Llandybie
Bancycapel
Llangendeirne
Gorslas
Penygroes
Brynaman
Glanaman
Abercraf
Crwbin
Drefach
Cwmmawr
Cwm-y-glo
Tumble
Cross Hands
Saron
Ammanford
Gwaun-Cae-Gurwen
Penller-Fedwen
Cwmllynfell
Pen Rhiwfawr
Cwmgiedd
Ystradgynlais
Onllwyn
Pontantwn
Bancffosfelen
Llandyfaelog
Pontyberem
Upper Tumble
Cwmgwili
Capel Hendre
Tycroes
Cwmgorse
Gurnos
Ferryside
Meinciau
River Towy
Wharley Point
Four Roads
Ponthenry
Llannon
Pontyates
Mynydd Sylen
Mynydd-y-Gwair
Lower Clydach River
River Egel
Ystalyfera
Mynydd Allt-y-grug
Farteg Hill
Godre'r-graig
Cilmaengwyn
Seven Sisters
Hir Fynydd
Llansaint
Pont Abraham
Craig-Fawr
Rhydyfro
R Gwendraeth
Kidwelly
Carway
Trimsaran
Fforest
Hendy
Cefn Drum
Pontardawe
Craig-Llangiwg
Cylibebyll
Gellinudd
Mynydd March Hywel
Crynant
Pembrey
Pontarddulais
Felindre
Alltwen
Rhos
Vale of Neath
Resolven
Archddu
Llangennech
Morlais R
Clydach
Faerdre
Ynystawel
Burry Port
Pwll
Furnace
Pemberton
Grovesend
Pontlliw
Swansea (West)
Glais
Bryn-côch
Cilfrew
Cadoxton-Juxta-Neath
Aberdulais Falls NT
Aberdulais
Clyne
Llanelli
Millennium Coastal Park
Machynys
Wetlands & Wildfowl Trust
Gorseinon
Loughor
Morriston
Llansamlet
Birchgrove
Tonna
Cefn Mawr
Pembury Scot
Burry Inlet
Mynydd-Bach
Neath
Cefn Marfydd
Cadle
Winsh-wen
Skewen
Cimla
Abercregan
Duffryn
Salthouse Point
Penclawdd
Gowerton
Fforest Fach
Landore
Efail-fach
Cynonville
Crofty
Waunarlwydd
Cockett
Cwmdu
Pentre-chwyth
Briton Ferry
Pont-rhyd-y-fen
Foel Mynyddau
Moel Trawsnant
Broughton Bay
Llanmadoc
Landimore
Weobley
Poundffald
Three Crosses
Dunvant
Swansea
Baglan
Pwll-y-glaw
Burry Holms
Cheriton
Oldwalls
Llanrhidian
Killay
Sketty
Brynmill
Llangennith
Burrygreen
Gower
Upper Killay
Cwmafan
Bryn
Maesteg
Rhossili Bay
Rhossili Downs
Arthur's Stone
Wildfowl Trust
Ilston
Swansea Bay
Reynoldston
Cefn-y-Bryn
Bishopston
Black Pill
West Cross
Port Talbot
Aberavon
Mynydd Margam
Llanddewi
Parkmill
Knelston
Penmaen
Pennard
Oystermouth
Rhossili
Nicholaston
Taibach
Llangynwyd
Worms Head
Middleton
Penrice
Southgate
Mumbles Head
The Mumbles
Margam
Moel Ton-Mawr
Oxwich
Oxwich Bay
Pwlldu Head
Paviland
Horton
Port Einon
Oxwich Green
Oxwich Castle
Oxwich Point
Margam Park
Overton
Culver Hole
Port Einon Point
Port Einon Bay
Gower Heritage Coast
Cork
Aton Kenfig
Pyle
North Cornelly
Mawdlam
Kenfig
South Cornelly
Newton Down
Rest Bay
Nottage
Newton
Porthcawl
Porthcawl Point
A40
A48
A484
A485
A486
A475
A476
A482
A483
A4069
A4068
A474
A4067
A4221
A4109
A4138
A4240
A4118
A465
A4107
A4229
A4106
M4
B4459
B4302
B4310
B4300
B4337
B4336
B4301
B4306
B4309
B4317
B4308
B4311
B4297
B4556
B4295
B4296
B4271
B4247
B4436
B4433
B4289
B4291
B4290
B4603
B4434
B4287
B4282
B4286
B4283
B4428
B4312
B4333
B4334
B4476

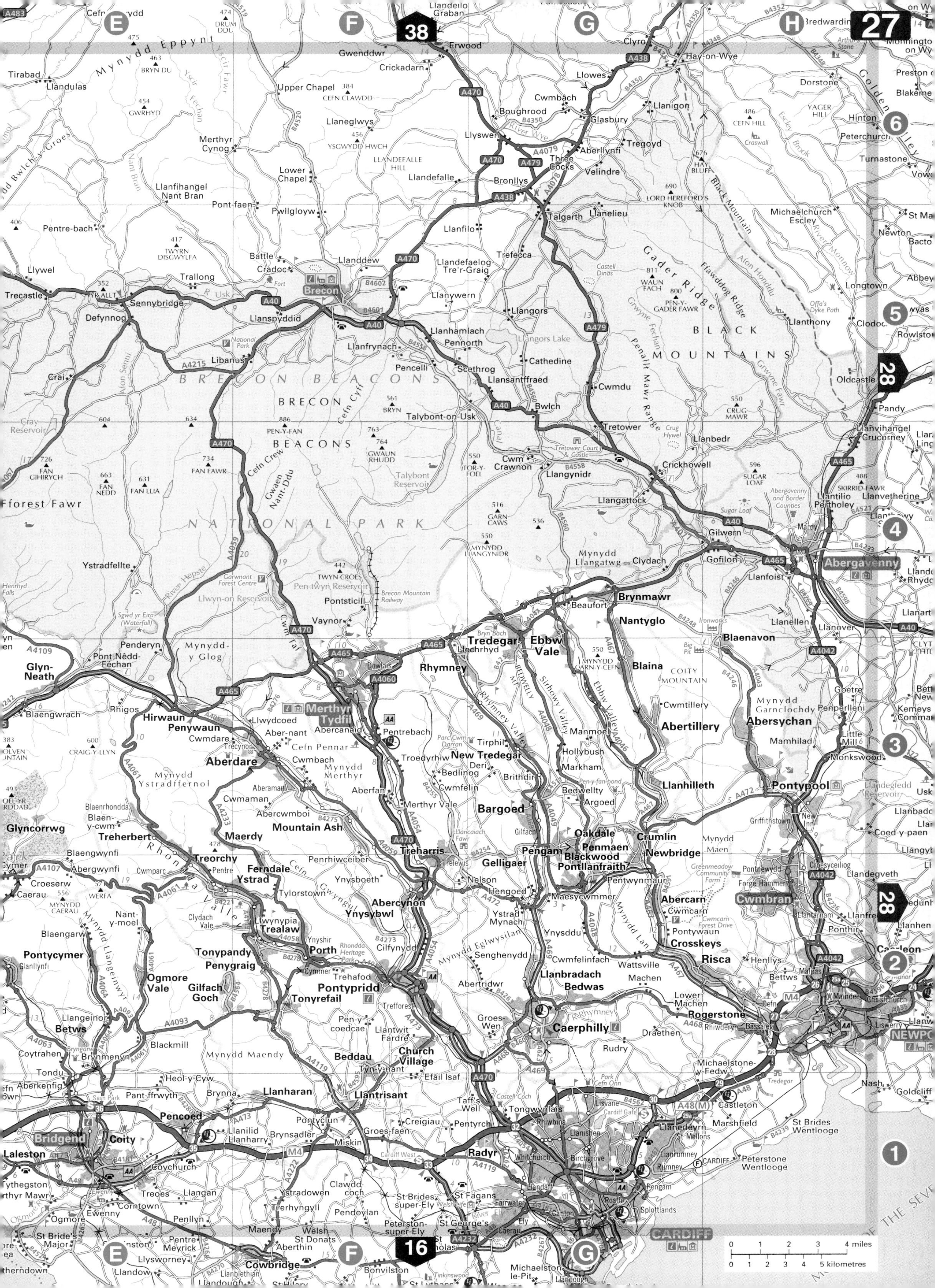
E
F
G
H
38
27
28
28
16
6
5
4
3
2
1
Mynydd Eppynt
Tirabad
Llandulas
Upper Chapel
Llaneglwys
Merthyr Cynog
Lower Chapel
Llanfihangel Nant Bran
Pont-faen
Pwllgloyw
Pentre-bach
Battle
Cradoc
Llywel
Trallong
Trecastle
Sennybridge
Defynnog
Llanspyddid
Brecon
Llanddew
Libanus
Crai
BRECON BEACONS
BRECON
BEACONS
NATIONAL PARK
Fforest Fawr
Ystradfellte
Penderyn
Pont-Nêdd-Fechan
Glyn-Neath
Hirwaun
Penywaun
Aberdare
Rhigos
Blaengwrach
Glyncorrwg
Treherbert
Treorchy
Ferndale
Ystrad
Maerdy
Mountain Ash
Tonypandy
Penygraig
Porth
Trealaw
Pontypridd
Tonyrefail
Ogmore Vale
Gilfach Goch
Pontycymer
Betws
Bridgend
Coity
Pencoed
Llanharan
Llantrisant
Laleston
Cowbridge
Llandow
Erwood
Gwenddwr
Crickadarn
Boughrood
Llyswen
Glasbury
Clyro
Hay-on-Wye
Llowes
Cwmbach
Llanigon
Tregoyd
Aberllynfi
Three Cocks
Velindre
Bronllys
Talgarth
Llanelieu
Llanfilo
Trefecca
Llandefaelog-Tre'r-Graig
Llanywern
Llangors
Llangors Lake
Llanhamlach
Pennorth
Llanfrynach
Pencelli
Scethrog
Cathedine
Llansantffraed
Cwmdu
Bwlch
Talybont-on-Usk
Tretower
Cwm Crawnon
Llangynidr
Crickhowell
Llangattock
Gilwern
Gofilon
Clydach
Brynmawr
Beaufort
Nantyglo
Tredegar
Ebbw Vale
Rhymney
Merthyr Tydfil
Blaina
Abertillery
Blaenavon
Abersychan
Pontypool
Cwmbran
Abergavenny
Llanfoist
Llanellen
Llanover
Gader Ridge
BLACK MOUNTAINS
Black Mountain
Llanthony
Michaelchurch Escley
Longtown
Pandy
Llanvihangel Crucorney
Llantilio Pertholey
Bargoed
Treharris
Abercynon
Ynysybwl
Nelson
Gelligaer
Pengam
Blackwood
Oakdale
Penmaen
Pontllanfraith
Crumlin
Newbridge
Abercarn
Crosskeys
Risca
Llanbradach
Bedwas
Caerphilly
Rogerstone
NEWPORT
Church Village
Beddau
Taff's Well
Tongwynlais
Radyr
Whitchurch
Llanishen
Pentyrch
Creigiau
St Fagans
St Brides super-Ely
Peterston-super-Ely
CARDIFF
Penarth
Castleton
Marshfield
St Brides Wentlooge
Peterstone Wentlooge
St Mellons
Llanrumney
Michaelstone-y-Fedw
Brecon Mountain Railway
Pen-y-fan 886
Talybont Reservoir
Llwyn-on Reservoir
Pontsticill
Vaynor
0 1 2 3 4 miles
0 1 2 3 4 5 kilometres

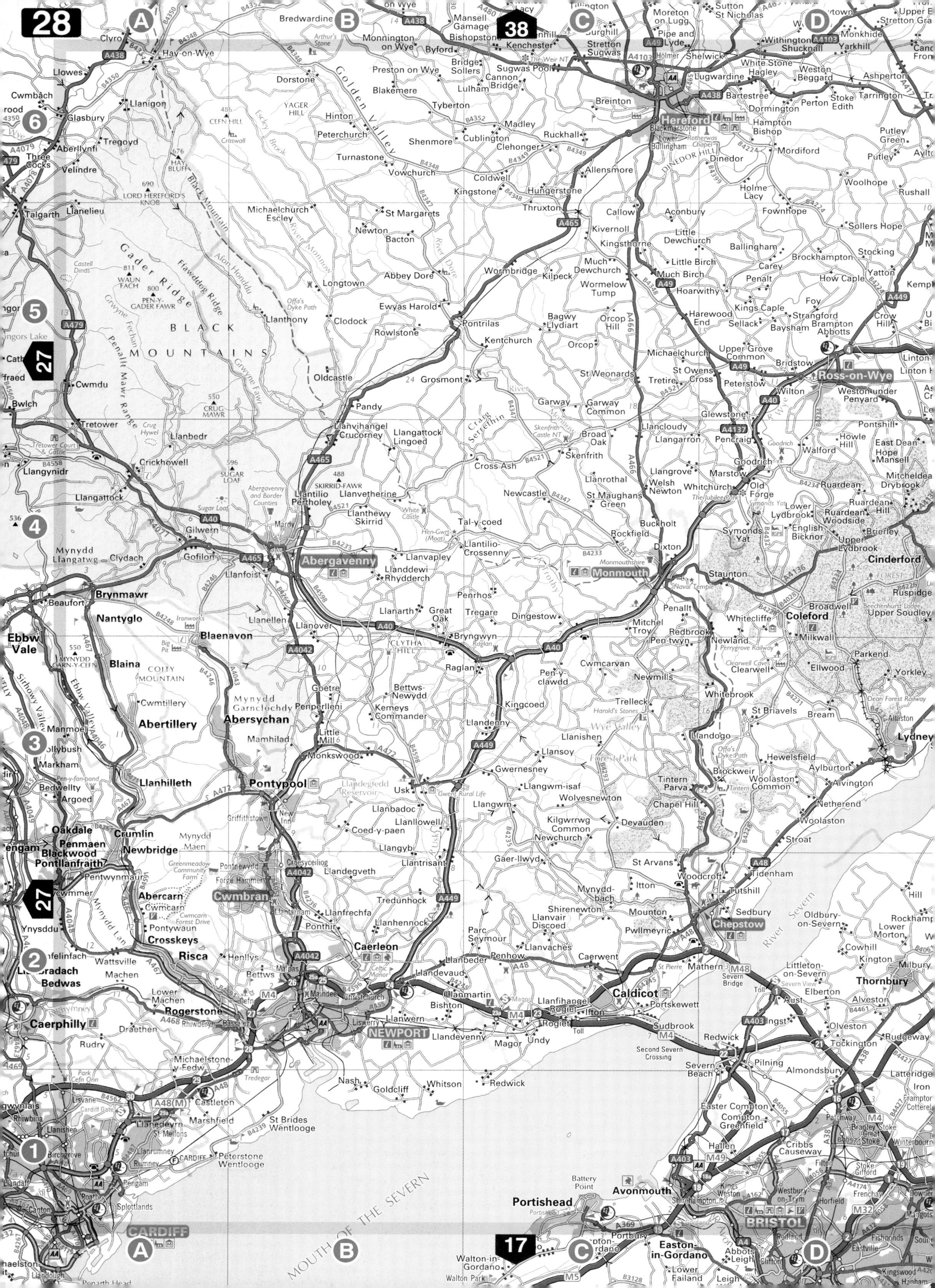
A
B
C
D
38
Clyro
Hay-on-Wye
Bredwardine
Mansell Gamage
Bishopstone
Kenchester
Tillington
Moreton on Lugg
Sutton St Nicholas
Upper Stretton Grandison
Arthur's Stone
Monnington on Wye
Byford
Bridge Sollers
Sugwas Pool
Stretton Sugwas
Burghill
Pipe and Lyde
Holmer
Shelwick
Withington
Shucknall
Monkhide
Yarkhill
Llowes
Dorstone
Preston on Wye
Blakemere
Cannon Bridge
Lulham
The Weir NT
White Stone
Hagley
Lugwardine
Weston Beggard
Ashperton
Cwmbach
Llanigon
Golden Valley
YAGER HILL
Tyberton
Breinton
Bartestree
Dormington
Perton
Stoke Edith
Tarrington
Glasbury
CEFN HILL
Hinton
Peterchurch
Madley
Cublington
Ruckhall
Hereford
Blackmarstone
Lower Bullingham
Rotherwas Chapel
Hampton Bishop
Mordiford
Putley Green
Putley
6
Tregoyd
Craswall
Escley Brook
Turnastone
Shenmore
Clehonger
DINEDOR HILL
Dinedor
Aberllynfi
Three Cocks
Velindre
HAY BLUFF
Vowchurch
Coldwell
Allensmore
Holme Lacy
Woolhope
Rushall
LORD HEREFORD'S KNOB
Black Mountain
Kingstone
Hungerstone
Thruxton
Callow
Aconbury
Fownhope
Talgarth
Llanelieu
Michaelchurch Escley
St Margarets
Newton
Bacton
Kivernoll
Little Dewchurch
Sollers Hope
Kingsthorne
Ballingham
River Monnow
River Dore
Afon Honddu
Much Dewchurch
Little Birch
Brockhampton
Stocking
Gader Ridge
Castell Dinas
WAUN FACH
Flawddog Ridge
Longtown
Abbey Dore
Wormbridge
Kilpeck
Much Birch
Carey
How Caple
Yatton
Kempley
PEN-Y-GADER FAWR
Offa's Dyke Path
Wormelow Tump
Hoarwithy
Penalt
Ewyas Harold
Harewood End
Kings Caple
Foy
Crow Hill
5
Llanthony
Clodock
Pontrilas
Bagwy Llydiart
Orcop Hill
Sellack
Strangford
Brampton Abbotts
Baysham
BLACK MOUNTAINS
Rowlstone
Kentchurch
Orcop
Michaelchurch
Upper Grove Common
Bridstow
Linton
Llangorse Lake
Grwyne Fechan
Penallt Mawr Range
Cathedine
27
Oldcastle
Grosmont
St Weonards
St Owens Cross
Tretire
Peterstow
Ross-on-Wye
Cwmdu
Wilton
Weston under Penyard
Bwlch
550 CRUG MAWR
Pandy
Garway
Garway Common
Glewstone
Tretower
Crug Hywel
Llanbedr
Llanvihangel Crucorney
Craig Serrethin
Llangattock Lingoed
Skenfrith Castle NT
Broad Oak
Llancloudy
Llangarron
Pencraig
Pontshill
Howle Hill
East Dean
Hope Mansell
Tretower Court & Castle
Crickhowell
SUGAR LOAF
Skenfrith
Cross Ash
Goodrich
Walford
Llangynidr
SKIRRID-FAWR
Llanrothal
Llangrove
Marstow
Welsh Newton
Whitchurch
Old Forge
Ruardean
Mitcheldean
Drybrook
Llangattock
Abergavenny and Border Counties
Llantilio Pertholey
Llanvetherine
Newcastle
St Maughans Green
The Jubilee Park
Symonds Yat
Lower Lydbrook
Ruardean Hill
Ruardean Woodside
Sugar Loaf
Llanthewy Skirrid
White Castle
Tal-y-coed
Buckholt
Symonds Yat
English Bicknor
Brierley
4
Gilwern
Mardy
Hen-Gwrt (Moat)
Llantilio-Crossenny
Rockfield
Upper Lydbrook
Mynydd Llangatwg
Clydach
Gofilon
Abergavenny
Llanvapley
Dixton
Cinderford
Llanfoist
Llanddewi Rhydderch
Monmouthshire
Monmouth
Naval Temple
Staunton
Beaufort
Brynmawr
Penrhos
Penallt
Ruspidge
Nantyglo
Ironworks
Llanellen
Llanarth
Great Oak
Tregare
Dingestow
Mitchel Troy
Whitecliffe
Coleford
Broadwell
Upper Soudley
Ebbw Vale
Blaenavon
Big Pit
Llanover
Bryngwyn
Raglan
Redbrook
Newland
Milkwall
MYNYDD CARN-Y-CEFN
CLYTHA HILL
Pen-twyn
Perrygrove Railway
Sirhowy Valley
Ebbw Valley
Blaina
COITY MOUNTAIN
Cwmcarvan
Clearwell Caves
Clearwell
Parkend
Ellwood
Yorkley
Pen-y-clawdd
Newmills
Goetre
Bettws-Newydd
Cwmtillery
Mynydd Garnclochdy
Kingcoed
Trelleck
Whitebrook
Dean Forest Railway
Harold's Stones
Abertillery
Abersychan
Penperlleni
Kemeys Commander
Llandenny
Wye Valley
St Briavels
Bream
Allaston
Manmoel
Little Mill
3
Llanishen
Llandogo
Lydney
Mamhilad
Hollybush
Monkswood
Llansoy
Forest Park
Offa's Dyke Path
Hewelsfield
Markham
Pen-y-fan-pond
Llandegfedd Reservoir
Gwernesney
Tintern Parva
Brockweir
Aylburton
Bedwellty
Llanhilleth
Pontypool
Usk
Gwent Rural Life
Llangwm-isaf
Woolaston Common
Alvington
Argoed
New Inn
Llanbadoc
Llangwm
Wolvesnewton
Chapel Hill
Netherend
Griffithstown
Llanllowell
Kilgwrrwg Common
Devauden
Woolaston
Oakdale
Crumlin
Mynydd Maen
Coed-y-paen
Newchurch
Penmaen
Blackwood
Newbridge
Llangybi
Stroat
Pontllanfraith
Greenmeadow Community Farm
Pontnewydd
Croesyceiliog
Llandegveth
Llantrisant
Gaer-llwyd
St Arvans
Tidenham
Pentwynmawr
Forge Hammer
Woodcroft
Itton
Mynydd-bach
Tutshill
Cwmfelinfach
Abercarn
Cwmbran
Tredunhock
Hill
Cwmcarn
Cwmcarn Forest Drive
Llantarnam
Llanfrechfa
Shirenewton
Mounton
Sedbury
Rockhampton
Mynydd Lan
Pontywaun
Llanvair Discoed
Chepstow
Oldbury-on-Severn
Ynysddu
Ponthir
Llanhennock
Pwllmeyric
River Severn
Lower Morton
Crosskeys
Parc Seymour
Cefn Mawr
Cowhill
Wattsville
Risca
Caerleon
Llanvaches
Henllys
Celtic Manor
Penhow
Caerwent
Kington
Milbury Heath
Bedwas
Machen
Malpas
Llanbeder
St Pierre
Mathern
Severn Bridge
Littleton-on-Severn
Thornbury
2
Bettws
Llandevaud
Caldicot
Severn View
Aust
Elberton
Alveston
Lower Machen
Maindee
Christchurch
Llanmartin
Magor
Llanfihangel Rogiet
Portskewett
Rogerstone
Bishton
Ifton
Caerphilly
Rhiwderyn
Bassaleg
Llanwern
Rogiet
Sudbrook
Ingst
Olveston
Draethen
Liswerry
NEWPORT
Llandevenny
Undy
Redwick
Rudry
Tockington
Rudgeway
Second Severn Crossing
Michaelstone-y-Fedw
Pilning
Severn Beach
Almondsbury
Park Cefn Onn
Tredegar
Nash
Goldcliff
Whitson
Redwick
Latteridge
Castleton
Lisvane
Cardiff Gate
Easter Compton
Compton Greenfield
Iron Acton
Rhiwbina
Llanedeyrn
St Mellons
Marshfield
St Brides Wentlooge
Patchway
Bradley Stoke
Great Stoke
Frampton Cotterell
Winterbourne
Llanishen
Hallen
Cribbs Causeway
1
Birchgrove
Llanrumney
CARDIFF
Peterstone Wentlooge
Filton
Rumney
Stoke Gifford
Llandaff
Battery Point
Avonmouth
Kings Weston
Westbury-on-Trym
Horfield
Frenchay
Downend
Pengam
Roath
Splottlands
Canton
Portishead
Shirehampton
Mangotsfield
CARDIFF
Portbury
Easton-in-Gordano
Redland
BRISTOL
Fishponds
Eastville
MOUTH OF THE SEVERN
Abbots Leigh
Clifton
Kingswood
Hanham
17
Walton-in-Gordano
Walton Park
Lower Failand
Leigh
Llandough
Penarth Head
Cardiff
A438
A480
A49
A4103
A465
A466
A479
A40
A4137
A449
A4136
A467
A472
A4042
A48
M48
M4
A403
M49
M5
M32
A4174
A369
A38
A469
A48(M)
B4350
B4348
B4352
B4349
B4224
B4399
B4347
B4521
B4233
B4293
B4228
B4231
B4234
B4246
B4248
B4598
B4235
B4245
B4239
B4562
B4055
B4061
B4461
B4427

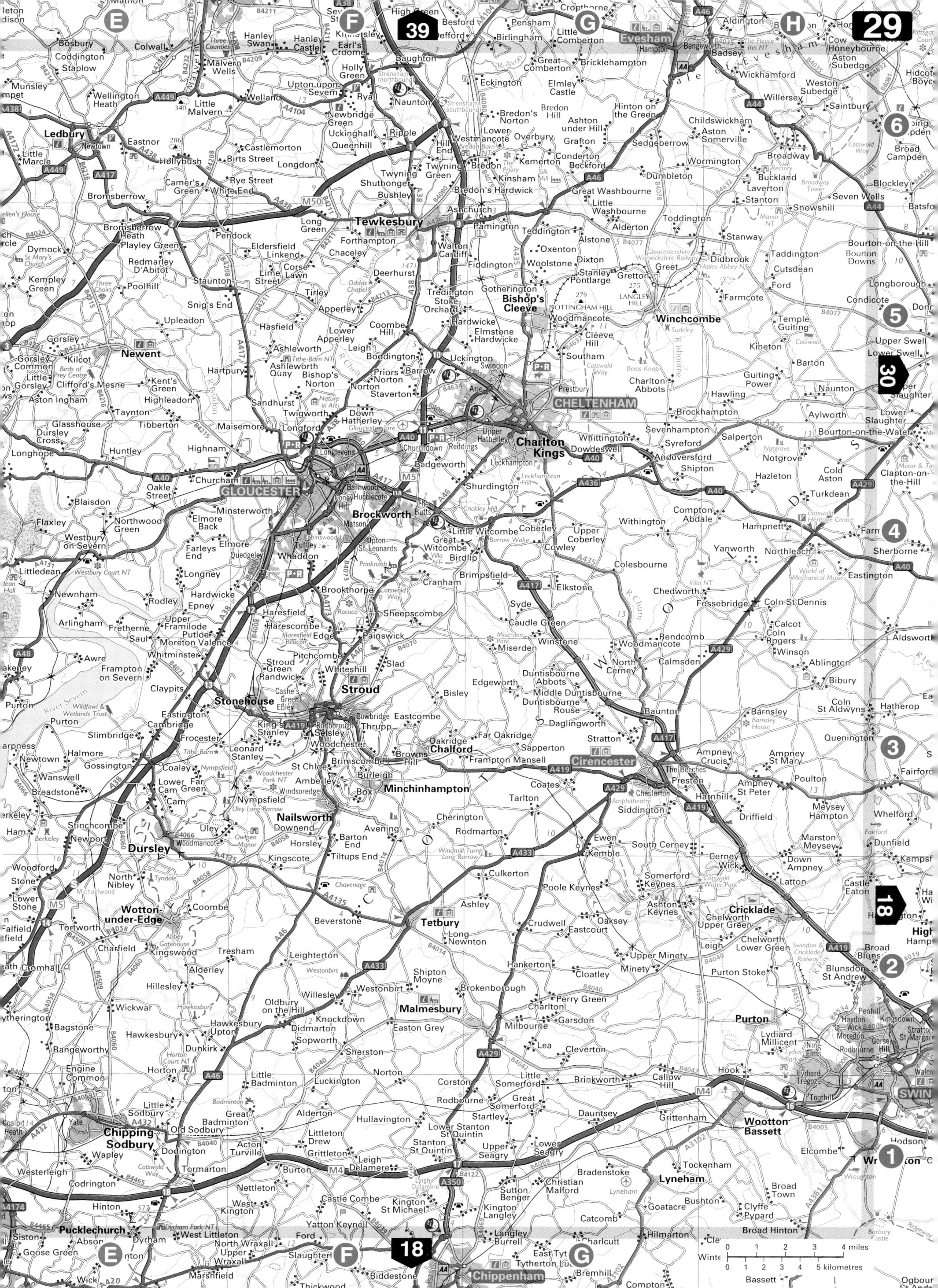

29
39
30
18
18
E
F
G
H
E
F
G
1
2
3
4
5
6
Evesham
Vale of Evesham
Tewkesbury
CHELTENHAM
GLOUCESTER
Charlton Kings
Bishop's Cleeve
Winchcombe
Brockworth
Stroud
Stonehouse
Dursley
Nailsworth
Minchinhampton
Chalford
Cirencester
Tetbury
Malmesbury
Wotton-under-Edge
Chipping Sodbury
Cricklade
Purton
Wootton Bassett
Lyneham
Chippenham
SWIN
Ledbury
Newent
Malvern Wells
Little Malvern
Hanley Swan
Hanley Castle
Upton upon Severn
Bredon
Ashchurch
Broadway
Snowshill
Stanway
Didbrook
Toddington
Prestbury
Southam
Shurdington
Birdlip
Painswick
Bisley
Sapperton
Fairford
Quenington
Bibury
Northleach
Andoversford
Chedworth
Withington
Yanworth
Hawling
Guiting Power
Naunton
Lower Slaughter
Bourton-on-the-Water
Bourton-on-the-Hill
Longborough
Upper Swell
Lower Swell
Condicote
Temple Guiting
Kineton
Ford
Cutsdean
Taddington
Snowshill
Buckland
Laverton
Stanton
Childswickham
Willersey
Saintbury
Weston Subedge
Aston Subedge
Honeybourne
Badsey
Bengeworth
Aldington
Wickhamford
Sedgeberrow
Ashton under Hill
Beckford
Kemerton
Overbury
Eckington
Birlingham
Great Comberton
Little Comberton
Cropthorne
Pensham
Elmley Castle
Bricklehampton
Kinsham
Alderton
Teddington
Dumbleton
Wormington
Great Washbourne
Little Washbourne
Gotherington
Woolstone
Oxenton
Stoke Orchard
Tredington
Walton Cardiff
Fiddington
Deerhurst
Tirley
Apperley
Hasfield
Ashleworth
Sandhurst
Maisemore
Highnam
Huntley
Longhope
Blaisdon
Flaxley
Westbury on Severn
Minsterworth
Elmore
Quedgeley
Hardwicke
Haresfield
Whitminster
Frampton on Severn
Arlingham
Newnham
Slimbridge
Cambridge
Eastington
Frocester
Leonard Stanley
King's Stanley
Coaley
Uley
North Nibley
Stinchcombe
Berkeley
Newport
Woodford
Stone
Tortworth
Charfield
Kingswood
Wickwar
Hawkesbury
Hawkesbury Upton
Badminton
Great Badminton
Little Badminton
Sherston
Luckington
Didmarton
Knockdown
Westonbirt
Shipton Moyne
Long Newnton
Easton Grey
Crudwell
Oaksey
Ashton Keynes
Somerford Keynes
South Cerney
Cerney Wick
Latton
Siddington
Preston
Ampney Crucis
Ampney St Mary
Ampney St Peter
Down Ampney
Meysey Hampton
Driffield
Kemble
Ewen
Coates
Tarlton
Rodmarton
Cherington
Avening
Horsley
Kingscote
Beverstone
Culkerton
Ashley
Hankerton
Minety
Upper Minety
Leigh
Charlton
Garsdon
Lea
Cleverton
Brinkworth
Little Somerford
Great Somerford
Startley
Dauntsey
Hullavington
Stanton St Quintin
Lower Stanton St Quintin
Grittleton
Alderton
Littleton Drew
Acton Turville
Tormarton
Dodington
Old Sodbury
Little Sodbury
Yate
Wapley
Westerleigh
Codrington
Pucklechurch
Dyrham
Hinton
West Littleton
Nettleton
Castle Combe
Yatton Keynell
Kington St Michael
West Kington
Ford
Slaughterford
North Wraxall
Upper Wraxall
Marshfield
Biddestone
Langley Burrell
Kington Langley
Sutton Benger
Christian Malford
Bradenstoke
Tockenham
Goatacre
Bushton
Clyffe Pypard
Broad Town
Broad Hinton
Hilmarton
Catcomb
Grittenham
Callow Hill
Hook
Lydiard Millicent
Lydiard Tregoze
Blunsdon St Andrew
Broad Blunsdon
Purton Stoke
Chelworth Upper Green
Chelworth Lower Green
Hodson
Elcombe
Wroughton
M4
M5
M50
A40
A46
A417
A419
A429
A433
A435
A436
A438
A38
A44
0 1 2 3 4 miles
0 1 2 3 4 5 kilometres

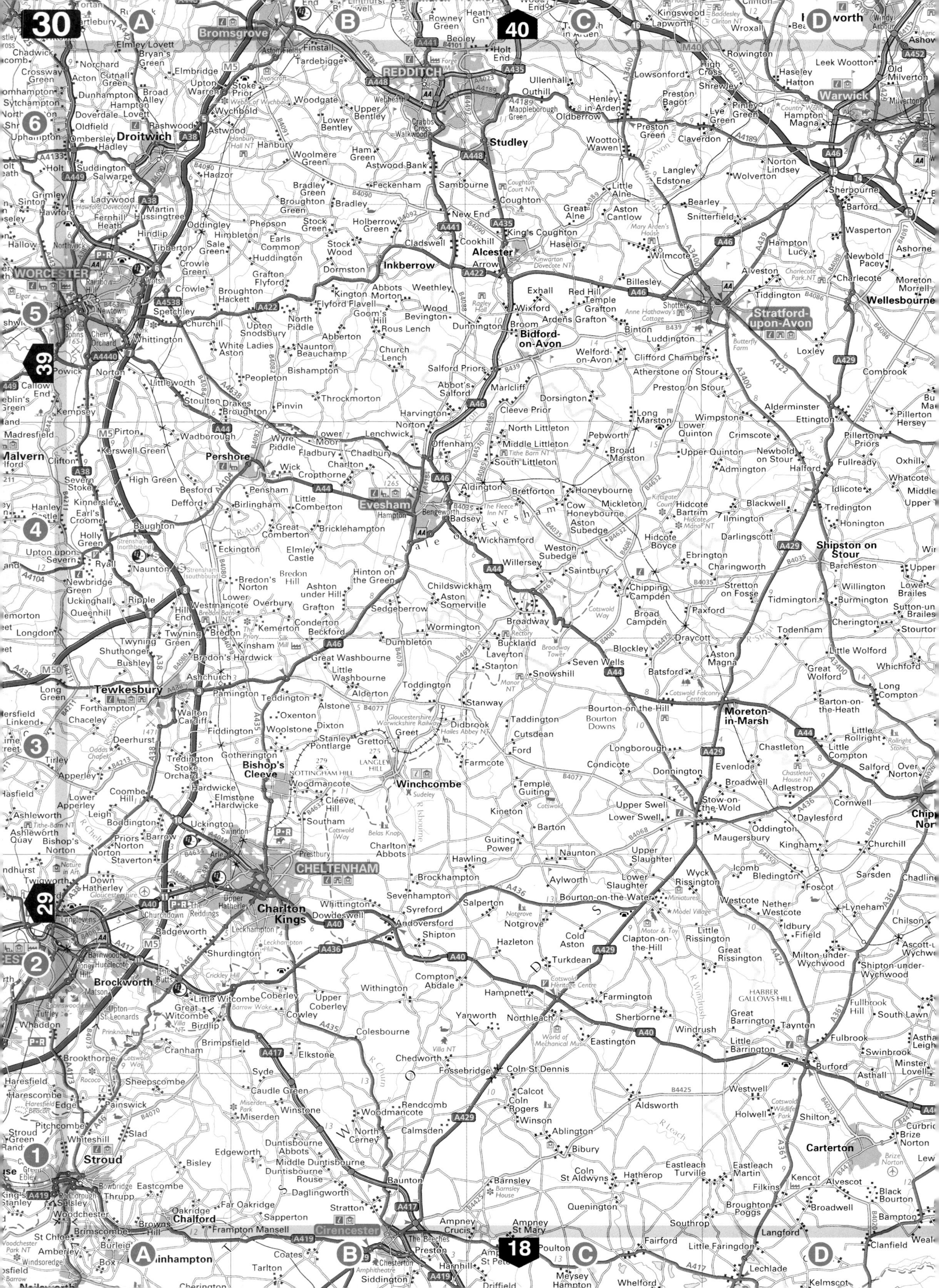
30
A
B
C
D
40
39
29
18
Bromsgrove
REDDITCH
Warwick
Droitwich
Studley
WORCESTER
Alcester
Inkberrow
Stratford-upon-Avon
Wellesbourne
Bidford-on-Avon
Pershore
Evesham
Malvern
Shipston on Stour
Tewkesbury
Moreton-in-Marsh
Bishop's Cleeve
Winchcombe
CHELTENHAM
Charlton Kings
Stow-on-the-Wold
Brockworth
Stroud
Chalford
Cirencester
Burford
Carterton
Northleach
Bourton-on-the-Water
Broadway
Chipping Campden
Hartlebury
Elmley Lovett
Bryan's Green
Finstall
Tardebigge
Rowney Green
Beoley
Holt End
Ullenhall
Henley-in-Arden
Lapworth
Kingswood
Rowington
Wroxall
Haseley
Hatton
Leek Wootton
Old Milverton
Chadwick
Norchard
Crossway Green
Elmbridge
Upton Warren
Stoke Prior
Woodgate
Upper Bentley
Lower Bentley
Wychbold
Astwood
Hanbury
Woolmere Green
Ham Green
Astwood Bank
Feckenham
Sambourne
Coughton
Great Alne
Little Alne
Aston Cantlow
Wootton Wawen
Preston Bagot
Claverdon
Langley
Edstone
Norton Lindsey
Wolverton
Sherbourne
Barford
Snitterfield
Bearley
Salwarpe
Hadzor
Ladywood
Martin Hussingtree
Oddingley
Phepson
Himbleton
Earls Common
Bradley Green
Broughton Green
Stock Green
Holberrow Green
Stock Wood
Dormston
Cladswell
Cookhill
New End
King's Coughton
Arrow
Haselor
Wilmcote
Billesley
Alveston
Hampton Lucy
Ashorne
Newbold Pacey
Charlecote
Tiddington
Moreton Morrell
Tibberton
Crowle
Huddington
Grafton Flyford
Broughton Hackett
Kington
Flyford Flavell
Abbots Morton
Weethley
Wood Bevington
Exhall
Wixford
Temple Grafton
Ardens Grafton
Binton
Luddington
Broom
Dunnington
Upton Snodsbury
North Piddle
Naunton Beauchamp
Abberton
Rous Lench
Church Lench
Bishampton
Salford Priors
Abbot's Salford
Marlcliff
Welford-on-Avon
Clifford Chambers
Atherstone on Stour
Preston on Stour
Loxley
Combrook
Whittington
Norton
Littleworth
Stoulton
Drakes Broughton
Peopleton
Pinvin
Throckmorton
Harvington
Cleeve Prior
Dorsington
Long Marston
Lower Quinton
Wimpstone
Alderminster
Ettington
Kempsey
Wadborough
Wyre Piddle
Lower Moor
Fladbury
Lenchwick
Chadbury
Offenham
North Littleton
Middle Littleton
South Littleton
Pebworth
Broad Marston
Upper Quinton
Crimscote
Newbold on Stour
Admington
Halford
Fullready
Pillerton Priors
Madresfield
Pirton
Kerswell Green
Clifton
Severn Stoke
High Green
Besford
Defford
Wick
Cropthorne
Charlton
Pensham
Birlingham
Little Comberton
Great Comberton
Bricklehampton
Aldington
Bretforton
Honeybourne
Cow Honeybourne
Mickleton
Hidcote Bartrim
Ilmington
Blackwell
Tredington
Honington
Badsey
Bengeworth
Hampton
Wickhamford
Aston Subedge
Weston Subedge
Hidcote Boyce
Ebrington
Darlingscott
Hanley Castle
Kinnersley
Earl's Croome
Holly Green
Baughton
Eckington
Elmley Castle
Upton upon Severn
Ryall
Naunton
Bredon's Norton
Bredon Hill
Ashton under Hill
Hinton on the Green
Childswickham
Aston Somerville
Willersey
Saintbury
Charingworth
Barcheston
Willington
Newbridge Green
Uckinghall
Ripple
Queenhill
Longdon
Westmancote
Lower Westmancote
Overbury
Grafton
Conderton
Beckford
Sedgeberrow
Wormington
Buckland
Laverton
Broad Campden
Paxford
Stretton on Fosse
Tidmington
Burmington
Todenham
Cherington
Twyning
Twyning Green
Shuthonger
Bushley
Bredon
Kemerton
Kinsham
Bredon's Hardwick
Great Washbourne
Little Washbourne
Dumbleton
Stanton
Snowshill
Seven Wells
Blockley
Draycott
Aston Magna
Little Wolford
Great Wolford
Whichford
Long Compton
Batsford
Long Green
Forthampton
Chaceley
Ashchurch
Pamington
Walton Cardiff
Teddington
Alston
Alderton
Oxenton
Woolstone
Dixton
Toddington
Stanway
Didbrook
Taddington
Cutsdean
Bourton-on-the-Hill
Bourton Downs
Barton-on-the-Heath
Little Rollright
Little Compton
Deerhurst
Tirley
Fiddington
Tredington
Gotherington
Stanley Pontlarge
Gretton
Greet
Farmcote
Ford
Longborough
Condicote
Donnington
Evenlode
Chastleton
Salford
Over Norton
Apperley
Stoke Orchard
Hardwicke
Coombe Hill
Elmstone Hardwicke
Woodmancote
Cleeve Hill
Southam
Temple Guiting
Kineton
Upper Swell
Lower Swell
Broadwell
Adlestrop
Cornwell
Lower Apperley
Leigh
Boddington
Uckington
Swindon
Prestbury
Charlton Abbots
Guiting Power
Barton
Naunton
Upper Slaughter
Lower Slaughter
Maugersbury
Oddington
Daylesford
Kingham
Churchill
Ashleworth
Priors Norton
Barrow
Staverton
Arle
Hawling
Brockhampton
Aylworth
Wyck Rissington
Icomb
Bledington
Foscot
Sarsden
Down Hatherley
Twigworth
Upper Hatherley
The Reddings
Churchdown
Sevenhampton
Whittington
Dowdeswell
Syreford
Andoversford
Salperton
Notgrove
Westcote
Nether Westcote
Lyneham
Chilson
Longlevens
Badgeworth
Leckhampton
Shipton
Hazleton
Cold Aston
Clapton-on-the-Hill
Little Rissington
Great Rissington
Idbury
Fifield
Milton-under-Wychwood
Shipton-under-Wychwood
Shurdington
Compton Abdale
Turkdean
Farmington
Hucclecote
Barnwood
Matson
Tuffley
Whaddon
Little Witcombe
Great Witcombe
Coberley
Upper Coberley
Cowley
Withington
Hampnett
Yanworth
Sherborne
Windrush
Great Barrington
Taynton
Little Barrington
Fulbrook
Swinbrook
Asthall
Birdlip
Brimpsfield
Cranham
Colesbourne
Chedworth
Fossebridge
Coln St Dennis
Eastington
Elkstone
Brookthorpe
Haresfield
Sheepscombe
Syde
Caudle Green
Painswick
Miserden
Winstone
Woodmancote
Rendcomb
Calmsden
North Cerney
Calcot
Coln Rogers
Winson
Ablington
Aldsworth
Westwell
Holwell
Shilton
Bibury
Pitchcombe
Whiteshill
Slad
Edgeworth
Bisley
Duntisbourne Abbots
Middle Duntisbourne
Duntisbourne Rouse
Daglingworth
Baunton
Barnsley
Coln St Aldwyns
Hatherop
Eastleach Turville
Eastleach Martin
Filkins
Kencot
Alvescot
Black Bourton
Broadwell
Broughton Poggs
Eastcombe
Bussage
Thrupp
Far Oakridge
Oakridge
Sapperton
Stratton
Ampney Crucis
Ampney St Mary
Quenington
Southrop
Langford
Bampton
Clanfield
Brimscombe
Frampton Mansell
Minchinhampton
Coates
Tarlton
Preston
Harnhill
Poulton
Fairford
Little Faringdon
Lechlade
Siddington
Driffield
Meysey Hampton
Whelford
Kelmscot
Woodchester
Amberley
St Chloe
Burleigh
Box
Selsley
Rodborough
Ebley
Stonehouse
Chesterton
Ampney St Peter
Vale of Evesham
M5
M40
M50
A38
A44
A46
A40
A429
A435
A436
A417
A419
A424
A361
A3400

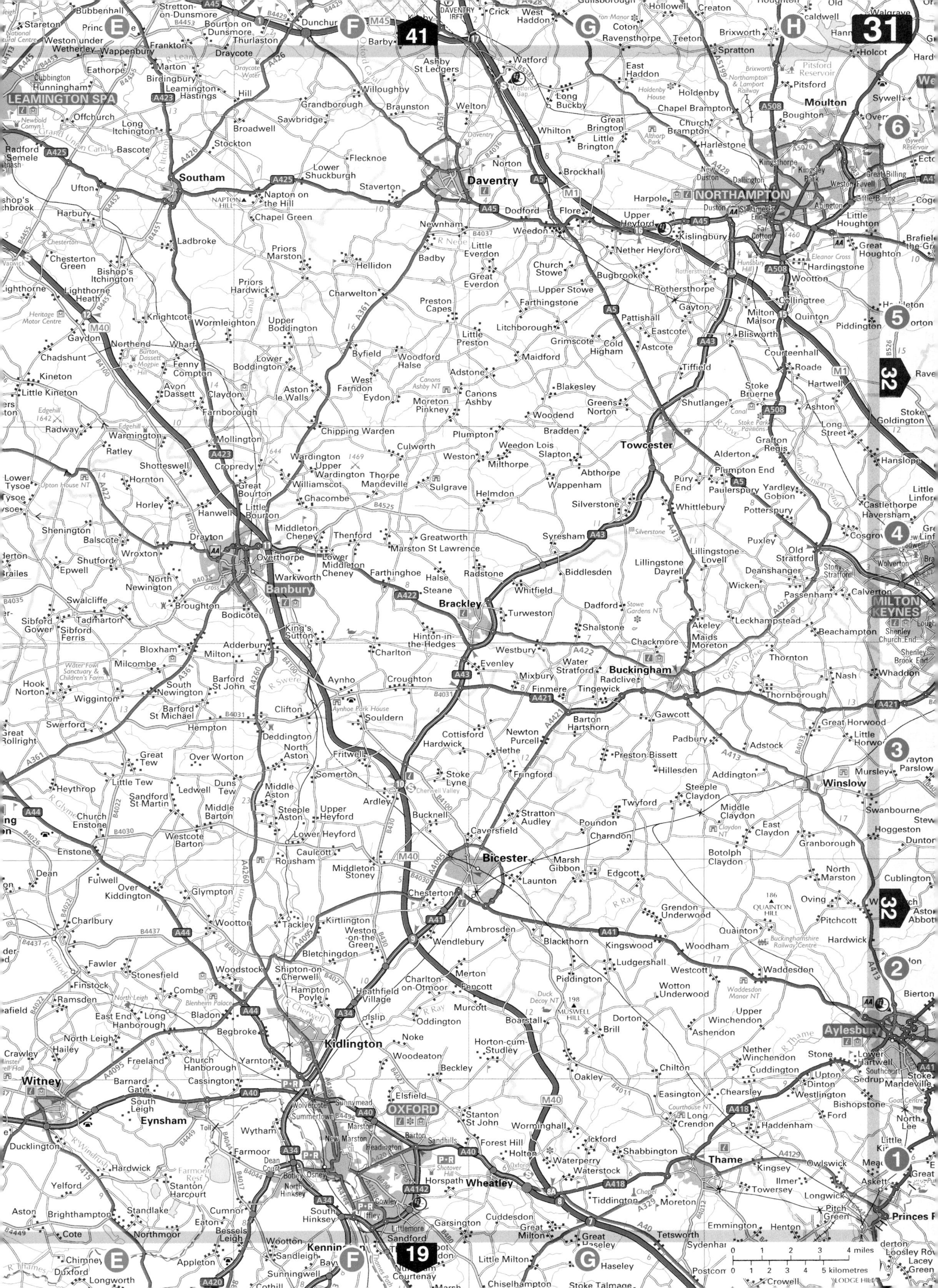

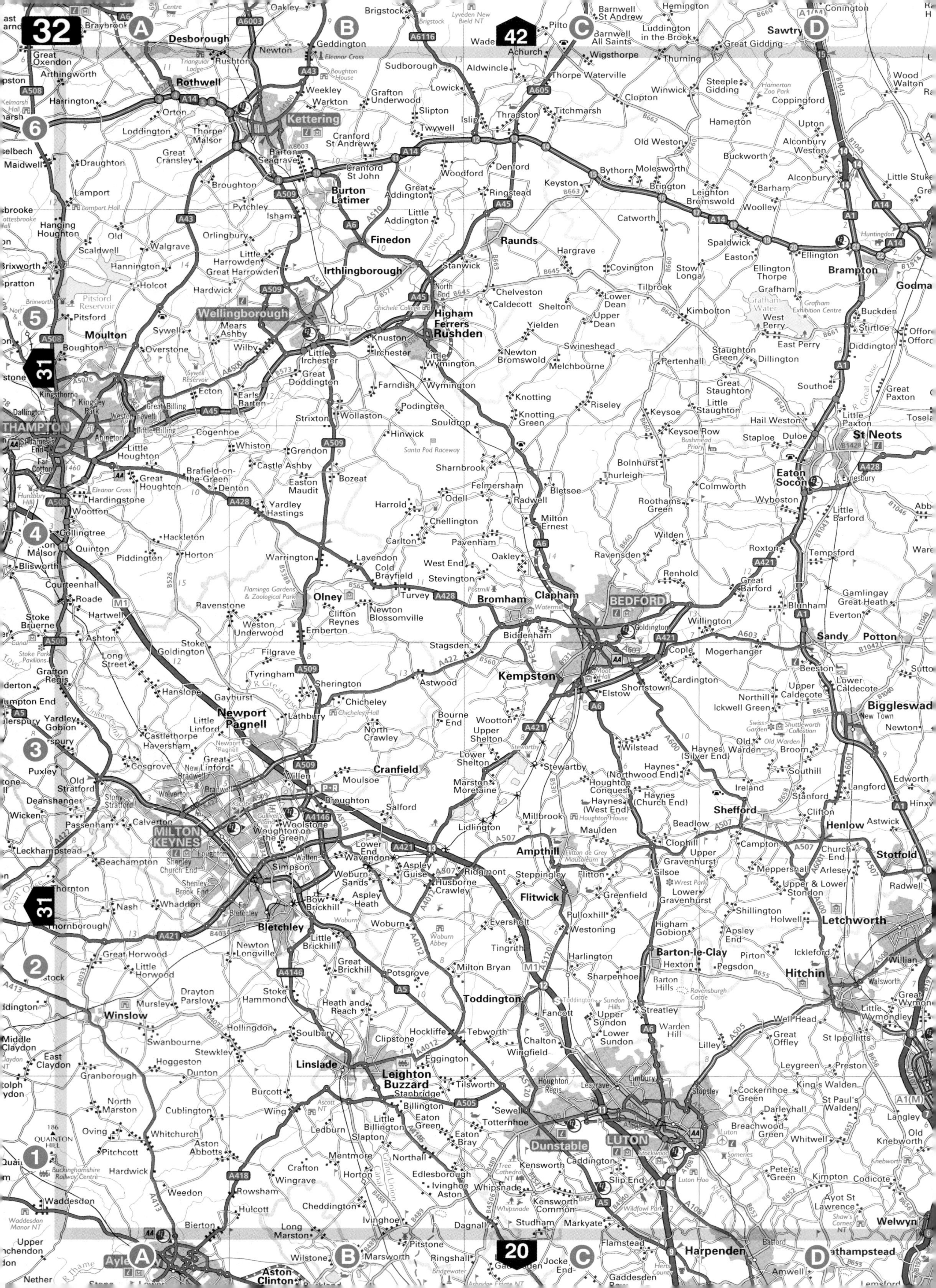

32
A
B
C
D
42
Desborough
Braybrooke
Oakley
Brigstock
Lyveden New Bield NT
Barnwell
St Andrew
Barnwell
All Saints
Hemington
Luddington
in the Brook
Conington
Sawtry
Geddington
Eleanor Cross
Newton
Rushton
Triangular Lodge
Great
Oxendon
Arthingworth
Rothwell
Sudborough
Boughton House
Wadenhoe
Pilton
Achurch
Wigsthorpe
Thurning
Great Gidding
Aldwincle
Thorpe Waterville
Lowick
Winwick
Steeple
Gidding
Hamerton
Zoo Park
Wood
Walton
Harrington
Orton
Kettering
Weekley
Warkton
Grafton
Underwood
Slipton
Twywell
Islip
Thrapston
Titchmarsh
Clopton
Coppingford
Loddington
Thorpe
Malsor
Cranford
St Andrew
Barton
Seagrave
Hamerton
Upton
Maidwell
Draughton
Great
Cransley
Cranford
St John
Woodford
Denford
Old Weston
Alconbury
Weston
Buckworth
Lamport
Lamport Hall
Broughton
Burton
Latimer
Great
Addington
Ringstead
Keyston
Bythorn
Molesworth
Brington
Leighton
Bromswold
Barham
Alconbury
Little Stukeley
Hanging
Houghton
Pytchley
Isham
Little
Addington
Woolley
Catworth
Orlingbury
Finedon
Raunds
Scaldwell
Old
Walgrave
Little
Harrowden
Great Harrowden
Spaldwick
Ellington
Huntingdon
Easton
Ellington
Thorpe
Brampton
Brixworth
Hannington
Holcot
Irthlingborough
Stanwick
Hargrave
Covington
Stow
Longa
Tilbrook
Hardwick
Pitsford
Reservoir
Wellingborough
Higham
Ferrers
Rushden
Chichele College
North End
Chelveston
Caldecott
Lower
Dean
Upper
Dean
Shelton
Kimbolton
Grafham
Water
Grafham
Exhibition Centre
West
Perry
Buckden
Stirtloe
Offord
Pitsford
Moulton
Sywell
Mears
Ashby
Wilby
Irchester
Knuston
Yielden
Swineshead
East Perry
Diddington
Boughton
Overstone
Sywell
Reservoir
Little
Irchester
Irchester
Little
Wymington
Newton
Bromswold
Melchbourne
Pertenhall
Staughton
Green
Dillington
Great
Doddington
Farndish
Wymington
Great
Staughton
Southoe
Kingsthorpe
Ecton
Kingsley Park
Great Billing
Earls
Barton
Knotting
Riseley
Little
Staughton
Great
Paxton
Dallington
Weston Favell
A45
Podington
Knotting
Green
Keysoe
Keysoe Row
Bushmead
Priory
Hail Weston
Little
Paxton
Toseland
NORTHAMPTON
Abington
Little Billing
Strixton
Wollaston
Souldrop
Staploe
Duloe
St Neots
Cogenhoe
Hinwick
Santa Pod Raceway
Far
Cotton
Little
Houghton
Whiston
Grendon
Sharnbrook
Bolnhurst
Thurleigh
Eaton
Socon
Eynesbury
Castle Ashby
Brafield-on-
the-Green
Easton
Maudit
Bozeat
Felmersham
Colmworth
Eleanor Cross
Hunsbury
Hill
Great
Houghton
Denton
Odell
Radwell
Bletsoe
Roothams
Green
Wyboston
Hardingstone
Yardley
Hastings
Harrold
Milton
Ernest
Little
Barford
Wootton
Chellington
Collingtree
Hackleton
Carlton
Pavenham
Wilden
Milton
Malsor
Quinton
Piddington
Horton
Warrington
Lavendon
Oakley
Ravensden
Roxton
Tempsford
Blisworth
Cold
Brayfield
West End
Stevington
Renhold
Great
Barford
Gamlingay
Great Heath
Courteenhall
Flamingo Gardens
& Zoological Park
Olney
Turvey
Postmill
Bromham
Clapham
BEDFORD
Blunham
Everton
Roade
Hartwell
Ravenstone
Clifton
Reynes
Newton
Blossomville
Watermill
Goldington
Willington
Stoke
Bruerne
Canal
Weston
Underwood
Emberton
Biddenham
Sandy
Potton
Ashton
Stoke Park
Pavilions
Stoke
Goldington
Filgrave
Stagsden
Cople
Mogerhanger
Long
Street
Tyringham
Kempston
Cardington
Beeston
Lower
Caldecote
Grafton
Regis
Moot Hall
Elstow
Shortstown
Hanslope
Gayhurst
Sherington
Astwood
Chicheley
Chicheley Hall
Northill
Ickwell Green
Upper
Caldecote
Biggleswade
New Town
Yardley
Gobion
Newport
Pagnell
Little
Linford
Lathbury
North
Crawley
Bourne
End
Wootton
Upper
Shelton
Stewartby
Wilstead
Haynes
(Silver End)
Old
Warden
Swiss
Garden
Shuttleworth
Collection
Old Warden
Broom
Newton
Castlethorpe
Haversham
Lower
Shelton
Stewartby
Haynes
(Northwood End)
Southill
Edworth
Puxley
Cosgrove
Great
Linford
New Linford
Bradwell
Willen
Cranfield
Moulsoe
Marston
Moretaine
Houghton
Conquest
Haynes
(Church End)
Ireland
Langford
Old
Stratford
Stony
Stratford
Wolverton
Bradwell
Broughton
Haynes
(West End)
Stanford
Deanshanger
Wicken
Passenham
Calverton
Gulliver's Land
Woolstone
Woughton on
the Green
Salford
Millbrook
Houghton House
Beadlow
Shefford
Clifton
Henlow
Astwick
Hinxworth
MILTON
KEYNES
Leckhampstead
Lidlington
Maulden
Clophill
Campton
Upper
Gravenhurst
Church
End
Arlesey
Stotfold
Beachampton
Shenley
Church End
Simpson
Walton
Lower
End
Wavendon
Aspley
Guise
Ridgmont
Ampthill
Flitton de Grey
Mausoleum
Flitton
Silsoe
Meppershall
Thornton
Shenley
Brook End
Woburn
Sands
Husborne
Crawley
Steppingley
Wrest Park
Upper & Lower
Stondon
Radwell
Nash
Whaddon
Far
Bletchley
Bow
Brickhill
Aspley
Heath
Flitwick
Greenfield
Lower
Gravenhurst
Shillington
Holwell
Letchworth
Thornborough
Bletchley
Woburn
Woburn
Abbey
Eversholt
Pulloxhill
Westoning
Higham
Gobion
Apsley
End
Great Horwood
Little
Brickhill
Tingrith
Harlington
Barton-le-Clay
Hexton
Pirton
Ickleford
Little
Horwood
Newton
Longville
Great
Brickhill
Potsgrove
Milton Bryan
Sharpenhoe
Pegsdon
Hitchin
Willian
Drayton
Parslow
Mursley
Stoke
Hammond
Heath and
Reach
Toddington
Toddington
Sundon Hills
Upper
Sundon
Lower
Sundon
Barton
Hills
Ravensburgh
Castle
Streatley
Walsworth
Great
Wymondley
Little
Wymondley
Winslow
Hollingdon
Soulbury
Hockliffe
Tebworth
Chalton
Warden
Hill
Well Head
Middle
Claydon
East
Claydon
Swanbourne
Stewkley
Clipstone
Wingfield
Lilley
Great
Offley
St Ippollitts
Hoggeston
Linslade
Eggington
Leighton
Buzzard
Stanbridge
Tilsworth
Houghton
Regis
Leagrave
Limbury
Leygreen
Preston
Granborough
Dunton
Burcott
Stopsley
Cockernhoe
Green
King's Walden
North
Marston
Cublington
Wing
Ascott
NT
Billington
Little
Billington
Eaton
Green
Sewell
Totternhoe
Darleyhall
St Paul's
Walden
Langley
Oving
Whitchurch
Ledburn
Slapton
Eaton
Bray
Dunstable
LUTON
Breachwood
Green
Whitwell
Knebworth
QUAINTON
HILL
Pitchcott
Aston
Abbotts
Mentmore
Northall
Tree
Cathedral
NT
Kensworth
Caddington
Stockwood
Luton
Luton Hoo
Someries
Knebworth
Hardwick
Buckinghamshire
Railway Centre
Crafton
Wingrave
Horton
Grand Union
Canal
Edlesborough
Slip End
Peter's
Green
Kimpton
Codicote
Weedon
Rowsham
Ivinghoe
Aston
Whipsnade
Whipsnade
Kensworth
Common
Markyate
Wildfowl Park
Ayot St
Lawrence
Shaw's
Corner
NT
Waddesdon
Waddesdon
Manor NT
Hulcott
Cheddington
Ivinghoe
Long
Marston
Dagnall
Studham
Bierton
Welwyn
Upper
Winchendon
Aylesbury
Wilstone
Pitstone
Marsworth
Ringshall
Bridgewater
20
Gaddesden
Jockey
End
Flamstead
Harpenden
Batford
Wheathampstead
Nether
Aston
Clinton
Ashridge Estate NT
Amwell
Gaddesden
Row
R. Nene
R. Great Ouse
R. Thame
R. Lea
Great Ouse
M1
A1
A1(M)
A5
A6
A14
A43
A45
A421
A428
A505
A507
A509
A603
A4146

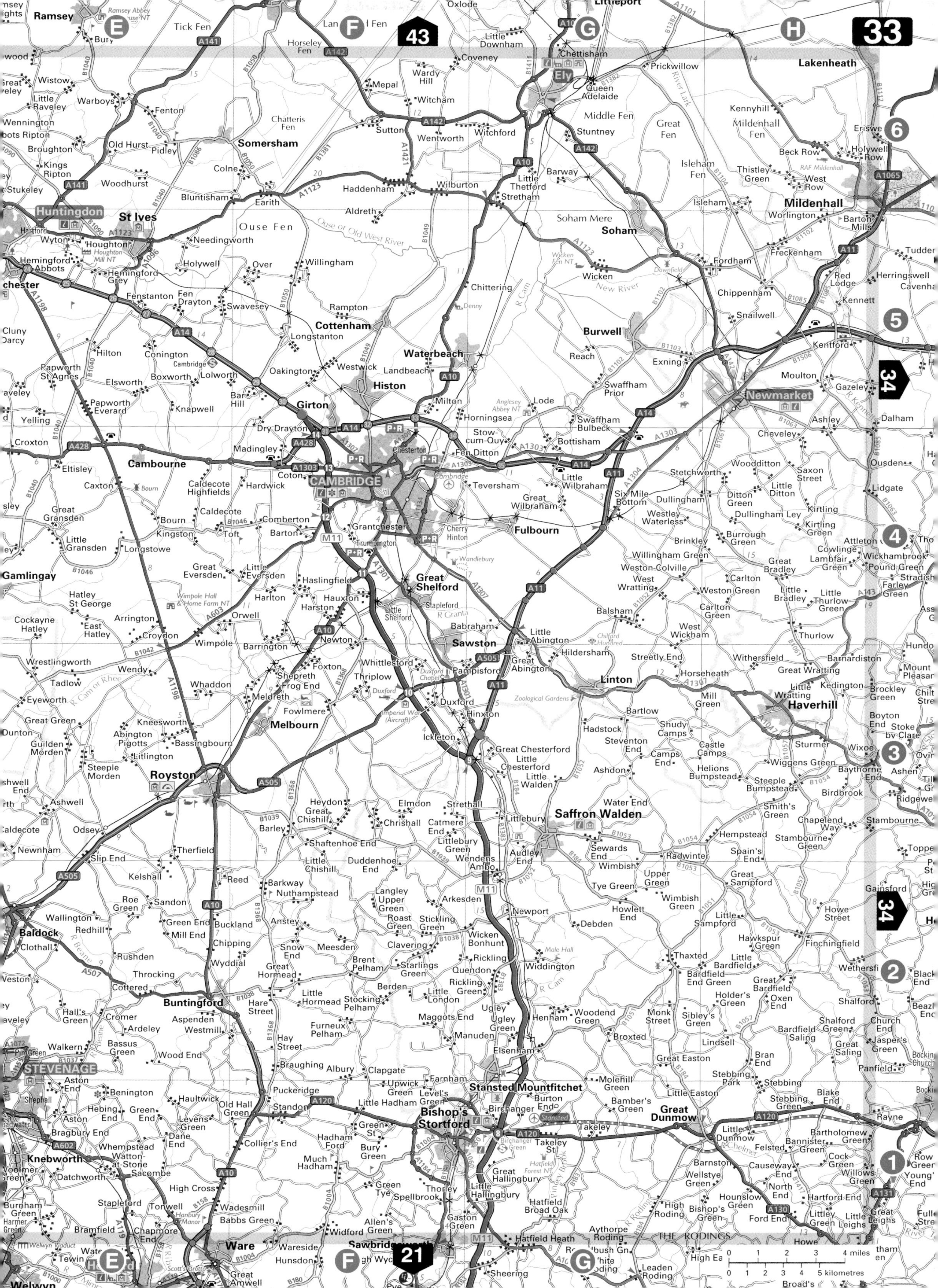

33
43
21
34
E
F
G
H
1
2
3
4
5
6
Ramsey
Ramsey Abbey Gatehouse NT
Bury
Tick Fen
Oxlode
Littleport
Little Downham
Horseley Fen
Coveney
Chettisham
Ely
Prickwillow
Lakenheath
Queen Adelaide
Wardy Hill
Mepal
Witcham
Wistow
Warboys
Little Raveley
Fenton
Chatteris Fen
Sutton
Wentworth
Witchford
Middle Fen
Stuntney
Great Fen
Kennyhill
Mildenhall Fen
Eriswell
Wennington
Kings Ripton
Broughton
Old Hurst
Pidley
Somersham
Colne
Woodhurst
Bluntisham
Earith
Haddenham
Wilburton
Little Thetford
Stretham
Barway
Isleham Fen
Thistley Green
West Row
Beck Row
Holywell Row
RAF Mildenhall
Mildenhall
Worlington
Barton Mills
Isleham
Huntingdon
Hartford
St Ives
Houghton
Wyton
Houghton Mill NT
Hemingford Abbots
Hemingford Grey
Needingworth
Holywell
Ouse Fen
Aldreth
Ouse or Old West River
Soham Mere
Soham
Fordham
Freckenham
Over
Willingham
Wicken Fen NT
Wicken
New River
Downfield
Chippenham
Red Lodge
Herringswell
Kennett
Cavenham
Fenstanton
Fen Drayton
Swavesey
Chittering
Denny
Rampton
Cottenham
Longstanton
Snailwell
Burwell
Kentford
Hilton
Conington
Cambridge
Papworth St Agnes
Elsworth
Boxworth
Lolworth
Oakington
Westwick
Waterbeach
Landbeach
Histon
Reach
Exning
Moulton
Gazeley
Swaffham Prior
Newmarket
Papworth Everard
Knapwell
Bar Hill
Girton
Milton
Horningsea
Anglesey Abbey NT
Lode
Swaffham Bulbeck
Ashley
Dalham
Yelling
Dry Drayton
Madingley
Stow-cum-Quy
Bottisham
Cheveley
Croxton
Cambourne
Coton
Chesterton
Fen Ditton
Little Wilbraham
Woodditton
Saxon Street
Ousden
Eltisley
Caxton
Bourn
Caldecote Highfields
Hardwick
CAMBRIDGE
Teversham
Great Wilbraham
Six Mile Bottom
Stetchworth
Dullingham
Ditton Green
Little Ditton
Lidgate
Great Gransden
Caldecote
Comberton
Westley Waterless
Dullingham Ley
Kirtling
Kirtling Green
Little Gransden
Kingston
Toft
Barton
Grantchester
Trumpington
Cherry Hinton
Fulbourn
Brinkley
Burrough Green
Attleton Green
Longstowe
Gamlingay
Great Eversden
Little Eversden
Haslingfield
Great Shelford
Stapleford
Wandlebury
Willingham Green
Weston Colville
Great Bradley
Cowlinge
Lambfair Green
Wickhambrook
Pound Green
Stradishall
Farley Green
Hatley St George
Wimpole Hall & Home Farm NT
Harlton
Hauxton
Harston
Little Shelford
R Granta
West Wratting
Weston Green
Carlton
Little Bradley
Little Thurlow Green
Carlton Green
Cockayne Hatley
East Hatley
Arrington
Croydon
Orwell
Wimpole
Barrington
Newton
Babraham
Sawston
Balsham
Little Abington
Chilford Hundred
West Wickham
Thurlow
Hundon
Wrestlingworth
Wendy
Foxton
Shepreth
Whittlesford
Thriplow
Duxford Chapel
Pampisford
Great Abington
Hildersham
Streetly End
Horseheath
Withersfield
Great Wratting
Barnardiston
Tadlow
Whaddon
Frog End
Meldreth
Duxford
Imperial War Museum (Aircraft)
Linton
Zoological Gardens
Little Wratting
Kedington
Haverhill
Brockley Green
Eyeworth
Fowlmere
Melbourn
Hinxton
Ickleton
Bartlow
Mill Green
Great Green
Kneesworth
Abington Pigotts
Bassingbourn
Hadstock
Steventon End
Shudy Camps
Castle Camps
Camps End
Boyton End
Stoke by Clare
Sturmer
Wixoe
Guilden Morden
Litlington
Great Chesterford
Little Chesterford
Little Walden
Ashdon
Helions Bumpstead
Wiggens Green
Steeple Bumpstead
Baythorne End
Steeple Morden
Royston
Heydon
Great Chishill
Elmdon
Strethall
Littlebury
Saffron Walden
Water End
Birdbrook
Smith's Green
Ashwell
Odsey
Barley
Chrishall
Catmere End
Littlebury Green
Hempstead
Chapelend Way
Stambourne
Stambourne Green
Newnham
Therfield
Shaftenhoe End
Little Chishill
Duddenhoe End
Wendens Ambo
Audley End
Sewards End
Wimbish
Radwinter
Spain's End
Great Sampford
Slip End
Kelshall
Reed
Barkway
Nuthampstead
Langley Upper Green
Arkesden
Newport
Tye Green
Upper Green
Wimbish Green
Howlett End
Gainsford End
Roe Green
Sandon
Anstey
Roast Green
Stickling Green
Debden
Little Sampford
Howe Street
Wallington
Green End
Buckland
Mill End
Chipping
Snow End
Meesden
Clavering
Wicken Bonhunt
Mole Hall
Hawkspur Green
Finchingfield
Baldock
Redhill
Clothall
Wyddial
Great Hormead
Brent Pelham
Starlings Green
Rickling
Quendon
Widdington
Thaxted
Little Bardfield
Bardfield End Green
Wethersfield
Rushden
Throcking
Cottered
Buntingford
Little Hormead
Hare Street
Berden
Stocking Pelham
Rickling Green
Little London
Ugley
Ugley Green
Henham
Woodend Green
Monk Street
Sibley's Green
Holder's Green
Great Bardfield
Oxen End
Shalford
Weston
Hall's Green
Cromer
Ardeley
Aspenden
Westmill
Furneux Pelham
Maggots End
Manuden
Broxted
Lindsell
Bardfield Saling
Shalford Green
Church End
Jasper's Green
Great Saling
Walkern
Bassus Green
Hay Street
Elsenham
Bran End
Great Easton
Panfield
Pin Green
Wood End
Braughing
Albury
Clapgate
Farnham
Stebbing Park
Stebbing
Stebbing Green
Blake End
STEVENAGE
Aston End
Benington
Upwick Green
Level's Green
Puckeridge
Stansted Mountfitchet
Molehill Green
Little Easton
Shephall
Haultwick
Old Hall Green
Standon
Little Hadham
Burton End
Birchanger
Bamber's Green
Great Dunmow
Hebing End
Green End
Aston
Levens Green
Green St
Bishop's Stortford
Stansted
Takeley
Rayne
Bragbury End
Whempstead
Dane End
Hadham Ford
Bury Green
Birchanger Green
Takeley St
Little Dunmow
Bartholomew Green
Bannister Green
Felsted
Knebworth
Watton-at-Stone
Sacombe
Collier's End
Much Hadham
Hatfield Forest NT
Great Hallingbury
Barnston
Causeway End
Cock Green
Willows Green
Datchworth
High Cross
Green Tye
Spellbrook
Thorley
Little Hallingbury
Wellstye Green
North End
Hartford End
Burnham Green
Stapleford
Tonwell
Wadesmill
Hanbury Manor
Babbs Green
Allen's Green
Gaston Green
Hatfield Broad Oak
High Roding
Hounslow Green
Bishop's Green
Ford End
Littley Green
Great Leighs
Little Leighs
Bramfield
Chapmore End
Ware
Wareside
Widford
Sawbridgeworth
Hatfield Heath
Aythorpe Roding
THE RODINGS
Welwyn Viaduct
Tewin
Hunsdon
Sheering
Leaden Roding
High Easter
Great Amwell
Scott's Grotto
Welwyn
Howe
River Cam
R Cam
R Rhee
R Beane
R Chelmer
Ouse
River Lark
A10
A11
A14
A141
A142
A1123
A1421
A428
A1303
A1307
A1301
A1134
A505
A603
A1198
A1096
A1101
A1065
A1304
A143
A1017
A507
A120
A602
A119
A1072
A131
A130
A1061
M11
B1040
B1050
B1086
B1381
B1049
B1411
B1382
B1104
B1102
B1085
B1506
B1063
B1103
B1046
B1042
B1039
B1368
B1052
B1053
B1054
B1057
B1051
B1383
B1038
B1037
B1004
B158
B1000
B184
B1008
B1417
B1256
B1090
B1112
B1106
B1061
B1085
B1109
B1183
B1004
B180
P+R
0 1 2 3 4 miles
0 1 2 3 4 5 kilometres

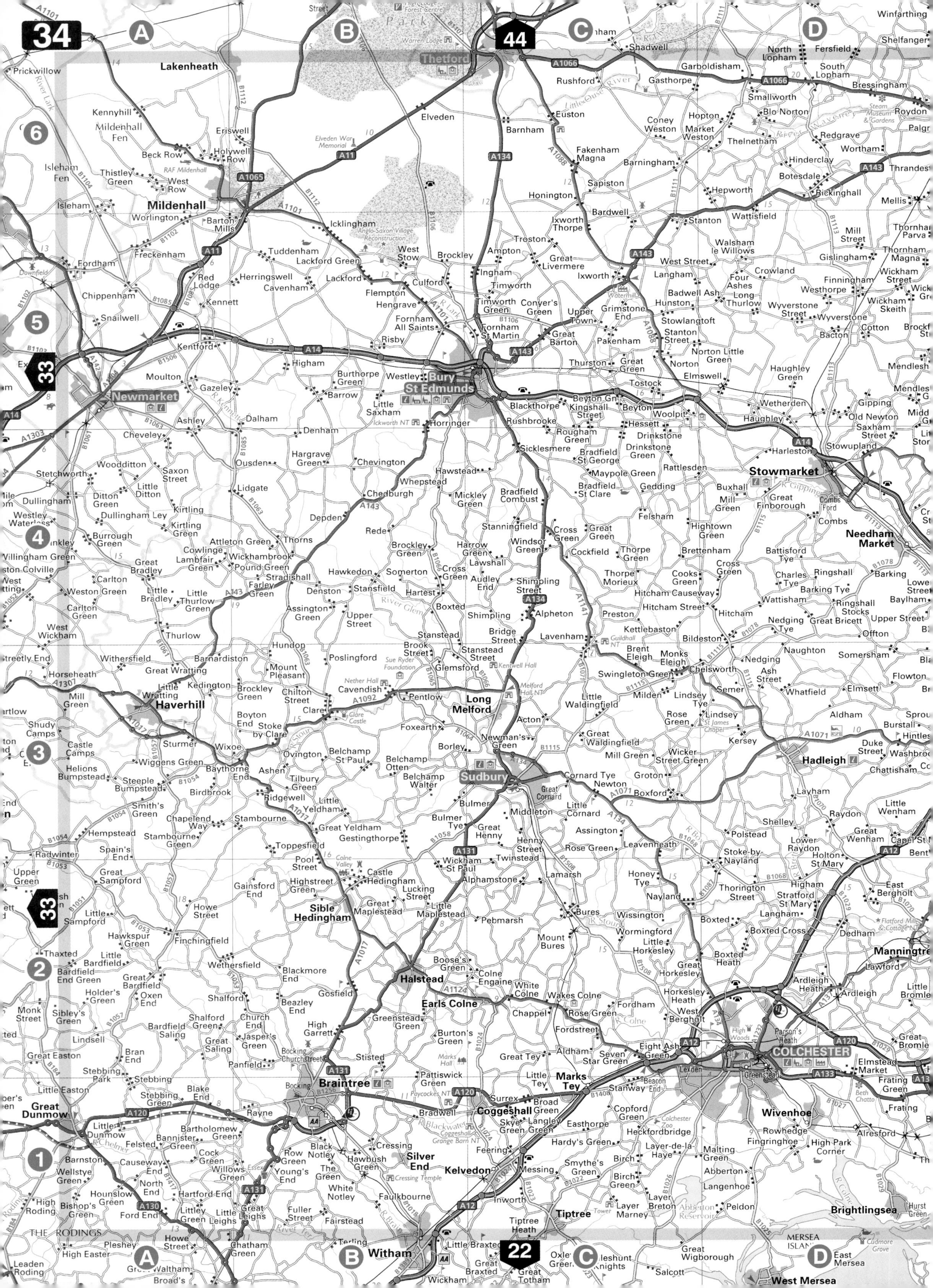

34
A
B
C
D
44
22
33
Lakenheath
Prickwillow
Thetford
Shadwell
North Lopham
Fersfield
Winfarthing
Shelfanger
South Lopham
Garboldisham
Rushford
Gasthorpe
Bressingham
Roydon
Smallworth
Blo Norton
Kennyhill
Mildenhall Fen
Eriswell
Elveden
Euston
Barnham
Coney Weston
Hopton
Market Weston
Thelnetham
Redgrave
Palgrave
Wortham
Beck Row
Holywell Row
Fakenham Magna
Barningham
Hinderclay
Botesdale
Thrandeston
Isleham Fen
Thistley Green
West Row
Sapiston
Hepworth
Rickinghall
Mellis
Isleham
Mildenhall
Worlington
Barton Mills
Icklingham
Honington
Bardwell
Stanton
Wattisfield
Ixworth Thorpe
Mill Street
Thornham Parva
Thornham Magna
Gislingham
Fordham
Freckenham
Tuddenham
Lackford Green
West Stow
Brockley
Ampton
Troston
Great Livermere
Walsham le Willows
West Street
Crowland
Langham
Ixworth
Ingham
Timworth
Lackford
Culford
Four Ashes
Finningham
Wickham Street
Chippenham
Red Lodge
Herringswell
Cavenham
Flempton
Hengrave
Timworth Green
Conyer's Green
Grimstone End
Badwell Ash
Long Thurlow
Hunston
Westhorpe
Wyverstone Street
Wickham Skeith
Kennett
Snailwell
Fornham All Saints
Fornham St Martin
Upper Town
Great Barton
Stowlangtoft
Stanton Street
Norton Little Green
Wyverstone
Bacton
Cotton
Kentford
Risby
Pakenham
Higham
Moulton
Gazeley
Burthorpe Green
Westley
Bury St Edmunds
Barrow
Thurston
Great Green
Norton
Elmswell
Haughley Green
Mendlesham
Newmarket
Tostock
Little Saxham
Blackthorpe
Beyton Gn
Kingshall Street
Beyton
Woolpit
Wetherden
Gipping
Old Newton
Ashley
Dalham
Denham
Horringer
Rushbrooke
Hessett
Drinkstone
Rougham Green
Haughley
Saxham Street
Cheveley
Hargrave Green
Chevington
Sicklesmere
Bradfield St George
Drinkstone Green
Rattlesden
Harleston
Stowupland
Stowmarket
Woodditton
Saxon Street
Stetchworth
Ditton Green
Little Ditton
Hawstead
Whepstead
Maypole Green
Bradfield St Clare
Gedding
Buxhall
Mill Green
Combs Ford
Dullingham
Kirtling
Chedburgh
Mickley Green
Bradfield Combust
Great Finborough
Dullingham Ley
Kirtling Green
Depden
Felsham
Combs
Westley Waterless
Burrough Green
Stanningfield
Cross Green
Great Green
Hightown Green
Needham Market
Rede
Attleton Green
Thorns
Windsor Green
Cowlinge
Brockley Green
Harrow Green
Cockfield
Thorpe Green
Brettenham
Battisford Tye
Willingham Green
Great Bradley
Lambfair Green
Wickhambrook
Pound Green
Lawshall
Carlton
Little Bradley
Stradishall
Farley Green
Hawkedon
Somerton
Cross Green
Audley End
Shimpling Street
Thorpe Morieux
Cooks Green
Charles Tye
Ringshall
Barking
Barking Tye
Weston Green
Little Thurlow Green
Denston
Stansfield
Hartest
Hitcham Causeway
Wattisham
Ringshall Stocks
Baylham
Carlton Green
Assington Green
Upper Street
Boxted
Shimpling
Alpheton
Preston
Hitcham Street
Hitcham
Nedging Tye
Great Bricett
Upper Street
West Wickham
Thurlow
River Glem
Stanstead
Bridge Street
Lavenham
Kettlebaston
Bildeston
Offton
Hundon
Brook Street
Stanstead Street
Brent Eleigh
Monks Eleigh
Naughton
Somersham
Withersfield
Barnardiston
Poslingford
Mount Pleasant
Glemsford
Chelsworth
Nedging
Ash Street
Horseheath
Great Wratting
Little Wratting
Kedington
Sue Ryder Foundation
Kentwell Hall
Melford Hall NT
Swingleton Green
Semer
Whatfield
Flowton
Elmsett
Mill Green
Haverhill
Brockley Green
Chilton Street
Cavendish
Nether Hall
Pentlow
Long Melford
Milden
Lindsey Tye
Clare
Glare Castle
Little Waldingfield
Boyton End
Stoke by Clare
Foxearth
Acton
Rose Green
Lindsey
Aldham
Sprou
Burstall
Shudy Camps
Castle Camps
Sturmer
Wixoe
Borley
Newman's Green
Great Waldingfield
St James Chapel
Kersey
Duke Street
Hintlesham
Washbrook
Helions Bumpstead
Wiggens Green
Baythorne End
Ovington
Belchamp St Paul
Belchamp Otten
Mill Green
Wicker Street Green
Hadleigh
Chattisham
Steeple Bumpstead
Ashen
Tilbury Green
Belchamp Walter
Sudbury
Cornard Tye
Newton
Groton
Boxford
Layham
Birdbrook
Ridgewell
Little Yeldham
Bulmer
Great Cornard
Little Cornard
Raydon
Little Wenham
Smith's Green
Chapelend Way
Stambourne
Great Yeldham
Bulmer Tye
Middleton
Shelley
Great Wenham
Hempstead
Stambourne Green
Gestingthorpe
Great Henny
Assington
Polstead
Lower Raydon
Capel St Mary
Bentley
Radwinter
Spain's End
Toppesfield
Henny Street
Twinstead
Rose Green
Leavenheath
Stoke-by-Nayland
Holton St Mary
Upper Green
Great Sampford
Pool Street
Wickham St Paul
Lamarsh
Colne Valley
Castle Hedingham
Honey Tye
Alphamstone
Highstreet Green
Gainsford End
Lucking Street
Nayland
Thorington Street
Higham
Stratford St Mary
East Bergholt
Howe Street
Sible Hedingham
Great Maplestead
Little Maplestead
Pebmarsh
Bures
Wissington
Boxted
Langham
Boxted Cross
Flatford Mill & Cottage NT
Dedham
Little Sampford
Hawkspur Green
Finchingfield
Mount Bures
Wormingford
Little Horkesley
Manningtree
Thaxted
Little Bardfield
Bardfield End Green
Wethersfield
Blackmore End
Halstead
Booser's Green
Colne Engaine
Boxted Heath
Great Horkesley
Lawford
Great Bardfield
Holder's Green
Oxen End
Gosfield
White Colne
Earls Colne
Wakes Colne
Horkesley Heath
Ardleigh Heath
Ardleigh
Little Bromley
Monk Street
Sibley's Green
Shalford
Beazley End
Shalford Green
Church End
Chappel
Rose Green
Fordham
West Bergholt
Bardfield Saling
Greenstead Green
Fordstreet
High Woods
Parson's Heath
Great Bromley
Lindsell
Great Saling
Jasper's Green
High Garrett
Burton's Green
Eight Ash Green
Colchester
Great Easton
Bran End
Panfield
Bocking Churchstreet
Stisted
Great Tey
Aldham
Seven Star Green
Lexden
Greenstead
Elmstead Market
Stebbing Park
Stebbing
Bocking
Braintree
Pattiswick Green
Marks Hall
Little Tey
Marks Tey
Broad Green
Beacon End
Stanway
Frating Green
Little Easton
Stebbing Green
Blake End
Paycocke's NT
Coggeshall
Surrex
Bradwell
Beth Chatto
Great Dunmow
Rayne
Little Dunmow
Bartholomew Green
Bannister Green
Felsted
Skye Green
Langley Green
Copford Green
Eastthorpe
Wivenhoe
Frating
Coggeshall Grange Barn NT
Colchester Zoo
Heckfordbridge
Rowhedge
Fingringhoe
Alresford
Cressing
Black Notley
Hawbush Green
Silver End
Hardy's Green
Layer-de-la-Haye
High Park Corner
Barnston
Causeway End
Cock Green
Willows Green
Row Green
Young's End
The Green
Cressing Temple
Feering
Kelvedon
Messing
Smythe's Green
Birch
Malting Green
Abberton
Wellstye Green
North End
White Notley
Birch Green
Langenhoe
Hounslow Green
Hartford End
Faulkbourne
Layer Breton
Layer Marney
Abberton Reservoir
Peldon
Brightlingsea
High Roding
Bishop's Green
Littley Green
Great Leighs
Little Leighs
Fuller Street
Fairstead
Inworth
Tiptree
Tower
Ford End
The Rodings
Howe Street
Chatham Green
Terling
Witham
Little Braxted
Tiptree Heath
Great Wigborough
Mersea Island
East Mersea
Cudmore Grove
Hurst Green
Pleshey
High Easter
Leaden Roding
Great Waltham
Broad's Green
Great Braxted
Wickham
Great Totham
Oxley Green
Tolleshunt Knights
Salcott
West Mersea
A11
A1065
A1101
A134
A143
A14
A1066
A1088
A1303
A1307
A142
A1017
A1092
A1141
A1071
A131
A1124
A120
A12
A133
A137
A130
A1304
B1085
B1063
B1061
B1054
B1053
B1057
B1058
B1064
B1065
B1066
B1115
B1078
B1070
B1068
B1087
B1029
B1027
B1024
B1023
B1022
B1026
B1025
B1018
B1256
B1417
B1008
B1102
B1104
B1106
B1112
B1113
B1111
B1506
B1508
B1508
B1050
B1051
B1071
1
2
3
4
5
6

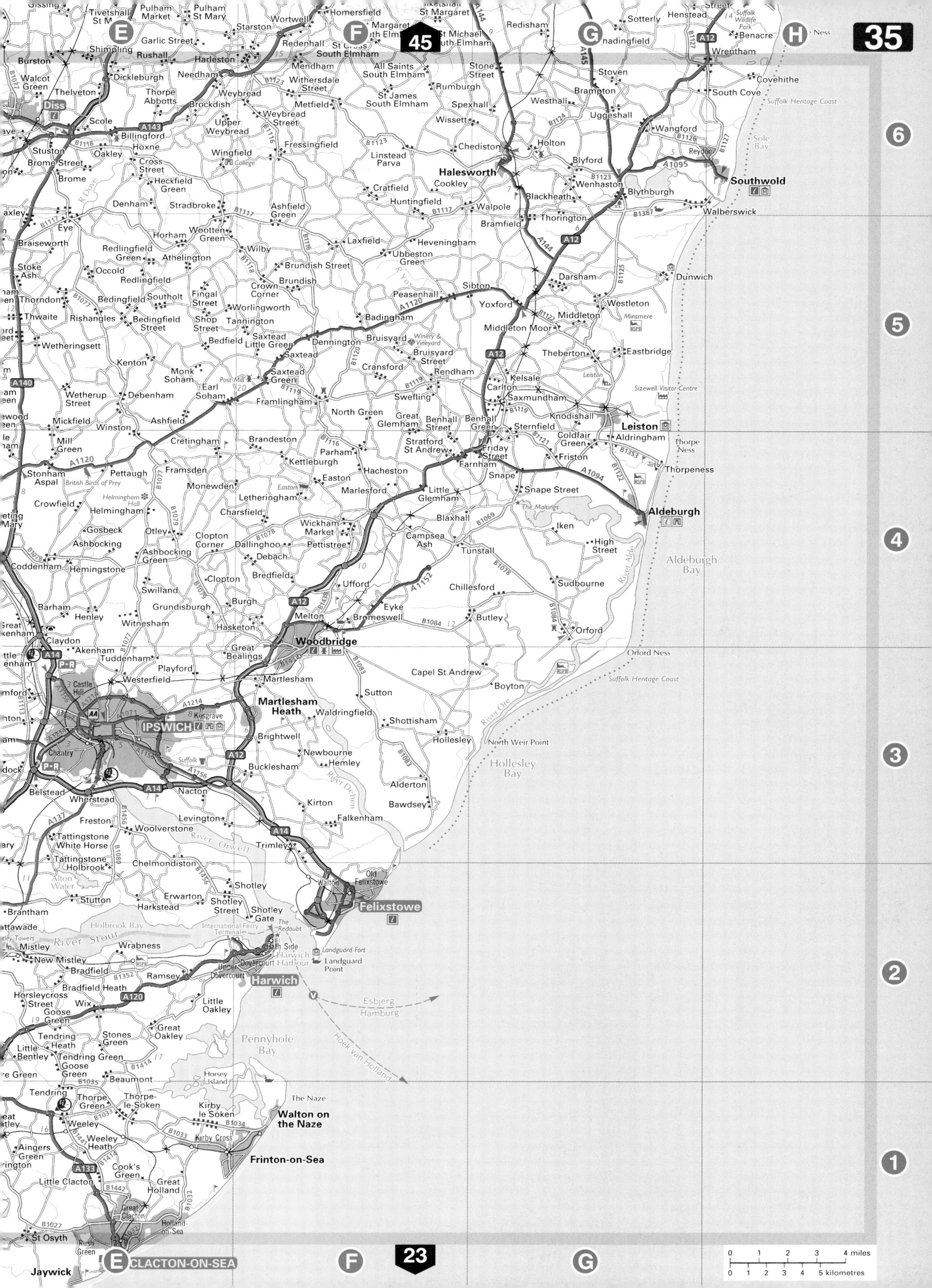
35
45
23
E
F
G
H
1
2
3
4
5
6
Tivetshall St M
Pulham Market
Pulham St Mary
Starston
Wortwell
Homersfield
St Margaret
Redisham
Sotterly
Henstead
Suffolk Wildlife Park
Benacre
Ness
Garlic Street
Redenhall
St Cross South Elmham
St Michael South Elmham
Wrentham
Burston
Shimpling
Rushall
Harleston
Mendham
All Saints South Elmham
Stone Street
Stoven
Covehithe
Walcot Green
Thelveton
Dickleburgh
Needham
Withersdale Street
Rumburgh
Brampton
South Cove
Suffolk Heritage Coast
Diss
Thorpe Abbotts
Weybread
St James South Elmham
Spexhall
Westhall
Uggeshall
Brockdish
Metfield
Scole
Upper Weybread
Weybread Street
Wissett
Wangford
Billingford
Hoxne
Holton
Sole Bay
Stuston
Oakley
Wingfield
Fressingfield
Chediston
Reydon
Brome Street
Cross Street
College
Linstead Parva
Blyford
Brome
Heckfield Green
Halesworth
Cookley
Wenhaston
Southwold
Blythburgh
Cratfield
Denham
Stradbroke
Ashfield Green
Huntingfield
Blackheath
Walpole
Thorington
Walberswick
Bramfield
Eye
Horham
Wootten Green
Laxfield
Heveningham
Braiseworth
Redlingfield Green
Athelington
Wilby
Ubbeston Green
Stoke Ash
Occold
Redlingfield
Brundish Street
Darsham
Dunwich
Brundish
Thorndon
Bedingfield
Southolt
Fingal Street
Crown Corner
Peasenhall
Sibton
Yoxford
Westleton
Worlingworth
Badingham
Middleton
Minsmere
Thwaite
Rishangles
Bedingfield Street
Shop Street
Tannington
Middleton Moor
Wetheringsett
Bedfield
Saxtead Little Green
Dennington
Bruisyard
Winery & Vineyard
Bruisyard Street
Theberton
Eastbridge
Saxtead
Kenton
Monk Soham
Cransford
Rendham
Post Mill
Saxtead Green
Kelsale
Leiston
Earl Soham
Carlton
Saxmundham
Sizewell Visitor Centre
Wetherup Street
Debenham
Framlingham
Swefling
Knodishall
North Green
Mickfield
Winston
Ashfield
Great Glemham
Benhall Street
Benhall Green
Sternfield
Coldfair Green
Aldringham
Mill Green
Cretingham
Brandeston
Stratford St Andrew
Friday Street
Thorpe Ness
Parham
Friston
Kettleburgh
Farnham
Thorpeness
Stonham Aspal
Pettaugh
Framsden
Hacheston
Snape
British Birds of Prey
Monewden
Easton
Marlesford
Little Glemham
Snape Street
Crowfield
Helmingham Hall
Letheringham
The Maltings
Helmingham
Charsfield
Aldeburgh
Blaxhall
Wickham Market
Iken
Gosbeck
Otley
Campsea Ash
High Street
Clopton Corner
Dallinghoo
Pettistree
Ashbocking
Tunstall
Ashbocking Green
Debach
Aldeburgh Bay
Coddenham
Hemingstone
Bredfield
River Alde
Clopton
Ufford
Chillesford
Sudbourne
Swilland
Barham
Henley
Grundisburgh
Burgh
Eyke
Melton
Bromeswell
Butley
Witnesham
Hasketon
Orford
Claydon
Akenham
Woodbridge
Great Bealings
Tuddenham
Orford Ness
Capel St Andrew
Playford
Westerfield
Martlesham
Boyton
Castle Hill
Sutton
Martlesham Heath
Kesgrave
Waldringfield
Shottisham
IPSWICH
Brightwell
Hollesley
North Weir Point
River Ore
Chantry
Suffolk
Newbourne
Hemley
Hollesley Bay
Bucklesham
Belstead
Wherstead
Nacton
Alderton
River Deben
Kirton
Bawdsey
Freston
Levington
Falkenham
Woolverstone
Tattingstone White Horse
River Orwell
Trimley
Tattingstone
Holbrook
Chelmondiston
Alton Water
Walton
Old Felixstowe
Shotley
Stutton
Erwarton
Felixstowe
Harkstead
Shotley Street
Shotley Gate
Brantham
Holbrook Bay
International Ferry Terminal
The Redoubt
River Stour
Mistley
Wrabness
Bath Side
Landguard Fort
Harwich Harbour
New Mistley
Dovercourt
Landguard Point
Bradfield
Ramsey
Upper Dovercourt
Harwich
Bradfield Heath
Horsleycross Street
Wix
Little Oakley
Esbjerg Hamburg
Goose Green
Great Oakley
Tendring Heath
Stones Green
Pennyhole Bay
Hoek van Holland
Little Bentley
Tendring Green
Goose Green
Beaumont
Horsey Island
Tendring
Thorpe Green
Thorpe-le-Soken
The Naze
Kirby le Soken
Walton on the Naze
Weeley
Weeley Heath
Kirby Cross
Aingers Green
Frinton-on-Sea
Cook's Green
Little Clacton
Great Holland
Great Clacton
Holland-on-Sea
St Osyth
Rush Green
CLACTON-ON-SEA
Jaywick
A12
A144
A145
A143
A140
A1120
A1095
A1094
A1152
A1214
A1156
A14
A137
A120
A133
B1123
B1124
B1126
B1127
B1387
B1125
B1122
B1116
B1117
B1118
B1077
B1119
B1121
B1069
B1078
B1079
B1353
B1084
B1083
B1438
B1456
B1080
B1352
B1414
B1035
B1033
B1034
B1441
B1442
B1032
B1027
B1113
B1071
0 1 2 3 4 miles
0 1 2 3 4 5 kilometres

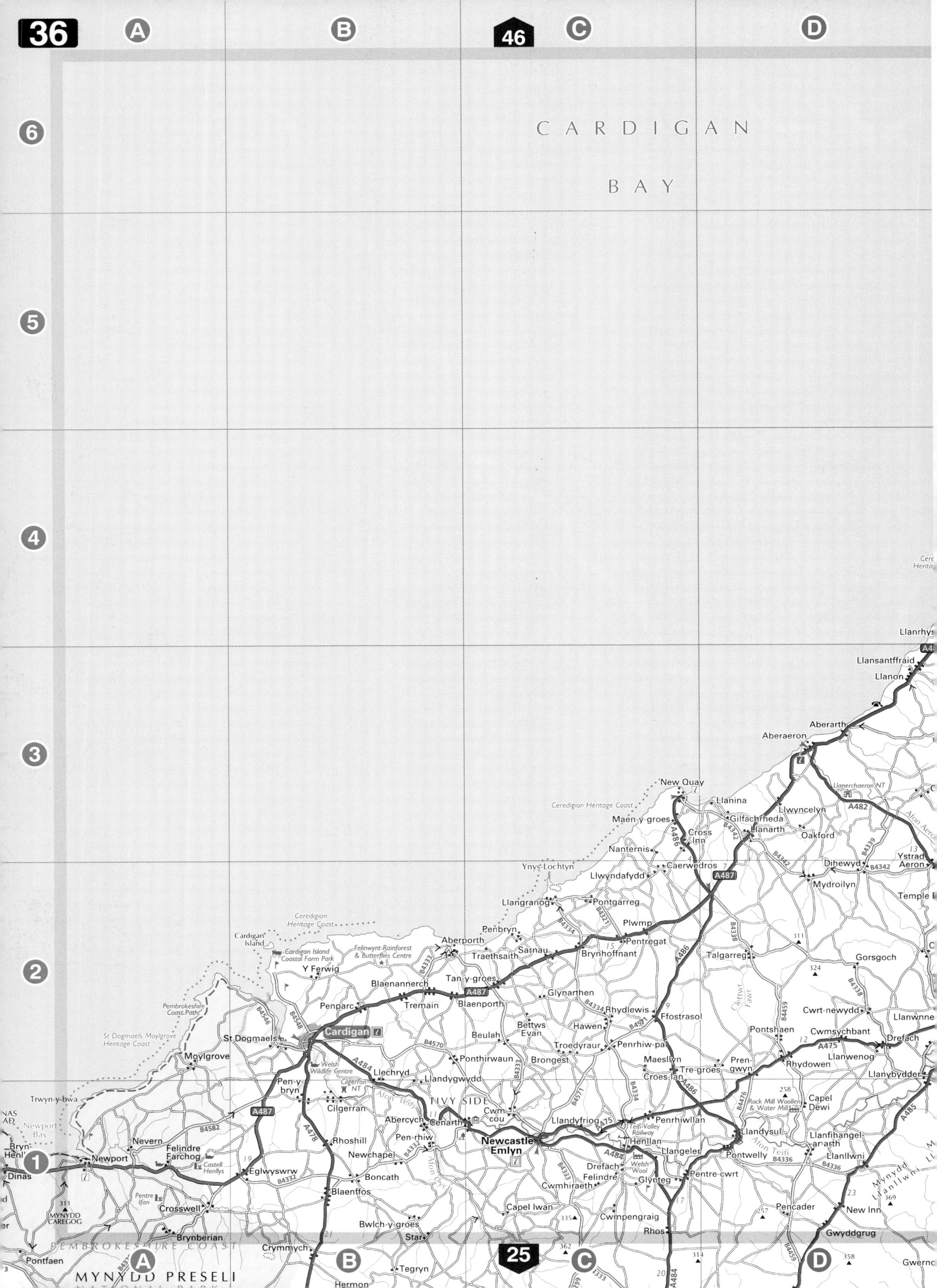

A   B   C   D

6

CARDIGAN

BAY

5

4

Cere
Herita

Llanrhys

A4
Llansantffraid

Llanon

3
Aberarth

Aberaeron
New Quay   Ulanerchaeron NT
Llanina   A482
Maen-y-groes   Llwyncelyn
Ceredigion Heritage Coast   Gilfachrheda
                    Cross   Llanarth   Oakford
Ynys-Lochtyn   Nanternis   Inn   Ystrad
                    Llwyndafydd   Caerwedros 7   Dihewyd   Aeron
Llangranog   A487   Mydroilyn
          Pontgarreg   Temple L

Penbryn   Plwmp
                              Pentregat
Aberporth   Sarnau   Brynhoffnant   Talgarreg   Gorsgoch
Ceredigion Heritage Coast   Traethsaith   311
Felinwynt Rainforest   324
& Butterflies Centre   Tan-y-groes   Glynarthen   B4338
Cardigan   Y Ferwig   Rhydlewis   9
Island   Blaenannerch   A487 Blaenporth   Ffostrasol   Cwrt-newydd   Llanwnne

2   Cardigan Island   Penparc   Tremain   Blaenporth   Hawen   Pontshaen   Cwmsychbant
Coastal Farm Park   Bettws   Drefach
                              Beulah Evan   Maesllyn Tre-groes Pren-   Rhydowen   Llanwenog
Pembrokeshire   Welsh   B4570   Ponthirwaun Troedyraur Penrhiw-pal   gwyn   Llanybydder
Coast Path   Wildlife Centre   Brongest   Croes-lan A486
St Dogmaels Moylgrove   St Dogmaels   Cilgerran   Llandygwydd   258   Rock Mill Woollen   Capel
Heritage Coast   Cardigan   NT   VY SIDE   258   & Water Mill   Dewi
Trwyn-y-bwa   Moylgrove   Pen-y-   Llechryd   Afon Teifi   Cwm-   Llandyfriog   Penrhiwllan   Llandysul Llanfihangel-
          bryn   cou   Teifi   ar-arth
NAS   Newport   Cilgerran   Abercych Cenarth   Teifi Valley   Henllan   Pontwelly Llanllwni
AD   Bay   A487   11   Railway   Clangeler
Bryn   Nevern Felindre   A478   Pen-rhiw   Newcastle   Welsh   Glynteg   Pentre-cwrt
Henl   Farchog   B4582   Rhoshill   Emlyn   A484 Wool   New Inn
Dinas   Newport   Castell   Newchapel   Drefach   Pencader
    Pontfaen   Henllys   B4332 Boncath   Felindre
311   Pentre   Eglwyswrw   Cwmhiraeth   257
MYNYDD   Ifan   B4332   Blaenffos   Capel Iwan 335   Cwmpengraig
CAREGOG   Crosswell   Rhos   314   358
PEMBROKESHIRE COAST   Brynberian   Bwlch-y-groes   362   Gwyddgrug
Pontfaen   Crymmych   Star   25 C   314   D
A   B   Hermon

MYNYDD PRESELI

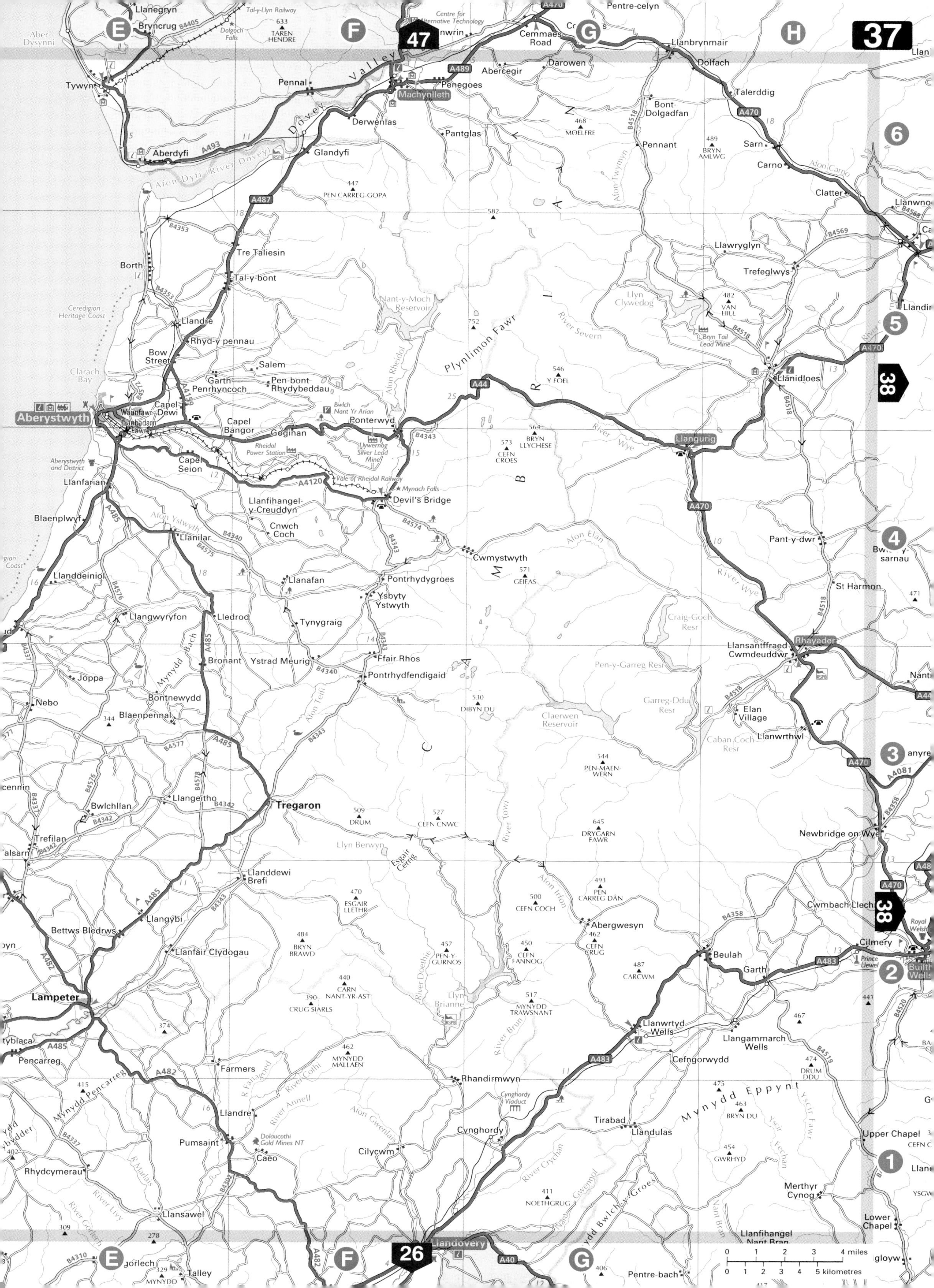

Llanegryn
Bryncrug
Tal-y-Llyn Railway
633 TAREN HENDRE
Dolgoch Falls
Centre for Alternative Technology
47
Pentre-celyn
Cemmaes Road
Llanbrynmair
Aber Dysynni
Tywyn
Pennal
Dovey Valley
Machynlleth
Penegoes
Abercegir
Darowen
Dolfach
Talerddig
Derwenlas
Pantglas
Bont-Dolgadfan
468 MOELFRE
489 BRYN AMLWG
Pennant
Sarn
Carno
Afon Carno
Clatter
Llanwnog
Aberdyfi
Glandyfi
Afon Dyfi (River Dovey)
447 PEN CARREG-GOPA
582
Afon Twymyn
Tre Taliesin
Borth
Tal-y-bont
Llawryglyn
Trefeglwys
Ceredigion Heritage Coast
Nant-y-Moch Reservoir
Llyn Clywedog
482 VAN HILL
Bryn Tail Lead Mine
Llandre
752
Plynlimon Fawr
River Severn
Rhyd-y pennau
Bow Street
Salem
Clarach Bay
Garth
Penrhyncoch
Pen-bont Rhydybeddau
Afon Rheidol
546 Y FOEL
Llanidloes
38
Aberystwyth
Waunfawr
Capel Dewi
Llanbadarn Fawr
Capel Bangor
Bwlch Nant Yr Arian
Ponterwyd
Goginan
Llywernog Silver Lead Mine
564 BRYN LLYCHESE
573 CEFN CROES
River Wye
Llangurig
Rheidol Power Station
Aberystwyth and District
Capel Seion
Vale of Rheidol Railway
Mynach Falls
Devil's Bridge
Llanfarian
Llanfihangel-y-Creuddyn
Blaenplwyf
Cnwch Coch
Afon Ystwyth
Llanilar
Cwmystwyth
Afon Elan
571 GEIFAS
Pant-y-dwr
Llanddeiniol
Llanafan
Pontrhydygroes
Ysbyty Ystwyth
St Harmon
471
Llangwyryfon
Lledrod
Tynygraig
Craig-Goch Resr
Mynydd Bach
Bronant
Ystrad Meurig
Ffair Rhos
Pontrhydfendigaid
Llansantffraed Cwmdeuddwr
Rhayader
Pen-y-Garreg Resr
Joppa
Nebo
Bontnewydd
Blaenpennal
344
530 DIBYN DU
Claerwen Reservoir
Garreg-Ddu Resr
Elan Village
Llanwrthwl
Afon Teifi
Caban Coch Resr
544 PEN-MAEN-WERN
Llangeitho
Bwlchllan
Tregaron
509 DRUM
527 CEFN CNWC
645 DRYGARN FAWR
Newbridge on Wye
Trefilan
Llyn Berwyn
Esgair Cerrig
River Towy
Llanddewi Brefi
470 ESGAIR LLEETHR
500 CEFN COCH
493 PEN CARREG-DÂN
Afon Irfon
Abergwesyn
462 CEFN CRUG
Cwmbach Llechryd
Royal Welsh
Bettws Bledrws
Llangybi
484 BRYN BRAWD
457 PEN-Y-GURNOS
450 CEFN FANNOG
Beulah
Cilmery
Llanfair Clydogau
River Doethie
487 CARCWM
Garth
Prince Llewelyn
Builth Wells
Lampeter
440 CARN NANT-YR-AST
390 CRUG SIARLS
Llyn Brianne
517 MYNYDD TRAWSNANT
441
374
River Brun
Llanwrtyd Wells
Llangammarch Wells
467
Pencarreg
Farmers
462 MYNYDD MALLAEN
Cefngorwydd
474 DRUM DDU
Mynydd Pencarreg
415
River Cothi
Rhandirmwyn
Cynghordy Viaduct
Mynydd Eppynt
475
463 BRYN DU
River Annell
Afon Gwenlais
Llandre
Tirabad
Llandulas
Dolaucothi Gold Mines NT
Pumsaint
Cynghordy
Caeo
Cilycwm
Upper Chapel
River Crychan
454 GWRHYD
Rhydcymerau
River Marlais
411 NOETHGRUG
Merthyr Cynog
River Livy
Llansawel
309
278
River Gorlech
Mynydd Bwlch-y-Groes
Nant Bran
Lower Chapel
Llanfihangel Nant Bran
26
Llandovery
Talley
329 MYNYDD
406
Pentre-bach
0 1 2 3 4 miles
0 1 2 3 4 5 kilometres
A470 A489 A493 A487 A4159 A44 A4120 A485 A482 A483 A40 A4081
B4405 B4353 B4343 B4574 B4340 B4575 B4576 B4577 B4578 B4342 B4337 B4518 B4569 B4568 B4358 B4519 B4302 B4310
E F G H
6 5 4 3 2 1

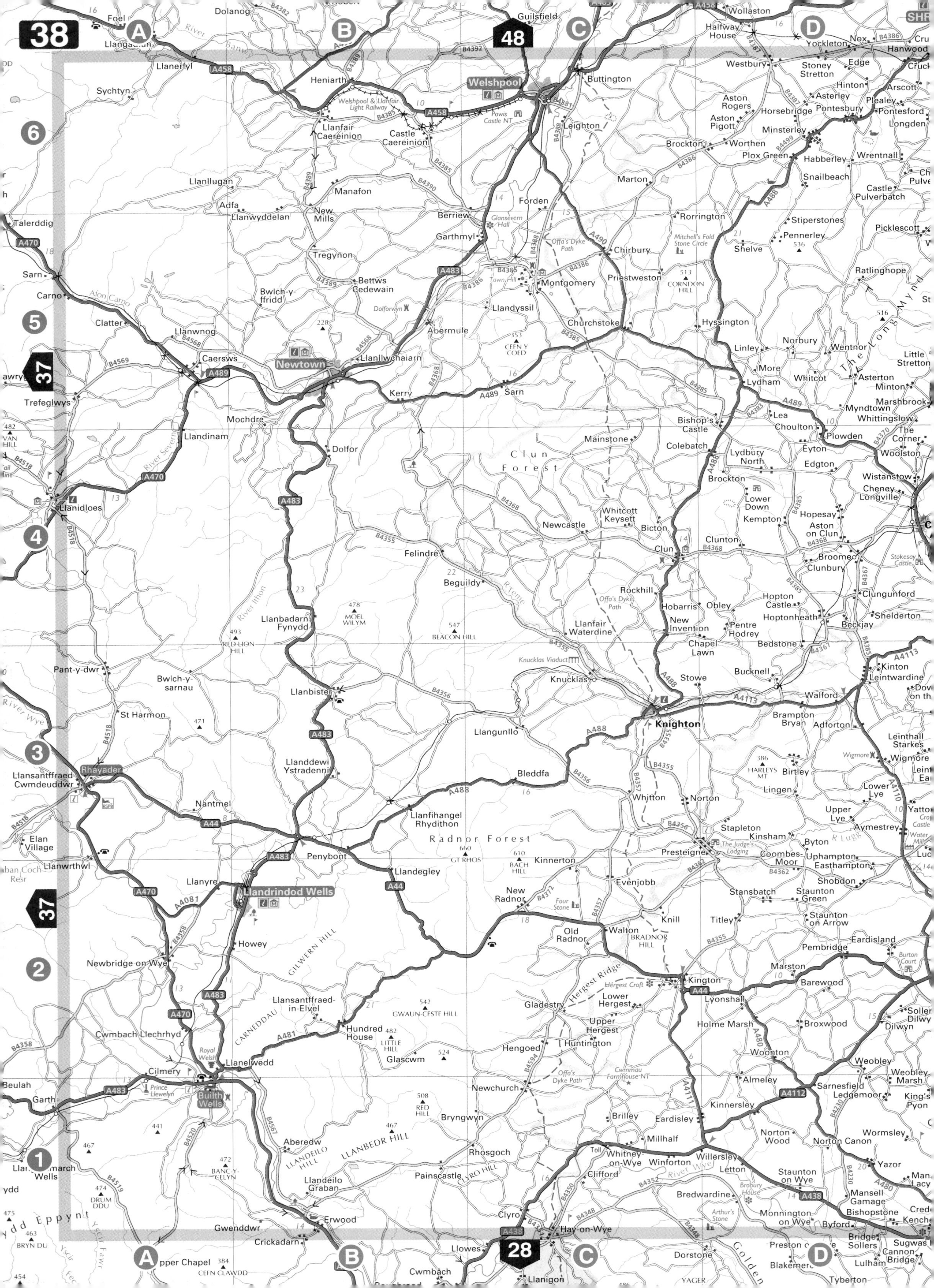
38
48
37
28
A
B
C
D
1
2
3
4
5
6
Foel
Llangadfan
Dolanog
Guilsfield
Wollaston
Halfway House
Yockleton
Nox
Cruckton
Hanwood
Llanerfyl
Heniarth
Welshpool
Buttington
Westbury
Stoney Stretton
Edge
Cruckmeole
Sychtyn
Welshpool & Llanfair Light Railway
Powis Castle NT
Aston Rogers
Hinton
Arscott
Llanfair Caereinion
Castle Caereinion
Leighton
Aston Pigott
Horsebridge
Asterley
Pontesbury
Pealey
Pontesford
Minsterley
Longden
Brockton
Worthen
Plox Green
Habberley
Wrentnall
Llanllugan
Manafon
Marton
Snailbeach
Castle Pulverbatch
Adfa
Llanwyddelan
New Mills
Berriew
Forden
Rorrington
Glansevern Hall
Stiperstones
Pennerley
Picklescott
Talerddig
Garthmyl
Offa's Dyke Path
Chirbury
Mitchell's Fold Stone Circle
Shelve
Tregynon
Montgomery
Priestweston
Corndon Hill
Ratlinghope
Sarn
Carno
Afon Carno
Bettws Cedewain
Bwlch-y-ffridd
Town Hill
Dolforwyn
Llandyssil
Churchstoke
Hyssington
The Long Mynd
Clatter
Abermule
Cefn y Coed
Norbury
Wentnor
Little Stretton
Llanwnog
Caersws
Newtown
Llanllwchaiarn
Linley
More
Whitcot
Asterton
Minton
Kerry
Lydham
Trefeglwys
Mochdre
Bishop's Castle
Lea
Choulton
Myndtown
Marshbrook
Whittingslow
Plowden
The Corner
Woolston
Landinam
Dolfor
Mainstone
Colebatch
Eyton
Clun Forest
Lydbury North
Edgton
River Severn
Llanidloes
Brockton
Wistanstow
Cheney Longville
Lower Down
Kempton
Hopesay
Aston on Clun
Whitcott Keysett
Newcastle
Bicton
Clun
Clunton
Broome
Clunbury
Stokesay Castle
Felindre
Beguildy
R Teme
Rockhill
Hobarris
Obley
Hopton Castle
Clungunford
Hoptonheath
Shelderton
Beckjay
Llanbadarn Fynydd
Moel Wilym
Beacon Hill
Llanfair Waterdine
New Invention
Pentre Hodrey
Chapel Lawn
Bedstone
River Ithon
Red Lion Hill
Knucklas Viaduct
Pant-y-dwr
Bwlch-y-sarnau
Knucklas
Stowe
Bucknell
Kinton
Leintwardine
River Wye
St Harmon
Llanbister
Walford
Knighton
Brampton Bryan
Adforton
Llangunllo
Leinthall Starkes
Wigmore
Rhayader
Llansantffraed-Cwmdeuddwr
Llanddewi Ystradenni
Bleddfa
Harley's Mt
Birtley
Lingen
Lower Lye
Upper Lye
Aymestrey
Whitton
Norton
Nantmel
Llanfihangel Rhydithon
Stapleton
Kinsham
Byton
R Lugg
Elan Village
Radnor Forest
Penybont
Presteigne
The Judge's Lodging
Coombes-Moor
Uphampton
Easthampton
Lucton
Caban Coch Resr
Llanwrthwl
Gt Rhos
Bach Hill
Kinnerton
Llandegley
Shobdon
Llanyre
Llandrindod Wells
Evenjobb
Stansbatch
Staunton Green
New Radnor
Four Stones
Knill
Titley
Staunton on Arrow
Old Radnor
Walton
Bradnor Hill
Eardisland
Howey
Gilwern Hill
Pembridge
Burton Court
Newbridge on Wye
Marston
Hergest Ridge
Hergest Croft
Kington
Barewood
Lyonshall
Lower Hergest
Gladestry
Llansantffraed-in-Elvel
Gwaun-Ceste Hill
Holme Marsh
Broxwood
Upper Hergest
Dilwyn
Cwmbach Llechrhyd
Carneddau
Hundred House
Little Hill
Hengoed
Huntington
Woonton
Royal Welsh
Llanelwedd
Glascwm
Cwmmau Farmhouse NT
Weobley
Weobley Marsh
Cilmery
Prince Llewelyn
Builth Wells
Newchurch
Almeley
Sarnesfield
Ledgemoor
Beulah
Garth
King's Pyon
Red Hill
Bryngwyn
Brilley
Eardisley
Kinnersley
Aberedw
Llanbedr Hill
Llandeilo Hill
Millhalf
Norton Wood
Norton Canon
Wormsley
Banc-y-Celyn
Rhosgoch
Whitney-on-Wye
Winforton
Willersley
Letton
Staunton on Wye
Yazor
Llanwrtyd Wells
Drum Ddu
Llandeilo Graban
Painscastle
Clyro Hill
Clifford
River Wye
Bredwardine
Bredwardine
Brobury House
Mansell Gamage
Mansell Lacy
Mynydd Eppynt
Erwood
Clyro
Arthur's Stone
Monnington on Wye
Bishopstone
Credenhill
Kenchester
Gwenddwr
Crickadarn
Hay-on-Wye
Byford
Bridge Sollers
Sugwas
Bryn Du
Upper Chapel
Cefn Clawdd
Llowes
Dorstone
Preston on Wye
Cannon Bridge
Blakemere
Lulham
Cwmbach
Llanigon
Yager
Golden Valley
Tyberton
A458
A470
A483
A489
A490
A488
A4113
A44
A4081
A481
A4112
A4111
A480
A438
A4110
B4382
B4392
B4385
B4381
B4388
B4386
B4387
B4499
B4389
B4390
B4568
B4569
B4518
B4368
B4355
B4356
B4357
B4362
B4372
B4358
B4594
B4567
B4520
B4519
B4350
B4352
B4348
B4230
B4367
B4365
B4383
B4370
B4385
660
610
547
542
524
508
513
536
516
493
478
482
474
475
472
471
467
463
454
441
386
384
353
228

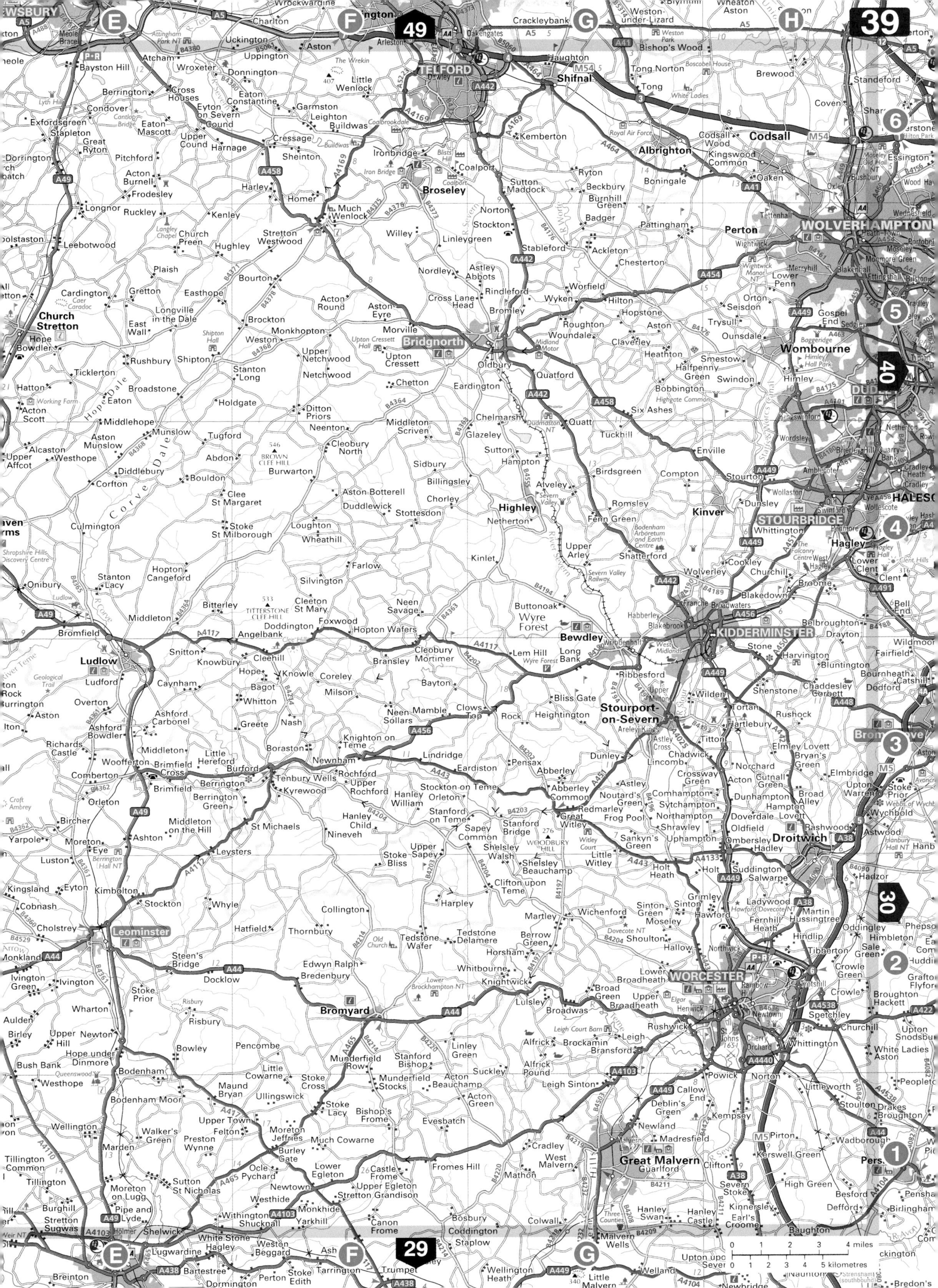

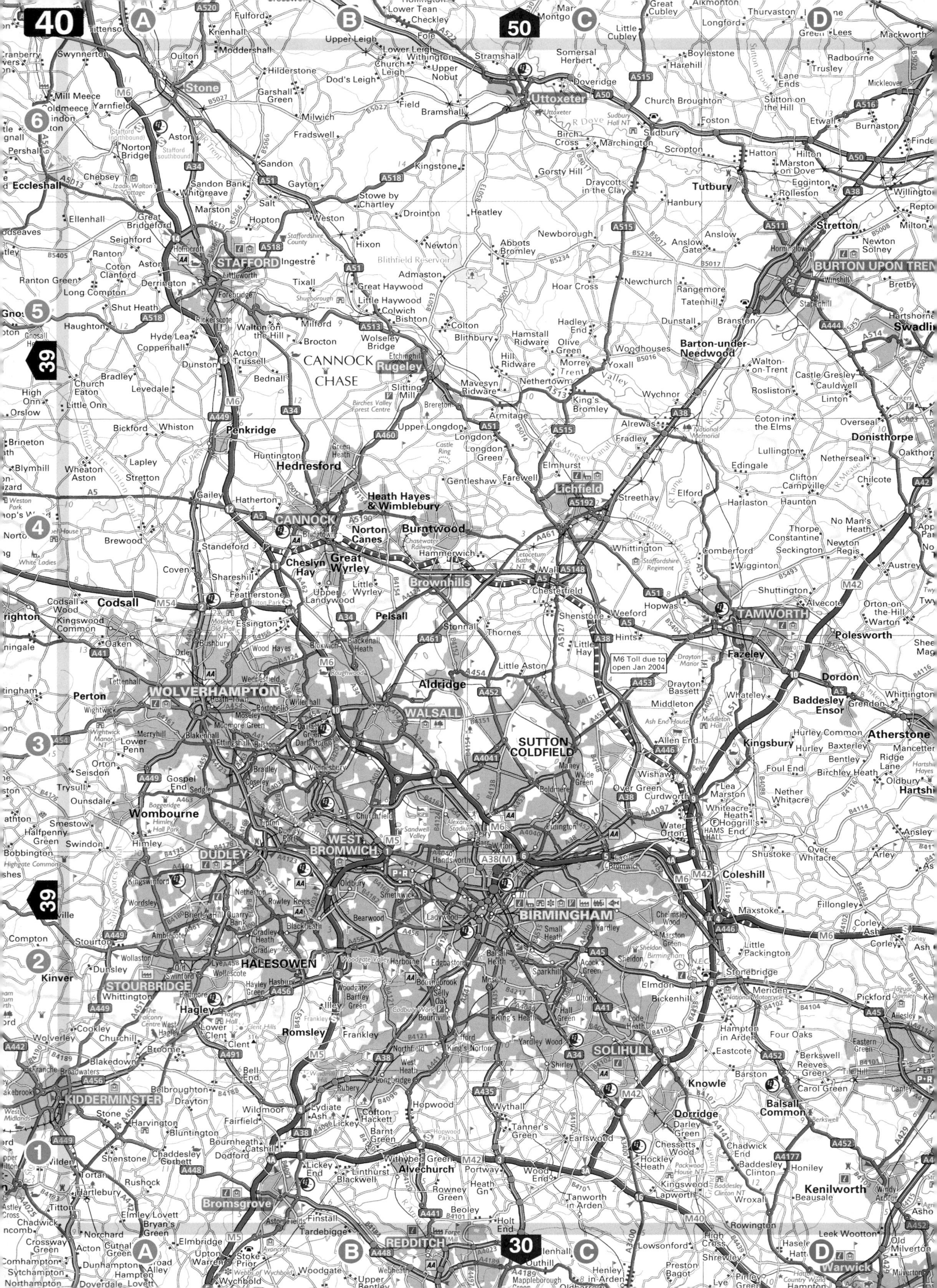

40
A
B
50
C
D
Tittensor
Fulford
Kenhall
Moddershall
Lower Tean
Checkley
Upper Leigh
Fole
Great Cubley
Alkmonton
Thurvaston
Longford
Little Cubley
Montgo
Swynnerton
Oulton
Hilderstone
Lower Leigh
Withington
Church Leigh
Upper Nobut
Stramshall
Somersal Herbert
Harehill
Boylestone
Radbourne
Trusley
Lane Ends
Mackworth
Mill Meece
Coldmeece
Yarnfield
Stone
Garshall Green
Dod's Leigh
Doveridge
Uttoxeter
Church Broughton
Sutton on the Hill
Mickleover
Etwall
Burnaston
Milwich
Field
Bramshall
Fradswell
Aston
Norton Bridge
Birch Cross
Marchington
Sudbury
Foston
Scropton
Hatton
Hilton
Marston on Dove
Egginton
Rolleston
Willington
Pershall
Eccleshall
Chebsey
Sandon
Kingstone
Gorsty Hill
Draycott in the Clay
Tutbury
Hanbury
Sandon Bank
Whitgreave
Gayton
Stowe by Chartley
Salt
Marston
Hopton
Weston
Drointon
Heatley
Ellenhall
Great Bridgeford
Seighford
Ranton
Newborough
Stretton
Repton
Milton
Abbots Bromley
Newton
Hixon
Anslow
Anslow Gate
Newton Solney
Coton Clanford
STAFFORD
Ingestre
Blithfield Reservoir
Burton upon Trent
Ranton Green
Derrington
Tixall
Admaston
Hoar Cross
Newchurch
Rangemore
Tatenhill
Long Compton
Great Haywood
Little Haywood
Colwich
Bishton
Bretby
Shut Heath
Haughton
Hyde Lea
Coppenhall
Walton-on-the-Hill
Milford
Brocton
Colton
Blithbury
Hamstall Ridware
Hadley End
Olive Green
Dunstall
Branston
Barton-under-Needwood
Hartshorne
Acton Trussell
Dunston
CANNOCK CHASE
Rugeley
Wolseley Bridge
Hill Ridware
Morrey
Yoxall
Woodhouses
Walton-on-Trent
Castle Gresley
Cauldwell
Bradley
Church Eaton
Levedale
Bednall
Slitting Mill
Mavesyn Ridware
Nethertown
King's Bromley
Wychnor
Rosliston
Linton
High Onn
Little Onn
Orslow
Penkridge
Brereton
Armitage
Alrewas
Coton in the Elms
Overseal
Donisthorpe
Bickford
Whiston
Upper Longdon
Longdon
Longdon Green
Fradley
Brineton
Lapley
Huntington
Hednesford
Lullington
Netherseal
Oakthorpe
Blymhill
Wheaton Aston
Stretton
Gentleshaw
Farewell
Elmhurst
Edingale
Clifton Campville
Chilcote
Lichfield
Elford
Gailey
Hatherton
Heath Hayes & Wimblebury
Streethay
Harlaston
Haunton
CANNOCK
Norton Canes
Burntwood
No Man's Heath
Brewood
Standeford
Hammerwich
Whittington
Thorpe Constantine
Newton Regis
Seckington
Comberford
Cheslyn Hay
Great Wyrley
Coven
Shareshill
Brownhills
Wigginton
Austrey
Featherstone
Little Wyrley
Upper Landywood
Chesterfield
Shuttington
Alvecote
Codsall
Codsall Wood
Kingswood Common
Essington
Pelsall
Shenstone
Weeford
Hopwas
TAMWORTH
Orton-on-the-Hill
Warton
Oaken
Bushbury
Wood Hayes
Blackenall Heath
Stonnall
Thornes
Hints
Little Hay
Fazeley
Polesworth
M6 Toll due to open Jan 2004
Tettenhall
Wednesfield
Little Aston
Drayton Bassett
Dordon
Perton
WOLVERHAMPTON
Aldridge
WALSALL
Whateley
Baddesley Ensor
Whittington
Grendon
Middleton
Atherstone
Lower Penn
Merryhill
Blakenhall
Ettingshall
Bilston
Darlaston
SUTTON COLDFIELD
Allen End
Kingsbury
Hurley Common
Hurley
Baxterley
Bentley
Mancetter
Orton
Seisdon
Gospel End
Sedgley
Bradley
Coseley
Wednesbury
Maney
Wylde Green
Boldmere
Wishaw
Over Green
Curdworth
Foul End
Birchley Heath
Ridge Lane
Oldbury
Trysull
Ounsdale
Wombourne
Lea Marston
Nether Whitacre
Whiteacre Heath
Hoggrill's End
Smestow
Halfpenny Green
Swindon
Himley
Tipton
Dudley Port
Churchfield
Erdington
Water Orton
Bobbington
DUDLEY
WEST BROMWICH
Handsworth
Castle Bromwich
Shustoke
Over Whitacre
Arley
Ansley
Kingswinford
Netherton
Oldbury
Smethwick
Coleshill
Rowley Regis
BIRMINGHAM
Fillongley
Wordsley
Brierley Hill
Quarry Bank
Blackheath
Bearwood
Ladywood
Small Heath
Yardley
Chelmsley Wood
Maxstoke
Corley
Compton
Stourton
Amblecote
Cradley Heath
Cradley
Marston Green
Corley Ash
Wollaston
Dunsley
Kinver
HALESOWEN
Harborne
Edgbaston
Balsall Heath
Sparkhill
Acock's Green
Sheldon
Little Packington
STOURBRIDGE
Lye
Wollescote
Hasbury
Hayley Green
Bournbrook
Selly Oak
Moseley
Elmdon
Stonebridge
Whittington
Pedmore
Hagley
Woodgate
Bartley Green
Illey
Bournville
King's Heath
Olton
Hall Green
Bickenhill
Meriden
Pickford
Allesley
Cookley
Lower Clent
Clent
Romsley
Frankley
Northfield
King's Norton
Yardley Wood
Solihull
Hampton in Arden
Four Oaks
Wolverley
Churchill
Broome
Blakedown
Eastcote
Berkswell
Reeves Green
KIDDERMINSTER
Bell End
West Heath
Longbridge
Shirley
Barston
Belbroughton
Drayton
Rubery
Knowle
Balsall Common
Carol Green
Stone
Wildmoor
Lydiate Ash
Lickey
Cofton Hackett
Hopwood
Wythall
Dorridge
Darley Green
Harvington
Fairfield
Bluntington
Barnt Green
Tanner's Green
Chadwick End
Shenstone
Chaddesley Corbett
Bournheath
Catshill
Dodford
Lickey End
Linthurst
Blackwell
Withybed Green
Alvechurch
Portway
Wood End
Earlswood
Chessetts Wood
Hockley Heath
Baddesley Clinton
Honiley
Rushock
Hartlebury
Elmley Lovett
Bromsgrove
Rowney Green
Beoley
Headley Heath
Tanworth in Arden
Kingswood
Lapworth
Wroxall
Kenilworth
Bryan's Green
Chadwick
Finstall
Tardebigge
Holt End
Rowington
Crossway Green
Acton
Elmbridge
Redditch
Leek Wootton
Old Milverton
Warwick
Dunhampton
Upton Warren
Stoke Prior
Woodgate
Lowsonford
High Cross
Shrewley
Preston Bagot
Henley-in-Arden
Hatton
30
39
1
2
3
4
5
6
M6
M5
M42
M54
A5
A34
A38
A51
A449
A456

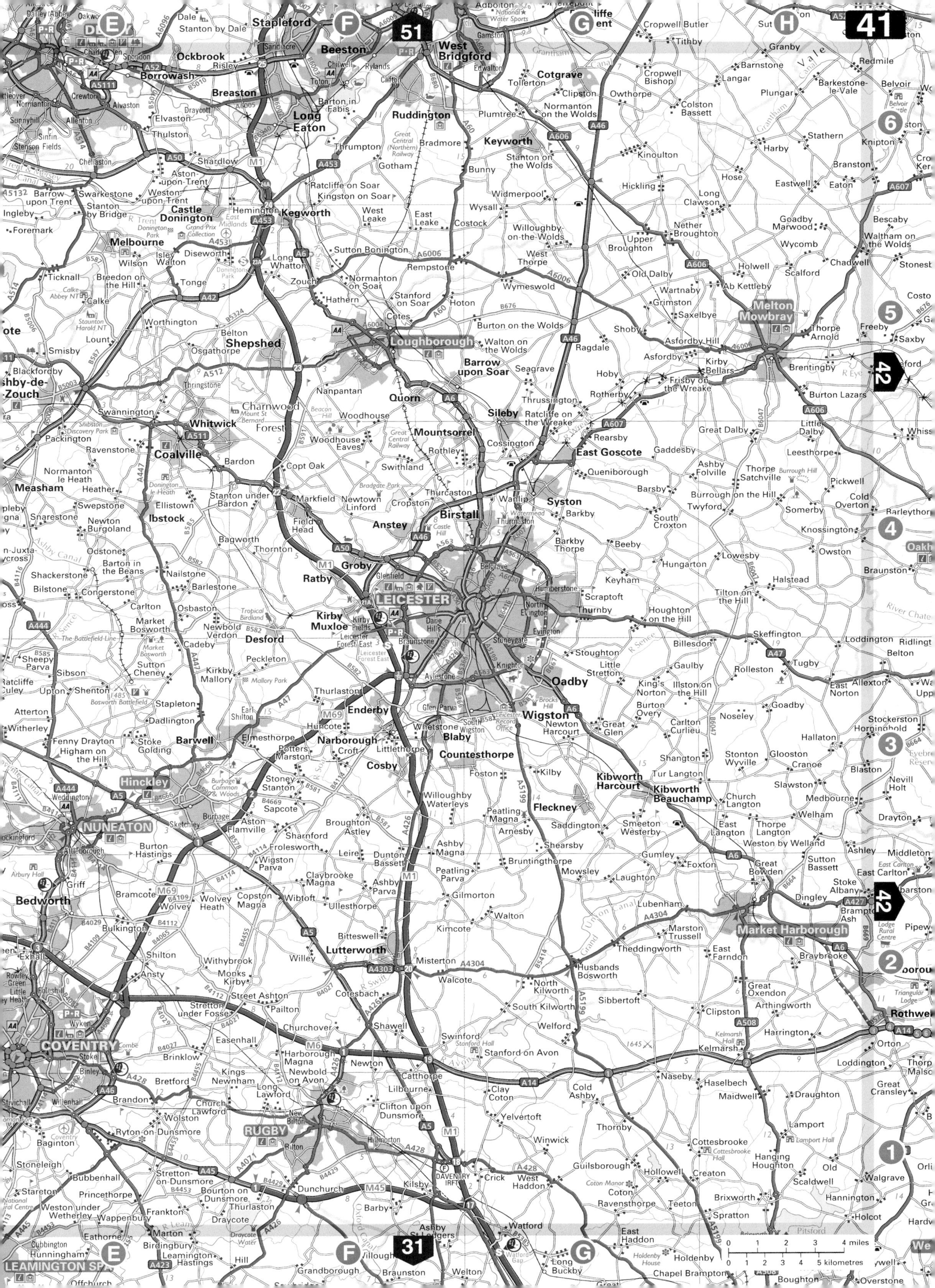
41
51
31
42
E
F
G
H
1
2
3
4
5
6
Stanton by Dale
Stapleford
Beeston
West Bridgford
Cropwell Butler
Tithby
Granby
Redmile
Ockbrook
Borrowash
Risley
Sandiacre
Chilwell
Rylands
Edwalton
Gamston
Cropwell Bishop
Barnstone
Langar
Barkestone-le-Vale
Belvoir
Spondon
Breaston
Toton
Clifton
Cotgrave
Tollerton
Clipston
Owthorpe
Plungar
Crewton
Alvaston
Draycott
Barton in Fabis
Long Eaton
Ruddington
Plumtree
Normanton on the Wolds
Colston Bassett
Normanton
Sunnyhill
Allenton
Elvaston
Thulston
Sinfin
Stenson Fields
Thrumpton
Bradmore
Keyworth
Stanton on the Wolds
Harby
Stathern
Knipton
Chellaston
Shardlow
Aston-upon-Trent
Weston-upon-Trent
Gotham
Bunny
Kinoulton
Hose
Branston
Eaton
Eastwell
Barrow upon Trent
Swarkestone
Stanton by Bridge
Castle Donington
Hemington
Kegworth
Ratcliffe on Soar
Kingston on Soar
Widmerpool
Hickling
Long Clawson
Ingleby
Foremark
East Midlands
Donington Park
Grand Prix Collection
West Leake
East Leake
Costock
Wysall
Willoughby-on-the-Wolds
Nether Broughton
Upper Broughton
Goadby Marwood
Bescaby
Waltham on the Wolds
Wycomb
Melbourne
Wilson
Isley Walton
Diseworth
Long Whatton
Sutton Bonington
Rempstone
West Thorpe
Holwell
Scalford
Chadwell
Ticknall
Breedon on the Hill
Calke Abbey NT
Calke
Tonge
Zouch
Normanton on Soar
Hathern
Stanford on Soar
Hoton
Wymeswold
Old Dalby
Wartnaby
Grimston
Saxelbye
Ab Kettleby
Melton Mowbray
Staunton Harold NT
Worthington
Belton
Shepshed
Osgathorpe
Lount
Smisby
Loughborough
Cotes
Burton on the Wolds
Walton on the Wolds
Barrow upon Soar
Seagrave
Shoby
Ragdale
Asfordby Hill
Asfordby
Kirby Bellars
Frisby on the Wreake
Thorpe Arnold
Freeby
Saxby
Brentingby
Burton Lazars
Blackfordby
Ashby-de-la-Zouch
Thringstone
Nanpantan
Quorn
Hoby
Rotherby
Swannington
Charnwood Forest
Mount St Bernard
Beacon Hill
Woodhouse
Woodhouse Eaves
Great Central Railway
Mountsorrel
Rothley
Sileby
Ratcliffe on the Wreake
Thrussington
Cossington
Rearsby
East Goscote
Gaddesby
Great Dalby
Little Dalby
Whitwick
Coalville
Bardon
Snibston Discovery Park
Packington
Ravenstone
Normanton le Heath
Measham
Heather
Donington le Heath
Copt Oak
Swithland
Bradgate Park
Thurcaston
Queniborough
Ashby Folville
Thorpe Satchville
Burrough Hill
Leesthorpe
Pickwell
Swepstone
Snarestone
Newton Burgoland
Ellistown
Ibstock
Stanton under Bardon
Markfield
Newtown Linford
Cropston
Wanlip
Syston
Barsby
Burrough on the Hill
Cold Overton
Somerby
Twyford
South Croxton
Field Head
Anstey
Birstall
Thurmaston
Watermead
Barkby
Barkby Thorpe
Knossington
Owston
Oakham
Bagworth
Thornton
Beeby
Lowesby
Hungarton
Braunston
Odstone
Barton in the Beans
Nailstone
Shackerstone
Bilstone
Congerstone
Barlestone
Groby
Ratby
Glenfield
Belgrave
Keyham
Halstead
Leicester
Humberstone
Scraptoft
Thurnby
North Evington
Evington
Tilton on the Hill
Carlton
Osbaston
Market Bosworth
Newbold Verdon
Tropical Birdland
Kirby Muxloe
Kirby Fields
Leicester Forest East
Dane Hills
Braunstone
Houghton on the Hill
Skeffington
Billesdon
Loddington
Belton
Sheepy Parva
Sibson
Cadeby
Desford
Peckleton
Kirby Mallory
Mallory Park
Sutton Cheney
Stoneygate
Knighton
Stoughton
Little Stretton
Gaulby
Rolleston
Tugby
Ratcliffe Culey
Upton
Shenton
Bosworth Battlefield
Stapleton
Earl Shilton
Thurlaston
Aylestone
Oadby
Brocks Hill
King's Norton
Illston on the Hill
East Norton
Allexton
Atterton
Witherley
Dadlington
Enderby
Glen Parva
Whetstone
South Wigston
Wigston
Newton Harcourt
Great Glen
Burton Overy
Carlton Curlieu
Noseley
Goadby
Stockerston
Fenny Drayton
Higham on the Hill
Stoke Golding
Barwell
Elmesthorpe
Huncote
Narborough
Croft
Potters Marston
Littlethorpe
Blaby
Countesthorpe
Cosby
Shangton
Stonton Wyville
Glooston
Cranoe
Hallaton
Blaston
Hinckley
Burbage Common & Woods
Stoney Stanton
Sapcote
Foston
Kilby
Tur Langton
Kibworth Harcourt
Kibworth Beauchamp
Church Langton
Nevill Holt
Slawston
Medbourne
Weddington
Nuneaton
Burbage
Aston Flamville
Sketchley
Broughton Astley
Willoughby Waterleys
Peatling Magna
Arnesby
Fleckney
Saddington
Smeeton Westerby
East Langton
Thorpe Langton
Welham
Drayton
Attleborough
Burton Hastings
Sharnford
Frolesworth
Leire
Dunton Bassett
Ashby Magna
Shearsby
Bruntingthorpe
Gumley
Foxton
Weston by Welland
Sutton Bassett
Ashley
Middleton
East Carlton
Arbury Hall
Griff
Wigston Parva
Claybrooke Magna
Ashby Parva
Peatling Parva
Mowsley
Laughton
Great Bowden
Stoke Albany
Bedworth
Bramcote
Wolvey
Wolvey Heath
Copston Magna
Wibtoft
Ullesthorpe
Gilmorton
Lubenham
Dingley
Brampton Ash
Walton
Marston Trussell
Market Harborough
Lodge Rural Centre
Bulkington
Bitteswell
Kimcote
Theddingworth
Great Farndon
Braybrooke
Exhall
Shilton
Withybrook
Monks Kirby
Willey
Lutterworth
Misterton
Walcote
Husbands Bosworth
North Kilworth
South Kilworth
Great Oxendon
Arthingworth
Rowley Green
Little Heath
Foleshill
Ansty
Street Ashton
Stretton under Fosse
Pailton
Cotesbach
Sibbertoft
Clipston
Triangular Lodge
Rothwell
Wyken
Coventry
Churchover
Shawell
Welford
Harrington
Kelmarsh Hall
Kelmarsh
Orton
Combe
Easenhall
Brinklow
Harborough Magna
Newton
Swinford
Stanford Hall
Stanford on Avon
Loddington
Stoke
Binley
Bretford
Kings Newnham
Newbold on Avon
Long Lawford
Catthorpe
Lilbourne
Cold Ashby
Naseby
Haselbech
Maidwell
Draughton
Great Cransley
Brandon
Willenhall
Church Lawford
Clifton upon Dunsmore
Clay Coton
Yelvertoft
Thornby
Wolston
New Bilton
Ryton-on-Dunsmore
Rugby
Hillmorton
Winwick
Cottesbrooke
Cottesbrooke Hall
Lamport
Lamport Hall
Baginton
Coventry
Bilton
Crick
Guilsborough
Hollowell
Creaton
Hanging Houghton
Old
Walgrave
Stoneleigh
Bubbenhall
Stretton-on-Dunsmore
Bourton on Dunsmore
Dunchurch
Daventry IRFT
Kilsby
West Haddon
Coton Manor
Coton
Ravensthorpe
Teeton
Brixworth
Scaldwell
Hannington
Holcot
Stareton
Princethorpe
Frankton
Thurlaston
Barby
Weston under Wetherley
Wappenbury
Draycote
Draycote Water
National Agricultural Centre
Marton
Birdingbury
Ashby St Ledgers
Watford
Watford Gap
East Haddon
Spratton
Pitsford
Cubbington
Hunningham
Leamington Hastings
Eathorpe
Leamington Spa
Hill
Grandborough
Willoughby
Braunston
Long Buckby
Holdenby
Holdenby House
Chapel Brampton
Welton
Offchurch
Overstone
Grand Union Canal
Oxford Canal
Ashby Canal
Trent & Mersey Canal
Grantham Canal
Vale of Belvoir
River Soar
River Wreake
River Sence
River Swift
River Avon
River Trent
River Eye
River Chater
River Leam
The Battlefield Line
1645
1485
0 1 2 3 4 miles
0 1 2 3 4 5 kilometres

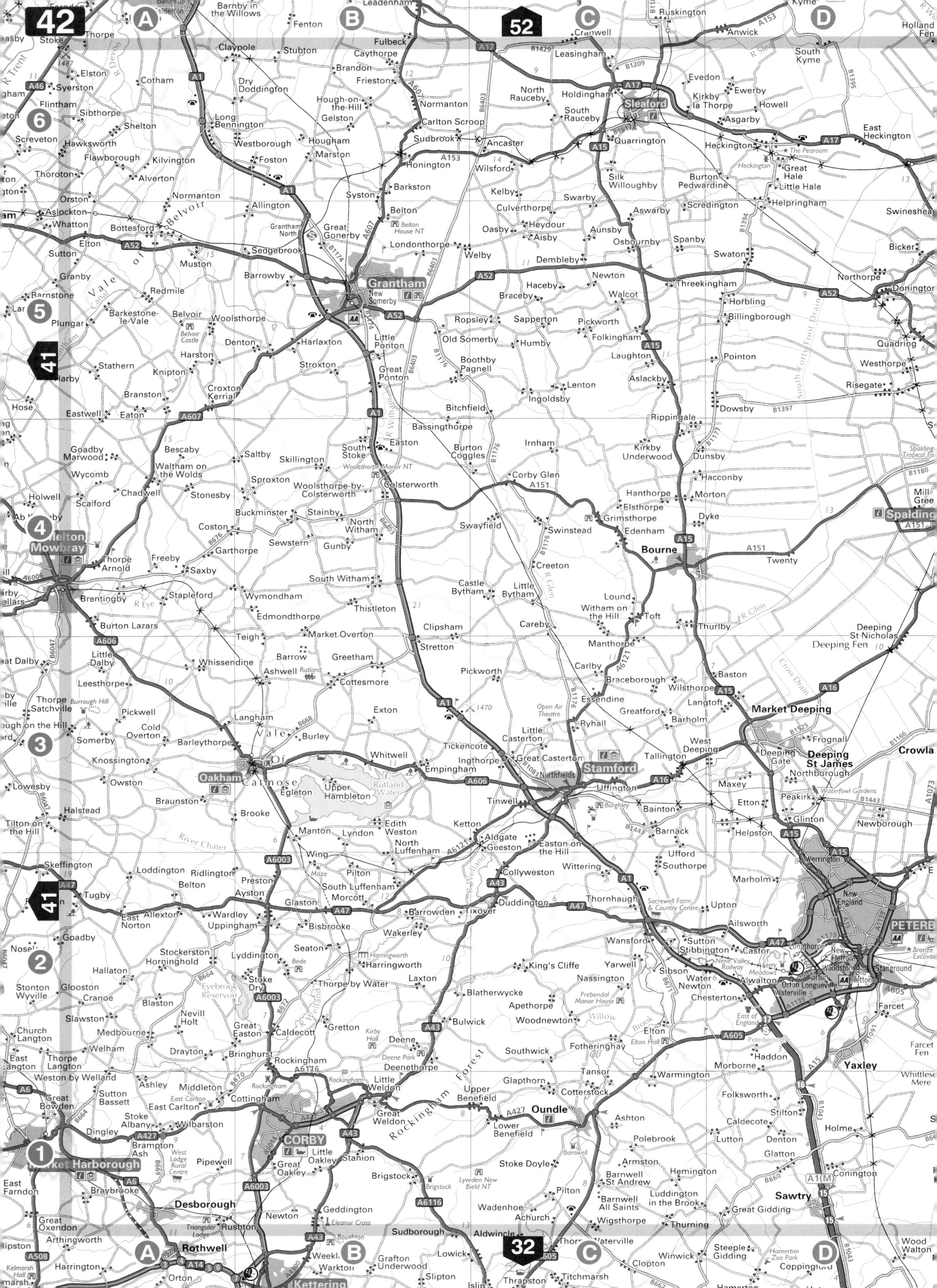

42
A
B
52
C
D
Barnby in the Willows
Fenton
Leadenham
Ruskington
Kyme
Holland Fen
Stoke
Thorpe
Claypole
Stubton
Fulbeck
Caythorpe
Cranwell
Anwick
South Kyme
Leasingham
A17
Elston
Syerston
Cotham
Brandon
Frieston
Dry Doddington
A46
A1
A607
Evedon
Ewerby
North Rauceby
Holdingham
Sleaford
Kirkby la Thorpe
Howell
Flintham
6
Sibthorpe
Shelton
Long Bennington
Hough-on-the-Hill
Gelston
Normanton
Carlton Scroop
South Rauceby
Asgarby
Screveton
Hawksworth
Westborough
Hougham
Sudbrook
Ancaster
Quarrington
A15
Heckington
East Heckington
The Pearoom
Flawborough
Kilvington
Foston
Marston
Honington
A153
Wilsford
Great Hale
Little Hale
Thoroton
Alverton
Orston
Normanton
Allington
Barkston
Syston
Kelby
Silk Willoughby
Burton Pedwardine
Helpringham
Aslockton
Whatton
Bottesford
Vale of Belvoir
Belton
Belton House NT
Culverthorpe
Swarby
Scredington
Swineshead
Heydour
Oasby
Aisby
Aunsby
Aswarby
Grantham North
Great Gonerby
Londonthorpe
Osbournby
Spanby
Bicker
Elton
A52
Sedgebrook
Welby
Dembleby
Swaton
Sutton
Muston
Granby
Barrowby
Grantham
New Somerby
A52
Newton
Threekingham
Northorpe
Donington
Barnstone
Redmile
Haceby
Braceby
Walcot
Horbling
5
Barkestone-le-Vale
Plungar
Belvoir
Belvoir Castle
Woolsthorpe
Ropsley
Sapperton
Pickworth
Billingborough
Denton
Harlaxton
Little Ponton
Old Somerby
Humby
Folkingham
Quadring
41
Harston
Stathern
Knipton
Stroxton
Great Ponton
Boothby Pagnell
Laughton
Pointon
Westhorpe
Aslackby
Risegate
Harby
Branston
Croxton Kerrial
Lenton
Ingoldsby
Dowsby
Hose
Eastwell
Eaton
A607
Bitchfield
Bassingthorpe
Rippingale
Goadby Marwood
Bescaby
Saltby
Skillington
South Stoke
Easton
Burton Coggles
Irnham
Kirkby Underwood
Dunsby
Wycomb
Waltham on the Wolds
Woolsthorpe Manor NT
Corby Glen
A151
Hacconby
Chadwell
Sproxton
Woolsthorpe-by-Colsterworth
Colsterworth
Hanthorpe
Morton
Holwell
Scalford
Stonesby
Elsthorpe
Grimsthorpe
Dyke
Spalding
Buckminster
Stainby
North Witham
Swayfield
Swinstead
Edenham
4
Melton Mowbray
Coston
Sewstern
Gunby
Bourne
Twenty
A151
Thorpe Arnold
Freeby
Garthorpe
Creeton
Saxby
South Witham
Castle Bytham
Little Bytham
Brentingby
Stapleford
Wymondham
Lound
Witham on the Hill
Toft
Thistleton
Edmondthorpe
Clipsham
Careby
Thurlby
Deeping St Nicholas
Deeping Fen
Burton Lazars
Teigh
Market Overton
Stretton
Manthorpe
A606
Little Dalby
Barrow
Greetham
Whissendine
Ashwell
Cottesmore
Pickworth
Carlby
Braceborough
Baston
Leesthorpe
Wilsthorpe
Langtoft
A16
Thorpe Satchville
Burrough Hill
Exton
Essendine
Greatford
Market Deeping
Pickwell
Langham
Open Air Theatre
Ryhall
Barholm
Cold Overton
Burley
Little Casterton
Frognall
3
Somerby
Barleythorpe
Tickencote
West Deeping
Deeping St James
Crowland
Knossington
Oakham
Whitwell
Ingthorpe
Great Casterton
Tallington
Deeping Gate
Northborough
Owston
Vale of Catmose
Empingham
Stamford
Northfields
Uffington
A16
Maxey
Lowesby
Egleton
Upper Hambleton
Rutland Water
A606
Tinwell
Bainton
Etton
Peakirk
Waterfowl Gardens
Halstead
Braunston
Brooke
Burghley
Helpston
Glinton
Newborough
Tilton on the Hill
Edith Weston
Ketton
Manton
Lyndon
Aldgate
Geeston
Easton on the Hill
Barnack
Werrington
River Chater
North Luffenham
Wing
A6121
Wittering
Ufford
Southorpe
Skeffington
Loddington
Ridlington
Pilton
Collyweston
Marholm
Belton
Preston
South Luffenham
A43
A1
New England
A47
Tugby
East Norton
Allexton
Wardley
Ayston
Glaston
Morcott
Duddington
Thornhaugh
Sacrewell Farm & Country Centre
Upton
Uppingham
Barrowden
Tixover
A47
Bisbrooke
Wakerley
Ailsworth
Goadby
Seaton
Wansford
Sutton
Stibbington
Castor
Longthorpe
PETERBOROUGH
Stockerton
Horninghold
Lyddington
Harringworth
King's Cliffe
Yarwell
Sibson
Nene Valley Railway
Ferry Meadows
Water Newton
Woodston
New Fletton
Stanground
Bronze Age Excavation
2
Hallaton
Bede
Stoke Dry
Thorpe by Water
Laxton
Nassington
Orton Longueville
Orton Waterville
Fletton
Glooston
Stonton Wyville
Cranoe
Eyebrook Reservoir
A6003
Blatherwycke
Apethorpe
Prebendal Manor House
Chesterton
Alwalton
Blaston
Willow Brook
A605
Farcet
Slawston
Nevill Holt
Bulwick
Woodnewton
East of England
Medbourne
Great Easton
Caldecott
Gretton
Kirby Hall
Elton
Elton Hall
A605
Church Langton
Welham
Drayton
Bringhurst
Deene
Deene Park
Southwick
Fotheringhay
Peterborough
Farcet Fen
East Langton
Thorpe Langton
Rockingham
Deenethorpe
Haddon
Morborne
Yaxley
Weston by Welland
A6116
Rockingham Forest
Tansor
Warmington
Whittlesey Mere
Great Bowden
Ashley
Middleton
Cottingham
Little Weldon
Glapthorn
Upper Benefield
Cotterstock
Folksworth
A6
Sutton Bassett
East Carlton
Great Weldon
A427
Oundle
Ashton
Stilton
Stoke Albany
Wilbarston
CORBY
Lower Benefield
Caldecote
Holme
Dingley
Brampton Ash
A427
Lutton
Denton
Polebrook
1
Market Harborough
A6
West Lodge Rural Centre
Pipewell
Little Oakley
Stanion
Great Oakley
A43
Glatton
Armston
Stoke Doyle
Barnwell
Hemington
Conington
A1(M)
East Farndon
Braybrooke
Brigstock
Lyveden New Bield NT
Barnwell St Andrew
Barnwell All Saints
Luddington in the Brook
Sawtry
Desborough
Geddington
Eleanor Cross
Pilton
Wadenhoe
Achurch
Great Gidding
Great Oxendon
Triangular Lodge
Rushton
Newton
Wigsthorpe
Thurning
Arthingworth
A6003
Sudborough
Aldwincle
Waterville
Wood Walton
Lipston
A508
Rothwell
A14
Weekley
Boughton
Grafton Underwood
Lowick
Winwick
Steeple Gidding
Hamerton Zoo Park
Kelmarsh Hall
Harrington
Orton
Kettering
Warkton
Slipton
Thrapston
Titchmarsh
Clopton
Coppingford
32

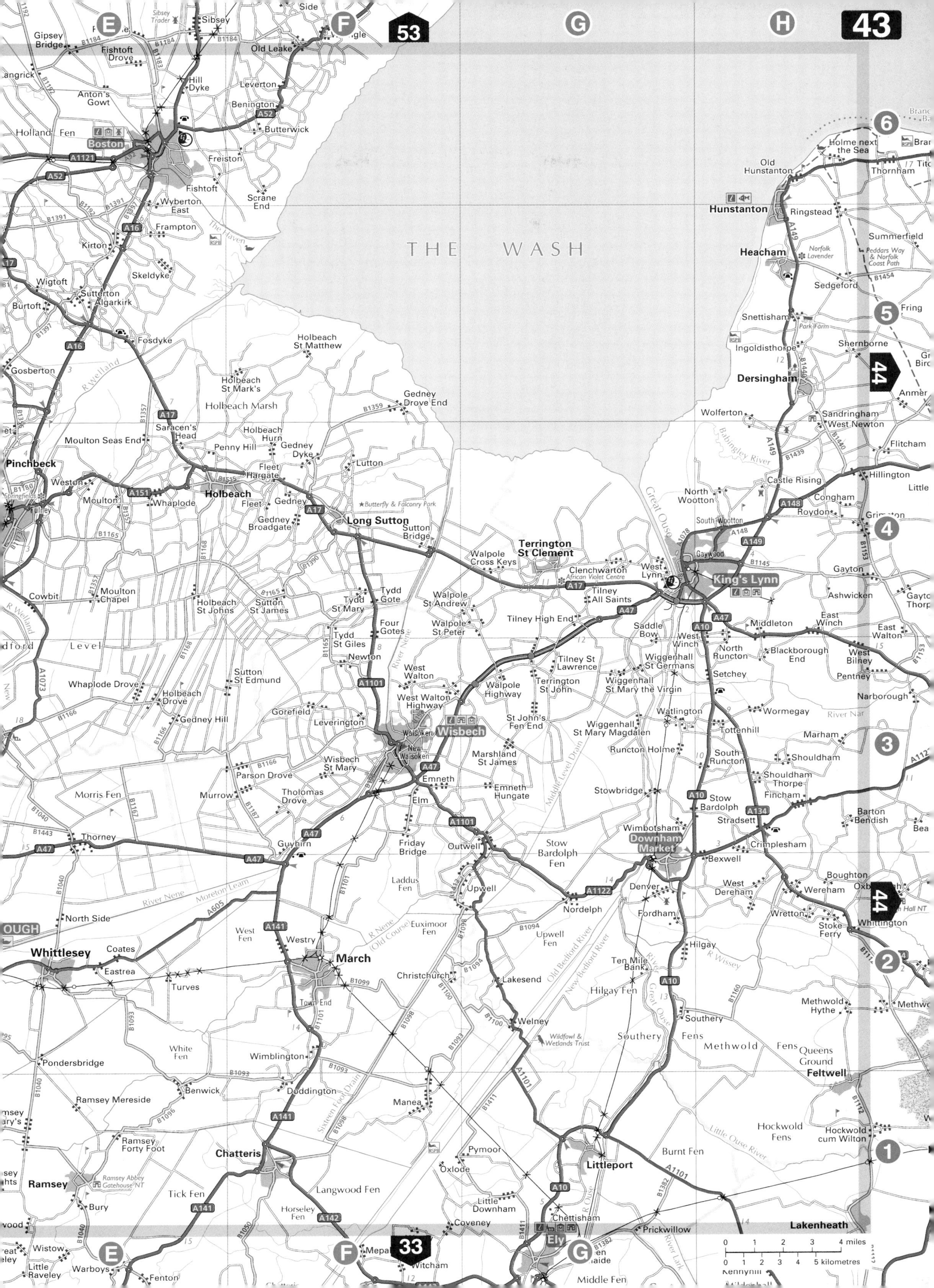

43
E
F
G
H
53
44
33
THE WASH
Sibsey
Side
Gipsey Bridge
Fishtoft Drove
Old Leake
Langrick
Hill Dyke
Leverton
Anton's Gowt
Benington
Butterwick
Holland Fen
Boston
Freiston
Fishtoft
Wyberton East
Scrane End
Frampton
The Haven
Kirton
Skeldyke
Wigtoft
Sutterton
Algarkirk
Burtoft
Fosdyke
Gosberton
R Welland
Holbeach St Matthew
Holbeach St Mark's
Holbeach Marsh
Gedney Drove End
Saracen's Head
Holbeach Hurn
Moulton Seas End
Penny Hill
Gedney Dyke
Lutton
Pinchbeck
Fleet Hargate
Weston
Moulton
Whaplode
Holbeach
Fleet
Gedney
Butterfly & Falconry Park
Spalding
Springfields
Pode Hole
Gedney Broadgate
Long Sutton
Sutton Bridge
Cowbit
Moulton Chapel
Holbeach St Johns
Sutton St James
Tydd Gote
Tydd St Mary
Four Gotes
Tydd St Giles
Newton
River Nene
Level
Whaplode Drove
Holbeach Drove
Sutton St Edmund
Gedney Hill
Gorefield
Leverington
West Walton
West Walton Highway
Wisbech
Walsoken
New Walsoken
Parson Drove
Wisbech St Mary
Murrow
Tholomas Drove
Morris Fen
Thorney
Guyhirn
Emneth
Elm
Friday Bridge
Outwell
Laddus Fen
Upwell
North Side
River Nene
Moreton Leam
Whittlesey
Coates
Eastrea
Turves
West Fen
Westry
March
Euximoor Fen
R Nene (Old Course)
Christchurch
Town End
Pondersbridge
White Fen
Wimblington
Benwick
Doddington
Ramsey Mereside
Manea
Sixteen Foot Drain
Ramsey Forty Foot
Chatteris
Ramsey
Ramsey Abbey Gatehouse NT
Bury
Tick Fen
Langwood Fen
Horseley Fen
Pymoor
Oxlode
Little Downham
Coveney
Chettisham
Ely
Wistow
Warboys
Little Raveley
Fenton
Mepal
Witcham
Middle Fen
Walpole Cross Keys
Terrington St Clement
Clenchwarton
African Violet Centre
West Lynn
Walpole St Andrew
Walpole St Peter
Tilney All Saints
Tilney High End
Tilney St Lawrence
Terrington St John
Walpole Highway
St John's Fen End
Marshland St James
Emneth Hungate
Stow Bardolph Fen
Middle Level Main Drain
Nordelph
Upwell Fen
Old Bedford River
New Bedford River
Lakesend
Welney
Wildfowl & Wetlands Trust
Ten Mile Bank
Hilgay Fen
Southery Fens
Littleport
Burnt Fen
Prickwillow
River Lark
Little Ouse River
Hockwold Fens
Hockwold cum Wilton
Lakenheath
Methwold Fens
Queens Ground
Feltwell
Methwold Hythe
Southery
Hilgay
Fordham
Denver
Downham Market
Wimbotsham
Stow Bardolph
Stradsett
Crimplesham
Bexwell
West Dereham
Wereham
Wretton
Stoke Ferry
Whittington
Oxborough
Boughton
Barton Bendish
Fincham
Shouldham Thorpe
Shouldham
Marham
Runcton Holme
Stowbridge
South Runcton
Tottenhill
Watlington
Wiggenhall St Mary Magdalen
Wiggenhall St Mary the Virgin
Wiggenhall St Germans
Saddle Bow
West Winch
North Runcton
Setchey
Wormegay
River Nar
Narborough
Pentney
West Bilney
East Walton
East Winch
Blackborough End
Middleton
Ashwicken
Gayton
Grimston
Roydon
Congham
Hillington
Flitcham
King's Lynn
Gaywood
South Wootton
North Wootton
Castle Rising
Babingley River
Great Ouse
Wolferton
Sandringham
West Newton
Anmer
Dersingham
Shernborne
Ingoldisthorpe
Park Farm
Snettisham
Fring
Sedgeford
Heacham
Norfolk Lavender
Peddars Way & Norfolk Coast Path
Summerfield
Ringstead
Hunstanton
Old Hunstanton
Holme next the Sea
Thornham
Titchwell
Brancaster
0 1 2 3 4 miles
0 1 2 3 4 5 kilometres

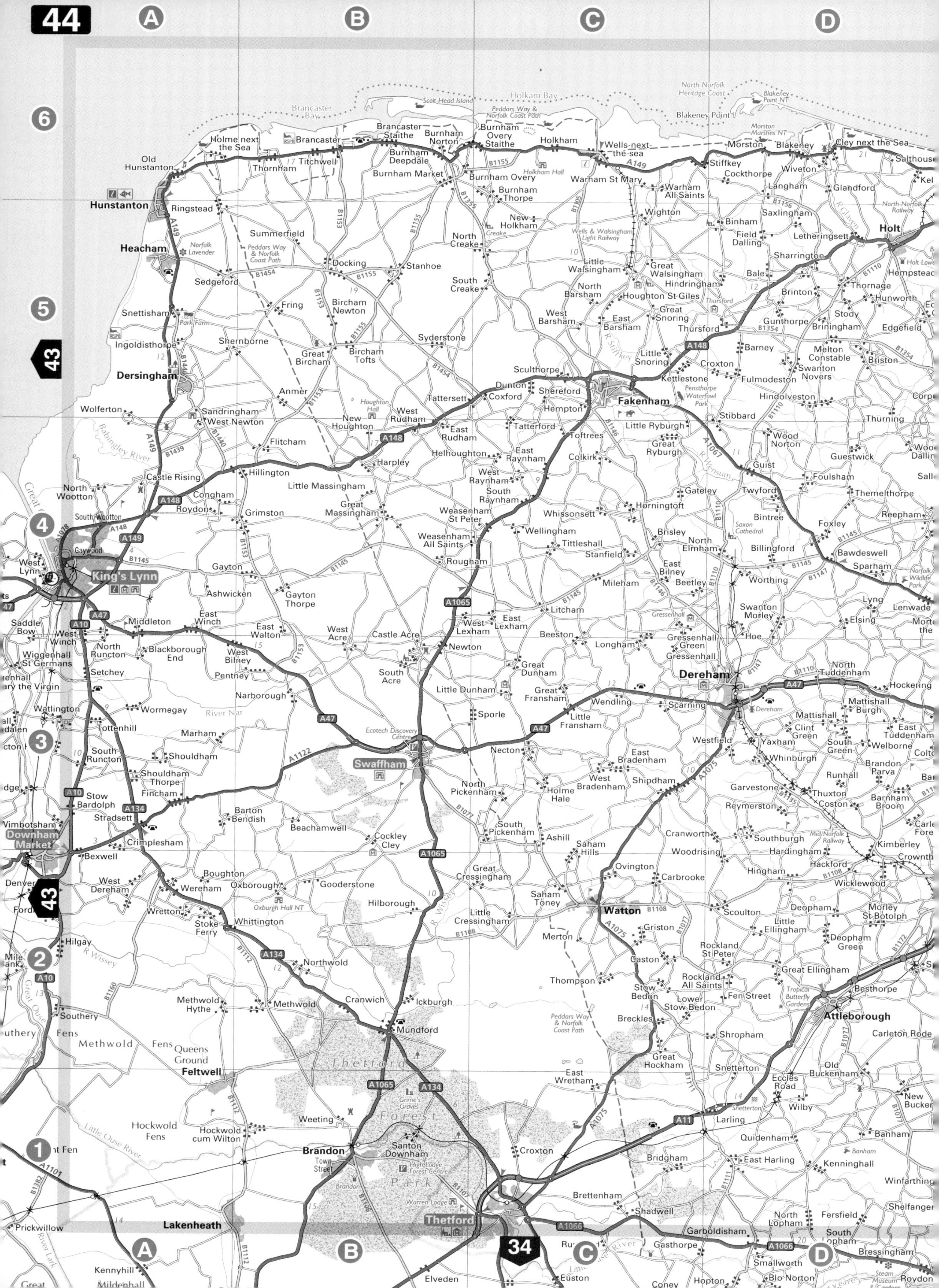
A
B
C
D
6
5
4
3
2
1
43
34
Brancaster Bay
Scolt Head Island
Holkam Bay
Peddars Way & Norfolk Coast Path
North Norfolk Heritage Coast
Blakeney Point NT
Blakeney Point
Morston Marshes NT
Holme next the Sea
Brancaster
Brancaster Staithe
Burnham Norton
Burnham Overy Staithe
Holkham
Wells-next-the-Sea
Morston
Blakeney
Cley next the Sea
Salthouse
Old Hunstanton
Thornham
Titchwell
Burnham Deepdale
Burnham Market
Burnham Overy
Holkham Hall
Warham St Mary
Stiffkey
Cockthorpe
Wiveton
Hunstanton
Ringstead
Burnham Thorpe
Warham All Saints
Langham
Glandford
Wighton
Binham
Saxlingham
North Norfolk Railway
New Holkham
Holt
Heacham
Norfolk Lavender
Summerfield
North Creake
Wells & Walsingham Light Railway
Field Dalling
Letheringsett
Docking
Stanhoe
Little Walsingham
Great Walsingham
Sharrington
Sedgeford
South Creake
Hindringham
Bale
Hempstead
North Barsham
Houghton St Giles
Thornage
Brinton
Hunworth
Snettisham
Fring
Bircham Newton
West Barsham
East Barsham
Great Snoring
Thursford
Gunthorpe
Stody
Briningham
Edgefield
Park Farm
Ingoldisthorpe
Shernborne
Syderstone
Barney
Great Bircham
Bircham Tofts
Little Snoring
Croxton
Melton Constable
Briston
Dersingham
Sculthorpe
Kettlestone
Swanton Novers
Fulmodeston
Dunton
Coxford
Shereford
Anmer
Tattersett
Fakenham
Pensthorpe Waterfowl Park
Hindolveston
Wolferton
Sandringham
West Newton
Houghton Hall
West Rudham
New Houghton
Hempton
East Rudham
Tatterford
Little Ryburgh
Stibbard
Thurning
Toftrees
Flitcham
Babingley River
Harpley
Helhoughton
East Raynham
Great Ryburgh
Wood Norton
Colkirk
Guestwick
Castle Rising
Hillington
West Raynham
Guist
Foulsham
North Wootton
Little Massingham
South Raynham
Gateley
Twyford
Themelthorpe
Congham
Great Massingham
Roydon
Weasenham St Peter
Horningtoft
South Wootton
Grimston
Whissonsett
Bintree
Reepham
Foxley
Wellingham
Saxon Cathedral
Weasenham All Saints
Tittleshall
Brisley
North Elmham
Gaywood
Stanfield
Billingford
Bawdeswell
West Lynn
King's Lynn
Gayton
Rougham
East Bilney
Beetley
Sparham
Worthing
Norfolk Wildlife Park
Ashwicken
Gayton Thorpe
Mileham
Lyng
Swanton Morley
Lenwade
Elsing
Saddle Bow
Middleton
East Winch
Litcham
West Lexham
East Lexham
Gressenhall
West Winch
East Walton
West Acre
Castle Acre
Beeston
Longham
Gressenhall Green
Hoe
North Runcton
Blackborough End
West Bilney
Newton
Wiggenhall St Germans
Great Dunham
North Tuddenham
Pentney
South Acre
Dereham
Hockering
Setchey
Wiggenhall St Mary the Virgin
Narborough
Little Dunham
Great Fransham
Wendling
Scarning
Mattishall Burgh
Mattishall
Watlington
Wormegay
River Nar
Sporle
Little Fransham
Clint Green
East Tuddenham
Tottenhill
Ecotech Discovery Centre
Westfield
Yaxham
South Green
Welborne
Marham
Necton
East Bradenham
Whinburgh
Shouldham
Swaffham
Brandon Parva
South Runcton
Shouldham Thorpe
North Pickenham
West Bradenham
Shipdham
Holme Hale
Runhall
Fincham
Garvestone
Thuxton
Stow Bardolph
Reymerston
Coston
Barnham Broom
Stradsett
Barton Bendish
South Pickenham
Ashill
Mid Norfolk Railway
Wimbotsham
Beachamwell
Cranworth
Southburgh
Downham Market
Crimplesham
Cockley Cley
Saham Hills
Woodrising
Hardingham
Kimberley
Crownthorpe
Bexwell
Great Cressingham
Ovington
Carbrooke
Hingham
Hackford
Denver
West Dereham
Boughton
Wereham
Oxborough
Gooderstone
Wicklewood
Oxburgh Hall NT
Hilborough
Saham Toney
Watton
Scoulton
Deopham
Morley St Botolph
Wretton
Stoke Ferry
Whittington
Little Cressingham
Griston
Little Ellingham
Hilgay
R Wissey
Merton
Deopham Green
Rockland St Peter
Northwold
Caston
Great Ellingham
Thompson
Rockland All Saints
Stow Bedon
Lower Stow Bedon
Fen Street
Tropical Butterfly Gardens
Besthorpe
Methwold Hythe
Methwold
Cranwich
Ickburgh
Attleborough
Southery
Peddars Way & Norfolk Coast Path
Breckles
Mundford
Shropham
Carleton Rode
Fens
Methwold Fens
Queens Ground
Great Hockham
Thetford
Old Buckenham
Feltwell
East Wretham
Snetterton
Eccles Road
Grime's Graves
Forest
New Buckenham
Hockwold Fens
Hockwold cum Wilton
Weeting
Shetterton
Wilby
Little Ouse River
Larling
Banham
Santon Downham
Quidenham
Brandon
Town Street
Croxton
Bridgham
East Harling
Kenninghall
Great Ouse
High Lodge Forest Centre
Park
Winfarthing
Warren Lodge
Brettenham
Prickwillow
Lakenheath
Shadwell
North Lopham
Shelfanger
Fersfield
River Lark
Thetford
Garboldisham
South Lopham
Gasthorpe
Bressingham
Kennyhill
Mildenhall
Euston
Smallworth
Steam Museum
Elveden
Coney
Hopton
Blo Norton
Roydon
Great
A149
A148
A1078
A47
A10
A134
A1122
A1065
A1067
A1075
A11
A1066
A1101
B1155
B1153
B1454
B1355
B1105
B1156
B1110
B1354
B1440
B1439
B1145
B1146
B1147
B1135
B1108
B1077
B1172
B1111
B1112
B1160
B1106
B1107
B1382

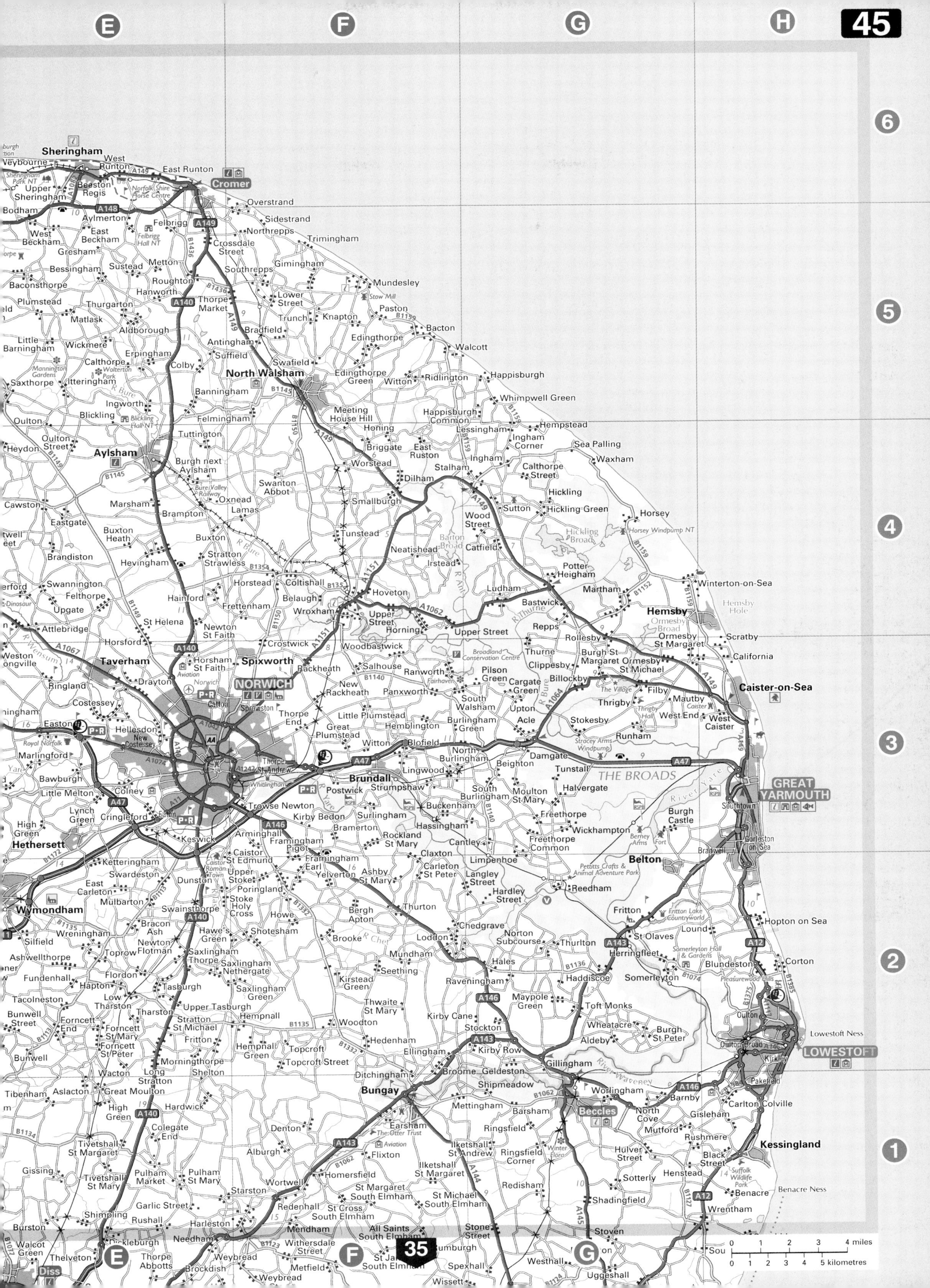

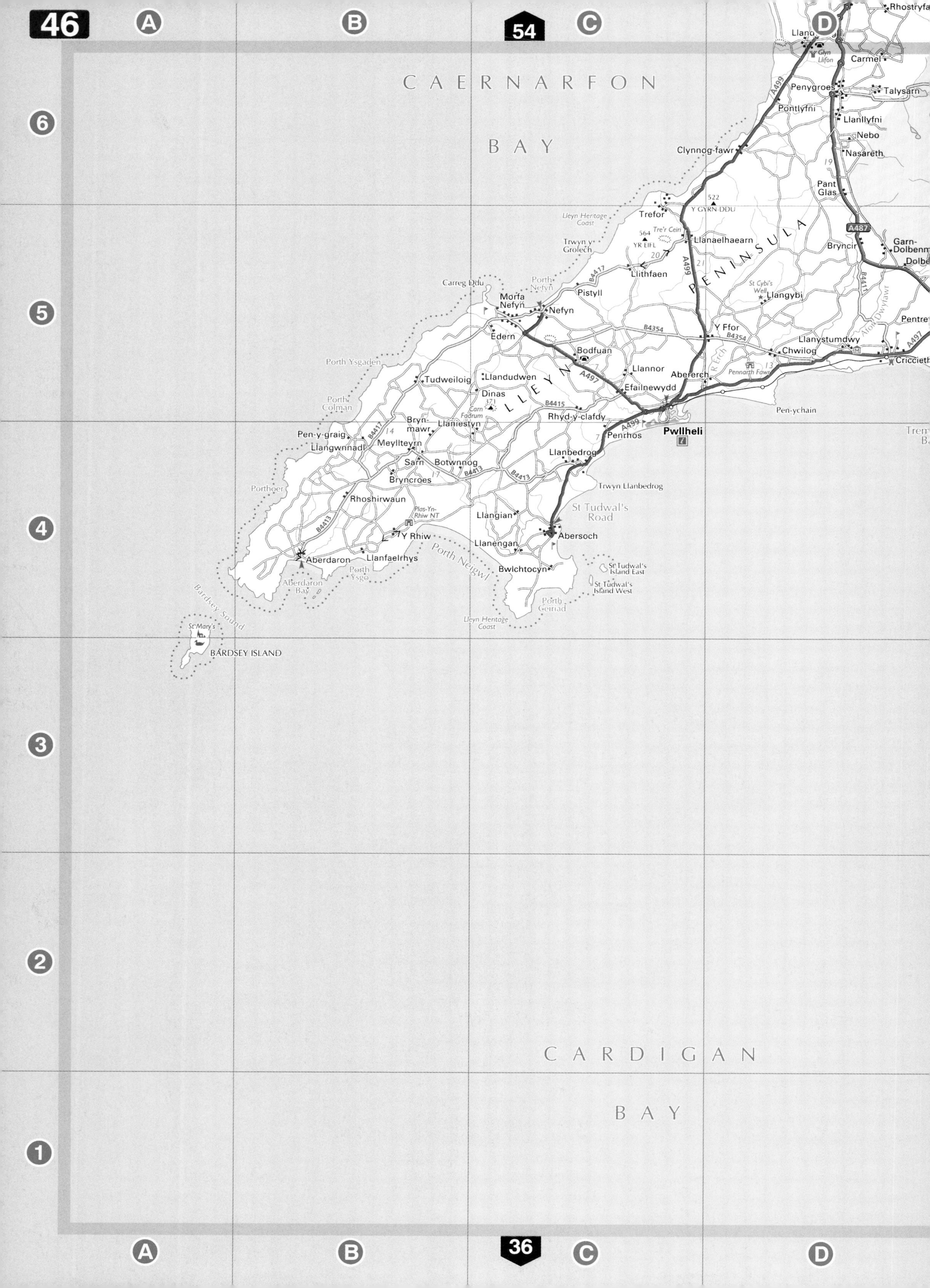

46
54
36
A
B
C
D
1
2
3
4
5
6
CAERNARFON BAY
CARDIGAN BAY
LLEYN PENINSULA
Rhostryfan
Llandwrog
Glyn Llifon
Carmel
Penygroes
Talysarn
Pontllyfni
Llanllyfni
Nebo
Nasareth
Clynnog-fawr
Pant Glas
Trefor
522
Y GYRN-DDU
Lleyn Heritage Coast
Trwyn y Gorlech
564
YR EIFL
Tre'r Ceiri
Llanaelhaearn
A487
Bryncir
Garn-Dolbenmaen
Dolben
Llithfaen
Carreg Ddu
Porth Nefyn
Pistyll
Morfa Nefyn
Nefyn
St Cybi's Well
Llangybi
Afon Dwyfawr
Pentre
B4354
Y Ffor
Edern
Bodfuan
Llanystumdwy
Chwilog
Criccieth
Porth Ysgaden
Llannor
Abererch
Pennarth Fawr
Tudweiloig
Llandudwen
Dinas
371
Carn Fadrun
Efailnewydd
Porth Colman
Bryn-mawr
Llaniestyn
B4415
Rhyd-y-clafdy
Pen-y-chain
A497
A499
B4417
B4413
B4411
Pen-y-graig
Llangwnnadl
Meyllteyrn
Penrhos
Pwllheli
Sarn
Botwnnog
Llanbedrog
Bryncroes
Trwyn Llanbedrog
Porthoer
Rhoshirwaun
St Tudwal's Road
Plas-Yn-Rhiw NT
Llangian
Y Rhiw
Abersoch
Llanengan
Porth Neigwl
Aberdaron
Llanfaelrhys
Bwlchtocyn
St Tudwal's Island East
St Tudwal's Island West
Porth Ysgo
Aberdaron Bay
Porth Ceiriad
Bardsey Sound
Lleyn Heritage Coast
St Mary's
BARDSEY ISLAND

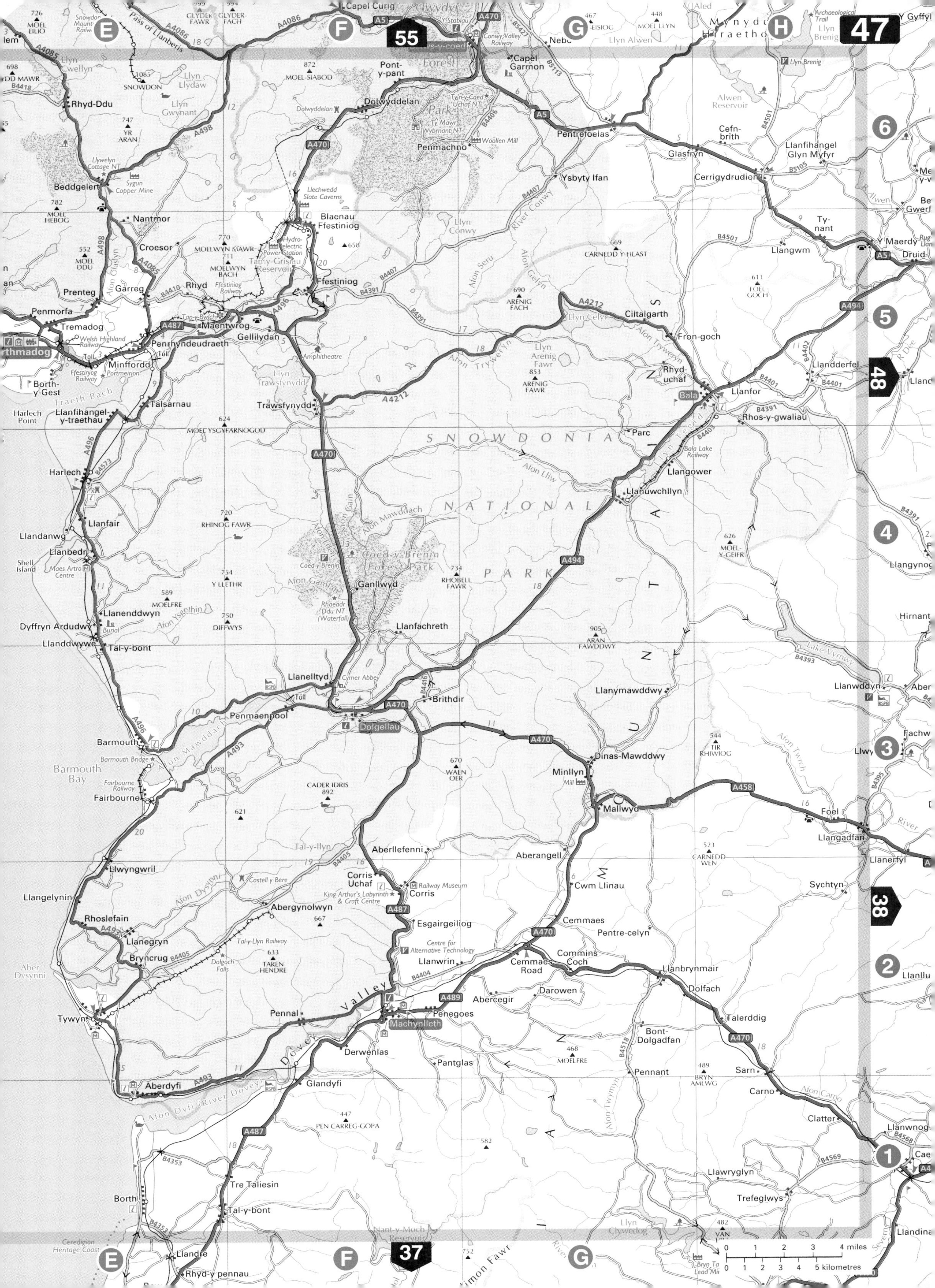

47
55
48
38
37
E
F
G
H
6
5
4
3
2
1
Capel Curig
Pass of Llanberis
A4086
GLYDER FAWR
GLYDER FACH
MOEL EILIO
Snowdon Mountain Railway
Llyn Cwellyn
Llyn Llydaw
SNOWDON
1085
Llyn Gwynant
Rhyd-Ddu
YR ARAN
Llywelyn Cottage NT
Sygun Copper Mine
Beddgelert
MOEL HEBOG
Nantmor
MOEL DDU
Croesor
MOELWYN MAWR
MOELWYN BACH
Tanygrisiau Reservoir
Hydro-electric Power Station
Ffestiniog Railway
Blaenau Ffestiniog
Llechwedd Slate Caverns
Ffestiniog
Rhyd
Garreg
Prenteg
Penmorfa
Tremadog
Welsh Highland Railway
Porthmadog
Tan-y-Bwlch
Maentwrog
Gellilydan
Penrhyndeudraeth
Minffordd
Portmeirion
Borth-y-Gest
Traeth Bach
Talsarnau
Harlech Point
Llanfihangel-y-traethau
Harlech
Llanfair
Llandanwg
Llanbedr
Shell Island
Maes Artro Centre
Llanenddwyn
Dyffryn Ardudwy
Llanddwywe
Tal-y-bont
Barmouth
Barmouth Bridge
Barmouth Bay
Fairbourne Railway
Fairbourne
Llwyngwril
Llangelynin
Rhoslefain
Llanegryn
Bryncrug
Dolgoch Falls
Aber Dysynni
Tywyn
Aberdyfi
Afon Dyfi (River Dovey)
Dovey Valley
Glandyfi
Derwenlas
Pennal
Machynlleth
Penegoes
Abercegir
Darowen
Llanwrin
Cemmaes Road
Commins Coch
Cemmaes
Llanbrynmair
Dolfach
Talerddig
Bont-Dolgadfan
Pennant
Sarn
Carno
Clatter
Llanwnog
Llawryglyn
Trefeglwys
Llyn Clywedog
Borth
Tre Taliesin
Tal-y-bont
Llandre
Rhyd-y pennau
Ceredigion Heritage Coast
Nant-y-Moch Reservoir
PEN CARREG-GOPA
Pantglas
MOELFRE
BRYN AMLWG
Esgairgeiliog
Centre for Alternative Technology
Corris
Corris Uchaf
Railway Museum
King Arthur's Labyrinth & Craft Centre
Abergynolwyn
Tal-y-Llyn Railway
TAREN HENDRE
Castell y Bere
Tal-y-llyn
Aberllefenni
CADER IDRIS
WAEN OER
Dinas-Mawddwy
Minllyn
Mallwyd
Aberangell
Cwm Llinau
Pentre-celyn
Foel
Llangadfan
Llanerfyl
Sychtyn
CARNEDD WEN
TIR RHIWIOG
Afon Twrch
Llanwddyn
Lake Vyrnwy
Hirnant
Llangynog
MOEL Y GEIFR
Llanymawddwy
ARAN FAWDDWY
Dolgellau
Brithdir
Penmaenpool
Llanelltyd
Cymer Abbey
Llanfachreth
Ganllwyd
Coed-y-Brenin Forest Park
Rhaeadr Ddu NT (Waterfall)
RHOBELL FAWR
Y LLETHR
MOELFRE
DIFFWYS
RHINOG FAWR
MOEL YSGYFARNOGOD
Trawsfynydd
Llyn Trawsfynydd
Amphitheatre
SNOWDONIA
NATIONAL
PARK
Afon Lliw
Llanuwchllyn
Llangower
Bala Lake Railway
Llyn Tegid
Parc
Bala
Rhyd-uchaf
Llanfor
Rhos-y-gwaliau
Llandderfel
Fron-goch
Ciltalgarth
Llyn Celyn
Afon Tryweryn
Llyn Arenig Fawr
ARENIG FAWR
ARENIG FACH
CARNEDD Y FILAST
FOEL GOCH
Llangwm
Ty-nant
Y Maerdy
Druid
Cerrigydrudion
Llanfihangel Glyn Myfyr
Cefn-brith
Glasfryn
Alwen Reservoir
Llyn Brenig
Pentrefoelas
Ysbyty Ifan
Llyn Conwy
Penmachno
Woollen Mill
Ty Mawr Wybrnant NT
Tyn-y-Coed Uchaf NT
Dolwyddelan
Pont-y-pant
MOEL-SIABOD
Capel Garmon
Conwy Valley Railway
Nebo
Llyn Alwen
MOEL LLYN
Mynydd Hiraethog
Archaeological Trail
A5
A470
A487
A493
A494
A496
A498
A4085
A4212
A458
A489
B4391
B4407
B4406
B4410
B4573
B4405
B4404
B4518
B4353
B4401
B4402
B4403
B4501
B5105
B4393
B4395
B4568
B4569
0 1 2 3 4 miles
0 1 2 3 4 5 kilometres

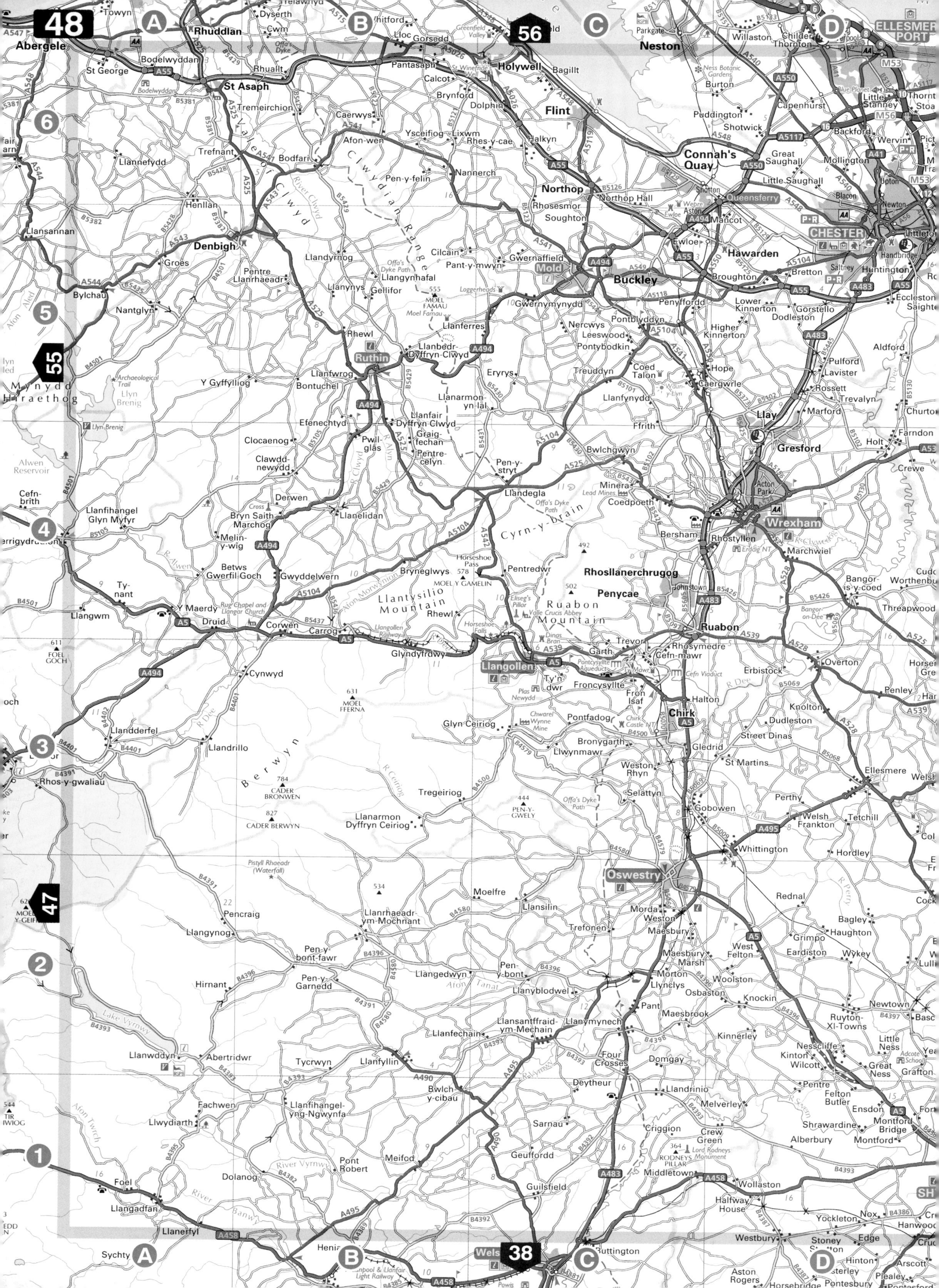

48
A
B
C
D
56
Towyn
Dyserth
Cwm
Rhuddlan
Abergele
Bodelwyddan
St George
Rhuallt
St Asaph
Tremeirchion
Trefnant
Llannefydd
Henllan
Llansannan
Denbigh
Groes
Pentre Llanrhaeadr
Bylchau
Nantglyn
Whitford
Lloc
Gorsedd
Pantasaph
Calcot
Holywell
Bagillt
Brynford
Dolphin
Flint
Caerwys
Ysceifiog
Lixwm
Rhes-y-cae
Halkyn
Afon-wen
Bodfari
Pen-y-felin
Nannerch
Northop
Northop Hall
Rhosesmor
Soughton
Clwydian Range
Vale of Clwyd
Cilcain
Pant-y-mwyn
Gwernaffield
Mold
Buckley
Llandyrnog
Llangynhafal
Gellifor
Llanynys
MOEL FAMAU
Loggerheads
Gwernymynydd
Llanferres
Rhewl
Ruthin
Llanbedr-Dyffryn-Clwyd
Eryrys
Llanfwrog
Bontuchel
Y Gyffylliog
Llanarmon-yn-Ial
Llanfair Dyffryn Clwyd
Efenechtyd
Graig-fechan
Pwll-glas
Pentre-celyn
Clocaenog
Clawdd-newydd
Pen-y-stryt
Derwen
Llanelidan
Bryn Saith Marchog
Llandegla
Parkgate
Neston
Willaston
Childer Thornton
ELLESMERE PORT
Ness Botanic Gardens
Burton
Puddington
Shotwick
Capenhurst
Great Saughall
Little Saughall
Backford
Mollington
Connah's Quay
Shotton
Queensferry
Ewloe
Mancot
Hawarden
CHESTER
Saltney
Broughton
Bretton
Handbridge
Huntington
Penyffordd
Lower Kinnerton
Dodleston
Higher Kinnerton
Pontblyddyn
Nercwys
Leeswood
Pontybodkin
Treuddyn
Coed Talon
Hope
Caergwrle
Llanfynydd
Ffrith
Llay
Rossett
Marford
Gresford
Pulford
Lavister
Trevalyn
Aldford
Holt
Farndon
Bwlchgwyn
Minera
Coedpoeth
Wrexham
Acton Park
Bersham
Rhostyllen
Marchwiel
Erddig
Mynydd Hiraethog
Llyn Brenig
Alwen Reservoir
Cefn-brith
Llanfihangel Glyn Myfyr
Cerrigydrudion
Melin-y-wig
Betws Gwerfil Goch
Gwyddelwern
Ty-nant
Llangwm
Y Maerdy
Druid
Corwen
Rug Chapel and Llangar Church
Carrog
Bryneglwys
Horseshoe Pass
MOEL Y GAMELIN
Llantysilio Mountain
Rhewl
Cyrn-y-brain
Pentredwr
Offa's Dyke Path
Rhosllanerchrugog
Penycae
Johnstown
Ruabon Mountain
Ruabon
Eliseg's Pillar
Valle Crucis Abbey
Dinas Bran
Llangollen Railway
Glyndyfrdwy
Llangollen
Garth
Trevor
Rhosymedre
Cefn-mawr
Pontcysyllte Aqueduct
Cefn Viaduct
Ty'n-dwr
Plas Newydd
Froncysyllte
Fron Isaf
Halton
Chirk
Chirk Castle NT
Bangor-is-y-coed
Bangor-on-Dee
Overton
Erbistock
Threapwood
Worthenbury
Penley
Knolton
Dudleston
Street Dinas
Ellesmere
FOEL GOCH
Cynwyd
Llandderfel
Bala
Llandrillo
Rhos-y-gwaliau
MOEL FFERNA
Berwyn
CADER BRONWEN
CADER BERWYN
Tregeiriog
Llanarmon Dyffryn Ceiriog
Glyn Ceiriog
Pontfadog
Chwarel Wynne Mine
Bronygarth
Llwynmawr
Weston Rhyn
St Martins
Gledrid
Selattyn
PEN-Y-GWELY
Gobowen
Perthy
Welsh Frankton
Tetchill
Whittington
Hordley
Oswestry
Pistyll Rhaeadr (Waterfall)
Moelfre
Llansilio
Llanrhaeadr-ym-Mochnant
Pencraig
Llangynog
Morda
Weston
Trefonen
Maesbury
Maesbury Marsh
Rednal
Bagley
Haughton
Grimpo
West Felton
Eardiston
Wykey
Pen-y-bont-fawr
Hirnant
Pen-y-Garnedd
Llangedwyn
Pen-y-bont
Llanyblodwel
Morton
Llynclys
Woolston
Osbaston
Knockin
Pant
Maesbrook
Ruyton-XI-Towns
Newtown
Lake Vyrnwy
Llanwddyn
Abertridwr
Llanfechain
Llansantffraid-ym-Mechain
Llanymynech
Kinnerley
Nesscliffe
Kinton
Wilcott
Little Ness
Great Ness
Tycrwyn
Llanfyllin
Four Crosses
Domgay
Bwlch-y-cibau
Deytheur
Llandrinio
Pentre
Felton Butler
Ensdon
Fachwen
Llanfihangel-yng-Ngwynfa
Llwydiarth
Melverley
Sarnau
Criggion
Crew Green
Shrawardine
Montford Bridge
Alberbury
Montford
RODNEYS PILLAR
Lord Rodneys Monument
Pont Robert
Meifod
Geuffordd
Dolanog
Foel
Llangadfan
Guilsfield
Middletown
Wollaston
Halfway House
Llanerfyl
Sychty
Heniarth
Welshpool & Llanfair Light Railway
Welshpool
38
Buttington
Westbury
Yockleton
Nox
Stoney Stretton
Edge
Hinton
Aston Rogers
Horsebridge
Pontesbury
Arscott
55
47
1
2
3
4
5
6

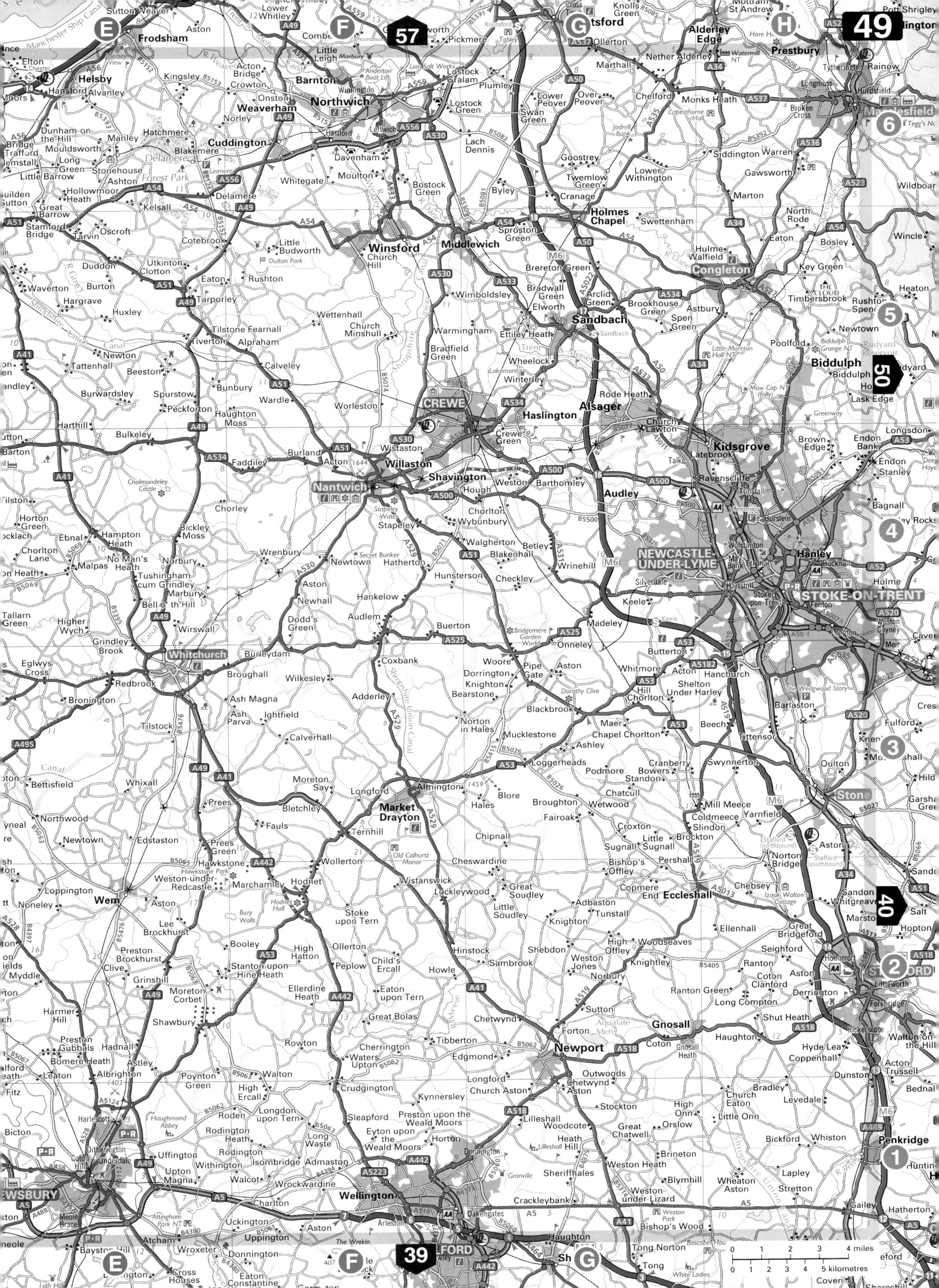

E
F
57
G
H
49
Sutton Weaver
Aston
Frodsham
Lower Whitley
Comberbach
Pickmere
Knutsford
Tatsford
Ollerton
Knolls Green
Alderley Edge
Mottram St Andrew
Pott Shrigley
Prestbury
Elton
Helsby
Hapsford
Alvanley
Kingsley
Acton Bridge
Crowton
Barnton
Little Leigh
Northwich
Weaverham
Onston
Norley
Lostock Gralam
Lostock Green
Plumley
Lower Peover
Over Peover
Swan Green
Chelford
Nether Alderley
Marthall
Monks Heath
Rainow
Macclesfield
6
Broken Cross
Dunham-on-the-Hill
Manley
Hatchmere
Cuddington
Mouldsworth
Delamere
Blakemere
Davenham
Hartford
Leftwich
Lach Dennis
Goostrey
Siddington
Warren
Gawsworth
Stonehouse
Ashton
Forest Park
Little Barrow
Moulton
Whitegate
Bostock Green
Byley
Cranage
Twemlow Green
Lower Withington
Marton
Wildboarclough
Hollowmoor Heath
Great Barrow
Kelsall
Stamford Bridge
Tarvin
Oscroft
Little Budworth
Winsford
Church Hill
Middlewich
Sproston Green
Holmes Chapel
Swettenham
North Rode
Wincle
Cotebrook
Oulton Park
Duddon
Utkinton
Clotton
Burton
Eaton
Rushton
Tarporley
Eaton
Bosley
Hulme Walfield
Congleton
Key Green
Brereton Green
Bradwall Green
Arclid Green
Elworth
Wimboldsley
Brookhouse Green
Astbury
Timbersbrook
Rushton Spencer
Heaton
5
Waverton
Hargrave
Huxley
Wettenhall
Church Minshull
Warmingham
Ettiley Heath
Sandbach
Spen Green
Newtown
Poolfold
Tilstone Fearnall
Tiverton
Alpraham
Bradfield Green
Biddulph
Rudyard Reservoir
50
Newton
Tattenhall
Beeston
Calveley
Wheelock
Winterley
Little Moreton Hall NT
Burwardsley
Bunbury
Spurstow
Peckforton
Wardle
Worleston
CREWE
Haslington
Rode Heath
Alsager
Mow Cop
Lask Edge
Harthill
Haughton Moss
Bulkeley
Church Lawton
Kidsgrove
Brown Edge
Endon Bank
Longsdon
Burland
Wistaston
Crewe Green
Latebrook
Talke
Faddiley
Acton
Willaston
Shavington
Weston
Barthomley
Ravenscliffe
Endon
Stanley
Cholmondeley Castle
Nantwich
Hough
Audley
Tunstall
Burslem
Bagnall
Horton Green
Chorley
Chorlton
Wybunbury
Stapeley Water
Stapeley
Hampton Heath
Bickley Moss
Ebnal
Walgherton
Betley
4
Chorlton Lane
No Man's Heath
Malpas
Wrenbury
Newtown
Secret Bunker
Hatherton
Blakenhall
Wrinehill
NEWCASTLE-UNDER-LYME
Hanley
Bucknall
Tushingham cum Grindley
Norbury
Marbury
Aston
Hunsterson
Checkley
Silverdale
Wolstanton
Etruria
Hartshill
STOKE-ON-TRENT
Hulme
Bell o' th' Hill
Newhall
Hankelow
Keele
Fenton
Tallarn Green
Higher Wych
Wirswall
Dodd's Green
Audlem
Buerton
Bridgemere Garden World
Madeley
Longton
Weston Coyney
Grindley Brook
Whitchurch
Burleydam
Onneley
Meir
Eglwys Cross
Redbrook
Broughall
Coxbank
Woore
Pipe Gate
Aston
Butterton
Whitmore
Acton
Hanchurch
Bronington
Wilkesley
Dorrington
Knighton
Bearstone
Shelton under Harley
Ash Magna
Adderley
Chorlton
Ash Parva
Ightfield
Blackbrook
Dorothy Clive
Barlaston
The Wedgwood Story
Tilstock
Norton in Hales
Maer
Beech
Calverhall
Mucklestone
Chapel Chorlton
Ashley
Tittensor
Fulford
3
Loggerheads
Cranberry
Swynnerton
Bettisfield
Whixall
Moreton Say
Longford
Almington
Blore
Podmore
Bowers
Standon
Oulton
Stone
Prees
Bletchley
Market Drayton
Hales
Broughton
Chatcull
Wetwood
Mill Meece
Coldmeece
Slindon
Yarnfield
Northwood
Fauls
Ternhill
Fairoak
Croxton
Newtown
Edstaston
Prees Green
Chipnall
Little Sugnall
Sugnall
Brockton
Aston
Old Colhurst Manor
Cheswardine
Bishop's Offley
Pershall
Norton Bridge
Hawkstone
Wollerton
Loppington
Weston-under-Redcastle
Marchamley
Hodnet
Wistanswick
Lockleywood
Great Soudley
Copmere End
Eccleshall
Chebsey
Sandon
Whitgreave
40
Noneley
Wem
Aston
Hodnet Hall
Adbaston
Tunstall
Little Soudley
Knighton
Marston
Stoke upon Tern
Lee Brockhurst
Ellenhall
Great Bridgeford
Hopton
Booley
High Offley
Woodseaves
Seighford
Preston Brockhurst
Clive
High Hatton
Ollerton
Child's Ercall
Hinstock
Shebdon
Weston Jones
Knightley
Ranton
Stanton upon Hine Heath
Peplow
Sambrook
Norbury
Coton Clanford
2
Grinshill
Moreton Corbet
Ellerdine Heath
Eaton upon Tern
Howle
Ranton Green
Derrington
Long Compton
Littleworth
Forebridge
Harmer Hill
Shawbury
Great Bolas
Chetwynd
Sutton
Shut Heath
Forton
Aqualate Mere
Gnosall
Haughton
Rickerscote
Walton-on-the-Hill
Preston Gubbals
Hadnall
Rowton
Cherrington
Tibberton
Newport
Coton
Gnosall Heath
Hyde Lea
Coppenhall
Bomere Heath
Astley
Albrighton
Waters Upton
Edgmond
Outwoods
Acton Trussell
Leaton
Poynton Green
Walton
Longford
Church Aston
Chetwynd Aston
Dunston
Fitz
High Ercall
Crudgington
Kynnersley
Church Eaton
Bradley
Levedale
Bednall
Harlescott
Haughmond Abbey
Roden
Longdon upon Tern
Sleapford
Preston upon the Weald Moors
Lilleshall
Stockton
High Onn
Little Onn
Rodington Heath
Eyton upon the Weald Moors
Long Waste
Woodcote
Great Chatwell
Orslow
Bicton
Rodington
Horton
Heath Hill
Bickford
Whiston
Penkridge
Uffington
Isombridge
Admaston
Donnington
Brineton
1
Upton Magna
Withington
Walcot
Granville
Sheriffhales
Weston Heath
Blymhill
Lapley
SHREWSBURY
Wrockwardine
Wellington
Wheaton Aston
Stretton
Charlton
Weston-under-Lizard
Crackleybank
Gailey
Hatherton
Meole Brace
Attingham Park NT
Uckington
Arleston
Oakengates
Weston Park
Bishop's Wood
Atcham
Uppington
Aston
The Wrekin
Haughton
Boscobel House
Bayston Hill
Wroxeter
Donnington
39
Tong Norton
Tong
White Ladies
Cross Houses
Eaton Constantine
0 1 2 3 4 miles
0 1 2 3 4 5 kilometres
M6
A49
A41
A51
A54
A50
A34
A500
A53
A519
A442
A518
A5

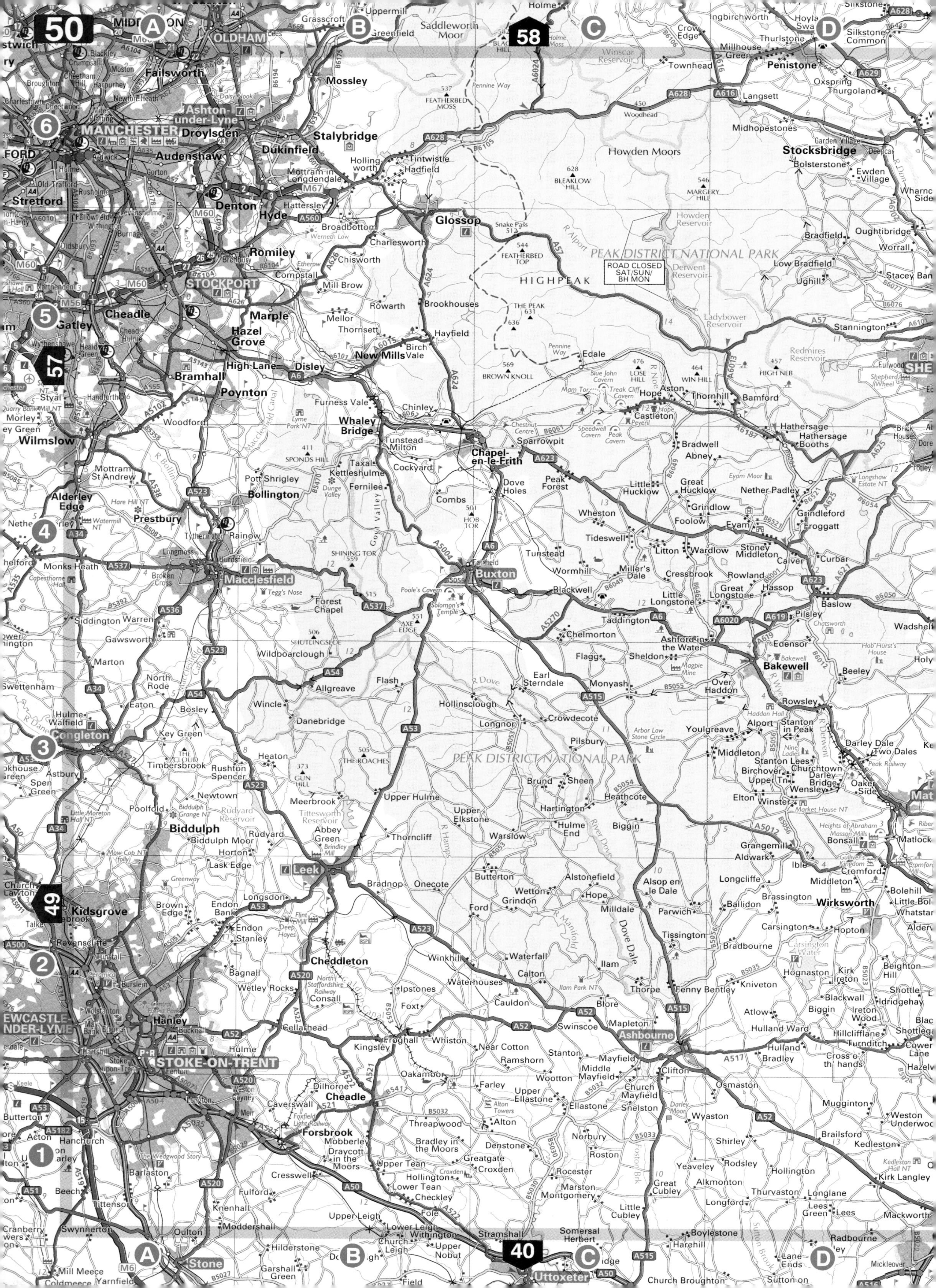
50
A
B
C
D
58
6
5
4
3
2
1
57
49
40
MIDDLETON
OLDHAM
Grasscroft
Greenfield
Uppermill
Saddleworth Moor
Holme
Crow Edge
Ingbirchworth
Silkstone
Silkstone Common
Thurlstone
Millhouse Green
Penistone
Townhead
Oxspring
Thurgoland
Langsett
Woodhead
Midhopestones
Stocksbridge
Bolsterstone
Ewden Village
Failsworth
Mossley
Ashton-under-Lyne
MANCHESTER
Droylsden
Audenshaw
Stalybridge
Dukinfield
Hollingworth
Tintwistle
Hadfield
Mottram in Longdendale
Denton
Hyde
Hattersley
Glossop
Broadbottom
Stretford
Romiley
Charlesworth
Chisworth
Compstall
Mill Brow
STOCKPORT
Cheadle
Gatley
Marple
Hazel Grove
Mellor
Thornsett
Rowarth
Brookhouses
Hayfield
Birch Vale
New Mills
Disley
High Lane
Bramhall
Poynton
Woodford
Wilmslow
Styal
Morley
Furness Vale
Whaley Bridge
Chinley
Tunstead Milton
Taxal
Kettleshulme
Fernilee
Cockyard
Chapel-en-le-Frith
Combs
Dove Holes
Sparrowpit
Peak Forest
Edale
Hope
Aston
Thornhill
Bamford
Castleton
Bradwell
Abney
Hathersage
Hathersage Booths
Howden Moors
Bleaklow Hill
Margery Hill
Featherbed Moss
Featherbed Top
Snake Pass
HIGH PEAK
The Peak
Brown Knoll
Lose Hill
Win Hill
High Neb
Howden Reservoir
Derwent Reservoir
Ladybower Reservoir
Redmires Reservoir
Bradfield
Oughtibridge
Worrall
Low Bradfield
Ughill
Stannington
PEAK DISTRICT NATIONAL PARK
ROAD CLOSED SAT/SUN/BH MON
Pennine Way
Mottram St Andrew
Alderley Edge
Prestbury
Pott Shrigley
Bollington
Rainow
Tytherington
Hurdsfield
Monks Heath
Macclesfield
Broken Cross
Siddington
Warren
Gawsworth
Marton
Forest Chapel
Wildboarclough
Shining Tor
Axe Edge
Buxton
Fairfield
Poole's Cavern
Solomon's Temple
Tunstead
Wormhill
Miller's Dale
Blackwell
Chelmorton
Taddington
Tideswell
Litton
Wardlow
Little Hucklow
Great Hucklow
Grindlow
Foolow
Eyam
Stoney Middleton
Calver
Curbar
Grindleford
Froggatt
Nether Padley
Cressbrook
Rowland
Hassop
Great Longstone
Little Longstone
Baslow
Pilsley
Ashford in the Water
Sheldon
Flagg
Monyash
Over Haddon
Bakewell
Edensor
Beeley
Rowsley
Earl Sterndale
Allgreave
Flash
Wincle
Danebridge
Hollinsclough
Longnor
Crowdecote
Swettenham
North Rode
Eaton
Bosley
Hulme Walfield
Congleton
Key Green
Timbersbrook
Astbury
Heaton
Rushton Spencer
Newtown
The Roaches
Gun Hill
Meerbrook
Upper Hulme
Tittesworth Reservoir
Pilsbury
Youlgreave
Alport
Stanton in Peak
Middleton
Darley Dale
Two Dales
Stanton Lees
Birchover
Churchtown
Upper Tn
Darley Bridge
Wensley
Oaker Side
Brund
Sheen
Hartington
Heathcote
Elton
Winster
Upper Elkstone
Hulme End
Biggin
Warslow
Poolfold
Biddulph
Biddulph Moor
Rudyard
Rudyard Reservoir
Horton
Lask Edge
Abbey Green
Thorncliff
Leek
Bradnop
Onecote
Butterton
Wetton
Grindon
Alstonefield
Hope
Milldale
Dove Dale
Alsop en le Dale
Parwich
Ballidon
Longcliffe
Grangemill
Aldwark
Ible
Bonsall
Matlock
Cromford
Middleton
Wirksworth
Brassington
Kidsgrove
Brown Edge
Endon Bank
Endon
Stanley
Longsdon
Ford
Tissington
Bradbourne
Carsington
Hopton
Ravenscliffe
Tunstall
Burslem
Bagnall
Wetley Rocks
Cheddleton
Consall
Winkhill
Waterfall
Calton
Ilam
Thorpe
Fenny Bentley
Kniveton
Hognaston
Kirk Ireton
Ipstones
Waterhouses
Foxt
Cauldon
Blore
Mapleton
Ashbourne
Atlow
Biggin
Hulland Ward
Hulland
Bradley
Newcastle-under-Lyme
Hanley
Cellarhead
Kingsley
Froghall
Whiston
Near Cotton
Swinscoe
Ramshorn
Stanton
Mayfield
Middle Mayfield
Clifton
Osmaston
Stoke-on-Trent
Hulme
Oakamoor
Farley
Wootton
Upper Ellastone
Ellastone
Church Mayfield
Snelston
Wyaston
Dilhorne
Cheadle
Caverswall
Forsbrook
Alton
Threapwood
Bradley in the Moors
Denstone
Norbury
Roston
Shirley
Brailsford
Mobberley
Draycott in the Moors
Upper Tean
Greatgate
Croxden
Rocester
Yeaveley
Rodsley
Hollington
Cresswell
Hollington
Lower Tean
Checkley
Marston Montgomery
Great Cubley
Alkmonton
Thurvaston
Longford
Longlane
Kirk Langley
Lees Green
Lees
Little Cubley
Mackworth
Barlaston
Fulford
Knenhall
Moddershall
Tittensor
Beech
Hanchurch
Acton
Trentham
Oulton
Upper Leigh
Fole
Lower Leigh
Withington
Church Leigh
Upper Nobut
Stramshall
Somersal Herbert
Boylestone
Harehill
Radbourne
Lane Ends
Swynnerton
Hilderstone
Stone
Garshall Green
Mill Meece
Yarnfield
Uttoxeter
Church Broughton
Sutton on
Mickleover
M60
M56
M67
M6
A6
A57
A623
A515
A52
A50
A53
A34
A523
A537
A54
A628
A616
A624
A5004
A5270
A6020
A619
A520
A521
A522
A5012
A517
A6187
A625
A621
A6013
A629
B5055
B5053
B5054
B5056
B5032
B5033
B5030
B6049
B6061

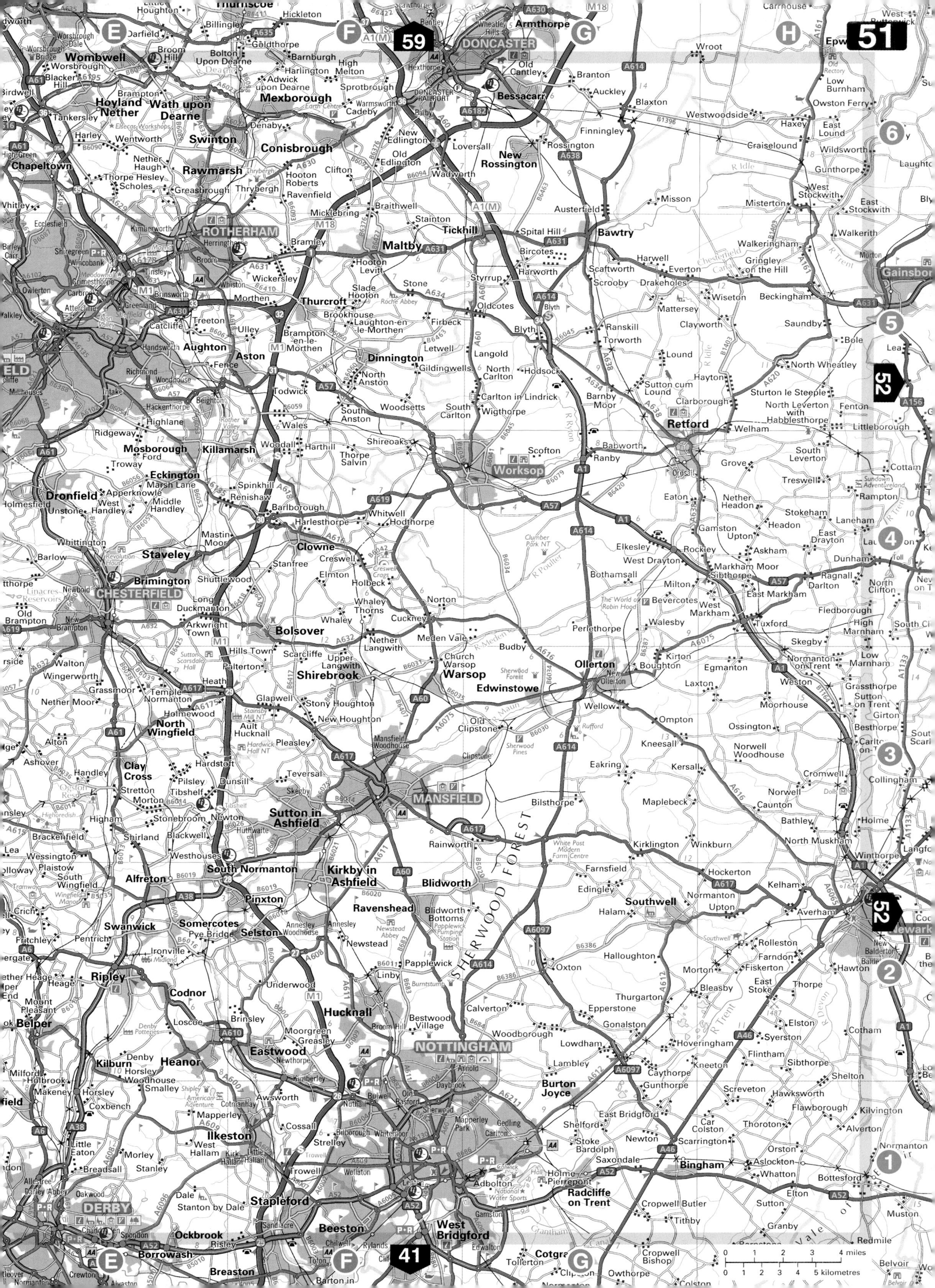

51
59
52
41
E
F
G
H
1
2
3
4
5
6
Houghton
Hickleton
Billingley
Darfield
Goldthorpe
Bentley
Armthorpe
DONCASTER
Wroot
Epworth
Wombwell
Broom Hill
Bolton upon Dearne
Barnburgh
High Melton
Harlington
Hexthorpe
Old Cantley
Branton
Worsbrough
Adwick upon Dearne
Sprotbrough
Auckley
Blaxton
Low Burnham
Owston Ferry
Hoyland Nether
Wath upon Dearne
Mexborough
Warmsworth
Cadeby
DONCASTER RAILPORT
Bessacarr
Westwoodside
Haxey
East Lound
Tankersley
Denaby
Balby
Finningley
Harley
Wentworth
Swinton
Conisbrough
New Edlington
Loversall
Rossington
Graiseland
Wildsworth
Chapeltown
Nether Haugh
Rawmarsh
Clifton
Old Edlington
New Rossington
Gunthorpe
Laughton
Thorpe Hesley
Scholes
Greasbrough
Hooton Roberts
Thrybergh
Wadworth
Ravenfield
West Stockwith
East Stockwith
Misson
Misterton
Braithwell
Micklebring
Stainton
Austerfield
Ecclesfield
ROTHERHAM
Tickhill
Spital Hill
Bawtry
Walkerith
Bramley
Maltby
Bircotes
Harwell
Walkeringham
Gringley on the Hill
Hooton Levitt
Scaftworth
Everton
Harworth
Wickersley
Styrrup
Scrooby
Drakeholes
Gainsborough
Whiston
Slade Hooton
Stone
Wiseton
Beckingham
Brinsworth
Thurcroft
Morthen
Oldcotes
Catcliffe
Treeton
Brookhouse
Laughton-en-le-Morthen
Firbeck
Blyth
Mattersey
Clayworth
Saundby
Ulley
Brampton-en-le-Morthen
Ranskill
Torworth
Bole
Aughton
Letwell
Langold
Lound
Aston
Dinnington
Gildingwells
North Carlton
Hodsock
North Wheatley
Fence
North Anston
Sutton cum Lound
Hayton
Richmond
Woodhouse
Todwick
Carlton in Lindrick
Barnby Moor
Clarborough
Sturton le Steeple
Intake
Beighton
Woodsetts
South Carlton
Wigthorpe
North Leverton with Habblesthorpe
Fenton
Hackenthorpe
South Anston
Retford
Welham
Littleborough
Highlane
Wales
Ridgeway
Harthill
Shireoaks
Babworth
South Leverton
Mosborough
Killamarsh
Woodall
Thorpe Salvin
Scofton
Ranby
Grove
Cottam
Troway
Worksop
Ordsall
Eckington
Marsh Lane
Spinkhill
Treswell
Dronfield
Apperknowle
Renishaw
Rampton
West Handley
Middle Handley
Eaton
Nether Headon
Unstone
Barlborough
Whitwell
Hodthorpe
Stokeham
Laneham
Harlesthorpe
Headon
Gamston
Upton
East Drayton
Whittington
Mastin Moor
Clowne
Clumber Park NT
Elkesley
Rockley
Askham
Staveley
Creswell
West Drayton
Markham Moor
Dunham
Barlow
Stanfree
Sibthorpe
Ragnall
Brimington
Shuttlewood
Elmton
Bothamsall
Milton
Darlton
North Clifton
CHESTERFIELD
Holbeck
East Markham
Long Duckmanton
Whaley Thorns
Norton
Bevercotes
The World of Robin Hood
West Markham
Fledborough
Old Brampton
Whaley
Cuckney
Walesby
New Brampton
Arkwright Town
Bolsover
Meden Vale
Perlethorpe
Tuxford
High Marnham
Hills Town
Scarcliffe
Nether Langwith
Budby
Skegby
Low Marnham
Walton
Church Warsop
Kirton
Normanton on Trent
Palterton
Upper Langwith
Warsop
Sherwood Forest
Ollerton
Boughton
Egmanton
Wingerworth
Shirebrook
New Ollerton
Weston
Heath
Edwinstowe
Laxton
Grassthorpe
Grassmoor
Temple Normanton
Sutton on Trent
Nether Moor
Holmewood
Glapwell
Stony Houghton
Wellow
Girton
Ompton
Moorhouse
North Wingfield
Stainsby Mill NT
New Houghton
Old Clipstone
Rufford
Besthorpe
Ault Hucknall
Alton
Hardwick Hall NT
Pleasley
Mansfield Woodhouse
Ossington
Kneesall
Carlton-on-Trent
Ashover
Clay Cross
Hardstoft
Sherwood Pines
Clipstone
Norwell Woodhouse
Handley
Pilsley
Teversal
Eakring
Kersall
Cromwell
Collingham
Stretton
Dunsill
Skegby
Norwell
Tibshelf
Caunton
Ogston Reservoir
Morton
MANSFIELD
Maplebeck
Bilsthorpe
Stonebroom
Newton
Sutton in Ashfield
Bathley
Holme
Higham
Huthwaite
Shirland
Blackwell
Rainworth
North Muskham
Brackenfield
Kirklington
Winkburn
Westhouses
White Post Modern Farm Centre
Winthorpe
Wessington
Plaistow
South Normanton
Kirkby in Ashfield
Farnsfield
Hockerton
South Wingfield
Alfreton
Blidworth
Edingley
Kelham
Wingfield Manor
Southwell
Normanton
Pinxton
Ravenshead
Upton
Averham
Crich
Blidworth Bottoms
Halam
Swanwick
Somercotes
Annesley
Annesley Woodhouse
Newark-on-Trent
Selston
Rolleston
Fritchley
Pye Bridge
Newstead Abbey
Farndon
Pentrich
Newstead
Balderton
Ironville
Halloughton
Fiskerton
Hawton
Papplewick
Oxton
Morton
Heage
Ripley
Linby
East Stoke
Thorpe
Underwood
Bleasby
Codnor
Hucknall
Thurgarton
Mount Pleasant
Calverton
Epperstone
Elston
Belper
Brinsley
Loscoe
Bestwood Village
Gonalston
Syerston
Cotham
Moorgreen
Greasley
Woodborough
Lowdham
Hoveringham
Flintham
Eastwood
Newthorpe
NOTTINGHAM
Kneeton
Sibthorpe
Kilburn
Denby
Heanor
Arnold
Lambley
Caythorpe
Shelton
Milford
Horsley Woodhouse
Holbrook
Kimberley
Daybrook
Burton Joyce
Gunthorpe
Screveton
Hawksworth
Makeney
Horsley
Smalley
Awsworth
Bulwell
Old Basford
Flawborough
Kilvington
Coxbench
Cotmanhay
Nuthall
Sherwood
East Bridgford
Car Colston
Thoroton
Alverton
Mapperley
Mapperley Park
Gedling
Shelford
Ilkeston
Cossall
Carlton
Newton
Scarrington
Orston
Normanton
Little Eaton
West Hallam
Strelley
Stoke Bardolph
Saxondale
Aslockton
Morley
Kirk Hallam
Trowell
Bingham
Breadsall
Stanley
Wollaton
Holme Pierrepont
Whatton
Bottesford
Allestree
Darley Abbey
Oakwood
Dale
Adbolton
National Water Sports
Elton
Stapleford
Radcliffe on Trent
Cropwell Butler
Stanton by Dale
Lenton
Gamston
Tithby
Sutton
Muston
DERBY
Beeston
West Bridgford
Granby
Spondon
Ockbrook
Risley
Sandiacre
Chilwell
Borrowash
Rylands
Edwalton
Cotgrave
Cropwell Bishop
Redmile
Breaston
Toton
Tollerton
Clipston
Owthorpe
Belvoir
Barton in Fabis
Crewton
Alvaston
Normanton
0
1
2
3
4 miles
0
1
2
3
4
5 kilometres

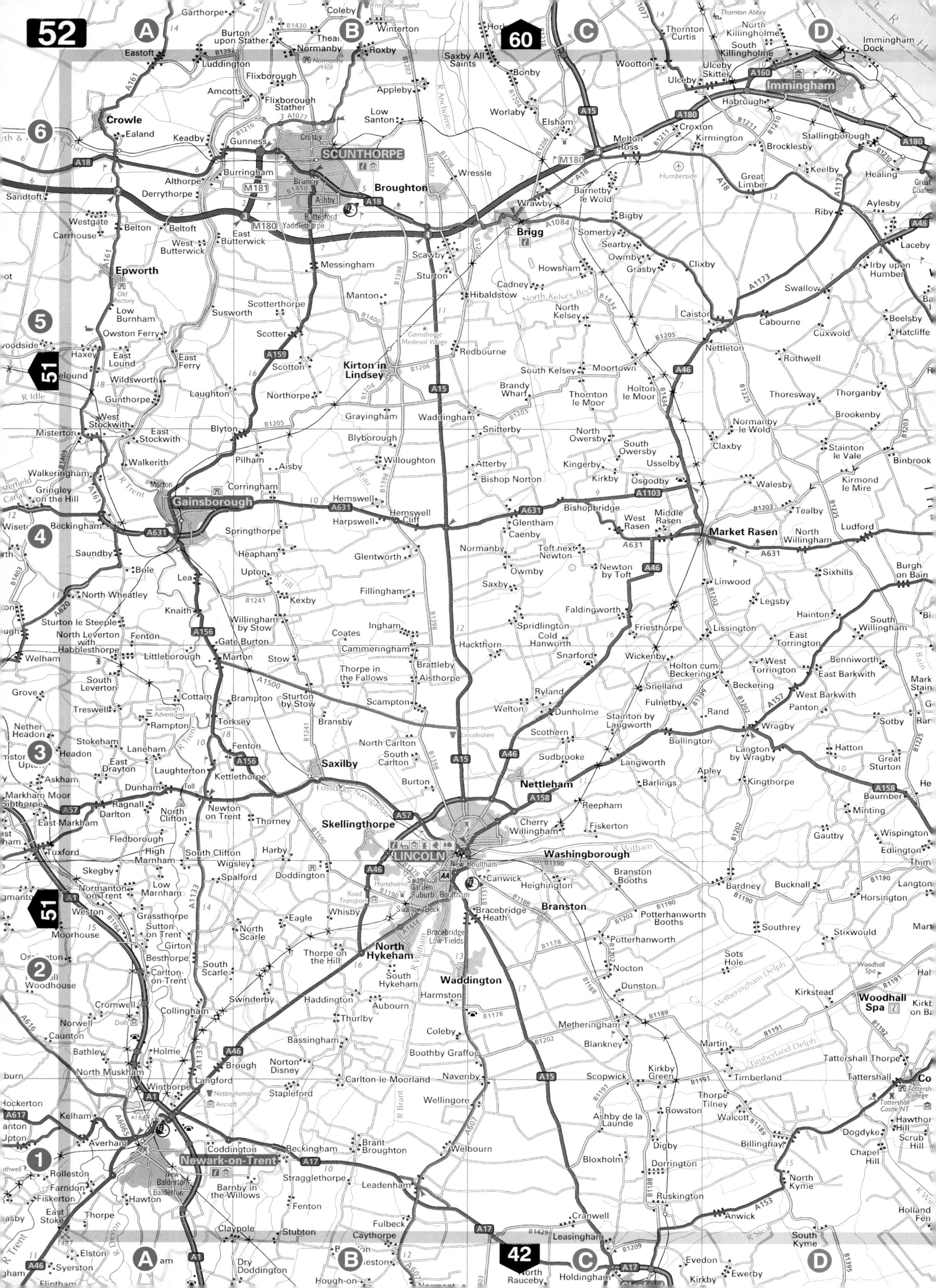
52
A
B
C
D
60
Garthorpe
Coleby
Winterton
Thornton Abbey
Thornton Curtis
North Killingholme
Immingham Dock
Burton upon Stather
Normanby
Roxby
Horkstow
Saxby All Saints
Eastoft
Luddington
Flixborough
Amcotts
Flixborough Stather
Appleby
Low Santon
Bonby
Wootton
Ulceby
Ulceby Skitter
South Killingholme
Immingham
Habrough
Worlaby
Elsham
Crowle
Ealand
Keadby
Gunness
Crosby
SCUNTHORPE
Croxton
Kirmington
Melton Ross
Stallingborough
Brocklesby
Wressle
Barnetby le Wold
Keelby
Healing
Great Limber
Humberside
Sandtoft
Althorpe
Burringham
Derrythorpe
Brumby
Ashby
Broughton
Wrawby
Brigg
Bigby
Aylesby
Riby
Westgate
Belton
Beltoft
East Butterwick
West Butterwick
Bottesford
Yaddlethorpe
Somerby
Searby
Owmby
Grasby
Laceby
Carrhouse
Messingham
Scawby
Sturton
Howsham
Clixby
Irby upon Humber
Epworth
Old Rectory
Low Burnham
Manton
Hibaldstow
Cadney
North Kelsey Beck
Swallow
Susworth
Scotterthorpe
North Kelsey
Caistor
Cabourne
Beelsby
Owston Ferry
Scotter
Gainsthorpe Medieval Village
Redbourne
Nettleton
Cuxwold
Hatcliffe
Haxey
East Lound
East Ferry
Scotton
Kirton in Lindsey
South Kelsey
Moortown
Rothwell
Westwoodside
Graizelound
Wildsworth
Laughton
Northorpe
Brandy Wharf
Thornton le Moor
Holton le Moor
Thoresway
Thorganby
R Idle
Gunthorpe
West Stockwith
Grayingham
Waddingham
Snitterby
North Owersby
Normanby le Wold
Brookenby
Misterton
East Stockwith
Blyton
Blyborough
South Owersby
Claxby
Stainton le Vale
Binbrook
Walkerith
Pilham
Aisby
Willoughton
Atterby
Kingerby
Usselby
Walkeringham
Morton
Corringham
Bishop Norton
Kirkby
Osgodby
Walesby
Kirmond le Mire
Gringley on the Hill
Gainsborough
Hemswell
Hemswell Cliff
Glentham
Bishopbridge
West Rasen
Middle Rasen
Market Rasen
Tealby
Ludford
North Willingham
Beckingham
Wiseton
Harpswell
Springthorpe
Caenby
Normanby
Toft next Newton
Saundby
Heapham
Glentworth
Owmby
Newton by Toft
Sixhills
Burgh on Bain
Bole
Lea
Upton
Linwood
Saxby
Legsby
North Wheatley
Kexby
Fillingham
Knaith
Faldingworth
Hainton
Sturton le Steeple
Willingham by Stow
Ingham
Spridlington
Friesthorpe
Lissington
South Willingham
North Leverton with Habblesthorpe
Fenton
Coates
Cold Hanworth
Hackthorn
East Torrington
Gate Burton
Cammeringham
Snarford
Wickenby
Welham
Littleborough
Marton
Stow
Thorpe in the Fallows
Brattleby
Aisthorpe
Holton cum Beckering
West Torrington
Benniworth
East Barkwith
South Leverton
Grove
Cottam
Brampton
Sturton by Stow
Scampton
Ryland
Snelland
Beckering
West Barkwith
Treswell
Sundown Adventureland
Rampton
Torksey
Bransby
Welton
Dunholme
Fulnetby
Rand
Panton
Stainton by Langworth
Wragby
Sotby
Nether Headon
Headon
Stokeham
Laneham
Fenton
North Carlton
South Carlton
Scothern
Bullington
Langton by Wragby
Hatton
Great Sturton
Upton
East Drayton
Laughterton
Kettlethorpe
Saxilby
Sudbrooke
Langworth
Apley
Askham
Dunham
Burton
Barlings
Kingthorpe
Markham Moor
Ragnall
Newton on Trent
Nettleham
Baumber
Sibthorpe
East Markham
Darlton
North Clifton
Thorney
Fossdyke Navigation
Skellingthorpe
Reepham
Minting
Cherry Willingham
Fiskerton
Gautby
Wispington
Fledborough
Tuxford
High Marnham
South Clifton
Harby
LINCOLN
Washingborough
Edlington
R Witham
Skegby
Wigsley
Doddington
New Boultham
Canwick
Heighington
Branston Booths
Bardney
Bucknall
Langton
Normanton on Trent
Low Marnham
Spalford
Hartsholme
Swanpool Garden Suburb
Boultham
Road Transport
Horsington
Weston
Grassthorpe
Eagle
Whisby
Swallow Beck
Bracebridge Heath
Branston
Potterhanworth Booths
Southrey
Sutton on Trent
North Scarle
Bracebridge Low Fields
Potterhanworth
Stixwould
Moorhouse
Girton
Thorpe on the Hill
North Hykeham
Nocton
Sots Hole
Ossington
Besthorpe
South Scarle
South Hykeham
Waddington
Woodhall Spa
Laxton Woodhouse
Carlton-on-Trent
Swinderby
Haddington
Dunston
Metheringham Delph
Kirkstead
Woodhall Spa
Kirkby on Bain
Cromwell
Collingham
Aubourn
Harmston
Thurlby
Metheringham
Norwell
Caunton
Coleby
Bassingham
Blankney
Martin
Dyke
Timberland Delph
Bathley
Holme
Brough
Norton Disney
Boothby Graffoe
Tattershall Thorpe
North Muskham
Langford
Carlton-le-Moorland
Navenby
Scopwick
Kirkby Green
Timberland
Tattershall
Winthorpe
Nottinghamshire Aircraft
Stapleford
Wellingore
Thorpe Tilney
Tattershall College
Tattershall Castle NT
Hockerton
Kelham
Rowston
Walcott
Hawthorn Hill
Averham
Coddington
Brant Broughton
Ashby de la Launde
Dogdyke
Scrub Hill
Newark-on-Trent
Beckingham
Welbourn
Digby
Billinghay
Chapel Hill
Rolleston
Barnby in the Willows
Stragglethorpe
Bloxholm
Dorrington
North Kyme
Farndon
Fiskerton
Balderton
Hawton
Leadenham
Ruskington
East Stoke
Thorpe
Fenton
Cranwell
Anwick
Holland Fen
Claypole
Fulbeck
Stubton
Caythorpe
Leasingham
South Kyme
Elston
Dry Doddington
42
North Rauceby
Holdingham
Evedon
Ewerby
Kirkby
Syerston
Flintham
Hough-on-the-Hill
A1
A46
A17
A15
A631
A156
A18
A180
A160
M180
M181
A159
A1103
A158
A157
A57
A1500
A153
A607
A1133
A616
A6075
A617
A620
A161
A1077
A1173
B1205
B1206
B1398
B1241
B1202
B1188
B1189
B1191
B1190
B1178
B1399
B1225
B1203
B1434
B1400
B1207
B1208
B1204
B1211
B1210
B1216
B1450
B1430
B1392
B1403
B1429
B1209
B1395
B1192
B1164
1
2
3
4
5
6
51

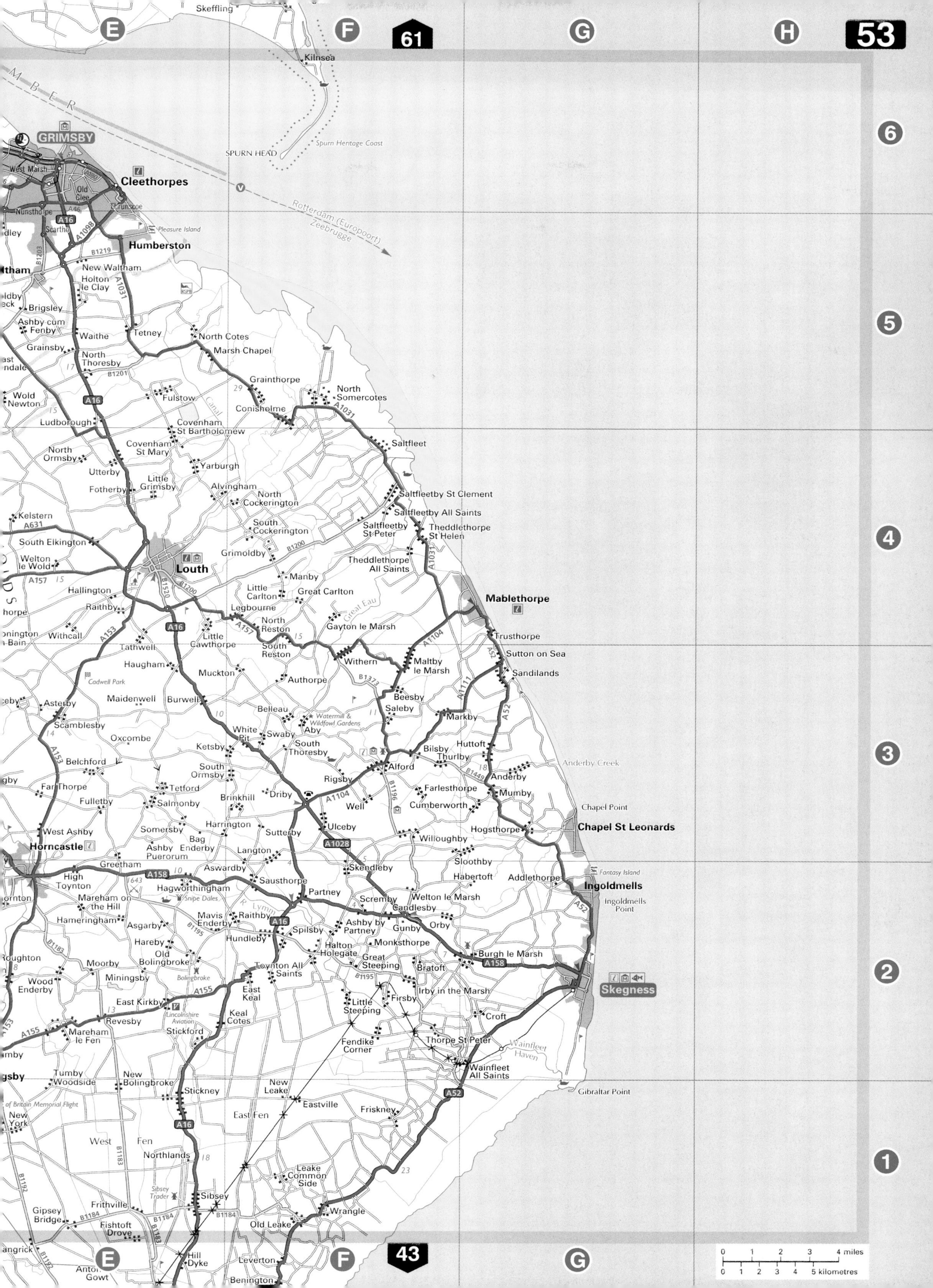

53
61
43
E
F
G
H
6
5
4
3
2
1
Skeffling
Kilnsea
SPURN HEAD
Spurn Heritage Coast
GRIMSBY
West Marsh
Cleethorpes
Old Clee
Nunsthorpe
Thrunscoe
Scartho
Rotterdam (Europoort) Zeebrugge
Pleasure Island
Humberston
New Waltham
Holton le Clay
Brigsley
Ashby cum Fenby
Waithe
Tetney
North Cotes
Marsh Chapel
Grainsby
North Thoresby
Grainthorpe
North Somercotes
Fulstow
Conisholme
Wold Newton
Ludborough
Covenham St Bartholomew
Covenham St Mary
North Ormsby
Utterby
Saltfleet
Yarburgh
Little Grimsby
Fotherby
Alvingham
North Cockerington
Saltfleetby St Clement
Saltfleetby All Saints
Kelstern
South Cockerington
Saltfleetby St Peter
Theddlethorpe St Helen
South Elkington
Grimoldby
Welton le Wold
Louth
Theddlethorpe All Saints
Manby
Little Carlton
Great Carlton
Mablethorpe
Hallington
Raithby
Legbourne
North Reston
Great Eau
Gayton le Marsh
Trusthorpe
Withcall
Little Cawthorpe
South Reston
Sutton on Sea
Tathwell
Withern
Maltby le Marsh
Sandilands
Haugham
Muckton
Authorpe
Cadwell Park
Beesby
Maidenwell
Burwell
Saleby
Asterby
Belleau
Watermill & Wildfowl Gardens
Markby
Scamblesby
Aby
White Pit
Swaby
Oxcombe
South Thoresby
Huttoft
Ketsby
Bilsby
Thurlby
Belchford
Anderby Creek
South Ormsby
Alford
Anderby
Rigsby
Farlesthorpe
Far Thorpe
Tetford
Driby
Mumby
Fulletby
Salmonby
Brinkhill
Well
Cumberworth
Chapel Point
Chapel St Leonards
Harrington
Ulceby
Hogsthorpe
West Ashby
Somersby
Bag Enderby
Sutterby
Willoughby
Horncastle
Ashby Puerorum
Langton
Sloothby
Greetham
Aswardby
Skendleby
Fantasy Island
High Toynton
Hagworthingham
Sausthorpe
Habertoft
Addlethorpe
Ingoldmells
Ingoldmells Point
Snipe Dales
Partney
Mareham on the Hill
Scremby
Welton le Marsh
Candlesby
Hameringham
Asgarby
Mavis Enderby
Raithby
Ashby by Partney
Orby
Spilsby
Gunby
Hareby
Hundleby
Halton Holegate
Monksthorpe
Old Bolingbroke
Burgh le Marsh
Moorby
Bolingbroke
Toynton All Saints
Great Steeping
Bratoft
Skegness
Wood Enderby
Miningsby
East Keal
Irby in the Marsh
Firsby
East Kirkby
Little Steeping
Lincolnshire Aviation
Croft
Revesby
Keal Cotes
Mareham le Fen
Stickford
Fendike Corner
Thorpe St Peter
Wainfleet Haven
Wainfleet All Saints
Tumby Woodside
New Bolingbroke
Stickney
New Leake
Gibraltar Point
of Britain Memorial Flight
Eastville
New York
East Fen
Friskney
West Fen
Northlands
Leake Common Side
Sibsey Trader
Sibsey
Frithville
Gipsey Bridge
Fishtoft Drove
Wrangle
Old Leake
Hill Dyke
Leverton
Anton Gowt
Benington
A16
A1098
A46
A180
B1219
B1203
A1031
B1201
A631
A157
B1520
B1200
A153
A1104
A52
A1111
B1373
B1449
B1196
A1028
A158
B1195
B1183
A155
B1184
B1192
A52
0 1 2 3 4 miles
0 1 2 3 4 5 kilometres

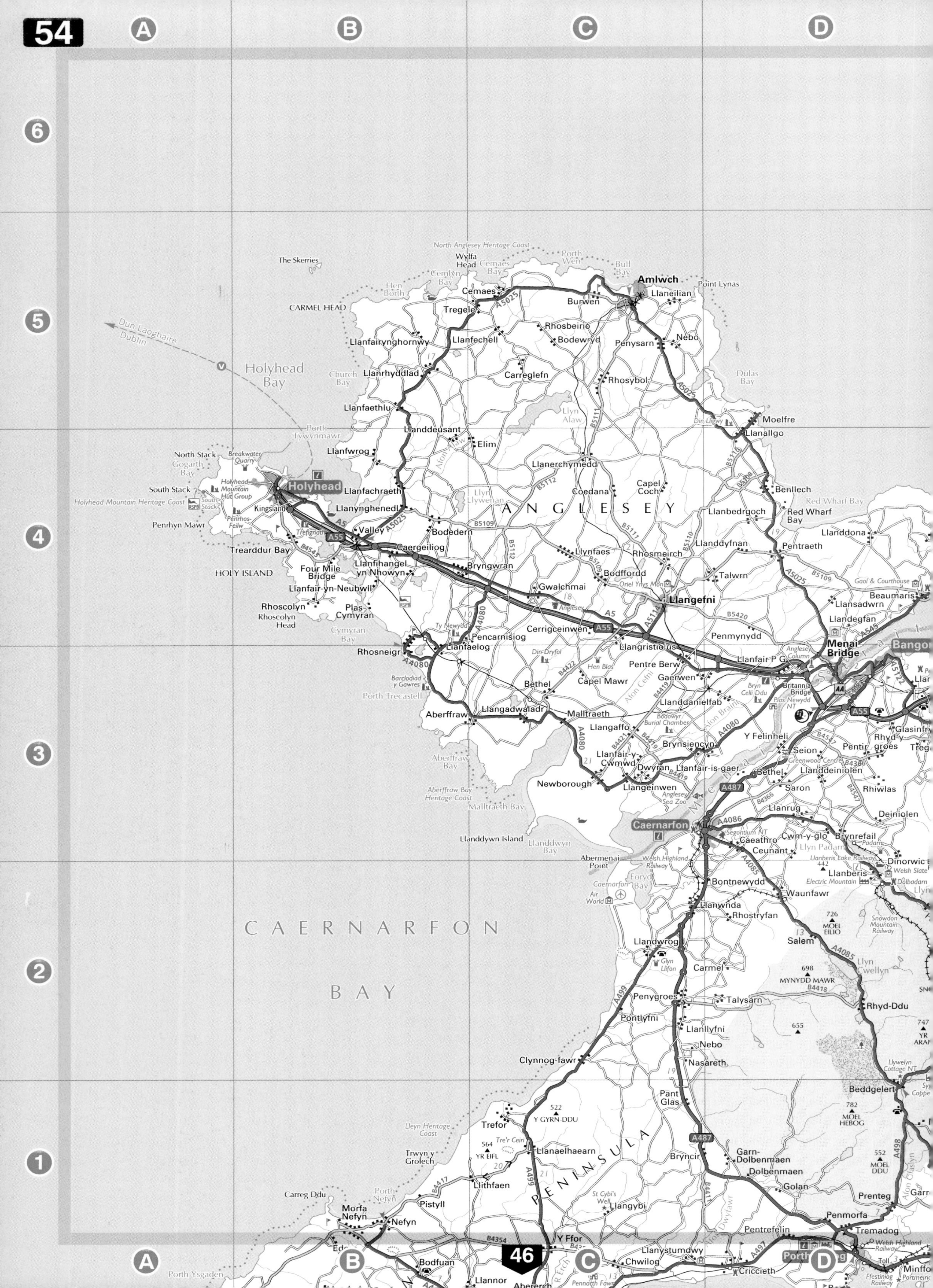
A
B
C
D
6
5
4
3
2
1
North Anglesey Heritage Coast
The Skerries
Wylfa Head
Cemaes Bay
Porth Wen
Bull Bay
Amlwch
Point Lynas
Llaneilian
Hen Borth
Cemlyn Bay
Cemaes
Burwen
CARMEL HEAD
Tregele
Rhosbeirio
Bodewryd
Penysarn
Nebo
Dun Laoghaire
Dublin
Llanfairynghornwy
Llanfechell
Holyhead Bay
Church Bay
Llanrhyddlad
Carreglefn
Rhosybol
Dulas Bay
Llanfaethlu
Llyn Alaw
Moelfre
Din Lligwy
Llanallgo
Porth Tywynmawr
Llanddeusant
Elim
North Stack
Breakwater Quarry
Gogarth Bay
Llanfwrog
Llanerchymedd
South Stack
Holyhead Mountain Hut Group
Holyhead
Llanfachraeth
Coedana
Capel Coch
Benllech
Holyhead Mountain Heritage Coast
South Stack
Llyn Llywenan
Red Wharf Bay
Kingsland
Llanynghenedl
ANGLESEY
Llanbedrgoch
Red Wharf Bay
Penrhyn Mawr
Penrhos Feilw
Trefignath
Valley
Bodedern
Llanddona
Trearddur Bay
Caergeiliog
Llynfaes
Rhosmeirch
Llanddyfnan
Pentraeth
HOLY ISLAND
Four Mile Bridge
Llanfihangel yn Nhowyn
Bryngwran
Bodffordd
Talwrn
Gaol & Courthouse
Beaumaris
Llanfair-yn-Neubwll
Gwalchmai
Oriel Ynys Mon
Llansadwrn
Rhoscolyn
Rhoscolyn Head
Plas Cymyran
Llangefni
Llandegfan
Ty Newydd
Cymyran Bay
Pencarnisiog
Cerrigceinwen
Penmynydd
Menai Bridge
Bangor
Rhosneigr
Llanfaelog
Din Dryfol
Llangristiolus
Anglesey Column
Llanfair P G
Barclodiad y Gawres
Hen Blas
Pentre Berw
Porth Trecastell
Bethel
Capel Mawr
Gaerwen
Bryn Celli Ddu
Britannia Bridge
Plas Newydd NT
Aberffraw
Llangadwaladr
Malltraeth
Llanddaniel fab
Bodowyr Burial Chamber
Llangaffo
Afon Braint
Afon Cefni
Y Felinheli
Glasinfryn
Aberffraw Bay
Brynsiencyn
Seion
Greenwood Centre
Pentir
Rhyd-y-groes
Llanfair-y-Cwmwd
Dwyran
Llanfair-is-gaer
Bethel
Llanddeiniolen
Newborough
Llangeinwen
Anglesey Sea Zoo
Saron
Rhiwlas
Aberffraw Bay Heritage Coast
Malltraeth Bay
Llanrug
Deiniolen
Caernarfon
Segontium NT
Caeathro
Cwm-y-glo
Brynrefail
Llanddwyn Island
Llanddwyn Bay
Ceunant
Llyn Padarn
Dinorwic
Abermenai Point
Welsh Highland Railway
Llanberis
Welsh Slate
Llanberis Lake Railway
Foryd Bay
Electric Mountain
Dolbadarn
Caernarfon Air World
Bontnewydd
Waunfawr
Llanwnda
Rhostryfan
MOEL EILIO
Snowdon Mountain Railway
CAERNARFON
Salem
BAY
Llandwrog
Glyn Llifon
Llyn Cwellyn
Carmel
MYNYDD MAWR
Penygroes
Talysarn
Rhyd-Ddu
Pontllyfni
Llanllyfni
Nebo
Nasareth
Clynnog-fawr
Llywelyn Cottage NT
Beddgelert
Pant Glas
Y GYRN-DDU
MOEL HEBOG
Lleyn Heritage Coast
Trefor
Tre'r Ceiri
YR EIFL
Llanaelhaearn
PENINSULA
Trwyn y Gorlech
Bryncir
Garn-Dolbenmaen
Dolbenmaen
MOEL DDU
Llithfaen
Golan
Prenteg
Carreg Ddu
Porth Nefyn
Pistyll
St Cybi's Well
Llangybi
Morfa Nefyn
Nefyn
Penmorfa
Pentrefelin
Tremadog
Welsh Highland Railway
Y Ffor
Llanystumdwy
Porthmadog
Bodfuan
Chwilog
Criccieth
Porth Ysgaden
Llannor
Abererch
Penarth Fawr
Ffestiniog Railway
Minffordd
46

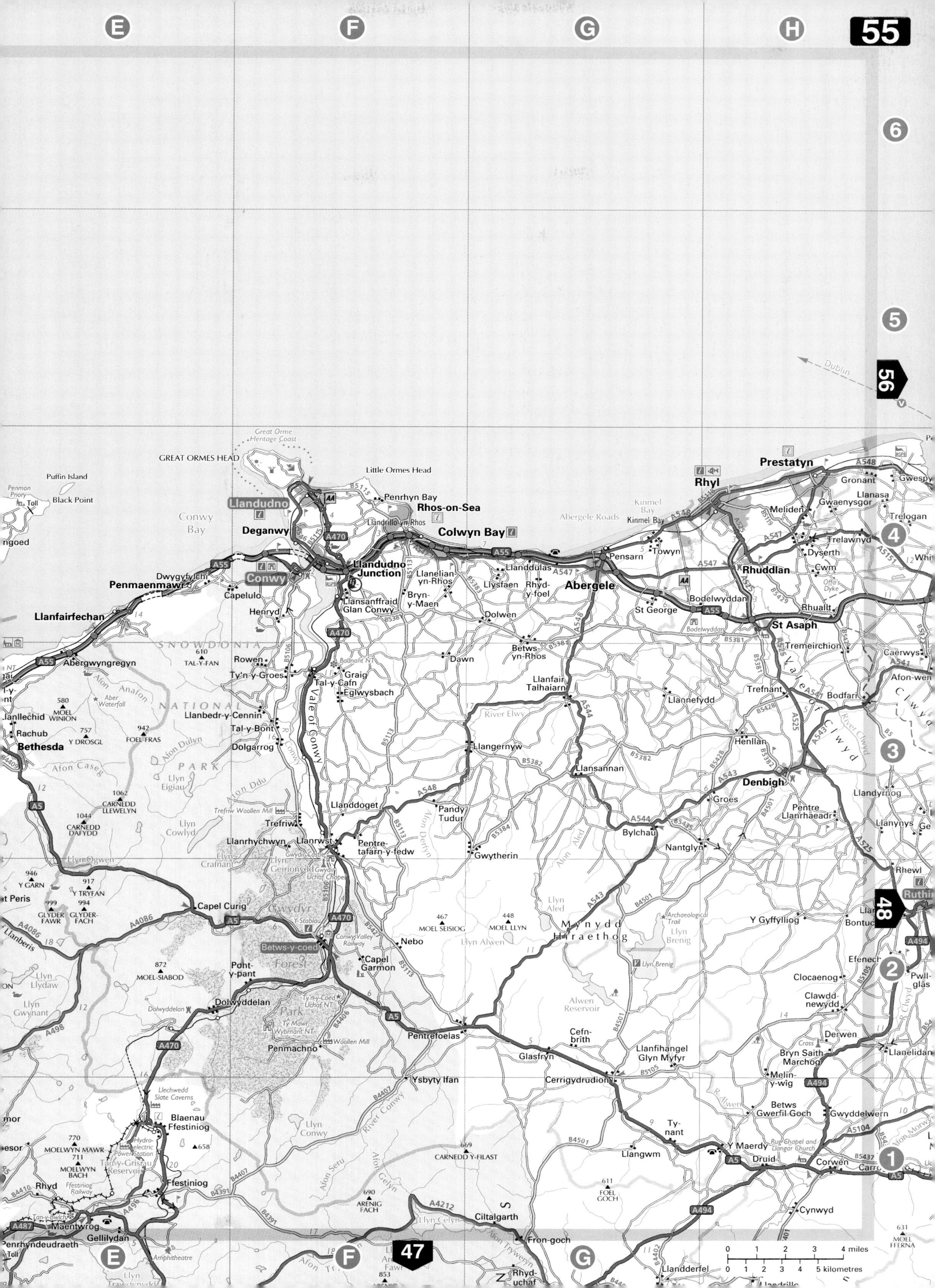

E
F
G
H
6
5
4
3
2
1
56
48
47
Dublin
GREAT ORMES HEAD
Great Orme Heritage Coast
Little Ormes Head
Puffin Island
Black Point
Llandudno
Conwy Bay
Deganwy
Penrhyn Bay
Rhos-on-Sea
Colwyn Bay
Llandudno Junction
Conwy
Penmaenmawr
Dwygyfylchi
Capelulo
Llanfairfechan
Henryd
Llansanffraid Glan Conwy
Llanelian-yn-Rhos
Bryn-y-Maen
Llysfaen
Llanddulas
Rhyd-y-foel
Abergele
Pensarn
Towyn
Kinmel Bay
Abergele Roads
Rhyl
Prestatyn
Meliden
Gronant
Llanasa
Gwaenysgor
Trelogan
Trelawnyd
Dyserth
Cwm
Rhuddlan
Bodelwyddan
St George
Rhuallt
St Asaph
Tremeirchion
Caerwys
Afon-wen
Bodfari
Trefnant
Vale of Clwyd
Llannefydd
Henllan
Denbigh
Llandyrnog
Pentre Llanrhaeadr
Llanynys
Rhewl
Groes
Nantglyn
Bylchau
Llansannan
Llanfair Talhaiarn
River Elwy
Llangernyw
Betws-yn-Rhos
Dolwen
Dawn
Graig
Tal-y-Cafn
Eglwysbach
Bodnant NT
Vale of Conwy
Rowen
Ty'n-y-Groes
Llanbedr-y-Cennin
Tal-y-Bont
Dolgarrog
SNOWDONIA NATIONAL PARK
Abergwyngregyn
Aber Waterfall
Afon Anafon
610 TAL-Y-FAN
580 MOEL WINION
757 Y DROSGL
942 FOEL-FRAS
Afon Dulyn
Afon Caseg
Llanllechid
Rachub
Bethesda
Llyn Eigiau
1062 CARNEDD LLEWELYN
1044 CARNEDD DAFYDD
Afon Ddu
Llyn Cowlyd
Trefriw Woollen Mill
Trefriw
Llanddoget
Llanrwst
Pandy Tudur
Pentre-tafarn-y-fedw
Gwytherin
Llanrhychwyn
Llyn Crafnant
Llyn Geirionydd
Gwydir Castle
Gwydir Uchaf Chapel
Llyn Ogwen
946 Y GARN
917 Y TRYFAN
999 GLYDER FAWR
994 GLYDER-FACH
Capel Curig
Gwydyr Forest
Y Stablau
Betws-y-coed
Conwy Valley Railway
Capel Garmon
Nebo
467 MOEL SEISIOG
448 MOEL LLYN
Llyn Aled
Llyn Alwen
Mynydd Hiraethog
Archaeological Trail
Llyn Brenig
Y Gyffylliog
Llanberis
872 MOEL-SIABOD
Pont-y-pant
Llyn Llydaw
Llyn Gwynant
Dolwyddelan
Ty'n-y-Coed Uchaf NT
Ty Mawr Wybrnant NT
Woollen Mill
Penmachno
Pentrefoelas
Alwen Reservoir
Cefn-brith
Glasfryn
Cerrigydrudion
Llanfihangel Glyn Myfyr
Clocaenog
Clawdd-newydd
Efenechtyd
Pwll-glas
Derwen
Bryn Saith Marchog
Llanelidan
Melin-y-wig
Betws Gwerfil Goch
Gwyddelwern
Ty-nant
Y Maerdy
Rug Chapel and Llangar Church
Druid
Corwen
Llangwm
Ysbyty Ifan
River Conwy
Llechwedd Slate Caverns
Blaenau Ffestiniog
Hydro-electric Power Station
770 MOELWYN MAWR
711 MOELWYN BACH
Tanygrisiau Reservoir
Ffestiniog
Rhyd
Ffestiniog Railway
Tan-y-Bwlch
Maentwrog
Gellilydan
Penrhyndeudraeth
Amphitheatre
Llyn Conwy
669 CARNEDD Y-FILAST
690 ARENIG FACH
611 FOEL GOCH
Llyn Celyn
Ciltalgarth
Fron-goch
Cynwyd
Llandderfel
631 MOEL FFERNA
A55
A470
A547
A548
A544
A543
A525
A5
A4086
A498
A496
A487
A4212
A494
A5104
B5381
B5382
B5383
B5384
B5113
B5106
B5105
B4501
B4407
B4391
B4406
0 1 2 3 4 miles
0 1 2 3 4 5 kilometres

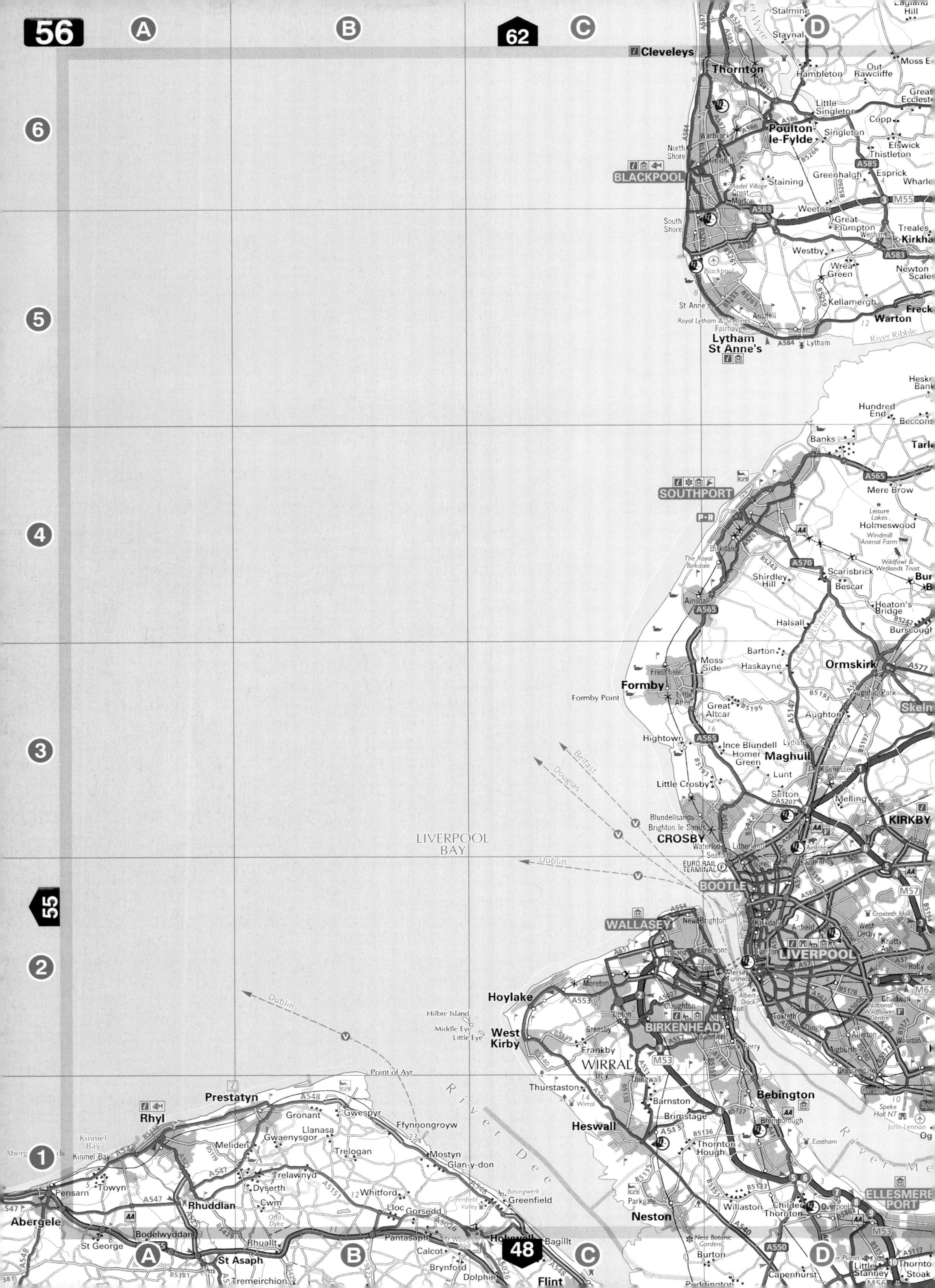

56
A
B
62
C
D
6
5
4
3
2
1
55
48
Cleveleys
Stalmine
Staynall
Thornton
Hambleton
Out Rawcliffe
Moss Edge
Great Eccleston
Little Singleton
Poulton-le-Fylde
Singleton
Copp
Elswick
Thistleton
North Shore
BLACKPOOL
Staining
Model Village
Great Marton
Greenhalgh
Esprick
Wharles
M55
Weeton
Great Plumpton
Wesham
Treales
Kirkham
South Shore
Westby
Wrea Green
Newton
Scales
Blackpool
Kellamergh
Warton
Freckleton
St Anne's
Royal Lytham & St Annes
Ansdell
Fairhaven
Lytham St Anne's
Lytham
River Ribble
Hesketh Bank
Hundred End
Becconsall
Banks
Tarleton
SOUTHPORT
Mere Brow
Leisure Lakes
Holmeswood
Windmill Animal Farm
Birkdale
The Royal Birkdale
Wildfowl & Wetlands Trust
Scarisbrick
Shirdley Hill
Bescar
Ainsdale
Heaton's Bridge
Halsall
Burscough
Barton
Moss Side
Haskayne
Ormskirk
Freshfield
Formby
Formby Point
Little Altcar
Great Altcar
Aughton Park
Aughton
Skelmersdale
Hightown
Ince Blundell
Lydiate
Homer Green
Maghull
Belfast
Douglas
Lunt
Little Crosby
Sefton
Melling
Blundellsands
Brighton le Sands
KIRKBY
CROSBY
LIVERPOOL BAY
Waterloo
Litherland
Aintree
Seaforth
EURO RAIL TERMINAL
Dublin
BOOTLE
Croxteth Hall
New Brighton
WALLASEY
Kirkdale
Anfield
West Derby
Knotty Ash
Liscard
Egremont
Everton
LIVERPOOL
Roby
Moreton
Mersey Tunnels
Toll
Hoylake
Albert Dock
Upton
Claughton
Childwall
National Wildflower Centre
Hilbre Island
Middle Eye
Little Eye
West Kirby
Greasby
BIRKENHEAD
Toxteth
Dingle
Allerton
Woolton
Frankby
Tranmere
Rock Ferry
Aigburth
WIRRAL
Irby
M53
Grassendale
Garston
Point of Ayr
Thurstaston
Thingwall
Bebington
Prestatyn
Wirral
Barnston
Speke Hall NT
John Lennon
Rhyl
Gronant
Gwespyr
Brimstage
Bromborough
Llanasa
Ffynnongroyw
Heswall
Kinmel Bay
Gwaenysgor
Meliden
Trelogan
Thornton Hough
Eastham
River Dee
River Mersey
Abergele Roads
Mostyn
Glan-y-don
Trelawnyd
Dyserth
Towyn
Whitford
Basingwerk Abbey
Greenfield
Pensarn
Rhuddlan
Cwm
Parkgate
Willaston
Childer Thornton
Overpool
ELLESMERE PORT
Lloc
Gorsedd
Offa's Dyke
Greenfield Valley
Neston
Abergele
Bodelwyddan
Pantasaph
Holywell
Bagillt
Ness Botanic Gardens
St George
Rhuallt
Calcot
Burton
Blue Planet
St Asaph
Brynford
Capenhurst
Little Stanney
Thornton-le-Moors
Stoak
Tremeirchion
Dolphin
Flint
Puddington

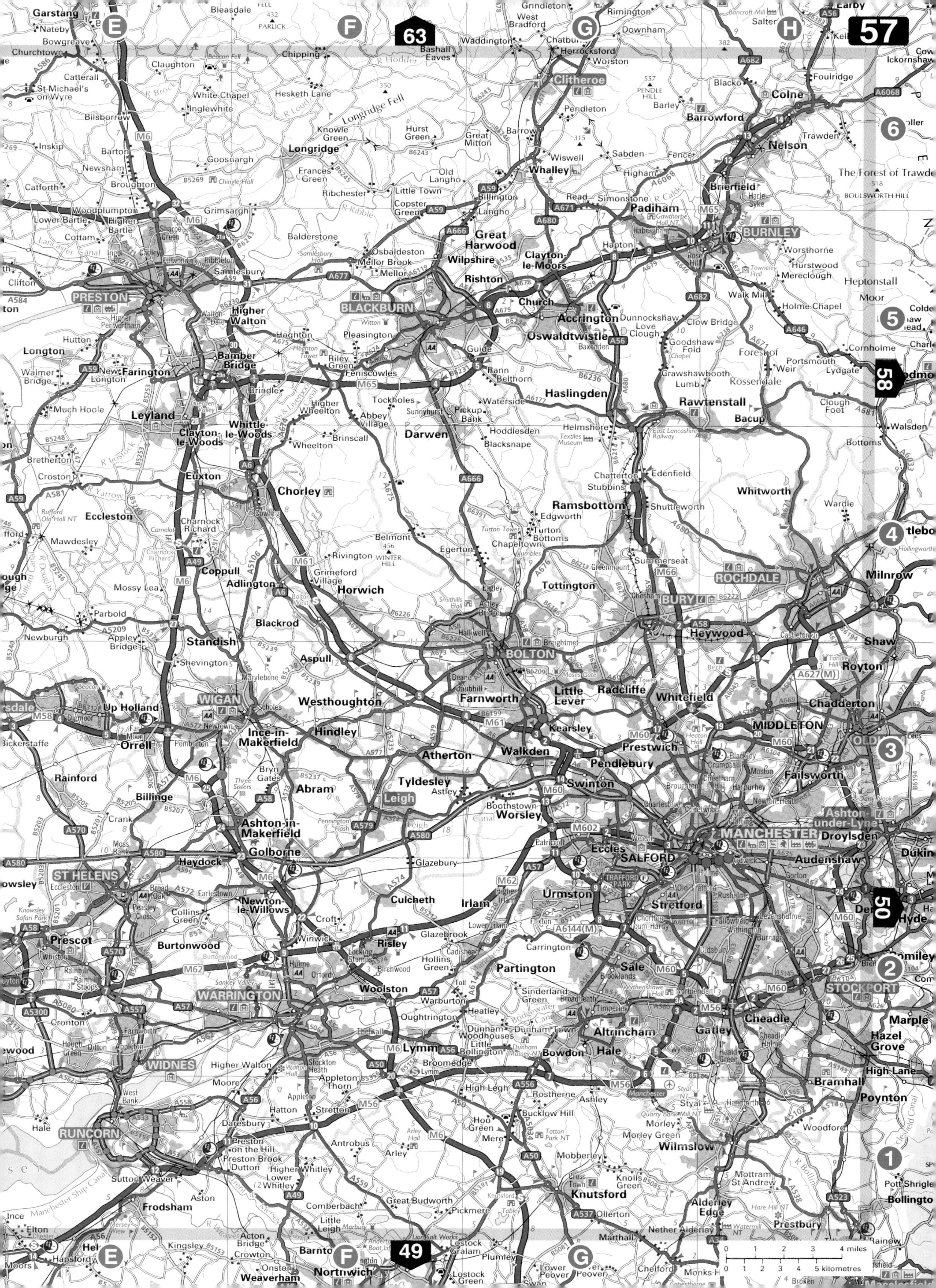

Garstang
Nateby
Bowgreave
Churchtown
Bleasdale
PARLICK
63
Grindleton
West Bradford
Waddington
Chatburn
Rimington
Downham
Horrocksford
Worston
Bashall Eaves
Salter
Earby
Kelbrook
Cowling
Ickornshaw
Catterall
St Michael's on Wyre
Claughton
Beacon Fell
Chipping
R Hodder
Clitheroe
White Chapel
Inglewhite
Hesketh Lane
Longridge Fell
PENDLE HILL
Pendleton
Blacko
Colne
Foulridge
Barley
Barrowford
Bilsborrow
Knowle Green
Hurst Green
Great Mitton
Barrow
Trawden
Nelson
Inskip
Barton
Goosnargh
Longridge
Wiswell
Whalley
Sabden
Fence
Higham
Newsham
Frances Green
Old Langho
Catforth
Broughton
Chingle Hall
Little Town
Ribchester
Billington
Brierfield
Harle Syke
The Forest of Trawden
BOULSWORTH HILL
Woodplumpton
Lower Bartle
Higher Bartle
Grimsargh
Copster Green
Langho
Read
Simonstone
Padiham
Gawthorpe Hall NT
Habergham
Cottam
Sharoe Green
Cadley
Fulwood
Ribbleton
Balderstone
Great Harwood
Clayton-le-Moors
Hapton
BURNLEY
Worsthorne
Hurstwood
Mereclough
Heptonstall Moor
Lancaster Canal
Ingol
Samlesbury
Osbaldeston
Mellor Brook
Mellor
Wilpshire
Rishton
Towneley Hall
Clifton
PRESTON
BLACKBURN
Church
Accrington
Oswaldtwistle
Walk Mill
Holme Chapel
Higher Penwortham
Walton-le-Dale
Higher Walton
Hoghton
Pleasington
Witton
Dunnockshaw
Love Clough
Clow Bridge
Goodshaw Fold
Goodshaw Chapel
Baxenden
Cornholme
Hutton
Longton
Bamber Bridge
Hoghton Tower
Riley Green
Guide
Forest of Rossendale
Portsmouth
Lydgate
Walmer Bridge
New Longton
Farington
Feniscowles
Rann
Belthorn
Crawshawbooth
Lumb
Weir
58
Brindle
Tockholes
Sunnyhurst
Pickup Bank
Waterside
Haslingden
Rawtenstall
Bacup
Clough Foot
Much Hoole
Leyland
Clayton-le-Woods
Whittle-le-Woods
Higher Wheelton
Abbey Village
Darwen
Hoddlesden
Blacksnape
Helmshore
Textiles Museum
East Lancashire Railway
Walsden
Bottoms
Bretherton
Wheelton
Brinscall
R Lostock
Croston
Euxton
Chatterton
Stubbins
Edenfield
Whitworth
R Yarrow
Chorley
Ramsbottom
Shuttleworth
Wardle
Rufford Old Hall NT
Eccleston
Charnock Richard
Cowling
Edgworth
Turton Tower
Turton Bottoms
Mawdesley
Belmont
WINTER HILL
Egerton
Chapeltown
Summerseat
Greenmount
Littleborough
Hollingworth
Coppull
Rivington
Grimeford Village
Tottington
ROCHDALE
Milnrow
Mossy Lea
Adlington
Horwich
Smithills Hall
Eagley
Astley Bridge
Chesham
BURY
Parbold
Blackrod
Halliwell
Heywood
Newburgh
Appley Bridge
Standish
Aspull
BOLTON
Breightmet
Castleton
Shaw
Shevington
Marylebone
Deane
Daubhill
Moses Gate
Birch
Royton
Beacon
Up Holland
Digmoor
WIGAN
Scholes
Newtown
Westhoughton
Farnworth
Little Lever
Radcliffe
Whitefield
Chadderton
Skelmersdale
Orrell
Pemberton
Ince-in-Makerfield
Hindley
Kearsley
Prestwich
MIDDLETON
Bickerstaffe
Walkden
Heaton Hall
Blackley
Crumpsall
Moston
OLDHAM
Rainford
Bryn Gates
Three Sisters
Abram
Atherton
Tyldesley
Astley
Leigh
Pendlebury
Swinton
Cheetham Hill
Harpurhey
Newton Heath
Failsworth
Billinge
Boothstown
Worsley
Broughton
Charlestown
Cheetwood
Ashton-under-Lyne
Crank
Ashton-in-Makerfield
Pennington Flash
Canal
Patricroft
MANCHESTER
Droylsden
Moss Bank
Haydock
Golborne
Eccles
SALFORD
Ardwick
Audenshaw
Dukinfield
ST HELENS
Eccleston
Glazebury
TRAFFORD PARK
Hulme
Old Trafford
Rusholme
Gorton
Denton
Hyde
Knowsley
Knowsley Safari Park
Broad Oak
Earlestown
Newton-le-Willows
Peasley Cross
Collins Green
Culcheth
Irlam
Higher Irlam
Urmston
Stretford
Chorlton-cum-Hardy
Fallowfield
Withington
Levenshulme
Prescot
Burtonwood
Croft
Winwick
Glazebrook
Lower Irlam
Flixton
Burnage
Whiston
Locking Stumps
Risley
Cadishead
Carrington
Didsbury
Bredbury
Romiley
Rainhill
Rainhill Stoops
Sankey Valley
Hulme
Orford
Birchwood
Hollins Green
Partington
Sale
Brooklands
WARRINGTON
Woolston
Warburton
Toll
Sinderland Green
Broadheath
Wythenshawe Hall
Northenden
STOCKPORT
Cronton
Farnworth
Appleton
Heatley
Oughtrington
Timperley
Cheadle
Marple
Bridgewater Canal
Dunham Town
Dunham Woodhouses
Altrincham
Gatley
Thelwall
Lymm
Little Bollington
Dunham Massey NT
Hale
Bowdon
Cheadle Hulme
Heald Green
Hazel Grove
Hough Green
Ditton
WIDNES
Higher Walton
Walton Hall
Stockton Heath
Appleton Thorn
Broomedge
Wythenshawe
High Lane
Bramhall
Manchester
Moore
West Bank
High Legh
Rostherne
Ashley
Styal NT
Styal
Handforth
Poynton
Hale
RUNCORN
Hatton
Stretton
Daresbury
Bucklow Hill
Quarry Bank Mill NT
Hoo Green
Mere
Tatton Park NT
Morley
Morley Green
Wilmslow
Woodford
Preston on the Hill
Preston Brook
Dutton
Antrobus
Arley Hall
Arley
Mobberley
Higher Whitley
Lower Whitley
Sutton Weaver
Aston
Great Budworth
Knutsford
Tabley
Cross Town
Knolls Green
Mottram St Andrew
Pott Shrigley
Bollington
Frodsham
Manchester Ship Canal
Comberbach
Pickmere
Alderley Edge
Hare Hill NT
Prestbury
Little Leigh
Marbury
Ollerton
Nether Alderley
Elton
Helsby
Acton Bridge
Crowton
Kingsley
Barnton
Anderton Boat Lift
Lion Salt Works
Lostock Gralam
Plumley
Marthall
Rainow
Hapsford
Moors
Onston
Weaverham
Northwich
Lostock Green
49
Lower Peover
Peover
Chelford
Monks Heath
Broken Cross
Macclesfield
0 1 2 3 4 miles
0 1 2 3 4 5 kilometres

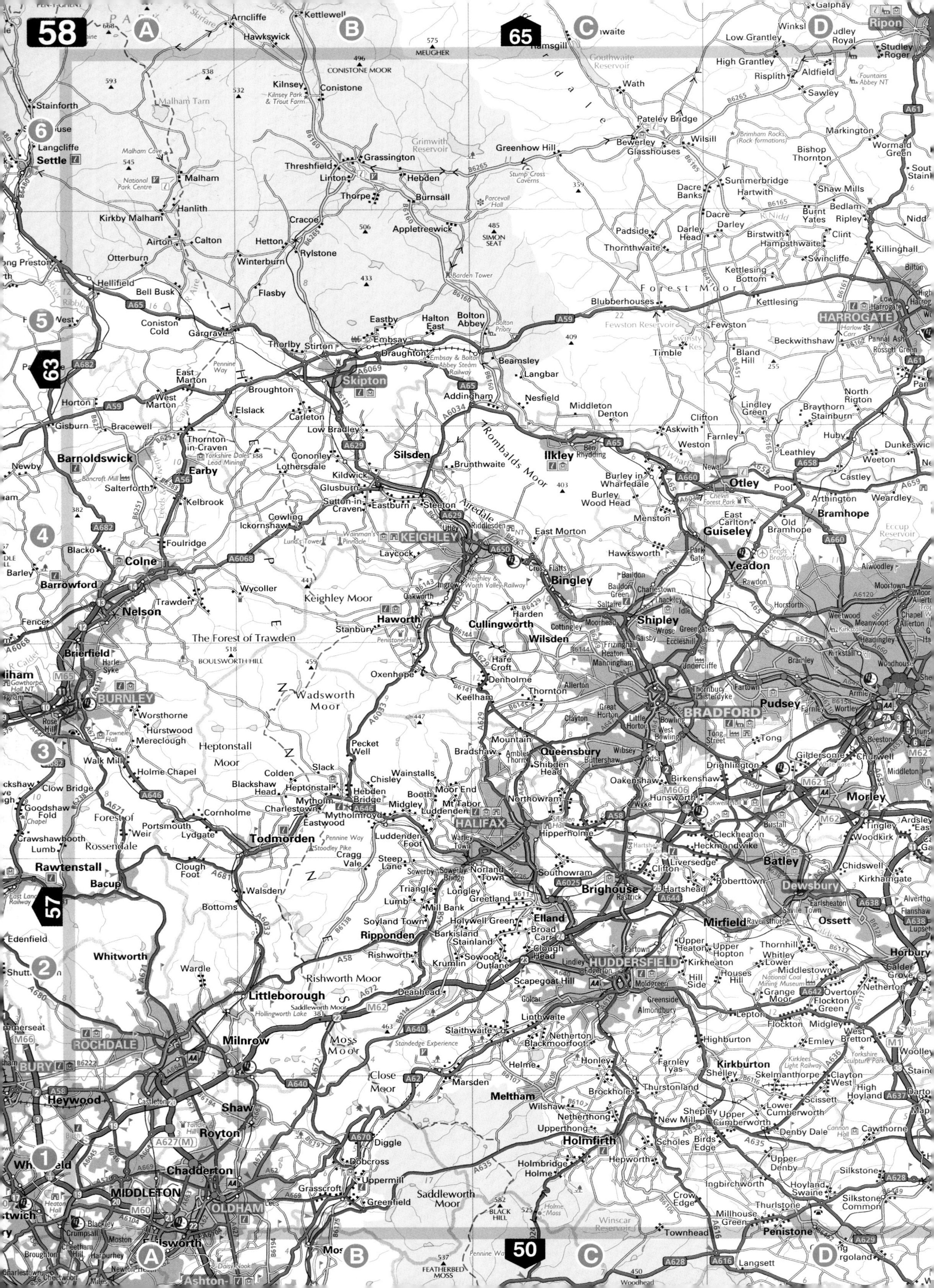

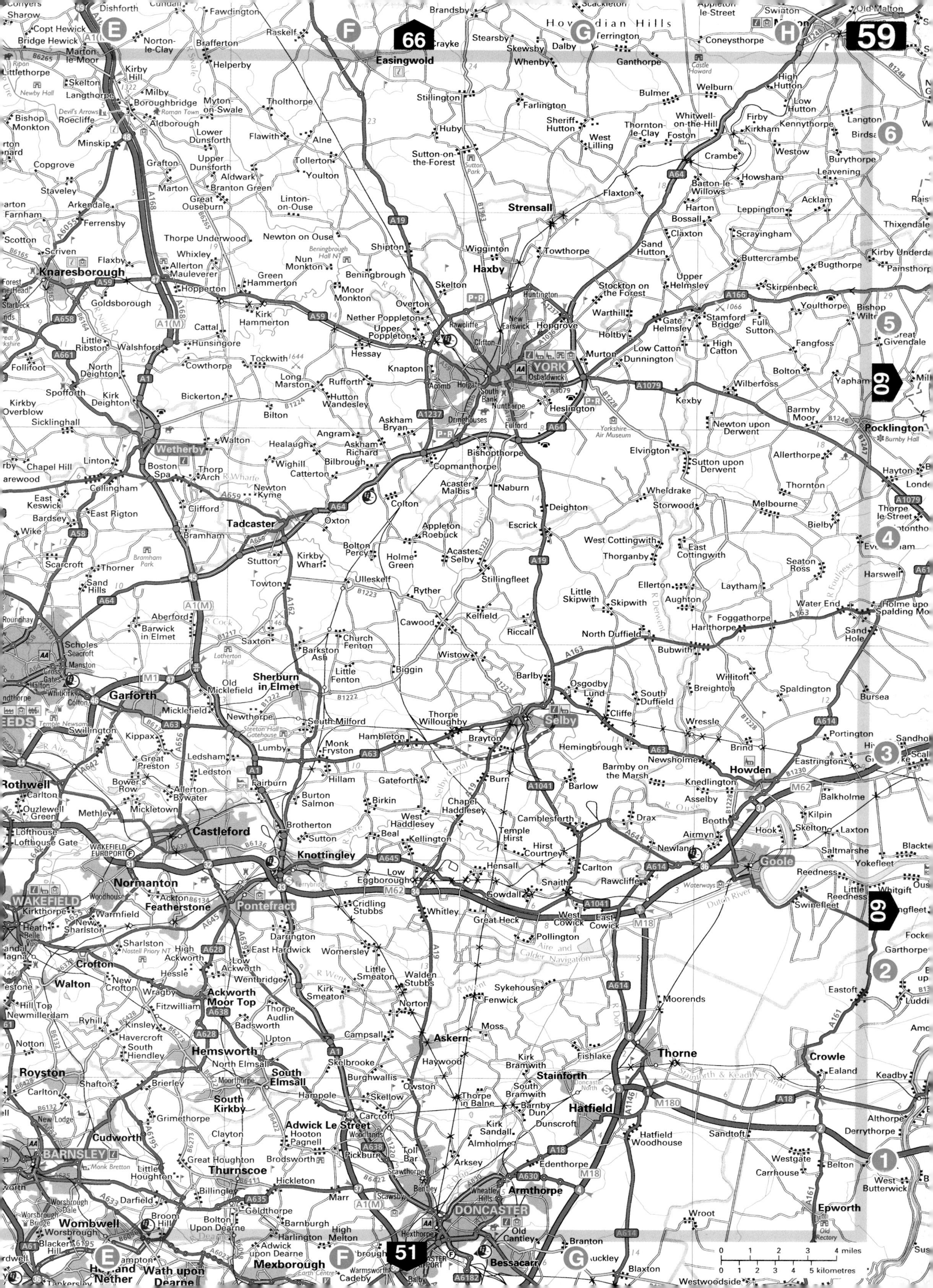

66
59
60
51
E
F
G
H
Dishforth
Sharow
Copt Hewick
Bridge Hewick
Marton-le-Moor
Norton-le-Clay
Brafferton
Fawdington
Raskelf
Brandsby
Crayke
Stearsby
Skewsby
Dalby
Terrington
Howardian Hills
Coneysthorpe
Easingwold
Helperby
Whenby
Ganthorpe
Castle Howard
Littlethorpe
Skelton
Newby Hall
Langthorpe
Kirby Hill
Milby
Boroughbridge
Roman Town
Devil's Arrows
Roecliffe
Aldborough
Myton-on-Swale
Tholthorpe
Stillington
Farlington
Bulmer
Welburn
High Hutton
Low Hutton
Bishop Monkton
Minskip
Lower Dunsforth
Upper Dunsforth
Flawith
Alne
Huby
Sheriff Hutton
West Lilling
Thornton-le-Clay
Whitwell-on-the-Hill
Foston
Firby
Kirkham
Kennythorpe
Langton
Birdsall
Copgrove
Grafton
Aldwark
Tollerton
Youlton
Sutton-on-the-Forest
Sutton Park
Crambe
Westow
Burythorpe
Leavening
Staveley
Marton
Branton Green
Great Ouseburn
Linton-on-Ouse
Strensall
Flaxton
Barton-le-Willows
Howsham
Acklam
Arkendale
Farnham
Ferrensby
Harton
Leppington
Bossall
Claxton
Scrayingham
Thixendale
Scotton
Thorpe Underwood
Newton on Ouse
Beningbrough Hall NT
Shipton
Wigginton
Towthorpe
Sand Hutton
Buttercrambe
Kirby Underdale
Bugthorpe
Scriven
Whixley
Flaxby
Knaresborough
Allerton Mauleverer
Green Hammerton
Nun Monkton
Beningbrough
Haxby
Upper Helmsley
Skirpenbeck
Goldsborough
Hopperton
Moor Monkton
Skelton
Stockton on the Forest
Huntington
Youlthorpe
Bishop Wilton
Kirk Hammerton
Overton
Nether Poppleton
Upper Poppleton
Rawcliffe
New Earswick
Hopgrove
Warthill
Gate Helmsley
Stamford Bridge
Full Sutton
Little Ribston
Walshford
Cattal
Hunsingore
Hessay
Clifton
Holtby
Low Catton
High Catton
Great Givendale
Fangfoss
Follifoot
North Deighton
Tockwith
Cowthorpe
Long Marston
Rufforth
Knapton
YORK
Murton
Dunnington
Osbaldwick
Bolton
Yapham
Spofforth
Kirk Deighton
Bickerton
Hutton Wandesley
Acomb
Holgate
South Bank
Nunthorpe
Heslington
Kexby
Wilberfoss
Kirkby Overblow
Bilton
Askham Bryan
Dringhouses
Fulford
Barmby Moor
Pocklington
Burnby Hall
Sicklinghall
Wetherby
Walton
Healaugh
Angram
Askham Richard
Bishopthorpe
Newton upon Derwent
Yorkshire Air Museum
Elvington
Linton
Boston Spa
Thorp Arch
Wighill
Bilbrough
Catterton
Copmanthorpe
Acaster Malbis
Naburn
Sutton upon Derwent
Allerthorpe
Hayton
Chapel Hill
Collingham
Newton Kyme
Colton
Wheldrake
Thornton
East Keswick
Clifford
Tadcaster
Oxton
Deighton
Storwood
Melbourne
Thorpe le Street
Bardsey
East Rigton
Bramham
Appleton Roebuck
Escrick
Bielby
Wike
Bramham Park
Bolton Percy
Holme Green
Acaster Selby
West Cottingwith
East Cottingwith
Thorganby
Scarcroft
Thorner
Stutton
Kirkby Wharfe
Stillingfleet
Seaton Ross
Sand Hills
Towton
Ulleskelf
Rytherr
Little Skipwith
Skipwith
Ellerton
Aughton
Laytham
Harswell
Aberford
Barwick in Elmet
Cawood
Kelfield
Riccall
North Duffield
Foggathorpe
Harlthorpe
Water End
Holme upon Spalding Moor
Sand Hole
Scholes
Seacroft
Manston
Saxton
Barkston Ash
Church Fenton
Little Fenton
Lotherton Hall
Biggin
Wistow
Bubwith
Cross Gates
Halton
Whitkirk
Old Micklefield
Sherburn in Elmet
Barlby
Osgodby
Lund
South Duffield
Willitoft
Breighton
Spaldington
Bursea
Garforth
Colton
Micklefield
Newthorpe
South Milford
Thorpe Willoughby
Cliffe
Temple Newsam
Swillington
Kippax
Steeton Hall Gatehouse
Lumby
Monk Fryston
Hambleton
Brayton
Selby
Hemingbrough
Wressle
Brind
Portington
Eastrington
Sandholme
Great Preston
Ledsham
Ledston
Hillam
Gateforth
Burn
Barmby on the Marsh
Newsholme
Knedlington
Howden
Rothwell
Bower's Row
Allerton Bywater
Fairburn
Burton Salmon
Birkin
Chapel Haddlesey
Barlow
Asselby
Balkholme
Carlton
Oulzewell Green
Mickletown
Methley
Brotherton
West Haddlesey
Camblesforth
Drax
Booth
Kilpin
Lofthouse
Lofthouse Gate
Castleford
Sutton
Beal
Kellington
Temple Hirst
Hirst Courtney
Airmyn
Hook
Skelton
Laxton
Wakefield Europort
Knottingley
Newland
Goole
Saltmarshe
Blacktoft
Yokefleet
Normanton
Ferrybridge
Low Eggborough
Hensall
Carlton
Rawcliffe
Reedness
Little Reedness
Whitgift
Ousefleet
Woodhouse
Ackton
Pontefract
Gowdall
Snaith
Waterways Museum
Dutch River
Swinefleet
WAKEFIELD
Kirkthorpe
Featherstone
Cridling Stubbs
Whitley
Great Heck
West Cowick
East Cowick
Warmfield
Heath
New Sharlston
Darrington
Pollington
Fockerby
Garthorpe
Sharlston
Nostell Priory NT
High Ackworth
East Hardwick
Womersley
Aire and Calder Navigation
Crofton
Low Ackworth
Little Smeaton
Walden Stubbs
Walton
Hessle
Wentbridge
Kirk Smeaton
Sykehouse
Eastoft
New Crofton
Wragby
Ackworth Moor Top
Fenwick
Moorends
Hill Top
Newmillerdam
Fitzwilliam
Thorpe Audlin
Norton
Ryhill
Kinsley
Badsworth
Campsall
Moss
Havercroft
Notton
South Hiendley
Upton
Askern
Crowle
Hemsworth
North Elmsall
Skelbrooke
Haywood
Kirk Bramwith
Fishlake
Thorne
Ealand
Keadby
Royston
Moorthorpe
South Elmsall
Burghwallis
Stainforth
Doncaster North
Stainforth & Keadby Canal
Shafton
Brierley
Hampole
Owston
Thorpe in Balne
South Bramwith
Carlton
South Kirkby
Skellow
Barnby Dun
Hatfield
Grimethorpe
Carcroft
Kirk Sandall
Dunscroft
Althorpe
New Lodge
Adwick Le Street
Woodlands
Hooton Pagnell
Clayton
Almholme
Hatfield Woodhouse
Sandtoft
Derrythorpe
Cudworth
BARNSLEY
Monk Bretton
Little Houghton
Great Houghton
Brodsworth
Pickburn
Toll Bar
Arksey
Edenthorpe
Westgate
Belton
Carrhouse
West Butterwick
Thurnscoe
Scawthorpe
Bentley
Wheatley Hills
Armthorpe
Hickleton
Billingley
Darfield
Goldthorpe
Marr
Scawsby
DONCASTER
Epworth
Worsbrough
Worsbrough Bridge
Wombwell
Broom Hill
Bolton upon Dearne
Barnburgh
High Melton
Hexthorpe
Old Cantley
Wroot
Old Rectory
Worsbrough Dale
Blacker Hill
Harlington
Adwick upon Dearne
Branton
Hemingfield
Wath upon Dearne
Mexborough
Earth Centre
Warmsworth
Cadeby
Bessacarr
Auckley
Blaxton
Westwoodside
Balby
Tankersley
Hoyland Nether
A1(M)
A1
A19
A64
A59
A168
A166
A1079
A1237
A163
A63
A645
A1041
A614
A162
A656
A659
A661
A658
A58
A628
A638
A639
A645
A614
A18
A630
A633
A635
A161
M1
M18
M62
M180
B1222
B1223
B1224
B1228
B1230
B1246
B1247
B1248
B1363
B6265
B6165
B1217
B6136
B6134
B6273
B6422
B6411
B6428
B6132
B6098
P+R
0 1 2 3 4 miles
0 1 2 3 4 5 kilometres

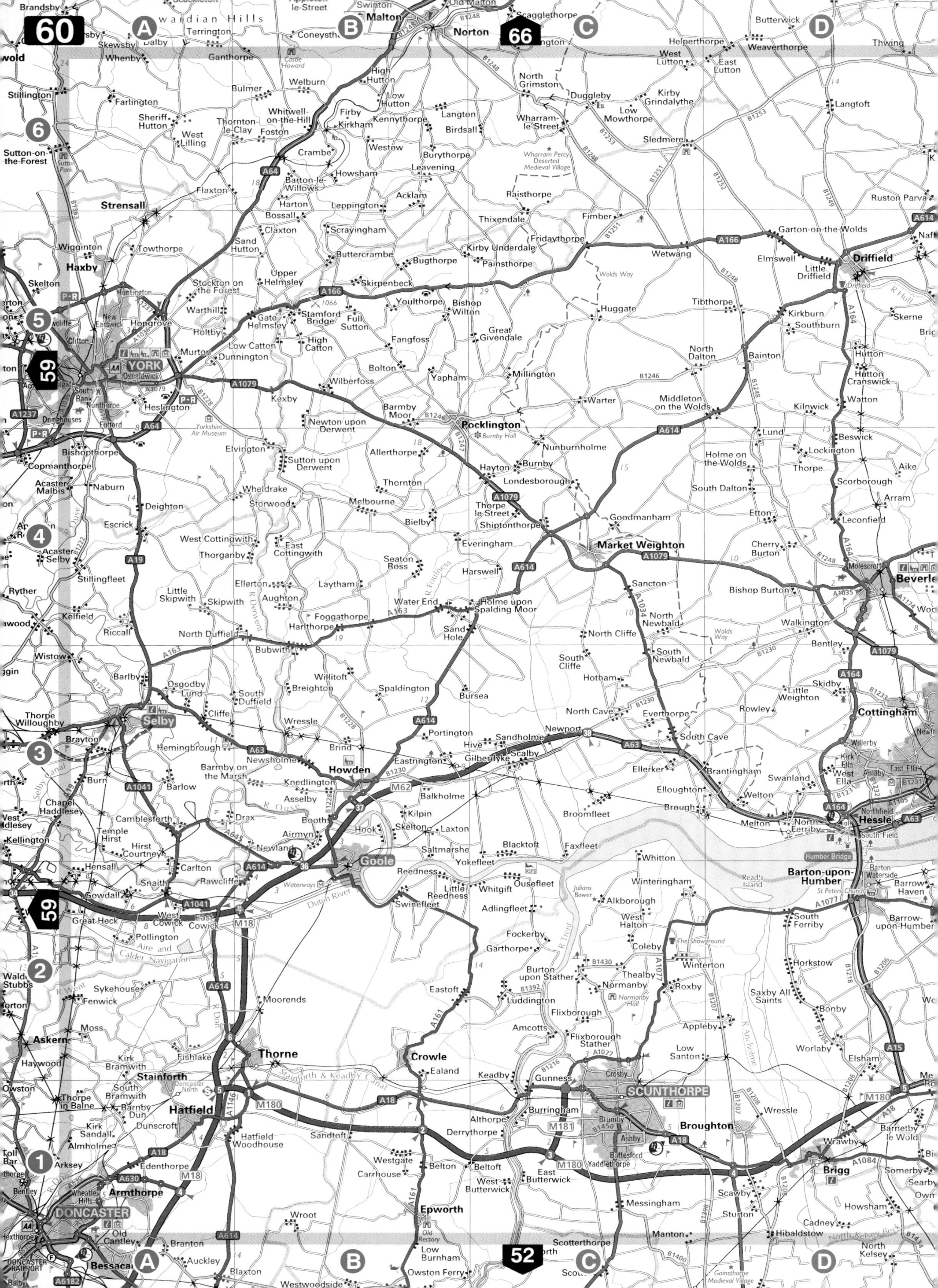

60
A
B
C
D
66
Howardian Hills
Brandsby
Skewsby
Dalby
Terrington
Coneysthorpe
Malton
Old Malton
Norton
Scagglethorpe
Swinton
Appleton-le-Street
Butterwick
Helperthorpe
Weaverthorpe
Thwing
West Lutton
East Lutton
Whenby
Ganthorpe
Castle Howard
Stillington
Farlington
Sheriff Hutton
West Lilling
Bulmer
Welburn
Whitwell-on-the-Hill
Thornton-le-Clay
Foston
High Hutton
Low Hutton
Firby
Kirkham
Kennythorpe
Langton
Birdsall
North Grimston
Duggleby
Kirby Grindalythe
Low Mowthorpe
Wharram-le-Street
Sledmere
Langtoft
6
Sutton-on-the-Forest
Sutton Park
Crambe
Westow
Burythorpe
Howsham
Barton-le-Willows
Leavening
Wharram Percy Deserted Medieval Village
Flaxton
Strensall
Harton
Acklam
Raisthorpe
Bossall
Leppington
Ruston Parva
Claxton
Scrayingham
Thixendale
Fimber
Garton-on-the-Wolds
Wigginton
Towthorpe
Sand Hutton
Buttercrambe
Fridaythorpe
Kirby Underdale
Painsthorpe
Bugthorpe
Wetwang
Elmswell
Little Driffield
Driffield
Haxby
Upper Helmsley
Stockton on the Forest
Skirpenbeck
Wolds Way
Skelton
Huntington
Youlthorpe
Bishop Wilton
Tibthorpe
Huggate
Kirkburn
Southburn
Skerne
5
Warthill
Gate Helmsley
Stamford Bridge
Full Sutton
High Catton
Great Givendale
Hopgrove
Holtby
New Earswick
Clifton
Fangfoss
North Dalton
Bainton
Hutton
Hutton Cranswick
59
YORK
Osbaldwick
Murton
Low Catton
Dunnington
Bolton
Millington
Yapham
Wilberfoss
Kexby
Heslington
Fulford
Dringhouses
South Bank
Nunthorpe
Barmby Moor
Newton upon Derwent
Pocklington
Burnby Hall
Warter
Middleton on the Wolds
Kilnwick
Watton
Yorkshire Air Museum
Bishopthorpe
Copmanthorpe
Elvington
Sutton upon Derwent
Allerthorpe
Nunburnholme
Lund
Beswick
Lockington
Holme on the Wolds
Thorpe
Aike
Hayton
Burnby
Londesborough
Scorborough
Acaster Malbis
Naburn
Thornton
Wheldrake
Storwood
Melbourne
South Dalton
Arram
Deighton
Thorpe le Street
Shiptonthorpe
Bielby
Goodmanham
Etton
Leconfield
Escrick
4
Acaster Selby
West Cottingwith
East Cottingwith
Thorganby
Seaton Ross
Everingham
Market Weighton
Cherry Burton
Stillingfleet
Molescroft
Beverley
Ellerton
Laytham
Harswell
Sancton
Bishop Burton
Ryther
Little Skipwith
Skipwith
Aughton
Water End
Holme upon Spalding Moor
Kelfield
Foggathorpe
Harlthorpe
North Newbald
Walkington
Riccall
North Duffield
Sand Hole
North Cliffe
Bentley
Wistow
Bubwith
South Cliffe
South Newbald
Barlby
Osgodby
Lund
Willitoft
Breighton
Spaldington
Bursea
Hotham
Skidby
Little Weighton
South Duffield
Cliffe
Thorpe Willoughby
Selby
Wressle
Portington
North Cave
Everthorpe
Rowley
Cottingham
Brayton
3
Hemingbrough
Newsholme
Brind
Hive
Sandholme
Newport
Gilberdyke
Scalby
Eastrington
South Cave
Willerby
Burn
Barmby on the Marsh
Barlow
Knedlington
Howden
Balkholme
Ellerker
Brantingham
Swanland
Kirk Ella
West Ella
Anlaby
Chapel Haddlesey
Asselby
Camblesforth
Drax
Booth
Kilpin
Elloughton
Welton
Brough
Melton
North Ferriby
Hessle
Temple Hirst
West Haddlesey
Kellington
Hirst Courtney
Airmyn
Newland
Hook
Skelton
Laxton
Saltmarshe
Broomfleet
Blacktoft
Faxfleet
Humber Bridge
South Field
Carlton
Snaith
Rawcliffe
Goole
Reedness
Yokefleet
Whitton
Hensall
Gowdall
Little Reedness
Whitgift
Ousefleet
Read's Island
Winteringham
Barton-upon-Humber
Barton Waterside
St Peters Church
Barrow Haven
Waterways
Dutch River
Swinefleet
Julians Bower
Alkborough
West Halton
South Ferriby
Barrow-upon-Humber
Great Heck
West Cowick
East Cowick
Adlingfleet
Pollington
Aire and Calder Navigation
Fockerby
Garthorpe
Coleby
The Showground
2
Walden Stubbs
R Went
Sykehouse
Fenwick
Burton upon Stather
Thealby
Normanby
Normanby Hall
Winterton
Roxby
Horkstow
Saxby All Saints
Moorends
Eastoft
Luddington
Flixborough
Bonby
Norton
Askern
Moss
Amcotts
Flixborough Stather
Appleby
Worlaby
Kirk Bramwith
Fishlake
Thorne
Crowle
Low Santon
Elsham
Haywood
Stainforth
Doncaster North
Ealand
Keadby
Gunness
Crosby
SCUNTHORPE
Owston
South Bramwith
Stainforth & Keadby Canal
Thorpe in Balne
Barnby Dun
Hatfield
Burringham
Brumby
Wressle
Broughton
Kirk Sandall
Dunscroft
Althorpe
Ashby
Barnetby le Wold
Almholme
Hatfield Woodhouse
Sandtoft
Derrythorpe
Bottesford
Yaddlethorpe
Wrawby
1
Toll Bar
Arksey
Edenthorpe
Westgate
Belton
Beltoft
East Butterwick
West Butterwick
Brigg
Somerby
Searby
Bentley
Wheatley Hills
Armthorpe
Carrhouse
Scawby
Messingham
Howsham
DONCASTER
Wroot
Epworth
Old Rectory
Sturton
Cadney
Hexthorpe
Old Cantley
Branton
Manton
Hibaldstow
North Kelsey Beck
North Kelsey
Doncaster Railport
Bessacarr
Auckley
Low Burnham
Scotterthorpe
Gainsthorpe Medieval Village
Balby
Blaxton
Westwoodside
Owston Ferry
52
A64
A166
A1079
A614
A163
A19
A63
A1041
A645
A614
M62
A1034
A164
A1035
A1174
A1079
A63
A1105
A164
A1077
A15
A18
M180
M181
A1146
M18
A630
A6182
A161
A1084
A1237
A1036
B1248
B1253
B1251
B1252
B1249
B1363
B1228
B1246
B1247
B1222
B1223
B1230
B1233
B1231
B1232
B1430
B1392
B1216
B1450
B1207
B1208
B1206
B1218
B1204
B1398
B1205
B1400
B1434
R Ouse
R Derwent
R Foulness
R Hull
R Trent
R Don
R Ancholme
Selby Canal

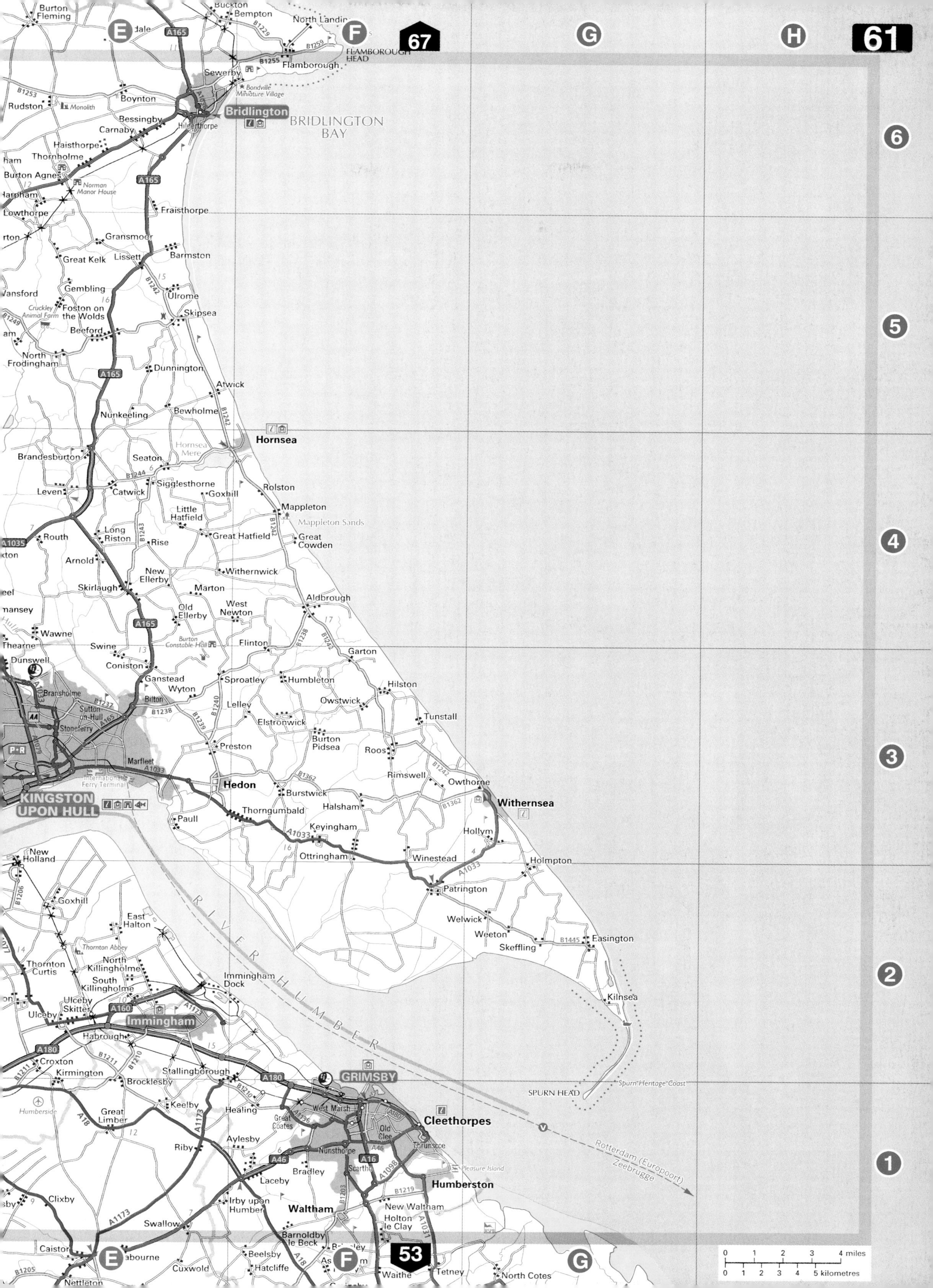

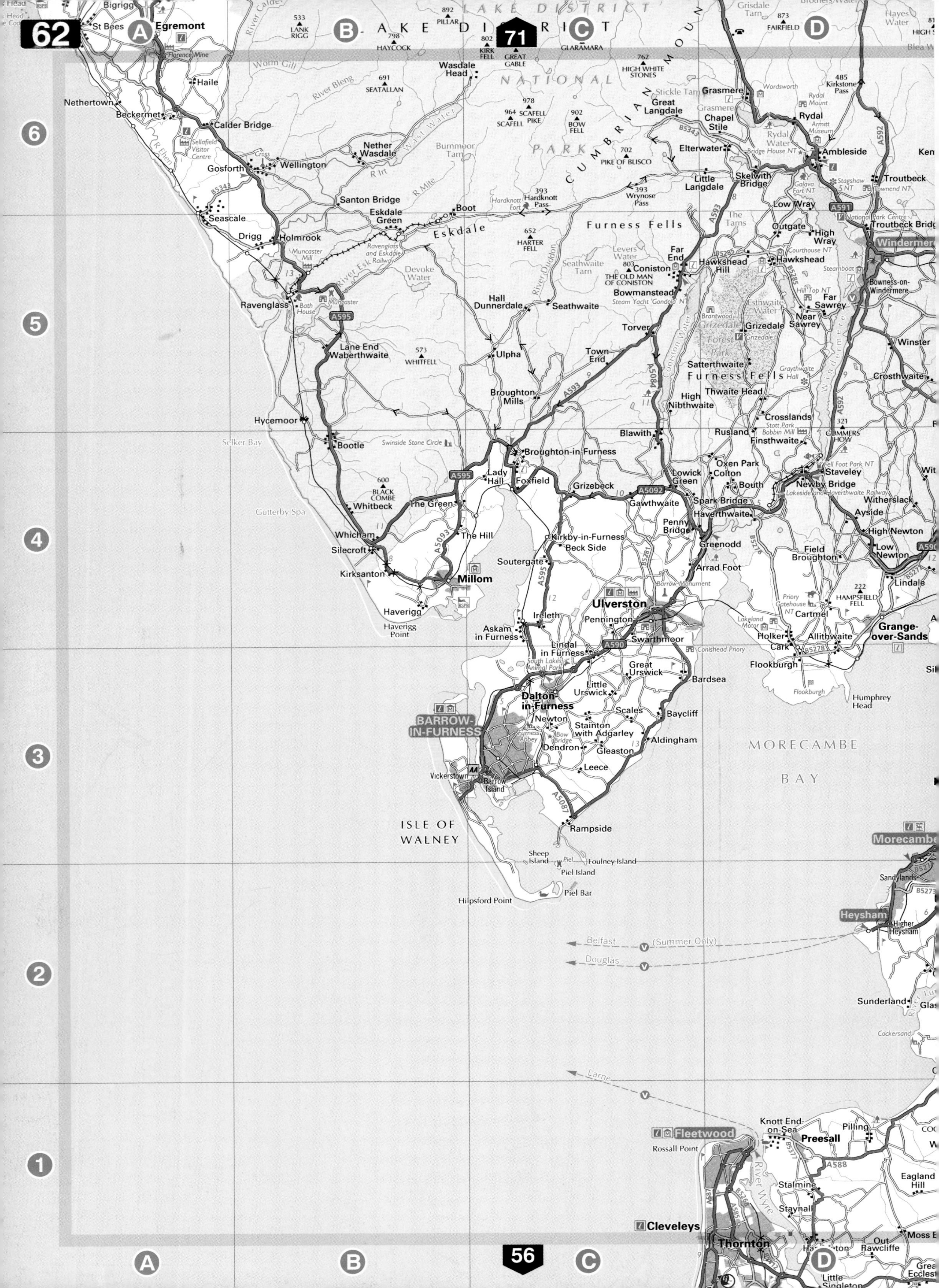
A
B
C
D
71
56
1
2
3
4
5
6
LAKE DISTRICT NATIONAL PARK
CUMBRIAN MOUNTAINS
St Bees
Bigrigg
Egremont
Florence Mine
Haile
Nethertown
Beckermet
Calder Bridge
Sellafield Visitor Centre
Gosforth
Wellington
Nether Wasdale
Wast Water
Burnmoor Tarn
Wasdale Head
533 LANK RIGG
798 HAYCOCK
892 PILLAR
802 KIRK FELL
GREAT GABLE
GLARAMARA
762 HIGH WHITE STONES
691 SEATALLAN
978 SCAFELL PIKE
964 SCAFELL
902 BOW FELL
702 PIKE OF BLISCO
393 Hardknott Pass
393 Wrynose Pass
Hardknott Fort
Grisdale Tarn
873 FAIRFIELD
Hayes Water
Grasmere
Wordsworth
Stickle Tarn
Great Langdale
Chapel Stile
Rydal
Rydal Mount
Rydal Water
Armitt Museum
485 Kirkstone Pass
Ambleside
Elterwater
Bridge House NT
Little Langdale
Skelwith Bridge
Troutbeck
Stagshaw NT
Townend NT
Galava Fort NT
Low Wray
National Park Centre
Troutbeck Bridge
Windermere
Outgate
High Wray
Courthouse NT
Hawkshead
Hawkshead Hill
Steamboat
Bowness-on-Windermere
Hill Top NT
Far Sawrey
Near Sawrey
Esthwaite Water
Grizedale
Grizedale Forest Park
Brantwood
Satterthwaite
Furness Fells
Graythwaite Hall
Winster
Crosthwaite
Seascale
Drigg
Holmrook
Santon Bridge
Eskdale Green
Boot
Eskdale
Muncaster Mill
Ravenglass and Eskdale Railway
Ravenglass
Bath House
Muncaster
River Esk
Devoke Water
652 HARTER FELL
Seathwaite Tarn
River Duddon
Levers Water
803 THE OLD MAN OF CONISTON
Coniston
Far End
Bowmanstead
Steam Yacht 'Gondola' NT
Coniston Water
Hall Dunnerdale
Seathwaite
Torver
Town End
Lane End Waberthwaite
573 WHITFELL
Ulpha
Broughton Mills
High Nibthwaite
Thwaite Head
Crosslands
Stott Park Bobbin Mill
Rusland
Finsthwaite
321 GUMMERS HOW
Fell Foot Park NT
Staveley
Newby Bridge
Lakeside and Haverthwaite Railway
Witherslack
Hycemoor
Selker Bay
Bootle
Swinside Stone Circle
Blawith
Broughton-in-Furness
Lady Hall
Foxfield
Grizebeck
Gawthwaite
Lowick Green
Oxen Park
Colton
Bouth
Spark Bridge
Haverthwaite
Ayside
High Newton
Low Newton
600 BLACK COMBE
Whitbeck
The Green
Gutterby Spa
Whicham
Silecroft
The Hill
Kirksanton
Millom
Haverigg
Haverigg Point
Kirkby-in-Furness
Beck Side
Soutergate
Penny Bridge
Greenodd
Arrad Foot
Field Broughton
Lindale
Barrow Monument
Ulverston
Pennington
Ireleth
Askam in Furness
Swarthmoor
Priory Gatehouse NT
Cartmel
222 HAMPSFIELD FELL
Lakeland Motor
Holker
Cark
Allithwaite
Grange-over-Sands
Conishead Priory
Flookburgh
Lindal in Furness
South Lakes Animal Park
Great Urswick
Bardsea
Little Urswick
Humphrey Head
Dalton-in-Furness
BARROW-IN-FURNESS
Newton
Furness Abbey
Bow Bridge
Stainton with Adgarley
Scales
Baycliff
Aldingham
Dendron
Gleaston
Leece
MORECAMBE BAY
Vickerstown
Barrow Island
ISLE OF WALNEY
Rampside
Sheep Island
Piel
Piel Island
Foulney Island
Piel Bar
Hilpsford Point
Morecambe
Sandylands
Heysham
Higher Heysham
Belfast (Summer Only)
Douglas
Larne
Sunderland
Cockersand
Fleetwood
Rossall Point
Knott End-on-Sea
Preesall
Pilling
Eagland Hill
River Wyre
Stalmine
Staynall
Cleveleys
Thornton
Out Rawcliffe
Moss Edge
Little Singleton
Great Eccleston
A595
A593
A5092
A5084
A5093
A590
A5087
A591
A592
A588
B5343
B5285
B5278
B5277
B5273
B5377
B5268

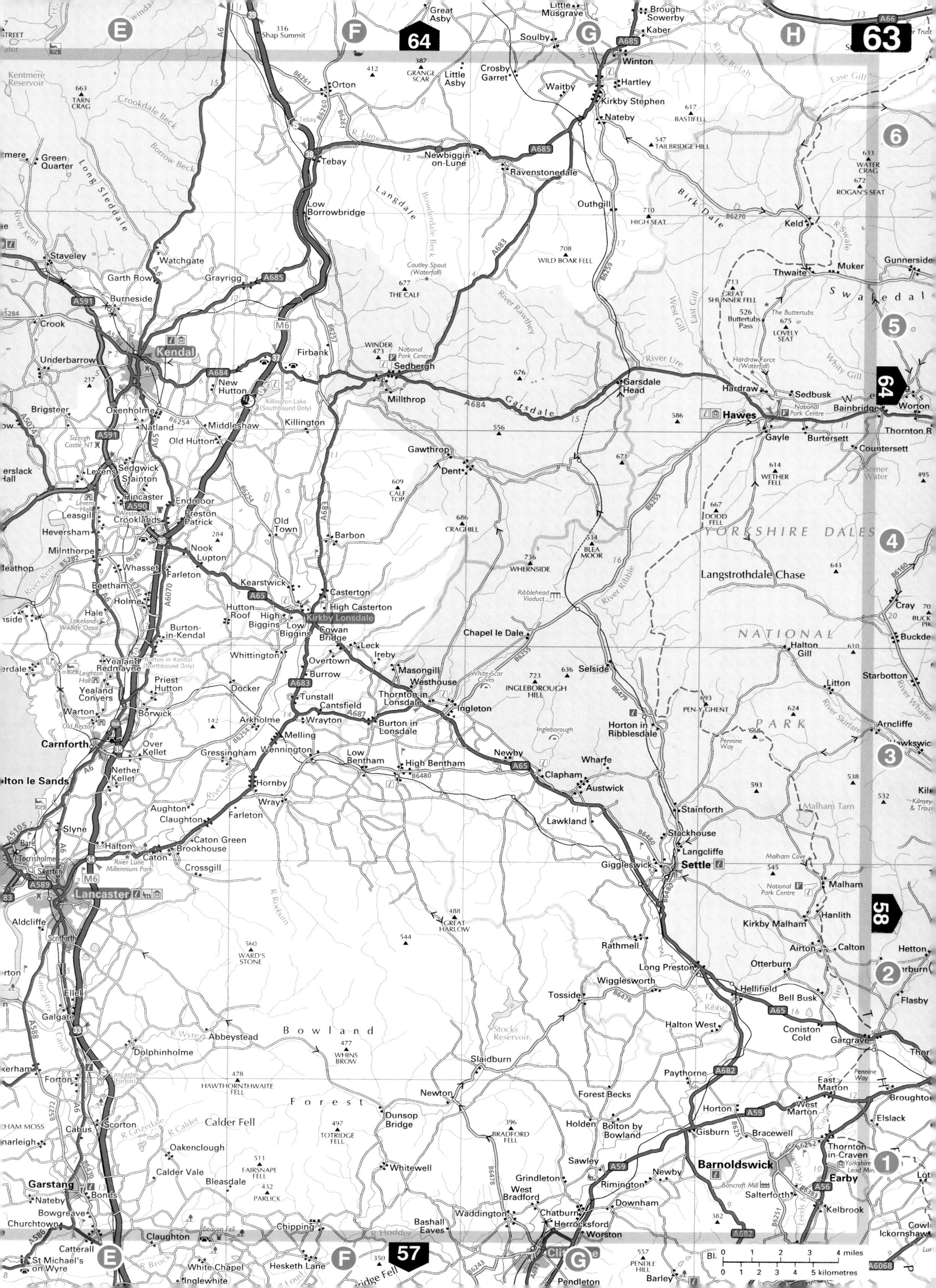

64
63
58
57
Kendal
Lancaster
Kirkby Lonsdale
Sedbergh
Hawes
Settle
Kirkby Stephen
Tebay
Orton
Shap Summit
Ravenstonedale
Garsdale Head
Dent
Ingleton
Clapham
Bentham
Hornby
Carnforth
Garstang
Slaidburn
Gisburn
Barnoldswick
Earby
Hellifield
Malham
Keld
Muker
Thwaite
YORKSHIRE DALES
NATIONAL PARK
Langstrothdale Chase
Bowland
Forest
Calder Fell
Whernside
Ingleborough Hill
Pen-y-Ghent

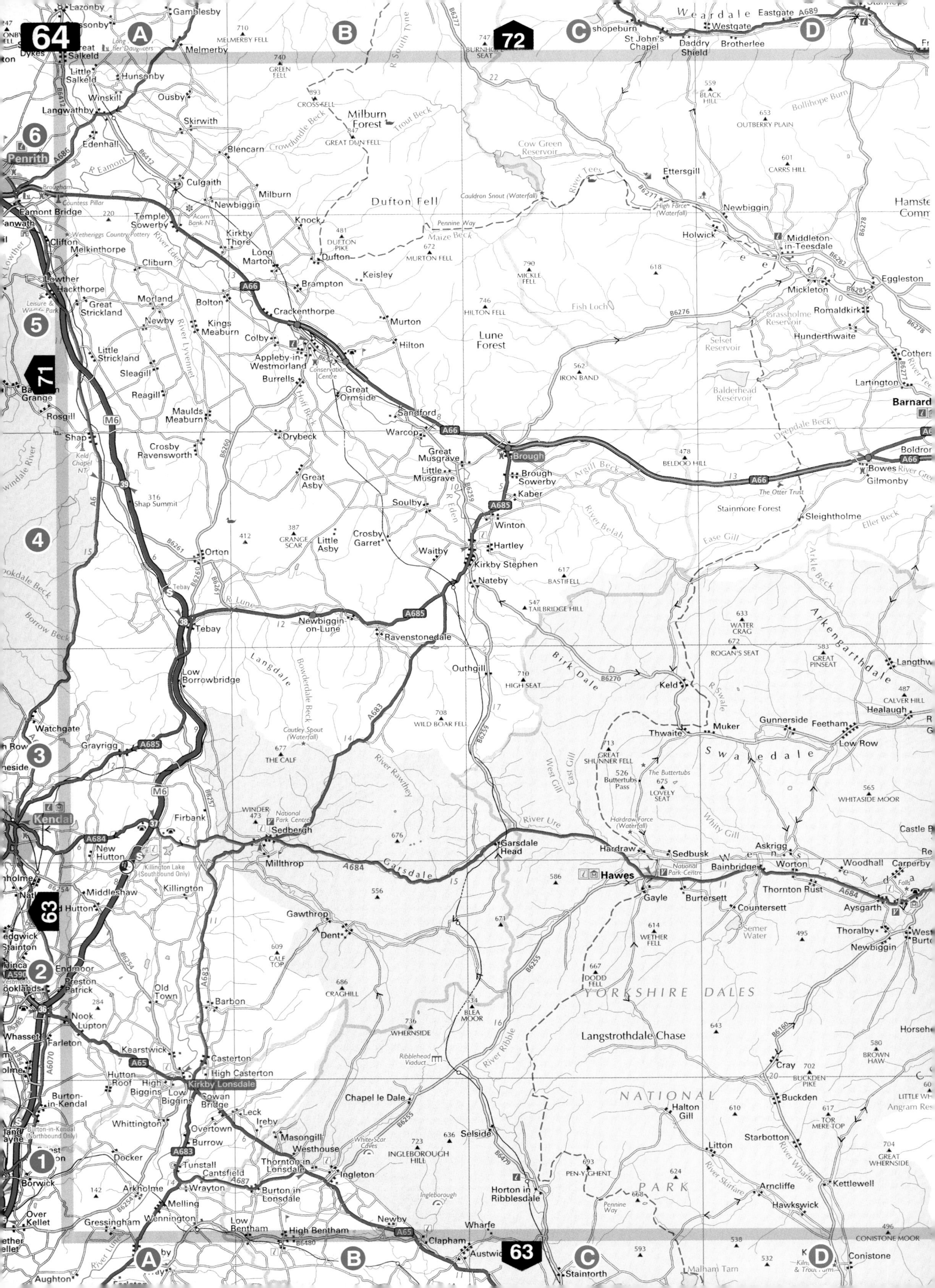

64
A
B
C
D
72
71
63
6
5
4
3
2
1
Lazonby
Gamblesby
Great Salkeld
Little Salkeld
Hunsonby
Melmerby
MELMERBY FELL
GREEN FELL
Winskill
Ousby
Langwathby
Skirwith
Edenhall
Penrith
Blencarn
Culgaith
Milburn
Newbiggin
Eamont Bridge
Brougham
Countess Pillar
Temple Sowerby
Acorn Bank NT
Clifton
Melkinthorpe
Kirkby Thore
Long Marton
Knock
DUFTON PIKE
Dufton
Cliburn
Lowther
Hackthorpe
Great Strickland
Morland
Bolton
Kings Meaburn
Newby
Brampton
Keisley
Crackenthorpe
Colby
Appleby-in-Westmorland
Conservation Centre
Murton
Hilton
Little Strickland
Sleagill
Reagill
Burrells
Great Ormside
Sandford
Maulds Meaburn
Bampton Grange
Rosgill
Shap
Keld Chapel NT
Shap Summit
Crosby Ravensworth
Drybeck
Warcop
Great Musgrave
Little Musgrave
Brough
Brough Sowerby
Kaber
Great Asby
Soulby
Winton
Hartley
Kirkby Stephen
Nateby
Waitby
Crosby Garrett
Little Asby
GRANGE SCAR
Orton
Tebay
Newbiggin-on-Lune
Ravenstonedale
Low Borrowbridge
Langdale
Bowderdale Beck
Cautley Spout (Waterfall)
THE CALF
Outhgill
HIGH SEAT
WILD BOAR FELL
Watchgate
Grayrigg
Kendal
Firbank
Sedbergh
National Park Centre
Millthrop
Garsdale
Garsdale Head
New Hutton
Killington Lake (Southbound Only)
Killington
Middleshaw
Gawthrop
Dent
CALF TOP
CRAGHILL
Endmoor
Preston Patrick
Old Town
Barbon
Nook
Lupton
Farleton
Kearstwick
Casterton
High Casterton
Kirkby Lonsdale
Cowan Bridge
Hutton Roof
High Biggins
Low Biggins
Burton-in-Kendal
Whittington
Leck
Ireby
Overtown
Burrow
Masongill
Westhouse
Tunstall
Cantsfield
Thornton in Lonsdale
Ingleton
Arkholme
Wrayton
Burton in Lonsdale
Borwick
Melling
Over Kellet
Gressingham
Wennington
Low Bentham
High Bentham
Newby
Clapham
Austwick
Stainforth
Wharfe
Horton in Ribblesdale
Ingleborough
INGLEBOROUGH HILL
White Scar Caves
Chapel le Dale
Selside
Ribblehead Viaduct
WHERNSIDE
BLEA MOOR
PEN-Y-GHENT
Pennine Way
Malham Tarn
Weardale
Eastgate
Westgate
St John's Chapel
Daddry Shield
Brotherlee
Ireshopeburn
BLACK HILL
OUTBERRY PLAIN
Bollihope Burn
CARRS HILL
Ettersgill
Cow Green Reservoir
River Tees
Cauldron Snout (Waterfall)
High Force (Waterfall)
Newbiggin
Holwick
Middleton-in-Teesdale
Eggleston
Mickleton
Romaldkirk
Grassholme Reservoir
Selset Reservoir
Hunderthwaite
Balderhead Reservoir
Cotherstone
Lartington
Barnard Castle
Milburn Forest
CROSS FELL
GREAT DUN FELL
Dufton Fell
MURTON FELL
MICKLE FELL
HILTON FELL
Fish Loch
Lune Forest
IRON BAND
Maize Beck
Deepdale Beck
BELDOO HILL
Bowes
Gilmonby
Boldron
The Otter Trust
Stainmore Forest
Sleightholme
Ellers Beck
Ease Gill
River Belah
Argill Beck
BASTIFELL
TAILBRIDGE HILL
Arkengarthdale
Langthwaite
WATER CRAG
ROGAN'S SEAT
GREAT PINSEAT
Birk Dale
Keld
CALVER HILL
Healaugh
Gunnerside
Feetham
Low Row
Thwaite
Muker
Swaledale
GREAT SHUNNER FELL
Buttertubs Pass
The Buttertubs
LOVELY SEAT
WHITASIDE MOOR
Hardraw Force (Waterfall)
Hardraw
Sedbusk
Askrigg
Hawes
Bainbridge
Worton
Woodhall
Carperby
Gayle
Burtersett
Countersett
Thornton Rust
Aysgarth
Semer Water
Thoralby
Newbiggin
WETHER FELL
DODD FELL
YORKSHIRE DALES
NATIONAL PARK
Langstrothdale Chase
BROWN HAW
Cray
BUCKDEN PIKE
Buckden
Halton Gill
TOR MERE TOP
Starbotton
GREAT WHERNSIDE
Litton
River Skirfare
Arncliffe
Kettlewell
Hawkswick
CONISTONE MOOR
Conistone
River Wharfe
M6
A66
A685
A683
A684
A65
A6
A686
A687
A689
B6277
B6276
B6259
B6255
B6479
B6160
B6254
B6480

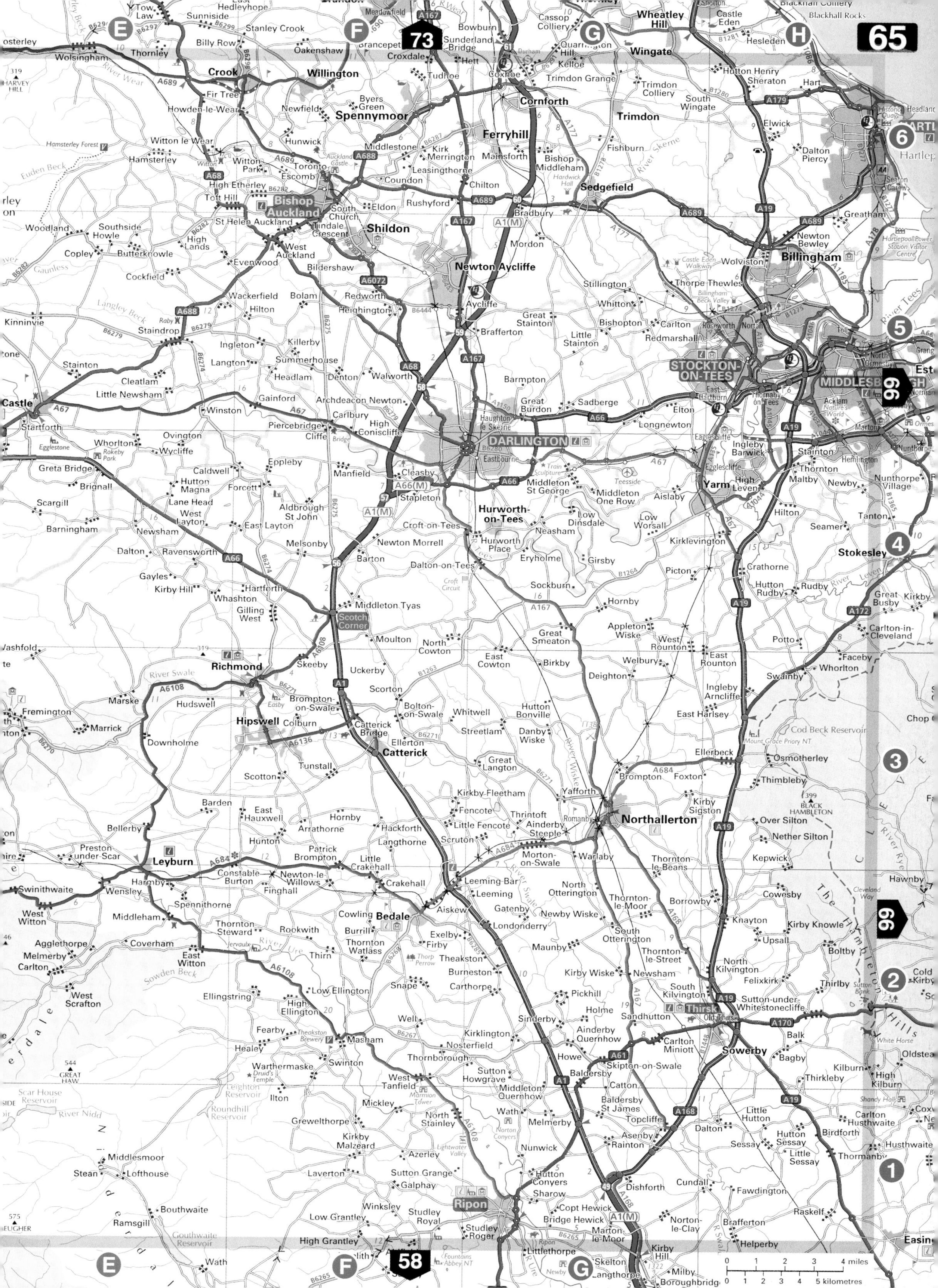
73
58
66
69
E
F
G
H
1
2
3
4
5
6
Darlington
Middlesbrough
Stockton-on-Tees
Bishop Auckland
Northallerton
Richmond
Ripon
Thirsk
Bedale
Leyburn
Yarm
Stokesley
Newton Aycliffe
Spennymoor
Ferryhill
Sedgefield
Billingham
Shildon
Crook
Willington
Catterick
Hipswell
Masham
Sowerby
Scotch Corner
Hurworth-on-Tees
0 1 2 3 4 miles
0 1 2 3 4 5 kilometres

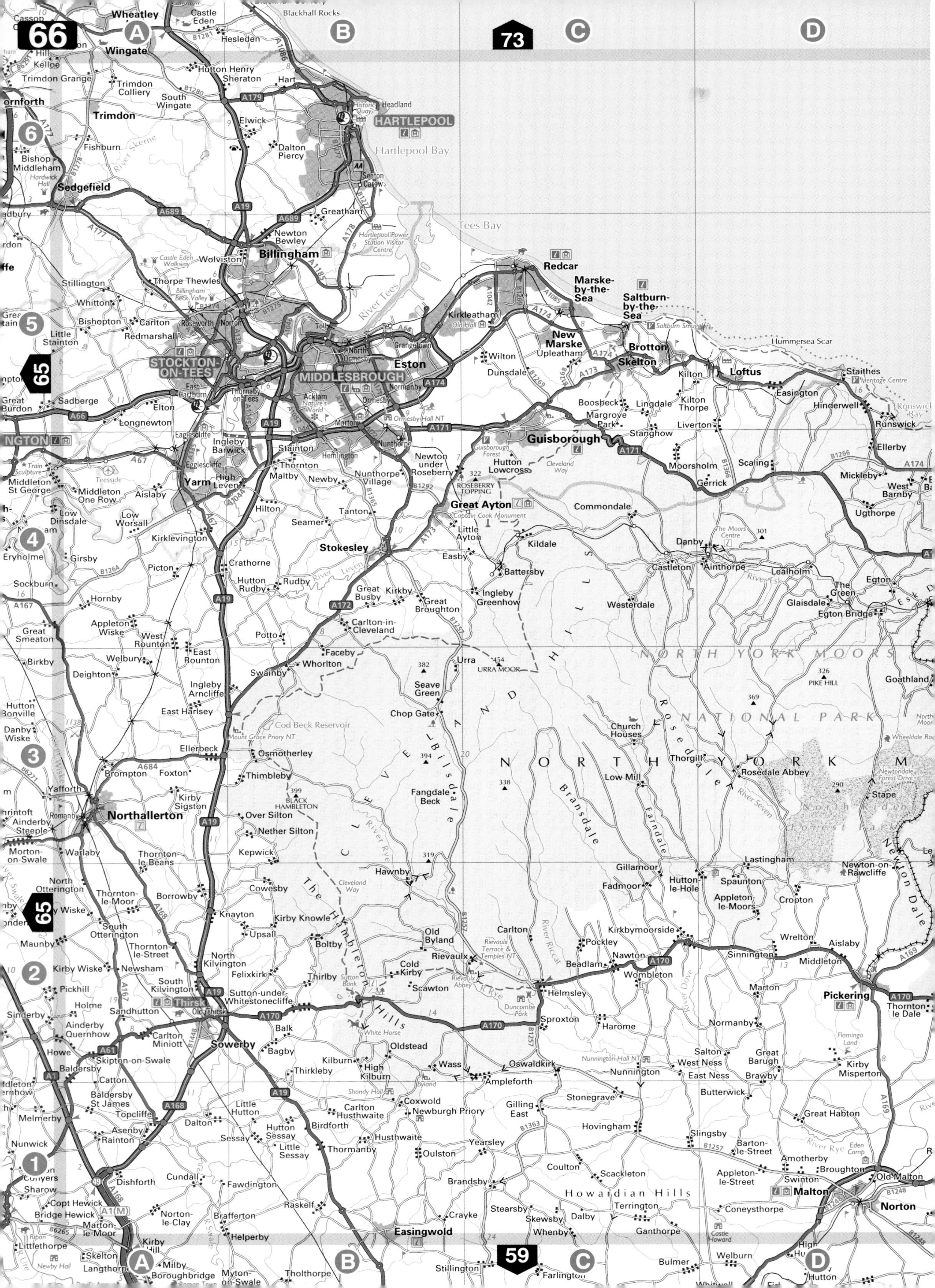

66
A
B
C
D
73
Wheatley
Wingate
Castle Eden
Hesleden
Blackhall Rocks
Hutton Henry
Sheraton
Hart
Trimdon Grange
Trimdon Colliery
South Wingate
Trimdon
Elwick
Headland
HARTLEPOOL
Hartlepool Bay
Fishburn
Dalton Piercy
Bishop Middleham
Hardwick Hall
Sedgefield
Seaton Carew
Greatham
Tees Bay
Newton Bewley
Hartlepool Power Station Visitor Centre
Billingham
Wolviston
Castle Eden Walkway
Thorpe Thewles
Billingham Beck Valley
Stillington
Whitton
Redcar
Marske-by-the-Sea
Saltburn-by-the-Sea
Saltburn Smugglers
Hummersea Scar
Bishopton
Carlton
Redmarshall
Little Stainton
Roseworth
Norton
River Tees
Kirkleatham
Old Hall
New Marske
Upleatham
Brotton
Skelton
Loftus
Staithes
Heritage Centre
STOCKTON-ON-TEES
MIDDLESBROUGH
Grangetown
North Ormesby
Eston
Wilton
Dunsdale
Kilton
Kilton Thorpe
Easington
Hinderwell
Runswick Bay
Runswick
Sadberge
Elton
East Hartburn
Thornaby on Tees
Acklam Nature's World
Normanby
Ormesby
Marton
Ormesby Hall NT
Boosbeck
Lingdale
Margrove Park
Liverton
Stanghow
Longnewton
Eaglescliffe
Ingleby Barwick
Stainton
Hemlington
Nunthorpe
Guisborough
Guisborough Forest
Cleveland Way
Moorsholm
Gerrick
Scaling
Ellerby
Mickleby
West Barnby
Ugthorpe
Middleton St George
Train Sculpture
Teesside
Middleton One Row
Yarm
High Leven
Thornton
Maltby
Newby
Nunthorpe Village
Newton under Roseberry
Hutton Lowcross
Roseberry Topping
322
Great Ayton
Captain Cook Monument
Commondale
Low Dinsdale
Low Worsall
Aislaby
Hilton
Tanton
Seamer
Little Ayton
Kildale
Danby
The Moors Centre
301
Castleton
Ainthorpe
Lealholm
River Esk
Egton
The Green
Glaisdale
Egton Bridge
Eryholme
Girsby
Kirklevington
Stokesley
Easby
Battersby
Sockburn
Picton
Crathorne
Hutton Rudby
Rudby
River Leven
Great Busby
Kirkby
Great Broughton
Ingleby Greenhow
Westerdale
Hornby
Appleton Wiske
West Rounton
East Rounton
Great Smeaton
Potto
Carlton-in-Cleveland
Faceby
Whorlton
Swainby
Birkby
Welbury
Deighton
Ingleby Arncliffe
Urra
382
454
URRA MOOR
Seave Green
NORTH YORK MOORS
326
PIKE HILL
Goathland
Hutton Bonville
East Harlsey
Chop Gate
369
NATIONAL PARK
Danby Wiske
Cod Beck Reservoir
Mount Grace Priory NT
Church Houses
Wheeldale Roman Road
Ellerbeck
Osmotherley
Thorgill
Rosedale Abbey
Brompton
Foxton
Thimbleby
394
338
Bilsdale
Bransdale
Rosedale
Low Mill
Newtondale Forest Drive
290
Stape
Yafforth
399
BLACK HAMBLETON
Kirby Sigston
Fangdale Beck
Farndale
River Seven
North Riding Forest Park
Romanby
Northallerton
Over Silton
Ainderby Steeple
Nether Silton
CLEVELAND HILLS
NORTH YORK
Morton-on-Swale
Warlaby
Thornton-le-Beans
Kepwick
319
River Rye
Lastingham
Newton-on-Rawcliffe
North Otterington
Thornton-le-Moor
Borrowby
Cowesby
Cleveland Way
Hawnby
Gillamoor
Fadmoor
Hutton-le-Hole
Spaunton
Appleton-le-Moors
Cropton
Newton Dale
Kirby Wiske
Knayton
The Hambleton Hills
Kirby Knowle
B1257
South Otterington
Upsall
Old Byland
Carlton
Kirkbymoorside
Maunby
Thornton-le-Street
Boltby
Rievaulx Terrace & Temples NT
River Riccal
Pockley
Wrelton
Aislaby
North Kilvington
Cold Kirby
Rievaulx
Beadlam
Nawton
Sinnington
Middleton
Newsham
Felixkirk
Thirlby
Sutton Bank
Rievaulx Abbey
Wombleton
River Dove
Pickhill
South Kilvington
Sutton-under-Whitestonecliffe
Scawton
Helmsley
Marton
Pickering
Thornton le Dale
Holme
Sinderby
Thirsk
Sandhutton
Old Thirsk
Duncombe Park
Sproxton
Harome
Normanby
Ainderby Quernhow
Carlton Miniott
Balk
White Horse
Flamingo Land
Howe
Sowerby
Bagby
Oldstead
Oswaldkirk
Salton
Great Barugh
Skipton-on-Swale
Kilburn
High Kilburn
Wass
Nunnington Hall NT
Nunnington
West Ness
East Ness
Kirby Misperton
Baldersby
Catton
Thirkleby
Ampleforth
Byland
Brawby
Baldersby St James
Shandy Hall
Little Hutton
Carlton Husthwaite
Coxwold
Newburgh Priory
Gilling East
Stonegrave
Butterwick
Topcliffe
Dalton
Hutton Sessay
Birdforth
Hovingham
Great Habton
Melmerby
Asenby
Rainton
Sessay
Little Sessay
Husthwaite
Yearsley
Slingsby
Nunwick
Thormanby
Oulston
Barton-le-Street
River Rye
Eden Camp
Amotherby
Conyers
Cundall
Dishforth
Coulston
Scackleton
Appleton-le-Street
Swinton
Broughton
Old Malton
Sharow
Fawdington
Brandsby
Howardian Hills
Malton
Norton
Copt Hewick
Bridge Hewick
Norton-le-Clay
Raskelf
Terrington
Marton le-Moor
Brafferton
Crayke
Stearsby
Skewsby
Dalby
Coneysthorpe
Ripon
Helperby
Easingwood
Whenby
Ganthorpe
Castle Howard
Littlethorpe
Kirby Hill
Skelton
Newby Hall
Langthorpe
Milby
Boroughbridge
Myton-on-Swale
Tholthorpe
Stillington
59
Farlington
Bulmer
Welburn
High Hutton
65
1
2
3
4
5
6
A1
A1(M)
A19
A168
A170
A171
A172
A173
A174
A179
A689
A66
A67
A684
A61
A169
A1086
A1085
A1042
A1185
A178
A177
A1044
A1032
A1130
A1045
A1046
A1053
B1280
B1281
B1274
B1275
B1277
B1269
B1268
B1266
B1366
B1292
B1365
B1264
B1257
B1363
B1448
B6265
B6271
B1248

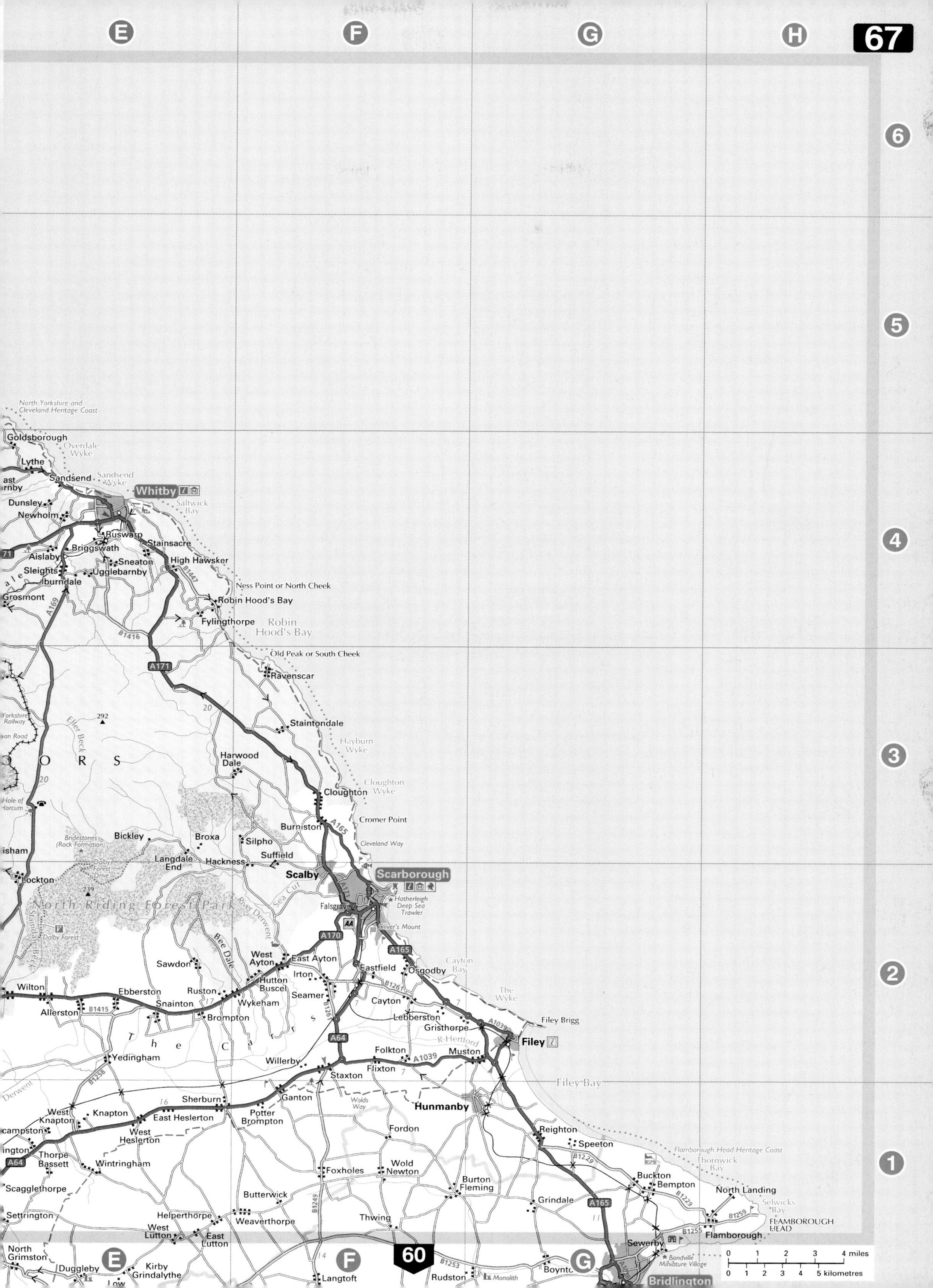

6

5

North Yorkshire and
Cleveland Heritage Coast

Goldsborough
Overdale
Wyke

Lythe
ast
rnby   Sandsend   Sandsend
Wyke
Whitby ☑ ⌂   Saltwick
Bay
Dunsley
Newholm
Ruswarp
Briggswath   Stainsacre
Aislaby
Sneaton   High Hawsker
Sleights   Ugglebarnby
Iburndale   Ness Point or North Cheek
Grosmont
Robin Hood's Bay
Fylingthorpe   Robin
Hood's Bay

Old Peak or South Cheek

A171

Ravenscar

Yorkshire
Railway   292
an Road   20

Staintondale

Harwood
Dale   Hayburn
Wyke

Hole of
larcum   Cloughton
Cloughton   Wyke

Bickley   Broxa   Burniston   Cromer Point
Bridestones
(Rock Formation)   Silpho   Cleveland Way
Langdale   Hackness   Suffield
isham   End
Scalby
Lockton
North Riding Forest Park   Falsgrave   **Scarborough** ☑ ⌂
Hatherleigh
Deep Sea
Trawler
AA
Oliver's Mount
A170

West   East Ayton   Cayton
Ayton   Bay
Sawdon   Eastfield   Osgodby
Irton   **A165**
Wilton   Ebberston   Ruston   Hutton   Seamer   The
Buscel   Wyke
Snainton   Wykeham   Cayton
Allerston   **B1415**   Brompton   Lebberston   Filey Brigg
Gristhorpe   **A1039**
Yedingham   Folkton   **Filey** ☑
Willerby   Muston
Flixton   R Hertford
B1258   Staxton
Sherburn   Ganton   Walds
West   Knapton   Way   Filey Bay
Knapton   East Heslerton   Potter   **Hunmanby**
campston   Brompton   Fordon
West   Reighton
A64   Thorpe   Heslerton   Speeton   Flamborough Head Heritage Coast
ington   Bassett   Wintringham   Thornwick
Bay
Scagglethorpe   Foxholes   Wold   Burton   Buckton
Newton   Fleming   Bempton   North Landing
Settrington   Butterwick   Grindale   Selwicks
Helperthorpe   Weaverthorpe   Thwing   **A165**   Bay
North   FLAMBOROUGH
Grimston   West   East   Sewerby   Flamborough   HEAD
Lutton   Lutton

4

3

2

1

Duggleby   Kirby
Grindalythe   Langtoft   Rudston   Monolith   Boyntc
Bondville
Miniature Village
Bridlington

0   1   2   3   4 miles
0 1 2 3 4 5 kilometres

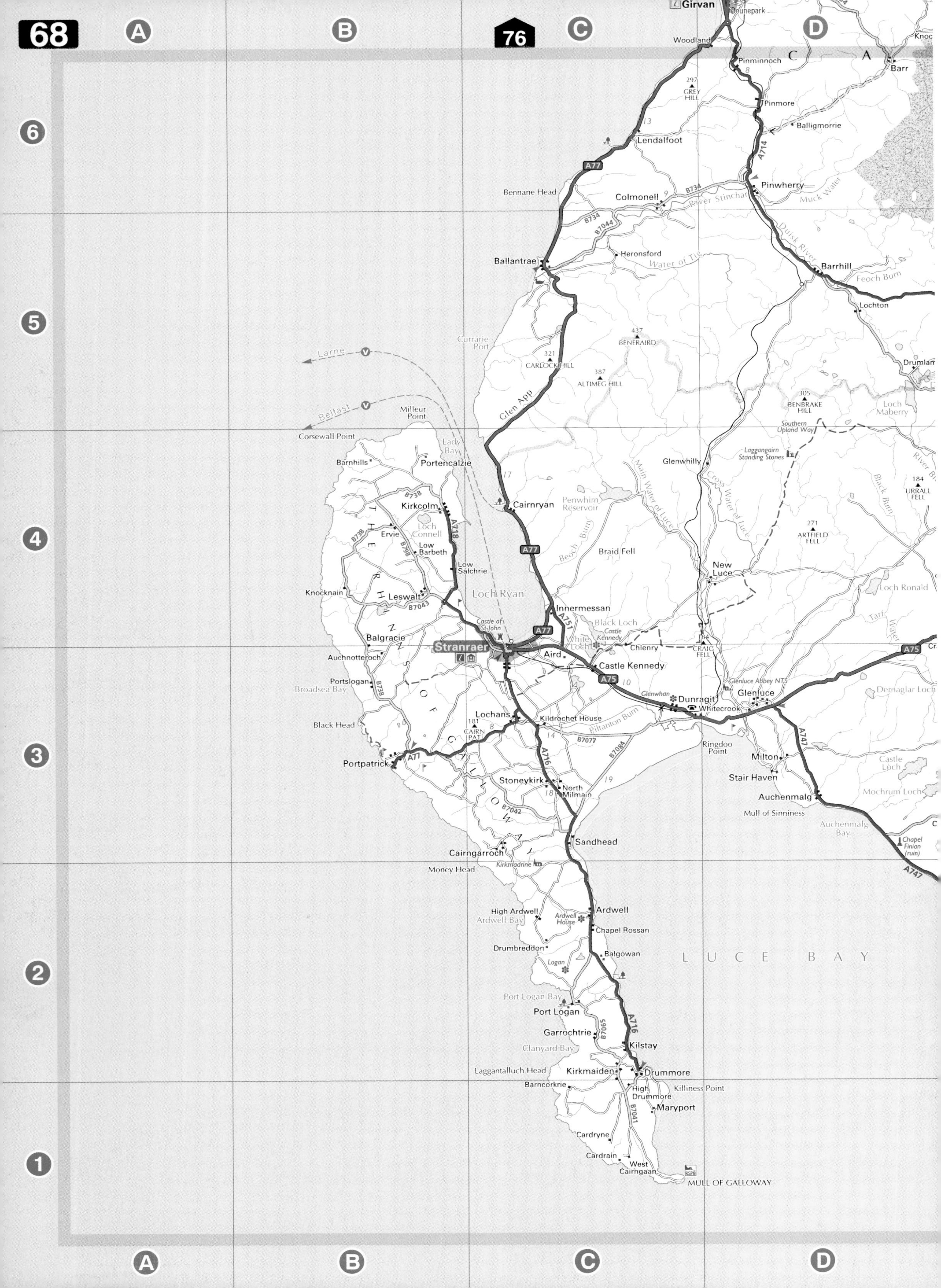

A
B
C
D
76
1
2
3
4
5
6
Girvan
Dounepark
Woodland
Pinminnoch
Barr
GREY HILL
Pinmore
Balligmorrie
Lendalfoot
A77
A714
Bennane Head
Colmonell
B734
River Stinchar
Pinwherry
Muck Water
B7044
Heronsford
Ballantrae
Water of Tig
Duisk River
Barrhill
Feoch Burn
Lochton
Currarie Port
BENERAIRD
CARLOCK HILL
ALTIMEG HILL
Drumlan
Larne
Belfast
Milleur Point
Glen App
BENBRAKE HILL
Loch Maberry
Southern Upland Way
Corsewall Point
Lady Bay
Barnhills
Portencalzie
Glenwhilly
Laggangairn Standing Stones
URRALL FELL
Black Burn
Kirkcolm
Cairnryan
Penwhirn Reservoir
Main Water of Luce
Cross Water of Luce
B738
Ervie
Loch Connell
A718
B798
Low Barbeth
Beoch Burn
Braid Fell
ARTFIELD FELL
Low Salchrie
New Luce
Knocknain
Leswalt
Loch Ryan
Loch Ronald
B7043
Innermessan
A751
Castle of St John
Black Loch
Castle Kennedy
Balgracie
White Loch
Chlenry
CRAIG FELL
Stranraer
Aird
A75
Auchnotteroch
Castle Kennedy
Portslogan
Broadsea Bay
Glenluce Abbey NTS
Glenwhan
Dunragit
Glenluce
Whitecrook
Dernaglar Loch
Black Head
Lochans
CAIRN PAT
Kildrochet House
Piltanton Burn
B7077
B7084
A747
Ringdoo Point
Milton
Castle Loch
Portpatrick
Stoneykirk
A716
North Milmain
Stair Haven
Auchenmalg
Mochrum Loch
B7042
Mull of Sinniness
Auchenmalg Bay
Sandhead
Chapel Finian (ruin)
Cairngarroch
Kirkmadrine
Money Head
THE RHINNS OF GALLOWAY
High Ardwell
Ardwell Bay
Ardwell House
Ardwell
Chapel Rossan
Drumbreddon
Balgowan
LUCE BAY
Logan
Port Logan Bay
Port Logan
Garrochtrie
B7065
Clanyard Bay
Kilstay
Laggantalluch Head
Kirkmaiden
Drummore
Barncorkrie
High Drummore
Killiness Point
Maryport
B7041
Cardryne
Cardrain
West Cairngaan
MULL OF GALLOWAY

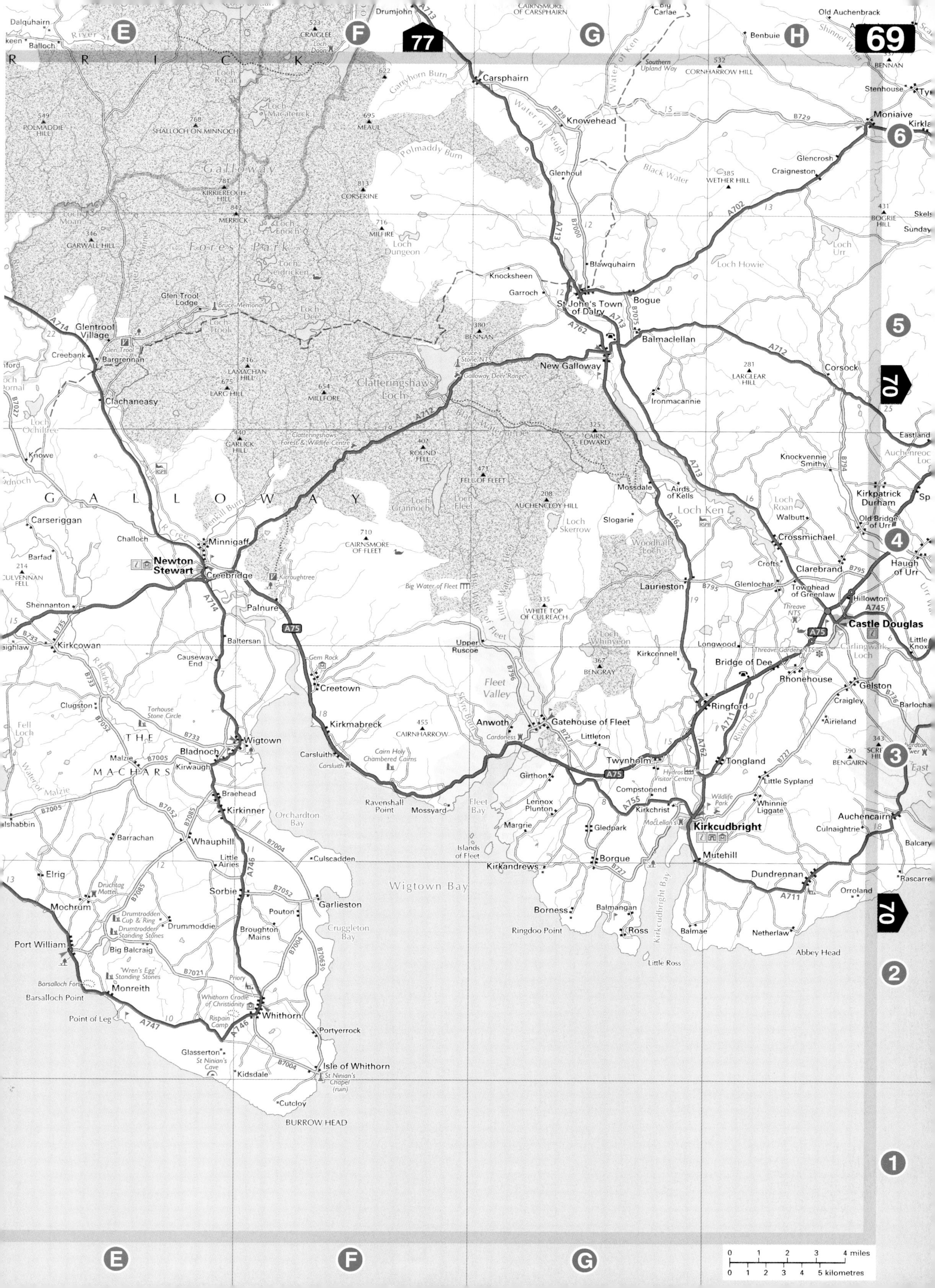
69
77
70
E
F
G
H
1
2
3
4
5
6
Newton Stewart
Castle Douglas
Kirkcudbright
Wigtown
Whithorn
Isle of Whithorn
Port William
Gatehouse of Fleet
New Galloway
St John's Town of Dalry
Carsphairn
Moniaive
Creetown
Galloway Forest Park
Wigtown Bay
Loch Ken
THE MACHARS
BURROW HEAD
0 1 2 3 4 miles
0 1 2 3 4 5 kilometres

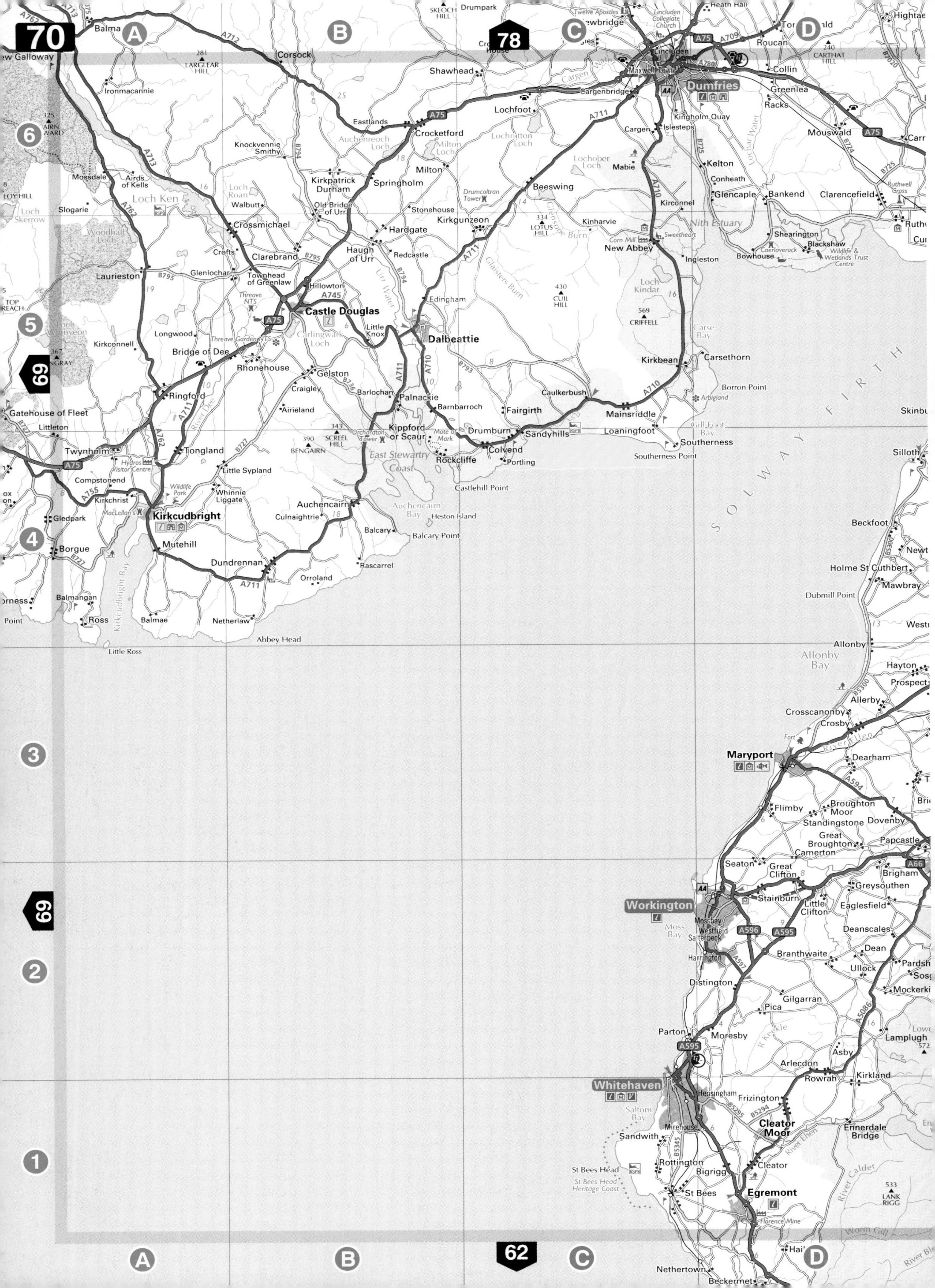

70
78
69
69
62
A
B
C
D
6
5
4
3
2
1
Balma
Corsock
LARGLEAR HILL
Ironmacannie
Shawhead
Lincluden
Maxwell Town
Dumfries
Cargenbridge
Lochfoot
Eastlands
Crocketford
Auchenreoch Loch
Knockvennie Smithy
Milton Loch
Milton
Lochrutton Loch
Lochaber Loch
Mabie
Kingholm Quay
Islesteps
Cargen
Mouswald
Roucan
Collin
Greenlea
Racks
Kelton
Conheath
Glencaple
Bankend
Clarencefield
Kirkconnel
Nith Estuary
Shearington
Blackshaw
Caerlaverock
Bowhouse
Wildlife & Wetlands Trust Centre
Ingleston
New Abbey
Sweetheart
Corn Mill
Kinharvie
Mossdale
Airds of Kells
Loch Ken
Slogarie
Walbutt
Loch Roan
Kirkpatrick Durham
Springholm
Old Bridge of Urr
Stonehouse
Drumcoltran Tower
Beeswing
Kirkgunzeon
LOTUS HILL
Crossmichael
Hardgate
Haugh of Urr
Redcastle
Clarebrand
Crofts
Glenlochar
Townhead of Greenlaw
Laurieston
Hillowton
Castle Douglas
Carlingwark Loch
Threave NTS
Threave Garden NTS
Edingham
CUIL HILL
Loch Kindar
CRIFFELL
Longwood
Kirkconnell
Bridge of Dee
Rhonehouse
Little Knox
Dalbeattie
Carse Bay
Kirkbean
Carsethorn
Gelston
Craigley
Barlochan
Palnackie
Airieland
Barnbarroch
Caulkerbush
Fairgirth
Mainsriddle
Borron Point
Arbigland
Ringford
Gatehouse of Fleet
Littleton
Twynholm
Tongland
River Dee
Hydros Visitor Centre
Compstonend
Kirkchrist
Little Sypland
Whinnie Liggate
Wildlife Park
MacLellan's
Kirkcudbright
SCREEL HILL
BENGAIRN
Orchardton Tower
Kippford or Scaur
Mote of Mark
Rockcliffe
Drumburn
Colvend
Sandyhills
Portling
Loaningfoot
Gill Foot Bay
Southerness
Southerness Point
East Stewartry Coast
Castlehill Point
SOLWAY FIRTH
Auchencairn
Auchencairn Bay
Heston Island
Culnaightrie
Balcary
Balcary Point
Gledpark
Borgue
Mutehill
Dundrennan
Rascarrel
Orroland
Kirkcudbright Bay
Balmangan
Ross
Balmae
Netherlaw
Abbey Head
Little Ross
Silloth
Skinburness
Beckfoot
Holme St Cuthbert
Mawbray
Dubmill Point
Allonby
Allonby Bay
Hayton
Allerby
Crosscanonby
Crosby
Maryport
River Ellen
Dearham
Flimby
Broughton Moor
Standingstone
Dovenby
Great Broughton
Camerton
Papcastle
Seaton
Great Clifton
Brigham
Greysouthen
Workington
Stainburn
Little Clifton
Eaglesfield
Moss Bay
Mossbay
Westfield
Salterbeck
Harrington
Deanscales
Dean
Branthwaite
Ullock
Distington
Gilgarran
Pica
Parton
Moresby
Lamplugh
Asby
Arlecdon
Rowrah
Kirkland
Whitehaven
Hensingham
Frizington
Saltom Bay
Mirehouse
Sandwith
Cleator Moor
Ennerdale Bridge
Cleator
Rottington
Bigrigg
St Bees Head
St Bees Head Heritage Coast
St Bees
Egremont
Florence Mine
LANK RIGG
Nethertown
Beckermet
A75
A711
A710
A712
A713
A762
A745
A755
A709
A780
A595
A596
A597
A594
A66
A5086
B794
B795
B727
B736
B793
B725
B724
B5300
B5345
B5294
B5295

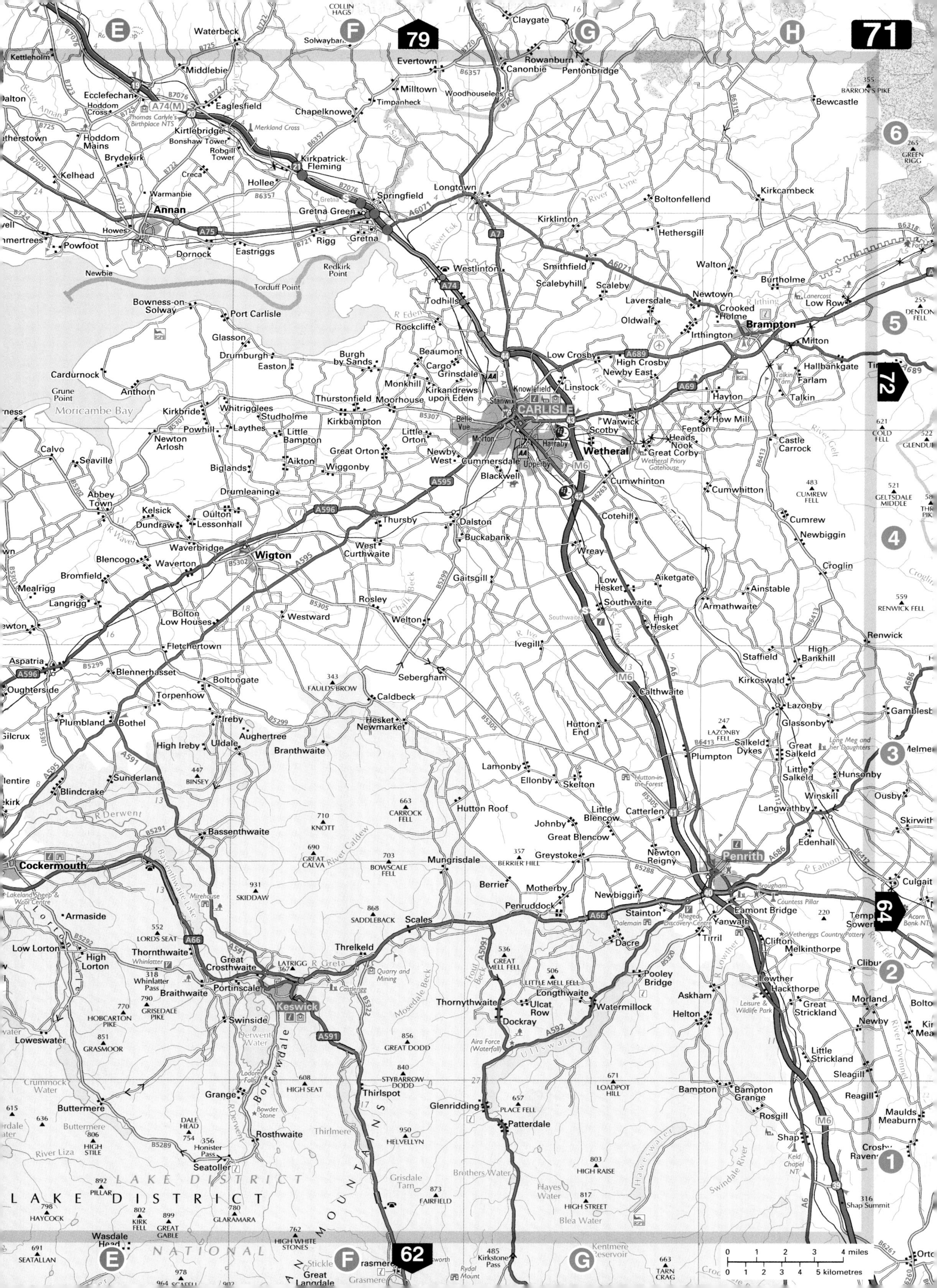

71
79
72
64
62
E
F
G
H
6
5
4
3
2
1
Waterbeck
Solwaybank
Collin Hags
Claygate
Kettleholm
Evertown
Rowanburn
Canonbie
Pentonbridge
Middlebie
Milltown
Woodhouselees
Timpanheck
Bewcastle
355 Barron's Pike
Dalton
Ecclefechan
Hoddom Cross
Eaglesfield
Thomas Carlyle's Birthplace NTS
Chapelknowe
Merkland Cross
Kirtlebridge
Bonshaw Tower
Hoddom Mains
Robgill Tower
265 Green Rigg
Brydekirk
Kirkpatrick-Fleming
Kelhead
Creca
Hollee
Springfield
Longtown
Kirkcambeck
Warmanbie
Gretna
Annan
Gretna Green
Boltonfellend
Howes
Powfoot
Rigg
Kirklinton
Hethersgill
Dornock
Eastriggs
Redkirk Point
Westlinton
Smithfield
Walton
Newbie
Torduff Point
Scalebyhill
Scaleby
Burtholme
Todhills
Laversdale
Newtown
Lanercost
Low Row
255 Denton Fell
Bowness-on-Solway
Port Carlisle
Rockcliffe
Oldwall
Crooked Holme
Brampton
Irthington
Glasson
Drumburgh
Burgh by Sands
Easton
Beaumont
Cargo
Grinsdale
Low Crosby
High Crosby
Newby East
Milton
Hallbankgate
Farlam
Talkin
Cardurnock
Anthorn
Grune Point
Monkhill
Kirkandrews upon Eden
Linstock
Knowlefield
Stanwix
Hayton
Moricambe Bay
Kirkbride
Whitrigglees
Studholme
Thurstonfield
Moorhouse
CARLISLE
Warwick
How Mill
Powhill
Laythes
Little Bampton
Kirkbampton
Belle Vue
Morton
Harraby
Scotby
Fenton
Heads Nook
Newton Arlosh
Great Orton
Little Orton
Wetheral
Great Corby
Castle Carrock
621 Cold Fell
522 Glendue
Calvo
Seaville
Aikton
Wiggonby
Newby West
Cummersdale
Upperby
Wetheral Priory Gatehouse
Biglands
Blackwell
Cumwhinton
Cumwhitton
483 Cumrew Fell
521 Geltsdale Middle
Abbey Town
Drumleaning
Kelsick
Oulton
Lessonhall
Dundraw
Thursby
Dalston
Cotehill
Cumrew
Newbiggin
Buckabank
Waverbridge
Wigton
West Curthwaite
Wreay
Blencogo
Waverton
Croglin
Bromfield
Mealrigg
Gaitsgill
Low Hesket
Aiketgate
Langrigg
Rosley
Southwaite
Ainstable
Armathwaite
559 Renwick Fell
Bolton Low Houses
Westward
Welton
High Hesket
Renwick
Fletchertown
Ivegill
Staffield
High Bankhill
Aspatria
Blennerhasset
Sebergham
Kirkoswald
Oughterside
Boltongate
343 Faulds Brow
Caldbeck
Calthwaite
Torpenhow
Lazonby
Plumbland
Bothel
Ireby
Hesket Newmarket
Hutton End
247 Lazonby Fell
Glassonby
Gamblesby
Gilcrux
Aughertree
Salkeld Dykes
Great Salkeld
Long Meg and her Daughters
Melmerby
High Ireby
Uldale
Branthwaite
Plumpton
447 Binsey
Lamonby
Little Salkeld
Hunsonby
Sunderland
Ellonby
Skelton
Hutton-in-the-Forest
Winskill
Ousby
Blindcrake
663 Carrock Fell
Hutton Roof
Little Blencow
Catterlen
Langwathby
Skirwith
710 Knott
Johnby
Great Blencow
Edenhall
Bassenthwaite
690 Great Calva
703 Bowscale Fell
357 Berrier Hill
Greystoke
Newton Reigny
Penrith
Mungrisdale
Cockermouth
Lakeland Sheep & Wool Centre
931 Skiddaw
Berrier
Motherby
Brougham
Culgaith
Mirehouse
Newbiggin
Countess Pillar
Armaside
868 Saddleback
Penruddock
Stainton
Eamont Bridge
220
Temple Sowerby
Acorn Bank NT
552 Lords Seat
Scales
Dalemain
Rheged Discovery Centre
Yanwath
Tirril
Wetheriggs Country Pottery
Clifton
Low Lorton
High Lorton
Thornthwaite
Threlkeld
536 Great Mell Fell
Dacre
Melkinthorpe
Cliburn
Whinlatter
Great Crosthwaite
Latrigg 367
Quarry and Mining
506 Little Mell Fell
Pooley Bridge
Lowther
Hackthorpe
318 Whinlatter Pass
Braithwaite
Portinscale
Castlerigg
Longthwaite
Askham
790 Grisedale Pike
Keswick
Thornythwaite
Ulcat Row
Watermillock
Morland
770 Hobcarton Pike
Swinside
Dockray
Helton
Leisure & Wildlife Park
Great Strickland
Newby
851 Grasmoor
Derwent Water
856 Great Dodd
Aira Force (Waterfall)
Ullswater
Loweswater
Little Strickland
840 Stybarrow Dodd
671 Loadpot Hill
Crummock Water
Lodore Falls
Borrowdale
608 High Seat
Thirlspot
Bampton
Bampton Grange
Sleagill
Grange
Glenridding
657 Place Fell
Reagill
615
Buttermere
636
Bowder Stone
Patterdale
Maulds Meaburn
Rosgill
Dale Head 754
806 High Stile
Rosthwaite
Thirlmere
950 Helvellyn
Shap
356 Honister Pass
Crosby Ravensworth
Keld Chapel NT
River Liza
Seatoller
803 High Raise
LAKE DISTRICT
Brothers Water
Grisdale Tarn
Hayes Water
892 Pillar
873 Fairfield
817 High Street
316 Shap Summit
798 Haycock
802 Kirk Fell
899 Great Gable
780 Glaramara
Blea Water
762 High White Stones
Wasdale Head
NATIONAL
MOUNTAINS
Kentmere Reservoir
691 Seatallan
Stickle
Grasmere
485 Kirkstone Pass
Rydal Mount
663 Tarn Crag
978 Scafell
Great Langdale
Orton
0 1 2 3 4 miles
0 1 2 3 4 5 kilometres

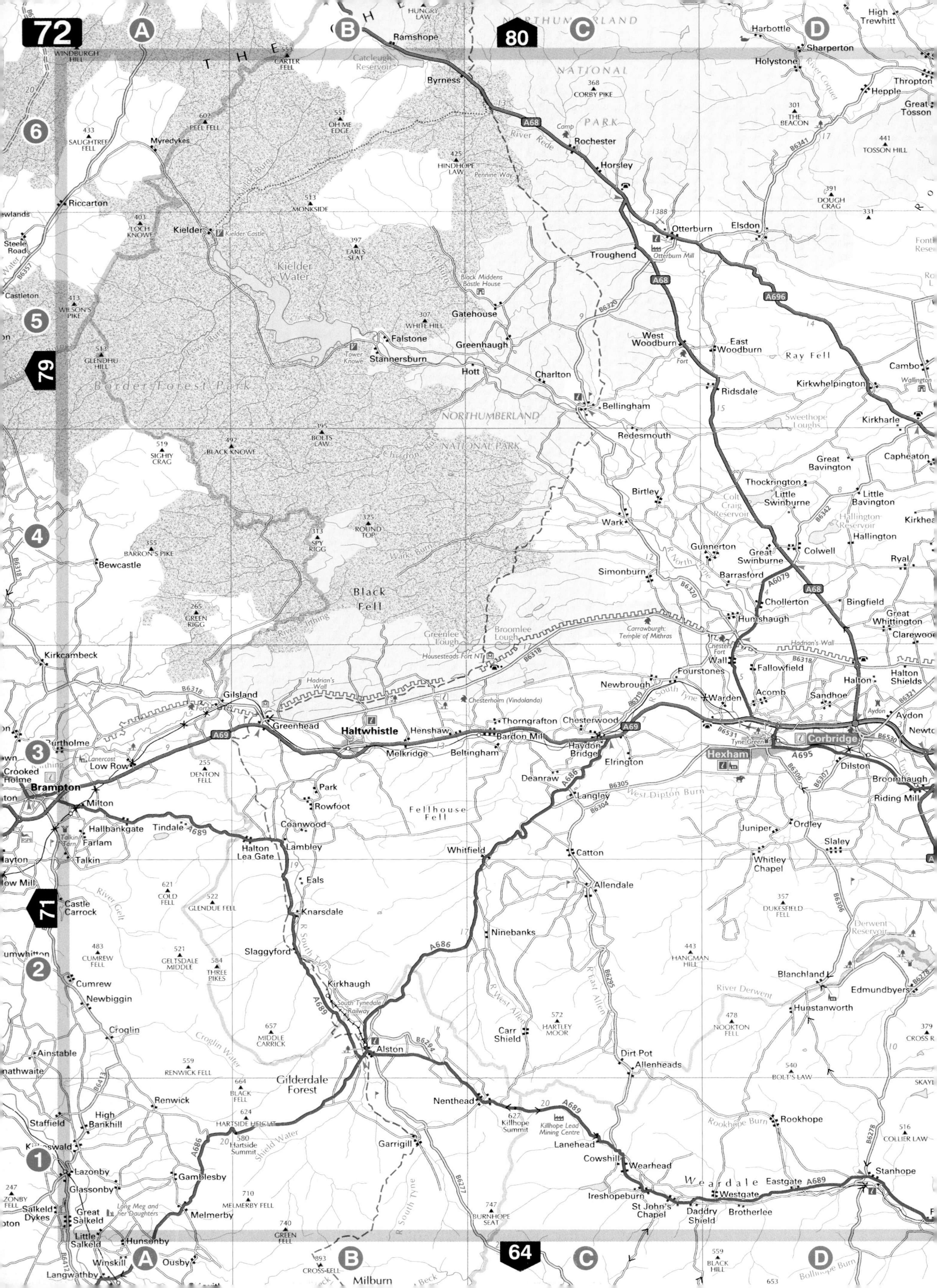

72
80
79
71
64
A
B
C
D
1
2
3
4
5
6
NORTHUMBERLAND NATIONAL PARK
Border Forest Park
Kielder Water
Black Fell
Fellhouse Fell
Gilderdale Forest
Weardale
Ray Fell
Ramshope
Byrness
Rochester
Horsley
Otterburn
Elsdon
Troughend
Harbottle
Sharperton
Holystone
Hepple
Thropton
Great Tosson
Riccarton
Kielder
Myredykes
Castleton
Steele Road
Gatehouse
Falstone
Stannersburn
Greenhaugh
Hott
Charlton
Bellingham
West Woodburn
East Woodburn
Ridsdale
Kirkwhelpington
Cambo
Kirkharle
Redesmouth
Great Bavington
Capheaton
Thockrington
Little Swinburne
Little Bavington
Birtley
Wark
Gunnerton
Great Swinburne
Colwell
Hallington
Simonburn
Barrasford
Chollerton
Bingfield
Humshaugh
Great Whittington
Clarewood
Wall
Fallowfield
Fourstones
Newbrough
Warden
Acomb
Sandhoe
Halton
Halton Shields
Aydon
Corbridge
Hexham
Dilston
Broomhaugh
Riding Mill
Haydon Bridge
Elrington
Chesterwood
Thorngrafton
Bardon Mill
Henshaw
Haltwhistle
Melkridge
Beltingham
Greenhead
Gilsland
Bewcastle
Kirkcambeck
Low Row
Brampton
Milton
Hallbankgate
Tindale
Farlam
Talkin
Halton Lea Gate
Lambley
Coanwood
Park
Rowfoot
Deanraw
Langley
Whitfield
Catton
Allendale
Juniper
Ordley
Slaley
Whitley Chapel
Eals
Knarsdale
Slaggyford
Kirkhaugh
Alston
Nenthead
Garrigill
Ninebanks
Carr Shield
Dirt Pot
Allenheads
Blanchland
Edmundbyers
Hunstanworth
Rookhope
Stanhope
Eastgate
Westgate
Wearhead
Cowshill
Lanehead
Ireshopeburn
St John's Chapel
Daddry Shield
Brotherlee
Castle Carrock
Cumrew
Newbiggin
Croglin
Ainstable
Renwick
High Bankhill
Staffield
Lazonby
Glassonby
Gamblesby
Melmerby
Great Salkeld
Little Salkeld
Hunsonby
Winskill
Ousby
Langwathby
Milburn
Crooked Holme
Burtholme
A68
A696
A69
A686
A689
A695
A6079
B6318
B6320
B6341
B6342
B6357
B6318
B6319
B6531
B6530
B6321
B6305
B6304
B6306
B6307
B6295
B6294
B6277
B6278
B6412
B6413

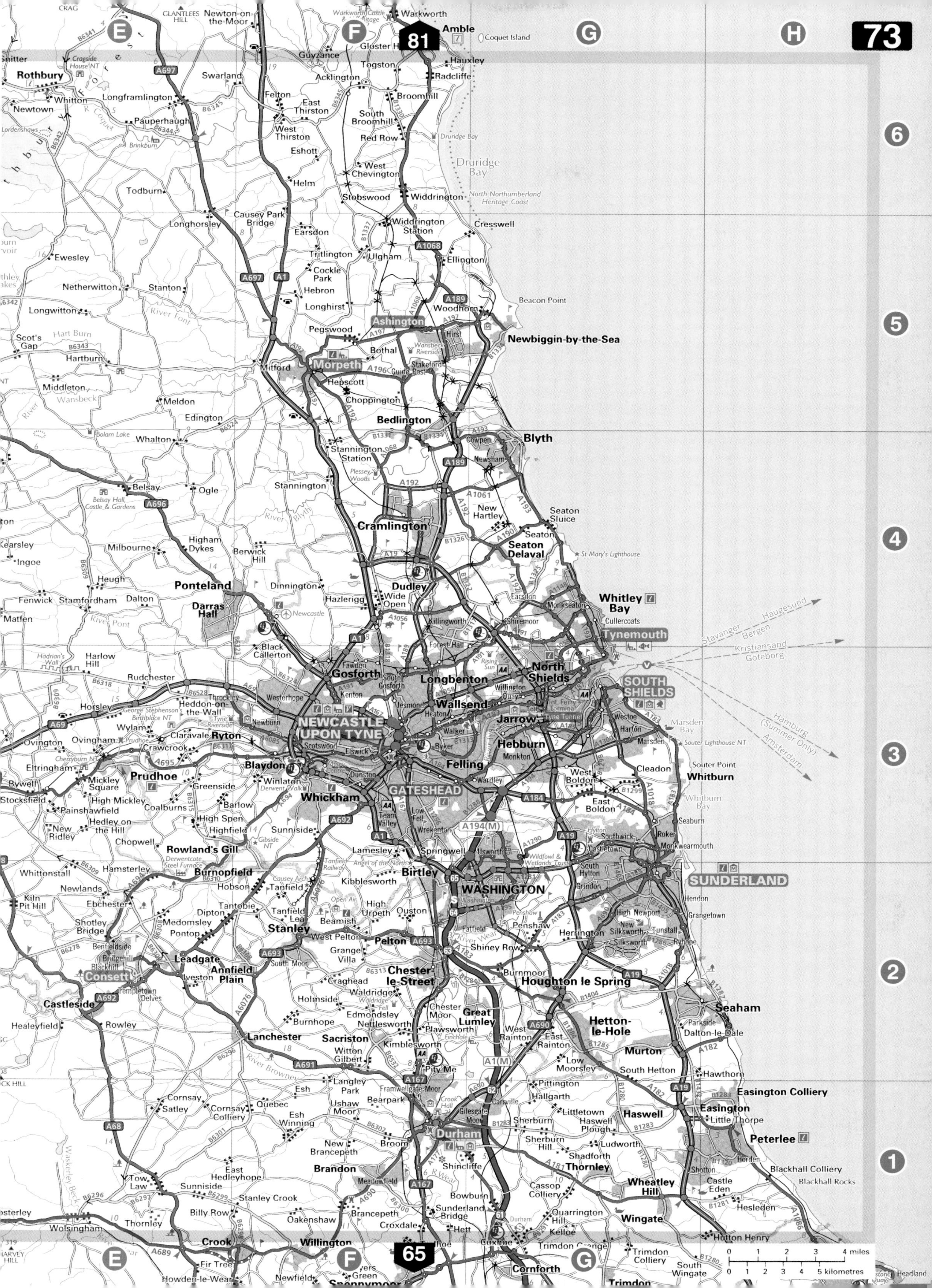
73
E
F
G
H
81
65
6
5
4
3
2
1
Warkworth
Amble
Coquet Island
Newton-on-the-Moor
Glantlees Hill
Guyzance
Togston
Hauxley
Radcliffe
Acklington
Broomhill
Rothbury
Cragside House NT
Swarland
Longframlington
Whitton
Newtown
Felton
East Thirston
South Broomhill
Pauperhaugh
Brinkburn
West Thirston
Red Row
Druridge Bay
Eshott
West Chevington
Helm
Todburn
Stobswood
Widdrington
North Northumberland Heritage Coast
Causey Park Bridge
Longhorsley
Widdrington Station
Cresswell
Earsdon
Tritlington
Ulgham
Ellington
Ewesley
Cockle Park
Hebron
Netherwitton
Stanton
Longhirst
Woodhorn
Beacon Point
Longwitton
River Font
Ashington
Pegswood
Scot's Gap
Hart Burn
Newbiggin-by-the-Sea
Hartburn
Bothal
Wansbeck Riverside
Morpeth
Mitford
Stakeford
Guide Post
Hepscott
Middleton
Wansbeck
Choppington
Meldon
Edington
Bedlington
Bolam Lake
Whalton
Blyth
Cowpen
Newsham
Stannington Station
Plessey Woods
Belsay
Belsay Hall, Castle & Gardens
Ogle
Stannington
New Hartley
Seaton Sluice
Cramlington
Seaton
Seaton Delaval
Higham Dykes
Milbourne
Berwick Hill
Kearsley
Ingoe
St Mary's Lighthouse
Heugh
Ponteland
Dinnington
Dudley
Fenwick
Stamfordham
Dalton
Wide Open
Hazlerigg
Earsdon
Whitley Bay
Darras Hall
Monkseaton
Matfen
Newcastle
Killingworth
Shiremoor
Cullercoats
Tynemouth
Stavanger
Haugesund
Bergen
Kristiansand
Goteborg
Hadrian's Wall
Harlow Hill
Black Callerton
Forest Hall
Rising Sun
North Shields
South Shields
Rudchester
Fawdon
Gosforth
South Gosforth
Longbenton
Willington Quay
Kenton
Westerhope
Jesmond
Wallsend
Horsley
Heddon-on-the-Wall
Throckley
George Stephenson's Birthplace NT
Newburn
Heaton
Int. Ferry Terminal
Tyne Tunnel
Jarrow
Westoe
Harton
Marsden Bay
Wylam
Claravale
Ryton
Newcastle upon Tyne
Walker
Byker
Hebburn
Marsden
Souter Lighthouse NT
Hamburg (Summer Only)
Amsterdam
Ovington
Ovingham
Prudhoe
Crawcrook
Scotswood
Elswick
Monkton
Cleadon
Souter Point
Whitburn
Eltringham
Cherryburn NT
Blaydon
Dunston
Felling
West Boldon
Bywell
Mickley Square
Prudhoe
Greenside
Winlaton
Derwent Walk
Gateshead
Wardley
Whitburn Bay
Stocksfield
Painshawfield
High Mickley
Coalburns
Barlow
Whickham
East Boldon
New Ridley
Hedley on the Hill
High Spen
Highfield
Sunniside
Team Valley
Low Fell
Wrekenton
Seaburn
Chopwell
Gibside NT
Hylton
Southwick
Roker
Rowland's Gill
Derwentcote Steel Furnace
Lamesley
Springwell
Usworth
Castletown
Monkwearmouth
Whittonstall
Hamsterley
Burnopfield
Tanfield Railway
Angel of the North
Birtley
Wildfowl & Wetlands Trust
South Hylton
Sunderland
Newlands
Hobson
Causey Arch
Tanfield
Kibblesworth
Washington
Grindon
Hendon
Kiln Pit Hill
Ebchester
Tantobie
Open Air
High Urpeth
Ouston
Penshaw
High Newport
Grangetown
Shotley Bridge
Dipton
Medomsley
Tanfield Lea
Beamish
Fatfield
Herrington
New Silksworth
Tunstall
Silksworth
Ryhope
Pontop
Stanley
West Pelton
Pelton
Shiney Row
Benfieldside
Bridgehill
Blackhill
Consett
Leadgate
Annfield Plain
Grange Villa
South Moor
Chester-le-Street
Burnmoor
Houghton le Spring
Templetown
Delves
Iveston
Craghead
Waldridge
Waldridge Fell
Castleside
Holmside
Chester Moor
Great Lumley
Hetton-le-Hole
Seaham
Parkside
Dalton-le-Dale
Healeyfield
Rowley
Edmondsley
Burnhope
Nettlesworth
Plawsworth
Finchale
West Rainton
East Rainton
Lanchester
Sacriston
Witton Gilbert
Kimblesworth
Murton
River Browney
Pity Me
Low Moorsley
South Hetton
Hawthorn
Langley Park
Framwellgate Moor
Pittington
Hallgarth
Easington Colliery
Cornsay
Satley
Quebec
Esh
Cornsay Colliery
Ushaw Moor
Bearpark
Crook Hall
Gilesgate Moor
Carrville
Littletown
Haswell
Easington
Little Thorpe
Esh Winning
Sherburn
Haswell Plough
Durham
Peterlee
Sherburn Hill
Ludworth
New Brancepeth
Broom
Shadforth
Horden
Waskerley Beck
Brandon
Shincliffe
Thornley
Shotton
Blackhall Colliery
Blackhall Rocks
Tow Law
East Hedleyhope
Meadowfield
Cassop Colliery
Wheatley Hill
Castle Eden
Sunniside
Stanley Crook
Bowburn
Hesleden
Billy Row
Brancepeth
Sunderland Bridge
Quarrington Hill
Wingate
Thornley
Oakenshaw
Croxdale
Hett
Kelloe
Wolsingham
Crook
Willington
Coxhoe
Trimdon Grange
Hutton Henry
Trimdon Colliery
South Wingate
Fir Tree
Cornforth
Howden-le-Wear
Newfield
Spennymoor
Trimdon
Headland
0 1 2 3 4 miles
0 1 2 3 4 5 kilometres

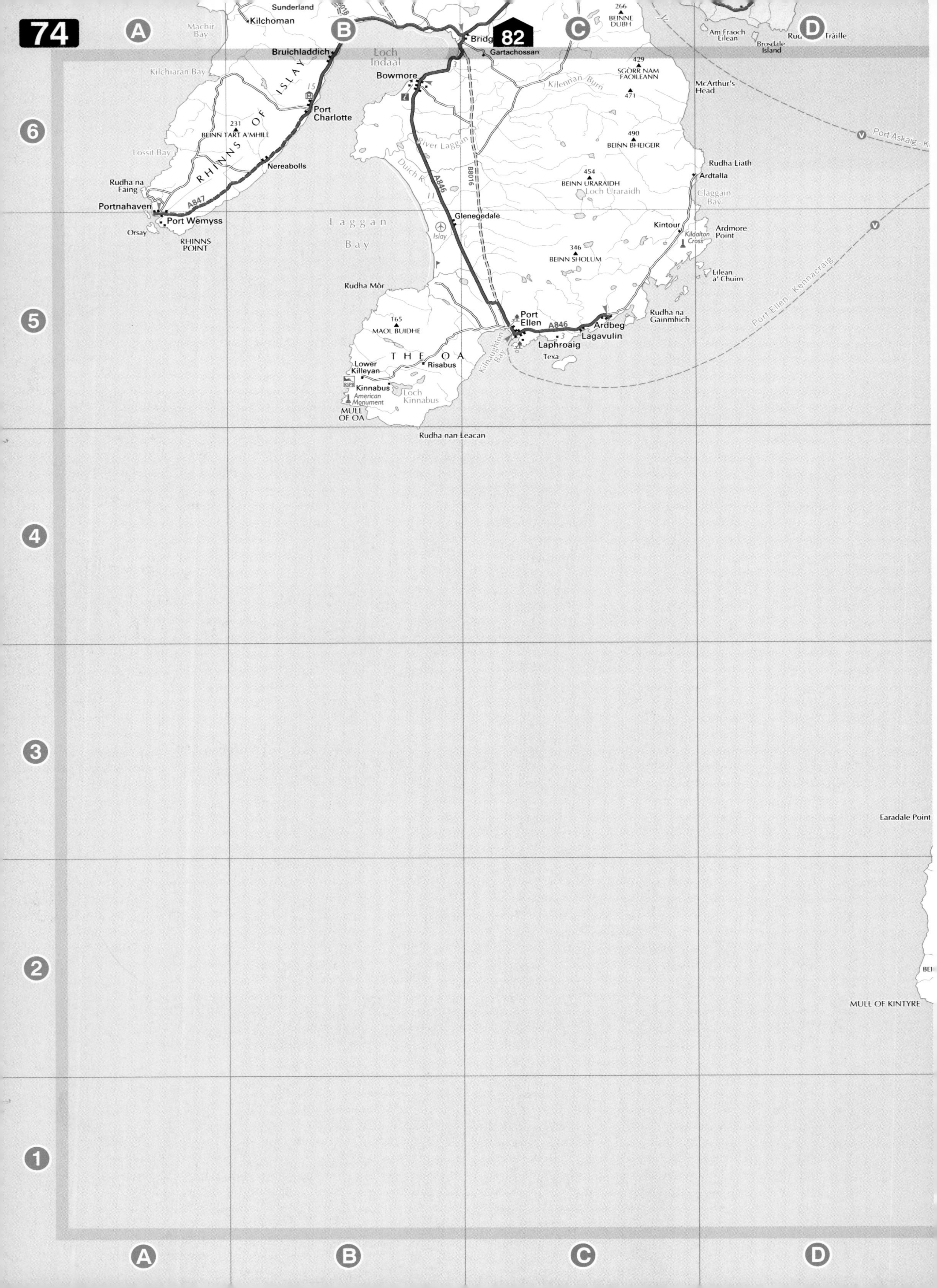

A   B   82   C   D

Machir Bay
Kilchoman
Sunderland

Bruichladdich
Loch Indaal
Bridg
Gartachossan

Kilchiaran Bay

RHINNS OF ISLAY

Bowmore

BEINNE DUBH

Am Fraoch Eilean
Brosdale Island
Rug   Fràille

SGORR NAM FAOILEANN

6

Port Charlotte

231
BEINN TART A'MHILE

Nereabolls

River Laggan

Kilennan Burn

471

McArthur's Head

Lossit Bay

Port Askaig

490
BEINN BHEIGEIR

Rudha Liath

Ardtalla

Rudha na Faing

A847

454
BEINN URARAIDH
Loch Uraraidh

Claggain Bay

Portnahaven

Duich R

A846

Port Wemyss

Orsay

RHINNS POINT

Laggan Bay

Islay

346
BEINN SHOLUM

Kintour

Kildalton Cross

Ardmore Point

Eilean a' Chuirn

Rudha Mòr

5

165
MAOL BUIDHE

Port Ellen

A846

Ardbeg
Lagavulin

Rudha na Gainmhich

Port Ellen - Kennacraig

THE OA

Risabus

Kilnaughton Bay

Laphroaig

Texa

Lower Killeyan

Kinnabus

American Monument

Loch Kinnabus

MULL OF OA

Rudha nan Leacan

4

3

Earadale Point

2

BEI

MULL OF KINTYRE

1

A   B   C   D

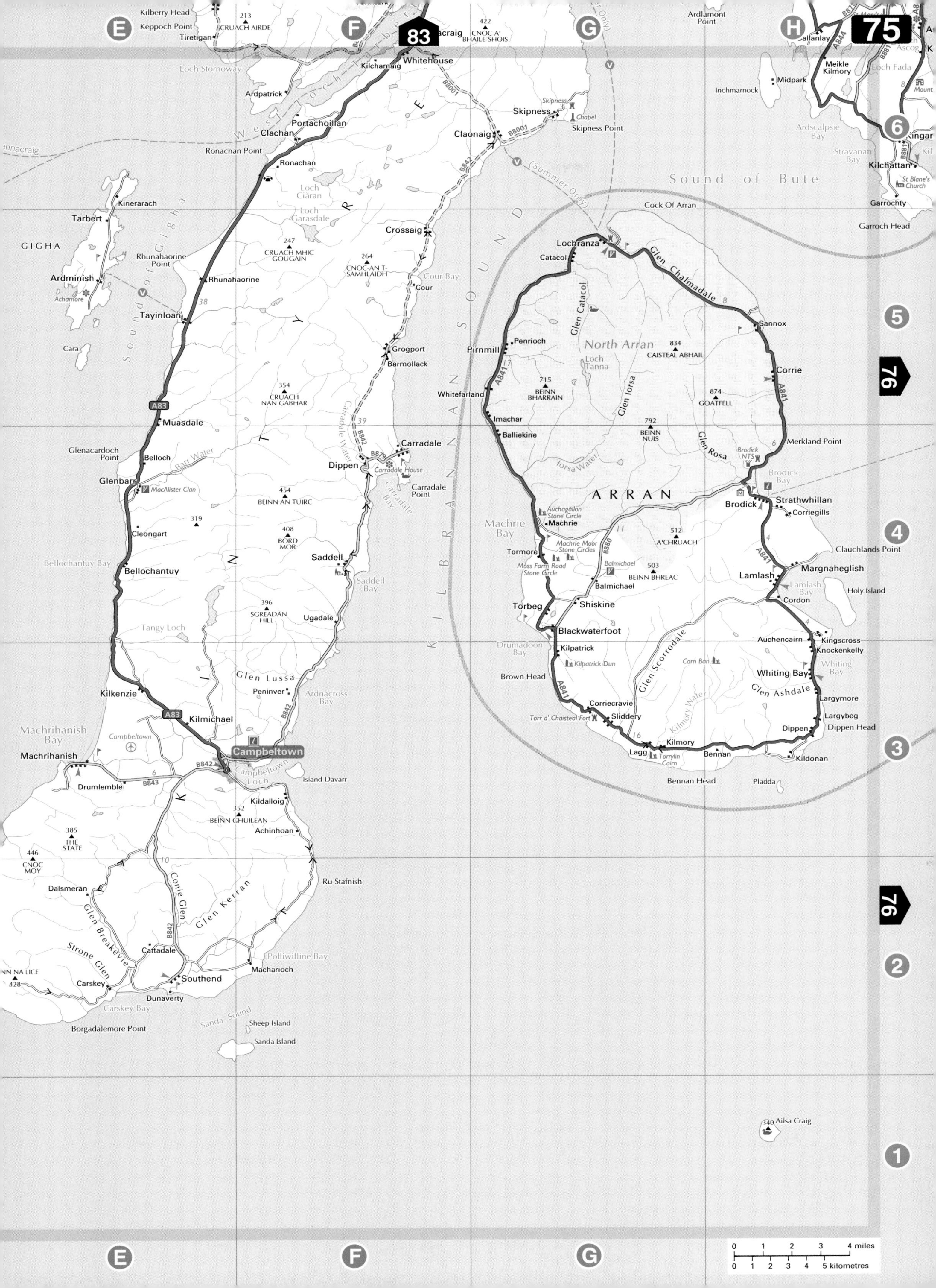

75
83
76
76
Campbeltown
Kintyre
Arran
North Arran
Sound of Bute
Kilbrannan Sound
Sound of Gigha
Gigha
Tarbert
Ardminish
Cara
Tayinloan
Rhunahaorine
Muasdale
Glenbarr
Bellochantuy
Kilkenzie
Kilmichael
Machrihanish
Drumlemble
Southend
Carskey
Dunaverty
Sanda Island
Sheep Island
Carradale
Dippen
Saddell
Ugadale
Peninver
Grogport
Barmollack
Crossaig
Claonaig
Skipness
Skipness Point
Whitehouse
Kilchamaig
Ardpatrick
Portachoillan
Clachan
Ronachan
Ronachan Point
Lochranza
Catacol
Pirnmill
Penrioch
Whitefarland
Imachar
Balliekine
Machrie
Tormore
Torbeg
Shiskine
Balmichael
Blackwaterfoot
Kilpatrick
Corriecravie
Sliddery
Lagg
Kilmory
Bennan
Kildonan
Dippen
Largybeg
Largymore
Whiting Bay
Knockenkelly
Kingscross
Auchencairn
Cordon
Lamlash
Margnaheglish
Corriegills
Strathwhillan
Brodick
Corrie
Sannox
Cock Of Arran
Holy Island
Pladda
Ailsa Craig
Island Davaar
Kildalloig
Achinhoan
Ru Stafnish
Machariоch
Cattadale
Dalsmeran
Goatfell
Caisteal Abhail
Beinn Nuis
Beinn Bharrain
A'Chruach
Beinn Bhreac
Kilchattan
Garrochty
Garroch Head
Midpark
Inchmarnock
Ardlamont Point
Meikle Kilmory
0 1 2 3 4 miles
0 1 2 3 4 5 kilometres

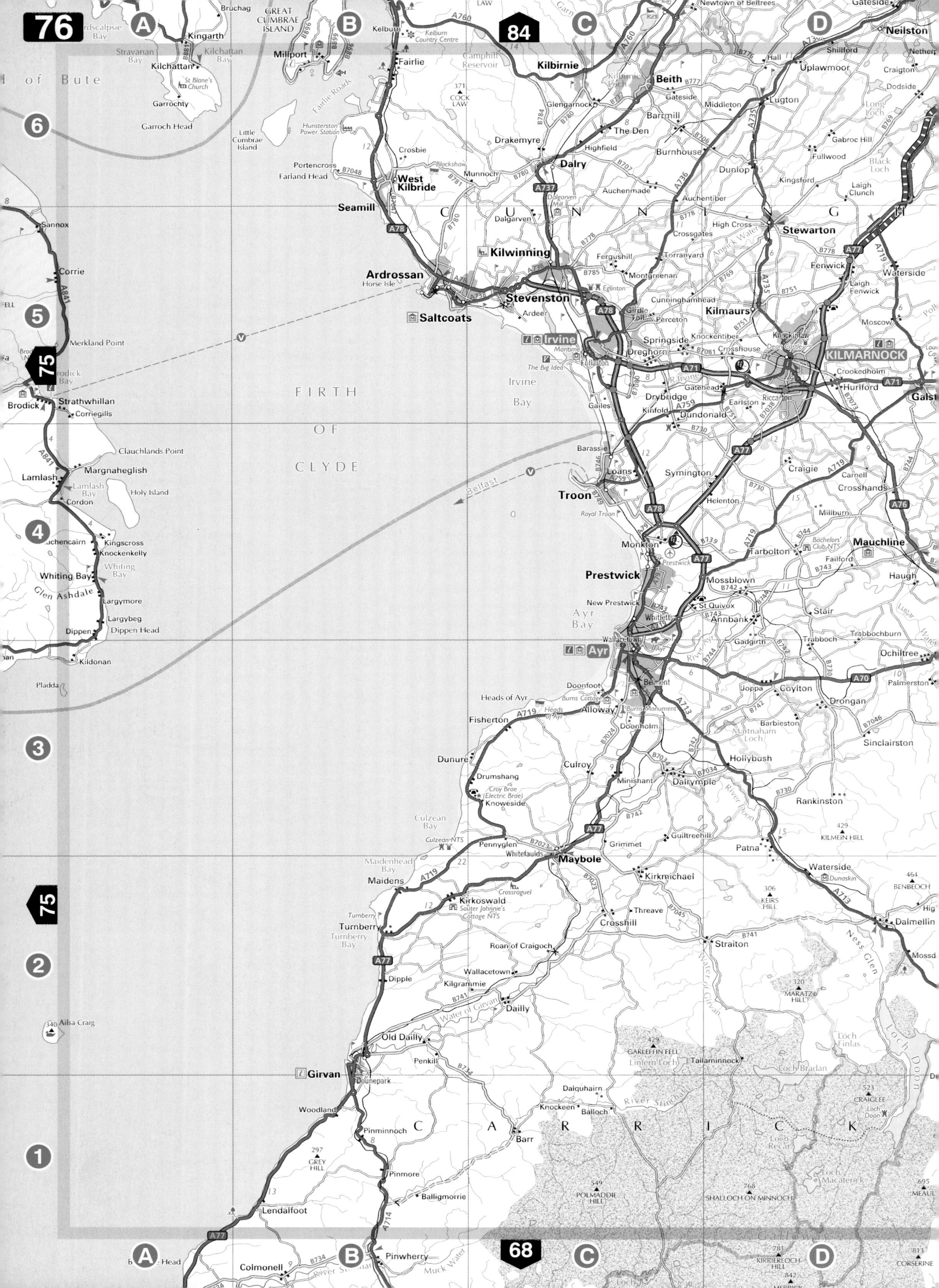

84
75
68
A
B
C
D
6
5
4
3
2
1
Bruchag
GREAT CUMBRAE ISLAND
Kingarth
Kilchattan
Kilchattan Bay
Stravanan Bay
St Blane's Church
Garrochty
Garroch Head
of Bute
Millport
Kelburn
Kelburn Country Centre
Fairlie
Fairlie Roads
Little Cumbrae Island
Hunsterston Power Station
Camphill Reservoir
Kilbirnie
Beith
Neilston
Shillford
Uplawmoor
Craigton
Dodside
Lugton
Gateside
Middleton
Barrmill
Glengarnock
The Den
Highfield
Drakemyre
Dalry
Burnhouse
Dunlop
Gabroc Hill
Fullwood
Kingsford
Laigh Clunch
Black Loch
Long Loch
371 COCK LAW
Crosbie
Portencross
Farland Head
West Kilbride
Munnoch
Seamill
Auchenmade
Auchentiber
Dalgarven Mill
Dalgarven
High Cross
Stewarton
Crossgates
Torranyard
Kilwinning
Fergushill
Montgreenan
Fenwick
Laigh Fenwick
Waterside
Ardrossan
Horse Isle
Saltcoats
Stevenston
Ardeer
Eglinton
Cunninghamhead
Kilmaurs
Girdle Toll
Perceton
Moscow
Irvine
Maritime
The Big Idea
Springside
Knockentiber
Knockinlaw
Dean Castle
KILMARNOCK
Dreghorn
Crosshouse
Fullarton
Crookedholm
Hurlford
Galston
Irvine Bay
FIRTH OF CLYDE
Drybridge
Gatehead
Kinfold
Dundonald
Earlston
Riccarton
Gailes
Barassie
Loans
Troon
Royal Troon
Symington
Craigie
Carnell
Crosshands
Hemington
Millburn
Monkton
Prestwick
Tarbolton
Bachelors' Club NTS
Mauchline
Failford
Haugh
Mossblown
St Quivox
New Prestwick
Ayr Bay
Whitletts
Annbank
Stair
Trabboch
Trabbochburn
Gadgirth
Wallacetown
Ayr
Ochiltree
Belmont
Joppa
Coylton
Palmerston
Doonfoot
Burns Cottage
Heads of Ayr
Alloway
Burns Monument
Doonholm
Drongan
Barbieston
Martnaham Loch
Sinclairston
Fisherton
Dunure
Culroy
Hollybush
Minishant
Dalrymple
Drumshang
Croy Brae (Electric Brae)
Knoweside
Rankinston
Culzean Bay
Culzean NTS
Pennyglen
Grimmet
Guiltreehill
Patna
429 KILMEIN HILL
Whitefaulds
Maybole
Maidenhead Bay
Maidens
Kirkmichael
Waterside
Dunaskin
464 BENBEOCH
Crossraguel
Kirkoswald
Souter Johnnie's Cottage NTS
306 KEIRS HILL
Turnberry
Turnberry Bay
Threave
Crosshill
Dalmellin
Straiton
Roan of Craigoch
Ness Glen
Mossdale
Wallacetown
Dipple
Kilgrammie
Dailly
320 MARATZ HILL
Water of Girvan
Ailsa Craig
Old Dailly
Penkill
429 GARLEFFIN FELL
Linfern Loch
Tallaminnock
Loch Finlas
Loch Doon
Loch Bradan
Girvan
Dounepark
Dalquhairn
523 CRAIGLEE
Loch Doon
River Stinchar
Woodland
Knockeen
Balloch
CARRICK
Pinminnoch
Barr
Loch Recar
297 GREY HILL
Pinmore
549 POLMADDIE HILL
768 SHALLOCH ON MINNOCH
Loch Macaterick
695 MEAUL
Balligmorrie
Lendalfoot
Pinwherry
Colmonell
781 KIRRIEREOCH HILL
813 CORSERINE
Sannox
Corrie
Merkland Point
Brodick
Brodick Bay
Strathwhillan
Corriegills
Clauchlands Point
Margnaheglish
Lamlash
Lamlash Bay
Holy Island
Cordon
Auchencairn
Kingscross
Knockenkelly
Whiting Bay
Glen Ashdale
Largymore
Largybeg
Dippen
Dippen Head
Kildonan
Pladda
Belfast
A77
A78
A71
A70
A76
A713
A719
A737
A736
A735
A760
A759
A841
A714
B7023
B7024
B7034
B7045
B741
B742
B730
B734
B743
B744
B751
B778
B7048
B7081

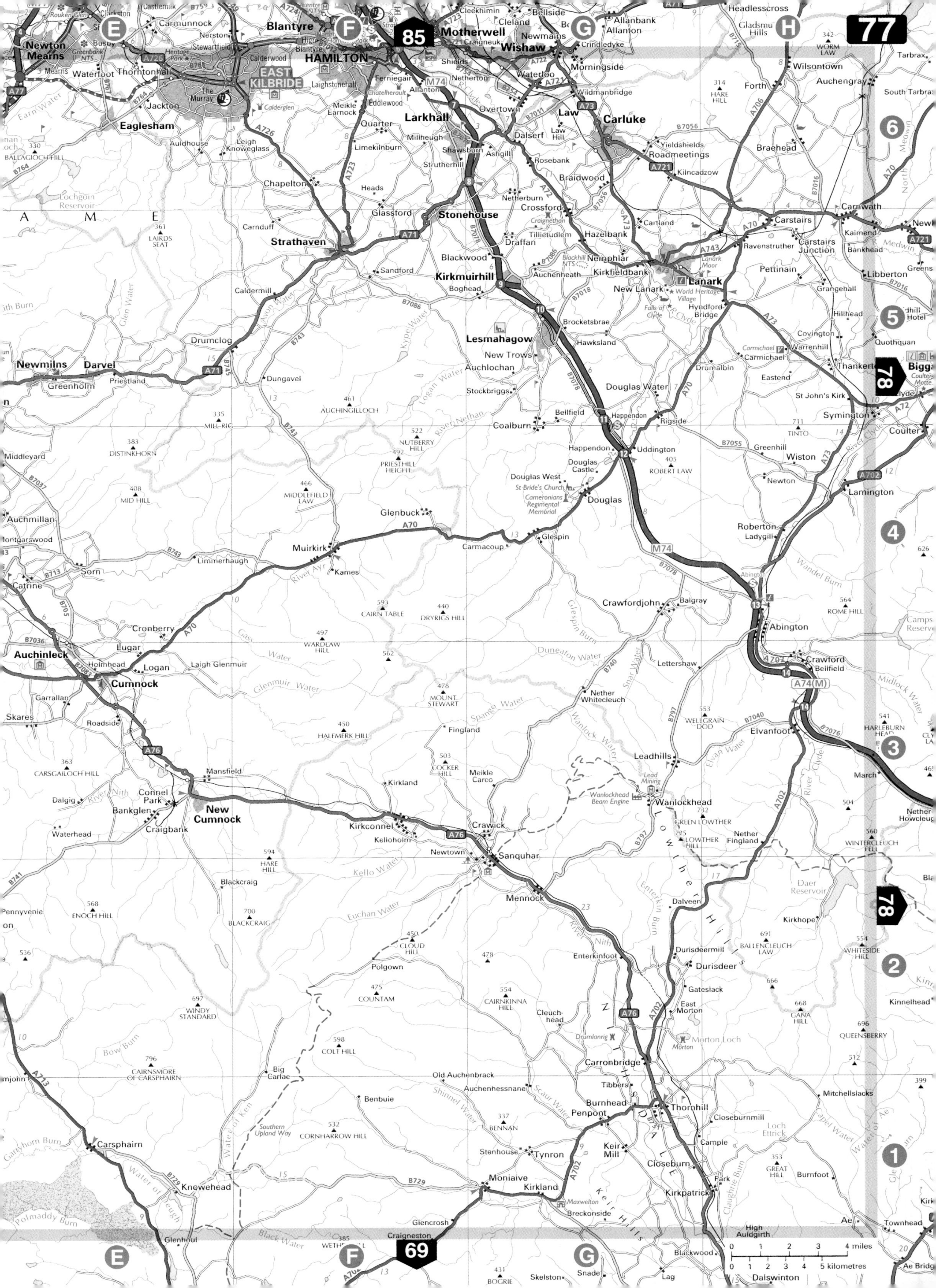
77
85
E
F
G
H
Newton Mearns
Busby
Carmunnock
Blantyre
Motherwell
Cleland
Bellside
Allanbank
Allanton
Headlesscross
Gladsmuir Hills
Newmains
Wishaw
Craigneuk
Crindledyke
HAMILTON
EAST KILBRIDE
Calderwood
Thorntonhall
Waterfoot
Stewartfield
Nerston
Ferniegair
Laighstonehall
Allanton
Shields
Netherton
Waterloo
Morningside
Wildmanbridge
Wilsontown
Forth
Auchengray
Tarbrax
South Tarbrax
342 WORM LAW
314 HARE HILL
Jackton
The Murray
Calderglen
Chatelherault
Eddlewood
Meikle Earnock
Eaglesham
Quarter
Larkhall
Overtown
Law
Carluke
Dalserf
Law Hill
Yieldshields
Roadmeetings
Kilncadzow
Braehead
Auldhouse
Leigh Knoweglass
Millheugh
Limekilnburn
Shawsburn
Ashgill
Rosebank
Braidwood
330 BALLAGIOCH HILL
Strutherhill
Chapelton
Lochgoin Reservoir
Heads
Netherburn
Crossford
Craignethan
Carnwath
Carstairs
Glassford
Stonehouse
Cartland
Kaimend
Bankhead
Carstairs Junction
Ravenstruther
361 LAIRDS SEAT
Carnduff
Strathaven
Tillietudlem
Draffan
Hazelbank
Blackwood
Blackhill NTS
Nemphlar
Lanark Moor
Pettinain
Libberton
Greens
Sandford
Kirkmuirhill
Auchenheath
Kirkfieldbank
Lanark
New Lanark
World Heritage Village
Grangehall
Caldermill
Boghead
Falls of Clyde
Hyndford Bridge
Hillhead
Lesmahagow
Brocketsbrae
Hawksland
Covington
Quothquan
Drumclog
Carmichael
Warrenhill
Thankerton
78
Newmilns
Darvel
Greenholm
Priestland
New Trows
Auchlochan
Drumalbin
Eastend
Dungavel
Stockbriggs
Douglas Water
St John's Kirk
461 AUCHINGILLOCH
Bellfield
Symington
Coulter
335 MILL RIG
Coalburn
Happendon
Rigside
711 TINTO
522 NUTBERRY HILL
383 DISTINKHORN
Middleyard
492 PRIESTHILL HEIGHT
Happendon
Uddington
Greenhill
Douglas Castle
405 ROBERT LAW
Wiston
Douglas West
St Bride's Church
Cameronians Regimental Memorial
Douglas
Newton
Lamington
466 MIDDLEFIELD LAW
408 MID HILL
Auchmillan
Glenbuck
Roberton
Ladygill
Montgarswood
Muirkirk
Carmacoup
Glespin
Limmerhaugh
Sorn
Kames
Catrine
Abington
593 CAIRN TABLE
440 DRYRIGS HILL
Crawfordjohn
Balgray
564 ROME HILL
Cronberry
497 WARDLAW HILL
Auchinleck
Lugar
Holmhead
Logan
Laigh Glenmuir
Cumnock
Lettershaw
Crawford
Belfield
Garrallan
Nether Whitecleuch
Skares
Roadside
478 MOUNT STEWART
553 WELLGRAIN DOD
541 HARLEBURN HEAD
Elvanfoot
450 HALFMERK HILL
Fingland
363 CARSGAILOCH HILL
Mansfield
503 COCKER HILL
Meikle Carco
Leadhills
Lead Mining
March
Dalgig
Connel Park
Kirkland
Wanlockhead Beam Engine
Wanlockhead
Bankglen
New Cumnock
Craigbank
732 GREEN LOWTHER
Waterhead
Kirkconnel
Kelloholm
Crawick
725 LOWTHER HILL
Nether Fingland
504
Nether Howcleugh
560 WINTERCLEUCH FELL
Newtown
Sanquhar
594 HARE HILL
Blackcraig
Mennock
Daer Reservoir
Dalveen
568 ENOCH HILL
700 BLACKCRAIG
Pennyvenie
Kirkhope
450 CLOUD HILL
Durisdeermill
Durisdeer
691 BALLENCLEUCH LAW
554 WHITESIDE HILL
Enterkinfoot
Polgown
478
475 COUNTAM
Gateslack
554 CAIRNKINNA HILL
East Morton
Kinnelhead
536
697 WINDY STANDARD
Cleuch-head
668 GANA HILL
696 QUEENSBERRY
Drumlanrig
Morton Loch
598 COLT HILL
796 CAIRNSMORE OF CARSPHAIRN
Carronbridge
512
Big Carlae
Old Auchenbrack
Auchenhessnane
Tibbers
Burnhead
Thornhill
Mitchellslacks
399
Benbuie
Penpont
Closeburnmill
Southern Upland Way
532 CORNHARROW HILL
337 BENNAN
Keir Mill
Cample
Loch Ettrick
Carsphairn
Stenhouse
Tynron
Closeburn
353 GREAT HILL
Burnfoot
Moniaive
Kirkland
Park
Knowehead
Kirkpatrick
Maxwelton
Breckonside
Glencrosh
Ae
Townhead
Craigneston
High Auldgirth
Glenhoul
385 WETHER HILL
69
Blackwood
Snade
431 BOGRIE
Skelston
Lag
Dalswinton
Ae Bridgend
0 1 2 3 4 miles
0 1 2 3 4 5 kilometres
1
2
3
4
5
6
A M E
L o w t h e r H i l l s
N I T H S D A L E
Keir Hills

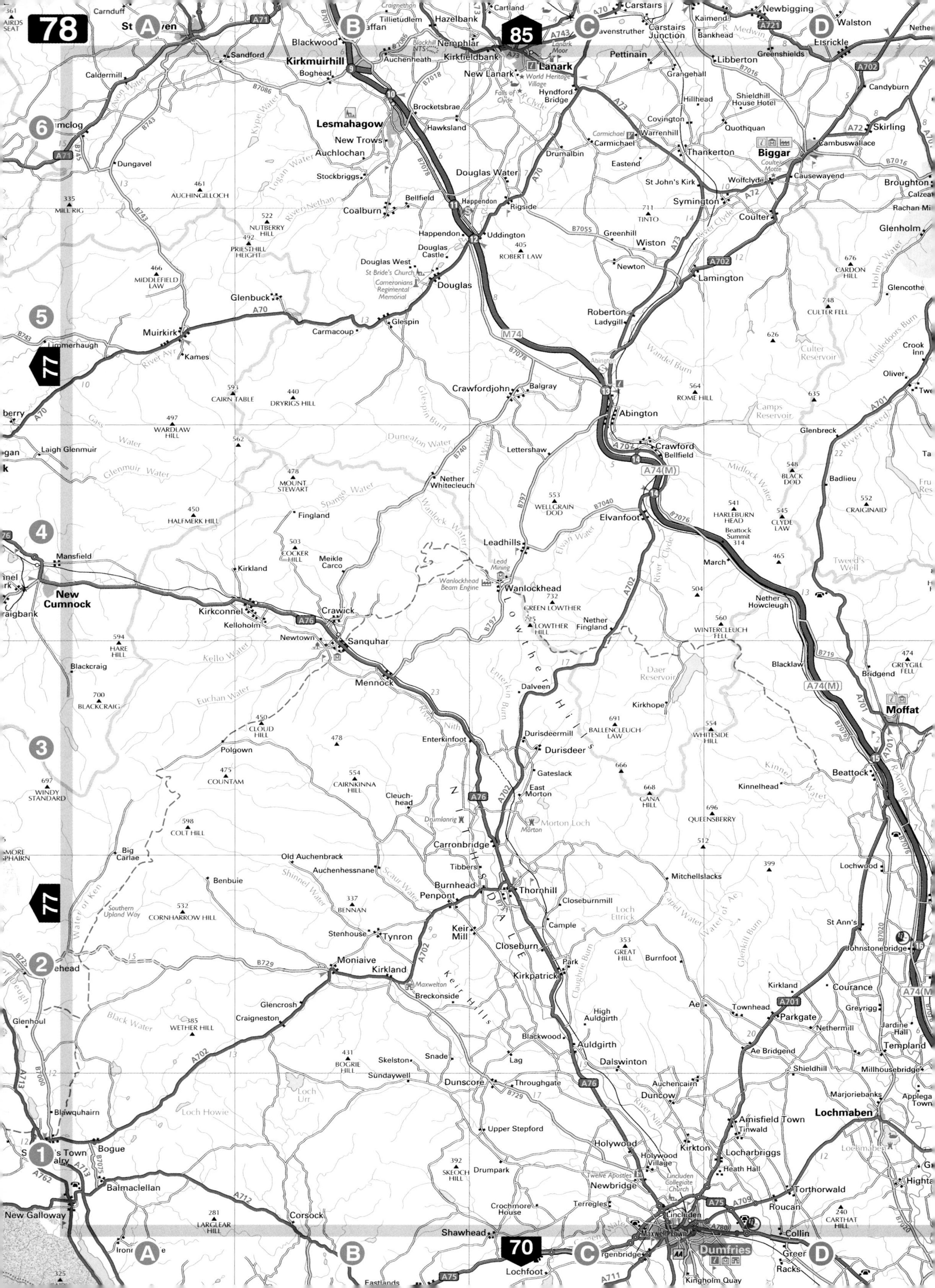
78
85
77
70
A
B
C
D
6
5
4
3
2
1
Carnduff
Tillietudlem
Hazelbank
Cartland
Carstairs
Kaimend
Newbigging
Walston
Blackwood
Nemphlar
Carstairs Junction
Bankhead
Elsrickle
Sandford
Kirkmuirhill
Auchenheath
Kirkfieldbank
Lanark
Pettinain
Libberton
Greenshields
Caldermill
Boghead
New Lanark
World Heritage Village
Grangehall
Candyburn
Falls of Clyde
Hyndford Bridge
Hillhead
Shieldhill House Hotel
Brocketsbrae
Covington
Quothquan
Skirling
Lesmahagow
Hawksland
Carmichael
Warrenhill
Cambuswallace
New Trows
Drumalbin
Thankerton
Biggar
Dungavel
Auchlochan
Eastend
Coulter Motte
Causewayend
Stockbriggs
Douglas Water
St John's Kirk
Wolfclyde
Broughton
461 AUCHINGILLOCH
Bellfield
Symington
335 MILL RIG
Coalburn
Happendon
Rigside
711 TINTO
Coulter
Rachan Mill
522 NUTBERRY HILL
492 PRIESTHILL HEIGHT
Happendon
Uddington
Greenhill
Wiston
Glenholm
Douglas Castle
405 ROBERT LAW
Newton
Lamington
676 CARDON HILL
466 MIDDLEFIELD LAW
Douglas West
St Bride's Church
Cameronians' Regimental Memorial
Douglas
Glencothe
Glenbuck
748 CULTER FELL
Roberton
Ladygill
Muirkirk
Carmacoup
Glespin
Limmerhaugh
Kames
River Ayr
626
Culter Reservoir
Crook Inn
Abington
Wandel Burn
Crawfordjohn
Balgray
Oliver
593 CAIRN TABLE
440 DRYRIGS HILL
564 ROME HILL
635
Abington
Camps Reservoir
497 WARDLAW HILL
562
Glespin Burn
Duneaton Water
Lettershaw
Crawford
Bellfield
Glenbreck
River Tweed
Laigh Glenmuir
Glenmuir Water
Gass Water
478 MOUNT STEWART
Nether Whitecleuch
Snar Water
Midlock Water
548 BLACK DOD
Badlieu
553 WELLGRAIN DOD
Elvanfoot
541 HARLEBURN HEAD
545 CLYDE LAW
552 CRAIGINAID
450 HALFMERK HILL
Fingland
Spango Water
Wanlock Water
Beattock Summit 314
Mansfield
503 COCKER HILL
Meikle Carco
Leadhills
Elvan Water
March
465
Tweed's Well
Kirkland
Lead Mining
Wanlockhead
Wanlockhead Beam Engine
504
New Cumnock
Kirkconnel
Crawick
732 GREEN LOWTHER
Nether Howcleugh
Kelloholm
725 LOWTHER HILL
Nether Fingland
560 WINTERCLEUCH FELL
594 HARE HILL
Newtown
Sanquhar
Lowther Hills
Kello Water
Blackcraig
Mennock
Daer Reservoir
Blacklaw
474 GREYGILL FELL
Bridgend
700 BLACKCRAIG
Euchan Water
Dalveen
Enterkin Burn
Kirkhope
Moffat
450 CLOUD HILL
691 BALLENCLEUCH LAW
554 WHITESIDE HILL
478
Enterkinfoot
River Nith
Durisdeermill
Polgown
Durisdeer
697 WINDY STANDARD
475 COUNTAM
554 CAIRNKINNA HILL
Gateslack
666
Beattock
Kinnelhead
Kinnel Water
East Morton
668 GANA HILL
Cleuchhead
Nithsdale
696 QUEENSBERRY
Drumlanrig
Morton Loch
Morton
598 COLT HILL
512
Carronbridge
Big Carlae
Old Auchenbrack
Auchenhessnane
Tibbers
399
Lochwood
Mitchellslacks
Benbuie
Shinnel Water
Scaur Water
Burnhead
Thornhill
Penpont
Closeburnmill
337 BENNAN
Loch Ettrick
Capel Water
Water of Ae
532 CORNHARROW HILL
Southern Upland Way
Water of Ken
Keir Mill
Cample
St Ann's
Stenhouse
Tynron
Closeburn
353 GREAT HILL
Burnfoot
Glenkill Burn
Johnstonebridge
Moniaive
Kirkland
Park
Kirkpatrick
Claughrie Burn
Keir Hills
Maxwelton
Breckonside
Kirkland
Courance
Glencrosh
Ae
Townhead
Parkgate
Greyrigg
Craigneston
High Auldgirth
Nethermill
Jardine Hall
Glenhoul
Black Water
385 WETHER HILL
Blackwood
Auldgirth
Templand
Ae Bridgend
431 BOGRIE HILL
Skelston
Snade
Lag
Dalswinton
Shieldhill
Millhousebridge
Sundaywell
Dunscore
Throughgate
Auchencairn
Duncow
River Nith
Marjoriebanks
Applegarth Town
Loch Urr
Lochmaben
Blawquhairn
Loch Howie
Amisfield Town
Tinwald
Upper Stepford
Holywood
Kirkton
Locharbriggs
Lochmaben
Bogue
Holywood Village
Heath Hall
392 SKEOCH HILL
Drumpark
Twelve Apostles
Lincluden Collegiate Church
Balmaclellan
Newbridge
Torthorwald
Hightae
Terregles
Roucan
240 CARTHAT HILL
New Galloway
Corsock
281 LARGLEAR HILL
Crochmore House
Lincluden
Shawhead
Maxwell Town
Dumfries
Collin
Cargenbridge
Greer
Racks
Lochfoot
Kingholm Quay
Eastlands
A71
A70
A73
A72
A702
A74(M)
M74
A76
A701
A713
A762
A712
A75
A709
A780
A711
B7078
B7086
B7018
B743
B745
B7055
B7016
B740
B797
B7040
B7076
B719
B729
B7000
B7075
B7020
B7016

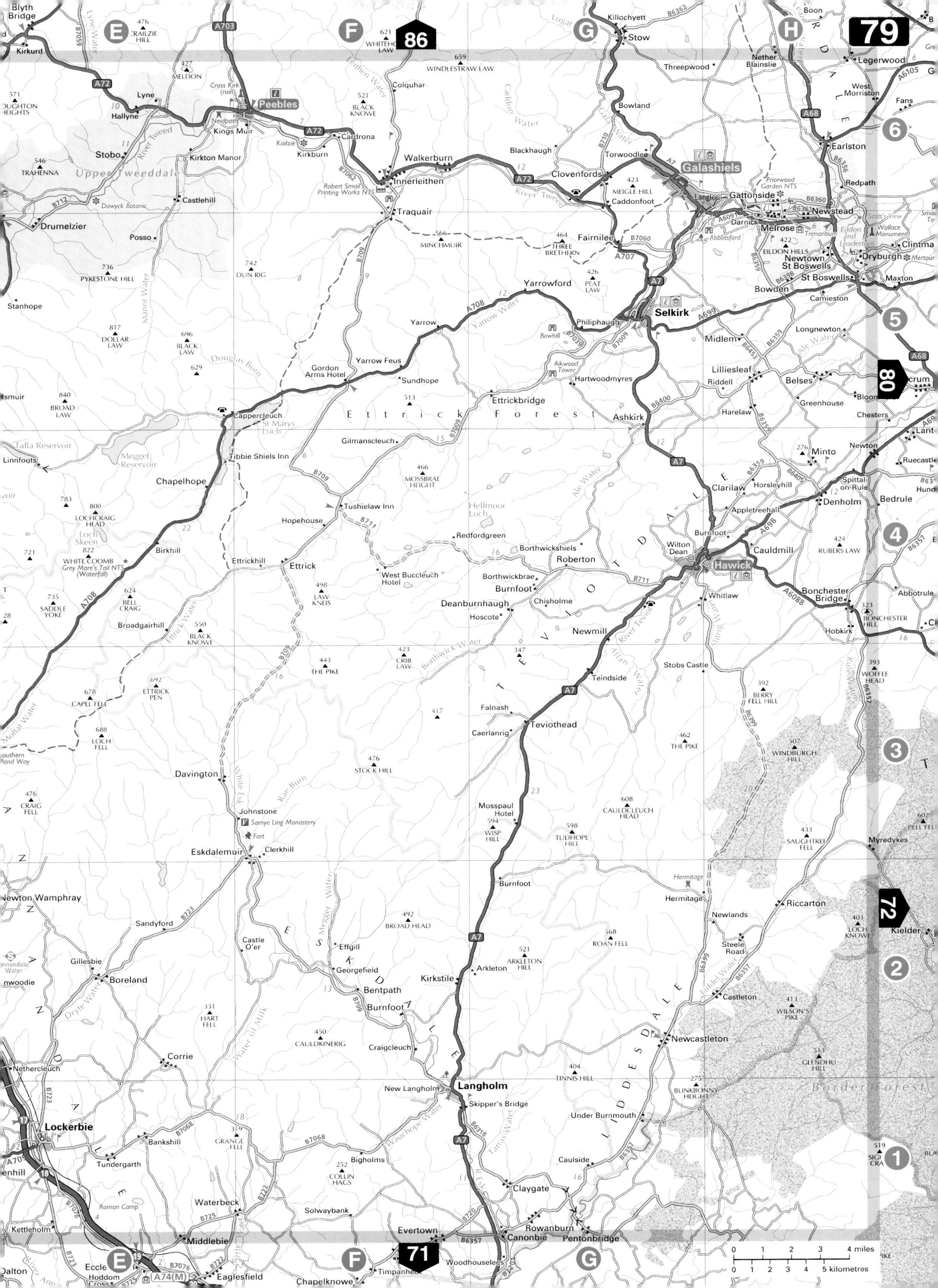

86
Blyth Bridge
Kirkurd
476 CRAILZIE HILL
A703
B7059
Lyne Water
621 WHITEHOPE LAW
Lugate
Killochyett
Stow
B6362
Boon
Legerwood
Nether Blainslie
Threepwood
659 WINDLESTRAW LAW
427 MELDON
A72
Lyne
Hallyne
Cross Kirk (ruin)
Peebles
Neidpath
Kings Muir
Colquhar
521 BLACK KNOWE
Leithen Water
Caddon Water
Bowland
West Morriston
Fans
A6105
A68
Earlston
571 DOUGHTON HEIGHTS
Stobo
546 TRAHENNA
Upper Tweeddale
River Tweed
Kailzie
Cardrona
Kirkburn
Kirkton Manor
Walkerburn
Blackhaugh
Torwoodlee
Gala Water
B710
A7
Galashiels
Redpath
Drumelzier
Dawyck Botanic
Castlehill
B712
B7062
Robert Smail's Printing Works NTS
Innerleithen
Traquair
Clovenfords
423 MEIGLE HILL
Caddonfoot
River Tweed
Priorwood Garden NTS
Gattonside
Langlee
Darnick
Melrose
Abbotsford
Newstead
B6360
B6361
A6091
Scott's View
Wallace Monument
Eildon and Leaderfoot
Trimontium
422 EILDON HILLS
Newtown St Boswells
St Boswells
Dryburgh
Mertoun
Clintmains
Maxton
Bowden
B6398
B6359
Posso
566 MINCHMUIR
464 THREE BRETHREN
Fairnilee
B7060
A707
736 PYKESTONE HILL
742 DUN RIG
B709
426 PEAT LAW
Yarrowford
A7
Selkirk
Camieston
A699
Stanhope
Manor Water
817 DOLLAR LAW
696 BLACK LAW
Douglas Burn
629
Yarrow
A708
Yarrow Water
Bowhill
Philiphaugh
B7039
B7009
Midlem
B6453
B6359
Longnewton
Ale Water
Yarrow Feus
Gordon Arms Hotel
Sundhope
Aikwood Tower
Hartwoodmyres
Lilliesleaf
Riddell
Belses
80
Ancrum
Bloomfield
Greenhouse
Chesters
840 BROAD LAW
Cappercleuch
St Marys Loch
513
Ettrick Forest
Ettrickbridge
Ashkirk
B6400
Harelaw
B6359
Talla Reservoir
Megget Reservoir
Linnfoots
Tibbie Shiels Inn
Gilmanscleuch
466 MOSSBRAE HEIGHT
Minto
Lanton
Newton
Ruecastle
Spittal-on-Rule
Chapelhope
783
800 LOCHCRAIG HEAD
Loch Skeen
B709
Tushielaw Inn
Hopehouse
B711
Hellmoor Loch
Ale Water
Clarilaw
Horsleyhill
B6405
Appletreehall
Denholm
Bedrule
Hundalee
721
822 WHITE COOMB
Grey Mare's Tail NTS (Waterfall)
Birkhill
Ettrickhill
Ettrick
Redfordgreen
Borthwickshiels
Wilton Dean
Burnfoot
A698
Cauldmill
424 RUBERS LAW
B6357
735 SADDLE YOKE
624 BELL CRAIG
498 LAW KNEIS
West Buccleuch Hotel
Roberton
Borthwickbrae
Burnfoot
Hawick
Whitlaw
Bonchester Bridge
Abbotrule
A6088
Deanburnhaugh
Hoscote
Chisholme
B711
Broadgairhill
550 BLACK KNOWE
Ettrick Water
Newmill
River Teviot
Slitrig Water
Hobkirk
323 BONCHESTER HILL
443 THE PIKE
423 CRIB LAW
Borthwick Water
347
Allan Water
Stobs Castle
393 WOFFEE HEAD
Rule Water
B6357
692 ETTRICK PEN
678 CAPEL FELL
Teindside
392 BERRY FELL HILL
B6399
Moffat Water
688 LOCH FELL
Southern Upland Way
417
Falnash
Teviothead
Caerlanrig
462 THE PIKE
507 WINDBURGH HILL
Davington
476 STOCK HILL
White Esk
Rae Burn
476 CRAIG FELL
Johnstone
Samye Ling Monastery
Fort
Mosspaul Hotel
594 WISP HILL
608 CAULDCLEUCH HEAD
598 TUDHOPE HILL
433 SAUGHTREE FELL
602 PEEL FELL
Myredykes
Eskdalemuir
Clerkhill
Burnfoot
Hermitage
Newton Wamphray
Sandyford
B723
Megget Water
492 BROAD HEAD
Newlands
Riccarton
72
403 LOCH KNOWE
Kielder
Castle O'er
Effgill
Georgefield
Eskdale
568 ROAN FELL
521 ARKLETON HILL
Arkleton
Kirkstile
Steele Road
Gillesbie
Boreland
Annandale Water
Dryfe Water
Bentpath
Burnfoot
B709
B6399
Liddel Water
B6357
Castleton
413 WILSON'S PIKE
331 HART FELL
450 CAULDKINERIG
Water of Milk
Craigcleuch
Newcastleton
Liddesdale
Corrie
Nethercleuch
404 TINNIS HILL
513 GLENDHU HILL
Langholm
New Langholm
275 BLINKBONNY HEIGHT
Border Forest
Skipper's Bridge
B723
Lockerbie
B7068
Bankshill
319 GRANGE FELL
B7068
Wauchope Water
B6318
Tarras Water
Under Burnmouth
Tundergarth
A709
252 COLLIN HAGS
Bigholms
Caulside
B6357
519 SIGHTY CRAG
Roman Camp
Waterbeck
B722
Claygate
B725
Solwaybank
B720
Evertown
Rowanburn
Canonbie
Penton Bridge
Kettleholm
Middlebie
B7076
B723
71
B6357
Eccle
Hoddom Cross
A74(M)
Eaglesfield
Dalton
Chapelknowe
Timpanheck
Woodhouselees
0 1 2 3 4 miles
0 1 2 3 4 5 kilometres

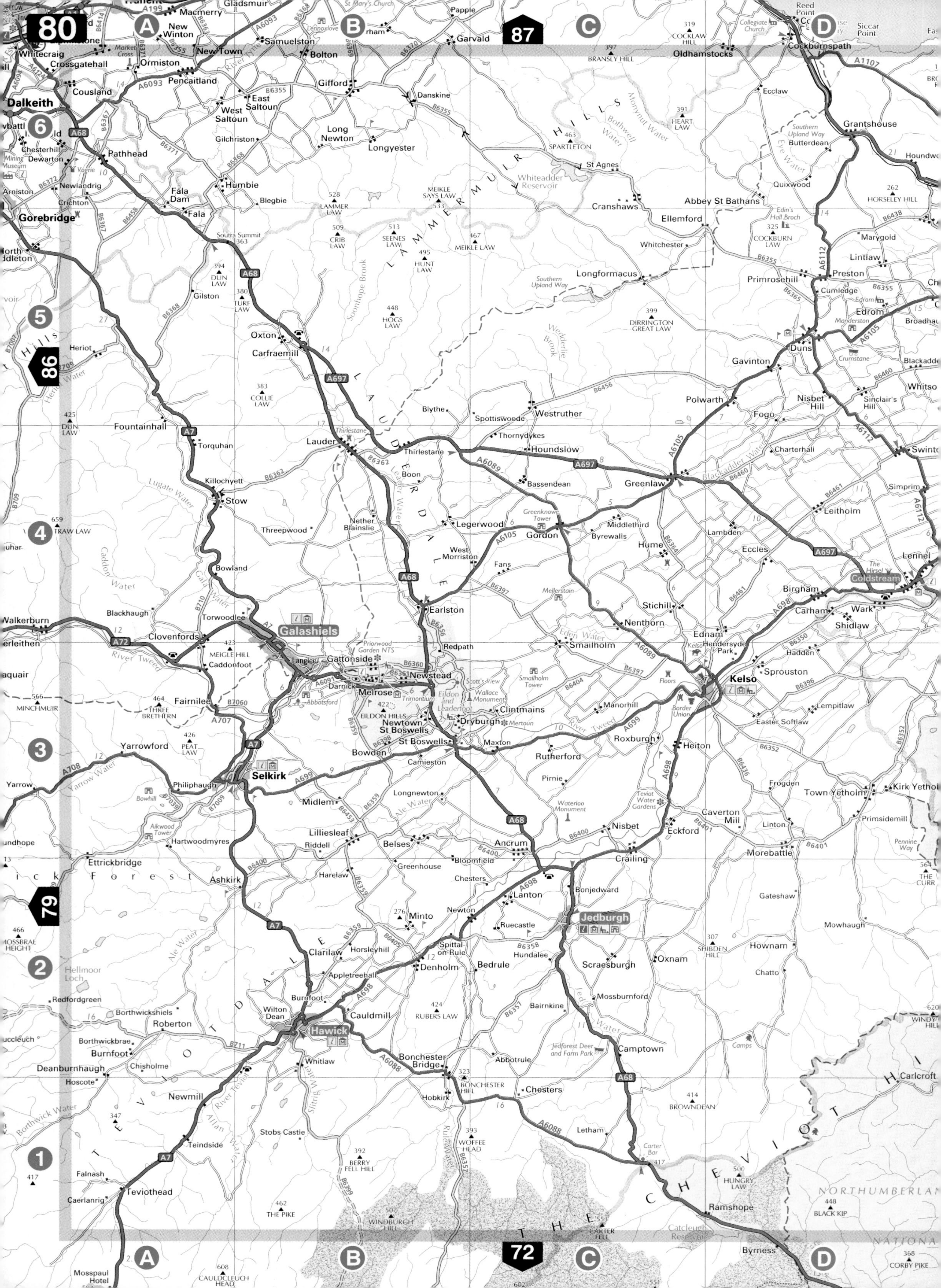
80
A
B
87
C
D
Gladsmuir
Macmerry
A199
New Winton
Samuelston
St Mary's Church
Papple
Garvald
Reed Point
Siccar Point
Collegiate Church
319 COCKLAW HILL
Whitecraig
Market Cross
New Town
Bolton
397 BRANSLY HILL
Oldhamstocks
Cockburnspath
A1107
Crossgatehall
Ormiston
A6093
A6124
Pencaitland
Cousland
East Saltoun
West Saltoun
Gifford
Danskine
B6355
Ecclaw
Dalkeith
6
A68
Long Newton
Longyester
Gilchriston
Chesterhill
Dewarton
Mining Museum
Pathhead
Vogrie
Newlandrig
Arniston
Crichton
Humbie
Fala Dam
Fala
Blegbie
Gorebridge
North Middleton
Soutra Summit 363
463 SPARTLETON
391 HEART LAW
Grantshouse
Southern Upland Way
Butterdean
Houndwood
St Agnes
Whiteadder Reservoir
L A M M E R M U I R   H I L L S
Bothwell Water
Monynut Water
Eye Water
Quixwood
262 HORSELEY HILL
528 LAMMER LAW
MEIKLE SAYS LAW 533
509 CRIB LAW
513 SEENES LAW
495 HUNT LAW
467 MEIKLE LAW
Cranshaws
Abbey St Bathans
Ellemford
Edin's Hall Broch
325 COCKBURN LAW
Marygold
Whitchester
B6438
A6112
Lintlaw
Preston
Primrosehill
B6355
B6365
Cumledge
Edrom
Manderston
Broadhaugh
394 DUN LAW
380 TURF LAW
Gilston
Longformacus
Southern Upland Way
399 DIRRINGTON GREAT LAW
Sootnhope Brook
448 HOGS LAW
5
Heriot
Oxton
Carfraemill
A697
86
Heriot Water
Duns
A6105
Crumstane
Blackadder
Gavinton
Watch Water
B6460
Whitsome
383 COLLIE LAW
L A U D E R D A L E
B6456
Polwarth
Nisbet Hill
Sinclair's Hill
Fogo
425 DUN LAW
Fountainhall
A7
Blythe
Spottiswoode
Westruther
Thirlestane
Lauder
Thornydykes
Torquhan
Houndslow
Charterhall
Swinton
A6089
B6362
Boon
Bassendean
Greenlaw
Blackadder Water
Simprim
Killochyett
Lugate Water
Stow
Leader Water
Greenknowe Tower
Legerwood
Middlethird
Leitholm
659 TRAW LAW
4
Threepwood
Nether Blainslie
Gordon
Byrewalls
Lambden
Hume
B6364
Eccles
West Morriston
Fans
A697
Lennel
Caddon Water
Bowland
The Hirsel
Coldstream
Birgham
Mellerstain
Carham
Wark
Walkerburn
Blackhaugh
B710
Torwoodlee
Gala Water
Galashiels
Earlston
Stichill
Nenthorn
Shidlaw
A72
Clovenfords
423 MEIGLE HILL
Caddonfoot
River Tweed
Priorwood Garden NTS
Redpath
Eden Water
Smailholm
Ednam
Kelso
Hendersyde Park
B6350
Hadden
Gattonside
Langlee
B6360
Newstead
A6091
Darnick
Melrose
Trimontium
Scott's View
Smailholm Tower
Floors
Sprouston
Eildon and Leaderfoot
Wallace Monument
Abbotsford
Border Union
B6396
566 MINCHMUIR
464 THREE BRETHREN
Fairnilee
B7060
A707
422 EILDON HILLS
Newtown St Boswells
Clintmains
Manorhill
Dryburgh
Mertoun
Lempitlaw
Easter Softlaw
426 PEAT LAW
St Boswells
Maxton
River Tweed
Roxburgh
Heiton
3
Yarrowford
Bowden
Camieston
Rutherford
B6352
A708
Yarrow Water
Philiphaugh
Selkirk
A699
Pirnie
Frogden
Town Yetholm
Kirk Yetholm
Yarrow
Bowhill
B7009
Midlem
Longnewton
Ale Water
Teviot Water Gardens
Caverton Mill
Linton
Primsidemill
Aikwood Tower
Hartwoodmyres
Lilliesleaf
Waterloo Monument
A68
Nisbet
Eckford
Pennine Way
Riddell
Belses
Ancrum
B6400
Crailing
Morebattle
Ettrickbridge
Ettrick Forest
Ashkirk
Harelaw
Greenhouse
Bloomfield
Chesters
564 THE CURR
79
Lanton
Bonjedward
Gateshaw
466 MOSSBRAE HEIGHT
Minto
Newton
Jedburgh
Ruecastle
Mowhaugh
2
Hellmoor Loch
Ale Water
Clarilaw
Horsleyhill
Spittal-on-Rule
Denholm
Hundalee
Bedrule
B6358
Scraesburgh
Oxnam
307 SHIBDEN HILL
Hownam
Chatto
Redfordgreen
Appletreehall
Burnfoot
Wilton Dean
A698
Cauldmill
Mossburnford
Bairnkine
424 RUBERS LAW
Borthwickshiels
Roberton
Hawick
Jed Water
Buccleuch
Borthwickbrae
Burnfoot
B711
Jedforest Deer and Farm Park
Camptown
Camps
620 WINDY HILL
Chisholme
Deanburnhaugh
Hoscote
Whitlaw
A6088
Bonchester Bridge
Abbotrule
T E V I O T D A L E
Newmill
River Teviot
Slitrig Water
323 BONCHESTER HILL
Hobkirk
Chesters
414 BROWNDEAN
Carlcroft
Borthwick Water
347
Allan Water
Stobs Castle
393 WOOFEE HEAD
Letham
Teindside
Rule Water
B6357
Carter Bar
417
1
417
392 BERRY FELL HILL
500 HUNGRY LAW
Falnash
Teviothead
C H E V I O T   H I L L S
NORTHUMBERLAND
Caerlanrig
B6399
462 THE PIKE
507 WINDBURGH HILL
THE
553 CARTER FELL
Ramshope
448 BLACK KIP
Catcleugh Reservoir
NATIONAL
72
Byrness
368 CORBY PIKE
Mosspaul Hotel
608 CAULDCLEUCH HEAD
602
551

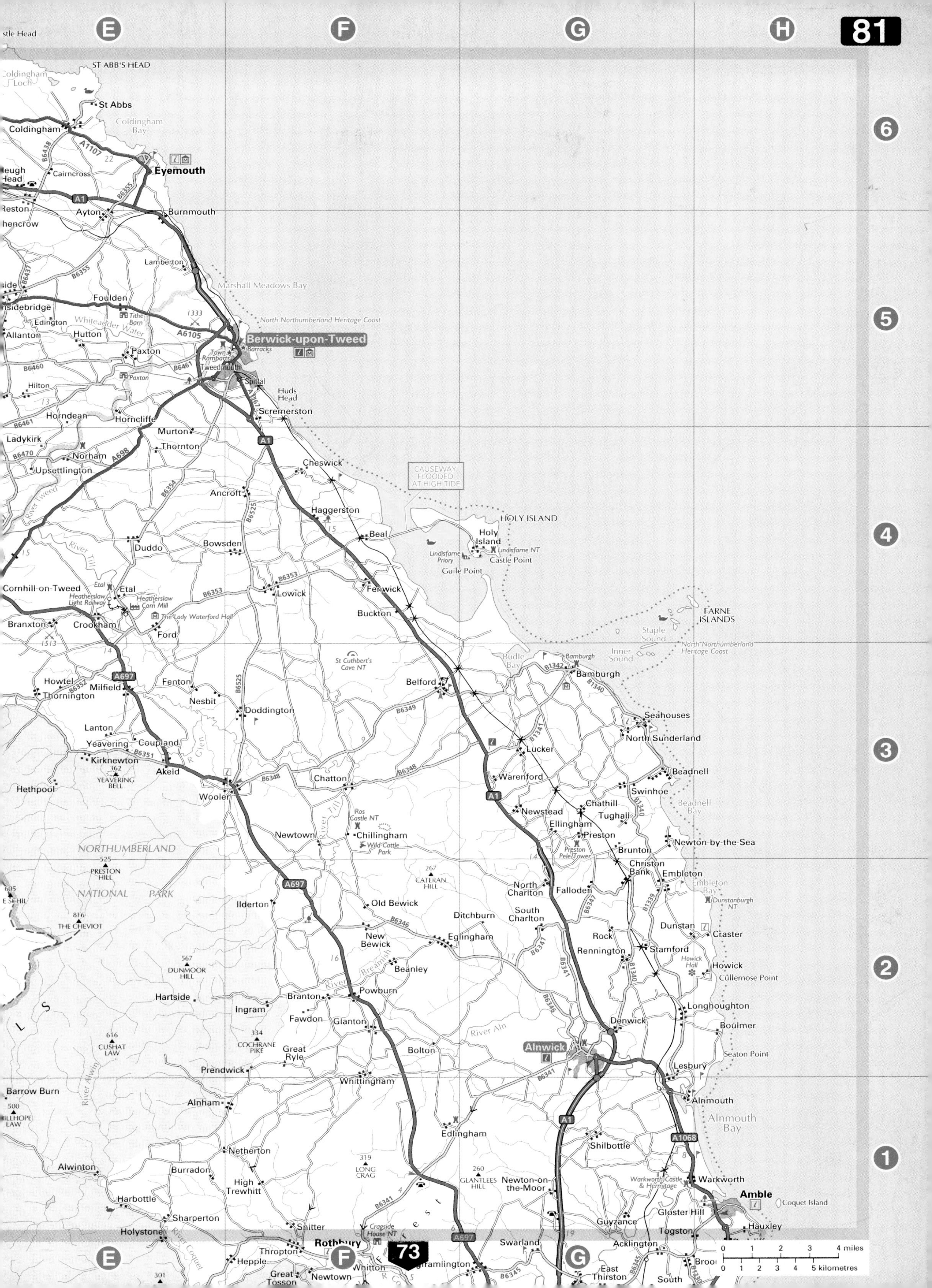
E
F
G
H
ST ABB'S HEAD
St Abbs
Coldingham
Coldingham Bay
Eyemouth
Cairncross
Burnmouth
Ayton
Lamberton
Marshall Meadows Bay
Foulden
North Northumberland Heritage Coast
Edington
Allanton
Hutton
Paxton
Berwick-upon-Tweed
Tweedmouth
Spittal
Huds Head
Scremerston
Horndean
Horncliffe
Ladykirk
Murton
Thornton
Norham
Upsettlington
Cheswick
CAUSEWAY FLOODED AT HIGH TIDE
Ancroft
Haggerston
HOLY ISLAND
Holy Island
Beal
Lindisfarne Priory
Lindisfarne NT
Castle Point
Guile Point
Duddo
Bowsden
Cornhill-on-Tweed
Etal
Lowick
Fenwick
Heatherslaw Corn Mill
Buckton
FARNE ISLANDS
Staple Sound
Inner Sound
Branxton
Crookham
The Lady Waterford Hall
Ford
St Cuthbert's Cave NT
Budle Bay
Bamburgh
Howtel
Milfield
Thornington
Fenton
Belford
Nesbit
Doddington
Seahouses
Lanton
Yeavering
Coupland
North Sunderland
Kirknewton
Lucker
Akeld
Beadnell
Hethpool
Wooler
Chatton
Warenford
Swinhoe
Newstead
Chathill
Tughall
Ellingham
Newtown
Chillingham
Preston
Newton-by-the-Sea
NORTHUMBERLAND
NATIONAL PARK
Brunton
Christon Bank
Embleton
Embleton Bay
North Charlton
Falloden
Dunstanburgh NT
Ilderton
Old Bewick
THE CHEVIOT
South Charlton
Ditchburn
Dunstan
Craster
New Bewick
Eglingham
Rock
Rennington
Stamford
Beanley
Howick
Cullernose Point
Hartside
Branton
Powburn
Longhoughton
Ingram
Fawdon
Glanton
Denwick
Boulmer
Great Ryle
Bolton
Alnwick
Seaton Point
Lesbury
Prendwick
Whittingham
Barrow Burn
Alnmouth
Alnham
Alnmouth Bay
Edlingham
Netherton
Shilbottle
Alwinton
Burradon
High Trewhitt
Newton-on-the-Moor
Warkworth
Amble
Coquet Island
Harbottle
Sharperton
Guyzance
Gloster Hill
Holystone
Snitter
Rothbury
Togston
Hauxley
Swarland
Acklington
Thropton
Hepple
Whitton
Framlington
East Thirston
Great Tosson
Newtown
South
73
0 1 2 3 4 miles
0 1 2 3 4 5 kilometres

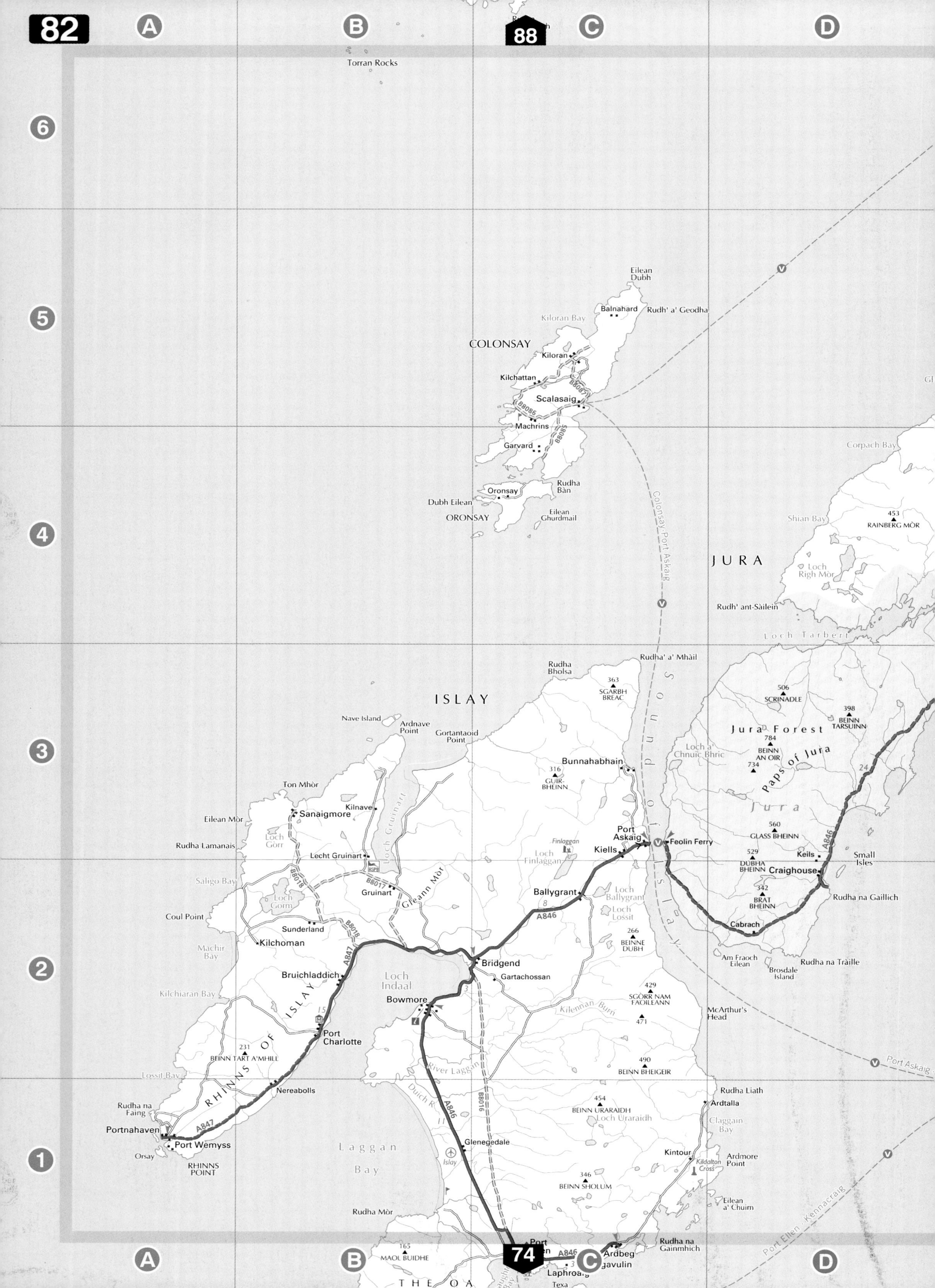
A
B
88
C
D
6
5
4
3
2
1
Torran Rocks
Eilean Dubh
Balnahard
Rudh' a' Geodha
Kiloran Bay
COLONSAY
Kiloran
Kilchattan
Scalasaig
B8086
B8087
B8085
Machrins
Garvard
Rudha Bàn
Oronsay
Dubh Eilean
ORONSAY
Eilean Ghurdmail
Colonsay-Port Askaig
Corpach Bay
Shian Bay
453
RAINBERG MÒR
JURA
Loch Righ Mòr
Rudh' ant-Sàilein
Loch Tarbert
Rudha' a' Mhàil
Rudha Bholsa
363
SGARBH BREAC
ISLAY
Sound of Islay
506
SCRINADLE
398
BEINN TARSUINN
Jura Forest
784
BEINN AN OIR
734
Paps of Jura
Loch a' Chnuic Bhric
Nave Island
Ardnave Point
Gortantaoid Point
Bunnahabhain
316
GUIR-BHEINN
Ton Mhòr
Kilnave
Loch Gruinart
Sanaigmore
Eilean Mòr
Loch Gòrr
Rudha Lamanais
Lecht Gruinart
Finlaggan
Loch Finlaggan
Port Askaig
Kiells
Feolin Ferry
560
GLASS BHEINN
529
DUBHA BHEINN
Keils
Craighouse
Small Isles
A846
Saligo Bay
B8018
B8017
Gruinart
Gleann Mòr
Ballygrant
Loch Ballygrant
Loch Lossit
342
BRAT BHEINN
Rudha na Gaillich
Cabrach
Coul Point
Loch Gorm
Sunderland
266
BEINNE DUBH
Kilchoman
Machir Bay
A847
Bridgend
Am Fraoch Eilean
Brosdale Island
Rudha na Tràille
Bruichladdich
Loch Indaal
Gartachossan
Kilchiaran Bay
Bowmore
429
SGÒRR NAM FAOILEANN
Kilennan Burn
471
McArthur's Head
RHINNS OF ISLAY
Port Charlotte
231
BEINN TART A'MHILL
River Laggan
490
BEINN BHEIGEIR
Port Askaig
Lossit Bay
Nereabolls
Rudha Liath
Duich R.
B8016
454
BEINN URARAIDH
Loch Uraraidh
Ardtalla
Claggain Bay
Rudha na Faing
Portnahaven
Port Wemyss
Orsay
RHINNS POINT
Laggan Bay
Glenegedale
Islay
Kintour
Kildalton Cross
Ardmore Point
346
BEINN SHOLUM
Eilean a' Chùirn
Port Ellen - Kennacraig
Rudha Mòr
165
MAOL BUIDHE
74
Ardbeg
Rudha na Gainmhich
Laphroaig
Texa
THE OA

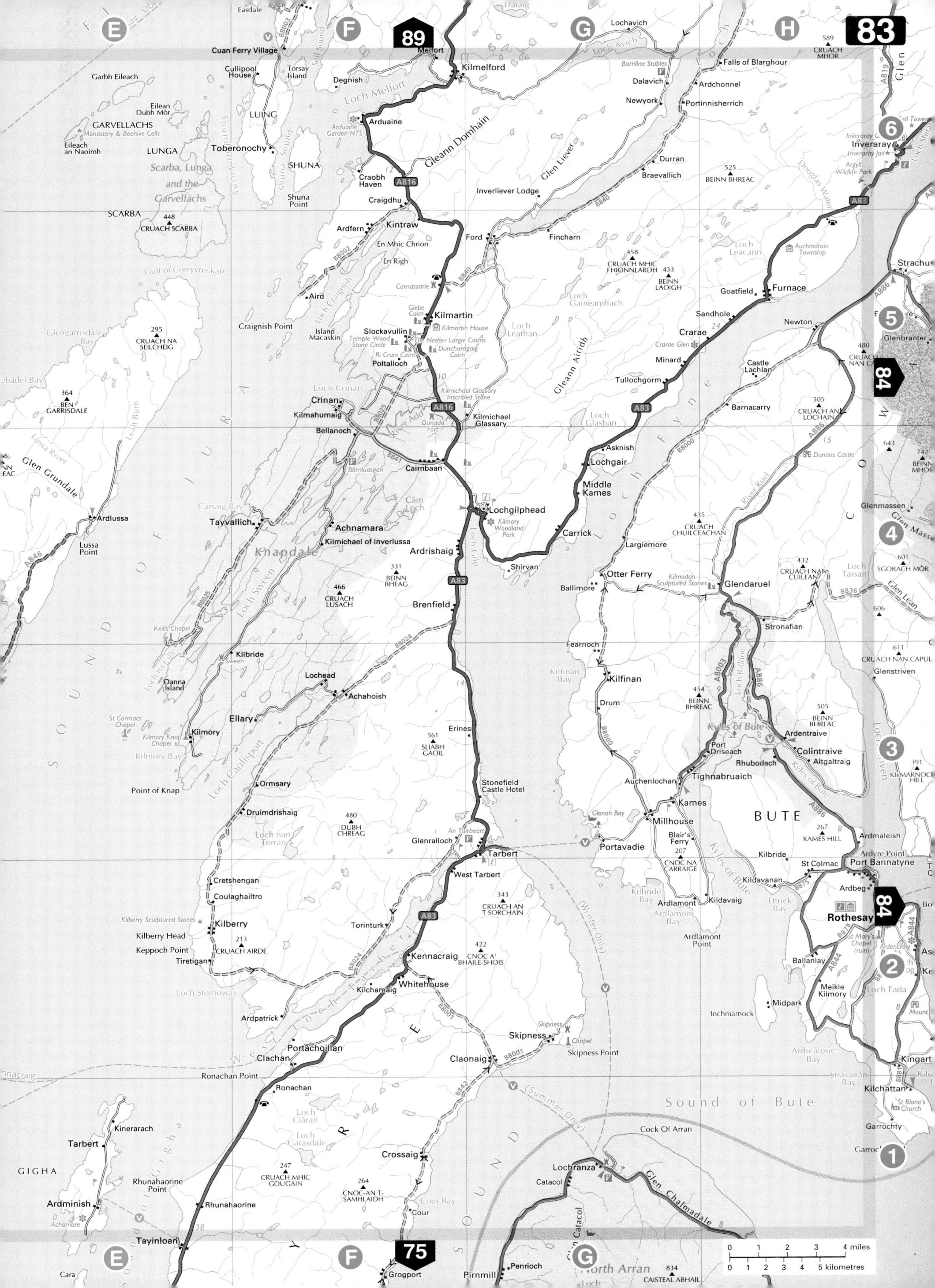

89
83
84
75
E
F
G
H
Cuan Ferry Village
Melfort
Kilmelford
Loch Melfort
Arduaine
Craobh Haven
Craigdhu
Kintraw
Ardfern
Kilmartin
Crinan
Lochgilphead
Ardrishaig
Achnamara
Tayvallich
Brenfield
Tarbert
West Tarbert
Kennacraig
Whitehouse
Clachan
Ronachan
Rhunahaorine
Tayinloan
Claonaig
Skipness
Crossaig
Lochranza
Catacol
Pirnmill
Grogport
Inveraray
Furnace
Strachur
Otter Ferry
Glendaruel
Kilfinan
Tighnabruaich
Portavadie
Colintraive
Port Bannatyne
Rothesay
Kingarth
Kilchattan
LUING
SCARBA
LUNGA
SHUNA
GIGHA
BUTE
Sound of Bute
Loch Fyne
Knapdale
0 1 2 3 4 miles
0 1 2 3 4 5 kilometres

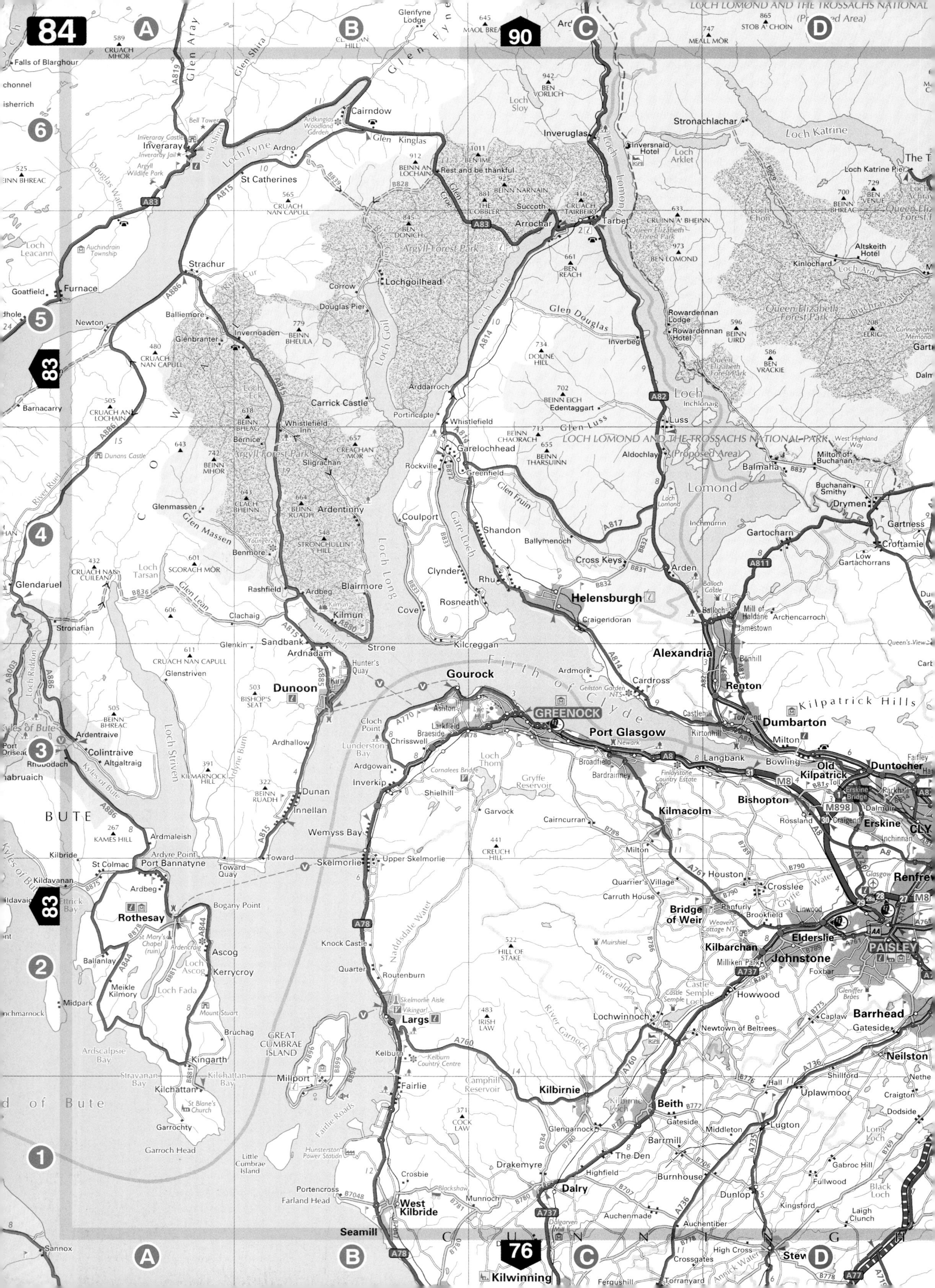
84
A
B
C
D
90
83
83
76
1
2
3
4
5
6
LOCH LOMOND AND THE TROSSACHS NATIONAL (Proposed Area)
Falls of Blarghour
Glen Aray
Glen Shira
Glen Fyne
Glenfyne Lodge
589 CRUACH MHOR
645 MAOL BREAC
865 STOB A' CHOIN
747 MEALL MOR
942 BEN VORLICH
Loch Sloy
Inveraray Castle
Inveraray
Inveraray Jail
Argyll Wildlife Park
Bell Tower
Cairndow
Ardkinglas Woodland Garden
Glen Kinglas
Loch Fyne
Ardno
St Catherines
525 BEINN BHREAC
Douglas Water
A83
A815
A819
B839
B828
565 CRUACH NAN CAPULL
912 BEINN AN LOCHAIN
1011 BEN IME
Rest and be thankful
925 BEINN NARNAIN
881 THE COBBLER
845 BEN DONICH
Succoth
416 CRUACH TAIRBEIRT
Arrochar
Tarbet
Inveruglas
Inversnaid Hotel
Loch Arklet
Stronachlachar
Loch Katrine
Loch Katrine Pier
729 BEN VENUE
700 BEINN BHREAC
633 CRUINN A' BHEINN
Queen Elizabeth Forest Park
973 BEN LOMOND
Loch Lomond
Altskeith Hotel
Kinlochard
Loch Ard
Duchray Water
208 ELRIG
Loch Leacann
Auchindrain Township
Strachur
River Cur
Argyll Forest Park
Corrow
Lochgoilhead
Douglas Pier
Loch Goil
Loch Long
661 BEN REACH
Glen Douglas
Inverbeg
Rowardennan Lodge
Rowardennan Hotel
596 BEINN UIRD
586 BEN VRACKIE
Goatfield
Furnace
Newton
Balliemore
A886
Invernoaden
Glenbranter
779 BEINN BHEULA
480 CRUACH NAN CAPULL
734 DOUNE HILL
702 BEINN EICH
Edentaggart
Arddarroch
A814
A82
Inchlonaig
Barnacarry
505 CRUACH AN LOCHAIN
Loch Eck
618 BEINN BHEAG
Carrick Castle
Portincaple
Whistlefield
Whistlefield Inn
Luss
Glen Luss
713 BEINN CHAORACH
655 BEINN THARSUINN
Aldochlay
West Highland Way
Balmaha
B837
Milton of Buchanan
643
742 BEINN MHOR
Bernice
Dunans Castle
657 CREACHAN MOR
Sligrachan
Garelochhead
Rockville
Greenfield
Glen Fruin
Buchanan Smithy
Drymen
River Ruel
C O W A L
Glenmassen
Glen Massen
643 CLACH BHEINN
664 BEINN RUADH
Ardentinny
Coulport
Gare Loch
Shandon
A817
Ballymenoch
Inchmurrin
Gartocharn
Gartness
Croftamie
548 STRONCHULLIN HILL
Benmore
Benmore Younger Botanic Garden
432 CRUACH NAN CUILEAN
601 SGORACH MOR
Loch Tarsan
Glendaruel
B836
Glen Lean
Rashfield
Ardbeg
Blairmore
Kilmun
Clynder
Rhu
Cross Keys
B831
B832
Arden
A811
Low Gartachorrans
Helensburgh
Balloch Castle
Balloch
Mill of Haldane
Archencarroch
Jamestown
Stronafian
606
Clachaig
A880
Holy Loch
Rosneath
Cove
Kilcreggan
Craigendoran
Strone
Glenkin
Sandbank
Ardnadam
A815
Hunter's Quay
Loch Riddon
A8003
611 CRUACH NAN CAPULL
Glenstriven
503 BISHOP'S SEAT
Dunoon
Kirn
Gourock
Firth of Clyde
Ardmore
Alexandria
Bonhill
Renton
Cardross
Geilston Garden NTS
Queen's View
Kilpatrick Hills
Kyles of Bute
505 BEINN BHREAC
Loch Striven
Ardentraive
Colintraive
Altgaltraig
Rhubodach
Port Driseach
Cloch Point
A770
Ashton
Lyle Hill
GREENOCK
Port Glasgow
Newark
Castlehill
Kirtonhill
Dumbarton
Milton
Bowling
Old Kilpatrick
Duntocher
Faifley
Ardhallow
Larkfield
Braeside
Chrisswell
Lunderston Bay
A78
A8
M8
Broadfield
Bardrainney
Langbank
Finlaystone Country Estate
Erskine Bridge
Parkhall
Dalmuir
M898
Erskine
Inchinnan
391 KILMARNOCK HILL
Ardyne Burn
322 BEINN RUADH
Dunan
Ardgowan
Inverkip
Cornalees Bridge
Loch Thom
Gryffe Reservoir
Shielhill
Garvock
Bishopton
Rossland
Craigend
Kilmacolm
BUTE
267 KAMES HILL
Ardmaleish
Innellan
Wemyss Bay
Cairncurran
Kilbride
Ardyne Point
Port Bannatyne
St Colmac
Toward
Toward Quay
Skelmorlie
Upper Skelmorlie
441 CREUCH HILL
Milton
B788
B789
Houston
B790
Crosslee
Quarrier's Village
Carruth House
Renfrew
Glasgow
Kildavanan
B875
Ardbeg
Bogany Point
Rothesay
St Mary's Chapel (ruin)
Ardencraig
A844
B878
Ascog
Loch Ascog
Kerrycroy
Ballanlay
Meikle Kilmory
B881
Loch Fada
Mount Stuart
Midpark
Bruchag
Knock Castle
Nadsdale Water
522 HILL OF STAKE
Muirshiel
Bridge of Weir
Ranfurly
Brookfield
Weavers' Cottage NTS
Linwood
Elderslie
PAISLEY
Kilbarchan
Milliken Park
Johnstone
Foxbar
A737
A761
B786
River Calder
Castle Semple Loch
Howwood
Quarter
Routenburn
Skelmorlie Aisle
Vikingar!
Largs
483 IRISH LAW
River Garnock
Lochwinnoch
Newtown of Beltrees
Gleniffer Braes
Caplaw
Barrhead
Gateside
B775
GREAT CUMBRAE ISLAND
Ardscalpsie Bay
Kingarth
Kilchattan Bay
Stravanan Bay
Kilchattan
St Blane's Church
Garrochty
Garroch Head
B896
B899
Millport
Kelburn
Kelburn Country Centre
A760
Campbill Reservoir
Kilbirnie
Kilbirnie Loch
Beith
B777
Neilston
A736
Shillford
Hall
Uplawmoor
Nether
Craigton
Dodside
B776
Fairlie
Fairlie Roads
371 COCK LAW
Glengarnock
Gateside
Middleton
Lugton
Long Loch
Barrmill
B784
B780
B706
A735
B769
Sound of Bute
Little Cumbrae Island
Hunterston Power Station
The Den
Highfield
Drakemyre
Gabroc Hill
Fullwood
Burnhouse
Crosbie
Blackshaw
Dalry
B707
Dunlop
Black Loch
Portencross
Farland Head
B7048
B781
Munnoch
West Kilbride
A737
Auchenmade
Kingsford
Laigh Clunch
Dalgarven Mill
Auchentiber
Seamill
CUNNINGHAME
A78
B780
B778
High Cross
Stewarton
Crossgates
Annick Water
A77
Kilwinning
Fergushill
Torranyard
Sannox
chonnel
isherrich
INN BHREAC
Kildavaig
Stravanan
abruaich
nchmarnock
The T
Gart
Dalm
Cunninghame Memorial

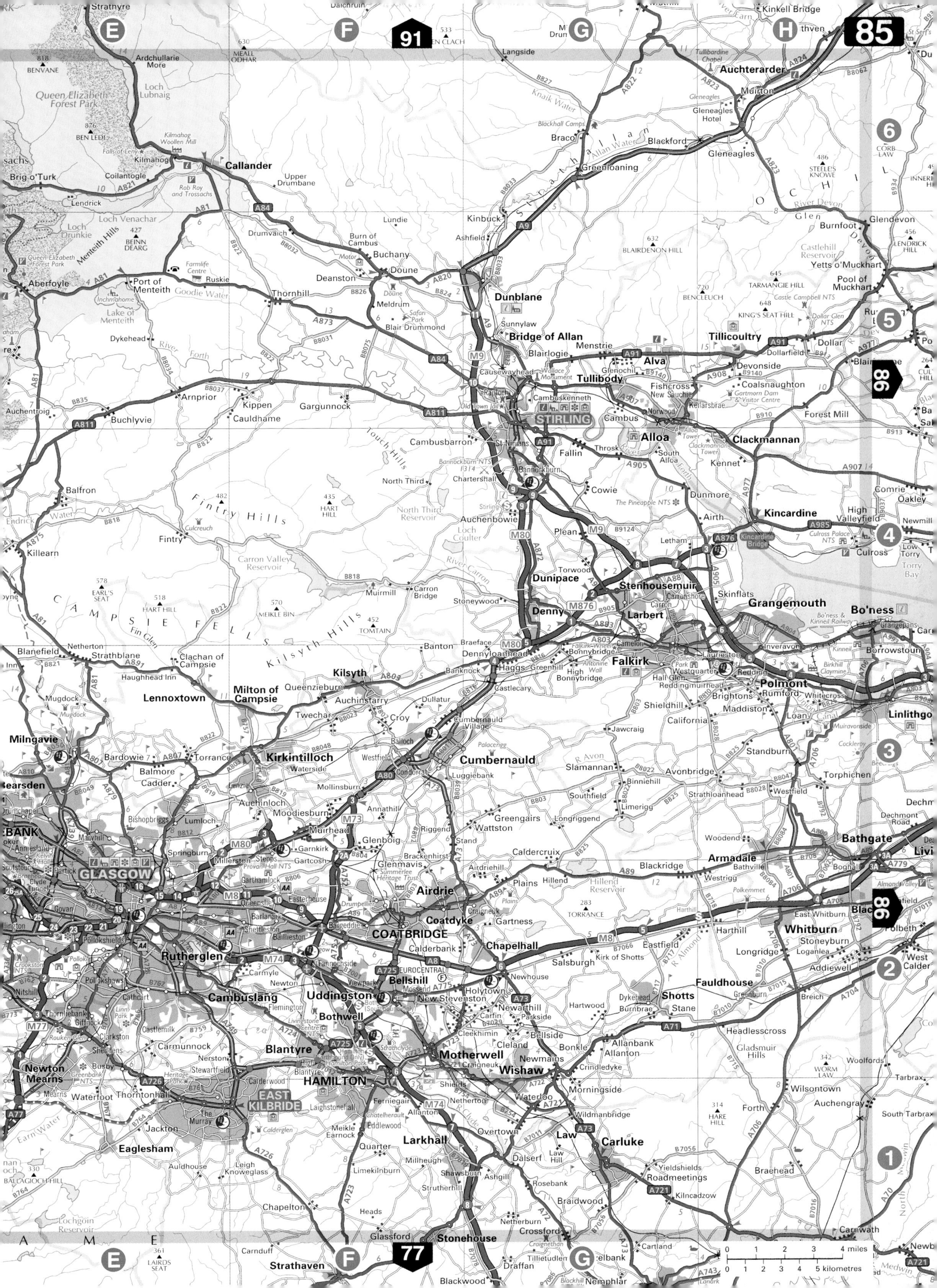

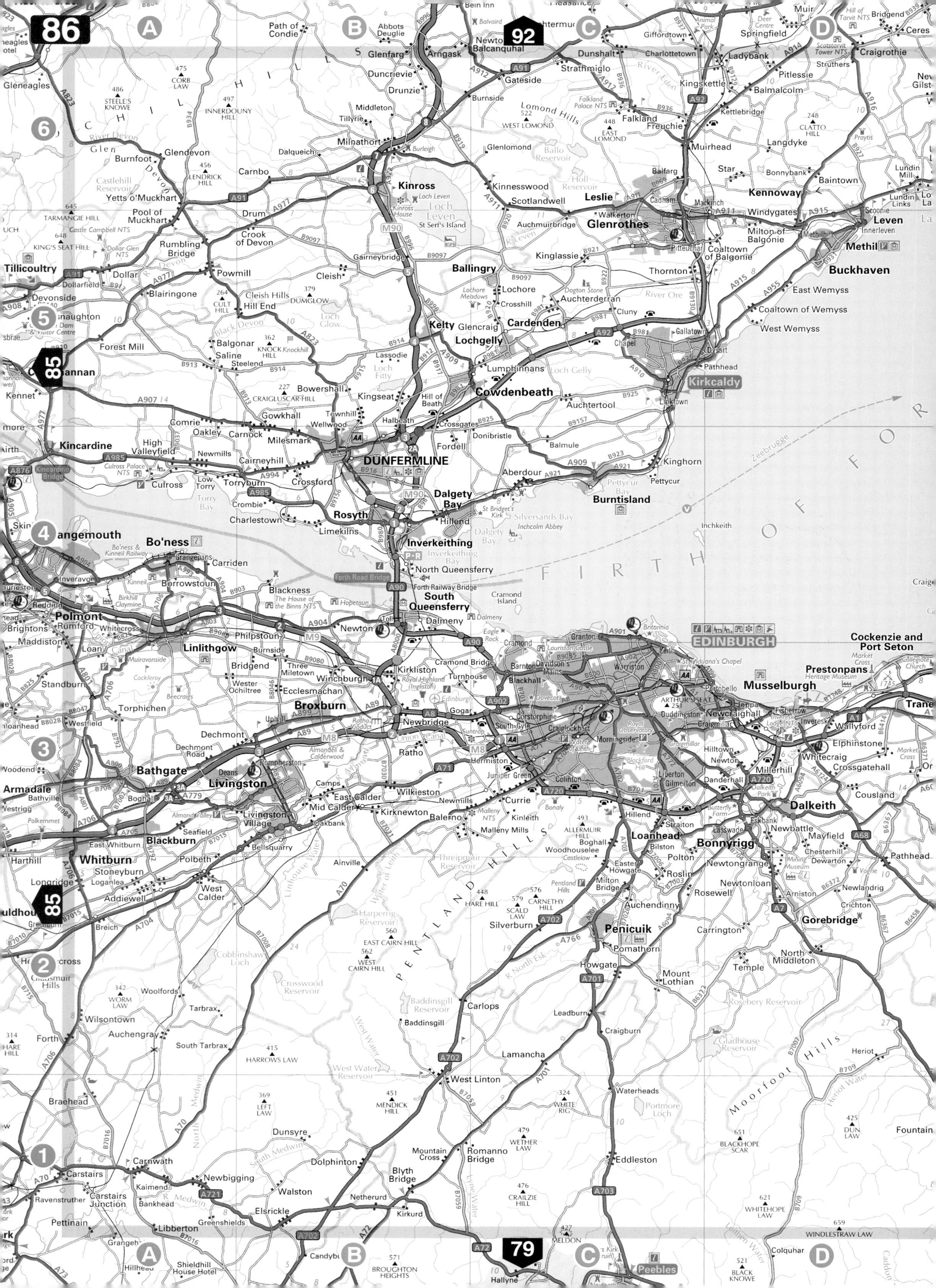

86
92
85
79
A
B
C
D
1
2
3
4
5
6
Path of Condie
Abbots Deuglie
Glenfarg
Arngask
Newton of Balcanquhal
Gateside
Strathmiglo
Dunshalt
Charlestown
Giffordtown
Springfield
Ladybank
Craigrothie
Pitlessie
Kingskettle
Balmalcolm
Gleneagles
Duncrievie
Drunzie
Burnside
Lomond Hills
Falkland
Freuchie
Kettlebridge
Middleton
Tillyrie
Milnathort
Glenlomond
Muirhead
Langdyke
Glendevon
Burnfoot
Dalqueich
Carnbo
Kinross
Kinnesswood
Leslie
Glenrothes
Kennoway
Baintown
Leven
Methil
Buckhaven
Yetts o'Muckhart
Pool of Muckhart
Scotlandwell
Auchmuirbridge
Windygates
Milton of Balgonie
Coaltown of Balgonie
Loch Leven
Drum
Crook of Devon
Rumbling Bridge
Tillicoultry
Dollar
Dollarfield
Powmill
Gairneybridge
Cleish
Ballingry
Kinglassie
Thornton
Lochore
Crosshill
Auchterderran
Cluny
East Wemyss
Coaltown of Wemyss
West Wemyss
Devonside
Blairingone
Cleish Hills
Hill End
Kelty
Glencraig
Cardenden
Lochgelly
Gallatown
Dysart
Pathhead
Kirkcaldy
Linktown
Forest Mill
Balgonar
Saline
Steelend
Lassodie
Lumphinnans
Cowdenbeath
Auchtertool
Kennet
Bowershall
Kingseat
Hill of Beath
Comrie
Oakley
Carnock
Gowkhall
Townhill
Wellwood
Halbeath
Crossgates
Donibristle
Fordell
Balmule
Kincardine
High Valleyfield
Newmills
Cairneyhill
Milesmark
DUNFERMLINE
Kinghorn
Culross
Low Torry
Torryburn
Crossford
Aberdour
Pettycur
Burntisland
Crombie
Charlestown
Rosyth
Dalgety Bay
Hillend
Limekilns
Inverkeithing
North Queensferry
Grangemouth
Bo'ness
Carriden
Borrowstoun
Blackness
South Queensferry
Cramond Island
Inchkeith
FIRTH OF FORTH
Polmont
Redding
Brightons
Rumford
Whitecross
Maddiston
Philpstoun
Newton
Dalmeny
Cramond
Granton
EDINBURGH
Cockenzie and Port Seton
Linlithgow
Burnside
Loan
Bridgend
Three Miletown
Kirkliston
Cramond Bridge
Barnton
Davidson's Mains
Leith
Warriston
Prestonpans
Musselburgh
Portobello
Standburn
Wester Ochiltree
Winchburgh
Ecclesmachan
Turnhouse
Blackhall
Arthur's Seat
Duddingston
Newcraighall
Craigmillar
Wallyford
Tranent
Torphichen
Westfield
Broxburn
Uphall
Gogar
Corstorphine
South Gyle
Craiglockhart
Morningside
Fisherrow
Inveresk
Elphinstone
Whitecraig
Dechmont
Newbridge
Ratho
Hermiston
Juniper Green
Colinton
Liberton
Gilmerton
Danderhall
Millerhill
Crossgatehall
Bathgate
Armadale
Livingston
Deans
Camps
East Calder
Mid Calder
Wilkieston
Kirknewton
Newmills
Currie
Balerno
Kinleith
Malleny Mills
Hillend
Straiton
Loanhead
Bilston
Dalkeith
Eskbank
Newbattle
Mayfield
Cousland
Livingston Village
Oakbank
Blackburn
Seafield
Bellsquarry
Whitburn
East Whitburn
Harthill
Polbeth
West Calder
Stoneyburn
Loganlea
Longridge
Addiewell
Breich
Ainville
Pentland Hills
Woodhouselee
Easter Howgate
Milton Bridge
Roslin
Polton
Bonnyrigg
Newtongrange
Newtonloan
Rosewell
Chesterhill
Pathhead
Dewarton
Newlandrig
Crichton
Arniston
Gorebridge
Auchendinny
Penicuik
Pomathorn
Carrington
Silverburn
Howgate
Temple
North Middleton
Mount Lothian
Woolfords
Tarbrax
Wilsontown
Auchengray
Forth
South Tarbrax
Carlops
Baddinsgill
Leadburn
Craigburn
Lamancha
West Linton
Braehead
Waterheads
Heriot
Dunsyre
Fountain
Carnwath
Carstairs
Carstairs Junction
Ravenstruther
Kaimend
Bankhead
Newbigging
Walston
Dolphinton
Mountain Cross
Romanno Bridge
Blyth Bridge
Eddleston
Pettinain
Libberton
Greenshields
Elsrickle
Netherurd
Kirkurd
Candybu
Hallyne
Shieldhill House Hotel
Grangehall
Colquhar
Peebles
Moorfoot Hills

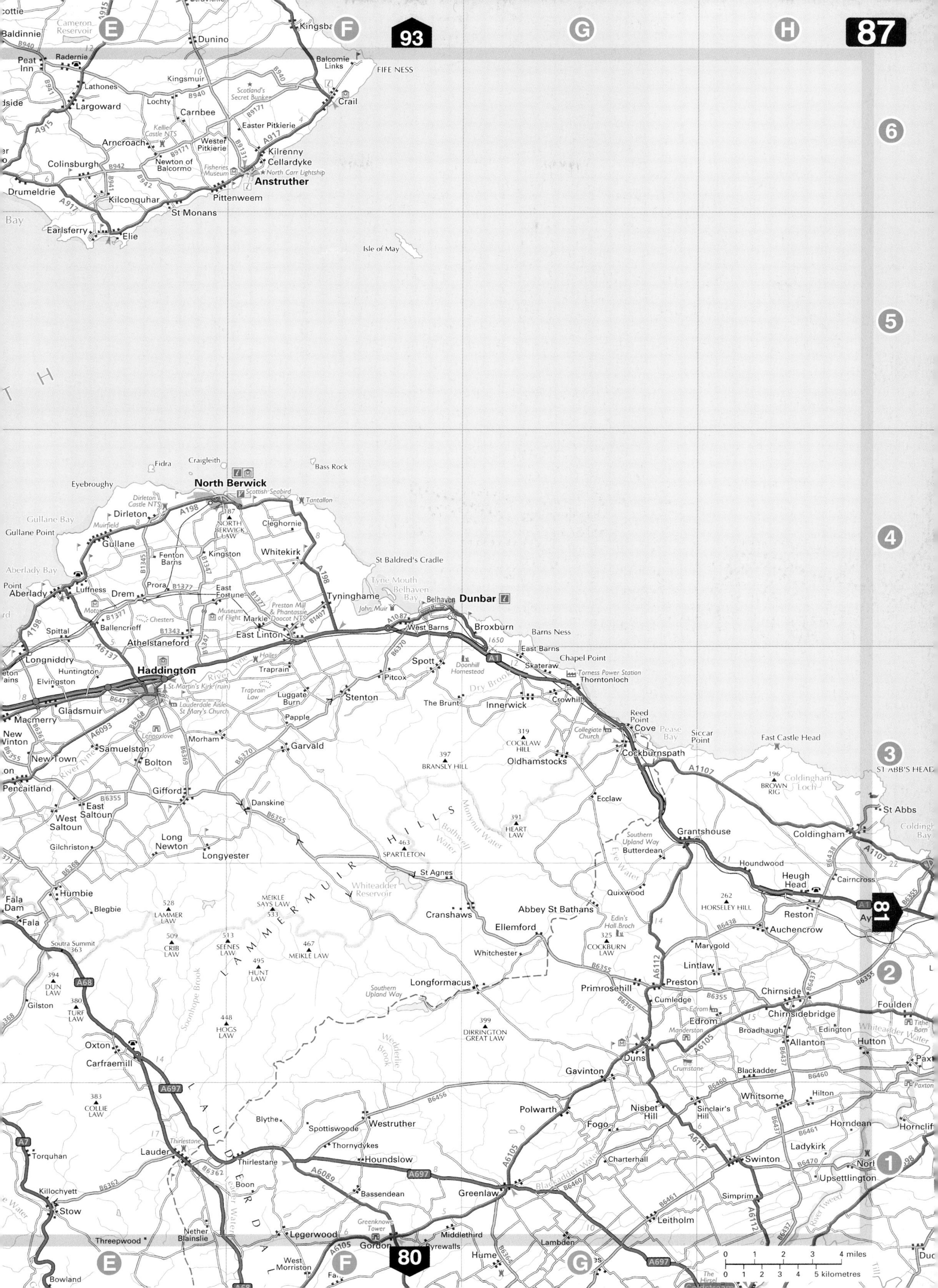
93
E
F
G
H
6
5
4
3
2
1
Kingsbarns
Dunino
Baldinnie
Cameron Reservoir
Peat Inn
Radernie
Balcomie Links
FIFE NESS
Crail
Kingsmuir
Scotland's Secret Bunker
Lathones
Largoward
Lochty
Carnbee
Easter Pitkierie
Kellie Castle NTS
Arncroach
Wester Pitkierie
Kilrenny
Cellardyke
North Carr Lightship
Colinsburgh
Newton of Balcormo
Fisheries Museum
Anstruther
Drumeldrie
Kilconquhar
Pittenweem
St Monans
Bay
Earlsferry
Elie
Isle of May
Fidra
Craigleith
Bass Rock
Eyebroughy
North Berwick
Scottish Seabird
Tantallon
Dirleton Castle NTS
Dirleton
Gullane Bay
Muirfield
Gullane Point
Gullane
NORTH BERWICK LAW
Cleghornie
Fenton Barns
Kingston
Whitekirk
St Baldred's Cradle
Aberlady Bay
Aberlady
Luffness
Drem
Prora
East Fortune
Tyne Mouth
Belhaven Bay
Tyninghame
Belhaven
Dunbar
Preston Mill & Phantassie Doocot NTS
John Muir
Chesters
Museum of Flight
Markle
Spittal
Ballencrieff
East Linton
West Barns
Broxburn
Barns Ness
Athelstaneford
East Barns
Chapel Point
Longniddry
Hailes
Spott
Skateraw
Doonhill Homestead
Torness Power Station
Thorntonloch
Huntington
Haddington
Traprain
Pitcox
Elvingston
St Martin's Kirk (ruin)
Traprain Law
Luggate Burn
Stenton
The Brunt
Innerwick
Crowhill
Dry Burn
Gladsmuir
Lauderdale Aisle St Mary's Church
Macmerry
Pappl
Reed Point
Cove
Pease Bay
Siccar Point
Lennoxlove
Collegiate Church
COCKLAW HILL
Fast Castle Head
New Winton
Morham
Garvald
Samuelston
Oldhamstocks
Cockburnspath
New Town
Bolton
BRANSLY HILL
ST ABB'S HEAD
River Tyne
BROWN RIG
Coldingham Loch
Pencaitland
Gifford
Ecclaw
East Saltoun
Danskine
St Abbs
West Saltoun
LAMMERMUIR HILLS
HEART LAW
Bothwell Water
Monynut Water
Grantshouse
Coldingham
Coldingham Bay
Long Newton
SPARTLETON
Southern Upland Way
Butterdean
Gilchriston
Longyester
Eye Water
Houndwood
Heugh Head
St Agnes
Cairncross
Humbie
Whiteadder Reservoir
Quixwood
Fala Dam
MEIKLE SAYS LAW
HORSELEY HILL
Blegbie
Cranshaws
Abbey St Bathans
Reston
Fala
LAMMER LAW
Edin's Hall Broch
Ayton
Ellemford
Auchencrow
Soutra Summit
CRIB LAW
SEENES LAW
COCKBURN LAW
MEIKLE LAW
Whitchester
Marygold
HUNT LAW
Lintlaw
DUN LAW
Longformacus
Primrosehill
Preston
Foulden
Gilston
Soonhope Brook
Chirnside
TURF LAW
Cumledge
Chirnsidebridge
Edrom
DIRRINGTON GREAT LAW
Manderston
Broadhaugh
Edington
Allanton
Hutton
Tithe Barn
Whiteadder Water
HOGS LAW
Oxton
Watch Water
Duns
Carfraemill
Crumstane
Paxton
Gavinton
Blackadder
COLLIE LAW
Whitsome
Hilton
Polwarth
Nisbet Hill
Sinclair's Hill
Blythe
Westruther
Fogo
Horndean
Spottiswoode
Hornclif
Torquhan
Thirlestane
Thornydykes
Ladykirk
Lauder
Houndslow
Charterhall
Swinton
Norham
Thirlestane
Upsettlington
Boon
Greenlaw
Blackadder Water
Killochyett
Bassendean
Simprim
River Tweed
Stow
Leader Water
LAUDERDALE
Greenknowe Tower
Leitholm
Nether Blainslie
Middlethird
Threepwood
Legerwood
Lambden
Gordon
Eyrewalls
Hume
West Morriston
Bowland
The Hirsel
80
81
A915
B940
B941
B942
B9171
B9131
A917
A198
B1345
B1347
B1377
B1371
B1343
B1407
A1087
B6370
A1
A6137
B6471
B6368
A6093
B6363
B6355
B6369
A1107
B6438
B6355
A6112
B6437
B6365
A68
A6105
A697
B6456
B6460
B6461
B6470
A6089
B6362
B6364
A7
0 1 2 3 4 miles
0 1 2 3 4 5 kilometres

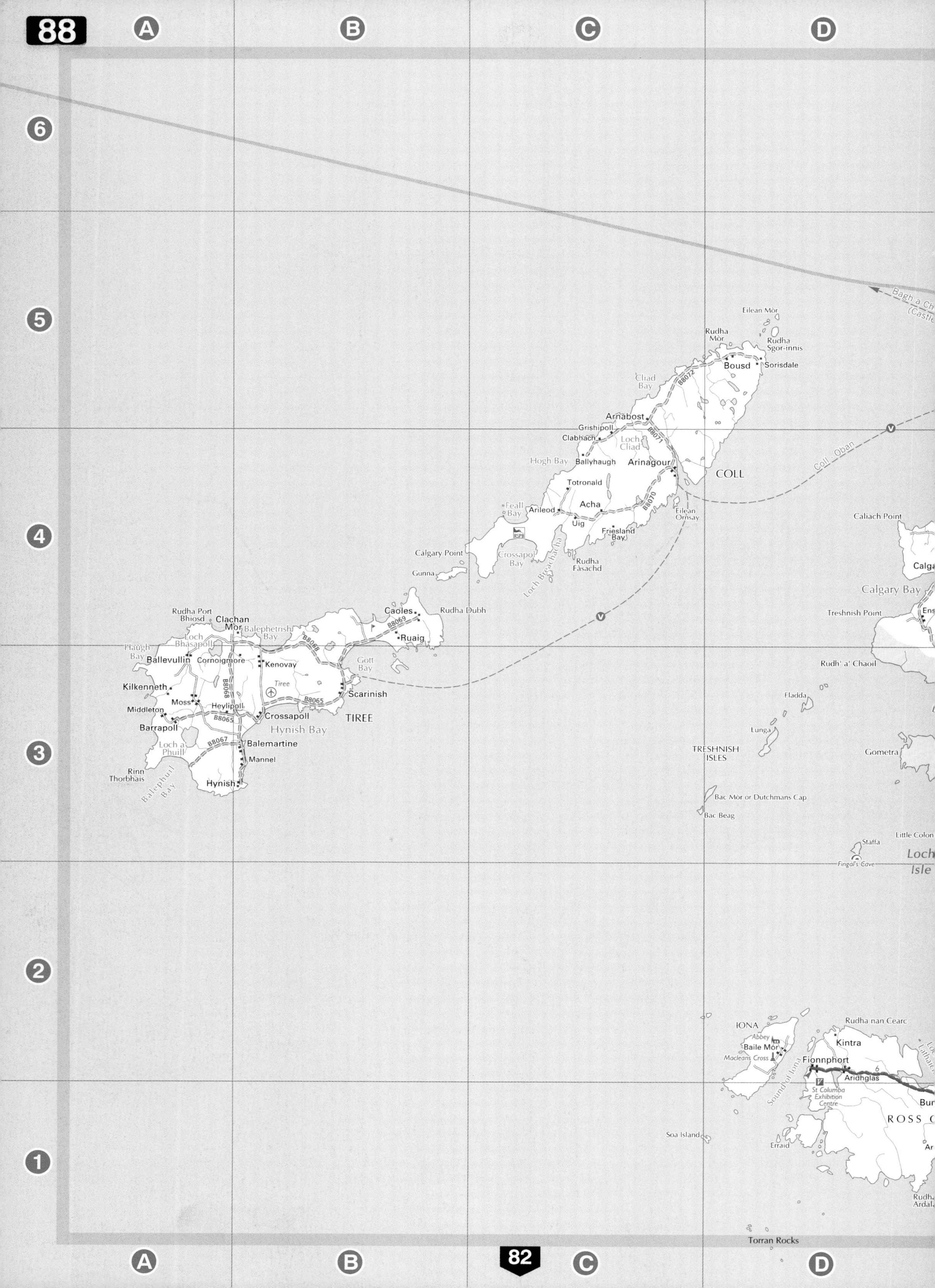

6

5

4

Eilean Mòr

Rudha Mòr

Rudha Sgor-innis

Bousd • Sorisdale

Cliad Bay

Arnabost

Grishipoll

Clabhach

Loch Cliad

Hogh Bay   Ballyhaugh   **Arinagour**

Totronald

COLL

Feall Bay

Arileod   **Acha**

Uig   Friesland Bay

Calgary Point

Crossapol Bay

Eilean Ornsay

Gunna

Rudha Fàsachd

Caliach Point

Calga

Calgary Bay

Loch Breachacha

Coll – Oban

Rudha Port Bhiosd

Clachan Mòr

Balephetrish Bay

Caoles

Rudha Dubh

Treshnish Point   Ens

Loch Bhasapoll

Ballevullin   Cornoigmore

Kenovay

Ruaig

Rudh' a' Chaoil

Flaugh Bay

Tiree

Gott Bay

Fladda

Kilkenneth

Moss   Heylipoll

Scarinish

Lunga

Middleton

Crossapoll

TIREE

TRESHNISH ISLES

Gometra

Barrapoll

Loch a' Phuill

Balemartine

Hynish Bay

Bac Mòr or Dutchmans Cap

3

Mannel

Rinn Thorbhais

Hynish

Bac Beag

Balephuil Bay

Staffa   Little Colon

Fingal's Cave

Loch Isle

2

IONA   Rudha nan Cearc

Abbey

Baile Mòr   Kintra

Macleans Cross

Fionnphort

Loch Lathaic

Aridhglas

Soa Island

St Columba Exhibition Centre

Bur

ROSS O

1

Errraid

Ar

Rudh. Ardal.

Torran Rocks

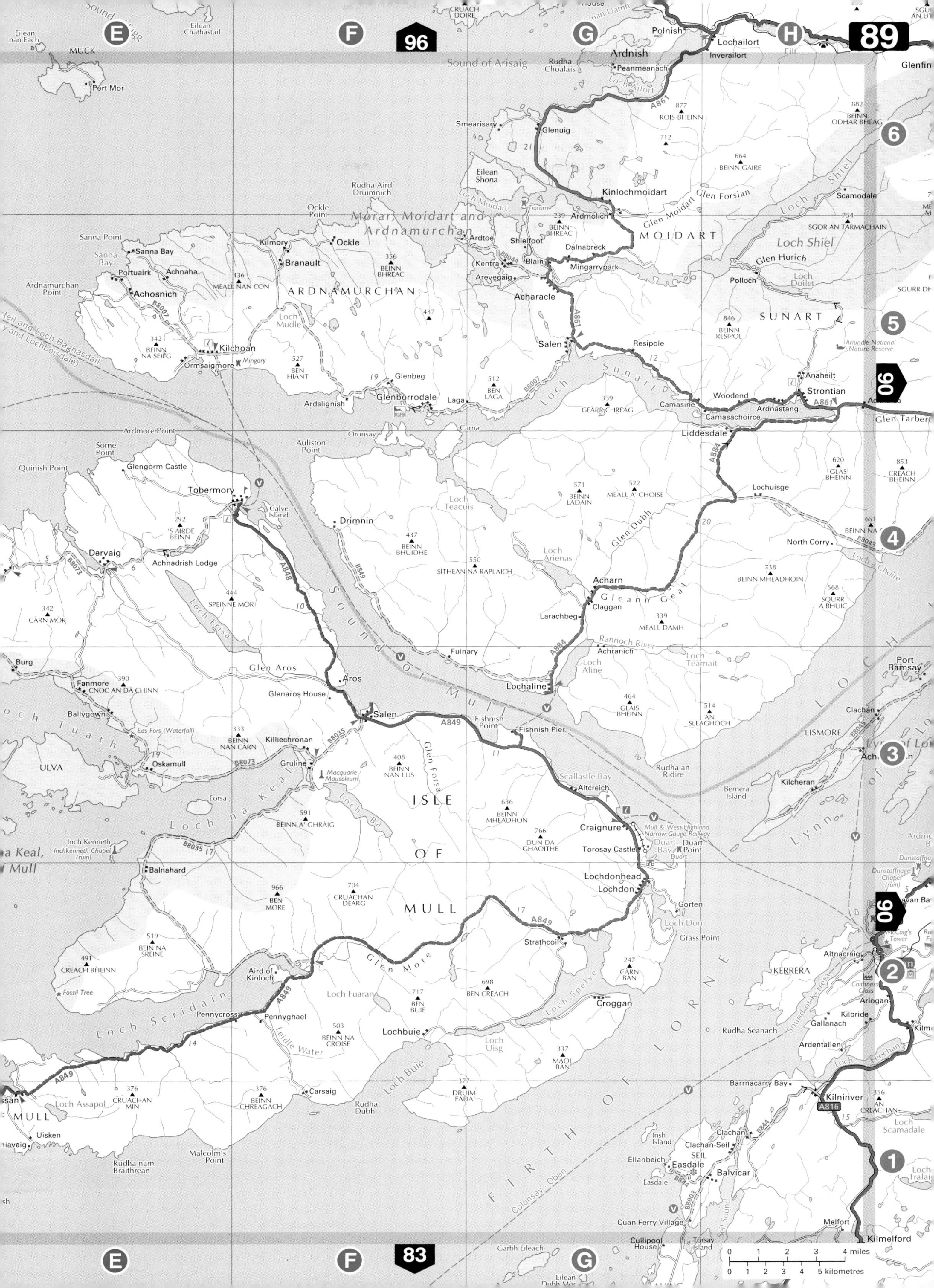

E
F
G
H
96
89
83
MUCK
Port Mor
Sound of Arisaig
Ardnish
Lochailort
Inveraillort
Polnish
Peanmeanach
Glenuig
Smearisary
Eilean Shona
Kinlochmoidart
MOIDART
Loch Shiel
Glen Hurich
Polloch
SUNART
Resipole
Salen
Acharacle
Strontian
Anaheilt
Ardnastang
Woodend
Camasine
Camasachoirce
Liddesdale
Glen Tarbert
Morar, Moidart and Ardnamurchan
ARDNAMURCHAN
Sanna Bay
Sanna Point
Portuairk
Achnaha
Achosnich
Ardnamurchan Point
Kilchoan
Ormsaigmore
Mingary
Kilmory
Branault
Ockle
Glenbeg
Glenborrodale
Laga
Ardslignish
Loch Sunart
Ardtoe
Shielfoot
Kentra
Arevegaig
Blain
Dalnabreck
Mingarrypark
Ardmolich
Glengorm Castle
Tobermory
Quinish Point
Sorne Point
Ardmore Point
Dervaig
Achnadrish Lodge
Drimnin
Auliston Point
Loch Teacuis
Loch Arienas
Glen Dubh
Lochuisge
North Corry
Acharn
Claggan
Larachbeg
Gleann Geal
Fuinary
Lochaline
Loch Aline
Rannoch River
Achranich
Loch Tearnait
Sound of Mull
Aros
Glen Aros
Glenaros House
Salen
Fishnish Point
Fishnish Pier
Burg
Fanmore
Ballygown
Eas Fors (Waterfall)
Killiechronan
Oskamull
Gruline
Macquarie Mausoleum
ULVA
Loch Tuath
Loch na Keal
Inch Kenneth
Inchkenneth Chapel (ruin)
Balnahard
ISLE OF MULL
Glen Forsa
Scallastle Bay
Altcreich
Craignure
Mull & West Highland Narrow Gauge Railway
Duart Bay
Duart Point
Torosay Castle
Lochdonhead
Lochdon
Gorten
Loch Don
Grass Point
Strathcoil
Glen More
Aird of Kinloch
Loch Scridain
Pennycross
Pennyghael
Loch Fuaran
Lochbuie
Loch Uisg
Loch Spelve
Croggan
Loch Buie
Carsaig
Rudha Dubh
Loch Assapol
Uisken
Malcolm's Point
Rudha nam Braithrean
Fossil Tree
FIRTH OF LORNE
Colonsay - Oban
LISMORE
Port Ramsay
Clachan
Kilcheran
Bernera Island
Rudha an Ridire
Lynn of Lorn
KERRERA
Altnacraig
McCaig's Tower
Ariogan
Kilbride
Gallanach
Ardentallen
Rudha Seanach
Sound of Kerrera
Loch Feochan
Barnacarry Bay
Kilninver
A816
Loch Scamadale
Insh Island
Clachan
Clachan-Seil
SEIL
Ellanbeich
Easdale
Balvicar
Cuan Ferry Village
Seil Sound
Melfort
Kilmelford
Cullipool House
Torsay Island
Garbh Eileach
A861
A884
A848
A849
B8007
B8073
B8035
B849
B8043
B844
B8003
0 1 2 3 4 miles
0 1 2 3 4 5 kilometres

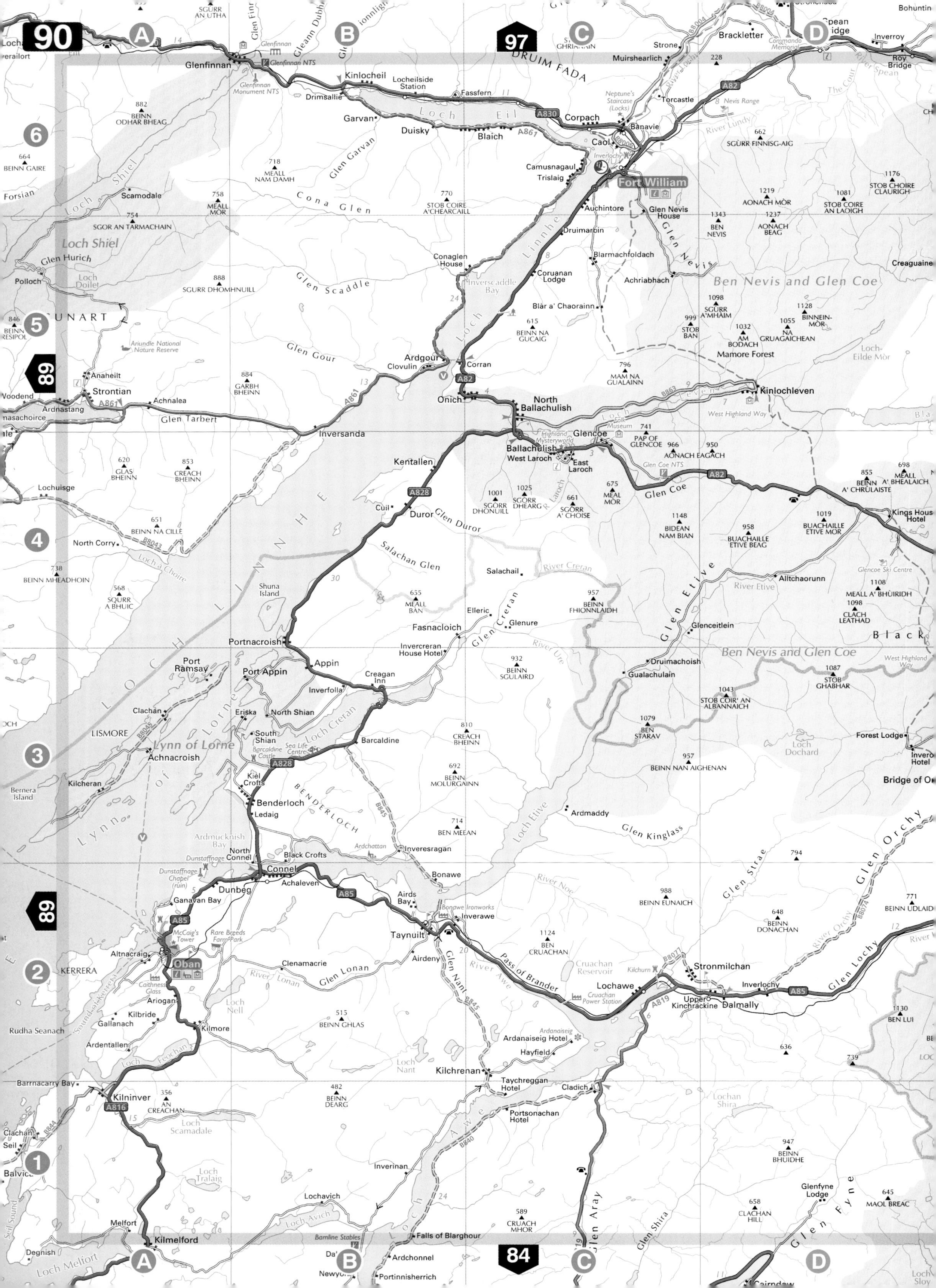

90
97
84
89
A
B
C
D
1
2
3
4
5
6
Glenfinnan
Kinlocheil
Locheilside Station
Fassfern
Drimsallie
Garvan
Duisky
Blaich
Corpach
Banavie
Caol
Fort William
Camusnagaul
Trislaig
Auchintore
Glen Nevis House
Druimarbin
Blarmachfoldach
Achriabhach
Coruanan Lodge
Conaglen House
Loch Shiel
Scamodale
Forsian
Polloch
Glen Hurich
Strontian
Anaheilt
Ardnastang
Achnalea
Glen Tarbert
Ardgour
Clovulin
Corran
Onich
North Ballachulish
Kinlochleven
Glencoe
Ballachulish
West Laroch
East Laroch
Kentallen
Inversanda
Cuil
Duror
Glen Duror
Salachan Glen
Glen Coe
Kings House Hotel
Ben Nevis and Glen Coe
Mamore Forest
Ben Nevis
Loch Linnhe
Lismore
Lynn of Lorne
Port Ramsay
Port Appin
Appin
Portnacroish
Creagan Inn
Inverfolla
Clachan
Eriska
North Shian
South Shian
Barcaldine
Loch Creran
Glen Creran
Elleric
Glenure
Fasnacloich
Invercreran House Hotel
Salachail
Glen Etive
Alltchaorunn
Glenceitlein
Druimachoish
Gualachulain
Forest Lodge
Bridge of Orchy
Achnacroish
Kilcheran
Bernera Island
Benderloch
Ledaig
Kiel Crofts
North Connel
Black Crofts
Connel
Achaleven
Dunbeg
Ganavan Bay
Inveresragan
Bonawe
Airds Bay
Inverawe
Taynuilt
Airdeny
Oban
Kerrera
Altnacraig
Clenamacrie
Glen Lonan
Loch Nell
Kilbride
Gallanach
Kilmore
Ardentallen
Rudha Seanach
Loch Feochan
Barnacarry Bay
Kilninver
Clachan
Seil
Balvicar
Loch Scamadale
Loch Tralaig
Lochavich
Loch Avich
Melfort
Kilmelford
Degnish
Loch Melfort
Glen Nant
Pass of Brander
Lochawe
Stronmilchan
Inverlochy
Dalmally
Upper Kinchrackine
Ardanaiseig Hotel
Hayfield
Kilchrenan
Taychreggan Hotel
Cladich
Portsonachan Hotel
Inverinan
Loch Awe
Falls of Blarghour
Ardchonnel
Portinnisherrich
Glen Aray
Glen Shira
Glen Fyne
Glenfyne Lodge
Glen Orchy
Glen Lochy
Glen Kinglass
Ardmaddy
Loch Etive
Cruachan Reservoir
Spean Bridge
Roy Bridge
Inverroy
Brackletter
Strone
Muirshearlich
Torcastle

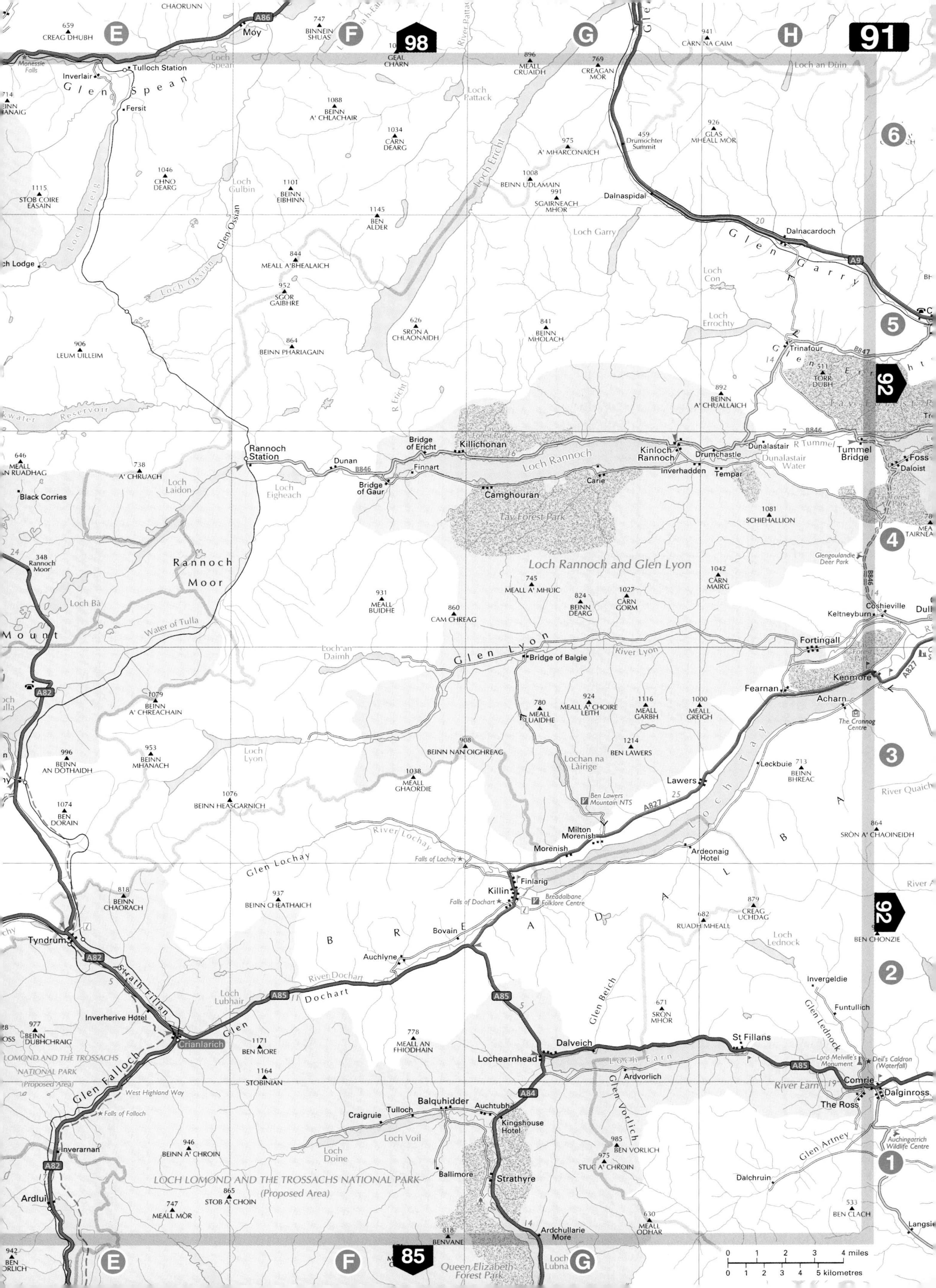

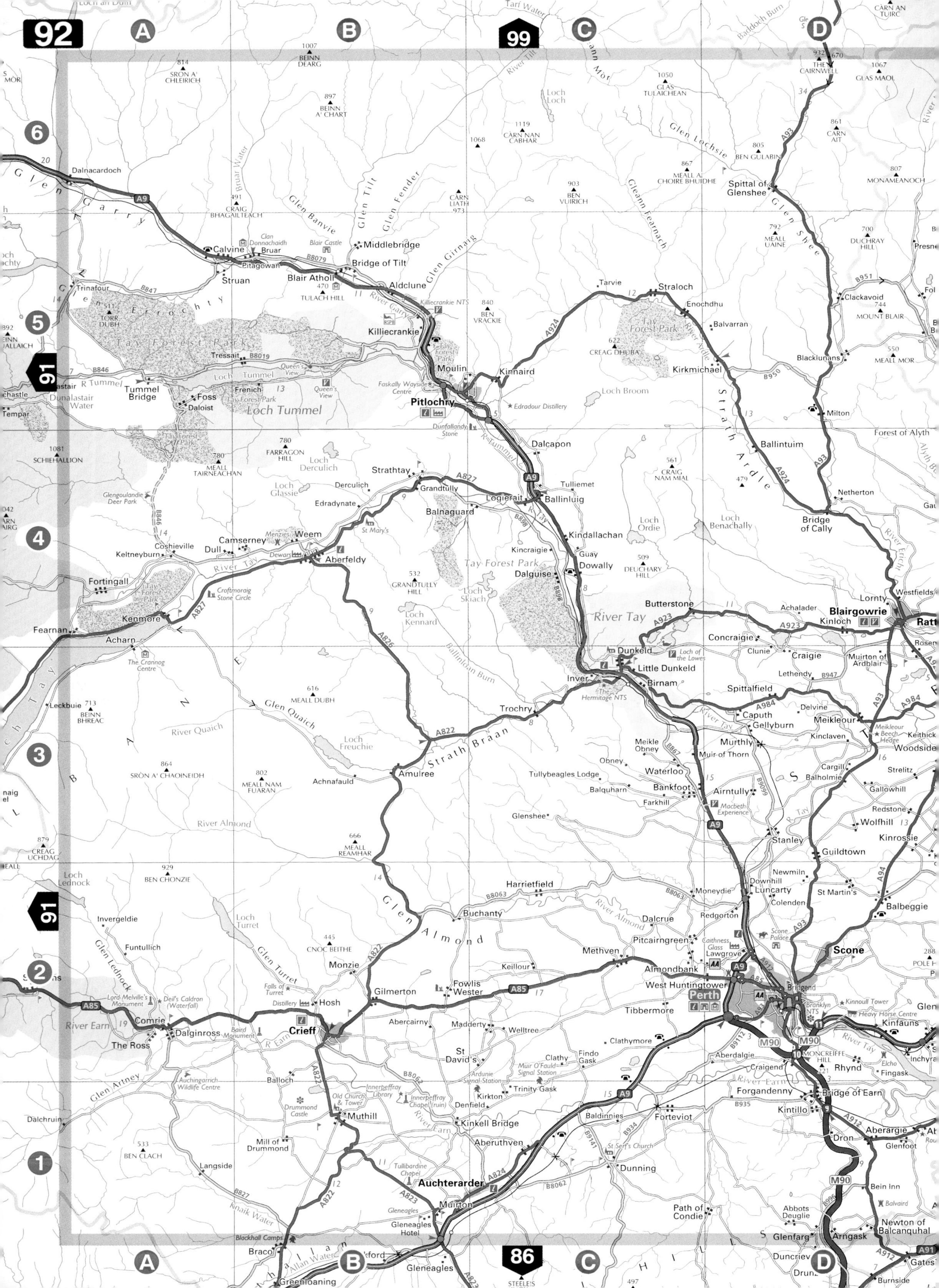
A
B
C
D
99
91
86
1
2
3
4
5
6
Tarf Water
Baddoch Burn
CÀRN AN TUIRC
1007 BEINN DEARG
814 SRÒN A' CHLEIRICH
897 BEINN A' CHAIT
River Tilt
Loch Loch
1050 GLAS TULAICHEAN
932 THE CAIRNWELL
1067 GLAS MAOL
1119 CÀRN NAN GABHAR
1068
Glen Lochsie
861 CÀRN AIT
805 BEN GULABIN
867 MEALL A' CHOIRE BHUIDHE
807 MONAMEANACH
Spittal of Glenshee
Glen Shee
Dalnacardoch
Glen Garry
A9
Bruar Water
491 CRAIG BHAGAILTEACH
Glen Banvie
Glen Tilt
Glen Fender
CARN LIATH 973
903 BEN VUIRICH
Gleann Fearnach
792 MEALL UAINE
700 DUCHRAY HILL
Calvine
Clan Donnachaidh
Bruar
Blair Castle
Middlebridge
Glen Girnaig
Pitagowan
B8079
Bridge of Tilt
Struan
Blair Atholl
Aldclune
Tarvie
Straloch
B951
Clackavoid
744 MOUNT BLAIR
Trinafour
B847
470 TULACH HILL
River Garry
Killiecrankie NTS
840 BEN VRACKIE
Enochdhu
Glen Errochty
Tay Forest Park
Killiecrankie
A924
Balvarran
Tay Forest Park
622 CREAG DHUBH
Blacklunans
550 MEALL MOR
Tressait
B8019
B846
Loch Tummel
Queen's View
Moulin
Kinnaird
River Ardle
Kirkmichael
B950
Tummel Bridge
R Tummel
Foss
Frenich
Faskally Wayside Centre
Loch Broom
Dunalastair Water
Daloist
Pitlochry
Edradour Distillery
Strath Ardle
Milton
Tempar
Dunfallandy Stone
Dalcapon
Ballintuim
Forest of Alyth
1081 SCHIEHALLION
780 FARRAGON HILL
Loch Derculich
780 MEALL TAIRNEACHAN
Strathtay
A827
Tulliemet
561 CRAIG NAM MIAL
A93
Derculich
Grandtully
Loch Glassie
Logierait
Ballinluig
479
Netherton
Glengoulandie Deer Park
Edradynate
Balnaguard
B898
Loch Ordie
Loch Benachally
Bridge of Cally
St Mary's
Menzies
Weem
Camserney
Dull
Kindallachan
Coshieville
Keltneyburn
Dewars
Aberfeldy
Kincraigie
Guay
Dowally
509 DEUCHARY HILL
River Tay
Tay Forest Park
532 GRANDTULLY HILL
Dalguise
River Ericht
Fortingall
Croftmoraig Stone Circle
Loch Skiach
Butterstone
Achalader
Lornty
Westfields
Loch Kennard
A826
River Tay
A923
Blairgowrie
Kinloch
Kenmore
Fearnan
Acharn
The Crannog Centre
Ballinloan Burn
Concraigie
Clunie
Craigie
Dunkeld
Loch of the Lowes
Little Dunkeld
Muirton of Ardblair
Inver
Birnam
Lethendy
B947
The Hermitage NTS
Leckbuie
713 BEINN BHREAC
616 MEALL DUBH
Glen Quaich
Trochry
Spittalfield
A984
Caputh
Delvine
Gellyburn
Meikleour
Meikleour Beech Hedge
Keithick
River Quaich
Loch Freuchie
A822
Strath Braan
Meikle Obney
B867
Murthly
Kinclaven
Woodside
Muir of Thorn
Obney
Cargill
Balholmie
Strelitz
864 SRÒN A' CHAOINEIDH
802 MEALL NAM FUARAN
Achnafauld
Amulree
Tullybeagles Lodge
Waterloo
Balquharn
Bankfoot
Airntully
B9099
Gallowhill
Farkhill
Macbeth Experience
Redstone
River Almond
Glenshee
Wolfhill
R Tay
879 CREAG UCHDAG
666 MEALL REAMHAR
Stanley
Kinrossie
Guildtown
Loch Lednock
929 BEN CHONZIE
Newmiln
Downhill
Harrietfield
B8063
Moneydie
Luncarty
A94
Colenden
St Martin's
Invergeldie
Loch Turret
Glen Almond
Buchanty
River Almond
Dalcrue
Redgorton
Balbeggie
Glen Lednock
Funtullich
445 CNOC BEITHE
Glen Turret
Pitcairngreen
Caithness Glass
Scone Palace
Scone
Methven
Lawgrove
Monzie
Keillour
Almondbank
Falls of Turret
West Huntingtower
Lord Melville's Monument
Deil's Caldron (Waterfall)
Fowlis Wester
A85
Bridgend
Distillery
Hosh
Gilmerton
Perth
Kinnoull Tower
Heavy Horse Centre
River Earn
Comrie
Tibbermore
Branklyn NTS
Kinfauns
Dalginross
Baird Monument
Crieff
Abercairny
Madderty
Welltree
The Ross
R Earn
Clathymore
M90
Moncreiffe Hill
River Tay
Inchyra
St David's
Clathy
Findo Gask
Aberdalgie
Elcho
Glen Artney
Auchingarrich Wildlife Centre
Balloch
Muir O'Fauld Signal Station
Ardunie Signal Station
Craigend
Rhynd
Fingask
Kirkton
Trinity Gask
Innerpeffray Library
Old Church & Tower
Innerpeffray Chapel (ruin)
Drummond Castle
River Earn
Forgandenny
Bridge of Earn
Denfield
B935
Kintillo
Dalchruin
Muthill
Kinkell Bridge
Baldinnies
Forteviot
A912
Aberargie
B934
Mill of Drummond
Aberuthven
St Serf's Church
Dron
Glenfoot
533 BEN CLACH
B9141
Langside
Tullibardine Chapel
Dunning
A824
Auchterarder
B8062
Bein Inn
B827
A823
Balvaird
Muirton
Path of Condie
Abbots Deuglie
Knaik Water
Gleneagles
Gleneagles Hotel
Newton of Balcanquhal
Blackhall Camps
Glenfarg
Arngask
Braco
Allan Water
Gleneagles
Duncrievie
Greenloaning
STEELE'S
497
Burnside
Gates
A91

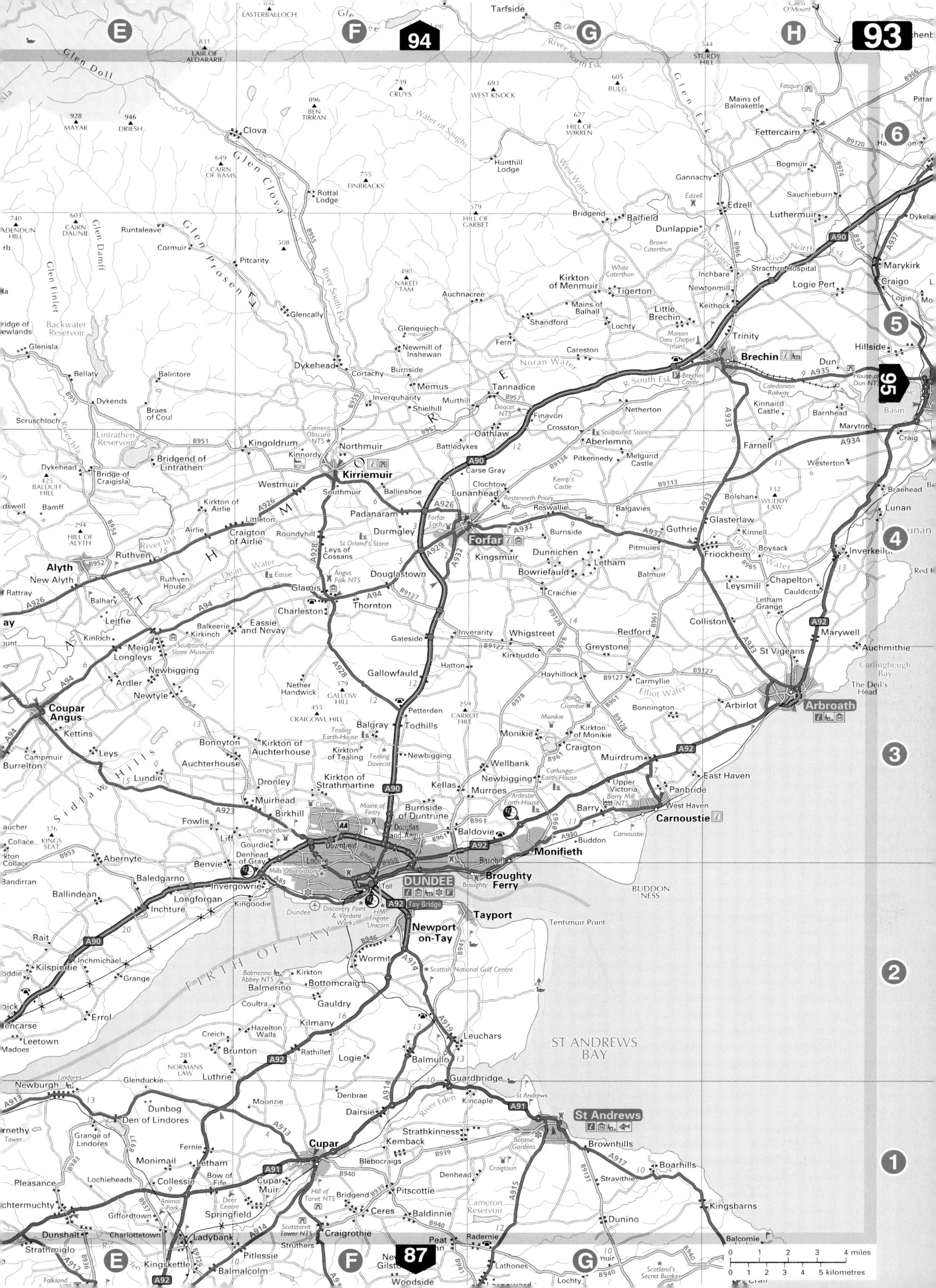

E
F
G
H
94
93
95
87
6
5
4
3
2
1
Tarfside
EASTERBALLOCH
831
LAIR OF ALDARARIE
Glen Doll
River North Esk
544
STURDY HILL
739
CRUYS
693
WEST KNOCK
605
BULG
896
BEN TIRRAN
928
MAYAR
946
DRIESH
Water of Saughs
677
HILL OF WIRREN
Glen Esk
Fasque
Mains of Balnakettle
Pittar
Fettercairn
B9120
B966
Clova
Glen Clova
649
CAIRN OF BAMS
755
FINBRACKS
Hunthill Lodge
West Water
Gannachy
Bogmuir
B974
Sauchieburn
Rottal Lodge
Edzell
740
603
CAIRN DAUNIE
579
HILL OF GARBET
Bridgend
Balfield
Luthermuir
Dunlappie
A90
A937
Runtaleave
Glen Prosen
Glen Damff
Cormuir
508
Pitcarity
B955
River South Esk
Brown Caterthun
White Caterthun
Inchbare
Stracathro Hospital
Marykirk
Craigo
490
NAKED TAM
Kirkton of Menmuir
Tigerton
Newtonmill
Logie Pert
Logie
Glen Finlet
Auchnacree
Mains of Balhall
Little Brechin
Keithock
Backwater Reservoir
Glencally
Shandford
Lochty
Glenisla
Glenquiech
Maison Dieu Chapel (ruin)
Trinity
Newmill of Inshewan
Fern
Careston
Noran Water
Brechin
Hillside
Dun
Dykehead
Cortachy
Burnside
A935
House of Dun NTS
Caledonian Railway
Bellaty
Balintore
Memus
Tannadice
B957
R South Esk
Brechin Castle
Kinnaird Castle
Barnhead
Inverquharity
Murthill
Netherton
Dykends
Braes of Coul
Shielhill
Doocot NTS
Finavon
A933
Maryton
Basin
Scruschloch
River Isla
Camera Obscura NTS
Crosston
Sculptured Stones
Craig
B951
Lintrathen Reservoir
Kingoldrum
Northmuir
Oathlaw
Aberlemno
Farnell
A934
Battledykes
Kinnordy
Bridgend of Lintrathen
Pitkennedy
Melgund Castle
Westerton
Dykehead
Bridge of Craigisla
Kirriemuir
Carse Gray
Kemp's Castle
425
BALDUFF HILL
Westmuir
Ballinshoe
Clochtow
B9113
Braehead
Southmuir
Lunanhead
Restenneth Priory
132
WUDDY LAW
Bolshan
Lunan
Bamff
Kirkton of Airlie
A926
Reswallie
Balgavies
Padanaram
Forfar Loch
Glasterlaw
Littleton
294
HILL OF ALYTH
Airlie
Craigton of Airlie
Roundyhill
Durmgley
Forfar
A932
Burnside
Guthrie
Kinnell
B954
St Orland's Stone
A929
Ruthven
Leys of Cossans
A928
Kingsmuir
Dunnichen
Pitmuies
Friockheim
Boysack
Inverkeilor
Alyth
B952
Letham
Lunan Water
B965
New Alyth
Dean Water
Eassie
Angus Folk NTS
Douglastown
Bowriefauld
Balmuir
Leysmill
Chapelton
Red
Rattray
Ruthven House
Glamis
Cauldcots
A94
B9127
Craichie
Letham Grange
Balhary
Charleston
Thornton
Colliston
Leitfie
Balkeerie
Kirkinch
Eassie and Nevay
Redford
Marywell
Inverarity
Whigstreet
A92
Kinloch
Meigle
Sculptured Stone Museum
Gateside
B9128
B961
Greystone
Auchmithie
Longleys
Kirkbuddo
St Vigeans
Carlingheugh Bay
Newbigging
Hatton
Hayhillock
Carmyllie
The Deil's Head
Ardler
Gallowfauld
379
GALLOW HILL
Elliot Water
Coupar Angus
Newtyle
Nether Handwick
Crombie
Bonnington
Arbirlot
Arbroath
Petterden
259
CARROT HILL
455
CRAIGOWL HILL
Balgray
Todhills
Monikie
Kettins
Teafing Earth-House
Kirkton of Monikie
Bonnyton
Kirkton of Auchterhouse
Kirkton of Tealing
Tealing Dovecot
Newbigging
Craigton
Leys
Sidlaw Hills
Wellbank
Muirdrum
Campmuir
Auchterhouse
Burrelton
East Haven
Newbigging
Carlungie Earth-House
Lundie
Dronley
Kirkton of Strathmartine
Kellas
Upper Victoria
Panbride
Murroes
Barry Mill NTS
Muirhead
Claypotts
Mains of Fintry
Ardestie Earth-House
Barry
West Haven
Carnoustie
A923
Birkhill
Burnside of Duntrune
A962
Fowlis
Camperdown
Douglas and Angus
Baldovie
Carnoustie
376
KINGS SEAT
Liff
A930
Buddon
Gourdie
Downfield
Monifieth
Collace
B953
Abernyte
Denhead of Gray
Lochee
Barnhill
Benvie
Mills Observatory
Broughty Ferry
Baledgarno
Invergowrie
DUNDEE
Toll
BUDDON NESS
A85
Ballindean
Longforgan
Kingoodie
A92 Tay Bridge
Inchture
Dundee
Discovery Point & Verdant Works
HM Frigate 'Unicorn'
Tayport
Tentsmuir Point
Newport-on-Tay
Rait
A90
FIRTH OF TAY
B946
B945
Inchmichael
Wormit
Kilspindie
A914
Scottish National Golf Centre
Balmerino Abbey NTS
Kirkton
Grange
Bottomcraig
Balmerino
Errol
Coultra
Gauldry
Hazelton Walls
Kilmany
Creich
A919
Leuchars
ST ANDREWS BAY
Leetown
Brunton
285
NORMANS LAW
A92
Rathillet
Logie
Balmullo
Lindores
Glenduckie
Luthrie
Guardbridge
Newburgh
A913
Denbrae
Moonzie
Dairsie
River Eden
Kincaple
St Andrews
A91
Dunbog
Den of Lindores
St Andrews
Grange of Lindores
Strathkinness
Fernie
Cupar
Kemback
Botanic Gardens
Brownhills
Monimail
Letham
B939
Blebocraigs
A917
Boarhills
Lochieheads
Bow of Fife
Cupar Muir
Collessie
B940
Denhead
Craigtoun
Stravithie
Pleasance
Hill of Tarvit NTS
Bridgend
Pitscottie
A915
B9131
Animal Park
Deer Centre
Cameron Reservoir
Kingsbarns
Giffordtown
Springfield
Ceres
Baldinnie
Dunino
Dunshalt
Charlottetown
Ladybank
Scotstarvit Tower NTS
Craigrothie
Radernie
Peat
Balcomie
Strathmiglo
Struthers
B941
Pitlessie
Kingskettle
Balmalcolm
Lathones
B9129
B936
A917
Falkland
Woodside
Lochty
B940
Scotland's Secret Bunker
0 1 2 3 4 miles
0 1 2 3 4 5 kilometres

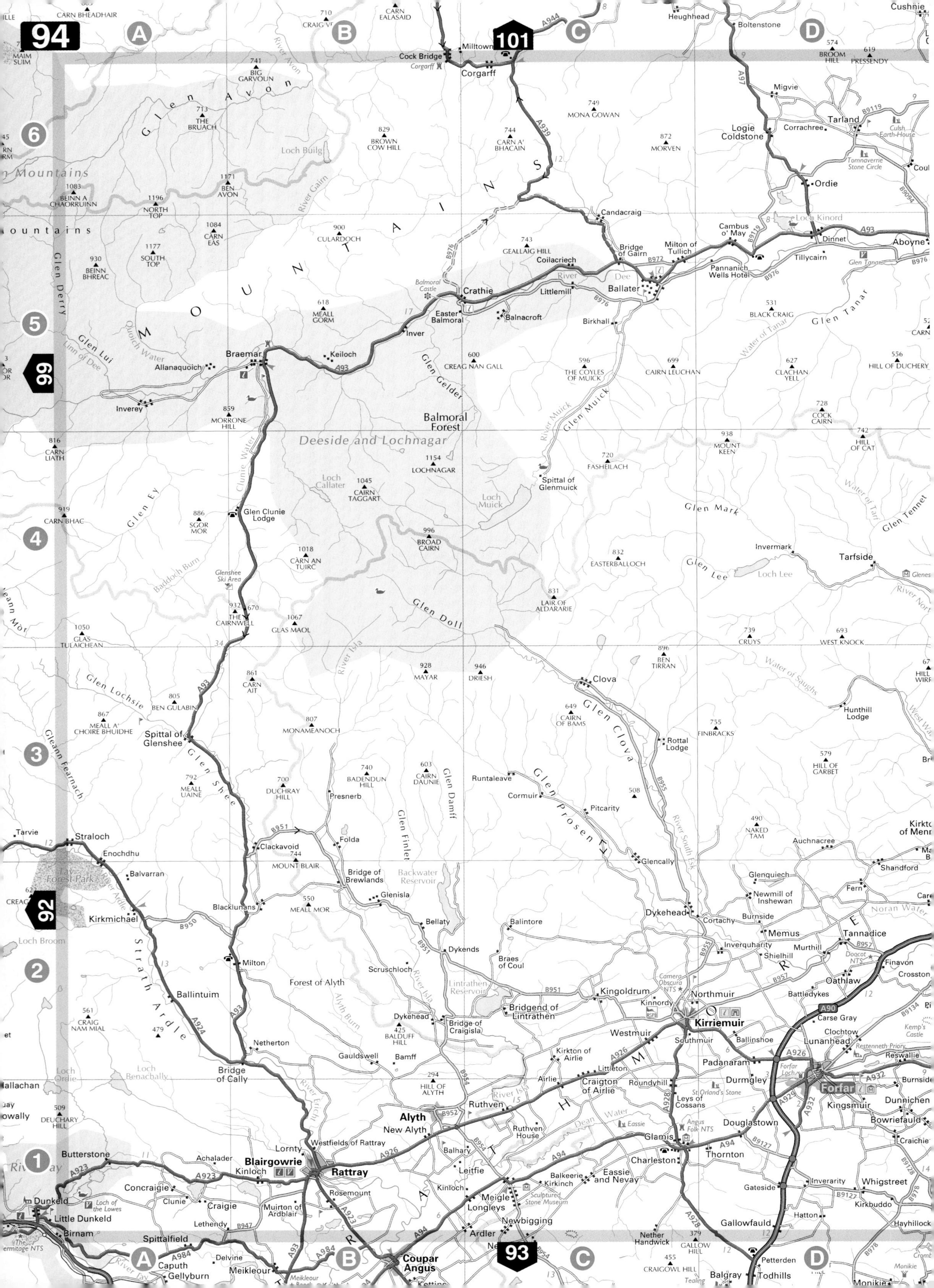

94
101
99
92
93
Cock Bridge
Corgarff
Milltown
Heughhead
Boltenstone
Migvie
Logie Coldstone
Tarland
Corrachree
Ordie
Candacraig
Cambus o' May
Dinnet
Aboyne
Bridge of Gairn
Milton of Tullich
Ballater
Crathie
Balmoral Castle
Easter Balmoral
Balnacroft
Littlemill
Coilacriech
Birkhall
Pannanich Wells Hotel
Tillycairn
Inver
Keiloch
Braemar
Allanaquoich
Inverey
MOUNTAINS
Balmoral Forest
Deeside and Lochnagar
LOCHNAGAR
BROAD CAIRN
Spittal of Glenmuick
Glen Clunie Lodge
Glenshee Ski Area
THE CAIRNWELL
GLAS MAOL
Glen Doll
Invermark
Tarfside
Loch Lee
Clova
Glen Clova
Rottal Lodge
Hunthill Lodge
Spittal of Glenshee
Glen Shee
Runtaleave
Cormuir
Pitcarity
Glen Prosen
Glencally
Presnerb
Folda
Clackavoid
Bridge of Brewlands
Glenisla
Blacklunans
Bellaty
Dykends
Balintore
Braes of Coul
Milton
Kirkmichael
Strath Ardle
Ballintuim
Straloch
Enochdhu
Balvarran
Tarvie
Forest of Alyth
Scruschloch
Lintrathen Reservoir
Bridgend of Lintrathen
Kingoldrum
Northmuir
Kirriemuir
Westmuir
Southmuir
Dykehead
Cortachy
Memus
Tannadice
Inverquharity
Shielhill
Finavon
Oathlaw
Forfar
Lunanhead
Padanaram
Douglastown
Glamis
Charleston
Thornton
Kingsmuir
Dunnichen
Bowriefauld
Netherton
Bridge of Cally
Dykehead
Bridge of Craigisla
Alyth
New Alyth
Ruthven
Airlie
Craigton of Airlie
Kirkton of Airlie
Blairgowrie
Rattray
Kinloch
Lornty
Westfields of Rattray
Butterstone
Dunkeld
Little Dunkeld
Birnam
Concraigie
Clunie
Craigie
Muirton of Ardblair
Rosemount
Meigle
Longleys
Newbigging
Ardler
Eassie and Nevay
Balkeerie
Kirkinch
Leitfie
Spittalfield
Caputh
Gellyburn
Meikleour
Coupar Angus
Delvine
Lethendy
Gallowfauld
Whigstreet
Inverarity
Kirkbuddo
Hatton
Petterden
Todhills
Balgray
Monikie
Nether Handwick
Gateside
Roundyhill
Leys of Cossans

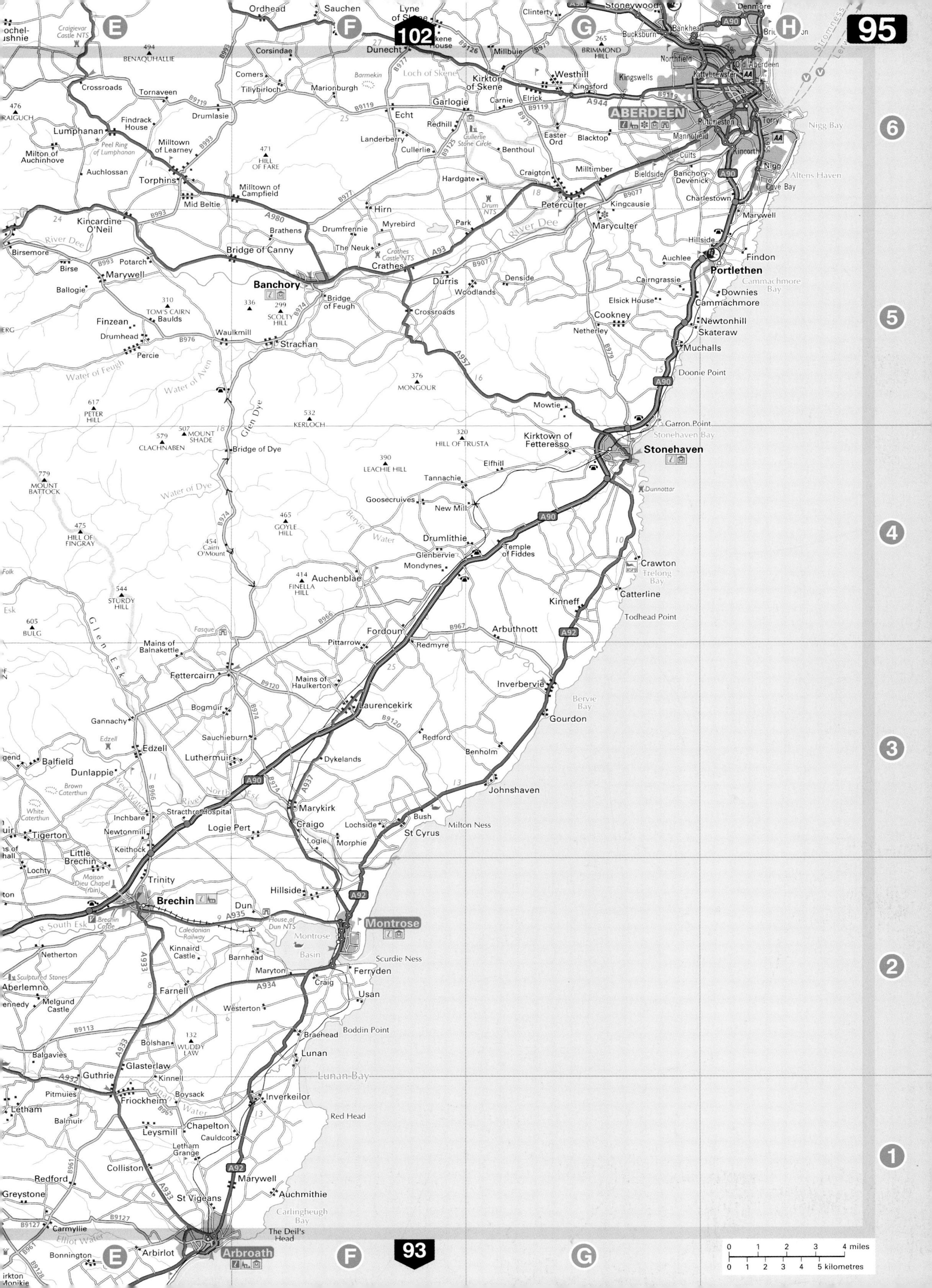
E
F
G
H
102
Ordhead
Sauchen
Clinterty
Stoneywood
Denmore
Craigievar Castle NTS
494 BENAQUHALLIE
Corsindae
Dunecht
Millbuie
265 BRIMMOND HILL
Bucksburn
Bankhead
Northfield
Comers
Tillybirloch
Barmekin
Loch of Skene
Kirkton of Skene
Westhill
Kingswells
Kittybrewster
Old Aberdeen
Crossroads
Tornaveen
Marionburgh
Kingsford
ABERDEEN
476
Drumlasie
Echt
Garlogie
Carnie
Elrick
Lumphanan
Findrack House
Redhill
Ruthrieston
Torry
Nigg Bay
Peel Ring of Lumphanan
Milltown of Learney
Landerberry
Cullerlie Stone Circle
Easter Ord
Blacktop
Mannofield
Milton of Auchinhove
471 HILL OF FARE
Cullerlie
Benthoul
Cults
Kincorth
Auchlossan
Torphins
Milltown of Campfield
Hardgate
Craigton
Milltimber
Bieldside
Banchory-Devenick
Nigg
Altens Haven
Cove Bay
Mid Beltie
Hirn
Drum NTS
Peterculter
Kingcausie
Charlestown
Kincardine O'Neil
Brathens
Myrebird
Park
Maryculter
Marywell
River Dee
Drumfrennie
Hillside
Findon
Birsemore
Bridge of Canny
The Neuk
Crathes Castle NTS
Crathes
Auchlee
Portlethen
Birse
Potarch
Marywell
Banchory
Durris
Denside
Cairngrassie
Cammachmore Bay
Ballogie
Bridge of Feugh
Woodlands
Downies
Elsick House
Cammachmore
310 TOM'S CAIRN
336
299 SCOLTY HILL
Crossroads
Cookney
Newtonhill
Baulds
Finzean
Netherley
Skateraw
Drumhead
Waulkmill
Strachan
Muchalls
Percie
Water of Feugh
Water of Aven
376 MONGOUR
Doonie Point
617 PETER HILL
532 KERLOCH
Glen Dye
Mowtie
Garron Point
Stonehaven Bay
579 CLACHNABEN
507 MOUNT SHADE
320 HILL OF TRUSTA
Kirktown of Fetteresso
Stonehaven
Bridge of Dye
390 LEACHIE HILL
Elfhill
779 MOUNT BATTOCK
Tannachie
Dunnottar
Water of Dye
Goosecruives
New Mill
465 GOYLE HILL
Bervie Water
475 HILL OF FINGRAY
454 Cairn O'Mount
Drumlithie
Glenbervie
Temple of Fiddes
Mondynes
Crawton
Trelong Bay
414 FINELLA HILL
Auchenblae
544 STURDY HILL
Catterline
Kinneff
605 BULG
Todhead Point
Fasque
Glen Esk
Fordoun
Arbuthnott
Mains of Balnakettle
Pittarrow
Redmyre
Fettercairn
Mains of Haulkerton
Inverbervie
Bervie Bay
Bogmuir
Laurencekirk
Gourdon
Gannachy
Edzell
Sauchieburn
Redford
Balfield
Luthermuir
Dykelands
Benholm
Dunlappie
Brown Caterthun
West Water
River North Esk
Johnshaven
White Caterthun
Inchbare
Stracathro Hospital
Marykirk
Logie Pert
Craigo
Lochside
Bush
Milton Ness
Tigerton
Newtonmill
St Cyrus
Logie
Morphie
Little Brechin
Keithock
Lochty
Maison Dieu Chapel (ruin)
Trinity
Hillside
Brechin
Dun
Brechin Castle
R. South Esk
House of Dun NTS
Montrose
Caledonian Railway
Montrose Basin
Netherton
Kinnaird Castle
Barnhead
Scurdie Ness
Sculptured Stones
Maryton
Ferryden
Aberlemno
Farnell
Craig
Usan
Melgund Castle
Westerton
Boddin Point
Bolshan
132 WUDDY LAW
Braehead
Balgavies
Lunan
Glasterlaw
Guthrie
Kinnell
Lunan Bay
Pitmuies
Boysack
Inverkeilor
Friockheim
Letham
Lunan Water
Balmuir
Red Head
Chapelton
Leysmill
Cauldcots
Letham Grange
Colliston
Redford
Marywell
Auchmithie
Greystone
St Vigeans
Carlingheugh Bay
Carmyllie
Elliot Water
The Deil's Head
Bonnington
Arbirlot
Arbroath
93
0 1 2 3 4 miles
0 1 2 3 4 5 kilometres
1
2
3
4
5
6

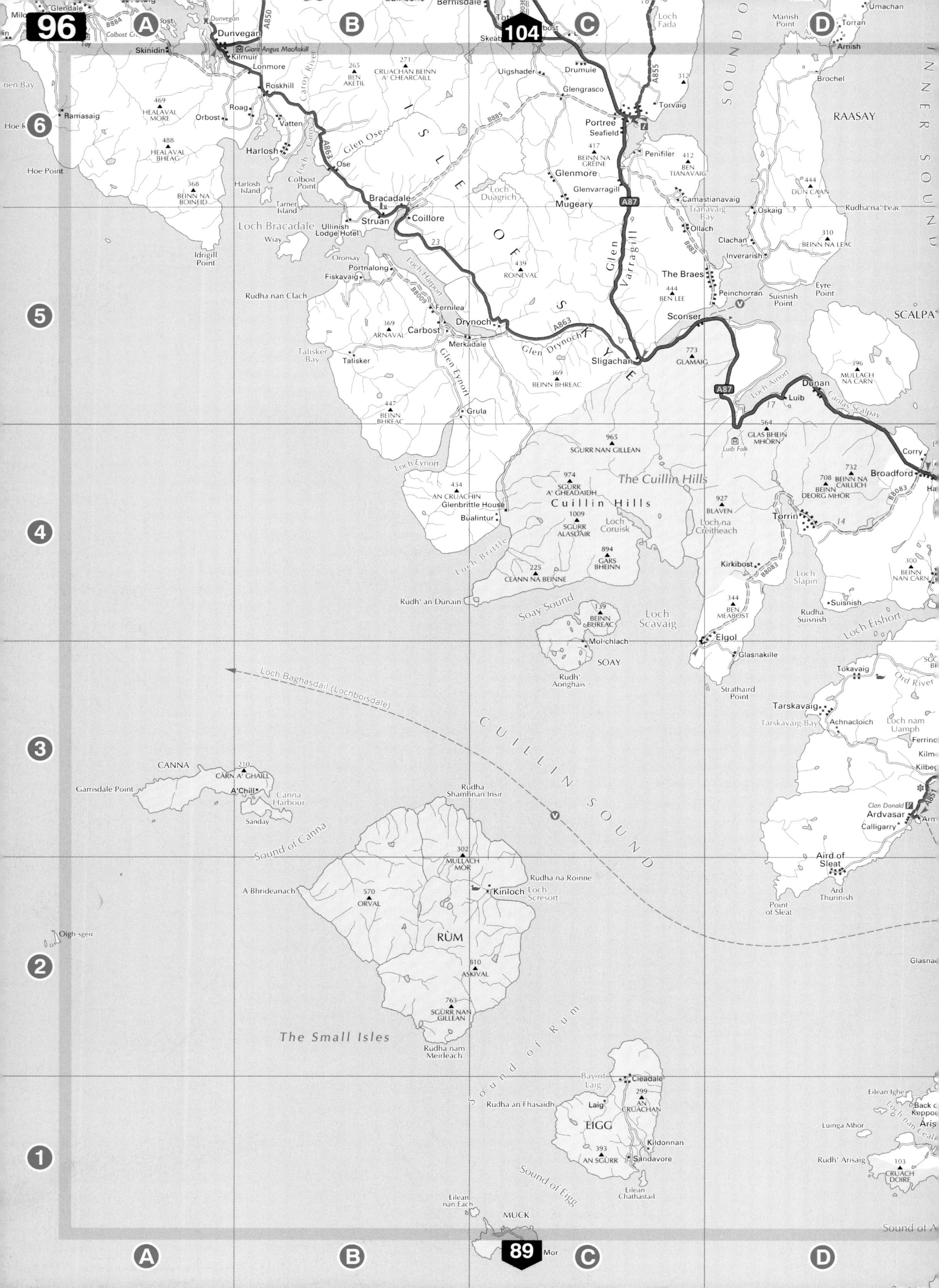
104
89
A
B
C
D
6
5
4
3
2
1
Glendale
Dunvegan
Skinidin
Kilmuir
Giant Angus MacAskill
Lonmore
Roskhill
Roag
Orbost
Vatten
Harlosh
Ramasaig
Hoe Point
469
HEALAVAL MORE
488
HEALAVAL BHEAG
368
BEINN NA BOINEID
265
BEN AKETIL
271
CRUACHAN BEINN A' CHEARCAILL
Caroy River
Glen Ose
Ose
Colbost Point
Harlosh Island
Tarner Island
Bracadale
Struan
Coillore
Loch Bracadale
Ullinish Lodge Hotel
Wiay
Idrigill Point
ISLE OF SKYE
Loch Duagrich
Uigshader
Drumuie
Glengrasco
Portree
Seafield
Torvaig
417
BEINN NA GREINE
Glenmore
Glenvarragill
Mugeary
Penifiler
412
BEN TIANAVAIG
Camastianavaig
Tianavaig Bay
Ollach
The Braes
444
BEN LEE
Peinchorran
Sconser
Glen Varragill
A87
A850
A855
A863
B885
B883
B8009
B8083
Loch Fada
SOUND OF RAASAY
INNER SOUND
RAASAY
Manish Point
Torran
Umachan
Arnish
Brochel
444
DUN CAAN
Oskaig
Rudha na' Leac
310
BEINN NA LEAC
Clachan
Inverarish
Eyre Point
Suisnish Point
SCALPAY
396
MULLACH NA CARN
Oronsay
Portnalong
Fiskavaig
Loch Harport
Fernilea
Rudha nan Clach
369
ARNAVAL
Carbost
Drynoch
Merkadale
Talisker Bay
Talisker
Glen Eynort
Glen Drynoch
439
ROINEVAL
Sligachan
773
GLAMAIG
369
BEINN BHREAC
447
BEINN BHREAC
Grula
Loch Ainort
Dunan
Luib
Caolas Scalpay
564
GLAS BHEIN MHÒRN
Luib Folk
965
SGURR NAN GILLEAN
Corry
Broadford
732
BEINN NA CAILLICH
708
BEINN DEORG MHOR
Loch Eynort
434
AN CRUACHIN
Glenbrittle House
Bualintur
974
SGURR A' GHEADAIDH
The Cuillin Hills
Cuillin Hills
1009
SGURR ALASDAIR
Loch Coruisk
927
BLAVEN
Loch na Creitheach
Torrin
Loch Brittle
225
CEANN NA BEINNE
894
GARS BHEINN
Kirkibost
Loch Slapin
300
BEINN NAN CARN
Rudh' an Dùnain
Soay Sound
139
BEINN BHREAC
Loch Scavaig
344
BEN MEABOST
Suisnish
Rudha Suisnish
Loch Eishort
Mol-chlach
SOAY
Elgol
Glasnakille
Rudh' Aonghais
Strathaird Point
Tokavaig
Ord River
Loch Baghasdail (Lochboisdale)
Tarskavaig
Tarskavaig Bay
Achnacloich
Loch nam Uamph
CUILLIN SOUND
CANNA
210
CARN A' GHAILL
Garrisdale Point
A'Chill
Canna Harbour
Sanday
Rudha Shamhnan Insir
Clan Donald
Ardvasar
Calligarry
Sound of Canna
302
MULLACH MOR
Rudha na Roinne
Kinloch
Loch Scresort
A Bhrideanach
570
ORVAL
Aird of Sleat
Ard Thurinish
Point of Sleat
Oigh-sgeir
RÙM
810
ASKIVAL
763
SGÙRR NAN GILLEAN
The Small Isles
Sound of Rum
Rudha nam Meirleach
Bay of Laig
Cleadale
299
AN CRUACHAN
Rudha an Fhasaidh
Laig
EIGG
Kildonnan
393
AN SGÙRR
Sandavore
Eilean Chathastail
Sound of Eigg
Eilean nan Each
MUCK
Eilean Ighe
Luinga Mhor
Rudh' Arisaig
103
CRUACH DOIRE
Sound of Arisaig

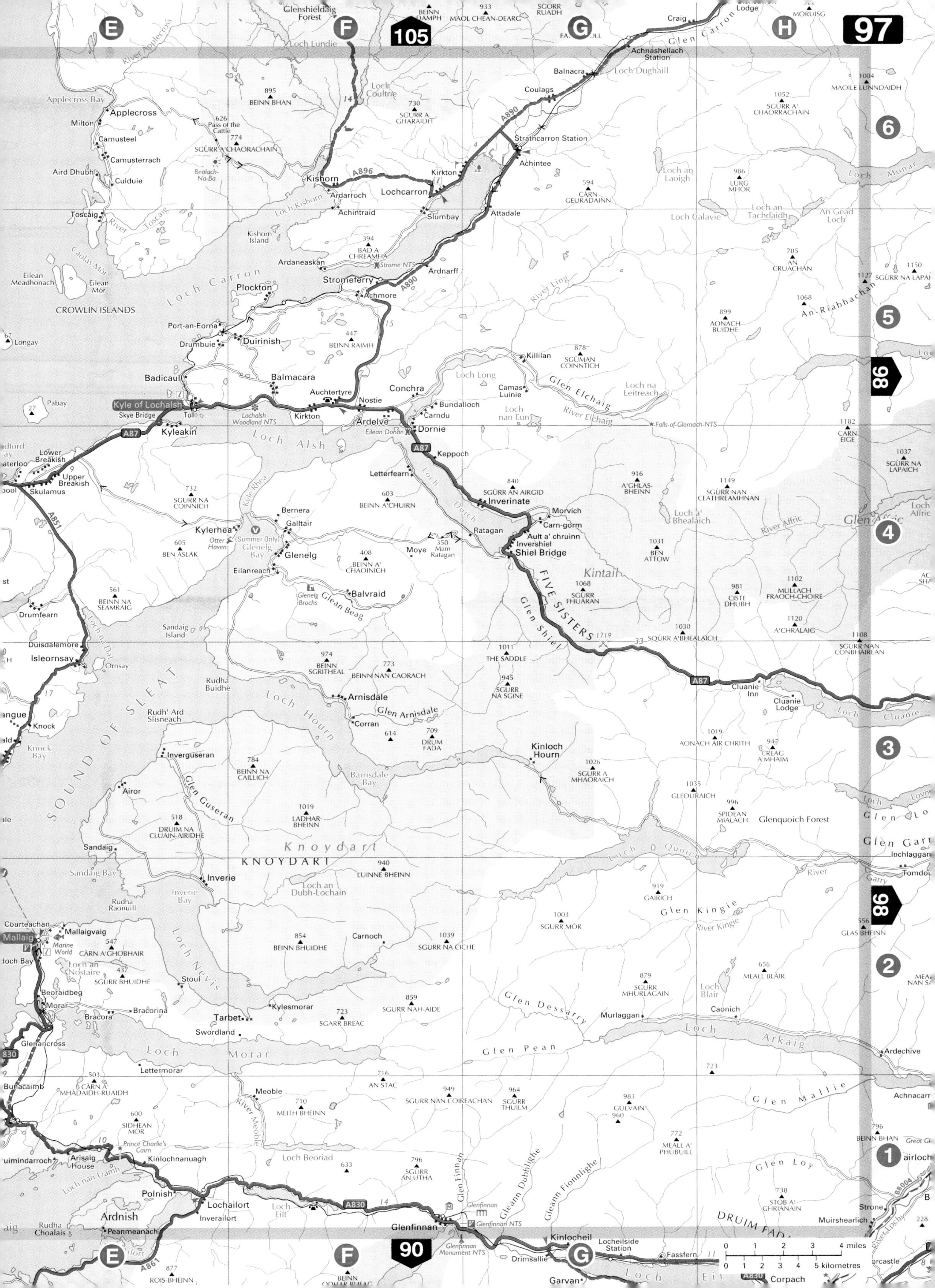

E
F
G
H
105
Applecross
Kishorn
Lochcarron
Plockton
Kyle of Lochalsh
Kyleakin
Dornie
Shiel Bridge
Glenelg
Arnisdale
Kinloch Hourn
Inverie
Mallaig
Morar
Glenfinnan
Lochailort
Arisaig
Achnashellach Station
Strathcarron Station
Stromeferry
Loch Carron
Loch Alsh
Loch Duich
Loch Hourn
Loch Nevis
Loch Morar
Loch Arkaig
Loch Quoich
Loch Cluanie
Sound of Sleat
Knoydart
Kintail
Five Sisters
Glen Shiel
Glen Elchaig
Glen Affric
Glen Garry
Glen Kingie
Glen Dessarry
Glen Pean
Glen Mallie
Glen Loy
Crowlin Islands
Isleornsay
Skye Bridge
Eilean Donan
Cluanie Inn
Glenfinnan Monument NTS
A87
A890
A896
A830
A851
A861
86
90
1
2
3
4
5
6
0 1 2 3 4 miles
0 1 2 3 4 5 kilometres

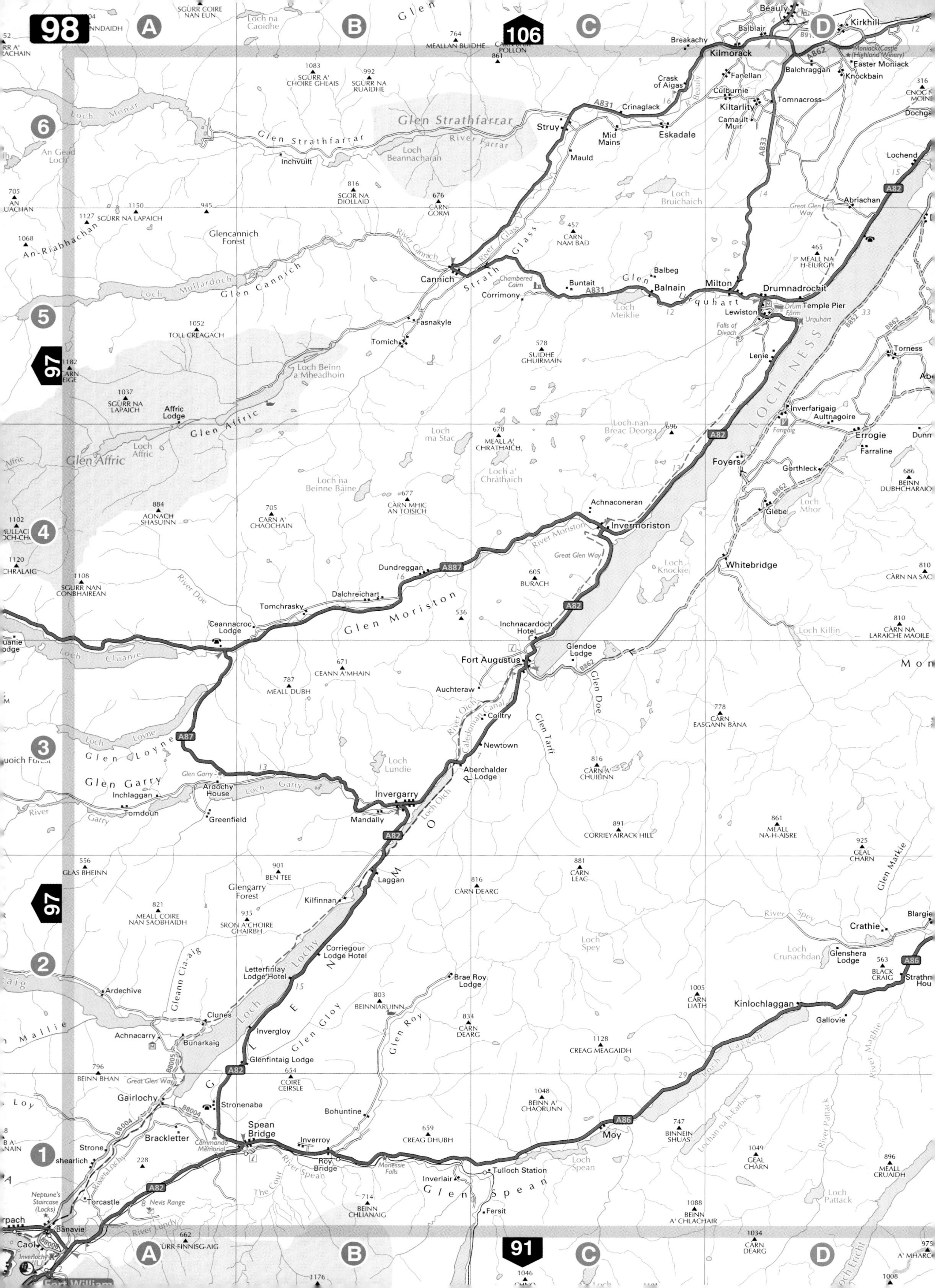

98
106
97
91
A
B
C
D
1
2
3
4
5
6
Beauly
Kirkhill
Balblair
Breakachy
Kilmorack
Moniack Castle (Highland Winery)
Easter Moniack
Balchraggan
Knockbain
Crask of Aigas
Fanellan
Culburnie
Kiltarlity
Tomnacross
Camault Muir
Crinaglack
Struy
Mid Mains
Eskadale
Mauld
Glen Strathfarrar
River Farrar
Loch Beannacharan
Loch Monar
An Gead Loch
Inchvuilt
Loch Bruichaich
Lochend
Abriachan
Great Glen Way
Glencannich Forest
River Cannich
Strath Glass
River Glass
Cannich
Chambered Cairn
Corrimony
Buntait
Balbeg
Glen Urquhart
Balnain
Milton
Drumnadrochit
Temple Pier
Lewiston
Drum Farm
Urquhart
Falls of Divach
Loch Meiklie
Loch Mullardoch
Glen Cannich
An-Riabhachan
Fasnakyle
Tomich
Loch Beinn a Mheadhoin
Affric Lodge
Glen Affric
Loch Affric
Lenie
Torness
LOCH NESS
Inverfarigaig
Aultnagoire
Errogie
Farraline
Foyers
Gorthleck
Glebe
Loch Mhor
Achnaconeran
Invermoriston
River Moriston
Loch Knockie
Whitebridge
Dundreggan
Dalchreichart
Tomchrasky
Ceannacroc Lodge
Glen Moriston
River Doe
Loch Cluanie
Inchnacardoch Hotel
Fort Augustus
Glendoe Lodge
Glen Doe
Loch Killin
Auchteraw
Caledonian Canal
River Oich
Coiltry
Glen Tarff
Newtown
Aberchalder Lodge
Loch Lundie
Loch Loyne
Glen Loyne
Glen Garry
Loch Garry
Ardochy House
Inchlaggan
Tomdoun
Greenfield
Invergarry
Mandally
Loch Oich
Laggan
Kilfinnan
Glengarry Forest
Loch Lochy
Corriegour Lodge Hotel
Letterfinlay Lodge Hotel
Ardechive
Gleann Cia-aig
Clunes
Achnacarry
Bunarkaig
Invergloy
Glen Gloy
Glen Roy
Brae Roy Lodge
Glenfintaig Lodge
Gairlochy
Stronenaba
Spean Bridge
Commando Memorial
Bohuntine
Brackletter
Strone
Inverroy
Roy Bridge
Monessie Falls
Tulloch Station
Inverlair
Glen Spean
River Spean
Fersit
Loch Treig
Loch Spey
River Spey
Crathie
Glenshera Lodge
Loch Crunachdan
Kinlochlaggan
Gallovie
Loch Laggan
Moy
Loch Pattack
River Pattack
Glen Markie
Torcastle
Neptune's Staircase (Locks)
Banavie
Caol
Fort William
Nevis Range
River Lundy
River Lochy
A82
A87
A831
A833
A862
A887
A86
B862
B852
B8004
B8005
B8006

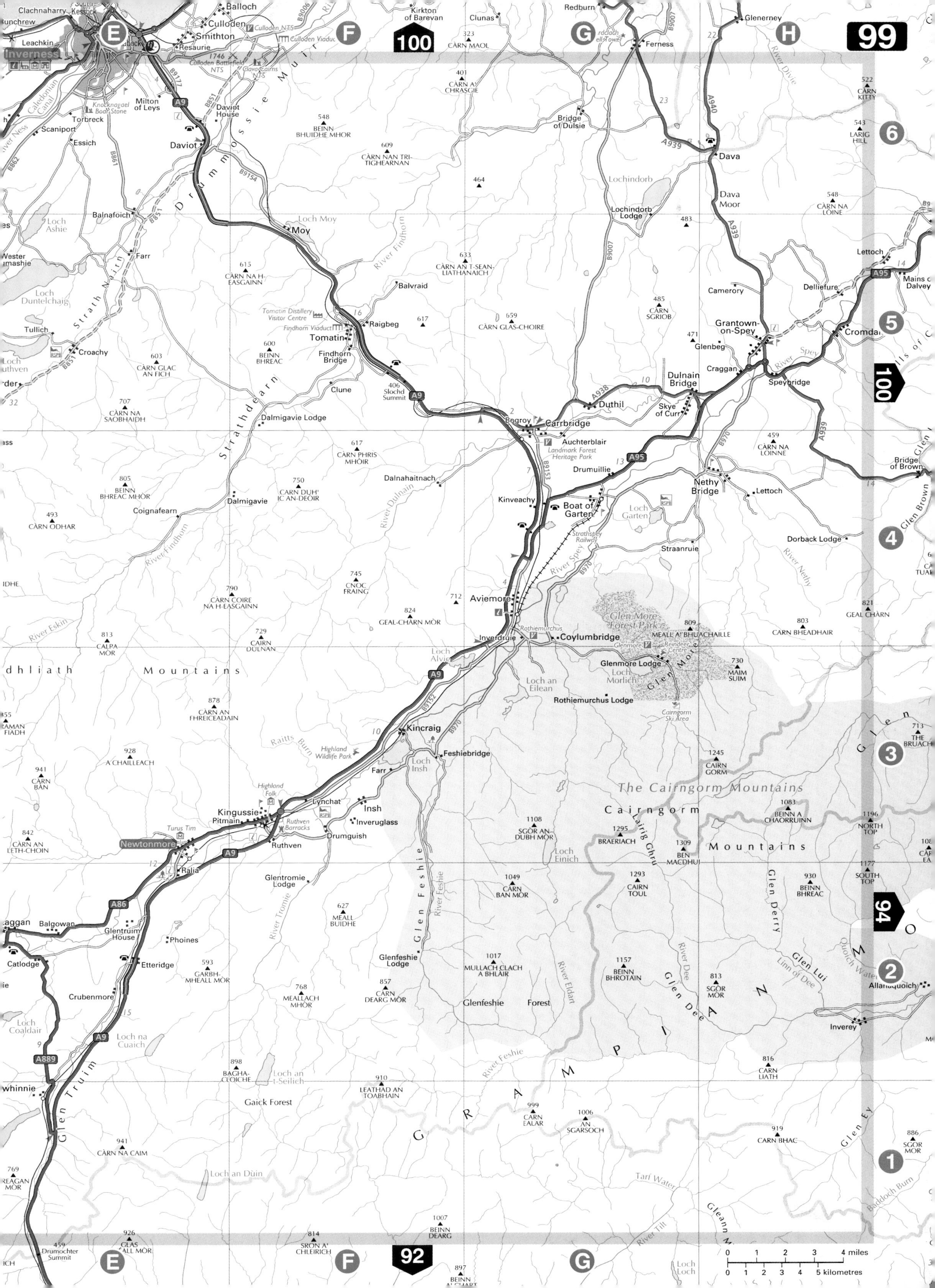

Clachnaharry
Bunchrew
Leachkin
Inverness
Balloch
Culloden
Smithton
Resaurie
Culloden NTS
Culloden Viaduct
1746 Culloden Battlefield NTS
Clava Cairns NTS
Kirkton of Barevan
Clunas
323 CÀRN MAOL
Redburn
Ferness
Glenerney
E
F
G
H
100
Milton of Leys
Knocknagael Boar Stone
Torbreck
Scaniport
Essich
Daviot House
Daviot
B9177
B851
B861
B862
B9154
B9006
B9007
A9
A939
A940
A938
A95
A86
A889
B970
B9152
B9153
401 CARN A' CHRASGIE
548 BEINN BHUIDHE MHOR
609 CÀRN NAN TRI-TIGHEARNAN
464
Bridge of Dulsie
Dava
Lochindorb
Lochindorb Lodge
Dava Moor
483
522 CARN KITTY
543 LARIG HILL
548 CÀRN NA LOINE
Drummossie Muir
Loch Ashie
Balnafoich
Loch Moy
Moy
Wester Aldourie
Farr
Loch Duntelchaig
Strath Nairn
Tullich
Croachy
Loch Ruthven
615 CÀRN NA H-EASGAINN
633 CÀRN AN T-SEAN-LIATHANAICH
River Findhorn
Balvraid
Tomatin Distillery Visitor Centre
Findhorn Viaduct
Raigbeg
617
659 CÀRN GLAS-CHOIRE
485 CÀRN SGRIOB
Camerory
Lettoch
Mains of Dalvey
Dellefure
Grantown-on-Spey
Glenbeg
471
Cromdale
Craggan
River Spey
Speybridge
Tomatin
Findhorn Bridge
600 BEINN BHREAC
603 CÀRN GLAC AN FHICH
Clune
406 Slochd Summit
Dulnain Bridge
Duthil
Skye of Curr
Carrbridge
Bogroy
Auchterblair
Landmark Forest Heritage Park
707 CÀRN NA SAOBHAIDH
Dalmigavie Lodge
Strathdearn
617 CÀRN PHRIS MHÒIR
459 CÀRN NA LOINNE
Bridge of Brown
Drumuillie
Dalnahaitnach
805 BEINN BHREAC MHÒR
750 CÀRN DUH' IC AN-DEOIR
Nethy Bridge
Lettoch
Kinveachy
Boat of Garten
Loch Garten
Dalmigavie
Coignafearn
493 CÀRN ODHAR
River Dulnain
Strathspey Railway
Straanruie
Dorback Lodge
Glen Brown
River Nethy
745 CNOC FRAING
790 CÀRN COIRE NA H-EASGAINN
712
Aviemore
824 GEAL-CHÀRN MÒR
Glen More Forest Park
809 MEALL A' BHUACHAILLE
821 GEAL CHÀRN
803 CARN BHEADHAIR
River Eskin
813 CALPA MÒR
729 CAIRN DULNAN
Loch Alvie
Inverdruie
Rothiemurchus
Coylumbridge
Glenmore
Reindeer Centre
Glenmore Lodge
Loch Morlich
Glen More
730 MAIM SUIM
Monadhliath Mountains
Loch an Eilean
Rothiemurchus Lodge
Cairngorm Ski Area
878 CÀRN AN FHREICEADAIN
Kincraig
Raitts Burn
Highland Wildlife Park
Feshiebridge
Loch Insh
Farr
713 THE BRUACH
Glen
928 A' CHAILLEACH
941 CÀRN BAN
1245 CAIRN GORM
The Cairngorm Mountains
Highland Folk
Kingussie
Pitmain
Lynchat
Insh
Inveruglass
Ruthven Barracks
Ruthven
Drumguish
1108 SGOR AN DUBH MÒR
Cairngorm Mountains
Lairig Ghru
1295 BRAERIACH
1309 BEN MACDHUI
1083 BEINN A' CHAORRUINN
1196 NORTH TOP
1177 SOUTH TOP
842 CÀRN AN LETH-CHOIN
Turus Tim
Newtonmore
Ralia
Loch Einich
Glentromie Lodge
1049 CÀRN BAN MÒR
1293 CAIRN TOUL
Glen Derry
930 BEINN BHREAC
94
Laggan
Balgowan
Glentruim House
Phoines
River Tromie
627 MEALL BUIDHE
Glen Feshie
River Feshie
Catlodge
Etteridge
593 GARBH-MHEALL MÒR
Glenfeshie Lodge
1017 MULLACH CLACH A' BHLAIR
River Eidart
1157 BEINN BHROTAIN
River Dee
Glen Lui
Linn of Dee
Quoich Water
Allanaquoich
813 SGOR MÒR
Glen Dee
Crubenmore
768 MEALLACH MHÒR
857 CÀRN DEARG MÒR
Glenfeshie Forest
Inverey
Loch Coaldair
Loch na Cuaich
898 BAGHA-CLOICHE
Loch an t-Seilich
River Feshie
GRAMPIAN MOUNTAINS
816 CÀRN LIATH
Dalwhinnie
Glen Truim
910 LEATHAD AN TOABHAIN
Gaick Forest
999 CÀRN EALAR
1006 AN SGARSOCH
919 CÀRN BHAC
886 SGOR MÒR
Glen Ey
941 CÀRN NA CAIM
769 MEALL A' CHAORAINN MÒR
Loch an Dùin
Tarf Water
Baddoch Burn
Gleann Mòr
River Tilt
459 Drumochter Summit
926 GLAS MHEALL MÒR
814 SRON A' CHLEIRICH
1007 BEINN DEARG
92
897 BEINN A' CHAIT
Loch Loch
1
2
3
4
5
6
0 1 2 3 4 miles
0 1 2 3 4 5 kilometres

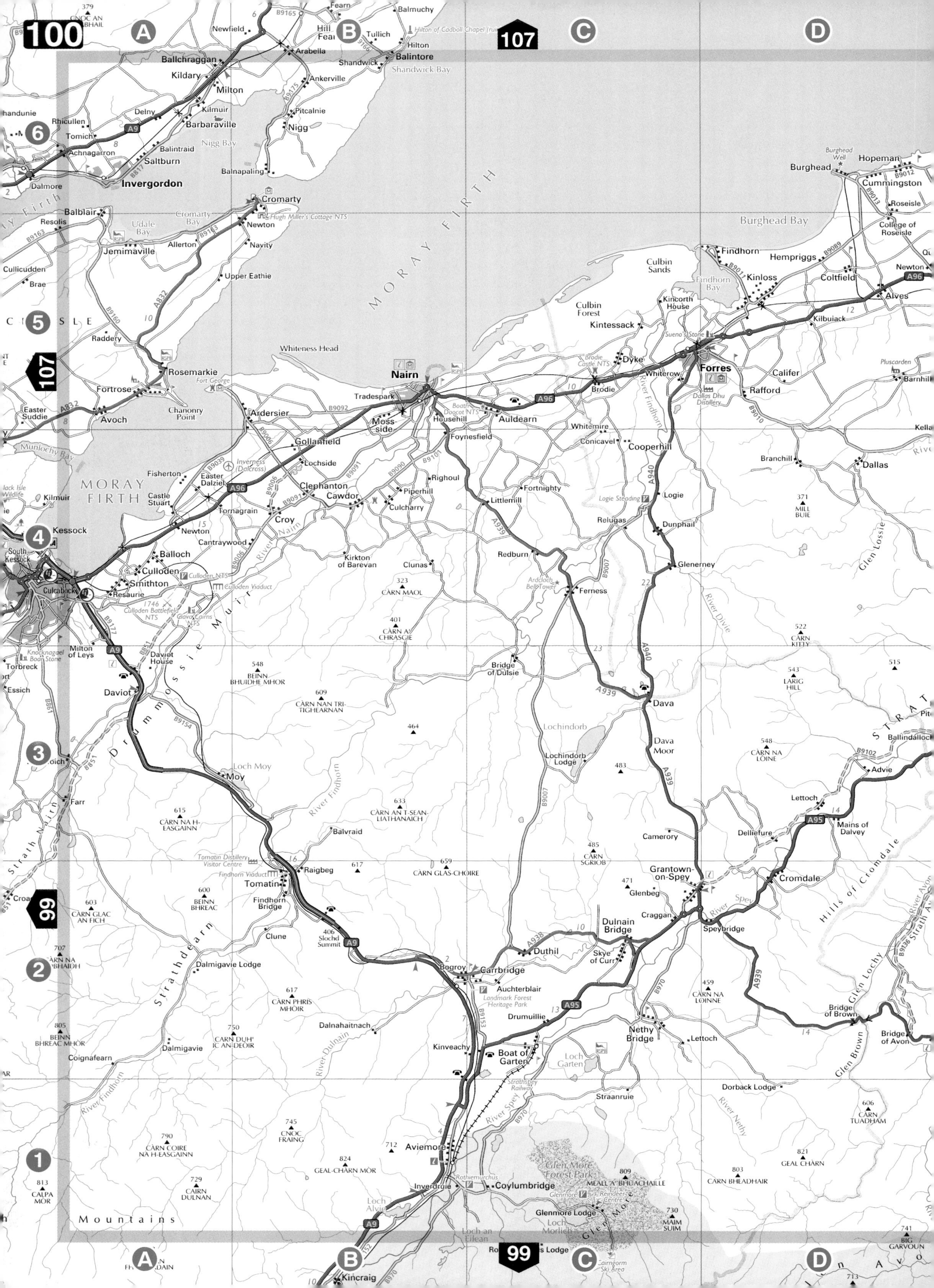
100
A
B
C
D
107
99
1
2
3
4
5
6
Newfield
Fearn
Balmuchy
Hill of Fearn
Tullich
Hilton of Cadboll Chapel
Hilton
Arabella
Balintore
Shandwick
Shandwick Bay
Ballchraggan
Kildary
Milton
Ankerville
Kilmuir
Delny
Barbaraville
Pitcalnie
Nigg
Rhicullen
Tomich
Achnagarron
Balintraid
Nigg Bay
Saltburn
Invergordon
Balnapaling
Dalmore
Cromarty
Cromarty Bay
Udale Bay
Hugh Miller's Cottage NTS
Balblair
Resolis
Newton
Navity
Jemimaville
Allerton
Cullicudden
Brae
Upper Eathie
MORAY FIRTH
Raddery
Rosemarkie
Fortrose
Chanonry Point
Fort George
Whiteness Head
Eastern Suddie
Avoch
Munlochy Bay
Ardersier
Nairn
Tradespark
Moss-side
Gollanfield
Lochside
Inverness (Dalcross)
Fisherton
Eastern Dalziel
Castle Stuart
Kilmuir
Kessock
South Kessock
Tornagrain
Croy
Clephanton
Cawdor
Piperhill
Culcharry
Righoul
Newton
Cantraywood
Balloch
Culloden
Culloden NTS
Culloden Viaduct
Smithton
Culcabock
Resaurie
1746 Culloden Battlefield NTS
Clava Cairns NTS
River Nairn
Kirkton of Barevan
Clunas
323 CÀRN MAOL
401 CÀRN A' CHRASGIE
Milton of Leys
Knocknagael Boar Stone
Torbreck
Essich
Daviot House
Daviot
548 BEINN BHUIDHE MHOR
609 CÀRN NAN TRI-TIGHEARNAN
464
Drummossie Muir
Loch Moy
Moy
Farr
Strath Nairn
615 CÀRN NA H-EASGAINN
River Findhorn
633 CÀRN AN T-SEAN-LIATHANAICH
Balvraid
Tomatin Distillery Visitor Centre
Findhorn Viaduct
Raigbeg
617
659 CÀRN GLAS-CHOIRE
Tomatin
Findhorn Bridge
600 BEINN BHREAC
603 CÀRN GLAC AN FHEIDH
Clune
406 Slochd Summit
707 CÀRN NA LOBHAIDH
Dalmigavie Lodge
Strathdearn
617 CÀRN PHRIS MHÒIR
805 BEINN BHREAC MHÒR
750 CÀRN DUBH' IC AN DEÒIR
Dalmigavie
Coignafearn
Dalnahaitnach
River Dulnain
790 CÀRN COIRE NA H-EASGAINN
745 CNOC FRAING
712
824 GEAL-CHÀRN MÒR
729 CAIRN DULNAN
813 CALPA MÒR
Monadhliath Mountains
Aviemore
Inverdruie
Rothiemurchus
Coylumbridge
Loch Alvie
Loch an Eilein
Kincraig
Culbin Sands
Culbin Forest
Kintessack
Findhorn
Findhorn Bay
Kincorth House
Sueno's Stone
Brodie Castle NTS
Dyke
Brodie
Whiterow
Forres
Dallas Dhu Distillery
Boath Doocot NTS
Auldearn
Househill
Foynesfield
Whitemire
Conicavel
Cooperhill
River Findhorn
Logie Steading
Logie
Fortnighty
Littlemill
Relugas
Dunphail
Redburn
Glenerney
Ardclach Bell Tower
Ferness
River Divie
Bridge of Dulsie
Dava
Lochindorb
Lochindorb Lodge
Dava Moor
483
485 CÀRN SGRIOB
Camerory
Grantown-on-Spey
471 Glenbeg
Craggan
Dulnain Bridge
Duthil
Skye of Curr
Bogroy
Carrbridge
Auchterblair
Landmark Forest Heritage Park
Drumuillie
Nethy Bridge
Lettoch
Kinveachy
Boat of Garten
Loch Garten
Strathspey Railway
River Spey
Straanruie
River Nethy
Glen More Forest Park
809 MEALL A' BHUACHAILLE
Glenmore
Reindeer Centre
Glenmore Lodge
Loch Morlich
Glen More
730 MAIM SUIM
Cairngorm Ski Area
Burghead Well
Burghead
Hopeman
Cummingston
Roseisle
College of Roseisle
Burghead Bay
Hempriggs
Kinloss
Coltfield
Newton
Alves
Kilbuiack
Pluscarden
Barnhill
Califer
Rafford
Branchill
Dallas
371 MILL BUIE
Glen Lossie
522 CÀRN KITTY
543 LARIG HILL
515
548 CÀRN NA LOINE
Ballindalloch
Advie
Lettoch
Dellefure
Mains of Dalvey
Cromdale
Hills of Cromdale
Speybridge
459 CÀRN NA LOINNE
Glen Lochy
Bridge of Brown
Bridge of Avon
Glen Brown
Dorback Lodge
606 CÀRN TUADHAM
821 GEAL CHÀRN
803 CÀRN BHEADHAIR
741 BIG GARVOUN
713
A9
A96
A832
A939
A940
A938
A95
B9165
B9175
B9176
B817
B9163
B9160
B9092
B9006
B9039
B9091
B9090
B9101
B9007
B9177
B851
B861
B9154
B9153
B970
B9012
B9013
B9089
B9011
B9010
B9102
B9136

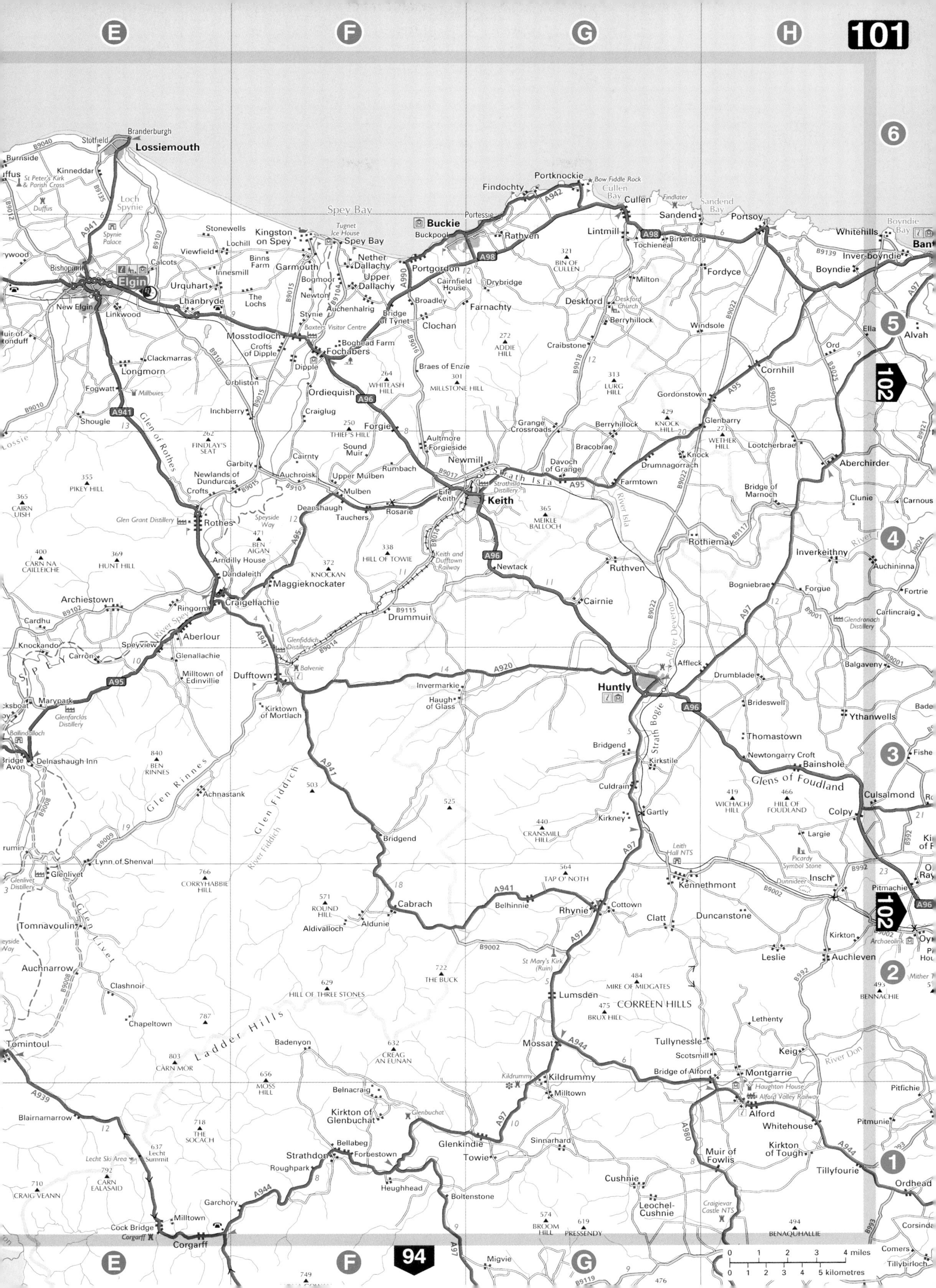
E
F
G
H
Lossiemouth
Branderburgh
Stotfield
Burnside
Kinneddar
St Peter's Kirk & Parish Cross
Duffus
Loch Spynie
Spynie Palace
Elgin
Bishopmill
New Elgin
Linkwood
Stonewells
Lochill
Kingston on Spey
Tugnet Ice House
Spey Bay
Viewfield
Innesmill
Binns Farm
Garmouth
Calcots
Urquhart
Lhanbryde
The Lochs
Bogmoor
Newton
Stynie
Auchenhalrig
Nether Dallachy
Upper Dallachy
Baxters Visitor Centre
Mosstodloch
Crofts of Dipple
Fochabers
Boghead Farm
Dipple
Clackmarras
Longmorn
Fogwatt
Millbuies
Orbliston
Inchberry
Shougle
Ordiequish
Craiglug
Buckie
Buckpool
Portessie
Portgordon
Rathven
Findochty
Portknockie
Bow Fiddle Rock
Cullen Bay
Cullen
Findlater
Sandend Bay
Sandend
Portsoy
Lintmill
Tochieneal
Birkenbog
Whitehills
Boyndie Bay
Inverboyndie
Boyndie
Fordyce
Milton
321 BIN OF CULLEN
Cairnfield House
Drybridge
Broadley
Bridge of Tynet
Clochan
Farnachty
Deskford
Deskford Church
Berryhillock
Windsole
Craibstone
272 ADDIE HILL
Braes of Enzie
301 MILLSTONE HILL
264 WHITEASH HILL
313 LURG HILL
Gordonstown
Cornhill
Ord
Ella
Alvah
429 KNOCK HILL
Glenbarry
271 WETHER HILL
Lootcherbrae
Knock
Aberchirder
Grange Crossroads
Berryhillock
Bracobrae
Drumnagorrach
Davoch of Grange
Farmtown
Bridge of Marnoch
Clunie
Carnousie
Forgie
250 THIEF'S HILL
Sound Muir
Aultmore
Forgieside
Newmill
Rumbach
Strathisla Distillery
Strath Isla
River Isla
Keith
Fife Keith
262 FINDLAY'S SEAT
Garbity
Cairnty
Auchroisk
Upper Mulben
Mulben
Newlands of Dundurcas
Crofts
355 PIKEY HILL
365 CAIRN UISH
Glen of Rothes
Glen Grant Distillery
Rothes
Speyside Way
Deanshaugh
Tauchers
Rosarie
365 MEIKLE BALLOCH
Rothiemay
Inverkeithny
Auchininna
Fortrie
471 BEN AIGAN
400 CARN NA CAILLEICHE
369 HUNT HILL
Arndilly House
372 KNOCKAN
338 HILL OF TOWIE
Keith and Dufftown Railway
Newtack
Ruthven
Bogniebrae
Forgue
Dandaleith
Maggieknockater
Cairnie
Glendronach Distillery
Carlincraig
Archiestown
Ringorm
Craigellachie
Drummuir
Cardhu
Aberlour
River Spey
Knockando
Speyview
Carron
Glenallachie
Glenfiddich Distillery
Balvenie
Milltown of Edinvillie
Dufftown
Invermarkie
Haugh of Glass
River Deveron
Affleck
Drumblade
Balgaveny
Huntly
Brideswell
Ythanwells
Marypark
Glenfarclas Distillery
Ballindalloch
Delnashaugh Inn
Bridge of Avon
Kirktown of Mortlach
840 BEN RINNES
Glen Rinnes
Achnastank
Glen Fiddich
River Fiddich
503
525
Strath Bogie
Bridgend
Kirkstile
Thomastown
Newtongarry Croft
Bainshole
Glens of Foudland
Culdrain
Gartly
Kirkney
440 CRANSMILL HILL
419 WICHACH HILL
466 HILL OF FOUDLAND
Culsalmond
Colpy
Largie
Bridgend
Lynn of Shenval
Glenlivet
Glenlivet Distillery
766 CORRYHABBIE HILL
564 TAP O' NOTH
Leith Hall NTS
Picardy Symbol Stone
Kennethmont
Insch
Dunnideer
Pitmachie
Cabrach
571 ROUND HILL
Aldunie
Aldivalloch
Belhinnie
Rhynie
Cottown
Clatt
Duncanstone
Kirkton
Archaeolink
Tomnavoulin
Glen Livet
Auchnarrow
Clashnoir
Chapeltown
629 HILL OF THREE STONES
722 THE BUCK
St Mary's Kirk (Ruin)
Lumsden
484 MIRE OF MIDGATES
475 BRUX HILL
CORREEN HILLS
Leslie
Auchleven
493 BENNACHIE
Mither Tap
Lethenty
787
Ladder Hills
Tomintoul
Badenyon
632 CREAG AN EUNAN
Mossat
Tullynessle
Scotsmill
Keig
River Don
803 CARN MOR
656 MOSS HILL
Kildrummy
Milltown
Bridge of Alford
Montgarrie
Haughton House
Alford Valley Railway
Alford
Whitehouse
Pitfichie
Pitmunie
Blairnamarrow
Belnacraig
Kirkton of Glenbuchat
Glenbuchat
718 THE SOCACH
637 Lecht Summit
Lecht Ski Area
Bellabeg
Strathdon
Forbestown
Glenkindie
Towie
Sinnarhard
Muir of Fowlis
Kirkton of Tough
Tillyfourie
Ordhead
792 CARN EALASAID
710 CRAIG VEANN
Roughpark
Heughhead
Boltenstone
Cushnie
Leochel-Cushnie
Craigievar Castle NTS
Garchory
Milltown
Cock Bridge
Corgarff
Corgarff Castle
574 BROOM HILL
619 PRESSENDY
494 BENAQUHALLIE
Corsindae
Comers
Tillybirloch
Migvie
749
476
0 1 2 3 4 miles
0 1 2 3 4 5 kilometres
A941
A96
A98
A95
A97
A920
A944
A939
A980
B9012
B9135
B9040
B9103
B9015
B9104
A990
B9016
B9018
B9022
B9023
B9025
B9139
B9010
B9017
B9014
B9115
B9102
B9009
B9008
B9002
B9117
B9001
B9024
B992
B9119
B993
102
94
1
2
3
4
5
6

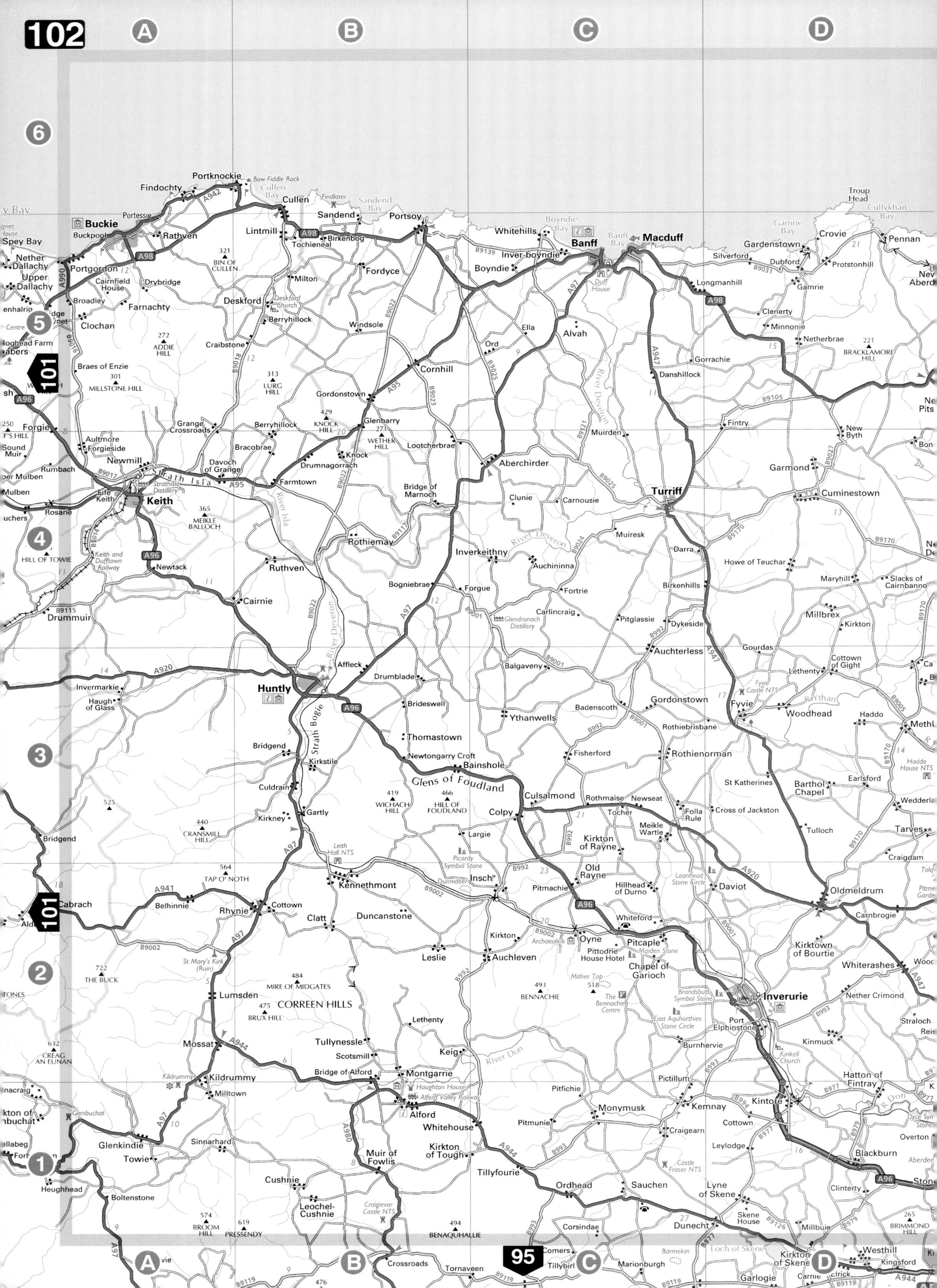

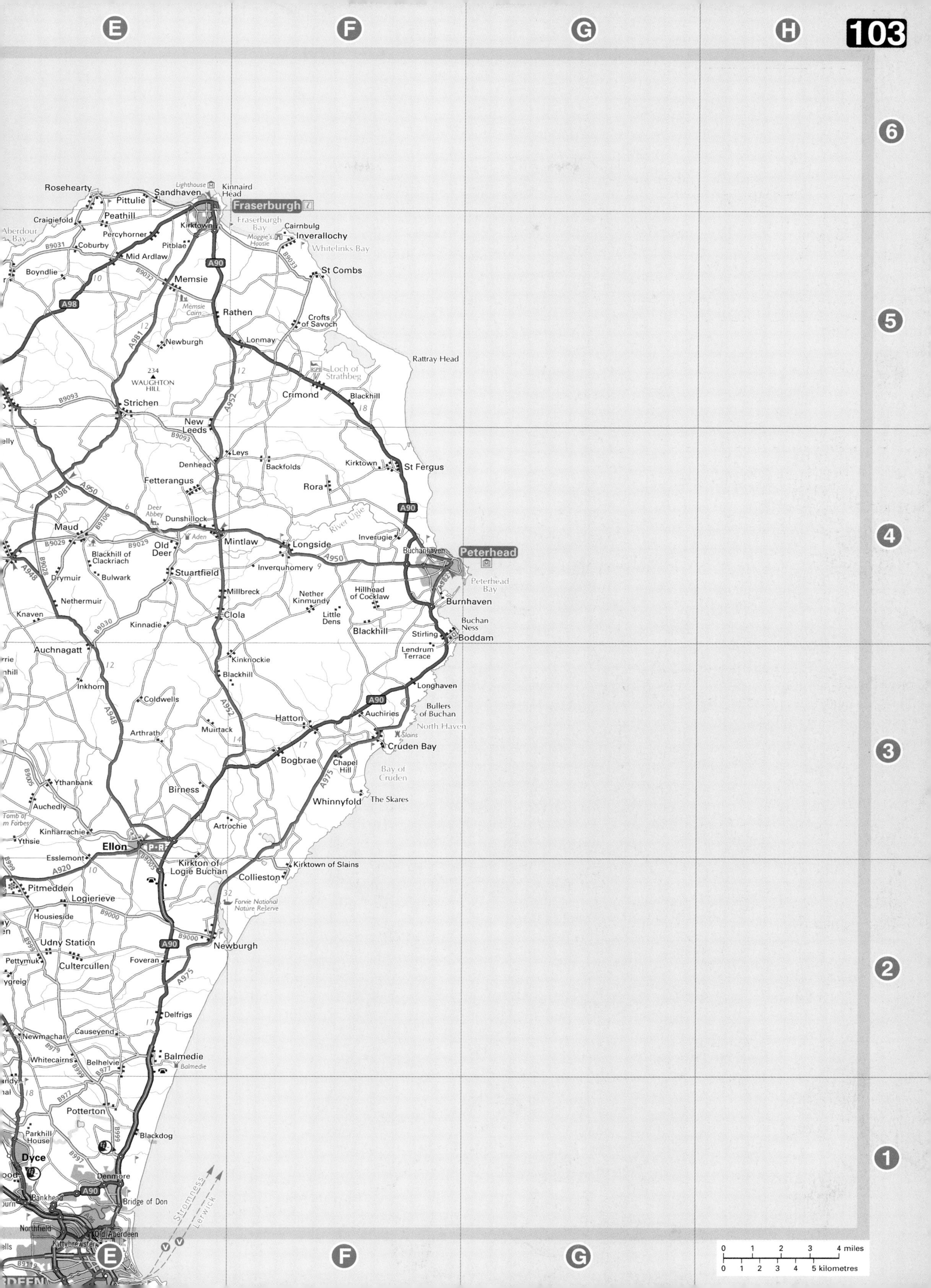
E
F
G
H
6
5
4
3
2
1
Rosehearty
Pittulie
Sandhaven
Lighthouse
Kinnaird Head
Fraserburgh
Craigiefold
Peathill
Aberdour Bay
Percyhorner
Kirktown
Fraserburgh Bay
Cairnbulg
Maggie's Hoosie
Inverallochy
Whitelinks Bay
B9031
Coburby
Pitblae
Mid Ardlaw
Boyndlie
B9032
Memsie
A90
B9033
St Combs
A98
Memsie Cairn
Rathen
Crofts of Savoch
A981
Newburgh
Lonmay
Rattray Head
234
WAUGHTON HILL
Loch of Strathbeg
A952
Crimond
Blackhill
B9093
Strichen
New Leeds
B9093
Leys
Denhead
Backfolds
Kirktown
St Fergus
Fetterangus
Rora
A981
A950
Deer Abbey
Dunshillock
River Ugie
Maud
B9106
Aden
Mintlaw
Inverugie
B9029
Old Deer
Longside
Buchanhaven
Peterhead
Blackhill of Clackriach
A950
B9028
Stuartfield
Inverquhomery
A948
Drymuir
Bulwark
Peterhead Bay
Millbreck
Hillhead of Cocklaw
Nether Kinmundy
Burnhaven
Nethermuir
Knaven
Clola
Little Dens
Buchan Ness
B9030
Kinnadie
Blackhill
Stirling
Boddam
Auchnagatt
Lendrum Terrace
Kinknockie
Blackhill
Longhaven
Inkhorn
A948
Coldwells
A90
A952
Bullers of Buchan
Auchiries
Hatton
North Haven
Arthrath
Muirtack
Slains
Cruden Bay
Bogbrae
Chapel Hill
Bay of Cruden
B9005
Ythanbank
A975
Birness
Whinnyfold
The Skares
Auchedly
Tomb of Forbes
Artrochie
Kinharrachie
Ythsie
Ellon
P+R
Esslemont
B9005
B999
A920
Kirkton of Logie Buchan
Kirktown of Slains
Collieston
Pitmedden
Logierieve
Forvie National Nature Reserve
Housieside
B9000
B9000
Udny Station
A90
Newburgh
B999
Pettymuk
Foveran
Cultercullen
A975
Delfrigs
Causeyend
Newmachar
B979
Whitecairns
Belhelvie
Balmedie
B999
B977
Balmedie
B977
Potterton
B999
Parkhill House
Blackdog
Dyce
B997
Denmore
A90
Bankhead
Stromness
Bridge of Don
Lerwick
Northfield
Old Aberdeen
Kittybrewster
B9119
F
G
0 1 2 3 4 miles
0 1 2 3 4 5 kilometres

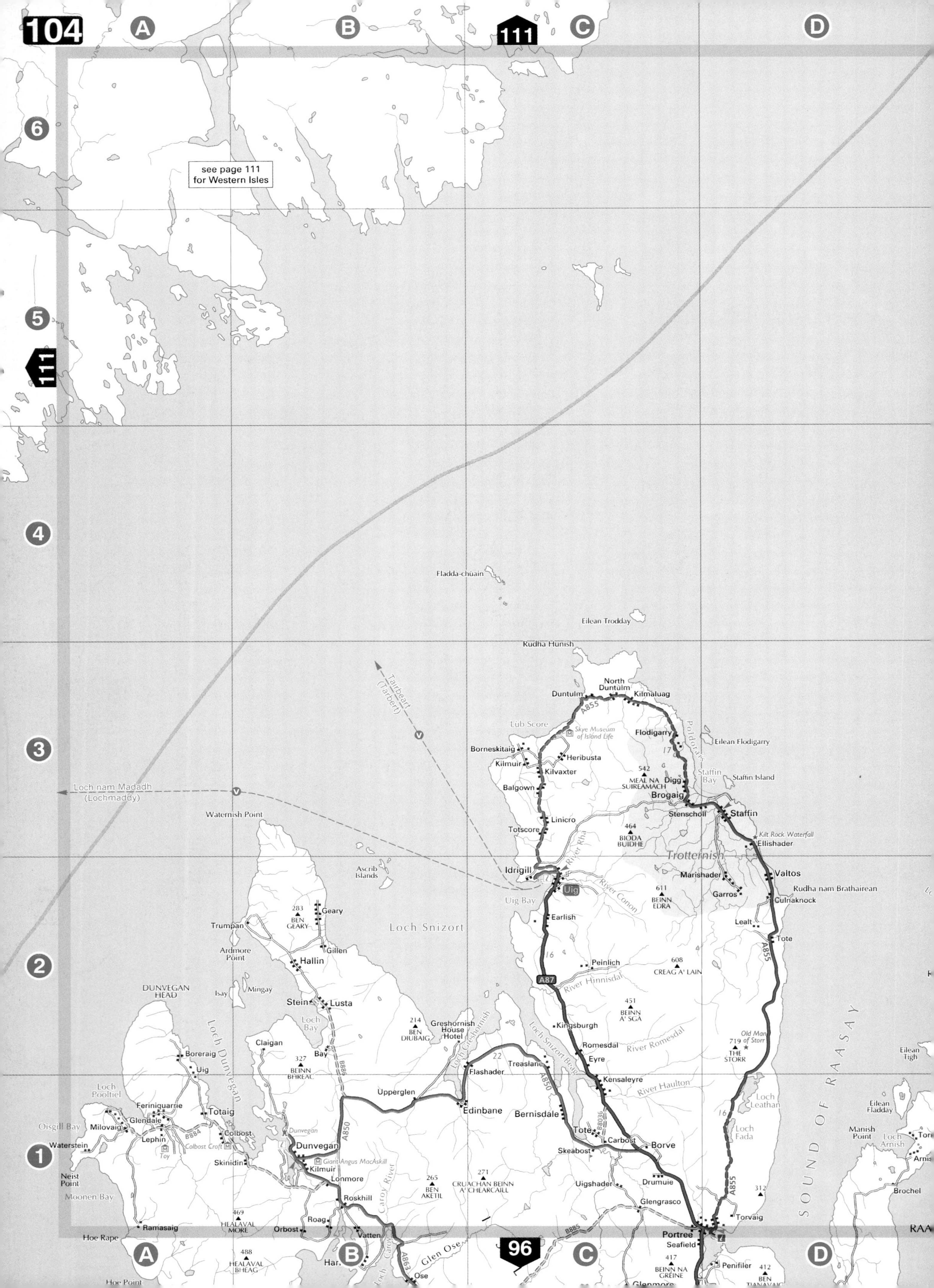

A B **111** C D

6

see page 111
for Western Isles

5

111

4

3

2

1

see page 111
for Western Isles

Hoe Point

96

A B C D

RAA

Tairbeart (Tarbert)

Loch nam Madadh (Lochmaddy)

Waternish Point

Rudha Hunish

Eilean Trodday

Fladda-chùain

North Duntulm
Duntulm
Kilmaluag
Skye Museum of Island Life
Lub Score
Flodigarry
Eilean Flodigarry
Borneskitaig
Heribusta
Kilmuir
Kilvaxter
542
Digg
MEAL NA SUIRLAMACH
Staffin Bay
Staffin Island
Balgown
Brogaig
Stenscholl
Staffin
Linicro
464
BIODA BUIDHE
Totscore
Kilt Rock Waterfall
Ellishader
Idrigill
Trotternish
Valtos
Uig Bay
River Rha
Marishader
611
Garros
Rudha nam Brathairean
Uig
River Conon
Culnaknock
BEINN EDRA
Earlish
Lealt
Tote
A855
16
Peinlich
608
CREAG A' LAIN
A87
River Hinnisdal
451
BEINN A' SGA
DUNVEGAN HEAD
283
BEN GEARY
Geary
Trumpan
Gillen
Ardmore Point
Hallin
Loch Snizort
Isay
Mingay
Stein
Lusta
Loch Bay
214
BEN DIUBAIG
Greshornish House Hotel
Kingsburgh
Romesdal
River Romesdal
Old Man of Storr
719
THE STORR
Claigan
Bay
327
BEINN BHREAC
Loch Greshornish
Eyre
Flashader
22
Treaslane
Kensaleyre
River Haulton
Loch Cleathan
Eilean Fladday
Upperglen
A850
Edinbane
Bernisdale
B8036
Tote
Eilean Tigh
Borreraig
Uig
Loch Pooltiel
Feriniquarrie
Glendale
Skeabost
Carbost
Borve
Loch Fada
Manish Point
Loch Arnish
Tor
Oisgill Bay
Milovaig
Lephin
B884
Colbost
Dunvegan
Giant Angus MacAskill
Uigshader
Drumuie
Brochel
Waterstein
Skinidin
Kilmuir
Lonmore
265
BEN AKETIL
271
CRUACHAN BEINN A' CHEARCAILL
Glengrasco
A855
312
SOUND OF RAASAY
Neist Point
Toy
Colbost Croft
Roskhill
Roag
Portree
Torvaig
Arnis
Moonen Bay
Ramasaig
469
HEALAVAL MORE
Orbost
Vatten
Seafield
Penifiler
Hoe Rape
488
HEALAVAL BHEAG
Har.
A863
Glen Ose
Ose
417
BEINN NA GREINE
412
BEN TIANAVAIG
Glenmore
B885
Dunvegan
Caroy River
River Snizort Beag
A850
Loch Snizort
Loch Dunvegan
A87
Portree
Ascrib Islands

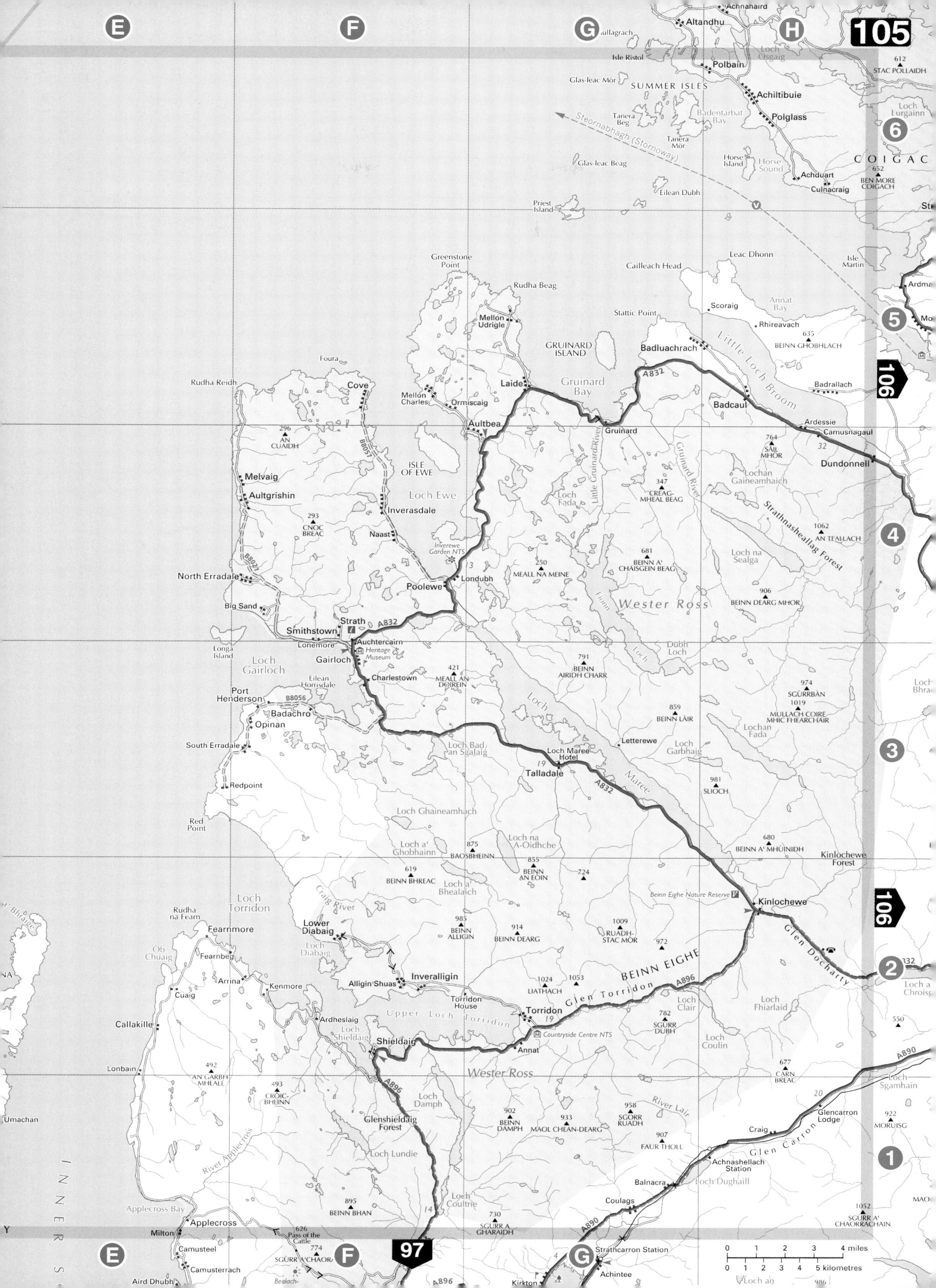

105
E
F
G
H
Achnahaird
Altandhu
Isle Ristol
Polbain
Loch Osgaig
612
STAC POLLAIDH
Glas-leac Mòr
SUMMER ISLES
Achiltibuie
Loch Lurgainn
Tanera Beg
Badentarbat Bay
Polglass
Steornabhagh (Stornoway)
Tanera Mòr
6
Horse Island
Horse Sound
Glas-leac Beag
COIGAC
652
BEN MORE COIGACH
Achduart
Culnacraig
Eilean Dubh
Priest Island
Greenstone Point
Cailleach Head
Leac Dhonn
Isle Martin
Rudha Beag
Scoraig
Annat Bay
Mellon Udrigle
Stattic Point
Rhireavach
5
635
BEINN GHOBHLACH
GRUINARD ISLAND
Badluachrach
Little Loch Broom
Foura
106
Rudha Reidh
Cove
Mellon Charles
Ormiscaig
Laide
Gruinard Bay
A832
Badcaul
Badrallach
Aultbea
Gruinard
Ardessie
Camusnagaul
296
AN CUAIDH
B8057
ISLE OF EWE
764
SAIL MHOR
32
Dundonnell
Melvaig
Little Gruinard River
Gruinard River
Lochan Gaineamhaich
Aultgrishin
Loch Ewe
Loch Fada
347
CREAG-MHEAL BEAG
Inverasdale
293
CNOC BREAC
Strathnasheallag Forest
1062
AN TEALLACH
4
Naast
Inverewe Garden NTS
B8021
13
250
MEALL NA MEINE
681
BEINN A' CHAISGEIN BEAG
Loch na Sealga
North Erradale
Londubh
Poolewe
Fionn
Wester Ross
906
BEINN DEARG MHOR
Big Sand
Strath
A832
Smithstown
Lonemore
Auchtercairn
Heritage Museum
Longa Island
Loch Gairloch
Gairloch
Dubh Loch
Loch
791
BEINN AIRIDH CHARR
421
MEALL AN DOIREIN
Charlestown
Eilean Horrisdale
974
SGÙRRBÀN
1019
MULLACH COIRE MHIC FHEARCHAIR
Port Henderson
B8056
Badachro
Opinan
Loch
859
BEINN LÀIR
Lochan Fada
South Erradale
Loch Bad an Sgalaig
Letterewe
Loch Garbhaig
3
Loch Maree Hotel
19
Talladale
A832
Maree
981
SLIOCH
Redpoint
Red Point
Loch Ghaineamhach
Loch na A-Oidhche
680
BEINN A' MHUINIDH
Loch a' Ghobhainn
875
BAOSBHEINN
855
BEINN AN EOIN
Kinlochewe Forest
619
BEINN BHREAC
Loch a' Bhealaich
724
Beinn Eighe Nature Reserve
Kinlochewe
Rudha na Fearn
Loch Torridon
Craig River
Lower Diabaig
985
BEINN ALLIGIN
914
BEINN DEARG
1009
RUADH-STAC MÒR
Glen Docharty
Fearnmore
972
Loch Diabaig
Òb Chuaig
Fearnbeg
BEINN EIGHE
2
Arrina
Inveralligin
1024
LIATHACH
1053
A896
Loch a Chroisg
Kenmore
Alligin Shuas
Glen Torridon
Cuaig
Torridon House
Loch Clair
Loch Fhiarlaid
Upper Loch Torridon
Torridon
Callakille
Ardheslaig
Loch Shieldaig
19
782
SGURR DUBH
550
Shieldaig
Countryside Centre NTS
Loch Coulin
Annat
A890
492
AN GARBH-MHEALL
677
CARN BREAC
Lonbain
Wester Ross
Loch Sgamhain
493
CROIC-BHEINN
A896
Loch Damph
20
Glencarron Lodge
River Lair
Umachan
Glenshieldaig Forest
902
BEINN DAMPH
933
MAOL CHEAN-DEARG
958
SGORR RUADH
922
MORUISG
Craig
Glen Carron
907
FAUR THOLL
River Applecross
Loch Lundie
Achnashellach Station
1
INNER
Balnacra
Loch Dughaill
Coulags
Loch Coultrie
895
BEINN BHAN
1052
SGURR A' CHAORACHAIN
Applecross Bay
14
730
SGURR A' GHARAIDH
Applecross
Milton
626
Pass of the Cattle
A890
97
E
F
G
Camusteel
774
SGÙRR A' CHAORA
Strathcarron Station
Camusterrach
0 1 2 3 4 miles
0 1 2 3 4 5 kilometres
Aird Dhubh
A896
Kirkton
Achintee
Loch an
986

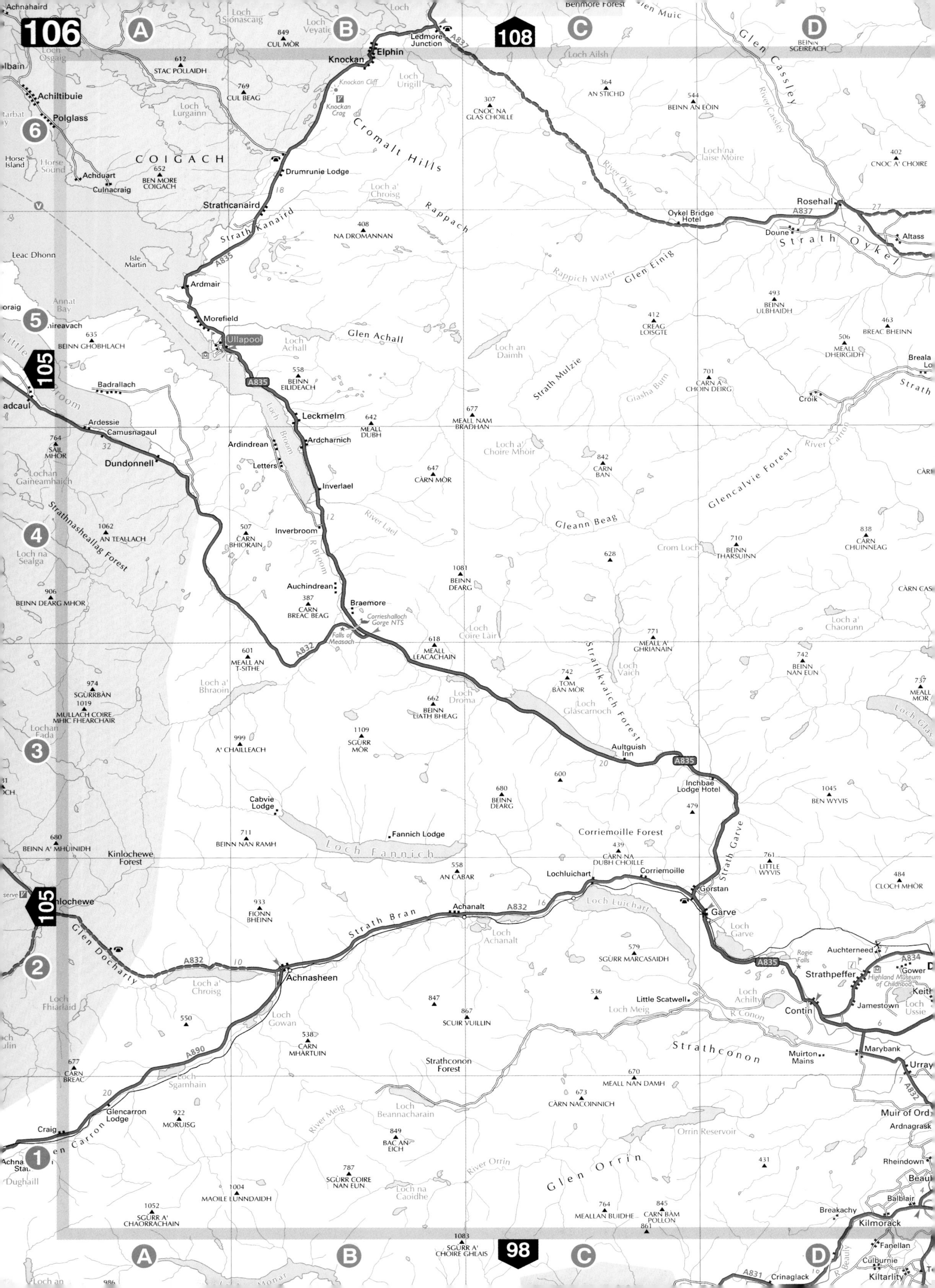
106
A
B
C
D
108
98
105
1
2
3
4
5
6
Achnahaird
Loch Sionascaig
849 CUL MÒR
Loch Veyatie
Loch
Ledmore Junction
A837
Benmore Forest
Glen Muic
BEINN SGEIREACH
Glen Cassley
Knockan
Elphin
Loch Osgaig
612 STAC POLLAIDH
Loch Ailsh
Achiltibuie
769 CUL BEAG
Knockan Cliff
Knockan Crag
Loch Urigill
307 CNOC NA GLAS CHOILLE
364 AN STICHD
544 BEINN AN EÒIN
River Cassley
Polglass
Loch Lurgainn
Cromalt Hills
Horse Island
Horse Sound
COIGACH
652 BEN MORE COIGACH
Achduart
Culnacraig
Drumrunie Lodge
Loch a' Choisg
River Oykel
Loch na Claise Moire
402 CNOC A' CHOIRE
Strathcanaird
Strath Kanaird
Rappach
408 NA DROMANNAN
Oykel Bridge Hotel
Rosehall
A837
Doune
Strath Oykel
Altass
Leac Dhonn
Isle Martin
A835
Ardmair
Rappich Water
Glen Einig
Annat Bay
Morefield
493 BEINN ULBHAIDH
412 CREAG LOISGTE
463 BREAC BHEINN
Ullapool
Little Loch Broom
635 BEINN GHOBHLACH
Loch Achall
Glen Achall
Loch an Daimh
506 MEALL DHEIRGIDH
Strath Mulzie
Glasha Burn
701 CARN A' CHOIN DEIRG
Croik
Badrallach
558 BEINN EILIDEACH
Loch Broom
Leckmelm
642 MEALL DUBH
677 MEALL NAM BRADHAN
Ardessie
Camusnagaul
764 SAIL MHÓR
Ardindrean
Ardcharnich
Loch a' Choire Mhòir
River Carron
Dundonnell
Letters
647 CÀRN MÒR
842 CARN BAN
Glencalvie Forest
Lochan Gaineamhaich
Inverlael
River Lael
Gleann Beag
Strathnasheallag Forest
1062 AN TEALLACH
507 CARN BHIORAIN
Inverbroom
Crom Loch
710 BEINN THARSUINN
838 CARN CHUINNEAG
Loch na Sealga
R Broom
628
1081 BEINN DEARG
906 BEINN DEARG MHOR
Auchindrean
387 CARN BREAC BEAG
Braemore
Corrieshalloch Gorge NTS
Falls of Measach
Loch Coire Làir
Loch a' Chaorunn
A832
601 MEALL AN T-SITHE
618 MEALL LEACACHAIN
771 MEALL A' GHRIANAIN
Strathvaich Forest
Loch Vaich
742 BEINN NAN EUN
974 SGÙRRBÀN
1019 MULLACH COIRE MHIC FHEARCHAIR
Loch a' Bhraoin
742 TOM BÀN MÒR
Loch Droma
662 BEINN LIATH BHEAG
Loch Glascarnoch
737 MEALL MÒR
Lochan Fada
999 A' CHAILLEACH
1109 SGÙRR MÒR
Aultguish Inn
A835
Inchbae Lodge Hotel
600
1045 BEN WYVIS
Cabvie Lodge
680 BEINN DEARG
479
711 BEINN NAN RAMH
Fannich Lodge
Loch Fannich
Corriemoille Forest
680 BEINN A' MHÙINIDH
Kinlochewe Forest
439 CÀRN NA DUBH CHOILLE
761 LITTLE WYVIS
558 AN CABAR
Lochluichart
Corriemoille
Strath Garve
484 CLOCH MHÒR
Gorstan
Kinlochewe
933 FIONN BHEINN
Achanalt
A832
Loch Luichart
Garve
Strath Bran
Loch Achanalt
Loch Garve
Glen Docherty
579 SGÙRR MARCASAIDH
Rogie Falls
Auchterneed
A834
A832
Achnasheen
Loch a' Chroisg
A835
Strathpeffer
Highland Museum of Childhood
Gower
Loch Fhiarlaid
847
536
Little Scatwell
Loch Achilty
Keith
Loch Gowan
867 SCUIR VUILLIN
Loch Meig
R Conon
Contin
Jamestown
Loch Ussie
550
A890
538 CARN MHARTUIN
Strathconon
Marybank
677 CARN BREAC
Strathconon Forest
Muirton Mains
Urray
Loch Sgamhain
670 MEALL NAN DAMH
A832
Glencarron Lodge
922 MORUISG
673 CÀRN NACOINNICH
Muir of Ord
Loch Beannacharain
River Meig
Orrin Reservoir
Ardnagrask
Craig
Glen Carron
849 BAC AN EICH
River Orrin
Glen Orrin
431
Rheindown
Dughaill
787 SGÙRR COIRE NAN EUN
1004 MAOILE LUNNDAIDH
Loch na Caoidhe
Beauly
Balblair
1052 SGÙRR A' CHAORRACHAIN
764 MEALLAN BUIDHE
845 CARN BÀN POLLON
861
Breakachy
Kilmorack
1083 SGÙRR A' CHOIRE GHLAIS
Fanellan
Culburnie
R Beauly
A831
Crinaglack
Kiltarlity
986

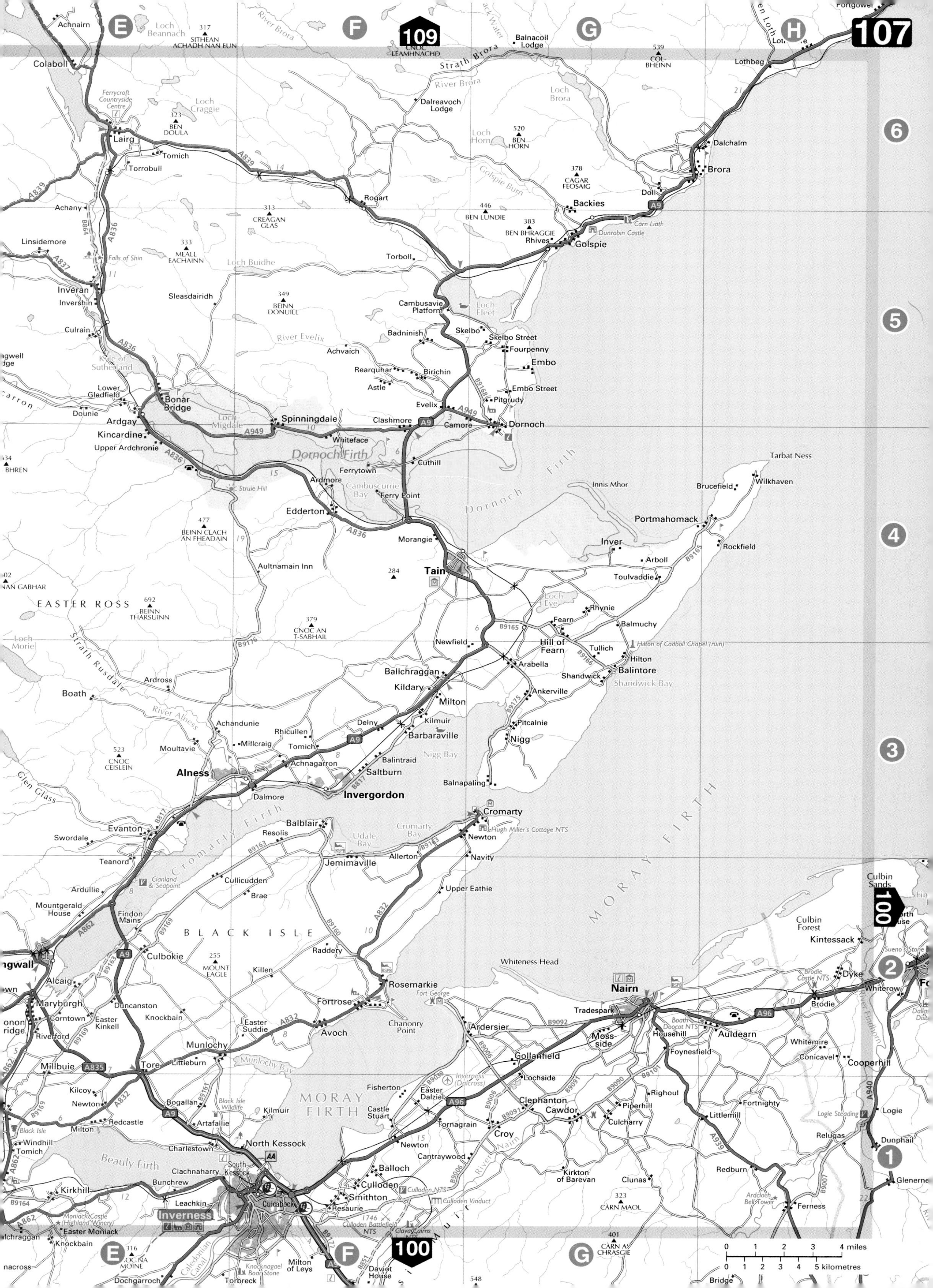

107
109
100
E
F
G
H
1
2
3
4
5
6
Achnairn
Loch Beannach
317 SITHEAN ACHADH NAN EUN
River Brora
CNOC LEAMHNACHD
Balnacoil Lodge
Strath Brora
539 COL-BHEINN
Lothbeg
Portgower
Colaboll
Ferrycroft Countryside Centre
Loch Craggie
323 BEN DOULA
River Brora
Dalreavoch Lodge
Loch Brora
Lairg
Tomich
Torrobull
A839
Loch Horn
520 BEN HORN
Dalchalm
Brora
Golspie Burn
378 CAGAR FEOSAIG
Rogart
Backies
Doll
A9
Achany
313 CREAGAN GLAS
446 BEN LUNDIE
383 BEN BHRAGGIE
Carn Liath
Dunrobin Castle
Rhives
Golspie
B864
A836
Linsidemore
333 MEALL EACHAINN
Falls of Shin
A837
Loch Buidhe
Torboll
Inveran
Invershin
Sleasdairidh
349 BEINN DONUILL
Cambusavie Platform
Loch Fleet
Culrain
River Evelix
Badninish
Skelbo
Skelbo Street
Fourpenny
Achvaich
Embo
Kyle of Sutherland
Rearquhar
Birichin
Astle
Embo Street
Lower Gledfield
B9168
Pitgrudy
Bonar Bridge
Evelix
A949
Dounie
Loch Migdale
Spinningdale
Clashmore
A9
Camore
Dornoch
Ardgay
A949
Kincardine
Whiteface
Upper Ardchronie
Dornoch Firth
A836
Cuthill
Tarbat Ness
Ferrytown
Struie Hill
Ardmore
Cambuscurrie Bay
Ferry Point
Innis Mhor
Brucefield
Wilkhaven
Edderton
Dornoch Firth
477 BEINN CLACH AN FHEADAIN
A836
Portmahomack
Morangie
Inver
Rockfield
Aultnamain Inn
284
Tain
Arboll
B9165
Toulvaddie
EASTER ROSS
692 BEINN THARSUINN
Loch Eye
Rhynie
Loch Morie
379 CNOC AN T-SABHAIL
Fearn
Balmuchy
B9165
Newfield
Hill of Fearn
Hilton of Cadboll Chapel (ruin)
B9176
Tullich
Hilton
Arabella
B9166
Strath Rusdale
Ballchraggan
Shandwick
Balintore
Shandwick Bay
Ardross
Kildary
Boath
Milton
Ankerville
B9175
River Alness
Kilmuir
Achandunie
Delny
Pitcalnie
Rhicullen
Barbaraville
Nigg
Millcraig
A9
Moultavie
Tomich
523 CNOC CEISLEIN
Balintraid
Nigg Bay
Achnagarron
Saltburn
Alness
B817
Balnapaling
Glen Glass
Invergordon
Dalmore
Cromarty
Hugh Miller's Cottage NTS
Cromarty Firth
Evanton
Balblair
Cromarty Bay
Swordale
Resolis
Udale Bay
Newton
B817
B9163
B9163
Teanord
Jemimaville
Allerton
Navity
MORAY FIRTH
Clanland & Seapoint
Cullicudden
Ardullie
Brae
Upper Eathie
Culbin Sands
Mountgerald House
A862
Findon Mains
B9169
A832
Culbin Forest
BLACK ISLE
B9160
Kintessack
Forres House
Sueno's Stone
Culbokie
255 MOUNT EAGLE
Raddery
Dingwall
Killen
Whiteness Head
Brodie Castle NTS
Dyke
Alcaig
B9163
Rosemarkie
Nairn
Whiterow
Maryburgh
Duncanston
Fort George
Brodie
Cornton
Easter Kinkell
Fortrose
Tradespark
A96
Knockbain
Conon Bridge
Riverford
Easter Suddie
A832
Avoch
Chanonry Point
Ardersier
B9092
Boath Doocot NTS
Moss-side
Househill
Auldearn
B9169
Munlochy
B9006
Whitemire
Millbuie
A835
Tore
Littleburn
Munlochy Bay
Gollanfield
Foynesfield
Conicavel
Cooperhill
A862
Lochside
B9101
Kilcoy
Inverness (Dalcross)
B9161
B9039
B9090
Fisherton
Easter Dalziel
Righoul
Newton
A832
MORAY FIRTH
Clephanton
Fortnighty
Bogallan
Black Isle Wildlife
A96
B9006
B9091
Kilmuir
Castle Stuart
Piperhill
Cawdor
Logie
Redcastle
Artafallie
B9091
Littlemill
Logie Steading
Milton
A9
Tornagrain
Culcharry
A940
Black Isle
Windhill
Croy
North Kessock
Newton
A939
Relugas
Tomich
Charlestown
River Nairn
Dunphail
Beauly Firth
Cantraywood
Balloch
Clachnaharry
South Kessock
Kirkton of Barevan
Cluanas
Redburn
Kirkhill
Bunchrew
Culloden
Culloden NTS
Glenerney
Smithton
B9006
Ardclach Bell Tower
B9007
B9164
Leachkin
Culcabock
Culloden Viaduct
323 CARN MAOL
Ferness
Moniack Castle (Highland Winery)
Inverness
Resaurie
A862
Easter Moniack
1746 Culloden Battlefield NTS
Clava Cairns NTS
Alchraggan
Knockbain
B9177
401 CARN A' CHRASGIE
316 LOCH NA MOINE
Milton of Leys
Caledonian Canal
Knocknagael Boar Stone
B851
Daviot House
548
Nacross
Dochgarroch
Torbreck
Bridge
0 1 2 3 4 miles
0 1 2 3 4 5 kilometres

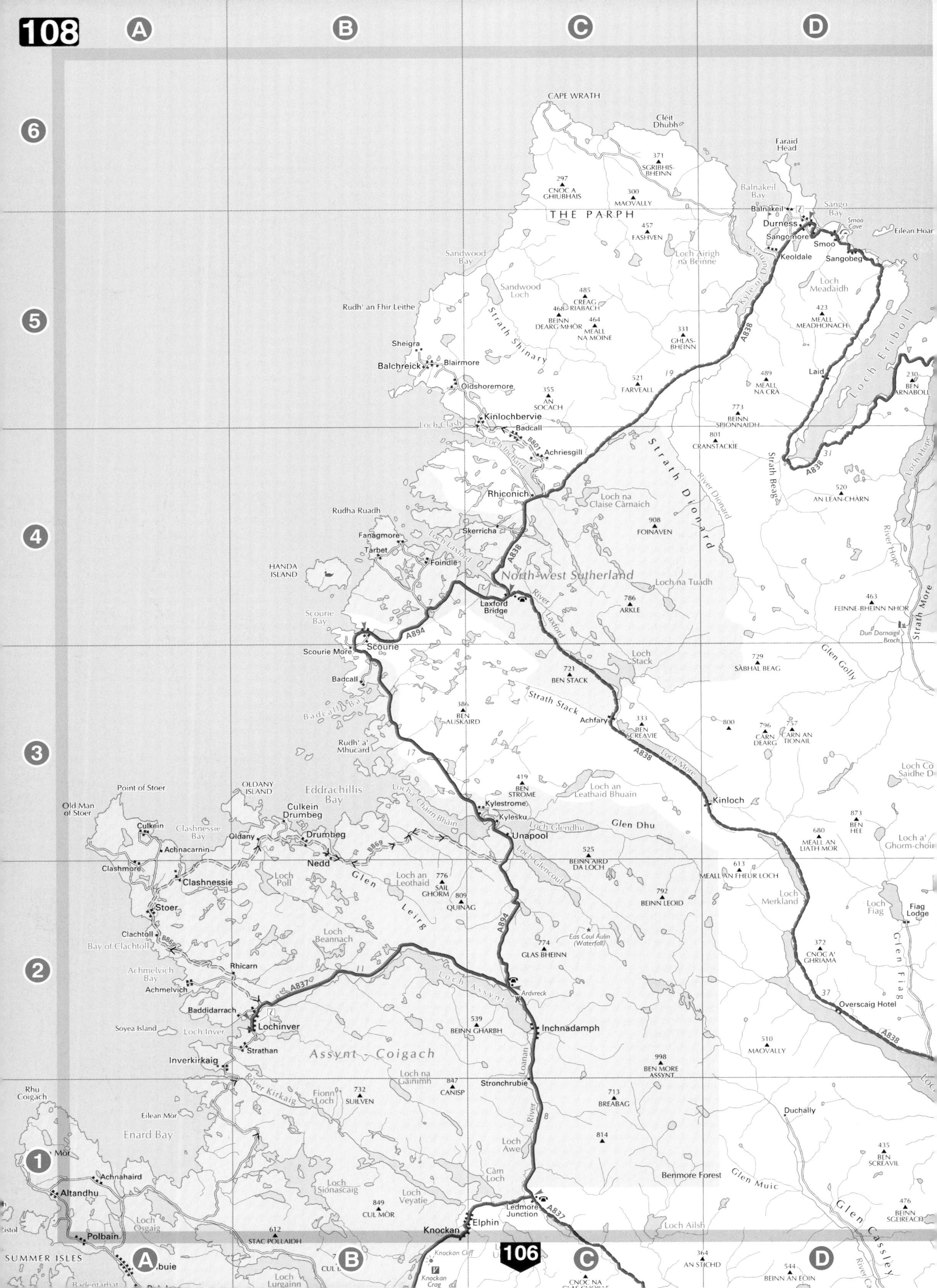
A
B
C
D
6
5
4
3
2
1
CAPE WRATH
Cléit Dhubh
Faraid Head
371 SGRIBHIS-BHEINN
297 CNOC A GHIUBHAIS
300 MAOVALLY
THE PARPH
457 FASHVEN
Balnakeil Bay
Balnakeil
Durness
Sango Bay
Smoo Cave
Eilean Hoan
Sangomore
Smoo
Keoldale
Sangobeg
Kyle of Durness
Loch Airigh na Beinne
Loch Meadaidh
Sandwood Bay
Sandwood Loch
485 CREAG RIABACH
468 BEINN DEARG MHÒR
464 MEALL NA MOINE
423 MEALL MEADHONACH
Rudh' an Fhir Leithe
Strath Shinary
331 GHLAS-BHEINN
A838
Loch Eriboll
Sheigra
Balchreick
Blairmore
Oldshoremore
355 AN SOCACH
521 FARVEALL
19
489 MEALL NA CRA
Laid
230 BEN ARNABOLL
Kinlochbervie
Loch Clash
Badcall
B801
Loch Inchard
Achriesgill
773 BEINN SPIONNAIDH
801 CRANSTACKIE
Strath Dionard
River Dionard
Strath Beag
31
Loch Hope
520 AN LEAN-CHÀRN
Rhiconich
Loch na Claise Càrnaich
Rudha Ruadh
Fanagmore
Skerricha
908 FOINAVEN
Tarbet
Loch Laxford
Foindle
River Hope
HANDA ISLAND
North-west Sutherland
Loch na Tuadh
Laxford Bridge
River Laxford
786 ARKLE
463 FEINNE-BHEINN NHOR
Strath More
Scourie Bay
7
A894
Dun Dornaigil Broch
Scourie
Scourie More
Loch Stack
Glen Golly
729 SÀBHAL BEAG
Badcall
721 BEN STACK
Badcall Bay
386 BEN AUSKAIRD
Strath Stack
Achfary
333 BEN SCREAVIE
800
796 CARN DEARG
757 CARN AN TIONAIL
Rudh' a' Mhucard
17
Loch More
Loch Coire nan Saidhe D
Point of Stoer
OLDANY ISLAND
Eddrachillis Bay
419 BEN STROME
Loch an Leathaid Bhuain
Kinloch
Old Man of Stoer
Culkein Drumbeg
Loch a' Chàirn Bhàin
Kylestrome
Kylesku
873 BEN HEE
Culkein
Clashnessie Bay
Oldany
Drumbeg
Loch Glendhu
Glen Dhu
Unapool
680 MEALL AN LIATH MOR
Loch a' Ghorm-choir
Achnacarnin
B869
525 BEINN AIRD DA LOCH
Clashmore
Nedd
Loch Glencoul
613 MEALL AN FHEUR LOCH
Clashnessie
Loch Poll
Glen Leirg
Loch an Leothaid
776 SAIL GHORM
809 QUINAG
792 BEINN LEOID
Loch Merkland
Stoer
Loch Fiag
Fiag Lodge
Clachtoll
Bay of Clachtoll
Loch Beannach
Eas Coul Aulin (Waterfall)
774 GLAS BHEINN
372 CNOC A' GHRIANA
Glen Fiag
Rhicarn
Achmelvich Bay
11
A837
Loch Assynt
Achmelvich
Ardvreck
37
Overscaig Hotel
Baddidarrach
Lochinver
539 BEINN GHARBH
Inchnadamph
Soyea Island
Loch Inver
Strathan
510 MAOVALLY
Assynt - Coigach
Loanan
998 BEN MORE ASSYNT
Inverkirkaig
Loch na Gainimh
847 CANISP
Stronchrubie
River Kirkaig
Fionn Loch
732 SUILVEN
713 BREABAG
Rhu Coigach
Duchally
Eilean Mòr
River
8
Enard Bay
814
Loch Awe
435 BEN SCREAVIL
Achnahaird
Càm Loch
Benmore Forest
Glen Muic
Altandhu
Loch Sionascaig
Loch Veyatie
Ledmore Junction
Glen Cassley
849 CUL MÒR
Elphin
476 BEINN SGEIREACH
Loch Osgaig
istol
612 STAC POLLAIDH
Loch Ailsh
Polbain
Knockan
SUMMER ISLES
buie
Knockan Cliff
Knockan Crag
364 AN STICHD
544 BEINN AN EOIN
River Cassley
CUL B
Loch Lurgainn
CNOC NA
Badentarbat

106

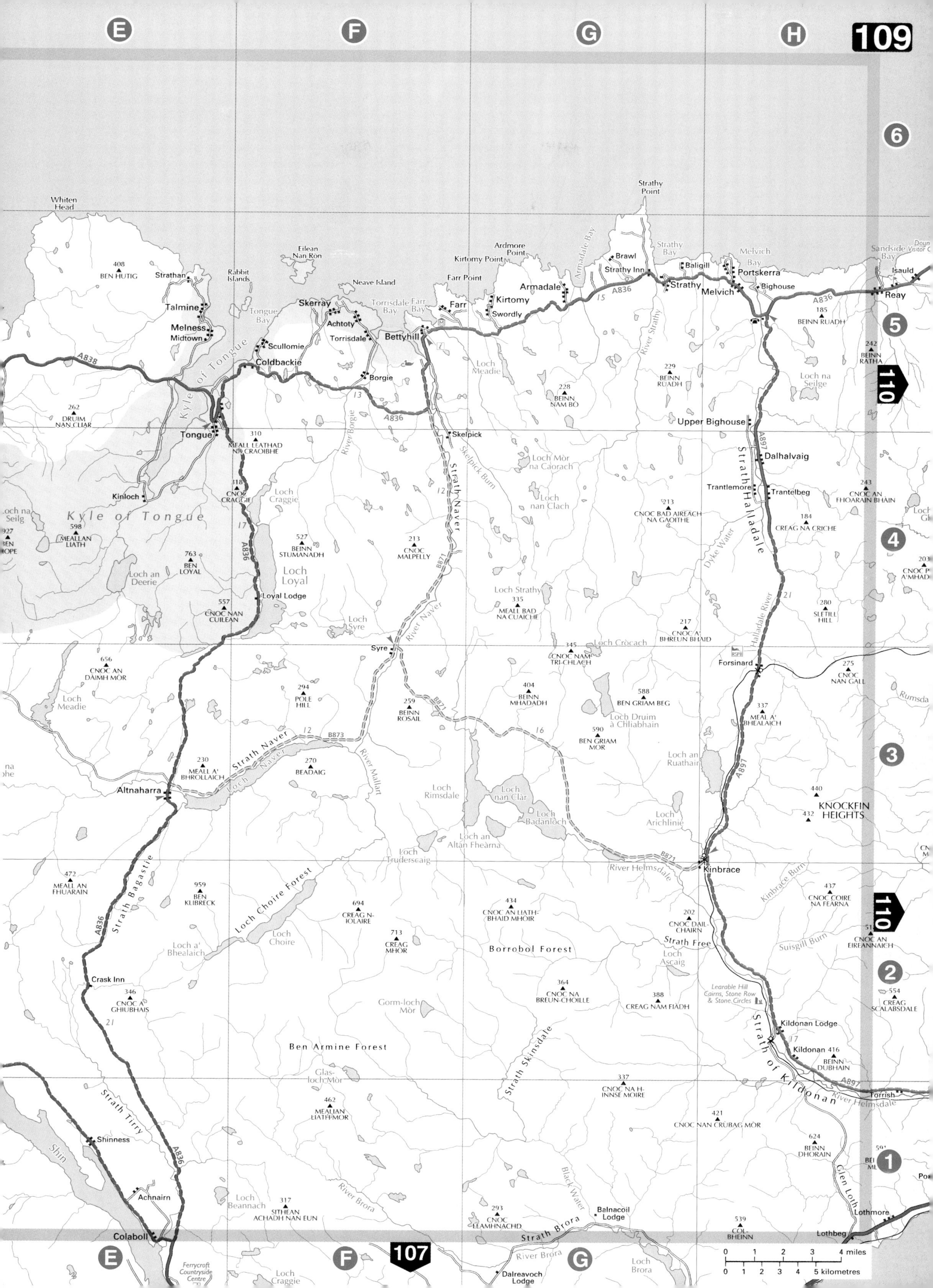

6

Whiten Head

408 ▲ BEN HUTIG
Strathan

Rabbit Islands

Eilean Nan Ron

Neave Island

Strathy Point

Ardmore Point

Strathy Bay

Brawl
Strathy Inn
Baligill
Melvich Bay

Melvich
Portskerra

Sandside Bay
Doun
Sandside Visitor C

Talmine

Skerray

Torrisdale Bay
Farr Bay

Farr Point

Kirtomy Point

A836
15

Bighouse

A836

Isauld

Reay

Melness
Midtown

Scullomie

Achtoty

Torrisdale

Farr

Kirtomy

Armadale

Armadale Bay

185 ▲ BEINN RUADH

203 ▲

Coldbackie

Bettyhill

Swordly

Strathy

242 ▲ BEINN RATHA

5

Borgie

A838

262 ▲ DRUIM NAN CLIAR

Tongue

Kyle of Tongue

Kinloch

Loch na Seilg

927 ▲ BEN HOPE

598 ▲ MEALLAN LIATH

Loch an Deerie

A836

310 ▲ MEALL LEATHAD NA CRAOIBHE

318 ▲ CNOC CRAGGIE

Loch Craggie

13

Loch Meadie

Loch na Caorach

River Strathy

Upper Bighouse

229 ▲ BEINN RUADH

228 ▲ BEINN NAM BO

Loch nan Clach

Dalhalvaig

Strath Halladale

A897

Trantlemore

Trantelbeg

243 ▲ CNOC AN FHOARAIN BHAIN

A836
17

763 ▲ BEN LOYAL

527 ▲ BEINN STUMANADH

Loch Loyal

213 ▲ CNOC MALPELLY

B871

213 ▲ CNOC BAD AIREACH NA GAOITHE

184 ▲ CREAG NA CRICHE

Loch Gl

4

557 ▲ CNOC NAN CUILEAN

Loyal Lodge

Loch Syre

River Naver

335 ▲ MEALL BAD NA CUAICHE

Loch Strathy

21

Halladale River

280 ▲ SLETILL HILL

203 ▲ CNOC A'MHAD

656 ▲ CNOC AN DAIMH MOR

Syre

294 ▲ POLE HILL

259 ▲ BEINN ROSAIL

B871

345 Loch Cròcach

217 ▲ CNOC A' BHREUN BHAID

CNOC NAM TRI-CHLACH

404 ▲ BEINN MHADADH

588 ▲ BEN GRIAM BEG

Forsinard

275 ▲ CNOC NAN GALL

Rumsda

337 ▲ MEAL A' BHEALAICH

3

Loch Meadie

Strath Naver

12 B873

230 ▲ MEALL A' BHROLLAICH

270 ▲ BEADAIG

River Mallart

16

590 ▲ BEN GRIAM MOR

Loch Druim à Chliabhain

Loch an Ruathair

440 ▲

432 ▲

KNOCKFIN HEIGHTS

Altnaharra

Loch Rimsdale

Loch nan Clàr

Loch Badanloch

Loch Arichlinie

A897

Loch Truderscaig

River Helmsdale

B871

Kinbrace

437 ▲ CNOC COIRE NA FEARNA

110

472 ▲ MEALL AN FHUARAIN

959 ▲ BEN KLIBRECK

694 ▲ CREAG N-IOLAIRE

434 ▲ CNOC AN LIATH-BHAID MHOIR

202 ▲ CNOC DAIL-CHAIRN

Strath Free

Loch Ascaig

Kinbrace Burn

Suisgill Burn

519 ▲ CNOC AN EIREANNAICH

2

Strath Bagastie

A836

Loch Choire Forest

346 ▲ CNOC A' GHIUBHAIS

Loch a' Bhealaich

Loch Choire

713 ▲ CREAG MHOR

Borrobol Forest

364 ▲ CNOC NA BREUN-CHOILLE

388 ▲ CREAG NAM FIADH

Learable Hill Cairns, Stone Row & Stone Circles

Kildonan Lodge

554 ▲ CREAG SCALABSDALE

Crask Inn

21

Gorm-loch Mòr

Ben Armine Forest

Strath Skinsdale

Strath of Kildonan

Kildonan
416 ▲ BEINN DUBHAIN

A897

Glas-loch Mòr

337 ▲ CNOC NA H-INNSE MOIRE

Kildonan

Torrish

River Helmsdale

1

Strath Tirry

Shinness

462 ▲ MEALLAN LIATH MOR

421 ▲ CNOC NAN CRUBAG MOR

624 ▲ BEINN DHORAIN

591 ▲ BEI ML

Glen Loth

Shin

Achnairn

Loch Beannach

317 ▲ SITHEAN ACHADH NAN EUN

293 ▲ CNOC LEAMHNACHD

Balnacoil Lodge

539 ▲ COL-BHEINN

Lothmore

Colaboll

River Brora

Strath Brora

A836

Loch Brora

Lothbeg

Ferrycroft Countryside Centre

Loch Craggie

Dalreavoch Lodge

River Brora

0 1 2 3 4 miles
0 1 2 3 4 5 kilometres

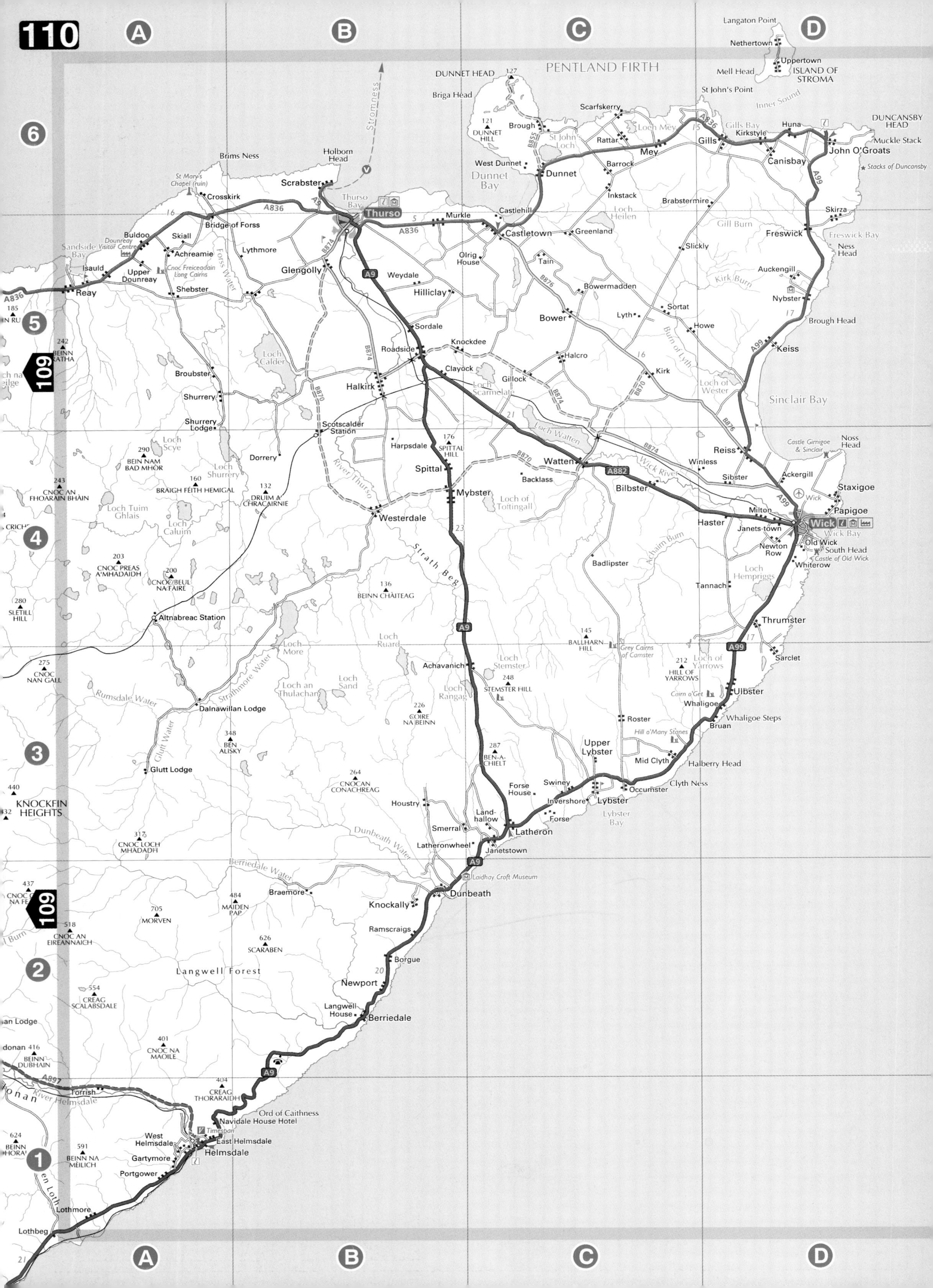
110
A
B
C
D
PENTLAND FIRTH
Langaton Point
Nethertown
Uppertown
ISLAND OF STROMA
Mell Head
St John's Point
Inner Sound
DUNNET HEAD
Briga Head
Stromness
Scarfskerry
DUNNET HILL
Brough
St John's Loch
Rattar
Loch Mey
Mey
Gills
Gills Bay
Huna
Kirkstyle
DUNCANSBY HEAD
Muckle Stack
John O'Groats
Canisbay
Stacks of Duncansby
West Dunnet
Dunnet
Dunnet Bay
Barrock
Inkstack
Brabstermire
Skirza
Loch Heilen
Gill Burn
Freswick
Freswick Bay
Ness Head
Brims Ness
Holborn Head
St Mary's Chapel (ruin)
Scrabster
Thurso Bay
Thurso
Crosskirk
Bridge of Forss
Murkle
Castlehill
Castletown
Greenland
Slickly
Dounreay
Buldoo
Skiall
Achreamie
Lythmore
Sandside Bay
Visitor Centre
Isauld
Upper Dounreay
Cnoc Freiceadain Long Cairns
Forss Water
Glengolly
Olrig House
Tain
Auckengill
Kirk Burn
Weydale
Reay
Shebster
Hilliclay
Bowermadden
Nybster
Sortat
Lyth
Bower
Howe
Brough Head
Sordale
Knockdee
Keiss
Roadside
Loch Calder
Halcro
Broubster
Clayock
Burn of Lyth
Kirk
Halkirk
Gillock
Loch Scarmclate
Loch of Wester
Sinclair Bay
Shurrery
Shurrery Lodge
Scotscalder Station
Loch Watten
Harpsdale
SPITTAL HILL
Loch Scye
BEINN NAM BAD MHÒR
Dorrery
Loch Shurrery
Spittal
Watten
Reiss
Castle Girnigoe & Sinclair
Noss Head
Wick River
Winless
Backlass
Ackergill
Bilbster
Sibster
CNOC AN FHOARAIN BHÀIN
BRAIGH FEITH HEMIGAL
DRUIM A' CHRACAIRNIE
Mybster
Loch of Tottingall
Staxigoe
Loch Tuim Ghlais
Milton
Papigoe
Westerdale
Haster
Wick
Loch Caluim
Janets-town
Wick Bay
Old Wick
Newton Row
South Head
Castle of Old Wick
Strath Beg
Achairn Burn
Whiterow
Badlipster
CNOC PREAS A'MHADAIDH
CNOC BEUL NA FAIRE
BEINN CHÀITEAG
Loch Hempriggs
Tannach
SLETILL HILL
Altnabreac Station
Thrumster
Loch Ruard
Loch More
BALLHARN HILL
Grey Cairns of Camster
Sarclet
CNOC NAN GALL
Achavanich
Loch Stemster
HILL OF YARROWS
Loch of Yarrows
Rumsdale Water
Strathmore Water
Loch an Thulachan
Loch Sand
Loch Rangag
STEMSTER HILL
Cairn o'Get
Ulbster
Whaligoe
Dalnawillan Lodge
COIRE NA BEINN
Whaligoe Steps
Bruan
Roster
Glutt Water
BEN ALISKY
Hill o'Many Stanes
Upper Lybster
BEN-A-CHIELT
Mid Clyth
Halberry Head
Glutt Lodge
CNOCAN CONACHREAG
Swiney
Forse House
Occumster
Clyth Ness
KNOCKFIN HEIGHTS
Houstry
Invershore
Lybster
Lybster Bay
Land-hallow
Forse
Smerral
Latheron
CNOC LOCH MHADADH
Dunbeath Water
Latheronwheel
Janetstown
Berriedale Water
Laidhay Croft Museum
Braemore
Dunbeath
MAIDEN PAP
Knockally
MORVEN
CNOC AN EIREANNAICH
SCARABEN
Ramscraigs
Borgue
Langwell Forest
Newport
CREAG SCALABSDALE
Langwell House
Berriedale
CNOC NA MAOILE
BEINN DUBHAIN
Torrish
River Helmsdale
CREAG THORARAIDH
Ord of Caithness
Navidale House Hotel
Timespan
West Helmsdale
East Helmsdale
Helmsdale
BEINN NA MEILICH
Gartymore
Portgower
Lothmore
Lothbeg
A836
A9
A882
A99
A897
B874
B855
B876
B870
109

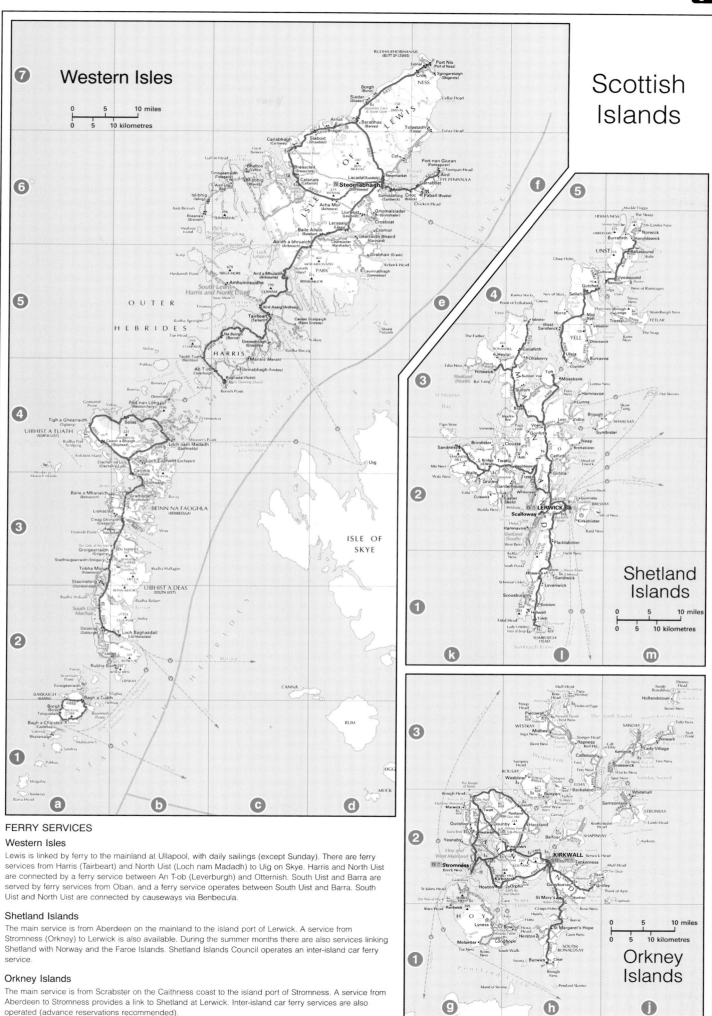

Western Isles

Scottish Islands

Shetland Islands

Orkney Islands

FERRY SERVICES

Western Isles

Lewis is linked by ferry to the mainland at Ullapool, with daily sailings (except Sunday). There are ferry services from Harris (Tairbeart) and North Uist (Loch nam Madadh) to Uig on Skye. Harris and North Uist are connected by a ferry service between An T-ob (Leverburgh) and Otternish. South Uist and Barra are served by ferry services from Oban, and a ferry service operates between South Uist and Barra. South Uist and North Uist are connected by causeways via Benbecula.

Shetland Islands

The main service is from Aberdeen on the mainland to the island port of Lerwick. A service from Stromness (Orkney) to Lerwick is also available. During the summer months there are also services linking Shetland with Norway and the Faroe Islands. Shetland Islands Council operates an inter-island car ferry service.

Orkney Islands

The main service is from Scrabster on the Caithness coast to the island port of Stromness. A service from Aberdeen to Stromness provides a link to Shetland at Lerwick. Inter-island car ferry services are also operated (advance reservations recommended).

A B C

Ireland

B3 Abbeydorney
B3 Abbeyfeale
D3 Abbeyleix
D3 Adamstown
B3 Adare
B2 Adrigole
C4 Ahascragh
E6 Ahoghill
A2 Allihies
A2 Anascaul
E5 Annalong
D2 Annestown
E6 Antrim
B3 Ardagh
C6 Ardara
E4 Ardcath
D5 Ardee
B3 Ardfert
C3 Ardfinnan
E5 Ardglass
A2 Ardgroom
E3 Arklow
D3 Arless
D6 Armagh
E7 Armoy
D2 Arthurstown
D5 Arvagh
E4 Ashbourne
E4 Ashford
B3 Askeaton
D5 Athboy
B3 Athea
C4 Athenry
C4 Athleague
C4 Athlone
D4 Athy
D6 Augher
D6 Aughnacloy
E3 Aughrim
E3 Avoca

D3 Bagenalstown (Muine Bheag)
D5 Bailieborough
E4 Balbriggan
B5 Balla
D3 Ballacolla
C5 Ballaghaderreen
C3 Ballina
B5 Ballina
C5 Ballinafad
D5 Ballinagh
D3 Ballinakill
C5 Ballinalee
D6 Ballinamallard
C5 Ballinamore
B2 Ballinascarty
C4 Ballinasloe
B5 Ballindine
B2 Ballineen
C3 Ballingarry
B3 Ballingarry
B2 Ballingeary (Béal Átha an Ghaorfthaidh)
C2 Ballinhassig
C5 Ballinlough
B5 Ballinrobe
C2 Ballinspittle
C5 Ballintober
C6 Ballintra
C4 Ballivor
D3 Ballon
C4 Ballybaun
D5 Ballybay
C6 Ballybofey
B3 Ballybunion
E3 Ballycanew
E6 Ballycarry
B6 Ballycastle
E7 Ballycastle
E6 Ballyclare
A4 Ballyconneely
C2 Ballycotton
C4 Ballycumber
B1 Ballydehob
B2 Ballydesmond
C2 Ballyduff
B3 Ballyduff
C5 Ballyfarnan
E5 Ballygalley
C4 Ballygar
D6 Ballygawley
E6 Ballygowan
D5 Ballyhaise
D3 Ballyhale
C5 Ballyhaunis
B5 Ballyhean
B3 Ballyheige
D5 Ballyjamesduff
C4 Ballykeeran
C3 Ballylanders
B3 Ballylongford
C3 Ballylooby
D3 Ballylynan
C4 Ballymahon
B2 Ballymakeery
E6 Ballymena
C5 Ballymoe
D7 Ballymoney
C4 Ballymore
D4 Ballymore Eustace
C5 Ballymote
E6 Ballynahinch
E6 Ballynure
C3 Ballyporeen
D3 Ballyragget
D4 Ballyroan
D6 Ballyronan
C5 Ballysadare
C6 Ballyshannon
B4 Ballyvaughan
E6 Ballywalter
E4 Balrothery
B1 Baltimore
D3 Baltinglass
C4 Banagher
E6 Banbridge
B2 Bandon
E6 Bangor
B5 Bangor Erris
C3 Bansha
B2 Banteer
B2 Bantry
B2 Beaufort
C6 Belcoo
E6 Belfast
C2 Belgooly
D6 Bellaghy
C6 Belleek
B6 Belmullet (Béal an Mhuirhead)
D5 Belturbet
D6 Benburb
D3 Bennett's Bridge
D6 Beragh
C4 Birr
C6 Blacklion
E3 Blackwater
C2 Blarney
D4 Blessington
B2 Boherbue
D3 Borris
C4 Borris-in-Ossory
C4 Borrisokane
C3 Borrisoleigh
C5 Boyle
D4 Bracknagh
E4 Bray
D2 Bridgetown
D4 Brittas
C3 Broadford
B3 Broadford
E6 Broughshane
C3 Bruff
C3 Bruree
D3 Bunclody
D7 Buncrana
C6 Bundoran
D2 Bunmahon
B6 Bunnahowen
B5 Bunnyconnellan
C2 Burnfort
D7 Bushmills
D5 Butler's Bridge
B2 Buttevant

C4 Cadamstown
C3 Caherconlish
A2 Caherdaniel
A2 Caherciveen
C3 Cahir
D6 Caledon
D3 Callan
C4 Caltra
A3 Camp
C3 Cappagh White
C3 Cappamore
C2 Cappoquin
D5 Carlanstown
E5 Carlingford
D3 Carlow
D7 Carndonagh
D3 Carnew
E7 Carnlough
C5 Carracastle
C6 Carrick (An Charraig)
E6 Carrickfergus
D5 Carrickmacross
D6 Carrickmore
C5 Carrick-on-Shannon
D3 Carrick-on-Suir
C4 Carrigahorig
C2 Carrigaline
D5 Carrigallen
B2 Carriganimmy
D7 Carrigans
C7 Carrigart (Carraig Airt)
C2 Carrigtohill
D7 Carrowkeel
E6 Carryduff
C3 Cashel
B5 Castlebar
E5 Castlebellingham
D5 Castleblayney
D3 Castlebridge
D3 Castlecomer
D6 Castlederg
D3 Castledermot
B3 Castleisland
B3 Castlemaine
C2 Castlemartyr
C5 Castleplunket
D5 Castlepollard
C5 Castlerea
D7 Castlerock
D5 Castleshane
D4 Castletown
A2 Castletown Bearhaven
C2 Castletownroche
B1 Castletownshend
E5 Castlewellan
B3 Causeway
D5 Cavan
D4 Celbridge
C5 Charlestown
B3 Charleville (Rath Luirc)
D6 Clady
D4 Clane
C4 Clara
B3 Clarecastle
B5 Claremorris
B4 Clarinbridge
C2 Clashmore
D7 Claudy
A4 Clifden
C6 Cliffoney
D3 Clogh
C4 Cloghan
C3 Clogheen
D6 Clogher
D3 Clohamon
B2 Clonakilty
D4 Clonard
D4 Clonaslee
D4 Clonbulloge
B5 Clonbur (An Fhairche)
E4 Clondalkin
D5 Clones
D7 Clonmany
C3 Clonmel
D5 Clonmellon
C3 Clonmore
C4 Clonony
C3 Clonoulty
D3 Clonroche
D5 Clontibret
C5 Cloondara
C5 Cloonlara
E6 Clough
C4 Cloughjordan
C2 Cloyne
D6 Coagh
D6 Coalisland
C2 Cobh
D7 Coleraine
D5 Collinstown
D5 Collon
C5 Collooney
E6 Comber
B5 Cong
C2 Conna
D6 Cookstown
D5 Coole
B3 Cooraclare
D5 Cootehill
C2 Cork
B4 Cornamona
B4 Corofin
B2 Courtmacsherry
E3 Courtown Harbour
E6 Craigavon
C4 Craughwell
C7 Creeslough
C5 Creggs
B3 Croagh
C7 Crolly (Croithlí)
D4 Crookenwood
B1 Crookhaven
B2 Crookstown
B3 Croom
D5 Crossakeel
B2 Cross Barry
C2 Crosshaven
D5 Crossmaglen
B5 Crossmolina
E6 Crumlin
B4 Crusheen
D7 Culdaff
E6 Culleybackey
D3 Curracloe
C4 Curraghboy
C5 Curry
E7 Cushendall

D4 Daingean
D5 Delvin
C6 Derrygonnelly
D5 Derrylin
E7 Dervock
A2 Dingle (An Daingean)
E6 Doagh
E6 Donaghadee
C3 Donaghmore
C6 Donegal
C2 Doneraile
C3 Doon
B3 Doonbeg
C2 Douglas
E6 Downpatrick
C5 Dowra
D6 Draperstown
B2 Drimoleague
B2 Dripsey
E5 Drogheda
C6 Dromahair
B3 Dromcolliher
C5 Dromod
E6 Dromore
D6 Dromore
C6 Dromore West
D5 Drum
C6 Drumcliff
D5 Drumconrath
C5 Drumkeeran
C5 Drumlish
D6 Drumquin
C5 Drumshanbo
C5 Drumsna
B3 Duagh
E4 Dublin
E5 Duleek
D4 Dunboyne
D2 Duncormick
E5 Dundalk
C2 Dunderrow
E5 Dundrum
C7 Dunfanaghy
D6 Dungannon
C2 Dungarvan
D3 Dungarvan
D7 Dungiven
C7 Dungloe (An Clochan Liath)
C2 Dungourney
C6 Dunkineely
E4 Dun Laoghaire
D4 Dunlavin
E5 Dunleer
E7 Dunloy
B2 Dunmanway
C5 Dunmore
D2 Dunmore East
E6 Dunmurry
D4 Dunshaughlin
D3 Durrow
B2 Durrus
C4 Dysart

B6 Easky
D4 Edenderry
D5 Edgeworthstown
D7 Eglinton
C5 Elphin
D6 Emyvale
D4 Enfield
B3 Ennis
D3 Enniscorthy
B6 Enniscrone
B2 Enniskean
D6 Enniskillen
B4 Ennistymon
C4 Eyrecourt
C5 Farnaght
B2 Farranfore
C4 Feakle
C5 Fenagh
C4 Ferbane
C2 Fermoy
D3 Ferns
D2 Fethard
C3 Fethard
D5 Finnea
D6 Fintona
D6 Fivemiletown
D4 Fontstown
B5 Foxford
B3 Foynes
B3 Freemount
C5 Frenchpark
D3 Freshford
C5 Fuerty

C3 Galbally
B4 Galway
C6 Garrison
E4 Garristown
D7 Garvagh
D4 Geashill
E6 Gilford
B1 Glandore
C2 Glanworth
D6 Glaslough
C4 Glassan
C5 Glenamaddy
E7 Glenarm
E6 Glenavy
A2 Glenbeigh
C6 Glencolumbkille (Gleann Cholm Cille)
E4 Glendalough
E3 Glenealy
B2 Glengarriff
D3 Glenmore
C6 Glenties
B3 Glin
B4 Glinsk (Glinsce)
C3 Golden
B1 Goleen
D3 Goresbridge
E3 Gorey
B4 Gort
D6 Gortin
D3 Gowran
D3 Graiguenamanagh
D5 Granard
C6 Grange
E6 Greyabbey
E4 Greystones
D6 Gulladuff

D3 Hacketstown
B4 Headford
C3 Herbertstown
E6 Hillsborough
E5 Hilltown
C3 Hospital
C3 Holycross
E6 Holywood
E4 Howth

A2 Inch
B2 Inchigeelagh
B2 Inishannon
D6 Irvinestown

C3 Johnstown

B2 Kanturk
C5 Keadue
D5 Keady
A5 Keel
C5 Keenagh
E6 Kells
D5 Kells
B2 Kenmare
C6 Kesh
D4 Kilbeggan
D5 Kilberry
B2 Kilbrittain
C6 Kilcar (Cill Charthaigh)
D4 Kilcock
B4 Kilcolgan
C4 Kilconnell
E4 Kilcoole
C4 Kilcormac
D4 Kilcullen
E5 Kilcurry
D4 Kildare
D3 Kildavin
C2 Kildorrery
B4 Kilfenora
B2 Kilgarvan
B3 Kilkee
E5 Kilkeel
C5 Kilkelly
D3 Kilkenny
B4 Kilkieran
B3 Kilkinlea
D2 Kill
B3 Killadysert
B6 Killala
C3 Killaloe
B2 Killarney
C5 Killashee
D4 Killeigh
C3 Killenaule
D5 Killashandra
B3 Killimer
C4 Killimor
E4 Killiney
D2 Killinick
B2 Killorglin
E5 Killough
D4 Killucan
C6 Killybegs
E6 Killyleagh
E4 Kilmacanoge
C7 Kilmacrenan
D2 Kilmacthomas
D3 Kilmaganny
B5 Kilmaine
C3 Kilmallock
D3 Kilmanagh
D2 Kilmeadan
D4 Kilmeage
B3 Kilmeedy
B2 Kilmichael
D2 Kilmore Quay
D5 Kilnaleck
D7 Kilrea
B3 Kilrush
C3 Kilsheelan
D3 Kiltealy
D3 Kiltegan
B5 Kiltimagh
C4 Kiltoom
D5 Kingscourt
C6 Kinlough
D4 Kinnegad
C4 Kinnitty
C2 Kinsale
B4 Kinvarra
E6 Kircubbin
B5 Knock
C4 Knockcroghery
C3 Knocklofty
D3 Knocktopher
B4 Lahinch
E4 Laragh
E6 Larne
A2 Lauragh
C4 Laurencetown
B2 Leap
B5 Leenane
D3 Leighlinbridge
C5 Leitrim
D4 Leixlip
C2 Lemybrien
B5 Letterfrack
D7 Letterkenny
D6 Lifford
D7 Limavady
C3 Limerick
D6 Lisbellaw
E6 Lisburn
B4 Liscanor
B3 Liscarroll
B4 Lisdoonvarna
C2 Lismore
D6 Lisnaskea
D5 Lisryan
B3 Listowel
B3 Loghill
D7 Londonderry
C5 Longford
E6 Loughbrickland
D6 Loughgall
C5 Loughglinn
C4 Loughrea
B5 Louisburgh
D4 Lucan
E6 Lurgan
E4 Lusk

B2 Macroom
E5 Maghera
D6 Maghera
D6 Magherafelt
D6 Maguiresbridge
E4 Malahide
D7 Malin
C6 Malin More
C2 Mallow
C6 Manorhamilton
D6 Markethill
D4 Maynooth
E6 Mazetown
D6 Middletown
C2 Midleton
D7 Milford
B2 Millstreet
B2 Milltown
B3 Milltown Malbay
C3 Mitchelstown
C4 Moate
C5 Mohill

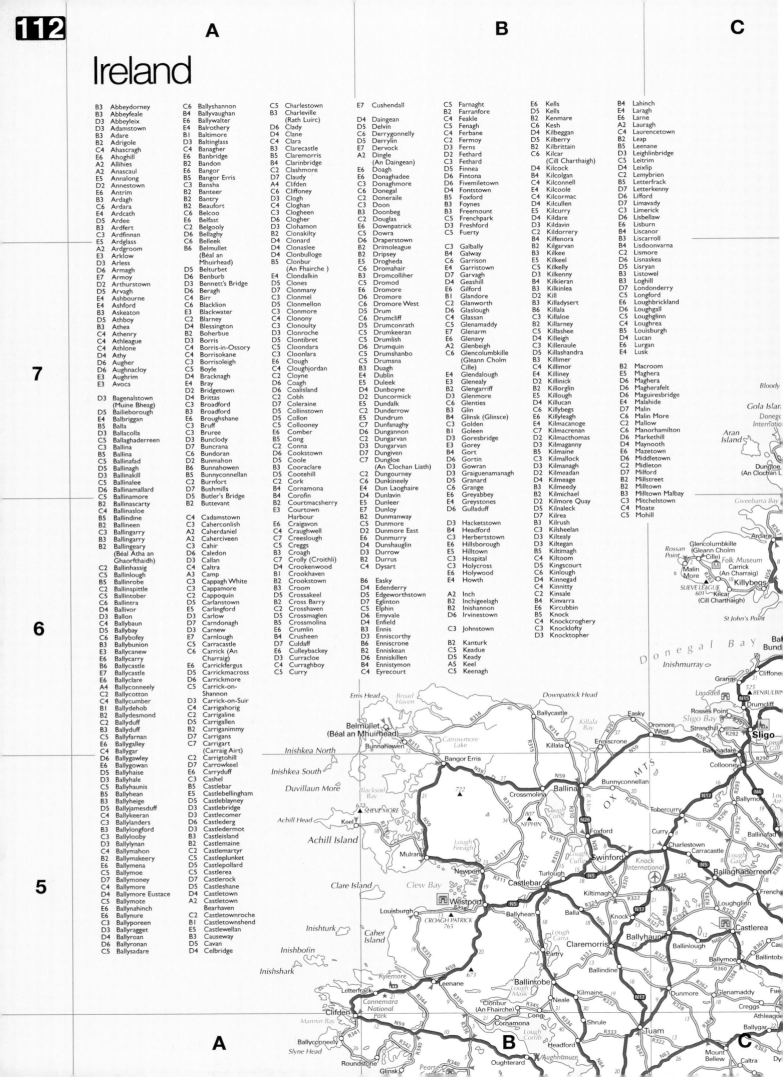

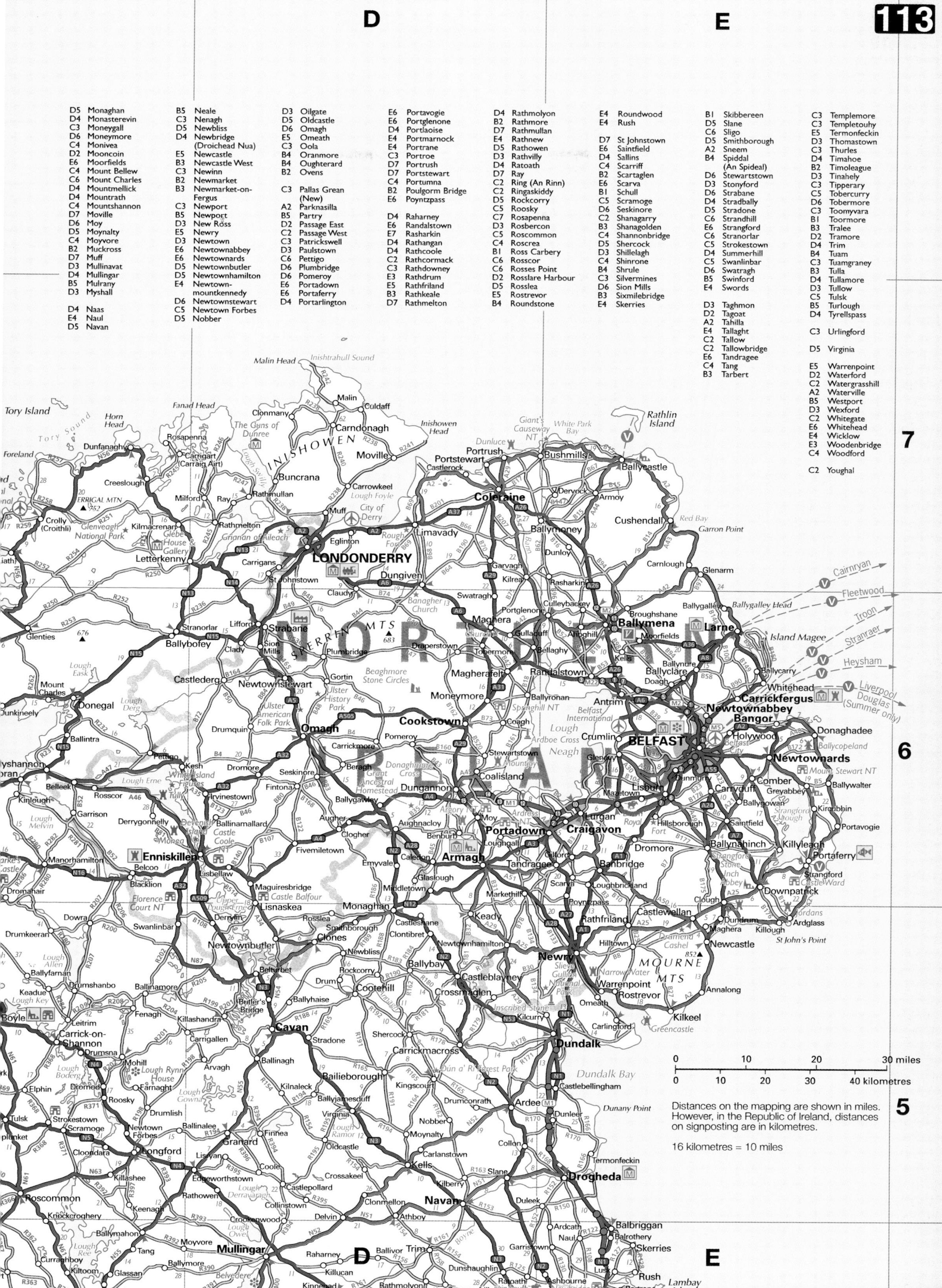

D5 Monaghan
D4 Monasterevin
C3 Moneygall
D6 Moneymore
C4 Monivea
D2 Mooncoin
E6 Moorfields
C4 Mount Bellew
C6 Mount Charles
D4 Mountmellick
C4 Mountrath
C4 Mountshannon
D7 Moville
D6 Moy
D5 Moynalty
C4 Moyvore
B2 Muckross
D7 Muff
D3 Mullinavat
D4 Mullingar
B5 Mulrany
D3 Myshall
D4 Naas
E4 Naul
D5 Navan

B5 Neale
C3 Nenagh
D5 Newbliss
D4 Newbridge (Droichead Nua)
E5 Newcastle
B3 Newcastle West
C3 Newinn
B2 Newmarket
B3 Newmarket-on-Fergus
C3 Newport
B5 Newport
D3 New Ross
E5 Newry
D3 Newtown
E6 Newtownabbey
E6 Newtownards
D5 Newtownbutler
D5 Newtownhamilton
E4 Newtown-mountkennedy
D6 Newtownstewart
C5 Newtown Forbes
D5 Nobber

D3 Oilgate
D5 Oldcastle
D6 Omagh
C3 Omeath
C3 Oola
B4 Oranmore
B4 Oughterard
B4 Ovens
C3 Pallas Green (New)
A2 Parknasilla
B5 Partry
D2 Passage East
C2 Passage West
C3 Patrickswell
D3 Paulstown
C6 Pettigo
D6 Plumbridge
D6 Pomeroy
E6 Portadown
D4 Portaferry
D4 Portarlington

E6 Portavogie
E6 Portglenone
D4 Portlaoise
E4 Portmarnock
E4 Portrane
C3 Portroe
D7 Portrush
D7 Portstewart
C4 Portumna
B2 Poulgorm Bridge
E6 Poyntzpass
D4 Raharney
E6 Randalstown
E7 Rasharkin
D4 Rathangan
D4 Rathcoole
C2 Rathcormack
C3 Rathdowney
E3 Rathdrum
E6 Rathfriland
B3 Rathkeale
D4 Rathmelton

D4 Rathmolyon
B2 Rathmore
D7 Rathmullan
E4 Rathnew
D5 Rathowen
D3 Rathvilly
D4 Ratoath
D7 Ray
C2 Ring (An Rinn)
C2 Ringaskiddy
D5 Rockcorry
C5 Roosky
C7 Rosapenna
D3 Rosbercon
C5 Roscommon
D5 Roscrea
B1 Ross Carbery
C6 Rosscor
C6 Rosses Point
D2 Rosslare Harbour
D5 Rosslea
E5 Rostrevor
B4 Roundstone

E4 Roundwood
E4 Rush
D7 St Johnstown
E6 Saintfield
C4 Sallins
C4 Scarriff
B2 Scartaglen
E6 Scarva
B1 Schull
C5 Scramoge
D6 Seskinore
C2 Shanagarry
B3 Shanagolden
C4 Shannonbridge
D5 Shercock
D3 Shillelagh
C4 Shinrone
B4 Shrule
C3 Silvermines
D6 Sion Mills
B3 Sixmilebridge
E4 Skerries

B1 Skibbereen
D5 Slane
C6 Sligo
D5 Smithborough
A2 Sneem
B4 Spiddal (An Spideal)
D6 Stewartstown
D3 Stonyford
D6 Strabane
D4 Stradbally
D5 Stradone
C6 Strandhill
E6 Strangford
C6 Stranorlar
C5 Strokestown
D4 Summerhill
C5 Swanlinbar
D6 Swatragh
B5 Swinford
E4 Swords
D3 Taghmon
D2 Tagoat
A2 Tahilla
E4 Tallaght
C2 Tallow
C2 Tallowbridge
E6 Tandragee
C4 Tang
B3 Tarbert

C3 Templemore
C3 Templetouhy
E5 Termonfeckin
D3 Thomastown
C3 Thurles
D4 Timahoe
B2 Timoleague
D3 Tinahely
C3 Tipperary
C5 Tobercurry
D6 Tobermore
C3 Toomyvara
B1 Toormore
B3 Tralee
D2 Tramore
D4 Trim
B4 Tuam
C3 Tuamgraney
B3 Tulla
D4 Tullamore
D3 Tullow
C5 Tulsk
B5 Turlough
D4 Tyrellspass

C3 Urlingford

D5 Virginia

E5 Warrenpoint
D2 Waterford
C2 Watergrasshill
A2 Waterville
B5 Westport
D3 Wexford
C2 Whitegate
E6 Whitehead
E4 Wicklow
E3 Woodenbridge
C4 Woodford

C2 Youghal

Distances on the mapping are shown in miles. However, in the Republic of Ireland, distances on signposting are in kilometres.

16 kilometres = 10 miles

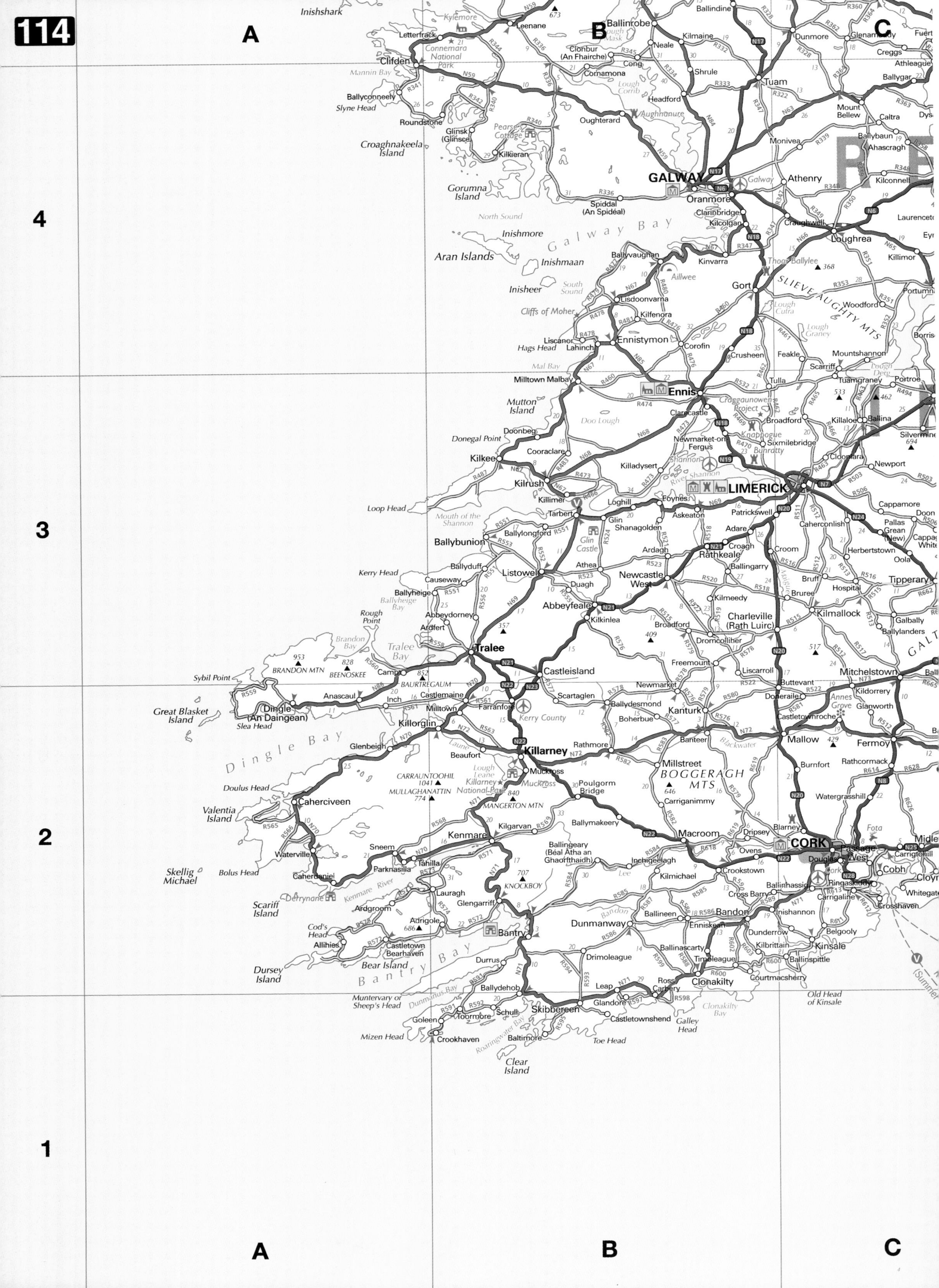

A
B
C
4
3
2
1
Inishshark
Kylemore
Leenane
Letterfrack
Connemara National Park
Clifden
Mannin Bay
Ballyconneely
Slyne Head
Roundstone
Glinsk (Glinsce)
Pearse's Cottage
Croaghnakeela Island
Kilkieran
Gorumna Island
Ballinrobe
Lough Mask
Clonbur (An Fhairche)
Cong
Cornamona
Lough Corrib
Neale
Kilmaine
Shrule
Headford
Oughterard
Aughnanure
Ballindine
Tuam
Dunmore
Glenamaddy
Creggs
Athleague
Ballygar
Mount Bellew
Caltra
Monivea
Ballybaun
Ahascragh
Kilconnell
Athenry
GALWAY
Galway
Oranmore
Spiddal (An Spidéal)
Clarinbridge
Kilcolgan
Craughwell
Loughrea
Laurencetown
Killimor
North Sound
Inishmore
Aran Islands
Inishmaan
Inisheer
Galway Bay
South Sound
Ballyvaughan
Aillwee
Kinvarra
Thoor Ballylee
Gort
SLIEVE AUGHTY MTS
Woodford
Portumna
Lisdoonvarna
Kilfenora
Cliffs of Moher
Lough Cutra
Lough Graney
Liscannor
Lahinch
Hags Head
Ennistymon
Corofin
Crusheen
Feakle
Mountshannon
Scarriff
Lough Derg
Tuamgraney
Portroe
Mal Bay
Milltown Malbay
Ennis
Tulla
Craggaunowen Project
Mutton Island
Doo Lough
Clarecastle
Knappogue
Broadford
Killaloe
Ballina
Silvermines
Doonbeg
Donegal Point
Kilkee
Cooraclare
Newmarket-on-Fergus
Sixmilebridge
Bunratty
Shannon
Cloonlara
Newport
Kilrush
Killadysert
River Shannon
LIMERICK
Killimer
Loop Head
Loghill
Foynes
Askeaton
Patrickswell
Cappamore
Doon
Tarbert
Mouth of the Shannon
Glin
Shanagolden
Adare
Caherconlish
Pallas Green (New)
Ballylongford
Glin Castle
Croagh
Croom
Herbertstown
Ballybunion
Ardagh
Rathkeale
Oola
Athea
Ballingarry
Kerry Head
Ballyduff
Listowel
Newcastle West
Bruff
Tipperary
Causeway
Duagh
Hospital
Ballyheige
Ballyheige Bay
Abbeyfeale
Kilmeedy
Bruree
Abbeydorney
Kilkinlea
Charleville (Rath Luirc)
Kilmallock
Galbally
Rough Point
Ardfert
Broadford
Ballylanders
Brandon Bay
Dromcolliher
Tralee Bay
Tralee
BRANDON MTN
BEENOSKEE
Castleisland
Freemount
Liscarroll
Mitchelstown
Sybil Point
Camp
BAURTREGAUM
Newmarket
Buttevant
Kildorrery
Anascaul
Inch
Castlemaine
Scartaglen
Doneraile
Annes Grove
Glanworth
Great Blasket Island
Dingle (An Daingean)
Milltown
Farranfore
Kerry County
Ballydesmond
Kanturk
Slea Head
Killorglin
Boherbue
Castletownroche
Dingle Bay
Glenbeigh
Beaufort
Killarney
Rathmore
Banteer
Blackwater
Mallow
Fermoy
Millstreet
Rathcormack
CARRAUNTOOHIL
Lough Leane
Killarney National Park
Muckross
BOGGERAGH MTS
Burnfort
Doulus Head
MULLAGHANATTIN
MANGERTON MTN
Poulgorm Bridge
Carriganimmy
Watergrasshill
Caherciveen
Valentia Island
Kilgarvan
Ballymakeery
Blarney
Fota
Midleton
Kenmare
Macroom
Dripsey
CORK
Waterville
Sneem
Tahilla
Ballingeary (Béal Atha an Ghaorfthaidh)
Ovens
Passage West
Carrigtohill
Skellig Michael
Bolus Head
Caherdaniel
Parknasilla
Inchigeelagh
Crookstown
Douglas
Cobh
Cloyne
Kenmare River
KNOCKBOY
Kilmichael
Whitegate
Derrynane
Lauragh
Ringaskiddy
Scariff Island
Ardgroom
Glengarriff
Cross Barry
Ballinhassig
Carrigaline
Crosshaven
Cod's Head
Adrigole
Ballineen
Bandon
Inishannon
Allihies
Castletown Bearhaven
Bantry
Dunmanway
Enniskean
Dunderrow
Belgooly
Kinsale
Bear Island
Kilbrittain
Ballinspittle
Dursey Island
Bantry Bay
Durrus
Drimoleague
Ballinascarty
Timoleague
Courtmacsherry
Ballydehob
Clonakilty
Muntervary or Sheep's Head
Dunmanus Bay
Leap
Ross Carbery
Old Head of Kinsale
Schull
Glandore
Clonakilty Bay
Goleen
Toormore
Skibbereen
Castletownshend
Galley Head
Crookhaven
Roaringwater Bay
Baltimore
Mizen Head
Toe Head
Clear Island
A
B
C

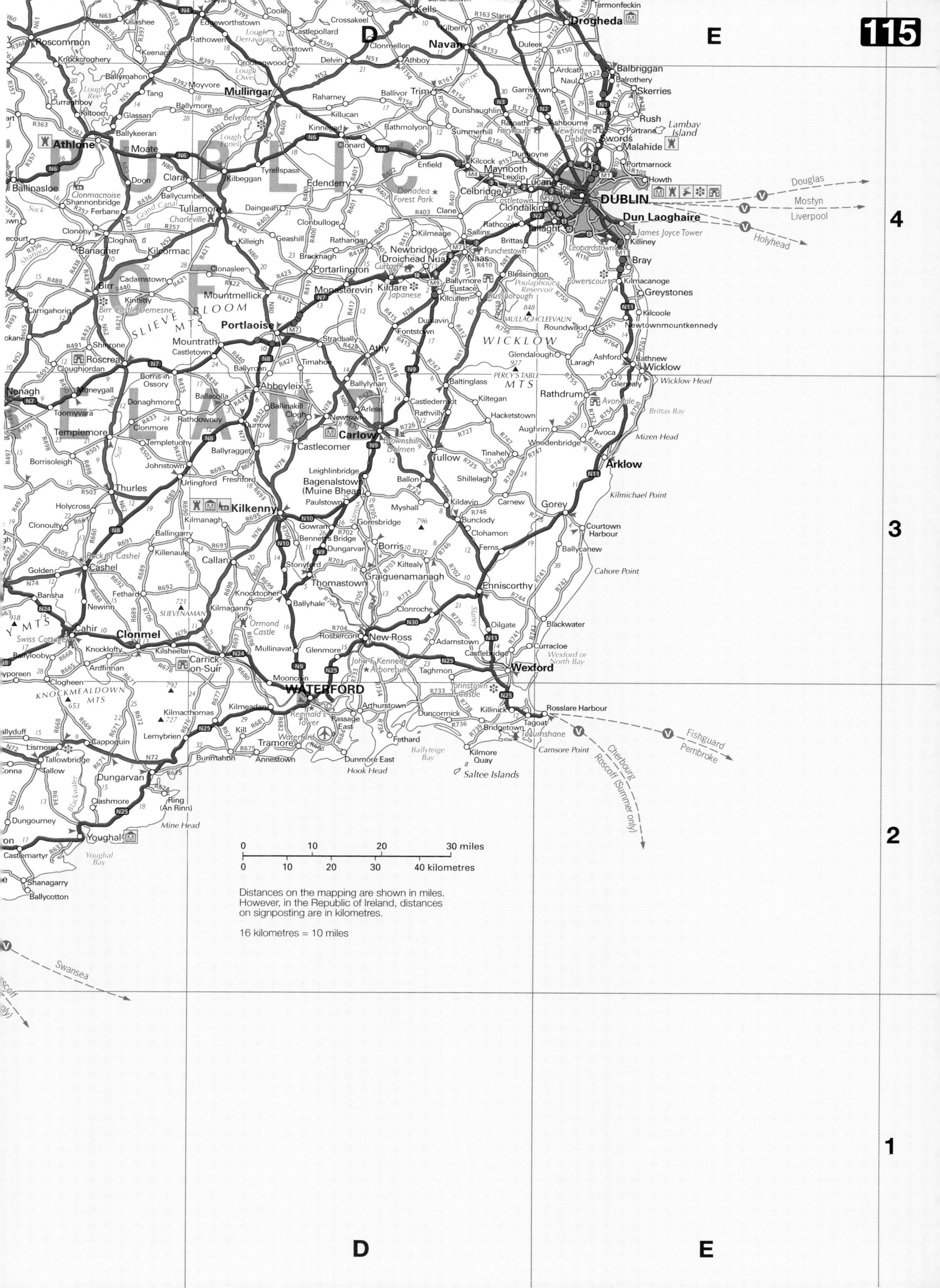
D
E
4
3
2
1
REPUBLIC OF IRELAND
Termonfeckin
Drogheda
Kells
Slane
Navan
Crossakeel
Castlepollard
Clonmellon
Athboy
Delvin
Collinstown
Edgeworthstown
Killashee
Roscommon
Knockcroghery
Keenagh
Rathowen
Lough Derravaragh
Crookedwood
Lough Owel
Mullingar
Moyvore
Ballymahon
Tang
Lough Ree
Curraghboy
Kiltoom
Glassan
Ballymore
Belvedere
Ballykeeran
Athlone
Moate
Lough Ennell
Kinnegad
Clonard
Killucan
Raharney
Ballivor
Trim
Rathmolyon
Summerhill
Dunshaughlin
Garristown
Duleek
Ardcath
Naul
Balbriggan
Balrothery
Skerries
Rush
Lusk
Lambay Island
Portrane
Ashbourne
Ratoath
Fairyhouse
Newbridge Demesne
Swords
Malahide
Portmarnock
Howth
Dunboyne
Kilcock
Maynooth
Leixlip
Lucan
Celbridge
Castletown
Clondalkin
Enfield
Tyrellspass
Kilbeggan
Clara
Doon
Ballinasloe
Clonmacnoise
Shannonbridge
Ferbane
Ballycumber
Grand Canal
Tullamore
Charleville
Daingean
Edenderry
Donadea Forest Park
Clane
DUBLIN
Dun Laoghaire
Douglas
Mostyn
Liverpool
Holyhead
James Joyce Tower
Killiney
Leopardstown
Tallaght
Rathcoole
Sallins
Brittas
Naas
Punchestown
Kilmeage
Clonbulloge
Rathangan
Geashill
Killeigh
Clonony
Cloghan
Banagher
Kilcormac
Birr
Birr Castle Demesne
Cadamstown
Kinnitty
Clonaslee
Mountmellick
Portarlington
Bracknagh
Monasterevin
Kildare
Japanese
Curragh
Newbridge (Droichead Nua)
Kilcullen
Ballymore Eustace
Blessington
Poulaphouca Reservoir
Russborough
Powerscourt
Bray
Kilmacanoge
Greystones
Kilcoole
Newtownmountkennedy
Roundwood
Mullaghcleevaun
Dunlavin
Fontstown
Athy
Stradbally
Portlaoise
Slieve Bloom Mts
Carrigahorig
Shinrone
Roscrea
Cloughjordan
Mountrath
Castletown
Borris-in-Ossory
Ballyroan
Timahoe
Abbeyleix
Ballylynan
Wicklow
Glendalough
Laragh
Ashford
Rathnew
Wicklow Head
Glenealy
Percy's Table
Wicklow Mts
Baltinglass
Kiltegan
Castledermot
Rathvilly
Hacketstown
Rathdrum
Avondale
Brittas Bay
Aughrim
Avoca
Woodenbridge
Mizen Head
Arklow
Tinahely
Shillelagh
Carlow
Brownshill Dolmen
Tullow
Newtown
Clogh
Ballinakill
Durrow
Ballacolla
Donaghmore
Rathdowney
Clonmore
Nenagh
Moneygall
Toomyvara
Templemore
Templetuohy
Ballyragget
Castlecomer
Johnstown
Urlingford
Freshford
Borrisoleigh
Thurles
Holycross
Clonoulty
Kilkenny
Kilmanagh
Leighlinbridge
Bagenalstown (Muine Bheag)
Paulstown
Ballon
Myshall
Kildavin
Bunclody
Clohamon
Carnew
Gorey
Kilmichael Point
Courtown Harbour
Ballycanew
Cahore Point
Gowran
Goresbridge
Bennett's Bridge
Dungarvan
Borris
Kiltealy
Ferns
Ballingarry
Killenaule
Callan
Rock of Cashel
Cashel
Golden
Bansha
Fethard
Newinn
Slievenaman
Stonyford
Thomastown
Graiguenamanagh
Enniscorthy
Knocktopher
Ballyhale
Kilmaganny
Ormond Castle
Clonroche
Oilgate
Blackwater
Cahir
Clonmel
Swiss Cottage
Knocklofty
Kilsheelan
Carrick-on-Suir
Mullinavat
Glenmore
Rosbercon
New Ross
Adamstown
Curracloe
Castlebridge
Wexford or North Bay
Wexford
John F Kennedy Arboretum
Taghmon
Ardfinnan
Clogheen
Knockmealdown Mts
Mooncoin
WATERFORD
Johnstown Castle
Killinick
Rosslare Harbour
Kilmacthomas
Kilmeadan
Reginald's Tower
Passage East
Arthurstown
Duncormick
Bridgetown
Tagoat
Tacumshane
Carnsore Point
Fishguard
Pembroke
Cherbourg
Roscoff (Summer only)
Lismore
Cappoquin
Lemybrien
Kill
Tramore
Waterford
Fethard
Ballyteige Bay
Kilmore Quay
Saltee Islands
Tallowbridge
Tallow
Dungarvan
Bunmahon
Annestown
Dunmore East
Hook Head
Ring (An Rinn)
Clashmore
Mine Head
Dungourney
Youghal
Youghal Bay
Castlemartyr
Shanagarry
Ballycotton
Swansea
0 10 20 30 miles
0 10 20 30 40 kilometres
Distances on the mapping are shown in miles. However, in the Republic of Ireland, distances on signposting are in kilometres.
16 kilometres = 10 miles

The Isle of Man

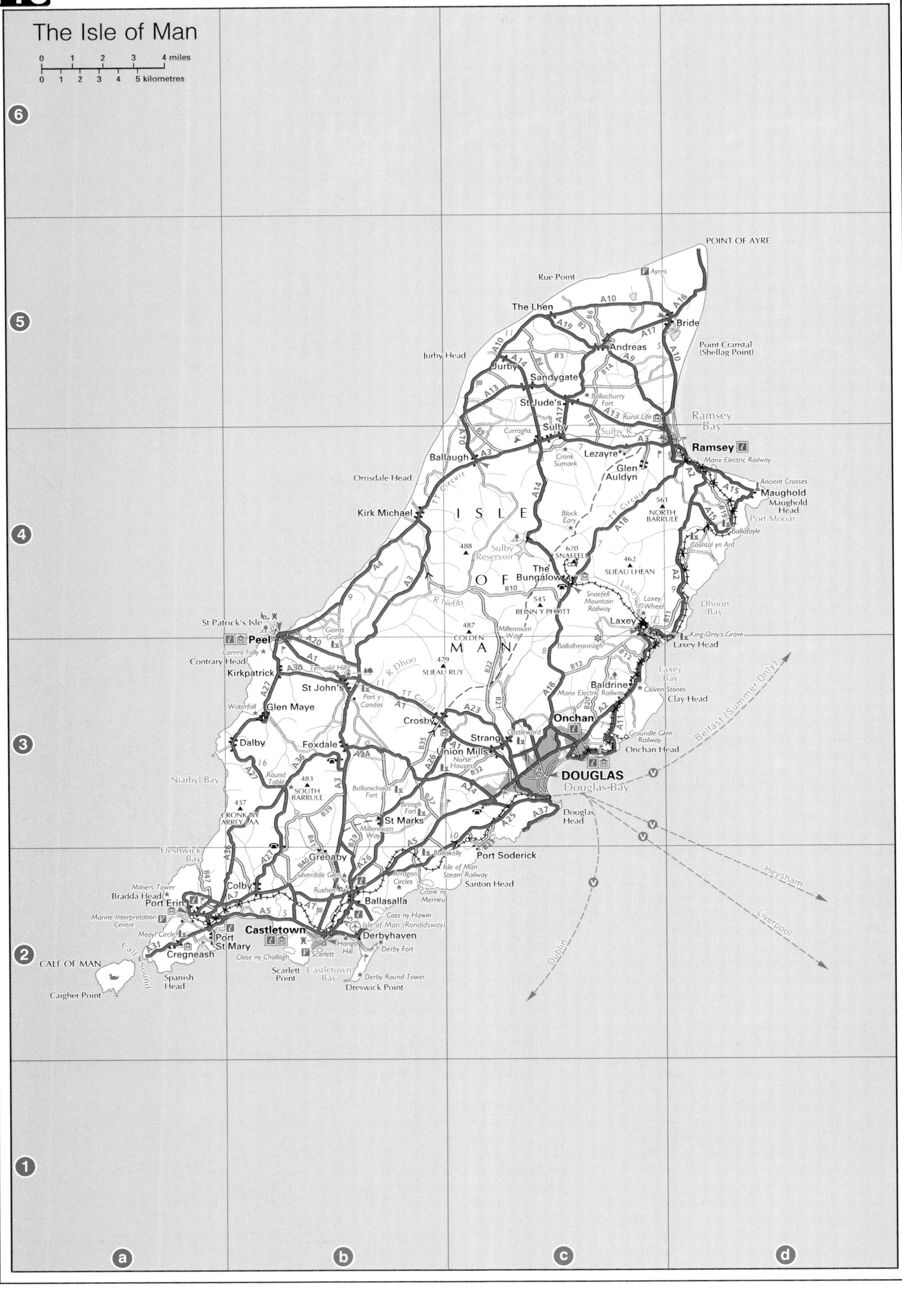

0 1 2 3 4 miles
0 1 2 3 4 5 kilometres

6

5

POINT OF AYRE

Rue Point

Ayres

The Lhen

A10

A16

Bride

A19 B2

Point Cranstal
(Shellag Point)

Jurby Head

A10 A14

Jurby

Andreas

A9

A17

B3

Sandygate

St Jude's

B14

Bollachurry
Fort

A13 Rural Life

Ramsey
Bay

A13

A10

Sulby

Sulby R.

Ramsey

Currophs

A10

A3

Cronk
Sumark

Lezayre

A3

Manx Electric Railway

A2

Ballaugh

Glen
Auldyn

561

Ancient Crosses

A14

Maughold

Orrisdale Head

Block
Eary

NORTH
BARRULE

A15

Maughold
Head

Port Mooar

ISLE

Kirk Michael

A18

Ballafayle

TT Circuit

488

Sulby
Reservoir

620
SNAEFELL

462

SLIEAU LHEAN

Cashtal yn Ard

A4

A3

OF

The
Bungalow

A9

Dhoon
Bay

St Patrick's Isle

Corrins Folly

Giants
Grave

545
BEINN Y PHOTT

B10

Snaefell
Mountain
Railway

Laxey
Wheel

Laxey

Peel

A20

A1

487
COLDEN

Millennium
Way

Ballalheannagh

Laxey Head

King Orry's Grave

Contrary Head

MAN

Laxey
Bay

Kirkpatrick

A30

Tynwald Hill

479

B12

Waterfall

St John's

SLIEAU RUY

B32

B12

Glen Maye

Port y
Candas

R. Dhoo

Baldrine

Manx Electric Railway

Crosby

A1

A23

A21

Cloven Stones

Dalby

Foxdale

A24

Union Mills

Strang

Castleward

Onchan

Clay Head

A27

16

Norse
Houses

B32

A18

Onchan Head

Niarbyl Bay

Round
Table

A36

A3

Ballanicholas
Fort

B35

A2

Groudle Glen
Railway

Belfast (Summer Only)

483
SOUTH
BARRULE

A5

B37

DOUGLAS

Douglas Bay

437
CRONK NY
ARREY LAA

B39

St Marks

Brough
Fort

A25

A37

Douglas
Head

Millennium
Way

A24

Fleshwick
Bay

B40

Grenaby

A26

B30

Silverdale Glen

Ballakelly

Isle of Man
Steam Railway

Port Soderick

Heysham

Milners Tower

Colby

A7

Rushen
Abbey

Arragon
Circles

Santon Head

Liverpool

Bradda Head

Port Erin

A5

Ballasalla

Cronk ny
Merriew

Cass ny Hawin

Marine Interpretation
Centre

Meayl Circle

A5

Derbyhaven

Isle of Man (Ronaldsway)

Dublin

31

Cregneash

Port
St Mary

Hango
Hill

Derby Fort

2

CALF OF MAN

Castletown

Close ny Chollogh

Scarlett

Derby Round Tower

Scarlett
Point

Castletown
Bay

Dreswick Point

Spanish
Head

Caigher Point

1

a b c d

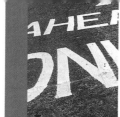

Key to town plans

Town plan legend

- M8 Motorway with number
- Primary Road
- A Road
- B Road
- Other road
- Restricted roads / pedestrians only
- COLLEGE Building of interest
- Church
- Park and open space
- P Car park
- Toilet
- One-way street
- Shopmobility
- P+ Park and ride
- M Metrolink station

Page 117.......... Aberdeen
117.......... Aberystwyth
118.......... Bath
118.......... Birmingham
118.......... Blackpool
118.......... Bradford
119.......... Brighton
119.......... Bristol
119.......... Cambridge
119.......... Canterbury
120.......... Cardiff
120.......... Carlisle
120.......... Chester
120.......... Coventry
121.......... Derby
121.......... Dundee
121.......... Edinburgh
121.......... Exeter
122.......... Glasgow
122.......... Ipswich
122.......... Kingston upon Hull
122.......... Leeds
123.......... Leicester
123.......... Liverpool
142-151.... LONDON

Page 123.......... Manchester
123.......... Middlesbrough
124.......... Milton Keynes
124.......... Newcastle upon Tyne
124.......... Newquay
124.......... Norwich
125.......... Nottingham
125.......... Oxford
125.......... Peterborough
125.......... Plymouth
126.......... Portsmouth
126.......... Reading
126.......... Salisbury
126.......... Sheffield
127.......... Shrewsbury
127.......... Southampton
127.......... Stratford-upon-Avon
127.......... Sunderland
128.......... Swansea
128.......... Taunton
128.......... Tunbridge Wells
128.......... Warwick
129.......... Watford
129.......... Winchester
129.......... Worcester
129.......... York

Central London

PADDINGTON 142 143
ISLINGTON 144 145
CITY
SOHO
150 151
KENSINGTON 146 147 148 149
SOUTHWARK
BERMONDSEY
WESTMINSTER
CHELSEA
KENNINGTON

Aberdeen
Aberystwyth

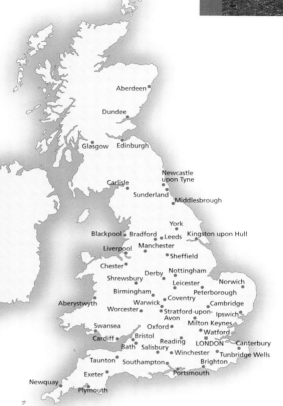

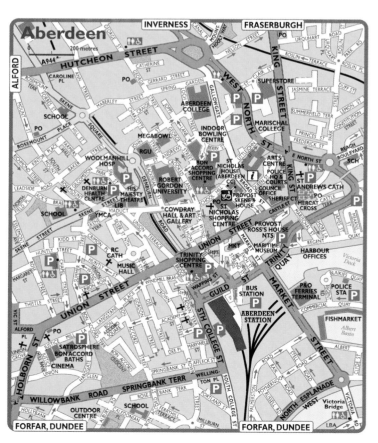

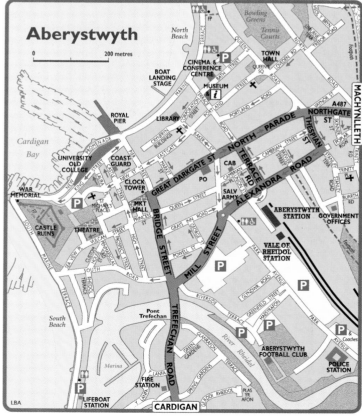

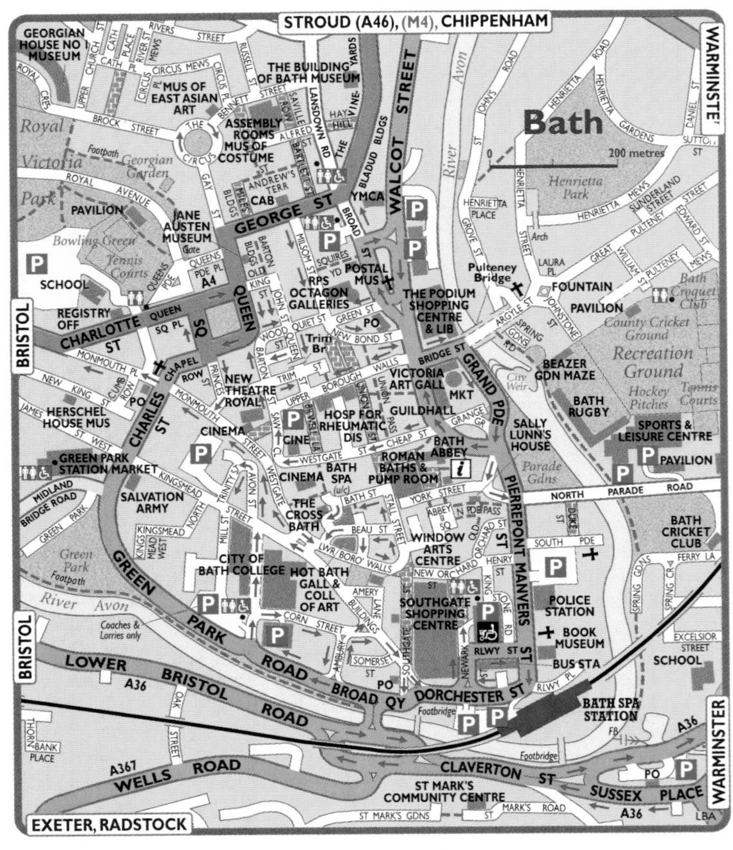
Bath
STROUD (A46), (M4), CHIPPENHAM
WARMINSTER
BRISTOL
EXETER, RADSTOCK
200 metres
GEORGIAN HOUSE NO 1 MUSEUM
THE BUILDING OF BATH MUSEUM
MUS OF EAST ASIAN ART
ASSEMBLY ROOMS MUS OF COSTUME
Royal Victoria Park
PAVILION
JANE AUSTEN MUSEUM
SCHOOL
REGISTRY OFFICE
CHARLOTTE ST
QUEEN SQ
GEORGE ST
WALCOT STREET
YMCA
POSTAL MUS
RPS OCTAGON GALLERIES
THE PODIUM SHOPPING CENTRE & LIB
Pulteney Bridge
FOUNTAIN
PAVILION
Recreation Ground
HERSCHEL HOUSE MUS
NEW THEATRE ROYAL
VICTORIA ART GALL
GUILDHALL
MKT
BEAZER GDN MAZE
BATH RUGBY
SPORTS & LEISURE CENTRE
HOSP FOR RHEUMATIC DIS
CINEMA
GREEN PARK STATION MARKET
SALLY LUNN'S HOUSE
BATH ABBEY
ROMAN BATHS & PUMP ROOM
BATH SPA
THE CROSS BATH
SALVATION ARMY
NORTH PARADE ROAD
BATH CRICKET CLUB
WINDOW ARTS CENTRE
CITY OF BATH COLLEGE
HOT BATH GALL & COLL OF ART
SOUTHGATE SHOPPING CENTRE
POLICE STATION
BOOK MUSEUM
BUS STA
SCHOOL
PIERREPONT MANVERS ST
GREEN PARK ROAD
LOWER BRISTOL ROAD
BROAD QY
DORCHESTER ST
BATH SPA STATION
WELLS ROAD
CLAVERTON ST
SUSSEX PLACE
ST MARK'S COMMUNITY CENTRE
A36
A367
LBA

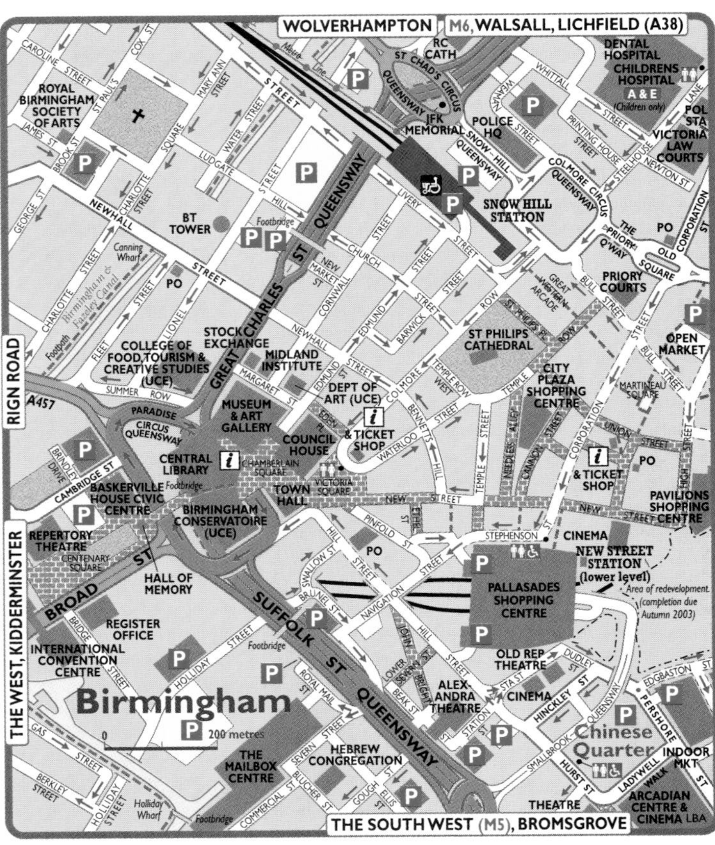
Birmingham
WOLVERHAMPTON M6, WALSALL, LICHFIELD (A38)
THE SOUTH WEST (M5), BROMSGROVE
THE WEST, KIDDERMINSTER
RIGN ROAD
200 metres
RC CATH
DENTAL HOSPITAL
CHILDRENS HOSPITAL
A & E (Children only)
POL STA
VICTORIA LAW COURTS
ROYAL BIRMINGHAM SOCIETY OF ARTS
JFK MEMORIAL
POLICE HQ
SNOW HILL STATION
BT TOWER
QUEENSWAY
PRIORY COURTS
OPEN MARKET
ST PHILIPS CATHEDRAL
CITY PLAZA SHOPPING CENTRE
COLLEGE OF FOOD, TOURISM & CREATIVE STUDIES (UCE)
STOCK EXCHANGE
MIDLAND INSTITUTE
GREAT CHARLES ST
MUSEUM & ART GALLERY
DEPT OF ART (UCE)
COUNCIL HOUSE
& TICKET SHOP
CENTRAL LIBRARY
TOWN HALL
BASKERVILLE HOUSE CIVIC CENTRE
BIRMINGHAM CONSERVATOIRE (UCE)
REPERTORY THEATRE
HALL OF MEMORY
BROAD ST
SUFFOLK ST QUEENSWAY
NEW STREET STATION (lower level)
PALLASADES SHOPPING CENTRE
PAVILIONS SHOPPING CENTRE
CINEMA
REGISTER OFFICE
INTERNATIONAL CONVENTION CENTRE
OLD REP THEATRE
ALEXANDRA THEATRE
THE MAILBOX CENTRE
HEBREW CONGREGATION
Chinese Quarter
INDOOR MKT
ARCADIAN CENTRE & CINEMA
THEATRE
A457
LBA

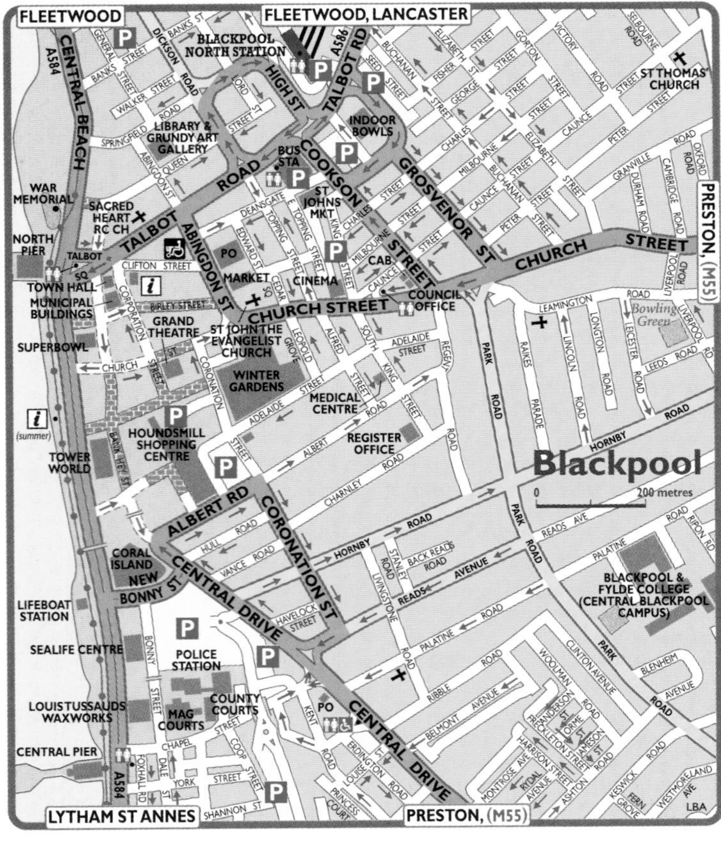
Blackpool
FLEETWOOD
FLEETWOOD, LANCASTER
PRESTON, (M55)
LYTHAM ST ANNES
200 metres
BLACKPOOL NORTH STATION
ST THOMAS' CHURCH
CENTRAL BEACH
A584
A586
TALBOT RD
HIGH ST
LIBRARY & GRUNDY ART GALLERY
INDOOR BOWLS
BUS STA
ST JOHNS MKT
COOKSON ST
GROSVENOR ST
WAR MEMORIAL
SACRED HEART RC CH
NORTH PIER
TOWN HALL
MUNICIPAL BUILDINGS
ABINGDON ST
MARKET
CINEMA
CAB
CHURCH STREET
COUNCIL OFFICE
GRAND THEATRE
ST JOHN THE EVANGELIST CHURCH
SUPERBOWL
WINTER GARDENS
MEDICAL CENTRE
REGISTER OFFICE
HOUNDSMILL SHOPPING CENTRE
TOWER WORLD
ALBERT RD
CORONATION ST
CORAL ISLAND
NEW BONNY ST
CENTRAL DRIVE
BLACKPOOL & FYLDE COLLEGE (CENTRAL BLACKPOOL CAMPUS)
LIFEBOAT STATION
SEALIFE CENTRE
POLICE STATION
LOUIS TUSSAUDS WAXWORKS
MAG COURTS
COUNTY COURTS
CENTRAL PIER
LBA

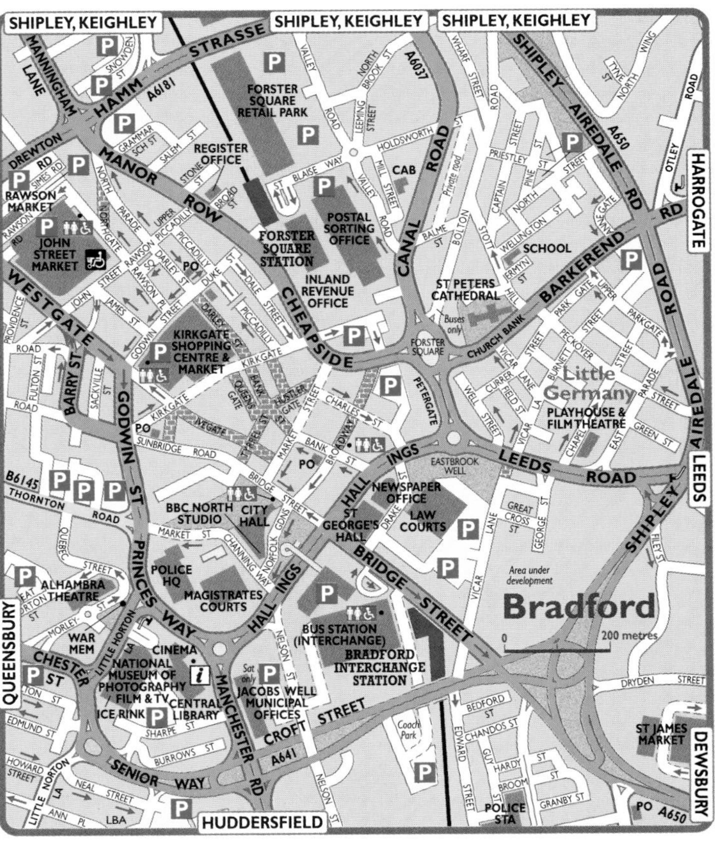
Bradford
SHIPLEY, KEIGHLEY
SHIPLEY, KEIGHLEY
SHIPLEY, KEIGHLEY
HARROGATE
LEEDS
DEWSBURY
HUDDERSFIELD
QUEENSBURY
200 metres
MANNINGHAM LANE
HAMM STRASSE
FORSTER SQUARE RETAIL PARK
A6181
A6037
A650
REGISTER OFFICE
MANOR ROW
RAWSON MARKET
JOHN STREET MARKET
CAB
POSTAL SORTING OFFICE
CANAL ROAD
FORSTER SQUARE STATION
INLAND REVENUE OFFICE
SCHOOL
ST PETERS CATHEDRAL
BARKEREND RD
AIREDALE RD
WESTGATE
CHEAPSIDE
KIRKGATE SHOPPING CENTRE & MARKET
Little Germany
PLAYHOUSE & FILM THEATRE
BARRY ST
GODWIN ST
LEEDS ROAD
HALL INGS
NEWSPAPER OFFICE
LAW COURTS
ST GEORGE'S HALL
BBC NORTH STUDIO
CITY HALL
POLICE HQ
MAGISTRATES COURTS
ALHAMBRA THEATRE
WAR MEM
BRIDGE STREET
BUS STATION (INTERCHANGE)
BRADFORD INTERCHANGE STATION
NATIONAL MUSEUM OF PHOTOGRAPHY FILM & TV
ICE RINK
CENTRAL LIBRARY
JACOBS WELL MUNICIPAL OFFICES
PRINCES WAY
MANCHESTER RD
CROFT STREET
SENIOR WAY
A641
CHESTER ST
ST JAMES MARKET
POLICE STA
B6145
THORNTON ROAD
LBA

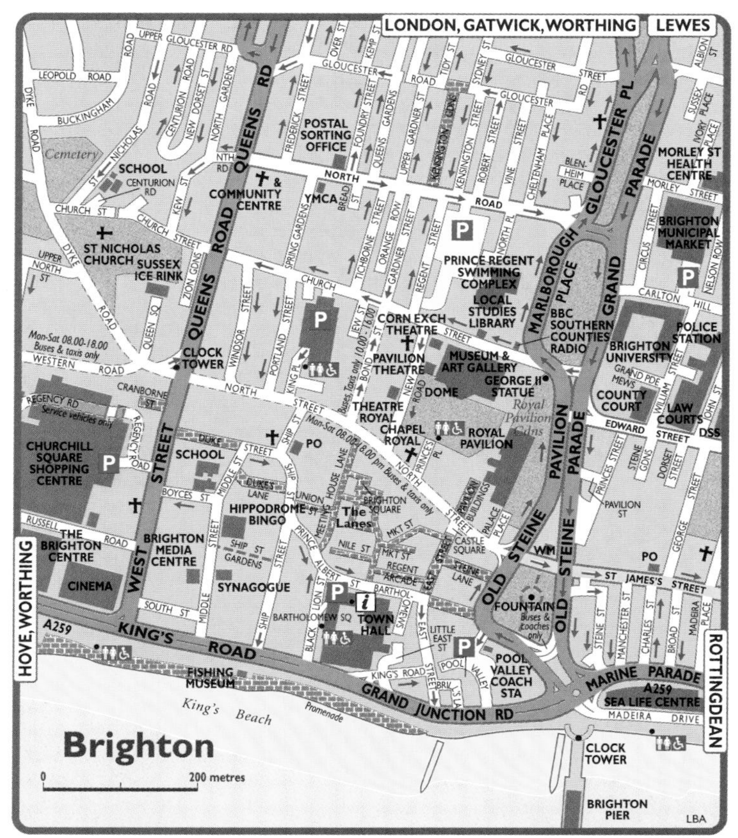
Brighton
LONDON, GATWICK, WORTHING
LEWES
HOVE, WORTHING
ROTTINGDEAN
200 metres
QUEENS ROAD
WEST STREET
KING'S ROAD
GRAND JUNCTION RD
MARINE PARADE
GLOUCESTER PL
GRAND PARADE
MARLBOROUGH PLACE
PAVILION PARADE
OLD STEINE
NORTH ROAD
CHURCH STREET
WESTERN ROAD
POSTAL SORTING OFFICE
COMMUNITY CENTRE
YMCA
SCHOOL
ST NICHOLAS CHURCH
SUSSEX ICE RINK
Cemetery
PRINCE REGENT SWIMMING COMPLEX
LOCAL STUDIES LIBRARY
BBC SOUTHERN COUNTIES RADIO
BRIGHTON MUNICIPAL MARKET
MORLEY ST HEALTH CENTRE
POLICE STATION
BRIGHTON UNIVERSITY
COUNTY COURT
LAW COURTS
DSS
CORN EXCH THEATRE
PAVILION THEATRE
MUSEUM & ART GALLERY
DOME
GEORGE II STATUE
Royal Pavilion Gdns
ROYAL PAVILION
THEATRE ROYAL
CHAPEL ROYAL
CLOCK TOWER
CHURCHILL SQUARE SHOPPING CENTRE
HIPPODROME BINGO
The Lanes
BRIGHTON MEDIA CENTRE
THE BRIGHTON CENTRE
CINEMA
SYNAGOGUE
TOWN HALL
FISHING MUSEUM
FOUNTAIN
POOL VALLEY COACH STA
SEA LIFE CENTRE
A259
CLOCK TOWER
BRIGHTON PIER
King's Beach
Promenade
Mon-Sat 08.00-18.00 Buses & taxis only
LBA

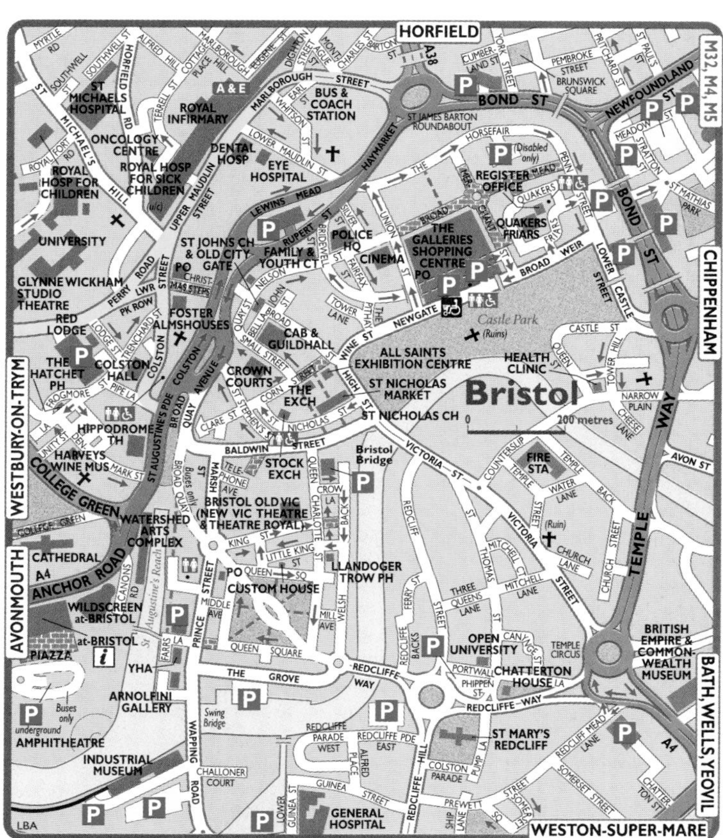
Bristol
HORFIELD
M32, M4, M5
CHIPPENHAM
BATH, WELLS, YEOVIL
WESTON-SUPER-MARE
AVONMOUTH
WESTBURY-ON-TRYM
200 metres
BOND ST
NEWFOUNDLAND ST
TEMPLE WAY
COLLEGE GREEN
ANCHOR ROAD
VICTORIA ST
REDCLIFFE WAY
THE GROVE
ST MICHAELS HOSPITAL
ROYAL INFIRMARY
BUS & COACH STATION
ONCOLOGY CENTRE
ROYAL HOSP FOR SICK CHILDREN
DENTAL HOSP
EYE HOSPITAL
ROYAL HOSP FOR CHILDREN
UNIVERSITY
GLYNNE WICKHAM STUDIO THEATRE
RED LODGE
THE HATCHET PH
COLSTON HALL
FOSTER ALMSHOUSES
ST JOHNS CH & OLD CITY GATE
FAMILY & YOUTH CT
POLICE HQ
CINEMA
THE GALLERIES SHOPPING CENTRE
REGISTER OFFICE
QUAKERS FRIARS
Castle Park
CAB & GUILDHALL
ALL SAINTS EXHIBITION CENTRE
ST NICHOLAS MARKET
HEALTH CLINIC
CROWN COURTS
THE EXCH
ST NICHOLAS CH
HIPPODROME TH
HARVEYS WINE MUS
STOCK EXCH
Bristol Bridge
FIRE STA
BRISTOL OLD VIC (NEW VIC THEATRE & THEATRE ROYAL)
WATERSHED ARTS COMPLEX
CATHEDRAL
LLANDOGER TROW PH
CUSTOM HOUSE
WILDSCREEN at-BRISTOL
at-BRISTOL
PIAZZA
YHA
ARNOLFINI GALLERY
OPEN UNIVERSITY
CHATTERTON HOUSE
BRITISH EMPIRE & COMMONWEALTH MUSEUM
AMPHITHEATRE
INDUSTRIAL MUSEUM
ST MARY'S REDCLIFF
GENERAL HOSPITAL
QUEEN SQUARE
A4
A38
LBA

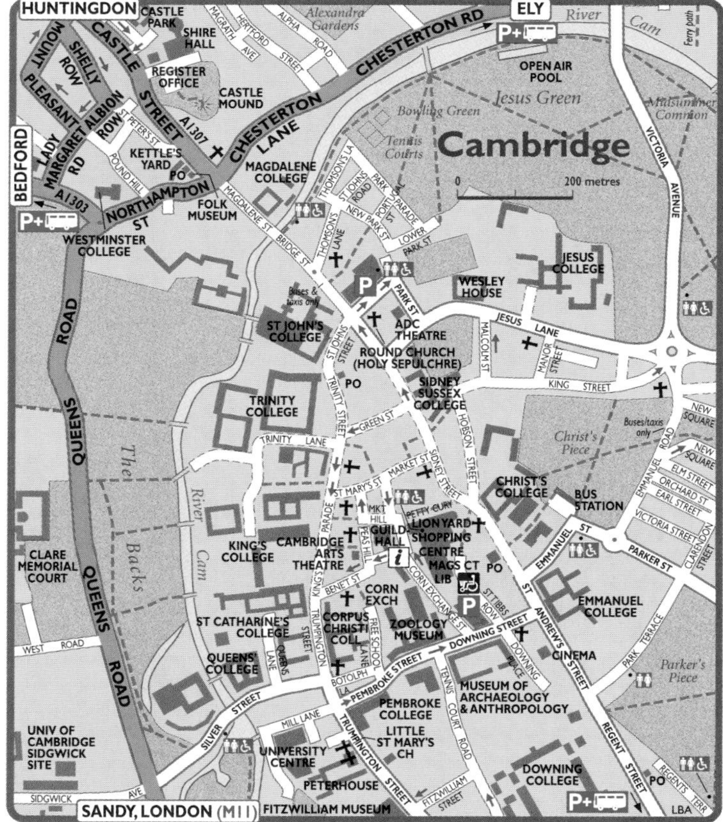
Cambridge
HUNTINGDON
ELY
BEDFORD
SANDY, LONDON (M11)
200 metres
CHESTERTON RD
CHESTERTON LANE
CASTLE STREET
QUEENS ROAD
NORTHAMPTON ST
JESUS LANE
KING STREET
REGENT STREET
River Cam
Jesus Green
Midsummer Common
Christ's Pieces
Parker's Piece
The Backs
SHIRE HALL
REGISTER OFFICE
CASTLE MOUND
KETTLE'S YARD
MAGDALENE COLLEGE
FOLK MUSEUM
WESTMINSTER COLLEGE
OPEN AIR POOL
JESUS COLLEGE
WESLEY HOUSE
ST JOHN'S COLLEGE
ADC THEATRE
ROUND CHURCH (HOLY SEPULCHRE)
SIDNEY SUSSEX COLLEGE
TRINITY COLLEGE
CHRIST'S COLLEGE
BUS STATION
LION YARD SHOPPING CENTRE
GUILD HALL
MAGS CT
LIB
KING'S COLLEGE
CAMBRIDGE ARTS THEATRE
CLARE MEMORIAL COURT
CORN EXCH
CORPUS CHRISTI COLL
ZOOLOGY MUSEUM
ST CATHARINE'S COLLEGE
QUEENS' COLLEGE
EMMANUEL COLLEGE
CINEMA
MUSEUM OF ARCHAEOLOGY & ANTHROPOLOGY
PEMBROKE COLLEGE
LITTLE ST MARY'S CH
UNIV OF CAMBRIDGE SIDGWICK SITE
UNIVERSITY CENTRE
PETERHOUSE
FITZWILLIAM MUSEUM
DOWNING COLLEGE
A1307
A1303
LBA

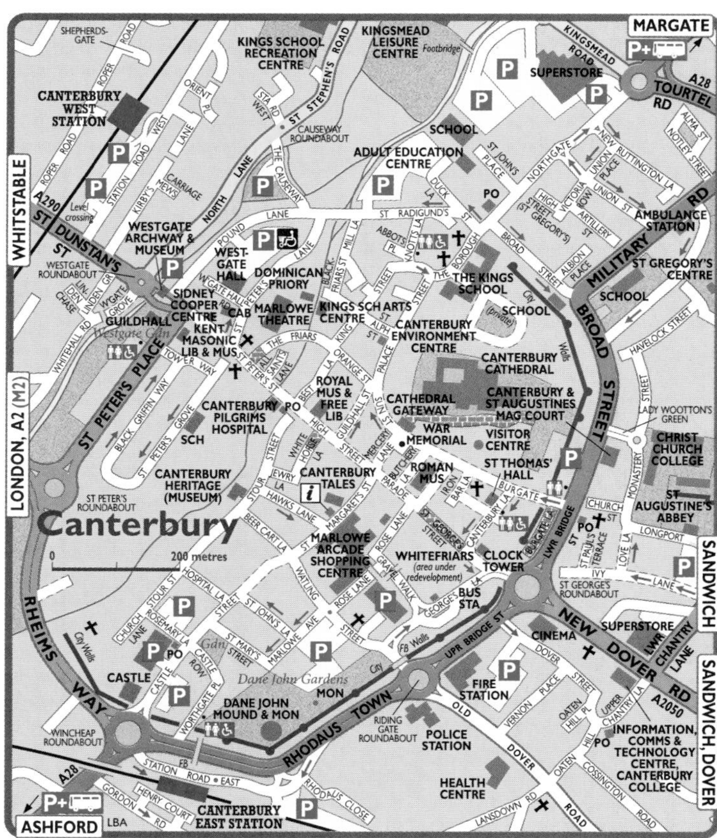
Canterbury
MARGATE
WHITSTABLE
LONDON, A2 (M2)
SANDWICH
SANDWICH, DOVER
ASHFORD
200 metres
ST DUNSTAN'S ST
ST PETER'S PLACE
RHEIMS WAY
RHODAUS TOWN
BROAD STREET
MILITARY RD
NEW DOVER RD
TOURTEL RD
A28
A290
A2050
KINGS SCHOOL RECREATION CENTRE
KINGSMEAD LEISURE CENTRE
SUPERSTORE
CANTERBURY WEST STATION
SCHOOL
ADULT EDUCATION CENTRE
AMBULANCE STATION
WESTGATE ARCHWAY & MUSEUM
WESTGATE HALL
DOMINICAN PRIORY
THE KINGS SCHOOL
ST GREGORY'S CENTRE
SIDNEY COOPER CENTRE
MARLOWE THEATRE
KINGS SCH ARTS CENTRE
CANTERBURY ENVIRONMENT CENTRE
GUILDHALL
KENT MASONIC LIB & MUS
CANTERBURY CATHEDRAL
CANTERBURY PILGRIMS HOSPITAL
ROYAL MUS & FREE LIB
CATHEDRAL GATEWAY
CANTERBURY & ST AUGUSTINES MAG COURT
WAR MEMORIAL
VISITOR CENTRE
LADY WOOTTON'S GREEN
CHRIST CHURCH COLLEGE
SCH
CANTERBURY HERITAGE (MUSEUM)
CANTERBURY TALES
ROMAN MUS
ST THOMAS' HALL
ST AUGUSTINE'S ABBEY
MARLOWE ARCADE SHOPPING CENTRE
WHITEFRIARS (area under redevelopment)
CLOCK TOWER
BUS STA
CINEMA
SUPERSTORE
CASTLE
DANE JOHN MOUND & MON
Dane John Gardens
FIRE STATION
POLICE STATION
INFORMATION, COMMS & TECHNOLOGY CENTRE, CANTERBURY COLLEGE
HEALTH CENTRE
CANTERBURY EAST STATION
WINCHEAP ROUNDABOUT
RIDING GATE ROUNDABOUT
ST GEORGE'S ROUNDABOUT
ST PETER'S ROUNDABOUT
WESTGATE ROUNDABOUT
City Walls
LBA

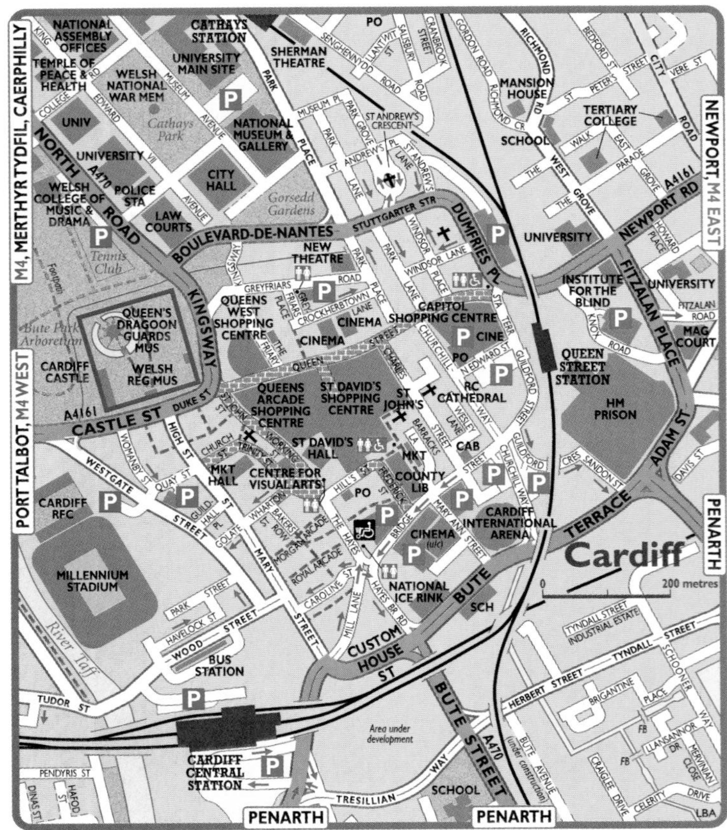
Cardiff
0
200 metres
M4, MERTHYR TYDFIL, CAERPHILLY
PORT TALBOT, M4 WEST
NEWPORT, M4 EAST
PENARTH
PENARTH
PENARTH
NATIONAL ASSEMBLY OFFICES
CATHAYS STATION
TEMPLE OF PEACE & HEALTH
UNIVERSITY MAIN SITE
SHERMAN THEATRE
WELSH NATIONAL WAR MEM
MANSION HOUSE
TERTIARY COLLEGE
UNIV
NATIONAL MUSEUM & GALLERY
Cathays Park
UNIVERSITY
SCHOOL
CITY HALL
WELSH COLLEGE OF MUSIC & DRAMA
POLICE STA
LAW COURTS
Gorsedd Gardens
NORTH ROAD
BOULEVARD-DE-NANTES
DUMFRIES PL
UNIVERSITY
NEWPORT RD
NEW THEATRE
INSTITUTE FOR THE BLIND
UNIVERSITY
QUEEN'S DRAGOON GUARDS MUS
QUEENS WEST SHOPPING CENTRE
CAPITOL SHOPPING CENTRE
CINE
MAG COURT
FITZALAN PLACE
Bute Park Arboretum
KINGSWAY
CINEMA
CINEMA
QUEEN STREET STATION
CARDIFF CASTLE
WELSH REG MUS
QUEENS ARCADE SHOPPING CENTRE
ST DAVID'S SHOPPING CENTRE
ST JOHN'S
RC CATHEDRAL
HM PRISON
CASTLE ST
ST DAVID'S HALL
MKT
CAB
ADAM ST
MKT HALL
CENTRE FOR VISUAL ARTS
COUNTY LIB
CARDIFF RFC
CARDIFF INTERNATIONAL ARENA
CINEMA
TERRACE
MILLENNIUM STADIUM
NATIONAL ICE RINK
BUTE
SCH
River Taff
CUSTOM HOUSE ST
BUS STATION
TUDOR ST
Area under development
CARDIFF CENTRAL STATION
BUTE STREET
TRESILLIAN
SCHOOL
LBA

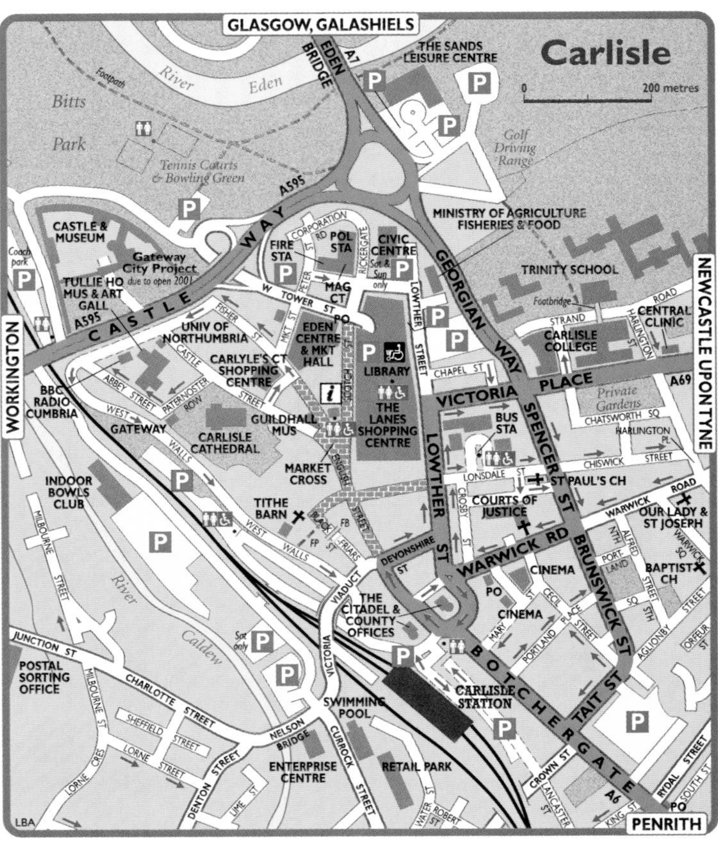
Carlisle
0
200 metres
GLASGOW, GALASHIELS
NEWCASTLE UPON TYNE
WORKINGTON
PENRITH
EDEN BRIDGE
THE SANDS LEISURE CENTRE
River Eden
Bitts Park
Golf Driving Range
Tennis Courts & Bowling Green
MINISTRY OF AGRICULTURE FISHERIES & FOOD
CASTLE & MUSEUM
Gateway City Project due to open 2001
FIRE STA
POL STA
CIVIC CENTRE
TRINITY SCHOOL
TULLIE HO MUS & ART GALL
MAG CT
GEORGIAN WAY
CENTRAL CLINIC
CASTLE WAY
UNIV OF NORTHUMBRIA
EDEN CENTRE & MKT HALL
LIBRARY
CARLISLE COLLEGE
CARLYLE'S CT SHOPPING CENTRE
THE LANES SHOPPING CENTRE
VICTORIA PLACE
Private Gardens
BBC RADIO CUMBRIA
GUILDHALL MUS
BUS STA
GATEWAY
CARLISLE CATHEDRAL
LOWTHER ST
SPENCER ST
MARKET CROSS
ST PAUL'S CH
INDOOR BOWLS CLUB
TITHE BARN
COURTS OF JUSTICE
OUR LADY & ST JOSEPH
WARWICK RD
BAPTIST CH
CINEMA
River Caldew
THE CITADEL & COUNTY OFFICES
CINEMA
POSTAL SORTING OFFICE
CARLISLE STATION
BOTCHERGATE
SWIMMING POOL
TAIT ST
ENTERPRISE CENTRE
RETAIL PARK
LBA

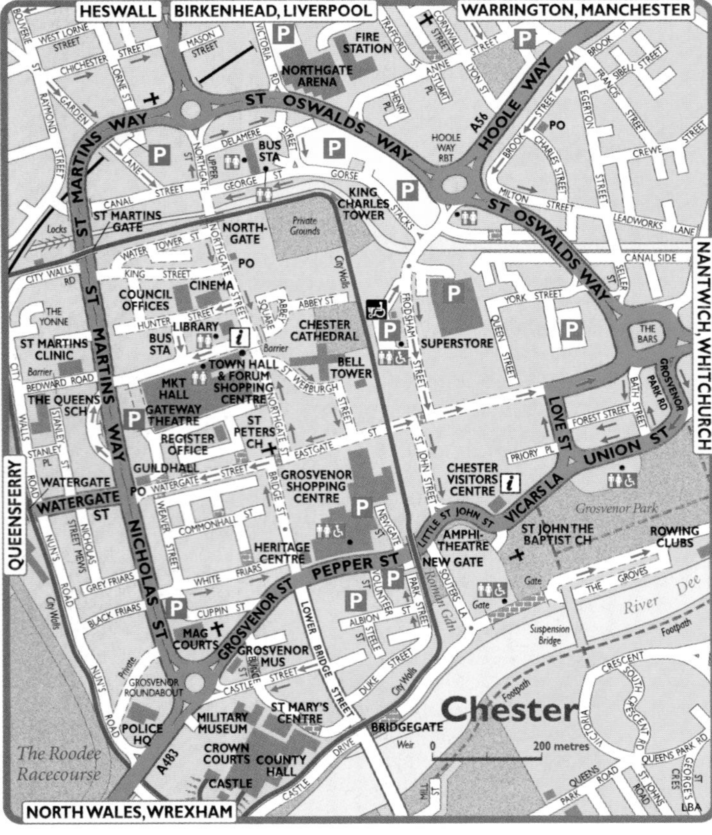
Chester
0
200 metres
HESWALL
BIRKENHEAD, LIVERPOOL
WARRINGTON, MANCHESTER
NANTWICH, WHITCHURCH
QUEENSFERRY
NORTH WALES, WREXHAM
FIRE STATION
NORTHGATE ARENA
HOOLE WAY
ST OSWALDS WAY
ST MARTINS WAY
BUS STA
HOOLE WAY RBT
KING CHARLES TOWER
ST MARTINS GATE
NORTH-GATE
Private Grounds
ST OSWALDS WAY
CINEMA
COUNCIL OFFICES
LIBRARY
CHESTER CATHEDRAL
SUPERSTORE
THE BARS
ST MARTINS CLINIC
BUS STA
TOWN HALL & FORUM SHOPPING CENTRE
BELL TOWER
MKT HALL
THE QUEENS SCH
GATEWAY THEATRE
ST PETERS CH
REGISTER OFFICE
LOVE ST
UNION ST
GUILDHALL
GROSVENOR SHOPPING CENTRE
CHESTER VISITORS CENTRE
WATERGATE
VICARS LA
Grosvenor Park
HERITAGE CENTRE
AMPHI-THEATRE
ST JOHN THE BAPTIST CH
ROWING CLUBS
NEW GATE
PEPPER ST
River Dee
NICHOLAS ST
GROSVENOR ST
MAG COURTS
GROSVENOR MUS
Suspension Bridge
GROSVENOR ROUNDABOUT
POLICE HQ
MILITARY MUSEUM
ST MARY'S CENTRE
BRIDGEGATE
The Roodee Racecourse
CROWN COURTS
COUNTY HALL
CASTLE
LBA

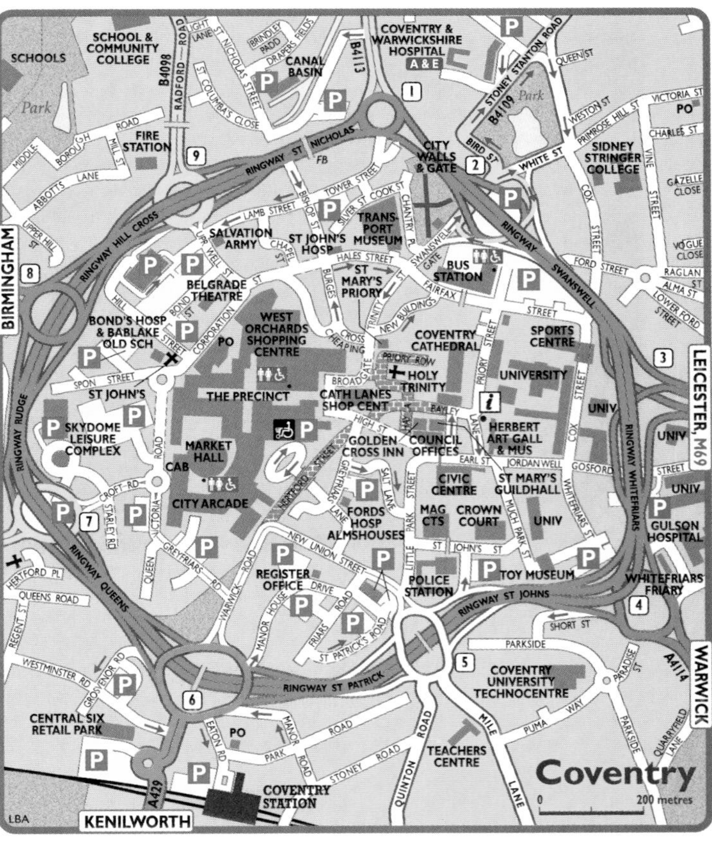
Coventry
0
200 metres
BIRMINGHAM
LEICESTER, M69
WARWICK
KENILWORTH
SCHOOLS
SCHOOL & COMMUNITY COLLEGE
COVENTRY & WARWICKSHIRE HOSPITAL A & E
CANAL BASIN
Park
FIRE STATION
RINGWAY ST NICHOLAS
CITY WALLS & GATE
SIDNEY STRINGER COLLEGE
RINGWAY HILL CROSS
SALVATION ARMY
ST JOHN'S HOSP
TRANS-PORT MUSEUM
BUS STATION
BELGRADE THEATRE
ST MARY'S PRIORY
RINGWAY SWANSWELL
BOND'S HOSP & BABLAKE OLD SCH
WEST ORCHARDS SHOPPING CENTRE
COVENTRY CATHEDRAL
SPORTS CENTRE
HOLY TRINITY
UNIVERSITY
ST JOHN'S
THE PRECINCT
CATH LANES SHOP CENT
SKYDOME LEISURE COMPLEX
HERBERT ART GALL & MUS
MARKET HALL
GOLDEN CROSS INN
COUNCIL OFFICES
UNIV
CAB
CIVIC CENTRE
ST MARY'S GUILDHALL
CITY ARCADE
FORDS HOSP ALMSHOUSES
MAG CTS
CROWN COURT
UNIV
GULSON HOSPITAL
RINGWAY WHITEFRIARS
RINGWAY QUEENS
REGISTER OFFICE
POLICE STATION
TOY MUSEUM
WHITEFRIARS FRIARY
RINGWAY ST JOHNS
RINGWAY ST PATRICK
COVENTRY UNIVERSITY TECHNOCENTRE
CENTRAL SIX RETAIL PARK
TEACHERS CENTRE
COVENTRY STATION
LBA

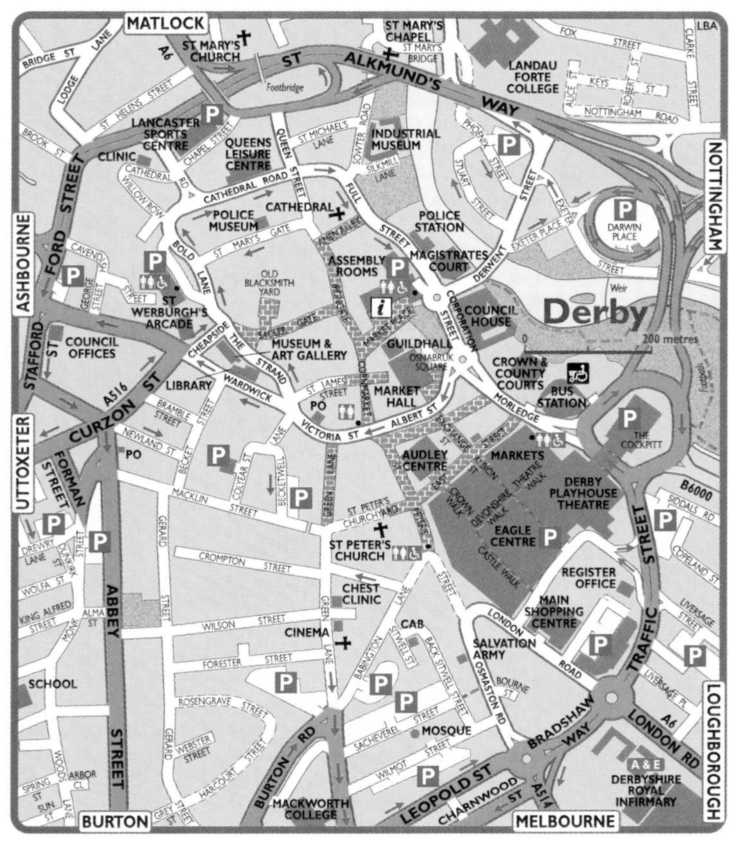
Derby
200 metres
MATLOCK
NOTTINGHAM
ASHBOURNE
UTTOXETER
BURTON
MELBOURNE
LOUGHBOROUGH
ST MARY'S CHURCH
ST MARY'S CHAPEL
ST ALKMUND'S WAY
LANDAU FORTE COLLEGE
LANCASTER SPORTS CENTRE
QUEENS LEISURE CENTRE
INDUSTRIAL MUSEUM
CLINIC
CATHEDRAL ROAD
CATHEDRAL
POLICE MUSEUM
POLICE STATION
MAGISTRATES COURT
ASSEMBLY ROOMS
DARWIN PLACE
ST WERBURGH'S ARCADE
COUNCIL OFFICES
COUNCIL HOUSE
MUSEUM & ART GALLERY
GUILDHALL
MARKET HALL
CROWN & COUNTY COURTS
BUS STATION
THE COCKPIT
LIBRARY
CURZON ST
FORD STREET
ABBEY STREET
VICTORIA ST
ALBERT ST
AUDLEY CENTRE
MARKETS
DERBY PLAYHOUSE THEATRE
EAGLE CENTRE
ST PETER'S CHURCH
CHEST CLINIC
REGISTER OFFICE
MAIN SHOPPING CENTRE
CINEMA
CAB
SALVATION ARMY
TRAFFIC STREET
SCHOOL
MOSQUE
BRADSHAW WAY
LEOPOLD ST
BURTON RD
LONDON RD
DERBYSHIRE ROYAL INFIRMARY
MACKWORTH COLLEGE
PO

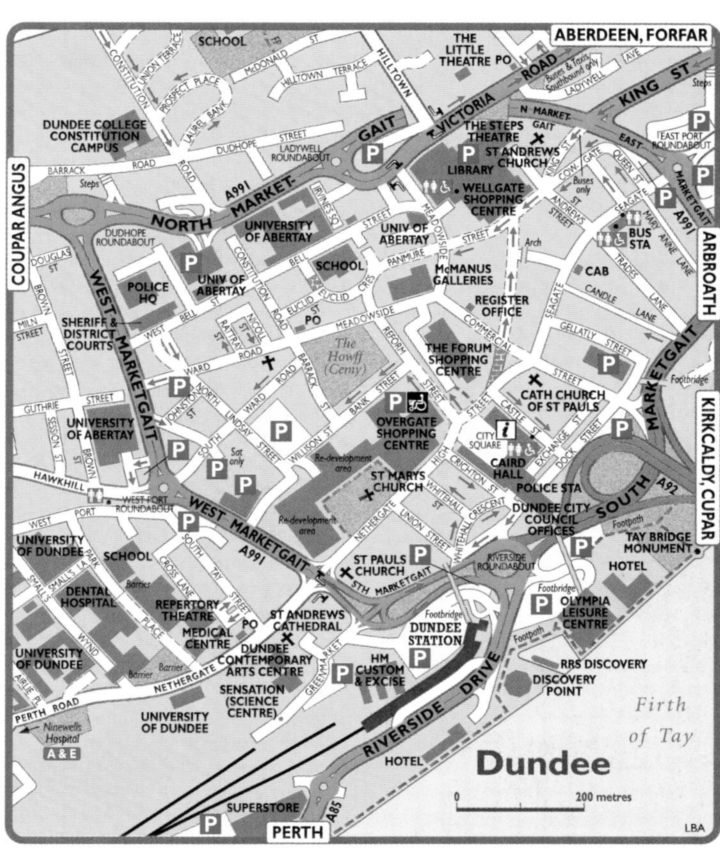
Dundee
200 metres
ABERDEEN, FORFAR
COUPAR ANGUS
ARBROATH
KIRKCALDY, CUPAR
PERTH
SCHOOL
THE LITTLE THEATRE
VICTORIA ROAD
KING ST
DUNDEE COLLEGE CONSTITUTION CAMPUS
NORTH MARKETGAIT
THE STEPS THEATRE
ST ANDREWS CHURCH
LIBRARY
WELLGATE SHOPPING CENTRE
BUS STA
UNIVERSITY OF ABERTAY
UNIV OF ABERTAY
McMANUS GALLERIES
POLICE HQ
SHERIFF & DISTRICT COURTS
REGISTER OFFICE
The Howff (Cemy)
THE FORUM SHOPPING CENTRE
CATH CHURCH OF ST PAULS
WEST MARKETGAIT
OVERGATE SHOPPING CENTRE
ST MARYS CHURCH
CAIRD HALL
POLICE STA
DUNDEE CITY COUNCIL OFFICES
TAY BRIDGE MONUMENT
HOTEL
UNIVERSITY OF DUNDEE
DENTAL HOSPITAL
REPERTORY THEATRE
MEDICAL CENTRE
ST PAULS CHURCH
ST ANDREWS CATHEDRAL
DUNDEE CONTEMPORARY ARTS CENTRE
DUNDEE STATION
HM CUSTOM & EXCISE
OLYMPIA LEISURE CENTRE
RRS DISCOVERY
DISCOVERY POINT
SENSATION (SCIENCE CENTRE)
NETHERGATE
PERTH ROAD
RIVERSIDE DRIVE
Firth of Tay
SUPERSTORE

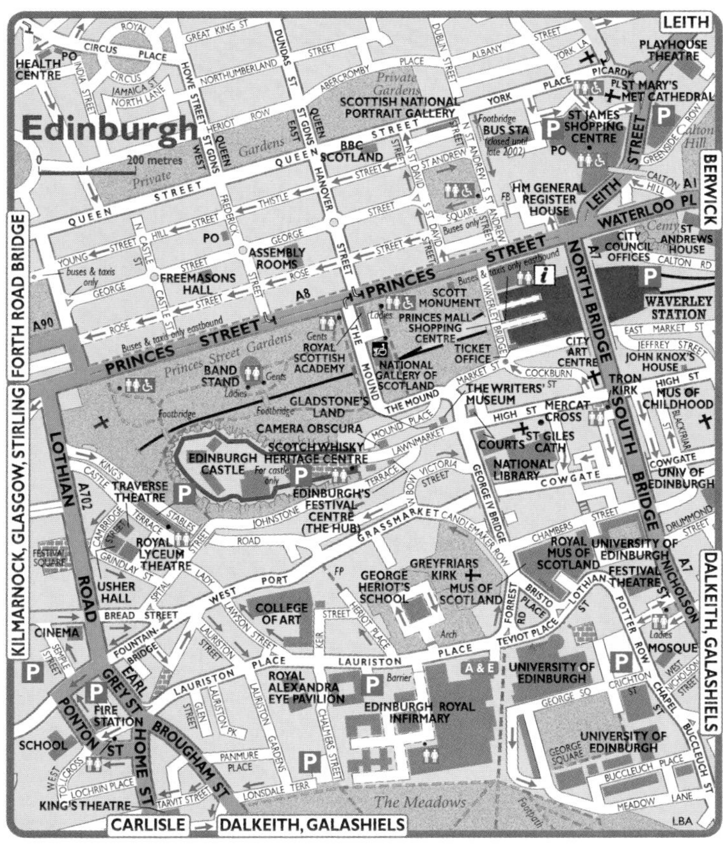
Edinburgh
200 metres
LEITH
BERWICK
FORTH ROAD BRIDGE
KILMARNOCK, GLASGOW, STIRLING
DALKEITH, GALASHIELS
CARLISLE
HEALTH CENTRE
PLAYHOUSE THEATRE
ST MARY'S MET CATHEDRAL
SCOTTISH NATIONAL PORTRAIT GALLERY
BUS STA
ST JAMES SHOPPING CENTRE
BBC SCOTLAND
QUEEN STREET
GEORGE STREET
HM GENERAL REGISTER HOUSE
WATERLOO PL
ST ANDREWS HOUSE
CITY COUNCIL OFFICES
ASSEMBLY ROOMS
FREEMASONS HALL
PRINCES STREET
SCOTT MONUMENT
PRINCES MALL SHOPPING CENTRE
WAVERLEY STATION
NORTH BRIDGE
ROYAL SCOTTISH ACADEMY
NATIONAL GALLERY OF SCOTLAND
TICKET OFFICE
CITY ART CENTRE
JOHN KNOX'S HOUSE
BAND STAND
THE WRITERS' MUSEUM
TRON KIRK
MUS OF CHILDHOOD
GLADSTONE'S LAND
MERCAT CROSS
CAMERA OBSCURA
SCOTCH WHISKY HERITAGE CENTRE
ST GILES CATH
COURTS
NATIONAL LIBRARY
EDINBURGH CASTLE
EDINBURGH'S FESTIVAL CENTRE (THE HUB)
UNIV OF EDINBURGH
TRAVERSE THEATRE
ROYAL LYCEUM THEATRE
GRASSMARKET
COWGATE
SOUTH BRIDGE
ROYAL MUS OF SCOTLAND
UNIVERSITY OF EDINBURGH
FESTIVAL THEATRE
USHER HALL
GREYFRIARS KIRK
GEORGE HERIOT'S SCHOOL
MUS OF SCOTLAND
COLLEGE OF ART
CINEMA
MOSQUE
LOTHIAN ROAD
ROYAL ALEXANDRA EYE PAVILION
EDINBURGH ROYAL INFIRMARY
FIRE STATION
SCHOOL
KING'S THEATRE
The Meadows

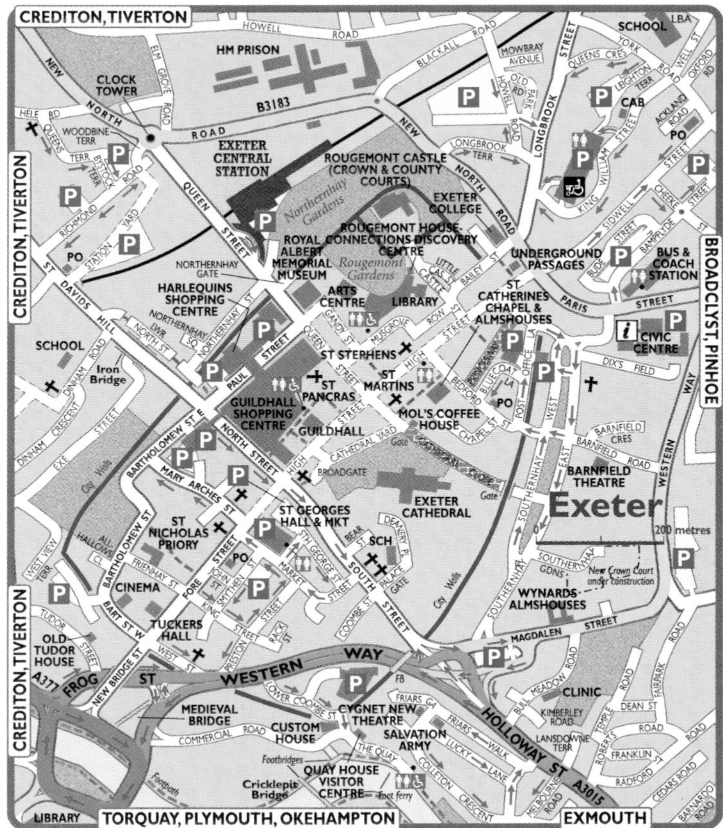
Exeter
200 metres
CREDITON, TIVERTON
BROADCLYST, PINHOE
TORQUAY, PLYMOUTH, OKEHAMPTON
EXMOUTH
HM PRISON
CLOCK TOWER
SCHOOL
EXETER CENTRAL STATION
ROUGEMONT CASTLE (CROWN & COUNTY COURTS)
EXETER COLLEGE
Northernhay Gardens
ROUGEMONT HOUSE
CONNECTIONS DISCOVERY CENTRE
ROYAL ALBERT MEMORIAL MUSEUM
Rougemont Gardens
UNDERGROUND PASSAGES
BUS & COACH STATION
HARLEQUINS SHOPPING CENTRE
ARTS CENTRE
LIBRARY
ST CATHERINES CHAPEL & ALMSHOUSES
CIVIC CENTRE
Iron Bridge
ST STEPHENS
ST MARTINS
ST PANCRAS
GUILDHALL SHOPPING CENTRE
GUILDHALL
MOL'S COFFEE HOUSE
EXETER CATHEDRAL
BARNFIELD THEATRE
ST GEORGES HALL & MKT
ST NICHOLAS PRIORY
CINEMA
New Crown Court under construction
WYNARDS ALMSHOUSES
TUCKERS HALL
OLD TUDOR HOUSE
WESTERN WAY
CYGNET NEW THEATRE
SALVATION ARMY
MEDIEVAL BRIDGE
CUSTOM HOUSE
QUAY HOUSE VISITOR CENTRE
Cricklepit Bridge
HOLLOWAY ST
CLINIC
LIBRARY

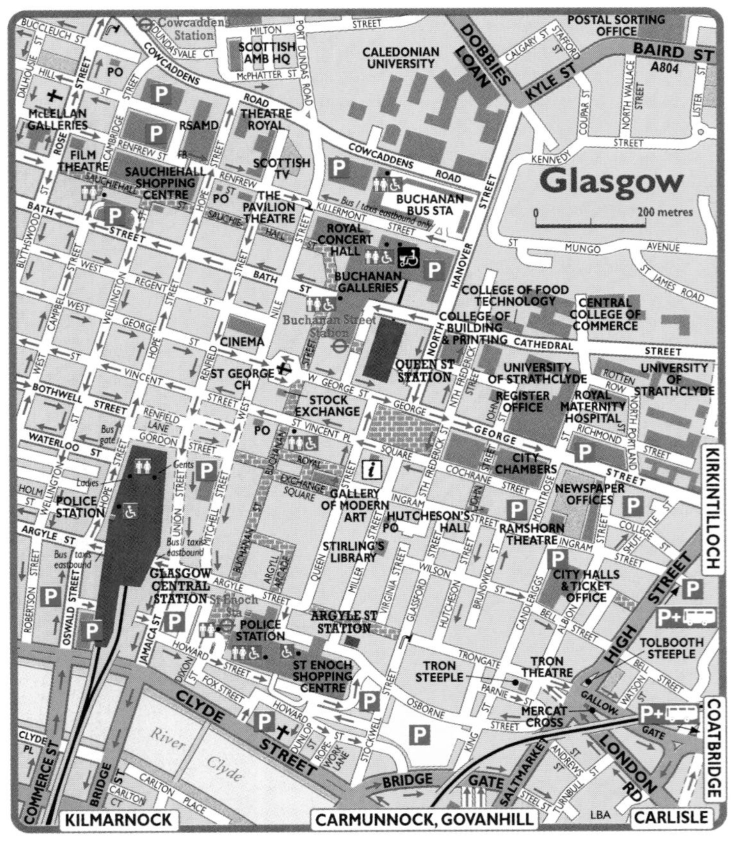
Glasgow
200 metres
KILMARNOCK
CARMUNNOCK, GOVANHILL
CARLISLE
COATBRIDGE
KIRKINTILLOCH
POSTAL SORTING OFFICE
BAIRD ST
A804
CALEDONIAN UNIVERSITY
DOBBIES LOAN
KYLE ST
SCOTTISH AMB HQ
Cowcaddens Station
COWCADDENS
McLELLAN GALLERIES
THEATRE ROYAL
RSAMD
FILM THEATRE
SAUCHIEHALL SHOPPING CENTRE
SCOTTISH TV
BUCHANAN BUS STA
THE PAVILION THEATRE
ROYAL CONCERT HALL
BUCHANAN GALLERIES
Buchanan Street Station
COLLEGE OF FOOD TECHNOLOGY
CENTRAL COLLEGE OF COMMERCE
COLLEGE OF BUILDING & PRINTING
CATHEDRAL
QUEEN ST STATION
UNIVERSITY OF STRATHCLYDE
CINEMA
ST GEORGE CH
STOCK EXCHANGE
REGISTER OFFICE
ROYAL MATERNITY HOSPITAL
CITY CHAMBERS
NEWSPAPER OFFICES
GALLERY OF MODERN ART
HUTCHESON'S HALL
RAMSHORN THEATRE
POLICE STATION
STIRLING'S LIBRARY
GLASGOW CENTRAL STATION
CITY HALLS & TICKET OFFICE
ARGYLE ST STATION
St Enoch
ST ENOCH SHOPPING CENTRE
TRON STEEPLE
TRON THEATRE
TOLBOOTH STEEPLE
MERCAT CROSS
HIGH STREET
CLYDE STREET
River Clyde
BRIDGE GATE
SALTMARKET
LONDON RD
LBA

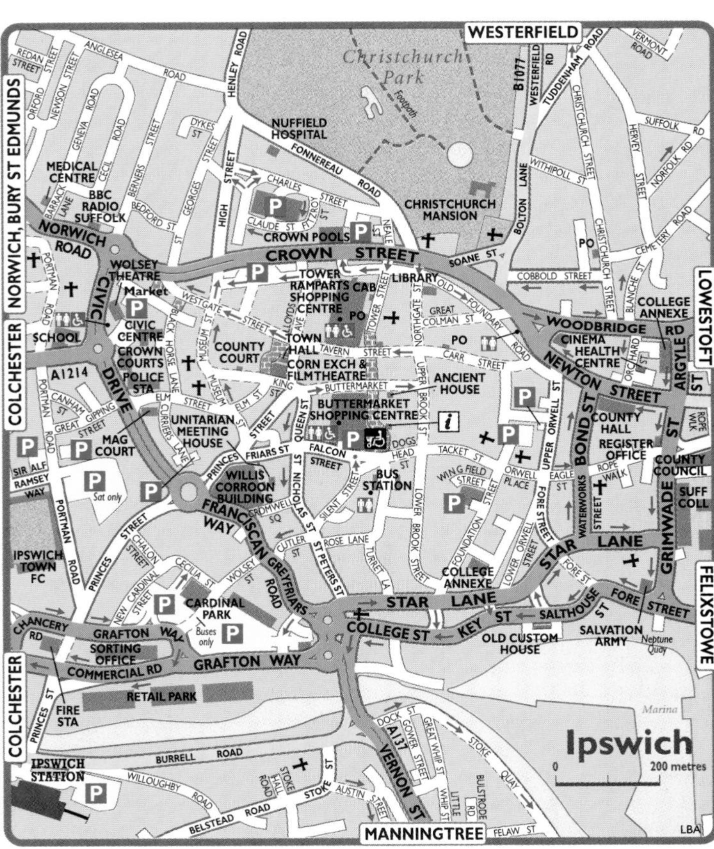
WESTERFIELD
Christchurch Park
NUFFIELD HOSPITAL
CHRISTCHURCH MANSION
MEDICAL CENTRE
BBC RADIO SUFFOLK
CROWN POOLS
NORWICH ROAD
CROWN STREET
WOLSEY THEATRE
TOWER RAMPARTS SHOPPING CENTRE
LIBRARY
SCHOOL
CIVIC CENTRE
CROWN COURTS
POLICE STA
COUNTY COURT
TOWN HALL
CORN EXCH & FILM THEATRE
ANCIENT HOUSE
BUTTERMARKET SHOPPING CENTRE
UNITARIAN MEETING HOUSE
MAG COURT
WILLIS CORROON BUILDING
BUS STATION
CIVIC DRIVE
FRANCISCAN WAY
GREYFRIARS ROAD
IPSWICH TOWN FC
CARDINAL PARK
GRAFTON WAY
SORTING OFFICE
COMMERCIAL RD
RETAIL PARK
FIRE STA
STAR LANE
COLLEGE ST
KEY ST
OLD CUSTOM HOUSE
SALVATION ARMY
COLLEGE ANNEXE
WOODBRIDGE RD
CINEMA
HEALTH CENTRE
NEWTON STREET
COUNTY HALL
REGISTER OFFICE
COUNTY COUNCIL
SUFF COLL
GRIMWADE ST
FELIXSTOWE
LOWESTOFT
COLCHESTER
NORWICH, BURY ST EDMUNDS
IPSWICH STATION
VERNON ST
MANNINGTREE
Ipswich
200 metres
LBA

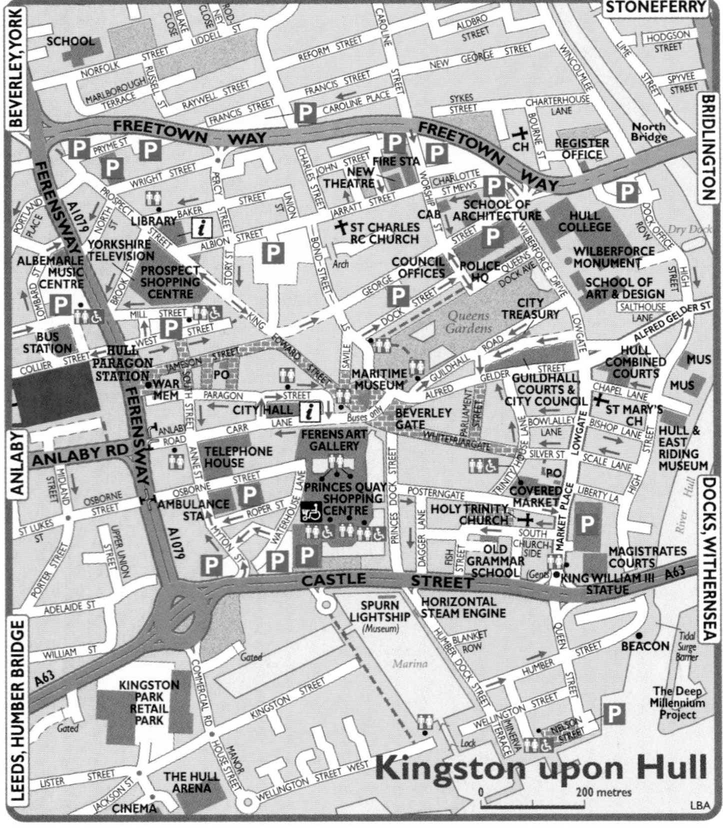
STONEFERRY
BEVERLEY, YORK
BRIDLINGTON
FREETOWN WAY
FIRE STA
NEW THEATRE
REGISTER OFFICE
North Bridge
LIBRARY
ST CHARLES RC CHURCH
SCHOOL OF ARCHITECTURE
HULL COLLEGE
YORKSHIRE TELEVISION
ALBEMARLE MUSIC CENTRE
PROSPECT SHOPPING CENTRE
COUNCIL OFFICES
POLICE HQ
WILBERFORCE MONUMENT
SCHOOL OF ART & DESIGN
CITY TREASURY
Queens Gardens
BUS STATION
HULL PARAGON STATION
WAR MEM
MARITIME MUSEUM
GUILDHALL COURTS & CITY COUNCIL
HULL COMBINED COURTS
CITY HALL
BEVERLEY GATE
ST MARY'S CH
HULL & EAST RIDING MUSEUM
ANLABY
ANLABY RD
FERENSWAY
TELEPHONE HOUSE
FERENS ART GALLERY
PRINCES QUAY SHOPPING CENTRE
AMBULANCE STA
HOLY TRINITY CHURCH
COVERED MARKET
OLD GRAMMAR SCHOOL
MAGISTRATES COURTS
KING WILLIAM III STATUE
CASTLE STREET
SPURN LIGHTSHIP
HORIZONTAL STEAM ENGINE
BEACON
The Deep Millennium Project
KINGSTON PARK RETAIL PARK
THE HULL ARENA
CINEMA
LEEDS, HUMBER BRIDGE
DOCKS, WITHERNSEA
Kingston upon Hull
200 metres
LBA

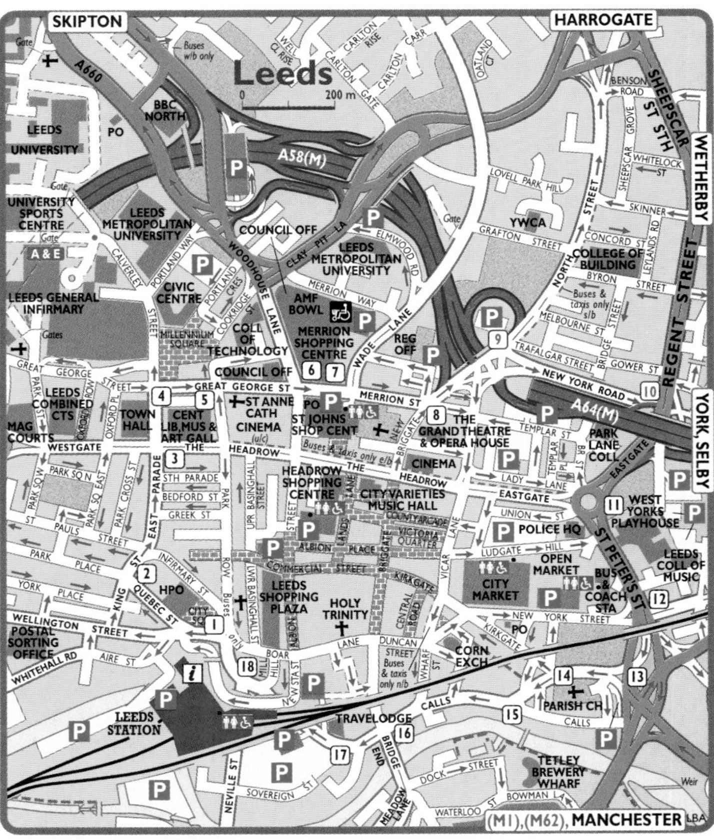
SKIPTON
HARROGATE
Leeds
200 m
A660
BBC NORTH
A58(M)
LEEDS UNIVERSITY
SHEEPSCAR ST STH
WETHERBY
UNIVERSITY SPORTS CENTRE
LEEDS METROPOLITAN UNIVERSITY
COUNCIL OFF
LEEDS METROPOLITAN UNIVERSITY
YWCA
COLLEGE OF BUILDING
A & E
LEEDS GENERAL INFIRMARY
CIVIC CENTRE
COLL OF TECHNOLOGY
AMF BOWL
MERRION SHOPPING CENTRE
REG OFF
COUNCIL OFF
REGENT STREET
YORK, SELBY
A64(M)
LEEDS COMBINED CTS
MAG COURTS
TOWN HALL
CENT LIB, MUS & ART GALL
ST ANNE CATH
CINEMA
ST JOHNS SHOP CENT
THE GRAND THEATRE & OPERA HOUSE
PARK LANE COLL
HEADROW SHOPPING CENTRE
CITY VARIETIES MUSIC HALL
CINEMA
WEST YORKS PLAYHOUSE
POLICE HQ
LEEDS COLL OF MUSIC
OPEN MARKET
CITY MARKET
BUS & COACH STA
HPO
POSTAL SORTING OFFICE
LEEDS SHOPPING PLAZA
HOLY TRINITY
CORN EXCH
PARISH CH
LEEDS STATION
TRAVELODGE
TETLEY BREWERY WHARF
(M1), (M62), MANCHESTER
LBA

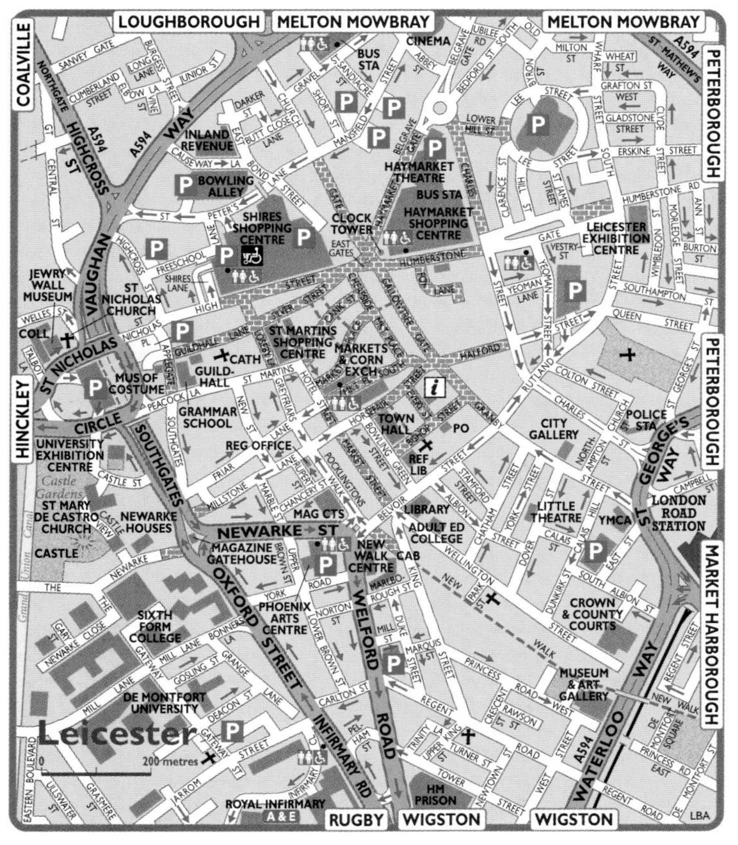
LOUGHBOROUGH
MELTON MOWBRAY
MELTON MOWBRAY
COALVILLE
PETERBOROUGH
PETERBOROUGH
HINCKLEY
MARKET HARBOROUGH
RUGBY
WIGSTON
WIGSTON
CINEMA
BUS STA
INLAND REVENUE
BOWLING ALLEY
HAYMARKET THEATRE
BUS STA
HAYMARKET SHOPPING CENTRE
CLOCK TOWER
SHIRES SHOPPING CENTRE
LEICESTER EXHIBITION CENTRE
JEWRY WALL MUSEUM
ST NICHOLAS CHURCH
COLL
ST MARTINS SHOPPING CENTRE
MARKETS & CORN EXCH
CATH
GUILD-HALL
MUS OF COSTUME
GRAMMAR SCHOOL
TOWN HALL
REF LIB
PO
CITY GALLERY
POLICE STA
UNIVERSITY EXHIBITION CENTRE
REG OFFICE
ST MARY DE CASTRO CHURCH
NEWARKE HOUSES
CASTLE
MAG CTS
LIBRARY
ADULT ED COLLEGE
LITTLE THEATRE
YMCA
LONDON ROAD STATION
MAGAZINE GATEHOUSE
NEW WALK CENTRE
CAB
PHOENIX ARTS CENTRE
SIXTH FORM COLLEGE
CROWN & COUNTY COURTS
MUSEUM & ART GALLERY
DE MONTFORT UNIVERSITY
HM PRISON
ROYAL INFIRMARY
A&E
Leicester
200 metres
LBA
VAUGHAN WAY
HIGHCROSS ST
NEWARKE ST
OXFORD STREET
WELFORD ROAD
INFIRMARY RD
SOUTHGATES
WATERLOO WAY
ST GEORGE'S WAY
CIRCLE
ST NICHOLAS

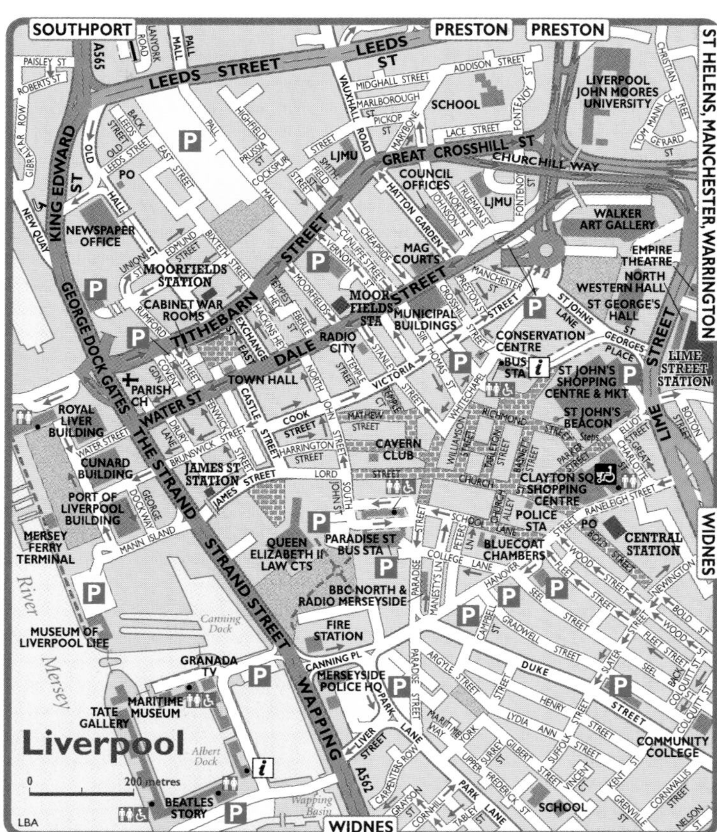
SOUTHPORT
PRESTON
PRESTON
ST HELENS, MANCHESTER, WARRINGTON
WIDNES
WIDNES
LEEDS STREET
KING EDWARD ST
GEORGE DOCK GATES
THE STRAND
STRAND STREET
WAPPING
TITHEBARN STREET
DALE STREET
GREAT CROSSHALL ST
CHURCHILL WAY
LIME STREET
SCHOOL
LIVERPOOL JOHN MOORES UNIVERSITY
LJMU
COUNCIL OFFICES
WALKER ART GALLERY
EMPIRE THEATRE
NORTH WESTERN HALL
ST GEORGE'S HALL
LIME STREET STATION
NEWSPAPER OFFICE
PO
MOORFIELDS STATION
CABINET WAR ROOMS
MOOR FIELDS STA
MUNICIPAL BUILDINGS
MAG COURTS
CONSERVATION CENTRE
BUS STA
ST JOHN'S SHOPPING CENTRE & MKT
ST JOHN'S BEACON
PARISH CH
TOWN HALL
RADIO CITY
ROYAL LIVER BUILDING
CUNARD BUILDING
PORT OF LIVERPOOL BUILDING
JAMES ST STATION
CAVERN CLUB
CLAYTON SQ SHOPPING CENTRE
POLICE STA
CENTRAL STATION
BLUECOAT CHAMBERS
MERSEY FERRY TERMINAL
QUEEN ELIZABETH II LAW CTS
PARADISE ST BUS STA
BBC NORTH & RADIO MERSEYSIDE
FIRE STATION
MUSEUM OF LIVERPOOL LIFE
River Mersey
Canning Dock
GRANADA TV
MERSEYSIDE POLICE HQ
MARITIME MUSEUM
TATE GALLERY
Albert Dock
BEATLES STORY
Wapping Basin
DUKE STREET
COMMUNITY COLLEGE
SCHOOL
Liverpool
200 metres
LBA

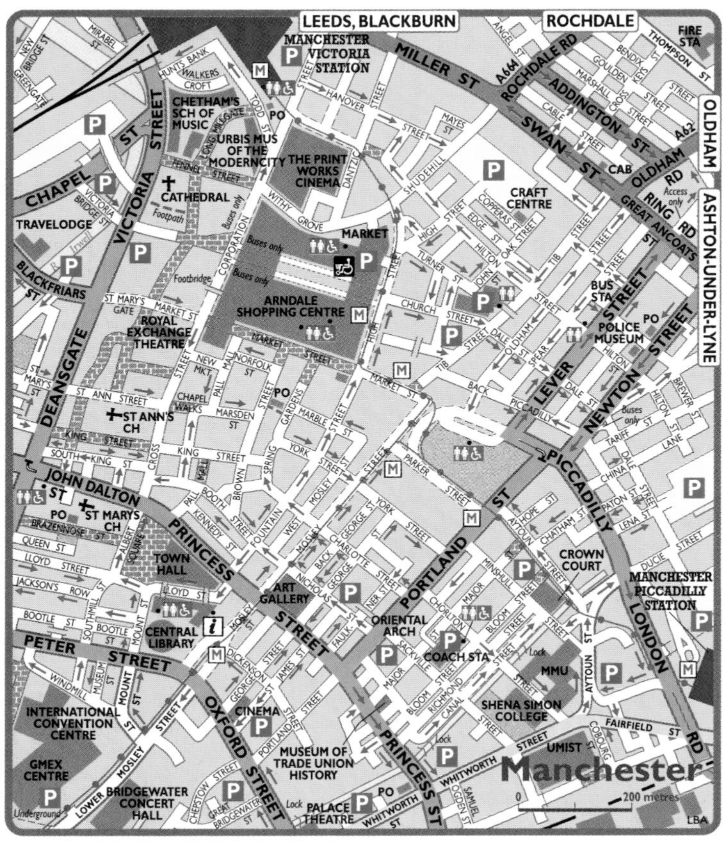
LEEDS, BLACKBURN
ROCHDALE
OLDHAM
ASHTON-UNDER-LYNE
FIRE STA
MANCHESTER VICTORIA STATION
MILLER ST
ROCHDALE RD
SWAN ST
OLDHAM RD
GREAT ANCOATS
RING RD
CHETHAM'S SCH OF MUSIC
URBIS MUS OF THE MODERNCITY
THE PRINT WORKS CINEMA
CRAFT CENTRE
CAB
CATHEDRAL
TRAVELODGE
CHAPEL ST
VICTORIA STREET
BLACKFRIARS
DEANSGATE
MARKET
ARNDALE SHOPPING CENTRE
ROYAL EXCHANGE THEATRE
BUS STA
POLICE MUSEUM
PO
ST ANN'S CH
JOHN DALTON ST
ST MARYS CH
TOWN HALL
ART GALLERY
PRINCESS STREET
PORTLAND ST
PICCADILLY
LEVER STREET
NEWTON STREET
LONDON RD
CROWN COURT
MANCHESTER PICCADILLY STATION
CENTRAL LIBRARY
PETER STREET
ORIENTAL ARCH
COACH STA
MMU
INTERNATIONAL CONVENTION CENTRE
CINEMA
SHENA SIMON COLLEGE
UMIST
GMEX CENTRE
MUSEUM OF TRADE UNION HISTORY
OXFORD STREET
PRINCESS ST
BRIDGEWATER CONCERT HALL
PALACE THEATRE
Manchester
200 metres
LBA

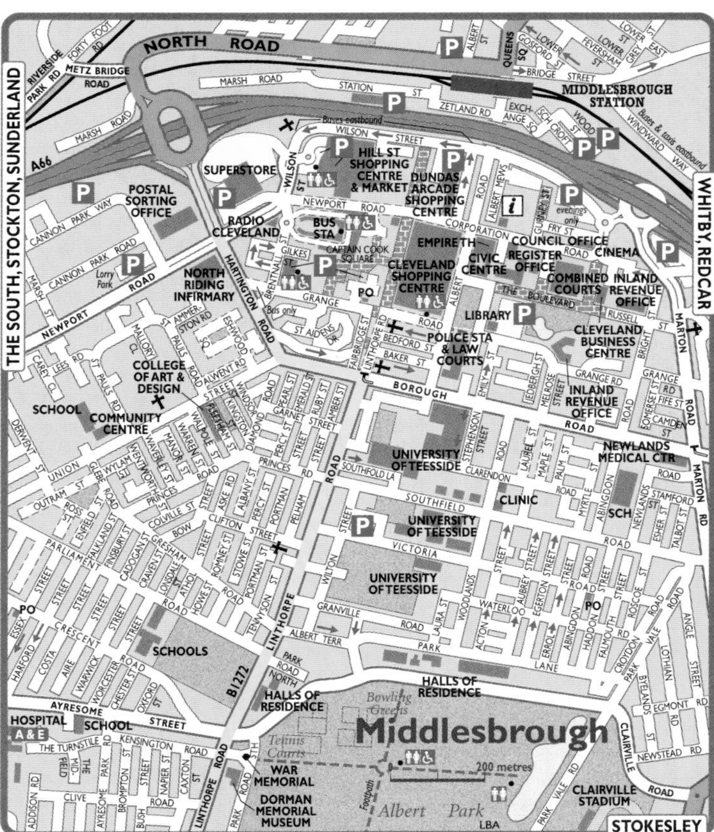
NORTH ROAD
THE SOUTH, STOCKTON, SUNDERLAND
WHITBY, REDCAR
STOKESLEY
MIDDLESBROUGH STATION
HILL ST SHOPPING CENTRE & MARKET
DUNDAS ARCADE SHOPPING CENTRE
SUPERSTORE
POSTAL SORTING OFFICE
RADIO CLEVELAND
BUS STA
CAPTAIN COOK SQUARE
EMPIRE TH
CIVIC CENTRE
COUNCIL OFFICE REGISTER OFFICE
CINEMA
CLEVELAND SHOPPING CENTRE
COMBINED COURTS
INLAND REVENUE OFFICE
NORTH RIDING INFIRMARY
LIBRARY
POLICE STA & LAW COURTS
CLEVELAND BUSINESS CENTRE
COLLEGE OF ART & DESIGN
INLAND REVENUE OFFICE
SCHOOL
COMMUNITY CENTRE
BOROUGH ROAD
UNIVERSITY OF TEESSIDE
NEWLANDS MEDICAL CTR
CLINIC
SCH
UNIVERSITY OF TEESSIDE
UNIVERSITY OF TEESSIDE
PO
PO
SCHOOLS
HALLS OF RESIDENCE
HALLS OF RESIDENCE
HOSPITAL A&E
SCHOOL
AYRESOME STREET
Middlesbrough
200 metres
WAR MEMORIAL
DORMAN MEMORIAL MUSEUM
Albert Park
CLAIRVILLE STADIUM
LINTHORPE ROAD
B1272
MARTON RD
LBA

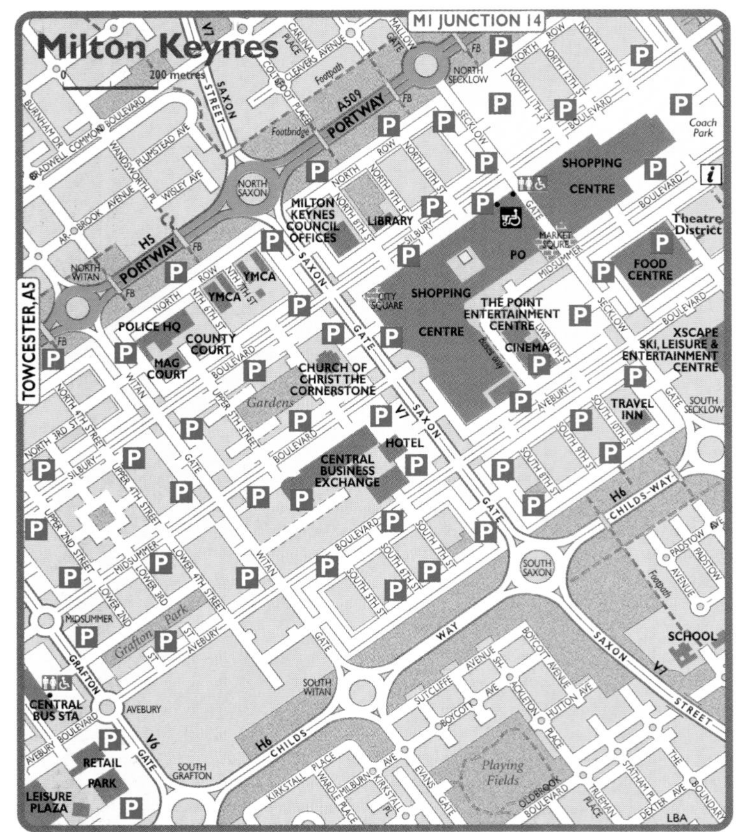
Milton Keynes
200 metres
M1 JUNCTION 14
TOWCESTER, A5
PORTWAY
A509
H5
SAXON
NORTH SAXON
NORTH WITAN
SHOPPING CENTRE
SHOPPING CENTRE
FOOD CENTRE
Theatre District
MILTON KEYNES COUNCIL OFFICES
LIBRARY
YMCA
POLICE HQ
COUNTY COURT
MAG COURT
CHURCH OF CHRIST THE CORNERSTONE
THE POINT ENTERTAINMENT CENTRE
CINEMA
XSCAPE SKI, LEISURE & ENTERTAINMENT CENTRE
TRAVEL INN
HOTEL
CENTRAL BUSINESS EXCHANGE
PO
Gardens
CHILDS WAY
H6
SOUTH SAXON
SCHOOL
V7
SOUTH WITAN
V6
CENTRAL BUS STA
RETAIL PARK
LEISURE PLAZA
SOUTH GRAFTON
Playing Fields
Grafton Park
MIDSUMMER
AVEBURY
LBA

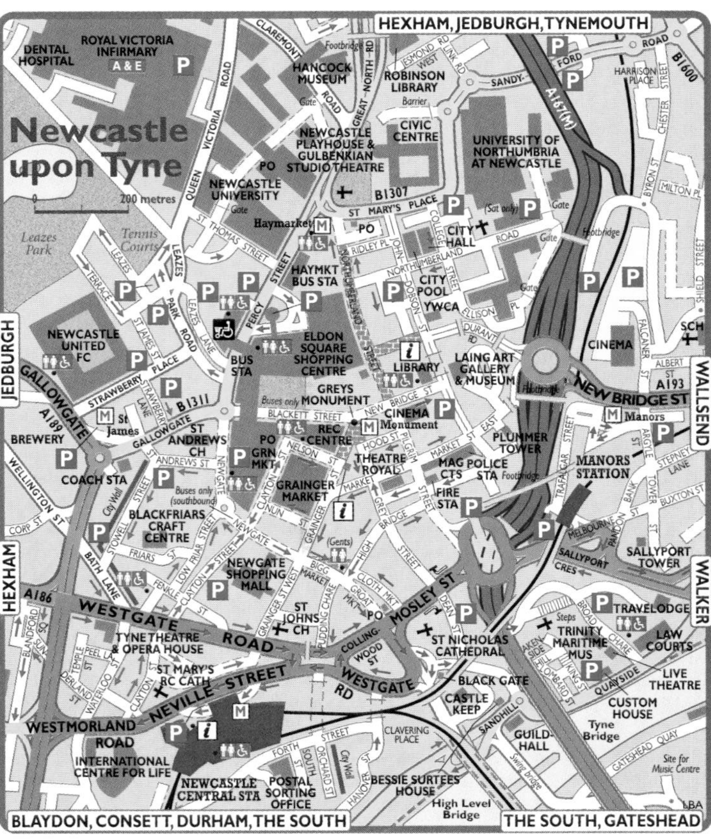
HEXHAM, JEDBURGH, TYNEMOUTH
Newcastle upon Tyne
200 metres
DENTAL HOSPITAL
ROYAL VICTORIA INFIRMARY A&E
HANCOCK MUSEUM
ROBINSON LIBRARY
NEWCASTLE PLAYHOUSE & GULBENKIAN STUDIO THEATRE
CIVIC CENTRE
UNIVERSITY OF NORTHUMBRIA AT NEWCASTLE
NEWCASTLE UNIVERSITY
A167(M)
B1600
B1307
Haymarket
CITY HALL
CITY POOL
YWCA
HAYMKT BUS STA
Leazes Park
Tennis Courts
NEWCASTLE UNITED FC
ELDON SQUARE SHOPPING CENTRE
BUS STA
LIBRARY
LAING ART GALLERY & MUSEUM
CINEMA
NEW BRIDGE ST
A193
Manors
JEDBURGH
GALLOWGATE
A189
BREWERY
St James
B1311
ST ANDREWS CH
GREYS MONUMENT
Monument
CINEMA
REC CENTRE
PLUMMER TOWER
MANORS STATION
WALLSEND
COACH STA
PO
GRN MKT
THEATRE ROYAL
MAG CTS
POLICE STA
FIRE STA
GRAINGER MARKET
BLACKFRIARS CRAFT CENTRE
NEWGATE SHOPPING MALL
SALLYPORT TOWER
HEXHAM
A186
WESTGATE ROAD
ST JOHNS CH
MOSLEY ST
TRAVELODGE
TRINITY MARITIME MUS
LAW COURTS
WALKER
TYNE THEATRE & OPERA HOUSE
ST MARY'S RC CATH
NEVILLE STREET
ST NICHOLAS CATHEDRAL
BLACK GATE
CASTLE KEEP
LIVE THEATRE
CUSTOM HOUSE
Tyne Bridge
WESTMORLAND ROAD
INTERNATIONAL CENTRE FOR LIFE
NEWCASTLE CENTRAL STA
POSTAL SORTING OFFICE
BESSIE SURTEES HOUSE
GUILD-HALL
High Level Bridge
Site for Music Centre
BLAYDON, CONSETT, DURHAM, THE SOUTH
THE SOUTH, GATESHEAD
LBA

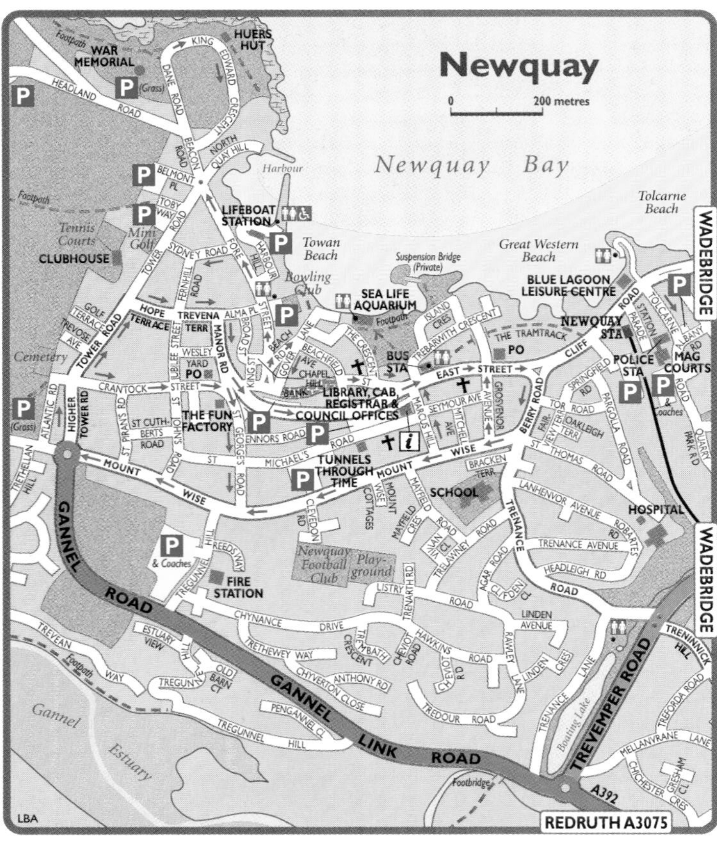
Newquay
200 metres
Newquay Bay
HUERS HUT
WAR MEMORIAL
Harbour
Tolcarne Beach
WADEBRIDGE
LIFEBOAT STATION
Towan Beach
Great Western Beach
Suspension Bridge (Private)
Tennis Courts
Mini Golf
CLUBHOUSE
Bowling Club
SEA LIFE AQUARIUM
BLUE LAGOON LEISURE CENTRE
NEWQUAY STA
Cemetery
BUS STA
PO
POLICE STA
MAG COURTS
LIBRARY, CAB, REGISTRAR & COUNCIL OFFICES
THE FUN FACTORY
TUNNELS THROUGH TIME
SCHOOL
HOSPITAL
FIRE STATION
Newquay Football Club
Play-ground
GANNEL ROAD
GANNEL LINK ROAD
TREVEMPER ROAD
Gannel Estuary
Boating Lake
A392
REDRUTH A3075
LBA

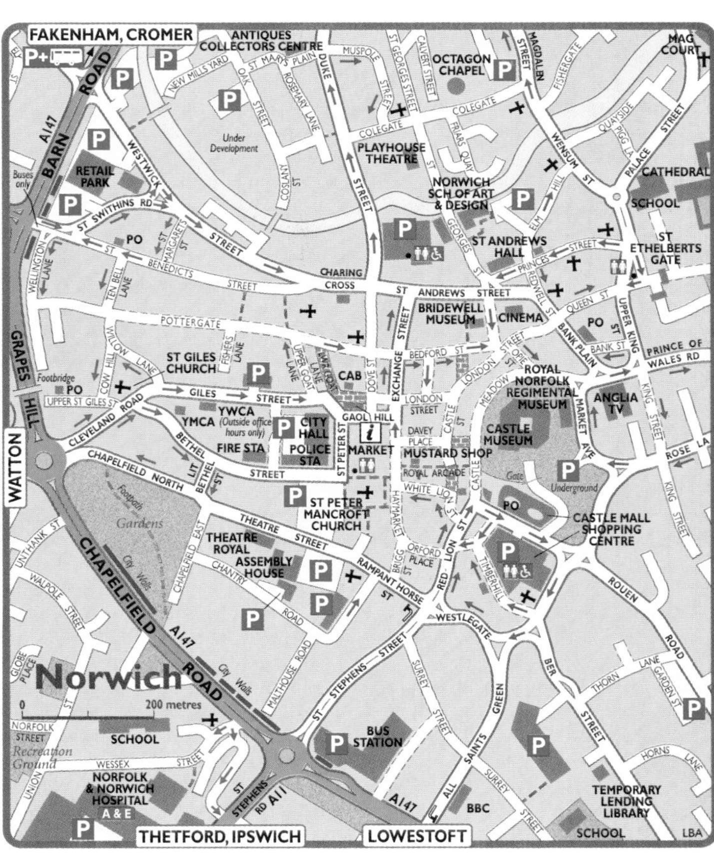
FAKENHAM, CROMER
ANTIQUES COLLECTORS CENTRE
OCTAGON CHAPEL
MAG COURT
A147
BARN ROAD
RETAIL PARK
Under Development
PLAYHOUSE THEATRE
NORWICH SCH OF ART & DESIGN
CATHEDRAL
SCHOOL
ST ANDREWS HALL
ST ETHELBERTS GATE
CHARING CROSS
BRIDEWELL MUSEUM
CINEMA
PO
PRINCE OF WALES RD
GRAPES HILL
ST GILES CHURCH
CAB
ROYAL NORFOLK REGIMENTAL MUSEUM
ANGLIA TV
YWCA
CITY HALL
POLICE STA
FIRE STA
MARKET
CASTLE MUSEUM
MUSTARD SHOP
WATTON
ST PETER MANCROFT CHURCH
CASTLE MALL SHOPPING CENTRE
Gardens
THEATRE ROYAL
ASSEMBLY HOUSE
CHAPELFIELD ROAD
Norwich
200 metres
SCHOOL
Recreation Ground
NORFOLK & NORWICH HOSPITAL A&E
BUS STATION
A11
BBC
TEMPORARY LENDING LIBRARY
SCHOOL
THETFORD, IPSWICH
LOWESTOFT
LBA

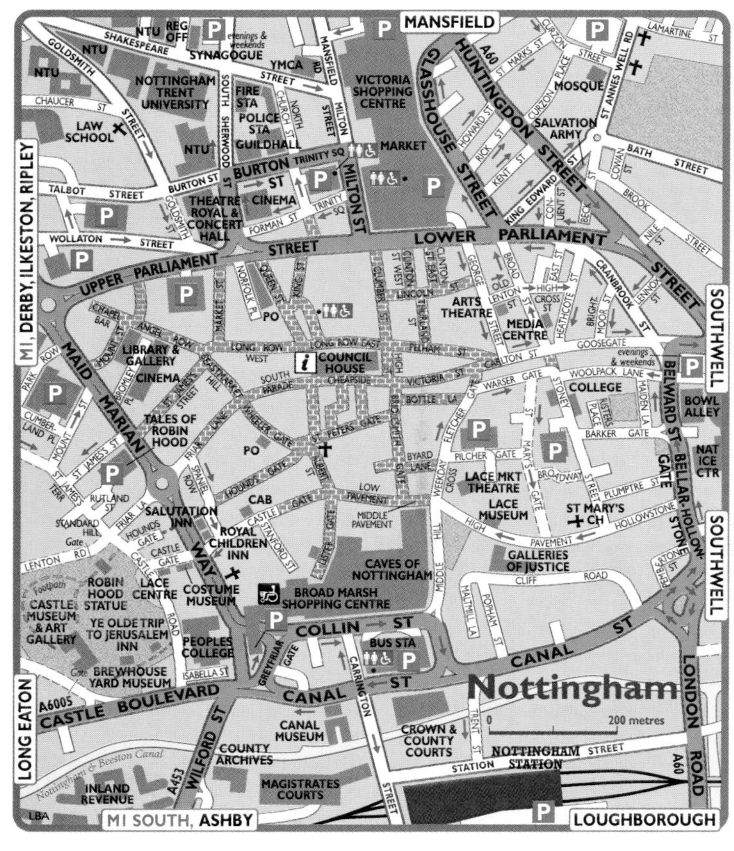
MANSFIELD
Nottingham
200 metres
NOTTINGHAM TRENT UNIVERSITY
VICTORIA SHOPPING CENTRE
UPPER PARLIAMENT STREET
LOWER PARLIAMENT STREET
MAID MARIAN WAY
COUNCIL HOUSE
LACE MKT THEATRE
GALLERIES OF JUSTICE
CAVES OF NOTTINGHAM
BROAD MARSH SHOPPING CENTRE
CASTLE MUSEUM & ART GALLERY
YE OLDE TRIP TO JERUSALEM INN
BREWHOUSE YARD MUSEUM
CANAL MUSEUM
NOTTINGHAM STATION
COUNTY ARCHIVES
MAGISTRATES COURTS
INLAND REVENUE
CROWN & COUNTY COURTS
CASTLE BOULEVARD
CANAL ST
COLLIN ST
LONDON ROAD
SOUTHWELL
M1, DERBY, ILKESTON, RIPLEY
LONG EATON
M1 SOUTH, ASHBY
LOUGHBOROUGH

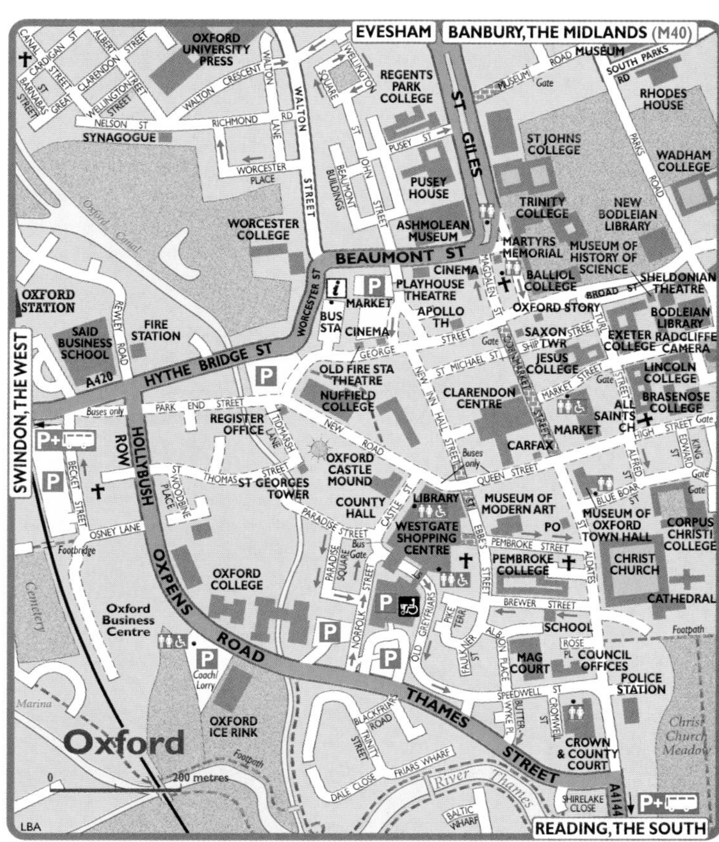
EVESHAM
BANBURY, THE MIDLANDS (M40)
Oxford
200 metres
OXFORD UNIVERSITY PRESS
WORCESTER COLLEGE
ASHMOLEAN MUSEUM
ST GILES
BEAUMONT ST
OXFORD STATION
SAID BUSINESS SCHOOL
HYTHE BRIDGE ST
NUFFIELD COLLEGE
OXFORD CASTLE MOUND
WESTGATE SHOPPING CENTRE
CARFAX
BALLIOL COLLEGE
TRINITY COLLEGE
ST JOHNS COLLEGE
NEW BODLEIAN LIBRARY
SHELDONIAN THEATRE
RADCLIFFE CAMERA
JESUS COLLEGE
EXETER COLLEGE
LINCOLN COLLEGE
BRASENOSE COLLEGE
MUSEUM OF OXFORD TOWN HALL
CORPUS CHRISTI COLLEGE
CHRIST CHURCH
CATHEDRAL
PEMBROKE COLLEGE
OXPENS ROAD
THAMES STREET
OXFORD ICE RINK
CROWN & COUNTY COURT
SWINDON, THE WEST
READING, THE SOUTH

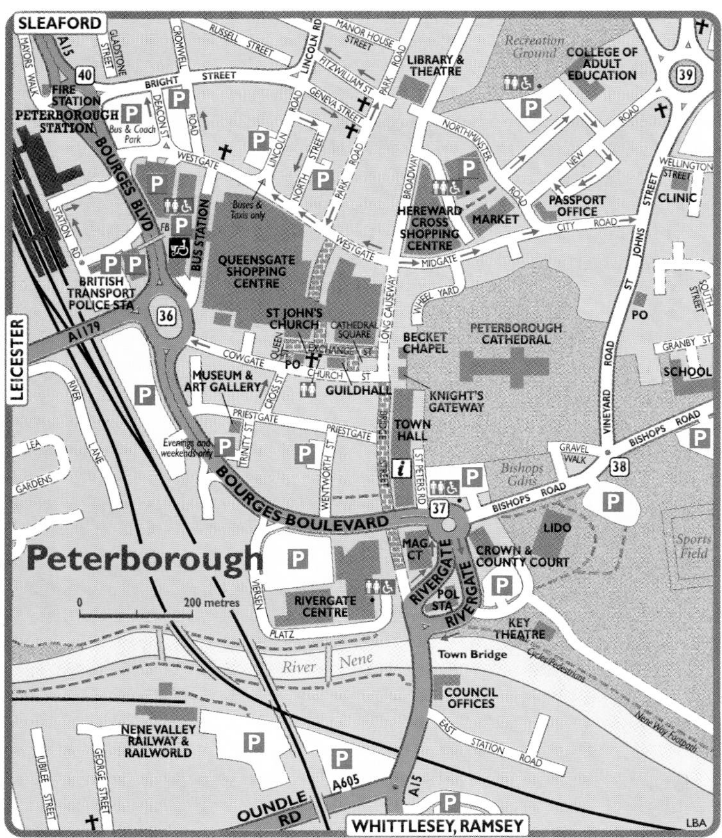
SLEAFORD
Peterborough
200 metres
PETERBOROUGH STATION
QUEENSGATE SHOPPING CENTRE
BUS STATION
BOURGES BLVD
ST JOHN'S CHURCH
CATHEDRAL SQUARE
GUILDHALL
PETERBOROUGH CATHEDRAL
MUSEUM & ART GALLERY
HEREWARD CROSS SHOPPING CENTRE
TOWN HALL
BOURGES BOULEVARD
RIVERGATE CENTRE
CROWN & COUNTY COURT
KEY THEATRE
LIDO
River Nene
Town Bridge
COUNCIL OFFICES
NENE VALLEY RAILWAY & RAILWORLD
OUNDLE RD
LEICESTER
WHITTLESEY, RAMSEY

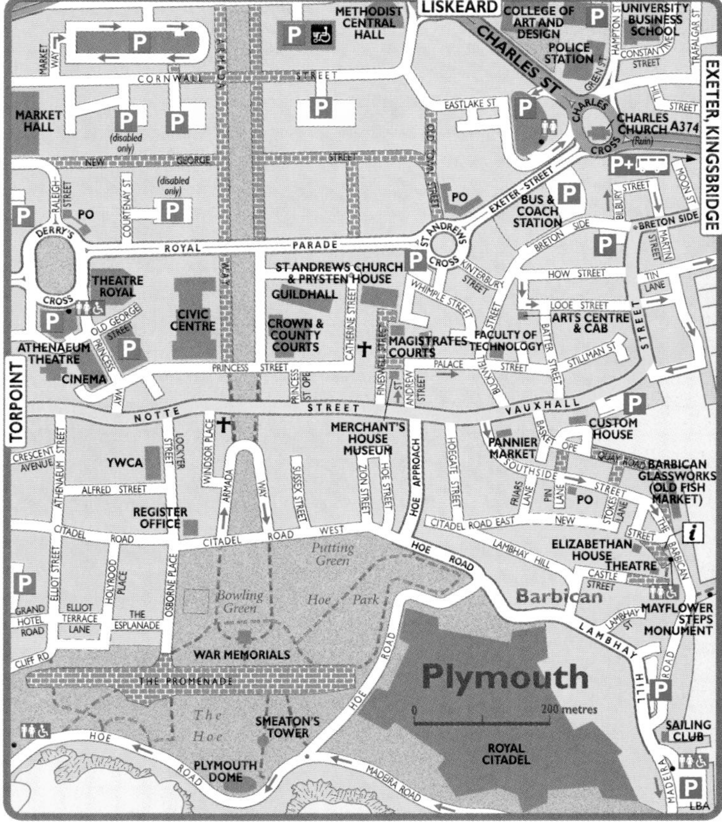
LISKEARD
Plymouth
200 metres
METHODIST CENTRAL HALL
COLLEGE OF ART AND DESIGN
UNIVERSITY BUSINESS SCHOOL
CHARLES ST
CHARLES CHURCH (Ruin)
MARKET HALL
ROYAL PARADE
THEATRE ROYAL
CIVIC CENTRE
GUILDHALL
ST ANDREWS CHURCH & PRYSTEN HOUSE
CROWN & COUNTY COURTS
MAGISTRATES COURTS
ATHENAEUM THEATRE
NOTTE STREET
VAUXHALL
MERCHANT'S HOUSE MUSEUM
YWCA
REGISTER OFFICE
BARBICAN GLASSWORKS (OLD FISH MARKET)
ELIZABETHAN HOUSE
MAYFLOWER STEPS MONUMENT
Barbican
WAR MEMORIALS
THE PROMENADE
The Hoe
SMEATON'S TOWER
PLYMOUTH DOME
ROYAL CITADEL
SAILING CLUB
TORPOINT
EXETER, KINGSBRIDGE

M275, SOUTHAMPTON(M27), CHICHESTER
Portsmouth
200 metres
MARY ROSE SHIP HALL
Historic Dockyard
HMS VICTORY
ACTION STATIONS! EXHIBITION
DOCKYARD APPRENTICE EXHIBITION
ROYAL NAVAL MUSEUM
MARY ROSE EXHIBITION
TICKET OFFICE & WARRIOR EXHIBITION
VICTORY/MAIN GATE
HMS WARRIOR
THE HARD INTERCHANGE BUS & COACH STATION
Passenger Ferry to Gosport
PORTSMOUTH HARBOUR STATION
SPINNAKER TOWER (under construction)
GUNWHARF QUAYS
Portsea
TREADGOLDS MUSEUM
JOHN POUNDS COMMUNITY CENTRE
HMS NELSON
ST JOHN'S RC CATHEDRAL
CATHEDRAL DISCOVERY CENTRE
CASCADES SHOPPING CENTRE
PORTSEA LIBRARY
PORTSMOUTH UNIVERSITY
AVIARY
PORTSMOUTH & SOUTHSEA STA
VICTORIA SWIMMING CENTRE
GUILD HALL
PORTSEA CLINIC
ST GEORGE'S CHURCH
UNIVERSITY
NEW THEATRE ROYAL
CEN LIB
REGISTER OFFICE
NUFFIELD CENTRE (PORTSMOUTH UNIVERSITY)
LAND REGISTRY
WINSTON CHURCHILL AVE
United Services Sports Ground
INDOOR TENNIS CENTRE
HMS TEMERAIRE
Victoria Stadium
ISLE OF WIGHT CAR FERRY TERMINAL
PORTSMOUTH GRAMMAR SCHOOL
Old Portsmouth
FISH MARKET
PRESERVED TRANSPORT DEPOT
ROUND TOWER
PORTSMOUTH GRAMMAR SCHOOL (Main building)
CITY MUSEUM & RECORDS OFFICE
SOUTHSEA COMMUNITY CENTRE
PORTSMOUTH CATHEDRAL
ST JUDE'S YOUTH CTR
SCHOOL
SQUARE TOWER
ROYAL GARRISON CHURCH
THE LONG CURTAIN (OLD TOWN DEFENCES)
Bowling Green
PORTSMOUTH HIGH SCH
SOUTHSEA
EASTNEY
ANGLESEA ROAD
CAMBRIDGE RD
HIGH STREET
BROAD ST
QUEEN STREET
LBA

WALLINGFORD, HENLEY
Reading
200 metres
River Thames
Reading Bridge
Kings Meadow
VASTERN RD
RETAIL PARK
SORTING OFFICE
READING STATION
FIRE STATION
SCHOOL
AUCTION MARKET
AMBULANCE STA
FRIARS WALK SHOPPING CENTRE
TOWN HALL & MUSEUM
FORBURY RETAIL PARK
FORBURY RD
Forbury Gardens
ABBEY REMAINS
ABBEY GATE
PRISON
COUNTY COURT
LIBRARY
BROAD ST MALL SHOPPING CENTRE
HEXAGON
CIVIC OFFICES
MAG CT
POLICE STA
ORACLE SHOPPING & LEISURE CENTRE
CINEMA
QUEENS ROAD
ARTS CENTRE
SCHOOL
LONDON RD
LONDON ST
SOUTHAMPTON ST
CROWN ST
MOUNT PLEASANT
ST DAVIDS HALL
GYOSEI INTL COLL
UNIVERSITY OF READING
THE ABBEY SCHOOL
REGISTER OFFICE
CASTLE HILL
SCH
OXFORD
NEWBURY
MAIDENHEAD, WOKINGHAM
BASINGSTOKE
NEWBURY
ALDERSHOT
LBA

AMESBURY
Salisbury
200 metres
FIRE STATION
SUPERSTORE
CHURCHILL WAY NORTH
CHURCHILL WAY WEST
CHURCHILL WAY EAST
CHURCHILL WAY SOUTH
SWIMMING POOL
BUS DEPOT
SALISBURY DISTRICT COUNCIL
ST EDMUND'S CHURCH (ART CENTRE)
HEALTH CLINIC
SALISBURY STATION
PLAYHOUSE THEATRE
CITY HALL
LIBRARY
BUS STA
MALTINGS SHOPPING CENTRE
CROSS KEYS SHOP CENT
POULTRY CROSS
OLD GEORGE MALL SHOP CENT
HEALTH CENTRE
MOMPESSON HOUSE
HIGH ST GATE
COURTS OF JUSTICE
MALMESBURY HOUSE
ST ANN'S GATE
THE WARDROBE (REGIMENTAL MUSEUM)
THE MEDIEVAL HALL (SECRETS OF SALISBURY)
SALISBURY CATHEDRAL
KINGS HOUSE (SALISBURY & SOUTH WILTSHIRE MUSEUM)
BISHOP'S PALACE (SCHOOL)
SCHOOL
SALISBURY COLLEGE
Queen Elizabeth Gdns
Churchill Gardens
River Avon
Nadder River
YHA
YEOVIL (A30), WARMINSTER, DEVIZES
BASINGSTOKE (A30), MARLBOROUGH
SOUTHAMPTON
BLANDFORD FORUM, RINGWOOD
LBA

THE NORTH, M1, ROTHERHAM
Sheffield
200 metres
BARNSLEY
GIBRALTAR STREET
CORPORATION ST
NURSERY ST
WICKER
LAW COURTS
POLICE STATION
WEST BAR
WEST BAR GREEN
BRIDGE ST
POLICE HQ
MAG COURT
CASTLEGATE
CASTLE MARKET
OPEN MARKET
SHEAF MARKET
CATHEDRAL
NEWSPAPER OFFICES
PARK SQUARE
VICTORIA HALL
ST MARIE RC CATH
POSTAL SORTING OFFICE
PONDS FORGE INTERNATIONAL SPORTS CENTRE
CITY HALL
RUSKIN GALLERIES
CRUCIBLE THEATRE
LYCEUM THEATRE
CINEMA
TOWN HALL
WAR MEM
CENTRAL LIB & GRAVES ART GALLERY
BUS AND COACH STATION
SHU
COUNCIL OFFICES
MILLENNIUM GALLERY & WINTER GARDEN
SHEFFIELD HALLAM UNIVERSITY
REGISTER OFFICE
S YORKS FIRE SERVICE HQ
SHEFFIELD MIDLAND STATION
YORKS TV STUDIO
NATIONAL MUSIC CENTRE
SCHOOL
GLOSSOP
THE SOUTH, M1, WORKSOP
CHESTERFIELD
LBA

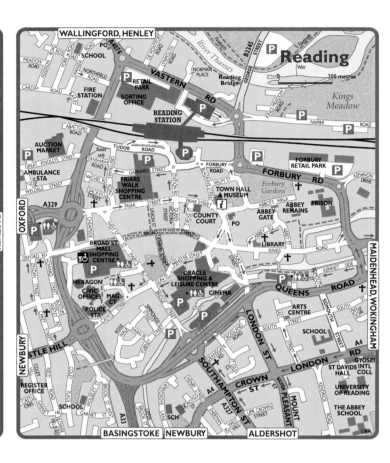

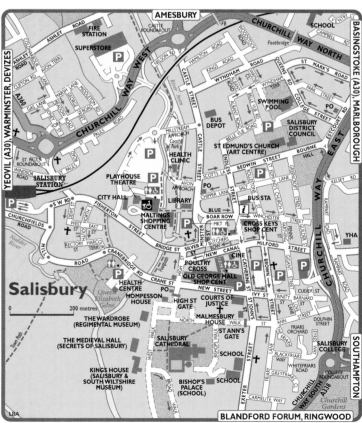

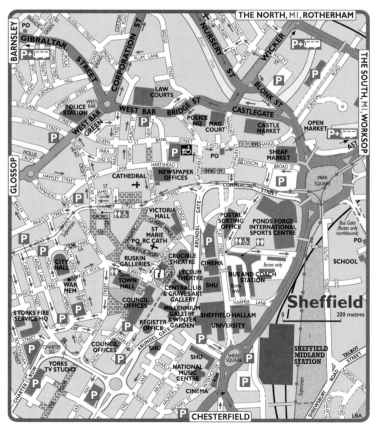

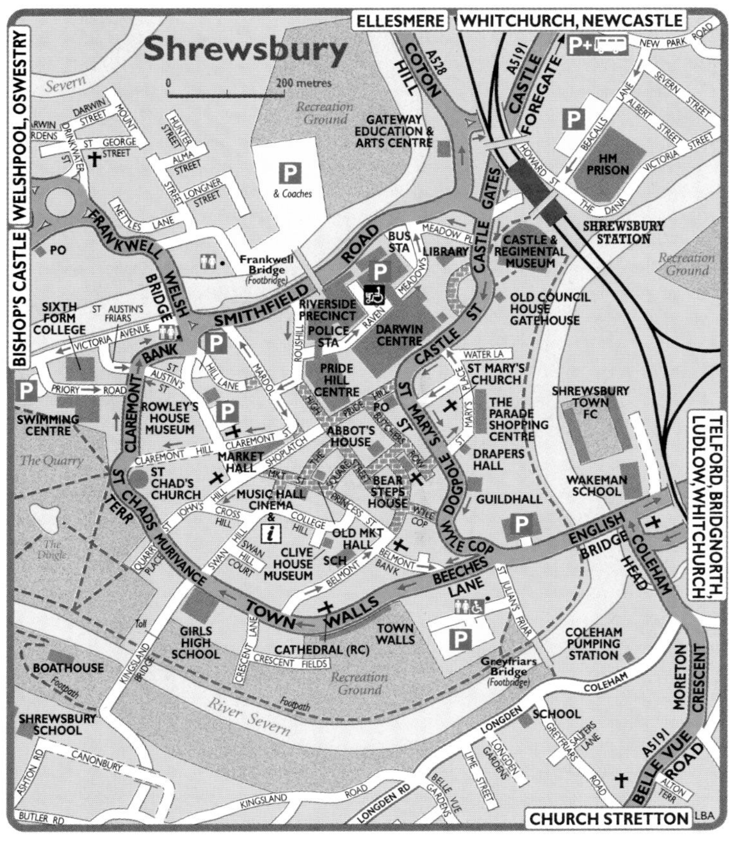
Shrewsbury
200 metres
ELLESMERE
WHITCHURCH, NEWCASTLE
BISHOP'S CASTLE
WELSHPOOL, OSWESTRY
TELFORD, BRIDGNORTH, LUDLOW, WHITCHURCH
CHURCH STRETTON
Recreation Ground
GATEWAY EDUCATION & ARTS CENTRE
HM PRISON
SHREWSBURY STATION
CASTLE & REGIMENTAL MUSEUM
OLD COUNCIL HOUSE GATEHOUSE
LIBRARY
BUS STA
Frankwell Bridge (Footbridge)
RIVERSIDE PRECINCT
POLICE STA
DARWIN CENTRE
PRIDE HILL CENTRE
ST MARY'S CHURCH
THE PARADE SHOPPING CENTRE
SHREWSBURY TOWN FC
SIXTH FORM COLLEGE
ROWLEY'S HOUSE MUSEUM
ABBOT'S HOUSE
MARKET HALL
DRAPERS HALL
SWIMMING CENTRE
The Quarry
ST CHAD'S CHURCH
MUSIC HALL CINEMA
BEAR STEPS HOUSE
GUILDHALL
WAKEMAN SCHOOL
OLD MKT HALL
CLIVE HOUSE MUSEUM
SCH
The Dingle
GIRLS HIGH SCHOOL
TOWN WALLS
CATHEDRAL (RC)
COLEHAM PUMPING STATION
BOATHOUSE
Greyfriars Bridge (Footbridge)
River Severn
SHREWSBURY SCHOOL
SCHOOL
FRANKWELL
WELSH BRIDGE
SMITHFIELD ROAD
CASTLE GATES
CASTLE FOREGATE
COTON HILL
CASTLE ST
ST MARY'S ST
DOGPOLE
WYLE COP
ENGLISH BRIDGE
COLEHAM HEAD
TOWN WALLS
BEECHES LANE
MURIVANCE
ST CHADS TERR
CLAREMONT BANK
MORETON CRESCENT
BELLE VUE ROAD
A5191
A528
LBA

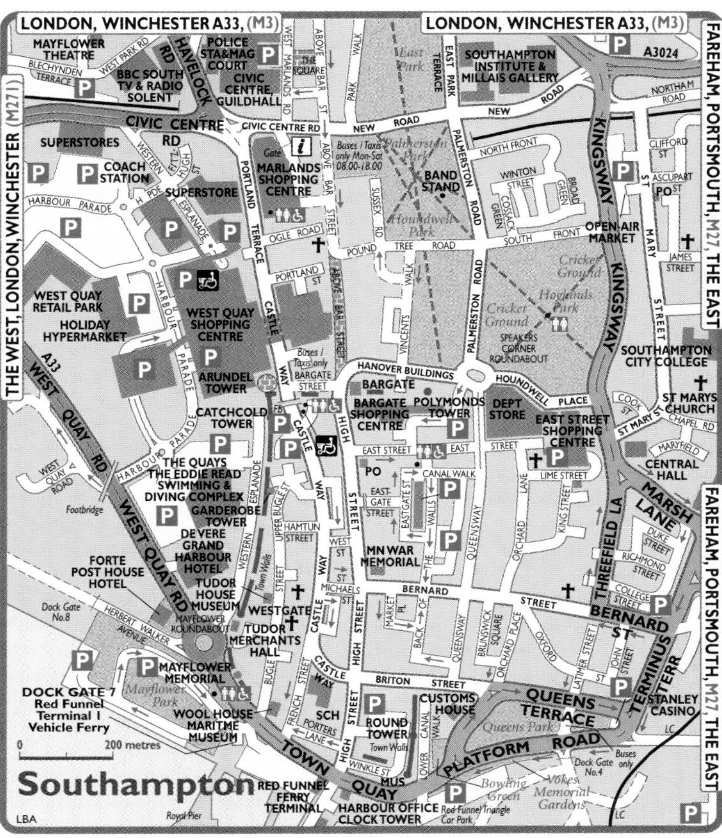
LONDON, WINCHESTER A33, (M3)
FAREHAM, PORTSMOUTH, M27, THE EAST
THE WEST, LONDON, WINCHESTER (M271)
MAYFLOWER THEATRE
BBC SOUTH TV & RADIO SOLENT
POLICE STA & MAG COURT
CIVIC CENTRE, GUILDHALL
SOUTHAMPTON INSTITUTE & MILLAIS GALLERY
East Park
SUPERSTORES
COACH STATION
SUPERSTORE
MARLANDS SHOPPING CENTRE
Buses / Taxis only Mon-Sat 08.00-18.00
Palmerston Park
BAND STAND
Houndwell Park
OPEN-AIR MARKET
WEST QUAY RETAIL PARK
HOLIDAY HYPERMARKET
WEST QUAY SHOPPING CENTRE
Cricket Ground
Hoglands Park
SPEAKERS CORNER ROUNDABOUT
SOUTHAMPTON CITY COLLEGE
ARUNDEL TOWER
BARGATE
BARGATE SHOPPING CENTRE
POLYMONDS TOWER
DEPT STORE
EAST STREET SHOPPING CENTRE
ST MARYS CHURCH
CATCHCOLD TOWER
CENTRAL HALL
THE QUAYS THE EDDIE READ SWIMMING & DIVING COMPLEX
GARDEROBE TOWER
DEVERE GRAND HARBOUR HOTEL
MN WAR MEMORIAL
FORTE POST HOUSE HOTEL
TUDOR HOUSE MUSEUM
WESTGATE
TUDOR MERCHANTS HALL
MAYFLOWER ROUNDABOUT
MAYFLOWER MEMORIAL
Mayflower Park
DOCK GATE 7 Red Funnel Terminal 1 Vehicle Ferry
WOOL HOUSE MARITIME MUSEUM
SCH
ROUND TOWER
CUSTOMS HOUSE
Queens Park
STANLEY CASINO
Southampton
200 metres
RED FUNNEL FERRY TERMINAL
HARBOUR OFFICE CLOCK TOWER
Royal Pier
Bowling Green
Vokes Memorial Gardens
Dock Gate No.4
Dock Gate No.8
KINGSWAY
WEST QUAY RD
TOWN QUAY
PLATFORM ROAD
QUEENS TERRACE
BERNARD ST
THREEFIELD LA
MARSH LANE
TERMINUS TERR
HIGH STREET
CIVIC CENTRE RD
HAVELOCK RD
PORTLAND TERRACE
A33
A3024
LBA

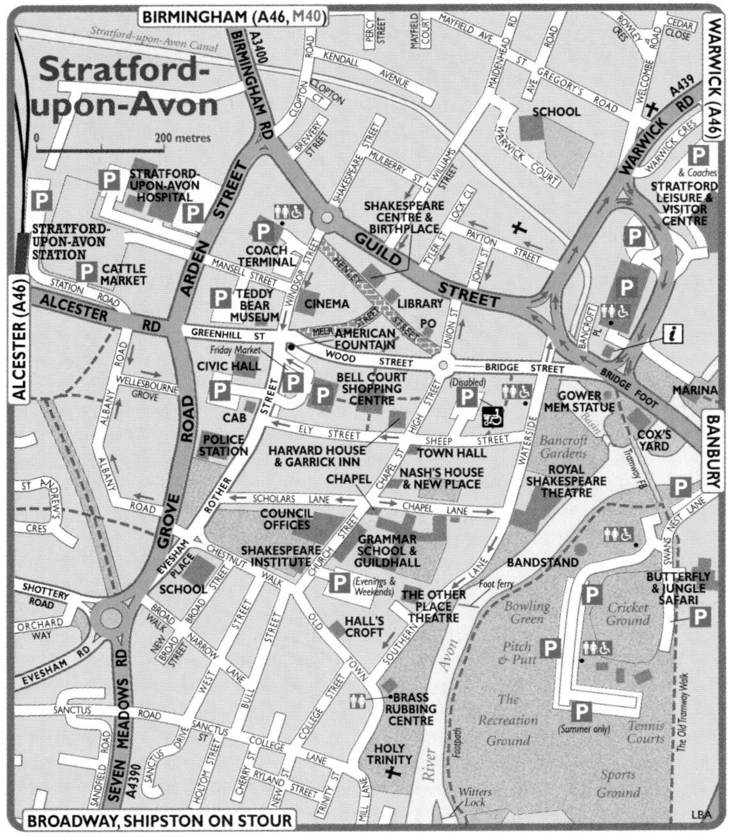
Stratford-upon-Avon
200 metres
BIRMINGHAM (A46, M40)
WARWICK (A46)
ALCESTER (A46)
BANBURY
BROADWAY, SHIPSTON ON STOUR
Stratford-upon-Avon Canal
SCHOOL
STRATFORD-UPON-AVON HOSPITAL
STRATFORD-UPON-AVON STATION
CATTLE MARKET
COACH TERMINAL
SHAKESPEARE CENTRE & BIRTHPLACE
STRATFORD LEISURE & VISITOR CENTRE
TEDDY BEAR MUSEUM
CINEMA
LIBRARY
AMERICAN FOUNTAIN
PO
Friday Market
CIVIC HALL
BELL COURT SHOPPING CENTRE
CAB
POLICE STATION
GOWER MEM STATUE
MARINA
COX'S YARD
HARVARD HOUSE & GARRICK INN
TOWN HALL
NASH'S HOUSE & NEW PLACE
CHAPEL
Bancroft Gardens
ROYAL SHAKESPEARE THEATRE
COUNCIL OFFICES
SHAKESPEARE INSTITUTE
GRAMMAR SCHOOL & GUILDHALL
BANDSTAND
BUTTERFLY & JUNGLE SAFARI
SCHOOL
THE OTHER PLACE THEATRE
HALL'S CROFT
Bowling Green
Cricket Ground
Pitch & Putt
The Recreation Ground
Tennis Courts
BRASS RUBBING CENTRE
HOLY TRINITY
Sports Ground
River Avon
Witters Lock
The Old Tramway Walk
GUILD STREET
ARDEN STREET
BIRMINGHAM RD
ALCESTER RD
GROVE ROAD
EVESHAM PLACE
SEVEN MEADOWS RD
WARWICK RD
BRIDGE STREET
WOOD STREET
A3400
A439
A4390
LBA

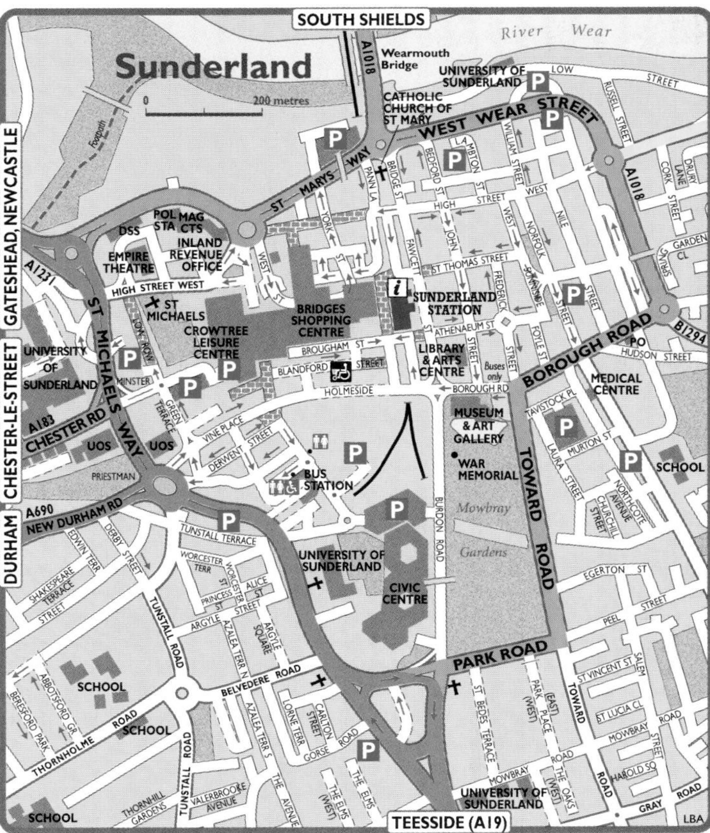
Sunderland
200 metres
SOUTH SHIELDS
GATESHEAD, NEWCASTLE
DURHAM
CHESTER-LE-STREET
TEESSIDE (A19)
River Wear
Wearmouth Bridge
UNIVERSITY OF SUNDERLAND
CATHOLIC CHURCH OF ST MARY
WEST WEAR STREET
ST MARYS WAY
POL STA
MAG CTS
DSS
INLAND REVENUE OFFICE
EMPIRE THEATRE
HIGH STREET WEST
ST MICHAELS
BRIDGES SHOPPING CENTRE
SUNDERLAND STATION
CROWTREE LEISURE CENTRE
UNIVERSITY OF SUNDERLAND
LIBRARY & ARTS CENTRE
BOROUGH ROAD
MEDICAL CENTRE
MUSEUM & ART GALLERY
WAR MEMORIAL
Mowbray Gardens
SCHOOL
UOS
BUS STATION
UNIVERSITY OF SUNDERLAND
CIVIC CENTRE
TOWARD ROAD
PARK ROAD
ST MICHAELS WAY
CHESTER RD
NEW DURHAM RD
SCHOOL
SCHOOL
UNIVERSITY OF SUNDERLAND
SCHOOL
A1018
A1231
A183
A690
B1294
LBA

Swansea
Taunton
Tunbridge Wells
Warwick

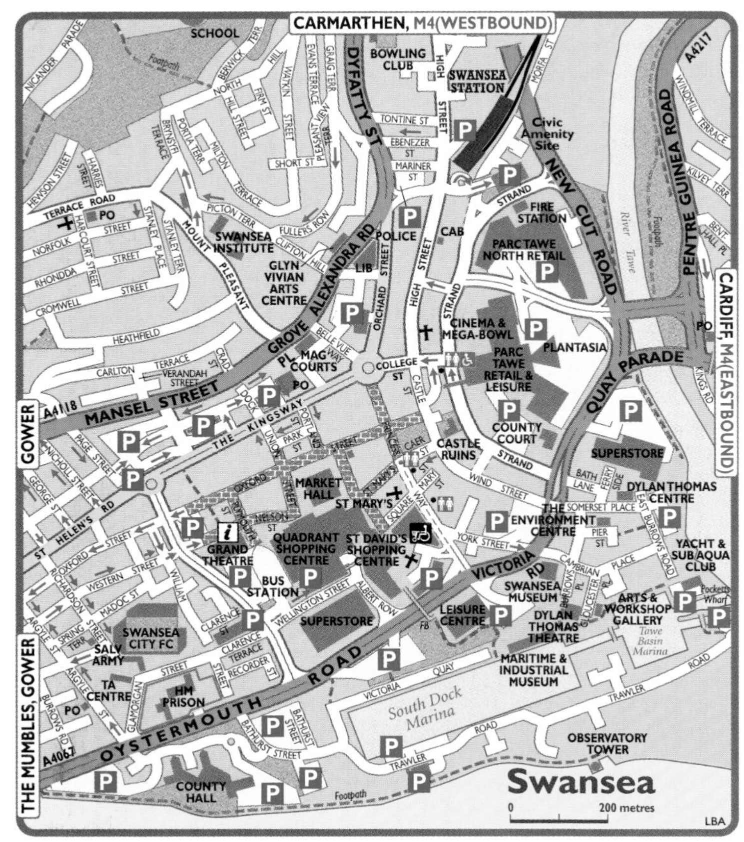
Swansea
CARMARTHEN, M4(WESTBOUND)
CARDIFF, M4(EASTBOUND)
GOWER
THE MUMBLES, GOWER
SCHOOL
BOWLING CLUB
SWANSEA STATION
Civic Amenity Site
NEW CUT ROAD
PENTRE GUINEA ROAD
FIRE STATION
PARC TAWE NORTH RETAIL
POLICE
CAB
SWANSEA INSTITUTE
GLYN VIVIAN ARTS CENTRE
LIB
CINEMA & MEGA-BOWL
PLANTASIA
PARC TAWE RETAIL & LEISURE
QUAY PARADE
MANSEL STREET
MAG COURTS
THE KINGSWAY
COUNTY COURT
CASTLE RUINS
SUPERSTORE
MARKET HALL
ST MARY'S
DYLAN THOMAS CENTRE
ENVIRONMENT CENTRE
GRAND THEATRE
QUADRANT SHOPPING CENTRE
ST DAVID'S SHOPPING CENTRE
YACHT & SUB AQUA CLUB
BUS STATION
VICTORIA RD
SWANSEA MUSEUM
ARTS & WORKSHOP GALLERY
SWANSEA CITY FC
SUPERSTORE
LEISURE CENTRE
DYLAN THOMAS THEATRE
Tawe Basin Marina
SALV ARMY
MARITIME & INDUSTRIAL MUSEUM
TA CENTRE
HM PRISON
OYSTERMOUTH ROAD
South Dock Marina
OBSERVATORY TOWER
COUNTY HALL
Footpath
200 metres
LBA

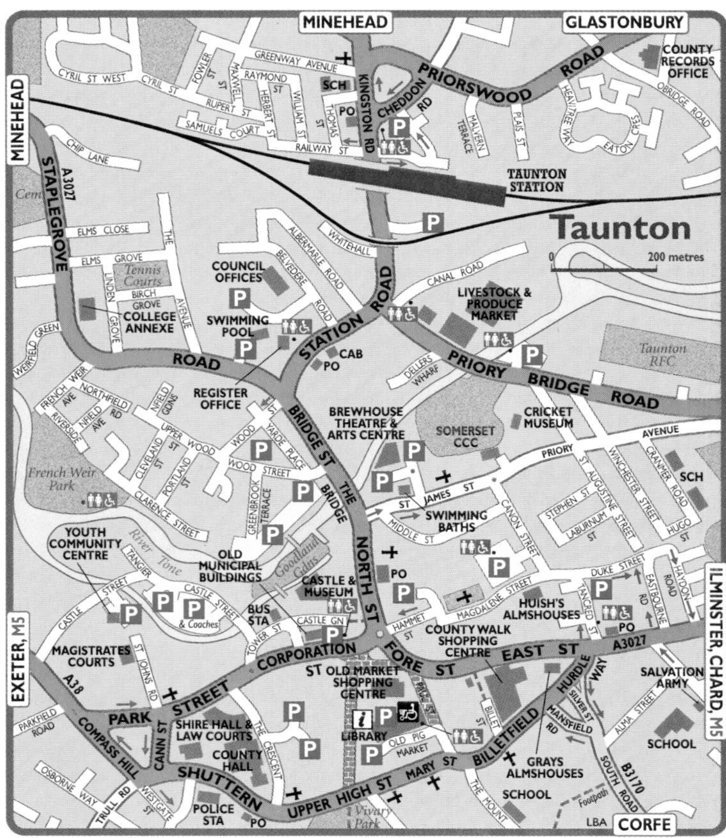
Taunton
MINEHEAD
GLASTONBURY
COUNTY RECORDS OFFICE
PRIORSWOOD ROAD
KINGSTON RD
TAUNTON STATION
STAPLEGROVE
COUNCIL OFFICES
COLLEGE ANNEXE
SWIMMING POOL
STATION ROAD
LIVESTOCK & PRODUCE MARKET
Taunton RFC
PRIORY BRIDGE ROAD
REGISTER OFFICE
CAB
BREWHOUSE THEATRE & ARTS CENTRE
CRICKET MUSEUM
SOMERSET CCC
French Weir Park
BRIDGE ST
NORTH ST
SWIMMING BATHS
SCH
YOUTH COMMUNITY CENTRE
River Tone
OLD MUNICIPAL BUILDINGS
CASTLE & MUSEUM
BUS STA
HUISH'S ALMSHOUSES
MAGISTRATES COURTS
CORPORATION ST
FORE ST
EAST ST
COUNTY WALK SHOPPING CENTRE
OLD MARKET SHOPPING CENTRE
PARK STREET
SHIRE HALL & LAW COURTS
COUNTY HALL
LIBRARY
SALVATION ARMY
GRAYS ALMSHOUSES
SCHOOL
SHUTTERN
UPPER HIGH ST
POLICE STA
Vivary Park
EXETER, M5
ILMINSTER, CHARD, M5
CORFE
200 metres
LBA

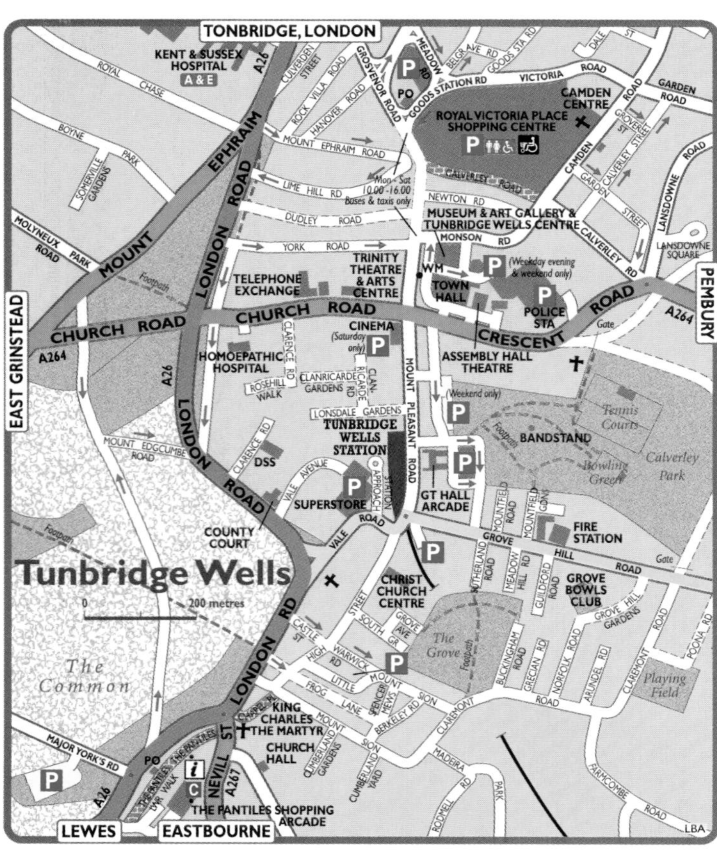
Tunbridge Wells
TONBRIDGE, LONDON
KENT & SUSSEX HOSPITAL
A&E
ROYAL VICTORIA PLACE SHOPPING CENTRE
CAMDEN CENTRE
MUSEUM & ART GALLERY & TUNBRIDGE WELLS CENTRE
TRINITY THEATRE & ARTS CENTRE
TELEPHONE EXCHANGE
TOWN HALL
POLICE STA
CHURCH ROAD
CRESCENT ROAD
CINEMA
HOMOEOPATHIC HOSPITAL
ASSEMBLY HALL THEATRE
TUNBRIDGE WELLS STATION
BANDSTAND
Tennis Courts
Calverley Park
DSS
SUPERSTORE
GT HALL ARCADE
FIRE STATION
COUNTY COURT
CHRIST CHURCH CENTRE
GROVE BOWLS CLUB
The Grove
The Common
Playing Field
KING CHARLES THE MARTYR CHURCH HALL
THE PANTILES SHOPPING ARCADE
LONDON ROAD
MOUNT EPHRAIM
EAST GRINSTEAD
PEMBURY
LEWES
EASTBOURNE
200 metres
LBA

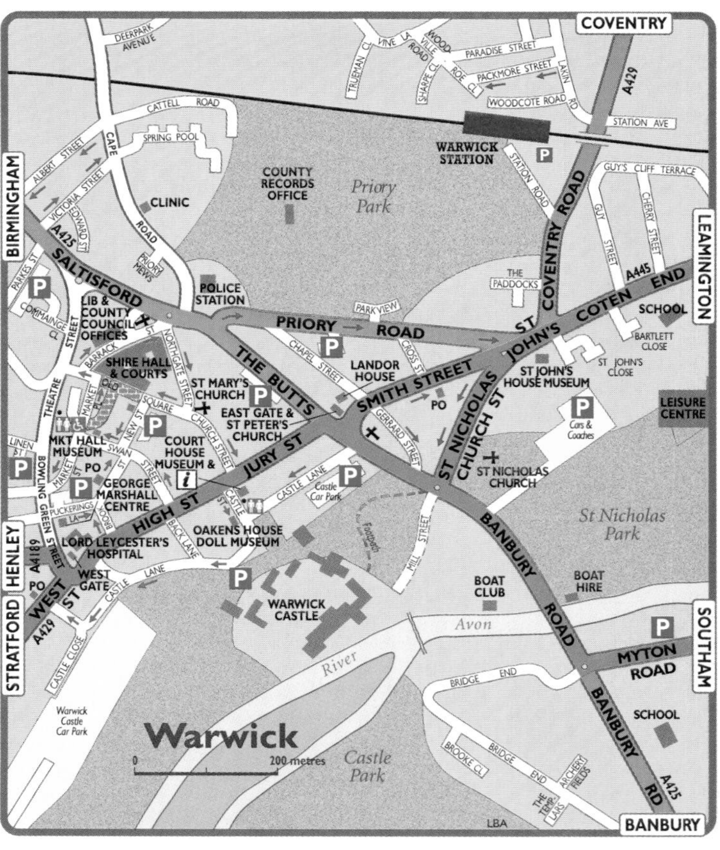
Warwick
COVENTRY
WARWICK STATION
COUNTY RECORDS OFFICE
Priory Park
CLINIC
BIRMINGHAM
LEAMINGTON
SALTISFORD
POLICE STATION
LIB & COUNTY COUNCIL OFFICES
PRIORY ROAD
COVENTRY ROAD
ST JOHN'S
COTEN END
SCHOOL
SHIRE HALL & COURTS
THE BUTTS
LANDOR HOUSE
SMITH STREET
ST JOHN'S HOUSE MUSEUM
ST MARY'S CHURCH
EAST GATE & ST PETER'S CHURCH
LEISURE CENTRE
MKT HALL MUSEUM
COURT HOUSE MUSEUM
JURY ST
ST NICHOLAS CHURCH ST
ST NICHOLAS CHURCH
GEORGE MARSHALL CENTRE
HIGH ST
OAKENS HOUSE DOLL MUSEUM
St Nicholas Park
LORD LEYCESTER'S HOSPITAL
WEST GATE
WEST ST
WARWICK CASTLE
BOAT CLUB
BOAT HIRE
Avon
River
MYTON ROAD
BANBURY ROAD
SCHOOL
Castle Park
STRATFORD
HENLEY
SOUTHAM
BANBURY
200 metres
LBA

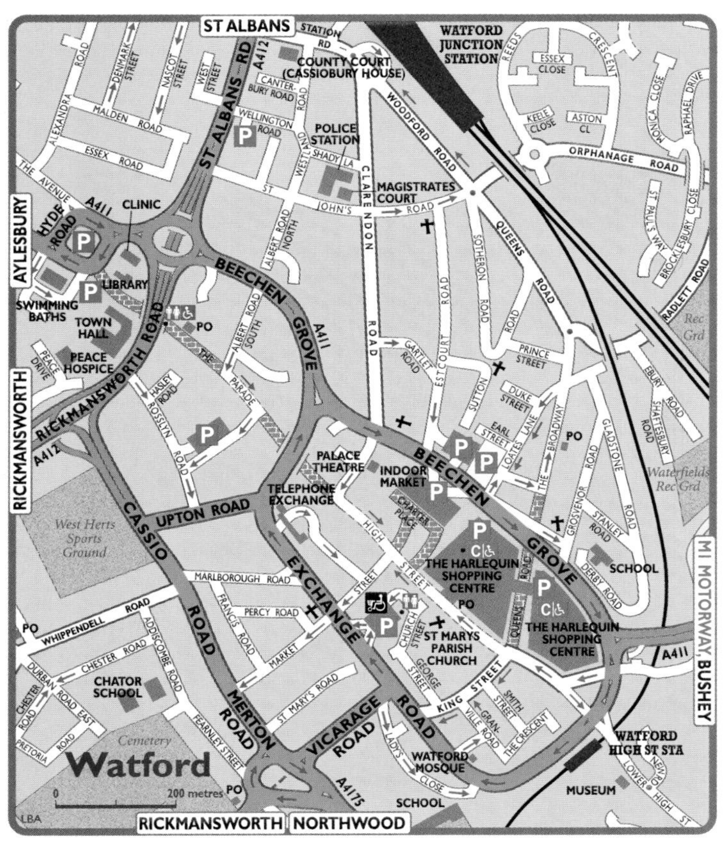
Watford
ST ALBANS
WATFORD JUNCTION STATION
COUNTY COURT (CASSIOBURY HOUSE)
POLICE STATION
MAGISTRATES COURT
ORPHANAGE ROAD
ST ALBANS RD
AYLESBURY
CLINIC
LIBRARY
SWIMMING BATHS
TOWN HALL
PEACE HOSPICE
RICKMANSWORTH
RICKMANSWORTH ROAD
BEECHEN GROVE
CASSIO ROAD
UPTON ROAD
West Herts Sports Ground
PALACE THEATRE
INDOOR MARKET
TELEPHONE EXCHANGE
EXCHANGE ROAD
THE HARLEQUIN SHOPPING CENTRE
ST MARYS PARISH CHURCH
SCHOOL
CHATOR SCHOOL
MERTON ROAD
VICARAGE ROAD
WATFORD MOSQUE
WATFORD HIGH ST STA
MUSEUM
M1 MOTORWAY, BUSHEY
Waterfields Rec Grd
Cemetery
RICKMANSWORTH
NORTHWOOD
200 metres

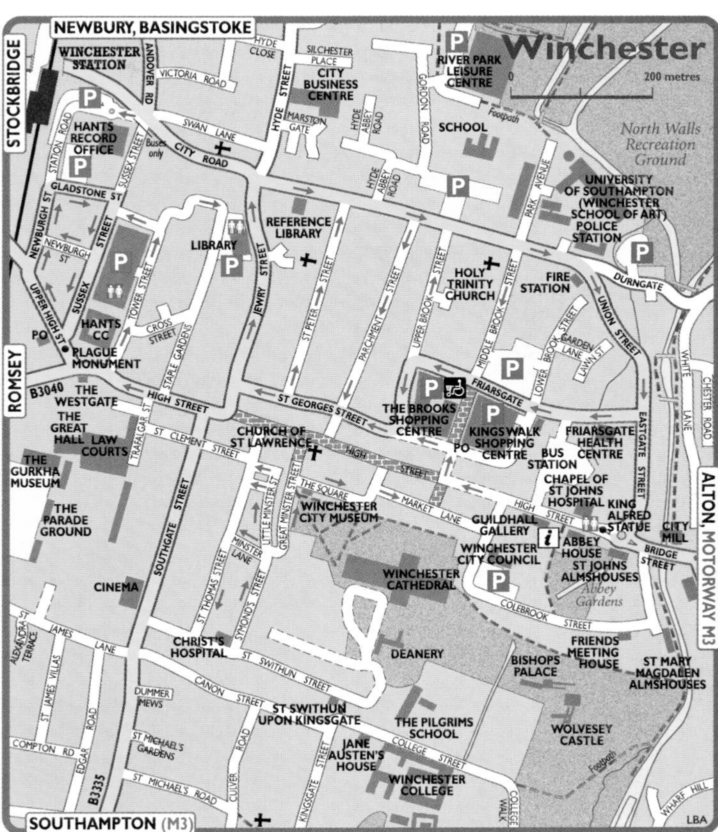
Winchester
NEWBURY, BASINGSTOKE
WINCHESTER STATION
STOCKBRIDGE
HANTS RECORD OFFICE
CITY BUSINESS CENTRE
RIVER PARK LEISURE CENTRE
SCHOOL
North Walls Recreation Ground
UNIVERSITY OF SOUTHAMPTON (WINCHESTER SCHOOL OF ART)
POLICE STATION
REFERENCE LIBRARY
LIBRARY
HOLY TRINITY CHURCH
FIRE STATION
HANTS CC
PLAGUE MONUMENT
ROMSEY
THE WESTGATE
THE GREAT HALL
LAW COURTS
THE GURKHA MUSEUM
THE PARADE GROUND
CHURCH OF ST LAWRENCE
THE BROOKS SHOPPING CENTRE
KINGSWALK SHOPPING CENTRE
FRIARSGATE HEALTH CENTRE
BUS STATION
CHAPEL OF ST JOHNS HOSPITAL
KING ALFRED STATUE
CITY MILL
ABBEY HOUSE
ST JOHNS ALMSHOUSES
Abbey Gardens
GUILDHALL GALLERY
WINCHESTER CITY COUNCIL
WINCHESTER CITY MUSEUM
WINCHESTER CATHEDRAL
CINEMA
CHRIST'S HOSPITAL
DEANERY
BISHOPS PALACE
FRIENDS MEETING HOUSE
ST MARY MAGDALEN ALMSHOUSES
ALTON, MOTORWAY M3
ST SWITHUN UPON KINGSGATE
THE PILGRIMS SCHOOL
WOLVESEY CASTLE
JANE AUSTEN'S HOUSE
WINCHESTER COLLEGE
SOUTHAMPTON (M3)
200 metres

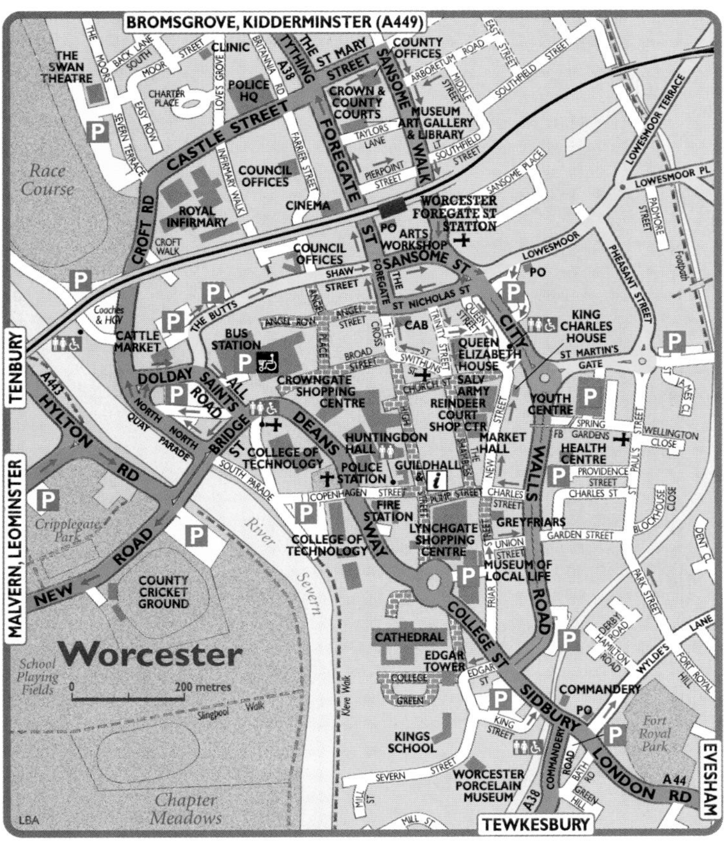
Worcester
BROMSGROVE, KIDDERMINSTER (A449)
THE SWAN THEATRE
CLINIC
POLICE HQ
COUNTY OFFICES
CROWN & COUNTY COURTS
MUSEUM ART GALLERY & LIBRARY
Race Course
CASTLE STREET
COUNCIL OFFICES
ROYAL INFIRMARY
CINEMA
FOREGATE
WORCESTER FOREGATE ST STATION
ARTS WORKSHOP
SANSOME ST
CATTLE MARKET
BUS STATION
KING CHARLES HOUSE
QUEEN ELIZABETH HOUSE
SALV ARMY REINDEER COURT SHOP CTR
CROWNGATE SHOPPING CENTRE
YOUTH CENTRE
TENBURY
HYLTON RD
HUNTINGDON HALL
COLLEGE OF TECHNOLOGY
POLICE STATION
GUILDHALL
MARKET HALL
HEALTH CENTRE
FIRE STATION
LYNCHGATE SHOPPING CENTRE
GREYFRIARS
MUSEUM OF LOCAL LIFE
MALVERN, LEOMINSTER
Cripplegate Park
River Severn
NEW ROAD
COUNTY CRICKET GROUND
CATHEDRAL
EDGAR TOWER
COMMANDERY
Fort Royal Park
KINGS SCHOOL
WORCESTER PORCELAIN MUSEUM
School Playing Fields
Chapter Meadows
SIDBURY
LONDON RD
EVESHAM
TEWKESBURY
200 metres

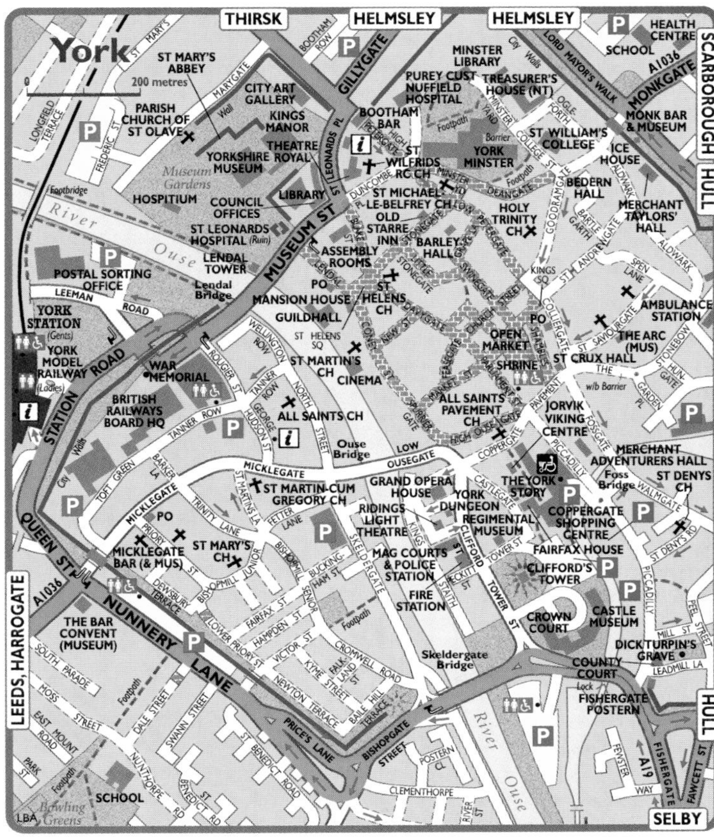
York
THIRSK
HELMSLEY
HELMSLEY
HEALTH CENTRE
SCHOOL
SCARBOROUGH
ST MARY'S ABBEY
CITY ART GALLERY
KINGS MANOR
MINSTER LIBRARY
PUREY CUST NUFFIELD HOSPITAL
TREASURER'S HOUSE (NT)
PARISH CHURCH OF ST OLAVE
THEATRE ROYAL
YORKSHIRE MUSEUM
BOOTHAM BAR
ST WILFRIDS RC CH
YORK MINSTER
ST WILLIAM'S COLLEGE
MONK BAR & MUSEUM
HOSPITIUM
COUNCIL OFFICES
LIBRARY
ST MICHAEL-LE-BELFREY CH
OLD STARRE INN
HOLY TRINITY CH
BEDERN HALL
MERCHANT TAYLORS' HALL
ST LEONARDS HOSPITAL (Ruin)
LENDAL TOWER
ASSEMBLY ROOMS
BARLEY HALL
POSTAL SORTING OFFICE
River Ouse
MANSION HOUSE
GUILDHALL
ST HELENS CH
YORK STATION
YORK MODEL RAILWAY
WAR MEMORIAL
ST MARTIN'S CH
CINEMA
OPEN MARKET
SHRINE
ST CRUX HALL
THE ARC (MUS)
AMBULANCE STATION
BRITISH RAILWAYS BOARD HQ
ALL SAINTS CH
ALL SAINTS PAVEMENT CH
JORVIK VIKING CENTRE
MERCHANT ADVENTURERS HALL
ST DENYS CH
ST MARTIN-CUM GREGORY CH
GRAND OPERA HOUSE
YORK DUNGEON
RIDINGS LIGHT THEATRE
REGIMENTAL MUSEUM
THE YORK STORY
COPPERGATE SHOPPING CENTRE
FAIRFAX HOUSE
MICKLEGATE BAR (& MUS)
ST MARY'S CH
MAG COURTS & POLICE STATION
FIRE STATION
CLIFFORD'S TOWER
CASTLE MUSEUM
CROWN COURT
THE BAR CONVENT (MUSEUM)
NUNNERY LANE
LEEDS, HARROGATE
Skeldergate Bridge
DICK TURPIN'S GRAVE
COUNTY COURT
FISHERGATE POSTERN
HULL
HULL
SCHOOL
SELBY
200 metres

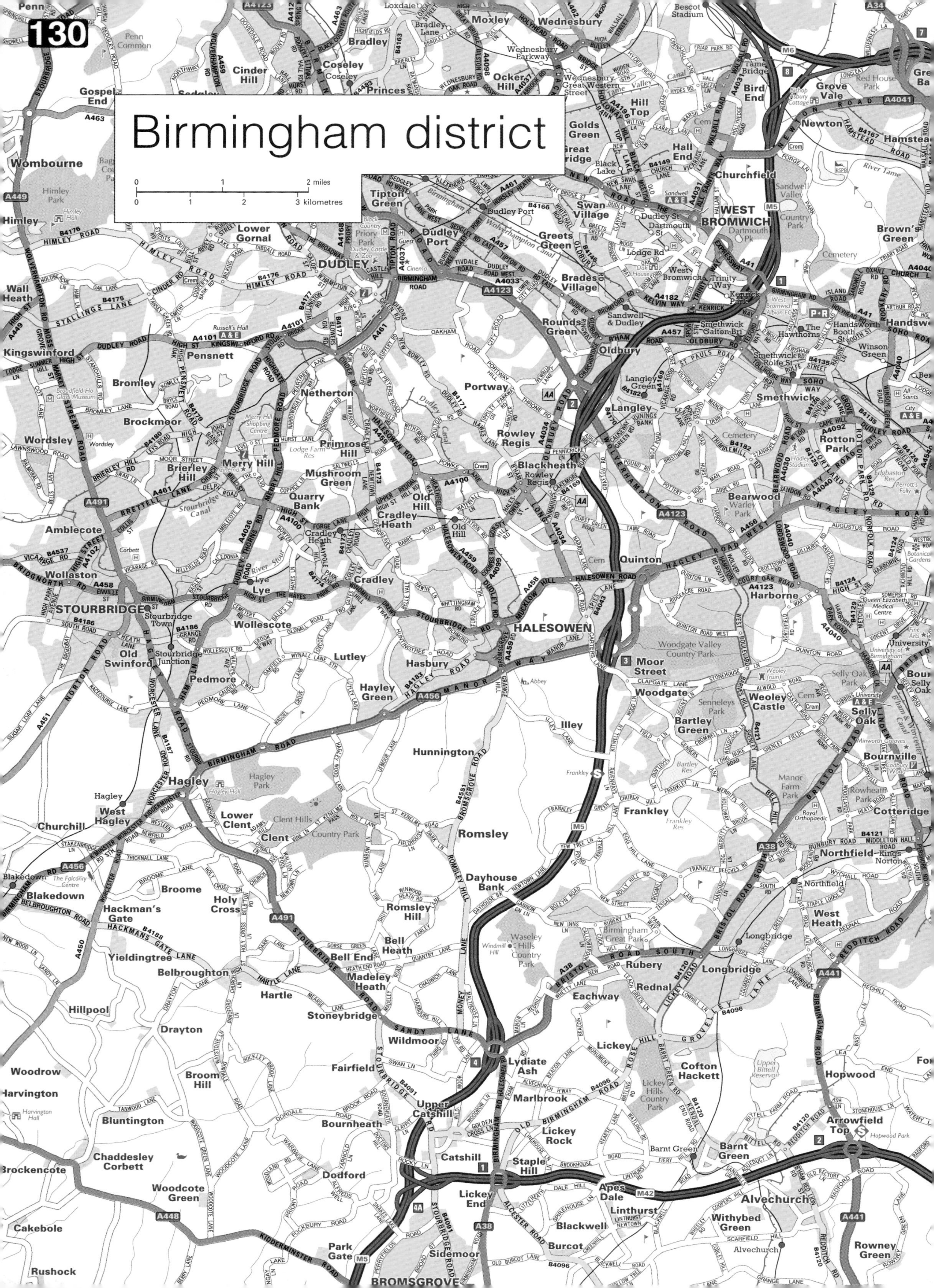

Birmingham district
0 1 2 miles
0 1 2 3 kilometres
Penn
Penn Common
Moxley
Wednesbury
Bescot Stadium
Bradley Lane
Bradley
Coseley
Cinder Hill
Princes End
Ocker Hill
Wednesbury Parkway
Wednesbury Great Western Street
Tame Bridge
Bird End
Grove Vale
Red House Park
Newton
Hamstead
Gospel End
Sedgley
Hill Top
Golds Green
Great Bridge
Black Lake
Hall End
Churchfield
Sandwell Valley
River Tame
Wombourne
Himley Park
Himley
Himley Hall
Tipton Green
Dudley Port
Swan Village
WEST BROMWICH
Dudley St
Dartmouth St
Dartmouth Pk
Country Park
Brown's Green
Lower Gornal
Black Country
Priory Park
Dudley Castle & Zoo
DUDLEY
Greets Green
Lodge Rd
West Bromwich
Trinity Way
Kenrick Park
Cemetery
Wall Heath
Brades Village
Rounds Green
Sandwell & Dudley
Smethwick Galton Bri
The Hawthorns
Handsworth Booth St
Handsworth
Winson Green
Kingswinford
Russell's Hall
Pensnett
Oldbury
Langley Green
Smethwick Rolfe St
Bromley
Broadfield Ho Glass Museum
Netherton
Portway
Smethwick
Brockmoor
Merry Hill Shopping Centre
Langley
Wordsley
Primrose Hill
Rowley Regis
Lodge Farm Res
Cemetery
Rotton Park
Merry Hill
Brierley Hill
Mushroom Green
Blackheath
Rowley Regis
Hadley Stadium
Edgbaston Res
Stourbridge Canal
Quarry Bank
Old Hill
Bearwood
Warley Park
Amblecote
Cradley Heath
Old Hill
Corbett
Quinton
Botanical Gardens
Wollaston
River Stour
Lye
Cradley
Harborne
STOURBRIDGE
Stourbridge Town
Queen Elizabeth Medical Centre
Wollescote
HALESOWEN
University of Birmingham
Old Swinford
Stourbridge Junction
Lutley
Woodgate Valley Country Park
Moor Street
Hasbury
Pedmore
Hayley Green
Abbey
Woodgate
Weoley Castle
Senneleys Park
Selly Oak Park
Selly Oak
Illey
Bartley Green
Hunnington
Bartley Res
Bournville
Frankley
Cadbury World
Hagley
Hagley Park
Hagley Hall
Manor Farm Park
Rowheath Park
Cotteridge
West Hagley
Lower Clent
Clent Hills Country Park
Frankley
Royal Orthopaedic
Churchill
Clent
Romsley
Frankley Res
Northfield
Kings Norton
Blakedown
The Falconry Centre
Dayhouse Bank
Northfield
Broome
Blakedown
Holy Cross
Hackman's Gate
Romsley Hill
West Heath
Birmingham Great Park
Bell Heath
Waseley Hills Country Park
Windmill Hill
Longbridge
Yieldingtree
Bell End
Rubery
Belbroughton
Madeley Heath
Longbridge
Rednal
Hartle
Eachway
Hillpool
Stoneybridge
Drayton
Wildmoor
Lickey
Cofton Hackett
Woodrow
Lydiate Ash
Fairfield
Broom Hill
Upper Bittell Reservoir
Hopwood
Harvington
Harvington Hall
Lickey Hills Country Park
Marlbrook
Upper Catshill
Bluntington
Bournheath
Lickey Rock
Arrowfield Top
Hopwood Park
Barnt Green
Barnt Green
Chaddesley Corbett
Catshill
Staple Hill
Brockencote
Dodford
Apes Dale
Alvechurch
Woodcote Green
Lickey End
Linthurst
Withybed Green
Blackwell
Cakebole
Alvechurch
Park Gate
Sidemoor
Burcot
Rowney Green
Rushock
BROMSGROVE

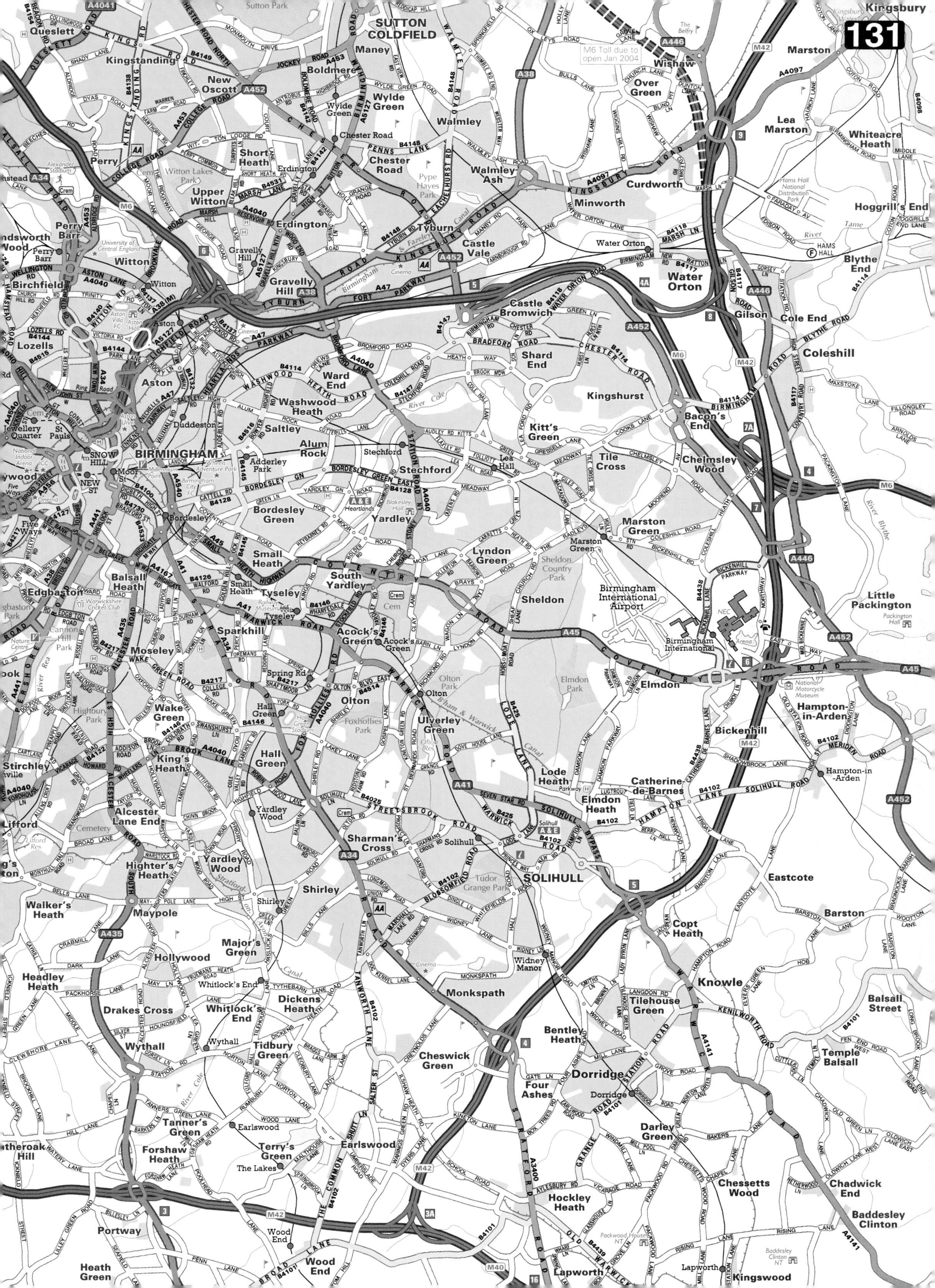

Kingsbury
Sutton Park
SUTTON COLDFIELD
Queslett
Maney
Kingstanding
Boldmere
New Oscott
Wylde Green
Over Green
Wishaw
Marston
M6 Toll due to open Jan 2004
The Belfry
Walmley
Lea Marston
Whiteacre Heath
Perry
Short Heath
Chester Road
Walmley Ash
Curdworth
Upper Witton
Erdington
Minworth
Hoggrill's End
Perry Barr
Tyburn
Castle Vale
Water Orton
Witton
Gravelly Hill
Blythe End
Birchfield
Castle Bromwich
Gilson
Cole End
Lozells
Shard End
Coleshill
Aston
Ward End
Kingshurst
Washwood Heath
Bacon's End
Saltley
Kitt's Green
Jewellery Quarter
St Pauls
Duddeston
Alum Rock
Stechford
Lea Hall
Tile Cross
Chelmsley Wood
BIRMINGHAM
Adderley Park
Bordesley Green
Yardley
Marston Green
Five Ways
Bordesley
Small Heath
Lyndon Green
Edgbaston
Balsall Heath
South Yardley
Tyseley
Sheldon
Birmingham International Airport
Little Packington
Sparkhill
Acock's Green
Birmingham International
Moseley
Elmdon
Hampton-in-Arden
Wake Green
Hall Green
Olton
Ulverley Green
Bickenhill
King's Heath
Lode Heath
Catherine-de-Barnes
Alcester Lane End
Yardley Wood
Elmdon Heath
Lifford
Sharman's Cross
Solihull
SOLIHULL
Highter's Heath
Shirley
Eastcote
Walker's Heath
Maypole
Barston
Copt Heath
Major's Green
Hollywood
Widney Manor
Headley Heath
Whitlock's End
Dickens Heath
Monkspath
Knowle
Balsall Street
Drakes Cross
Tilehouse Green
Bentley Heath
Wythall
Tidbury Green
Cheswick Green
Temple Balsall
Dorridge
Four Ashes
Tanner's Green
Earlswood
Darley Green
Forshaw Heath
Terry's Green
The Lakes
Chessetts Wood
Chadwick End
Hockley Heath
Portway
Wood End
Baddesley Clinton
Heath Green
Lapworth
Kingswood

Glasgow district

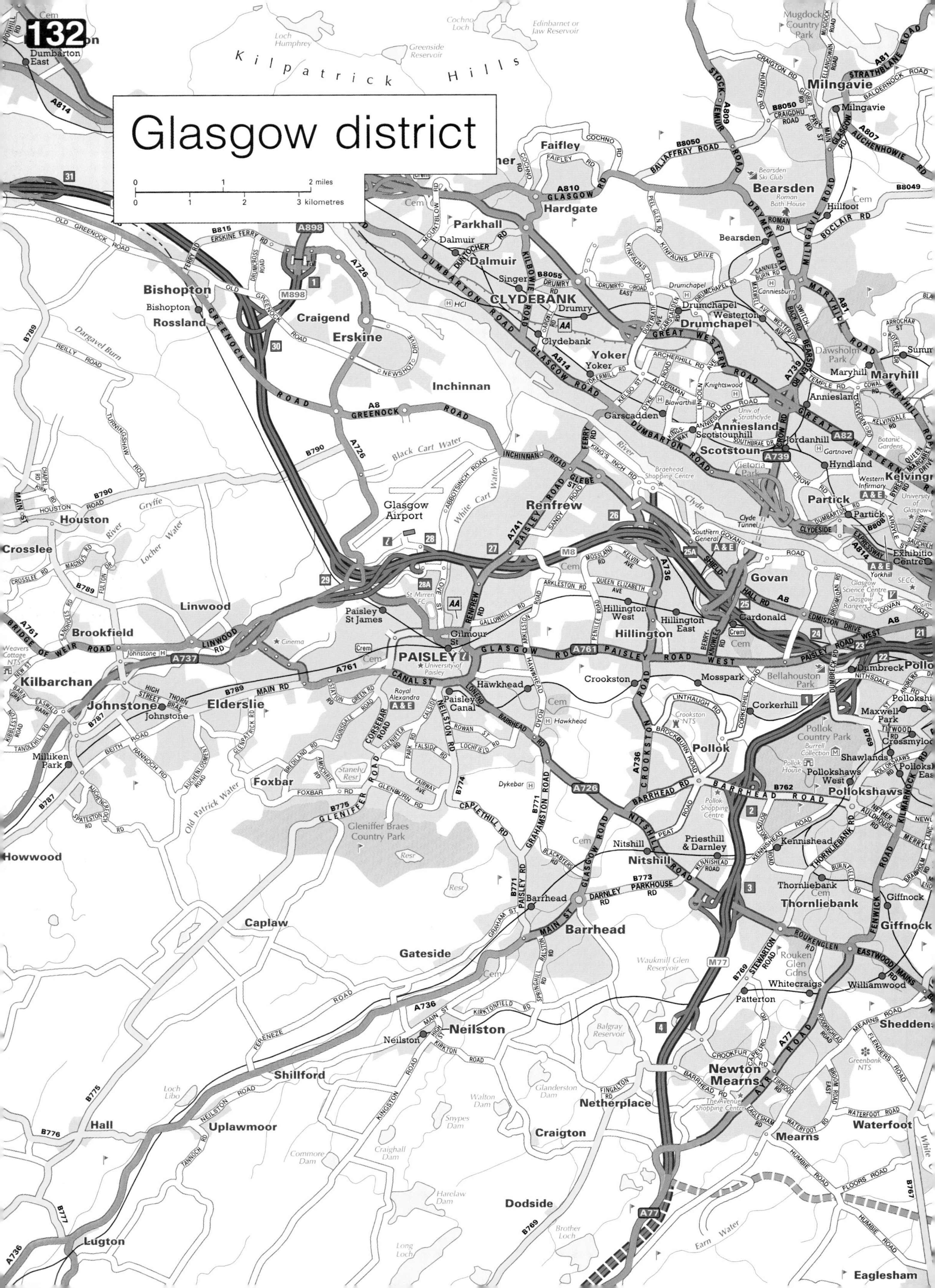
0 1 2 miles
0 1 2 3 kilometres
Kilpatrick Hills
Dumbarton East
Faifley
Milngavie
Bearsden
Hardgate
Parkhall
Dalmuir
CLYDEBANK
Drumchapel
Bishopton
Rossland
Craigend
Erskine
Yoker
Inchinnan
Maryhill
Anniesland
Scotstoun
Partick
Houston
Crosslee
Glasgow Airport
Renfrew
Govan
Linwood
Brookfield
Kilbarchan
Johnstone
Elderslie
PAISLEY
Hillington
Cardonald
Crookston
Mosspark
Pollok
Pollokshaws
Foxbar
Gleniffer Braes Country Park
Howwood
Nitshill
Priesthill & Darnley
Thornliebank
Giffnock
Barrhead
Caplaw
Gateside
Neilston
Shillford
Patterton
Whitecraigs
Williamwood
Newton Mearns
Netherplace
Hall
Uplawmoor
Craigton
Mearns
Waterfoot
Dodside
Lugton
Eaglesham

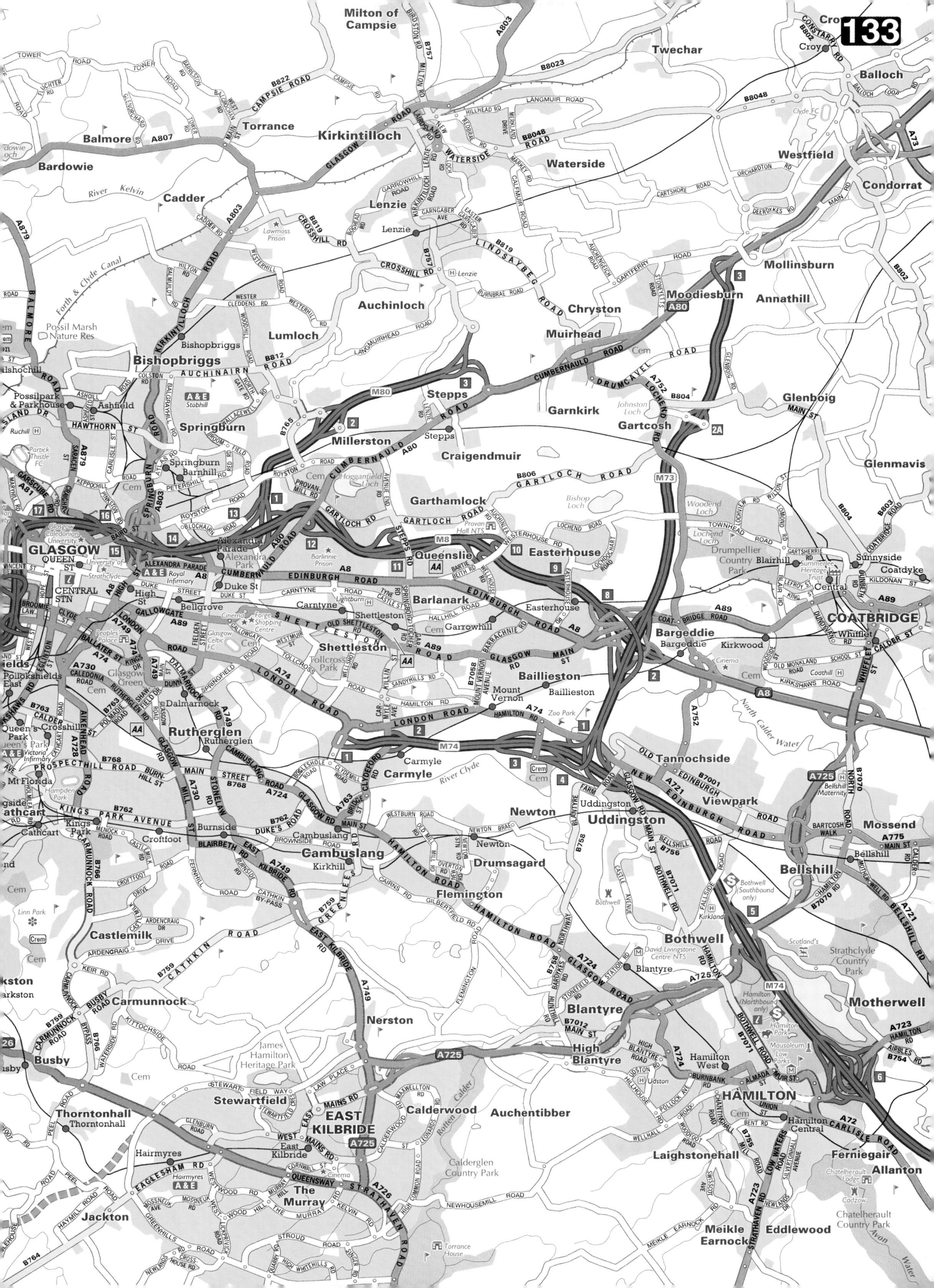
Milton of Campsie
Twechar
Croy
Balloch
Torrance
Kirkintilloch
Balmore
Bardowie
Waterside
Westfield
Condorrat
Cadder
Lenzie
Mollinsburn
Auchinloch
Moodiesburn
Annathill
Chryston
Lumloch
Muirhead
Bishopbriggs
Possil Marsh Nature Res
Stepps
Garnkirk
Glenboig
Springburn
Millerston
Gartcosh
Craigendmuir
Glenmavis
Garthamlock
GLASGOW
Queenslie
Easterhouse
Drumpellier Country Park
Barlanark
Shettleston
Bargeddie
COATBRIDGE
Baillieston
Mount Vernon
Rutherglen
Carmyle
Tannochside
Viewpark
Newton
Uddingston
Mossend
Gambuslang
Drumsagard
Bellshill
Flemington
Castlemilk
Bothwell
Strathclyde Country Park
Blantyre
Carmunnock
Motherwell
Nerston
High Blantyre
James Hamilton Heritage Park
Busby
HAMILTON
Stewartfield
Calderwood
Auchentibber
Thorntonhall
EAST KILBRIDE
Laighstonehall
Ferniegair
Allanton
Hairmyres
Calderglen Country Park
The Murray
Jackton
Meikle Earnock
Eddlewood
Chatelherault Country Park

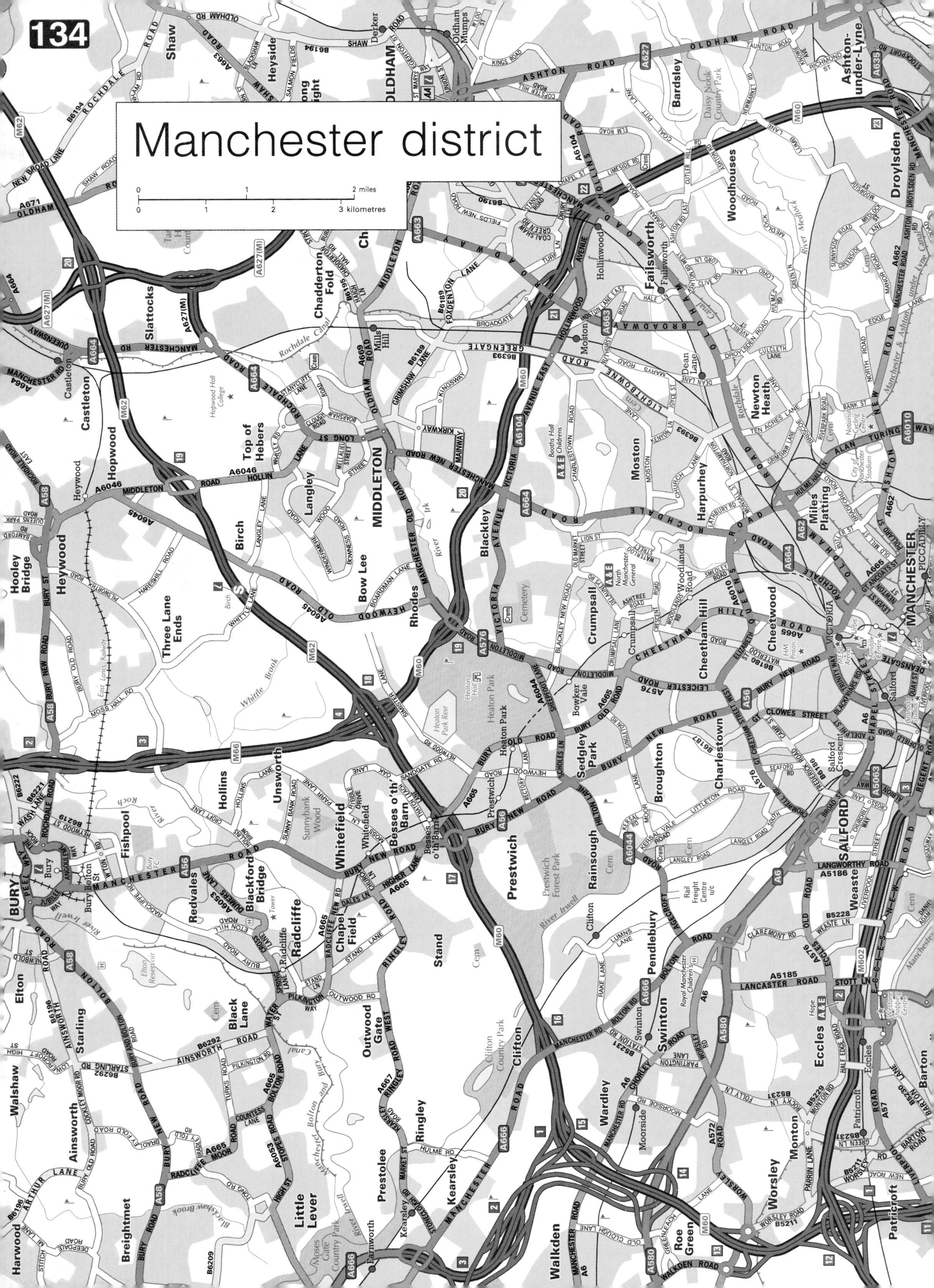
Manchester district
0 1 2 miles
0 1 2 3 kilometres
OLDHAM
Shaw
Heyside
Oldham Mumps
Derker
Ashton-under-Lyne
Bardsley
Daisy Nook Country Park
Woodhouses
Droylsden
Failsworth
Hollinwood
Chadderton Fold
Slattocks
Mills Hill
Moston
Dean Lane
Newton Heath
Castleton
Hopwood
Top of Hebers
Heywood
MIDDLETON
Langley
Birch
Blackley
Harpurhey
Miles Platting
MANCHESTER
PICCADILLY
Hooley Bridge
Bow Lee
Rhodes
Three Lane Ends
Crumpsall
Woodlands Road
Cheetham Hill
Cheetwood
VICTORIA
Heaton Park
Bowker Vale
Sedgley Park
Broughton
Charlestown
Salford Crescent
SALFORD
Hollins
Unsworth
Whitefield
Besses o'th' Barn
Prestwich
Fishpool
BURY
Redvales
Blackford Bridge
Radcliffe
Chapel Field
Stand
Rainsough
Clifton
Pendlebury
Weaste
Eccles
Elton
Starling
Black Lane
Outwood Gate
Swinton
Walshaw
Ainsworth
Prestolee
Ringley
Kearsley
Wardley
Moorside
Monton
Worsley
Patricroft
Barton
Breightmet
Little Lever
Farnworth
Walkden
Roe Green
Harwood
Rochdale Canal
River Irwell
Clifton Country Park
Prestwich Forest Park
Moses Gate Country Park

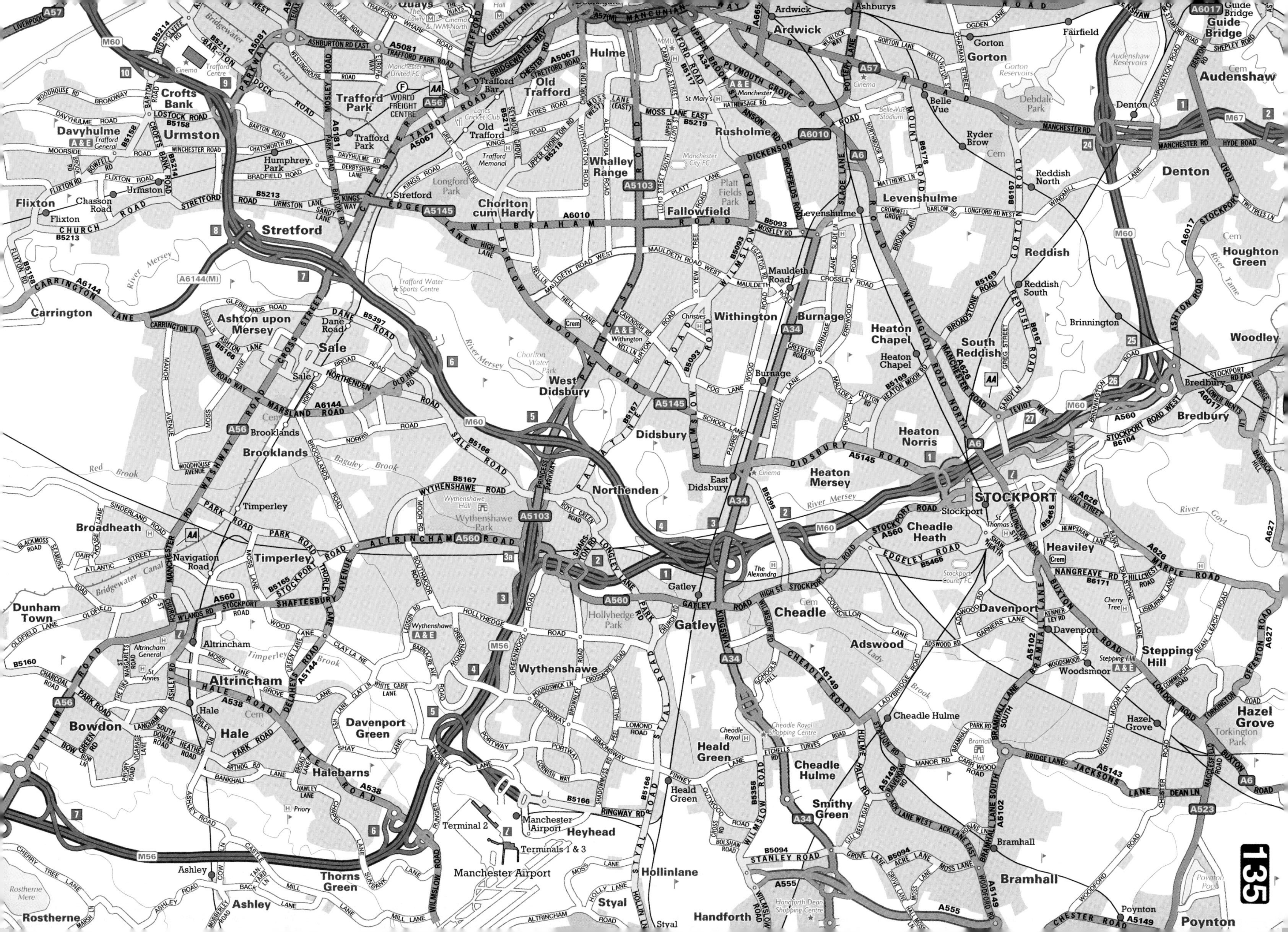

Ardwick
Ashburys
Guide Bridge
Fairfield
Gorton
Audenshaw
Hulme
Old Trafford
Trafford Bar
Crofts Bank
Trafford Park
WORLD FREIGHT CENTRE
Davyhulme
Urmston
Rusholme
Belle Vue
Denton
Ryder Brow
Humphrey Park
Whalley Range
Reddish North
Flixton
Chasson Road
Longford Park
Chorlton cum Hardy
Fallowfield
Levenshulme
Stretford
Reddish
Houghton Green
Mauldeth Road
Reddish South
Carrington
Ashton upon Mersey
Sale
Withington
Burnage
Heaton Chapel
South Reddish
Brinnington
Woodley
West Didsbury
Bredbury
Brooklands
Didsbury
Heaton Norris
Heaton Mersey
East Didsbury
Northenden
STOCKPORT
Timperley
Broadheath
Navigation Road
Cheadle Heath
Heaviley
Dunham Town
Gatley
Cheadle
Davenport
Wythenshawe Park
Adswood
Stepping Hill
Altrincham
Wythenshawe
Woodsmoor
Bowdon
Hale
Davenport Green
Cheadle Hulme
Hazel Grove
Torkington Park
Heald Green
Halebarns
Smithy Green
Manchester Airport
Terminal 2
Terminals 1 & 3
Heyhead
Bramhall
Ashley
Thorns Green
Hollinlane
Rostherne
Styal
Handforth
Poynton
M60
M56
M67
A6
A34
A560
A5103
A5145
A56
A57
A6010
A6144
A555
A5149
A5102
A523
A626
A627
A6017
WILMSLOW ROAD
KINGSWAY
PRINCESS PARKWAY
MANCHESTER ROAD
STOCKPORT ROAD
BUXTON ROAD
WELLINGTON ROAD NORTH
HYDE ROAD
BARLOW MOOR ROAD
WASHWAY ROAD
CROSS STREET
DUNHAM ROAD
HALE ROAD
STYAL ROAD
CHEADLE ROAD
BRAMHALL LANE

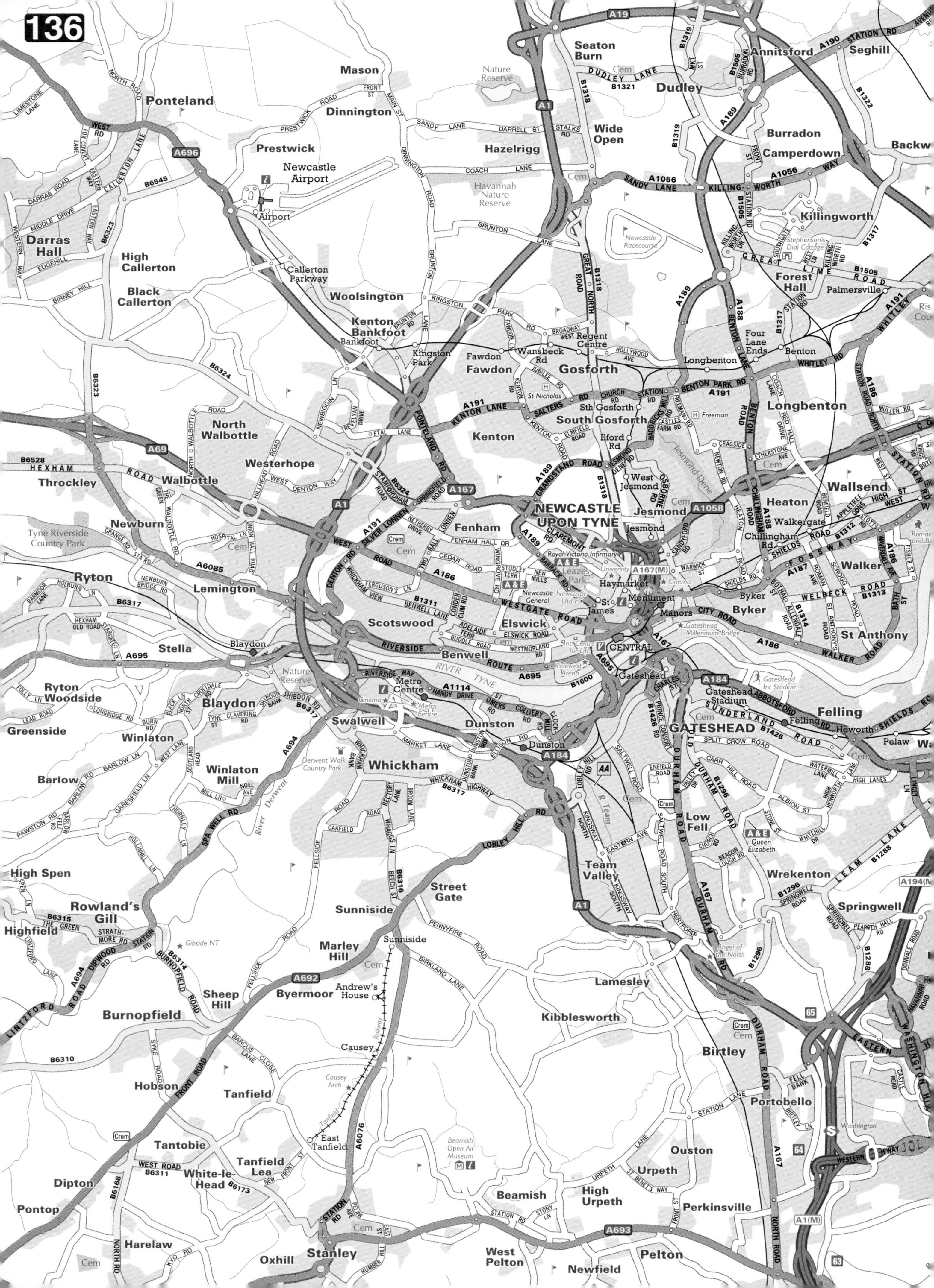

Seaton Burn
Annitsford
Seghill
Mason
Ponteland
Dinnington
Dudley
Wide Open
Prestwick
Hazelrigg
Burradon
Camperdown
Newcastle Airport
Havannah Nature Reserve
Killingworth
Darras Hall
High Callerton
Black Callerton
Callerton Parkway
Woolsington
Newcastle Racecourse
Forest Hall
Palmersville
Kenton Bankfoot
Kingston Park
Fawdon
Wansbeck Rd
Regent Centre
Gosforth
Four Lane Ends
Longbenton
Benton
Sth Gosforth
South Gosforth
Kenton
North Walbottle
Westerhope
Walbottle
Throckley
Ilford Rd
West Jesmond
Jesmond
Wallsend
Heaton
Walkergate
Chillingham Rd
Newburn
Tyne Riverside Country Park
Fenham
NEWCASTLE UPON TYNE
Ryton
Lemington
Royal Victoria Infirmary
Haymarket
Monument
Walker
Byker
Scotswood
Elswick
St James
Manors
St Anthony
Stella
Blaydon
Benwell
CENTRAL
Gateshead Millennium Bridge
Ryton Woodside
Metro Centre
Gateshead
Gateshead Stadium
Gateshead Int Stadium
Felling
Heworth
Pelaw
Greenside
Blaydon
Winlaton
Swalwell
Dunston
GATESHEAD
Barlow
Winlaton Mill
Whickham
Derwent Walk Country Park
Low Fell
Queen Elizabeth
High Spen
Team Valley
Wrekenton
Rowland's Gill
Highfield
Street Gate
Sunniside
Springwell
Gibside NT
Marley Hill
Angel of the North
Sheep Hill
Byermoor
Andrew's House
Lamesley
Burnopfield
Kibblesworth
Causey
Birtley
Hobson
Tanfield
Causey Arch
Portobello
Washington
Tantobie
East Tanfield
Beamish Open Air Museum
Ouston
Tanfield Lea
White-le-Head
Urpeth
Dipton
Beamish
High Urpeth
Perkinsville
Pontop
Harelaw
Oxhill
Stanley
West Pelton
Newfield
Pelton

Tyne & Wear district

0 1 2 miles
0 1 2 3 kilometres

Seaton Delaval
Holywell
St Mary's Lighthouse
Crem
Cem
Burn
B1325
A192
A193
Earsdon
Whitley Bay
The Links
Claremont Rd
A1148
Monkseaton Drive
West Monkseaton
Monkseaton
Earsdon Rd
Norham Rd
East Parade
Promenade
Whitley Rd
Whitley Bay
Cullercoats
Cullercoats
A186
B1322
Station Rd
Shiremoor
Shiremoor
Park Lane
A192
Shields Rd
Hillheads Rd
Marden Rd
Road Sth
Broadway
Mast Ln
Grand Parade
Murton
The Aquarium
Murton Ln
New York
A191
Rake Lane
A&E
North Tyneside General
Hartington Rd
Hart-burn Rd
Beach Rd
Broadway
Percy Park
Manor Rd
Front St
Tynemouth Castle & Priory
Sun Park
A19
Stephenson Railway Museum
Middle Engine Lane
Norham Road North
Billy Mill Lane
B1316
Lynn Rd
A1058
Crem
Cem
Walton Ave
Preston Rd
A192
King Edward Rd
Trevor Terr
Tynemouth
Tynemouth Rd
Tynemouth
Cinema
Coast Road
A1108
Billy Mill Ave
Hawkeys Lane
Albion Road
A193
North Shields
North Shields
Norham Road
Churchill St
Coach Ln
Prudhoe St
Hill Drive
Road
Wallsend Rd
Waterville Road
Howdon
A193
St Peter's Road
B1315
Archer St
Cem
Hunter
Tynemouth Rd
Meadow Well
Howdon Rd
A187
Percy Main
Hadrian Road
Howdon
Howdon Ln
Willington Quay
A187
Toll
Designer Outlet Village
Coble Dene
Royal Quays
International Ferry Terminal
River Tyne
Tyne Tunnel
Harbour Drive
Arbeia Roman Fort
South Shields
Beach Rd
Bents Park Rd
Cem
Cross Gate
Westoe Rd
Mowbray Rd
South Shields
A183
The Broadway
Commercial Road
Chichester
Horsley Hill Rd
Cheviot Rd
B1301
Westoe
Cemetery
Approach
B1297
Wagonway Rd
Blackett St
Chaytor St
Jarrow
Bedesworld
Jarrow Priory
Church Bank
Jarrow
Lyon St
Hedgeley Road
Station Rd
Hebburn
Victoria Road East
Jarrow Rd
A185
Western
Tyne Dock
Hudson St
Stanhope
Mortimer Road
Sunderland Rd
King George Rd
Temple Park Rd
Marsden Rd
Centenary Ave
Marsden
Marsden Lane
Marsden Bay
Marsden Rock NT
Harton
Harton Ln
A1300
Prince Edward Road
Bede
Bede Burn Road
Springwell
A19
Newcastle Rd
Hebburn
Campbell Park Rd
York Ave
Cemetery
A185
Victoria Road West
Hadrian Rd
Wenlock Rd
Boldon Ln
A&E
South Tyneside District
Green Ln
Whiteleas Way
A1300
John Reid Rd
Lizard Lane
Mill Lane
Lizard Point
Souter Lighthouse NT
Crem
Nevison Ave
Sunderland Rd
Road
Monkton
Brockley Whins
Shields Road
Benton Road
B1298
Cleadon
Cleadon Lane
Lizard Lane
Souter Point
Whitburn
B1306
Hedworth Lane
A194
Cotswold Ln
Boldon Colliery
Abingdon Way
Tileshed Ln
Boldon Ln
Front St
B1299
Whitburn Rd
Cleadon Ln
Boldon Flats Nature Res
Sunderland Road
A1018
Moor Lane
Front St
Leam Lane
New Road
West Boldon
Henley Way
North Rd
Cinema
Boker Ln
East Boldon
Station Rd
East Boldon
Moor Lane
A184
Addison Rd
Front St
Dipe Ln
Cem
A184
Sunderland Road
Shields Road
A183
Whitburn Bay
Follinsby Lane
Downhill Ln
Hylton Lane
Dovedale Rd
Cemetery
Dykelands Rd
Seaburn
Seaburn
River Don
Sea Rd
Roker
Fulwell Rd
Ramsgate Rd
Wiltshire Rd
Southwick
Sta
Newcastle Road
Thompson Rd
B1291
Monkwearmouth
Whitburn Road
Washington Rd
Rotherfield Rd
Aircraft
North Hylton Rd
Monkwearmouth
A195
Ferryboat Ln
Craig-avon Rd
Hylton Castle
Castletown
Works
A1290
Southwick Rd
A1290
Sunderland FC
Monkwearmouth Railway
Dame Dorothy St
National Glass Centre
Sulgrave Road
Hylton Castle Rd
Ringway
River Wear
Pallion
European Way
Queen Alexandra Bridge
A1231
St Peter's
B1293
Vermont
Works
Pallion Road
South Hylton
St Lukes Road
Front Rd
B1405
Kayll Rd
University
Sunderland
Sans St
High St
Sunderland
'F' Pit
A1231
Millfield
Museum & Art Gallery
Cem
Washington Old Hall NT
South Hylton
Hylton Bank
Hylton Road
Chester Rd
University
Park Lane
Park Rd
Galleries Shopping Centre
Parkway
Wildfowl & Wetland Trust
A19
Crem
Cem
A&E
Royal
Thornholme Rd
Ormonde Street
Road
Eye Infirmary
B1522
Commercial Road
Hendon
Hylton Road
Washington
Grindon
Penny Well Rd
Broadway
A183
Chester Rd
Durham Road
Queen
Tunstall
Alexandra B1405
Ryhope Road
A1018
Offerton
Grindon Lane
Grindon Hall
Premier Road
Lane
Road
Grangetown
A195
James Steel Country Park
Penshaw Monument
Road
A690
Silksworth Sports Complex & Ski Centre
Essen Way
Silksworth Lane
High Newport
Leechmere Road
Cem
Fatfield
North Moor Ln
Durham Rd
Chester Road
A183
Langdale Road
Penshaw
Allendale Road
New Silksworth
Herrington
B1286
Ryhope Road
New Herrington
Ryhope St S
Ryhope
A182
Silksworth Rd
Park Side
Silksworth
Hill Brow
Tunstall
Burdon Ln
Shiney Row
B1286
B1286

Stavanger
Haugesund
Bergen
Kristiansand
Goteborg
Hamburg (Summer Only)
Amsterdam

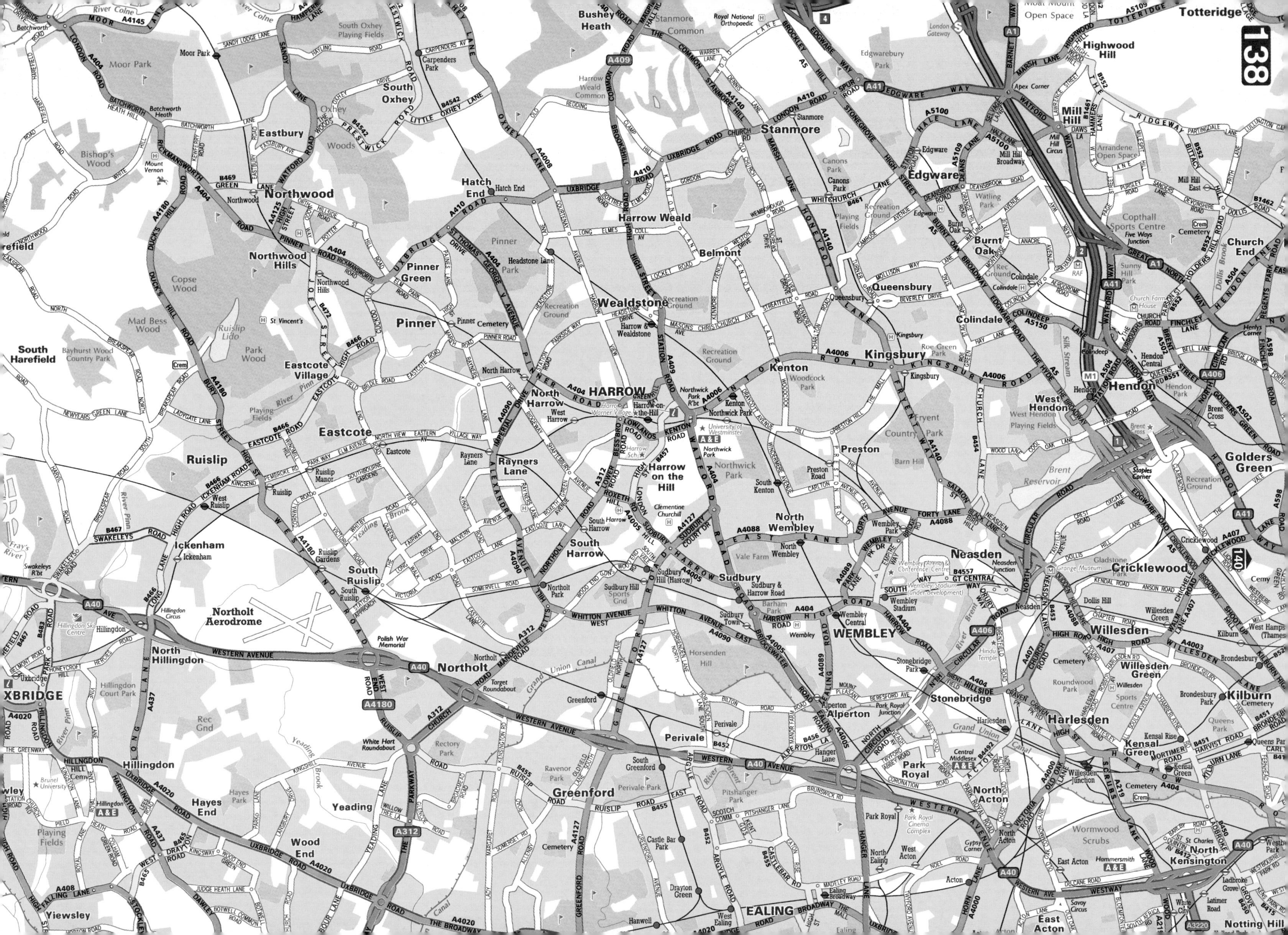
Totteridge
Highwood Hill
Mill Hill
Church End
Golders Green
Hendon
West Hendon
Cricklewood
Willesden
Willesden Green
Kilburn
Kensal Green
Harlesden
North Kensington
Notting Hill
Edgware
Burnt Oak
Colindale
Queensbury
Kingsbury
Neasden
Stonebridge
North Acton
Park Royal
East Acton
Stanmore
Canons Park
Preston
Wembley
WEMBLEY
Alperton
Kenton
North Wembley
Belmont
Harrow Weald
Wealdstone
Sudbury
Harrow on the Hill
HARROW
Perivale
EALING
Bushey Heath
Stanmore Common
North Harrow
South Harrow
Greenford
Hatch End
Rayners Lane
Northolt
Pinner
Pinner Green
South Oxhey
Eastcote
South Ruislip
Northwood
Northwood Hills
Eastcote Village
Eastbury
Ruislip
Northolt Aerodrome
Yeading
Wood End
Hayes End
Ickenham
North Hillingdon
Hillingdon
Moor Park
Copse Wood
Mad Bess Wood
Park Wood
Ruislip Lido
Bishop's Wood
South Harefield
Yiewsley
Wormwood Scrubs
Brent Reservoir
Horsenden Hill
Grand Union Canal
River Pinn
Silk Stream
Western Avenue
Watford Way
Edgware Road
Uxbridge Road
XBRIDGE
140
1
2
4

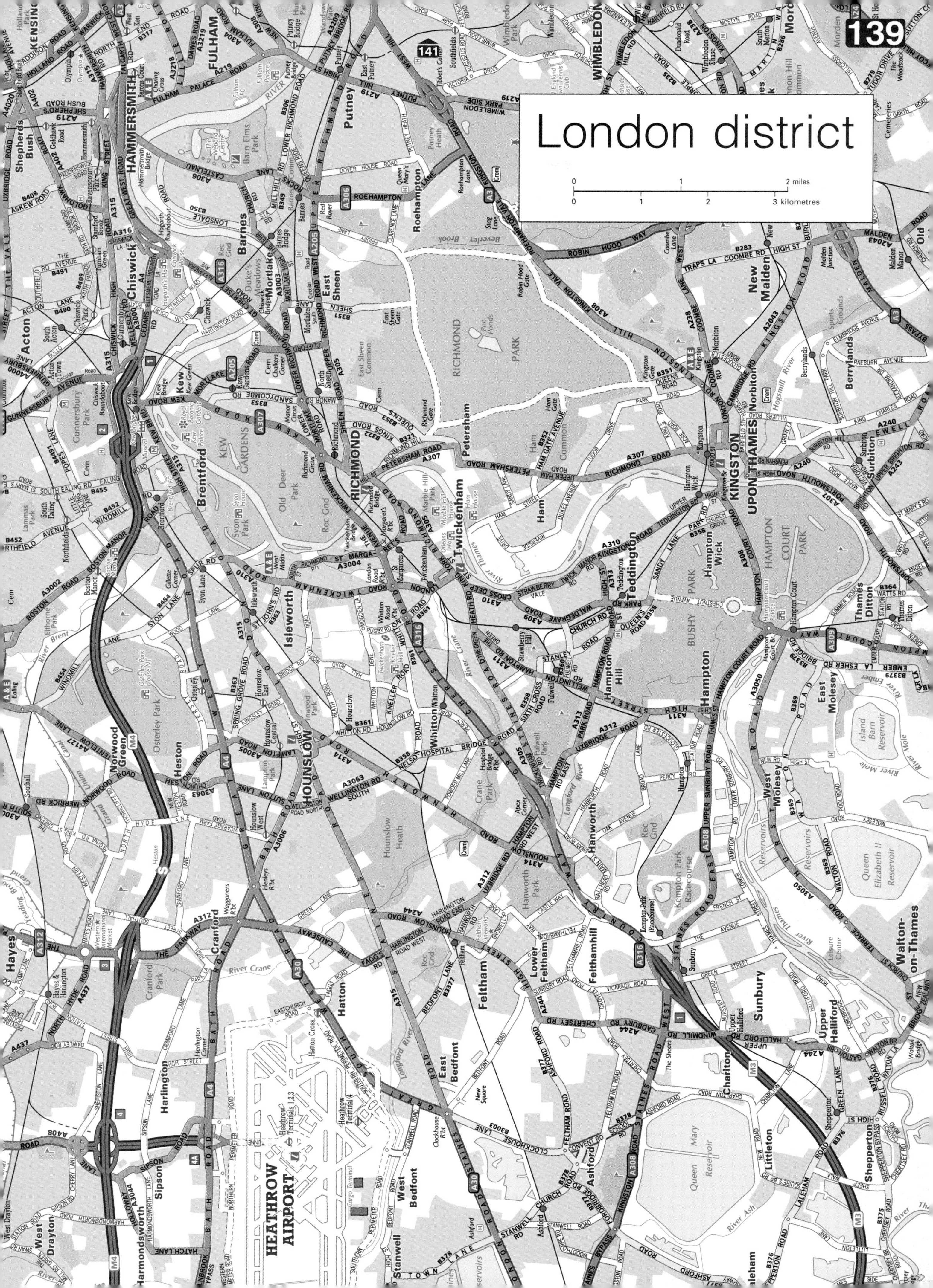

139
London district
0
1
2 miles
0
1
2
3 kilometres
141
HAMMERSMITH
FULHAM
Putney
WIMBLEDON
Shepherds Bush
Chiswick
Barnes
Mortlake
East Sheen
Roehampton
Acton
South Acton
Kew
RICHMOND PARK
KEW GARDENS
Brentford
RICHMOND
Petersham
Twickenham
Ham
Ham Common
KINGSTON UPON THAMES
Norbiton
New Malden
Berrylands
Surbiton
Old Deer Park
Isleworth
Hounslow
HOUNSLOW
Teddington
Hampton Wick
HAMPTON COURT PARK
BUSHY PARK
Thames Ditton
East Molesey
West Molesey
Hampton
Hampton Hill
Hanworth
Whitton
Heston
Norwood Green
Osterley Park
Southall
Hounslow Heath
Cranford
Hayes
Feltham
Lower Feltham
Felthamhill
Hatton
East Bedfont
Sunbury
Kempton Park Racecourse
Walton-on-Thames
Upper Halliford
Charlton
Shepperton
Littleton
Queen Mary Reservoir
Queen Elizabeth II Reservoir
Island Barn Reservoir
Harlington
Sipson
Harmondsworth
West Drayton
HEATHROW AIRPORT
West Bedfont
Stanwell
Ashford
River Thames
River Crane
River Brent
Grand Union Canal

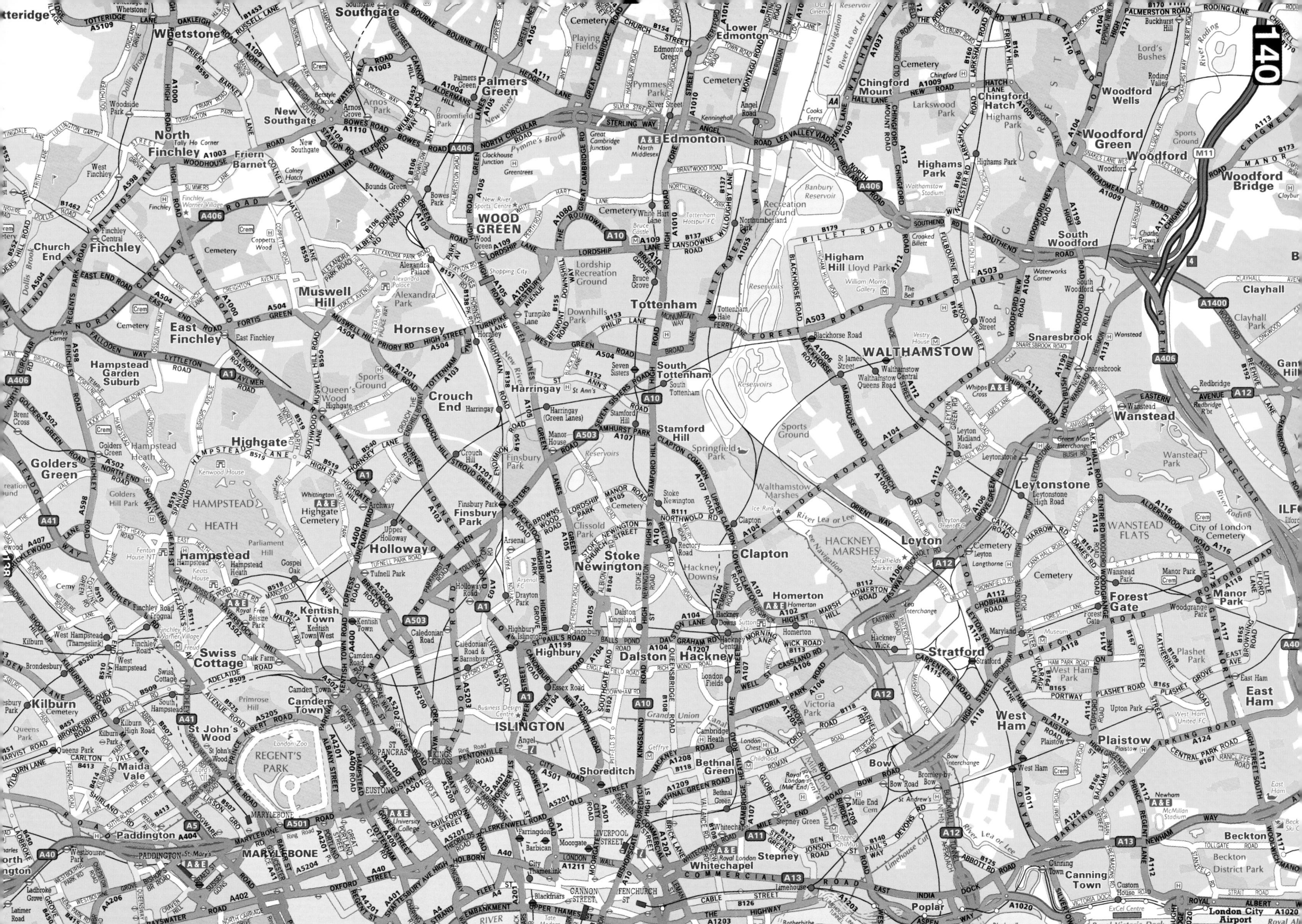

Whetstone
Southgate
Lower Edmonton
Palmers Green
New Southgate
North Finchley
Friern Barnet
Edmonton
Chingford Mount
Chingford Hatch
Higham Park
Woodford Wells
Woodford Green
Woodford
Woodford Bridge
WOOD GREEN
Church End
Finchley
Muswell Hill
Tottenham
Higham Hill
South Woodford
Clayhall
East Finchley
Hornsey
Snaresbrook
WALTHAMSTOW
Hampstead Garden Suburb
South Tottenham
Harringay
Crouch End
Wanstead
Stamford Hill
Highgate
Golders Green
Finsbury Park
Leytonstone
Holloway
Stoke Newington
Clapton
Leyton
HAMPSTEAD HEATH
HACKNEY MARSHES
WANSTEAD FLATS
Hampstead
Forest Gate
Manor Park
Homerton
Kentish Town
Swiss Cottage
Highbury
Dalston
Hackney
Stratford
East Ham
Kilburn
Camden Town
St John's Wood
ISLINGTON
West Ham
Plaistow
REGENT'S PARK
Maida Vale
Shoreditch
Bethnal Green
Bow
Paddington
MARYLEBONE
Whitechapel
Stepney
Beckton
Canning Town
Poplar
Wapping
London City Airport
Notting Hill
Mayfair
138

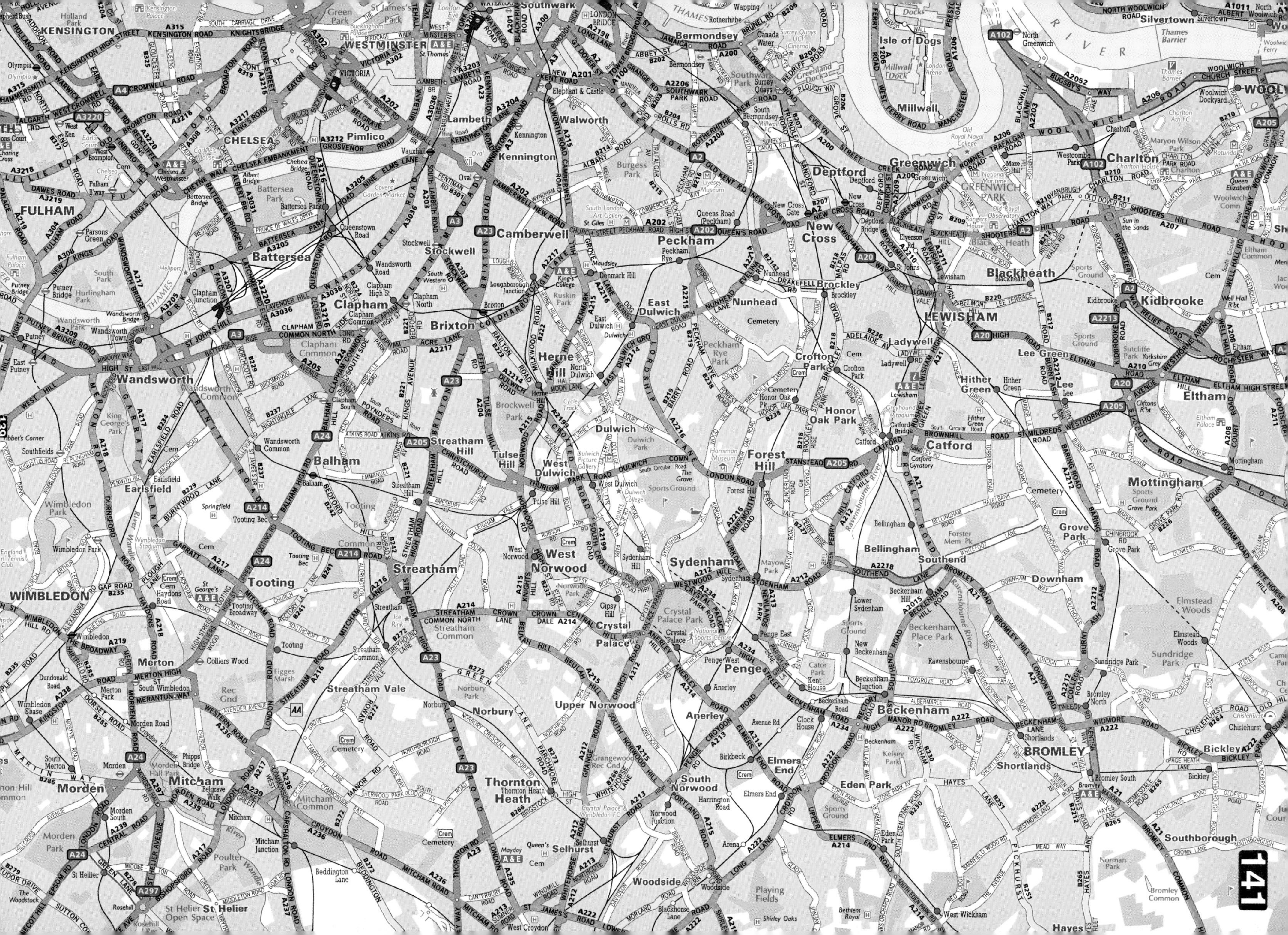
KENSINGTON
WESTMINSTER
VICTORIA
Southwark
Bermondsey
Rotherhithe
Isle of Dogs
Millwall
Silvertown
Thames Barrier
RIVER THAMES
Woolwich
Charlton
Greenwich
Deptford
New Cross
Kidbrooke
Eltham
Blackheath
LEWISHAM
Lee Green
Lee
Mottingham
Hither Green
Catford
Ladywell
Brockley
Crofton Park
Honor Oak Park
Nunhead
Peckham
Camberwell
Walworth
Kennington
Lambeth
Pimlico
CHELSEA
FULHAM
Battersea
Stockwell
Clapham
Brixton
Herne Hill
East Dulwich
Dulwich
West Dulwich
Tulse Hill
Forest Hill
Sydenham
Bellingham
Southend
Downham
Grove Park
Elmstead Woods
Sundridge Park
Chislehurst
Bickley
BROMLEY
Shortlands
Southborough
Hayes
West Wickham
Eden Park
Beckenham
Elmers End
Penge
Anerley
Crystal Palace
West Norwood
Streatham Hill
Streatham
Balham
Wandsworth
Earlsfield
Tooting
WIMBLEDON
Merton
Morden
Mitcham
St Helier
Streatham Vale
Norbury
Upper Norwood
South Norwood
Thornton Heath
Selhurst
Woodside
West Croydon
River Wandle
Ravensbourne River

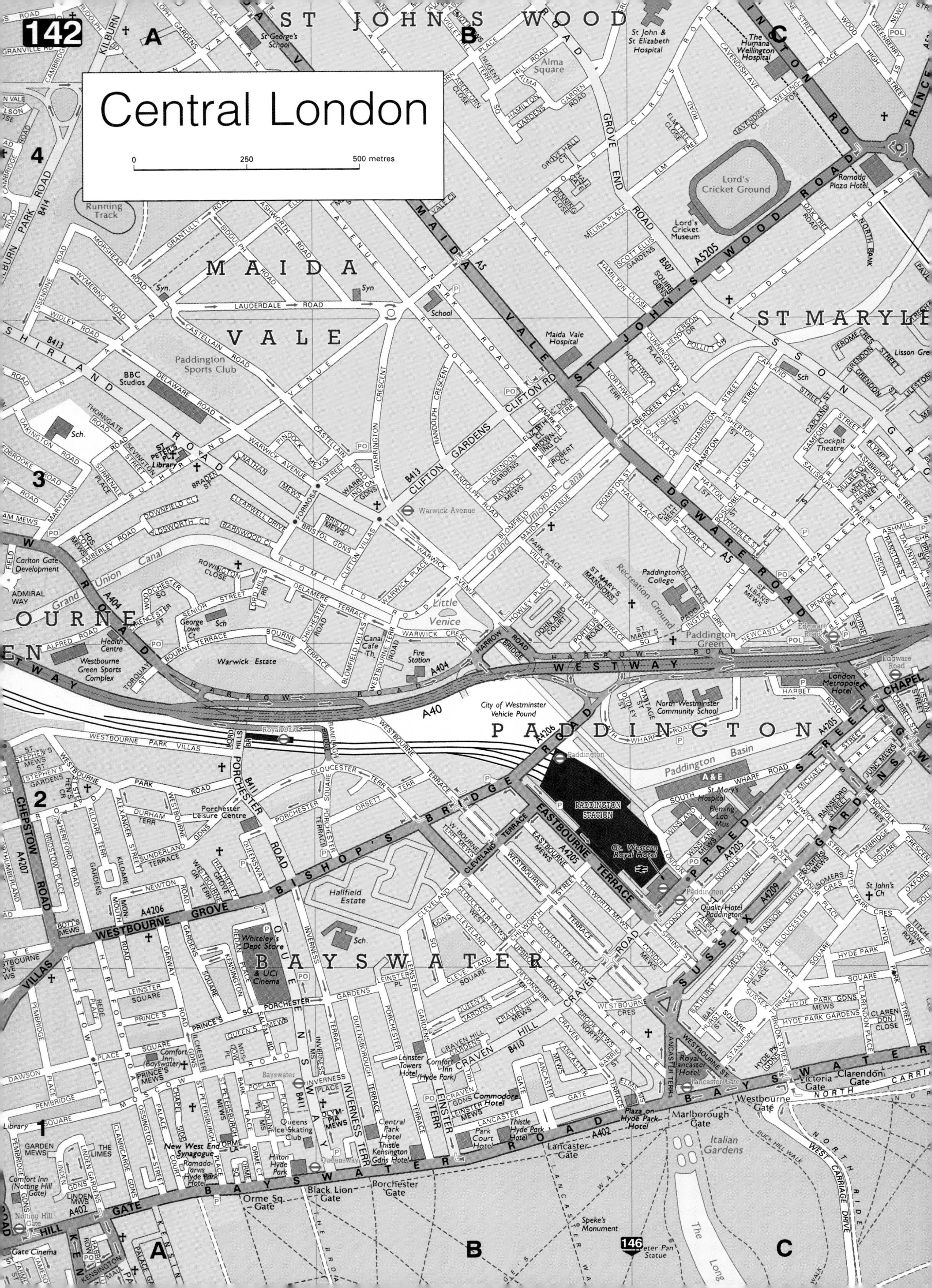

142
Central London
0
250
500 metres
ST JOHN'S WOOD
MAIDA VALE
ST MARYLEBONE
PADDINGTON
BAYSWATER
A
B
C
1
2
3
4
St George's School
St John & St Elizabeth Hospital
The Humana Wellington Hospital
Alma Square
Lord's Cricket Ground
Lord's Cricket Museum
Ramada Plaza Hotel
Running Track
Paddington Sports Club
BBC Studios
Maida Vale Hospital
Warwick Avenue
Little Venice
Grand Union Canal
Paddington College
Recreation Ground
Paddington Green
Edgware Road
London Metropole Hotel
Cockpit Theatre
Carlton Gate Development
Health Centre
Westbourne Green Sports Complex
Warwick Estate
Canal Cafe Th.
Fire Station
City of Westminster Vehicle Pound
North Westminster Community School
WESTWAY
A40
Royal Oak
Paddington
Paddington Basin
PADDINGTON STATION
Gt. Western Royal Hotel
St Mary's Hospital
Fleming Lab Mus
Quality Hotel Paddington
Porchester Leisure Centre
Hallfield Estate
Whiteley's Dept Store & UCI Cinema
Comfort Inn (Bayswater)
Leinster Towers Hotel
Comfort Inn (Hyde Park)
Commodore Hotel
Central Park Hotel
Thistle Kensington Gdns Hotel
Park Court Hotel
Thistle Hyde Park Hotel
Plaza on Hyde Park Hotel
Royal Lancaster Hotel
Queens Ice Skating Club
Hilton Hyde Park
New West End Synagogue
Ramada-Jarvis Hyde Park Hotel
Comfort Inn (Notting Hill Gate)
Bayswater
Queensway
Lancaster Gate
Notting Hill Gate
Gate Cinema
Library
St John's Ch
Victoria Gate
Clarendon Gate
Westbourne Gate
Marlborough Gate
Italian Gardens
Black Lion Gate
Porchester Gate
Orme Sq. Gate
Speke's Monument
Peter Pan Statue
146
EDGWARE ROAD
MAIDA VALE
ST JOHN'S WOOD ROAD
BAYSWATER ROAD
BISHOP'S BRIDGE ROAD
WESTBOURNE GROVE
PRAED STREET
SUSSEX GARDENS
HARROW ROAD
CLIFTON GARDENS
WARWICK AVENUE
SUTHERLAND AVENUE
ELGIN AVENUE
GROVE END ROAD
LISSON GROVE
EASTBOURNE TERRACE
QUEENSWAY
PORCHESTER ROAD
CHEPSTOW ROAD
WESTBOURNE TERRACE
NORTH CARRIAGE DRIVE
WEST CARRIAGE DRIVE

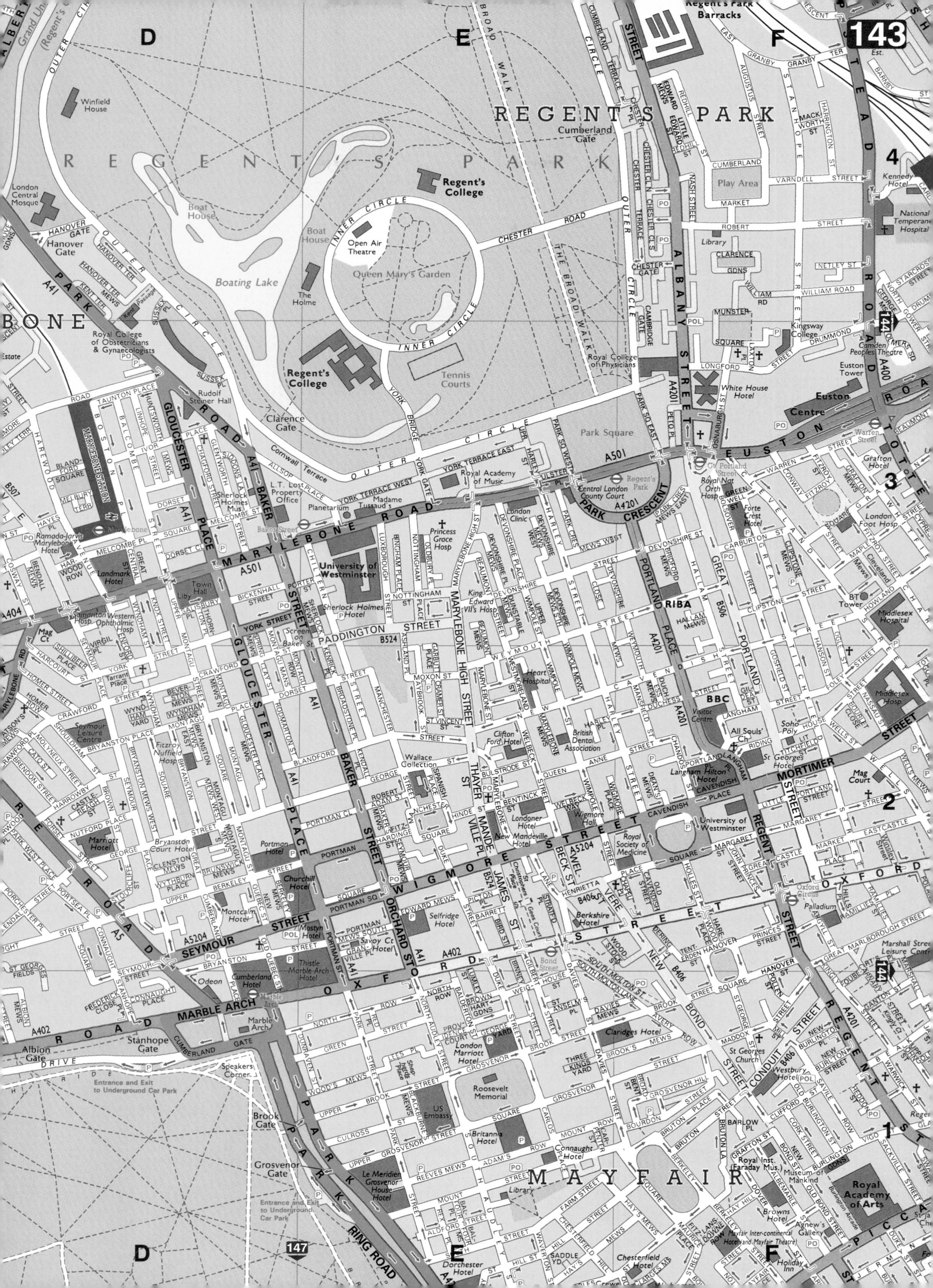
D
E
F
REGENT'S PARK
REGENT'S PARK
Regent's Park Barracks
Winfield House
London Central Mosque
Hanover Gate
Boat House
Boating Lake
The Holme
Open Air Theatre
Queen Mary's Garden
INNER CIRCLE
OUTER CIRCLE
Regent's College
Tennis Courts
Clarence Gate
Cumberland Gate
CHESTER ROAD
THE BROAD WALK
Royal College of Physicians
Royal College of Obstetricians & Gynaecologists
Rudolf Steiner Hall
Park Square
PARK CRESCENT
EUSTON ROAD
Euston Centre
Euston Tower
White House Hotel
Kingsway College
Library
Play Area
National Temperance Hospital
Kennedy Hotel
Camden Peoples Theatre
Regent's Park
Great Portland Street
Warren Street
Grafton Hotel
Royal Nat Orth Hosp
Forte Crest Hotel
London Foot Hosp
BT Tower
Middlesex Hospital
Middlesex Hosp
Central London County Court
Royal Academy of Music
Madame Tussaud's
Planetarium
L.T. Lost Property Office
Sherlock Holmes Mus
MARYLEBONE STATION
Marylebone
Baker Street
MARYLEBONE ROAD
Ramada-Jarvis Marylebone Hotel
Landmark Hotel
Town Hall
Liby
Samaritan Hosp
Western Ophthalmic Hosp
University of Westminster
Sherlock Holmes Hotel
Screen on Baker St
London Clinic
Princess Grace Hosp
King Edward VII's Hosp
Heart Hospital
PADDINGTON STREET
MARYLEBONE HIGH STREET
PORTLAND PLACE
RIBA
BBC
Visitor Centre
All Souls' Ch
Langham Hilton Hotel
St Georges Hotel
Soho Poly
British Dental Association
Clifton Ford Hotel
Wallace Collection
Seymour Leisure Centre
Fitzroy Nuffield Hosp
Marriott Hotel
Bryanston Court Hotel
Portman Hotel
Churchill Hotel
Montcalm Hotel
Londoner Hotel
New Mandeville Hotel
Wigmore Hall
Royal Society of Medicine
University of Westminster
WIGMORE STREET
MORTIMER STREET
OXFORD STREET
Oxford Circus
Palladium
Marshall Street Leisure Centre
Mag Court
SEYMOUR STREET
Mostyn Hotel
Selfridge Hotel
Savoy Ct Hotel
Thistle Marble Arch Hotel
Cumberland Hotel
Marble Arch
Odeon
Berkshire Hotel
Bond Street
MARBLE ARCH
Stanhope Gate
Albion Gate
Speakers Corner
Entrance and Exit to Underground Car Park
Brook Gate
Grosvenor Gate
PARK LANE
London Marriott Hotel
Roosevelt Memorial
US Embassy
Britannia Hotel
Claridges Hotel
Connaught Hotel
Le Meridien Grosvenor House Hotel
Library
MAYFAIR
St Georges Church
Westbury Hotel
Royal Inst. (Faraday Mus.)
Museum of Mankind
Royal Academy of Arts
Browns Hotel
Agnew's Gallery
Mayfair Inter-continental Hotel and Mayfair Theatre
Chesterfield Hotel
Dorchester Hotel
Holiday Inn
RING ROAD
NEW BOND STREET
REGENT STREET
1
2
3
4
144
147

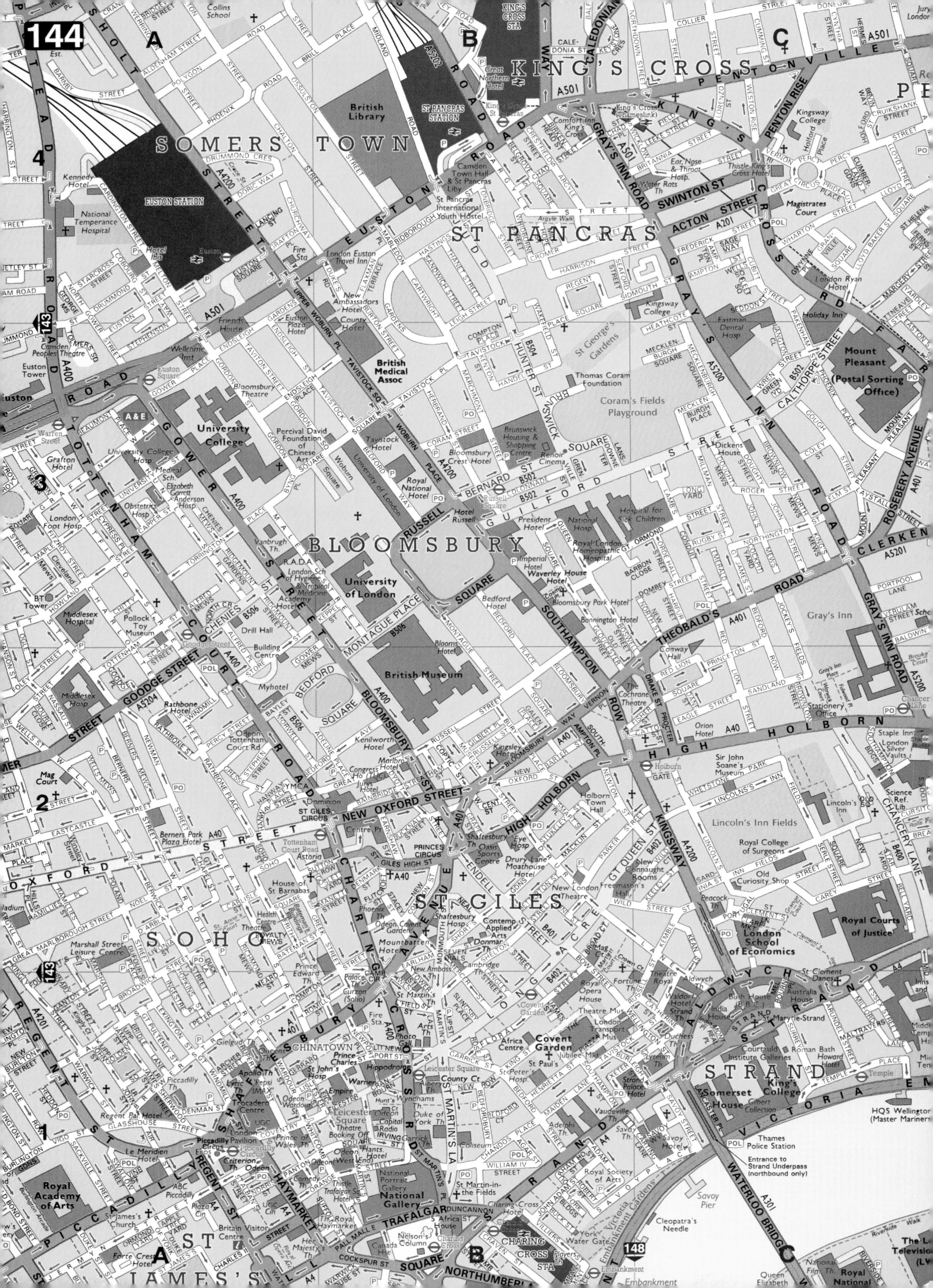

144
A
B
C
4
3
2
1
KING'S CROSS
SOMERS TOWN
ST PANCRAS
BLOOMSBURY
ST GILES
SOHO
STRAND
CHINATOWN
King's Cross Sta
St Pancras Station
Euston Station
British Library
Great Northern Hotel
Camden Town Hall & St Pancras Liby
St Pancras International Youth Hostel
London Euston Travel Inn
National Temperance Hospital
Kennedy Hotel
Hotel Ibis
Euston Square
Euston Tower
Friends House
Wellcome Inst
New Ambassadors Hotel
Euston Plaza Hotel
County Hotel
British Medical Assoc
St George's Gardens
Thomas Coram Foundation
Coram's Fields Playground
Brunswick Housing & Shopping Centre
Renoir Cinema
Kingsway College
Eastman Dental Hosp
Holiday Inn
Mount Pleasant (Postal Sorting Office)
Magistrates Court
Thistle King's Cross Hotel
Ear, Nose & Throat Hosp.
Water Rats Th
Comfort Inn King's Cross
London Ryan Hotel
University College
University College Hosp
Percival David Foundation of Chinese Art
Tavistock Hotel
Royal National Hotel
Bloomsbury Crest Hotel
Bloomsbury Theatre
Hotel Russell
President Hotel
National Hosp
Royal London Homeopathic Hospital
Hospital for Sick Children
Dickens House
Grafton Hotel
Obstetrics Hosp
London Foot Hosp
BT Tower
Middlesex Hospital
Pollock's Toy Museum
Drill Hall
Building Centre
R.A.D.A.
Vanbrugh Th.
London Sch of Hygiene & Tropical Medicine
University of London
British Museum
Imperial Hotel
Waverley House Hotel
Bedford Hotel
Bloomsbury Park Hotel
Bonnington Hotel
Conway Hall
Gray's Inn
Myhotel
Rathbone Hotel
Odeon Tottenham Court Rd
Kenilworth Hotel
Marlboro Hotel
Congress Ho (TUC)
Kingsley Hotel
Holborn Town Hall
Sir John Soane's Museum
Lincoln's Inn Fields
Lincoln's Inn
Royal College of Surgeons
Old Curiosity Shop
London School of Economics
Royal Courts of Justice
Science Ref. Lib
Staple Inn
London Silver Vaults
Orion Hotel
Stationery Office
The Cochrane Theatre
Mag Court
Berners Park Plaza Hotel
Astoria
House of St Barnabas
Marshall Street Leisure Centre
Shaftesbury Th
Oasis Sports Centre
Drury Lane Moathouse Hotel
New London Theatre
Freemason's Hall
New Connaught Rooms
Peacock Th
Mountbatten Hotel
Donmar Th
Cambridge Th
Prince Edward Th
Palace Th
Royal Opera House
Theatre Royal
Fortune Th
Aldwych Th
Waldorf Hotel
Strand Th
Bush House (B.B.C.)
India House
Australia House
St Mary-le-Strand
St Clement Danes
Courtauld Institute Galleries
Roman Bath
Howard Hotel
King's College
Somerset House
Gilbert Collection
Thames Police Station
Entrance to Strand Underpass (northbound only)
HQS Wellington (Master Mariners)
Savoy Pier
Cleopatra's Needle
London Transport Mus
Theatre Mus
Covent Garden
Jubilee Mkt
St Paul's
Africa Centre
Strand Palace Hotel
Savoy Hotel
Vaudeville Th
Adelphi Th
Royal Society of Arts
York Water Gate
Victoria Embankment Gardens
Charing Cross Sta
Charing Cross Hotel
St Martin-in-the Fields
National Gallery
National Portrait Gallery
Coliseum
Duke of York Th
Wyndhams Th
Albery Th
Garrick Th
Hippodrome
Leicester Square
Empire
Warner
Odeon West End
Prince of Wales Th
Prince Charles
St John's Hosp
Apollo Th
Lyric Th
Trocadero Centre
Piccadilly Circus
Criterion Th
Regent Pal. Hotel
Le Meridien Hotel
Royal Academy of Arts
St James's Church
Britain Visitor Centre
Her Majesty's Th
Nelson's Column
S Africa House
Canada Hse
Forte Crest Hotel
Gielgud Th
Queens Th
Fire Sta.
A501
A5200
A201
A401
A4200
A400
A40
A4
A4201
A5201
A5204
A301
B502
B504
B506
B401
B402
EUSTON ROAD
PENTONVILLE ROAD
CALEDONIAN ROAD
GRAY'S INN ROAD
KING'S CROSS ROAD
TOTTENHAM COURT ROAD
GOWER STREET
HIGH HOLBORN
NEW OXFORD STREET
OXFORD STREET
KINGSWAY
ALDWYCH
STRAND
VICTORIA EMBANKMENT
WATERLOO BRIDGE
SHAFTESBURY AVENUE
CHARING CROSS ROAD
PICCADILLY
REGENT STREET
HAYMARKET
TRAFALGAR SQUARE
THEOBALD'S ROAD
SOUTHAMPTON ROW
RUSSELL SQUARE
BLOOMSBURY STREET
GOODGE STREET
ROSEBERY AVENUE
FARRINGDON ROAD
CLERKENWELL
143
148

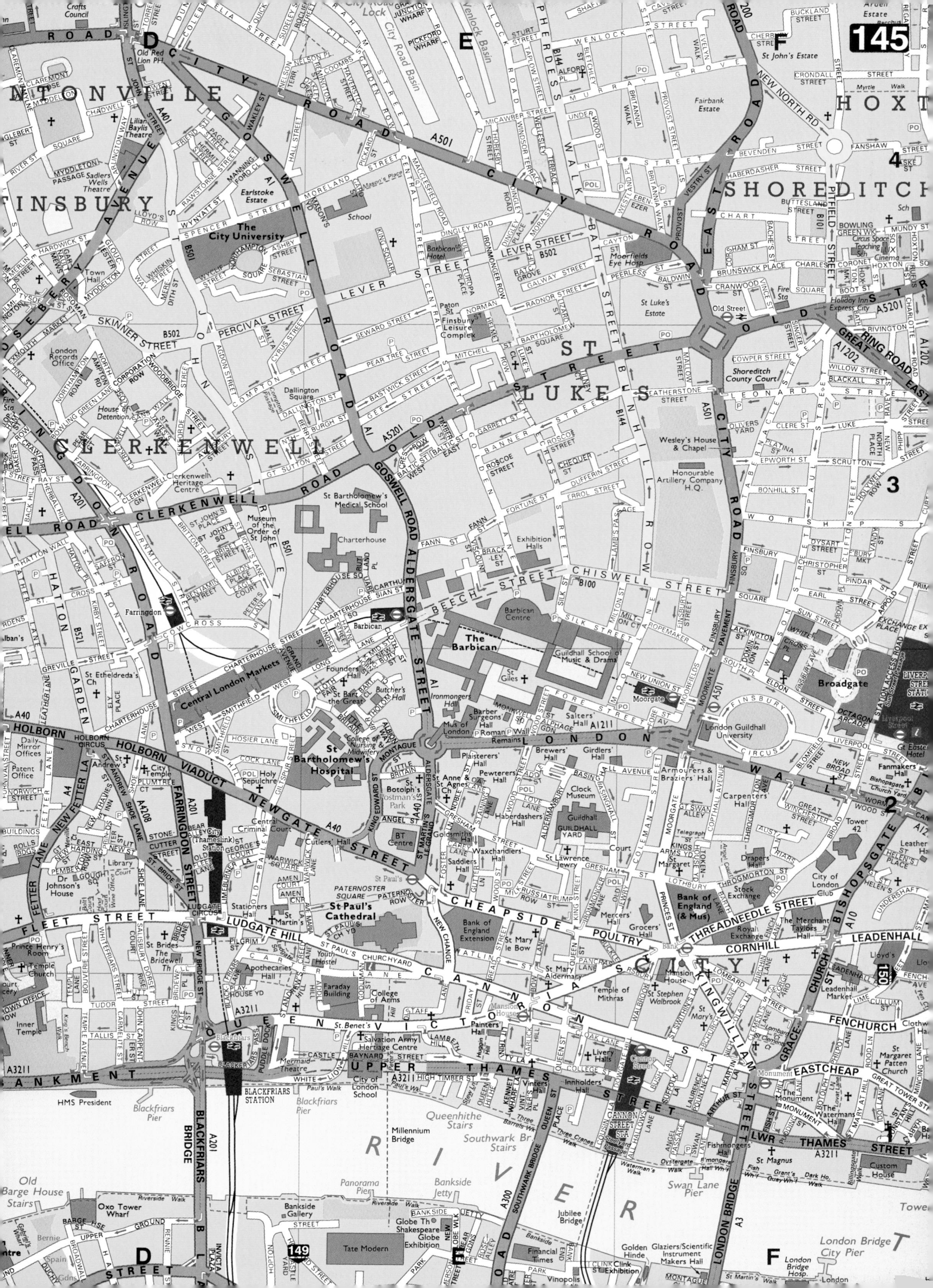
D
E
F
4
3
2
NTONVILLE
FINSBURY
CLERKENWELL
ST LUKES
SHOREDITCH
HOXT
CITY
RIVER
City Road Basin
Wenlock Basin
Crafts Council
Old Red Lion PH
Lilian Baylis Theatre
Sadlers Wells Theatre
Earlstoke Estate
The City University
Town Hall
London Records Office
House of Detention
Dallington Square
Clerkenwell Heritage Centre
St Bartholomew's Medical School
Museum of the Order of St John
Charterhouse
Barbican Hotel
Finsbury Leisure Complex
Moorfields Eye Hosp
St Luke's Estate
Fairbank Estate
St John's Estate
Old Street
Shoreditch County Court
Wesley's House & Chapel
Honourable Artillery Company H.Q.
Exhibition Halls
Barbican Centre
The Barbican
Guildhall School of Music & Drama
St Giles
Moorgate
Broadgate
Liverpool Street
Farringdon
Barbican
Central London Markets
St Etheldreda's Ch
St Bart the Great
Founders' Hall
Butcher's Hall
Ironmongers Hall
Barber Surgeons' Hall
Mus of London
Roman Wall Remains
Salters' Hall
London Guildhall University
Daily Mirror Offices
Patent Office
St Andrew's
City Temple
Holy Sepulchre
St Bartholomew's Hospital
College of Nursing & Midwifery
Postman's Park
BT Centre
Central Criminal Court
City (Thameslink) Station
Cutlers' Hall
Dr Johnson's House
Library
Stationers Hall
St Paul's Cathedral
St Martin's
Plaisterers' Hall
Pewterers' Hall
Brewers' Hall
Girdlers' Hall
Haberdashers' Hall
Clock Museum
Guildhall
Goldsmiths' Hall
Waxchandlers' Hall
Saddlers Hall
St Lawrence Jewry
Mercers' Hall
Grocers' Hall
Armourers & Braziers' Hall
Carpenters' Hall
Drapers' Hall
Stock Exchange
Bank of England (& Mus)
City of London Club
Tower 42
Royal Exchange
The Merchant Taylors Hall
Lloyd's
Leadenhall Market
Bank of England Extension
St Mary le Bow
St Brides
The Bridewell Th
Prince Henry's Room
Temple Church
Inner Temple
Youth Hostel
Apothecaries' Hall
Faraday Building
College of Arms
Temple of Mithras
St Stephen Walbrook
Mansion House
St Mary Aldermary
St Mary's
Salvation Army Heritage Centre
Mermaid Theatre
City of London School
Painters' Hall
Vintners' Hall
Innholders' Hall
Livery Halls
Cannon Street
Fishmongers Hall
St Magnus
Monument
The Monument
The Watermans Hall
St Margaret Patten Church
Custom House
Blackfriars Station
HMS President
Blackfriars Pier
Millennium Bridge
Queenhithe Stairs
Southwark Br. Stairs
Old Barge House Stairs
Oxo Tower Wharf
Bankside Gallery
Panorama Pier
Bankside Jetty
Globe Th Shakespeare Globe Exhibition
Tate Modern
Jubilee Bridge
Swan Lane Pier
Golden Hinde
Glaziers/Scientific Instrument Makers Hall
Clink Exhibition
Vinopolis
Financial Times
London Bridge City Pier
London Bridge Hosp.
149
150
CITY ROAD
GOSWELL ROAD
OLD STREET
CLERKENWELL ROAD
ALDERSGATE STREET
FARRINGDON ROAD
FARRINGDON STREET
HOLBORN VIADUCT
NEWGATE STREET
FLEET STREET
LUDGATE HILL
CHEAPSIDE
POULTRY
CORNHILL
THREADNEEDLE STREET
LEADENHALL
BISHOPSGATE
LONDON WALL
CANNON STREET
QUEEN VICTORIA STREET
UPPER THAMES STREET
LWR THAMES STREET
EASTCHEAP
FENCHURCH
KING WILLIAM STREET
LONDON BRIDGE
SOUTHWARK BRIDGE
BLACKFRIARS BRIDGE
CHISWELL STREET
FINSBURY PAVEMENT
EAST ROAD
NEW NORTH RD
GREAT EASTERN STREET
RING ROAD
ROSEBERY AVENUE
ST JOHN STREET
BEECH STREET
LEVER STREET
GRACECHURCH
A1
A40
A201
A401
A501
A5201
A1211
A3211
A300
A3
A10
B501
B502
B100
B144

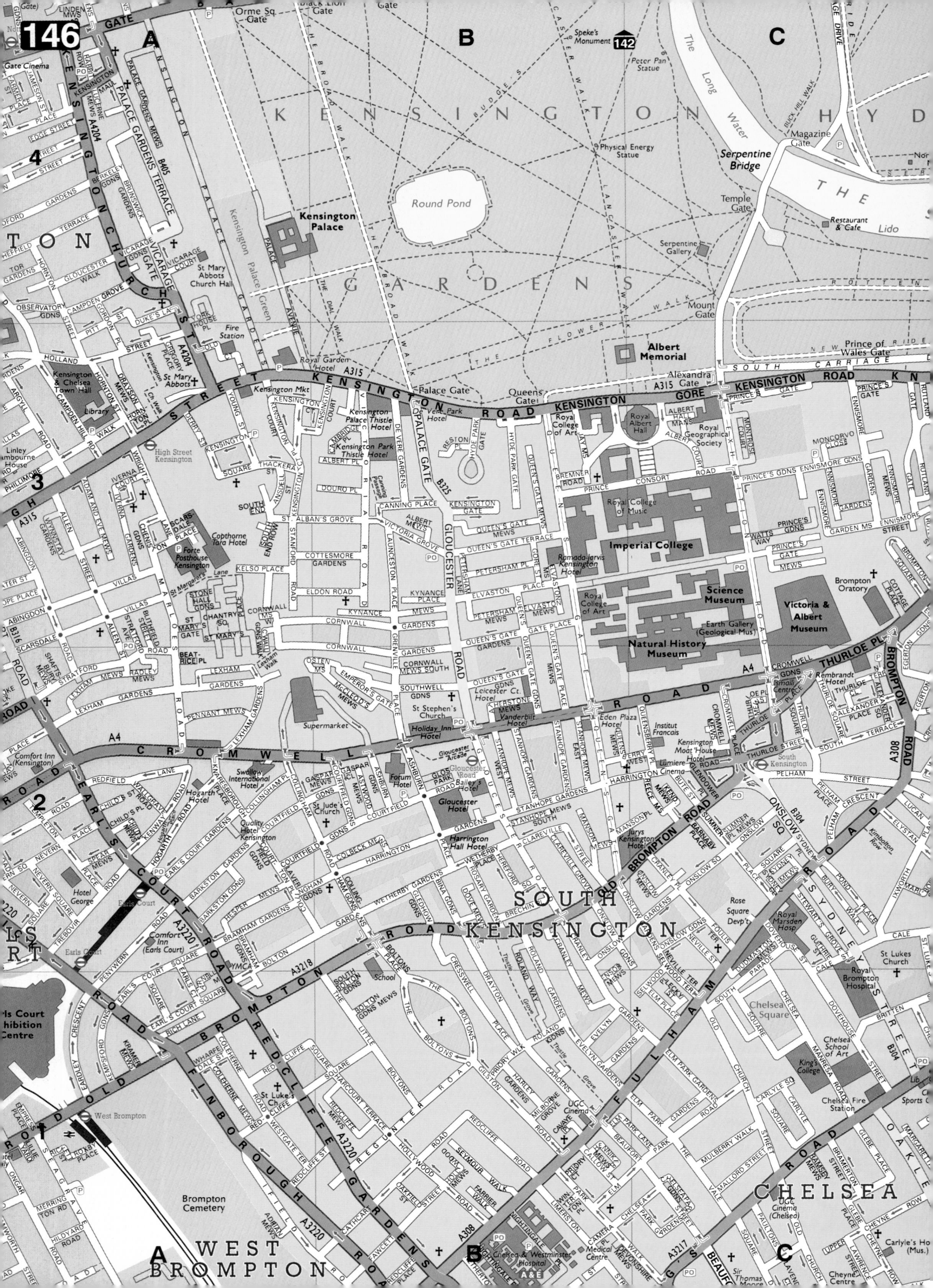
A
B
C
4
3
2
1
KENSINGTON GARDENS
Round Pond
Kensington Palace
Speke's Monument
142
Peter Pan Statue
The Long Water
Physical Energy Statue
Magazine Gate
Serpentine Bridge
Temple Gate
Restaurant & Cafe
Lido
Serpentine Gallery
Mount Gate
Albert Memorial
Prince of Wales Gate
Alexandra Gate
Queens Gate
Palace Gate
Royal Garden Hotel
KENSINGTON ROAD
KENSINGTON GORE
Royal Albert Hall
Royal College of Art
Royal Geographical Society
Royal College of Music
Imperial College
Science Museum
Victoria & Albert Museum
Natural History Museum
Earth Gallery (Geological Mus)
Brompton Oratory
Kensington & Chelsea Town Hall
Library
High Street Kensington
Copthorne Tara Hotel
Forte Posthouse Kensington
Kensington Mkt
St Mary Abbots Church Hall
Fire Station
CROMWELL ROAD
A4
Supermarket
Holiday Inn Hotel
Vanderbilt Hotel
Gloucester Road
Gloucester Hotel
Harrington Hall Hotel
Forum Hotel
Swallow International Hotel
Hogarth Hotel
Comfort Inn (Kensington)
Quality Hotel Kensington
Hotel George
Earls Court
Comfort Inn (Earls Court)
Earls Court Exhibition Centre
South Kensington
Institut Français
Lumière Cinema
Rembrandt Hotel
Jurys Kensington Hotel
SOUTH KENSINGTON
Rose Square Devp't
Royal Marsden Hosp
St Lukes Church
Royal Brompton Hospital
Chelsea Square
Chelsea School of Art
King's College
Chelsea Fire Station
FULHAM ROAD
OLD BROMPTON ROAD
BROMPTON ROAD
REDCLIFFE GARDENS
FINBOROUGH ROAD
A3220
A3218
A308
A3217
School
St Luke's Ch
UGC Cinema
West Brompton
Brompton Cemetery
WEST BROMPTON
Chelsea & Westminster Hospital
A&E
CHELSEA
UGC Cinema (Chelsea)
Carlyle's House (Mus.)
Cheyne Centre
Sir Thomas Moore

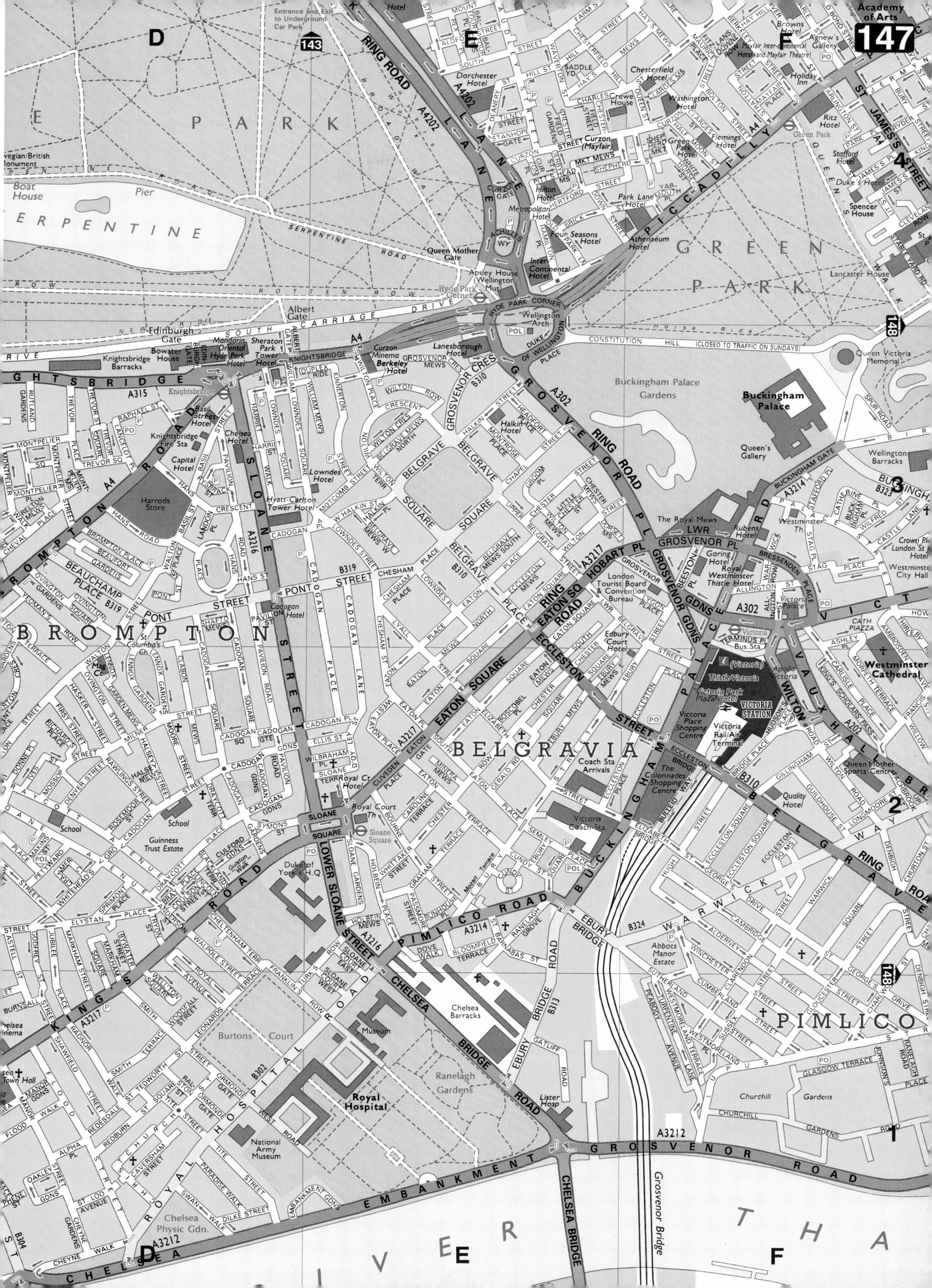
D
E
F
143
148
4
3
2
1
PARK
SERPENTINE
Boat House
Pier
SERPENTINE ROAD
ROTTEN ROW
SOUTH CARRIAGE DRIVE
Queen Mother Gate
Albert Gate
Edinburgh Gate
Entrance and Exit to Underground Car Park
RING ROAD
PARK LANE
A4202
Dorchester Hotel
Hilton Hotel
Metropolitan Hotel
Four Seasons Hotel
Inter-Continental Hotel
Apsley House (Wellington Mus)
Hyde Park Corner
HYDE PARK CORNER
Wellington Arch
Achilles Wy
Curzon Gate
CURZON STREET
Curzon (Mayfair)
Chesterfield Hotel
Crewe House
Washington Hotel
Green Park Hotel
Flemings Hotel
Park Lane Hotel
Athenaeum Hotel
Ritz Hotel
Holiday Inn
Browns Hotel
Mayfair Inter-Continental Hotel (and Mayfair Theatre)
Agnew's Gallery
Academy of Arts
Stafford Hotel
Duke's Hotel
Spencer House
Lancaster House
PICCADILLY
A4
Green Park
GREEN PARK
ST JAMES'S STREET
QUEEN'S WALK
CONSTITUTION HILL (CLOSED TO TRAFFIC ON SUNDAYS)
Horse Ride
Queen Victoria Memorial
Buckingham Palace Gardens
Buckingham Palace
Queen's Gallery
Wellington Barracks
BIRDCAGE WALK
BUCKINGHAM GATE
The Royal Mews
Rubens Hotel
Goring Hotel
Royal Westminster Thistle Hotel
Westminster Th.
Crown Pl London St James Hotel
Westminster City Hall
VICTORIA STREET
Victoria Palace
Victoria
Victoria Station
Thistle Victoria
Victoria Park Plaza Hotel
Victoria Place Shopping Centre
Victoria Rail/Air Terminal
Apollo Victoria
Westminster Cathedral
VAUXHALL BRIDGE ROAD
A202
Queen Mother Sports Centre
Quality Hotel
BELGRAVE ROAD
RING ROAD
KNIGHTSBRIDGE
Knightsbridge
A315
Knightsbridge Barracks
Bowater House
Mandarin Oriental Hyde Park Hotel
Sheraton Park Tower Hotel
Curzon Minema
Berkeley Hotel
Lanesborough Hotel
DUKE OF WELLINGTON PLACE
GROSVENOR CRES
GROSVENOR PLACE
A302
RING ROAD
Halkin Hotel
Basil Street Hotel
Knightsbridge Fire Sta
Chelsea Hotel
Capital Hotel
Harrods Store
Lowndes Hotel
Hyatt-Carlton Tower Hotel
BELGRAVE SQUARE
BROMPTON ROAD
SLOANE STREET
A3216
PONT STREET
B319
Cadogan Hotel
BROMPTON
BEAUCHAMP PLACE
St Columba's Ch
CADOGAN PLACE
EATON PLACE
EATON SQUARE
A3217
B310
BELGRAVIA
ECCLESTON STREET
HOBART PL
GROSVENOR GDNS
GROSVENOR PL
BRESSENDEN PLACE
London Tourist Board & Convention Bureau
Ebury Court Hotel
Terminus Pl
Bus Sta
BUCKINGHAM PALACE ROAD
Coach Sta Arrivals
The Colonnades Shopping Centre
Victoria Coach Sta
ECCLESTON BRIDGE
Royal Ct Hotel
Royal Court Th
SLOANE SQUARE
Sloane Square
Guinness Trust Estate
School
Duke of York's H.Q.
LOWER SLOANE STREET
PIMLICO ROAD
A3214
Chelsea Barracks
EBURY BRIDGE
B324
WARWICK WAY
Abbots Manor Estate
PIMLICO
Churchill Gardens
KING'S ROAD
A3217
Burtons Court
Museum
Ranelagh Gardens
Royal Hospital
National Army Museum
ROYAL HOSPITAL ROAD
B302
CHELSEA BRIDGE ROAD
Lister Hosp
GROSVENOR ROAD
A3212
CHELSEA EMBANKMENT
CHELSEA BRIDGE
Grosvenor Bridge
Chelsea Physic Gdn.
RIVER THAMES

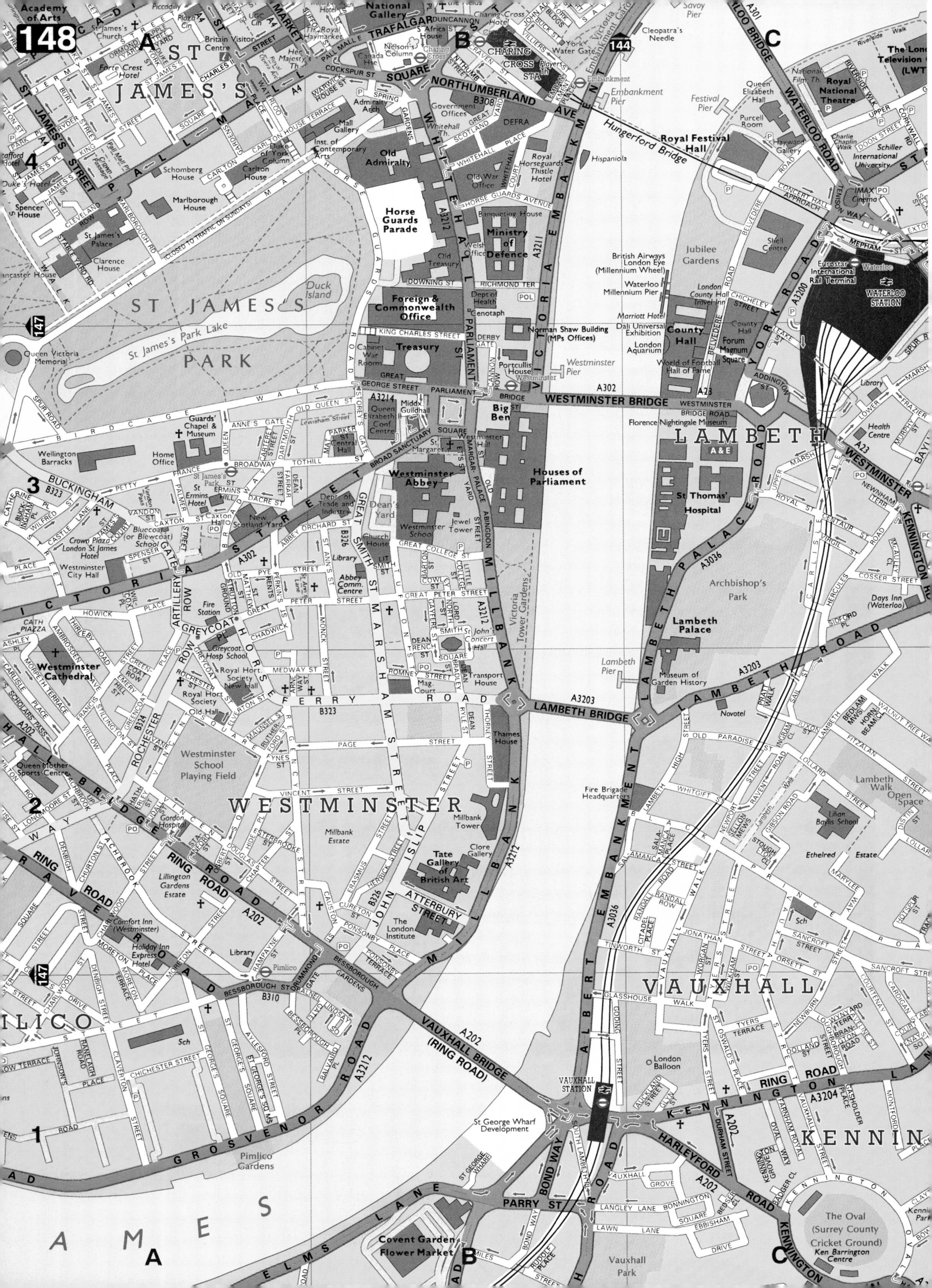
A
B
C
4
3
2
1
144
147
147
ST JAMES'S
ST JAMES'S PARK
St James's Park Lake
Duck Island
Academy of Arts
National Gallery
TRAFALGAR SQUARE
Nelson's Column
Charing Cross
CHARING CROSS STA
Embankment
Embankment Pier
Cleopatra's Needle
Savoy Pier
Festival Pier
Hungerford Bridge
Royal Festival Hall
Queen Elizabeth Hall
Purcell Room
Hayward Gallery
Royal National Theatre
National Film Th
The London Television Centre (LWT)
IMAX Cinema
International University
Charlie Chaplin Walk
Schiller International University
WATERLOO ROAD
WATERLOO STATION
Eurostar International Rail Terminal
Shell Centre
Jubilee Gardens
British Airways London Eye (Millennium Wheel)
Waterloo Millennium Pier
London County Hall Travel Inn
Marriott Hotel
Dali Universal Exhibition
London Aquarium
County Hall
Forum Magnum Square
World of Football Hall of Fame
Hispaniola
St James's Church
Britain Visitor Centre
Forte Crest Hotel
PALL MALL
THE MALL
Admiralty Arch
Mall Gallery
Inst. of Contemporary Arts
Duke of York Column
Carlton House
Schomberg House
Marlborough House
Spencer House
St James's Palace
Clarence House
Lancaster House
Queen Victoria Memorial
Old Admiralty
Horse Guards Parade
Government Offices
Whitehall Th.
DEFRA
Old War Office
Royal Horseguards Thistle Hotel
Banqueting House
Ministry of Defence
Welsh Office
Old Treasury
DOWNING ST
RICHMOND TER
Dept of Health
Cenotaph
Foreign & Commonwealth Office
KING CHARLES STREET
Treasury
Cabinet War Rooms
Norman Shaw Building (MPs Offices)
Portcullis House
Westminster Pier
NORTHUMBERLAND AVE
VICTORIA EMBANKMENT
WHITEHALL
PARLIAMENT ST
WESTMINSTER BRIDGE
Big Ben
Houses of Parliament
Middx Guildhall
Queen Elizabeth II Conf Centre
Methodist Central Hall
St Margaret's
Westminster Abbey
Dean's Yard
Jewel Tower
Westminster School
Church House
Dept of Trade and Industry
New Scotland Yard
Home Office
Guards' Chapel & Museum
Wellington Barracks
BIRDCAGE WALK
BUCKINGHAM GATE
St Ermins Hotel
Caxton Hall
Bluecoat (or Blewcoat) School
Crown Plaza London St James Hotel
Westminster City Hall
VICTORIA STREET
BROADWAY
Florence Nightingale Museum
LAMBETH
St Thomas' Hospital
A & E
Archbishop's Park
Lambeth Palace
Museum of Garden History
LAMBETH PALACE ROAD
LAMBETH BRIDGE
LAMBETH ROAD
Lambeth Pier
Novotel
Health Centre
Days Inn (Waterloo)
Victoria Tower Gardens
MILLBANK
Thames House
St John's Concert Hall
Transport House
Westminster Cathedral
Greycoat Hosp School
Royal Hort. Society New Hall
Royal Hort Society Old Hall
Fire Station
Westminster School Playing Field
Queen Mother Sports Centre
Gordon Hospital
WESTMINSTER
Millbank Estate
Millbank Tower
Tate Gallery of British Art
Clore Gallery
The London Institute
Lillington Gardens Estate
Comfort Inn (Westminster)
Holiday Inn Express Hotel
Library
Pimlico
VAUXHALL BRIDGE (RING ROAD)
VAUXHALL BRIDGE ROAD
GROSVENOR ROAD
Pimlico Gardens
St George Wharf Development
VAUXHALL STATION
Fire Brigade Headquarters
ALBERT EMBANKMENT
Lambeth Walk Open Space
Lilian Baylis School
Ethelred Estate
VAUXHALL
London Balloon
KENNINGTON LANE
HARLEYFORD ROAD
KENNINGTON
The Oval (Surrey County Cricket Ground)
Ken Barrington Centre
Vauxhall Park
Covent Garden Flower Market
NINE ELMS LANE
PARRY ST
BOND WAY
THAMES

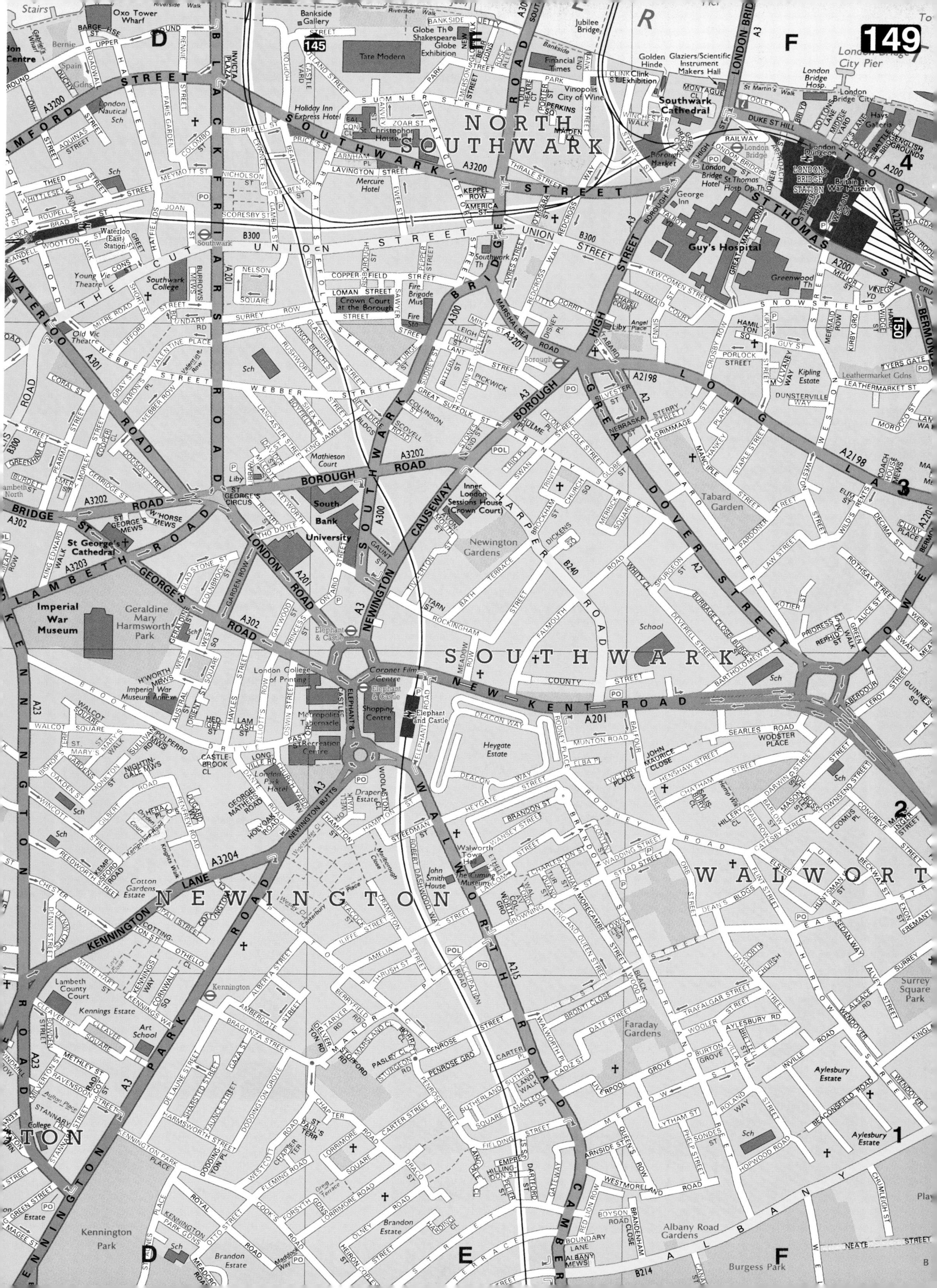
D
E
F
1
2
3
4
145
150
NORTH SOUTHWARK
SOUTHWARK
NEWINGTON
WALWORTH
Oxo Tower Wharf
Bankside Gallery
Tate Modern
Globe Theatre Shakespeare Globe Exhibition
Jubilee Bridge
Financial Times
Golden Hinde
Glaziers/Scientific Instrument Makers Hall
Clink Exhibition
Vinopolis City of Wine
Southwark Cathedral
London Bridge City Pier
London Bridge Hosp.
London Bridge City
Hays Galleria
London Dungeon
LONDON BRIDGE STATION
Britain at War Museum
Borough Market
London Bridge Hotel
St.Thomas' Hosp Op Th
George Inn
Guy's Hospital
Greenwood Th
Holiday Inn Express Hotel
St Christopher House
Mercure Hotel
London Nautical Sch
Waterloo (East) Station
Southwark
Young Vic Theatre
Southwark College
Old Vic Theatre
Crown Court at the Borough
Fire Brigade Mus
Southwark Th
Kipling Estate
Leathermarket Gdns
Mathieson Court
South Bank University
Inner London Sessions House (Crown Court)
Newington Gardens
St George's Cathedral
Imperial War Museum
Geraldine Mary Harmsworth Park
Elephant & Castle
London College of Printing
Coronet Film Centre
Elephant & Castle Shopping Centre
Metropolitan Tabernacle
Heygate Estate
Tabard Garden
School
Imperial War Museum Annexe
London Park Hotel
Draper Estate
Walworth Town Hall
The Cuming Museum
John Smith House
Cotton Gardens Estate
Lambeth County Court
Kennings Estate
Art School
Kennington
Faraday Gardens
Surrey Square Park
Aylesbury Estate
Brandon Estate
Kennington Park
Albany Road Gardens
Burgess Park
BLACKFRIARS ROAD
SOUTHWARK STREET
STAMFORD STREET
UNION STREET
BOROUGH HIGH STREET
SOUTHWARK BRIDGE ROAD
BOROUGH ROAD
LONG LANE
TOOLEY STREET
ST THOMAS STREET
GREAT DOVER STREET
NEWINGTON CAUSEWAY
LONDON ROAD
ST GEORGE'S ROAD
LAMBETH ROAD
WATERLOO ROAD
THE CUT
KENNINGTON ROAD
KENNINGTON LANE
KENNINGTON PARK ROAD
NEWINGTON BUTTS
NEW KENT ROAD
WALWORTH ROAD
CAMBERWELL ROAD
ALBANY ROAD
OLD KENT ROAD
TOWER BRIDGE ROAD
EAST STREET
PORTLAND STREET
THURLOW STREET
RODNEY ROAD
HARPER ROAD
A3
A2
A23
A200
A201
A215
A300
A301
A302
A2198
A3200
A3202
A3203
A3204
B214
B240
B300

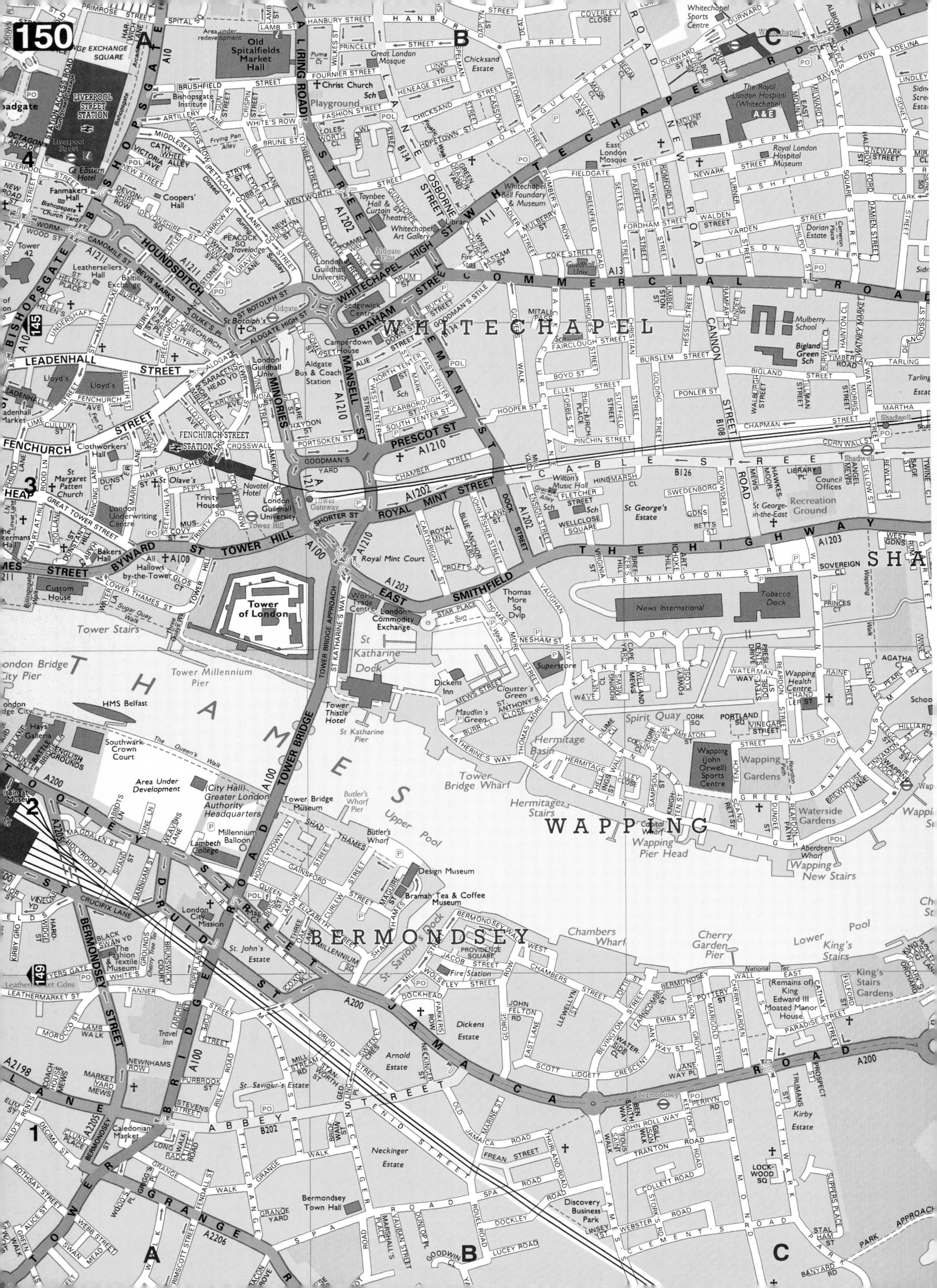
A
B
C
4
3
2
1
145
149
Old Spitalfields Market Hall
Area under redevelopment
Liverpool Street Station
Bishopsgate Institute
Christ Church
Playground
Great London Mosque
Chicksand Estate
Whitechapel Sports Centre
The Royal London Hospital (Whitechapel)
A&E
Royal London Hospital Museum
East London Mosque
Whitechapel Bell Foundary & Museum
Toynbee Hall & Curtain Theatre
Whitechapel Art Gallery
London Guildhall University
Aldgate East
Guildhall Univ
Dorian Estate
WHITECHAPEL
Mulberry School
Bigland Green Sch
Sedgewick Centre
Camperdown House
Aldgate Bus & Coach Station
Lloyd's
Fenchurch Street Station
Clothworkers' Hall
St Margaret Pattens Church
London Underwriting Centre
Trinity House
Novotel Hotel
Tower Gateway
Tower Hill
Royal Mint Court
All Hallows by-the-Tower
Custom House
Tower of London
Tower Stairs
World Trade Centre
London Commodity Exchange
St Katharine Dock
Thomas More Sq Dvlp
Wilton's Music Hall
St George's Estate
St George-in-the-East
Recreation Ground
Council Offices
News International
Tobacco Dock
Superstore
Dickens Inn
Tower Thistle Hotel
St Katharine Pier
Tower Millennium Pier
London Bridge City Pier
HMS Belfast
Hays Galleria
Southwark Crown Court
THAMES
Area Under Development
(City Hall) Greater London Authority Headquarters
Millennium Balloon
Lambeth College
Tower Bridge Museum
Butler's Wharf Pier
Butler's Wharf
Upper Pool
Design Museum
Bramah Tea & Coffee Museum
Hermitage Basin
Tower Bridge Wharf
Hermitage Stairs
Spirit Quay
Wapping (John Orwell) Sports Centre
Wapping Gardens
WAPPING
Wapping Health Centre
Waterside Gardens
Capital Wharf
Wapping Pier Head
Aberdeen Wharf
Wapping New Stairs
BERMONDSEY
London City Mission
St. John's Estate
The Fashion & Textile Museum
Chambers Wharf
Cherry Garden Pier
Lower Pool
King's Stairs
King's Stairs Gardens
(Remains of) King Edward III Moated Manor House
Fire Station
Dickens Estate
Arnold Estate
Travel Inn
St. Saviour's Estate
Caledonian Market
Neckinger Estate
Bermondsey Town Hall
Discovery Business Park
Kirby Estate
Bermondsey
Shadwell
WHITECHAPEL ROAD
COMMERCIAL ROAD
THE HIGHWAY
CABLE STREET
EAST SMITHFIELD
ROYAL MINT STREET
TOWER BRIDGE
TOWER BRIDGE ROAD
TOWER BRIDGE APPROACH
JAMAICA ROAD
TOOLEY STREET
BERMONDSEY STREET
DRUID STREET
GRANGE ROAD
ABBEY STREET
SPA ROAD
BISHOPSGATE
HOUNDSDITCH
LEADENHALL STREET
FENCHURCH STREET
MINORIES
MANSELL ST
LEMAN ST
COMMERCIAL STREET
OSBORNE STREET
NEW ROAD
CANNON STREET ROAD
PRESCOT ST
ALDGATE HIGH ST
TOWER HILL
BYWARD ST
WAPPING LANE
WAPPING HIGH ST
SOUTHWARK PARK ROAD
PARK APPROACH

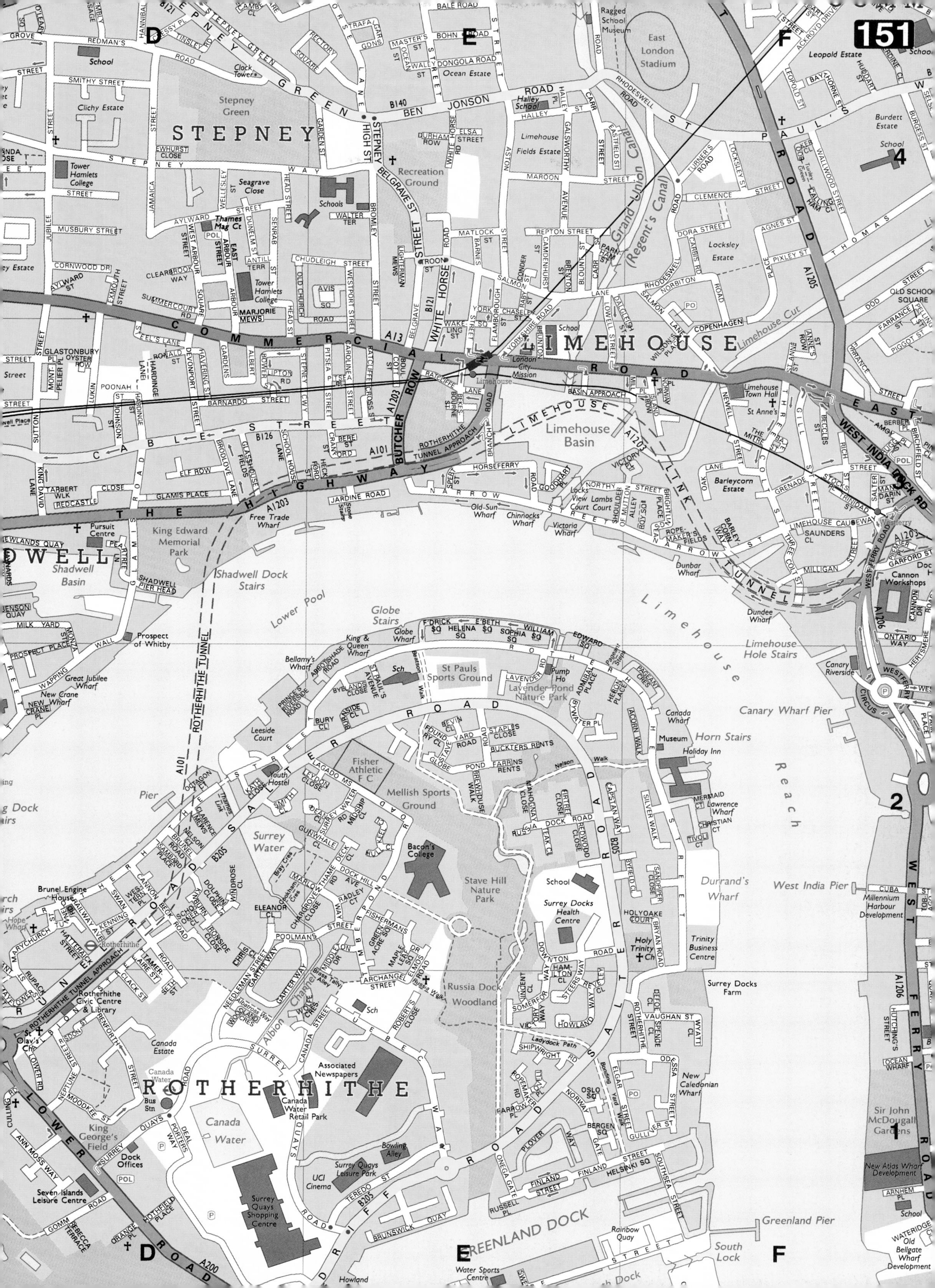
D
E
F
STEPNEY
LIMEHOUSE
ROTHERHITHE
Stepney Green
East London Stadium
Ragged School Museum
Clock Tower
Ben Jonson Road
Commercial Road
The Highway
Cable Street
Stepney Way
Tower Hamlets College
Schools
Recreation Ground
Limehouse Fields Estate
Halley School
Ocean Estate
Clichy Estate
Grand Union Canal
(Regent's Canal)
Limehouse Cut
Locksley Estate
Leopold Estate
Burdett Estate
London City Mission
Limehouse
Limehouse Basin
Limehouse Link
Limehouse Town Hall
St Anne's
Barleycorn Estate
West India Dock Rd
Narrow Street
Rotherhithe Tunnel Approach
Rotherhithe Tunnel
King Edward Memorial Park
Shadwell Basin
Shadwell Dock Stairs
Shadwell Pier Head
Pursuit Centre
Free Trade Wharf
Old Sun Wharf
Chinnocks' Wharf
Victoria Wharf
Dunbar Wharf
Dundee Wharf
Lower Pool
Limehouse Reach
Limehouse Hole Stairs
Cannon Workshops
Canary Riverside
Canary Wharf Pier
Westferry Circus
Globe Stairs
Globe Wharf
King & Queen Wharf
Bellamy's Wharf
Prospect of Whitby
Great Jubilee Wharf
New Crane Wharf
Wapping Wall
Rotherhithe Street
Salter Road
St Pauls Sports Ground
Lavender Pond Nature Park
Pump Ho
Canada Wharf
Museum
Horn Stairs
Holiday Inn
Lawrence Wharf
Youth Hostel
Fisher Athletic F C
Mellish Sports Ground
Surrey Water
Bacon's College
Stave Hill Nature Park
Russia Dock Woodland
Durrand's Wharf
West India Pier
Millennium Harbour Development
School
Surrey Docks Health Centre
Holy Trinity Ch
Trinity Business Centre
Surrey Docks Farm
Brunel Engine House
Rotherhithe
Rotherhithe Civic Centre & Library
Canada Estate
Canada Water
Associated Newspapers
Canada Water Retail Park
King George's Field
Dock Offices
Seven Islands Leisure Centre
Surrey Quays Shopping Centre
Surrey Quays Leisure Park
UCI Cinema
Bowling Alley
New Caledonian Wharf
Sir John McDougall Gardens
New Atlas Wharf Development
Greenland Dock
Greenland Pier
Rainbow Quay
South Lock
Water Sports Centre
Old Bellgate Wharf Development
Lower Road
Westferry Road
A13
A1203
A1205
A1206
A101
A200
B205
B126
B121
B140
1
2
4

Central London street index

In the index the street names are listed in alphabetical order and written in full, but may be abbreviated on the map. Postal codes are listed where information is available. A proportion of street names and their references are also followed by the name of another street in italics. These entries do not appear on the map due to insufficient space but can be located adjacent to the name of the road in italics.

A

148 B3 Abbey Orchard Street SW1
150 A1 Abbey Street SE1
146 A3 Abbots Gardens W8
St Mary's Place
150 A2 Abbots Lane SE1
146 A3 Abbots Walk W8
St Mary's Place
151 E2 Abbotshade Road SE16
145 F1 Abchurch Lane EC4
142 B4 Abercorn Close NW8
142 B4 Abercorn Place NW8
142 C3 Aberdeen Place NW8
149 F2 Aberdour Street SE1
146 A3 Abingdon Road W8
148 B3 Abingdon Street SW1
146 A3 Abingdon Villas W8
147 E4 Achilles Way W1
151 F4 Ackroyd Drive E3
151 F2 Acorn Walk SE16
144 C4 Acton Street WC1
143 E1 Adam and Eve Court W1
Oxford Street
146 A3 Adam And Eve Mews W8
148 B1 Adam Street WC2
143 E1 Adam's Row W1
148 C3 Addington Street SE1
145 E1 Addle Hill EC4
145 E2 Addle Street EC2
144 B1 Adelaide Street WC2
William IV Street
150 D4 Adelina Grove E1
144 B2 Adeline Place WC1
144 B1 Adelphi Terrace WC2
Adams Street
150 B4 Adler Street E1
151 E2 Admiral Place SE16
142 A3 Admiral Way W9
142 C3 Adpar Street W2
146 A1 Adrian Mews SW10
144 B1 Agar Street WC2
150 C2 Agatha Close E1
145 D3 Agdon Street EC1
151 F4 Agnes Street E14
151 D1 Ainstey Street SE16
Brunel Road
144 A1 Air Street W1
148 C4 Alaska Street SE1
149 E1 Albany Mews SE5
149 E1 Albany Road SE5
143 F4 Albany Street NW1
151 D1 Albatross Way SE16
143 F1 Albemarle Street W1
144 C3 Albemarle Way EC1
Clerkenwell Road
146 C3 Albert Court SW7
148 B1 Albert Embankment SE1
151 D3 Albert Gardens E1
146 C3 Albert Hall Mansions SW7
146 B3 Albert Mews W8
146 B3 Albert Place W8
149 D1 Alberta Street SE17
143 D1 Albion Close W2
143 D1 Albion Mews W2
145 D3 Albion Place EC1
151 D1 Albion Street SE16
143 D1 Albion Street W2
145 E2 Albion Way EC1
150 C4 Albion Yard E1
143 E2 Aldburgh Mews W1
Wigmore Street
144 A4 Aldenham Street NW1
145 E2 Aldermanbury EC2
145 E2 Aldermanbury Square EC2
Aldermanbury
147 F2 Alderney Street SW1
145 E3 Aldersgate Street EC1
143 E1 Alford Street W1
150 A3 Aldgate EC3
150 A3 Aldgate High Street EC3
142 A3 Aldsworth Close W9
144 C1 Aldwych WC2
146 C2 Alexander Place SW7
146 C2 Alexander Square SW3
142 A2 Alexander Street W2
145 E4 Alford Place N1
144 A3 Alfred Mews W1
144 A3 Alfred Place WC1
142 A2 Alfred Road W2
149 F3 Alice Street SE1
150 B3 Alie Street E1
145 F1 All Hallows Lane EC4
143 F2 All Soul's Place W1
Langham Street
146 A3 Allen Street W8
147 F3 Allington Street SW1
143 D3 Allsop Place NW1
142 B4 Alma Square NW8
147 D1 Alpha Place SW3
149 F1 Alsace Road SE17
149 B1 Alscot Road SE1
151 F2 Alvey Street SE17
149 D1 Ambergate Street SE17
142 A3 Amberley Road W9
148 A3 Ambrosden Avenue SW1
149 E2 Amelia Street SE17
145 D2 Amen Corner EC4
145 D2 Amen Court EC4
150 A3 America Square EC3
149 E4 America Street SE1
151 F3 Amoy Place E14
144 C4 Ampton Place WC1
144 C4 Ampton Street WC1
144 C4 Amwell Street EC1
147 D2 Anderson Street SW3
144 B2 Andrew Borde Street WC2
Charing Cross Road
145 F2 Angel Court EC2
148 A4 Angel Court SW1
King Street
150 C3 Angel Mews E1
145 F1 Angel Passage EC4
149 E4 Angel Place SE1
145 E2 Angel Street EC1
151 D1 Ann Moss Way SE16
146 A3 Ansdell Street W8
151 D4 Antill Terrace E1
145 D2 Apothecary Street EC4
New Bridge Street
144 A1 Apple Tree Yard SW1
145 F3 Appold Street EC2
149 D4 Aquinas Street SE1
151 D4 Arbour Square E1
151 E1 Archangel Street SE16
144 A1 Archer Street W1
149 E4 Argent Street SE1
Loman Street
144 B4 Argyle Square WC1
144 B4 Argyle Street WC1
144 B4 Argyle Walk WC1
146 A3 Argyll Road W8
143 F2 Argyll Street W1
147 F4 Arlington Street SW1
145 D4 Arlington Way EC1
144 B2 Arne Street WC2
148 A2 Arneway Street SW1
149 E1 Arnside Street SE17
145 F1 Arthur Street EC4
150 C3 Artichoke Hill E1
150 A4 Artillery Lane E1
150 A4 Artillery Passage E1
Artillery Lane
148 A3 Artillery Row SW1
150 A4 Artizan Street E1
Harrow Place
144 C1 Arundel Street WC2
142 C3 Ashbridge Street NW8
146 B2 Ashburn Gardens SW7
146 B2 Ashburn Mews SW7
146 B2 Ashburn Place SW7
145 D4 Ashby Street EC1
150 B3 Asher Drive E1
151 D4 Ashfield Road E1
Ashfield Street
150 C4 Ashfield Street E1
151 D4 Ashfield Yard E1
Ashfield Street
142 E3 Ashland Place W1
147 F3 Ashley Place SW1
142 C3 Ashmill Street NW1
142 A4 Ashworth Road W9
145 F4 Aske Street N1
149 E2 Asolando Drive SE17
King & Queen Street
150 B4 Assam Street E1
151 D4 Assembly Passage E1
147 D2 Astell Street SW3
151 E4 Aston Street E14
146 B2 Astwood Mews SW7
146 B2 Atherstone Mews SW7
148 B2 Atterbury Street SW1
144 C4 Attneave Street WC1
142 B4 Aubrey Place NW8
148 C1 Auckland Street SE11
143 F4 Augustus Street NW1
149 D1 Aulton Place SE11
145 F2 Austin Friars EC2
145 F2 Austin Friars Square EC2
Austin Friars
149 D2 Austral Street SE11
145 E2 Ave Maria Lane EC4
148 C1 Aveline Street SE11
143 F1 Avery Row W1
151 E4 Avis Square E1
149 E3 Avon Place SE1
149 E3 Avonmouth Street SE1
143 E2 Aybrook Street W1
149 F1 Aylesbury Road SE17
145 D3 Aylesbury Street EC1
148 A1 Aylesford Street SW1
151 D4 Aylward Street E1
149 E4 Ayres Street SE1

B

148 A4 Babmaes Street SW1
Jermyn Street
145 F4 Bacchus Walk N1
145 F4 Bache's Street N1
150 B4 Back Church Lane E1
145 D3 Back Hill EC1
150 A1 Bacon Grove SE1
148 C1 Badger Close SE11
144 B2 Bainbridge Street WC1
143 D3 Baker Street W1 & NW1
143 E2 Baker's Mews W1
145 F3 Baker's Row EC1
145 D3 Baker's Yard EC1
Baker's Row
150 A3 Bakers Hall Court EC3
Harp Lane
143 D3 Balcombe Street NW1
143 E1 Balderton Street W1
145 F4 Baldwin Street EC1
144 C3 Baldwin's Gardens EC1
151 F4 Bale Road E1
144 B4 Balfe Street N1
143 E1 Balfour Mews W1
143 E1 Balfour Place W1
149 F2 Balfour Street SE17
148 A1 Balneil Gate SW1
145 E3 Baltic Street East EC1
145 E3 Baltic Street West EC1
148 B2 Balvaird Place SW1
148 C1 Bancroft Road E1
149 E4 Bank End SE1
149 E4 Bankside SE1
145 E1 Bankside Jetty SE1
145 E3 Banner Street EC1
150 C1 Banyard Road SE16
144 C3 Barbon Close WC1
145 D1 Barge House Street SE1
142 A1 Bark Place W2
146 A2 Barkston Gardens SW5
151 F3 Barleycorn Way E14
143 F1 Barlow Place W1
149 F2 Barlow Street SE17
146 C2 Barnaby Place SW7
151 D3 Barnardo Street E1
144 A4 Barnby Street NW1
151 E4 Barnes Street E14
150 A2 Barnham Street SE1
142 A3 Barnwood Close W9
149 D3 Baron's Place SE1
143 E2 Barrett Street W1
142 B1 Barrie Street W2
142 C4 Barrow Hill Road NW8
St Johns Wood High Street
144 B2 Barter Street WC1
145 F2 Barth Lane EC2
145 E2 Bartholomew Close EC1
145 E3 Bartholomew Square EC1
149 F2 Bartholomew Street SE1
148 B3 Barton Street SW1
147 D3 Basil Street SW3
151 E3 Basin Approach E14
145 E2 Basinghall Avenue EC2
145 E2 Basinghall Street EC2
145 E3 Bastwick Street EC1
151 F3 Bate Street E14
144 A2 Bateman Street W1
144 A2 Bateman's Buildings W1
144 C3 Bath Court EC1
Warner Street
145 F4 Bath Place N1
145 E4 Bath Street EC1
149 E3 Bath Terrace SE1
142 C1 Bathurst Mews W2
142 C1 Bathurst Street W2
149 F4 Battle Bridge Lane SE1
150 B4 Batty Street E1
144 A2 Bayley Street WC1
148 C3 Baylis Road SE1
142 A1 Bayswater Road W2
151 F4 Baythorne Street E3
149 F1 Beaconsfield Road SE17
144 A1 Beak Street W1
145 D2 Bear Alley EC4
Farringdon Street
145 E1 Bear Gardens SE1
149 D4 Bear Lane SE1
144 B1 Bear Street WC2
Cranbourn Street
146 A2 Beatrice Place W8
147 D3 Beauchamp Place SW3
145 D3 Beauchamp Street EC1
Brooke Street
147 D3 Beaufort Gardens SW3
146 B1 Beaufort Street SW3
143 E2 Beaumont Mews W1
144 A3 Beaumont Place W1
143 E3 Beaumont Street W1
151 F3 Beccles Street E14
149 F2 Beckway Street SE17
149 E3 Bedale Street SE1
Borough High Street
144 B2 Bedford Avenue WC1
144 B1 Bedford Court WC2
146 A4 Bedford Gardens W8
144 B3 Bedford Place WC1
144 C3 Bedford Row WC1
144 B2 Bedford Square WC1
144 B1 Bedford Street WC2
144 B3 Bedford Way WC1
144 B1 Bedfordbury WC2
148 C2 Bedlam Mews SE11
148 C1 Bedser Close SE11
145 E3 Beech Street EC2
145 F3 Beeston Place SW1
151 E3 Bekesbourne Street E14
147 E3 Belgrave Mews North SW1
147 E3 Belgrave Mews South SW1
147 E3 Belgrave Mews West SW1
147 E3 Belgrave Place SW1
147 F2 Belgrave Road SW1
147 E3 Belgrave Square SW1
151 E3 Belgrave Street E1
144 B4 Belgrove Street WC1
150 A4 Bell Lane E1
142 C3 Bell Street NW1
144 C2 Bell Yard WC2
149 E3 Belvedere Buildings SE1
148 C4 Belvedere Road SE1
151 E4 Ben Jonson Road E1
150 C1 Ben Smith Way SE16
143 D3 Bendall Mews W1
145 E1 Bennet's Hill EC4
Castle Baynard Street
151 D3 Benson Quay E1
143 E2 Bentinck Mews W1
Marylebone Lane
143 E2 Bentinck Street W1
151 E3 Bere Street E1
151 E1 Bergen Square SE16
146 A4 Berkeley Gardens W8
143 D2 Berkeley Mews W1
143 F1 Berkeley Square W1
143 F1 Berkeley Street W1
145 E2 Bermondsey Square SE1
Long Lane
150 A2 Bermondsey Street SE1
150 B1 Bermondsey Wall East SE16
150 B2 Bermondsey Wall West SE16
144 B3 Bernard Street WC1
144 A2 Berners Mews W1
144 A2 Berners Street W1
145 E3 Berry Street EC1
149 E1 Berryfield Road SE17
144 A2 Berwick Street W1
148 B2 Bessborough Gardens SW1
148 A1 Bessborough Place SW1
148 A1 Bessborough Street SW1
144 B2 Betterton Street WC2
150 C3 Betts Street E1
145 F4 Bevenden Street N1
143 D2 Beverston Mews W1
151 E2 Bevin Close SE16
144 C4 Bevin Way WC1
150 A1 Bevington Path SE1
Tanner Street
150 B1 Bevington Street SE16
150 A4 Bevis Marks EC3
150 C3 Bewley Street E1
143 D3 Bickenhall Street W1
144 B4 Bidborough Street WC1
142 A4 Biddulph Road W9
150 C3 Bigland Street E1
150 A3 Billiter Square EC3
Fenchurch Avenue
150 A3 Billiter Street EC3
146 B2 Bina Gardens SW5
143 E3 Bingham Place W1
143 E1 Binney Street W1
151 E3 Birchfield Street E14
145 F1 Birchin Lane EC3
143 E2 Bird Street W1
148 A3 Birdcage Walk SW1
144 B4 Birkenhead Street WC1
145 D2 Bishop's Court EC4
Old Bailey
144 C2 Bishop's Court WC2
Chancery Lane
149 D2 Bishop's Terrace SE11
142 B2 Bishops Bridge Road W2
145 F2 Bishopsgate EC2
150 A4 Bishopsgate Arcade EC2
145 F2 Bishopsgate Churchyard EC2
149 E3 Bittern Street SE1
148 C2 Black Prince Road SE1 & SE11
150 A2 Black Swan Yard SE1
145 F3 Blackall Street EC2
143 E1 Blackburne's Mews W1
145 D1 Blackfriars Bridge EC4 & SE1
145 D1 Blackfriars Lane EC4
145 D1 Blackfriars Passage EC4
149 D4 Blackfriars Road SE1
147 D2 Blacklands Terrace SW3
149 F1 Blackwood Street SE17
143 D3 Blandford Square NW1
143 F2 Blandford Street W1
145 D2 Bleeding Heart Yard EC1
Greville Street
143 F1 Blenheim Street W1
New Bond Street
145 E4 Bletchley Street N1
146 A3 Blithfield Street W8
142 A3 Blomfield Road W9
145 F2 Blomfield Street EC2
142 B2 Blomfield Villas W2
147 F2 Bloomburg Street SW1
Vauxhall Bridge Road
143 F1 Bloomfield Place W1
Bourdon Street
147 E2 Bloomfield Terrace SW1
144 B2 Bloomsbury Court WC1
High Holborn
144 B3 Bloomsbury Place WC1
Southampton Row
144 B2 Bloomsbury Square WC1
144 B2 Bloomsbury Street WC1
144 B2 Bloomsbury Way WC1
151 E4 Blount Street E14
150 B3 Blue Anchor Yard E1
148 A4 Blue Ball Yard SW1
St James's Street
151 F4 Bohn Road E1
143 F3 Bolsover Street W1
145 D2 Bolt Court EC4
146 A2 Bolton Gardens SW5
146 B1 Bolton Gardens Mews SW10
147 F4 Bolton Street W1
146 B2 Boltons Place SW10
148 B1 Bond Way SW8
151 E1 Bonding Yard Walk SE16
145 F3 Bonhill Street EC2
148 C1 Bonnington Square SW8
151 F4 Booker Close E14
145 F4 Boot Street N1
143 F2 Booth's Place W1
Wells Street
145 E4 Boreas Walk N1
Nelson Place
149 E3 Borough High Street SE1
149 E3 Borough Road SE1
149 E1 Borrett Close SE17
147 E2 Boscobel Place SW1
142 C3 Boscobel Street NW8
150 A2 Boss Street SE1
142 D3 Boston Place NW1
144 B3 Boswell Court WC1
Boswell Street
144 B3 Boswell Street WC1
145 F1 Botolph Lane EC3
142 A2 Bott's Mews W2
151 E3 Boulcott Street E1
149 E1 Boundary Lane SE17
149 D4 Boundary Road SE1
143 F1 Bourdon Street W1
143 F2 Bourlet Close W1
147 E2 Bourne Street SW1
142 A2 Bourne Terrace W2
145 D1 Bouverie Street EC4
145 E1 Bow Lane EC4
144 B2 Bow Street WC2
149 D1 Bowden Street SE11
151 D3 Bower Street E1
145 D3 Bowling Green Lane EC1
149 F4 Bowling Green Place SE1
Newcomen Street
148 C1 Bowling Green Street SE11
145 F4 Bowling Green Walk N1
150 B3 Boyd Street E1
149 D3 Boyfield Street SE1
143 F1 Boyle Street W1
Savile Row
149 E1 Boyson Road SE17
145 E3 Brackley Street EC1
149 D4 Brad Street SE1
142 A3 Braden Street W9
149 F1 Bradenham Close SE17
149 D1 Braganza Street SE17
150 B3 Braham Street E1
146 C1 Bramerton Street SW3
146 A2 Bramham Gardens SW5
151 E3 Branch Road E14
149 E2 Brandon Street SE17
148 C1 Brangton Road SE11
151 E1 Brass Tally Alley SE16
151 D2 Bray Crescent SE16
147 D2 Bray Place SW3
145 E1 Bread Street EC4
144 C2 Bream's Buildings EC
146 B2 Brechin Place SW7
150 C3 Breezer's Hill E1
146 B3 Bremner Road SW7
143 D2 Brendon Street W1
151 E4 Brenton Street E14
147 F3 Bressenden Place SW1
149 F1 Brettell Street SE17
144 A1 Brewer Street W1
148 A3 Brewers' Green SW1
Caxton Street
150 C2 Brewhouse Lane E1
151 E2 Brewhouse Walk SE16
144 C2 Brick Court EC4
Middle Temple Lane
147 E4 Brick Street W1
145 D2 Bride Lane EC4
150 B1 Bridewain Street SE1
145 D1 Bridewell Place EC4
143 F3 Bridford Mews W1
147 F2 Bridge Place SW1
148 B3 Bridge Street SW1
149 F4 Bridge Yard SE1
150 B2 Bridgeport Place E1
Kennet Street
145 E3 Bridgewater Square EC2
Beech Street
145 E3 Bridgewater Street EC2
Beech Street
144 A2 Bridgeway Street NW1
144 A1 Bridle Lane W1
142 A2 Bridstow Place W2
151 F3 Brightlingsea Place E14
144 A4 Brill Place NW1
145 D3 Briset Street EC1
142 A3 Bristol Gardens W9
142 B3 Bristol Mews W9
144 C4 Britannia Street WC1
145 F4 Britannia Walk N1
146 C1 Britten Street SW3
145 D3 Britton Street EC1
144 B2 Broad Court WC2
148 B3 Broad Sanctuary SW1
147 E4 Broad Walk W2
143 F1 Broadbent Street W1
142 C4 Broadley Street NW8
143 D3 Broadley Terrace NW1
143 E2 Broadstone Place W1
149 D4 Broadwall SE1
148 A3 Broadway SW1
144 A1 Broadwick Street W1
149 E3 Brockham Street SE1
151 D3 Brodlove Lane E1
151 E4 Bromley Street E1
147 D3 Brompton Place SW3
147 D3 Brompton Road SW3
146 C3 Brompton Square SW3
149 E1 Bronti Close SE17
149 D2 Brook Drive SE11
143 E1 Brook Gate W1
142 B1 Brook Mews North W2
143 E1 Brook Street W1
142 C1 Brook Street W2
143 F1 Brook's Mews W1
145 D2 Brooke Street EC1
144 C2 Brooke's Court EC1
145 D2 Brooke's Market EC1
Brooke Street
143 E1 Brown Hart Gardens W1
143 D2 Brown Street W1
142 B3 Browning Close W9
149 E2 Browning Street SE17
144 C3 Brownlow Mews WC1

Brownlow Street - Dorrington Street 153

144 C2 Brownlow Street WC1
150 A4 Brune Street E1
151 D1 Brunel Road SE16
146 A4 Brunswick Gardens W8
143 D2 Brunswick Mews W1
145 F4 Brunswick Place N1
151 E1 Brunswick Quay SE16
144 B3 Brunswick Square WC1
151 E3 Brunton Place E14
150 A4 Brushfield Street E1
143 F1 Bruton Lane W1
143 F1 Bruton Place W1
143 F1 Bruton Street W1
151 F2 Bryan Road SE16
143 D2 Bryanston Mews East W1
143 D2 Bryanston Mews West W1
143 D2 Bryanston Place W1
143 D2 Bryanston Square W1
143 D2 Bryanston Street W1
142 C1 Buck Hill Walk W2
144 B1 Buck Street WC2
147 F3 Buckingham Gate SW1
147 F2 Buckingham Palace Road SW1
147 F3 Buckingham Place SW1
145 F4 Buckland Street N1
150 B4 Buckle Street E1
145 E2 Bucklersbury EC4
144 B2 Bucknall Street WC2
151 E2 Buckters Rents SE16
142 B4 Budge's Walk W2
147 F2 Bulleid Way SW1
143 E2 Bulstrode Place W1 *Marylebone Lane*
143 E2 Bulstrode Street W1
145 F3 Bunhill Row EC1
147 E2 Bunhouse Place SW1
149 F3 Burbage Close SE1
149 D3 Burdett Street SE1
149 F3 Burge Street SE1
151 F4 Burgess Street E14
145 E2 Burgon Street EC4 *Carter Lane*
144 B1 Burleigh Street WC2
143 F1 Burlington Arcade W1
143 F1 Burlington Gardens W1
142 C3 Burne Street NW1
147 D1 Burnsall Street SW3
151 E2 Burnside Close SE16
150 B2 Burr Close E1
149 D4 Burrell Street SE1
149 D4 Burrows Mews SE1
150 A2 Bursar Street SE1 *Tooley Street*
150 C3 Burslem Street E1
149 F1 Burton Grove SE17
144 B4 Burton Street WC1
150 C3 Burwell Close E1
143 D2 Burwood Place W2
151 E2 Bury Close SE16
150 A4 Bury Court EC3
144 B2 Bury Place WC1
150 A3 Bury Street EC3
148 A4 Bury Street SW1
146 C2 Bury Walk SW3
145 E1 Bush Lane EC4
150 B2 Bushell Street E1 *Wapping High Street*
151 E3 Butcher Row E1
146 C1 Bute Street SW7
147 F3 Butler Place SW1 *Buckingham Gate*
150 C1 Butterfield Close SE16
145 F4 Buttesland Street N1
151 E2 Byelands Close SE16
151 F2 Byfield Close SE16
144 A3 Byng Place WC1
150 A3 Byward Street EC3
151 E2 Bywater Place SE16
147 D2 Bywater Street SW3

C

142 C2 Cabbell Street NW1
150 B3 Cable Street E1
149 E1 Cadiz Street SE17
147 D2 Cadogan Gardens SW3
147 D2 Cadogan Gate SW1
147 E3 Cadogan Lane SW1
147 E2 Cadogan Place SW1
147 D2 Cadogan Square SW1
147 D2 Cadogan Street SW3
145 E3 Cahill Street EC1 *Dufferin Street*
146 C2 Cale Street SW3
149 E4 Caleb Street SE1 *Marshalsea Road*
144 B4 Caledonia Street N1
144 B4 Caledonian Road N1 & N7
151 F4 Callingham Close E14
146 B1 Callow Street SW3
144 C3 Calthorpe Street WC1
149 E1 Camberwell Road SE5
144 B1 Cambridge Circus WC2
143 F3 Cambridge Gate NW1
143 F4 Cambridge Gate Mews NW1 *Albany Street*
146 B3 Cambridge Place W8
142 A4 Cambridge Road NW6
142 C2 Cambridge Square W2
147 F2 Cambridge Street SW1
144 F4 Cambridge Terrace Mews NW1 *Chester Gate*
151 E4 Camdenhurst Street E14
146 B1 Camera Place SW10
150 C4 Cameron Place E1
150 A4 Camomile Street EC3
146 A4 Campden Grove W8
146 A3 Campden Hill Road W8
150 B3 Camperdown Street E1
151 E1 Canada Street SE16
149 F1 Canal Street SE5
143 F2 Candover Street W1 *Foley Street*
146 B3 Canning Passage W8
146 B3 Canning Place W8
151 D2 Cannon Beck Road SE16
151 F3 Cannon Drive E14
148 B3 Cannon Row SW1
145 E2 Cannon Street EC4
150 C3 Cannon Street Road E1
149 E2 Canterbury Place SE17
149 E4 Canvey Street SE1
150 B3 Cape Yard E1
142 C3 Capland Street NW8
144 A3 Capper Street WC1
151 E2 Capstan Way SE16
151 F4 Carbis Road E14
143 F3 Carburton Street W1
148 C1 Cardigan Street SE11
144 A4 Cardington Street NW1
145 E2 Carey Lane EC2
144 C2 Carey Street WC2
150 A3 Carlisle Avenue EC3
148 C3 Carlisle Lane SE1
147 F2 Carlisle Place SW1
144 A2 Carlisle Street W1
143 E1 Carlos Place W1
148 A4 Carlton Gardens SW1
148 A4 Carlton House Terrace SW1
142 A4 Carlton Vale NW6
146 C1 Carlyle Square SW3
145 D1 Carmelite Street EC4
144 A1 Carnaby Street W1
142 A1 Caroline Place Mews W2
151 E3 Caroline Street E1
147 E2 Caroline Terrace SW1
143 E1 Carpenter Street W1
151 E4 Carr Street E14
147 E4 Carrington Street W1 *Shepherd Street*
145 E2 Carter Lane EC4
149 E1 Carter Place SE17
149 E1 Carter Street SE17
148 A3 Carteret Street SW1
145 E3 Carthusian Street EC1
144 C1 Carting Lane WC2
144 B4 Cartwright Gardens WC1
150 B3 Cartwright Street E1
150 B4 Casson Street E1
142 A3 Castellain Road W9
145 E1 Castle Baynard Street EC4
148 A3 Castle Lane SW1
149 D4 Castle Yard SE1
149 D2 Castlebrook Close SE11
143 D2 Castlereagh Street W1
149 F2 Catesby Street SE17
150 C1 Cathay Street SE16
146 B1 Cathcart Road SW10
147 F3 Cathedral Piazza SW1
149 F4 Cathedral Street SE1 *Winchester Walk*
147 F3 Catherine Place SW1
144 C1 Catherine Street WC2
150 A4 Catherine Wheel Alley E1
148 A4 Catherine Wheel Yard SW1 *Little St James's Street*
143 D2 Cato Street W1
144 C2 Catton Street WC1
148 B2 Causton Street SW1
146 B1 Cavaye Place SW10
150 C4 Cavell Street E1
142 C4 Cavendish Avenue NW8
142 C4 Cavendish Close NW8
143 F3 Cavendish Mews North W1 *Hallam Street*
143 F2 Cavendish Mews South W1 *Hallam Street*
143 F2 Cavendish Place W1
143 F2 Cavendish Square W1
147 D1 Caversham Street SW3
148 A3 Caxton Street SW1
145 E4 Cayton Place EC1 *Cayton Street*
145 E4 Cayton Street EC1
144 B1 Cecil Court WC2 *St Martin's Lane*
148 C3 Centaur Street SE1
145 E4 Central Street EC1
145 D4 Chadwell Street EC1
148 A3 Chadwick Street SW1
143 D3 Chagford Street NW1
144 A4 Chalton Street NW1
150 B3 Chamber Street E1
150 B1 Chambers Street SE16
149 D4 Chancel Street SE1
144 C2 Chancery Lane WC2
150 C2 Chandler Street E1
144 B1 Chandos Place WC2
143 F2 Chandos Street W1
146 A3 Chantry Square W8
149 E4 Chapel Court SE1
143 F2 Chapel Place W1
142 A1 Chapel Side W2
142 C2 Chapel Street NW1
147 E3 Chapel Street SW1
150 C3 Chapman Street E1
149 E1 Chapter Road SE17
148 A2 Chapter Street SW1
149 D1 Chapter Terrace SE17
151 D2 Chargrove Close SE16
144 B2 Charing Cross Road WC2
148 A4 Charles II Street SW1
145 F4 Charles Square N1
147 F4 Charles Street W1
149 E2 Charleston Street SE17
148 C4 Charlie Chaplin Walk SE1
144 A2 Charlotte Place W1 *Goodge Street*
147 F2 Charlotte Place SW1 *Wilton Road*
145 F4 Charlotte Road EC2
144 A3 Charlotte Street W1
148 A1 Charlwood Street SW1
145 F4 Chart Street N1
145 E2 Charterhouse Square EC1
145 D2 Charterhouse Street EC1
151 E4 Chaseley Street E14
149 F2 Chatham Street SE17
145 E2 Cheapside EC4
147 E1 Chelsea Bridge SW1 & SW8
147 E1 Chelsea Bridge Road SW1
147 D1 Chelsea Embankment SW3
147 D1 Chelsea Manor Gardens SW3
147 D1 Chelsea Manor Street SW3
146 C1 Chelsea Park Gardens SW3
146 C1 Chelsea Square SW3
147 D2 Cheltenham Terrace SW3
144 A3 Chenies Mews WC1
144 E3 Chenies Street WC1
146 A3 Cheniston Gardens W8
142 A1 Chepstow Place W2
142 A2 Chepstow Road W2
145 E3 Chequer Street EC1
145 F4 Cherbury Street N1
150 C1 Cherry Garden Street SE16
150 A2 Cherry Tree Terrace SE1
147 E3 Chesham Place SW1
147 E3 Chesham Street SW1
143 F4 Chester Close North NW1
143 F4 Chester Close South NW1
143 F4 Chester Court NW1 *Albany Street*
143 F4 Chester Gate NW1
147 E3 Chester Mews SW1
143 F4 Chester Place NW1
147 E2 Chester Row SW1
147 E2 Chester Square SW1
147 E3 Chester Street SW1
143 F4 Chester Terrace NW1
149 D2 Chester Way SE11
147 E4 Chesterfield Gardens W1
143 E1 Chesterfield Hill W1
147 E4 Chesterfield Street W1
147 D3 Cheval Place SW7
146 D1 Cheyne Gardens SW3
146 C1 Cheyne Walk SW3 & SW10
148 C4 Chicheley Street SE1
144 C2 Chichester Rents WC2 *Chancery Lane*
142 A3 Chichester Road W2
148 A1 Chichester Street SW1
150 B4 Chicksand Street E1
150 C3 Chigwell Hill E1 *The Highway*
146 A2 Child's Place SW5
146 A2 Child's Street SW5
146 A2 Childs Mews SW5
143 E3 Chiltern Street W1
142 B2 Chilworth Mews W2
142 B2 Chilworth Street W2
145 E3 Chiswell Street EC1
144 A3 Chitty Street W1
147 D1 Christchurch Street SW3
151 F2 Christian Court SE16
150 C3 Christian Street E1
150 D1 Christopher Close SE16
145 F3 Christopher Street EC2
151 E4 Chudleigh Street E1
149 F1 Chumleigh Street SE5
147 F4 Church Place SW1 *Piccadilly*
142 C3 Church Street NW8
149 D2 Church Yard Row SE11
147 F1 Churchill Gardens Road SW1
144 A4 Churchway NW1
148 A2 Churton Street SW1
150 C2 Cinnamon Street E1
143 D3 Circus Mews W1 *Enford Street*
145 F2 Circus Place EC2 *Finsbury Circus*
142 C4 Circus Road NW8
142 A3 Cirencester Street W2
148 C2 Citadel Place SE11
145 E4 City Garden Row N1
145 F3 City Road EC1
147 D2 Clabon Mews SW1
151 D1 Clack Street SE16
142 A1 Clanricarde Gardens W2
144 C2 Clare Market WC2
145 D4 Claremont Close N1
145 D4 Claremont Square N1
143 F4 Clarence Gardens NW1
151 D2 Clarence Mews SE16
142 C1 Clarendon Close W2
142 B3 Clarendon Gardens W9
142 C1 Clarendon Place W2
147 F1 Clarendon Road W11
147 F1 Clarendon Street SW1
142 B3 Clarendon Terrace W9
146 B2 Clareville Grove SW7
146 B2 Clareville Street SW7
147 F4 Clarges Mews W1
147 F4 Clarges Street W1
150 C4 Clark Street E1
150 C1 Clark's Orchard SE16
150 C2 Clave Street E1
148 A1 Claverton Street SW1
143 D2 Clay Street W1
148 C1 Clayton Street SE11
151 D4 Clearbrook Way E1
142 A3 Clearwell Drive W9
149 D1 Cleaver Square SE11
149 D1 Cleaver Street SE11
150 C2 Clegg Street E1
151 F4 Clemence Street E14
144 C2 Clement's Inn WC2
150 C1 Clement's Road SE16
145 F1 Clements Lane EC4
143 D2 Clenston Mews W1
145 F3 Clere Street EC2
145 D3 Clerkenwell Close EC1
145 D3 Clerkenwell Green EC1
144 C3 Clerkenwell Road EC1
142 B2 Cleveland Gardens W2
143 F3 Cleveland Mews W1
148 A4 Cleveland Place SW1 *King Street*
148 A4 Cleveland Row SW1
142 B2 Cleveland Square W2
143 F3 Cleveland Street W1
142 B2 Cleveland Terrace W2
143 F1 Clifford Street W1
142 B3 Clifton Gardens W9
142 C1 Clifton Place W2
142 B3 Clifton Road W9
145 F3 Clifton Street EC2
142 B3 Clifton Villas W9
149 E4 Clink Street SE1
151 D2 Clipper Close SE16 *Kinburn Street*
143 F3 Clipstone Mews W1
143 F3 Clipstone Street W1
147 E2 Cliveden Place SW1
145 E1 Cloak Lane EC4
145 E2 Cloth Fair EC1
145 E3 Cloth Street EC1
145 F4 Clunbury Street N1 *Cherbury Street*
149 F3 Cluny Place SE1
143 F1 Coach & Horses Yard W1 *Old Burlington Street*
149 F3 Coach House Mews SE1
150 A4 Cobb Street E1
144 A4 Cobourg Street NW1
145 D2 Cock Lane EC1
144 C3 Cockpit Yard WC1
148 B4 Cockspur Street SW1
150 C1 Codling Close E1
149 D4 Coin Street SE1
150 B4 Coke Street E1
146 B2 Colbeck Mews SW7
150 B4 Colchester Street E1 *Drum Street*
144 C3 Coldbath Square EC1
149 E3 Cole Street SE1
145 D1 Colebrooke Row N1
148 A1 Coleherne Mews SW10
146 A1 Coleherne Road SW10
145 E2 Coleman Street EC2
144 C3 Coley Street WC1
145 E1 College Hill EC4 *College Street*
145 E1 College Street EC4
150 C1 Collett Road SE16
144 C4 Collier Street N1
146 A2 Collingham Gardens SW5
146 A2 Collingham Place SW4
146 A2 Collingham Road SW5
149 E3 Collinson Street SE1
149 D3 Colnbrook Street SE1
149 D4 Colombo Street SE1
144 B3 Colonnade WC1
149 E2 Colworth Grove SE17
150 B4 Commercial Road E1 & E14
150 A4 Commercial Street E1
145 D3 Compton Passage EC1
144 B3 Compton Place WC1
145 D3 Compton Street EC1
149 F2 Comus Place SE17
148 C4 Concert Hall Approach SE1
151 E4 Conder Street E14
142 C4 Conduit Mews W2
142 C2 Conduit Place W2
143 F1 Conduit Street W1
149 F2 Congreve Street SE17
143 D1 Connaught Place W2
143 D2 Connaught Square W2
142 C2 Connaught Street W2
149 D4 Cons Street SE1
147 E3 Constitution Hill SW1
149 E2 Content Street SE17
143 F3 Conway Street W1
149 D1 Cook's Road E15
151 D2 Cookham Crescent SE16
145 E4 Coombs Street N1
149 D3 Cooper Close SE1
150 A3 Cooper's Row EC3
146 A3 Cope Place W8
151 F3 Copenhagen Place E14
149 E1 Copley Close SE17
149 E4 Copperfield Street SE1
145 F2 Copthall Avenue EC2
144 B2 Coptic Street WC1
149 D3 Coral Street SE1
144 B3 Coram Street WC1
150 C2 Cork Square E1
143 F1 Cork Street W1
142 C3 Corlett Street NW1 *Bell Street*
148 B4 Corner House Street WC2 *Northumberland Street*
145 F2 Cornhill EC3
146 B3 Cornwall Gardens SW7
146 A2 Cornwall Gardens Walk SW7
146 B2 Cornwall Mews South SW7
146 A3 Cornwall Mews West SW7
148 C4 Cornwall Road SE1
149 D1 Cornwall Square SE11
150 C3 Cornwall Street E1
143 D3 Cornwall Terrace NW1
151 D4 Cornwood Drive E1
145 F4 Coronet Street N1
145 D3 Corporation Row EC1
145 F4 Corsham Street N1
144 B3 Cosmo Place WC1
148 C3 Cosser Street SE1
143 D3 Cosway Street NW1
149 E2 Cotham Street SE17
146 C3 Cottage Place SW3
149 D3 Cottesloe Mews SE1
146 B3 Cottesmore Gardens W8
149 D2 Cottingham Close SE11
149 D2 Cottington Street SE11
149 F4 Cottons Lane SE1
149 F4 Counter Street SE1
149 E2 County Street SE1
150 C4 Court Street E1
148 C1 Courtenay Square SE11
148 C1 Courtenay Street SE11
146 A2 Courtfield Gardens SW5
146 B2 Courtfield Road SW7
145 F1 Cousin Lane EC4
144 A1 Coventry Street W1
150 B4 Coverley Close E1
145 D3 Cowcross Street EC1
148 B3 Cowley Street SW1
145 F3 Cowper Street EC2
150 A1 Coxon Place SE1
144 A4 Crace Street NW1
149 F2 Crail Row SE17
143 E2 Cramer Street W1
149 C2 Crampton Street SE17
144 B1 Cranbourn Street WC2
151 E3 Cranford Street E1
146 B2 Cranley Gardens SW7
146 B2 Cranley Mews SW7
146 C2 Cranley Place SW7
147 D2 Cranmer Court SW3
145 F4 Cranwood Street EC1
142 B1 Craven Hill W2
142 B1 Craven Hill Gardens W2
142 B1 Craven Hill Mews W2
142 B1 Craven Road W2
144 B1 Craven Street WC2
142 B1 Craven Terrace W2
145 D3 Crawford Passage EC1
143 D2 Crawford Place W1
143 D2 Crawford Street W1
149 F3 Creasy Street SE1 *Swan Mead*
150 A3 Creechurch Lane EC3
150 A3 Creechurch Place EC3
145 E2 Creed Lane EC4
150 A3 Crescent EC3 *America Square*
147 D2 Crescent Place SW3
145 E3 Crescent Row EC1
146 B1 Cresswell Place SW10
151 D4 Cressy Place E1
144 B4 Crestfield Street WC1
149 D1 Cricketers' Court SE11 *Kennington Park Road*
150 A1 Crimscott Street SE1
143 E3 Cripplegate Street EC1 *Viscount Street*
150 A4 Crispin Street E1
150 B3 Crofts Street E1
144 B3 Cromer Street WC1
142 B3 Crompton Street W2
146 C2 Cromwell Mews SW7
146 C2 Cromwell Place SW7
146 A1 Cromwell Road SW7 & SW5
145 F4 Crondall Street N1
149 F3 Crosby Row SE1
145 F2 Crosby Square EC3 *Great St Helen's*
143 E2 Cross Keys Close W1 *Marylebone Lane*
150 A3 Cross Lane EC3 *St Dunstan's Hill*
149 F2 Crosslet Street SE17
150 A3 Crosswall EC3
150 C3 Crowder Street E1
144 B2 Crown Court WC2
145 D1 Crown Office Row EC4
148 A4 Crown Passage SW1
145 F3 Crown Place EC2
150 A2 Crucifix Lane SE1
144 C4 Cruikshank Street WC1
150 A3 Crutched Friars EC3
144 C4 Cubitt Street WC1
144 B1 Cubitts Yard WC2 *James Street*
147 D2 Culford Gardens SW3
151 D1 Culling Road SE16
150 A3 Cullum Street EC3
143 E1 Culross Street W1
142 C4 Culworth Street NW8
144 C4 Cumberland Gardens WC1 *Great Percy Street*
143 D1 Cumberland Gate W1 & W2
143 F4 Cumberland Market NW1
147 F1 Cumberland Street SW1
143 E4 Cumberland Terrace NW1
143 F4 Cumberland Terrace Mews NW1 *Albany Street*
144 C4 Cumming Street N1
147 E2 Cundy Street SW1
142 C3 Cunningham Place NW8
148 B2 Cureton Street SW1
150 B2 Curlew Street SE1
144 C2 Cursitor Street EC4
147 E4 Curzon Gate W1
147 E4 Curzon Place W1
147 E4 Curzon Street W1
142 C3 Cuthbert Street W2
150 A4 Cutler Street E1
144 C4 Cynthia Street N1
144 A3 Cypress Place W1
145 D3 Cyrus Street EC1

D

144 A2 D'Arblay Street W1
147 E2 D'Oyley Street SW1
148 A3 Dacre Street SW1
151 E4 Dalgleish Street E14
145 E3 Dallington Square EC1
145 D3 Dallington Street EC1
150 C4 Damien Street E1
144 C2 Dane Street WC1
149 D2 Dante Road SE11
150 B4 Daplyn Street E1
145 F1 Dark House Walk EC3
149 E1 Dartford Street SE17
148 A3 Dartmouth Street SW1
149 F2 Darwin Street SE17
149 E1 Date Street SE17
150 B4 Davenant Street E1
142 C3 Daventry Street NW1
149 D3 Davidge Street SE1
143 E1 Davies Mews W1
143 E1 Davies Street W1
149 F2 Dawes Street SE17
142 A1 Dawson Place W2
149 D1 De Laune Street SE17
146 B3 De Vere Gardens W8
143 E2 De Walden Street W1 *Westmorland Street*
149 E2 Deacon Way SE17
151 D1 Deal Porters Way SE16
150 B4 Deal Street E1
148 B2 Dean Bradley Street SW1
151 E2 Dean Close SE16
148 A3 Dean Farrar Street SW1
148 B2 Dean Ryle Street SW1
148 B2 Dean Stanley Street SW1 *Millbank*
144 A2 Dean Street W1
148 B3 Dean Trench Street SW1
149 F2 Dean's Buildings SE17
145 E2 Dean's Court EC4 *Carter Lane*
143 F2 Dean's Mews W1
150 C3 Deancross Street E1
147 E4 Deanery Street W1
149 F3 Decima Street SE1
151 E2 Deck Close SE16
151 F1 Defoe Close SE16
142 A3 Delamere Terrace W2
142 A3 Delaware Road W9
150 C3 Dellow Street E1
149 E1 Delverton Road SE17
148 A2 Denbigh Street SW1
144 A1 Denman Street W1
144 B2 Denmark Place WC2 *Charing Cross Road*
144 B2 Denmark Street WC2
142 B4 Denning Close NW8
149 D2 Denny Crescent SE11
149 D2 Denny Street SE11
147 D2 Denyer Street SW3
148 B3 Derby Gate SW1
147 E4 Derby Street W1
143 F2 Dering Street W1
149 F3 Deverell Street SE1
144 B1 Devereux Court WC2 *Strand*
151 D3 Devonport Street E1
143 F3 Devonshire Close W1
146 B1 Devonshire Mews SW10 *Park Walk*
143 E3 Devonshire Mews South W1
143 E3 Devonshire Mews West W1
143 E3 Devonshire Place W1
146 A3 Devonshire Place W8 *St Mary's Place*
143 E3 Devonshire Place Mews W1
150 A4 Devonshire Row EC2
150 A4 Devonshire Square EC2
143 E3 Devonshire Street W1
142 B1 Devonshire Terrace W2
144 A2 Diadem Court W1 *Dean Street*
149 E3 Dickens Square SE1
147 D1 Dilke Street SW3
145 E4 Dingley Place EC1
145 E4 Dingley Road EC1
149 E3 Disney Place SE1
149 E4 Disney Street SE1 *Redcross Way*
145 E1 Distaff Lane EC4
148 C2 Distin Street SE11
150 C1 Dixon's Alley SE16 *West Lane*
151 E2 Dock Hill Avenue SE16
150 B3 Dock Street E1
150 B1 Dockhead SE1
150 B1 Dockley Road SE16
151 F4 Dod Street E14
149 D1 Doddington Grove SE17
149 D1 Doddington Place SE17
149 D3 Dodson Street SE1
149 D4 Dolben Street SE1
148 C1 Dolland Street SE11
151 D2 Dolphin Close SE16
144 C3 Dombey Street WC1
145 E3 Domingo Street EC1 *Old Street*
145 F2 Dominion Street EC2
144 C4 Donegal Street N1
151 F4 Dongola Road E1
147 D2 Donne Place SW3
148 C4 Doon Street SE1
151 F4 Dora Street E14
144 A4 Doric Way NW1
145 D3 Dorrington Street EC1 *Brooke Street*

154 Dorset Close - Harrington Road

143 D3 Dorset Close NW1
147 E3 Dorset Mews SW1
145 D1 Dorset Rise EC4
143 D3 Dorset Square NW1
143 D2 Dorset Street W1
144 C3 Doughty Mews WC1
144 C3 Doughty Street WC1
148 A2 Douglas Place SW1
Douglas Street
148 A2 Douglas Street SW1
146 B3 Douro Place W8
146 B2 Dove Mews SW5
147 E2 Dove Walk SW1
146 C1 Dovehouse Street SW3
143 F1 Dover Street W1
145 F1 Dowgate Hill EC4
147 E4 Down Street W1
142 A3 Downfield Close W9
148 B4 Downing Street SW1
151 E2 Downton Road SE16
149 E4 Doyce Street SE1
149 E1 Draco Street SE17
144 C2 Drake Street WC1
147 D2 Draycott Avenue SW3
147 D2 Draycott Place SW3
147 D2 Draycott Terrace SW3
146 A3 Drayson Mews W8
146 B1 Drayton Gardens SW10
150 A2 Druid Street SE1
150 B4 Drum Street E1
144 A4 Drummond Crescent NW1
148 A1 Drummond Gate SW1
150 C1 Drummond Road SE16
143 F3 Drummond Street NW1
144 B2 Drury Lane WC2
149 D2 Dryden Court SE11
143 F2 Duchess Mews W1
143 F2 Duchess Street W1
149 D4 Duchy Street SE1
144 A2 Duck Lane W1
142 B2 Dudley Street W2
146 C2 Dudmaston Mews SW3
145 E3 Dufferin Street EC1
144 A4 Dufour's Place W1
149 D2 Dugard Way SE11
Renfrew Road
147 E3 Duke of Wellington Place SW1
144 A1 Duke of York Street SW1
143 E2 Duke Street W1
149 F4 Duke Street Hill SE1
146 A4 Duke's Lane W8
150 A4 Duke's Place EC3
144 B4 Duke's Road WC1
143 E2 Duke's Yard W1
Duke Street
144 B1 Duncannon Street WC2
150 C2 Dundee Street E1
151 F3 Dundee Wharf E14
151 D4 Dunelm Street E1
150 B1 Dunlop Place SE16
143 E1 Dunraven Street W1
143 E3 Dunstable Mews W1
150 A3 Dunster Court EC3
149 F3 Dunsterville Way SE1
147 E3 Duplex Ride SW1
144 B1 Durham House Street WC2
151 E4 Durham Row E1
148 C1 Durham Street SE11
142 E2 Durham Terrace W2
150 C4 Durward Street E1
143 D2 Durweston Street W1
Crawford Street
144 B2 Dyott Street WC1
145 F3 Dysart Street EC2

E

145 D3 Eagle Court EC1
144 A4 Eagle Place SW1 *Piccadilly*
144 C2 Eagle Street WC2
146 A1 Eardley Crescent SW5
145 F3 Earl Street EC2
146 A2 Earl's Court Gardens SW5
146 A1 Earl's Court Square SW5
144 B2 Earlham Street WC2
146 A2 Earls Court Road W8
145 D4 Earlstoke Street EC1
Spencer Street
144 B2 Earnshaw Street WC2
143 E2 Easley's Mews W1
Wigmore Street
151 D4 East Arbour Street E1
145 D2 East Harding Street EC4
145 D2 East India Dock Wall Road E14
150 B1 East Lane SE16
150 C4 East Mount Street E1
145 F4 East Road N1
150 B3 East Smithfield E1
149 E1 East Street SE17
150 B3 East Tenter Street E1
142 B2 Eastbourne Mews W2
142 B2 Eastbourne Terrace W2
144 A2 Eastcastle Street W1
145 F1 Eastcheap EC3
151 E4 Eastfield Street E14
144 C3 Easton Street WC1
147 E2 Eaton Gate SW1
147 E2 Eaton Mews North SW1
147 E2 Eaton Mews South SW1
147 E2 Eaton Place SW1
147 E2 Eaton Square SW1
147 E2 Eaton Terrace SW1
148 C1 Ebbisham Drive SW8
145 F4 Ebenezer Street N1
147 E2 Ebury Bridge SW1
147 E1 Ebury Bridge Road SW1
147 E2 Ebury Mews SW1
147 E2 Ebury Mews East SW1
147 E2 Ebury Square SW1
147 E2 Ebury Street SW1
147 F2 Eccleston Bridge SW1
147 E3 Eccleston Mews SW1
147 E2 Eccleston Place SW1
147 F2 Eccleston Square SW1
147 F2 Eccleston Square Mews SW1
147 E2 Eccleston Street SW1
142 A3 Edbrooke Road W9
146 A4 Edge Street W8
142 C3 Edgware Road W2
143 F4 Edward Mews NW1
143 E2 Edward Mews W1
151 E3 Edward Square SE16
147 D2 Egerton Crescent SW3
146 C2 Egerton Gardens SW3
147 D3 Egerton Terrace SW3
149 E2 Elba Place SE17
146 B3 Eldon Road W8
145 F2 Eldon Street EC2
151 D2 Eleanor Close SE16
149 E2 Elephant and Castle SE1
150 C2 Elephant Lane SE16
149 E2 Elephant Road SE17
151 D3 Elf Row E1
151 F1 Elgar Street SE16
142 A3 Elgin Avenue W9
142 A4 Elgin Mews North W9
142 B4 Elgin Mews South W9
145 D4 Elia Street N1
149 F3 Elim Street SE1
142 B4 Eliot Mews NW8
147 F2 Elizabeth Bridge SW1
142 B3 Elizabeth Close W9
151 E3 Elizabeth Square SE16
147 E2 Elizabeth Street SW1
150 B3 Ellen Street E1
149 D2 Elliott Road SE9
147 E2 Ellis Street SW1
146 C1 Elm Park Gardens SW10
146 B1 Elm Park Lane SW3
146 B1 Elm Park Road SW3
146 C1 Elm Place SW7
144 C3 Elm Street WC1
142 C4 Elm Tree Close NW8
142 C4 Elm Tree Road NW8
142 A3 Elmfield Way W9
151 E1 Elmos Road SE16
142 C1 Elms Mews W2
142 A3 Elnathan Mews W9
151 E4 Elsa Street E1
149 F2 Elsted Street SE17
146 B3 Elvaston Mews SW7
146 B3 Elvaston Place SW7
148 A2 Elverton Street SW1
145 D2 Ely Place EC1
146 C2 Elystan Place SW3
146 C2 Elystan Street SW3
150 C1 Emba Street SE16
147 D1 Embankment Gardens SW3
148 B4 Embankment Place WC2
144 C3 Emerald Street WC1
149 E4 Emerson Street SE1
148 A2 Emery Hill Street SW1
149 D3 Emery Street SE1
151 F3 Emmett Street E14
146 B2 Emperor's Gate SW7
146 A1 Empress Place SW6
149 E1 Empress Street SE17
144 B2 Endell Street WC2
144 A3 Endsleigh Gardens WC1
144 A3 Endsleigh Place WC1
144 A3 Endsleigh Street WC1
143 D3 Enford Street W1
150 A2 English Grounds SE1
150 B1 Enid Street SE16
146 C3 Ennismore Garden Mews SW7
146 C3 Ennismore Gardens SW7
146 C3 Ennismore Mews SW7
146 C3 Ennismore Street SW7
150 B3 Ensign Street E1
146 B1 Ensor Mews SW7
145 F3 Epworth Street EC2
148 B2 Erasmus Street SW1
145 E3 Errol Street EC1
142 A4 Essendine Road W9
144 C1 Essex Street WC2
148 A2 Esterbrooke Street SW1
149 E2 Ethel Street SE17
145 E4 Europa Place EC1
143 F3 Euston Road NW1
144 A4 Euston Square NW1
144 A4 Euston Street NW1
148 B1 Evelyn Gardens SW7
145 F4 Evelyn Walk N1
144 A2 Evelyn Yard W1
Gresse Street
144 A4 Eversholt Street NW1
149 E4 Ewer Street SE1
151 D4 Ewhurst Close E1
150 A4 Exchange Place EC2
150 A4 Exchange Square EC2
144 B1 Exeter Street WC2
146 C3 Exhibition Road SW7
145 D3 Exmouth Market EC1
151 D4 Exmouth Street E1
149 F2 Exon Street SE17
148 C4 Exton Street SE1
145 D3 Eyre Street Hill EC1

F

150 A2 Fair Street SE1
150 B3 Fairclough Street E1
149 E4 Falcon Close SE1
144 A2 Falconberg Mews W1
Sutton Row
149 E3 Falmouth Road SE1
145 E3 Fann Street EC1
145 F4 Fanshaw Street N1
144 B1 Fareham Street W1
Dean Street
143 E1 Farm Street W1
146 A4 Farmer Street W8
150 C1 Farncombe Street SE16
146 A1 Farnell Mews SW5
149 E4 Farnham Place SE1
148 C1 Farnham Royal SE11
151 F3 Farrance Street E14
146 B1 Farrier Walk SW10
145 D3 Farringdon Lane EC1
144 C3 Farringdon Road EC1
145 D2 Farringdon Street EC4
151 E2 Farrins Rents SE16
151 E1 Farrow Place SE16
150 B1 Farthing Alley SE1
Wolseley Street
150 C2 Farthing Fields E1
Raine Street
150 B4 Fashion Street E1
149 D1 Faunce Street SE17
146 B1 Fawcett Street SW10
145 F3 Featherstone Street EC1
150 A3 Fen Court EC3
150 A3 Fenchurch Avenue EC3
145 F1 Fenchurch Buildings EC3
Fenchurch Street
145 F1 Fenchurch Place EC3
Fenchurch Street
145 F1 Fenchurch Street EC3
150 A1 Fendall Street SE1
149 F4 Fenning Street SE1
St Thomas Street
144 A2 Fennings Circus W1
144 C4 Fernsbury Street WC1
145 D2 Fetter Lane EC4
144 C4 Field Street WC1
150 B4 Fieldgate Street E1
149 E1 Fielding Street SE17
146 A1 Finborough Road SW10
145 F2 Finch Lane EC3
151 E1 Finland Street SE16
145 F2 Finsbury Avenue EC2
145 F2 Finsbury Circus EC2
145 F3 Finsbury Market EC2
145 F3 Finsbury Pavement EC2
145 F3 Finsbury Square EC2
145 F3 Finsbury Street EC2
147 D2 First Street SW3
151 E2 Firtree Close SE16
145 F1 Fish Street Hill EC3
145 F1 Fish Wharf EC3
144 C2 Fisher Street WC1
151 E2 Fishermans Drive SE16
142 C3 Fisherton Street NW8
145 F1 Fishmongers' Hall Wharf EC4
148 C2 Fitzalan Street SE11
143 E2 Fitzhardinge Street W1
143 F1 Fitzmaurice Place W1
143 F3 Fitzroy Square W1
143 F3 Fitzroy Street WC1
151 E3 Flamborough Street E14
150 B3 Flank Street E1
144 B4 Flaxman Terrace WC1
144 C4 Fleet Square WC1
145 D2 Fleet Street EC4
149 D1 Fleming Road SE17
150 B3 Fletcher Street E1
149 F2 Flint Street SE17
144 B2 Flitcroft Street WC2
147 D1 Flood Street SW3
147 D1 Flood Walk SW3
144 B1 Floral Street WC2
150 B4 Flower and Dean Walk E1
Thrawl Street
143 F2 Foley Street W1
150 B3 Forbes Street E1
150 C4 Ford Square E1
150 C4 Fordham Street E1
145 E2 Fore Street EC2
145 E2 Fore Street Avenue EC2
142 A3 Formosa Street W9
143 D2 Forset Street W1
149 D1 Forsyth Gardens SE17
150 A4 Fort Street E1
Artillery Lane
145 E3 Fortune Street EC1
142 A3 Foscote Mews W9
145 E2 Foster Lane EC2
143 F1 Foubert's Place W1
146 C2 Foulis Terrace SW7
151 E2 Foundry Close SE16
150 C1 Fountain Green Square SE16 *Loftie Street*
150 B4 Fournier Street E1
150 C2 Fowey Close E1
145 E2 Fox and Knot Street EC1
Charterhouse Square
142 C3 Frampton Street NW8
148 A2 Francis Street SW1
147 D1 Franklin's Row SW3
148 C3 Frazier Street SE1
150 B1 Frean Street SE16
143 D1 Frederick Close W2
149 E1 Frederick Road SE17
151 E3 Frederick Square SE16
144 C4 Frederick Street WC1
145 D4 Fredericks Row EC1
Goswell Road
149 F2 Fremantle Street SE17
150 A3 French Ordinary Court EC3 *Hart Street*
145 E2 Friar Street EC4
Carter Lane
145 E1 Friday Street EC4
145 D4 Friend Street EC1
144 A2 Frith Street W1
150 B4 Frostic Walk E1
150 A4 Frying Pan Alley E1
150 C4 Fulbourne Street E1
150 C1 Fulford Street SE16
146 C1 Fulham Road SW3, SW6 & SW10
144 C2 Fulwood Place WC1
145 D2 Furnival Street EC4
148 A2 Fynes Street SW1

G

149 D4 Gabriels Wharf SE1
150 A2 Gainsford Street SE1
144 B2 Galen Place WC1
151 D2 Galleon Close SE16
Kinburn Street
151 E4 Galsworthy Avenue E14
145 E4 Galway Street EC1
149 D4 Gambia Street SE1
144 A1 Ganton Street W1
143 E2 Garbutt Place W1
145 E4 Gard Street EC1
142 A1 Garden Mews W2
142 B4 Garden Road NW8
149 D3 Garden Row SE1
151 E4 Garden Street E1
145 E1 Gardeners Lane EC4
High Timber Street
151 F3 Garford Street E14
145 F1 Garlick Hill EC4
145 D4 Garnault Mews EC1
150 C3 Garnet Street E1
145 E3 Garrett Street EC1
144 B1 Garrick Street WC2
151 D1 Garter Way SE16
142 A2 Garway Road W2
148 C1 Gasholder Place SE11
146 B2 Gaspar Close SW5
146 B2 Gaspar Mews SW5
144 C2 Gate Street WC2
149 E1 Gateway SE17
147 E1 Gatliff Road SW1
149 E3 Gaunt Street SE1
149 F2 Gavel Street SE17
148 B3 Gayfere Street SW1
149 D3 Gaywood Street SE1
149 D1 Gaza Street SE17
150 B1 Gedling Place SE1
145 E3 Gee Street EC1
143 E2 Gees Court W1
149 D2 George Mathers Road SE11
144 A4 George Mews NW1
150 B1 George Row SE16
143 D2 George Street W1
145 F1 George Yard EC3
143 E1 George Yard W1
147 E2 Gerald Road SW1
149 D3 Geraldine Street SE11
144 B1 Gerrard Place W1
Gerrard Street
144 A1 Gerrard Street W1
149 D3 Gerridge Street SE1
149 D3 Gibson Road SE11
144 B2 Gilbert Place WC1
149 D2 Gilbert Road SE11
143 E1 Gilbert Street W1
143 F2 Gildea Street W1
151 F3 Gill Street E14
147 F2 Gillingham Street SW1
150 C1 Gillison Walk SE16
142 B2 Gilpin Close W2
Porteus Road
146 B1 Gilston Road SW10
145 D2 Giltspur Street EC1
149 D3 Gladstone Street SE1
151 D3 Glamis Place E1
151 D3 Glamis Road E1
147 F1 Glasgow Terrace SW1
149 E3 Glasshill Street SE1
151 D3 Glasshouse Fields E1
144 A1 Glasshouse Street W1
148 B1 Glasshouse Walk SE11
151 D3 Glastonbury Place E1
146 C1 Glebe Place SW3
146 B2 Gledhow Gardens SW5
146 C2 Glendower Place SW7
143 D3 Glentworth Street NW1
151 E2 Globe Pond Road SE16
149 E3 Globe Street SE1
146 B2 Gloucester Arcade SW7
150 A3 Gloucester Court EC3
144 F4 Gloucester Gate Mews NW1 *Albany Street*
142 B2 Gloucester Mews W2
142 B2 Gloucester Mews West W2
146 B2 Gloucester Park SW7
143 D3 Gloucester Place NW1 & W1
143 D2 Gloucester Place Mews W1
146 B3 Gloucester Road SW7
142 C2 Gloucester Square W2
147 F1 Gloucester Street SW1
142 B2 Gloucester Terrace W2
146 A4 Gloucester Walk W8
145 D4 Gloucester Way EC1
148 C1 Glyn Street SE11
150 A2 Goat Street SE1
Lafone Street
147 D2 Godfrey Street SW3
148 B1 Goding Street SE11
145 E1 Godliman Street EC4
145 E3 Golden Lane EC1
144 A1 Golden Square W1
150 C3 Golding Street E1
151 D1 Gomm Road SE16
144 A2 Goodge Place W1
144 A2 Goodge Street W1
151 E3 Goodhart Place E14
150 B4 Goodman's Stile E1
150 B3 Goodman's Yard E1
150 B1 Goodwin Close SE16
145 F1 Gophir Lane EC4 *Bush Lane*
146 A4 Gordon Place W8
144 A3 Gordon Square WC1
144 A3 Gordon Street WC1
146 B3 Gore Street SW7
150 A4 Goring Street E1
Bevis Marks
143 F2 Gosfield Street W1
144 B2 Goslett Yard WC2
145 D4 Goswell Road EC1
145 D2 Gough Square EC4
144 C3 Gough Street WC1
150 B4 Goulston Street E1
144 A2 Gower Mews WC1
144 A3 Gower Place WC1
144 A3 Gower Street WC1
150 B3 Gowers Walk E1
150 B3 Grace's Alley E1
145 F1 Gracechurch Street EC3
142 B4 Graces Mews NW8
143 F3 Grafton Mews W1
144 A4 Grafton Place NW1
143 F1 Grafton Street W1
143 A3 Grafton Way W1
145 E4 Graham Street N1
147 E2 Graham Terrace SW1
143 F4 Granby Terrace NW1
145 D2 Grand Avenue EC1
145 E4 Grand Junction Wharf N1
144 C2 Grange Court WC2
150 A1 Grange Road SE1
150 A1 Grange Walk SE1
150 A1 Grange Yard SE1
145 F1 Grant's Quay Wharf EC3
142 A4 Grantully Road W9
143 E2 Granville Place W1
142 A4 Granville Road NW6
144 C4 Granville Square WC1
144 C4 Granville Street WC1
Granville Square
144 B2 Grape Street WC2
150 A4 Gravel Lane E1
149 D3 Gray Street SE1
144 C2 Gray's Inn Place WC1
144 B4 Gray's Inn Road WC1
143 F2 Great Castle Street W1
143 D3 Great Central Street NW1
144 A2 Great Chapel Street W1
143 D1 Great College Street SW1
Seymour Street
143 D2 Great Cumberland Place W1
149 F3 Great Dover Street SE1
145 F3 Great Eastern Street EC2
148 B3 Great George Street SW1
149 E4 Great Guildford Street SE1
144 C3 Great James Street WC1
143 F2 Great Marlborough Street W1
149 F4 Great Maze Pond SE1
145 D2 Great New Street EC4
144 B1 Great Newport Street WC2
Charing Cross Road
144 C3 Great Ormond Street WC1
144 C4 Great Percy Street WC1
148 A3 Great Peter Street SW1
143 F3 Great Portland Street W1
144 A1 Great Pulteney Street W1
144 B2 Great Queen Street WC2
144 B2 Great Russell Street WC1
148 B4 Great Scotland Yard SW1
148 B3 Great Smith Street SW1
145 F2 Great St Helen's EC3
145 E1 Great St Thomas Apostle EC4 *Queen Street*
149 E3 Great Suffolk Street SE1
145 D3 Great Sutton Street EC1
145 F2 Great Swan Alley EC2
150 A3 Great Tower Street EC3
145 E1 Great Trinity Lane EC4
Garlick Hill
144 B2 Great Turnstile WC1
High Holborn
145 F2 Great Winchester Street EC2
144 A1 Great Windmill Street W1
150 B4 Greatorex Street E1
144 B2 Greek Street W1
150 C2 Green Bank E1
149 F4 Green Dragon Court SE1
150 B4 Green Dragon Yard E1
143 E1 Green Street W1
149 F3 Green Walk SE1
144 C3 Green Yard WC1
151 E2 Greenacre Square SE16
142 C4 Greenberry Street NW8
148 A2 Greencoat Place SW1
148 A2 Greencoat Row SW1
150 B4 Greenfield Road E1
149 D3 Greenham Close SE1
143 F3 Greenwell Street W1
149 D4 Greet Street SE1
146 A3 Gregory Place W8
149 E1 Greig Terrace SE17
151 F3 Grenade Street E14
142 C3 Grendon Street NW8
146 B2 Grenville Place SW7
144 B3 Grenville Street WC1
145 E2 Gresham Street EC2
144 A2 Gresse Street W1
145 D2 Greville Street EC1
148 A3 Greycoat Place SW1
148 A2 Greycoat Street SW1
145 D2 Greystoke Place EC4
Fetter Lane
150 A1 Grigg's Place SE1
147 E3 Groom Place SW1
147 E3 Grosvenor Crescent SW1
147 E3 Grosvenor Crescent Mews SW1
147 F3 Grosvenor Gardens SW1
143 E1 Grosvenor Gate W1
Park Lane
143 F1 Grosvenor Hill W1
147 E3 Grosvenor Place SW1
147 F1 Grosvenor Road SW1
143 E1 Grosvenor Square W1
143 E1 Grosvenor Street W1
142 B4 Grove End Road NW8
143 D4 Grove Gardens NW8
142 B4 Grove Hall Court NW8
145 E2 Guildhall Buildings EC2
Basinghall Street
145 E2 Guildhall Yard EC2
147 F2 Guildhouse Street SW1
144 B3 Guilford Place WC1
Guilford Street
144 B3 Guilford Street WC1
149 F2 Guinness Square SE1
151 F1 Gulliver Street SE16
147 D2 Gulston Walk SW3
150 A4 Gun Street E1
150 B4 Gunthorpe Street E1
151 E2 Gunwhale Close SE16
146 C2 Guthrie Street SW3
145 E2 Gutter Lane EC2
149 F3 Guy Street SE1
144 C4 Gwynne Place WC1

H

145 F4 Haberdasher Street N1
150 C3 Hainton Close E1
150 C4 Halcrow Street E1
145 E2 Half Moon Court EC1
Bartholomew Close
147 F4 Half Moon Street W1
147 E3 Halkin Place SW1
147 E3 Halkin Street SW1
142 B4 Hall Gate NW8
142 C3 Hall Place W2
142 B4 Hall Road NW8
145 D4 Hall Street EC1
143 F3 Hallam Mews W1
143 F3 Hallam Street W1
151 E4 Halley Place E14
151 E4 Halley Street E14
147 D2 Halsey Mews SW3
147 D2 Halsey Street SW3
142 B4 Hamilton Close NW8
151 E1 Hamilton Close SE16
142 B4 Hamilton Gardens NW8
147 E4 Hamilton Place W1
149 F3 Hamilton Square SE1
142 B4 Hamilton Terrace NW8
150 A3 Hammett Street EC3
America Square
143 F4 Hampstead Road NW1
149 E2 Hampton Street SE1 & SE17
150 B4 Hanbury Street E1
144 B3 Handel Street WC1
149 F3 Hankey Place SE1
151 D4 Hannibal Road E1
144 B1 Hanover Place WC2
Long Acre
143 F2 Hanover Square W1
143 F2 Hanover Street W1
143 D4 Hanover Terrace NW1
143 D4 Hanover Terrace Mews NW1
147 D3 Hans Crescent SW1
147 D3 Hans Place SW1
147 D3 Hans Road SW3
147 D3 Hans Street SW1
143 F2 Hanson Street W1
144 A2 Hanway Place W1
144 A2 Hanway Street W1
142 C2 Harbert Road W2
143 D2 Harcourt Street W1
146 B1 Harcourt Terrace SW10
149 E1 Harding Close SE17
151 D3 Hardinge Lane E1
Hardinge Street
151 D3 Hardinge Street E1
145 D4 Hardwick Street EC1
144 C4 Hardwicke Mews WC1
Lloyd Baker Street
149 F4 Hardwidge Street SE1
143 D3 Harewood Avenue NW1
143 F2 Harewood Place W1
146 B1 Harley Gardens SW10
143 E2 Harley Place W1
143 E3 Harley Street W1
148 C1 Harleyford Road SE11
149 D2 Harmsworth Mews SE11
West Square
149 D1 Harmsworth Street SE17
145 D2 Harp Alley EC4
Farringdon Street
150 A3 Harp Lane EC3
149 E3 Harper Road SE1
144 C3 Harpur Street WC1
147 D3 Harriet Street SW1
147 D3 Harriet Walk SW1
146 B2 Harrington Gardens SW7
146 C2 Harrington Road SW7

Harrington Street - Maunsel Street 155

143 F4 **Harrington Street** NW1
144 B4 **Harrison Street** WC1
150 A4 **Harrow Place** E1
142 B2 **Harrow Road** W2, W9, W10 & NW10
142 B2 **Harrow Road Bridge** W2
143 D2 **Harrowby Street** W1
150 A3 **Hart Street** EC3
150 A4 **Harwich Lane** EC2
143 D3 **Harwood Row** NW1
147 D2 **Hasker Street** SW3
144 B4 **Hastings Street** WC1
149 D4 **Hatfields** SE1
142 A2 **Hatherley Grove** W2
148 A2 **Hatherley Street** SW1
151 D2 **Hatteraick Street** SE16
145 D3 **Hatton Garden** EC1
145 D3 **Hatton Place** EC1
145 D3 **Hatton Place** EC1
142 C3 **Hatton Street** NW8
145 D3 **Hatton Wall** EC1
142 C1 **Haunch of Venison Yard** W1 *Brook Street*
151 D3 **Havering Street** E1
145 E4 **Haverstock Street** N1
150 C3 **Hawkesmoor Mews** E1
143 F1 **Hay Hill** W1
149 F4 **Hay's Lane** SE1
143 F1 **Hay's Mews** W1
143 D3 **Hayes Place** NW1
149 D2 **Hayles Street** SE11
144 A1 **Haymarket** SW1
145 E3 **Hayne Street** EC1
145 D3 **Hayward's Place** EC1
147 E3 **Headfort Place** SW1
144 C3 **Heathcote Street** WC1
151 E3 **Heckford Street** E1
143 F1 **Heddon Street** W1
149 D2 **Hedger Street** SE11
149 E1 **Heiron Street** SE17
151 E3 **Helena Square** SE16
150 B2 **Hellings Street** E1
145 E3 **Helmet Row** EC1
151 E3 **Helsinki Square** SE16
149 F2 **Hemp Walk** SE17
142 C3 **Henderson Drive** NW8
150 A4 **Heneage Lane** EC3
150 A4 **Heneage Place** EC3
150 B4 **Heneage Street** E1
146 B1 **Henniker Mews** SW3
143 E2 **Henrietta Place** W1
144 B1 **Henrietta Street** WC2
150 B4 **Henriques Street** E1
149 F2 **Henshaw Street** SE17
149 D2 **Herald's Place** SE11
145 D3 **Herbal Hill** EC1
144 B3 **Herbrand Street** WC1
148 C3 **Hercules Road** SE1
142 A3 **Hereford Road** W2
146 B2 **Hereford Square** SW7
144 C4 **Hermes Street** N1
145 D4 **Hermit Street** EC1
142 C2 **Hermitage Street** W2
150 B2 **Hermitage Wall** E1
151 E2 **Heron Place** SE16
148 B2 **Herrick Street** SW1
147 E4 **Hertford Street** W1
146 A2 **Hesper Mews** SW5
150 C3 **Hessel Street** E1
149 E2 **Heygate Street** SE17
148 A2 **Hide Place** SW1
144 B2 **High Holborn** WC1
145 E1 **High Timber Street** EC4
146 A1 **Hildyard Road** SW6
142 B4 **Hill Road** W9
143 F2 **Hill Street** W1
149 F2 **Hillery Close** SE17
150 C2 **Hilliard's Court** E1
149 E1 **Hillingdon Street** SE5 & SE17 *Peller Street*
145 D2 **Hind Court** EC4
143 E2 **Hinde Street** W1
150 B3 **Hindmarsh Close** E1
147 F3 **Hobart Place** SW1
145 F1 **Hogarth Court** EC3 *Fenchurch Street*
146 A2 **Hogarth Place** SW5
146 A2 **Hogarth Road** SW5
147 E2 **Holbein Mews** SW1
147 E2 **Holbein Place** SW1
145 D2 **Holborn** EC1
145 D2 **Holborn Circus** EC1
145 D2 **Holborn Viaduct** EC1
144 C4 **Holford Place** WC1
144 C4 **Holford Street** WC1
149 D4 **Holland Street** SE1
146 A3 **Holland Street** W8
144 A2 **Hollen Street** W1 *Wardour Street*
143 F2 **Holles Street** W1
146 B1 **Holley Mews** SW10 *Drayton Gardens*
146 B1 **Hollywood Mews** SW10
146 B1 **Hollywood Road** SW10
149 D2 **Holyoak Road** SE11
151 F2 **Holyoake Court** SE16
150 A2 **Holyrood Street** SE1
145 F3 **Holywell Row** EC2
143 D2 **Homer Row** W1
143 D2 **Homer Street** W1
145 E3 **Honduras Street** EC1 *Old Street*
150 B3 **Hooper Street** E1
144 B1 **Hop Gardens** WC2 *St Martin's Lane*
151 D2 **Hope Wharf** SE16
150 B4 **Hopetown Street** E1
144 A1 **Hopkins Street** W1
149 D4 **Hopton Street** SE1
149 F1 **Hopwood Road** SE17
151 D2 **Horley Crescent** SE16 *Marlow Way*
148 C2 **Hornbeam Close** SE11
146 A3 **Hornton Place** W8
146 A3 **Hornton Street** W8
148 B4 **Horse Guards Avenue** SW1
148 B4 **Horse Guards Road** SW1
147 F3 **Horse Ride** SW1
151 E3 **Horseferry Road** E14
148 A3 **Horseferry Road** SW1
150 A2 **Horselydown Lane** SE1
145 D2 **Hosier Lane** EC1
151 D1 **Hothfield Place** SE16
148 C2 **Hotspur Street** SE11
144 C1 **Houghton Street** WC2 *Aldwych*
150 A4 **Houndsditch** EC3
144 A2 **Howard Place** SW1 *Carlisle Street*
149 E2 **Howell Walk** SE1
148 A3 **Howick Place** SW1
144 A3 **Howland Street** W1
151 E1 **Howland Way** SE16
142 B3 **Howley Place** W2
145 F4 **Hoxton Market** N1
145 F4 **Hoxton Square** N1
151 F4 **Huddart Street** E3
147 F2 **Hudson's Place** SW1
145 E1 **Huggin Hill** EC4
147 F2 **Hugh Street** SW1
151 E2 **Hull Close** SE16
145 E4 **Hull Street** EC1
149 E3 **Hulme Place** SE1
144 B1 **Hunt's Court** WC2
149 F3 **Hunter Close** SE1 *Prioress Street*
144 B3 **Hunter Street** WC1
144 A3 **Huntley Street** WC1
149 F2 **Huntsman Street** SE17
143 D3 **Huntsworth Mews** NW1
145 D1 **Hutton Street** EC4
147 E4 **Hyde Park Corner** W1
142 C2 **Hyde Park Crescent** W2
142 C1 **Hyde Park Gardens** W2
142 C1 **Hyde Park Gardens Mews** W2
146 B3 **Hyde Park Gate** SW7
142 C2 **Hyde Park Square** W2
142 C2 **Hyde Park Street** W2

I

150 A3 **Idol Lane** EC3
146 A1 **Ifield Road** SW10
142 A1 **Ilchester Gardens** W2
149 E2 **Iliffe Street** SE17
144 C1 **India Place** WC2 *Montreal Place*
150 A3 **India Street** EC3
144 A1 **Ingestre Place** W1
145 D4 **Inglebert Street** EC1
148 C2 **Ingram Close** SE11
144 B1 **Inigo Place** WC2 *Bedford Street*
145 D2 **Inner Temple Lane** EC4
146 A4 **Inverness Gardens** W8 *Palace Garden Terrace*
142 B1 **Inverness Mews** W2
142 B1 **Inverness Place** W2
142 B1 **Inverness Terrace** W2
149 D4 **Invicta Plaza** SE1
149 F1 **Inville Road** SE17
145 D1 **Ireland Yard** EC4 *St Andrew's Hill*
145 E2 **Ironmonger Lane** EC2
145 E4 **Ironmonger Row** EC1
151 D2 **Ironside Close** SE16
144 B1 **Irving Street** WC2
151 D2 **Isambard Place** SE16
151 F3 **Island Row** E14
146 A3 **Iverna Court** W8
146 A3 **Iverna Gardens** W8
147 D2 **Ives Street** SW3
143 D3 **Ivor Place** NW1
146 C2 **Ixworth Place** SW3

J

150 B2 **Jacob Street** SE1
150 B1 **Jamaica Road** SE1 & SE16
151 D4 **Jamaica Street** E1
143 E2 **James Street** W1
144 B1 **James Street** WC2 *Long Acre*
146 A4 **Jameson Street** W8
150 C1 **Janeway Place** SE16
150 C1 **Janeway Street** SE16
151 E3 **Jardine Road** E1
146 B3 **Jay Mews** SW7
148 A4 **Jermyn Street** SW1
146 C3 **Jerome Crescent** NW8
150 A3 **Jewry Street** EC3
149 D4 **Joan Street** SE1
144 C3 **Jockey's Fields** WC1
144 B1 **John Adam Street** WC2
142 B3 **John Aird Court** W2
145 D1 **John Carpenter Street** EC4
150 B1 **John Felton Road** SE16
150 B3 **John Fisher Street** E1
148 B2 **John Islip** Street
149 F2 **John Maurice Close** SE17
143 F2 **John Princes Street** W1
150 C1 **John Roll Way** SE16
144 C3 **John Street** WC1
144 C3 **John's Mews** WC1
151 D3 **Johnson Street** E1
148 A1 **Johnson's Place** SW1
149 F4 **Joiner Street** SE1
148 C2 **Jonathan Street** SE11
143 F1 **Jones Street** W1 *Bourdon Street*
147 D2 **Jubilee Place** SW3
151 D4 **Jubilee Street** E1
144 B4 **Judd Street** WC1
142 C2 **Junction Mews** W2
148 C2 **Juxon Street** SE11

K

151 D2 **Katherine Close** SE16
144 C2 **Kean Street** WC2
151 E2 **Keel Close** SE16
144 C2 **Keeley Street** WC2
150 C1 **Keeton's Road** SE16
146 A3 **Kelso Place** W8
144 C2 **Kemble Street** WC2
146 A1 **Kempsford Gardens** SW5
149 D2 **Kempsford Road** SE11
150 C4 **Kempton Court** E1 *Durward Street*
143 C2 **Kendal Street** W2
143 D2 **Kendall Place** W1
146 C2 **Kendrick Mews** SW7
146 C2 **Kendrick Place** SW7 *Reece Mews*
150 B2 **Kennet Street** E1
145 E1 **Kennet Wharf Lane** EC4
151 D2 **Kenning Street** SE16
149 D1 **Kennings Way** SE11
149 D1 **Kennington Green** SE11
148 C1 **Kennington Grove** SE11
148 C1 **Kennington Lane** SE11
148 C1 **Kennington Oval** SE11
149 D1 **Kennington Park Gardens** SE11
149 D1 **Kennington Park Place** SE11
149 D1 **Kennington Park Road** SE11
148 C3 **Kennington Road** SE1 & SE11
143 E2 **Kenrick Place** W1
146 A4 **Kensington Church Street** W8
146 A3 **Kensington Church Walk** W8
146 A3 **Kensington Court** W8
146 A3 **Kensington Court Place** W8
142 A2 **Kensington Gardens Square** W2
146 B3 **Kensington Gate** W8
146 B3 **Kensington Gore** SW7
146 A3 **Kensington High Street** W8 & W14
146 A4 **Kensington Mall** W8
146 A4 **Kensington Palace Gardens** W8
146 B3 **Kensington Road** W8 & SW7
146 A3 **Kensington Square** W8
143 D4 **Kent Passage** NW1
143 D4 **Kent Terrace** NW1
143 B3 **Kenton Street** WC1
145 A2 **Kenway Road** SW5
149 E4 **Keppel Row** SE1
144 B3 **Keppel Street** WC1
150 B1 **Keyse Road** SE1
144 B4 **Keystone Crescent** N1
149 D3 **Keyworth Street** SE1
142 A4 **Kilburn Park Road** NW6
142 A2 **Kildare Gardens** W2
142 A2 **Kildare Terrace** W2
146 C2 **Kimbolton Row** SW3 *Fulham Road*
151 D2 **Kinburn Street** SE16
150 C3 **Kinder Street** E1
149 E2 **King and Queen Street** SE17
148 B3 **King Charles Street** SW1
151 D3 **King David Lane** E1
150 C1 **King Edward III Mews** SE16 *Paradise Street*
145 E2 **King Edward Street** EC1
149 D3 **King Edward Walk** SE1
149 E3 **King James Street** SE1
145 E4 **King Square** EC1
145 E2 **King Street** EC2
148 A4 **King Street** SW1
144 B1 **King Street** WC2
145 E1 **King William Street** EC4
145 D1 **King's Bench Walk** EC4
144 C4 **King's Cross Road** WC1
144 C3 **King's Mews** WC1
147 D1 **King's Road** SW3, SW6 & SW10
147 F2 **King's Scholars' Passage** SW1
150 C2 **King's Stairs Close** SE16
145 E3 **Kinghorn Street** EC1
149 F2 **Kinglake Street** SE17
144 A1 **Kingly Court** W1
143 F1 **Kingly Street** W1
145 F2 **Kings Arms Yard** EC2
149 D3 **Kings Bench Street** SE1
145 D1 **Kingscote Street** EC4
144 C2 **Kingsway** WC2
147 E3 **Kinnerton Street** SW1
149 F4 **Kipling Street** SE1
149 F3 **Kirby Grove** SE1
145 D3 **Kirby Street** EC1
146 A2 **Knaresborough Place** SW5
149 D2 **Knight's Walk** SE11
150 C2 **Knighten Street** E1
145 E1 **Knightrider Street** EC4 *Godliman Street*
147 D3 **Knightsbridge** SW1 & SW7
147 D3 **Knightsbridge Green** SW1 *Brompton Road*
143 D3 **Knox Street** W1
146 A1 **Kramer Mews** SW5
146 B3 **Kynance Mews** SW7

L

145 F3 **Lackington Street** EC2
150 A2 **Lafone Street** SE1
151 E2 **Lagado Mews** SE16
150 A4 **Lamb Street** E1
149 F3 **Lamb Walk** SE1
144 C3 **Lamb's Conduit Street** WC1
145 F3 **Lamb's Passage** EC1
148 B2 **Lambeth Bridge** SW1 & SE11
148 C2 **Lambeth High Street** SE1
145 E1 **Lambeth Hill** EC4
148 C2 **Lambeth Palace Road** SE1
148 C2 **Lambeth Road** SE1
148 C2 **Lambeth Walk** SE11
149 D2 **Lamlash Street** SE11
149 B3 **Lanark Place** W9
142 A4 **Lanark Road** W9
142 B1 **Lancaster Gate** W2
142 B1 **Lancaster Mews** W2
147 D3 **Lancaster Place** WC2
149 D3 **Lancaster Street** SE1
142 C1 **Lancaster Terrace** W2
142 B1 **Lancaster Walk** W2
147 D3 **Lancelot Place** SW7
144 A4 **Lancing Street** NW1
147 D3 **Landon Place** SW1
149 E1 **Langdale Close** SE17
143 F2 **Langham Place** W1
143 F2 **Langham Street** W1
148 B1 **Langley Lane** SW8
144 B1 **Langley Street** WC2
149 C3 **Langton Close** WC1
143 F1 **Lansdowne Row** W1
144 B3 **Lansdowne Terrace** WC1
149 E3 **Lant Street** SE1
149 E2 **Larcom Street** SE17
142 A4 **Lauderdale Road** W9
148 C3 **Launcelot Street** SE1 *Lower Marsh*
146 B3 **Launceston Place** W8
145 F1 **Laurence Pountney Lane** EC4
146 C1 **Lavender Close** SW3
151 E2 **Lavender Road** SE16
146 A2 **Laverton Place** SW5
149 E4 **Lavington Street** SE1
149 F3 **Law Street** SE1
148 B1 **Lawn Lane** SW8
145 E2 **Lawrence Lane** EC2 *Trump Street*
146 C1 **Lawrence Street** SW3
143 F3 **Laxton Place** NW1
144 C3 **Laystall Street** EC1
149 E4 **Layton's Buildings** SE1 *Borough High Street*
145 F1 **Leadenhall Place** EC3
145 F2 **Leadenhall Street** EC3
148 C3 **Leake Street** SE1
145 D3 **Leather Lane** EC1
149 F3 **Leathermarket Court** SE1 *Leathermarket Street*
149 F3 **Leathermarket Street** SE1
146 C1 **Lecky Street** SW7
143 E1 **Lees Place** W1
144 B1 **Leicester Court** WC2 *Cranbourn Street*
144 A1 **Leicester Place** WC2 *Lisle Street*
144 B1 **Leicester Square** WC2
144 B1 **Leicester Street** WC2
149 E3 **Leigh Hunt Street** SE1
144 B4 **Leigh Street** WC1
142 B1 **Leinster Gardens** W2
142 B1 **Leinster Mews** W2
142 B1 **Leinster Place** W2
142 A1 **Leinster Square** W2
142 B1 **Leinster Terrace** W2
150 B3 **Leman Street** E1
147 D2 **Lennox Gardens** SW1
147 D2 **Lennox Gardens Mews** SW1
145 F3 **Leonard Street** EC2
151 F4 **Leopold Street** E3
149 F2 **Leroy Street** SE1
145 E4 **Lever Street** EC1
147 D2 **Leverett Street** SW3 *Mossop Street*
148 B3 **Lewisham Street** SW1
146 A2 **Lexham Gardens** W8
146 A2 **Lexham Mews** W8
146 A2 **Lexham Walk** W8
144 A1 **Lexington Street** W1
150 A4 **Leyden Street** E1
151 E2 **Leydon Close** SE16
150 C3 **Library Place** E1
149 D3 **Library Street** SE1
151 E4 **Lighterman Mews** E1
142 C3 **Lilestone Street** NW8
150 B2 **Lilley Close** E1
146 A1 **Lillie Yard** SW6
150 B2 **Lime Close** E1
145 F1 **Lime Street** EC3
145 F1 **Lime Street Passage** EC3 *Lime Street*
145 D2 **Limeburner Lane** EC4
151 F3 **Limehouse Causeway** E14
151 E3 **Limehouse Link Tunnel** E14
146 B1 **Limerston Street** SW10
147 D2 **Lincoln Street** SW3
144 C2 **Lincoln's Inn Fields** WC2
142 A1 **Linden Gardens** W2
142 A1 **Linden Mews** W2
150 C4 **Lindley Street** E1
148 B2 **Lindsay Square** SW1
145 E3 **Lindsey Street** EC1
142 D3 **Linhope Street** NW1
150 B4 **Links Yard** E1
150 B1 **Linsey Street** SE16
151 D3 **Lipton Road** E1
144 A1 **Lisle Street** W1
142 C3 **Lisson Grove** NW1 & NW8
142 C3 **Lisson Street** NW1
144 B1 **Litchfield Street** WC2
148 A2 **Little Argyll Street** W1 *Regent Street*
145 E2 **Little Britain** EC1
147 E3 **Little Chester Street** SW1
148 B3 **Little College Street** SW1
149 E4 **Little Dorrit Close** SE1
143 F4 **Little Edward Street** NW1
148 B3 **Little George Street** SW1 *Great George Street*
150 B1 **Little London Court** SE1 *Mill Street*
150 B1 **Little London Court** SE1 *Mill Street*
143 F1 **Little Marlborough Street** W1 *Kingly Street*
145 D2 **Little New Street** EC4 *New Street Square*
144 B1 **Little Newport Street** WC2
143 F2 **Little Portland Street** W1
144 B2 **Little Russell Street** WC1
148 B3 **Little Sanctuary** SW1 *Broad Sanctuary*
148 B3 **Little Smith Street** SW1
148 A3 **Little Somerset Street** E1
148 A4 **Little St James's Street** SW1
143 F2 **Little Titchfield Street** W1
145 E1 **Little Trinity Lane** EC4
149 E1 **Liverpool Grove** SE17
145 F2 **Liverpool Street** EC2
144 A2 **Livonia Street** W2
145 E4 **Lizard Street** EC1
150 B1 **Llewellyn Street** SE16
144 C4 **Lloyd Baker Street** WC1
144 C4 **Lloyd Square** WC1
144 C4 **Lloyd Street** WC1
150 A3 **Lloyd's Avenue** EC3
145 D4 **Lloyd's Row** EC1
151 F4 **Locksley Street** E14
150 C1 **Lockwood Square** SE16
142 C4 **Lodge Road** NW8
150 B1 **Loftie Street** SE16
150 B4 **Lolesworth Close** E1
148 C2 **Lollard Street** SE11
149 E4 **Loman Street** SE1
150 C4 **Lomas Street** E1
145 F1 **Lombard Court** EC4
145 A2 **Lombard Lane** EC4 *Temple Lane*
145 F1 **London Bridge** EC4 & SE1
149 F4 **London Bridge Street** SE1
149 D3 **London Road** SE1
150 A3 **London Street** EC3
142 C2 **London Street** W2
145 E2 **London Wall** EC2
144 B1 **Long Acre** WC2
145 E2 **Long Lane** EC1
149 F3 **Long Lane** SE1
150 A1 **Long Walk** SE1
144 C3 **Long Yard** WC1
143 F3 **Longford Street** NW1
147 F2 **Longmoore Street** SW1
149 D2 **Longville Road** SE11
142 A2 **Lord Hill's Bridge** W2
142 A3 **Lord Hill's Road** W2
148 B3 **Lord North Street** SW1
146 C1 **Lordship Place** SW3 *Lawrence Street*
144 C4 **Lorenzo Street** WC1
149 E1 **Lorrimore Road** SE17
149 E1 **Lorrimore Square** SE17
145 F2 **Lothbury** EC2
148 C1 **Loughborough Street** SE11
145 F1 **Lovat Lane** EC3
145 E2 **Love Lane** EC2
151 E1 **Lovell Place** SE16
147 E4 **Lovers' Walk** W1
151 E4 **Lowell Street** E14
147 E3 **Lower Belgrave Street** SW1
147 F3 **Lower Grosvenor Place** SW1
144 A1 **Lower James Street** W1
144 A1 **Lower John Street** W1
148 C3 **Lower Marsh** SE1
151 D1 **Lower Road** SE8 & SE16
144 B1 **Lower Robert Street** WC2 *Savoy Place*
147 E1 **Lower Sloane Street** SW1
145 F1 **Lower Thames Street** EC3
147 E3 **Lowndes Place** SW1
147 D3 **Lowndes Square** SW1
147 E3 **Lowndes Street** SW1
150 C3 **Lowood Street** E1 *Bewley Street*
144 B3 **Loxham Street** WC1 *Cromer Street*
146 C2 **Lucan Place** SW3
146 A4 **Lucerne Mews** W8
150 B1 **Lucey Road** SE16
145 D2 **Ludgate Broadway** EC4 *Pilgrim Street*
145 D2 **Ludgate Circus** EC4
145 D2 **Ludgate Square** EC4
145 F3 **Luke Street** EC2
151 D3 **Lukin Street** E1
143 E1 **Lumley Street** W1 *Brown Hart Garden*
147 F1 **Lupus Street** SW1
142 C3 **Luton Street** NW8
143 E3 **Luxborough Street** W1
147 E3 **Lyall Street** SW1
147 F3 **Lygon Place** SW1
142 C3 **Lyons Place** NW8
149 F1 **Lytham Street** SE17

M

144 B4 **Mabledon Place** WC1
145 E4 **Macclesfield Road** EC1
144 B2 **Macklin Street** WC2
143 F4 **Mackworth Street** NW1
149 E1 **Macleod Street** SE17
149 D1 **Maddock Way** SE17
143 F1 **Maddox Street** W1
150 A2 **Magdalen Street** SE1
149 D1 **Magee Street** SE11
150 B2 **Maguire Street** SE1
151 E2 **Mahognay Close** SE16
142 B3 **Maida Avenue** W2
142 B4 **Maida Vale** W9
144 B1 **Maiden Lane** WC2
149 E4 **Maiden Lane** SE1
150 D2 **Makins Street** SW3
144 A3 **Malet Street** WC1
146 C1 **Mallord Street** SW3
142 C3 **Mallory Street** NW8
145 F3 **Mallow Street** EC1
145 D3 **Malta Street** EC1
150 A1 **Maltby Street** SE1
144 C1 **Maltravers Street** WC2
143 E2 **Manchester Square** W1
143 E2 **Manchester Street** W1
149 F3 **Manciple Street** SE1
151 F3 **Mandarin Street** E14
143 E2 **Mandeville Place** W1
144 B2 **Manette Street** W1
145 D4 **Manningford Close** EC1
150 B4 **Manningtree Street** E1 *Commercial Road*
149 E1 **Manor Place** SE17
146 C1 **Manresa Road** SW3
150 B3 **Mansell Street** E1
143 F2 **Mansfield Mews** W1 *Mansfield Street*
143 F2 **Mansfield Street** W1
145 A1 **Mansion House Place** EC4 *St Swithun's Lane*
146 B2 **Manson Mews** SW7
146 C2 **Manson Place** SW7
151 E2 **Maple Leaf Square** SE16
143 F3 **Maple Street** W1
150 C4 **Maples Place** E1
143 D1 **Marble Arch** W1
144 B3 **Marchmont Street** WC1
143 F2 **Margaret Court** W1 *Margaret Street*
143 F2 **Margaret Street** W1
146 C1 **Margaretta Terrace** SW3
144 C4 **Margery Street** WC1
150 C1 **Marigold Street** SE16
151 D4 **Marjorie Mews** E1
150 A3 **Mark Lane** EC3
143 E1 **Market Court** W1 *Oxford Street*
147 E4 **Market Mews** W1
143 F2 **Market Place** W1
150 A1 **Market Yard Mews** SE1
147 D2 **Markham Place** SW3 *Elystan Place*
147 D2 **Markham Square** SW3
147 D2 **Markham Street** SW3
149 E2 **Marlborough Close** SE17
148 A4 **Marlborough Road** SW1
146 C2 **Marlborough Street** SW3
146 A3 **Marloes Road** W8
151 D2 **Marlow Way** SE16
150 B1 **Marne Street** W10
151 E4 **Maroon Street** E14
144 A1 **Marshall Street** W1
150 B1 **Marshall's Place** SE16
149 E4 **Marshalsea Road** SE1
148 B3 **Marsham Street** SW1
149 E1 **Marsland Close** SE17
150 C3 **Martha Street** E1
145 F1 **Martin Lane** EC4
144 B1 **Martin's Street** WC2
144 B2 **Martlett Court** WC2
142 A3 **Marylands Road** W9
143 E3 **Marylebone High Street** W1
143 E2 **Marylebone Lane** W1
143 E2 **Marylebone Mews** W1
143 D3 **Marylebone Road** NW1
143 E2 **Marylebone Street** W1
148 C2 **Marylee Way** SE11
149 F2 **Mason Street** SE17
143 F1 **Mason's Arms Mews** W1 *Maddox Street*
145 E4 **Mason's Place** EC1
143 E2 **Mason's Yard** SW1 *Duke Street*
145 E4 **Mason's Yard** EC1
149 F2 **Massinger Street** SE17
151 E4 **Master's Street** E1
151 E4 **Matlock Street** E14
148 B3 **Matthew Parker Street** SW1
148 A2 **Maunsel Street** SW1

144 B1 **May's Court** WC2
St Martin's Lane
147 F4 **Mayfair Place** W1
151 D1 **Mayflower Street** SE16
150 C3 **Maynards Quay** E1
148 C3 **McAuley Close** SE1
146 B2 **McCleod's Mews** SW7
149 D3 **Mead Row** SE1
149 D1 **Meadcroft Road** SE11
149 E2 **Meadow Row** SE1
144 A2 **Meard Street** W1
144 A2 **Mecklenburgh Place** WC1
144 C3 **Mecklenburgh Square** WC1
144 C3 **Mecklenburgh Street** WC1
Mecklenburgh Square
148 A2 **Medway Street** SW1
143 D3 **Melbury Terrace** NW1
143 D3 **Melcombe Place** NW1
143 D3 **Melcombe Street** NW1
142 B4 **Melina Place** NW8
149 F4 **Melior Place** SE1
Snowsfields
146 A4 **Melon Place** W8
Kensington Church Street
144 A4 **Melton Street** NW1
145 E3 **Memel Court** EC1
Baltic Street
148 C4 **Mepham Street** SE1
144 B1 **Mercer Street** WC2
145 D4 **Meredith Street** EC1
145 D4 **Merlin Street** WC1
149 F4 **Mermaid Court** SE1
151 F2 **Mermaid Court** SE16
149 F3 **Mermaid Row** SE1
149 E3 **Merrick Square** SE1
146 A1 **Merrington Road** SW6
149 E1 **Merrow Street** SE17
149 D1 **Methley Street** SE11
150 B2 **Mews Street** E1
149 D4 **Meymott Street** SE1
145 E4 **Micawber Street** N1
145 E2 **Middle Street** EC1
144 C2 **Middle Temple Lane** EC4
149 F4 **Middle Yard** SE1
150 A4 **Middlesex Street** E1
151 E2 **Middleton Drive** SE16
144 A3 **Midford Place** W1
Tottenham Court Road
144 B4 **Midhope Street** WC1
144 B4 **Midland Road** NW1
151 E2 **Midship Close** SE16
146 B1 **Milborne Grove** SW10
149 D3 **Milcote Street** SE1
150 C4 **Mile End Road** E1
148 B1 **Miles Street** SW8
144 C1 **Milford Lane** WC2
145 E2 **Milk Street** EC2
151 D3 **Milk Yard** E1
151 F3 **Mill Place** E14
150 B1 **Mill Street** SE1
143 F1 **Mill Street** W1
150 B3 **Mill Yard** E1
148 B2 **Millbank** SW1
150 B2 **Millennium Square** SE1
151 F3 **Milligan Street** E14
144 C3 **Millman Street** WC1
150 A1 **Millstream Road** SE1
147 D2 **Milner Street** SW3
145 F3 **Milton Court** EC2
145 F3 **Milton Street** EC2
149 D1 **Milverton Street** SE11
150 C4 **Milward Street** E1
150 A3 **Mincing Lane** EC3
147 E2 **Minera Mews** SW1
150 A3 **Minories** EC3
149 E3 **Mint Street** SE1
150 C4 **Miranda Close** E1
150 B4 **Mitali Passage** E1
145 E3 **Mitchell Street** EC1
149 D3 **Mitre Road** SE1
150 A3 **Mitre Square** EC3
Mitre Street
150 A3 **Mitre Street** EC3
143 D2 **Molyneux Street** W1
148 B3 **Monck Street** SW1
146 C3 **Moncorvo Close** SW7
149 D2 **Monkton Street** SE11
145 E2 **Monkwell Square** EC2
142 A2 **Monmouth Road** W2
144 B1 **Monmouth Street** WC2
143 D3 **Montagu Mansions** W1
143 D2 **Montagu Mews North** W1
143 D2 **Montagu Mews South** W1
143 D2 **Montagu Mews West** W1
143 D2 **Montagu Place** W1
143 D2 **Montagu Row** W1
143 D2 **Montagu Square** W1
143 D2 **Montagu Street** W1
149 F4 **Montague Close** SE1
144 D3 **Montague Place** WC1
145 E2 **Montague Street** EC1
144 B3 **Montague Street** WC1
148 C1 **Montford Place** SE11
147 D3 **Montpelier Mews** SW7
147 D3 **Montpelier Place** SW7
151 D3 **Montpelier Place** E1
147 D3 **Montpelier Square** SW7
147 D3 **Montpelier Street** SW7
147 D3 **Montpelier Walk** SW7
144 C3 **Montreal Place** WC2
146 C3 **Montrose Court** SW7
147 E3 **Montrose Place** SW1
145 F1 **Monument Street** EC3
151 D3 **Monza Street** E1
151 D1 **Moodkee Street** SE16
145 F2 **Moor Lane** EC2
145 F2 **Moor Place** EC2 *Moorfields*
144 A1 **Moore Street** SW3
Old Compton Street
147 E2 **Moorfields** EC2
145 F2 **Moorgate** EC2
145 E4 **Mora Street** EC1
151 D4 **Morecambe Close** E1
149 E2 **Morecambe Street** SE17
145 E4 **Moreland Street** EC1
146 A2 **Moreton Mews** SW5
Earl's Court Gardens
148 A2 **Moreton Place** SW1
148 A2 **Moreton Street** SW1
148 A1 **Moreton Terrace** SW1
149 D3 **Morley Street** SE1
149 F3 **Morocco Street** SE1
147 F2 **Morpeth Terrace** SW1
150 C3 **Morris Street** E1
142 A4 **Morshead Road** W9
144 A3 **Mortimer Market** WC1
Capper Street
143 F2 **Mortimer Street** W1
146 A2 **Morton Mews** SW5
Earl's Court Gardens
148 C3 **Morton Place** SE1
Cosser Street
144 A2 **Morwell Street** WC1

142 A1 **Moscow Place** W2
142 A1 **Moscow Road** W2
150 B4 **Moss Close** E1
147 D2 **Mossop Street** SW3
147 E3 **Motcomb Street** SW1
144 C3 **Mount Pleasant** WC1
143 E1 **Mount Row** W1
143 E1 **Mount Street** W1
150 C4 **Mount Terrace** E1
143 E2 **Moxon Street** W1
147 E2 **Mozart Terrace** SW1
150 B4 **Mulberry Street** E1
146 C1 **Mulberry Walk** SW3
142 C3 **Mulready Street** NW8
149 F3 **Mulvaney Way** SE1
145 E2 **Mumford Court** EC2
Milk Street
145 F1 **Mundy Street** N1
143 F4 **Munster Square** NW1
149 E2 **Munton Road** SE17
148 C3 **Murphy Street** SE1
145 E4 **Murray Grove** N1
151 D1 **Musbury Street** E1
150 A3 **Muscovy Street** EC3
144 B3 **Museum Street** WC1
145 D4 **Myddelton Passage** EC1
145 D4 **Myddelton Square** EC1
145 D4 **Myddelton Street** EC1
145 D4 **Mylne Street** EC1
150 C4 **Myrdle Street** E1
145 F4 **Myrtle Walk** N1

N

144 C4 **Naoroji Street** WC1
151 E3 **Narrow Street** E14
143 F4 **Nash Street** NW1
143 F2 **Nassau Street** W1
150 B4 **Nathaniel Close** E1
Thrawl Street
150 C1 **National Terrace** SE16
Bermondsey Wall East
144 B2 **Neal Street** WC2
147 F2 **Neathouse Place** SW1
Wilton Road
149 E3 **Nebraska Street** SE1
150 B1 **Neckinger** SE1
150 B1 **Neckinger Street** SE1
151 D2 **Nelson Court** SE16
145 E4 **Nelson Passage** EC1
Mora Street
145 E4 **Nelson Place** N1
149 D4 **Nelson Square** SE1
150 C4 **Nelson Street** E1
150 C4 **Nelson Terrace** N1
151 E2 **Nelson Walk** SE16
151 D1 **Neptune Street** SE16
150 B3 **Nesham Street** E1
146 B1 **Netherton Grove** SW10
143 F4 **Netley Street** NW1
146 A2 **Nevern Place** SW5
146 A2 **Nevern Square** SW5
145 D2 **Neville Court** EC4
146 C2 **Neville Street** SW7
146 C1 **Neville Terrace** SW7
143 F1 **New Bond Street** W1
145 D2 **New Bridge Street** EC4
145 F2 **New Broad Street** EC2
150 A3 **New Burlington Mews** W1
Hart Street
143 F1 **New Burlington Place** W1
143 F1 **New Burlington Street** W1
143 E2 **New Cavendish Street** W1
145 E2 **New Change** EC4
144 B2 **New Compton Street** WC2
151 D2 **New Crane Place** E1
145 D2 **New Fetter Lane** EC4
150 B4 **New Globe Walk** SE1
150 A4 **New Goulston Street** E1
149 E2 **New Kent Road** SE1
145 F3 **New North Place** EC2
145 F4 **New North Road** N1
144 C3 **New North Street** WC1
144 B2 **New Oxford Street** WC1
143 D2 **New Quebec Street** W1
146 C3 **New Ride** SW7
150 C4 **New Road** E1
144 B1 **New Row** WC2
148 B1 **New Spring Gardens Walk** SE11 *Goding Street*
144 C2 **New Square** WC2
150 A4 **New Street** EC2
145 D2 **New Street Square** EC4
144 B2 **New Turnstile** WC1
High Holborn
145 F2 **New Union Street** EC2
150 C4 **Newark Street** E1
144 F1 **Newburgh Street** W1
Foubert's Place
148 C1 **Newburn Street** SE11
145 E2 **Newbury Street** EC1
142 C3 **Newcastle Place** W2
149 F4 **Newcomen Street** SE1
151 F3 **Newell Street** E14
145 D2 **Newgate Street** EC1
149 D2 **Newington Butts** SE1 & SE11
149 E3 **Newington Causeway** SE1
151 D3 **Newlands Quay** E1
144 A2 **Newman Street** W1
144 C2 **Newman's Row** WC2
Lincoln's Inn Fields
148 C3 **Newnham Terrace** SE1
150 A1 **Newnhams Row** SE1
144 B1 **Newport Place** WC2
148 C3 **Newport Street** SE11
142 A2 **Newton Road** W2
144 B2 **Newton Street** WC2
145 F1 **Nicholas Lane** EC4
149 D4 **Nicholson Street** SE1
149 D2 **Nightingale Mews** SE11
146 B1 **Nightingale Place** SW10
145 E4 **Nile Street** N1
148 A1 **Nine Elms Lane** SW8
145 E2 **Noble Street** EC2
144 A2 **Noel Street** W1
151 F4 **Norbiton Road** E14
142 C2 **Norfolk Crescent** W2
142 C2 **Norfolk Place** W2
142 C2 **Norfolk Square** W2
145 E4 **Norman Street** EC1
144 A1 **Norris Street** SW1
143 E1 **North Audley Street** W1
142 C4 **North Bank** NW8
144 A1 **North Crescent** W1
150 B1 **North Flockton Street** SE16 *Chambers Street*
144 A4 **North Gower Street** NW1
144 C3 **North Mews** WC1
142 B2 **North Ride** W2
143 E1 **North Row** W1
150 B3 **North Tenter Street** E1

146 C3 **North Terrace** SW3
142 B2 **North Wharf Road** W2
145 D3 **Northampton Road** EC1
145 D3 **Northampton Row** EC1
Exmouth Market
145 D4 **Northampton Square** EC1
145 D3 **Northburgh Street** EC1
149 F2 **Northchurch** SE17
144 C4 **Northdown Street** N1
144 C3 **Northington Street** WC1
150 A3 **Northumberland Alley** EC3
148 B4 **Northumberland Avenue** WC2
148 B4 **Northumberland Street** WC2
142 B3 **Northwick Close** NW8
142 B3 **Northwick Terrace** NW8
151 E3 **Northy Street** E14
150 A4 **Norton Folgate** E1
151 E1 **Norway Gate** SE16
151 E4 **Norway Place** E14
145 D2 **Norwich Street** EC4
142 A1 **Notting Hill Gate** W11
143 E3 **Nottingham Place** W1
143 E3 **Nottingham Street** W1
142 B4 **Nugent Terrace** NW8

O

151 D4 **O'Leary Square** E1
149 E4 **O'Meara Street** SE1
151 F3 **Oak Lane** E14
142 C4 **Oak Tree Road** NW8
149 D2 **Oakden Street** SE11
146 B1 **Oakfield Street** SW10
142 A3 **Oakington Road** W9
145 E4 **Oakley Crescent** EC1
147 D1 **Oakley Gardens** SW3
146 C1 **Oakley Street** SW3
145 E2 **Oat Lane** EC2
146 A4 **Observatory Gardens** W8
149 E1 **Occupation Road** SE17
151 E4 **Ocean Street** E1
145 F2 **Octagon Arcade** EC2
151 D2 **Octagon Court** SE16
151 F1 **Odessa Street** SE16
143 F2 **Ogle Street** W1
145 F1 **Old Bailey** EC4
145 F1 **Old Bond Street** W1
145 F2 **Old Broad Street** EC2
146 A1 **Old Brompton Road** SW5 & SW7
143 F1 **Old Burlington Street** W1
150 B4 **Old Castle Street** E1
143 F2 **Old Cavendish Street** W1
151 D4 **Old Church Road** E1
146 C1 **Old Church Street** SW3
144 A1 **Old Compton Street** W1
146 A3 **Old Court Place** W8
145 D2 **Old Fleet Lane** EC4
144 B3 **Old Gloucester Street** WC1
150 B1 **Old Jamaica Road** SE16
145 F1 **Old Jewry** EC2
143 D2 **Old Marylebone Road** NW1
145 D2 **Old Mitre Court** EC4
Fleet Street
150 B4 **Old Montagu Street** E1
144 C3 **Old North Street** WC1
Theobalds Road
148 B3 **Old Palace Yard** SW1
148 C2 **Old Paradise Street** SE11
147 E4 **Old Park Lane** W1
148 A3 **Old Pye Street** SW1
143 D2 **Old Quebec Street** W1
148 A3 **Old Queen Street** SW1
151 F4 **Old School Square** E14
Pelling Street
144 C2 **Old Square** WC2
145 E3 **Old Street** EC1
149 E4 **Old Theatre Court** SE1
143 E3 **Oldbury Place** W1
145 F3 **Olivers Yard** EC1
149 E1 **Olney Road** SE7
142 B1 **Olympia Mews** W2
151 E1 **Onega Gate** SE16
146 A1 **Ongar Road** SW6
146 B2 **Onslow Gardens** SW7
146 C2 **Onslow Mews** SW7
146 C2 **Onslow Square** SW7
145 D3 **Onslow Street** EC1
Saffron Street
149 E3 **Ontario Street** SE1
149 D2 **Opal Street** SE11
151 D2 **Orange Place** SE16
144 B1 **Orange Street** WC2
149 F2 **Orb Street** SE17
143 E2 **Orchard Street** W1
142 C3 **Orchardson Street** NW8
144 C3 **Orde Hall Street** WC1
145 D2 **Orient Street** SE11
142 A1 **Orme Court** W2
142 A1 **Orme Lane** W2
142 A1 **Orme Square** W2
144 A1 **Ormond Yard** SW1
147 D1 **Ormonde Gate** SW3
142 B2 **Orsett Terrace** W2
150 B2 **Orton Street** E1
Wapping High Street
148 A2 **Osbert Street** SW1
150 B4 **Osborne Street** E1
151 E1 **Oslo Square** SE16
143 F3 **Osnaburgh Street** NW1
143 F4 **Osnaburgh Terrace** NW1
Albany Street
143 E2 **Ossington Buildings** W1
Moxon Street
142 A1 **Ossington Street** W2
144 A4 **Ossulston Street** NW1
146 B2 **Osten Mews** SW7
149 D2 **Oswin Street** SE11
149 D2 **Othello Close** SE11
149 D1 **Otto Street** SE17
148 C1 **Oval Way** SE11
147 D3 **Ovington Gardens** SW3
147 D3 **Ovington Square** SW3
147 D2 **Ovington Street** SW3
145 D4 **Owen Street** EC1
144 A1 **Oxendon Street** SW1
Coventry Street
143 F2 **Oxford Circus** W1
Regent Street
150 A2 **Oxford Drive** SE1
Magdalen Street
142 C2 **Oxford Square** W2
143 E1 **Oxford Street** W1
151 D3 **Oyster Row** E1
145 F1 **Oystergate Walk** EC4

P

142 C3 **Paddington Green** W2
143 E3 **Paddington Street** W1
148 B2 **Page Street** SW1
151 F2 **Pageant Crescent** SE16
151 E2 **Pageant Steps** SE16
145 D2 **Pageantmaster Court** EC4
Ludgate Hill
145 D4 **Paget Street** EC1
144 C4 **Pakenham Street** WC1
146 A4 **Palace Avenue** W8
142 A1 **Palace Court** W2
146 A4 **Palace Gardens Mews** W8
146 A4 **Palace Gardens Terrace** W8
146 B3 **Palace Gate** W8
147 F3 **Palace Street** SW1
148 A4 **Pall Mall** SW1
148 A4 **Pall Mall East** SW1
148 A4 **Pall Mall Place** SW1
145 E2 **Palmer Street** SW1
145 E2 **Pancras Lane** EC4
144 A1 **Panton Street** SW1
150 C1 **Paradise Street** SE16
143 D1 **Paradise Walk** SW3
149 F2 **Paragon Mews** SE1
Searles Road
149 F3 **Pardoner Street** SE1
150 C4 **Parfetts Street** E1
149 D4 **Paris Garden** SE1
150 C1 **Park Approach** SE16
143 E3 **Park Crescent** W1
143 F3 **Park Crescent Mews East** W1
143 E3 **Park Crescent Mews West** W1
143 E3 **Park Lane** W1
147 F4 **Park Place** SW1
142 B3 **Park Place Villas** W2
143 E3 **Park Road** NW1 & NW8
143 E3 **Park Square East** NW1
143 E3 **Park Square Mews** NW1
Harley Street
143 E3 **Park Square West** NW1
149 E4 **Park Street** SE1
143 E1 **Park Street** W1
146 B1 **Park Walk** SW10
143 D2 **Park West Place** W2
144 B2 **Parker Street** WC2
150 B1 **Parkers Row** SE1
148 B3 **Parliament Square** SW1
148 B4 **Parliament Street** SW1
151 E4 **Parnham Street** E14
148 B1 **Parry Street** SW8
149 E1 **Pasley Close** SE17
147 E2 **Passmore Street** SW1
149 D2 **Pastor Street** SE11
146 A3 **Pater Street** W8
145 E2 **Paternoster Row** EC4
145 E3 **Paternoster Square** EC4
145 E3 **Paton Street** EC1
145 E1 **Paul's Walk** EC4
146 C1 **Paultons Square** SW3
142 C1 **Paveley Street** NW8
147 D2 **Pavilion Road** SW1
147 D3 **Pavilion Street** SW1
147 F1 **Peabody Avenue** SW1
149 E2 **Peacock Street** SE17
145 D3 **Pear Tree Court** EC1
145 E1 **Pear Tree Street** EC1
150 C2 **Pearl Street** E1
149 D3 **Pearman Street** SE1
151 D3 **Peartree Lane** E1
145 E4 **Peerless Street** EC1
146 C2 **Pelham Crescent** SW7
146 C2 **Pelham Place** SW7
146 C2 **Pelham Street** SW7
151 F4 **Pelier Street** SE17
151 F4 **Pelling Street** E14
145 D2 **Pemberton Row** EC4
142 A1 **Pembridge Gardens** W2
142 A1 **Pembridge Place** W2
142 A1 **Pembridge Road** W11
142 A1 **Pembridge Square** W2
146 A2 **Pembroke Mews** W8
Earls Court Road
150 C2 **Penang Street** E1
142 C3 **Penfold Place** NW1
142 C3 **Penfold Street** NW1 & NW8
146 A2 **Pennant Mews** W8
150 C3 **Pennington Street** E1
149 E1 **Penrose Grove** SE17
149 E1 **Penrose Street** SE17
146 A2 **Penryn Street** NW1
149 E2 **Penton Place** SE17
144 C4 **Penton Rise** WC1
144 C4 **Pentonville Road** N1
149 E4 **Pepper Street** SE1
150 A3 **Pepys Street** EC3
144 C4 **Percival Street** EC1
144 A2 **Percy Circus** WC1
144 A2 **Percy Street** W1
148 A3 **Perkin's Rents** SW1
149 E4 **Perkins Square** SE1
144 A2 **Perry's Place** W1
150 C1 **Perryn Road** SE16
144 A1 **Peter Street** W1
145 E2 **Peter's Hill** EC4
146 B3 **Peter's Lane** EC1
146 B3 **Petersham Lane** SW7
146 B3 **Petersham Mews** SW7
146 B3 **Petersham Place** SW7
143 F5 **Peto Place** NW1
150 A4 **Petticoat Lane** E1
150 A4 **Petticoat Square** E1
148 A3 **Petty France** SW1
147 D2 **Petyward** SW3
149 F2 **Phelp Street** SE17
147 D1 **Phene Street** SW3
150 B3 **Philchurch Place** E1
146 A3 **Phillimore Walk** W8
146 C2 **Philpot Lane** EC3
150 C4 **Philpot Street** E1
145 F3 **Phipp Street** EC2
151 D3 **Phoenix Place** WC1
144 A4 **Phoenix Road** NW1
144 B2 **Phoenix Street** WC2
Charing Cross Road
144 A1 **Piccadilly** W1
148 A4 **Piccadilly Arcade** SW1
Piccadilly
144 A1 **Piccadilly Circus** W1
144 A1 **Piccadilly Place** W1
Vine Street
145 E4 **Pickard Street** EC1
145 E4 **Pickford Wharf** N1
143 E2 **Pickwick Street** SE1
143 E2 **Picton Place** W1
151 F2 **Piggot Street** E14
145 D2 **Pilgrim Street** EC4
149 F3 **Pilgrimage Street** SE1
147 E2 **Pimlico Road** SW1

150 B3 **Pinchin Street** E1
145 F3 **Pindar Street** EC2
142 A3 **Pindock Mews** W9
145 D3 **Pine Street** E1
145 F4 **Pitfield Street** N1
151 E1 **Pitsea Place** E1
151 E3 **Pitsea Street** E1
146 A3 **Pitt Street** W8
147 E4 **Pitt's Head Mews** W1
151 F4 **Pixley Street** E14
143 F3 **Platina Street** EC2
145 D1 **Playhouse Yard** EC4
145 D1 **Pleydell Street** EC4
Bouverie Street
145 D2 **Plough Place** EC4
Fetter Lane
151 E1 **Plover Way** SE16
151 B4 **Plumber's Row** E1
145 D2 **Plumtree Court** EC4
149 D3 **Plympton Street** NW8
149 D3 **Pocock Street** SE1
144 A2 **Poland Street** W1
143 F1 **Pollen Street** W1
142 C3 **Pollitt Drive** NW8
149 D2 **Polperro Mews** SE11
144 A4 **Polygon Road** NW1
150 B4 **Pomwell Way** E1
146 C2 **Pond Place** SW3
150 C3 **Ponler Street** E1
148 B2 **Ponsonby Place** SW1
148 B2 **Ponsonby Terrace** SW1
147 D3 **Pont Street** SW1
147 D3 **Pont Street Mews** SW1
151 F2 **Poolmans Street** SE16
151 D3 **Poonah Street** E1
150 A1 **Pope Street** SE1
142 A1 **Poplar Place** W2
145 D2 **Poppins Court** EC4
Fleet Street
143 A1 **Porchester Gardens** W2
143 A1 **Porchester Place** W2
142 A2 **Porchester Road** W2
142 A2 **Porchester Square** W2
142 B1 **Porchester Terrace** W2
149 F3 **Porlock Street** SE1
143 E3 **Porter Street** W1
149 E4 **Porter Street** SE1
145 B2 **Porteus Road** W2
144 C3 **Portland Mews** W1
D'Arblay Street
143 F2 **Portland Place** W1
150 C2 **Portland Square** E1
149 F1 **Portland Street** SE17
143 E2 **Portman Close** W1
143 E2 **Portman Mews South** W1
143 E2 **Portman Square** W1
143 E2 **Portman Street** W1
144 C3 **Portpool Lane** EC1
144 D2 **Portsea Place** W2
144 C2 **Portsmouth Street** WC2
Portugal Street
150 A3 **Portsoken Street** EC3
144 C2 **Portugal Street** WC2
149 F3 **Potier Street** SE1
150 C1 **Pottery Street** SE16
145 E2 **Poultry** EC2
142 C2 **Praed Street** W2
148 C2 **Pratt Walk** SE11
150 B3 **Prescot Street** E1
145 E4 **President Street** EC1
Central Street
150 C2 **Presidents Drive** E1
145 E4 **Prestwood Street** N1
Wenlock Road
144 C4 **Price's Street** SE1
144 C4 **Prideaux Place** WC1
145 D1 **Primrose Hill** EC4
Hutton Street
150 A4 **Primrose Street** EC2
142 C4 **Prince Albert Road** NW1 & NW8
146 C3 **Prince Consort Road** SW7
146 C3 **Prince of Wales Terrace** W8 *Kensington Road*
146 C3 **Prince's Gardens** SW7
146 C3 **Prince's Gate** SW7
146 C3 **Prince's Gate Mews** SW7
142 A1 **Prince's Mews** W2
142 A1 **Prince's Square** W2
150 B4 **Princelet Street** E1
148 A4 **Princes Arcade** SW1
Piccadilly
144 B2 **Princes Circus** WC2
150 C3 **Princes Court** E1
151 E1 **Princes Riverside Road** SE16
145 F2 **Princes Street** EC2
143 F2 **Princes Street** W1
149 D3 **Princess Street** SE1
144 C2 **Princeton Street** WC1
145 D2 **Printer Street** EC4
149 F3 **Prioress Street** SE1
146 B1 **Priory Walk** SW10
144 C2 **Procter Street** WC1
151 E1 **Prospect Place** E1
150 C1 **Prospect Street** SE16
143 E2 **Providence Court** W1
150 B2 **Providence Square** SE1
145 F4 **Provost Street** N1
150 C2 **Prusom Street** E1
145 F1 **Pudding Lane** EC3
145 D1 **Puddle Dock** EC4
150 B4 **Puma Court** E1
151 D1 **Pump House Close** SE16
Renforth Street
150 A1 **Purbrook Street** SE1

Q

143 D2 **Quarley Way** SE15
New Quebec Street
151 E1 **Quebec Way** SE16
143 F2 **Queen Anne Mews** W1
Chandos Street
142 E2 **Queen Anne Street** W1
148 A3 **Queen Anne's Gate** SW1
150 A2 **Queen Elizabeth Street** SE1
144 B3 **Queen Square** WC1
145 E1 **Queen Street** EC4
145 F4 **Queen Street** W1
145 E1 **Queen Street Place** EC4
145 D1 **Queen Victoria Street** EC4
147 F3 **Queen's Gardens** SW1
142 B1 **Queen's Gardens** W2
146 B3 **Queen's Gate** SW7
146 B2 **Queen's Gate Gardens** SW7
146 B3 **Queen's Gate Mews** SW7
146 B3 **Queen's Gate Place** SW7
146 B2 **Queen's Gate Place Mews** SW7

146 B3 Queen's Gate Terrace SW7
142 A1 Queen's Mews W2
149 E1 Queen's Row SE17
147 F4 Queen's Walk SW1
145 C1 Queenhithe EC4
146 B2 Queensberry Mews West SW7
143 F4 Queensberry Place SW7
Harrington Street
142 B1 Queensborough Terrace W2
142 A2 Queensway W2
145 D4 Quick Street N1

R

146 A4 Rabbit Row W8
151 E4 Raby Street E14
150 A1 Radcliffe Road SE1
149 D1 Radcot Street SE11
151 E2 Radley Court SE16
146 A2 Radley Mews W8
142 C2 Radnor Mews W2
142 C2 Radnor Place W2
145 D3 Radnor Street EC1
147 D1 Ralston Street SW3
149 F4 Railway Approach SE1
151 E2 Railway Avenue SE16
150 C2 Raine Street E1
142 C2 Rainsford Street W2
147 D1 Ralston Street SW3
143 F2 Ramillies Place W1
144 A1 Ramillies Street W1
150 C4 Rampart Street E1
148 A2 Rampayne Street SW1
146 C1 Ramsey Mews SW3
148 C2 Randall Road SE11
148 C2 Randall Row SE11
142 A4 Randolph Avenue W9
142 B3 Randolph Crescent W9
142 B3 Randolph Mews W9
142 B3 Randolph Road W9
142 B2 Ranelagh Bridge W2
147 E2 Ranelagh Grove SW1
148 A1 Ranelagh Road SW1
150 A3 Rangoon Street EC3
Jewry Street
142 A3 Ranston Street NW1
147 D3 Raphael Street SW7
145 E4 Ratcliff Grove EC1
151 E3 Ratcliffe Cross Street E1
151 E3 Ratcliffe Lane E14
144 A2 Rathbone Place W1
150 C4 Raven Row E1
149 D1 Ravensdon Street SE11
148 C2 Ravent Road SE11
145 F3 Ravey Street EC2
147 D2 Rawlings Street SW3
145 D4 Rawstorne Place EC1
Rawstorne Street
145 D4 Rawstorne Street EC1
145 D3 Ray Street EC1
150 C2 Reardon Path E1
150 C2 Reardon Street E1
151 D1 Rebecca Terrace SE16
151 E4 Rectory Square E1
149 E1 Red Lion Row SE17
144 C2 Red Lion Square WC1
144 C2 Red Lion Street WC1
142 A2 Redan Place W2
147 D1 Redburn Street SW3
151 D3 Redcastle Close E1
146 A1 Redcliffe Gardens SW10 & SW5
146 B1 Redcliffe Mews SW10
146 B1 Redcliffe Place SW10
146 B1 Redcliffe Road SW10
146 A1 Redcliffe Square SW10
146 B1 Redcliffe Street SW10
149 E4 Redcross Way SE1
142 A1 Rede Place W2
147 D1 Redesdale Street SW3
146 A2 Redfield Lane SW5
143 F4 Redhill Street NW1
151 D4 Redman's Road E1
150 B2 Redmead Lane E1
Wapping High Street
151 E4 Redriff Road SE16
151 E2 Redwood Close SE16
146 C1 Reece Mews SW7
149 D2 Reedworth Street SE11
143 E1 Reeves Mews W1
150 C4 Regal Close E1
145 F4 Regan Way N1
148 A2 Regency Street SW1
144 B4 Regent Square WC1
143 F2 Regent Street W1 & SW1
144 A4 Regnart Buildings NW1
Euston Street
147 D3 Relton Mews SW7
145 E4 Remington Street N1
144 C2 Remnant Street WC2
Kingsway
151 D1 Renforth Street SE16
149 D2 Renfrew Road SE11
145 D3 Rennie Street SE1
149 F3 Rephidim Street SE1
151 E4 Repton Street E14
146 B3 Reston Place SW7
151 E1 Reveley Close SE16
143 E1 Rex Place W1
151 F4 Rhodeswell Road E14
146 A1 Rich Lane SW5
151 F3 Rich Street E14
147 D2 Richard's Place SW3
144 C2 Richbell Place WC1
Emerald Street
144 A2 Richmond Buildings W1
Dean Street
144 A2 Richmond Mews W1
148 B4 Richmond Terrace SW1
146 A1 Rickett Street SW6
144 A4 Ridgmount Gardens WC1
144 A3 Ridgmount Street WC1
143 F2 Riding House Street W1
150 A1 Riley Road SE1
149 E4 Risborough Street SE1
151 D1 Risdon Street SE16
145 D4 River Street EC1
148 C4 Riverside Walk SE1
145 F3 Rivington Street EC2
143 E2 Robert Adam Street W1
143 F4 Robert Street NW1
144 B1 Robert Street WC2
151 E1 Roberts Close SE16
145 D3 Roberts Place EC1
Bowling Green Lane
147 D1 Robinson Street SW3
Flood Street

148 A2 Rochester Row SW1
148 A2 Rochester Street SW1
149 E3 Rockingham Street SE1
145 E4 Rocliffe Street N1
150 B2 Roding Mews E1
143 D2 Rodmarton Street W1
149 E2 Rodney Place SE17
149 E2 Rodney Road SE17
144 C3 Roger Street WC1
146 B1 Roland Gardens SW7
151 D4 Roland Mews E1
149 F1 Roland Way SE17
146 B1 Roland Way SW7
145 D2 Rolls Buildings EC4
144 C2 Rolls Passage EC4
150 C4 Romford Street E1
144 A1 Romilly Street W1
143 E3 Romney Mews W1
Chiltern Street
148 B2 Romney Street SW1
151 D3 Ronald Street E1
145 F1 Rood Lane EC3
151 E1 Rope Street SE16
151 E1 Ropemaker Road SE16
145 F3 Ropemaker Street EC2
151 F3 Ropemaker's Fields E14
150 A1 Roper Lane SE1
146 B2 Rosary Gardens SW7
145 E3 Roscoe Street EC1
148 A4 Rose & Crown Yard SW1
King Street
149 E4 Rose Alley SE1
144 B1 Rose Street WC2
147 D3 Rosebery Avenue EC1
147 D2 Rosemoor Street SW3
145 D4 Rosoman Place EC1
Rosoman Street
145 D4 Rosoman Street EC1
143 D3 Rossmore Road NW1
149 D3 Rotary Street SE1
151 D2 Rotherhithe Street SE16
151 E3 Rotherhithe Tunnel Approach E14
151 F1 Rotherhithe Tunnel Approach SE16
149 F3 Rothsay Street SE1
146 C4 Rotten Row SW7 & SW1
150 B1 Rouel Road SE16
149 D4 Roupell Street SE1
142 A3 Rowington Close W2
146 A1 Roxby Place SW6
151 F3 Roy Square E14
147 D1 Royal Avenue SW3
145 F2 Royal Exchange Buildings EC3 *Cornhill*
147 D1 Royal Hospital Road SW3
150 B3 Royal Mint Place E1
150 B3 Royal Mint Street E1
148 A4 Royal Opera Arcade SW1
149 E1 Royal Road SE17
148 C3 Royal Street SE1
144 A2 Royalty Mews W1
144 A2 Royalty Mews W1
148 B1 Rudolf Place SW8
142 A4 Rudolph Road NW6
145 F4 Rufus Street N1
144 C3 Rugby Street WC1
151 F3 Rugg Street E14
150 C3 Rum Close E1
151 D1 Rupack Street SE16
144 A1 Rupert Street W1
149 D3 Rushworth Street SE1
148 A4 Russell Court SW1
Cleveland Row
151 E1 Russell Place SE16
144 B3 Russell Square WC1
144 C1 Russell Street WC2
151 E2 Russia Dock Road SE16
145 E2 Russia Row EC2
151 E1 Russia Walk SE16
148 A2 Rutherford Street SW1
147 D3 Rutland Gardens SW7
146 C3 Rutland Gate SW7
146 C3 Rutland Gate Mews SW7
Rutland Gate
146 C3 Rutland Mews East SW7
Ennismore Street
146 C3 Rutland Mews South SW7
Ennismore Street
145 E3 Rutland Place EC1
146 C3 Rutland Street SW7
147 D3 Rysbrack Street SW3

S

144 A1 Sackville Street W1
147 E4 Saddle Yard W1
145 D3 Saffron Hill EC1
145 D3 Saffron Street EC1
150 C3 Sage Street E1
144 C4 Sage Way WC1
148 C2 Sail Street SE11
149 D1 St Agnes Place SE11
146 A3 St Alban's Grove W8
148 A3 St Alban's Street SW1
142 C3 St Albans Mews W2
145 D2 St Alphage Garden EC2
145 D1 St Andrew Street EC4
145 D1 St Andrew's Hill EC4
148 A3 St Ann's Lane SW1
151 F3 St Ann's Row E14
148 B3 St Ann's Street SW1
151 F3 St Anne Street E14
144 A2 St Anne's Court W1
143 E1 St Anselm's Place W1
150 B2 St Anthony's Close E1
147 E2 St Barnabas Street SW1
150 A4 St Botolph Street EC3
145 D2 St Bride Street EC4
147 D2 St Catherines Mews SW3
Milner Street
144 B4 St Chad's Place WC1
144 B4 St Chad's Street WC1
143 E2 St Christoper's Place W1
150 A3 St Clare Street EC3
145 D1 St Clement's Lane WC2
145 F1 St Clements Court EC4
145 E1 St Cross Street EC1
145 D2 St Dunstan's Court EC4
Fleet Street
145 F1 St Dunstan's Lane EC3
St Mary at Hill
150 A3 St Dunstans Alley EC3
St Dunstans Hill
150 A3 St Dunstans Hill EC3
145 A3 St Ermins Hill SW1
143 F1 St George Street W1
148 B1 St George Wharf SW8
150 D3 St George's Circus SE1
145 D2 St George's Court EC4
147 F2 St George's Drive SW1
149 D3 St George's Fields W2

149 D3 St George's Road SE1
148 A1 St George's Square SW1
151 E3 St George's Square E14
148 A1 St George's Square Mews SW1
143 D1 St Georges Fields W2
144 B2 St Giles High Street WC2
145 F2 St Helen's Place EC3
144 C4 St Helena Street WC1
148 A3 St James's Court SW1
144 A1 St James's Market SW1
Haymarket
147 F4 St James's Place SW1
150 B1 St James's Road SE1 & SE16
145 D3 St James's Row EC1
St James's Walk
148 A4 St James's Square SW1
148 A4 St James's Street SW1
145 D3 St James's Walk EC1
145 D4 St John Street EC1
145 D3 St John's Lane EC1
145 D3 St John's Place EC1
145 D3 St John's Square EC1
146 A3 St John's Villas W8
St Mary's Place
142 C4 St John's Wood High Street NW8
142 C4 St John's Wood Road NW8
145 F1 St Katherine's Row EC3
Fenchurch Street
150 B1 St Katherine's Way E1
147 D1 St Leonard's Terrace SW3
147 D1 St Loo Avenue SW3
145 E3 St Luke's Close EC1
146 C1 St Luke's Street SW3
146 A3 St Margaret's Lane W8
148 B3 St Margaret's Street SW1
150 B3 St Mark Street E1
144 B1 St Martin's Court WC2
St Martin's Lane
144 B1 St Martin's Lane WC2
144 B1 St Martin's Place WC2
144 B1 St Martin's Street WC2
145 E2 St Martin's-le-Grand EC1
145 F1 St Mary at Hill EC3
150 A3 St Mary Axe EC3
145 D2 St Mary's Gardens SE11
146 A3 St Mary's Gate W8
142 B3 St Mary's Mansions W2
146 A3 St Mary's Place W8
142 C3 St Mary's Square W2
142 B3 St Mary's Terrace W2
149 D2 St Mary's Walk SE11
151 D1 St Marychurch Street SE16
148 A3 St Matthew Street SW1
142 C2 St Michael's Street W2
151 D1 St Olav's Square SE16
Lower Road
148 C1 St Oswald's Place SE11
151 E2 St Paul's Avenue SE16
145 E2 St Paul's Churchyard EC4
149 E1 St Paul's Terrace SE17
151 F4 St Paul's Way E3
142 A3 St Peter's Place W9
142 A1 St Petersburgh Mews W2
142 A1 St Petersburgh Place W2
142 A2 St Stephen's Crescent W2
142 A2 St Stephen's Gardens W2
142 A2 St Stephen's Mews W2
151 F1 St Swithin's Lane EC4
149 F4 St Thomas Street SE1
143 E2 St Vincent Street W1
148 C2 Salamanca Place SE1
148 C2 Salamanca Street SE1 & SE11
142 A1 Salem Road W2
149 F2 Salisbury Close SE17
145 D2 Salisbury Court EC4
143 D3 Salisbury Place W1
145 D2 Salisbury Square EC4
Salisbury Court
142 C3 Salisbury Street NW8
151 E4 Salmon Lane E14
151 E1 Salter Road SE16
151 F3 Salter Street E14
142 C3 Samford Street NW8
150 C2 Sampson Street E1
148 C2 Sancroft Street SE11
149 E4 Sanctuary Street SE1
Marshalsea Road
149 D4 Sandell Street SE1
144 C2 Sandland Street WC1
151 F2 Sandpiper Close SE16
144 B4 Sandwich Street WC1
150 A4 Sandys Row E1
147 D3 Sans Walk EC1
150 A3 Saracens Head Yard EC3
144 C2 Sardinia Street WC2
151 F3 Saunders Court E14
Limehouse Causeway
150 A3 Savage Gardens EC3
Pepys Street
143 F1 Savile Row W1
144 C1 Savoy Buildings WC2
144 C1 Savoy Hill WC2 *Savoy Way*
144 B1 Savoy Place WC2
144 C1 Savoy Row WC2
Savoy Street
144 C1 Savoy Steps WC2
Savoy Way
144 C1 Savoy Street WC2
144 C1 Savoy Way WC2
149 E4 Sawyer Street SE1
144 A2 Scala Street W1
150 C2 Scandrett Street E1
150 B3 Scarborough Street E1
146 A3 Scarsdale Place W8
146 A3 Scarsdale Villas W8
151 D3 School House Lane E1
151 D2 Schooner Close SE16
149 D4 Scoresby Street SE1
147 D3 Scotswood Street EC1
Sans Walk
142 B4 Scott Ellis Gardens NW8
150 B4 Scott Lidgett Crescent SE16
149 E3 Scovell Road SE1
145 E2 Scrutton Street EC2
146 A1 Seagrave Road SW6
149 F2 Searles Road SE1
145 D4 Sebastian Street EC1
145 C4 Secker Street SE1
149 E2 Sedan Way SE17
147 E2 Sedding Street SW1
Sloane Square
144 C4 Seddon Street WC1
143 F2 Sedley Place W1
Woodstock Street
150 A3 Seething Lane EC3
145 D3 Sekforde Street EC1
148 C2 Sellon Mews SE11
151 F4 Selsey Street E14
146 C2 Selwood Terrace SW7

146 C1 Selwood Place SW7
147 E2 Semley Place SW1
142 A3 Senior Street W9
151 D4 Senrab Street E1
144 C2 Serle Street WC2
146 C1 Serpentine Road W2
151 D1 Seth Street SE16
150 C4 Settles Street E1
144 B2 Seven Dials WC2
147 D3 Seville Street SW1
Knightsbridge
142 A3 Sevington Street W9
145 E3 Seward Street EC1
143 E2 Seymour Mews W1
143 D2 Seymour Place W1
143 D1 Seymour Street W2
146 B1 Seymour Walk SW10
150 A2 Shad Thames SE1
151 D3 Shadwell Pier Head E1
150 C3 Shadwell Place E1
144 A1 Shaftesbury Avenue W1 & WC2
146 A2 Shaftesbury Mews W8
147 D3 Shafto Mews SW1
150 A2 Shand Street SE1
149 D1 Sharsted Street SE17
147 D1 Shawfield Street SW3
144 C2 Sheffield Street WC2
Portugal Street
146 A4 Sheffield Terrace W8
151 F4 Shelmerdine Close E3
144 B2 Shelton Street WC2
147 E4 Shepherd Market W1
147 E4 Shepherd Street W1
143 E1 Shepherd's Place W1
145 E4 Shepherdess Place N1
Shepherdess Walk
145 E4 Shepherdess Walk N1
144 A2 Sheraton Street W1
Wardour Street
143 E3 Sherlock Mews W1
144 A1 Sherwood Street W1
143 D2 Shillibeer Place W1
151 E1 Shipwright Road SE16
142 A3 Shirland Road W9
145 D2 Shoe Lane EC4
149 D4 Short Street SE1
144 B2 Short's Gardens WC2
150 B3 Shorter Street E1
151 F2 Shoulder of Mutton Alley E14
143 D2 Shouldham Street W1
142 C3 Shroton Street NW1
144 B2 Sicilian Avenue WC1
Vernon Place
143 D3 Siddons Lane NW1
148 C2 Sidford Place SE1
144 C4 Sidmouth Street WC1
151 D4 Sidney Square E1
150 C4 Sidney Street E1
149 D3 Silex Street SE1
145 E3 Silk Street EC2
151 F2 Silver Walk SE16
149 E3 Silvester Street SE1
143 F3 Singer Street EC2
145 E2 Sise Lane EC4 *Pancras Lane*
145 D3 Skinner Street EC1
145 F4 Skinners Lane EC4
Queen Street
144 B4 Sleaford Street SW8
144 B1 Slingsby Place WC2
150 C1 Slippers Place SE16
147 D2 Sloane Avenue SW3
147 E2 Sloane Court East SW3
147 E1 Sloane Court West SW3
147 E2 Sloane Gardens SW1
147 E2 Sloane Square SW1
147 D3 Sloane Street SW1
147 E2 Sloane Terrace SW1
150 C3 Sly Street E1
Cannon Street Road
144 B2 Smart's Place WC2
150 B2 Smeaton Street E1
151 D2 Smith Close SE16
148 B3 Smith Square SW1
147 D1 Smith Street SW3
147 D1 Smith Terrace SW3
145 D2 Smithfield Street EC1
151 D4 Smithy Street E1
145 D2 Snow Hill EC1
149 F4 Snowsfields SE1
144 A2 Soho Square W1
144 A2 Soho Street W1
151 E1 Somerford Way SE16
142 C2 Somers Crescent W2
142 C2 Somers Mews W2
149 F1 Sondes Street SE17
151 E3 Sophia Square SE16
143 E1 South Audley Street W1
146 B1 South Bolton Gardens SW5
146 C3 South Carriage Drive SW1 & SW7
144 A2 South Crescent WC1
Store Street
147 E2 South Eaton Place SW1
146 A3 South End W8
146 A3 South End Row W8
148 B1 South Lambeth Place SW8
143 E1 South Molton Lane W1
143 E2 South Molton Street W1
146 C1 South Parade SW3
145 E2 South Place EC2
147 E4 South Street W1
150 B3 South Tenter Street E1
146 C2 South Terrace SW7
142 C2 South Wharf Road W2
149 F3 Southall Place SE1
Long Lane
144 C2 Southampton Buildings WC2
144 B2 Southampton Place WC1
144 B1 Southampton Row WC1
144 B1 Southampton Street WC2
151 F1 Southsea Street SE16
145 E1 Southwark Bridge EC4 & SE1
149 E3 Southwark Bridge Road SE1
150 C1 Southwark Park Road SE16
149 D4 Southwark Street SE1
146 B2 Southwell Gardens SW7
142 C2 Southwick Street W2
Hyde Park Crescent
150 C2 Sovereign Close E1
150 B1 Spa Road SE16
143 E2 Spanish Place W1
146 A2 Spear Mews SW5
150 B4 Spelman Street E1
151 F1 Spence Close SE16
145 D4 Spencer Street EC1
148 A3 Spenser Street SW1
151 E4 Spert Street E14

150 A4 Spital Square E1
150 B4 Spital Street E1
147 D2 Sprimont Place SW3
148 B4 Spring Gardens SW1
143 D3 Spring Mews W1
142 C2 Spring Street W2
147 F3 Spur Road SW1
148 C3 Spur Road SE1
Lower Marsh
149 F3 Spurgeon Street SE1
142 C4 Squire Gardens NW8
148 A4 Stable Yard Road SW1
148 C1 Stables Way SE11
144 B2 Stacey Street WC2
145 F4 Staff Street EC1
Vince Street
147 F3 Stafford Place SW1
147 F3 Stag Place SW1
149 F4 Stainer Street SE1
145 E2 Staining Lane EC2
142 C3 Stalbridge Street NW1
150 C1 Stalham Street SE16
148 C4 Stamford Street SE1
146 A3 Stamford Road W8
148 A2 Stanford Street SW1
146 B2 Stanhope Gardens SW7
147 E4 Stanhope Gate W1
Hertford Street
146 B2 Stanhope Mews East SW7
146 B2 Stanhope Mews South SW7
146 B2 Stanhope Mews West SW7
146 B2 Stanhope Place W2
143 F4 Stanhope Street NW1
142 C1 Stanhope Terrace W2
149 D1 Stannary Place SE11
149 D1 Stannary Street SE11
150 B1 Stanworth Street SE1
144 C2 Staple Inn Buildings WC1
149 F3 Staple Street E1
151 E1 Staples Close SE16
150 B3 Star Place E1
142 C2 Star Street W2
144 C2 Star Yard WC2
144 A3 Starcross Street NW1
145 F2 Station Acces Road EC2
151 E2 Stave Yard Road SE16
149 E2 Stead Street SE17
144 B2 Stedham Place WC1 *New Oxford Street*
149 E2 Steedman Street SE17
151 D3 Steel's Lane E1
145 E1 Steelyard Passage EC4
151 E1 Steers Way SE16
144 A2 Stephen Mews W1
Gresse Street
144 A2 Stephen Street W1
145 F1 Stephen's Row EC4
Walbrook
144 A3 Stephenson Way NW1
151 D3 Stepney Causeway E1
151 D4 Stepney Green E1
151 E4 Stepney High Street E1
150 C4 Stepney Way E1
147 D3 Sterling Street SW7
Montpelier Place
149 F3 Sterry Street SE1
150 C4 Stevedore Street E1
150 A1 Stevens Street SE1
145 E2 Stew Lane EC4
146 C2 Stewart's Grove SW3
148 A2 Stillington Street SW1
150 B2 Stockholm Way E1
Vaughan Way
151 F3 Stocks Place E14
144 C2 Stone Buildings WC2
Chancery Lane
146 A3 Stone Hall Gardens W8
146 A3 Stone Hall Place W8
Stone Hall Gardens
151 E3 Stone Stairs E1
145 D2 Stonecutter Street EC4
149 E3 Stones End Street SE1
150 A4 Stoney Lane E1
149 F4 Stoney Street SE1
149 E1 Stopford Road SE17
144 A2 Store Street WC1
148 B3 Storey's Gate SW1
150 C1 Stork's Road SE16
148 C2 Stoughton Close SE11
143 D2 Stourcliffe Street W1
144 B1 Strand WC2
146 A3 Stratford Avenue W8
143 E2 Stratford Place W1
146 A2 Stratford Road W8
142 C2 Strathearn Place W2
Hyde Park Square
146 A4 Strathmore Gardens W8
Palace Gardens Terrace
147 F4 Stratton Street W1
144 B2 Streatham Street WC1
Dyott Street
148 A3 Strutton Ground SW1
150 A4 Strype Street E1
144 B2 Stukeley Street WC2
149 E3 Sturge Street SE1
149 E1 Sturgeon Road SE17
145 E4 Sturt Street N1
150 B3 Stutfield Street E1
145 D4 Sudeley Street N1
149 E3 Sudrey Street SE1
145 F1 Suffolk Lane EC4
144 B1 Suffolk Place SW1
Suffolk Street
144 B1 Suffolk Street SW1
150 A3 Sugar Quay Walk EC3
149 D2 Sullivan Road E1
151 D4 Summercourt Road E1
145 D3 Summers Street EC1
Back Hill
146 C2 Sumner Place SW7
146 C2 Sumner Place Mews SW7
145 E4 Sumner Street SE1
145 F3 Sun Street EC2
145 F2 Sun Street Passage EC2
150 B3 Sun Walk E1
142 A2 Sunderland Terrace W2
146 A2 Sunningdale Gardens W8
Stratford Road
142 A3 Surrendale Place W9
151 D1 Surrey Quays Road SE16
149 D4 Surrey Row SE1
149 F2 Surrey Square SE17
144 C1 Surrey Street WC2
151 E2 Surrey Water Road SE16
142 C1 Sussex Gardens W2
143 D1 Sussex Mews NW1
142 C1 Sussex Place W2
142 C1 Sussex Square W2
148 A1 Sussex Street SW1
147 F1 Sussex Street SW1
142 A3 Sutherland Avenue W9
147 F1 Sutherland Row SW1
Sutherland Street
149 E1 Sutherland Square SE17

147 F1 Sutherland Street SW1
149 E1 Sutherland Walk SE17
144 B2 Sutton Row W1
144 A1 Swallow Street W1
145 F1 Swan Lane EC4
149 F3 Swan Mead SE1
151 D2 Swan Road SE16
149 E3 Swan Street SE1
147 D1 Swan Walk SW3
151 E1 Sweden Gate SE16
150 C3 Swedenborg Gardens E1
150 B3 Sweeney Crescent SE1
144 C4 Swinton Street WC1
144 B1 Swiss Court WC2
　Leicester Square
145 E3 Sycamore Street EC1
　Old Street
146 C2 Sydney Close SW3
146 C2 Sydney Mews SW3
146 C2 Sydney Street SW3
145 F4 Syminster Mews N1
　Coronet Street
147 D2 Symons Street SW3

T

149 F3 Tabard Street SE1
145 F3 Tabernacle Street EC2
148 A2 Tachbrook Street SW1
150 B4 Tailworth Street E1
　Chicksand Street
142 C2 Talbot Square W2
149 F4 Talbot Yard SE1
145 D1 Tallis Street EC4
151 D2 Tameraire Street SE16
145 A1 Tamworth Street SW6
144 B4 Tankerton Street WC1
　Cromer Street
150 A1 Tanner Street SE1
145 E4 Taplow Street N1
151 D3 Tarbert Walk E1
150 C3 Tarling Street E1
149 E3 Tarn Street SE1
149 E1 Tarver Road SE17
149 F2 Tatum Street SE17
143 D3 Taunton Mews NW1
　Balcombe Street
143 D3 Taunton Place NW1
144 B3 Tavistock Place WC1
144 B3 Tavistock Square WC1
144 B1 Tavistock Street WC2
144 A3 Taviton Street WC1
149 D2 Tavy Close SE11
151 E2 Teak Close SE16
147 D1 Tedworth Square SW3
145 F2 Telegraph Street EC2
145 D1 Temple Avenue EC4
145 A2 Temple Lane EC4
144 C1 Temple Place WC2
145 D1 Templeton Place SW5
150 C2 Tench Street E1
143 F2 Tenison Court W1
　Regent Street
148 C4 Tenison Way SE1
149 F3 Tennis Street SE1
150 A4 Tenter Ground E1
　White's Row
143 F2 Tenterden Street W1
151 E1 Teredo Street SE16
147 F3 Terminus Place SW1
146 A3 Thackeray Street W8
151 E2 Thame Road SE16
151 D2 Thames Link SE16
144 B4 Thanet Street WC1
145 D2 Thavies Inn EC4
143 E2 Thayer Street W1
146 B1 The Boltons SW10
143 E4 The Broad Walk NW1
146 B4 The Broad Walk W8
149 D4 The Cut SE1
146 B4 The Dial Walk W8
148 A4 The Economist Plaza SW1
　Bury Street
146 B3 The Flower Walk SW7
150 A1 The Grange SE1
150 C3 The Highway E1 & E14
142 A1 The Limes W2
145 B1 The Little Boltons SW10 & SW5
148 A4 The Mall SW1
151 F3 The Mitre E14
144 B1 The Piazza WC2
146 C1 The Vale SW3
149 D4 Theed Street SE1
149 F2 Theobald Street SE1
　New Kent Road
144 C3 Theobald's Road WC1
145 E4 Theseus Walk N1
　Rocliffe Street
148 A3 Thirleby Road SW1
146 B1 Thistle Grove SW10
149 D3 Thomas Doyle Street SE1
150 B2 Thomas More Street E1
146 A3 Thomas Place W8
　St Mary's Place
151 F4 Thomas Road E14
145 E4 Thoresby Street N1
148 B2 Thorney Street SW1
142 A3 Thorngate Road W9
143 D3 Thornton Place W1
149 E4 Thrale Street SE1
150 B4 Thrawl Street E1
145 F2 Threadneedle Street EC2
151 F3 Three Colt Street E14
145 E1 Three Cranes Walk EC4
143 E1 Three Kings Yard W1
150 A2 Three Oak Lane SE1
145 F2 Throgmorton Avenue EC2
145 F2 Throgmorton Street EC2
149 E1 Thrush Street SE17
150 B1 Thurland Road SE16
146 C2 Thurloe Close SW7
146 C2 Thurloe Place SW7
146 C2 Thurloe Place Mews SW7
146 C2 Thurloe Square SW7
146 C2 Thurloe Street SW7
149 F2 Thurlow Street SE17
150 C3 Tillman Street E1
145 E3 Tilney Court EC1
147 E3 Tilney Street W1
145 E3 Timber Street EC1
150 C3 Timberland Road E1
151 E2 Timberpond Road SE16
151 D4 Tinsley Road E1
148 B2 Tinworth Street SE11
142 C2 Titchborne Row W2
147 D1 Tite Street SW3
149 E3 Tiverton Street SE1
151 F1 Tivoli Court SE16
145 F2 Tokenhouse Yard EC2
144 A3 Tolmers Square NW1
144 B4 Tonbridge Street WC1

144 C2 Took's Court EC4
150 A2 Tooley Street SE1
145 D3 Topham Street EC1
146 A4 Tor Gardens W8
142 A2 Torquay Street W2
145 D4 Torrens Street EC1
150 C1 Torrington Place E1
144 A3 Torrington Place WC1
148 A3 Tothill Street SW1
144 A3 Tottenham Court Road W1
144 A3 Tottenham Street W1
149 E3 Toulmin Street SE1
150 B1 Toussaint Walk SE16
150 A2 Tower Bridge E1 & SE1
150 B2 Tower Bridge Approach E1
150 A1 Tower Bridge Road SE1
144 B1 Tower Court WC2
　Monmouth Street
150 A3 Tower Hill EC3
150 A3 Tower Hill Terrace EC3
　Gloucester Close
144 B1 Tower Street WC2
149 E2 Townley Street SE17
149 F2 Townsend Street SE17
150 B4 Toynbee Street E1
148 C2 Tracey Street SE11
151 E4 Trafalgar Gardens E1
146 A3 Trafalgar Gardens W8
　South End Row
144 B1 Trafalgar Square WC2
149 F1 Trafalgar Street SE17
150 C1 Tranton Road SE16
147 E4 Trebeck Street W1
　Curzon Street
146 A2 Trebovir Road SW5
146 B1 Tregunter Road SW10
142 C4 Tresham Crescent NW8
149 D4 Treveris Street SE1
　Bear Lane
147 D3 Trevor Place SW7
147 D3 Trevor Square SW7
147 D3 Trevor Street SW7
149 D1 Triangle Estate SE11
　Kennington Lane
151 F3 Trinidad Street E14
149 E3 Trinity Church Square SE1
150 A3 Trinity Place EC3
　Trinity Square
150 A3 Trinity Square EC3
149 E3 Trinity Street SE1
149 E3 Trio Place SE1
151 E4 Troon Street E1
150 C1 Trumans Street SE16
145 E2 Trump Street EC2
147 D2 Tryon Street SW3
145 D1 Tudor Street EC4
148 B3 Tufton Street SW1
151 F4 Tunley Green E14
151 D2 Tunnel Road SE16
147 E1 Turk's Row SW3
150 C4 Turner Street E1
145 D3 Turnmill Street EC1
147 F1 Turpentine Lane SW1
149 E2 Turquand Street SE17
150 C3 Twine Court E1
144 C2 Twyford Place WC2
　Kingsway
149 F3 Tyers Gate SE1
148 C1 Tyers Street SE11
148 C1 Tyers Terrace SE11
150 B4 Tyne Street E1
145 D4 Tysoe Street EC1

U

148 A2 Udall Street SW1
149 D3 Ufford Street SE1
143 E3 Ulster Place NW1
150 C4 Umberston Street E1
145 F2 Undershaft EC3
145 E4 Underwood Row N1
　Shepherdess Walk
145 E4 Underwood Street N1
149 D4 Union Street SE1
144 A3 University Street WC1
142 B2 Upbrook Mews W2
147 E3 Upper Belgrave Street SW1
143 D2 Upper Berkeley Street W1
143 E1 Upper Brook Street W1
146 C1 Upper Cheyne Row SW3
143 E1 Upper Grosvenor Street W1
145 D1 Upper Ground SE1
143 E3 Upper Harley Street NW1
144 A1 Upper James Street W1
144 A1 Upper John Street W1
148 C3 Upper Marsh SE1
143 D3 Upper Montagu Street W1
144 B1 Upper St Martin's Lane WC2
148 A2 Upper Tachbrook Street SW1
145 E1 Upper Thames Street EC4
143 E3 Upper Wimpole Street W1
144 B3 Upper Woburn Place WC1

V

142 B4 Vale Close W9
149 D3 Valentine Place SE1
149 D3 Valentine Row SE1
148 A3 Vandon Passage SW1
148 A3 Vandon Street SW1
145 F3 Vandy Street EC2
148 A2 Vane Street SW1
150 C4 Varden Street E1
143 F4 Varndell Street NW1
150 B1 Vauban Street SE16
151 F1 Vaughan Street SE16
143 E4 Vaughan Way E1
148 B2 Vauxhall Bridge SW1 & SE1
147 F2 Vauxhall Bridge Road SW1
148 B1 Vauxhall Grove SW8
148 C2 Vauxhall Street SE11
142 C2 Vauxhall Walk SE11
142 C3 Venables Street NW8
143 E2 Vere Street W1
144 B2 Vernon Place WC1
144 C4 Vernon Rise WC1
144 C4 Vernon Square WC1
　Penton Rise
144 C4 Vernon Street W14
144 C3 Verulam Street WC1
145 F4 Vestry Street N1
146 A4 Vicarage Court W8
146 A4 Vicarage Gardens W8
146 A4 Vicarage Gate W8
150 A4 Victoria Avenue EC2
144 C1 Victoria Embankment SW1, WC2 & EC4

146 B3 Victoria Grove W8
146 B3 Victoria Road W8
147 F3 Victoria Street SW1
149 F2 Victory Place SE17
151 E3 Victory Place E1
151 E3 Victory Way SE16
144 A1 Vigo Street W1
149 E1 Villa Street SE17
144 B1 Villiers Street WC2
145 F4 Vince Street N1
151 E1 Vincent Close SE16
148 A2 Vincent Square SW1
148 A2 Vincent Street SW1
150 C4 Vine Court E1
150 A2 Vine Lane SE1
150 A3 Vine Street EC3
144 A1 Vine Street W1
145 D3 Vine Street Bridge EC1
　Farringdon Lane
150 C2 Vinegar Street E1
149 F4 Vinegar Yard SE1
　St Thomas Street
145 D3 Vineyard Walk EC1
　Pine Street
145 E1 Vintner's Place EC4
142 B4 Violet Hill NW8
143 D2 Virgil Place W1
　Seymour Place
148 C3 Virgil Street SE1
150 B3 Virginia Street E1
145 E3 Viscount Street EC1

W

149 E2 Wadding Street SE17
145 D2 Waithman Street EC4
　Pilgrim Street
144 B4 Wakefield Mews WC1
　Wakefield Street
144 B4 Wakefield Street WC1
151 E3 Wakeling Street E14
145 D4 Wakley Street EC1
145 F1 Walbrook EC4
150 C3 Walburgh Street E1
149 E2 Walcorde Avenue SE17
149 D2 Walcot Square SE11
150 C4 Walden Street E1
151 E4 Waley Street E1
146 A2 Wallgrave Road SW5
151 F4 Wallwood Street E14
143 D3 Walmer Street W1
148 C2 Walnut Tree Walk SE11
147 D2 Walpole Street SW3
151 E4 Walter Terrace E1
147 D3 Walton Place SW3
147 D3 Walton Street SW3
143 D2 Walton's Mews W1
149 E1 Walworth Place SE17
149 E2 Walworth Road SE1 & SE17
149 E2 Wansey Street SE17
150 C2 Wapping Dock Street E1
150 B2 Wapping High Street E1
150 C2 Wapping Lane E1
150 C2 Wapping Walk E1
151 D2 Wapping Wall E1
144 A2 Wardour Street W1
144 C3 Warner Street EC1
143 F3 Warren Street W1
142 B3 Warrington Crescent W9
142 B3 Warrington Gardens W9
142 A3 Warwick Avenue W9
144 C2 Warwick Court WC1
142 B3 Warwick Crescent W2
148 B4 Warwick House Street SW1
145 E2 Warwick Lane EC4
145 D2 Warwick Passage EC4
　Warwick Square
142 B3 Warwick Place W9
147 F3 Warwick Row SW1
147 F2 Warwick Square SW1
145 D2 Warwick Square EC4
144 A1 Warwick Street W1
147 F2 Warwick Way SW1
150 A3 Water Lane EC3
145 E1 Watergate EC4
　New Bridge Street
144 B1 Watergate Walk WC2
　Villiers Street
144 C1 Waterloo Bridge WC2 & SE1
148 A4 Waterloo Place SW1
148 C4 Waterloo Road SE1
150 C4 Waterman Way E1
145 F1 Waterman's Walk EC4
150 C4 Waterside Close SE16
145 E2 Watling Street EC4
150 C4 Watney Market E1
150 C3 Watney Street E1
150 C2 Watson's Street SE8
146 C3 Watts Way SW7
150 B2 Waveney Close E1
147 E4 Waverton Street W1
150 A2 Weavers Lane SE1
149 F3 Webb Street SE1
149 D3 Webber Row SE1
149 D3 Webber Street SE1
150 C1 Webster Road SE16
143 E1 Weighouse Street W1
143 E2 Welbeck Street W1
143 E2 Welbeck Way W1
145 E1 Well Court EC4
　Queen Street
150 C1 Welland Mews E1
150 B3 Wellclose Square E1
150 C3 Wellclose Street E1
　The Highway
149 E3 Weller Street SE1
151 D4 Wellesley Street E1
145 E4 Wellesley Terrace N1
142 B2 Wellington Place NW8
142 C4 Wellington Road NW8
147 D1 Wellington Square SW3
147 C2 Wellington Street WC2
144 A2 Wells Mews W1
144 A2 Wells Square WC1
143 F2 Wells Street W1
145 E4 Wendover N1
145 E4 Wenlock Road N1
145 E4 Wenlock Street N1
150 B4 Wentworth Market E1
　Wentworth Street
150 B4 Wentworth Street E1
144 A4 Werrington Street NW1
149 D2 Wesley Close SE17
143 E2 Wesley Street W1
　Weymouth Street
151 D4 West Arbour Street E1
144 B1 West Central Street WC1
147 E2 West Eaton Place SW1
150 C3 West Gardens E1

147 E3 West Halkin Street SW1
151 F3 West India Dock Road E14
150 C1 West Lane SE16
147 F2 West Mews SW1
　Warwick Way
145 D2 West Poultry Avenue EC1
　West Smithfield
147 D1 West Road SW4
145 D2 West Smithfield EC1
149 D2 West Square SE11
144 B1 West Street WC2
150 B1 West Tenter Street E1
142 B1 Westbourne Crescent W2
142 A2 Westbourne Gardens W2
142 A2 Westbourne Grove W2 & W11
142 A2 Westbourne Grove Terrace W2
142 A1 Westbourne Park Road W2 & W11
142 A1 Westbourne Park Villas W2
142 C1 Westbourne Street W2
142 B2 Westbourne Terrace W2
142 B2 Westbourne Terrace Mews W2
142 B2 Westbourne Terrace Road W2
149 D1 Westcott Road SE17
151 D2 Western Place SE16
146 A1 Westgate Terrace SW10
145 F4 Westland Place N1
145 B3 Westminster Bridge SW1 & SE1
148 F3 Westminster Bridge Road SE1
147 F1 Westmoreland Place SW1
149 E1 Westmoreland Road SE17
143 E1 Westmoreland Street W1
147 F1 Westmoreland Terrace SW1
144 C4 Weston Rise WC1
149 F3 Weston Street SE1
151 E4 Westport Street E1
142 B2 Westway W12
145 B2 Wetherby Gardens SW5
146 A2 Wetherby Mews SW5
　Earls Court Road
146 B2 Wetherby Place SW7
143 F2 Weymouth Mews W1
143 E2 Weymouth Street W1
145 E4 Wharf Road N1
146 A1 Wharfedale Street SW10
144 C4 Wharton Street WC1
143 E2 Wheatley Street W1
　Marylebone Street
144 C2 Whetstone Park WC2
144 B4 Whidborne Street WC1
145 D4 Whiskin Street EC1
144 A1 Whitcomb Street WC2
150 B4 White Church Lane E1
145 E1 White Hart Street SE11
151 E4 White Horse Lane E1
149 D3 White Horse Mews SE1
151 E3 White Horse Road E1
147 F4 White Horse Street W1
150 A4 White Kennet Street E1
145 E1 White Lion Hill EC4
150 A1 White's Grounds SE1
150 A4 White's Row E1
150 B4 Whitechapel High Street E1
150 B4 Whitechapel Road E1
145 F3 Whitecross Place EC2
145 E3 Whitecross Street EC1
145 D2 Whitefriars Street EC4
148 B4 Whitehall SW1
148 B4 Whitehall Court SW1
148 B4 Whitehall Place SW1
142 C3 Whitehaven Street NW8
147 D2 Whitehead's Grove SW3
144 A3 Whitfield Place W1
　Whitfield Street
144 A3 Whitfield Street W1
148 C2 Whitgift Street SE11
147 E2 Whittaker Street SW1
147 F2 Whittington Avenue EC3
　Leadenhall Street
149 E1 Whittlesey Street SE1
149 F3 Whity Close SE1
148 C1 Wickham Street SE11
144 C1 Wicklow Street WC1
150 A4 Widegate Street E1
　Middlesex Street
142 A4 Widley Road W9
143 E2 Wigmore Place W1
143 E2 Wigmore Street W1
148 A3 Wilbraham Place SW1
148 A3 Wilcox Place SW1
144 C1 Wild Court WC2
144 B2 Wild Street WC2
149 F3 Wild's Rents SE1
147 F3 Wilfred Street SW1
150 B4 Wilkes Street E1
144 B1 William IV Street WC2
147 E3 William Mews SW1
143 E4 William Road NW1
151 E3 William Square SE16
147 D3 William Street SW1
144 B2 Willoughby Street WC1
　Streatham Street
148 A3 Willow Place SW1
145 F3 Willow Street EC2
145 D4 Wilmington Square WC1
145 D4 Wilmington Street WC1
150 C1 Wilson Grove SE16
145 F2 Wilson Street EC2
151 F3 Wilson's Place E14
147 E3 Wilton Crescent SW1
147 E3 Wilton Mews SW1
147 E3 Wilton Place SW1
147 F2 Wilton Road SW1
147 E3 Wilton Row SW1
147 E3 Wilton Street SW1
147 E3 Wilton Terrace SW1
143 E2 Wimpole Mews W1
143 E2 Wimpole Street W1
149 E2 Winchester Close SE17
149 F4 Winchester Square SE1
　Winchester Walk
147 F2 Winchester Street SW1
149 F4 Winchester Walk SE1
149 D2 Wincott Street SE11
149 D1 Windmill Row SE11
148 A2 Windmill Street W1
149 D4 Windmill Walk SE1
151 D2 Windrose Close SE16
145 E4 Windsor Terrace N1
150 C2 Wine Close E1
145 E1 Wine Office Court EC4
144 A1 Winnett Street W1
　Rupert Street
142 C2 Winsland Mews W2
142 C2 Winsland Street W2

144 A2 Winsley Street W1
146 B1 Winterton Place SW10
144 B3 Woburn Place WC1
144 B3 Woburn Square WC1
144 B3 Woburn Walk WC1
　Upper Woburn Place
151 D1 Wolfe Crescent SE16
150 D1 Wolseley Street SE1
145 E2 Wood Street EC2
143 E1 Wood's Mews W1
150 A1 Wood's Place SE1
145 D3 Woodbridge Street EC1
142 A3 Woodchester Square W2
147 D1 Woodfall Street SW3
151 D1 Woodland Crescent SE16
143 E2 Woodstock Mews W1
　Westmoreland Street
143 F2 Woodstock Street W1
149 E1 Woolaston Close SE17
149 F1 Wooler Street SE17
149 D2 Wooster Place SE1
149 D4 Wootton Street SE1
148 C2 Worgan Street SE11
145 F2 Wormwood Street EC2
145 F3 Worship Street EC2
144 C3 Wren Street WC1
146 A3 Wright's Lane W8
151 E1 Wyatt Close SE16
143 E2 Wybert Street NW1
　Laxton Place
145 D4 Wyclif Street EC1
142 A4 Wymering Road W9
143 D2 Wyndham Mews W1
143 D2 Wyndham Place W1
143 D2 Wyndham Street W1
143 D2 Wyndham Yard W1
146 A3 Wynnstay Gardens W8
148 C1 Wynyard Terrace SE11
143 D2 Wynyatt Street EC1
143 D2 Wythburn Place W1

Y

144 C4 Yardley Street WC1
147 E4 Yarmouth Place W1
145 B3 Yeoman's Row SW3
144 B1 York Buildings WC2
146 A4 York Gate NW1
146 A4 York House Place W8
148 C3 York Road SE1
151 E4 York Square E14
145 D3 York Street W1
143 E3 York Terrace East NW1
143 E3 York Terrace West NW1
151 E3 Yorkshire Road E14
146 A3 Young Street W8

Z

149 E4 Zoar Street SE1

Index to place names

Place names are listed alphabetically. Each entry is followed by its county or administrative area. Each place name is preceded by the page number and the grid reference to the square in which the name is found. A map of counties, unitary authorities and administrative areas is given below, together with the abbreviated forms used in the index.

100 places of interest are indexed in red. Airports are indexed in blue.

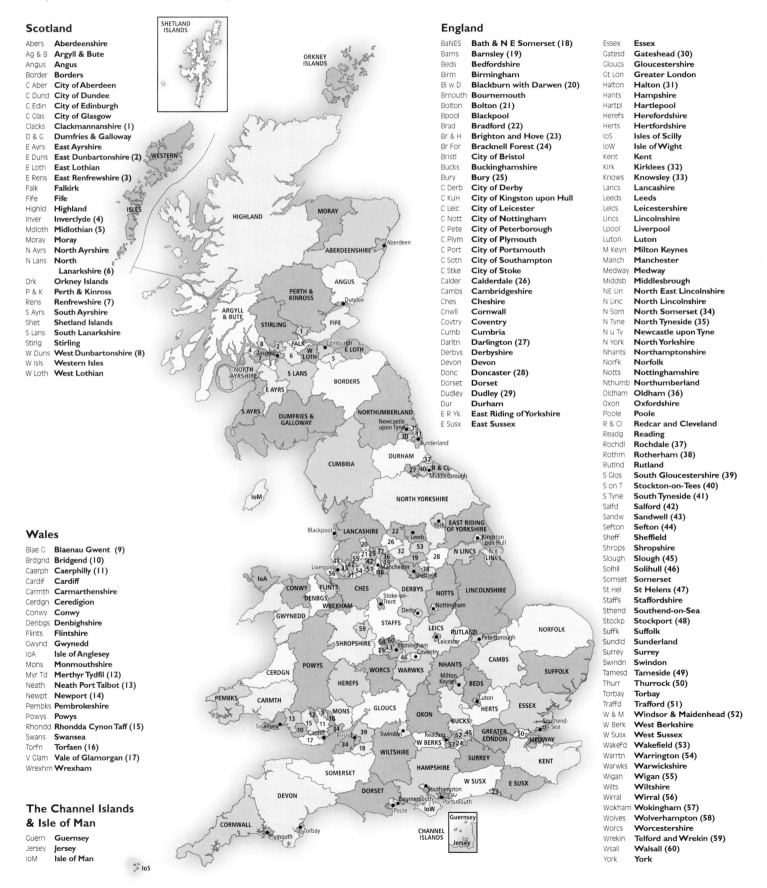

Scotland

Abers	**Aberdeenshire**
Ag & B	**Argyll & Bute**
Angus	**Angus**
Border	**Borders**
C Aber	**City of Aberdeen**
C Dund	**City of Dundee**
C Edin	**City of Edinburgh**
C Glas	**City of Glasgow**
Clacks	**Clackmannanshire (1)**
D & G	**Dumfries & Galloway**
E Ayrs	**East Ayrshire**
E Duns	**East Dunbartonshire (2)**
E Loth	**East Lothian**
E Rens	**East Renfrewshire (3)**
Falk	**Falkirk**
Fife	**Fife**
Highld	**Highland**
Inver	**Inverclyde (4)**
Mdloth	**Midlothian (5)**
Moray	**Moray**
N Ayrs	**North Ayrshire**
N Lans	**North Lanarkshire (6)**
Ork	**Orkney Islands**
P & K	**Perth & Kinross**
Rens	**Renfrewshire (7)**
S Ayrs	**South Ayrshire**
Shet	**Shetland Islands**
S Lans	**South Lanarkshire**
Stirlg	**Stirling**
W Duns	**West Dunbartonshire (8)**
W Isls	**Western Isles**
W Loth	**West Lothian**

Wales

Blae G	**Blaenau Gwent (9)**
Brdgnd	**Bridgend (10)**
Caerph	**Caerphilly (11)**
Cardif	**Cardiff**
Carmth	**Carmarthenshire**
Cerdgn	**Ceredigion**
Conwy	**Conwy**
Denbgs	**Denbighshire**
Flints	**Flintshire**
Gwynd	**Gwynedd**
IoA	**Isle of Anglesey**
Mons	**Monmouthshire**
Myr Td	**Merthyr Tydfil (12)**
Neath	**Neath Port Talbot (13)**
Newpt	**Newport (14)**
Pembks	**Pembrokeshire**
Powys	**Powys**
Rhondd	**Rhondda Cynon Taff (15)**
Swans	**Swansea**
Torfn	**Torfaen (16)**
V Glam	**Vale of Glamorgan (17)**
Wrexhm	**Wrexham**

The Channel Islands & Isle of Man

Guern	**Guernsey**
Jersey	**Jersey**
IoM	**Isle of Man**

England

BaNES	**Bath & N E Somerset (18)**
Barns	**Barnsley (19)**
Beds	**Bedfordshire**
Birm	**Birmingham**
Bl w D	**Blackburn with Darwen (20)**
Bmouth	**Bournemouth**
Bolton	**Bolton (21)**
Bpool	**Blackpool**
Brad	**Bradford (22)**
Br & H	**Brighton and Hove (23)**
Br For	**Bracknell Forest (24)**
Bristl	**City of Bristol**
Bucks	**Buckinghamshire**
Bury	**Bury (25)**
C Derb	**City of Derby**
C KuH	**City of Kingston upon Hull**
C Leic	**City of Leicester**
C Nott	**City of Nottingham**
C Pete	**City of Peterborough**
C Plym	**City of Plymouth**
C Port	**City of Portsmouth**
C Sotn	**City of Southampton**
C Stke	**City of Stoke**
Calder	**Calderdale (26)**
Cambs	**Cambridgeshire**
Ches	**Cheshire**
Cnwll	**Cornwall**
Covtry	**Coventry**
Cumb	**Cumbria**
Darltn	**Darlington (27)**
Derbys	**Derbyshire**
Devon	**Devon**
Donc	**Doncaster (28)**
Dorset	**Dorset**
Dudley	**Dudley (29)**
Dur	**Durham**
E R Yk	**East Riding of Yorkshire**
E Susx	**East Sussex**

Essex	**Essex**
Gatesd	**Gateshead (30)**
Gloucs	**Gloucestershire**
Halton	**Halton (31)**
Hants	**Hampshire**
Hartpl	**Hartlepool**
Herefs	**Herefordshire**
Herts	**Hertfordshire**
IoS	**Isles of Scilly**
IoW	**Isle of Wight**
Kent	**Kent**
Kirk	**Kirklees (32)**
Knows	**Knowsley (33)**
Lancs	**Lancashire**
Leeds	**Leeds**
Leics	**Leicestershire**
Lincs	**Lincolnshire**
Lpool	**Liverpool**
Luton	**Luton**
M Keyn	**Milton Keynes**
Manch	**Manchester**
Medway	**Medway**
Middsb	**Middlesbrough**
NE Lin	**North East Lincolnshire**
N Linc	**North Lincolnshire**
N Som	**North Somerset (34)**
N Tyne	**North Tyneside (35)**
N u Ty	**Newcastle upon Tyne**
N York	**North Yorkshire**
Nhants	**Northamptonshire**
Norfk	**Norfolk**
Notts	**Nottinghamshire**
Nthumb	**Northumberland**
Oldham	**Oldham (36)**
Oxon	**Oxfordshire**
Poole	**Poole**
R & Cl	**Redcar and Cleveland**
Readg	**Reading**
Rochdl	**Rochdale (37)**
Rothm	**Rotherham (38)**
Rutlnd	**Rutland**
S Glos	**South Gloucestershire (39)**
S on T	**Stockton-on-Tees (40)**
S Tyne	**South Tyneside (41)**
Salfd	**Salford (42)**
Sandw	**Sandwell (43)**
Sefton	**Sefton (44)**
Sheff	**Sheffield**
Shrops	**Shropshire**
Slough	**Slough (45)**
Solhll	**Solihull (46)**
Somset	**Somerset**
St Hel	**St Helens (47)**
Staffs	**Staffordshire**
Sthend	**Southend-on-Sea**
Stockp	**Stockport (48)**
Suffk	**Suffolk**
Sundld	**Sunderland**
Surrey	**Surrey**
Swindn	**Swindon**
Tamesd	**Tameside (49)**
Thurr	**Thurrock (50)**
Torbay	**Torbay**
Traffd	**Trafford (51)**
W & M	**Windsor & Maidenhead (52)**
W Berk	**West Berkshire**
W Susx	**West Sussex**
Wakefd	**Wakefield (53)**
Warrtn	**Warrington (54)**
Warwks	**Warwickshire**
Wigan	**Wigan (55)**
Wilts	**Wiltshire**
Wirral	**Wirral (56)**
Wokham	**Wokingham (57)**
Wolves	**Wolverhampton (58)**
Worcs	**Worcestershire**
Wrekin	**Telford and Wrekin (59)**
Wsall	**Walsall (60)**
York	**York**

160 A'Chill - Arkendale

A

96 B3 **A'Chill** Highld
41 H5 **Ab Kettleby** Leics
17 H2 **Abbas Combe** Somset
39 G3 **Abberley** Worcs
39 G3 **Abberley Common** Worcs
34 D1 **Abberton** Essex
30 B5 **Abberton** Worcs
22 B6 **Abbess Roding** Essex
28 B5 **Abbey Dore** Herefs
50 B3 **Abbey Green** Staffs
87 G2 **Abbey St Bathans** Border
71 E4 **Abbey Town** Cumb
57 F5 **Abbey Village** Lancs
21 G3 **Abbey Wood** Gt Lon
50 D5 **Abbeydale** Sheff
63 E2 **Abbeystead** Lancs
30 C5 **Abbot's Salford** Warwks
80 C2 **Abbotrule** Border
14 D2 **Abbots Bickington** Devon
40 C5 **Abbots Bromley** Staffs
92 D1 **Abbots Deuglie** P & K
20 D5 **Abbots Langley** Herts
17 F6 **Abbots Leigh** N Som
30 B5 **Abbots Morton** Worcs
32 D6 **Abbots Ripton** Cambs
9 G6 **Abbots Worthy** Hants
7 G4 **Abbotsbury** Dorset
14 D4 **Abbotsham** Devon
6 A3 **Abbotskerswell** Devon
32 D4 **Abbotsley** Cambs
8 C3 **Abbott Street** Dorset
19 E1 **Abbotts Ann** Hants
39 F4 **Abdon** Shrops
27 F3 **Aber-nant** Rhondd
36 D3 **Aberaeron** Cerdgn
27 F5 **Aberaman** Rhondd
47 G3 **Aberangell** Gwynd
99 E5 **Aberarder** Highld
92 D1 **Aberargie** P & K
36 D3 **Aberarth** Cerdgn
26 D2 **Aberavon** Neath
92 B2 **Abercairny** P & K
27 F3 **Abercanaid** Myr Td
27 G2 **Abercarn** Caerph
24 C5 **Abercastle** Pembks
47 G2 **Abercegir** Powys
98 B3 **Aberchalder Lodge** Highld
102 C4 **Aberchirder** Abers
26 D4 **Abercraf** Powys
26 D2 **Abercregan** Neath
27 F3 **Abercwmboi** Rhondd
36 B1 **Abercych** Pembks
27 F2 **Abercynon** Rhondd
92 D2 **Aberdalgie** P & K
27 F3 **Aberdare** Rhondd
46 B4 **Aberdaron** Gwynd
95 H6 **Aberdeen** C Aber
103 E1 **Aberdeen Airport** C Aber
86 C4 **Aberdour** Fife
26 D3 **Aberdulais** Neath
47 E1 **Aberdyfi** Gwynd
38 B1 **Aberedw** Powys
24 C5 **Abereiddy** Pembks
46 D5 **Abererch** Gwynd
27 F3 **Aberfan** Myr Td
92 B4 **Aberfeldy** P & K
54 C3 **Aberffraw** IOA
53 E4 **Aberford** Leeds
85 E5 **Aberfoyle** Stirlg
28 B6 **Abergavenny** Mons
55 G4 **Abergele** Conwy
26 B5 **Abergorlech** Carmth
37 G2 **Abergwesyn** Powys
25 H4 **Abergwili** Carmth
27 E2 **Abergwynfi** Neath
55 E3 **Abergwyngregyn** Gwynd
47 F2 **Abergynolwyn** Gwynd
27 E1 **Aberkenfig** Brdgnd
87 E4 **Aberlady** E Loth
93 G4 **Aberlemno** Angus
47 F3 **Aberllefenni** Powys
27 G6 **Aberllynfi** Powys
101 E4 **Aberlour** Moray
38 B5 **Abermule** Powys
25 G5 **Abernant** Carmth
92 D1 **Abernethy** P & K
93 E3 **Abernyte** P & K
36 B2 **Aberporth** Cerdgn
46 C4 **Abersoch** Gwynd
28 A3 **Abersychan** Torfn
16 B6 **Aberthin** V Glam
27 G3 **Abertillery** Blae G
27 G2 **Abertridwr** Caerph
48 A2 **Abertridwr** Powys
92 C1 **Aberuthven** P & K
37 E5 **Aberystwyth** Cerdgn
19 G6 **Abingdon** Oxon
10 D6 **Abinger** Surrey
10 D6 **Abinger Hammer** Surrey
32 A4 **Abington** Nhants
78 C5 **Abington** S Lans
33 E3 **Abington Pigotts** Cambs
30 C1 **Ablington** Gloucs
50 D4 **Abney** Derbys
95 E5 **Aboyne** Abers
57 F3 **Abram** Wigan
98 D6 **Abriachan** Highld
21 G5 **Abridge** Essex
17 H6 **Abson** S Glos
31 G4 **Abthorpe** Nhants
53 F3 **Aby** Lincs
59 G4 **Acaster Malbis** York
59 F4 **Acaster Selby** N York
57 G5 **Accrington** Lancs
82 C4 **Acha** Ag & B
111 d6 **Acha Mor** W Isls
83 F3 **Achahoish** Ag & B
92 D4 **Achalader** P & K
90 B2 **Achaleven** Ag & B
106 B2 **Achanalt** Highld
107 E3 **Achandunie** Highld
107 E5 **Achany** Highld
89 G5 **Acharacle** Highld
89 G4 **Acharn** Highld
92 A4 **Acharn** P & K
110 C3 **Achavanich** Highld
105 H6 **Achduart** Highld
108 C3 **Achfary** Highld
105 H6 **Achiltibuie** Highld
75 F3 **Achinhoan** Ag & B
97 G6 **Achintee** Highld
97 F6 **Achintraid** Highld
108 A2 **Achmelvich** Highld
97 F5 **Achmore** Highld
111 d6 **Achmore** W Isls
108 A3 **Achnacarnin** Highld
98 A2 **Achnacarry** Highld
96 D3 **Achnacloich** Highld
98 C4 **Achnaconeran** Highld
90 A3 **Achnacroish** Ag & B
89 E4 **Achnadrish Lodge** Ag & B
92 B3 **Achnafauld** P & K
107 F3 **Achnagarron** Highld
89 E5 **Achnaha** Highld
108 A1 **Achnahaird** Highld
109 E1 **Achnairn** Highld
90 A5 **Achnalea** Highld
83 F4 **Achnamara** Ag & B
106 B2 **Achnasheen** Highld
105 H1 **Achnashellach Station** Highld
101 E3 **Achnastank** Moray
89 E5 **Achosnich** Highld
89 G4 **Achranich** Highld
110 A5 **Achreamie** Highld
90 C5 **Achriabhach** Highld
108 C4 **Achriesgill** Highld
109 F5 **Achtoty** Highld
42 C1 **Achurch** Nhants
107 F5 **Achvaich** Highld
110 D4 **Ackergill** Highld
66 B5 **Acklam** Middsb
60 B6 **Acklam** N York
39 G5 **Ackleton** Shrops
73 F6 **Acklington** Nthumb
59 E2 **Ackton** Wakefd
59 E2 **Ackworth Moor Top** Wakefd
45 G3 **Acle** Norfk
40 C2 **Acock's Green** Birm
23 G2 **Acol** Kent
72 D3 **Acomb** Nthumb
59 F5 **Acomb** York
28 C5 **Aconbury** Herefs
49 F4 **Acton** Ches
21 E3 **Acton** Gt Lon
49 G3 **Acton** Staffs
34 C3 **Acton** Suffk
39 H3 **Acton** Worcs
39 F1 **Acton Beauchamp** Herefs
49 F6 **Acton Bridge** Ches
39 E6 **Acton Burnell** Shrops
39 F1 **Acton Green** Herefs
48 D4 **Acton Park** Wrexhm
39 F5 **Acton Round** Shrops
39 E5 **Acton Scott** Shrops
40 B5 **Acton Trussell** Staffs
18 A4 **Acton Turville** S Glos
49 G2 **Adbaston** Staffs
17 G1 **Adber** Dorset
51 G1 **Adbolton** Notts
31 F3 **Adderbury** Oxon
49 F3 **Adderley** Shrops
86 A2 **Addiewell** W Loth
58 C5 **Addingham** Brad
31 H3 **Addington** Bucks
22 B2 **Addington** Kent
21 F2 **Addiscombe** Gt Lon
20 D2 **Addlestone** Surrey
53 G2 **Addlethorpe** Lincs
20 D6 **Adeyfield** Herts
38 B6 **Adfa** Powys
38 D3 **Adforton** Herefs
23 G1 **Adisham** Kent
30 D3 **Adlestrop** Gloucs
60 C2 **Adlingfleet** E R Yk
57 F4 **Adlington** Lancs
40 B5 **Admaston** Staffs
49 F1 **Admaston** Wrekin
30 D4 **Admington** Warwks
16 D2 **Adsborough** Somset
16 D3 **Adscombe** Somset
31 H3 **Adstock** Bucks
10 D4 **Adversane** W Susx
100 D3 **Advie** Highld
59 F1 **Adwick Le Street** Donc
51 F6 **Adwick upon Dearne** Donc
78 D2 **Ae** D & G
78 D2 **Ae Bridgend** D & G
26 D3 **Afan Forest Park** Neath
102 B3 **Affleck** Abers
8 A3 **Affpuddle** Dorset
98 A4 **Affric Lodge** Highld
48 B6 **Afon-wen** Flints
65 E2 **Agglethorpe** N York
56 D2 **Aigburth** Lpool
60 D4 **Aike** E R Yk
71 G4 **Aiketgate** Cumb
71 F4 **Aikton** Cumb
42 D2 **Ailsworth** C Pete
65 G2 **Ainderby Quernhow** N York
65 G3 **Ainderby Steeple** N York
35 E1 **Aingers Green** Essex
56 C4 **Ainsdale** Sefton
71 H4 **Ainstable** Cumb
66 D4 **Ainthorpe** N York
86 B2 **Ainville** W Loth
83 F5 **Aird** Ag & B
68 C3 **Aird** D & G
111 e6 **Aird** W Isls
111 c5 **Aird a Mhulaidh** W Isls
111 c5 **Aird Asaig** W Isls
97 E6 **Aird Dhubh** Highld
89 F2 **Aird of Kinloch** Ag & B
96 D2 **Aird of Sleat** Highld
111 c6 **Aird Uig** W Isls
90 B2 **Airdeny** Ag & B
85 F2 **Airdrie** N Lans
85 G2 **Airdriehill** N Lans
90 B2 **Airds Bay** Ag & B
69 G4 **Airds of Kells** D & G
111 c5 **Airidh a bhruaich** W Isls
70 B5 **Airieland** D & G
93 E4 **Airlie** Angus
60 B3 **Airmyn** E R Yk
92 D3 **Airntully** P & K
97 E3 **Airor** Highld
85 H4 **Airth** Falk
58 A5 **Airton** N York
52 B4 **Aisby** Lincs
42 C5 **Aisby** Lincs
5 G3 **Aish** Devon
6 A2 **Aish** Devon
16 D3 **Aisholt** Somset
65 F2 **Aiskew** N York
67 E4 **Aislaby** N York
66 D2 **Aislaby** N York
65 G4 **Aislaby** S on T
52 B3 **Aisthorpe** Lincs
111 I2 **Aith** Shet
81 E3 **Akeld** Nthumb
31 G4 **Akeley** Bucks
35 E3 **Akenham** Suffk
5 E4 **Albaston** Devon
48 D1 **Alberbury** Shrops
11 E4 **Albourne** W Susx
49 E2 **Albrighton** Shrops
39 G6 **Albrighton** Shrops
45 F1 **Alburgh** Norfk
33 F2 **Albury** Herts
10 D6 **Albury** Surrey
10 D6 **Albury Heath** Surrey
107 E2 **Alcaig** Highld
39 E4 **Alcaston** Shrops
30 C5 **Alcester** Warwks
11 G3 **Alciston** E Susx
32 D6 **Alconbury** Cambs
32 D6 **Alconbury Weston** Cambs
59 E6 **Aldborough** N York
45 E5 **Aldborough** Norfk
19 E4 **Aldbourne** Wilts
61 F4 **Aldbrough** E R Yk
65 F4 **Aldbrough St John** N York
20 C6 **Aldbury** Herts
63 E2 **Aldcliffe** Lancs
92 B5 **Aldclune** P & K
35 G4 **Aldeburgh** Suffk
45 G2 **Aldeby** Norfk
21 E5 **Aldenham** Herts
8 D6 **Alderbury** Wilts
45 E4 **Alderford** Norfk
8 D4 **Alderholt** Dorset
29 E2 **Alderley** Gloucs
57 H1 **Alderley Edge** Ches
19 G3 **Aldermaston** W Berk
30 D5 **Alderminster** Warwks
20 B1 **Aldershot** Hants
30 B3 **Alderton** Gloucs
31 H4 **Alderton** Nhants
35 F3 **Alderton** Suffk
18 B5 **Alderton** Wilts
50 D2 **Alderwasley** Derbys
58 D6 **Aldfield** N York
48 D5 **Aldford** Ches
42 C3 **Aldgate** Rutlnd
34 C2 **Aldham** Essex
34 D3 **Aldham** Suffk
10 C3 **Aldingbourne** W Susx
62 C3 **Aldingham** Cumb
13 E5 **Aldington** Kent
30 C4 **Aldington** Worcs
13 E5 **Aldington Corner** Kent
101 F2 **Aldivalloch** Moray
84 C4 **Aldochlay** Ag & B
33 F5 **Aldreth** Cambs
40 B3 **Aldridge** Wsall
35 G4 **Aldringham** Suffk
30 C1 **Aldsworth** Gloucs
101 F2 **Aldunie** Moray
50 D3 **Aldwark** Derbys
59 F6 **Aldwark** N York
10 C2 **Aldwick** W Susx
32 C6 **Aldwincle** Nhants
19 G4 **Aldworth** W Berk
84 D3 **Alexandria** W Duns
16 D3 **Aley** Somset
6 C5 **Alfington** Devon
10 D5 **Alfold** Surrey
10 D5 **Alfold Crossways** Surrey
102 B1 **Alford** Abers
53 F3 **Alford** Lincs
17 G2 **Alford** Somset
51 E2 **Alfreton** Derbys
39 G2 **Alfrick** Worcs
39 G2 **Alfrick Pound** Worcs
11 G2 **Alfriston** E Susx
43 E5 **Algarkirk** Lincs
17 G3 **Alhampton** Somset
60 C2 **Alkborough** N Linc
13 G6 **Alkham** Kent
50 C1 **Alkmonton** Derbys
18 C3 **All Cannings** Wilts
35 F6 **All Saints South Elmham** Suffk
39 E5 **All Stretton** Shrops
5 H2 **Allaleigh** Devon
94 A5 **Allanaquoich** Abers
85 G2 **Allanbank** N Lans
81 E5 **Allanton** Border
85 G2 **Allanton** N Lans
85 F1 **Allanton** S Lans
28 D3 **Allaston** Gloucs
9 F5 **Allbrook** Hants
40 C3 **Allen End** Warwks
33 F1 **Allen's Green** Herts
72 C2 **Allendale** Nthumb
72 C2 **Allenheads** Nthumb
28 C6 **Allensmore** Herefs
41 E6 **Allenton** C Derb
15 G3 **Aller** Devon
17 E2 **Aller** Somset
70 D3 **Allerby** Cumb
6 C5 **Allercombe** Devon
16 A4 **Allerford** Somset
67 E2 **Allerston** N York
60 B4 **Allerthorpe** E R Yk
58 C3 **Allerton** Brad
107 F3 **Allerton** Highld
56 D2 **Allerton** Lpool
59 E3 **Allerton Bywater** Leeds
59 E5 **Allerton Mauleverer** N York
40 D2 **Allesley** Covtry
51 E1 **Allestree** C Derb
42 A2 **Allexton** Leics
50 B3 **Allgreave** Ches
22 D3 **Allhallows** Medway
105 F2 **Alligin Shuas** Highld
7 F5 **Allington** Dorset
42 B5 **Allington** Lincs
18 B4 **Allington** Wilts
18 C3 **Allington** Wilts
18 D1 **Allington** Wilts
62 D4 **Allithwaite** Cumb
85 G5 **Alloa** Clacks
70 D3 **Allonby** Cumb
76 C3 **Alloway** S Ayrs
17 E1 **Allowenshay** Somset
90 D4 **Alltchaorunn** Highld
25 H5 **Alltwalis** Carmth
26 D3 **Alltwen** Neath
36 D2 **Alltyblaca** Cerdgn
17 G1 **Allweston** Dorset
38 D1 **Almeley** Herefs
59 G1 **Almholme** Donc
49 G3 **Almington** Staffs
92 C2 **Almondbank** P & K
58 C2 **Almondbury** Kirk
28 D1 **Almondsbury** S Glos
59 F6 **Alne** N York
107 F3 **Alness** Highld
81 F1 **Alnham** Nthumb
81 G1 **Alnmouth** Nthumb
81 G2 **Alnwick** Nthumb
21 E4 **Alperton** Gt Lon
34 C2 **Alphamstone** Essex
34 C4 **Alpheton** Suffk
6 B4 **Alphington** Devon
50 D3 **Alport** Derbys
49 F5 **Alpraham** Ches
34 D1 **Alresford** Essex
40 C4 **Alrewas** Staffs
49 G5 **Alsager** Ches
50 C2 **Alsop en le Dale** Derbys
72 B2 **Alston** Cumb
7 E5 **Alston** Devon
17 E4 **Alston Sutton** Somset
29 G5 **Alstone** Gloucs
50 C2 **Alstonefield** Staffs
15 F3 **Alswear** Devon
108 A1 **Altandhu** Highld
4 C5 **Altarnun** Cnwll
106 D5 **Altass** Highld
89 G3 **Altcreich** Ag & B
83 H3 **Altgaltraig** Ag & B
22 D5 **Althorne** Essex
60 C1 **Althorpe** N Linc
110 A4 **Altnabreac Station** Highld
90 A2 **Altnacraig** Ag & B
109 E3 **Altnaharra** Highld
51 E3 **Alton** Derbys
10 A5 **Alton** Hants
50 C1 **Alton** Staffs
18 D3 **Alton Barnes** Wilts
7 H5 **Alton Pancras** Dorset
18 D3 **Alton Priors** Wilts
50 C1 **Alton Towers** Staffs
57 G2 **Altrincham** Traffd
84 D5 **Altskeith Hotel** Stirlg
85 G5 **Alva** Clacks
102 C5 **Alvah** Abers
49 E6 **Alvanley** Ches
41 E5 **Alvaston** C Derb
40 B1 **Alvechurch** Worcs
40 D4 **Alvecote** Warwks
8 C5 **Alvediston** Wilts
39 G4 **Alveley** Shrops
15 E3 **Alverdiscott** Devon
9 G3 **Alverstoke** Hants
9 G2 **Alverstone** IOW
58 D2 **Alverthorpe** Wakefd
42 A6 **Alverton** Notts
100 D5 **Alves** Moray
30 D1 **Alvescot** Oxon
28 D2 **Alveston** Gloucs
30 D5 **Alveston** Warwks
53 E4 **Alvingham** Lincs
28 D3 **Alvington** Gloucs
42 D2 **Alwalton** Cambs
81 E1 **Alwinton** Nthumb
58 D4 **Alwoodley** Leeds
93 E4 **Alyth** P & K
51 E2 **Ambergate** Derbys
29 F3 **Amberley** Gloucs
10 D3 **Amberley** W Susx
81 H1 **Amble** Nthumb
40 A2 **Amblecote** Dudley
58 C3 **Ambler Thorn** Brad
62 D6 **Ambleside** Cumb
24 D5 **Ambleston** Pembks
31 G2 **Ambrosden** Oxon
60 C2 **Amcotts** N Linc
20 C5 **Amersham** Bucks
18 D1 **Amesbury** Wilts
111 c5 **Amhuinnsuidhe** W Isls
78 D1 **Amisfield Town** D & G
54 C5 **Amlwch** IOA
26 C4 **Ammanford** Carmth
66 D1 **Amotherby** N York
9 F5 **Ampfield** Hants
66 C2 **Ampleforth** N York
18 C6 **Ampney Crucis** Gloucs
18 D6 **Ampney St Mary** Gloucs
18 C6 **Ampney St Peter** Gloucs
19 E1 **Amport** Hants
32 C3 **Ampthill** Beds
34 C5 **Ampton** Suffk
25 E3 **Amroth** Pembks
92 B3 **Amulree** P & K
21 E6 **Amwell** Herts
111 c4 **An T-ob** W Isls
89 H5 **Anaheilt** Highld
42 C6 **Ancaster** Lincs
81 F4 **Ancroft** Nthumb
80 C3 **Ancrum** Border
53 G3 **Anderby** Lincs
19 F2 **Andover** Hants
30 B2 **Andoversford** Gloucs
116 c5 **Andreas** IOM
21 F2 **Anerley** Gt Lon
56 D2 **Anfield** Lpool
2 C3 **Angarrack** Cnwll
39 F3 **Angelbank** Shrops
16 D1 **Angersleigh** Somset
24 C3 **Angle** Pembks
54 C4 **Anglesey** IOA
10 D3 **Angmering** W Susx
59 F4 **Angram** N York
107 G3 **Ankerville** Highld
60 D3 **Anlaby** E R Yk
44 B5 **Anmer** Norfk
9 H4 **Anmore** Hants
19 F1 **Anna Valley** Hants
71 E5 **Annan** D & G
105 G2 **Annat** Highld
85 F3 **Annathill** N Lans
76 D4 **Annbank** S Ayrs
30 C5 **Anne Hathaway's Cottage** Warwks
51 F2 **Annesley** Notts
51 F2 **Annesley Woodhouse** Notts
73 F2 **Annfield Plain** Dur
85 E3 **Anniesland** C Glas
56 D5 **Ansdell** Lancs
17 G2 **Ansford** Somset
40 D3 **Ansley** Warwks
40 D5 **Anslow** Staffs
40 D5 **Anslow Gate** Staffs
33 F2 **Anstey** Herts
41 F4 **Anstey** Leics
87 F6 **Anstruther** Fife
11 F4 **Ansty** W Susx
41 E2 **Ansty** Warwks
8 C5 **Ansty** Wilts
71 E5 **Anthorn** Cumb
45 F5 **Antingham** Norfk
43 E6 **Anton's Gowt** Lincs
5 E3 **Antony** Cnwll
57 F1 **Antrobus** Ches
52 D1 **Anwick** Lincs
69 G3 **Anwoth** D & G
21 G2 **Aperfield** Gt Lon
42 C2 **Apethorpe** Nhants
52 D3 **Apley** Lincs
51 E4 **Apperknowle** Derbys
29 F5 **Apperley** Gloucs
90 B3 **Appin** Ag & B
60 D2 **Appleby** N Linc
40 D4 **Appleby Magna** Leics
40 D4 **Appleby Parva** Leics
64 B5 **Appleby-in-Westmorland** Cumb
97 E6 **Applecross** Highld
14 D4 **Appledore** Devon
16 C1 **Appledore** Devon
13 E5 **Appledore** Kent
19 G5 **Appleford** Oxon
78 D1 **Applegarth Town** D & G
19 E2 **Appleshaw** Hants
57 E2 **Appleton** Halton
19 F6 **Appleton** Oxon
57 F1 **Appleton** Warrtn
59 F4 **Appleton Roebuck** N York
57 F1 **Appleton Thorn** Warrtn
65 G4 **Appleton Wiske** N York
66 D2 **Appleton-le-Moors** N York
66 D1 **Appleton-le-Street** N York
80 B2 **Appletreehall** Border
58 B5 **Appletreewick** N York
16 C2 **Appley** Somset
57 E3 **Appley Bridge** Lancs
9 G2 **Apse Heath** IOW
32 D2 **Apsley End** Beds
10 B2 **Apuldram** W Susx
107 G3 **Arabella** Highld
93 H3 **Arbirlot** Angus
107 G4 **Arboll** Highld
20 B2 **Arborfield** Wokham
20 B2 **Arborfield Cross** Wokham
93 H3 **Arbroath** Angus
95 G4 **Arbuthnott** Abers
25 H3 **Archddu** Carmth
65 F5 **Archdeacon Newton** Darltn
84 D4 **Archencarroch** W Duns
101 E4 **Archiestown** Moray
7 c2 **Archirondel** Jersey
49 G5 **Arclid Green** Ches
90 C2 **Ardanaiseig Hotel** Ag & B
97 F5 **Ardaneaskan** Highld
97 F6 **Ardarroch** Highld
74 C5 **Ardbeg** Ag & B
84 A2 **Ardbeg** Ag & B
84 B4 **Ardbeg** Ag & B
106 B4 **Ardcharnich** Highld
89 E1 **Ardchiavaig** Ag & B
83 G6 **Ardchonnel** Ag & B
85 E6 **Ardchullarie More** Stirlg
84 B5 **Arddarroch** Ag & B
98 A2 **Ardechive** Highld
76 C5 **Ardeer** N Ayrs
33 E2 **Ardeley** Herts
97 F5 **Ardelve** Highld
84 C4 **Arden** Ag & B
30 C5 **Ardens Grafton** Warwks
90 A2 **Ardentallen** Ag & B
84 B4 **Ardentinny** Ag & B
83 H3 **Ardentraive** Ag & B
91 G3 **Ardeonaig Hotel** Stirlg
107 G2 **Ardersier** Highld
105 H4 **Ardessie** Highld
83 F5 **Ardfern** Ag & B
107 E5 **Ardgay** Highld
90 B5 **Ardgour** Highld
84 B3 **Ardgowan** Inver
84 B3 **Ardhallow** Ag & B
111 c5 **Ardhasig** W Isls
105 F2 **Ardheslaig** Highld
106 B4 **Ardindrean** Highld
11 F5 **Ardingly** W Susx
19 F5 **Ardington** Oxon
83 G2 **Ardlamont** Ag & B
34 D2 **Ardleigh** Essex
34 D2 **Ardleigh Heath** Essex
93 E3 **Ardler** P & K
31 F3 **Ardley** Oxon
91 E1 **Ardlui** Ag & B
83 E4 **Ardlussa** Ag & B
90 C3 **Ardmaddy** Ag & B
106 A5 **Ardmair** Highld
84 A3 **Ardmaleish** Ag & B
75 E5 **Ardminish** Ag & B
89 G6 **Ardmolich** Highld
84 C3 **Ardmore** Ag & B
107 F4 **Ardmore** Highld
84 B3 **Ardnadam** Ag & B
106 D1 **Ardnagrask** Highld
97 F5 **Ardnarff** Highld
89 H5 **Ardnastang** Highld
84 B6 **Ardno** Ag & B
98 A3 **Ardochy House** Highld
83 F2 **Ardpatrick** Ag & B
83 F4 **Ardrishaig** Ag & B
107 E3 **Ardross** Highld
76 B5 **Ardrossan** N Ayrs
58 D3 **Ardsley East** Leeds
89 F5 **Ardslignish** Highld
82 D1 **Ardtalla** Ag & B
89 F5 **Ardtoe** Highld
83 F6 **Arduaine** Ag & B
107 E2 **Ardullie** Highld
96 D3 **Ardvasar** Highld
91 G2 **Ardvorlich** P & K
111 c5 **Ardvourlie** W Isls
68 C2 **Ardwell** D & G
57 H2 **Ardwick** Manch
39 G3 **Areley Kings** Worcs
89 G5 **Arevegaig** Highld
10 B5 **Arford** Hants
27 G3 **Argoed** Caerph
84 B5 **Argyll Forest Park** Ag & B
111 c5 **Aribruach** W Isls
88 D2 **Aridhglas** Ag & B
88 C4 **Arileod** Ag & B
88 C4 **Arinagour** Ag & B
90 A2 **Ariogan** Ag & B
97 E1 **Arisaig** Highld
97 E1 **Arisaig House** Highld
59 E6 **Arkendale** N York

Arkesden - Barford St John 161

33 F2 **Arkesden** Essex
63 F3 **Arkholme** Lancs
79 G2 **Arkleton** D & G
21 E5 **Arkley** Gt Lon
59 F1 **Arksey** Donc
51 E4 **Arkwright Town** Derbys
29 G5 **Arle** Gloucs
70 D2 **Arlecdon** Cumb
32 D2 **Arlesey** Beds
49 F1 **Arleston** Wrekin
57 F1 **Arley** Ches
40 D3 **Arley** Warwks
29 E4 **Arlingham** Gloucs
15 E5 **Arlington** Devon
12 A3 **Arlington** E Susx
109 G5 **Armadale** Highld
96 D3 **Armadale** Highld
85 H3 **Armadale** W Loth
71 E2 **Armaside** Cumb
71 H4 **Armathwaite** Cumb
45 F3 **Arminghall** Norfk
40 C5 **Armitage** Staffs
58 D3 **Armley** Leeds
42 C1 **Armston** Nhants
59 G1 **Armthorpe** Donc
88 C5 **Arnabost** Ag & B
64 D1 **Arncliffe** N York
87 E6 **Arncroach** Fife
101 E4 **Arndilly House** Moray
8 C2 **Arne** Dorset
41 G3 **Arnesby** Leics
92 D1 **Arngask** P & K
97 F3 **Arnisdale** Highld
104 D1 **Arnish** Highld
86 D2 **Arniston** Mdloth
111 d7 **Arnol** W Isls
61 E4 **Arnold** E R Yk
51 G2 **Arnold** Notts
85 E5 **Arnprior** Stirlg
63 E4 **Arnside** Cumb
89 F3 **Aros** Ag & B
62 C4 **Arrad Foot** Cumb
60 D4 **Arram** E R Yk
75 G4 **Arran** N Ayrs
65 F3 **Arrathorne** N York
9 G2 **Arreton** IOW
105 F2 **Arrina** Highld
33 E4 **Arrington** Cambs
84 C5 **Arrochar** Ag & B
30 C5 **Arrow** Warwks
38 D6 **Arscott** Shrops
107 E1 **Artafallie** Highld
58 D4 **Arthington** Leeds
41 H2 **Arthingworth** Nhants
103 E3 **Arthrath** Abers
103 F3 **Artrochie** Abers
10 D3 **Arundel** W Susx
70 D2 **Asby** Cumb
84 A2 **Ascog** Ag & B
20 C2 **Ascot** W & M
30 D2 **Ascott-under-Wychwood** Oxon
65 G1 **Asenby** N York
41 G5 **Asfordby** Leics
41 H5 **Asfordby Hill** Leics
42 D6 **Asgarby** Lincs
53 E2 **Asgarby** Lincs
22 B2 **Ash** Kent
23 G2 **Ash** Kent
17 F1 **Ash** Somset
20 C1 **Ash** Surrey
20 C1 **Ash Green** Surrey
41 E2 **Ash Green** Warwks
49 E3 **Ash Magna** Shrops
15 G3 **Ash Mill** Devon
49 F3 **Ash Parva** Shrops
16 C2 **Ash Priors** Somset
34 D3 **Ash Street** Suffk
6 B6 **Ash Thomas** Devon
20 C1 **Ash Vale** Surrey
19 G4 **Ashampstead** W Berk
35 E4 **Ashbocking** Suffk
35 E4 **Ashbocking Green** Suffk
50 C2 **Ashbourne** Derbys
16 C1 **Ashbrittle** Somset
5 G4 **Ashburton** Devon
15 E1 **Ashbury** Devon
19 E5 **Ashbury** Oxon
52 B6 **Ashby** N Linc
53 F2 **Ashby by Partney** Lincs
53 E5 **Ashby cum Fenby** NE Lin
52 C1 **Ashby de la Launde** Lincs
41 G4 **Ashby Folville** Leics
41 F2 **Ashby Magna** Leics
41 F2 **Ashby Parva** Leics
53 E3 **Ashby Puerorum** Lincs
31 F6 **Ashby St Ledgers** Nhants
45 F2 **Ashby St Mary** Norfk
41 E5 **Ashby-de-la-Zouch** Leics
29 G5 **Ashchurch** Gloucs
6 B4 **Ashcombe** Devon
17 E5 **Ashcombe** N Som
17 F3 **Ashcott** Somset
33 G3 **Ashdon** Essex
19 G2 **Ashe** Hants
23 E5 **Asheldham** Essex
34 B3 **Ashen** Essex
31 G2 **Ashendon** Bucks
20 C5 **Asheridge** Bucks
85 G5 **Ashfield** Stirlg
35 E5 **Ashfield** Suffk
35 F5 **Ashfield Green** Suffk
15 E4 **Ashford** Devon
5 G2 **Ashford** Devon
13 E6 **Ashford** Kent
20 D3 **Ashford** Surrey
39 E3 **Ashford Bowdler** Shrops
39 E3 **Ashford Carbonel** Shrops
19 G3 **Ashford Hill** Hants
50 D4 **Ashford in the Water** Derbys
77 G6 **Ashgill** S Lans
6 C6 **Ashill** Devon
44 C3 **Ashill** Norfk
17 E1 **Ashill** Somset
22 D4 **Ashingdon** Essex
73 F5 **Ashington** Nthumb
17 G1 **Ashington** Somset
11 E3 **Ashington** W Susx
79 G5 **Ashkirk** Border
29 F5 **Ashleworth** Gloucs
29 F5 **Ashleworth Quay** Gloucs
34 A4 **Ashley** Cambs
57 G1 **Ashley** Ches
15 F2 **Ashley** Devon
29 G2 **Ashley** Gloucs
9 F6 **Ashley** Hants
9 E3 **Ashley** Hants
13 G6 **Ashley** Kent
42 A1 **Ashley** Nhants
49 G3 **Ashley** Staffs
18 A3 **Ashley** Wilts
20 C5 **Ashley Green** Bucks
19 F3 **Ashmansworth** Hants
14 C3 **Ashmansworthy** Devon
8 B5 **Ashmore** Dorset
19 G4 **Ashmore Green** W Berk
30 D5 **Ashorne** Warwks
51 E3 **Ashover** Derbys
40 D1 **Ashow** Warwks
28 D6 **Ashperton** Herefs
5 H3 **Ashprington** Devon
15 F2 **Ashreigney** Devon
21 E2 **Ashtead** Surrey
49 E6 **Ashton** Ches
2 C2 **Ashton** Cnwll
6 A4 **Ashton** Devon
39 E3 **Ashton** Herefs
84 B3 **Ashton** Inver
31 H5 **Ashton** Nhants
42 C1 **Ashton** Nhants
18 B3 **Ashton Common** Wilts
18 C6 **Ashton Keynes** Wilts
30 B4 **Ashton under Hill** Worcs
57 F3 **Ashton-in-Makerfield** Wigan
50 B6 **Ashton-under-Lyne** Tamesd
9 E4 **Ashurst** Hants
11 G5 **Ashurst** Kent
11 E4 **Ashurst** W Susx
11 G5 **Ashurstwood** W Susx
5 E6 **Ashwater** Devon
33 E3 **Ashwell** Herts
42 B3 **Ashwell** Rutlnd
33 E3 **Ashwell End** Herts
45 E2 **Ashwellthorpe** Norfk
17 G4 **Ashwick** Somset
44 A4 **Ashwicken** Norfk
62 C4 **Askam in Furness** Cumb
59 F2 **Askern** Donc
7 F5 **Askerswell** Dorset
20 B5 **Askett** Bucks
71 H2 **Askham** Cumb
51 H4 **Askham** Notts
59 F4 **Askham Bryan** York
59 F4 **Askham Richard** York
83 G4 **Asknish** Ag & B
64 D3 **Askrigg** N York
58 C4 **Askwith** N York
42 C5 **Aslackby** Lincs
45 E1 **Aslacton** Norfk
51 H1 **Aslockton** Notts
71 E3 **Aspatria** Cumb
33 E2 **Aspenden** Herts
32 B2 **Aspley Guise** Beds
32 B2 **Aspley Heath** Beds
57 F3 **Aspull** Wigan
60 B3 **Asselby** E R Yk
34 C3 **Assington** Suffk
34 B4 **Assington Green** Suffk
49 H5 **Astbury** Ches
31 G5 **Astcote** Nhants
53 E3 **Asterby** Lincs
38 D6 **Asterley** Shrops
38 D5 **Asterton** Shrops
30 D2 **Asthall** Oxon
30 D2 **Asthall Leigh** Oxon
107 F5 **Astle** Highld
49 E2 **Astley** Shrops
40 D2 **Astley** Warwks
57 F3 **Astley** Wigan
39 G3 **Astley** Worcs
39 G5 **Astley Abbots** Shrops
57 G4 **Astley Bridge** Bolton
39 G3 **Astley Cross** Worcs
57 E1 **Aston** Ches
49 F4 **Aston** Ches
50 C5 **Aston** Derbys
48 C5 **Aston** Flints
39 E3 **Aston** Herefs
33 E1 **Aston** Herts
31 E1 **Aston** Oxon
51 F5 **Aston** Rothm
49 E2 **Aston** Shrops
39 G5 **Aston** Shrops
49 G3 **Aston** Staffs
40 A5 **Aston** Staffs
40 A6 **Aston** Staffs
20 B4 **Aston** Wokham
49 F1 **Aston** Wrekin
32 B1 **Aston Abbotts** Bucks
39 F4 **Aston Botterell** Shrops
30 C5 **Aston Cantlow** Warwks
20 C6 **Aston Clinton** Bucks
29 E5 **Aston Crews** Herefs
33 E1 **Aston End** Herts
40 B1 **Aston Fields** Worcs
41 F3 **Aston Flamville** Leics
29 E5 **Aston Ingham** Herefs
31 F5 **Aston le Walls** Nhants
30 D3 **Aston Magna** Gloucs
39 E4 **Aston Munslow** Shrops
38 D4 **Aston on Clun** Shrops
38 D6 **Aston Pigott** Shrops
38 D6 **Aston Rogers** Shrops
20 A5 **Aston Rowant** Oxon
30 B4 **Aston Somerville** Worcs
30 C4 **Aston Subedge** Gloucs
19 G5 **Aston Tirrold** Oxon
19 G5 **Aston Upthorpe** Oxon
39 F5 **Aston-Eyre** Shrops
41 E6 **Aston-upon-Trent** Derbys
32 D3 **Astwick** Beds
32 B3 **Astwood** M Keyn
30 B6 **Astwood** Worcs
30 B6 **Astwood Bank** Worcs
42 C5 **Aswarby** Lincs
53 F2 **Aswardby** Lincs
39 E6 **Atcham** Shrops
8 A3 **Athelhampton** Dorset
35 E5 **Athelington** Suffk
17 E2 **Athelney** Somset
87 E4 **Athelstaneford** E Loth
15 E3 **Atherington** Devon
40 D3 **Atherstone** Warwks
30 D5 **Atherstone on Stour** Warwks
57 F3 **Atherton** Wigan
50 D2 **Atlow** Derbys
97 G5 **Attadale** Highld
52 C4 **Atterby** Lincs
51 E5 **Attercliffe** Sheff
41 E3 **Atterton** Leics
44 D2 **Attleborough** Norfk
41 E3 **Attleborough** Warwks
45 E4 **Attlebridge** Norfk
34 B4 **Attleton Green** Suffk
61 E5 **Atwick** E R Yk
18 B3 **Atworth** Wilts
52 B2 **Aubourn** Lincs
103 E3 **Auchedly** Abers
95 F4 **Auchenblae** Abers
85 G4 **Auchenbowie** Stirlg
70 B4 **Auchencairn** D & G
78 C1 **Auchencairn** D & G
75 H4 **Auchencairn** N Ayrs
87 H2 **Auchencrow** Border
86 C2 **Auchendinny** Mdloth
86 A2 **Auchengray** S Lans
101 F5 **Auchenhalrig** Moray
77 G5 **Auchenheath** S Lans
77 G1 **Auchenhessnane** D & G
83 G3 **Auchenlochan** Ag & B
76 C6 **Auchenmade** N Ayrs
68 D3 **Auchenmalg** D & G
76 C6 **Auchentiber** N Ayrs
85 E5 **Auchentroig** Stirlg
106 B4 **Auchindrean** Highld
102 C4 **Auchininna** Abers
77 E3 **Auchinleck** E Ayrs
85 F3 **Auchinloch** N Lans
85 F3 **Auchinstarry** N Lans
90 C6 **Auchintore** Highld
103 F3 **Auchiries** Abers
95 G5 **Auchlee** Abers
102 C5 **Auchleven** Abers
77 G5 **Auchlochan** S Lans
95 E6 **Auchlossan** Abers
91 F2 **Auchlyne** Stirlg
77 E4 **Auchmillan** E Ayrs
93 H4 **Auchmithie** Angus
86 C5 **Auchmuirbridge** Fife
94 D3 **Auchnacree** Angus
103 E3 **Auchnagatt** Abers
101 E2 **Auchnarrow** Moray
68 B3 **Auchnotteroch** D & G
101 F4 **Auchroisk** Moray
92 C1 **Auchterarder** P & K
98 C3 **Auchteraw** Highld
99 G4 **Auchterblair** Highld
105 F3 **Auchtercairn** Highld
86 C5 **Auchterderran** Fife
93 F3 **Auchterhouse** Angus
102 C3 **Auchterless** Abers
93 E1 **Auchtermuchty** Fife
106 D2 **Auchterneed** Highld
86 C5 **Auchtertool** Fife
97 F5 **Auchtertyre** Highld
91 G1 **Auchtubh** Stirlg
110 D5 **Auckengill** Highld
51 G6 **Auckley** Donc
50 A6 **Audenshaw** Tamesd
49 F4 **Audlem** Ches
49 G4 **Audley** Staffs
33 G3 **Audley End** Essex
33 G3 **Audley End** Essex
34 C4 **Audley End** Suffk
71 F3 **Aughertree** Cumb
60 B4 **Aughton** E R Yk
56 D3 **Aughton** Lancs
63 E3 **Aughton** Lancs
51 F5 **Aughton** Rothm
19 E2 **Aughton** Wilts
56 D3 **Aughton Park** Lancs
100 C5 **Auldearn** Highld
39 E2 **Aulden** Herefs
78 C2 **Auldgirth** D & G
77 E6 **Auldhouse** S Lans
97 G4 **Ault a' chruinn** Highld
51 F3 **Ault Hucknall** Derbys
105 G4 **Aultbea** Highld
105 F4 **Aultgrishin** Highld
106 C3 **Aultguish Inn** Highld
101 F4 **Aultmore** Moray
98 D5 **Aultnagoire** Highld
107 F4 **Aultnamain Inn** Highld
42 C5 **Aunsby** Lincs
28 D2 **Aust** S Glos
51 G6 **Austerfield** Donc
40 D4 **Austrey** Warwks
63 G3 **Austwick** N York
53 F3 **Authorpe** Lincs
18 D4 **Avebury** Wilts
22 B3 **Aveley** Thurr
29 F3 **Avening** Gloucs
51 H2 **Averham** Notts
5 G2 **Aveton Gifford** Devon
99 G4 **Aviemore** Highld
19 F3 **Avington** W Berk
107 F2 **Avoch** Highld
8 D3 **Avon** Dorset
31 E5 **Avon Dassett** Warwks
85 H3 **Avonbridge** Falk
28 C1 **Avonmouth** Bristl
5 G3 **Avonwick** Devon
9 E5 **Awbridge** Hants
6 C5 **Awliscombe** Devon
29 E3 **Awre** Gloucs
51 F1 **Awsworth** Notts
17 F4 **Axbridge** Somset
19 H1 **Axford** Hants
19 E4 **Axford** Wilts
6 D5 **Axminster** Devon
6 D4 **Axmouth** Devon
65 F5 **Aycliffe** Dur
72 D3 **Aydon** Nthumb
28 D3 **Aylburton** Gloucs
6 B5 **Aylesbeare** Devon
20 B6 **Aylesbury** Bucks
52 D5 **Aylesby** NE Lin
22 C2 **Aylesford** Kent
23 G1 **Aylesham** Kent
41 F3 **Aylestone** C Leic
45 E5 **Aylmerton** Norfk
45 E4 **Aylsham** Norfk
28 D6 **Aylton** Gloucs
30 C2 **Aylworth** Gloucs
38 D3 **Aymestrey** Herefs
31 F3 **Aynho** Nhants
32 D1 **Ayot St Lawrence** Herts
76 C3 **Ayr** S Ayrs
64 D2 **Aysgarth** N York
16 C1 **Ayshford** Devon
62 D4 **Ayside** Cumb
42 B2 **Ayston** Rutlnd
22 B6 **Aythorpe Roding** Essex
81 E5 **Ayton** Border
65 F1 **Azerley** N York

B

6 B2 **Babbacombe** Torbay
33 F1 **Babbs Green** Herts
17 G2 **Babcary** Somset
17 H4 **Babington** Somset
33 G4 **Babraham** Cambs
51 G4 **Babworth** Notts
97 E1 **Back of Keppoch** Highld
111 h3 **Backaland** Ork
103 F4 **Backfolds** Abers
48 D6 **Backford** Ches
107 G5 **Backies** Highld
110 C4 **Backlass** Highld
17 F5 **Backwell** N Som
45 E5 **Baconsthorpe** Norfk
28 B5 **Bacton** Herefs
45 F5 **Bacton** Norfk
34 D5 **Bacton** Suffk
57 H5 **Bacup** Lancs
105 F3 **Badachro** Highld
18 D4 **Badbury** Swindn
31 F5 **Badby** Nhants
108 B3 **Badcall** Highld
108 C4 **Badcall** Highld
105 H5 **Badcaul** Highld
40 D1 **Baddesley Clinton** Warwks
40 D3 **Baddesley Ensor** Warwks
108 B2 **Baddidarrach** Highld
86 B2 **Baddinsgill** Border
102 C3 **Badenscoth** Abers
101 F2 **Badenyon** Abers
39 G5 **Badger** Shrops
29 F4 **Badgeworth** Gloucs
17 E4 **Badgworth** Somset
97 E5 **Badicaul** Highld
35 F5 **Badingham** Suffk
23 E1 **Badlesmere** Kent
78 D4 **Badlieu** Border
110 C4 **Badlipster** Highld
105 G5 **Badluachrach** Highld
107 F5 **Badninish** Highld
105 H5 **Badrallach** Highld
30 C4 **Badsey** Worcs
10 B6 **Badshot Lea** Surrey
59 F2 **Badsworth** Wakefd
34 D5 **Badwell Ash** Suffk
53 E3 **Bag Enderby** Lincs
17 H1 **Bagber** Dorset
66 B2 **Bagby** N York
111 a1 **Bagh a Chaisteil** W Isls
111 a1 **Bagh a Tuath** W Isls
48 C6 **Bagillt** Flints
41 E1 **Baginton** Warwks
26 D2 **Baglan** Neath
48 D2 **Bagley** Shrops
17 F3 **Bagley** Somset
19 H2 **Bagmore** Hants
50 A2 **Bagnall** Staffs
39 F3 **Bagot** Shrops
20 C2 **Bagshot** Surrey
29 E2 **Bagstone** S Glos
41 E4 **Bagworth** Leics
28 C5 **Bagwy Llydiart** Herefs
58 C4 **Baildon** Brad
58 C4 **Baildon Green** Brad
111 b3 **Baile a Mhanaich** W Isls
111 d6 **Baile Ailein** W Isls
88 D2 **Baile Mor** Ag & B
85 F2 **Baillieston** C Glas
64 D2 **Bainbridge** N York
102 B3 **Bainshole** Abers
42 C3 **Bainton** C Pete
60 D5 **Bainton** E R Yk
86 D6 **Baintown** Fife
80 C2 **Bairnkine** Border
50 D3 **Bakewell** Derbys
47 H5 **Bala** Gwynd
111 d6 **Balallan** W Isls
98 C5 **Balbeg** Highld
92 D2 **Balbeggie** P & K
106 D1 **Balblair** Highld
107 F3 **Balblair** Highld
51 F6 **Balby** Donc
70 B4 **Balcary** D & G
98 D6 **Balchraggan** Highld
108 B5 **Balchreick** Highld
11 F5 **Balcombe** W Susx
87 F6 **Balcomie Links** Fife
65 G2 **Baldersby** N York
65 G1 **Baldersby St James** N York
57 F5 **Balderstone** Lancs
52 A1 **Balderton** Notts
93 F1 **Baldinnie** Fife
92 C1 **Baldinnies** P & K
33 E2 **Baldock** Herts
93 F3 **Baldovie** C Dund
116 c3 **Baldrine** IOM
12 C3 **Baldslow** E Susx
44 D5 **Bale** Norfk
93 E2 **Baledgarno** P & K
88 B3 **Balemartine** Ag & B
86 B3 **Balerno** C Edin
86 C6 **Balfarg** Fife
95 E3 **Balfield** Angus
111 h2 **Balfour** Ork
85 E4 **Balfron** Stirlg
102 C3 **Balgaveny** Abers
93 G4 **Balgavies** Angus
86 A5 **Balgonar** Fife
68 C2 **Balgowan** D & G
99 E2 **Balgowan** Highld
104 C3 **Balgown** Highld
68 B3 **Balgracie** D & G
93 F3 **Balgray** Angus
78 C5 **Balgray** S Lans
21 F3 **Balham** Gt Lon
93 E4 **Balhary** P & K
92 D3 **Balholmie** P & K
109 G5 **Baligill** Highld
93 E5 **Balintore** Angus
107 G3 **Balintore** Highld
107 F3 **Balintraid** Highld
111 b3 **Balivanich** W Isls
66 B2 **Balk** N York
93 E4 **Balkeerie** Angus
60 B3 **Balkholme** E R Yk
90 C4 **Ballachulish** Highld
83 H2 **Ballanlay** Ag & B
68 C5 **Ballantrae** S Ayrs
116 b2 **Ballasalla** IOM
94 C5 **Ballater** Abers
116 c4 **Ballaugh** IOM
107 F3 **Ballchraggan** Highld
87 E4 **Ballencrieff** E Loth
88 A3 **Ballevullin** Ag & B
50 D2 **Ballidon** Derbys
75 G4 **Balliekine** N Ayrs
84 A5 **Balliemore** Ag & B
68 D6 **Balligmorrie** S Ayrs
83 G4 **Ballimore** Ag & B
91 F1 **Ballimore** Stirlg
101 E3 **Ballindalloch** Moray
93 E2 **Ballindean** P & K
20 C5 **Ballinger Common** Bucks
28 D5 **Ballingham** Herefs
86 C5 **Ballingry** Fife
92 C4 **Ballinluig** P & K
93 F4 **Ballinshoe** Angus
92 D4 **Ballintuim** P & K
107 F1 **Balloch** Highld
85 F3 **Balloch** N Lans
92 B2 **Balloch** P & K
76 C1 **Balloch** S Ayrs
84 D4 **Balloch** W Duns
95 E5 **Ballogie** Abers
10 C4 **Balls Cross** W Susx
11 G5 **Balls Green** E Susx
89 E3 **Ballygown** Ag & B
82 C2 **Ballygrant** Ag & B
88 C4 **Ballyhaugh** Ag & B
84 C4 **Ballymenoch** Ag & B
97 F5 **Balmacara** Highld
69 G5 **Balmaclellan** D & G
69 G2 **Balmae** D & G
84 D4 **Balmaha** Stirlg
86 D6 **Balmalcolm** Fife
69 G2 **Balmangan** D & G
103 E2 **Balmedie** Abers
93 F2 **Balmerino** Fife
75 G4 **Balmichael** N Ayrs
94 B5 **Balmoral Castle Grounds** Abers
85 E3 **Balmore** E Duns
107 G4 **Balmuchy** Highld
93 G4 **Balmuir** Angus
86 C4 **Balmule** Fife
93 F2 **Balmullo** Fife
109 G1 **Balnacoil Lodge** Highld
105 G1 **Balnacra** Highld
94 C5 **Balnacroft** Abers
99 E6 **Balnafoich** Highld
92 C4 **Balnaguard** P & K
89 E2 **Balnahard** Ag & B
82 C5 **Balnahard** Ag & B
98 C5 **Balnain** Highld
108 D5 **Balnakeil** Highld
107 G3 **Balnapaling** Highld
92 C3 **Balquharn** P & K
91 F1 **Balquhidder** Stirlg
40 D1 **Balsall Common** Solhll
40 C2 **Balsall Heath** Birm
31 E4 **Balscote** Oxon
33 G4 **Balsham** Cambs
111 m4 **Baltasound** Shet
111 m4 **Baltasound Airport** Shet
69 E4 **Baltersan** D & G
17 F3 **Baltonsborough** Somset
94 A2 **Balvarran** P & K
89 H1 **Balvicar** Ag & B
97 F4 **Balvraid** Highld
99 F5 **Balvraid** Highld
57 E5 **Bamber Bridge** Lancs
33 G1 **Bamber's Green** Essex
81 G3 **Bamburgh** Nthumb
81 G3 **Bamburgh Castle** Nthumb
93 E4 **Bamff** P & K
50 D5 **Bamford** Derbys
71 H1 **Bampton** Cumb
16 B2 **Bampton** Devon
30 D1 **Bampton** Oxon
71 H1 **Bampton Grange** Cumb
90 C6 **Banavie** Highld
31 F4 **Banbury** Oxon
26 B4 **Bancffosfelen** Carmth
95 F5 **Banchory** Abers
95 G6 **Banchory-Devenick** Abers
25 G4 **Bancycapel** Carmth
25 G4 **Bancyfelin** Carmth
93 E2 **Bandirran** P & K
102 C5 **Banff** Abers
54 D3 **Bangor** Gwynd
48 D4 **Bangor-is-y-coed** Wrexhm
14 B1 **Bangors** Cnwll
44 D1 **Banham** Norfk
9 E4 **Bank** Hants
70 D6 **Bankend** D & G
92 C3 **Bankfoot** P & K
77 E3 **Bankglen** E Ayrs
103 E1 **Bankhead** C Aber
86 A1 **Bankhead** S Lans
85 G3 **Banknock** Falk
56 D4 **Banks** Lancs
79 E1 **Bankshill** D & G
45 E5 **Banningham** Norfk
34 A1 **Bannister Green** Essex
85 G4 **Bannockburn** Stirlg
21 E2 **Banstead** Surrey
5 G2 **Bantham** Devon
85 F3 **Banton** N Lans
17 E5 **Banwell** N Som
22 D2 **Bapchild** Kent
18 C1 **Bapton** Wilts
33 F5 **Bar Hill** Cambs
111 d7 **Barabhas** W Isls
76 C4 **Barassie** S Ayrs
107 F3 **Barbaraville** Highld
76 D3 **Barbieston** S Ayrs
63 F4 **Barbon** Cumb
15 F5 **Barbrook** Devon
41 F1 **Barby** Nhants
90 B3 **Barcaldine** Ag & B
30 D4 **Barcheston** Warwks
11 G3 **Barcombe** E Susx
11 G4 **Barcombe Cross** E Susx
65 E3 **Barden** N York
12 B6 **Barden Park** Kent
33 H2 **Bardfield End Green** Essex
34 A2 **Bardfield Saling** Essex
52 D2 **Bardney** Lincs
41 E4 **Bardon** Leics
72 C3 **Bardon Mill** Nthumb
85 E3 **Bardowie** E Duns
84 C3 **Bardrainney** Inver
62 C3 **Bardsea** Cumb
59 E4 **Bardsey** Leeds
34 C5 **Bardwell** Suffk
63 E5 **Bare** Lancs
38 D2 **Barewood** Herefs
69 E4 **Barfad** D & G
45 E3 **Barford** Norfk
30 D6 **Barford** Warwks
31 E3 **Barford St John** Oxon

8 C6 Barford St Martin Wilts
31 E3 Barford St Michael Oxon
23 G1 Barfrestone Kent
85 F2 Bargeddie N Lans
27 G3 Bargoed Caerph
69 E5 Bargrennan D & G
32 D6 Barham Cambs
23 G1 Barham Kent
35 E4 Barham Suffk
42 C3 Barholm Lincs
41 G4 Barkby Leics
41 G4 Barkby Thorpe Leics
41 H6 Barkestone-le-Vale Leics
20 B2 Barkham Wokham
21 G4 Barking Gt Lon
34 D4 Barking Suffk
34 D4 Barking Tye Suffk
21 G4 Barkingside Gt Lon
58 B2 Barkisland Calder
2 D4 Barkla Shop Cnwll
42 B6 Barkston Lincs
59 F3 Barkston Ash N York
33 F2 Barkway Herts
85 F2 Barlanark C Glas
50 A1 Barlaston Staffs
10 C4 Barlavington W Susx
51 F4 Barlborough Derbys
59 G3 Barlby N York
41 E4 Barlestone Leics
33 F3 Barley Herts
57 G6 Barley Lancs
42 B3 Barleythorpe Rutlnd
22 D4 Barling Essex
52 C3 Barlings Lincs
70 B5 Barlochan D & G
51 E4 Barlow Derbys
73 E3 Barlow Gatesd
59 G3 Barlow N York
60 B5 Barmby Moor E R Yk
59 G3 Barmby on the Marsh E R Yk
75 F5 Barmollack Ag & B
47 E3 Barmouth Gwynd
65 G5 Barmpton Darltn
61 E5 Barmston E R Yk
83 H5 Barnacarry Ag & B
42 C3 Barnack C Pete
65 E5 Barnard Castle Dur
31 E1 Barnard Gate Oxon
34 A3 Barnardiston Suffk
70 B5 Barnbarroch D & G
59 F1 Barnburgh Donc
45 G1 Barnby Suffk
59 G1 Barnby Dun Donc
52 B1 Barnby in the Willows Notts
51 G5 Barnby Moor Notts
68 C1 Barncorkrie D & G
21 E3 Barnes Gt Lon
12 B6 Barnes Street Kent
21 E5 Barnet Gt Lon
52 C6 Barnetby le Wold N Linc
44 D5 Barney Norfk
34 C6 Barnham Suffk
10 C3 Barnham W Susx
44 D3 Barnham Broom Norfk
93 H5 Barnhead Angus
93 G3 Barnhill C Dund
100 D5 Barnhill Moray
68 B4 Barnhills D & G
65 E4 Barningham Dur
34 C6 Barningham Suffk
52 D5 Barnoldby le Beck NE Lin
63 H1 Barnoldswick Lancs
10 D4 Barns Green W Susx
59 E1 Barnsley Barns
30 C1 Barnsley Gloucs
15 E4 Barnstaple Devon
33 H1 Barnston Essex
56 C1 Barnston Wirral
41 H6 Barnstone Notts
40 B1 Barnt Green Worcs
86 C3 Barnton C Edin
49 F6 Barnton Ches
42 C1 Barnwell All Saints Nhants
42 C1 Barnwell St Andrew Nhants
29 F4 Barnwood Gloucs
76 C1 Barr S Ayrs
111 a2 Barra Airport W Isls
69 E3 Barrachan D & G
88 A3 Barrapoll Ag & B
72 D4 Barrasford Nthumb
84 D2 Barrhead E Rens
68 D5 Barrhill S Ayrs
33 F4 Barrington Cambs
17 E1 Barrington Somset
2 C3 Barripper Cnwll
84 C1 Barrmill N Ayrs
89 H1 Barrnacarry Bay Ag & B
110 C6 Barrock Highld
29 F5 Barrow Gloucs
57 G6 Barrow Lancs
42 B3 Barrow Rutlnd
17 H2 Barrow Somset
34 B5 Barrow Suffk
81 E1 Barrow Burn Nthumb
17 F5 Barrow Gurney N Som
60 D2 Barrow Haven N Linc
62 C3 Barrow Island Cumb
41 F5 Barrow upon Soar Leics
41 E6 Barrow upon Trent Derbys
62 C3 Barrow-in-Furness Cumb
60 D2 Barrow-upon-Humber N Linc
42 B5 Barrowby Lincs
42 B2 Barrowden Rutlnd
57 H6 Barrowford Lancs
93 G3 Barry Angus
16 C5 Barry V Glam
41 G4 Barsby Leics
45 G1 Barsham Suffk
40 D2 Barston Solhll
28 D6 Bartestree Herefs
102 D3 Barthol Chapel Abers
34 B1 Bartholomew Green Essex
49 G4 Barthomley Ches
9 E4 Bartley Hants
40 B2 Bartley Green Birm
33 G3 Bartlow Cambs
33 F4 Barton Cambs
49 E4 Barton Ches
30 C3 Barton Gloucs
56 D3 Barton Lancs
57 E6 Barton Lancs
65 F4 Barton N York
31 F1 Barton Oxon
6 B3 Barton Torbay
44 A3 Barton Bendish Norfk
29 F3 Barton End Gloucs
31 G3 Barton Hartshorn Bucks
41 F6 Barton in Fabis Notts
41 E4 Barton in the Beans Leics
34 B5 Barton Mills Suffk
32 B6 Barton Seagrave Nhants
17 F2 Barton St David Somset
19 F1 Barton Stacey Hants
15 F5 Barton Town Devon
60 D2 Barton Waterside N Linc
32 C2 Barton-le-Clay Beds
66 D1 Barton-le-Street N York
60 B6 Barton-le-Willows N York
9 E3 Barton-on-Sea Hants
30 D3 Barton-on-the-Heath Warwks
40 C5 Barton-under-Needwood Staffs
60 D2 Barton-upon-Humber N Linc
111 d7 Barvas W Isls
33 G6 Barway Cambs
41 E3 Barwell Leics
15 E2 Barwick Devon
17 F1 Barwick Somset
59 E4 Barwick in Elmet Leeds
48 D2 Baschurch Shrops
31 E6 Bascote Warwks
63 F1 Bashall Eaves Lancs
22 C4 Basildon Essex
19 H2 Basingstoke Hants
50 D4 Baslow Derbys
17 E3 Bason Bridge Somset
28 B2 Bassaleg Newpt
80 C4 Bassendean Border
71 E3 Bassenthwaite Cumb
9 F5 Bassett C Sotn
33 E3 Bassingbourn Cambs
52 B2 Bassingham Lincs
42 B4 Bassingthorpe Lincs
33 E2 Bassus Green Herts
42 D3 Baston Lincs
45 G4 Bastwick Norfk
20 D4 Batchworth Herts
7 G5 Batcombe Dorset
17 H3 Batcombe Somset
21 E6 Batford Herts
17 H5 Bath BaNES
35 F2 Bath Side Essex
18 A3 Bathampton BaNES
16 C2 Bathealton Somset
18 A3 Batheaston BaNES
18 A3 Bathford BaNES
86 A3 Bathgate W Loth
51 H3 Bathley Notts
4 D4 Bathpool Cnwll
16 D2 Bathpool Somset
85 H2 Bathville W Loth
17 G4 Bathway Somset
58 D3 Batley Kirk
30 C3 Batsford Gloucs
66 C4 Battersby N York
21 F3 Battersea Gt Lon
34 D4 Battisford Tye Suffk
12 C3 Battle E Susx
27 F5 Battle Powys
52 D1 Battle of Britain Memorial Flight Lincs
93 F4 Battledykes Angus
22 C4 Battlesbridge Essex
16 B2 Battleton Somset
29 F6 Baughton Worcs
19 G3 Baughurst Hants
95 E5 Baulds Abers
19 E5 Baulking Oxon
52 D3 Baumber Lincs
30 B1 Baunton Gloucs
8 C6 Baverstock Wilts
45 E3 Bawburgh Norfk
44 D4 Bawdeswell Norfk
17 E3 Bawdrip Somset
35 F3 Bawdsey Suffk
51 G5 Bawtry Donc
57 G5 Baxenden Lancs
40 D3 Baxterley Warwks
104 B2 Bay Highld
111 e6 Bayble W Isls
9 G5 Baybridge Hants
62 C3 Baycliff Cumb
19 E4 Baydon Wilts
21 F6 Bayford Herts
17 H2 Bayford Somset
111 a4 Bayhead W Isls
34 D4 Baylham Suffk
28 D5 Baysham Herefs
39 E6 Bayston Hill Shrops
34 B3 Baythorne End Essex
39 F3 Bayton Worcs
19 G6 Bayworth Oxon
31 H4 Beachampton Bucks
44 B3 Beachamwell Norfk
12 B2 Beachy Head E Susx
6 D6 Beacon Devon
34 C1 Beacon End Essex
20 B5 Beacon's Bottom Bucks
20 C4 Beaconsfield Bucks
66 C2 Beadlam N York
32 C3 Beadlow Beds
81 G3 Beadnell Nthumb
15 E3 Beaford Devon
59 F3 Beal N York
81 F4 Beal Nthumb
4 D4 Bealsmill Cnwll
7 F5 Beaminster Dorset
73 F2 Beamish Dur
58 C5 Beamsley N York
18 B3 Beanacre Wilts
81 F2 Beanley Nthumb
5 F5 Beardon Devon
6 B5 Beare Devon
11 E6 Beare Green Surrey
30 C5 Bearley Warwks
73 F1 Bearpark Dur
85 E3 Bearsden E Duns
22 C1 Bearsted Kent
49 G3 Bearstone Shrops
40 B2 Bearwood Birm
8 C3 Bearwood Poole
78 D3 Beattock D & G
22 B6 Beauchamp Roding Essex
27 G4 Beaufort Blae G
9 F3 Beaulieu Hants
9 F4 Beaulieu House Hants
107 E1 Beauly Highld
54 D4 Beaumaris IOA
71 F5 Beaumont Cumb
35 E2 Beaumont Essex
7 b1 Beaumont Jersey
40 D1 Beausale Warwks
9 G5 Beauworth Hants
13 E6 Beaver Green Kent
14 D1 Beaworthy Devon
34 B2 Beazley End Essex
56 D1 Bebington Wirral
45 G1 Beccles Suffk
57 E5 Becconsall Lancs
34 A6 Beck Row Suffk
62 C4 Beck Side Cumb
39 G6 Beckbury Shrops
21 F2 Beckenham Gt Lon
52 D3 Beckering Lincs
62 A6 Beckermet Cumb
70 D4 Beckfoot Cumb
29 G6 Beckford Worcs
18 D3 Beckhampton Wilts
52 B1 Beckingham Lincs
51 H5 Beckingham Notts
18 A2 Beckington Somset
38 D4 Beckjay Shrops
12 D4 Beckley E Susx
31 F2 Beckley Oxon
21 G3 Beckton Gt Lon
58 D5 Beckwithshaw N York
21 G4 Becontree Gt Lon
7 b2 Becquet Vincent Jersey
65 F2 Bedale N York
8 B5 Bedchester Dorset
27 F2 Beddau Rhondd
54 D1 Beddgelert Gwynd
11 G3 Beddingham E Susx
21 F2 Beddington Gt Lon
21 F2 Beddington Corner Gt Lon
35 E5 Bedfield Suffk
32 C4 Bedford Beds
10 A3 Bedhampton Hants
35 E5 Bedingfield Suffk
35 E5 Bedingfield Street Suffk
58 D6 Bedlam N York
12 D6 Bedlam Lane Kent
73 F4 Bedlington Nthumb
27 F3 Bedlinog Myr Td
17 G6 Bedminster Bristl
17 G5 Bedminster Down Bristl
20 D5 Bedmond Herts
40 B5 Bednall Staffs
80 C2 Bedrule Border
38 D3 Bedstone Shrops
27 G2 Bedwas Caerph
27 G3 Bedwellty Caerph
41 E2 Bedworth Warwks
41 G4 Beeby Leics
10 A5 Beech Hants
49 H3 Beech Staffs
20 A2 Beech Hill W Berk
18 D3 Beechingstoke Wilts
19 G4 Beedon W Berk
19 G4 Beedon Hill W Berk
61 E5 Beeford E R Yk
50 D3 Beeley Derbys
52 D5 Beelsby NE Lin
19 G3 Beenham W Berk
6 D4 Beer Devon
17 E2 Beer Somset
7 G6 Beer Hackett Dorset
17 E1 Beercrocombe Somset
5 H1 Beesands Devon
53 F3 Beesby Lincs
5 H1 Beeson Devon
32 D3 Beeston Beds
49 E5 Beeston Ches
58 D3 Beeston Leeds
44 C3 Beeston Norfk
51 F1 Beeston Notts
45 E6 Beeston Regis Norfk
70 C6 Beeswing D & G
63 E4 Beetham Cumb
6 D6 Beetham Somset
44 C6 Beetley Norfk
31 F2 Begbroke Oxon
25 E3 Begelly Pembks
38 C4 Beguildy Powys
45 G3 Beighton Norfk
51 E5 Beighton Sheff
50 D2 Beighton Hill Derbys
92 D1 Bein Inn P & K
84 C1 Beith N Ayrs
23 F1 Bekesbourne Kent
45 F4 Belaugh Norfk
40 A1 Belbroughton Worcs
8 A4 Belchalwell Dorset
8 A4 Belchalwell Street Dorset
34 B3 Belchamp Otten Essex
34 B3 Belchamp St Paul Essex
34 B3 Belchamp Walter Essex
53 E3 Belchford Lincs
81 F3 Belford Nthumb
41 G4 Belgrave C Leic
87 F4 Belhaven E Loth
103 E2 Belhelvie Abers
101 G2 Belhinnie Abers
58 A5 Bell Busk N York
40 B1 Bell End Worcs
49 E4 Bell o' th' Hill Ches
101 F1 Bellabeg Abers
83 F4 Bellanoch Ag & B
93 E5 Bellaty Angus
71 F5 Belle Vue Cumb
59 E2 Belle Vue Wakefd
53 F3 Belleau Lincs
65 E3 Bellerby N York
78 B6 Bellfield S Lans
78 C4 Bellfield S Lans
20 C5 Bellingdon Bucks
72 C5 Bellingham Nthumb
75 E4 Belloch Ag & B
75 E4 Bellochantuy Ag & B
12 B5 Bells Yew Green E Susx
85 F2 Bellshill N Lans
85 G2 Bellside N Lans
86 B3 Bellsquarry W Loth
17 G5 Belluton BaNES
57 F4 Belmont Bl w D
21 E2 Belmont Gt Lon
76 C3 Belmont S Ayrs
111 m4 Belmont Shet
101 F1 Belnacraig Abers
51 E2 Belper Derbys
51 E2 Belper Lane End Derbys
73 E4 Belsay Nthumb
80 B3 Belses Border
5 G3 Belsford Devon
20 D5 Belsize Herts
35 E3 Belstead Suffk
5 F6 Belstone Devon
57 G5 Belthorn Lancs
23 F2 Beltinge Kent
72 C3 Beltingham Nthumb
52 A5 Beltoft N Linc
41 E5 Belton Leics
42 B5 Belton Lincs
52 A5 Belton N Linc
45 G2 Belton Norfk
42 A2 Belton Rutlnd
21 G3 Belvedere Gt Lon
42 A5 Belvoir Leics
42 A5 Belvoir Castle Leics
9 H2 Bembridge IOW
8 D6 Bemerton Wilts
67 G1 Bempton E R Yk
90 D5 Ben Nevis Highld
58 C4 Ben Rhydding Brad
45 H1 Benacre Suffk
111 b3 Benbecula Airport W Isls
77 F1 Benbuie D & G
90 B3 Benderloch Ag & B
12 C5 Benenden Kent
73 E2 Benfieldside Dur
30 B4 Bengeworth Worcs
35 G4 Benhall Green Suffk
35 F4 Benhall Street Suffk
95 G3 Benholm Abers
59 F5 Beningbrough N York
33 E1 Benington Herts
43 F6 Benington Lincs
54 D4 Benllech IOA
84 B4 Benmore Ag & B
4 D6 Bennacott Cnwll
75 H3 Bennan N Ayrs
52 D3 Benniworth Lincs
12 C6 Benover Kent
19 H5 Benson Oxon
95 G6 Benthoul C Aber
59 F1 Bentley Donc
60 D3 Bentley E R Yk
10 B6 Bentley Hants
35 E3 Bentley Suffk
40 D3 Bentley Warwks
15 F4 Benton Devon
79 F2 Bentpath D & G
15 F4 Bentwichen Devon
19 H1 Bentworth Hants
93 E3 Benvie Angus
7 F5 Benville Dorset
43 E1 Benwick Cambs
40 C1 Beoley Worcs
97 E2 Beoraidbeg Highld
10 B4 Bepton W Susx
33 F2 Berden Essex
5 E4 Bere Alston Devon
5 E3 Bere Ferrers Devon
8 B3 Bere Regis Dorset
24 C5 Berea Pembks
45 F2 Bergh Apton Norfk
19 G6 Berinsfield Oxon
29 E3 Berkeley Gloucs
20 C6 Berkhamsted Herts
18 A2 Berkley Somset
40 D2 Berkswell Solhll
21 F3 Bermondsey Gt Lon
97 F4 Bernera Highld
84 B4 Bernice Ag & B
104 C1 Bernisdale Highld
19 H6 Berrick Prior Oxon
19 H5 Berrick Salome Oxon
110 B2 Berriedale Highld
71 G2 Berrier Cumb
38 C6 Berriew Powys
39 E6 Berrington Shrops
39 F3 Berrington Worcs
39 F3 Berrington Green Worcs
16 D4 Berrow Somset
39 G2 Berrow Green Worcs
5 H3 Berry Pomeroy Devon
101 G4 Berryhillock Moray
101 G5 Berryhillock Moray
15 E5 Berrynarbor Devon
48 C4 Bersham Wrexhm
11 G3 Berwick E Susx
18 D4 Berwick Bassett Wilts
73 F4 Berwick Hill Nthumb
18 C1 Berwick St James Wilts
8 B5 Berwick St John Wilts
8 B6 Berwick St Leonard Wilts
81 F5 Berwick-upon-Tweed Nthumb
42 A4 Bescaby Leics
56 D4 Bescar Lancs
30 A4 Besford Worcs
51 G6 Bessacarr Donc
19 F6 Bessels Leigh Oxon
61 E6 Bessingby E R Yk
45 E5 Bessingham Norfk
44 D2 Besthorpe Norfk
52 A2 Besthorpe Notts
51 F2 Bestwood Village Notts
60 D4 Beswick E R Yk
21 E1 Betchworth Surrey
34 D1 Beth Chatto Garden Essex
53 D3 Bethel Gwynd
54 C3 Bethel IOA
13 D5 Bethersden Kent
55 E3 Bethesda Gwynd
25 E4 Bethesda Pembks
26 C5 Bethlehem Carmth
21 F4 Bethnal Green Gt Lon
49 G4 Betley Staffs
22 B3 Betsham Kent
23 G1 Betteshanger Kent
7 E5 Bettiscombe Dorset
49 E3 Bettisfield Wrexhm
28 B2 Bettws Newpt
37 E2 Bettws Bledrws Cerdgn
38 B5 Bettws Cedewain Powys
36 C2 Bettws Evan Cerdgn
28 B3 Bettws-Newydd Mons
109 F5 Bettyhill Highld
27 E2 Betws Brdgnd
48 A4 Betws Gwerfil Goch Denbgs
55 F2 Betws-y-coed Conwy
55 G4 Betws-yn-Rhos Conwy
36 C2 Beulah Cerdgn
37 H2 Beulah Powys
51 G4 Bevercotes Notts
60 D4 Beverley E R Yk
29 F2 Beverstone Gloucs
71 H6 Bewcastle Cumb
39 G3 Bewdley Worcs
58 C6 Bewerley N York
61 E5 Bewholme E R Yk
12 C3 Bexhill E Susx
21 G3 Bexley Gt Lon
21 G3 Bexleyheath Gt Lon
43 H2 Bexwell Norfk
34 C5 Beyton Suffk
34 C5 Beyton Green Suffk
111 c6 Bhaltos W Isls
111 a1 Bhatarsaigh W Isls
30 C1 Bibury Gloucs
31 G2 Bicester Oxon
40 C2 Bickenhill Solhll
42 D5 Bicker Lincs
57 E3 Bickerstaffe Lancs
59 E5 Bickerton N York
40 A4 Bickford Staffs
15 E4 Bickington Devon
5 H4 Bickington Devon
6 B6 Bickleigh Devon
5 F3 Bickleigh Devon
21 G2 Bickley Gt Lon
67 E3 Bickley N York
49 E4 Bickley Moss Ches
22 C5 Bicknacre Essex
16 C3 Bicknoller Somset
22 D2 Bicknor Kent
49 E1 Bicton Shrops
38 C4 Bicton Shrops
12 B6 Bidborough Kent
12 D5 Biddenden Kent
32 C4 Biddenham Beds
18 B4 Biddestone Wilts
17 E4 Biddisham Somset
31 G4 Biddlesden Bucks
50 A3 Biddulph Staffs
50 A3 Biddulph Moor Staffs
14 D4 Bideford Devon
30 C5 Bidford-on-Avon Warwks
60 B4 Bielby E R Yk
95 G6 Bieldside C Aber
9 G2 Bierley IOW
20 B6 Bierton Bucks
69 E2 Big Balcraig D & G
77 F2 Big Carlae D & G
27 G3 Big Pit Blaenavon Torfn
105 F4 Big Sand Highld
5 G2 Bigbury Devon
5 G2 Bigbury-on-Sea Devon
52 C5 Bigby Lincs
78 D6 Biggar S Lans
50 D2 Biggin Derbys
50 C3 Biggin Derbys
59 F3 Biggin N York
21 G2 Biggin Hill Gt Lon
21 G2 Biggin Hill Airport Gt Lon
32 D3 Biggleswade Beds
79 F1 Bigholms D & G
109 H5 Bighouse Highld
9 H6 Bighton Hants
71 F4 Biglands Cumb
10 C3 Bignor W Susx
70 D1 Bigrigg Cumb
51 F1 Bilborough C Nott
16 B3 Bilbrook Somset
59 F4 Bilbrough N York
110 C4 Bilbster Highld
65 F5 Bildershaw Dur
34 D4 Bildeston Suffk
22 B4 Billericay Essex
41 H3 Billesdon Leics
30 C5 Billesley Warwks
42 D5 Billingborough Lincs
57 E3 Billinge St Hel
44 D4 Billingford Norfk
35 E6 Billingford Norfk
66 B5 Billingham S on T
52 D1 Billinghay Lincs
59 E1 Billingley Barns
10 D4 Billingshurst W Susx
39 G4 Billingsley Shrops
32 B1 Billington Beds
57 G6 Billington Lancs
45 G3 Billockby Norfk
73 F1 Billy Row Dur
57 E6 Bilsborrow Lancs
53 F3 Bilsby Lincs
10 C2 Bilsham W Susx
13 E5 Bilsington Kent
51 G3 Bilsthorpe Notts
86 C3 Bilston Mdloth
40 B3 Bilston Wolves
41 E4 Bilstone Leics
61 E3 Bilton E R Yk
59 F5 Bilton N York
58 D5 Bilton N York
41 F1 Bilton Warwks
52 D4 Binbrook Lincs
7 G4 Bincombe Dorset
17 G4 Binegar Somset
20 B3 Binfield Br For
20 B3 Binfield Heath Oxon
72 D4 Bingfield Nthumb
51 G1 Bingham Notts
8 A3 Bingham's Melcombe Dorset
58 C4 Bingley Brad
44 D5 Binham Norfk
41 E2 Binley Covtry
19 F2 Binley Hants
8 B2 Binnegar Dorset
85 G3 Binniehill Falk
101 F5 Binns Farm Moray
10 C6 Binscombe Surrey
9 G3 Binstead IOW
10 B6 Binsted Hants
10 C3 Binsted W Susx
30 C5 Binton Warwks
44 D4 Bintree Norfk
34 C1 Birch Essex
40 C6 Birch Cross Staffs
34 C1 Birch Green Essex
50 B5 Birch Vale Derbys
16 D1 Birch Wood Somset
44 B5 Bircham Newton Norfk
44 B5 Bircham Tofts Norfk
33 G1 Birchanger Essex
39 E3 Bircher Herefs
27 G1 Birchgrove Cardif
11 G5 Birchgrove E Susx
26 C3 Birchgrove Swans
23 G2 Birchington Kent
40 D3 Birchley Heath Warwks
50 D3 Birchover Derbys
57 F2 Birchwood Warrtn
51 G5 Bircotes Notts

34 A3 **Birdbrook** Essex
66 B1 **Birdforth** N York
10 B2 **Birdham** W Susx
31 E6 **Birdingbury** Warwks
29 G4 **Birdlip** Gloucs
58 D1 **Birds Edge** Kirk
22 B6 **Birds Green** Essex
60 C6 **Birdsall** N York
39 G4 **Birdsgreen** Shrops
7 E5 **Birdsmoorgate** Dorset
51 E6 **Birdwell** Barns
80 D4 **Birgham** Border
107 F5 **Birichin** Highld
65 G3 **Birkby** N York
56 D4 **Birkdale** Sefton
102 B5 **Birkenbog** Abers
56 D2 **Birkenhead** Wirral
102 C4 **Birkenhills** Abers
58 D3 **Birkenshaw** Kirk
94 C5 **Birkhall** Abers
93 F3 **Birkhill** Angus
79 E4 **Birkhill** D & G
59 F3 **Birkin** N York
39 E2 **Birley** Herefs
51 E5 **Birley Carr** Sheff
22 B2 **Birling** Kent
30 B4 **Birlingham** Worcs
40 C2 **Birmingham** Birm
40 C2 Birmingham Airport Solhll
92 C3 **Birnam** P & K
103 E3 **Birness** Abers
95 E5 **Birse** Abers
95 E5 **Birsemore** Abers
58 D3 **Birstall** Kirk
41 G4 **Birstall** Leics
58 D5 **Birstwith** N York
73 F2 **Birtley** Gatesd
38 D3 **Birtley** Herefs
72 C4 **Birtley** Nthumb
29 E6 **Birts Street** Worcs
42 B2 **Bisbrooke** Rutlnd
52 D4 **Biscathorpe** Lincs
15 F3 **Bish Mill** Devon
20 B4 **Bisham** W & M
30 B5 **Bishampton** Worcs
65 F6 **Bishop Auckland** Dur
60 D4 **Bishop Burton** E R Yk
65 G6 **Bishop Middleham** Dur
59 E6 **Bishop Monkton** N York
52 C4 **Bishop Norton** Lincs
17 G5 **Bishop Sutton** BaNES
58 D6 **Bishop Thornton** N York
60 B5 **Bishop Wilton** E R Yk
38 D5 **Bishop's Castle** Shrops
17 H1 **Bishop's Caundle** Dorset
29 G5 **Bishop's Cleeve** Gloucs
39 F1 **Bishop's Frome** Herefs
33 H1 **Bishop's Green** Essex
31 E5 **Bishop's Itchington** Warwks
29 F5 **Bishop's Norton** Gloucs
15 G3 **Bishop's Nympton** Devon
49 G2 **Bishop's Offley** Staffs
33 F1 **Bishop's Stortford** Herts
9 H6 **Bishop's Sutton** Hants
30 D6 **Bishop's Tachbrook** Warwks
15 E4 **Bishop's Tawton** Devon
9 G5 **Bishop's Waltham** Hants
49 H1 **Bishop's Wood** Staffs
52 C4 **Bishopbridge** Lincs
85 E3 **Bishopbriggs** E Duns
101 E5 **Bishopmill** Moray
18 C3 **Bishops Cannings** Wilts
16 D2 **Bishops Hull** Somset
16 D2 **Bishops Lydeard** Somset
23 F1 **Bishopsbourne** Kent
6 A3 **Bishopsteignton** Devon
9 F5 **Bishopstoke** Hants
26 B2 **Bishopston** Swans
20 B6 **Bishopstone** Bucks
11 G2 **Bishopstone** E Susx
38 D1 **Bishopstone** Herefs
23 G2 **Bishopstone** Kent
19 E5 **Bishopstone** Swindn
8 C5 **Bishopstone** Wilts
18 B1 **Bishopstrow** Wilts
6 D6 **Bishopswood** Somset
17 G5 **Bishopsworth** Bristl
59 G4 **Bishopthorpe** York
65 G5 **Bishopton** Darltn
84 D3 **Bishopton** Rens
28 B2 **Bishton** Newpt
40 B5 **Bishton** Staffs
29 F3 **Bisley** Gloucs
20 C2 **Bisley** Surrey
2 D3 **Bissoe** Cnwll
8 D3 **Bisterne** Hants
42 C5 **Bitchfield** Lincs
15 E5 **Bittadon** Devon
5 G3 **Bittaford** Devon
39 E4 **Bitterley** Shrops
9 F4 **Bitterne** C Sotn
41 F2 **Bitteswell** Leics
17 G5 **Bitton** S Glos
20 A4 **Bix** Oxon
41 F3 **Blaby** Leics
30 D1 **Black Bourton** Oxon
73 F3 **Black Callerton** N u Ty
91 E4 **Black Corries** Highld
90 B3 **Black Crofts** Ag & B
15 G2 **Black Dog** Devon
34 B1 **Black Notley** Essex
26 C2 **Black Pill** Swans
45 H1 **Black Street** Suffk
14 D2 **Black Torrington** Devon
80 D5 **Blackadder** Border
5 H2 **Blackawton** Devon
6 C6 **Blackborough** Devon
43 H3 **Blackborough End** Norfk
11 H4 **Blackboys** E Susx
51 E2 **Blackbrook** Derbys
49 G3 **Blackbrook** Staffs
102 D1 **Blackburn** Abers
57 F5 **Blackburn** Bl w D
86 A3 **Blackburn** W Loth
77 E2 **Blackcraig** E Ayrs
103 E1 **Blackdog** Abers
7 E5 **Blackdown** Dorset
40 B3 **Blackenall Heath** Wsall
51 E6 **Blacker Hill** Barns
21 G3 **Blackfen** Gt Lon
9 F3 **Blackfield** Hants
85 G6 **Blackford** P & K
17 E4 **Blackford** Somset
17 G2 **Blackford** Somset
41 E5 **Blackfordby** Leics
86 C3 **Blackhall** C Edin
73 H1 **Blackhall Colliery** Dur
79 G6 **Blackhaugh** Border
21 F3 **Blackheath** Gt Lon
40 B2 **Blackheath** Sandw
35 G6 **Blackheath** Suffk
10 D6 **Blackheath** Surrey
103 F3 **Blackhill** Abers
103 F5 **Blackhill** Abers
103 F4 **Blackhill** Abers
73 E2 **Blackhill** Dur
103 E4 **Blackhill of Clackriach** Abers
6 B5 **Blackhorse** Devon
78 D3 **Blacklaw** D & G
57 H3 **Blackley** Manch
94 B2 **Blacklunans** P & K
28 C6 **Blackmarstone** Herefs
27 E2 **Blackmill** Brdgnd
10 B5 **Blackmoor** Hants
17 F5 **Blackmoor** N Som
58 C2 **Blackmoorfoot** Kirk
22 B5 **Blackmore** Essex
34 B2 **Blackmore End** Essex
86 B4 **Blackness** Falk
10 B6 **Blacknest** Hants
57 H6 **Blacko** Lancs
56 C6 **Blackpool** Bpool
6 A1 **Blackpool** Devon
56 D5 Blackpool Airport Lancs
85 G2 **Blackridge** W Loth
57 F4 **Blackrod** Bolton
101 E3 **Blacksboat** Moray
70 D5 **Blackshaw** D & G
58 B3 **Blackshaw Head** Calder
57 G4 **Blacksnape** Bl w D
11 E4 **Blackstone** W Susx
31 G2 **Blackthorn** Oxon
34 C5 **Blackthorpe** Suffk
60 C3 **Blacktoft** E R Yk
95 G6 **Blacktop** C Aber
50 D2 **Blackwall** Derbys
2 D4 **Blackwater** Cnwll
20 B2 **Blackwater** Hants
9 G2 **Blackwater** IOW
16 D1 **Blackwater** Somset
75 G4 **Blackwaterfoot** N Ayrs
71 G4 **Blackwell** Cumb
50 C4 **Blackwell** Derbys
51 E3 **Blackwell** Derbys
30 D4 **Blackwell** Warwks
40 B1 **Blackwell** Worcs
27 G3 **Blackwood** Caerph
78 C2 **Blackwood** D & G
77 G5 **Blackwood** S Lans
48 D6 **Blacon** Ches
69 E3 **Bladnoch** D & G
31 E2 **Bladon** Oxon
25 G5 **Blaen-y-Coed** Carmth
27 E3 **Blaen-y-cwm** Rhondd
36 B2 **Blaenannerch** Cerdgn
47 F5 **Blaenau Ffestiniog** Gwynd
27 H3 **Blaenavon** Torfn
25 F6 **Blaenffos** Pembks
27 E2 **Blaengarw** Brdgnd
27 E3 **Blaengwrach** Neath
27 E2 **Blaengwynfi** Neath
37 E3 **Blaenpennal** Cerdgn
37 E4 **Blaenplwyf** Cerdgn
36 B2 **Blaenporth** Cerdgn
27 E3 **Blaenrhondda** Rhondd
25 F5 **Blaenwaun** Carmth
17 F5 **Blagdon** N Som
16 D1 **Blagdon** Somset
6 A2 **Blagdon** Torbay
16 D1 **Blagdon Hill** Somset
90 C6 **Blaich** Highld
89 G5 **Blain** Highld
27 G3 **Blaina** Blae G
92 B5 **Blair Atholl** P & K
85 F5 **Blair Drummond** Stirlg
83 G3 **Blair's Ferry** Ag & B
92 D4 **Blairgowrie** P & K
86 A5 **Blairingone** P & K
85 G4 **Blairlogie** Stirlg
84 B4 **Blairmore** Ag & B
108 B5 **Blairmore** Highld
101 E1 **Blairnamarrow** Moray
29 E4 **Blaisdon** Gloucs
34 A1 **Blake End** Essex
39 G4 **Blakebrook** Worcs
39 H4 **Blakedown** Worcs
49 E6 **Blakemere** Ches
28 B6 **Blakemere** Herefs
29 E3 **Blakeney** Gloucs
44 D6 **Blakeney** Norfk
49 G4 **Blakenhall** Ches
40 A3 **Blakenhall** Wolves
31 G5 **Blakesley** Nhants
72 D2 **Blanchland** Nthumb
50 B5 **Bland Hill** N York
8 B4 **Blandford Forum** Dorset
8 B4 **Blandford St Mary** Dorset
85 E3 **Blanefield** Stirlg
52 C2 **Blankney** Lincs
85 F2 **Blantyre** S Lans
90 C5 **Blar a' Chaorainn** Highld
98 D2 **Blargie** Highld
90 C5 **Blarmachfoldach** Highld
42 A2 **Blaston** Leics
42 B2 **Blatherwycke** Nhants
62 C4 **Blawith** Cumb
69 G5 **Blawquhairn** D & G
35 F4 **Blaxhall** Suffk
51 G6 **Blaxton** Donc
73 F3 **Blaydon** Gatesd
17 F3 **Bleadney** Somset
17 E4 **Bleadon** N Som
23 F2 **Blean** Kent
51 H2 **Bleasby** Notts
63 F1 **Bleasdale** Lancs
93 F1 **Blebocraigs** Fife
38 C3 **Bleddfa** Powys
30 D2 **Bledington** Gloucs
20 B5 **Bledlow** Bucks
20 B5 **Bledlow Ridge** Bucks
87 E2 **Blegbie** E Loth
64 A6 **Blencarn** Cumb
71 E4 **Blencogo** Cumb
10 A3 **Blendworth** Hants
71 E3 **Blennerhasset** Cumb
31 F2 **Bletchingdon** Oxon
21 F1 **Bletchingley** Surrey
32 B2 **Bletchley** M Keyn
49 F3 **Bletchley** Shrops
25 E4 **Bletherston** Pembks
32 C4 **Bletsoe** Beds
19 G5 **Blewbury** Oxon
45 E5 **Blickling** Norfk
51 G2 **Blidworth** Notts
51 G2 **Blidworth Bottoms** Notts
71 E3 **Blindcrake** Cumb
11 F6 **Blindley Heath** Surrey
4 B4 **Blisland** Cnwll
39 G3 **Bliss Gate** Worcs
8 D4 **Blissford** Hants
31 H5 **Blisworth** Nhants
40 C5 **Blithbury** Staffs
34 D6 **Blo Norton** Norfk
30 C3 **Blockley** Gloucs
45 F3 **Blofield** Norfk
80 B3 **Bloomfield** Border
49 G3 **Blore** Staffs
50 C2 **Blore** Staffs
31 E3 **Bloxham** Oxon
52 C1 **Bloxholm** Lincs
40 B3 **Bloxwich** Wsall
8 B3 **Bloxworth** Dorset
58 C5 **Blubberhouses** N York
16 B3 **Blue Anchor** Somset
22 C2 **Blue Bell Hill** Kent
50 C5 Blue John Cavern Derbys
56 C3 **Blundellsands** Sefton
45 H2 **Blundeston** Suffk
32 D4 **Blunham** Beds
18 D5 **Blunsdon St Andrew** Swindn
40 A1 **Bluntington** Worcs
33 E6 **Bluntisham** Cambs
52 B4 **Blyborough** Lincs
35 G6 **Blyford** Suffk
49 G1 **Blymhill** Staffs
51 G5 **Blyth** Notts
73 G4 **Blyth** Nthumb
86 B1 **Blyth Bridge** Border
35 G6 **Blythburgh** Suffk
80 B5 **Blythe** Border
52 B4 **Blyton** Lincs
86 A4 **Bo'ness** Falk
93 G1 **Boarhills** Fife
9 G4 **Boarhunt** Hants
31 G2 **Boarstall** Bucks
99 G4 **Boat of Garten** Highld
107 E3 **Boath** Highld
22 D2 **Bobbing** Kent
39 G5 **Bobbington** Staffs
34 B1 **Bocking** Essex
34 B2 **Bocking Churchstreet** Essex
103 F4 **Boddam** Abers
111 I1 **Boddam** Shet
29 F5 **Boddington** Gloucs
54 B4 **Bodedern** IOA
55 H4 **Bodelwyddan** Denbgs
39 E1 **Bodenham** Herefs
8 D5 **Bodenham** Wilts
39 E1 **Bodenham Moor** Herefs
54 C5 **Bodewryd** IOA
48 B6 **Bodfari** Denbgs
54 C4 **Bodffordd** IOA
46 C5 **Bodfuan** Gwynd
45 E5 **Bodham** Norfk
12 C4 **Bodiam** E Susx
12 C4 Bodiam Castle E Susx
31 F4 **Bodicote** Oxon
4 C2 **Bodinnick** Cnwll
12 B3 **Bodle Street Green** E Susx
3 G5 **Bodmin** Cnwll
4 C4 **Bodmin Moor** Cnwll
55 F3 Bodnant Garden Conwy
13 F6 **Bodsham Green** Kent
3 F5 **Bodwen** Cnwll
107 E1 **Bogallan** Highld
103 F3 **Bogbrae** Abers
86 C3 **Boghall** Mdloth
86 A3 **Boghall** W Loth
77 G5 **Boghead** S Lans
101 F5 **Boghead Farm** Moray
101 F5 **Bogmoor** Moray
95 E3 **Bogmuir** Abers
102 B4 **Bogniebrae** Abers
10 C2 **Bognor Regis** W Susx
99 G5 **Bogroy** Highld
69 G5 **Bogue** D & G
3 E3 **Bohortha** Cnwll
98 B1 **Bohuntine** Highld
65 F5 **Bolam** Dur
5 G1 **Bolberry** Devon
40 C3 **Boldmere** Birm
9 E3 **Boldre** Hants
65 E4 **Boldron** Dur
52 A4 **Bole** Notts
50 D2 **Bolehill** Derbys
16 B1 **Bolham** Devon
6 C6 **Bolham Water** Devon
2 D4 **Bolingey** Cnwll
50 B4 **Bollington** Ches
11 F4 **Bolney** W Susx
32 C4 **Bolnhurst** Beds
93 H4 **Bolshan** Angus
51 F4 **Bolsover** Derbys
50 D6 **Bolsterstone** Sheff
66 B2 **Boltby** N York
101 F1 **Boltenstone** Abers
57 G3 **Bolton** Bolton
64 A5 **Bolton** Cumb
87 E3 **Bolton** E Loth
60 B5 **Bolton** E R Yk
81 F2 **Bolton** Nthumb
58 C5 **Bolton Abbey** N York
63 G1 **Bolton by Bowland** Lancs
63 E3 **Bolton le Sands** Lancs
71 E4 **Bolton Low Houses** Cumb
59 F4 **Bolton Percy** N York
51 F6 **Bolton Upon Dearne** Barns
65 F3 **Bolton-on-Swale** N York
71 G6 **Boltonfellend** Cumb
71 E3 **Boltongate** Cumb
4 C4 **Bolventor** Cnwll
49 E2 **Bomere Heath** Shrops
107 E5 **Bonar Bridge** Highld
90 B2 **Bonawe** Ag & B
60 D2 **Bonby** N Linc
25 F6 **Boncath** Pembks
80 B2 **Bonchester Bridge** Border
15 F2 **Bondleigh** Devon
63 E1 **Bonds** Lancs
84 D3 **Bonhill** W Duns
39 G6 **Boningale** Shrops
80 C2 **Bonjedward** Border
85 G2 **Bonkle** N Lans
93 G3 **Bonnington** Angus
13 E5 **Bonnington** Kent
86 D6 **Bonnybank** Fife
85 G3 **Bonnybridge** Falk
102 D4 **Bonnykelly** Abers
86 D3 **Bonnyrigg** Mdloth
93 F3 **Bonnyton** Angus
50 D3 **Bonsall** Derbys
71 E6 **Bonshaw Tower** D & G
47 G2 **Bont-Dolgadfan** Powys
37 E3 **Bontnewydd** Cerdgn
54 D2 **Bontnewydd** Gwynd
48 B5 **Bontuchel** Denbgs
16 C6 **Bonvilston** V Glam
15 E4 **Boode** Devon
6 A1 **Boohay** Devon
20 B4 **Booker** Bucks
49 E2 **Booley** Shrops
80 B4 **Boon** Border
66 C5 **Boosbeck** R & Cl
34 C2 **Boose's Green** Essex
62 B5 **Boot** Cumb
58 B3 **Booth** Calder
60 B3 **Booth** E R Yk
52 C2 **Boothby Graffoe** Lincs
42 B5 **Boothby Pagnell** Lincs
57 G3 **Boothstown** Salfd
62 B4 **Bootle** Cumb
56 D2 **Bootle** Sefton
39 F3 **Boraston** Shrops
6 c2 **Bordeaux** Guern
22 D2 **Borden** Kent
72 A5 **Border Forest Park**
10 B5 **Bordon** Hants
22 C6 **Boreham** Essex
18 B1 **Boreham** Wilts
12 B3 **Boreham Street** E Susx
21 E5 **Borehamwood** Herts
79 E2 **Boreland** D & G
104 A2 **Boreraig** Highld
111 d7 **Borgh** W Isls
111 a1 **Borgh** W Isls
109 F5 **Borgie** Highld
69 G2 **Borgue** D & G
110 B2 **Borgue** Highld
34 C3 **Borley** Essex
104 C3 **Borneskitaig** Highld
69 G2 **Borness** D & G
22 B1 **Borough Green** Kent
59 E6 **Boroughbridge** N York
41 E6 **Borrowash** Derbys
65 H2 **Borrowby** N York
86 A4 **Borrowstoun** Falk
22 C2 **Borstal** Medway
37 E5 **Borth** Cerdgn
47 E5 **Borth-y-Gest** Gwynd
79 G4 **Borthwickbrae** Border
79 G4 **Borthwickshiels** Border
104 C1 **Borve** Highld
111 d7 **Borve** W Isls
111 a1 **Borve** W Isls
111 c5 **Borve** W Isls
63 E3 **Borwick** Lancs
39 F1 **Bosbury** Herefs
4 B5 **Boscastle** Cnwll
8 D3 **Boscombe** Bmouth
18 D1 **Boscombe** Wilts
10 B3 **Bosham** W Susx
24 D2 **Bosherston** Pembks
50 A3 **Bosley** Ches
3 E5 **Bosoughan** Cnwll
60 B5 **Bossall** N York
4 B5 **Bossiney** Cnwll
13 F6 **Bossingham** Kent
16 A4 **Bossington** Somset
49 F6 **Bostock Green** Ches
43 E6 **Boston** Lincs
59 E4 **Boston Spa** Leeds
3 F3 **Boswinger** Cnwll
2 A3 **Botallack** Cnwll
93 G1 Botanic Gardens Fife
21 F5 **Botany Bay** Gt Lon
34 D6 **Botesdale** Suffk
73 F5 **Bothal** Nthumb
19 G4 **Bothampstead** W Berk
51 G4 **Bothamsall** Notts
71 E3 **Bothel** Cumb
7 F4 **Bothenhampton** Dorset
85 F2 **Bothwell** S Lans
20 C5 **Botley** Bucks
9 G4 **Botley** Hants
31 F1 **Botley** Oxon
31 H3 **Botolph Claydon** Bucks
11 E3 **Botolphs** W Susx
42 A5 **Bottesford** Leics
52 B5 **Bottesford** N Linc
33 G4 **Bottisham** Cambs
93 F2 **Bottomcraig** Fife
58 A2 **Bottoms** Calder
5 E3 **Botusfleming** Cnwll
46 B4 **Botwnnog** Gwynd
11 G6 **Bough Beech** Kent
27 G6 **Boughrood** Powys
31 H6 **Boughton** Nhants
44 A2 **Boughton** Norfk
51 G3 **Boughton** Notts
13 E6 **Boughton Aluph** Kent
22 C1 **Boughton Green** Kent
22 D1 **Boughton Malherbe** Kent
22 C1 **Boughton Monchelsea** Kent
23 E2 **Boughton Street** Kent
39 E4 **Bouldon** Shrops
81 H2 **Boulmer** Nthumb
52 B2 **Boultham** Lincs
33 E4 **Bourn** Cambs
42 C4 **Bourne** Lincs
32 B3 **Bourne End** Beds
20 C4 **Bourne End** Bucks
20 D5 **Bourne End** Herts
21 G4 **Bournebridge** Essex
40 B2 **Bournebrook** Birm
8 D3 **Bournemouth** Bmouth
8 D3 Bournemouth Airport Dorset
22 D4 **Bournes Green** Sthend
40 B1 **Bournheath** Worcs
40 B2 **Bournville** Birm
8 A6 **Bourton** Dorset
19 E5 **Bourton** Oxon
39 F5 **Bourton** Shrops
18 C3 **Bourton** Wilts
41 E1 **Bourton on Dunsmore** Warwks
30 C3 **Bourton-on-the-Hill** Gloucs
30 C2 **Bourton-on-the-Water** Gloucs
88 D5 **Bousd** Ag & B
62 D4 **Bouth** Cumb
65 E1 **Bouthwaite** N York
91 F2 **Bovain** Stirlg
8 C5 **Boveridge** Dorset
5 H4 **Bovey Tracey** Devon
20 D5 **Bovingdon** Herts
8 B2 Bovington Tank Museum Dorset
15 F2 **Bow** Devon
21 F4 **Bow** Gt Lon
111 h1 **Bow** Ork
32 B2 **Bow Brickhill** M Keyn
93 E1 **Bow of Fife** Fife
37 E5 **Bow Street** Cerdgn
29 F3 **Bowbridge** Gloucs
73 G1 **Bowburn** Dur
9 F2 **Bowcombe** IOW
6 C4 **Bowd** Devon
80 B3 **Bowden** Border
18 B3 **Bowden Hill** Wilts
57 G2 **Bowdon** Traffd
110 C5 **Bower** Highld
59 E3 **Bower's Row** Leeds
8 C5 **Bowerchalke** Wilts
110 C5 **Bowermadden** Highld
49 G3 **Bowers** Staffs
22 C4 **Bowers Gifford** Essex
86 B5 **Bowershall** Fife
64 D4 **Bowes** Dur
63 E1 **Bowgreave** Lancs
70 D5 **Bowhouse** D & G
79 G6 **Bowland** Border
39 E2 **Bowley** Herefs
10 C5 **Bowlhead Green** Surrey
58 C3 **Bowling** Brad
84 D3 **Bowling** W Duns
62 C5 **Bowmanstead** Cumb
82 B2 **Bowmore** Ag & B
71 E5 **Bowness-on-Solway** Cumb
62 D5 **Bowness-on-Windermere** Cumb
93 G4 **Bowriefauld** Angus
81 F4 **Bowsden** Nthumb
29 F3 **Box** Gloucs
18 B3 **Box** Wilts
34 C3 **Boxford** Suffk
19 F4 **Boxford** W Berk
10 C3 **Boxgrove** W Susx
22 C2 **Boxley** Kent
20 D5 **Boxmoor** Herts
34 D2 **Boxted** Essex
34 B4 **Boxted** Suffk
34 D2 **Boxted Cross** Essex
34 D2 **Boxted Heath** Essex
33 E5 **Boxworth** Cambs
23 G2 **Boyden Gate** Kent
40 C6 **Boylestone** Derbys
102 C5 **Boyndie** Abers
103 E5 **Boyndlie** Abers
61 E6 **Boynton** E R Yk
93 H4 **Boysack** Angus
4 D6 **Boyton** Cnwll
35 G3 **Boyton** Suffk
18 B1 **Boyton** Wilts
22 B6 **Boyton Cross** Essex
34 B3 **Boyton End** Suffk
32 B4 **Bozeat** Nhants
13 F6 **Brabourne** Kent
13 F5 **Brabourne Lees** Kent
110 D6 **Brabstermire** Highld
96 B6 **Bracadale** Highld
42 C3 **Braceborough** Lincs
52 C2 **Bracebridge Heath** Lincs
52 B2 **Bracebridge Low Fields** Lincs
42 C5 **Braceby** Lincs
63 H1 **Bracewell** Lancs
51 E3 **Brackenfield** Derbys
85 F3 **Brackenhirst** N Lans
98 A1 **Brackletter** Highld
31 G4 **Brackley** Nhants
20 C2 **Bracknell** Br For
85 G6 **Braco** P & K
101 G4 **Bracobrae** Moray
45 E2 **Bracon Ash** Norfk
97 E2 **Bracora** Highld
97 E2 **Bracorina** Highld
50 D2 **Bradbourne** Derbys
65 G6 **Bradbury** Dur
31 G4 **Bradden** Nhants
20 B5 **Bradenham** Bucks
18 C4 **Bradenstoke** Wilts
6 C6 **Bradfield** Devon
35 E2 **Bradfield** Essex
45 F5 **Bradfield** Norfk
50 D5 **Bradfield** Sheff
19 G4 **Bradfield** W Berk
34 C4 **Bradfield Combust** Suffk
49 F5 **Bradfield Green** Ches
35 E2 **Bradfield Heath** Essex
34 C4 **Bradfield St Clare** Suffk
34 C4 **Bradfield St George** Suffk
58 C3 **Bradford** Brad
14 D2 **Bradford** Devon
17 G1 **Bradford Abbas** Dorset
18 B3 **Bradford Leigh** Wilts
7 G5 **Bradford Peverell** Dorset
18 B3 **Bradford-on-Avon** Wilts
16 D2 **Bradford-on-Tone** Somset
15 E4 **Bradiford** Devon
9 H2 **Brading** IOW
50 D2 **Bradley** Derbys
19 H1 **Bradley** Hants
53 E5 **Bradley** NE Lin
49 H1 **Bradley** Staffs
40 B3 **Bradley** Wolves
30 B6 **Bradley** Worcs
30 B6 **Bradley Green** Worcs
50 B1 **Bradley in the Moors** Staffs
28 D1 **Bradley Stoke** S Glos
41 G6 **Bradmore** Notts
6 B5 **Bradninch** Devon
50 B2 **Bradnop** Staffs
7 F5 **Bradpole** Dorset
58 C3 **Bradshaw** Calder
4 D5 **Bradstone** Devon
49 G5 **Bradwall Green** Ches
50 C4 **Bradwell** Derbys
34 B1 **Bradwell** Essex
32 A3 **Bradwell** M Keyn
45 H3 **Bradwell** Norfk
23 E6 **Bradwell Waterside** Essex
23 E5 **Bradwell-on-Sea** Essex
14 C3 **Bradworthy** Devon
107 F2 **Brae** Highld

111 I3 Brae Shet
98 B2 Brae Roy Lodge Highld
85 G3 Braeface Falk
95 F2 Braehead Angus
69 E3 Braehead D & G
77 H6 Braehead S Lans
94 B5 Braemar Abers
110 B2 Braemore Highld
106 B4 Braemore Highld
93 E5 Braes of Coul Angus
101 F5 Braes of Enzie Moray
84 B3 Braeside Inver
111 j3 Braeswick Ork
83 G6 Braevallich Ag & B
65 G5 Brafferton Darltn
66 A1 Brafferton N York
32 A4 Brafield-on-the-Green Nhants
111 d7 Bragar W Isls
33 E1 Bragbury End Herts
77 G6 Braidwood S Lans
50 D1 Brailsford Derbys
34 B1 Braintree Essex
35 E5 Braiseworth Suffk
9 F5 Braishfield Hants
71 E2 Braithwaite Cumb
51 F6 Braithwell Donc
11 E3 Bramber W Susx
41 E1 Bramcote Warwks
9 H6 Bramdean Hants
45 F3 Bramerton Norfk
21 F6 Bramfield Herts
35 G5 Bramfield Suffk
35 E3 Bramford Suffk
50 A5 Bramhall Stockp
59 E4 Bramham Leeds
58 D4 Bramhope Leeds
19 H3 Bramley Hants
58 D3 Bramley Leeds
51 F5 Bramley Rothm
10 D6 Bramley Surrey
19 H3 Bramley Corner Hants
23 G1 Bramling Kent
6 B5 Brampford Speke Devon
32 D5 Brampton Cambs
71 H5 Brampton Cumb
64 B5 Brampton Cumb
52 A3 Brampton Lincs
45 E4 Brampton Norfk
51 E6 Brampton Rothm
35 G6 Brampton Suffk
28 D5 Brampton Abbotts Herefs
42 A1 Brampton Ash Nhants
38 D3 Brampton Bryan Herefs
51 F5 Brampton-en-le-Morthen Rothm
40 B6 Bramshall Staffs
9 E5 Bramshaw Hants
10 B5 Bramshott Hants
17 F2 Bramwell Somset
33 H2 Bran End Essex
89 F5 Branault Highld
44 B6 Brancaster Norfk
44 B6 Brancaster Staithe Norfk
73 F1 Brancepeth Dur
100 D4 Branchill Moray
101 E6 Branderburgh Moray
61 E4 Brandesburton E R Yk
35 F4 Brandeston Suffk
45 E4 Brandiston Norfk
73 F1 Brandon Dur
42 B6 Brandon Lincs
44 B1 Brandon Suffk
41 E1 Brandon Warwks
44 D3 Brandon Parva Norfk
66 C1 Brandsby N York
52 C5 Brandy Wharf Lincs
8 C3 Branksome Poole
8 C3 Branksome Park Poole
19 F1 Bransbury Hants
52 B3 Bransby Lincs
6 D4 Branscombe Devon
39 G2 Bransford Worcs
8 D3 Bransgore Hants
61 E3 Bransholme C KuH
39 F3 Bransley Shrops
42 A5 Branston Leics
52 C2 Branston Lincs
40 D5 Branston Staffs
52 C2 Branston Booths Lincs
9 G2 Branstone IOW
52 B1 Brant Broughton Lincs
35 E2 Brantham Suffk
70 D2 Branthwaite Cumb
71 F3 Branthwaite Cumb
60 D3 Brantingham E R Yk
51 G6 Branton Donc
81 F2 Branton Nthumb
59 E6 Branton Green N York
81 E4 Branxton Nthumb
50 D2 Brassington Derbys
21 G1 Brasted Kent
21 G1 Brasted Chart Kent
95 F5 Brathens Abers
53 F2 Bratoft Lincs
52 B3 Brattleby Lincs
18 B2 Bratton Wilts
5 E6 Bratton Clovelly Devon
15 F4 Bratton Fleming Devon
17 G2 Bratton Seymour Somset
33 F2 Braughing Herts
31 F6 Braunston Nhants
42 A3 Braunston Rutlnd
41 F4 Braunstone Leics
14 D4 Braunton Devon
66 D1 Brawby N York
109 G5 Brawl Highld
20 C3 Bray W & M
4 D4 Bray Shop Cnwll
41 H2 Braybrooke Nhants
15 F4 Brayford Devon
58 D5 Braythorn N York
59 G3 Brayton N York
20 C3 Braywick W & M
32 D1 Breachwood Green Herts
51 E1 Breadsall Derbys
29 E3 Breadstone Gloucs
2 C2 Breage Cnwll
106 D1 Breakachy Highld
106 D5 Brealangwell Lodge Highld
28 D3 Bream Gloucs
8 D5 Breamore Hants
16 D4 Brean Somset
111 b6 Breanais W Isls
58 D5 Brearton N York
111 c6 Breascleit W Isls
111 c6 Breasclete W Isls
41 F6 Breaston Derbys
26 B5 Brechfa Carmth
95 E2 Brechin Angus
44 C2 Breckles Norfk
78 B2 Breckonside D & G
27 F5 Brecon Powys
27 F5 Brecon Beacons National Park
50 A5 Bredbury Stockp
12 D4 Brede E Susx
39 F2 Bredenbury Herefs
35 F4 Bredfield Suffk
22 D2 Bredgar Kent
22 C2 Bredhurst Kent
29 G6 Bredon Worcs
29 F6 Bredon's Hardwick Worcs
29 G6 Bredon's Norton Worcs
38 D1 Bredwardine Herefs
41 E5 Breedon on the Hill Leics
85 H2 Breich W Loth
57 G3 Breightmet Bolton
60 B3 Breighton E R Yk
28 C6 Breinton Herefs
18 C4 Bremhill Wilts
12 B6 Brenchley Kent
15 G5 Brendon Devon
83 F4 Brenfield Ag & B
111 b6 Brenish W Isls
34 C3 Brent Eleigh Suffk
17 E4 Brent Knoll Somset
5 G3 Brent Mill Devon
33 F2 Brent Pelham Herts
21 E3 Brentford Gt Lon
42 A4 Brentingby Leics
22 B4 Brentwood Essex
13 E4 Brenzett Kent
13 E5 Brenzett Green Kent
40 B5 Brereton Staffs
49 G5 Brereton Green Ches
34 D6 Bressingham Norfk
40 D5 Bretby Derbys
41 E1 Bretford Warwks
30 C4 Bretforton Worcs
57 E4 Bretherton Lancs
111 I2 Brettabister Shet
44 C1 Brettenham Norfk
34 C4 Brettenham Suffk
48 D5 Bretton Flints
40 A4 Brewood Staffs
8 A3 Briantspuddle Dorset
50 D4 Brick Houses Sheff
21 F6 Brickendon Herts
20 D5 Bricket Wood Herts
29 G6 Bricklehampton Worcs
116 d5 Bride IOM
71 E3 Bridekirk Cumb
5 F5 Bridestowe Devon
102 B3 Brideswell Abers
5 H5 Bridford Devon
2 D4 Bridge Cnwll
23 F1 Bridge Kent
65 G1 Bridge Hewick N York
102 B2 Bridge of Alford Abers
85 G5 Bridge of Allan Stirlg
101 E3 Bridge of Avon Moray
100 D2 Bridge of Avon Moray
91 G3 Bridge of Balgie P & K
94 B2 Bridge of Brewlands Angus
100 D2 Bridge of Brown Highld
92 D4 Bridge of Cally P & K
95 E5 Bridge of Canny Abers
93 E4 Bridge of Craigisla Angus
70 B5 Bridge of Dee D & G
103 E1 Bridge of Don C Aber
100 C3 Bridge of Dulsie Highld
95 E4 Bridge of Dye Abers
92 D1 Bridge of Earn P & K
91 F4 Bridge of Ericht P & K
95 F5 Bridge of Feugh Abers
110 A5 Bridge of Forss Highld
94 C5 Bridge of Gairn Abers
91 F4 Bridge of Gaur P & K
102 B4 Bridge of Marnoch Abers
91 E3 Bridge of Orchy Ag & B
92 B5 Bridge of Tilt P & K
101 F5 Bridge of Tynet Moray
111 k2 Bridge of Walls Shet
84 D2 Bridge of Weir Rens
28 C6 Bridge Sollers Herefs
34 C4 Bridge Street Suffk
49 E6 Bridge Trafford Ches
17 G2 Bridgehampton Somset
73 E2 Bridgehill Dur
9 G4 Bridgemary Hants
101 G3 Bridgend Abers
82 C2 Bridgend Ag & B
95 E3 Bridgend Angus
27 E1 Bridgend Brdgnd
78 D3 Bridgend D & G
5 F2 Bridgend Devon
93 F1 Bridgend Fife
101 F3 Bridgend Moray
92 D2 Bridgend P & K
86 B3 Bridgend W Loth
93 E4 Bridgend of Lintrathen Angus
14 C2 Bridgerule Devon
16 B2 Bridgetown Somset
44 C1 Bridgham Norfk
39 G5 Bridgnorth Shrops
40 B4 Bridgtown Staffs
16 D3 Bridgwater Somset
61 E6 Bridlington E R Yk
7 F5 Bridport Dorset
28 D5 Bridstow Herefs
57 H6 Brierfield Lancs
59 E1 Brierley Barns
28 D4 Brierley Gloucs
40 A2 Brierley Hill Dudley
85 E6 Brig o'Turk Stirlg
52 C5 Brigg N Linc
45 F4 Briggate Norfk
67 E4 Briggswath N York
70 D2 Brigham Cumb
61 E5 Brigham E R Yk
58 C2 Brighouse Calder
9 F2 Brighstone IOW
31 E1 Brighthampton Oxon
15 E1 Brightley Devon
12 B4 Brightling E Susx
34 D1 Brightlingsea Essex
11 F3 Brighton Br & H
56 C3 Brighton le Sands Sefton
85 H3 Brightons Falk
19 F4 Brightwalton W Berk
35 F3 Brightwell Suffk
19 H6 Brightwell Baldwin Oxon
19 H6 Brightwell Upperton Oxon
19 G5 Brightwell-cum-Sotwell Oxon
65 E4 Brignall Dur
53 E5 Brigsley NE Lin
63 E5 Brigsteer Cumb
42 B1 Brigstock Nhants
31 G2 Brill Bucks
2 D2 Brill Cnwll
38 C1 Brilley Herefs
39 E3 Brimfield Herefs
39 E3 Brimfield Cross Herefs
51 E4 Brimington Derbys
5 H4 Brimley Devon
29 G4 Brimpsfield Gloucs
19 G3 Brimpton W Berk
29 F3 Brimscombe Gloucs
56 C1 Brimstage Wirral
51 E5 Brincliffe Sheff
60 B3 Brind E R Yk
111 k2 Brindister Shet
57 F5 Brindle Lancs
49 G1 Brineton Staffs
42 A2 Bringhurst Leics
32 C6 Brington Cambs
44 D5 Brininghham Norfk
53 F3 Brinkhill Lincs
33 H4 Brinkley Cambs
41 E2 Brinklow Warwks
18 C5 Brinkworth Wilts
57 F4 Brinscall Lancs
51 F2 Brinsley Notts
51 E5 Brinsworth Rothm
44 D5 Brinton Norfk
111 h2 Brinyan Ork
44 C4 Brisley Norfk
17 G5 Brislington Bristl
12 D5 Brissenden Green Kent
17 G6 Bristol Bristl
17 F5 Bristol Airport N Som
17 G6 Bristol Zoo Bristl
44 D5 Briston Norfk
8 D6 Britford Wilts
27 G3 Brithdir Caerph
47 F3 Brithdir Gwynd
22 C1 British Legion Village Kent
26 D2 Briton Ferry Neath
19 H5 Britwell Salome Oxon
6 B2 Brixham Torbay
5 F2 Brixton Devon
21 F3 Brixton Gt Lon
18 B1 Brixton Deverill Wilts
41 H1 Brixworth Nhants
30 D1 Brize Norton Oxon
30 D1 Brize Norton Airport Oxon
30 A6 Broad Alley Worcs
18 D5 Broad Blunsdon Swindn
30 C4 Broad Campden Gloucs
58 C2 Broad Carr Calder
8 C5 Broad Chalke Wilts
34 C1 Broad Green Essex
39 G2 Broad Green Worcs
24 C4 Broad Haven Pembks
18 D4 Broad Hinton Wilts
19 F3 Broad Laying Hants
30 C4 Broad Marston Worcs
12 D4 Broad Oak E Susx
12 B4 Broad Oak E Susx
28 C4 Broad Oak Herefs
23 F2 Broad Oak Kent
57 E2 Broad Oak St Hel
12 D4 Broad Street E Susx
22 D1 Broad Street Kent
18 D4 Broad Town Wilts
22 C6 Broad's Green Essex
50 B5 Broadbottom Tamesd
10 B3 Broadbridge W Susx
11 E5 Broadbridge Heath W Susx
6 B5 Broadclyst Devon
84 C3 Broadfield Inver
96 D4 Broadford Highld
10 D4 Broadford Bridge W Susx
79 E4 Broadgairhill Border
81 E5 Broadhaugh Border
57 G2 Broadheath Traffd
6 C6 Broadhembury Devon
5 H3 Broadhempston Devon
12 D4 Broadland Row E Susx
101 F5 Broadley Moray
7 H4 Broadmayne Dorset
25 E3 Broadmoor Pembks
7 F5 Broadoak Dorset
23 H2 Broadstairs Kent
8 C3 Broadstone Poole
39 E5 Broadstone Shrops
39 G2 Broadwas Worcs
33 E1 Broadwater Herts
11 E3 Broadwater W Susx
39 H4 Broadwaters Worcs
24 C4 Broadway Pembks
17 E1 Broadway Somset
30 C4 Broadway Worcs
30 D3 Broadwell Gloucs
30 D1 Broadwell Oxon
31 F6 Broadwell Warwks
7 F5 Broadwindsor Dorset
15 E2 Broadwood Kelly Devon
5 E5 Broadwoodwidger Devon
104 D1 Brochel Highld
39 G2 Brockamin Worcs
9 H5 Brockbridge Hants
35 E6 Brockdish Norfk
9 E3 Brockenhurst Hants
78 B6 Brocketsbrae S Lans
35 E5 Brockford Street Suffk
31 G6 Brockhall Nhants
21 E1 Brockham Surrey
30 B2 Brockhampton Gloucs
10 A3 Brockhampton Hants
28 D5 Brockhampton Herefs
58 C1 Brockholes Kirk
61 E1 Brocklesby Lincs
17 F5 Brockley N Som
34 B5 Brockley Suffk
34 B3 Brockley Green Suffk
34 B4 Brockley Green Suffk
38 D6 Brockton Shrops
38 D4 Brockton Shrops
39 F5 Brockton Shrops
49 G3 Brockton Staffs
28 D3 Brockweir Gloucs
29 F4 Brockworth Gloucs
40 B5 Brocton Staffs
75 H4 Brodick N Ayrs
100 C5 Brodie Moray
59 F1 Brodsworth Donc
104 C3 Brogaig Highld
50 A4 Broken Cross Ches
18 B5 Brokenborough Wilts
18 B2 Brokerswood Wilts
56 D1 Bromborough Wirral
35 E6 Brome Suffk
35 E6 Brome Street Suffk
35 F4 Bromeswell Suffk
71 E4 Bromfield Cumb
39 E4 Bromfield Shrops
32 C4 Bromham Beds
18 C3 Bromham Wilts
21 G2 Bromley Gt Lon
39 G5 Bromley Shrops
22 C2 Brompton Medway
65 G3 Brompton N York
67 E2 Brompton N York
16 C2 Brompton Ralph Somset
16 B2 Brompton Regis Somset
65 F3 Brompton-on-Swale N York
29 E5 Bromsberrow Gloucs
29 E5 Bromsberrow Heath Gloucs
40 B1 Bromsgrove Worcs
39 F2 Bromyard Herefs
37 E3 Bronant Cerdgn
36 C2 Brongest Cerdgn
49 E3 Bronington Wrexhm
27 G6 Bronllys Powys
25 G5 Bronwydd Carmth
48 C3 Bronygarth Shrops
9 E4 Brook Hants
9 F2 Brook IOW
13 E6 Brook Kent
10 C5 Brook Surrey
9 E4 Brook Hill Hants
22 B4 Brook Street Essex
12 D5 Brook Street Kent
34 B3 Brook Street Suffk
45 F2 Brooke Norfk
42 B3 Brooke Rutlnd
52 D5 Brookenby Lincs
84 D2 Brookfield Rens
17 G2 Brookhampton Somset
63 E3 Brookhouse Lancs
51 F5 Brookhouse Rothm
49 G5 Brookhouse Green Ches
50 B5 Brookhouses Derbys
13 E4 Brookland Kent
57 G2 Brooklands Traffd
21 E5 Brookmans Park Herts
29 F4 Brookthorpe Gloucs
20 C1 Brookwood Surrey
32 D3 Broom Beds
73 F1 Broom Dur
51 E5 Broom Rothm
30 C5 Broom Warwks
51 E6 Broom Hill Barns
51 F2 Broom Hill Notts
23 E2 Broom Street Kent
45 F2 Broome Norfk
38 D4 Broome Shrops
40 A2 Broome Worcs
57 G2 Broomedge Warrtn
22 C6 Broomfield Essex
22 D1 Broomfield Kent
23 F2 Broomfield Kent
16 D2 Broomfield Somset
60 C3 Broomfleet E R Yk
72 D3 Broomhaugh Nthumb
73 F6 Broomhill Nthumb
107 G6 Brora Highld
39 F6 Broseley Shrops
72 D1 Brotherlee Dur
59 F3 Brotherton N York
66 C5 Brotton R & Cl
110 A5 Broubster Highld
64 C4 Brough Cumb
60 C3 Brough E R Yk
110 C6 Brough Highld
52 A2 Brough Notts
111 I3 Brough Shet
111 m4 Brough Lodge Shet
64 C4 Brough Sowerby Cumb
49 E3 Broughall Shrops
78 D6 Broughton Border
33 E6 Broughton Cambs
48 D5 Broughton Flints
9 E6 Broughton Hants
57 E6 Broughton Lancs
32 B3 Broughton M Keyn
52 B6 Broughton N Linc
58 B5 Broughton N York
66 D1 Broughton N York
32 A6 Broughton Nhants
31 E4 Broughton Oxon
57 G3 Broughton Salfd
49 G3 Broughton Staffs
16 B5 Broughton V Glam
41 F3 Broughton Astley Leics
18 B3 Broughton Gifford Wilts
30 B6 Broughton Green Worcs
30 A5 Broughton Hackett Worcs
69 F2 Broughton Mains D & G
62 C5 Broughton Mills Cumb
70 D3 Broughton Moor Cumb
30 D1 Broughton Poggs Oxon
62 C4 Broughton-in-Furness Cumb
93 G2 Broughty Ferry C Dund
19 G1 Brown Candover Hants
50 A2 Brown Edge Staffs
102 D3 Brownhill Abers
93 G1 Brownhills Fife
40 B4 Brownhills Wsall
19 G3 Browninghill Green Hants
29 F3 Browns Hill Gloucs
14 C3 Brownsham Devon
5 G2 Brownston Devon
67 E3 Broxa N York
21 F5 Broxbourne Herts
87 G4 Broxburn E Loth
86 B3 Broxburn W Loth
33 G2 Broxted Essex
38 D2 Broxwood Herefs
110 D3 Bruan Highld
92 B5 Bruar P & K
107 H4 Brucefield Highld
82 A2 Bruchag Ag & B
82 B2 Bruichladdich Ag & B
35 F5 Bruisyard Suffk
35 F5 Bruisyard Street Suffk
52 B6 Brumby N Linc
50 C3 Brund Staffs
45 F3 Brundall Norfk
35 F5 Brundish Suffk
35 F5 Brundish Street Suffk
58 B4 Brunthwaite Brad
41 G2 Bruntingthorpe Leics
93 E2 Brunton Fife
81 G3 Brunton Nthumb
19 E2 Brunton Wilts
16 B2 Brushford Somset
15 F2 Brushford Barton Devon
17 G3 Bruton Somset
30 A6 Bryan's Green Worcs
8 B4 Bryanston Dorset
71 E6 Brydekirk D & G
17 F1 Brympton Somset
26 D2 Bryn Neath
57 F3 Bryn Gates Wigan
48 B4 Bryn Saith Marchog Denbgs
26 D3 Bryn-coch Neath
24 D6 Bryn-Henllan Pembks
46 B4 Bryn-mawr Gwynd
55 F4 Bryn-y-Maen Conwy
26 C4 Brynaman Carmth
25 E6 Brynberian Pembks
46 D5 Bryncir Gwynd
46 B4 Bryncroes Gwynd
47 E2 Bryncrug Gwynd
48 B4 Bryneglwys Denbgs
48 B6 Brynford Flints
54 B4 Bryngwran IOA
28 B3 Bryngwyn Mons
38 C1 Bryngwyn Powys
36 C2 Brynhoffnant Cerdgn
27 G4 Brynmawr Blae G
27 E2 Brynmenyn Brdgnd
26 C2 Brynmill Swans
27 F1 Brynna Rhondd
54 D3 Brynrefail Gwynd
27 F1 Brynsadler Rhondd
54 C3 Brynsiencyn IOA
96 C4 Bualintur Highld
41 E1 Bubbenhall Warwks
60 B3 Bubwith E R Yk
84 D4 Buchanan Smithy Stirlg
103 F4 Buchanhaven Abers
92 B2 Buchanty P & K
85 F5 Buchany Stirlg
85 E5 Buchlyvie Stirlg
14 C3 Buck's Cross Devon
14 C3 Buck's Mills Devon
71 F4 Buckabank Cumb
32 D5 Buckden Cambs
64 D1 Buckden N York
45 F3 Buckenham Norfk
6 C5 Buckerell Devon
5 G4 Buckfast Devon
5 G3 Buckfastleigh Devon
86 D5 Buckhaven Fife
28 C4 Buckholt Mons
17 H2 Buckhorn Weston Dorset
21 G4 Buckhurst Hill Essex
101 F5 Buckie Moray
31 G3 Buckingham Bucks
20 C6 Buckland Bucks
5 G2 Buckland Devon
30 C3 Buckland Gloucs
33 E2 Buckland Herts
13 G6 Buckland Kent
19 E6 Buckland Oxon
21 E1 Buckland Surrey
14 D3 Buckland Brewer Devon
20 C5 Buckland Common Bucks
17 H4 Buckland Dinham Somset
14 D2 Buckland Filleigh Devon
5 G4 Buckland in the Moor Devon
5 E4 Buckland Monachorum Devon
7 G6 Buckland Newton Dorset
7 G4 Buckland Ripers Dorset
16 D1 Buckland St Mary Somset
5 G2 Buckland-Tout-Saints Devon
19 G4 Bucklebury W Berk
9 F3 Bucklers Hard Hants
35 F3 Bucklesham Suffk
48 C5 Buckley Flints
57 G1 Bucklow Hill Ches
42 B4 Buckminster Leics
50 A2 Bucknall C Stke
52 D2 Bucknall Lincs
31 F3 Bucknell Oxon
38 D3 Bucknell Shrops
101 F5 Buckpool Moray
10 D5 Bucks Green W Susx
10 B6 Bucks Horn Oak Hants
103 E1 Bucksburn C Aber
67 G1 Buckton E R Yk
81 F4 Buckton Nthumb
32 D6 Buckworth Cambs
51 G4 Budby Notts
14 C2 Budd's Titson Cnwll
93 G3 Buddon Angus
14 B2 Bude Cnwll
4 D3 Budge's Shop Cnwll
6 C4 Budleigh Salterton Devon
2 D2 Budock Water Cnwll
49 F4 Buerton Ches
31 G5 Bugbrooke Nhants
3 F5 Bugle Cnwll
8 A5 Bugley Dorset
60 B5 Bugthorpe E R Yk
39 F6 Buildwas Shrops
38 A1 Builth Wells Powys
8 D6 Bulbridge Wilts
110 A5 Buldoo Highld
18 D1 Bulford Wilts
49 E4 Bulkeley Ches
41 E2 Bulkington Warwks
18 B3 Bulkington Wilts
14 D3 Bulkworthy Devon
20 C2 Bullbrook Br For
19 F1 Bullington Hants
52 C3 Bullington Lincs
34 B3 Bulmer Essex
60 B6 Bulmer N York
34 B3 Bulmer Tye Essex
22 B4 Bulphan Thurr
103 E4 Bulwark Abers
51 F1 Bulwell C Nott
42 B2 Bulwick Nhants
21 G5 Bumble's Green Essex
97 E1 Bunacaimb Highld
98 A2 Bunarkaig Highld
49 E5 Bunbury Ches

107 E1 Bunchrew Highld
97 F5 Bundalloch Highld
89 E1 Bunessan Ag & B
45 F1 Bungay Suffk
82 C3 Bunnahabhain Ag & B
41 G6 Bunny Notts
98 C5 Buntait Highld
33 E2 Buntingford Herts
45 E2 Bunwell Norfk
45 E2 Bunwell Street Norfk
41 E3 Burbage Leics
19 E3 Burbage Wilts
20 B3 Burchett's Green W & M
8 C6 Burcombe Wilts
32 B1 Burcott Bucks
34 C2 Bures Essex
30 D2 Burford Oxon
39 F3 Burford Shrops
89 E3 Burg Ag & B
10 B5 Burgates Hants
11 F4 Burgess Hill W Susx
35 E4 Burgh Suffk
71 F5 Burgh by Sands Cumb
45 G3 Burgh Castle Norfk
21 E2 Burgh Heath Surrey
53 G2 Burgh le Marsh Lincs
45 E4 Burgh next Aylsham Norfk
52 D4 Burgh on Bain Lincs
45 G3 Burgh St Margaret Norfk
45 G2 Burgh St Peter Norfk
19 F3 Burghclere Hants
100 D6 Burghead Moray
19 H3 Burghfield W Berk
19 H3 Burghfield Common W Berk
39 E1 Burghill Herefs
59 F2 Burghwallis Donc
22 C2 Burham Kent
10 B4 Buriton Hants
49 F4 Burland Ches
3 F6 Burlawn Cnwll
20 C2 Burleigh Br For
29 F3 Burleigh Gloucs
16 C1 Burlescombe Devon
8 A3 Burleston Dorset
8 D4 Burley Hants
42 B3 Burley Rutlnd
39 F1 Burley Gate Herefs
58 C4 Burley in Wharfedale Brad
8 D4 Burley Street Hants
58 C4 Burley Wood Head Brad
49 F3 Burleydam Ches
45 F3 Burlingham Green Norfk
49 E2 Burlton Shrops
13 F5 Burmarsh Kent
30 D4 Burmington Warwks
59 G3 Burn N York
85 F5 Burn of Cambus Stirlg
57 H2 Burnage Manch
40 D6 Burnaston Derbys
85 G2 Burnbrae N Lans
60 C4 Burnby E R Yk
63 E5 Burneside Cumb
65 G2 Burneston N York
17 G5 Burnett BaNES
79 G4 Burnfoot Border
80 B2 Burnfoot Border
78 C2 Burnfoot D & G
79 F2 Burnfoot D & G
79 G2 Burnfoot D & G
86 A6 Burnfoot P & K
20 C3 Burnham Bucks
44 B6 Burnham Deepdale Norfk
33 E1 Burnham Green Herts
44 B6 Burnham Market Norfk
44 B6 Burnham Norton Norfk
44 B6 Burnham Overy Norfk
44 B6 Burnham Overy Staithe Norfk
44 C6 Burnham Thorpe Norfk
23 E5 Burnham-on-Crouch Essex
17 E4 Burnham-on-Sea Somset
103 F4 Burnhaven Abers
78 C2 Burnhead D & G
102 C2 Burnhervie Abers
39 G5 Burnhill Green Staffs
73 F2 Burnhope Dur
76 D6 Burnhouse N Ayrs
67 F3 Burniston N York
57 H5 Burnley Lancs
73 G2 Burnmoor Dur
81 E5 Burnmouth Border
73 F2 Burnopfield Dur
58 B6 Burnsall N York
93 G4 Burnside Angus
93 F5 Burnside Angus
86 B6 Burnside Fife
101 E6 Burnside Moray
86 B3 Burnside W Loth
93 F3 Burnside of Duntrune Angus
58 D6 Burnt Yates N York
86 C4 Burntisland Fife
40 B4 Burntwood Staffs
16 D1 Burnworthy Somset
20 D1 Burpham Surrey
10 D3 Burpham W Susx
81 E1 Burradon Nthumb
111 m4 Burrafirth Shet
111 l3 Burravoe Shet
64 B5 Burrells Cumb
92 D3 Burrelton P & K
7 E6 Burridge Devon
9 G4 Burridge Hants
65 F2 Burrill N York
52 A6 Burringham N Linc
15 F3 Burrington Devon
38 D3 Burrington Herefs
17 F5 Burrington N Som
33 H4 Burrough Green Cambs
41 H4 Burrough on the Hill Leics
63 F3 Burrow Lancs
16 B3 Burrow Somset
17 E2 Burrow Bridge Somset
20 C2 Burrowhill Surrey
25 H3 Burry Port Carmth
26 A2 Burrygreen Swans
56 D4 Burscough Lancs
57 E4 Burscough Bridge Lancs
60 B3 Bursea E R Yk
9 G4 Bursledon Hants
49 H4 Burslem C Stke
34 D3 Burstall Suffk
7 E5 Burstock Dorset
45 E1 Burston Norfk
11 F6 Burstow Surrey
61 F3 Burstwick E R Yk
64 C2 Burtersett N York
71 H5 Burtholme Cumb
34 B5 Burthorpe Green Suffk
43 E5 Burtoft Lincs
48 D6 Burton Ches
49 E5 Burton Ches
8 D3 Burton Dorset
52 B3 Burton Lincs
24 D3 Burton Pembks
16 D3 Burton Somset
18 A4 Burton Wilts
61 E6 Burton Agnes E R Yk
7 F4 Burton Bradstock Dorset
42 C4 Burton Coggles Lincs
61 E3 Burton Constable Hall E R Yk
33 G1 Burton End Essex
67 F1 Burton Fleming E R Yk
41 E2 Burton Hastings Warwks
63 F3 Burton in Lonsdale N York
51 G1 Burton Joyce Notts
32 B6 Burton Latimer Nhants
41 H5 Burton Lazars Leics
59 E6 Burton Leonard N York
41 G5 Burton on the Wolds Leics
41 G3 Burton Overy Leics
42 D6 Burton Pedwardine Lincs
61 F3 Burton Pidsea E R Yk
59 F3 Burton Salmon N York
60 C2 Burton upon Stather N Linc
40 D5 Burton upon Trent Staffs
34 B2 Burton's Green Essex
63 E3 Burton-in-Kendal Cumb
57 E2 Burtonwood Warrtn
49 E5 Burwardsley Ches
39 F4 Burwarton Shrops
12 B4 Burwash E Susx
12 B4 Burwash Common E Susx
12 B4 Burwash Weald E Susx
33 G5 Burwell Cambs
53 E3 Burwell Lincs
54 C5 Burwen IOA
111 h1 Burwick Ork
57 G4 Bury Bury
43 E1 Bury Cambs
16 B2 Bury Somset
10 D3 Bury W Susx
33 F1 Bury Green Herts
34 C5 Bury St Edmunds Suffk
60 B6 Burythorpe N York
85 E2 Busby E Rens
19 E6 Buscot Wilts
95 F3 Bush Abers
32 E2 Bush Bank Herefs
21 F5 Bush Hill Park Gt Lon
40 A3 Bushbury Wolves
21 E5 Bushey Herts
21 E4 Bushey Heath Herts
29 F6 Bushley Worcs
18 C4 Bushton Wilts
17 E3 Bussex Somset
17 F5 Butcombe N Som
17 F2 Butleigh Somset
17 F3 Butleigh Wootton Somset
30 D5 Butlers Marston Warwks
35 G4 Butley Suffk
60 B5 Buttercrambe N York
87 G3 Butterdean Border
65 E5 Butterknowle Dur
6 B6 Butterleigh Devon
71 E1 Buttermere Cumb
58 C3 Buttershaw Brad
92 C4 Butterstone P & K
49 G3 Butterton Staffs
50 C2 Butterton Staffs
43 F6 Butterwick Lincs
66 D1 Butterwick N York
67 F1 Butterwick N York
38 C6 Buttington Powys
39 G4 Buttonoak Shrops
34 D4 Buxhall Suffk
11 G4 Buxted E Susx
50 B4 Buxton Derbys
45 E4 Buxton Norfk
45 E4 Buxton Heath Norfk
27 G5 Bwlch Powys
48 B1 Bwlch-y-cibau Powys
38 B5 Bwlch-y-ffridd Powys
25 F6 Bwlch-y-groes Pembks
38 A3 Bwlch-y-sarnau Powys
48 C4 Bwlchgwyn Wrexhm
25 E3 Bwlchllan Cerdgn
46 C4 Bwlchtocyn Gwynd
65 F6 Byers Green Dur
31 F5 Byfield Nhants
20 D2 Byfleet Surrey
38 D1 Byford Herefs
73 F3 Byker N u Ty
55 G3 Bylchau Conwy
49 G6 Byley Ches
80 C4 Byrewalls Border
72 B6 Byrness Nthumb
6 B4 Bystock Devon
32 C6 Bythorn Cambs
38 D3 Byton Herefs
73 E3 Bywell Nthumb
10 C4 Byworth W Susx

C

52 D5 Cabourne Lincs
82 D2 Cabrach Ag & B
101 F2 Cabrach Moray
63 E1 Cabus Lancs
106 B3 Cabvie Lodge Highld
6 B6 Cadbury Devon
85 E3 Cadder E Duns
32 C1 Caddington Beds
79 G6 Caddonfoot Border
12 B4 Cade Street E Susx
51 F6 Cadeby Donc
41 E3 Cadeby Leics
6 B6 Cadeleigh Devon
2 D1 Cadgwith Cnwll
86 C6 Cadham Fife
57 G2 Cadishead Salfd
26 C2 Cadle Swans
57 E5 Cadley Lancs
18 D3 Cadley Wilts
19 E2 Cadley Wilts
20 B4 Cadmore End Bucks
9 E4 Cadnam Hants
52 C5 Cadney N Linc
16 C5 Cadoxton V Glam
26 D3 Cadoxton Juxta-Neath Neath
54 D3 Caeathro Gwynd
52 C4 Caenby Lincs
37 F1 Caeo Carmth
24 C5 Caer Farchell Pembks
27 E2 Caerau Brdgnd
16 C6 Caerau Cardif
54 B4 Caergeiliog IOA
48 C5 Caergwrle Flints
79 G3 Caerlanrig Border
28 B2 Caerleon Newpt
54 C3 Caernarfon Gwynd
54 C2 Caernarfon Airport Gwynd
54 C3 Caernarfon Castle Gwynd
27 G2 Caerphilly Caerph
38 A5 Caersws Powys
36 C2 Caerwedros Cerdgn
28 C2 Caerwent Mons
48 B6 Caerwys Flints
111 b3 Cairinis W Isls
83 F4 Cairnbaan Ag & B
103 F5 Cairnbulg Abers
81 E6 Cairncross Border
84 C3 Cairncurran Inver
84 B6 Cairndow Ag & B
86 B4 Cairneyhill Fife
101 F5 Cairnfield House Moray
68 C3 Cairngarroch D & G
99 H3 Cairngorm Mountains
95 G5 Cairngrassie Abers
101 G4 Cairnie Abers
102 D3 Cairnorrie Abers
68 C4 Cairnryan D & G
101 F4 Cairnty Moray
45 H3 Caister-on-Sea Norfk
52 D5 Caistor Lincs
45 E3 Caistor St Edmund Norfk
111 c6 Calanais W Isls
9 F2 Calbourne IOW
48 B6 Calcot Flints
30 C1 Calcot Gloucs
19 H4 Calcot Row W Berk
101 E5 Calcots Moray
71 F3 Caldbeck Cumb
42 D1 Caldecote Cambs
33 E4 Caldecote Cambs
33 E3 Caldecote Herts
33 E4 Caldecote Highfields Cambs
32 C5 Caldecott Nhants
19 G6 Caldecott Oxon
42 B2 Caldecott Rutlnd
62 A6 Calder Bridge Cumb
58 D2 Calder Grove Wakefd
63 E1 Calder Vale Lancs
85 F2 Calderbank N Lans
85 G2 Caldercruix N Lans
77 F5 Caldermill S Lans
85 F1 Calderwood S Lans
28 C2 Caldicot Mons
65 F4 Caldwell N York
111 h3 Calfsound Ork
89 E4 Calgary Ag & B
100 D5 Califer Moray
85 H3 California Falk
45 H3 California Norfk
41 E5 Calke Derbys
105 E2 Callakille Highld
85 E6 Callander Stirlg
111 c6 Callanish W Isls
2 D4 Callestick Cnwll
96 D3 Calligarry Highld
4 D4 Callington Cnwll
28 C6 Callow Herefs
39 H1 Callow End Worcs
18 C5 Callow Hill Wilts
9 E4 Calmore Hants
30 B1 Calmsden Gloucs
18 C4 Calne Wilts
9 G3 Calshot Hants
5 E4 Calstock Cnwll
18 C3 Calstone Wellington Wilts
45 E5 Calthorpe Norfk
45 G4 Calthorpe Street Norfk
71 G3 Calthwaite Cumb
58 A5 Calton N York
50 C2 Calton Staffs
49 F5 Calveley Ches
50 D4 Calver Derbys
49 F3 Calverhall Shrops
16 B1 Calverleigh Devon
32 A3 Calverton M Keyn
51 G2 Calverton Notts
92 A5 Calvine P & K
71 E4 Calvo Cumb
78 D6 Calzeat Border
29 E3 Cam Gloucs
97 G5 Camas Luinie Highld
89 H5 Camasachoirce Highld
89 G5 Camasine Highld
96 C6 Camastianavaig Highld
98 D6 Camault Muir Highld
13 E4 Camber E Susx
20 C2 Camberley Surrey
21 F3 Camberwell Gt Lon
59 G3 Camblesforth N York
72 D5 Cambo Nthumb
2 C3 Camborne Cnwll
33 E4 Cambourne Cambs
33 F4 Cambridge Cambs
29 E3 Cambridge Gloucs
33 F4 Cambridge Airport Cambs
2 D4 Cambrose Cnwll
85 G5 Cambus Clacks
94 D5 Cambus o' May Abers
107 F5 Cambusavie Platform Highld
85 G4 Cambusbarron Stirlg
85 G5 Cambuskenneth Stirlg
85 F2 Cambuslang S Lans
78 D6 Cambuswallace S Lans
21 F4 Camden Town Gt Lon
17 G4 Cameley BaNES
4 B5 Camelford Cnwll
85 G4 Camelon Falk
29 E6 Camer's Green Worcs
100 C3 Camerory Highld
17 G4 Camerton BaNES
70 D3 Camerton Cumb
91 G4 Camghouran P & K
80 B3 Camieston Border
95 G5 Cammachmore Abers
52 B3 Cammeringham Lincs
107 G5 Camore Highld
75 E3 Campbeltown Ag & B
75 E3 Campbeltown Airport Ag & B
78 C2 Cample D & G
93 E3 Campmuir Angus
86 B3 Camps W Loth
33 G3 Camps End Cambs
59 F2 Campsall Donc
35 F4 Campsea Ash Suffk
32 D3 Campton Beds
80 C2 Camptown Border
24 D4 Camrose Pembks
92 B4 Camserney P & K
105 H4 Camusnagaul Highld
90 C6 Camusnagaul Highld
97 E6 Camusteel Highld
97 E6 Camusterrach Highld
9 E5 Canada Hants
94 C5 Candacraig Abers
53 F2 Candlesby Lincs
78 D6 Candyburn Border
20 A3 Cane End Oxon
22 D4 Canewdon Essex
8 C2 Canford Cliffs Poole
8 C3 Canford Heath Poole
8 C3 Canford Magna Poole
110 D6 Canisbay Highld
40 D1 Canley Covtry
8 B5 Cann Dorset
98 B5 Cannich Highld
21 G3 Canning Town Gt Lon
16 D3 Cannington Somset
40 B4 Cannock Staffs
40 B5 Cannock Chase Staffs
28 C6 Cannon Bridge Herefs
39 F1 Canon Frome Herefs
39 E1 Canon Pyon Herefs
71 G6 Canonbie D & G
31 F5 Canons Ashby Nhants
2 B3 Canonstown Cnwll
23 F1 Canterbury Kent
23 F2 Canterbury Cathedral Kent
45 G3 Cantley Norfk
16 C6 Canton Cardif
107 G1 Cantraywood Highld
63 F3 Cantsfield Lancs
22 C4 Canvey Island Essex
52 C2 Canwick Lincs
4 C6 Canworthy Water Cnwll
90 C6 Caol Highld
111 c5 Caolas Scalpaigh W Isls
88 B4 Caoles Ag & B
97 H2 Caonich Highld
12 B6 Capel Kent
11 E6 Capel Surrey
37 E4 Capel Bangor Cerdgn
54 C4 Capel Coch IOA
55 E2 Capel Curig Conwy
26 B4 Capel Dewi Carmth
36 D1 Capel Dewi Cerdgn
55 F2 Capel Garmon Conwy
26 C4 Capel Hendre Carmth
25 F6 Capel Iwan Carmth
13 G5 Capel le Ferne Kent
54 C3 Capel Mawr IOA
37 E4 Capel Seion Cerdgn
35 G3 Capel St Andrew Suffk
34 D3 Capel St Mary Suffk
37 E5 Capel-Dewi Cerdgn
6 c2 Capelles Guern
55 F4 Capelulo Conwy
48 D6 Capenhurst Ches
73 E4 Capheaton Nthumb
84 D2 Caplaw E Rens
79 E5 Cappercleuch Border
5 H2 Capton Devon
92 D3 Caputh P & K
51 H1 Car Colston Notts
85 E3 Carbeth Inn Stirlg
2 B3 Carbis Bay Cnwll
96 B5 Carbost Highld
104 C1 Carbost Highld
51 E5 Carbrook Sheff
44 C2 Carbrooke Norfk
59 F1 Carcroft Donc
86 C5 Cardenden Fife
101 E4 Cardhu Moray
16 D6 Cardiff Cardif
16 C5 Cardiff Airport V Glam
36 B2 Cardigan Cerdgn
32 C3 Cardington Beds
39 E5 Cardington Shrops
4 B4 Cardinham Cnwll
68 C1 Cardrain D & G
79 F6 Cardrona Border
84 C3 Cardross Ag & B
68 C1 Cardryne D & G
71 E5 Cardurnock Cumb
42 C4 Careby Lincs
95 E2 Careston Angus
24 D3 Carew Pembks
24 D3 Carew Cheriton Pembks
24 D3 Carew Newton Pembks
28 D5 Carey Herefs
85 G2 Carfin N Lans
80 B5 Carfraemill Border
45 G3 Cargate Green Norfk
70 C6 Cargen D & G
70 C6 Cargenbridge D & G
92 D3 Cargill P & K
71 F5 Cargo Cumb
5 E3 Cargreen Cnwll
80 D4 Carham Nthumb
16 B3 Carhampton Somset
2 D3 Carharrack Cnwll
91 G4 Carie P & K
111 b3 Carinish W Isls
9 G2 Carisbrooke IOW
62 D4 Cark Cumb
5 E3 Carkeel Cnwll
111 c6 Carlabhagh W Isls
65 F5 Carlbury Darltn
42 C3 Carlby Lincs
80 D1 Carlcroft Nthumb
2 C2 Carleen Cnwll
58 B5 Carleton N York
44 D3 Carleton Forehoe Norfk
44 D2 Carleton Rode Norfk
45 F2 Carleton St Peter Norfk
102 C4 Carlincraig Abers
17 H4 Carlingcott BaNES
71 G5 Carlisle Cumb
71 G5 Carlisle Airport Cumb
86 B2 Carlops Border
111 c6 Carloway W Isls
59 E1 Carlton Barns
32 B4 Carlton Beds
33 H4 Carlton Cambs
59 E3 Carlton Leeds
41 E4 Carlton Leics
65 E2 Carlton N York
66 C2 Carlton N York
59 G2 Carlton N York
51 G1 Carlton Notts
65 G5 Carlton S on T
35 G5 Carlton Suffk
45 H1 Carlton Colville Suffk
41 G3 Carlton Curlieu Leics
33 H4 Carlton Green Cambs
66 B1 Carlton Husthwaite N York
51 G5 Carlton in Lindrick Notts
65 G2 Carlton Miniott N York
42 B6 Carlton Scroop Lincs
66 B4 Carlton-in-Cleveland N York
52 B2 Carlton-le-Moorland Lincs
52 A2 Carlton-on-Trent Notts
77 G6 Carluke S Lans
77 G4 Carmacoup S Lans
25 G4 Carmarthen Carmth
26 B4 Carmel Carmth
54 D2 Carmel Gwynd
78 C6 Carmichael S Lans
85 E2 Carmunnock C Glas
85 F2 Carmyle C Glas
93 G3 Carmyllie Angus
2 D3 Carn Brea Cnwll
97 G4 Carn-gorm Highld
61 E6 Carnaby E R Yk
87 E6 Carnbee Fife
86 B6 Carnbo P & K
102 D2 Carnbrogie Abers
97 F5 Carndu Highld
77 F5 Carnduff S Lans
76 D4 Carnell E Ayrs
63 E3 Carnforth Lancs
2 C3 Carnhell Green Cnwll
95 G6 Carnie Abers
2 D3 Carnkie Cnwll
47 H1 Carno Powys
97 F2 Carnoch Highld
86 B5 Carnock Fife
3 E3 Carnon Downs Cnwll
102 C4 Carnousie Abers
93 G3 Carnoustie Angus
86 A1 Carnwath S Lans
40 D1 Carol Green Solhll
64 D2 Carperby N York
58 D3 Carr Gate Wakefd
72 C2 Carr Shield Nthumb
75 F4 Carradale Ag & B
99 G5 Carrbridge Highld
7 b2 Carrefour Jersey
54 C5 Carreglefn IOA
60 B1 Carrhouse N Linc
83 G4 Carrick Ag & B
84 B5 Carrick Castle Ag & B
86 A4 Carriden Falk
86 D2 Carrington Mdloth
57 G2 Carrington Traffd
48 B4 Carrog Denbgs
85 G4 Carron Falk
101 E3 Carron Moray
85 F4 Carron Bridge Stirlg
78 C3 Carronbridge D & G
85 G4 Carronshore Falk
84 C2 Carruth House Inver
70 D6 Carrutherstown D & G
73 G1 Carrville Dur
89 F1 Carsaig Ag & B
93 F4 Carse Gray Angus
69 E4 Carseriggan D & G
70 D5 Carsethorn D & G
21 F2 Carshalton Gt Lon
50 D2 Carsington Derbys
75 E2 Carskey Ag & B
69 F3 Carsluith D & G
77 E1 Carsphairn D & G
77 H5 Carstairs S Lans
77 H5 Carstairs Junction S Lans
30 D1 Carterton Oxon
3 F4 Carthew Cnwll
65 G2 Carthorpe N York
77 G5 Cartland S Lans
62 D4 Cartmel Cumb
26 B3 Carway Carmth
29 F3 Cashe's Green Gloucs
31 F1 Cassington Oxon
73 G1 Cassop Colliery Dur
63 F4 Casterton Lancs
44 B3 Castle Acre Norfk
32 B4 Castle Ashby Nhants
65 E3 Castle Bolton N York
40 C2 Castle Bromwich Solhll
42 C4 Castle Bytham Lincs
38 B6 Castle Caereinion Powys
33 G3 Castle Camps Cambs
71 H4 Castle Carrock Cumb
17 G2 Castle Cary Somset
18 B4 Castle Combe Wilts
41 E5 Castle Donington Leics
70 B5 Castle Douglas D & G
18 D6 Castle Eaton Swindn
73 H1 Castle Eden Dur
39 F1 Castle Frome Herefs
40 D5 Castle Gresley Derbys
34 B2 Castle Hedingham Essex
35 E3 Castle Hill Suffk
68 C3 Castle Kennedy D & G
83 H5 Castle Lachlan Ag & B
79 F2 Castle O'er D & G
38 D6 Castle Pulverbatch Shrops
43 H4 Castle Rising Norfk
107 F1 Castle Stuart Highld
111 a1 Castlebay W Isls
24 D5 Castlebythe Pembks
85 G3 Castlecary Falk
59 E3 Castleford Wakefd
79 E6 Castlehill Border
110 C5 Castlehill Highld
84 D3 Castlehill W Duns
24 C3 Castlemartin Pembks
85 E2 Castlemilk C Glas
29 F6 Castlemorton Worcs
71 F2 Castlerigg Cumb
73 E2 Castleside Dur
32 A3 Castlethorpe M Keyn
79 H2 Castleton Border
50 C5 Castleton Derbys
66 C4 Castleton N York
27 H1 Castleton Newpt

58 A1 Castleton Rochdl
110 C5 Castletown Highld
116 b2 Castletown IOM
73 G3 Castletown Sundld
58 D4 Castley N York
44 C2 Caston Norfk
42 D2 Castor C Pete
75 G5 Catacol N Ayrs
51 E5 Catcliffe Rothm
18 C4 Catcomb Wilts
17 E3 Catcott Somset
17 E3 Catcott Burtle Somset
6 b1 Catel Guern
21 F1 Caterham Surrey
45 G4 Catfield Norfk
111 I2 Catfirth Shet
21 F3 Catford Gt Lon
57 E6 Catforth Lancs
85 E2 Cathcart C Glas
27 G5 Cathedine Powys
10 A3 Catherington Hants
7 E5 Catherston Leweston Dorset
9 G4 Catisfield Hants
99 E2 Catlodge Highld
33 F3 Catmere End Essex
19 F4 Catmore W Berk
63 E3 Caton Lancs
63 E3 Caton Green Lancs
77 E4 Catrine E Ayrs
12 C3 Catsfield E Susx
17 F2 Catsgore Somset
40 B1 Catshill Worcs
75 E2 Cattadale Ag & B
59 E5 Cattal N York
34 D2 Cattawade Suffk
57 E6 Catterall Lancs
65 F3 Catterick N York
65 F3 Catterick Bridge N York
71 G4 Catterlen Cumb
95 G4 Catterline Abers
59 E4 Catterton N York
10 C6 Catteshall Surrey
41 F2 Catthorpe Leics
7 G5 Cattistock Dorset
72 C2 Catton Cumb
65 G1 Catton N York
45 G4 Catton Norfk
61 E4 Catwick E R Yk
32 C1 Catworth Cambs
29 G4 Caudle Green Gloucs
31 F3 Caulcott Oxon
93 H4 Cauldcots Angus
85 G4 Cauldhame Stirlg
80 B2 Cauldmill Border
50 C2 Cauldon Staffs
40 D5 Cauldwell Derbys
70 C6 Caulkerbush D & G
79 C1 Caulside D & G
17 G1 Caundle Marsh Dorset
51 H3 Caunton Notts
69 E3 Causeway End D & G
34 A1 Causeway End Essex
78 D6 Causewayend S Lans
85 G5 Causewayhead Stirlg
73 F6 Causey Park Bridge Nthumb
103 E2 Causeyend Abers
34 B5 Cavendish Suffk
34 B5 Cavenham Suffk
31 F3 Caversfield Oxon
20 A3 Caversham Readg
50 B1 Caverswall Staffs
80 D3 Caverton Mill Border
100 B4 Cawdor Highld
59 F4 Cawood N York
5 E2 Cawsand Cnwll
45 E4 Cawston Norfk
58 D1 Cawthorne Barns
33 E4 Caxton Cambs
39 E3 Caynham Shrops
42 B6 Caythorpe Lincs
51 G2 Caythorpe Notts
67 F2 Cayton N York
111 a4 Ceann a Bhaigh W Isls
98 B4 Ceannacroc Lodge Highld
111 d6 Cearsiadar W Isls
28 B2 Cefn Newpt
27 E1 Cefn Cribwr Brdgnd
55 G2 Cefn-brith Conwy
48 C3 Cefn-mawr Wrexhm
25 F5 Cefn-y-pant Carmth
37 G2 Cefngorwydd Powys
87 F6 Cellardyke Fife
50 B2 Cellarhead Staffs
54 C5 Cemaes IOA
47 E2 Cemmaes Powys
47 G2 Cemmaes Road Powys
36 C1 Cenarth Cerdgn
93 F1 Ceres Fife
7 G5 Cerne Abbas Dorset
18 C6 Cerney Wick Gloucs
54 C4 Cerrigceinwen IOA
55 G1 Cerrigydrudion Conwy
54 D3 Ceunant Gwynd
29 F5 Chaceley Gloucs
2 D4 Chacewater Cnwll
31 G3 Chackmore Bucks
31 F4 Chacombe Nhants
30 B4 Chadbury Worcs
58 A1 Chadderton Oldham
51 E1 Chaddesden C Derb
40 A1 Chaddesley Corbett Worcs
5 E4 Chaddlehanger Devon
19 F4 Chaddleworth W Berk
31 E2 Chadlington Oxon
31 E5 Chadshunt Warwks
42 A4 Chadwell Leics
21 G4 Chadwell Heath Gt Lon
22 B3 Chadwell St Mary Thurr
39 H3 Chadwick Worcs
40 D1 Chadwick End Solhll
7 E6 Chaffcombe Somset
5 G5 Chagford Devon
11 G4 Chailey E Susx
12 C6 Chainhurst Kent
21 F1 Chaldon Surrey
9 G1 Chale IOW
9 G2 Chale Green IOW
20 D4 Chalfont Common Bucks
20 C4 Chalfont St Giles Bucks
20 D4 Chalfont St Peter Bucks
29 F3 Chalford Gloucs
18 B2 Chalford Wilts
19 H6 Chalgrove Oxon
22 B3 Chalk Kent

22 D2 Chalkwell Kent
15 F5 Challacombe Devon
69 E4 Challoch D & G
23 E1 Challock Kent
32 C2 Chalton Beds
10 A4 Chalton Hants
20 C3 Chalvey Slough
11 G3 Chalvington E Susx
20 D5 Chandler's Cross Herts
9 F5 Chandler's Ford Hants
17 H4 Chantry Somset
35 E3 Chantry Suffk
86 C5 Chapel Fife
58 D4 Chapel Allerton Leeds
17 E4 Chapel Allerton Somset
3 F6 Chapel Amble Cnwll
31 H6 Chapel Brampton Nhants
49 G3 Chapel Chorlton Staffs
31 F5 Chapel Green Warwks
59 F3 Chapel Haddlesey N York
103 F3 Chapel Hill Abers
52 D1 Chapel Hill Lincs
18 D3 Chapel Hill Mons
59 E4 Chapel Hill N York
38 D4 Chapel Lawn Shrops
64 B1 Chapel le Dale N York
16 C2 Chapel Leigh Somset
102 C2 Chapel of Garioch Abers
68 C2 Chapel Rossan D & G
19 G4 Chapel Row W Berk
53 G3 Chapel St Leonards Lincs
62 D6 Chapel Stile Cumb
50 B4 Chapel-en-le-Frith Derbys
34 A3 Chapelend Way Essex
85 G2 Chapelhall N Lans
79 E4 Chapelhope Border
71 F6 Chapelknowe D & G
93 H4 Chapelton Angus
15 E4 Chapelton Devon
77 F6 Chapelton S Lans
57 G4 Chapeltown Bl w D
101 E2 Chapeltown Moray
51 E6 Chapeltown Sheff
4 D6 Chapmans Well Devon
18 B2 Chapmanslade Wilts
33 E1 Chapmore End Herts
34 C2 Chappel Essex
7 E6 Chard Somset
7 E6 Chard Junction Somset
7 E6 Chardleigh Green Somset
7 E6 Chardstock Devon
29 E2 Charfield S Glos
23 E1 Charing Kent
30 D4 Charingworth Gloucs
31 E2 Charlbury Oxon
17 H5 Charlcombe BaNES
18 C4 Charlcutt Wilts
30 D5 Charlecote Warwks
15 F4 Charles Devon
34 D4 Charles Tye Suffk
93 F4 Charleston Angus
58 C4 Charlestown Brad
95 H6 Charlestown C Aber
58 B3 Charlestown Calder
3 F4 Charlestown Cnwll
86 B4 Charlestown Fife
105 F3 Charlestown Highld
107 E1 Charlestown Highld
57 F3 Charlestown Salfd
50 B5 Charlesworth Derbys
16 D3 Charlinch Somset
93 F1 Charlottetown Fife
21 G3 Charlton Gt Lon
31 F3 Charlton Nhants
72 C5 Charlton Nthumb
19 F5 Charlton Oxon
16 D2 Charlton Somset
17 G4 Charlton Somset
10 C3 Charlton W Susx
8 B5 Charlton Wilts
18 B2 Charlton Wilts
18 D2 Charlton Wilts
30 B4 Charlton Worcs
49 F1 Charlton Wrekin
30 B3 Charlton Abbots Gloucs
17 F2 Charlton Adam Somset
17 G2 Charlton Horethorne Somset
29 G4 Charlton Kings Gloucs
17 F2 Charlton Mackrell Somset
8 B4 Charlton Marshall Dorset
17 H2 Charlton Musgrove Somset
8 B4 Charlton on the Hill Dorset
8 D5 Charlton-all-Saints Wilts
31 F2 Charlton-on-Otmoor Oxon
10 A5 Charlwood Hants
11 E6 Charlwood Surrey
7 G5 Charminster Dorset
7 E5 Charmouth Dorset
31 G3 Charndon Bucks
19 F6 Charney Bassett Oxon
57 E4 Charnock Richard Lancs
35 F4 Charsfield Suffk
22 C1 Chart Sutton Kent
19 G3 Charter Alley Hants
80 B4 Charterhall Border
17 H4 Charterhouse Somset
85 G4 Chartershall Stirlg
23 F1 Chartham Kent
23 F1 Chartham Hatch Kent
20 C5 Chartridge Bucks
20 B3 Charvil Wokham
31 F5 Charwelton Nhants
30 D3 Chastleton Oxon
14 C2 Chasty Devon
63 G1 Chatburn Lancs
49 G3 Chatcull Staffs
22 C2 Chatham Medway
22 C2 Chatham Green Essex
81 G3 Chathill Nthumb
50 D6 Chatsworth House Derbys
22 C3 Chattenden Medway
43 F1 Chatteris Cambs
57 G4 Chatterton Lancs
34 D3 Chattisham Suffk
80 D2 Chatto Border
81 F3 Chatton Nthumb
15 F2 Chawleigh Devon
10 A5 Chawton Hants
50 B1 Cheadle Staffs
57 H2 Cheadle Stockp
57 H2 Cheadle Hulme Stockp
21 E2 Cheam Gt Lon
31 H1 Chearsley Bucks

49 H2 Chebsey Staffs
19 H5 Checkendon Oxon
49 G4 Checkley Ches
50 B1 Checkley Staffs
34 B4 Chedburgh Suffk
17 F4 Cheddar Somset
31 H2 Cheddington Bucks
50 B2 Cheddleton Staffs
16 D2 Cheddon Fitzpaine Somset
45 F2 Chedgrave Norfk
17 F6 Chedington Dorset
35 F6 Chediston Suffk
30 B2 Chedworth Gloucs
17 E3 Chedzoy Somset
57 H3 Cheetham Hill Manch
57 G3 Cheetwood Salfd
15 F2 Cheldon Devon
49 G6 Chelford Ches
41 E6 Chellaston C Derb
32 B4 Chellington Beds
39 G4 Chelmarsh Shrops
35 E3 Chelmondiston Suffk
50 C4 Chelmorton Derbys
22 C5 Chelmsford Essex
40 C2 Chelmsley Wood Solhll
21 F3 Chelsea Gt Lon
21 G2 Chelsfield Gt Lon
34 D3 Chelsworth Suffk
29 G5 Cheltenham Gloucs
32 C5 Chelveston Nhants
17 F5 Chelvey N Som
17 G5 Chelwood BaNES
11 G5 Chelwood Gate E Susx
18 D5 Chelworth Lower Green Wilts
18 C5 Chelworth Upper Green Wilts
38 D4 Cheney Longville Shrops
20 D5 Chenies Bucks
28 D2 Chepstow Mons
18 C4 Cherhill Wilts
29 F3 Cherington Gloucs
30 D4 Cherington Warwks
9 G6 Cheriton Hants
13 F5 Cheriton Kent
26 A2 Cheriton Swans
5 G6 Cheriton Bishop Devon
15 G2 Cheriton Fitzpaine Devon
24 D3 Cheriton or Stackpole Elidor Pembks
49 E2 Cherrington Wrekin
60 D4 Cherry Burton E R Yk
33 F4 Cherry Hinton Cambs
39 H2 Cherry Orchard Worcs
52 C3 Cherry Willingham Lincs
20 D2 Chertsey Surrey
8 A3 Cheselbourne Dorset
20 C5 Chesham Bucks
57 G4 Chesham Bury
20 C5 Chesham Bois Bucks
21 F5 Cheshunt Herts
7 G4 Chesil Beach Dorset
40 B4 Cheslyn Hay Staffs
40 C1 Chessetts Wood Warwks
21 E2 Chessington Surrey
21 E2 Chessington World of Adventure Gt Lon
48 D5 Chester Ches
48 D5 Chester Cathedral Ches
73 F2 Chester Moor Dur
48 D6 Chester Zoo Ches
73 F2 Chester-le-Street Dur
17 G3 Chesterblade Somset
51 E4 Chesterfield Derbys
40 C4 Chesterfield Staffs
86 D3 Chesterhill Mdloth
80 C2 Chesters Border
80 C1 Chesters Border
42 D2 Chesterton Cambs
33 F4 Chesterton Cambs
18 C6 Chesterton Gloucs
31 F2 Chesterton Oxon
39 G5 Chesterton Shrops
31 E5 Chesterton Green Warwks
72 C3 Chesterwood Nthumb
23 F2 Chestfield Kent
5 G3 Cheston Devon
49 G2 Cheswardine Shrops
81 F4 Cheswick Nthumb
7 G6 Chetnole Dorset
43 G1 Chettisham Cambs
8 B4 Chettle Dorset
39 F5 Chetton Shrops
31 G3 Chetwode Bucks
49 G2 Chetwynd Wrekin
49 G1 Chetwynd Aston Wrekin
34 A4 Cheveley Cambs
21 G1 Chevening Kent
34 B4 Chevington Suffk
80 D1 Cheviot Hills
16 B1 Chevithorne Devon
17 G5 Chew Magna BaNES
17 F5 Chew Stoke BaNES
17 G5 Chewton Keynsham BaNES
17 G4 Chewton Mendip Somset
32 B3 Chicheley M Keyn
10 B3 Chichester W Susx
7 G6 Chickerell Dorset
8 B6 Chicklade Wilts
9 H5 Chidden Hants
10 C5 Chiddingfold Surrey
12 A3 Chiddingly E Susx
11 G6 Chiddingstone Kent
11 H6 Chiddingstone Causeway Kent
7 E5 Chideock Dorset
10 B3 Chidham W Susx
58 D2 Chidswell Kirk
19 F5 Chieveley W Berk
22 B6 Chignall Smealy Essex
22 B6 Chignall St James Essex
21 G4 Chigwell Essex
19 F1 Chilbolton Hants
9 G6 Chilcomb Hants
7 F6 Chilcombe Dorset
17 G5 Chilcompton Somset
40 D4 Chilcote Leics
8 A4 Child Okeford Dorset
49 F2 Child's Ercall Shrops
56 D1 Childer Thornton Ches
19 F5 Childrey Oxon
30 C4 Childswickham Worcs
56 D2 Childwall Lpool
7 G5 Chilfrome Dorset
10 B3 Chilgrove W Susx

23 E1 Chilham Kent
5 E5 Chillaton Devon
23 G1 Chillenden Kent
9 G2 Chillerton IOW
35 G4 Chillesford Suffk
81 F3 Chillingham Nthumb
5 H2 Chillington Devon
7 E6 Chillington Somset
8 C6 Chilmark Wilts
13 E5 Chilmington Green Kent
30 D2 Chilson Oxon
5 E4 Chilsworthy Cnwll
14 C2 Chilsworthy Devon
20 B5 Chiltern Hills
17 F1 Chilthorne Domer Somset
31 G2 Chilton Bucks
65 F6 Chilton Dur
19 G5 Chilton Oxon
19 G1 Chilton Candover Hants
17 G2 Chilton Cantelo Somset
19 E4 Chilton Foliat Wilts
17 E3 Chilton Polden Somset
34 B3 Chilton Street Suffk
16 D3 Chilton Trinity Somset
41 F6 Chilwell Notts
9 F5 Chilworth Hants
10 D6 Chilworth Surrey
19 F6 Chimney Oxon
21 H2 Chineham Hants
21 F4 Chingford Gt Lon
50 B5 Chinley Derbys
20 B5 Chinnor Oxon
49 G3 Chipnall Shrops
33 H5 Chippenham Cambs
18 A4 Chippenham Wilts
20 D5 Chipperfield Herts
33 E2 Chipping Herts
63 F1 Chipping Lancs
30 C4 Chipping Campden Gloucs
30 D3 Chipping Norton Oxon
22 A5 Chipping Ongar Essex
29 E1 Chipping Sodbury S Glos
31 F4 Chipping Warden Nhants
16 C2 Chipstable Somset
21 G1 Chipstead Kent
21 F1 Chipstead Surrey
38 C3 Chirbury Shrops
48 C3 Chirk Wrexhm
81 E5 Chirnside Border
80 D5 Chirnsidebridge Border
18 C3 Chirton Wilts
19 E3 Chisbury Wilts
17 F1 Chiselborough Somset
18 D4 Chiseldon Swindn
19 G6 Chiselhampton Oxon
79 G6 Chisholme Border
21 G2 Chislehurst Gt Lon
23 G2 Chislet Kent
58 B3 Chisley Calder
21 E5 Chiswell Green Herts
21 E3 Chiswick Gt Lon
50 B5 Chisworth Derbys
10 B4 Chithurst W Susx
33 F5 Chittering Cambs
18 C1 Chitterne Wilts
15 F3 Chittlehamholt Devon
15 F3 Chittlehampton Devon
15 F2 Chittlehampton Devon
18 C3 Chittoe Wilts
5 H1 Chivelstone Devon
68 C4 Chlenry D & G
20 C2 Chobham Surrey
19 E1 Cholderton Wilts
20 C5 Cholesbury Bucks
72 D4 Chollerton Nthumb
19 G5 Cholsey Oxon
39 E2 Cholstrey Herefs
66 B3 Chop Gate N York
73 F5 Choppington Nthumb
73 E3 Chopwell Gatesd
49 E4 Chorley Ches
57 F4 Chorley Lancs
39 F4 Chorley Shrops
20 D5 Chorleywood Herts
20 D5 Chorleywood West Herts
49 G4 Chorlton Ches
49 E4 Chorlton Lane Ches
57 G2 Chorlton-cum-Hardy Manch
38 D4 Choulton Shrops
49 G5 Chowley Ches
33 F3 Chrishall Essex
84 B3 Chrisswell Inver
43 F2 Christchurch Cambs
8 D3 Christchurch Dorset
28 B2 Christchurch Mons
18 C4 Christian Malford Wilts
49 E5 Christleton Ches
17 E4 Christon N Som
81 G2 Christon Bank Nthumb
5 H5 Christow Devon
6 A4 Chudleigh Devon
6 A3 Chudleigh Knighton Devon
15 F3 Chulmleigh Devon
57 G5 Church Lancs
49 G1 Church Aston Wrekin
31 H6 Church Brampton Nhants
40 D6 Church Broughton Derbys
20 B1 Church Crookham Hants
49 H1 Church Eaton Staffs
32 D3 Church End Beds
34 B2 Church End Essex
21 E4 Church End Gt Lon
19 H2 Church End Hants
31 E3 Church Enstone Oxon
59 F4 Church Fenton N York
6 D5 Church Green Devon
31 E2 Church Hanborough Oxon
49 F5 Church Hill Ches
66 C3 Church Houses N York
8 B2 Church Knowle Dorset
41 H3 Church Langton Leics
41 F1 Church Lawford Warwks
49 G5 Church Lawton Ches
49 H6 Church Leigh Staffs
30 B5 Church Lench Worcs
50 C1 Church Mayfield Staffs
49 F5 Church Minshull Ches
10 C2 Church Norton W Susx
39 G4 Church Preen Shrops
38 D6 Church Pulverbatch Shrops
31 G5 Church Stowe Nhants
22 C3 Church Street Kent
39 E4 Church Stretton Shrops
27 F2 Church Village Rhondd

51 F3 Church Warsop Notts
29 E4 Churcham Gloucs
29 F4 Churchdown Gloucs
23 E4 Churchend Essex
40 B3 Churchfield Birm
6 D5 Churchill Devon
17 F5 Churchill N Som
30 D3 Churchill Oxon
39 H4 Churchill Worcs
30 A5 Churchill Worcs
6 D6 Churchinford Somset
41 F2 Churchover Warwks
16 D1 Churchstanton Somset
38 C5 Churchstoke Powys
5 G2 Churchstow Devon
50 D3 Churchtown Derbys
63 E1 Churchtown Lancs
6 A2 Churston Ferrers Torbay
10 B5 Churt Surrey
48 B5 Churton Ches
58 D3 Churwell Leeds
46 D5 Chwilog Gwynd
2 B2 Chyandour Cnwll
2 B3 Chysauster Cnwll
48 B5 Cilcain Flints
36 B3 Cilcennin Cerdgn
26 D3 Cilfrew Neath
27 F2 Cilfynydd Rhondd
36 B1 Cilgerran Pembks
26 D3 Cilmaengwyn Neath
38 A1 Cilmery Powys
26 C2 Cilsan Carmth
47 G5 Ciltalgarth Gwynd
37 F1 Cilycwm Carmth
26 D2 Cimla Neath
28 D4 Cinderford Gloucs
20 C3 Cippenham Slough
18 C6 Cirencester Gloucs
21 F3 City Gt Lon
21 G3 City Airport Gt Lon
88 C4 Clabhach Ag & B
84 A4 Clachaig Ag & B
89 H1 Clachan Ag & B
90 A3 Clachan Ag & B
83 F2 Clachan Ag & B
96 D5 Clachan Highld
88 B4 Clachan Mor Ag & B
111 b4 Clachan na Luib W Isls
85 E3 Clachan of Campsie E Duns
111 b4 Clachan-a-Luib W Isls
89 H1 Clachan-Seil Ag & B
69 E5 Clacheasny D & G
107 E1 Clachnaharry Highld
108 A2 Clachtoll Highld
94 B3 Clackavoid P & K
85 H4 Clackmannan Stirlg
101 E5 Clackmarras Moray
23 F6 Clacton-on-Sea Essex
90 C1 Cladich Ag & B
30 B5 Cladswell Worcs
89 G4 Claggan Highld
104 B2 Claigan Highld
10 A4 Clanfield Hants
19 E6 Clanfield Oxon
19 E1 Clanville Hants
17 G2 Clanville Somset
83 G2 Claonaig Ag & B
33 F2 Clapgate Herts
32 C4 Clapham Beds
21 F3 Clapham Gt Lon
63 G3 Clapham N York
10 D3 Clapham W Susx
7 E6 Clapton Somset
17 G4 Clapton Somset
17 F6 Clapton-in-Gordano N Som
30 C2 Clapton-on-the-Hill Gloucs
73 E3 Claravale Gatesd
25 E4 Clarbeston Pembks
24 D4 Clarbeston Road Pembks
51 H5 Clarborough Notts
34 B3 Clare Suffk
70 B5 Clarebrand D & G
70 B5 Clarencefield D & G
72 D4 Clarewood Nthumb
80 B2 Clarilaw Border
85 E2 Clarkston E Rens
108 A2 Clashmore Highld
107 F4 Clashmore Highld
108 A2 Clashnessie Highld
101 E2 Clashnoir Moray
92 C2 Clathy P & K
92 C2 Clathymore P & K
102 B2 Clatt Abers
38 A5 Clatter Powys
16 C2 Clatworthy Somset
57 E6 Claughton Lancs
63 E3 Claughton Lancs
56 C2 Claughton Wirral
30 D6 Claverdon Warwks
17 F5 Claverham N Som
33 F2 Clavering Essex
39 G5 Claverley Shrops
18 A3 Claverton BaNES
27 F1 Clawdd-coch V Glam
48 B4 Clawdd-newydd Denbgs
14 C1 Clawton Devon
52 D4 Claxby Lincs
59 G5 Claxton N York
45 F2 Claxton Norfk
41 G1 Clay Coton Nhants
51 E3 Clay Cross Derbys
41 F2 Claybrooke Magna Leics
31 F5 Claydon Oxon
35 E4 Claydon Suffk
79 G1 Claygate D & G
12 C6 Claygate Kent
21 E2 Claygate Surrey
21 F5 Clayhall Gt Lon
16 B2 Clayhanger Devon
16 C1 Clayhidon Devon
12 D4 Clayhill E Susx
110 B5 Claypits Gloucs
29 E3 Claypits Gloucs
42 B6 Claypole Lincs
58 C3 Clayton Brad
59 F1 Clayton Donc
11 F3 Clayton W Susx
58 D1 Clayton West Kirk
57 G5 Clayton-le-Moors Lancs
57 G5 Clayton-le-Woods Lancs
51 H5 Clayworth Notts
96 C1 Cleadale Highld
73 G2 Cleadon S Tyne
5 F3 Clearbrook Devon
28 D3 Clearwell Gloucs

Cleasby - Coxtie Green 167

65 F4 **Cleasby** N York
111 h1 **Cleat** Ork
65 E5 **Cleatlam** Dur
70 D1 **Cleator** Cumb
70 D1 **Cleator Moor** Cumb
58 C3 **Cleckheaton** Kirk
39 E4 **Clee St Margaret** Shrops
39 F3 **Cleehill** Shrops
85 F2 **Cleekhimin** N Lans
53 E6 **Cleethorpes** NE Lin
39 F4 **Cleeton St Mary** Shrops
17 F5 **Cleeve** N Som
19 H4 **Cleeve** Oxon
29 G5 **Cleeve Hill** Gloucs
30 C5 **Cleeve Prior** Worcs
87 F4 **Cleghornie** E Loth
28 C6 **Clehonger** Herefs
86 B5 **Cleish** P & K
85 G2 **Cleland** N Lans
90 B2 **Clenamacrie** Ag & B
43 G4 **Clenchwarton** Norfk
102 D5 **Clenerty** Abers
40 A2 **Clent** Worcs
39 F3 **Cleobury Mortimer** Shrops
39 F4 **Cleobury North** Shrops
75 E4 **Cleongart** Ag & B
107 G1 **Clephanton** Highld
79 F3 **Clerkhill** D & G
78 B3 **Cleuch-head** D & G
18 C4 **Clevancy** Wilts
17 E6 **Clevedon** N Som
56 D6 **Cleveleys** Lancs
18 C5 **Cleverton** Wilts
17 F4 **Clewer** Somset
44 D6 **Cley next the Sea** Norfk
64 A5 **Cliburn** Cumb
19 H2 **Cliddesden** Hants
12 D4 **Cliff End** E Susx
22 C3 **Cliffe** Medway
65 F4 **Cliffe** N York
59 G3 **Cliffe** N York
22 C3 **Cliffe Woods** Medway
38 C1 **Clifford** Herefs
59 E4 **Clifford** Leeds
30 D5 **Clifford Chambers** Warwks
29 E5 **Clifford's Mesne** Gloucs
32 D3 **Clifton** Beds
17 G6 **Clifton** Bristl
41 F6 **Clifton** C Nott
58 C2 **Clifton** Calder
71 H2 **Clifton** Cumb
50 C1 **Clifton** Derbys
51 F6 **Clifton** Donc
57 E5 **Clifton** Lancs
58 C4 **Clifton** N York
31 F3 **Clifton** Oxon
39 H1 **Clifton** Worcs
59 G5 **Clifton** York
40 D4 **Clifton Campville** Staffs
19 G6 **Clifton Hampden** Oxon
32 B4 **Clifton Reynes** M Keyn
41 F1 **Clifton upon Dunsmore** Warwks
39 G2 **Clifton upon Teme** Worcs
23 H3 **Cliftonville** Kent
10 C2 **Climping** W Susx
18 A2 **Clink** Somset
58 D5 **Clint** N York
44 D3 **Clint Green** Norfk
102 D1 **Clinterty** C Aber
80 C3 **Clintmains** Border
45 G3 **Clippesby** Norfk
42 B4 **Clipsham** Rutlnd
41 H2 **Clipston** Nhants
41 G6 **Clipston** Notts
32 B2 **Clipstone** Beds
51 G3 **Clipstone** Notts
57 G6 **Clitheroe** Lancs
49 E2 **Clive** Shrops
52 C5 **Clixby** Lincs
29 G2 **Cloatley** Wilts
48 B4 **Clocaenog** Denbgs
101 F5 **Clochan** Moray
93 G4 **Clochtow** Angus
28 B5 **Clodock** Herefs
103 E4 **Clola** Abers
32 C3 **Clophill** Beds
32 C6 **Clopton** Nhants
35 E4 **Clopton** Suffk
35 E4 **Clopton Corner** Suffk
6 C2 **Clos du Valle** Guern
78 C2 **Closeburn** D & G
78 C2 **Closeburnmill** D & G
7 G6 **Closworth** Somset
33 E2 **Clothall** Herts
49 E5 **Clotton** Ches
58 A2 **Clough Foot** Calder
58 C2 **Clough Head** Calder
67 F3 **Cloughton** N York
111 k2 **Clousta** Shet
94 C3 **Clova** Angus
14 C3 **Clovelly** Devon
79 G6 **Clovenfords** Border
90 B5 **Clovulin** Highld
57 G5 **Clow Bridge** Lancs
51 F4 **Clowne** Derbys
39 G3 **Clows Top** Worcs
97 H3 **Cluanie Inn** Highld
97 H3 **Cluanie Lodge** Highld
69 E3 **Clugston** D & G
38 C4 **Clun** Shrops
100 B4 **Clunas** Highld
38 D4 **Clunbury** Shrops
99 F5 **Clune** Highld
98 A2 **Clunes** Highld
38 D4 **Clungunford** Shrops
102 C4 **Clunie** Abers
92 D4 **Clunie** P & K
38 D4 **Clunton** Shrops
86 C5 **Cluny** Fife
17 G5 **Clutton** BaNES
49 E4 **Clutton** Ches
17 G5 **Clutton Hill** BaNES
27 G4 **Clydach** Mons
26 C3 **Clydach** Swans
27 E2 **Clydach Vale** Rhondd
84 D3 **Clydebank** W Duns
18 C4 **Clyffe Pypard** Wilts
84 B4 **Clynder** Ag & B
25 E4 **Clynderwen** Carmth
26 D3 **Clyne** Neath
54 C2 **Clynnog-fawr** Gwynd
38 C1 **Clyro** Powys
6 B5 **Clyst Honiton** Devon
6 B5 **Clyst Hydon** Devon
6 B4 **Clyst St George** Devon
6 B5 **Clyst St Lawrence** Devon
6 B4 **Clyst St Mary** Devon
111 d6 **Cnoc** W Isls
37 F4 **Cnwch Coch** Cerdgn
4 D4 **Coad's Green** Cnwll
78 B6 **Coalburn** S Lans
73 E3 **Coalburns** Gatesd
29 E3 **Coaley** Gloucs
22 C5 **Coalhill** Essex
29 E1 **Coalpit Heath** S Glos
39 F6 **Coalport** Wrekin
85 H5 **Coalsnaughton** Clacks
86 D5 **Coaltown of Balgonie** Fife
86 D5 **Coaltown of Wemyss** Fife
41 E4 **Coalville** Leics
72 B3 **Coanwood** Nthumb
17 F1 **Coat** Somset
85 F2 **Coatbridge** N Lans
85 F2 **Coatdyke** N Lans
18 D5 **Coate** Swindn
18 C3 **Coate** Wilts
43 E2 **Coates** Cambs
29 G3 **Coates** Gloucs
52 B4 **Coates** Lincs
10 C4 **Coates** W Susx
15 E4 **Cobbaton** Devon
29 G4 **Coberley** Gloucs
22 B2 **Cobham** Kent
20 D2 **Cobham** Surrey
39 E2 **Cobnash** Herefs
6 b2 **Cobo** Guern
103 E5 **Coburby** Abers
101 E1 **Cock Bridge** Abers
22 C5 **Cock Clarks** Essex
34 A1 **Cock Green** Essex
12 D4 **Cock Marling** E Susx
33 E4 **Cockayne Hatley** Beds
87 G3 **Cockburnspath** Border
86 D3 **Cockenzie and Port Seton** E Loth
63 E2 **Cockerham** Lancs
71 E2 **Cockermouth** Cumb
32 D1 **Cockernhoe Green** Herts
26 C2 **Cockett** Swans
65 E5 **Cockfield** Dur
34 C4 **Cockfield** Suffk
21 F5 **Cockfosters** Gt Lon
10 C4 **Cocking** W Susx
10 C4 **Cocking Causeway** W Susx
6 A2 **Cockington** Torbay
17 F4 **Cocklake** Somset
73 F5 **Cockle Park** Nthumb
44 B3 **Cockley Cley** Norfk
20 B3 **Cockpole Green** Wokham
48 D2 **Cockshutt** Shrops
44 D6 **Cockthorpe** Norfk
6 B4 **Cockwood** Devon
50 B4 **Cockyard** Derbys
35 E4 **Coddenham** Suffk
29 E6 **Coddington** Herefs
52 A1 **Coddington** Notts
18 C1 **Codford St Mary** Wilts
18 C1 **Codford St Peter** Wilts
32 D1 **Codicote** Herts
10 D4 **Codmore Hill** W Susx
51 E2 **Codnor** Derbys
29 E1 **Codrington** S Glos
39 H6 **Codsall** Staffs
39 H6 **Codsall Wood** Staffs
48 C5 **Coed Talon** Flints
28 B3 **Coed-y-paen** Mons
54 C4 **Coedana** IOA
48 C4 **Coedpoeth** Wrexhm
6 A3 **Coffinswell** Devon
6 B4 **Cofton** Devon
40 B1 **Cofton Hackett** Worcs
16 D6 **Cogan** V Glam
32 A4 **Cogenhoe** Nhants
34 C1 **Coggeshall** Essex
99 E4 **Coignafearn** Highld
94 C5 **Coilacriech** Abers
85 E6 **Coilantogle** Stirlg
96 B5 **Coillore** Highld
98 C3 **Coiltry** Highld
27 E1 **Coity** Brdgnd
111 d6 **Col** W Isls
107 E6 **Colaboll** Highld
3 E5 **Colan** Cnwll
6 C4 **Colaton Raleigh** Devon
104 A1 **Colbost** Highld
65 F3 **Colburn** N York
64 B5 **Colby** Cumb
116 b2 **Colby** IOM
45 E5 **Colby** Norfk
34 D2 **Colchester** Essex
19 G4 **Cold Ash** W Berk
41 G1 **Cold Ashby** Nhants
17 H6 **Cold Ashton** S Glos
30 C2 **Cold Aston** Gloucs
32 B4 **Cold Brayfield** M Keyn
52 C4 **Cold Hanworth** Lincs
31 G5 **Cold Higham** Nhants
66 B2 **Cold Kirby** N York
22 D5 **Cold Norton** Essex
42 A3 **Cold Overton** Leics
109 F5 **Coldbackie** Highld
11 F3 **Coldean** Br & H
5 H4 **Coldeast** Devon
58 B3 **Colden** Calder
9 G5 **Colden Common** Hants
35 G4 **Coldfair Green** Suffk
11 E6 **Coldharbour** Surrey
81 E6 **Coldingham** Border
49 H3 **Coldmeece** Staffs
13 G6 **Coldred** Kent
15 F2 **Coldridge** Devon
80 D4 **Coldstream** Border
10 D4 **Coldwaltham** W Susx
28 C6 **Coldwell** Herefs
103 E3 **Coldwells** Abers
17 G2 **Cole** Somset
38 D4 **Colebatch** Shrops
6 B6 **Colebrook** Devon
15 G1 **Colebrooke** Devon
52 B2 **Coleby** Lincs
60 C2 **Coleby** N Linc
15 G1 **Coleford** Devon
28 D4 **Coleford** Gloucs
17 G4 **Coleford** Somset
16 C3 **Coleford Water** Somset
45 E1 **Colegate End** Norfk
8 C3 **Colehill** Dorset
11 G5 **Coleman's Hatch** E Susx
48 D3 **Colemere** Shrops
10 A5 **Colemore** Hants
92 D2 **Colenden** P & K
18 A4 **Colerne** Wilts
30 B2 **Colesbourne** Gloucs
20 C5 **Coleshill** Bucks
19 E5 **Coleshill** Oxon
40 D2 **Coleshill** Warwks
17 G4 **Coley** BaNES
11 E5 **Colgate** W Susx
87 E6 **Colinsburgh** Fife
86 C3 **Colinton** C Edin
83 H3 **Colintraive** Ag & B
44 C4 **Colkirk** Norfk
93 E3 **Collace** P & K
111 l3 **Collafirth** Shet
5 G1 **Collaton** Devon
6 A2 **Collaton St Mary** Torbay
100 D5 **College of Roseisle** Moray
20 B2 **College Town** Br For
93 E1 **Collessie** Fife
21 G4 **Collier Row** Gt Lon
12 C6 **Collier Street** Kent
33 F1 **Collier's End** Herts
103 F2 **Collieston** Abers
70 D6 **Collin** D & G
19 E2 **Collingbourne Ducis** Wilts
19 E2 **Collingbourne Kingston** Wilts
59 E4 **Collingham** Leeds
52 A2 **Collingham** Notts
39 F2 **Collington** Herefs
31 H5 **Collingtree** Nhants
57 E2 **Collins Green** Warrtn
93 H4 **Colliston** Angus
6 C6 **Colliton** Devon
42 C2 **Collyweston** Nhants
68 C6 **Colmonell** S Ayrs
32 C4 **Colmworth** Beds
30 C1 **Coln Rogers** Gloucs
30 C1 **Coln St Aldwyns** Gloucs
30 C1 **Coln St Dennis** Gloucs
20 D3 **Colnbrook** Slough
33 F6 **Colne** Cambs
58 A4 **Colne** Lancs
34 C2 **Colne Engaine** Essex
45 E3 **Colney** Norfk
21 E5 **Colney Heath** Herts
102 C3 **Colpy** Abers
79 F6 **Colquhar** Border
42 B4 **Colsterworth** Lincs
41 G6 **Colston Bassett** Notts
12 B6 **Colt's Hill** Kent
100 D5 **Coltfield** Moray
45 F4 **Coltishall** Norfk
62 D4 **Colton** Cumb
59 E3 **Colton** Leeds
59 F4 **Colton** N York
44 D3 **Colton** Norfk
40 B5 **Colton** Staffs
70 C4 **Colvend** D & G
29 E6 **Colwall** Herefs
72 D4 **Colwell** Nthumb
40 B5 **Colwich** Staffs
16 B6 **Colwinston** V Glam
10 C2 **Colworth** W Susx
55 F4 **Colwyn Bay** Conwy
6 D5 **Colyford** Devon
6 D5 **Colyton** Devon
31 E2 **Combe** Oxon
19 F3 **Combe** W Berk
18 A3 **Combe Down** BaNES
6 A2 **Combe Fishacre** Devon
16 C2 **Combe Florey** Somset
17 H5 **Combe Hay** BaNES
15 E5 **Combe Martin** Devon
6 C5 **Combe Raleigh** Devon
7 E6 **Combe St Nicholas** Somset
6 A3 **Combeinteignhead** Devon
57 F1 **Comberbach** Ches
40 C4 **Comberford** Staffs
33 F4 **Comberton** Cambs
39 E3 **Comberton** Herefs
30 D5 **Combrook** Warwks
50 B4 **Combs** Derbys
34 D4 **Combs** Suffk
34 D4 **Combs Ford** Suffk
16 D3 **Combwich** Somset
95 F6 **Comers** Abers
39 H3 **Comhampton** Worcs
25 E4 **Commercial** Pembks
47 G2 **Commins Coch** Powys
4 C4 **Common Moor** Cnwll
66 C4 **Commondale** N York
50 B5 **Compstall** Stockp
69 G3 **Compstonend** D & G
6 A2 **Compton** Devon
9 F5 **Compton** Hants
39 G4 **Compton** Staffs
10 C6 **Compton** Surrey
19 G4 **Compton** W Berk
10 B3 **Compton** W Susx
18 D2 **Compton** Wilts
8 B5 **Compton Abbas** Dorset
30 B2 **Compton Abdale** Gloucs
18 C4 **Compton Bassett** Wilts
19 E5 **Compton Beauchamp** Oxon
17 E4 **Compton Bishop** Somset
8 C6 **Compton Chamberlayne** Wilts
17 G5 **Compton Dando** BaNES
17 F2 **Compton Dundon** Somset
17 E1 **Compton Durville** Somset
28 D1 **Compton Greenfield** S Glos
17 F4 **Compton Martin** BaNES
17 G2 **Compton Pauncefoot** Somset
7 G5 **Compton Valence** Dorset
86 A5 **Comrie** Fife
92 A2 **Comrie** P & K
90 C5 **Conaglen House** Highld
97 F5 **Conchra** Highld
92 D4 **Concraigie** P & K
29 G6 **Conderton** Worcs
30 C3 **Condicote** Gloucs
85 F3 **Condorrat** N Lans
39 E6 **Condover** Shrops
29 F4 **Coney Hill** Gloucs
34 C6 **Coney Weston** Suffk
10 D4 **Coneyhurst Common** W Susx
66 D1 **Coneysthorpe** N York
4 D4 **Congdon's Shop** Cnwll
41 E4 **Congerstone** Leics
44 A4 **Congham** Norfk
49 H5 **Congleton** Ches
17 F5 **Congresbury** N Som
70 D6 **Conheath** D & G
100 C4 **Conicavel** Moray
52 D1 **Coningsby** Lincs
42 D1 **Conington** Cambs
33 E5 **Conington** Cambs
51 F6 **Conisbrough** Donc
53 F5 **Conisholme** Lincs
62 C5 **Coniston** Cumb
61 E3 **Coniston** E R Yk
58 A5 **Coniston Cold** N York
58 B6 **Conistone** N York
48 C6 **Connah's Quay** Flints
90 B2 **Connel** Ag & B
77 E3 **Connel Park** E Ayrs
2 C3 **Connor Downs** Cnwll
107 E2 **Conon Bridge** Highld
58 B4 **Cononley** N York
50 B2 **Consall** Staffs
73 E2 **Consett** Dur
65 F3 **Constable Burton** N York
2 D2 **Constantine** Cnwll
106 D2 **Contin** Highld
55 F4 **Conwy** Conwy
34 C5 **Conyer's Green** Suffk
12 C3 **Cooden** E Susx
35 E1 **Cook's Green** Essex
14 D2 **Cookbury** Devon
20 C4 **Cookham** W & M
20 B4 **Cookham Dean** W & M
20 C4 **Cookham Rise** W & M
30 B5 **Cookhill** Warwks
35 F6 **Cookley** Suffk
39 H4 **Cookley** Worcs
20 A4 **Cookley Green** Oxon
95 G5 **Cookney** Abers
34 D4 **Cooks Green** Suffk
22 B5 **Cooksmill Green** Essex
10 D4 **Coolham** W Susx
22 C3 **Cooling** Medway
6 B3 **Coombe** Devon
6 C5 **Coombe** Devon
29 E2 **Coombe** Gloucs
9 H5 **Coombe** Hants
8 D5 **Coombe Bissett** Wilts
6 A3 **Coombe Cellars** Devon
16 B2 **Coombe End** Somset
29 F5 **Coombe Hill** Gloucs
8 B2 **Coombe Keynes** Dorset
6 B2 **Coombe Pafford** Torbay
38 D2 **Coombes-Moor** Herefs
100 C4 **Cooperhill** Moray
21 G5 **Coopersale Common** Essex
21 G5 **Coopersale Street** Essex
23 G2 **Cop Street** Kent
35 E3 **Copdock** Suffk
34 C1 **Copford Green** Essex
59 E6 **Copgrove** N York
111 l3 **Copister** Shet
32 C3 **Cople** Beds
65 E5 **Copley** Dur
59 F4 **Copmanthorpe** York
49 G2 **Copmere End** Staffs
56 D6 **Copp** Lancs
14 B1 **Coppathorne** Cnwll
40 A5 **Coppenhall** Staffs
2 C3 **Copperhouse** Cnwll
32 D6 **Coppingford** Cambs
15 G2 **Copplestone** Devon
57 E4 **Coppull** Lancs
11 E4 **Copsale** W Susx
57 F5 **Copster Green** Lancs
41 F2 **Copston Magna** Warwks
65 G1 **Copt Hewick** N York
41 F4 **Copt Oak** Leics
11 F5 **Copthorne** W Susx
9 E4 **Copythorne** Hants
22 B4 **Corbets Tey** Gt Lon
7 a1 **Corbiere** Jersey
72 D3 **Corbridge** Nthumb
42 B1 **Corby** Nhants
42 C4 **Corby Glen** Lincs
75 H4 **Cordon** N Ayrs
39 F3 **Coreley** Shrops
16 D1 **Corfe** Somset
8 C2 **Corfe Castle** Dorset
8 C3 **Corfe Mullen** Dorset
39 E4 **Corfton** Shrops
94 C6 **Corgarff** Abers
9 H5 **Corhampton** Hants
40 D2 **Corley** Warwks
40 D2 **Corley Ash** Warwks
94 C3 **Cormuir** Angus
34 C3 **Cornard Tye** Suffk
65 G6 **Cornforth** Dur
102 B5 **Cornhill** Abers
81 E4 **Cornhill-on-Tweed** Nthumb
58 A3 **Cornholme** Calder
88 B3 **Cornoigmore** Ag & B
73 E1 **Cornsay** Dur
73 F1 **Cornsay Colliery** Dur
107 E2 **Corntown** Highld
27 E1 **Corntown** V Glam
30 D3 **Cornwell** Oxon
5 F3 **Cornwood** Devon
5 H3 **Cornworthy** Devon
90 C6 **Corpach** Highld
45 E5 **Corpusty** Norfk
94 D6 **Corrachree** Abers
97 F3 **Corran** Highld
90 B5 **Corran** Highld
79 E2 **Corrie** D & G
75 H5 **Corrie** N Ayrs
75 G3 **Corriecravie** N Ayrs
75 H4 **Corriegills** N Ayrs
98 B2 **Corriegour Lodge Hotel** Highld
106 C2 **Corriemoille** Highld
98 C5 **Corrimony** Highld
52 B4 **Corringham** Lincs
22 C4 **Corringham** Thurr
47 F2 **Corris** Gwynd
47 F2 **Corris Uchaf** Gwynd
84 B5 **Corrow** Ag & B
96 D4 **Corry** Highld
15 F1 **Corscombe** Devon
7 F6 **Corscombe** Dorset
29 F5 **Corse Lawn** Gloucs
18 B4 **Corsham** Wilts
102 C1 **Corsindae** Abers
18 B2 **Corsley** Wilts
18 A2 **Corsley Heath** Wilts
78 B1 **Corsock** D & G
17 H5 **Corston** BaNES
18 B5 **Corston** Wilts
86 C3 **Corstorphine** C Edin
94 C2 **Cortachy** Angus
45 H2 **Corton** Suffk
18 B1 **Corton** Wilts
17 G2 **Corton Denham** Somset
90 C5 **Coruanan Lodge** Highld
48 B4 **Corwen** Denbgs
5 E5 **Coryton** Devon
22 C4 **Coryton** Thurr
41 F3 **Cosby** Leics
40 B3 **Coseley** Dudley
32 A3 **Cosgrove** Nhants
9 H4 **Cosham** C Port
24 D3 **Cosheston** Pembks
92 A4 **Coshieville** P & K
51 F1 **Cossall** Notts
41 G4 **Cossington** Leics
17 E3 **Cossington** Somset
45 E3 **Costessey** Norfk
41 F5 **Costock** Notts
42 A4 **Coston** Leics
44 D3 **Coston** Norfk
19 F6 **Cote** Oxon
49 F5 **Cotebrook** Ches
71 G4 **Cotehill** Cumb
41 F5 **Cotes** Leics
41 F2 **Cotesbach** Leics
41 G6 **Cotgrave** Notts
102 D1 **Cothal** Abers
42 A6 **Cotham** Notts
64 D5 **Cotherstone** Dur
19 F6 **Cothill** Oxon
6 D5 **Cotleigh** Devon
51 F1 **Cotmanhay** Derbys
33 F4 **Coton** Cambs
41 G1 **Coton** Nhants
49 G2 **Coton** Staffs
49 H2 **Coton Clanford** Staffs
49 E1 **Coton Hill** Shrops
40 D5 **Coton in the Elms** Derbys
30 B1 **Cotswolds**
5 H3 **Cott** Devon
57 E5 **Cottam** Lancs
52 A3 **Cottam** Notts
33 F5 **Cottenham** Cambs
33 E2 **Cottered** Herts
42 C1 **Cotterstock** Nhants
41 G1 **Cottesbrooke** Nhants
42 B3 **Cottesmore** Rutlnd
60 D3 **Cottingham** E R Yk
42 A1 **Cottingham** Nhants
58 C4 **Cottingley** Brad
31 G3 **Cottisford** Oxon
34 D5 **Cotton** Suffk
101 G2 **Cottown** Abers
102 D1 **Cottown** Abers
102 D3 **Cottown of Gight** Abers
5 E3 **Cotts** Devon
30 C5 **Coughton** Warwks
83 E2 **Coulaghailtro** Ag & B
97 G6 **Coulags** Highld
94 D6 **Coull** Abers
84 B4 **Coulport** Ag & B
21 F2 **Coulsdon** Gt Lon
18 B2 **Coulston** Wilts
78 D5 **Coulter** S Lans
66 C1 **Coulton** N York
93 F2 **Coultra** Fife
39 E6 **Cound** Shrops
65 F6 **Coundon** Dur
64 D2 **Countersett** N York
6 B4 **Countess Wear** Devon
41 G3 **Countesthorpe** Leics
15 F5 **Countisbury** Devon
93 E3 **Coupar Angus** P & K
81 E3 **Coupland** Nthumb
75 F5 **Cour** Ag & B
78 D2 **Courance** D & G
26 B5 **Court Henry** Carmth
97 E2 **Courteachan** Highld
31 H5 **Courteenhall** Nhants
23 E4 **Courtsend** Essex
16 D3 **Courtway** Somset
86 D3 **Cousland** Mdloth
12 B5 **Cousley Wood** E Susx
84 B4 **Cove** Ag & B
87 G3 **Cove** Border
16 B1 **Cove** Devon
20 B1 **Cove** Hants
105 F5 **Cove** Highld
95 H6 **Cove Bay** C Aber
35 H6 **Covehithe** Suffk
40 A4 **Coven** Staffs
33 F6 **Coveney** Cambs
53 E4 **Covenham St Bartholomew** Lincs
53 E4 **Covenham St Mary** Lincs
41 E2 **Coventry** Covtry
41 E1 Coventry Airport Warwks
2 D1 **Coverack** Cnwll
2 D2 **Coverack Bridges** Cnwll
65 E2 **Coverham** N York
32 C5 **Covington** Cambs
78 C6 **Covington** S Lans
30 C4 **Cow Honeybourne** Worcs
63 F3 **Cowan Bridge** Lancs
12 B3 **Cowbeech** E Susx
43 E4 **Cowbit** Lincs
16 B6 **Cowbridge** V Glam
11 G5 **Cowden** Kent
86 B5 **Cowdenbeath** Fife
50 D2 **Cowers Lane** Derbys
9 G3 **Cowes** IOW
66 B2 **Cowesby** N York
11 E4 **Cowfold** W Susx
28 D2 **Cowhill** S Glos
85 G4 **Cowie** Stirlg
6 A5 **Cowley** Devon
29 G4 **Cowley** Gloucs
20 D3 **Cowley** Gt Lon
31 F1 **Cowley** Oxon
57 F4 **Cowling** Lancs
58 B4 **Cowling** N York
65 F2 **Cowling** N York
34 A4 **Cowlinge** Suffk
73 G4 **Cowpen** Nthumb
10 A3 **Cowplain** Hants
72 C1 **Cowshill** Dur
17 F5 **Cowslip Green** N Som
59 E5 **Cowthorpe** N York
49 F3 **Coxbank** Ches
51 E1 **Coxbench** Derbys
14 B1 **Coxford** Cnwll
44 C5 **Coxford** Norfk
22 C1 **Coxheath** Kent
65 G6 **Coxhoe** Dur
17 F3 **Coxley** Somset
17 F3 **Coxley Wick** Somset
22 B5 **Coxtie Green** Essex

66 B1 **Coxwold** N York
27 E1 **Coychurch** Brdgnd
76 D3 **Coylton** S Ayrs
99 G4 **Coylumbridge** Highld
27 E2 **Coytrahen** Brdgnd
30 B6 **Crabbs Cross** Worcs
11 E4 **Crabtree** W Susx
64 B5 **Crackenthorpe** Cumb
14 B1 **Crackington Haven** Cnwll
49 G1 **Crackleybank** Shrops
58 B5 **Cracoe** N York
6 C6 **Craddock** Devon
40 B2 **Cradley** Dudley
39 G1 **Cradley** Herefs
40 B2 **Cradley Heath** Sandw
27 F5 **Cradoc** Powys
4 D2 **Crafthole** Cnwll
32 B1 **Crafton** Bucks
58 B2 **Cragg Vale** Calder
100 C2 **Craggan** Highld
73 F2 **Craghead** Dur
27 E5 **Crai** Powys
101 G5 **Craibstone** Moray
93 G4 **Craichie** Angus
95 F2 **Craig** Angus
105 H1 **Craig** Highld
26 D3 **Craig Llangiwg** Neath
77 E3 **Craigbank** E Ayrs
86 C2 **Craigburn** Border
79 F2 **Craigcleuch** D & G
102 D3 **Craigdam** Abers
83 F6 **Craigdhu** Ag & B
102 C1 **Craigearn** Abers
101 E4 **Craigellachie** Moray
92 D2 **Craigend** P & K
84 D3 **Craigend** Rens
84 C4 **Craigendoran** Ag & B
69 E4 **Craighlaw** D & G
82 D2 **Craighouse** Ag & B
92 D3 **Craigie** P & K
76 D4 **Craigie** S Ayrs
103 E5 **Craigiefold** Abers
70 B5 **Craigley** D & G
86 C3 **Craiglockhart** C Edin
101 F5 **Craiglug** Moray
86 D3 **Craigmillar** C Edin
78 B2 **Craigneston** D & G
85 G2 **Craigneuk** N Lans
85 G2 **Craigneuk** N Lans
89 G3 **Craignure** Ag & B
95 F3 **Craigo** Angus
93 F1 **Craigrothie** Fife
91 F1 **Craigruie** Stirlg
93 G3 **Craigton** Angus
95 G6 **Craigton** C Aber
84 D1 **Craigton** E Rens
93 E4 **Craigton of Airlie** Angus
87 F6 **Crail** Fife
80 C3 **Crailing** Border
51 H6 **Craiselound** N Linc
65 F2 **Crakehall** N York
60 B6 **Crambe** N York
73 H4 **Cramlington** Nthumb
86 C3 **Cramond** C Edin
86 C3 **Cramond Bridge** C Edin
49 G6 **Cranage** Ches
49 G3 **Cranberry** Staffs
8 C4 **Cranborne** Dorset
12 C5 **Cranbrook** Kent
32 B3 **Cranfield** Beds
20 D3 **Cranford** Gt Lon
32 B6 **Cranford St Andrew** Nhants
32 B6 **Cranford St John** Nhants
29 F4 **Cranham** Gloucs
57 E3 **Crank** St Hel
10 D5 **Cranleigh** Surrey
17 G3 **Cranmore** Somset
41 H3 **Cranoe** Leics
35 F5 **Cransford** Suffk
87 G2 **Cranshaws** Border
2 D5 **Crantock** Cnwll
52 C1 **Cranwell** Lincs
44 B2 **Cranwich** Norfk
44 D3 **Cranworth** Norfk
83 F6 **Craobh Haven** Ag & B
83 H5 **Crarae** Ag & B
109 E2 **Crask Inn** Highld
98 C6 **Crask of Aigas** Highld
81 H2 **Craster** Nthumb
35 H6 **Cratfield** Suffk
95 F5 **Crathes** Abers
95 F5 **Crathes Castle** Abers
94 C5 **Crathie** Abers
98 D2 **Crathie** Highld
66 A4 **Crathorne** N York
38 A4 **Craven Arms** Shrops
73 E3 **Crawcrook** Gatesd
78 C4 **Crawford** S Lans
78 C5 **Crawfordjohn** S Lans
77 G3 **Crawick** D & G
9 F6 **Crawley** Hants
31 E2 **Crawley** Oxon
11 F5 **Crawley** W Susx
11 F5 **Crawley Down** W Susx
57 G5 **Crawshawbooth** Lancs
95 G4 **Crawton** Abers
64 D2 **Cray** N York
21 G3 **Crayford** Gt Lon
66 B1 **Crayke** N York
22 C4 **Crays Hill** Essex
16 B1 **Craze Lowman** Devon
15 G3 **Creacombe** Devon
111 b3 **Creag Ghoraidh** W Isls
90 B3 **Creagan Inn** Ag & B
111 b3 **Creagorry** W Isls
91 E5 **Creaguaineach Lodge** Highld
41 G1 **Creaton** Nhants
71 E6 **Creca** D & G
39 E1 **Credenhill** Herefs
15 G1 **Crediton** Devon
69 E5 **Creebank** D & G
69 E4 **Creebridge** D & G
16 D2 **Creech Heathfield** Somset
16 D2 **Creech St Michael** Somset
3 F4 **Creed** Cnwll
21 G3 **Creekmouth** Gt Lon
34 D4 **Creeting St Mary** Suffk
42 C4 **Creeton** Lincs
69 F3 **Creetown** D & G
116 a2 **Cregneash** IOM
93 E2 **Creich** Fife
27 F1 **Creigiau** Cardif
5 F5 **Cremyll** Cnwll
39 F6 **Cressage** Shrops
50 C4 **Cressbrook** Derbys

25 E3 **Cresselly** Pembks
20 B4 **Cressex** Bucks
34 B3 **Cressing** Essex
73 G5 **Cresswell** Nthumb
25 E3 **Cresswell** Pembks
50 B1 **Cresswell** Staffs
51 F4 **Creswell** Derbys
35 E4 **Cretingham** Suffk
83 E2 **Cretshengan** Ag & B
48 D1 **Crew Green** Powys
48 D4 **Crewe** Ches
49 G5 **Crewe** Ches
49 G4 **Crewe Green** Ches
7 F6 **Crewkerne** Somset
41 E6 **Crewton** C Derb
91 E2 **Crianlarich** Stirlg
36 D2 **Cribyn** Cerdgn
46 D5 **Criccieth** Gwynd
51 E2 **Crich** Derbys
86 D2 **Crichton** Mdloth
41 G1 **Crick** Nhants
27 F6 **Crickadarn** Powys
7 E6 **Cricket St Thomas** Somset
27 G4 **Crickhowell** Powys
18 D5 **Cricklade** Wilts
21 E4 **Cricklewood** Gt Lon
59 F2 **Cridling Stubbs** N York
92 B2 **Crieff** P & K
48 C1 **Criggion** Powys
58 D2 **Crigglestone** Wakefd
103 F5 **Crimond** Abers
43 H3 **Crimplesham** Norfk
30 D4 **Crimscote** Warwks
98 C6 **Crinaglack** Highld
83 F5 **Crinan** Ag & B
85 G2 **Crindledyke** N Lans
45 E3 **Cringleford** Norfk
25 E4 **Crinow** Pembks
99 E5 **Croachy** Highld
78 C1 **Crochmore House** D & G
21 G2 **Crockenhill** Kent
20 A4 **Crocker End** Oxon
5 G6 **Crockernwell** Devon
18 B1 **Crockerton** Wilts
70 B6 **Crocketford** D & G
21 G1 **Crockham Hill** Kent
24 C5 **Croes-goch** Pembks
36 C2 **Croes-lan** Cerdgn
27 E2 **Croeserw** Neath
47 E5 **Croesor** Gwynd
25 G4 **Croesyceiliog** Carmth
28 B2 **Croesyceiliog** Torfn
41 F3 **Croft** Leics
53 G2 **Croft** Lincs
57 F2 **Croft** Warrtn
65 F4 **Croft-on-Tees** N York
84 D4 **Croftamie** Stirlg
59 E2 **Crofton** Wakefd
70 B5 **Crofts** D & G
101 E4 **Crofts** Moray
101 F5 **Crofts of Dipple** Moray
103 F5 **Crofts of Savoch** Abers
26 B2 **Crofty** Swans
89 G2 **Croggan** Ag & B
71 H4 **Croglin** Cumb
106 B6 **Croik** Highld
107 G3 **Cromarty** Highld
86 B4 **Crombie** Fife
100 D2 **Cromdale** Highld
33 F2 **Cromer** Herts
45 E6 **Cromer** Norfk
50 D4 **Cromford** Derbys
29 E2 **Cromhall** S Glos
111 d6 **Cromor** W Isls
52 A2 **Cromwell** Notts
77 E4 **Cronberry** E Ayrs
10 B6 **Crondall** Hants
57 E2 **Cronton** Knows
63 E5 **Crook** Cumb
65 F6 **Crook** Dur
78 D5 **Crook Inn** Border
86 B5 **Crook of Devon** P & K
71 H5 **Crooked Holme** Cumb
76 D5 **Crookedholm** E Ayrs
51 E5 **Crookes** Sheff
81 E4 **Crookham** Nthumb
19 G3 **Crookham** W Berk
20 B1 **Crookham Village** Hants
63 E4 **Crooklands** Cumb
31 F4 **Cropredy** Oxon
41 F4 **Cropston** Leics
30 B4 **Cropthorne** Worcs
66 D2 **Cropton** N York
41 G6 **Cropwell Bishop** Notts
51 G1 **Cropwell Butler** Notts
111 e7 **Cros** W Isls
76 B6 **Crosbie** N Ayrs
111 d6 **Crosbost** W Isls
70 D3 **Crosby** Cumb
116 B3 **Crosby** IOM
60 C2 **Crosby** N Linc
56 D3 **Crosby** Sefton
63 G6 **Crosby Garret** Cumb
64 A4 **Crosby Ravensworth** Cumb
17 G3 **Croscombe** Somset
17 E4 **Cross** Somset
28 C4 **Cross Ash** Mons
58 C4 **Cross Flatts** Brad
59 E4 **Cross Gates** Leeds
34 C4 **Cross Green** Suffk
34 C4 **Cross Green** Suffk
34 D4 **Cross Green** Suffk
26 B4 **Cross Hands** Carmth
39 E6 **Cross Houses** Shrops
12 B4 **Cross in Hand** E Susx
36 C3 **Cross Inn** Cerdgn
84 C4 **Cross Keys** Ag & B
9 G2 **Cross Lane** IOW
39 G5 **Cross Lane Head** Shrops
50 D2 **Cross o' th' hands** Derbys
102 D3 **Cross of Jackston** Abers
35 E6 **Cross Street** Suffk
57 G1 **Cross Town** Ches
75 F5 **Crossaig** Ag & B
88 B3 **Crossapoll** Ag & B
70 D3 **Crosscanonby** Cumb
45 E5 **Crossdale Street** Norfk
86 B4 **Crossford** Fife
77 G5 **Crossford** S Lans
86 D3 **Crossgatehall** E Loth
76 D5 **Crossgates** E Ayrs
86 B4 **Crossgates** Fife
63 E2 **Crossgill** Lancs
76 D3 **Crosshands** E Ayrs
86 C5 **Crosshill** Fife

76 C2 **Crosshill** S Ayrs
76 D5 **Crosshouse** E Ayrs
27 D5 **Crosskeys** Caerph
110 A6 **Crosskirk** Highld
62 D5 **Crosslands** Cumb
84 D2 **Crosslee** Rens
70 B2 **Crossmichael** D & G
95 E6 **Crossroads** Abers
95 F5 **Crossroads** Abers
93 G4 **Crosston** Angus
39 H3 **Crossway Green** Worcs
8 A2 **Crossways** Dorset
25 E2 **Crosswell** Pembks
62 D5 **Crosthwaite** Cumb
57 E4 **Croston** Lancs
45 F3 **Crostwick** Norfk
21 F4 **Crouch End** Gt Lon
7 H6 **Crouch Hill** Dorset
8 C5 **Croucheston** Wilts
31 F3 **Croughton** Nhants
102 D4 **Crovie** Abers
58 C1 **Crow Edge** Barns
28 E3 **Crow Hill** Herefs
2 C1 **Crowan** Cnwll
11 G5 **Crowborough** E Susx
16 C3 **Crowcombe** Somset
50 C3 **Crowdecote** Derbys
20 B5 **Crowell** Oxon
35 E4 **Crowfield** Suffk
87 G3 **Crowhill** E Loth
12 C3 **Crowhurst** E Susx
11 F6 **Crowhurst** Surrey
43 E3 **Crowland** Lincs
34 D5 **Crowland** Suffk
2 B3 **Crowlas** Cnwll
60 B2 **Crowle** N Linc
30 A5 **Crowle** Worcs
19 H5 **Crowle Green** Worcs
19 F4 **Crowmarsh Gifford** Oxon
35 F5 **Crown Corner** Suffk
5 C5 **Crownhill** C Plym
44 D2 **Crownthorpe** Norfk
2 C2 **Crowntown** Cnwll
2 A2 **Crows-an-Wra** Cnwll
20 A2 **Crowthorne** Wokham
49 F6 **Crowton** Ches
73 F1 **Croxdale** Dur
50 C1 **Croxden** Staffs
20 D5 **Croxley Green** Herts
33 E4 **Croxton** Cambs
61 E2 **Croxton** N Linc
44 D5 **Croxton** Norfk
44 C1 **Croxton** Norfk
49 G3 **Croxton** Staffs
42 A5 **Croxton Kerrial** Leics
107 G1 **Croy** Highld
85 F3 **Croy** N Lans
5 G6 **Croyde** Devon
33 E4 **Croydon** Cambs
21 F2 **Croydon** Gt Lon
99 E2 **Crubenmore** Highld
38 D6 **Cruckmeole** Shrops
48 D1 **Cruckton** Shrops
103 F3 **Cruden Bay** Abers
49 F1 **Crudgington** Wrekin
29 G2 **Crudwell** Wilts
27 G3 **Crumlin** Caerph
4 C2 **Crumplehorn** Cnwll
57 H3 **Crumpsall** Manch
13 E6 **Crundale** Kent
25 F4 **Crunwear** Pembks
19 F2 **Crux Easton** Hants
25 B4 **Crwbin** Carmth
20 C5 **Cryers Hill** Bucks
25 F6 **Crymmych** Pembks
26 D3 **Crynant** Neath
21 F3 **Crystal Palace** Gt Lon
105 E2 **Cuaig** Highld
89 G1 **Cuan Ferry Village** Ag & B
31 E6 **Cubbington** Warwks
2 D5 **Cubert** Cnwll
32 A1 **Cublington** Bucks
28 C6 **Cublington** Herefs
11 F4 **Cuckfield** W Susx
17 H2 **Cucklington** Somset
51 H4 **Cuckney** Notts
31 G1 **Cuddesdon** Oxon
31 H1 **Cuddington** Bucks
49 F6 **Cuddington** Ches
49 E4 **Cuddington Heath** Ches
21 G2 **Cudham** Gt Lon
5 F5 **Cudliptown** Devon
8 C3 **Cudnell** Bmouth
59 E1 **Cudworth** Barns
7 E6 **Cudworth** Somset
21 F5 **Cuffley** Herts
90 B4 **Cuil** Highld
96 C4 **Cuillin Hills** Highld
107 E2 **Culbokie** Highld
98 D6 **Culburnie** Highld
107 F1 **Culcabock** Highld
100 B4 **Culcharry** Highld
57 F2 **Culcheth** Warrtn
101 E4 **Culdrain** Abers
97 E6 **Culduie** Highld
34 B5 **Culford** Suffk
64 A6 **Culgaith** Cumb
19 G6 **Culham** Oxon
108 A3 **Culkein** Highld
108 B3 **Culkein Drumbeg** Highld
29 G2 **Culkerton** Gloucs
101 G6 **Cullen** Moray
73 G4 **Cullercoats** N Tyne
95 F6 **Cullerlie** Abers
107 E2 **Cullicudden** Highld
58 C4 **Cullingworth** Brad
83 F6 **Cullipool House** Ag & B
111 I4 **Cullivoe** Shet
107 H1 **Culloden** Highld
6 B6 **Cullompton** Devon
16 C1 **Culm Davy** Devon
39 E4 **Culmington** Shrops
16 C1 **Culmstock** Devon
106 A6 **Culnacraig** Highld
70 B4 **Culnaightrie** D & G
104 D2 **Culnaknock** Highld
107 E5 **Culrain** Highld
86 A4 **Culross** Fife
76 C3 **Culroy** S Ayrs
102 C3 **Culsalmond** Abers
69 G3 **Culscadden** D & G
69 E3 **Culshabbin** D & G
111 k2 **Culswick** Shet
103 E2 **Cultercullen** Abers
95 G6 **Cults** C Aber
22 B2 **Culverstone Green** Kent
42 C5 **Culverthorpe** Lincs

31 F4 **Culworth** Nhants
76 B3 **Culzean Castle** S Ayrs
85 F3 **Cumbernauld** N Lans
85 F3 **Cumbernauld Village** N Lans
53 G3 **Cumberworth** Lincs
102 D4 **Cuminestown** Abers
80 D5 **Cumledge** Border
71 G4 **Cummersdale** Cumb
71 E5 **Cummertrees** D & G
100 D6 **Cummingston** Moray
77 E3 **Cumnock** E Ayrs
31 F1 **Cumnor** Oxon
71 H4 **Cumrew** Cumb
78 D2 **Cumrue** D & G
71 G4 **Cumwhinton** Cumb
71 H4 **Cumwhitton** Cumb
65 H1 **Cundall** N York
76 D3 **Cunninghamhead** N Ayrs
93 F1 **Cupar** Fife
93 F1 **Cupar Muir** Fife
50 D4 **Curbar** Derbys
9 G4 **Curbridge** Hants
31 E1 **Curbridge** Oxon
9 G4 **Curdridge** Hants
40 C3 **Curdworth** Warwks
16 D1 **Curland** Somset
19 G4 **Curridge** W Berk
86 C2 **Currie** C Edin
17 E2 **Curry Mallet** Somset
17 E2 **Curry Rivel** Somset
12 C5 **Curtisden Green** Kent
5 G2 **Curtisknowle** Devon
2 D2 **Cury** Cnwll
102 B1 **Cushnie** Abers
69 F1 **Cutcloy** D & G
16 B3 **Cutcombe** Somset
107 F4 **Cuthill** Highld
39 H3 **Cutnall Green** Worcs
30 C3 **Cutsdean** Gloucs
51 E4 **Cutthorpe** Derbys
19 H6 **Cuxham** Oxon
22 C2 **Cuxton** Medway
52 D5 **Cuxwold** Lincs
56 B1 **Cwm** Denbgs
27 G4 **Cwm Crawnon** Powys
47 G2 **Cwm Llinau** Powys
36 C1 **Cwm-cou** Cerdgn
26 D1 **Cwm-y-glo** Carmth
54 D3 **Cwm-y-glo** Gwynd
26 D2 **Cwmafan** Neath
27 F3 **Cwmaman** Rhondd
25 E3 **Cwmbach** Carmth
27 G6 **Cwmbach** Powys
27 F6 **Cwmbach** Rhondd
38 A2 **Cwmbach Llechrhyd** Powys
28 B2 **Cwmbran** Torfn
28 C3 **Cwmcarn** Caerph
28 C3 **Cwmcarvan** Mons
27 G5 **Cwmdare** Rhondd
27 G5 **Cwmdu** Powys
26 C2 **Cwmdu** Swans
25 G4 **Cwmduad** Carmth
27 F3 **Cwmfelin** Brdgnd
27 F3 **Cwmfelin** Myr Td
25 F4 **Cwmfelin Boeth** Carmth
25 G2 **Cwmfelinfach** Caerph
25 G4 **Cwmffrwd** Carmth
26 D4 **Cwmgiedd** Powys
26 C4 **Cwmgorse** Carmth
26 B4 **Cwmgwili** Carmth
25 G6 **Cwmhiraeth** Carmth
26 B4 **Cwmmawr** Carmth
28 C3 **Cwmparc** Rhondd
25 G6 **Cwmpengraig** Carmth
36 D2 **Cwmsychbant** Cerdgn
27 G3 **Cwmtillery** Blae G
37 G4 **Cwmystwyth** Cerdgn
36 D2 **Cwrt-newydd** Cerdgn
27 E2 **Cymer** Neath
27 F2 **Cymmer** Rhondd
37 G1 **Cynghordy** Carmth
26 D4 **Cynonville** Neath
48 B3 **Cynwyd** Denbgs
25 G5 **Cynwyl Elfed** Carmth

D

6 A3 **Daccombe** Devon
71 G2 **Dacre** Cumb
58 C5 **Dacre** N York
58 D6 **Dacre Banks** N York
72 C1 **Daddry Shield** Dur
31 G4 **Dadford** Bucks
41 G3 **Dadlington** Leics
21 G4 **Dagenham** Gt Lon
30 B1 **Daglingworth** Gloucs
32 C1 **Dagnall** Bucks
76 C2 **Dailly** S Ayrs
93 F1 **Dairsie** Fife
111 a2 **Dalabrog** W Isls
83 G6 **Dalavich** Ag & B
70 B5 **Dalbeattie** D & G
116 b3 **Dalby** IOM
66 C1 **Dalby** N York
92 C4 **Dalcapon** P & K
107 H6 **Dalchalm** Highld
98 B4 **Dalchreichart** Highld
91 H1 **Dalchruin** P & K
92 C2 **Dalcrue** P & K
6 C4 **Dalditch** Devon
51 E1 **Dale** Derbys
24 C3 **Dale** Pembks
76 C5 **Dalgarven** N Ayrs
86 C4 **Dalgety Bay** Fife
77 G2 **Dalgig** E Ayrs
92 A2 **Dalginross** P & K
92 C4 **Dalguise** P & K
109 H4 **Dalhalvaig** Highld
34 B5 **Dalham** Suffk
111 a2 **Daliburgh** W Isls
86 D3 **Dalkeith** Mdloth
100 D4 **Dallas** Moray
35 F4 **Dallinghoo** Suffk
12 B4 **Dallington** E Susx
31 H6 **Dallington** Nhants
90 D2 **Dalmally** Ag & B
85 E4 **Dalmary** Stirlg
76 D2 **Dalmellington** E Ayrs
86 C3 **Dalmeny** C Edin
99 F4 **Dalmigavie** Highld
99 F5 **Dalmigavie Lodge** Highld

107 F3 **Dalmore** Highld
84 D3 **Dalmuir** W Duns
89 G5 **Dalnabreck** Highld
99 H5 **Dalnacardoch** P & K
99 F4 **Dalnahaitnach** Highld
91 G6 **Dalnaspidal** P & K
110 A3 **Dalnawillan Lodge** Highld
92 A5 **Daloist** P & K
86 B6 **Dalqueich** P & K
76 C1 **Dalquhairn** S Ayrs
107 F6 **Dalreavoch Lodge** Highld
76 C6 **Dalry** N Ayrs
76 C3 **Dalrymple** E Ayrs
77 G6 **Dalserf** S Lans
75 F4 **Dalsmeran** Ag & B
71 F4 **Dalston** Cumb
21 F4 **Dalston** Gt Lon
78 C2 **Dalswinton** D & G
70 D6 **Dalton** D & G
65 E4 **Dalton** N York
66 A1 **Dalton** N York
73 E4 **Dalton** Nthumb
66 B6 **Dalton Piercy** Hartpl
62 C3 **Dalton-in-Furness** Cumb
65 H4 **Dalton-le-Dale** Dur
65 G4 **Dalton-on-Tees** N York
78 E3 **Dalveen** D & G
91 G2 **Dalveich** Stirlg
99 E1 **Dalwhinnie** Highld
6 D5 **Dalwood** Devon
8 D5 **Damerham** Hants
45 G3 **Damgate** Norfk
66 D4 **Danby** N York
66 D4 **Danby Wiske** N York
101 E6 **Dandaleith** Moray
86 D3 **Danderhall** Mdloth
33 E1 **Dane End** Herts
41 H6 **Dane Hills** C Leic
23 E1 **Dane Street** Kent
50 B3 **Danebridge** Ches
11 G4 **Danehill** E Susx
102 C5 **Danshillock** Abers
87 F3 **Danskine** E Loth
22 B3 **Darenth** Kent
57 F1 **Daresbury** Halton
59 E1 **Darfield** Barns
23 F2 **Dargate** Kent
4 D4 **Darite** Cnwll
40 B3 **Darlaston** Wsall
40 B3 **Darlaston Green** Wsall
58 D5 **Darley** N York
51 E1 **Darley Abbey** C Derb
50 D3 **Darley Bridge** Derbys
50 D3 **Darley Dale** Derbys
40 C1 **Darley Green** Solhll
58 D5 **Darley Head** N York
32 D1 **Darleyhall** Herts
30 D4 **Darlingscott** Warwks
65 F4 **Darlington** Darltn
51 H4 **Darlton** Notts
80 B3 **Darnick** Border
47 G2 **Darowen** Powys
102 C4 **Darra** Abers
14 D5 **Darracott** Devon
14 D5 **Darracott** Devon
73 E4 **Darras Hall** Nthumb
59 F2 **Darrington** Wakefd
35 G5 **Darsham** Suffk
17 G3 **Darshill** Somset
22 A3 **Dartford** Kent
5 H3 **Dartington** Devon
5 G5 **Dartmoor National Park** Devon
6 A1 **Dartmouth** Devon
58 D1 **Darton** Barns
77 E5 **Darvel** E Ayrs
57 F5 **Darwen** Bl w D
20 C3 **Datchet** W & M
33 E1 **Datchworth** Herts
57 F3 **Daubhill** Bolton
18 C5 **Dauntsey** Wilts
100 C4 **Dava** Highld
49 F6 **Davenham** Ches
31 F6 **Daventry** Nhants
86 C3 **Davidson's Mains** C Edin
4 C5 **Davidstow** Cnwll
79 E3 **Davington** D & G
23 E2 **Davington Hill** Kent
102 D2 **Daviot** Abers
99 E6 **Daviot** Highld
99 F1 **Daviot House** Highld
101 G4 **Davoch of Grange** Moray
11 E6 **Dawesgreen** Surrey
39 F6 **Dawley** Wrekin
6 B3 **Dawlish** Devon
6 B3 **Dawlish Warren** Devon
55 F3 **Dawn** Conwy
51 F1 **Daybrook** Notts
30 D3 **Daylesford** Gloucs
23 H1 **Deal** Kent
70 D2 **Dean** Cumb
15 F5 **Dean** Devon
5 G3 **Dean** Devon
9 F6 **Dean** Hants
9 G5 **Dean** Hants
31 E2 **Dean** Somset
17 G3 **Dean** Somset
22 B2 **Dean Bottom** Kent
31 F1 **Dean Court** Oxon
5 G3 **Dean Prior** Devon
79 G4 **Deanburnhaugh** Border
5 G3 **Deancombe** Devon
57 F3 **Deane** Bolton
19 G2 **Deane** Hants
58 B2 **Deanhead** Kirk
8 C5 **Deanland** Dorset
72 C3 **Deanraw** Nthumb
86 A3 **Deans** W Loth
70 D2 **Deanscales** Cumb
86 D5 **Deanshanger** Nhants
101 F4 **Deanshaugh** Moray
85 F5 **Deanston** Stirlg
70 D3 **Dearham** Cumb
35 F4 **Debach** Suffk
33 G2 **Debden** Essex
21 G5 **Debden** Essex
35 E5 **Debenham** Suffk
39 G1 **Deblin's Green** Worcs
86 B3 **Dechmont** W Loth
86 A3 **Dechmont Road** W Loth
31 F3 **Deddington** Oxon
34 D2 **Dedham** Essex
20 C3 **Dedworth** W & M
42 B3 **Deene** Nhants
42 B2 **Deenethorpe** Nhants
50 D6 **Deepcar** Sheff

42 D3 **Deeping Gate** C Pete
42 D3 **Deeping St James** Lincs
42 D3 **Deeping St Nicholas** Lincs
29 F5 **Deerhurst** Gloucs
30 A4 **Defford** Worcs
27 E5 **Defynnog** Powys
55 F4 **Deganwy** Conwy
83 F6 **Degnish** Ag & B
65 G3 **Deighton** N York
59 G4 **Deighton** York
54 D3 **Deiniolen** Gwynd
4 B5 **Delabole** Cnwll
49 E6 **Delamere** Ches
103 E2 **Delfrigs** Abers
10 B3 **Dell Quay** W Susx
100 D3 **Delliefure** Highld
101 E3 **Delnashaugh Inn** Moray
107 F3 **Delny** Highld
73 E2 **Delves** Dur
92 D3 **Delvine** P & K
42 C5 **Dembleby** Lincs
93 E1 **Den of Lindores** Fife
51 F6 **Denaby** Donc
48 B5 **Denbigh** Denbgs
93 F1 **Denbrae** Fife
5 H4 **Denbury** Devon
51 E2 **Denby** Derbys
58 D1 **Denby Dale** Kirk
19 F5 **Denchworth** Oxon
62 C3 **Dendron** Cumb
92 C1 **Denfield** P & K
32 C6 **Denford** Nhants
23 E5 **Dengie** Essex
20 D4 **Denham** Bucks
34 B4 **Denham** Suffk
35 E6 **Denham** Suffk
20 D4 **Denham Green** Bucks
103 E4 **Denhead** Abers
93 G1 **Denhead** Fife
93 F3 **Denhead of Gray** C Dund
80 B2 **Denholm** Border
58 C3 **Denholme** Brad
9 H4 **Denmead** Hants
103 E1 **Denmore** C Aber
35 F5 **Dennington** Suffk
85 G4 **Denny** Falk
85 G3 **Dennyloanhead** Falk
95 G5 **Denside** Abers
13 G6 **Densole** Kent
34 B4 **Denston** Suffk
50 C1 **Denstone** Staffs
23 F2 **Denstroude** Kent
63 G4 **Dent** Cumb
42 D1 **Denton** Cambs
65 F5 **Denton** Darltn
11 G2 **Denton** E Susx
13 G6 **Denton** Kent
42 B5 **Denton** Lincs
58 C5 **Denton** N York
32 A4 **Denton** Nhants
45 F1 **Denton** Norfk
50 A6 **Denton** Tamesd
43 G2 **Denver** Norfk
81 G2 **Denwick** Nthumb
44 D2 **Deopham** Norfk
44 D2 **Deopham Green** Norfk
34 B4 **Depden** Suffk
21 F3 **Deptford** Gt Lon
18 C1 **Deptford** Wilts
41 E6 **Derby** C Derb
15 E4 **Derby** Devon
116 b2 **Derbyhaven** IOM
92 B4 **Derculich** P & K
44 D3 **Dereham** Norfk
27 G3 **Deri** Caerph
23 F1 **Derringstone** Kent
40 A5 **Derrington** Staffs
18 C4 **Derry Hill** Wilts
52 A6 **Derrythorpe** N Linc
44 A5 **Dersingham** Norfk
89 E4 **Dervaig** Ag & B
48 B4 **Derwen** Denbgs
47 F2 **Derwenlas** Powys
71 F2 **Derwent Water** Cumb
42 A1 **Desborough** Nhants
41 F4 **Desford** Leics
101 G5 **Deskford** Moray
22 C2 **Detling** Kent
28 C3 **Devauden** Mons
37 F4 **Devil's Bridge** Cerdgn
18 C3 **Devizes** Wilts
5 E3 **Devonport** C Plym
85 H5 **Devonside** Clacks
2 D3 **Devoran** Cnwll
86 D2 **Dewarton** Mdloth
8 A3 **Dewlish** Dorset
58 D2 **Dewsbury** Kirk
48 C1 **Deytheur** Powys
11 E4 **Dial Post** W Susx
9 F4 **Dibden** Hants
9 F4 **Dibden Purlieu** Hants
35 E6 **Dickleburgh** Norfk
30 B3 **Didbrook** Gloucs
19 G5 **Didcot** Oxon
19 G5 **Didcot Railway Centre** Oxon
32 D5 **Diddington** Cambs
39 E4 **Diddlebury** Shrops
10 B4 **Didling** W Susx
18 A5 **Didmarton** Gloucs
57 H2 **Didsbury** Manch
52 C1 **Digby** Lincs
104 C3 **Digg** Highld
58 B1 **Diggle** Oldham
57 E3 **Digmoor** Lancs
36 D2 **Dihewyd** Cerdgn
45 F4 **Dilham** Norfk
50 B1 **Dilhorne** Staffs
32 D5 **Dillington** Cambs
72 D3 **Dilston** Nthumb
18 B2 **Dilton** Wilts
18 B2 **Dilton Marsh** Wilts
38 D2 **Dilwyn** Herefs
46 C5 **Dinas** Gwynd
24 D6 **Dinas** Pembks
16 C6 **Dinas Powys** V Glam
47 G3 **Dinas-Mawddwy** Gwynd
17 G3 **Dinder** Somset
28 D6 **Dinedor** Herefs
28 C4 **Dingestow** Mons
56 D2 **Dingle** Lpool
41 H2 **Dingley** Nhants
107 E2 **Dingwall** Highld
94 D5 **Dinnet** Abers
73 F4 **Dinnington** N u Ty
51 F5 **Dinnington** Rothm
17 E1 **Dinnington** Somset
54 D3 **Dinorwic** Gwynd
31 H1 **Dinton** Bucks
8 C6 **Dinton** Wilts
78 D2 **Dinwoodie** D & G
14 C3 **Dinworthy** Devon
16 D2 **Dipford** Somset
75 F4 **Dippen** Ag & B
75 H3 **Dippen** N Ayrs
5 E5 **Dippertown** Devon
101 F5 **Dipple** Moray
76 B2 **Dipple** S Ayrs
5 G3 **Diptford** Devon
73 E2 **Dipton** Dur
87 E4 **Dirleton** E Loth
72 C2 **Dirt Pot** Nthumb
41 F5 **Diseworth** Leics
65 G1 **Dishforth** N York
50 B5 **Disley** Ches
35 E6 **Diss** Norfk
70 D2 **Distington** Cumb
8 D6 **Ditchampton** Wilts
81 G2 **Ditchburn** Nthumb
17 G3 **Ditcheat** Somset
45 F1 **Ditchingham** Norfk
11 F3 **Ditchling** E Susx
49 E1 **Ditherington** Shrops
18 A4 **Ditteridge** Wilts
6 A2 **Dittisham** Devon
57 E2 **Ditton** Halton
22 C2 **Ditton** Kent
33 H4 **Ditton Green** Cambs
39 F5 **Ditton Priors** Shrops
29 G5 **Dixton** Gloucs
28 C4 **Dixton** Mons
58 B1 **Dobcross** Oldham
4 C3 **Dobwalls** Cnwll
5 H5 **Doccombe** Devon
99 E6 **Dochgarroch** Highld
63 F3 **Docker** Lancs
44 B5 **Docking** Norfk
39 E2 **Docklow** Herefs
71 G2 **Dockray** Cumb
40 B6 **Dod's Leigh** Staffs
49 F4 **Dodd's Green** Ches
22 B5 **Doddinghurst** Essex
43 F1 **Doddington** Cambs
22 D1 **Doddington** Kent
52 B2 **Doddington** Lincs
81 F3 **Doddington** Nthumb
39 F4 **Doddington** Shrops
6 A4 **Doddiscombsleigh** Devon
31 G5 **Dodford** Nhants
31 B1 **Dodford** Worcs
29 E1 **Dodington** S Glos
16 D3 **Dodington** Somset
48 D5 **Dodleston** Ches
84 D1 **Dodside** E Rens
58 D1 **Dodworth** Barns
52 D1 **Dogdyke** Lincs
20 B1 **Dogmersfield** Hants
48 B1 **Dolanog** Powys
46 D5 **Dolbenmaen** Gwynd
47 G2 **Dolfach** Powys
38 B4 **Dolfor** Powys
55 F3 **Dolgarrog** Conwy
47 F3 **Dolgellau** Gwynd
107 G6 **Doll** Highld
85 H5 **Dollar** Clacks
85 H5 **Dollarfield** Clacks
48 C6 **Dolphin** Flints
63 E2 **Dolphinholme** Lancs
86 B1 **Dolphinton** S Lans
15 E2 **Dolton** Devon
55 G4 **Dolwen** Conwy
55 E2 **Dolwyddelan** Conwy
62 C2 **Domgay** Powys
59 F1 **Doncaster** Donc
8 B5 **Donhead St Andrew** Wilts
8 B5 **Donhead St Mary** Wilts
86 C4 **Donibristle** Fife
16 C3 **Doniford** Somset
42 D5 **Donington** Lincs
52 D3 **Donington on Bain** Lincs
40 D4 **Donisthorpe** Leics
30 C3 **Donnington** Gloucs
39 F6 **Donnington** Shrops
19 F3 **Donnington** W Berk
10 B2 **Donnington** W Susx
49 G1 **Donnington** Wrekin
17 E1 **Donyatt** Somset
76 C3 **Doonfoot** S Ayrs
76 C3 **Doonholm** S Ayrs
100 D1 **Dorback Lodge** Highld
7 H4 **Dorchester** Dorset
19 G6 **Dorchester** Oxon
40 D3 **Dordon** Warwks
50 D4 **Dore** Sheff
98 D5 **Dores** Highld
21 E1 **Dorking** Surrey
11 G6 **Dormans Land** Surrey
28 D6 **Dormington** Herefs
30 B5 **Dormston** Worcs
20 C3 **Dorney** Bucks
97 F4 **Dornie** Highld
107 G5 **Dornoch** Highld
71 E5 **Dornock** D & G
110 B4 **Dorrery** Highld
40 C1 **Dorridge** Solhll
52 C1 **Dorrington** Lincs
39 E6 **Dorrington** Shrops
49 G3 **Dorrington** Shrops
30 C5 **Dorsington** Warwks
28 B6 **Dorstone** Herefs
31 G2 **Dorton** Bucks
116 c3 **Douglas** IOM
78 B5 **Douglas** S Lans
93 F3 **Douglas and Angus** C Dund
78 B5 **Douglas Castle** S Lans
84 B5 **Douglas Pier** Ag & B
78 C6 **Douglas Water** S Lans
78 B5 **Douglas West** S Lans
93 F4 **Douglastown** Angus
17 G3 **Doulting** Somset
111 g2 **Dounby** Ork
106 D5 **Doune** Highld
85 F5 **Doune** Stirlg
76 B1 **Dounepark** S Ayrs
107 E5 **Dounie** Highld
5 F4 **Dousland** Devon
50 C4 **Dove Holes** Derbys
70 D3 **Dovenby** Cumb
13 G6 **Dover** Kent
13 G6 **Dover Castle** Kent
35 F2 **Dovercourt** Essex
39 H3 **Doverdale** Worcs
40 C6 **Doveridge** Derbys
11 E6 **Doversgreen** Surrey
92 C4 **Dowally** P & K
30 B2 **Dowdeswell** Gloucs
27 F3 **Dowlais** Myr Td
15 E2 **Dowland** Devon
7 E6 **Dowlish Wake** Somset
18 D6 **Down Ampney** Gloucs
29 F5 **Down Hatherley** Gloucs
15 F2 **Down St Mary** Devon
5 E2 **Down Thomas** Devon
4 D2 **Downderry** Cnwll
21 G2 **Downe** Gt Lon
29 F3 **Downend** Gloucs
28 D1 **Downend** S Glos
93 F3 **Downfield** C Dund
4 D4 **Downgate** Cnwll
4 D4 **Downgate** Cnwll
22 C5 **Downham** Essex
21 F3 **Downham** Gt Lon
63 G1 **Downham** Lancs
43 G2 **Downham Market** Norfk
17 G2 **Downhead** Somset
17 H3 **Downhead** Somset
92 D2 **Downhill** P & K
65 E3 **Downholme** N York
95 H5 **Downies** Abers
20 B5 **Downley** Bucks
20 D2 **Downside** Surrey
9 E3 **Downton** Hants
8 D5 **Downton** Wilts
38 D3 **Downton on the Rock** Herefs
42 D5 **Dowsby** Lincs
17 H6 **Doynton** S Glos
27 G2 **Draethen** Caerph
77 G5 **Draffan** S Lans
51 G5 **Drakeholes** Notts
76 C6 **Drakemyre** N Ayrs
30 A5 **Drakes Broughton** Worcs
58 B5 **Draughton** N York
41 H1 **Draughton** Nhants
59 G3 **Drax** N York
41 E1 **Draycote** Warwks
41 E6 **Draycott** Derbys
30 C3 **Draycott** Gloucs
17 F4 **Draycott** Somset
40 C6 **Draycott in the Clay** Staffs
50 B1 **Draycott in the Moors** Staffs
9 H4 **Drayton** C Port
42 A2 **Drayton** Leics
45 E3 **Drayton** Norfk
31 E4 **Drayton** Oxon
19 G6 **Drayton** Oxon
17 E2 **Drayton** Somset
40 A1 **Drayton** Worcs
40 D3 **Drayton Bassett** Staffs
20 C6 **Drayton Beauchamp** Bucks
40 D3 **Drayton Manor Park** Staffs
32 A2 **Drayton Parslow** Bucks
19 G6 **Drayton St Leonard** Oxon
24 D4 **Dreen Hill** Pembks
25 G6 **Drefach** Carmth
26 B4 **Drefach** Carmth
36 D2 **Drefach** Cerdgn
76 C5 **Dreghorn** N Ayrs
13 G6 **Drellingore** Kent
87 E4 **Drem** E Loth
5 G5 **Drewsteignton** Devon
53 F3 **Driby** Lincs
60 D5 **Driffield** E R Yk
18 C6 **Driffield** Gloucs
2 B2 **Drift** Cnwll
62 B5 **Drigg** Cumb
58 D3 **Drighlington** Leeds
89 F4 **Drimnin** Highld
7 E6 **Drimpton** Dorset
90 B6 **Drimsallie** Highld
59 G5 **Dringhouses** York
34 C4 **Drinkstone** Suffk
34 C4 **Drinkstone Green** Suffk
40 B5 **Drointon** Staffs
30 A6 **Droitwich** Worcs
92 D1 **Dron** P & K
51 E4 **Dronfield** Derbys
76 D3 **Drongan** E Ayrs
93 F3 **Dronley** Angus
7 H6 **Droop** Dorset
9 H5 **Droxford** Hants
50 A6 **Droylsden** Tamesd
48 A4 **Druid** Denbgs
24 C4 **Druidston** Pembks
90 C3 **Druimachoish** Highld
90 C5 **Druimarbin** Highld
83 F3 **Druimdrishaig** Ag & B
97 E1 **Druimindarroch** Highld
83 G3 **Drum** Ag & B
86 B5 **Drum** P & K
78 C6 **Drumalbin** S Lans
108 B3 **Drumbeg** Highld
102 B3 **Drumblade** Abers
68 C2 **Drumbreddon** D & G
97 E5 **Drumbuie** Highld
71 F5 **Drumburgh** Cumb
70 C4 **Drumburn** D & G
85 E3 **Drumchapel** C Glas
91 H4 **Drumchastle** P & K
77 F5 **Drumclog** S Lans
87 E6 **Drumeldrie** Fife
79 E5 **Drumelzier** Border
97 E4 **Drumfearn** Highld
95 F5 **Drumfrennie** Abers
99 F3 **Drumguish** Highld
95 E5 **Drumhead** Abers
101 E3 **Drumin** Moray
77 E2 **Drumjohn** D & G
68 D5 **Drumlamford** S Ayrs
95 E6 **Drumlasie** Abers
71 F4 **Drumleaning** Cumb
75 E3 **Drumlemble** Ag & B
95 G4 **Drumlithie** Abers
69 E2 **Drummoddie** D & G
68 C2 **Drummore** D & G
101 F4 **Drummuir** Moray
98 D5 **Drumnadrochit** Highld
102 B4 **Drumnagorrach** Moray
78 C1 **Drumpark** D & G
106 B6 **Drumrunie Lodge** Highld
76 C3 **Drumshang** S Ayrs
104 C1 **Drumuie** Highld
99 G4 **Drumuillie** Highld
85 F5 **Drumvaich** Stirlg
86 B6 **Drunzie** P & K
42 B6 **Dry Doddington** Lincs
33 F5 **Dry Drayton** Cambs
64 B4 **Drybeck** Cumb
101 G5 **Drybridge** Moray
76 C5 **Drybridge** N Ayrs
28 D4 **Drybrook** Gloucs
80 B3 **Dryburgh** Border
2 C3 **Drym** Cnwll
84 D4 **Drymen** Stirlg
103 E4 **Drymuir** Abers
96 C5 **Drynoch** Highld
102 D5 **Dubford** Abers
108 D1 **Duchally** Highld
31 E1 **Ducklington** Oxon
33 F2 **Duddenhoe End** Essex
86 C3 **Duddingston** C Edin
42 C2 **Duddington** Nhants
16 D1 **Duddlestone** Somset
39 F4 **Duddlewick** Shrops
81 E4 **Duddo** Nthumb
49 E5 **Duddon** Ches
48 D3 **Dudleston** Shrops
40 B2 **Dudley** Dudley
73 F4 **Dudley** N Tyne
40 B3 **Dudley Port** Sandw
8 C3 **Dudsbury** Dorset
51 E1 **Duffield** Derbys
26 D2 **Duffryn** Neath
101 F3 **Dufftown** Moray
101 E6 **Duffus** Moray
64 B5 **Dufton** Cumb
60 C6 **Duggleby** N York
97 F5 **Duirinish** Highld
97 E3 **Duisdalemore** Highld
90 B6 **Duisky** Highld
34 D3 **Duke Street** Suffk
50 B6 **Dukinfield** Tamesd
17 G3 **Dulcote** Somset
6 C6 **Dulford** Devon
92 A4 **Dull** P & K
85 F3 **Dullatur** N Lans
33 H4 **Dullingham** Cambs
33 H4 **Dullingham Ley** Cambs
99 G5 **Dulnain Bridge** Highld
32 D4 **Duloe** Beds
4 C3 **Duloe** Cnwll
16 B2 **Dulverton** Somset
21 F3 **Dulwich** Gt Lon
84 D3 **Dumbarton** W Duns
30 B3 **Dumbleton** Gloucs
70 C6 **Dumfries** D & G
85 E4 **Dumgoyne** Stirlg
19 G2 **Dummer** Hants
23 H2 **Dumpton** Kent
95 F2 **Dun** Angus
91 H4 **Dunalastair** P & K
84 B3 **Dunan** Ag & B
96 D5 **Dunan** Highld
91 F4 **Dunan** P & K
75 E2 **Dunaverty** Ag & B
17 E3 **Dunball** Somset
87 F4 **Dunbar** E Loth
110 B2 **Dunbeath** Highld
90 A2 **Dunbeg** Ag & B
85 G5 **Dunblane** Stirlg
93 E1 **Dunbog** Fife
107 E2 **Duncanston** Highld
102 B2 **Duncanstone** Abers
6 A4 **Dunchideock** Devon
41 F1 **Dunchurch** Warwks
78 C1 **Duncow** D & G
86 B6 **Duncrievie** P & K
10 C4 **Duncton** W Susx
93 F2 **Dundee** C Dund
93 F2 **Dundee Airport** C Dund
17 F2 **Dundon** Somset
76 C4 **Dundonald** S Ayrs
106 A4 **Dundonnell** Highld
71 E4 **Dundraw** Cumb
98 B4 **Dundreggan** Highld
70 B4 **Dundrennan** D & G
17 G5 **Dundry** N Som
102 D1 **Dunecht** Abers
86 B4 **Dunfermline** Fife
18 D6 **Dunfield** Gloucs
77 F5 **Dungavel** S Lans
13 F4 **Dungeness** Kent
52 A3 **Dunham** Notts
57 G2 **Dunham Town** Traffd
57 G2 **Dunham Woodhouses** Traffd
49 E6 **Dunham-on-the-Hill** Ches
39 H3 **Dunhampton** Worcs
52 C3 **Dunholme** Lincs
93 G1 **Dunino** Fife
85 G4 **Dunipace** Falk
22 B1 **Dunk's Green** Kent
92 C3 **Dunkeld** P & K
17 H5 **Dunkerton** BaNES
6 C6 **Dunkeswell** Devon
58 D4 **Dunkeswick** N York
23 F2 **Dunkirk** Kent
18 A5 **Dunkirk** S Glos
95 E3 **Dunlappie** Angus
39 G3 **Dunley** Worcs
76 D6 **Dunlop** E Ayrs
98 D4 **Dunmaglass** Highld
85 G4 **Dunmore** Falk
110 C6 **Dunnet** Highld
93 G4 **Dunnichen** Angus
92 C1 **Dunning** P & K
61 E5 **Dunnington** E R Yk
30 C5 **Dunnington** Warwks
59 G5 **Dunnington** York
57 G5 **Dunnockshaw** Lancs
84 B3 **Dunoon** Ag & B
100 C4 **Dunphail** Moray
68 C3 **Dunragit** D & G
80 D5 **Duns** Border
31 F3 **Duns Tew** Oxon
42 C4 **Dunsby** Lincs
78 C1 **Dunscore** D & G
59 G1 **Dunscroft** Donc
66 C5 **Dunsdale** R & Cl
20 A3 **Dunsden Green** Oxon
14 C2 **Dunsdon** Devon
10 D5 **Dunsfold** Surrey
5 H5 **Dunsford** Devon
93 E1 **Dunshalt** Fife
103 E4 **Dunshillock** Abers
51 F3 **Dunsill** Notts
67 E4 **Dunsley** N York
39 H4 **Dunsley** Staffs
20 B5 **Dunsmore** Bucks
63 F1 **Dunsop Bridge** Lancs
32 C1 **Dunstable** Beds
40 C5 **Dunstall** Staffs
81 H2 **Dunstan** Nthumb
16 B3 **Dunster** Somset
73 F3 **Dunston** Gatesd
52 C2 **Dunston** Lincs
45 E2 **Dunston** Norfk
40 A5 **Dunston** Staffs
5 F2 **Dunstone** Devon
5 G4 **Dunstone** Devon
61 E3 **Dunswell** E R Yk
86 B1 **Dunsyre** S Lans
4 D5 **Dunterton** Devon
29 G3 **Duntisbourne Abbots** Gloucs
29 G3 **Duntisbourne Rouse** Gloucs
7 H6 **Duntish** Dorset
84 D3 **Duntocher** W Duns
33 E3 **Dunton** Beds
32 A1 **Dunton** Bucks
44 C5 **Dunton** Norfk
41 F3 **Dunton Bassett** Leics
21 G1 **Dunton Green** Kent
104 C3 **Duntulm** Highld
76 C3 **Dunure** S Ayrs
26 B2 **Dunvant** Swans
104 B1 **Dunvegan** Highld
35 G5 **Dunwich** Suffk
2 D2 **Durgan** Cnwll
73 F1 **Durham** Dur
73 F1 **Durham Cathedral** Dur
78 C3 **Durisdeer** D & G
78 C3 **Durisdeermill** D & G
16 D3 **Durleigh** Somset
9 G5 **Durley** Hants
19 E3 **Durley** Wilts
9 G5 **Durley Street** Hants
23 G2 **Durlock** Kent
23 G2 **Durlock** Kent
93 F4 **Durmgley** Angus
108 D5 **Durness** Highld
90 B4 **Duror** Highld
83 G6 **Durran** Ag & B
10 D3 **Durrington** W Susx
18 D2 **Durrington** Wilts
95 F5 **Durris** Abers
29 E3 **Dursley** Gloucs
29 E4 **Dursley Cross** Gloucs
16 D2 **Durston** Somset
8 B4 **Durweston** Dorset
31 H6 **Duston** Nhants
99 G5 **Duthil** Highld
57 F1 **Dutton** Ches
33 F3 **Duxford** Cambs
19 F6 **Duxford** Oxon
33 F3 **Duxford Aircraft Museum** Cambs
55 E4 **Dwygyfylchi** Conwy
54 C3 **Dwyran** IOA
103 E1 **Dyce** C Aber
47 E4 **Dyffryn Ardudwy** Gwynd
27 E4 **Dyffryn Cellwen** Neath
42 C4 **Dyke** Lincs
100 C5 **Dyke** Moray
93 E4 **Dykehead** Angus
94 C2 **Dykehead** Angus
85 G2 **Dykehead** N Lans
85 E5 **Dykehead** Stirlg
95 F3 **Dykelands** Abers
93 E5 **Dykends** Angus
102 C4 **Dykeside** Abers
13 F5 **Dymchurch** Kent
29 E5 **Dymock** Gloucs
17 H6 **Dyrham** S Glos
86 D5 **Dysart** Fife
56 B1 **Dyserth** Denbgs

E

62 D1 **Eagland Hill** Lancs
52 B2 **Eagle** Lincs
65 H4 **Eaglescliffe** S on T
70 D2 **Eaglesfield** Cumb
71 E6 **Eaglesfield** D & G
85 E1 **Eaglesham** E Rens
57 G4 **Eagley** Bolton
51 G3 **Eakring** Notts
60 B2 **Ealand** N Linc
21 E3 **Ealing** Gt Lon
72 B2 **Eals** Nthumb
71 H2 **Eamont Bridge** Cumb
58 A4 **Earby** Lancs
39 G5 **Eardington** Shrops
38 D2 **Eardisland** Herefs
38 C1 **Eardisley** Herefs
48 D2 **Eardiston** Shrops
39 F3 **Eardiston** Worcs
33 F6 **Earith** Cambs
41 F3 **Earl Shilton** Leics
35 E5 **Earl Soham** Suffk
50 C3 **Earl Sterndale** Derbys
29 F6 **Earl's Croome** Worcs
57 F2 **Earlestown** St Hel
20 B3 **Earley** Wokham
104 C2 **Earlish** Highld
32 B5 **Earls Barton** Nhants
34 C2 **Earls Colne** Essex
30 B5 **Earls Common** Worcs
40 D1 **Earlsdon** Covtry
87 E5 **Earlsferry** Fife
21 E3 **Earlsfield** Gt Lon
102 D3 **Earlsford** Abers
58 D2 **Earlsheaton** Kirk
80 B4 **Earlston** Border
76 D5 **Earlston** E Ayrs
21 F1 **Earlswood** Surrey
40 C1 **Earlswood** Warwks
10 B2 **Earnley** W Susx
73 G4 **Earsdon** N Tyne
73 F5 **Earsdon** Nthumb
45 F1 **Earsham** Norfk
10 C3 **Eartham** W Susx
66 C4 **Easby** N York
89 G1 **Easdale** Ag & B
10 C4 **Easebourne** W Susx
41 F2 **Easenhall** Warwks
10 C6 **Eashing** Surrey
31 G1 **Easington** Bucks
73 G1 **Easington** Dur
61 G2 **Easington** E R Yk
66 D5 **Easington** R & Cl
73 H1 **Easington Colliery** Dur
66 B1 **Easingwold** N York
93 F4 **Eassie and Nevay** Angus
16 B5 **East Aberthaw** V Glam
5 G2 **East Allington** Devon
15 G4 **East Anstey** Devon
9 G2 **East Ashey** IOW

10 B3 East Ashling W Susx
67 F2 East Ayton N York
52 D3 East Barkwith Lincs
22 C1 East Barming Kent
66 D4 East Barnby N York
21 F5 East Barnet Gt Lon
87 G3 East Barns E Loth
44 C5 East Barsham Norfk
45 E5 East Beckham Norfk
20 D3 East Bedfont Gt Lon
34 D2 East Bergholt Suffk
44 C4 East Bilney Norfk
11 G2 East Blatchington E Susx
73 G3 East Boldon S Tyne
9 F3 East Boldre Hants
44 C3 East Bradenham Norfk
17 E4 East Brent Somset
51 G1 East Bridgford Notts
15 F4 East Buckland Devon
6 C4 East Budleigh Devon
52 A5 East Butterwick N Linc
86 B3 East Calder W Loth
45 E2 East Carleton Norfk
58 D4 East Carlton Leeds
42 A1 East Carlton Nhants
8 A2 East Chaldon (Chaldon Herring) Dorset
19 F5 East Challow Oxon
5 G2 East Charleton Devon
7 F6 East Chelborough Dorset
11 F3 East Chiltington E Susx
17 F1 East Chinnock Somset
18 D2 East Chisenbury Wilts
20 D1 East Clandon Surrey
31 H3 East Claydon Bucks
7 F6 East Coker Somset
16 C2 East Combe Somset
17 G3 East Compton Somset
6 A2 East Cornworthy Devon
60 B4 East Cottingwith E R Yk
9 G3 East Cowes IOW
59 G2 East Cowick E R Yk
65 G4 East Cowton N York
17 G3 East Cranmore Somset
8 B2 East Creech Dorset
12 B2 East Dean E Susx
28 D4 East Dean Gloucs
9 E3 East Dean Hants
10 C3 East Dean W Susx
15 E5 East Down Devon
51 H4 East Drayton Notts
21 F3 East Dulwich Gt Lon
17 G5 East Dundry N Som
60 D3 East Ella C KuH
19 F3 East End Hants
9 F3 East End Hants
12 D5 East End Kent
31 E2 East End Oxon
17 G4 East End Somset
18 D2 East Everleigh Wilts
22 C1 East Farleigh Kent
41 H2 East Farndon Nhants
52 A5 East Ferry Lincs
87 E4 East Fortune E Loth
19 F4 East Garston W Berk
41 G4 East Goscote Leics
19 E3 East Grafton Wilts
9 E6 East Grimstead Wilts
11 G5 East Grinstead W Susx
12 D4 East Guldeford E Susx
31 G6 East Haddon Nhants
19 G5 East Hagbourne Oxon
61 E2 East Halton N Linc
21 G4 East Ham Gt Lon
19 F5 East Hanney Oxon
22 C5 East Hanningfield Essex
59 F2 East Hardwick Wakefd
44 D1 East Harling Norfk
65 H3 East Harlsey N York
8 D6 East Harnham Wilts
17 G4 East Harptree BaNES
65 H5 East Hartburn S on T
10 B4 East Harting W Susx
8 B6 East Hatch Wilts
33 E4 East Hatley Cambs
65 F3 East Hauxwell N York
93 G3 East Haven Angus
42 D6 East Heckington Lincs
73 E1 East Hedleyhope Dur
110 A1 East Helmsdale Highld
19 F5 East Hendred Oxon
67 E1 East Heslerton N York
11 H4 East Hoathly E Susx
8 B2 East Holme Dorset
17 G4 East Horrington Somset
20 D1 East Horsley Surrey
8 C3 East Howe Bmouth
17 E3 East Huntspill Somset
19 G4 East Ilsley W Berk
53 F2 East Keal Lincs
18 D3 East Kennett Wilts
59 E4 East Keswick Leeds
85 E1 East Kilbride S Lans
53 E2 East Kirkby Lincs
8 A2 East Knighton Dorset
8 B6 East Knoyle Wilts
17 F1 East Lambrook Somset
13 G6 East Langdon Kent
41 H3 East Langton Leics
90 C4 East Larach Highld
10 B3 East Lavant W Susx
10 C4 East Lavington W Susx
65 F4 East Layton N York
41 F5 East Leake Notts
15 F2 East Leigh Devon
5 G3 East Leigh Devon
44 C4 East Lexham Norfk
87 F4 East Linton E Loth
19 F5 East Lockinge Oxon
52 A5 East Lound N Linc
8 B2 East Lulworth Dorset
60 D6 East Lutton N York
17 G2 East Lydford Somset
22 C1 East Malling Kent
10 B3 East Marden W Susx
51 H4 East Markham Notts
8 C5 East Martin Hants
58 A5 East Marton N York
10 A4 East Meon Hants
23 E6 East Mersea Essex
41 E5 East Midlands Airport Leics
21 E2 East Molesey Surrey
8 B3 East Morden Dorset
58 C4 East Morton Brad
78 C3 East Morton D & G
66 C2 East Ness N York
42 A2 East Norton Leics
5 H4 East Ogwell Devon
8 B5 East Orchard Dorset
12 B6 East Peckham Kent
24 D3 East Pennar Pembks
17 G3 East Pennard Somset
32 D5 East Perry Cambs
5 G1 East Portlemouth Devon
5 H1 East Prawle Devon
10 D2 East Preston W Susx
7 H6 East Pulham Dorset
14 D3 East Putford Devon
16 C3 East Quantoxhead Somset
73 G2 East Rainton Sundld
52 D5 East Ravendale NE Lin
44 C4 East Raynham Norfk
59 E4 East Rigton Leeds
65 H4 East Rounton N York
44 B4 East Rudham Norfk
45 E6 East Runton Norfk
45 F4 East Ruston Norfk
87 E3 East Saltoun E Loth
21 E3 East Sheen Gt Lon
19 F4 East Shefford W Berk
52 A4 East Stockwith Lincs
8 B2 East Stoke Dorset
51 H2 East Stoke Notts
8 A5 East Stour Dorset
23 G2 East Stourmouth Kent
15 F4 East Stowford Devon
19 G1 East Stratton Hants
23 G1 East Studdal Kent
4 C3 East Taphouse Cnwll
73 F6 East Thirston Nthumb
22 B3 East Tilbury Thurr
10 A5 East Tisted Hants
52 D4 East Torrington Lincs
44 D3 East Tuddenham Norfk
9 E6 East Tytherley Hants
18 C4 East Tytherton Wilts
15 G2 East Village Devon
39 E5 East Wall Shrops
44 B4 East Walton Norfk
17 F4 East Water Somset
5 G6 East Week Devon
9 E5 East Wellow Hants
86 D5 East Wemyss Fife
85 H2 East Whitburn W Loth
21 G3 East Wickham Gt Lon
25 E3 East Williamston Pembks
44 A4 East Winch Norfk
9 E6 East Winterslow Wilts
10 B2 East Wittering W Susx
65 E2 East Witton N York
72 D5 East Woodburn Nthumb
19 F3 East Woodhay Hants
10 B5 East Worldham Hants
44 C1 East Wretham Norfk
14 C3 East Youlstone Devon
14 D4 East-the-Water Devon
65 G4 Eastbourne Darltn
12 B2 Eastbourne E Susx
35 G5 Eastbridge Suffk
58 B4 Eastburn Brad
20 D4 Eastbury Herts
19 E4 Eastbury W Berk
58 B5 Eastby N York
23 E3 Eastchurch Kent
29 G3 Eastcombe Gloucs
20 D4 Eastcote Gt Lon
31 G5 Eastcote Nhants
40 D2 Eastcote Solhll
18 C2 Eastcott Wilts
29 G2 Eastcourt Wilts
19 E3 Eastcourt Wilts
22 D4 Eastend Essex
78 C6 Eastend S Lans
94 C5 Easter Balmoral Abers
28 D1 Easter Compton S Glos
107 F1 Easter Dalziel Highld
86 C2 Easter Howgate Mdloth
107 E2 Easter Kinkell Highld
98 D6 Easter Moniack Highld
95 G6 Easter Ord Abers
87 F6 Easter Pitkierie Fife
111 I2 Easter Skeld Shet
80 D3 Easter Softlaw Border
107 F2 Easter Suddie Highld
10 C3 Eastergate W Susx
85 F2 Easterhouse C Glas
40 D2 Eastern Green Covtry
18 C2 Easterton Wilts
85 G2 Eastfield N Lans
67 F2 Eastfield N York
72 D1 Eastgate Dur
45 E4 Eastgate Norfk
20 B2 Easthampstead Br For
38 D2 Easthampton Herefs
39 E5 Easthope Shrops
34 C1 Easthorpe Essex
15 F2 Eastington Devon
30 C2 Eastington Gloucs
29 E3 Eastington Gloucs
70 B6 Eastlands D & G
30 D1 Eastleach Martin Gloucs
30 D1 Eastleach Turville Gloucs
14 D4 Eastleigh Devon
9 F5 Eastleigh Hants
23 E1 Eastling Kent
9 H3 Eastney C Port
29 E6 Eastnor Herefs
60 B2 Eastoft N Linc
32 D5 Easton Cambs
71 F5 Easton Cumb
5 G5 Easton Devon
7 H3 Easton Dorset
9 G6 Easton Hants
42 B4 Easton Lincs
45 E3 Easton Norfk
17 F4 Easton Somset
35 F4 Easton Suffk
18 B4 Easton Wilts
18 B5 Easton Grey Wilts
32 B4 Easton Maudit Nhants
42 C3 Easton on the Hill Nhants
18 D3 Easton Royal Wilts
17 F6 Easton-in-Gordano N Som
43 E2 Eastrea Cambs
71 F5 Eastriggs D & G
60 B3 Eastrington E R Yk
18 D5 Eastrop Swindn
23 G1 Eastry Kent
17 G6 Eastville Bristl
53 F1 Eastville Lincs
41 H6 Eastwell Leics
21 G6 Eastwick Herts
58 B3 Eastwood Calder
51 F2 Eastwood Notts
22 D4 Eastwood Sthend
31 E6 Eathorpe Warwks
49 F5 Eaton Ches
49 H5 Eaton Ches
42 A5 Eaton Leics
45 E3 Eaton Norfk
51 G4 Eaton Notts
31 E1 Eaton Oxon
39 E5 Eaton Shrops
32 B1 Eaton Bray Beds
39 F6 Eaton Constantine Shrops
32 B1 Eaton Green Beds
19 E6 Eaton Hastings Oxon
39 E6 Eaton Mascott Shrops
32 D4 Eaton Socon Cambs
49 F2 Eaton upon Tern Shrops
67 E2 Ebberston N York
8 C5 Ebbesborne Wake Wilts
27 G4 Ebbw Vale Blae G
73 E2 Ebchester Dur
6 B4 Ebford Devon
29 F3 Ebley Gloucs
49 E4 Ebnal Ches
30 C4 Ebrington Gloucs
19 G3 Ecchinswell Hants
87 G3 Ecclaw Border
71 E6 Ecclefechan D & G
80 D4 Eccles Border
22 C2 Eccles Kent
57 G3 Eccles Salfd
44 D1 Eccles Road Norfk
50 D5 Ecclesall Sheff
51 E5 Ecclesfield Sheff
49 G2 Eccleshall Staffs
58 C3 Eccleshill Brad
86 B3 Ecclesmachan W Loth
48 D5 Eccleston Ches
57 E4 Eccleston Lancs
57 E2 Eccleston St Hel
95 F6 Echt Abers
80 C3 Eckford Border
51 E4 Eckington Derbys
29 G6 Eckington Worcs
32 A5 Ecton Nhants
50 C5 Edale Derbys
111 h3 Eday Airport Ork
11 E3 Edburton W Susx
107 F4 Edderton Highld
86 C1 Eddleston Border
85 F1 Eddlewood S Lans
21 F2 Eden Park Gt Lon
11 G6 Edenbridge Kent
57 G4 Edenfield Lancs
71 H3 Edenhall Cumb
42 C4 Edenham Lincs
50 D4 Edensor Derbys
84 C5 Edentaggart Ag & B
59 G1 Edenthorpe Donc
46 C5 Edern Gwynd
40 B2 Edgbaston Birm
31 G2 Edgcott Bucks
15 G5 Edgcott Somset
29 F4 Edge Gloucs
38 D6 Edge Shrops
44 D5 Edgefield Norfk
44 D5 Edgefield Green Norfk
58 C2 Edgerton Kirk
29 G3 Edgeworth Gloucs
49 G2 Edgmond Wrekin
38 D4 Edgton Shrops
21 E4 Edgware Gt Lon
57 G4 Edgworth Bl w D
104 B1 Edinbane Highld
86 C3 Edinburgh C Edin
86 B3 Edinburgh Airport C Edin
86 C3 Edinburgh Castle C Edin
86 C3 Edinburgh Zoo C Edin
40 D4 Edingale Staffs
70 B5 Edingham D & G
51 G2 Edingley Notts
45 F5 Edingthorpe Norfk
45 F5 Edingthorpe Green Norfk
81 E5 Edington Border
73 E5 Edington Nthumb
17 E3 Edington Somset
18 B2 Edington Wilts
17 E3 Edington Burtle Somset
17 E4 Edingworth Somset
42 B3 Edith Weston Rutlnd
17 E4 Edithmead Somset
32 B1 Edlesborough Bucks
81 F1 Edlingham Nthumb
52 D3 Edlington Lincs
8 C4 Edmondsham Dorset
73 F2 Edmondsley Dur
42 B4 Edmondthorpe Leics
21 F4 Edmonton Gt Lon
72 D2 Edmundbyers Dur
80 D4 Ednam Border
92 B4 Edradynate P & K
80 D5 Edrom Border
49 E3 Edstaston Shrops
30 C6 Edstone Warwks
41 G6 Edwalton Notts
51 G3 Edwinstowe Notts
32 D3 Edworth Beds
39 F2 Edwyn Ralph Herefs
95 E3 Edzell Angus
27 F1 Efail Isaf Rhondd
26 D2 Efail-fach Neath
46 C5 Efailnewydd Gwynd
25 E5 Efailwen Carmth
48 B5 Efenechtyd Denbgs
79 F2 Effgill D & G
20 D1 Effingham Surrey
15 H1 Efford Devon
57 G4 Egerton Bolton
12 D6 Egerton Kent
5 E3 Eggbuckland C Plym
15 F2 Eggesford Devon
32 B2 Eggington Beds
40 D6 Egginton Derbys
65 G4 Egglescliffe S on T
64 D5 Eggleston Dur
20 D3 Egham Surrey
42 B3 Egleton Rutlnd
81 F2 Eglingham Nthumb
3 F6 Egloshayle Cnwll
4 D5 Egloskerry Cnwll
49 E3 Eglwys Cross Wrexhm
55 F3 Eglwysbach Conwy
25 E6 Eglwyswrw Pembks
51 H3 Egmanton Notts
70 D1 Egremont Cumb
56 D2 Egremont Wirral
66 D4 Egton N York
66 D4 Egton Bridge N York
34 C2 Eight Ash Green Essex
97 F4 Eilanreach Highld
37 H3 Elan Village Powys
28 D2 Elberton S Glos
5 F2 Elburton C Plym
18 D4 Elcombe Swindn
29 F5 Eldersfield Worcs
84 D2 Elderslie Rens
65 F6 Eldon Dur
95 G4 Elfhill Abers
40 C4 Elford Staffs
101 E5 Elgin Moray
96 D4 Elgol Highld
13 F6 Elham Kent
87 E5 Elie Fife
54 C4 Elim IOA
9 F4 Eling Hants
51 G4 Elkesley Notts
29 G4 Elkstone Gloucs
102 C5 Ella Abers
6 B2 Ellacombe Torbay
89 G1 Ellanbeich Ag & B
58 C2 Elland Calder
83 F3 Ellary Ag & B
50 C1 Ellastone Staffs
63 E2 Ellel Lancs
87 G2 Ellemford Border
10 D5 Ellen's Green Surrey
49 H2 Ellenhall Staffs
66 A3 Ellerbeck N York
66 D4 Ellerby N York
49 F2 Ellerdine Heath Wrekin
90 C4 Elleric Ag & B
60 C3 Ellerker E R Yk
60 B4 Ellerton E R Yk
65 F3 Ellerton N York
20 B5 Ellesborough Bucks
48 D3 Ellesmere Shrops
56 D1 Ellesmere Port Ches
45 F2 Ellingham Norfk
81 G3 Ellingham Nthumb
65 F2 Ellingstring N York
32 D5 Ellington Cambs
73 F5 Ellington Nthumb
18 A2 Elliots Green Somset
19 H2 Ellisfield Hants
104 D3 Ellishader Highld
41 E4 Ellistown Leics
103 E3 Ellon Abers
71 G3 Ellonby Cumb
60 D3 Elloughton E R Yk
28 D3 Ellwood Gloucs
43 F3 Elm Cambs
21 H4 Elm Park Gt Lon
30 A6 Elmbridge Worcs
33 F3 Elmdon Essex
40 C2 Elmdon Solhll
21 F2 Elmers End Gt Lon
41 F3 Elmesthorpe Leics
40 C4 Elmhurst Staffs
29 G6 Elmley Castle Worcs
39 H3 Elmley Lovett Worcs
29 E4 Elmore Gloucs
29 E4 Elmore Back Gloucs
34 D3 Elmsett Suffk
34 D2 Elmstead Market Essex
13 F6 Elmsted Court Kent
23 G2 Elmstone Kent
29 F5 Elmstone Hardwicke Gloucs
60 D5 Elmswell E R Yk
34 D5 Elmswell Suffk
51 F4 Elmton Derbys
108 C1 Elphin Highld
86 D3 Elphinstone E Loth
95 G6 Elrick Abers
69 E2 Elrig D & G
72 C3 Elrington Nthumb
72 D5 Elsdon Nthumb
33 G2 Elsenham Essex
31 F1 Elsfield Oxon
60 D2 Elsham N Linc
95 G5 Elsick House Abers
44 D4 Elsing Norfk
58 A5 Elslack N York
9 G3 Elson Hants
86 B1 Elsrickle S Lans
10 C6 Elstead Surrey
10 B4 Elsted W Susx
42 C4 Elsthorpe Lincs
51 H2 Elston Notts
15 F3 Elstone Devon
32 C3 Elstow Beds
21 E5 Elstree Herts
61 F3 Elstronwick E R Yk
56 D6 Elswick Lancs
73 F3 Elswick N u Ty
33 E5 Elsworth Cambs
62 D6 Elterwater Cumb
21 G3 Eltham Gt Lon
33 E4 Eltisley Cambs
42 C2 Elton Cambs
49 E6 Elton Ches
50 D3 Elton Derbys
39 E3 Elton Herefs
51 H1 Elton Notts
65 G5 Elton S on T
73 E3 Eltringham Nthumb
78 C4 Elvanfoot S Lans
41 E6 Elvaston Derbys
34 B6 Elveden Suffk
20 B1 Elvetham Heath Hants
87 E3 Elvingston E Loth
23 G1 Elvington Kent
60 B4 Elvington York
66 B6 Elwick Hartpl
49 G5 Elworth Ches
16 C3 Elworthy Somset
33 G6 Ely Cambs
16 C6 Ely Cardif
32 B4 Emberton M Keyn
81 G2 Embleton Nthumb
107 G5 Embo Highld
107 G5 Embo Street Highld
17 G4 Emborough Somset
58 B5 Embsay N York
9 E4 Emery Down Hants
58 D2 Emley Kirk
20 B5 Emmington Oxon
43 F3 Emneth Cambs
43 G3 Emneth Hungate Norfk
42 B3 Empingham Rutlnd
10 B5 Empshott Hants
10 B3 Emsworth Hants
19 F3 Enborne W Berk
19 F3 Enborne Row W Berk
41 F3 Enderby Leics
63 E4 Endmoor Cumb
50 A2 Endon Staffs
50 A2 Endon Bank Staffs
21 F5 Enfield Gt Lon
21 F5 Enfield Lock Gt Lon
21 F5 Enfield Wash Gt Lon
18 D2 Enford Wilts
29 E1 Engine Common S Glos
19 H4 Englefield W Berk
20 C3 Englefield Green Surrey
28 D4 English Bicknor Gloucs
49 E2 English Frankton Shrops
17 H5 Englishcombe BaNES
19 F2 Enham-Alamein Hants
16 D3 Enmore Somset
8 B5 Enmore Green Dorset
70 D1 Ennerdale Bridge Cumb
92 C5 Enochdhu P & K
88 D4 Ensay Ag & B
8 C3 Ensbury Bmouth
48 D1 Ensdon Shrops
15 E4 Ensis Devon
31 E3 Enstone Oxon
78 C3 Enterkinfoot D & G
39 G4 Enville Staffs
111 a2 Eolaigearraidh W Isls
29 E4 Epney Gloucs
51 G2 Epperstone Notts
21 G5 Epping Essex
21 G5 Epping Green Essex
21 G5 Epping Upland Essex
65 F4 Eppleby N York
21 E2 Epsom Surrey
31 E4 Epwell Oxon
52 A5 Epworth N Linc
48 D3 Erbistock Wrexhm
40 C3 Erdington Birm
12 A5 Eridge Green E Susx
83 G3 Erines Ag & B
90 B3 Eriska Ag & B
34 B6 Eriswell Suffk
21 G3 Erith Gt Lon
18 C2 Erlestoke Wilts
5 F2 Ermington Devon
45 E5 Erpingham Norfk
98 D4 Errogie Highld
93 E2 Errol P & K
84 D3 Erskine Rens
68 B4 Ervie D & G
35 E2 Erwarton Suffk
38 B1 Erwood Powys
65 G4 Eryholme N York
48 C5 Eryrys Denbgs
65 F6 Escomb Dur
59 G4 Escrick York
47 F2 Esgairgeiliog Powys
73 F1 Esh Dur
73 F1 Esh Winning Dur
21 E2 Esher Surrey
73 F6 Eshott Nthumb
98 C6 Eskadale Highld
86 D3 Eskbank Mdloth
62 B5 Eskdale Green Cumb
79 F3 Eskdalemuir D & G
56 D6 Esprick Lancs
42 C3 Essendine Rutlnd
21 F6 Essendon Herts
99 E6 Essich Highld
40 B4 Essington Staffs
103 E3 Esslemont Abers
66 B5 Eston R & Cl
81 E4 Etal Nthumb
18 C3 Etchilhampton Wilts
12 C4 Etchingham E Susx
13 F5 Etchinghill Kent
40 B5 Etchinghill Staffs
20 C3 Eton W & M
20 C3 Eton Wick W & M
49 H4 Etruria C Stke
99 E2 Etteridge Highld
64 C6 Ettersgill Dur
49 G5 Ettiley Heath Ches
40 A3 Ettingshall Wolves
30 D5 Ettington Warwks
42 D3 Etton C Pete
60 D4 Etton E R Yk
79 F4 Ettrick Border
79 G5 Ettrickbridge Border
79 F4 Ettrickhill Border
40 D6 Etwall Derbys
34 C6 Euston Suffk
57 E4 Euxton Lancs
107 E3 Evanton Highld
42 C6 Evedon Lincs
107 F5 Evelix Highld
38 C2 Evenjobb Powys
31 G3 Evenley Oxon
30 D3 Evenlode Gloucs
65 E5 Evenwood Dur
17 G3 Evercreech Somset
60 B4 Everingham E R Yk
18 D2 Everleigh Wilts
32 C2 Eversholt Beds
7 G6 Evershot Dorset
20 B2 Eversley Hants
20 B2 Eversley Cross Hants
60 C3 Everthorpe E R Yk
32 D4 Everton Beds
9 E3 Everton Hants
56 D2 Everton Lpool
51 G5 Everton Notts
71 F6 Evertown D & G
39 F1 Evesbatch Herefs
30 B4 Evesham Worcs
41 G4 Evington C Leic
50 D6 Ewden Village Sheff
21 E2 Ewell Surrey
13 G6 Ewell Minnis Kent
19 H5 Ewelme Oxon
18 C6 Ewen Gloucs
27 E1 Ewenny V Glam
42 D6 Ewerby Lincs
73 E5 Ewesley Nthumb
10 D5 Ewhurst Surrey
12 C4 Ewhurst Green E Susx
10 D5 Ewhurst Green Surrey
48 C5 Ewloe Flints
5 E6 Eworthy Devon
20 B1 Ewshot Hants
28 B5 Ewyas Harold Herefs
15 G2 Exbourne Devon
9 F3 Exbury Hants
16 B2 Exebridge Somset
65 G2 Exelby N York
6 B5 Exeter Devon

6 B5 Exeter Airport Devon
15 G4 Exford Somset
39 E6 Exfordsgreen Shrops
30 C5 Exhall Warwks
41 E2 Exhall Warwks
19 H5 Exlade Street Oxon
6 B4 Exminster Devon
15 G4 Exmoor National Park
6 B4 Exmouth Devon
33 G5 Exning Suffk
13 F6 Exted Kent
6 B4 Exton Devon
9 H5 Exton Hants
42 B3 Exton Rutlnd
16 B2 Exton Somset
6 A5 Exwick Devon
50 D4 Eyam Derbys
31 F5 Eydon Nhants
42 D2 Eye C Pete
39 E3 Eye Herefs
35 E5 Eye Suffk
81 E6 Eyemouth Border
33 E3 Eyeworth Beds
22 D1 Eyhorne Street Kent
35 F4 Eyke Suffk
32 D4 Eynesbury Cambs
22 A2 Eynsford Kent
31 E1 Eynsham Oxon
7 F4 Eype Dorset
104 C2 Eyre Highld
23 G1 Eythorne Kent
39 E2 Eyton Herefs
48 D2 Eyton Shrops
38 D4 Eyton Shrops
39 F6 Eyton on Severn Shrops
49 F1 Eyton upon the Weald Moors Wrekin

F

19 F3 Faccombe Hants
66 B3 Faceby N York
48 A1 Fachwen Powys
49 F4 Faddiley Ches
66 C2 Fadmoor N York
26 C3 Faerdre Swans
84 D3 Faifley W Duns
17 F6 Failand N Som
76 D4 Failford S Ayrs
50 A6 Failsworth Oldham
9 G5 Fair Oak Hants
19 H3 Fair Oak Green Hants
47 E3 Fairbourne Gwynd
59 F3 Fairburn N York
50 C4 Fairfield Derbys
40 B1 Fairfield Worcs
18 D6 Fairford Gloucs
70 C5 Fairgirth D & G
56 D5 Fairhaven Lancs
84 B1 Fairlie N Ayrs
12 D3 Fairlight E Susx
6 C5 Fairmile Devon
20 D2 Fairmile Surrey
79 G5 Fairmilee Border
49 G3 Fairoak Staffs
22 B2 Fairseat Kent
34 B1 Fairstead Essex
11 G4 Fairwarp E Susx
27 G1 Fairwater Cardif
14 D3 Fairy Cross Devon
44 C5 Fakenham Norfk
34 C6 Fakenham Magna Suffk
87 E2 Fala Mdloth
87 E2 Fala Dam Mdloth
52 C4 Faldingworth Lincs
7 C1 Faldouet Jersey
29 E2 Falfield S Glos
35 F3 Falkenham Suffk
85 G3 Falkirk Falk
86 C6 Falkland Fife
85 G4 Fallin Stirlg
81 G2 Falloden Nthumb
57 H2 Fallowfield Manch
72 D3 Fallowfield Nthumb
83 H6 Falls of Blarghour Ag & B
11 F3 Falmer E Susx
3 E3 Falmouth Cnwll
79 G2 Falnash Border
67 F2 Falsgrave N York
72 B5 Falstone Nthumb
108 B4 Fanagmore Highld
32 C2 Fancott Beds
98 D6 Fanellan Highld
66 B3 Fangdale Beck N York
60 B5 Fangfoss E R Yk
89 E3 Fanmore Ag & B
106 B3 Fannich Lodge Highld
80 C4 Fans Border
32 B2 Far Bletchley M Keyn
31 H5 Far Cotton Nhants
62 C5 Far End Cumb
29 G3 Far Green Gloucs
57 E3 Far Moor Wigan
29 G3 Far Oakridge Gloucs
62 D5 Far Sawrey Cumb
53 E3 Far Thorpe Lincs
42 D2 Farcet Cambs
9 G4 Fareham Hants
40 C4 Farewell Staffs
19 E6 Faringdon Oxon
57 E5 Farington Lancs
92 C3 Farkhill P & K
71 H5 Farlam Cumb
17 F5 Farleigh N Som
21 F2 Farleigh Surrey
18 A3 Farleigh Hungerford Somset
19 H2 Farleigh Wallop Hants
53 F3 Farlesthorpe Lincs
63 E4 Farleton Cumb
63 F3 Farleton Lancs
50 C1 Farley Staffs
9 E6 Farley Wilts
34 B4 Farley Green Suffk
10 D6 Farley Green Surrey
20 B2 Farley Hill Wokham
29 E4 Farleys End Gloucs
10 A3 Farlington C Port
59 G6 Farlington N York
39 F4 Farlow Shrops
17 G5 Farmborough BaNES
30 B3 Farmcote Gloucs
37 E2 Farmers Carmth
30 C2 Farmington Gloucs
31 F1 Farmoor Oxon
101 G4 Farmtown Moray
101 G5 Farnachty Moray
21 G2 Farnborough Gt Lon
20 C1 Farnborough Hants
19 F5 Farnborough W Berk
31 E5 Farnborough Warwks
20 C1 Farnborough Park Hants
20 C1 Farnborough Street Hants
10 C6 Farncombe Surrey
32 B5 Farndish Beds
48 D4 Farndon Ches
51 H2 Farndon Notts
81 H4 Farne Islands Nthumb
93 H4 Farnell Angus
8 C5 Farnham Dorset
33 F1 Farnham Essex
59 E5 Farnham N York
35 F4 Farnham Suffk
10 B6 Farnham Surrey
20 C4 Farnham Common Bucks
20 C4 Farnham Royal Bucks
22 A2 Farningham Kent
58 D4 Farnley Leeds
58 D3 Farnley Leeds
58 C2 Farnley Tyas Kirk
51 G2 Farnsfield Notts
57 G3 Farnworth Bolton
57 H4 Farnworth Halton
109 F5 Farr Highld
99 E5 Farr Highld
99 E5 Farr Highld
98 A1 Farraline Highld
6 B4 Farringdon Devon
17 G4 Farrington Gurney BaNES
31 F4 Farthinghoe Nhants
31 G5 Farthingstone Nhants
58 C2 Fartown Kirk
58 D3 Fartown Leeds
6 D5 Farway Street Devon
90 B4 Fasnacloich Ag & B
98 B5 Fasnakyle Highld
90 B6 Fassfern Highld
73 G2 Fatfield Sundld
85 H2 Fauldhouse W Loth
34 B1 Faulkbourne Essex
17 H4 Faulkland Somset
49 F3 Fauls Shrops
23 E2 Faversham Kent
66 A1 Fawdington N York
73 F3 Fawdon N u Ty
81 F2 Fawdon Nthumb
22 B2 Fawkham Green Kent
31 E2 Fawler Oxon
20 B4 Fawley Bucks
9 F4 Fawley Hants
19 F4 Fawley W Berk
60 C3 Faxfleet E R Yk
11 E5 Faygate W Susx
56 D2 Fazakerley Lpool
40 D3 Fazeley Staffs
65 F2 Fearby N York
107 G4 Fearn Highld
91 H3 Fearnan P & K
105 F2 Fearnbeg Highld
105 E2 Fearnmore Highld
83 G3 Fearnoch Ag & B
40 B4 Featherstone Staffs
59 E2 Featherstone Wakefd
30 B6 Feckenham Worcs
34 C1 Feering Essex
64 D3 Feetham N York
11 F5 Felbridge Surrey
45 E5 Felbrigg Norfk
11 F6 Felcourt Surrey
26 B5 Felin gwm Isaf Carmth
26 B5 Felin gwm Uchaf Carmth
26 B4 Felindre Carmth
25 G6 Felindre Carmth
38 B4 Felindre Powys
26 C3 Felindre Swans
36 A1 Felindre Farchog Pembks
66 B2 Felixkirk N York
35 F2 Felixstowe Suffk
73 F3 Felling Gatesd
32 C4 Felmersham Beds
45 F5 Felmingham Norfk
10 C2 Felpham W Susx
34 C4 Felsham Suffk
34 A1 Felsted Essex
20 D3 Feltham Gt Lon
20 D3 Felthamhill Gt Lon
45 E4 Felthorpe Norfk
39 F1 Felton Herefs
17 F5 Felton N Som
73 F6 Felton Nthumb
48 D1 Felton Butler Shrops
44 A1 Feltwell Norfk
33 F4 Fen Ditton Cambs
33 E5 Fen Drayton Cambs
44 D2 Fen Street Norfk
57 E6 Fence Lancs
51 E5 Fence Rothm
65 F3 Fencote N York
31 F2 Fencott Oxon
53 F2 Fendike Corner Lincs
57 F5 Feniscowles Bl w D
6 C5 Feniton Devon
39 G4 Fenn Green Shrops
22 C3 Fenn Street Medway
50 C2 Fenny Bentley Derbys
6 C5 Fenny Bridges Devon
31 E5 Fenny Compton Warwks
41 E3 Fenny Drayton Leics
33 E5 Fenstanton Cambs
50 A1 Fenton C Stke
33 E6 Fenton Cambs
71 H5 Fenton Cumb
52 B1 Fenton Lincs
52 A4 Fenton Notts
81 E3 Fenton Nthumb
54 A4 Fenton Barns E Loth
59 G2 Fenwick Donc
76 D5 Fenwick E Ayrs
81 F4 Fenwick Nthumb
73 E4 Fenwick Nthumb
3 E3 Feock Cnwll
82 A6 Feolin Ferry Ag & B
76 C5 Fergushill N Ayrs
104 A1 Feriniquarrie Highld
6 c1 Fermain Bay Guern
94 D2 Fern Angus
27 F2 Ferndale Rhondd
8 C3 Ferndown Dorset
100 C4 Ferness Moray
19 E5 Fernham Oxon
39 H2 Fernhill Heath Worcs
10 C5 Fernhurst W Susx
93 E1 Fernie Fife
85 F1 Ferniegair S Lans
96 B5 Fernilea Highld
50 B4 Fernilee Derbys
59 E5 Ferrensby N York
97 E3 Ferrindonald Highld
10 D2 Ferring W Susx
107 F4 Ferry Point Highld
95 F2 Ferryden Angus
65 F6 Ferryhill Dur
25 G4 Ferryside Carmth
107 F4 Ferrytown Highld
44 D1 Fersfield Norfk
91 E6 Fersit Highld
99 F3 Feshiebridge Highld
21 E1 Fetcham Surrey
103 E4 Fetterangus Abers
95 E3 Fettercairn Abers
58 D5 Fewston N York
37 E3 Ffair Rhos Cerdgn
26 C4 Ffairfach Carmth
47 F5 Ffestiniog Gwynd
47 E5 Ffestiniog Railway Gwynd
26 B3 Fforest Carmth
26 C2 Fforest Fach Swans
36 C2 Ffostrasol Cerdgn
48 C5 Ffrith Flints
56 B1 Ffynnongroyw Flints
108 D2 Fiag Lodge Highld
21 F2 Fickleshole Surrey
29 G5 Fiddington Gloucs
16 D3 Fiddington Somset
8 A4 Fiddleford Dorset
3 E4 Fiddlers Green Cnwll
40 B6 Field Staffs
62 D4 Field Broughton Cumb
44 D5 Field Dalling Norfk
41 F4 Field Head Leics
101 F4 Fife Keith Moray
8 A5 Fifehead Magdalen Dorset
8 A4 Fifehead Neville Dorset
8 A4 Fifehead St Quintin Dorset
30 D2 Fifield Oxon
20 C3 Fifield W & M
18 D2 Figheldean Wilts
45 G3 Filby Norfk
67 G2 Filey N York
32 B3 Filgrave M Keyn
30 D1 Filkins Oxon
15 F4 Filleigh Devon
15 F2 Filleigh Devon
52 B4 Fillingham Lincs
40 D2 Fillongley Warwks
28 D1 Filton S Glos
60 C5 Fimber E R Yk
93 G5 Finavon Angus
44 A3 Fincham Norfk
20 B2 Finchampstead Wokham
83 G5 Fincharn Ag & B
10 A3 Finchdean Hants
34 A2 Finchingfield Essex
21 F4 Finchley Gt Lon
40 D6 Findern Derbys
100 D5 Findhorn Moray
99 F5 Findhorn Bridge Highld
92 C2 Findo Gask P & K
101 G6 Findochty Moray
95 H5 Findon Abers
10 D3 Findon W Susx
107 F4 Findon Mains Highld
95 E6 Findrack House Abers
32 B5 Finedon Nhants
35 E3 Fingal Street Suffk
92 D2 Fingask P & K
20 B4 Fingest Bucks
65 F2 Finghall N York
77 F3 Fingland D & G
23 G1 Finglesham Kent
34 D1 Fingringhoe Essex
91 G2 Finlarig Stirlg
31 G3 Finmere Oxon
91 F4 Finnart P & K
34 D5 Finningham Suffk
51 G6 Finningley Donc
111 c4 Finsbay W Isls
40 B1 Finstall Worcs
62 D4 Finsthwaite Cumb
31 E2 Finstock Oxon
111 h2 Finstown Ork
102 D5 Fintry Abers
85 E4 Fintry Stirlg
95 E5 Finzean Abers
88 D2 Fionnphort Ag & B
111 c4 Fionnsbhagh W Isls
65 E6 Fir Tree Dur
63 F5 Firbank Cumb
51 F5 Firbeck Rothm
65 F2 Firby N York
60 B6 Firby N York
53 F2 Firsby Lincs
9 G3 Fishbourne IOW
10 B3 Fishbourne W Susx
10 B3 Fishbourne Roman Palace W Susx
65 G6 Fishburn Dur
85 G5 Fishcross Clacks
9 G5 Fisher's Pond Hants
102 C3 Fisherford Abers
86 D3 Fisherrow E Loth
107 F1 Fisherton Highld
76 C3 Fisherton S Ayrs
18 C1 Fisherton de la Mere Wilts
24 D6 Fishguard Pembks
59 G2 Fishlake Donc
89 G3 Fishnish Pier Ag & B
17 G6 Fishponds Bristl
43 E6 Fishtoft Lincs
43 E6 Fishtoft Drove Lincs
96 B5 Fiskavaig Highld
52 C3 Fiskerton Lincs
51 H2 Fiskerton Notts
18 D2 Fittleton Wilts
10 D4 Fittleworth W Susx
49 E1 Fitz Shrops
16 C2 Fitzhead Somset
59 E2 Fitzwilliam Wakefd
11 G4 Five Ash Down E Susx
12 A4 Five Ashes E Susx
12 B6 Five Oak Green Kent
7 c1 Five Oaks Jersey
10 D5 Five Oaks W Susx
16 D2 Fivehead Somset
4 C5 Fivelanes Cnwll
20 C4 Flackwell Heath Bucks
30 B4 Fladbury Worcs
111 I2 Fladdabister Shet
50 C3 Flagg Derbys
67 H1 Flamborough E R Yk
67 H1 Flamborough Head E R Yk
66 D2 Flamingo Land Theme Park N York
20 D6 Flamstead Herts
10 C2 Flansham W Susx
58 D2 Flanshaw Wakefd
58 B5 Flasby N York
50 B3 Flash Staffs
104 B2 Flashader Highld
20 D5 Flaunden Herts
42 A6 Flawborough Notts
59 F6 Flawith N York
17 F5 Flax Bourton N Som
59 E5 Flaxby N York
29 E4 Flaxley Gloucs
16 C3 Flaxpool Somset
59 G6 Flaxton N York
41 G3 Fleckney Leics
31 F6 Flecknoe Warwks
52 A3 Fledborough Notts
7 G4 Fleet Dorset
20 B1 Fleet Hants
43 F4 Fleet Lincs
43 F4 Fleet Hargate Lincs
62 D1 Fleetwood Lancs
16 B5 Flemington V Glam
85 F2 Flemington S Lans
34 B5 Flempton Suffk
71 E3 Fletchertown Cumb
11 G4 Fletching E Susx
14 B2 Flexbury Cnwll
20 C1 Flexford Surrey
70 D3 Flimby Cumb
12 C5 Flimwell E Susx
48 C6 Flint Flints
51 H2 Flintham Notts
61 F3 Flinton E R Yk
44 B4 Flitcham Norfk
32 C3 Flitton Beds
32 C2 Flitwick Beds
60 C2 Flixborough N Linc
60 C2 Flixborough Stather N Linc
67 F2 Flixton N York
45 F1 Flixton Suffk
57 G2 Flixton Traffd
58 D2 Flockton Kirk
58 D2 Flockton Green Kirk
104 C3 Flodigarry Highld
62 D3 Flookburgh Cumb
45 E2 Flordon Norfk
31 G5 Flore Nhants
34 D3 Flowton Suffk
3 E3 Flushing Cnwll
6 C5 Fluxton Devon
30 B5 Flyford Flavell Worcs
22 C4 Fobbing Thurr
101 F5 Fochabers Moray
60 C2 Fockerby N Linc
17 G2 Foddington Somset
48 A1 Foel Powys
60 B4 Foggathorpe E R Yk
80 D5 Fogo Border
101 E5 Fogwatt Moray
108 B4 Foindle Highld
94 B3 Folda Angus
50 B1 Fole Staffs
41 E2 Foleshill Covtry
17 G1 Folke Dorset
13 G5 Folkestone Kent
42 C5 Folkingham Lincs
12 B3 Folkington E Susx
42 D1 Folksworth Cambs
67 F2 Folkton N York
102 C3 Folla Rule Abers
59 E5 Follifoot N York
15 E1 Folly Gate Devon
8 B6 Fonthill Bishop Wilts
8 B6 Fonthill Gifford Wilts
8 B5 Fontmell Magna Dorset
8 A4 Fontmell Parva Dorset
10 C3 Fontwell W Susx
50 C4 Foolow Derbys
101 F1 Forbestown Abers
65 F4 Forcett N York
83 G5 Ford Ag & B
31 H1 Ford Bucks
51 E4 Ford Derbys
14 D3 Ford Devon
5 E4 Ford Devon
30 C3 Ford Gloucs
81 E4 Ford Nthumb
16 C2 Ford Somset
50 C2 Ford Staffs
10 C3 Ford W Susx
18 B4 Ford Wilts
34 A1 Ford End Essex
16 C1 Ford Street Somset
11 H5 Fordcombe Kent
86 B4 Fordell Fife
38 C6 Forden Powys
5 H4 Forder Green Devon
33 H5 Fordham Cambs
34 C2 Fordham Essex
43 G2 Fordham Norfk
8 D4 Fordingbridge Hants
67 F1 Fordon E R Yk
95 E4 Fordoun Abers
34 C2 Fordstreet Essex
23 F2 Fordwich Kent
102 B5 Fordyce Abers
40 A5 Forebridge Staffs
41 E5 Foremark Derbys
6 b1 Forest Guern
63 G1 Forest Becks Lancs
50 B4 Forest Chapel Ches
28 D4 Forest of Dean Gloucs
21 G4 Forest Gate Gt Lon
10 D6 Forest Green Surrey
73 F4 Forest Hall N Tyne
21 F3 Forest Hill Gt Lon
31 G1 Forest Hill Oxon
59 F4 Forest Lane Head N York
90 D3 Forest Lodge Ag & B
85 H5 Forest Mill Clacks
11 G5 Forest Row E Susx
10 B3 Forestside W Susx
93 H4 Forfar Angus
92 D1 Forgandenny P & K
27 F4 Forge Hammer Torfn
101 F5 Forgie Moray
101 F4 Forgieside Moray
102 B4 Forgue Abers
56 C3 Formby Sefton
45 E2 Forncett End Norfk
45 E2 Forncett St Mary Norfk
45 E2 Forncett St Peter Norfk
34 B5 Fornham All Saints Suffk
34 C5 Fornham St Martin Suffk
100 C5 Forres Moray
50 B1 Forsbrook Staffs
110 C3 Forse Highld
110 C3 Forse House Highld
109 H3 Forsinard Highld
98 C3 Fort Augustus Highld
6 b2 Fort Hommet Guern
6 c2 Fort le Marchant Guern
90 C6 Fort William Highld
92 C1 Forteviot P & K
85 H1 Forth S Lans
29 F5 Forthampton Gloucs
91 H4 Fortingall P & K
100 C4 Fortnighty Highld
19 F1 Forton Hants
63 E1 Forton Lancs
48 D1 Forton Shrops
7 E6 Forton Somset
49 G2 Forton Staffs
102 C4 Fortrie Abers
107 F2 Fortrose Highld
7 G3 Fortuneswell Dorset
21 F5 Forty Hill Gt Lon
19 E3 Fosbury Wilts
30 D2 Foscot Oxon
43 E5 Fosdyke Lincs
92 A5 Foss P & K
30 C1 Fossebridge Gloucs
21 G6 Foster Street Essex
40 C6 Foston Derbys
41 G3 Foston Leics
42 B6 Foston Lincs
59 G6 Foston N York
61 E5 Foston on the Wolds E R Yk
53 E4 Fotherby Lincs
42 C2 Fotheringhay Nhants
40 D3 Foul End Warwks
81 E5 Foulden Border
58 A4 Foulridge Lancs
44 D4 Foulsham Norfk
87 E1 Fountainhall Border
34 D5 Four Ashes Suffk
6 b1 Four Cabots Guern
48 C2 Four Crosses Powys
11 G6 Four Elms Kent
16 D3 Four Forks Somset
43 F4 Four Gotes Cambs
2 D3 Four Lanes Cnwll
9 H6 Four Marks Hants
54 B4 Four Mile Bridge IOA
40 D2 Four Oaks Solhll
25 H3 Four Roads Carmth
12 C5 Four Throws Kent
107 G5 Fourpenny Highld
72 C3 Fourstones Nthumb
8 C6 Fovant Wilts
103 E2 Foveran Abers
4 B2 Fowey Cnwll
12 C6 Fowlhall Kent
93 E3 Fowlis Angus
92 B2 Fowlis Wester P & K
33 F5 Fowlmere Cambs
28 D5 Fownhope Herefs
84 D2 Foxbar Rens
17 H4 Foxcote Somset
116 B3 Foxdale IOM
34 B3 Foxearth Essex
62 C4 Foxfield Cumb
3 F4 Foxhole Cnwll
67 F1 Foxholes N York
44 D4 Foxley Norfk
50 B2 Foxt Staffs
33 F3 Foxton Cambs
41 G2 Foxton Leics
65 H3 Foxton N York
39 F4 Foxwood Shrops
28 D5 Foy Herefs
98 D4 Foyers Highld
100 B4 Foynesfield Highld
3 G5 Fraddon Cnwll
40 C4 Fradley Staffs
40 B6 Fradswell Staffs
61 E6 Fraisthorpe E R Yk
11 G4 Framfield E Susx
45 F2 Framingham Earl Norfk
45 F2 Framingham Pigot Norfk
35 F5 Framlingham Suffk
7 G5 Frampton Dorset
43 E5 Frampton Lincs
29 E1 Frampton Cotterell S Glos
29 G3 Frampton Mansell Gloucs
29 E3 Frampton on Severn Gloucs
35 E4 Framsden Suffk
73 F1 Framwellgate Moor Dur
57 F6 Frances Green Lancs
39 G4 Franche Worcs
56 C2 Frankby Wirral
40 B2 Frankley Worcs
41 E1 Frankton Warwks
12 B5 Frant E Susx
103 E6 Fraserburgh Abers
34 D1 Frating Essex
34 D1 Frating Green Essex
9 H3 Fratton C Port
5 E2 Freathy Cnwll
33 H5 Freckenham Suffk
56 D5 Freckleton Lancs
42 A4 Freeby Leics
19 G2 Freefolk Hants
31 E2 Freeland Oxon
45 G3 Freethorpe Norfk
45 G3 Freethorpe Common Norfk
43 F6 Freiston Lincs
15 E4 Fremington Devon
65 E3 Fremington N York
28 D1 Frenchay S Glos
92 B5 Frenich P & K
10 B6 Frensham Surrey
56 C3 Freshfield Sefton
18 A3 Freshford Wilts
9 E2 Freshwater IOW
35 F6 Fressingfield Suffk
35 E3 Freston Suffk
110 D5 Freswick Highld
29 E4 Fretherne Gloucs
45 F4 Frettenham Norfk
86 C6 Freuchie Fife
24 D4 Freystrop Pembks

43	F3	Friday Bridge Cambs
35	E4	Friday Street Suffk
60	C5	Fridaythorpe E R Yk
21	F1	Friern Barnet Gt Lon
88	C4	Friesland Bay Ag & B
52	C5	Friesthorpe Lincs
42	B6	Frieston Lincs
20	B4	Frieth Bucks
19	F6	Frilford Oxon
19	G4	Frilsham W Berk
20	C4	Frimley Surrey
22	C2	Frindsbury Medway
44	B5	Fring Norfk
31	G3	Fringford Oxon
22	D1	Frinsted Kent
35	E1	Frinton-on-Sea Essex
93	H4	Friockheim Angus
41	G5	Frisby on the Wreake Leics
53	F1	Friskney Lincs
12	A1	Friston E Susx
35	G4	Friston Suffk
51	E2	Fritchley Derbys
9	A4	Fritham Hants
14	D3	Frithelstock Devon
14	D3	Frithelstock Stone Devon
53	E1	Frithville Lincs
12	C6	Frittenden Kent
5	H2	Frittiscombe Devon
45	G2	Fritton Norfk
45	E2	Fritton Norfk
31	F3	Fritwell Oxon
58	C3	Frizinghall Brad
70	D1	Frizington Cumb
29	E3	Frocester Gloucs
39	E6	Frodesley Shrops
57	E1	Frodsham Ches
33	F3	Frog End Cambs
39	G3	Frog Pool Worcs
80	D3	Frogden Border
50	B4	Froggatt Derbys
50	B2	Froghall Staffs
5	G5	Frogmore Devon
42	D3	Frognall Lincs
4	D2	Frogwell Cnwll
41	F3	Frolesworth Leics
18	A2	Frome Somset
7	G5	Frome St Quintin Dorset
39	F1	Fromes Hill Herefs
48	C3	Fron Isaf Wrexhm
47	C3	Fron-goch Gwynd
48	C3	Froncysyllte Denbgs
72	D1	Frosterley Dur
19	E3	Froxfield Wilts
10	A4	Froxfield Green Hants
9	F5	Fryern Hill Hants
22	B5	Fryerning Essex
89	F3	Fuinary Highld
52	B1	Fulbeck Lincs
33	G4	Fulbourn Cambs
30	D2	Fulbrook Oxon
9	F6	Fulflood Hants
16	D2	Fulford Somset
50	B1	Fulford Staffs
59	G5	Fulford York
21	E3	Fulham Gt Lon
11	E3	Fulking W Susx
60	B5	Full Sutton E R Yk
76	C5	Fullarton N Ayrs
34	B1	Fuller Street Essex
19	F1	Fullerton Hants
53	E3	Fulletby Lincs
30	D4	Fullready Warwks
76	D6	Fullwood E Ayrs
20	C4	Fulmer Bucks
44	D5	Fulmodeston Norfk
52	C3	Fulnetby Lincs
43	E4	Fulney Lincs
53	E5	Fulstow Lincs
31	E2	Fulwell Oxon
73	G3	Fulwell Sundld
57	E1	Fulwood Lancs
50	D5	Fulwood Sheff
45	E2	Fundenhall Norfk
10	B3	Funtington W Susx
92	A2	Funtullich P & K
6	D6	Furley Devon
83	H5	Furnace Ag & B
26	B3	Furnace Carmth
50	B5	Furness Vale Derbys
33	F2	Furneux Pelham Herts
9	F5	Furzley Hants
22	B5	Fyfield Essex
19	E2	Fyfield Hants
19	F6	Fyfield Oxon
18	D3	Fyfield Wilts
18	D3	Fyfield Wilts
67	E4	Fylingthorpe N York
10	B4	Fyning W Susx
102	D3	Fyvie Abers

G

76	D6	Gabroc Hill E Ayrs
41	G4	Gaddesby Leics
20	D6	Gaddesden Row Herts
76	D4	Gadgirth S Ayrs
28	C2	Gaer-llwyd Mons
54	C3	Gaerwen IOA
76	C5	Gailes N Ayrs
40	A4	Gailey Staffs
65	F5	Gainford Dur
52	A4	Gainsborough Lincs
34	B2	Gainsford End Essex
105	F3	Gairloch Highld
98	A1	Gairlochy Highld
86	B5	Gairneybridge P & K
58	C4	Gaisby Brad
71	G4	Gaitsgill Cumb
80	B3	Galashiels Border
63	E2	Galgate Lancs
17	G2	Galhampton Somset
90	A2	Gallanach Ag & B
86	D5	Gallatown Fife
22	C5	Galleywood Essex
98	D3	Gallovie Highld
69	F5	Galloway Forest Park
93	F3	Gallowfauld Angus
92	D3	Gallowhill P & K
97	F4	Galltair Highld
5	G1	Galmpton Devon
5	H5	Galmpton Torbay
65	F1	Galphay N York
76	D5	Galston E Ayrs
8	A2	Galton Dorset
72	A1	Gamblesby Cumb
33	E4	Gamlingay Cambs
32	D4	Gamlingay Great Heath Beds
102	D5	Gamrie Abers
51	G4	Gamston Notts
51	G1	Gamston Notts
90	A2	Ganavan Bay Ag & B
47	F4	Ganllwyd Gwynd
95	E3	Gannachy Angus
61	E3	Ganstead E R Yk
66	C1	Ganthorpe N York
67	F1	Ganton N York
101	F4	Garbity Moray
34	D6	Garboldisham Norfk
101	F1	Garchory Abers
50	D6	Garden Village Sheff
20	B2	Gardeners Green Wokham
102	D5	Gardenstown Abers
111	I2	Garderhouse Shet
18	A1	Gare Hill Somset
84	B4	Garelochhead Ag & B
19	F6	Garford Oxon
59	E3	Garforth Leeds
58	A5	Gargrave N York
85	F5	Gargunnock Stirlg
45	E1	Garlic Street Norfk
69	F2	Garlieston D & G
23	G2	Garlinge Kent
23	F1	Garlinge Green Kent
95	F6	Garlogie Abers
102	D4	Garmond Abers
101	F5	Garmouth Moray
39	F6	Garmston Shrops
46	D5	Garn-Dolbenmaen Gwynd
85	F3	Garnkirk N Lans
111	e6	Garrabost W Isls
77	E3	Garrallan E Ayrs
2	D2	Garras Cnwll
47	E5	Garreg Gwynd
72	B1	Garrigill Cumb
69	G5	Garroch D & G
68	C2	Garrochtrie D & G
84	A1	Garrochty Ag & B
104	D2	Garros Highld
64	C3	Garsdale Head Cumb
18	C5	Garsdon Wilts
40	B6	Garshall Green Staffs
19	G6	Garsington Oxon
63	E1	Garstang Lancs
20	D5	Garston Herts
56	D1	Garston Lpool
82	C2	Gartachossan Ag & B
85	F2	Gartcosh N Lans
48	C3	Garth Denbgs
37	H2	Garth Powys
37	E5	Garth Penrhyncoch Cerdgn
63	E5	Garth Row Cumb
85	F2	Garthamlock C Glas
38	C5	Garthmyl Powys
42	A4	Garthorpe Leics
60	C2	Garthorpe N Linc
102	B3	Gartly Abers
85	E5	Gartmore Stirlg
85	G2	Gartness N Lans
84	D4	Gartness Stirlg
84	D4	Gartocharn W Duns
61	F3	Garton E R Yk
60	D5	Garton-on-the-Wolds E R Yk
110	A1	Gartymore Highld
87	F3	Garvald E Loth
90	B6	Garvan Highld
82	C4	Garvard Ag & B
106	D2	Garve Highld
44	D3	Garvestone Norfk
84	C3	Garvock Inver
28	C5	Garway Herefs
28	C5	Garway Common Herefs
111	d6	Garyvard W Isls
8	A6	Gasper Wilts
18	B3	Gastard Wilts
34	C6	Gasthorpe Norfk
33	G1	Gaston Green Essex
9	G2	Gatcombe IOW
52	A3	Gate Burton Lincs
59	G5	Gate Helmsley N York
59	F3	Gateforth N York
76	D5	Gatehead E Ayrs
72	C5	Gatehouse Nthumb
69	G3	Gatehouse of Fleet D & G
44	C4	Gateley Norfk
65	G2	Gatenby N York
80	D2	Gateshaw Border
73	F3	Gateshead Gatesd
93	F4	Gateside Angus
84	D2	Gateside E Rens
86	C6	Gateside Fife
84	C1	Gateside N Ayrs
78	C3	Gateslack D & G
57	H2	Gatley Stockp
80	B3	Gattonside Border
11	F6	Gatwick Airport W Susx
41	G3	Gaulby Leics
93	F2	Gauldry Fife
93	E4	Gauldswell P & K
52	D3	Gautby Lincs
80	D5	Gavinton Border
31	G3	Gawcott Bucks
50	A4	Gawsworth Ches
57	F4	Gawthrop Cumb
62	C4	Gawthwaite Cumb
31	E5	Gaydon Warwks
32	B3	Gayhurst M Keyn
64	C2	Gayle N York
65	E4	Gayles N York
31	G5	Gayton Nhants
44	B4	Gayton Norfk
40	B6	Gayton Staffs
53	F4	Gayton le Marsh Lincs
44	B4	Gayton Thorpe Norfk
44	B4	Gaywood Norfk
34	B5	Gazeley Suffk
111	d6	Gearraidh Bhaird W Isls
104	B2	Geary Highld
34	C4	Gedding Suffk
13	G6	Geddinge Kent
42	B1	Geddington Nhants
51	G1	Gedling Notts
43	F4	Gedney Lincs
43	F4	Gedney Broadgate Lincs
43	F4	Gedney Drove End Lincs
43	F4	Gedney Dyke Lincs
43	E3	Gedney Hill Lincs
42	C3	Geeston Rutlnd
45	G2	Geldeston Norfk
48	B5	Gellifor Denbgs
27	G2	Gelligaer Caerph
47	F5	Gellilydan Gwynd
26	D3	Gellinudd Neath
92	D3	Gellyburn P & K
25	F5	Gellywen Carmth
70	B5	Gelston D & G
42	B6	Gelston Lincs
61	E5	Gembling E R Yk
40	B4	Gentleshaw Staffs
20	B4	George Green Bucks
15	F3	George Nympton Devon
79	F2	Georgefield D & G
14	D5	Georgeham Devon
111	h2	Georth Ork
5	E6	Germansweek Devon
3	E3	Gerrans Cnwll
20	D4	Gerrards Cross Bucks
66	D4	Gerrick R & Cl
34	B3	Gestingthorpe Essex
48	C1	Geuffordd Powys
21	H4	Gidea Park Gt Lon
85	E2	Giffnock E Rens
87	E3	Gifford E Loth
93	E1	Giffordtown Fife
63	G2	Giggleswick N York
60	C5	Gilberdyke E R Yk
87	E3	Gilchriston E Loth
70	D3	Gilcrux Cumb
58	D3	Gildersome Leeds
51	F5	Gildingwells Rothm
73	G1	Gilesgate Moor Dur
16	B5	Gileston V Glam
27	G3	Gilfach Caerph
27	E2	Gilfach Goch Brdgnd
36	D3	Gilfachrheda Cerdgn
70	D2	Gilgarran Cumb
66	C2	Gillamoor N York
104	B2	Gillen Highld
79	E2	Gillesbie D & G
66	C1	Gilling East N York
65	F4	Gilling West N York
8	A5	Gillingham Dorset
22	C2	Gillingham Medway
45	G2	Gillingham Norfk
110	C5	Gillock Highld
110	D6	Gills Highld
79	H4	Gilmanscleuch Border
86	C3	Gilmerton C Edin
92	B2	Gilmerton P & K
64	D4	Gilmonby Dur
41	F2	Gilmorton Leics
72	A3	Gilsland Nthumb
87	E2	Gilston Mdloth
27	H4	Gilwern Mons
45	F5	Gimingham Norfk
34	D5	Gipping Suffk
53	E1	Gipsey Bridge Lincs
76	C5	Girdle Toll N Ayrs
111	I2	Girlsta Shet
65	G4	Girsby N York
69	G3	Girthon D & G
33	F5	Girton Cambs
52	A2	Girton Notts
76	B2	Girvan S Ayrs
63	G1	Gisburn Lancs
45	H1	Gisleham Suffk
34	D5	Gislingham Suffk
45	E1	Gissing Norfk
6	C5	Gittisham Devon
38	C2	Gladestry Powys
87	E3	Gladsmuir E Loth
26	C3	Glais Swans
66	D4	Glaisdale N York
93	F4	Glamis Angus
56	B1	Glan-y-don Flints
26	C4	Glanaman Carmth
44	D6	Glandford Norfk
25	F6	Glandwr Pembks
47	F1	Glandyfi Cerdgn
27	E2	Glanllynfi Brdgnd
81	F2	Glanton Nthumb
7	G6	Glanvilles Wootton Dorset
42	C1	Glapthorn Nhants
51	F3	Glapwell Derbys
27	G6	Glasbury Powys
38	B2	Glascwm Powys
55	G2	Glasfryn Conwy
85	E2	Glasgow C Glas
84	D2	Glasgow Airport Rens
85	E2	Glasgow Science Centre C Glas
54	D3	Glasinfryn Gwynd
97	E2	Glasnacardoch Bay Highld
96	D3	Glasnakille Highld
69	E2	Glasserton D & G
77	F6	Glassford S Lans
29	E4	Glasshouse Gloucs
58	C6	Glasshouses N York
71	F5	Glasson Cumb
63	E2	Glasson Lancs
72	A1	Glassonby Cumb
93	H4	Glasterlaw Angus
42	B2	Glaston Rutlnd
17	F3	Glastonbury Somset
42	D1	Glatton Cambs
57	F2	Glazebrook Warrtn
57	F2	Glazebury Warrtn
39	G4	Glazeley Shrops
62	C3	Gleaston Cumb
98	D4	Glebe Highld
58	D4	Gledhow Leeds
69	G3	Gledpark D & G
48	C3	Gledrid Shrops
34	B3	Glemsford Suffk
116	c4	Glen Auldyn IOM
94	B4	Glen Clunie Lodge Abers
116	b3	Glen Maye IOM
90	C6	Glen Nevis House Highld
41	F5	Glen Parva Leics
69	E5	Glen Trool Lodge D & G
101	E3	Glenallachie Highld
97	E2	Glenancross Highld
89	F3	Glenaros House Ag & B
75	E4	Glenbarr Ag & B
102	B5	Glenbarry Abers
89	F5	Glenbeg Highld
100	C2	Glenbeg Highld
95	H4	Glenborrodale Highld
84	A5	Glenbranter Ag & B
78	D4	Glenbreck Border
96	C4	Glenbrittle House Highld
77	H4	Glenbuck E Ayrs
94	C3	Glencally Angus
70	D6	Glencaple D & G
105	H1	Glencarron Lodge Highld
92	D2	Glencarse P & K
90	C4	Glenceitlein Highld
90	C4	Glencoe Highld
78	D2	Glencothe Border
86	C5	Glencraig Fife
78	B2	Glencrosh D & G
104	A1	Glendale Highld
83	H4	Glendaruel Ag & B
86	A6	Glendevon P & K
98	C3	Glendoe Lodge Highld
93	E2	Glendoick Fife
93	E1	Glenduckie Fife
85	H6	Gleneagles P & K
85	H6	Gleneagles Hotel P & K
74	B5	Glenegedale Ag & B
97	F4	Glenelg Highld
100	C4	Glenerney Moray
92	D1	Glenfarg P & K
99	F2	Glenfeshie Lodge Highld
41	F4	Glenfield Leics
97	F1	Glenfinnan Highld
98	B2	Glenfintaig Lodge Highld
92	D1	Glenfoot P & K
90	D1	Glenfyne Lodge Ag & B
84	C1	Glengarnock N Ayrs
110	B5	Glengolly Highld
89	E4	Glengorm Castle Ag & B
96	C6	Glengrasco Highld
78	D5	Glenholm Border
69	G6	Glenhoul D & G
94	B2	Glenisla Angus
84	B3	Glenkin Ag & B
101	G1	Glenkindie Abers
101	E2	Glenlivet Moray
70	B5	Glenlochar D & G
86	C6	Glenlomond P & K
68	D3	Glenluce D & G
84	A4	Glenmassan Ag & B
85	F2	Glenmavis N Lans
96	C6	Glenmore Highld
99	G3	Glenmore Lodge Highld
94	D2	Glenquiech Angus
83	F3	Glenralloch Ag & B
71	G1	Glenridding Cumb
86	C5	Glenrothes Fife
92	C5	Glenshee P & K
98	D2	Glenshera Lodge Highld
84	A3	Glenstriven Ag & B
52	C4	Glentham Lincs
99	F2	Glentromie Lodge Highld
69	E5	Glentrool Village D & G
99	E2	Glentruim House Highld
52	B4	Glentworth Lincs
89	G6	Glenuig Highld
90	C4	Glenure Ag & B
96	C6	Glenvarragill Highld
68	D4	Glenwhilly D & G
78	B5	Glespin S Lans
78	D5	Glewstone Herefs
42	D3	Glinton C Pete
41	H3	Glooston Leics
50	B5	Glossop Derbys
81	H1	Gloster Hill Nthumb
29	F4	Gloucester Gloucs
29	F4	Gloucestershire Airport Gloucs
58	B4	Glusburn N York
110	A3	Glutt Lodge Highld
3	E5	Gluvian Cnwll
31	E2	Glympton Oxon
48	C3	Glyn Ceiriog Wrexhm
27	E3	Glyn-Neath Neath
36	C2	Glynarthen Cerdgn
27	E3	Glyncorrwg Neath
11	G3	Glynde E Susx
48	B3	Glyndyfrdwy Denbgs
26	D4	Glyntawe Powys
25	G6	Glynteg Carmth
49	G2	Gnosall Staffs
49	G2	Gnosall Heath Staffs
41	H3	Goadby Leics
41	H5	Goadby Marwood Leics
18	C4	Goatacre Wilts
83	H5	Goatfield Ag & B
17	G1	Goathill Dorset
67	E3	Goathland N York
16	D3	Goathurst Somset
48	C3	Gobowen Shrops
10	C6	Godalming Surrey
12	D5	Goddard's Green Kent
33	E5	Godmanchester Cambs
7	G5	Godmanstone Dorset
23	E1	Godmersham Kent
17	F3	Godney Somset
2	C2	Godolphin Cross Cnwll
26	D3	Godre'r-graig Neath
9	G2	Godshill IOW
21	F1	Godstone Surrey
28	B3	Goetre Mons
21	F5	Goff's Oak Herts
28	A4	Gofilon Mons
86	C3	Gogar C Edin
37	E5	Goginan Cerdgn
46	D5	Golan Gwynd
4	B3	Golant Cnwll
4	D4	Golberdon Cnwll
57	F3	Golborne Wigan
58	C2	Golcar Kirk
28	B1	Goldcliff Newpt
12	B6	Golden Green Kent
10	A6	Golden Pot Hants
21	E4	Golders Green Gt Lon
22	D6	Goldhanger Essex
32	C4	Goldington Beds
67	E4	Goldsborough N York
59	E5	Goldsborough N York
2	C2	Goldsithney Cnwll
20	C2	Goldsworth Park Surrey
59	F1	Goldthorpe Barns
14	D3	Goldworthy Devon
107	G2	Gollanfield Highld
107	G5	Golspie Highld
8	D6	Gomeldon Wilts
10	D6	Gomshall Surrey
51	G2	Gonalston Notts
111	I3	Gonfirth Shet
22	B6	Good Easter Essex
44	B2	Gooderstone Norfk
15	E4	Goodleigh Devon
60	C4	Goodmanham E R Yk
21	G4	Goodmayes Gt Lon
23	E2	Goodnestone Kent
23	G1	Goodnestone Kent
28	D4	Goodrich Herefs
28	D4	Goodrich Castle Herefs
6	A2	Goodrington Torbay
57	G5	Goodshaw Fold Lancs
24	D6	Goodwick Pembks
19	F1	Goodworth Clatford Hants
60	B2	Goole E R Yk
30	B5	Goom's Hill Worcs
2	D4	Goonbell Cnwll
2	D4	Goonhavern Cnwll
2	D4	Goonvrea Cnwll
35	E2	Goose Green Essex
35	E2	Goose Green Essex
17	G6	Goose Green S Glos
95	F4	Goosecruives Abers
5	G6	Gooseford Devon
19	F5	Goosey Oxon
57	E6	Goosnargh Lancs
49	G6	Goostrey Ches
80	C4	Gordon Border
79	F3	Gordon Arms Hotel Border
102	B5	Gordonstown Abers
102	C3	Gordonstown Abers
86	D2	Gorebridge Mdloth
43	F3	Gorefield Cambs
18	D3	Gores Wilts
7	c1	Gorey Jersey
19	G4	Goring Oxon
10	D2	Goring-by-Sea W Susx
45	H3	Gorleston on Sea Norfk
102	C5	Gorrachie Abers
3	F3	Gorran Cnwll
3	F3	Gorran Haven Cnwll
18	D5	Gorse Hill Swindn
56	B1	Gorsedd Flints
26	B3	Gorseinon Swans
36	D2	Gorsgoch Cerdgn
26	B4	Gorslas Carmth
29	E5	Gorsley Gloucs
29	E5	Gorsley Common Gloucs
106	C2	Gorstan Highld
48	C2	Gorstello Ches
40	C6	Gorsty Hill Staffs
89	G2	Gorten Ag & B
98	D4	Gorthleck Highld
50	A6	Gorton Manch
35	E4	Gosbeck Suffk
43	E5	Gosberton Lincs
34	B2	Gosfield Essex
62	B6	Gosforth Cumb
73	F3	Gosforth N u Ty
40	A3	Gospel End Staffs
9	H3	Gosport Hants
29	E3	Gossington Gloucs
41	F6	Gotham Notts
29	G5	Gotherington Gloucs
16	D2	Gotton Somset
12	C5	Goudhurst Kent
53	E3	Goulceby Lincs
102	D3	Gourdas Abers
93	F3	Gourdie Angus
95	G3	Gourdon Abers
84	B3	Gourock Inver
85	E2	Govan C Glas
5	G2	Goveton Devon
59	G2	Gowdall E R Yk
106	D2	Gower Highld
26	B2	Gower Swans
26	B2	Gowerton Swans
86	B4	Gowkhall Fife
61	E4	Goxhill E R Yk
61	G1	Goxhill N Linc
111	d5	Grabhair W Isls
10	C4	Graffham W Susx
32	D5	Grafham Cambs
10	D6	Grafham Surrey
59	E6	Grafton N York
19	E6	Grafton Oxon
48	D2	Grafton Shrops
29	G6	Grafton Worcs
30	B5	Grafton Flyford Worcs
31	H4	Grafton Regis Nhants
32	B6	Grafton Underwood Nhants
12	D6	Grafty Green Kent
55	F5	Graig Conwy
48	B4	Graig-fechan Denbgs
22	D3	Grain Medway
53	E5	Grainsby Lincs
53	F5	Grainthorpe Lincs
3	F4	Grampound Cnwll
3	E4	Grampound Road Cnwll
111	b3	Gramsdal W Isls
111	b3	Gramsdale W Isls
31	H3	Granborough Bucks
41	H6	Granby Notts
7	c1	Grand Chemins Jersey
41	E5	Grand Prix Collection Donington Leics
31	F6	Grandborough Warwks
6	b2	Grandes Rocques Guern
92	B4	Grandtully P & K
71	F2	Grange Cumb
22	C2	Grange Medway
93	E2	Grange P & K
101	G5	Grange Crossroads Moray
100	D5	Grange Hall Moray
21	G4	Grange Hill Gt Lon
58	D2	Grange Moor Kirk
93	F1	Grange of Lindores Fife
73	F2	Grange Villa Dur
62	D4	Grange-over-Sands Cumb
78	C6	Grangehall S Lans
50	D3	Grangemill Derbys
85	H4	Grangemouth Falk
86	A4	Grangepans Falk
66	B5	Grangetown R & Cl
73	G2	Grangetown Sundld
61	E5	Gransmoor E R Yk
24	C6	Granston Pembks
33	F4	Grantchester Cambs
42	B5	Grantham Lincs
86	C4	Granton C Edin
100	C2	Grantown-on-Spey Highld
87	G3	Grantshouse Border
52	C5	Grasby Lincs
62	D6	Grasmere Cumb
58	B1	Grasscroft Oldham
56	D1	Grassendale Lpool
58	B6	Grassington N York
51	E3	Grassmoor Derbys
52	A2	Grassthorpe Notts
19	E1	Grateley Hants
33	E5	Graveley Cambs
32	D2	Graveley Herts
23	F2	Graveney Kent
22	B3	Gravesend Kent
111	d5	Gravir W Isls

Grayingham - Hardisworthy 173

52 B5 Grayingham Lincs
63 F5 Grayrigg Cumb
22 B3 Grays Thurr
10 C5 Grayshott Hants
10 C5 Grayswood Surrey
51 E6 Greasbrough Rothm
56 C2 Greasby Wirral
51 F2 Greasley Notts
33 G3 Great Abington Cambs
32 B6 Great Addington Nhants
30 C5 Great Alne Warwks
56 D3 Great Altcar Lancs
21 F6 Great Amwell Herts
64 B4 Great Asby Cumb
66 B4 Great Ayton N York
22 C5 Great Baddow Essex
18 A5 Great Badminton S Glos
34 A2 Great Bardfield Essex
32 D4 Great Barford Beds
30 D2 Great Barrington Gloucs
49 E6 Great Barrow Ches
34 C5 Great Barton Suffk
66 D4 Great Barugh N York
72 D4 Great Bavington Nthumb
35 E3 Great Bealings Suffk
19 E3 Great Bedwyn Wilts
35 E1 Great Bentley Essex
32 A5 Great Billing Nhants
44 B5 Great Bircham Norfk
35 E4 Great Blakenham Suffk
71 G3 Great Blencow Cumb
49 F2 Great Bolas Wrekin
21 E1 Great Bookham Surrey
2 B3 Great Bosullow Cnwll
31 F4 Great Bourton Oxon
41 H2 Great Bowden Leics
34 A4 Great Bradley Suffk
22 D6 Great Braxted Essex
34 D4 Great Bricett Suffk
32 B2 Great Brickhill Bucks
40 A5 Great Bridgeford Staffs
31 G6 Great Brington Nhants
34 D2 Great Bromley Essex
70 D3 Great Broughton Cumb
66 B4 Great Broughton N York
57 F1 Great Budworth Ches
65 G5 Great Burdon Darltn
22 B4 Great Burstead Essex
66 B4 Great Busby N York
53 F4 Great Carlton Lincs
42 C3 Great Casterton Rutlnd
18 B3 Great Chalfield Wilts
13 E6 Great Chart Kent
49 G1 Great Chatwell Staffs
33 G3 Great Chesterford Essex
18 C2 Great Cheverell Wilts
33 F3 Great Chishill Cambs
35 E1 Great Clacton Essex
70 D2 Great Clifton Cumb
61 F1 Great Coates NE Lin
29 G6 Great Comberton Worcs
71 G4 Great Corby Cumb
34 C3 Great Cornard Suffk
61 F4 Great Cowden E R Yk
19 E5 Great Coxwell Oxon
32 A6 Great Cransley Nhants
44 C2 Great Cressingham Norfk
71 F2 Great Crosthwaite Cumb
50 C1 Great Cubley Derbys
41 H4 Great Dalby Leics
32 B5 Great Doddington Nhants
44 C3 Great Dunham Norfk
33 H1 Great Dunmow Essex
18 D1 Great Durnford Wilts
33 G2 Great Easton Essex
42 B2 Great Easton Leics
56 D6 Great Eccleston Lancs
44 D2 Great Ellingham Norfk
17 H4 Great Elm Somset
5 H3 Great Englebourne Devon
31 G5 Great Everdon Nhants
33 E4 Great Eversden Cambs
34 D4 Great Finborough Suffk
44 C3 Great Fransham Norfk
20 D6 Great Gaddesden Herts
42 D1 Great Gidding Cambs
60 C5 Great Givendale E R Yk
35 F5 Great Glemham Suffk
41 G3 Great Glen Leics
42 B5 Great Gonerby Lincs
33 E4 Great Gransden Cambs
33 E3 Great Green Cambs
34 C4 Great Green Suffk
34 C5 Great Green Suffk
66 D1 Great Habton N York
42 D6 Great Hale Lincs
33 G1 Great Hallingbury Essex
32 B5 Great Harrowden Nhants
57 G5 Great Harwood Lancs
19 H6 Great Haseley Oxon
61 E4 Great Hatfield E R Yk
40 B5 Great Haywood Staffs
59 G2 Great Heck N York
34 C3 Great Henny Essex
18 B3 Great Hinton Wilts
44 C2 Great Hockham Norfk
35 E1 Great Holland Essex
34 C2 Great Horkesley Essex
33 F2 Great Hormead Herts
58 C3 Great Horton Brad
31 H3 Great Horwood Bucks
59 E1 Great Houghton Barns
32 A4 Great Houghton Nhants
50 C4 Great Hucklow Derbys
61 E5 Great Kelk E R Yk
20 B5 Great Kimble Bucks
20 C5 Great Kingshill Bucks
62 C6 Great Langdale Cumb
65 G3 Great Langton N York
34 B1 Great Leighs Essex
52 D6 Great Limber Lincs
32 B3 Great Linford M Keyn
34 C5 Great Livermere Suffk
50 D4 Great Longstone Derbys
73 G2 Great Lumley Dur
39 G1 Great Malvern Worcs
34 B2 Great Maplestead Essex
56 D6 Great Marton Bpool
44 B4 Great Massingham Norfk
31 G1 Great Milton Oxon
20 C5 Great Missenden Bucks
57 G6 Great Mitton Lancs
23 H1 Great Mongeham Kent
45 E1 Great Moulton Norfk
64 B4 Great Musgrave Cumb
48 D2 Great Ness Shrops
28 B4 Great Oak Mons
35 E2 Great Oakley Essex
42 B1 Great Oakley Nhants
32 D2 Great Offley Herts
64 B5 Great Ormside Cumb
71 F4 Great Orton Cumb
59 E6 Great Ouseburn N York
41 H2 Great Oxendon Nhants
22 B5 Great Oxney Green Essex
32 D5 Great Paxton Cambs
56 D5 Great Plumpton Lancs
45 F3 Great Plumstead Norfk
42 B5 Great Ponton Lincs
59 E3 Great Preston Leeds
33 E6 Great Raveley Cambs
30 D2 Great Rissington Gloucs
31 E3 Great Rollright Oxon
44 C4 Great Ryburgh Norfk
81 F2 Great Ryle Nthumb
39 E6 Great Ryton Shrops
34 A2 Great Saling Essex
71 H3 Great Salkeld Cumb
33 H2 Great Sampford Essex
48 D6 Great Saughall Ches
19 F4 Great Shefford W Berk
33 F4 Great Shelford Cambs
65 G4 Great Smeaton N York
44 C5 Great Snoring Norfk
18 C5 Great Somerford Wilts
49 G2 Great Soudley Shrops
65 G5 Great Stainton Darltn
22 D4 Great Stambridge Essex
32 D5 Great Staughton Cambs
53 F2 Great Steeping Lincs
28 D1 Great Stoke S Glos
71 H2 Great Strickland Cumb
32 D6 Great Stukeley Cambs
52 D3 Great Sturton Lincs
72 D4 Great Swinburne Nthumb
31 E3 Great Tew Oxon
34 C2 Great Tey Essex
15 E3 Great Torrington Devon
72 D6 Great Tosson Nthumb
22 D6 Great Totham Essex
22 D6 Great Totham Essex
62 C3 Great Urswick Cumb
22 D4 Great Wakering Essex
34 C3 Great Waldingfield Suffk
44 C5 Great Walsingham Norfk
22 C6 Great Waltham Essex
22 B4 Great Warley Essex
29 G6 Great Washbourne Gloucs
5 G5 Great Weeke Devon
42 B1 Great Weldon Nhants
34 D3 Great Wenham Suffk
72 D4 Great Whittington Nthumb
23 E6 Great Wigborough Essex
33 G4 Great Wilbraham Cambs
8 C6 Great Wishford Wilts
29 F4 Great Witcombe Gloucs
39 G3 Great Witley Worcs
30 D3 Great Wolford Warwks
34 A3 Great Wratting Essex
32 D2 Great Wymondley Herts
40 B4 Great Wyrley Staffs
45 H3 Great Yarmouth Norfk
34 B3 Great Yeldham Essex
42 C3 Greatford Lincs
50 B1 Greatgate Staffs
10 B5 Greatham Hants
66 B5 Greatham Hartpl
10 D4 Greatham W Susx
13 F4 Greatstone-on-Sea Kent
31 F4 Greatworth Nhants
33 E1 Green End Herts
33 E2 Green End Herts
59 F5 Green Hammerton N York
40 B4 Green Heath Staffs
17 G4 Green Ore Somset
63 E6 Green Quarter Cumb
33 F1 Green Street Herts
21 E5 Green Street Herts
22 B3 Green Street Green Kent
33 F1 Green Tye Herts
85 H2 Greenburn W Loth
84 B4 Greenfield Ag & B
32 C2 Greenfield Beds
56 C1 Greenfield Flints
98 A3 Greenfield Highld
58 B1 Greenfield Oldham
21 E3 Greenford Gt Lon
85 G3 Greengairs N Lans
58 D4 Greengates Brad
56 D6 Greenhalgh Lancs
16 C1 Greenham Somset
72 C5 Greenhaugh Nthumb
78 D1 Greenhill D & G
85 G3 Greenhill Falk
23 F2 Greenhill Kent
78 C5 Greenhill S Lans
22 B3 Greenhithe Kent
77 E5 Greenholm E Ayrs
80 B2 Greenhouse Border
58 C6 Greenhow Hill N York
110 C5 Greenland Highld
51 E5 Greenland Sheff
80 C4 Greenlaw Border
70 D6 Greenlea D & G
85 G6 Greenloaning P & K
57 G4 Greenmount Bury
84 C3 Greenock Inver
62 B4 Greenodd Cumb
31 G5 Greens Norton Nhants
86 A1 Greenshields S Lans
73 E3 Greenside Gatesd
58 C2 Greenside Kirk
34 D2 Greenstead Essex
34 B2 Greenstead Green Essex
17 E2 Greenway Somset
21 F3 Greenwich Gt Lon
30 B3 Greet Gloucs
39 F3 Greete Shrops
53 E3 Greetham Lincs
42 B3 Greetham Rutlnd
58 C2 Greetland Calder
17 E3 Greinton Somset
116 b2 Grenaby IOM
32 B4 Grendon Nhants
40 D3 Grendon Warwks
31 G2 Grendon Underwood Bucks
51 E5 Grenoside Sheff
111 c5 Greosabhagh W Isls
48 D4 Gresford Wrexhm
45 E5 Gresham Norfk
104 B2 Greshornish House Hotel Highld
44 C3 Gressenhall Norfk
44 C4 Gressenhall Green Norfk
63 E3 Gressingham Lancs
65 E4 Greta Bridge Dur
71 F5 Gretna D & G
71 F6 Gretna Green D & G
30 B3 Gretton Gloucs
42 B2 Gretton Nhants
39 E5 Gretton Shrops
65 F1 Grewelthorpe N York
78 D2 Greyrigg D & G
20 A4 Greys Green Oxon
70 D2 Greysouthen Cumb
71 G3 Greystoke Cumb
93 G3 Greystone Angus
20 A1 Greywell Hants
41 E2 Griff Warwks
28 B3 Griffithstown Torfn
57 F4 Grimeford Village Lancs
51 E5 Grimesthorpe Sheff
59 E1 Grimethorpe Barns
39 H2 Grimley Worcs
76 C3 Grimmet S Ayrs
53 F4 Grimoldby Lincs
48 D2 Grimpo Shrops
57 F5 Grimsargh Lancs
61 F1 Grimsby NE Lin
31 G5 Grimscote Nhants
14 C2 Grimscott Cnwll
111 d6 Grimshader W Isls
42 C4 Grimsthorpe Lincs
41 G5 Grimston Leics
44 B4 Grimston Norfk
7 G5 Grimstone Dorset
34 C5 Grimstone End Suffk
67 G1 Grindale E R Yk
50 D4 Grindleford Derbys
63 G1 Grindleton Lancs
49 E3 Grindley Brook Shrops
50 C4 Grindlow Derbys
50 C2 Grindon Staffs
73 G2 Grindon Sundld
51 H5 Gringley on the Hill Notts
71 F5 Grinsdale Cumb
49 E2 Grinshill Shrops
65 E3 Grinton N York
111 d6 Griomaisiader W Isls
111 b3 Griomsaigh W Isls
88 C4 Grishipoll Ag & B
67 F2 Gristhorpe N York
44 C2 Griston Norfk
111 h2 Gritley Ork
18 C5 Grittenham Wilts
18 B4 Grittleton Wilts
62 C4 Grizebeck Cumb
62 D5 Grizedale Cumb
41 F4 Groby Leics
55 H3 Groes Conwy
27 F1 Groes-faen Rhondd
27 G2 Groes-Wen Caerph
111 a3 Grogarry W Isls
75 F5 Grogport Ag & B
111 a3 Groigearraidh W Isls
56 B1 Gronant Flints
11 H5 Groombridge E Susx
111 c5 Grosebay W Isls
28 C5 Grosmont Mons
67 E4 Grosmont N York
34 C3 Groton Suffk
7 c1 Grouville Jersey
51 H4 Grove Notts
19 F5 Grove Oxon
21 G3 Grove Park Gt Lon
26 B3 Grovesend Swans
105 G5 Gruinard Highld
82 B2 Gruinart Ag & B
96 B5 Grula Highld
89 F3 Gruline Ag & B
35 E4 Grundisburgh Suffk
111 k2 Gruting Shet
90 C3 Gualachulain Highld
93 F1 Guardbridge Fife
39 G1 Guarlford Worcs
92 C4 Guay P & K
6 b1 Guernsey Airport Guern
12 D3 Guestling Green E Susx
12 D4 Guestling Thorn E Susx
44 D4 Guestwick Norfk
57 G5 Guide Bl w D
73 F5 Guide Post Nthumb
33 E3 Guilden Morden Cambs
49 E6 Guilden Sutton Ches
20 C1 Guildford Surrey
92 D3 Guildtown P & K
41 G1 Guilsborough Nhants
48 C1 Guilsfield Powys
76 C3 Guiltreehill S Ayrs
15 E4 Guineaford Devon
66 C5 Guisborough R & Cl
58 D4 Guiseley Leeds
44 D4 Guist Norfk
30 C3 Guiting Power Gloucs
87 E4 Gullane E Loth
2 B2 Gulval Cnwll
5 E4 Gulworthy Devon
25 E3 Gumfreston Pembks
41 G2 Gumley Leics
12 B3 Gun Hill E Susx
42 B4 Gunby Lincs
53 F2 Gunby Lincs
9 H6 Gundleton Hants
15 F4 Gunn Devon
64 D3 Gunnerside N York
72 D4 Gunnerton Nthumb
60 C1 Gunness N Linc
5 E4 Gunnislake Cnwll
111 l2 Gunnista Shet
52 A5 Gunthorpe N Linc
44 D5 Gunthorpe Norfk
51 G1 Gunthorpe Notts
2 C2 Gunwalloe Cnwll
9 G3 Gurnard IOW
17 G4 Gurney Slade Somset
26 D3 Gurnos Powys
8 C4 Gussage All Saints Dorset
8 C4 Gussage St Andrew Dorset
8 C4 Gussage St Michael Dorset
13 G6 Guston Kent
111 l4 Gutcher Shet
93 G4 Guthrie Angus
43 F3 Guyhirn Cambs
81 G1 Guyzance Nthumb
56 B1 Gwaenysgor Flints
54 C4 Gwalchmai IOA
26 C4 Gwaun-Cae-Gurwen Carmth
2 D2 Gweek Cnwll
38 B1 Gwenddwr Powys
2 D3 Gwennap Cnwll
48 C5 Gwernaffield Flints
28 C3 Gwernesney Mons
26 B5 Gwernogle Carmth
48 C5 Gwernymynydd Flints
56 B1 Gwespyr Flints
2 C3 Gwinear Cnwll
2 C3 Gwithian Cnwll
48 B4 Gwyddelwern Denbgs
26 B6 Gwyddgrug Carmth
55 G3 Gwytherin Conwy

H

38 D6 Habberley Shrops
39 G4 Habberley Worcs
57 G5 Habergham Lancs
53 G2 Habertoft Lincs
61 E2 Habrough NE Lin
42 C4 Hacconby Lincs
42 C5 Haceby Lincs
35 F4 Hacheston Suffk
21 F2 Hackbridge Gt Lon
51 E5 Hackenthorpe Sheff
44 D2 Hackford Norfk
65 F3 Hackforth N York
111 h2 Hackland Ork
32 A4 Hackleton Nhants
23 H1 Hacklinge Kent
67 F2 Hackness N York
21 F4 Hackney Gt Lon
52 C3 Hackthorn Lincs
71 H2 Hackthorpe Cumb
80 D3 Hadden Border
20 A6 Haddenham Bucks
33 F6 Haddenham Cambs
87 E3 Haddington E Loth
52 B2 Haddington Lincs
45 G2 Haddiscoe Norfk
102 D3 Haddo Abers
42 D2 Haddon Cambs
50 B6 Hadfield Derbys
53 F1 Hadham Ford Herts
22 C4 Hadleigh Essex
34 D3 Hadleigh Suffk
39 H3 Hadley Worcs
40 C5 Hadley End Staffs
21 F5 Hadley Wood Gt Lon
22 B1 Hadlow Kent
11 H4 Hadlow Down E Susx
49 E2 Hadnall Shrops
33 G3 Hadstock Essex
30 A6 Hadzor Worcs
81 F4 Haggerston Nthumb
85 G3 Haggs Falk
28 D6 Hagley Herefs
40 A2 Hagley Worcs
53 E2 Hagworthingham Lincs
32 D5 Hail Weston Cambs
62 A6 Haile Cumb
31 E2 Hailey Oxon
12 B3 Hailsham E Susx
21 G4 Hainault Gt Lon
45 E4 Hainford Norfk
52 D4 Hainton Lincs
61 E6 Haisthorpe E R Yk
24 C3 Hakin Pembks
51 G2 Halam Notts
86 B4 Halbeath Fife
16 B1 Halberton Devon
110 C5 Halcro Highld
63 E4 Hale Cumb
57 E1 Hale Halton
8 D5 Hale Hants
10 B6 Hale Surrey
57 G2 Hale Traffd
12 A3 Hale Green E Susx
22 B1 Hale Street Kent
45 G2 Hales Norfk
49 G3 Hales Staffs
23 F2 Hales Place Kent
40 B2 Halesowen Dudley
35 G6 Halesworth Suffk
57 E2 Halewood Knows
5 H4 Halford Devon
30 D4 Halford Warwks
39 G5 Halfpenny Green Staffs
48 D1 Halfway House Shrops
22 D3 Halfway Houses Kent
58 C3 Halifax Calder
110 B5 Halkirk Highld
48 C6 Halkyn Flints
84 D1 Hall E Rens
62 C5 Hall Dunnerdale Cumb
85 G3 Hall Glen Falk
40 C2 Hall Green Birm
33 E2 Hall's Green Herts
11 G4 Halland E Susx
42 A2 Hallaton Leics
17 G4 Hallatrow BaNES
72 A3 Hallbankgate Cumb
28 D1 Hallen S Glos
73 G1 Hallgarth Dur
104 B2 Hallin Highld
22 C2 Halling Medway
53 E4 Hallington Lincs
72 D4 Hallington Nthumb
57 F4 Halliwell Bolton
51 G2 Halloughton Notts
39 G2 Hallow Worcs
5 H1 Hallsands Devon
79 E6 Hallyne Border
29 E3 Halmore Gloucs
10 C3 Halnaker W Susx
56 D4 Halsall Lancs
31 F4 Halse Nhants
16 C2 Halse Somset
2 B3 Halsetown Cnwll
61 F3 Halsham E R Yk
34 B2 Halstead Essex
21 G2 Halstead Kent
41 H4 Halstead Leics
7 F6 Halstock Dorset
16 C3 Halsway Somset
53 E2 Haltham Lincs
20 C6 Halton Bucks
63 E3 Halton Lancs
59 E3 Halton Leeds
72 D3 Halton Nthumb
48 C3 Halton Wrexhm
58 B5 Halton East N York
64 C1 Halton Gill N York
53 F2 Halton Holegate Lincs
72 B3 Halton Lea Gate Nthumb
72 D3 Halton Shields Nthumb
63 H2 Halton West N York
72 B3 Haltwhistle Nthumb
45 G3 Halvergate Norfk
5 H2 Halwell Devon
14 D1 Halwill Devon
14 D1 Halwill Junction Devon
6 D5 Ham Devon
29 E3 Ham Gloucs
21 E3 Ham Gt Lon
23 G1 Ham Kent
16 D2 Ham Somset
19 E3 Ham Wilts
30 B6 Ham Green Worcs
17 F3 Ham Street Somset
9 G4 Hamble-le-Rice Hants
20 B4 Hambleden Bucks
9 H5 Hambledon Hants
10 C5 Hambledon Surrey
56 D6 Hambleton Lancs
59 F3 Hambleton N York
17 E2 Hambridge Somset
10 B3 Hambrook W Susx
53 E2 Hameringham Lincs
32 D6 Hamerton Cambs
85 F1 Hamilton S Lans
7 G6 Hamlet Dorset
21 E3 Hammersmith Gt Lon
40 C4 Hammerwich Staffs
8 A4 Hammoon Dorset
111 l2 Hamnavoe Shet
111 l3 Hamnavoe Shet
12 B2 Hampden Park E Susx
20 B5 Hampden Row Bucks
30 C2 Hampnett Gloucs
59 F1 Hampole Donc
8 C3 Hampreston Dorset
21 F4 Hampstead Gt Lon
19 G4 Hampstead Norrey's W Berk
58 D5 Hampsthwaite N York
21 E2 Hampton Gt Lon
23 F2 Hampton Kent
39 G4 Hampton Shrops
18 D5 Hampton Swindn
30 B4 Hampton Worcs
28 D6 Hampton Bishop Herefs
21 E2 Hampton Court Palace & Gardens Gt Lon
49 E4 Hampton Heath Ches
40 D2 Hampton in Arden Solhll
30 A6 Hampton Lovett Worcs
30 D5 Hampton Lucy Warwks
30 D6 Hampton Magna Warwks
31 F2 Hampton Poyle Oxon
21 E2 Hampton Wick Gt Lon
9 E5 Hamptworth Wilts
11 G3 Hamsey E Susx
40 C5 Hamstall Ridware Staffs
19 F3 Hamstead Marshall W Berk
73 E2 Hamsterley Dur
65 E6 Hamsterley Dur
13 E5 Hamstreet Kent
8 C3 Hamworthy Poole
40 C6 Hanbury Staffs
30 B6 Hanbury Worcs
49 H3 Hanchurch Staffs
6 C5 Hand and Pen Devon
48 D5 Handbridge Ches
11 F5 Handcross W Susx
57 H1 Handforth Ches
49 E5 Handley Ches
51 E3 Handley Derbys
40 B2 Handsworth Birm
51 E5 Handsworth Sheff
41 H1 Hanging Houghton Nhants
18 C1 Hanging Langford Wilts
11 F3 Hangleton Br & H
17 G6 Hanham S Glos
49 F4 Hankelow Ches
29 G2 Hankerton Wilts
50 A2 Hanley C Stke
29 F6 Hanley Castle Worcs
39 F3 Hanley Child Worcs
39 G1 Hanley Swan Worcs
39 F3 Hanley William Worcs
58 A6 Hanlith N York
49 E3 Hanmer Wrexhm
15 E4 Hannaford Devon
19 G2 Hannington Hants
32 A5 Hannington Nhants
18 D5 Hannington Swindn
18 D6 Hannington Wick Swindn
32 A3 Hanslope M Keyn
42 C4 Hanthorpe Lincs
21 E3 Hanwell Gt Lon
31 E4 Hanwell Oxon
49 E1 Hanwood Shrops
20 D3 Hanworth Gt Lon
45 E5 Hanworth Norfk
78 C5 Happendon S Lans
45 G5 Happisburgh Norfk
45 G5 Happisburgh Common Norfk
49 E6 Hapsford Ches
57 G5 Hapton Lancs
45 E2 Hapton Norfk
5 H3 Harberton Devon
5 H3 Harbertonford Devon
23 F2 Harbledown Kent
40 B2 Harborne Birm
41 F2 Harborough Magna Warwks
81 E1 Harbottle Nthumb
5 G3 Harbourneford Devon
31 E5 Harbury Warwks
41 H6 Harby Leics
52 B3 Harby Notts
6 A4 Harcombe Devon
6 C4 Harcombe Devon
7 E5 Harcombe Bottom Devon
58 C4 Harden Brad
95 G6 Hardgate Abers
70 B5 Hardgate D & G
84 D3 Hardgate W Duns
10 D4 Hardham W Susx
44 D3 Hardingham Norfk
31 H5 Hardingstone Nhants
17 H4 Hardington Somset
7 F6 Hardington Mandeville Somset
7 F6 Hardington Marsh Somset
7 F6 Hardington Moor Somset
14 C3 Hardisworthy Devon

9 F4 **Hardley** Hants
45 G2 **Hardley Street** Norfk
64 C3 **Hardraw** N York
51 E3 **Hardstoft** Derbys
9 H3 **Hardway** Hants
17 H3 **Hardway** Somset
32 A1 **Hardwick** Bucks
33 F4 **Hardwick** Cambs
32 B5 **Hardwick** Nhants
45 E1 **Hardwick** Norfk
31 E1 **Hardwick** Oxon
31 F3 **Hardwick** Oxon
29 F4 **Hardwicke** Gloucs
29 F5 **Hardwicke** Gloucs
34 C1 **Hardy's Green** Essex
58 C3 **Hare Croft** Brad
34 D2 **Hare Green** Essex
20 B3 **Hare Hatch** Wokham
21 G6 **Hare Street** Essex
33 F2 **Hare Street** Herts
53 E2 **Hareby** Lincs
20 D4 **Harefield** Gt Lon
40 C6 **Harehill** Derbys
59 E3 **Harehills** Leeds
80 B2 **Harelaw** Border
79 G1 **Harelaw** D & G
29 F4 **Harescombe** Gloucs
29 F4 **Haresfield** Gloucs
9 F6 **Harestock** Hants
58 D4 **Harewood** Leeds
28 C5 **Harewood End** Herefs
5 F3 **Harford** Devon
49 E5 **Hargrave** Ches
32 C5 **Hargrave** Nhants
34 B4 **Hargrave Green** Suffk
35 E2 **Harkstead** Suffk
40 D4 **Harlaston** Staffs
42 B5 **Harlaxton** Lincs
57 H6 **Harle Syke** Lancs
47 E4 **Harlech** Gwynd
49 E1 **Harlescott** Shrops
21 E4 **Harlesden** Gt Lon
51 F4 **Harlesthorpe** Derbys
5 H2 **Harleston** Devon
45 F1 **Harleston** Norfk
34 D4 **Harleston** Suffk
31 G6 **Harlestone** Nhants
51 E6 **Harley** Rothm
39 F6 **Harley** Shrops
32 C2 **Harlington** Beds
51 F6 **Harlington** Donc
20 D3 **Harlington** Gt Lon
96 B6 **Harlosh** Highld
21 G6 **Harlow** Essex
73 E3 **Harlow Hill** Nthumb
60 B4 **Harlthorpe** E R Yk
33 F4 **Harlton** Cambs
3 E6 **Harlyn Bay** Cnwll
8 C2 **Harman's Cross** Dorset
65 E2 **Harmby** N York
33 E1 **Harmer Green** Herts
49 E2 **Harmer Hill** Shrops
52 B2 **Harmston** Lincs
39 E6 **Harnage** Shrops
18 C6 **Harnhill** Gloucs
21 H4 **Harold Hill** Gt Lon
22 A4 **Harold Wood** Gt Lon
24 C4 **Haroldston West** Pembks
111 m4 **Haroldswick** Shet
66 C2 **Harome** N York
21 E6 **Harpenden** Herts
6 C4 **Harpford** Devon
61 E6 **Harpham** E R Yk
44 B4 **Harpley** Norfk
39 F2 **Harpley** Worcs
31 G6 **Harpole** Nhants
110 B4 **Harpsdale** Highld
52 B4 **Harpswell** Lincs
57 H3 **Harpurhey** Manch
71 G4 **Harraby** Cumb
15 E4 **Harracott** Devon
97 E4 **Harrapool** Highld
92 C2 **Harrietfield** P & K
22 D1 **Harrietsham** Kent
21 F4 **Harringay** Gt Lon
70 D2 **Harrington** Cumb
53 F3 **Harrington** Lincs
41 H2 **Harrington** Nhants
42 B2 **Harringworth** Nhants
58 D5 **Harrogate** N York
32 B4 **Harrold** Beds
21 E4 **Harrow** Gt Lon
34 C4 **Harrow Green** Suffk
21 E4 **Harrow on the Hill** Gt Lon
21 E4 **Harrow Weald** Gt Lon
5 E4 **Harrowbarrow** Cnwll
33 F4 **Harston** Cambs
42 A5 **Harston** Leics
60 C4 **Harswell** E R Yk
66 B6 **Hart** Hartpl
73 E5 **Hartburn** Nthumb
34 B4 **Hartest** Suffk
11 G5 **Hartfield** E Susx
33 E5 **Hartford** Cambs
49 F6 **Hartford** Ches
34 A1 **Hartford End** Essex
20 B2 **Hartfordbridge** Hants
65 F4 **Hartforth** N York
8 B5 **Hartgrove** Dorset
49 E5 **Harthill** Ches
85 H2 **Harthill** N Lans
51 F4 **Harthill** Rothm
50 C3 **Hartington** Derbys
14 C3 **Hartland** Devon
14 B3 **Hartland Quay** Devon
39 H3 **Hartlebury** Worcs
66 B6 **Hartlepool** Hartpl
64 C4 **Hartley** Cumb
22 B2 **Hartley** Kent
12 C5 **Hartley** Kent
20 A2 **Hartley Wespall** Hants
20 B1 **Hartley Wintney** Hants
22 D2 **Hartlip** Kent
60 B6 **Harton** N York
73 G3 **Harton** S Tyne
29 F5 **Hartpury** Gloucs
58 C2 **Hartshead** Kirk
49 H4 **Hartshill** C Stke
41 E3 **Hartshill** Warwks
41 E5 **Hartshorne** Derbys
81 E2 **Hartside** Nthumb
32 A4 **Hartwell** Nhants
58 D6 **Hartwith** N York
85 G2 **Hartwood** N Lans
79 G5 **Hartwoodmyres** Border
22 B2 **Harvel** Kent
39 H3 **Harvington** Worcs
30 B5 **Harvington** Worcs
51 G5 **Harwell** Notts
19 G5 **Harwell** Oxon
35 F2 **Harwich** Essex
67 F3 **Harwood Dale** N York
51 G5 **Harworth** Notts
40 B2 **Hasbury** Dudley
10 D5 **Hascombe** Surrey
41 G1 **Haselbech** Nhants
7 F6 **Haselbury Plucknett** Somset
30 D6 **Haseley** Warwks
30 C5 **Haselor** Warwks
29 F5 **Hasfield** Gloucs
56 D3 **Haskayne** Lancs
35 F4 **Hasketon** Suffk
10 C5 **Haslemere** Surrey
57 G5 **Haslingden** Lancs
33 F4 **Haslingfield** Cambs
49 G5 **Haslington** Ches
45 G3 **Hassingham** Norfk
11 F3 **Hassocks** W Susx
50 D4 **Hassop** Derbys
110 D4 **Haster** Highld
13 F6 **Hastingleigh** Kent
12 D3 **Hastings** E Susx
21 G6 **Hastingwood** Essex
20 C6 **Hastoe** Herts
73 G1 **Haswell** Dur
73 G1 **Haswell Plough** Dur
17 E1 **Hatch Beauchamp** Somset
21 E4 **Hatch End** Gt Lon
49 E6 **Hatchmere** Ches
52 D5 **Hatcliffe** NE Lin
59 G1 **Hatfield** Donc
39 F2 **Hatfield** Herefs
21 E6 **Hatfield** Herts
33 G1 **Hatfield Broad Oak** Essex
21 H6 **Hatfield Heath** Essex
22 C6 **Hatfield Peverel** Essex
59 G1 **Hatfield Woodhouse** Donc
19 E6 **Hatford** Oxon
19 E2 **Hatherden** Hants
15 E2 **Hatherleigh** Devon
41 F5 **Hathern** Leics
30 C1 **Hatherop** Gloucs
50 D4 **Hathersage** Derbys
50 D4 **Hathersage Booths** Derbys
49 F4 **Hatherton** Ches
40 B4 **Hatherton** Staffs
33 E4 **Hatley St George** Cambs
5 E3 **Hatt** Cnwll
50 B6 **Hattersley** Tamesd
103 F3 **Hatton** Abers
93 G3 **Hatton** Angus
40 D6 **Hatton** Derbys
20 D3 **Hatton** Gt Lon
52 D3 **Hatton** Lincs
39 E5 **Hatton** Shrops
57 F1 **Hatton** Warrtn
30 D6 **Hatton** Warwks
102 D1 **Hatton of Fintray** Abers
76 D4 **Haugh** E Ayrs
101 F3 **Haugh of Glass** Moray
70 B5 **Haugh of Urr** D & G
53 E3 **Haugham** Lincs
85 E3 **Haughhead Inn** E Duns
34 D5 **Haughley** Suffk
34 D5 **Haughley Green** Suffk
48 D2 **Haughton** Shrops
39 G6 **Haughton** Shrops
49 H2 **Haughton** Staffs
65 G5 **Haughton le Skerne** Darltn
49 F5 **Haughton Moss** Ches
33 E1 **Haultwick** Herts
40 D6 **Haunton** Staffs
7 b2 **Hautes Croix** Jersey
73 F6 **Hauxley** Nthumb
33 F4 **Hauxton** Cambs
10 A3 **Havant** Hants
9 G3 **Havenstreet** IOW
59 E2 **Havercroft** Wakefd
24 D4 **Haverfordwest** Pembks
33 H3 **Haverhill** Suffk
62 B4 **Haverigg** Cumb
21 G4 **Havering-atte-Bower** Essex
32 A3 **Haversham** M Keyn
62 D4 **Haverthwaite** Cumb
17 F5 **Havyat** N Som
48 D5 **Hawarden** Flints
34 B1 **Hawbush Green** Essex
45 F2 **Hawe's Green** Norfk
36 C2 **Hawen** Cerdgn
64 C2 **Hawes** N York
39 H2 **Hawford** Worcs
80 C2 **Hawick** Border
7 E5 **Hawkchurch** Devon
34 B4 **Hawkedon** Suffk
18 B2 **Hawkeridge** Wilts
18 A5 **Hawkesbury** S Glos
18 A5 **Hawkesbury Upton** S Glos
12 C5 **Hawkhurst** Kent
13 G5 **Hawkinge** Kent
10 B5 **Hawkley** Hants
15 G4 **Hawkridge** Somset
62 D5 **Hawkshead** Cumb
62 D5 **Hawkshead Hill** Cumb
78 B6 **Hawksland** S Lans
33 H2 **Hawkspur Green** Essex
49 F2 **Hawkstone** Shrops
64 D1 **Hawkswick** N York
58 C4 **Hawksworth** Leeds
51 H1 **Hawksworth** Notts
22 D4 **Hawkwell** Essex
20 B2 **Hawley** Hants
30 C2 **Hawling** Gloucs
66 B2 **Hawnby** N York
58 B4 **Haworth** Brad
34 C4 **Hawstead** Suffk
73 G2 **Hawthorn** Dur
52 D1 **Hawthorn Hill** Lincs
52 A1 **Hawton** Notts
59 G5 **Haxby** York
51 H6 **Haxey** N Linc
33 F2 **Hay Street** Herts
27 G6 **Hay-on-Wye** Powys
57 E2 **Haydock** St Hel
72 C3 **Haydon Bridge** Nthumb
18 D5 **Haydon Wick** Swindn
20 D3 **Hayes** Gt Lon
21 G2 **Hayes** Gt Lon
20 D3 **Hayes End** Gt Lon
90 C2 **Hayfield** Ag & B
50 B5 **Hayfield** Derbys
93 G3 **Hayhillock** Angus
2 C3 **Hayle** Cnwll
40 B2 **Hayley Green** Dudley
10 A2 **Hayling Island** Hants
16 B1 **Hayne** Devon
5 G5 **Hayne** Devon
32 C3 **Haynes (Church End)** Beds
32 C3 **Haynes (Northwood End)** Beds
32 C3 **Haynes (Silver End)** Beds
32 C3 **Haynes (West End)** Beds
24 C5 **Hayscastle** Pembks
24 C5 **Hayscastle Cross** Pembks
70 D3 **Hayton** Cumb
71 H5 **Hayton** Cumb
60 C4 **Hayton** E R Yk
51 H5 **Hayton** Notts
5 G4 **Haytor Vale** Devon
14 D3 **Haytown** Devon
11 F4 **Haywards Heath** W Susx
59 G2 **Haywood** Donc
50 A5 **Hazel Grove** Stockp
77 G5 **Hazelbank** S Lans
7 H6 **Hazelbury Bryan** Dorset
22 D5 **Hazeleigh** Essex
93 F2 **Hazelton Walls** Fife
51 E2 **Hazelwood** Derbys
20 C5 **Hazlemere** Bucks
73 F4 **Hazlerigg** N u Ty
30 C2 **Hazleton** Gloucs
44 A5 **Heacham** Norfk
9 G6 **Headbourne Worthy** Hants
12 D6 **Headcorn** Kent
58 D3 **Headingley** Leeds
31 F1 **Headington** Oxon
65 F5 **Headlam** Dur
66 B6 **Headland** Hartpl
85 H2 **Headlesscross** N Lans
19 G3 **Headley** Hants
10 B5 **Headley** Hants
21 E1 **Headley** Surrey
51 H4 **Headon** Notts
77 F6 **Heads** S Lans
71 G4 **Heads Nook** Cumb
51 E2 **Heage** Derbys
64 D3 **Healaugh** N York
59 F4 **Healaugh** N York
57 H2 **Heald Green** Stockp
16 D1 **Heale** Somset
17 E2 **Heale** Somset
65 F2 **Healey** N York
73 E2 **Healeyfield** Dur
61 F1 **Healing** NE Lin
2 B2 **Heamoor** Cnwll
51 E2 **Heanor** Derbys
15 E4 **Heanton Punchardon** Devon
52 B4 **Heapham** Lincs
15 F4 **Heasley Mill** Devon
96 D4 **Heast** Highld
51 E3 **Heath** Derbys
59 E2 **Heath** Wakefd
32 B2 **Heath and Reach** Beds
10 B6 **Heath End** Surrey
40 C1 **Heath Green** Worcs
78 D1 **Heath Hall** D & G
40 B4 **Heath Hayes & Wimblebury** Staffs
49 G1 **Heath Hill** Shrops
40 A3 **Heath Town** Wolves
50 C3 **Heathcote** Derbys
41 E4 **Heather** Leics
12 B4 **Heathfield** E Susx
16 C2 **Heathfield** Somset
20 D3 Heathrow Airport Gt Lon
39 G5 **Heathton** Shrops
40 C5 **Heatley** Staffs
57 G2 **Heatley** Warrtn
58 C3 **Heaton** Brad
73 F3 **Heaton** N u Ty
50 B3 **Heaton** Staffs
56 D4 **Heaton's Bridge** Lancs
22 B2 **Heaverham** Kent
6 B5 **Heavitree** Devon
73 G3 **Hebburn** S Tyne
58 B6 **Hebden** N York
58 B3 **Hebden Bridge** Calder
33 E1 **Hebing End** Herts
25 F5 **Hebron** Carmth
73 F5 **Hebron** Nthumb
20 A2 **Heckfield** Hants
35 E6 **Heckfield Green** Suffk
34 C1 **Heckfordbridge** Essex
42 D6 **Heckington** Lincs
58 C3 **Heckmondwike** Kirk
18 C3 **Heddington** Wilts
73 E3 **Heddon-on-the-Wall** Nthumb
45 F2 **Hedenham** Norfk
9 G4 **Hedge End** Hants
20 C4 **Hedgerley** Bucks
17 E2 **Hedging** Somset
73 E3 **Hedley on the Hill** Nthumb
40 B4 **Hednesford** Staffs
61 E3 **Hedon** E R Yk
20 C4 **Hedsor** Bucks
111 I2 **Heglibister** Shet
65 F5 **Heighington** Darltn
52 C2 **Heighington** Lincs
39 G3 **Heightington** Worcs
80 C3 **Heiton** Border
15 E5 **Hele** Devon
6 B5 **Hele** Devon
16 D2 **Hele** Somset
84 C4 **Helensburgh** Ag & B
76 D4 **Helenton** S Ayrs
2 D2 **Helford** Cnwll
2 D2 **Helford Passage** Cnwll
44 C4 **Helhoughton** Norfk
33 H3 **Helions Bumpstead** Essex
3 G6 **Helland** Cnwll
4 D5 **Hellescott** Cnwll
45 E3 **Hellesdon** Norfk
31 F5 **Hellidon** Nhants
63 H2 **Hellifield** N York
12 B3 **Hellingly** E Susx
73 F6 **Helm** Nthumb
31 G4 **Helmdon** Nhants
58 C2 **Helme** Kirk
35 E4 **Helmingham** Suffk
110 A1 **Helmsdale** Highld
57 G4 **Helmshore** Lancs
66 C2 **Helmsley** N York
59 E6 **Helperby** N York
67 E1 **Helperthorpe** N York
42 D5 **Helpringham** Lincs
42 D3 **Helpston** C Pete
49 E6 **Helsby** Ches
2 C2 **Helston** Cnwll
4 B5 **Helstone** Cnwll
71 H2 **Helton** Cumb
45 F3 **Hemblington** Norfk
20 D6 **Hemel Hempstead** Herts
5 F3 **Hemerdon** Devon
59 G3 **Hemingbrough** N York
53 E3 **Hemingby** Lincs
33 E5 **Hemingford Abbots** Cambs
33 E5 **Hemingford Grey** Cambs
35 E4 **Hemingstone** Suffk
41 F6 **Hemington** Leics
42 C1 **Hemington** Nhants
17 H4 **Hemington** Somset
35 F3 **Hemley** Suffk
66 B4 **Hemlington** Middsb
45 F2 **Hempnall** Norfk
45 F2 **Hempnall Green** Norfk
100 D5 **Hempriggs** Moray
33 H3 **Hempstead** Essex
44 D5 **Hempstead** Norfk
45 G4 **Hempstead** Norfk
44 C5 **Hempton** Norfk
31 E3 **Hempton** Oxon
45 G4 **Hemsby** Norfk
52 B4 **Hemswell** Lincs
52 B4 **Hemswell Cliff** Lincs
59 E2 **Hemsworth** Wakefd
16 C1 **Hemyock** Devon
80 D3 **Hendersyde Park** Border
21 E4 **Hendon** Gt Lon
73 G2 **Hendon** Sundld
26 B3 **Hendy** Carmth
11 E4 **Henfield** W Susx
27 G2 **Hengoed** Caerph
38 C2 **Hengoed** Powys
34 B5 **Hengrave** Suffk
33 G2 **Henham** Essex
22 B2 **Henhurst** Kent
38 B6 **Heniarth** Powys
16 D2 **Henlade** Somset
7 H6 **Henley** Dorset
17 F2 **Henley** Somset
35 E4 **Henley** Suffk
10 C4 **Henley** W Susx
12 C3 **Henley's Down** E Susx
30 C6 **Henley-in-Arden** Warwks
20 B4 **Henley-on-Thames** Oxon
36 C1 **Henllan** Cerdgn
55 H3 **Henllan** Denbgs
28 A2 **Henllys** Torfn
32 D3 **Henlow** Beds
5 H5 **Hennock** Devon
34 C3 **Henny Street** Essex
24 D5 **Henry's Moat (Castell Hendre)** Pembks
55 F4 **Henryd** Conwy
59 G2 **Hensall** N York
72 B3 **Henshaw** Nthumb
70 D1 **Hensingham** Cumb
45 G1 **Henstead** Suffk
9 G5 **Hensting** Hants
17 H1 **Henstridge** Somset
17 H1 **Henstridge Ash** Somset
20 B5 **Henton** Oxon
17 F3 **Henton** Somset
39 H2 **Henwick** Worcs
4 D4 **Henwood** Cnwll
27 E1 **Heol-y-Cyw** Brdgnd
72 D6 **Hepple** Nthumb
73 F5 **Hepscott** Nthumb
58 B3 **Heptonstall** Calder
58 C1 **Hepworth** Kirk
34 D6 **Hepworth** Suffk
24 C3 **Herbrandston** Pembks
28 C6 **Hereford** Herefs
23 H2 **Hereson** Kent
104 C3 **Heribusta** Highld
86 D2 **Heriot** Border
86 C3 **Hermiston** C Edin
79 G2 **Hermitage** Border
7 G6 **Hermitage** Dorset
19 G4 **Hermitage** W Berk
25 F5 **Hermon** Pembks
23 F2 **Herne** Kent
23 F2 **Herne Bay** Kent
21 F3 **Herne Hill** Gt Lon
22 B1 **Herne Pound** Kent
15 E4 **Herner** Devon
23 E2 **Hernhill** Kent
4 C3 **Herodsfoot** Cnwll
68 C5 **Heronsford** S Ayrs
19 H2 **Herriard** Hants
45 G2 **Herringfleet** Suffk
34 B5 **Herringswell** Suffk
51 E5 **Herringthorpe** Rothm
73 G2 **Herrington** Sundld
23 F2 **Hersden** Kent
20 D2 **Hersham** Surrey
12 B3 **Herstmonceux** E Susx
111 h1 **Herston** Ork
21 F6 **Hertford** Herts
21 F6 **Hertford Heath** Herts
21 F6 **Hertingfordbury** Herts
71 F3 **Hesket Newmarket** Cumb
57 E5 **Hesketh Bank** Lancs
57 F6 **Hesketh Lane** Lancs
73 H1 **Hesleden** Dur
59 G5 **Heslington** York
59 F5 **Hessay** York
4 D3 **Hessenford** Cnwll
34 C5 **Hessett** Suffk
60 D3 **Hessle** E R Yk
59 E2 **Hessle** Wakefd
20 D3 **Heston** Gt Lon
111 g2 **Hestwall** Ork
56 C1 **Heswall** Wirral
31 G3 **Hethe** Oxon
45 E3 **Hethersett** Norfk
71 G5 **Hethersgill** Cumb
81 E3 **Hethpool** Nthumb
73 F1 **Hett** Dur
58 B5 **Hetton** N York
73 G2 **Hetton-le-Hole** Sundld
73 E4 **Heugh** Nthumb
87 H2 **Heugh Head** Border
101 F1 **Heughhead** Abers
35 F5 **Heveningham** Suffk
11 G6 **Hever** Kent
63 E4 **Heversham** Cumb
45 E4 **Hevingham** Norfk
3 F4 **Hewas Water** Cnwll
28 D3 **Hewelsfield** Gloucs
7 E6 **Hewish** Somset
7 E5 **Hewood** Dorset
72 D3 **Hexham** Nthumb
21 G3 **Hextable** Kent
51 F6 **Hexthorpe** Donc
32 C2 **Hexton** Herts
4 D5 **Hexworthy** Cnwll
5 G4 **Hexworthy** Devon
22 D6 **Heybridge** Essex
22 B5 **Heybridge** Essex
5 E2 **Heybrook Bay** Devon
33 F3 **Heydon** Cambs
45 E4 **Heydon** Norfk
42 C5 **Heydour** Lincs
88 A3 **Heylipoll** Ag & B
111 k3 **Heylor** Shet
62 D2 **Heysham** Lancs
10 C4 **Heyshott** W Susx
18 B1 **Heytesbury** Wilts
31 E3 **Heythrop** Oxon
57 H4 **Heywood** Rochdl
18 B2 **Heywood** Wilts
52 B5 **Hibaldstow** N Linc
59 F1 **Hickleton** Donc
45 G4 **Hickling** Norfk
41 G6 **Hickling** Notts
45 G4 **Hickling Green** Norfk
11 F4 **Hickstead** W Susx
30 C4 **Hidcote Bartrim** Gloucs
30 C4 **Hidcote Boyce** Gloucs
59 E2 **High Ackworth** Wakefd
68 C2 **High Ardwell** D & G
78 C2 **High Auldgirth** D & G
71 H3 **High Bankhill** Cumb
21 G5 **High Beach** Essex
63 F3 **High Bentham** N York
15 E3 **High Bickington** Devon
63 F4 **High Biggins** Cumb
85 F2 **High Blantyre** S Lans
85 G3 **High Bonnybridge** Falk
15 F4 **High Bray** Devon
12 B6 **High Brooms** Kent
63 F4 **High Casterton** Cumb
60 B5 **High Catton** E R Yk
65 F4 **High Coniscliffe** Darltn
71 G5 **High Crosby** Cumb
76 D5 **High Cross** E Ayrs
10 A4 **High Cross** Hants
33 E1 **High Cross** Herts
30 D6 **High Cross** Warwks
68 C1 **High Drummore** D & G
22 B6 **High Easter** Essex
65 F2 **High Ellington** N York
49 F1 **High Ercall** Wrekin
65 F6 **High Etherley** Dur
34 B2 **High Garrett** Essex
65 F1 **High Grantley** N York
45 E3 **High Green** Norfk
45 E1 **High Green** Norfk
51 E6 **High Green** Sheff
39 H1 **High Green** Worcs
12 D5 **High Halden** Kent
22 C3 **High Halstow** Medway
17 E2 **High Ham** Somset
58 D5 **High Harrogate** N York
49 F2 **High Hatton** Shrops
67 E4 **High Hawsker** N York
71 G4 **High Hesket** Cumb
58 D1 **High Hoyland** Barns
11 G4 **High Hurstwood** E Susx
60 B6 **High Hutton** N York
71 E3 **High Ireby** Cumb
66 B2 **High Kilburn** N York
65 E5 **High Lands** Dur
50 B5 **High Lane** Stockp
2 C3 **High Lanes** Cnwll
57 F1 **High Legh** Ches
66 B4 **High Leven** S on T
17 G4 **High Littleton** BaNES
71 E2 **High Lorton** Cumb
52 A2 **High Marnham** Notts
51 F6 **High Melton** Donc
73 E3 **High Mickley** Nthumb
73 G2 **High Newport** Sundld
62 D4 **High Newton** Cumb
62 C5 **High Nibthwaite** Cumb
49 G2 **High Offley** Staffs
22 B5 **High Ongar** Essex
49 G1 **High Onn** Staffs
34 D1 **High Park Corner** Essex
76 D2 **High Pennyvenie** E Ayrs
33 G1 **High Roding** Essex
10 D3 **High Salvington** W Susx
73 E3 **High Spen** Gatesd
3 F4 **High Street** Cnwll
35 G4 **High Street** Suffk
53 E2 **High Toynton** Lincs
81 F1 **High Trewhitt** Nthumb
73 F2 **High Urpeth** Dur
86 A4 **High Valleyfield** Fife
62 D5 **High Wray** Cumb
21 G6 **High Wych** Herts
20 B4 **High Wycombe** Bucks
58 D1 **Higham** Barns
51 E3 **Higham** Derbys
12 B6 **Higham** Kent
22 C3 **Higham** Kent
57 G6 **Higham** Lancs
34 B5 **Higham** Suffk
34 D2 **Higham** Suffk
73 E4 **Higham Dykes** Nthumb
32 B5 **Higham Ferrers** Nhants
32 C2 **Higham Gobion** Beds
21 F4 **Higham Hill** Gt Lon
41 E3 **Higham on the Hill** Leics
14 D2 **Highampton** Devon
21 F4 **Highams Park** Gt Lon
17 E4 **Highbridge** Somset
11 F5 **Highbrook** W Susx
58 C2 **Highburton** Kirk
21 F4 **Highbury** Gt Lon
17 H4 **Highbury** Somset
19 F3 **Highclere** Hants
8 D3 **Highcliffe** Dorset
8 A4 **Higher Ansty** Dorset
57 E5 **Higher Bartle** Lancs
7 H5 **Higher Bockhampton** Dorset
6 B2 **Higher Brixham** Torbay
7 E6 **Higher Chillington** Somset
16 A2 **Higher Combe** Somset
6 B3 **Higher Gabwell** Devon
62 D2 **Higher Heysham** Lancs
57 G2 **Higher Irlam** Salfd
48 D5 **Higher Kinnerton** Flints

15 E4 Higher Muddiford Devon
57 E5 Higher Penwortham Lancs
3 E4 Higher Town Cnwll
3 F5 Higher Town Cnwll
2 b2 Higher Town IOS
57 F5 Higher Walton Lancs
57 F2 Higher Walton Warrtn
6 D6 Higher Wambrook Somset
7 H5 Higher Waterston Dorset
57 F5 Higher Wheelton Lancs
57 F1 Higher Whitley Ches
7 G5 Higher Wraxhall Dorset
49 E4 Higher Wych Ches
73 E3 Highfield Gatesd
76 C6 Highfield N Ayrs
21 F4 Highgate Gt Lon
99 F3 Highland Wildlife Park Highld
51 E5 Highlane Derbys
29 E5 Highleadon Gloucs
10 B2 Highleigh W Susx
39 G4 Highley Shrops
20 A4 Highmoor Oxon
20 A4 Highmoor Cross Oxon
29 E4 Highnam Gloucs
22 D2 Highsted Kent
23 F2 Highstreet Kent
34 B2 Highstreet Green Essex
10 C5 Highstreet Green Surrey
78 D1 Hightae D & G
56 C3 Hightown Sefton
34 C4 Hightown Green Suffk
6 A3 Highweek Devon
21 E4 Highwood Hill Gt Lon
18 D5 Highworth Swindn
44 B2 Hilborough Norfk
12 B6 Hilden Park Kent
12 B6 Hildenborough Kent
33 G3 Hildersham Cambs
40 B6 Hilderstone Staffs
61 E6 Hilderthorpe E R Yk
7 G6 Hilfield Dorset
43 G2 Hilgay Norfk
28 D2 Hill S Glos
31 F6 Hill Warwks
10 B4 Hill Brow Hants
49 G3 Hill Choriton Staffs
16 C2 Hill Common Somset
43 E6 Hill Dyke Lincs
86 B5 Hill End Fife
29 F6 Hill End Gloucs
22 D2 Hill Green Kent
9 G4 Hill Head Hants
86 B5 Hill of Beath Fife
107 G4 Hill of Fearn Highld
40 C5 Hill Ridware Staffs
58 C2 Hill Side Kirk
93 F1 Hill of Tarvit Mansion House Fife
59 E2 Hill Top Wakefd
59 F3 Hillam N York
8 C3 Hillbutts Dorset
50 D2 Hillclifflane Derbys
18 D3 Hillcott Wilts
86 B4 Hillend Fife
86 C3 Hillend Mdloth
85 G2 Hillend N Lans
31 G3 Hillesden Bucks
29 E2 Hillesley Gloucs
16 C2 Hillfarrance Somset
78 C6 Hillhead S Lans
103 F4 Hillhead of Cocklaw Abers
102 D2 Hillhead of Durno Abers
110 B5 Hilliclay Highld
20 D4 Hillingdon Gt Lon
85 E2 Hillington C Glas
44 B4 Hillington Norfk
41 F1 Hillmorton Warwks
70 B5 Hillowton D & G
51 F4 Hills Town Derbys
95 H5 Hillside Abers
95 F2 Hillside Angus
9 E5 Hillstreet Hants
111 k3 Hillswick Shet
5 F5 Hilltown Devon
86 D3 Hilltown E Loth
111 I1 Hillwell Shet
18 C4 Hilmarton Wilts
18 B3 Hilperton Wilts
9 H4 Hilsea C Port
61 E7 Hilston E R Yk
81 E5 Hilton Border
33 E5 Hilton Cambs
64 B5 Hilton Cumb
40 D6 Hilton Derbys
8 A4 Hilton Dorset
65 F5 Hilton Dur
107 G3 Hilton Highld
66 B3 Hilton S on T
39 G5 Hilton Shrops
30 B5 Himbleton Worcs
40 A3 Himley Staffs
63 E4 Hincaster Cumb
21 E2 Hinchley Wood Surrey
41 E4 Hinckley Leics
34 D6 Hinderclay Suffk
66 D5 Hinderwell N York
10 C5 Hindhead Surrey
57 F3 Hindley Wigan
39 H2 Hindlip Worcs
44 D5 Hindolveston Norfk
8 B6 Hindon Wilts
44 D5 Hindringham Norfk
44 D2 Hingham Norfk
49 F2 Hinstock Shrops
34 D3 Hintlesham Suffk
28 B6 Hinton Herefs
17 H6 Hinton S Glos
38 D6 Hinton Shrops
9 G6 Hinton Ampner Hants
17 G4 Hinton Blewett BaNES
18 A3 Hinton Charterhouse BaNES
8 C4 Hinton Martell Dorset
30 B4 Hinton on the Green Worcs
19 E5 Hinton Parva Swindn
7 E6 Hinton St George Somset
8 A5 Hinton St Mary Dorset
19 F6 Hinton Waldrist Oxon
31 F4 Hinton-in-the-Hedges Nhants
40 C4 Hints Staffs
32 B4 Hinwick Beds
13 E6 Hinxhill Kent
33 F3 Hinxton Cambs

32 D3 Hinxworth Herts
58 C3 Hipperholme Calder
65 F3 Hipswell N York
95 H6 Hirn Abers
48 A2 Hirnant Powys
73 F5 Hirst Nthumb
59 G3 Hirst Courtney N York
27 E3 Hirwaun Rhondd
15 E3 Hiscott Devon
33 F5 Histon Cambs
34 D4 Hitcham Suffk
34 D4 Hitcham Causeway Suffk
34 D4 Hitcham Street Suffk
32 D2 Hitchin Herts
21 F3 Hither Green Gt Lon
5 G6 Hittisleigh Devon
60 C3 Hive E R Yk
40 B5 Hixon Staffs
23 G2 Hoaden Kent
40 C5 Hoar Cross Staffs
28 D5 Hoarwithy Herefs
23 F2 Hoath Kent
38 C4 Hobarris Shrops
80 B1 Hobkirk Border
73 F2 Hobson Dur
41 G5 Hoby Leics
44 D3 Hockering Norfk
51 H2 Hockerton Notts
22 D4 Hockley Essex
40 C1 Hockley Heath Solhll
32 B2 Hockliffe Beds
44 B1 Hockwold cum Wilton Norfk
16 B1 Hockworthy Devon
21 F6 Hoddesdon Herts
57 G5 Hoddlesden Bl w D
71 E6 Hoddom Cross D & G
71 E6 Hoddom Mains D & G
24 D3 Hodgeston Pembks
49 F2 Hodnet Shrops
22 B2 Hodsall Street Kent
51 G5 Hodsock Notts
18 D4 Hodson Swindn
51 F4 Hodthorpe Derbys
44 D4 Hoe Norfk
23 E1 Hogben's Hill Kent
32 A2 Hoggeston Bucks
40 D3 Hoggrill's End Warwks
57 F5 Hoghton Lancs
50 D2 Hognaston Derbys
53 G3 Hogsthorpe Lincs
43 E4 Holbeach Lincs
43 E4 Holbeach Drove Lincs
43 E4 Holbeach Hurn Lincs
43 E4 Holbeach St Johns Lincs
43 F5 Holbeach St Mark's Lincs
43 F5 Holbeach St Matthew Lincs
51 F4 Holbeck Notts
30 B5 Holberrow Green Worcs
5 F2 Holbeton Devon
21 F3 Holborn Gt Lon
51 E1 Holbrook Derbys
35 E2 Holbrook Suffk
9 F4 Holbury Hants
6 B3 Holcombe Devon
17 G4 Holcombe Somset
16 C1 Holcombe Rogus Devon
32 A5 Holcot Nhants
63 G1 Holden Lancs
31 G6 Holdenby Nhants
33 H2 Holder's Green Essex
39 E5 Holdgate Shrops
42 C6 Holdingham Lincs
7 E5 Holditch Dorset
14 D2 Hole Devon
16 C3 Holford Somset
59 G5 Holgate York
62 D4 Holker Cumb
44 C4 Holkham Norfk
14 C6 Holkham Hall Norfk
14 D6 Hollacombe Devon
52 D1 Holland Fen Lincs
35 E1 Holland-on-Sea Essex
111 j3 Hollandstoun Ork
71 F6 Hollee D & G
35 F3 Hollesley Suffk
6 A2 Hollicombe Torbay
22 D1 Hollingbourne Kent
12 C2 Hollingbury Br & H
32 B2 Hollingdon Bucks
50 D1 Hollington Derbys
50 B1 Hollington Staffs
58 B6 Hollingworth Tamesd
57 F2 Hollins Green Warrtn
50 C3 Hollinsclough Staffs
15 F2 Hollocombe Devon
21 F4 Holloway Gt Lon
41 G1 Hollowell Nhants
49 E6 Hollowmoor Heath Ches
79 G1 Hollows D & G
27 G6 Holly Green Worcs
76 D3 Hollybush E Ayrs
29 E6 Hollybush Herefs
61 G3 Hollym E R Yk
58 C1 Holmbridge Kirk
10 D6 Holmbury St Mary Surrey
3 F4 Holmbush Cnwll
40 A5 Holmcroft Staffs
42 D1 Holme Cambs
63 E4 Holme Cumb
58 C1 Holme Kirk
65 G2 Holme N York
52 A2 Holme Notts
57 H5 Holme Chapel Lancs
59 F4 Holme Green N York
44 C3 Holme Hale Norfk
28 D6 Holme Lacy Herefs
38 D2 Holme Marsh Herefs
44 A6 Holme next the Sea Norfk
60 D4 Holme on the Wolds E R Yk
51 G1 Holme Pierrepont Notts
70 D4 Holme St Cuthbert Cumb
60 B4 Holme upon Spalding Moor E R Yk
28 C6 Holmer Herefs
20 C5 Holmer Green Bucks
49 G5 Holmes Chapel Ches
50 D4 Holmesfield Derbys
56 D4 Holmeswood Lancs
21 F1 Holmethorpe Surrey
51 E3 Holmewood Derbys
58 C1 Holmfirth Kirk
77 E3 Holmhead E Ayrs

61 G2 Holmpton E R Yk
62 B5 Holmrook Cumb
73 F2 Holmside Dur
5 G4 Holne Devon
7 G6 Holnest Dorset
16 B4 Holnicote Somset
14 C2 Holsworthy Devon
14 D2 Holsworthy Beacon Devon
8 C4 Holt Dorset
44 D5 Holt Norfk
18 B3 Holt Wilts
39 G2 Holt Worcs
48 D4 Holt Wrexhm
40 C1 Holt End Worcs
39 G2 Holt Heath Worcs
59 G5 Holtby York
31 G1 Holton Oxon
17 G2 Holton Somset
35 G6 Holton Suffk
52 D3 Holton cum Beckering Lincs
53 E5 Holton le Clay Lincs
52 C5 Holton le Moor Lincs
34 D3 Holton St Mary Suffk
7 H6 Holwell Dorset
32 D2 Holwell Herts
41 H5 Holwell Leics
30 D1 Holwell Oxon
64 D5 Holwick Dur
81 G4 Holy Island Nthumb
10 A6 Holybourne Hants
54 B4 Holyhead IOA
51 E3 Holymoorside Derbys
20 C3 Holyport W & M
72 D6 Holystone Nthumb
85 F2 Holytown N Lans
33 E5 Holywell Cambs
2 D5 Holywell Cnwll
7 G6 Holywell Dorset
48 C6 Holywell Flints
58 C2 Holywell Green Calder
16 C1 Holywell Lake Somset
34 A6 Holywell Row Suffk
78 D1 Holywood D & G
78 C1 Holywood Village D & G
39 F6 Homer Shrops
56 D3 Homer Green Sefton
45 F1 Homersfield Suffk
8 D5 Homington Wilts
34 C2 Honey Tye Suffk
30 C4 Honeybourne Worcs
15 F2 Honeychurch Devon
18 D3 Honeystreet Wilts
40 D1 Honiley Warwks
45 F4 Honing Norfk
44 D3 Honingham Norfk
42 B6 Honington Lincs
34 C6 Honington Suffk
30 D4 Honington Warwks
6 C5 Honiton Devon
58 C2 Honley Kirk
51 G1 Hoo Green Ches
22 C3 Hoo St Werburgh Medway
5 E2 Hooe C Plym
12 C3 Hooe E Susx
56 D6 Hoohill Bpool
60 B3 Hook E R Yk
20 A1 Hook Hants
22 B3 Hook Kent
24 D4 Hook Pembks
21 E2 Hook Surrey
18 C5 Hook Wilts
12 B5 Hook Green Kent
31 E3 Hook Norton Oxon
7 F5 Hooke Dorset
15 G1 Hookway Devon
51 F5 Hooton Levitt Rothm
59 F1 Hooton Pagnell Donc
51 F6 Hooton Roberts Rothm
50 C5 Hope Derbys
5 G1 Hope Devon
48 C5 Hope Flints
39 F3 Hope Shrops
50 C2 Hope Staffs
39 E5 Hope Bowdler Shrops
28 D4 Hope Mansell Herefs
39 E2 Hope under Dinmore Herefs
79 F4 Hopehouse Border
100 D6 Hopeman Moray
38 D4 Hopesay Shrops
59 G5 Hopgrove York
59 E5 Hopperton N York
39 G5 Hopstone Shrops
50 D2 Hopton Derbys
40 B5 Hopton Staffs
34 D6 Hopton Suffk
39 F4 Hopton Cangeford Shrops
38 D4 Hopton Castle Shrops
45 H2 Hopton on Sea Norfk
39 F4 Hopton Wafers Shrops
38 D4 Hoptonheath Shrops
40 C4 Hopwas Staffs
40 B1 Hopwood Worcs
12 B4 Horam E Susx
42 D5 Horbling Lincs
58 D2 Horbury Wakefd
73 H1 Horden Dur
9 E3 Hordle Hants
48 D3 Hordley Shrops
17 G6 Horfield Bristl
35 E5 Horham Suffk
34 D2 Horkesley Heath Essex
60 D2 Horkstow N Linc
31 E4 Horley Oxon
11 F6 Horley Surrey
17 G2 Hornblotton Green Somset
63 F3 Hornby Lancs
65 G4 Hornby N York
65 F3 Hornby N York
53 E2 Horncastle Lincs
21 H4 Hornchurch Gt Lon
81 E5 Horncliffe Nthumb
81 E5 Horndean Border
10 A3 Horndean Hants
5 F5 Horndon Devon
22 B4 Horndon on the Hill Thurr
11 F6 Horne Surrey
16 A3 Horner Somset
45 F4 Horning Norfk
42 A2 Horninghold Leics
40 D5 Horninglow Staffs
33 F5 Horningsea Cambs
18 A1 Horningsham Wilts
44 C4 Horningtoft Norfk

14 D3 Horns Cross Devon
61 E4 Hornsea E R Yk
21 F4 Hornsey Gt Lon
31 E4 Hornton Oxon
111 I4 Horra Shet
5 E4 Horrabridge Devon
5 G4 Horridge Devon
34 B5 Horringer Suffk
63 G1 Horrocksford Lancs
5 E4 Horsebridge Devon
12 B3 Horsebridge E Susx
9 F6 Horsebridge Hants
38 D6 Horsebridge Shrops
33 G3 Horseheath Cambs
65 E2 Horsehouse N York
20 C2 Horsell Surrey
49 E3 Horseman's Green Wrexhm
45 G4 Horsey Norfk
17 E3 Horsey Somset
45 E4 Horsford Norfk
58 D4 Horsforth Leeds
11 E5 Horsham W Susx
39 G2 Horsham Worcs
45 E3 Horsham St Faith Norfk
52 D2 Horsington Lincs
17 H2 Horsington Somset
51 E1 Horsley Derbys
29 F3 Horsley Gloucs
72 C6 Horsley Nthumb
73 E3 Horsley Nthumb
51 E1 Horsley Woodhouse Derbys
35 E2 Horsleycross Street Essex
80 B2 Horsleyhill Border
12 C6 Horsmonden Kent
31 F1 Horspath Oxon
45 F4 Horstead Norfk
11 F4 Horsted Keynes W Susx
32 B1 Horton Bucks
8 C4 Horton Dorset
63 H1 Horton Lancs
32 A4 Horton Nhants
18 A5 Horton S Glos
17 E1 Horton Somset
50 B3 Horton Staffs
26 B2 Horton Swans
20 D3 Horton W & M
18 C3 Horton Wilts
49 F1 Horton Wrekin
49 E4 Horton Green Ches
64 C1 Horton in Ribblesdale N York
22 B2 Horton Kirby Kent
31 G2 Horton-cum-Studley Oxon
57 F4 Horwich Bolton
15 E4 Horwood Devon
79 G4 Hoscote Border
41 H6 Hose Leics
92 B2 Hosh P & K
111 I1 Hoswick Shet
60 C3 Hotham E R Yk
13 E6 Hothfield Kent
41 F5 Hoton Leics
72 C5 Hott Nthumb
49 G4 Hough Ches
57 E2 Hough Green Halton
42 B6 Hough-on-the-Hill Lincs
42 B6 Hougham Lincs
33 E5 Houghton Cambs
9 E6 Houghton Hants
24 D3 Houghton Pembks
10 D3 Houghton W Susx
32 C3 Houghton Conquest Beds
12 D4 Houghton Green E Susx
73 G2 Houghton le Spring Sundld
41 G4 Houghton on the Hill Leics
32 C1 Houghton Regis Beds
44 C5 Houghton St Giles Norfk
20 A2 Hound Green Hants
80 C4 Houndslow Border
87 H2 Houndwood Border
21 E3 Hounslow Gt Lon
33 H1 Hounslow Green Essex
100 B5 Househill Highld
58 D2 Houses Hill Kirk
72 C3 Housesteads Roman Fort Nthumb
103 E2 Housieside Abers
84 D2 Houston Rens
110 B3 Houstry Highld
111 g2 Houton Ork
11 F3 Hove Br & H
51 G2 Hoveringham Notts
45 F4 Hoveton Norfk
66 C1 Hovingham N York
28 D5 How Caple Herefs
71 H5 How Mill Cumb
60 B3 Howden E R Yk
73 F2 Howden-le-Wear Dur
110 C5 Howe Highld
65 G2 Howe N York
45 F4 Howe Norfk
22 C5 Howe Green Essex
102 D4 Howe of Teuchar Abers
22 C6 Howe Street Essex
34 A2 Howe Street Essex
22 D5 Howegreen Essex
42 B6 Howell Lincs
71 E5 Howes D & G
38 B2 Howey Powys
86 C2 Howgate Mdloth
81 H2 Howick Nthumb
65 E5 Howle Dur
49 F2 Howle Wrekin
28 D4 Howle Hill Herefs
33 G4 Howlett End Essex
6 D6 Howley Somset
111 a3 Howmore W Isls
80 D2 Hownam Border
52 C5 Howsham N Linc
60 B6 Howsham N York
81 E5 Howtel Nthumb
84 D2 Howwood Rens
35 E6 Hoxne Suffk
56 C2 Hoylake Wirral
51 E6 Hoyland Nether Barns
58 D1 Hoyland Swaine Barns
24 C3 Hubberston Pembks
58 D4 Huby N York
59 F6 Huby N York
29 E4 Hucclecote Gloucs
22 D2 Hucking Kent
51 F2 Hucknall Notts

58 C2 Huddersfield Kirk
30 B5 Huddington Worcs
65 E3 Hudswell N York
60 C5 Huggate E R Yk
2 b2 Hugh Town IOS
20 B5 Hughenden Valley Bucks
39 E5 Hughley Shrops
15 E2 Huish Devon
18 D3 Huish Wilts
16 C2 Huish Champflower Somset
17 F2 Huish Episcopi Somset
32 B1 Hulcott Bucks
6 B4 Hulham Devon
50 D2 Hulland Derbys
50 D2 Hulland Ward Derbys
18 B5 Hullavington Wilts
22 C5 Hullbridge Essex
57 H2 Hulme Manch
50 B2 Hulme S Laffs
57 F2 Hulme Warrtn
50 C3 Hulme End Staffs
49 H5 Hulme Walfield Ches
45 G5 Hulver Street Suffk
9 F2 Hulverstone IOW
61 E1 Humberside Airport N Linc
53 E5 Humberston NE Lin
41 G4 Humberstone C Leic
87 E2 Humbie E Loth
61 F3 Humbleton E R Yk
42 C5 Humby Lincs
80 C4 Hume Border
72 D4 Humshaugh Nthumb
110 D6 Huna Highld
41 F3 Huncote Leics
80 C2 Hundalee Border
64 D5 Hunderthwaite Dur
53 F2 Hundleby Lincs
24 D3 Hundleton Pembks
34 B3 Hundon Suffk
56 D5 Hundred End Lancs
38 B2 Hundred House Powys
41 G4 Hungarton Leics
16 C3 Hungerford Somset
19 E3 Hungerford W Berk
19 F4 Hungerford Newtown W Berk
28 C6 Hungerstone Herefs
67 G1 Hunmanby N York
31 E6 Hunningham Warwks
21 G6 Hunsdon Herts
59 E5 Hunsingore N York
58 D3 Hunslet Leeds
64 A6 Hunsonby Cumb
43 H5 Hunstanton Norfk
72 D2 Hunstanworth Dur
49 F4 Hunsterson Ches
34 C5 Hunston Suffk
10 B2 Hunston W Susx
17 G5 Hunstrete BaNES
58 C3 Hunsworth Kirk
84 B3 Hunter's Quay Ag & B
17 E2 Huntham Somset
94 D3 Hunthill Lodge Angus
33 E5 Huntingdon Cambs
35 F6 Huntingfield Suffk
48 D5 Huntington Ches
87 E3 Huntington E Loth
38 C2 Huntington Herefs
40 B4 Huntington Staffs
59 G5 Huntington York
29 E4 Huntley Gloucs
102 B3 Huntly Abers
19 G1 Hunton Hants
22 C1 Hunton Kent
65 F3 Hunton N York
16 B3 Huntscott Somset
16 B1 Huntsham Devon
15 E3 Huntshaw Devon
17 E3 Huntspill Somset
16 D2 Huntstile Somset
17 E3 Huntworth Somset
65 F6 Hunwick Dur
44 D5 Hunworth Norfk
8 D6 Hurdcott Wilts
50 A4 Hurdsfield Ches
20 B4 Hurley W & M
40 D3 Hurley Warwks
40 D3 Hurley Common Warwks
76 D5 Hurlford E Ayrs
8 D3 Hurn Dorset
9 F5 Hursley Hants
20 B3 Hurst Wokham
12 C4 Hurst Green E Susx
34 D1 Hurst Green Essex
57 F6 Hurst Green Lancs
21 G1 Hurst Green Surrey
19 F2 Hurstbourne Priors Hants
19 F2 Hurstbourne Tarrant Hants
11 F4 Hurstpierpoint W Susx
57 H5 Hurstwood Lancs
111 h2 Hurtiso Ork
65 G4 Hurworth Place Darltn
65 G4 Hurworth-on-Tees Darltn
41 G2 Husbands Bosworth Leics
32 B3 Husborne Crawley Beds
66 B1 Husthwaite N York
51 F3 Huthwaite Notts
53 G3 Huttoft Lincs
81 E5 Hutton Border
60 D5 Hutton E R Yk
22 B5 Hutton Essex
57 E5 Hutton Lancs
17 E5 Hutton N Som
65 G3 Hutton Bonville N York
67 F2 Hutton Buscel N York
65 G1 Hutton Conyers N York
60 D5 Hutton Cranswick E R Yk
71 E4 Hutton End Cumb
65 H6 Hutton Henry Dur
66 C4 Hutton Lowcross R & Cl
65 E4 Hutton Magna Dur
71 F3 Hutton Roof Cumb
63 E4 Hutton Roof Cumb
66 B4 Hutton Rudby N York
66 B1 Hutton Sessay N York
59 F5 Hutton Wandesley N York
66 D2 Hutton-le-Hole N York
6 B5 Huxham Devon
49 E5 Huxley Ches
57 E2 Huyton Knows
62 B5 Hycemoor Cumb
50 B6 Hyde Tamesd
20 C5 Hyde Heath Bucks
40 A5 Hyde Lea Staffs

176 Hyndford Bridge - King's Norton

78 C6 Hyndford Bridge S Lans
88 B3 Hynish Ag & B
38 C5 Hyssington Powys
9 F4 Hythe Hants
13 F5 Hythe Kent
20 D3 Hythe End W & M

I

8 A4 Ibberton Dorset
50 D2 Ible Derbys
8 D4 Ibsley Hants
41 E4 Ibstock Leics
20 B4 Ibstone Bucks
19 F2 Ibthorpe Hants
67 E4 Iburndale N York
19 G2 Ibworth Hants
44 B2 Ickburgh Norfk
20 D4 Ickenham Gt Lon
31 G1 Ickford Bucks
23 G2 Ickham Kent
32 D2 Ickleford Herts
12 D4 Icklesham E Susx
33 F3 Ickleton Cambs
34 B5 Icklingham Suffk
58 B4 Ickornshaw N York
32 D3 Ickwell Green Beds
34 B5 Ickworth Suffk
30 D2 Icomb Gloucs
30 D2 Idbury Oxon
15 E2 Iddesleigh Devon
6 A4 Ide Devon
21 G1 Ide Hill Kent
6 A3 Ideford Devon
12 D4 Iden E Susx
12 C5 Iden Green Kent
12 C5 Iden Green Kent
58 C4 Idle Brad
3 E4 Idless Cnwll
30 D4 Idlicote Warwks
18 D1 Idmiston Wilts
50 D2 Idridgehay Derbys
104 C2 Idrigill Highld
19 E5 Idstone Oxon
31 F1 Iffley Oxon
11 E5 Ifield W Susx
8 D3 Iford Bmouth
11 G3 Iford E Susx
28 C2 Ifton Mons
49 F3 Ightfield Shrops
22 B1 Ightham Kent
35 G4 Iken Suffk
50 C2 Ilam Staffs
17 F2 Ilchester Somset
81 F2 Ilderton Nthumb
21 G4 Ilford Gt Lon
17 E1 Ilford Somset
15 E5 Ilfracombe Devon
51 F1 Ilkeston Derbys
45 G1 Ilketshall St Andrew Suffk
45 F1 Ilketshall St Margaret Suffk
58 C4 Ilkley Brad
4 D4 Illand Cnwll
40 B2 Illey Dudley
2 D3 Illogan Cnwll
41 G3 Illston on the Hill Leics
20 B5 Ilmer Bucks
30 D4 Ilmington Warwks
17 E1 Ilminster Somset
5 H4 Ilsington Devon
26 B2 Ilston Swans
65 F1 Ilton N York
17 E1 Ilton Somset
75 G5 Imachar N Ayrs
61 E2 Immingham NE Lin
61 E2 Immingham Dock NE Lin
57 E1 Ince Ches
56 D3 Ince Blundell Sefton
57 F3 Ince-in-Makerfield Wigan
106 D3 Inchbae Lodge Hotel Highld
95 E3 Inchbare Angus
101 F5 Inchberry Moray
84 D3 Inchinnan Rens
98 A3 Inchlaggan Highld
93 E2 Inchmichael P & K
98 C4 Inchnacardoch Hotel Highld
108 C2 Inchnadamph Highld
93 E2 Inchture P & K
98 B6 Inchvuilt Highld
92 D2 Inchyra P & K
3 E5 Indian Queens Cnwll
22 B5 Ingatestone Essex
58 D1 Ingbirchworth Barns
40 B5 Ingestre Staffs
52 B4 Ingham Lincs
45 G4 Ingham Norfk
34 C5 Ingham Suffk
45 G4 Ingham Corner Norfk
41 E5 Ingleby Derbys
66 B3 Ingleby Arncliffe N York
66 B4 Ingleby Barwick S on T
66 C4 Ingleby Greenhow N York
15 E2 Ingleigh Green Devon
17 H5 Inglesbatch BaNES
18 D6 Inglesham Swindn
70 C5 Ingleston D & G
65 F5 Ingleton Dur
63 F3 Ingleton N York
57 E6 Inglewhite Lancs
73 E4 Ingoe Nthumb
57 E5 Ingol Lancs
44 A5 Ingoldisthorpe Norfk
53 G2 Ingoldmells Lincs
42 C5 Ingoldsby Lincs
81 F2 Ingram Nthumb
22 B4 Ingrave Essex
58 B4 Ingrow Brad
28 D2 Ingst S Glos
42 C3 Ingthorpe Lincs
45 E5 Ingworth Norfk
30 B5 Inkberrow Worcs
103 E3 Inkhorn Abers
19 F3 Inkpen W Berk
110 C6 Inkstack Highld
84 B3 Innellan Ag & B
79 F6 Innerleithen Border
86 D5 Innerleven Fife
68 C4 Innermessan D & G
87 G3 Innerwick E Loth
101 E5 Innesmill Moray
102 C2 Insch Abers
99 F3 Insh Highld
57 E6 Inskip Lancs
14 D4 Instow Devon
51 E5 Intake Sheff
94 B5 Inver Abers
107 G4 Inver Highld
92 C3 Inver P & K
102 C5 Inver-boyndie Abers
97 E1 Inverailort Highld
105 F2 Inveralligin Highld
103 F5 Inverallochy Abers
107 E5 Inveran Highld
84 A6 Inveraray Ag & B
96 D5 Inverarish Highld
93 F4 Inverarity Angus
91 E1 Inverarnan Stirlg
105 F4 Inverasdale Highld
85 H3 Inveravon Falk
90 B2 Inverawe Ag & B
84 C5 Inverbeg Ag & B
95 G3 Inverbervie Abers
106 B4 Inverbroom Highld
90 B3 Invercreran House Hotel Ag & B
99 G4 Inverdruie Highld
86 D3 Inveresk E Loth
90 B3 Inveresragan Ag & B
105 F4 Inverewe Garden Highld
94 A5 Inverey Abers
98 D5 Inverfarigaig Highld
90 B3 Inverfolla Ag & B
98 B3 Invergarry Highld
91 H2 Invergeldie P & K
98 B2 Invergloy Highld
107 F3 Invergordon Highld
93 F2 Invergowrie P & K
97 E3 Inverguseran Highld
91 G4 Inverhadden P & K
91 E2 Inverherive Hotel Stirlg
97 E2 Inverie Highld
90 B1 Inverinan Ag & B
97 G4 Inverinate Highld
93 H4 Inverkeilor Angus
86 B4 Inverkeithing Fife
102 C4 Inverkeithny Abers
84 B3 Inverkip Inver
108 A2 Inverkirkaig Highld
106 B4 Inverlael Highld
98 B1 Inverlair Highld
83 G6 Inverliever Lodge Ag & B
90 D2 Inverlochy Ag & B
94 D4 Invermark Angus
101 F3 Invermarkie Abers
98 C4 Invermoriston Highld
107 F1 Inverness Highld
107 F1 Inverness Dalcross Airport Highld
84 B5 Invernoaden Ag & B
90 D3 Inveroran Hotel Ag & B
93 F5 Inverquharity Angus
103 F4 Inverquhomery Abers
98 B1 Inverroy Highld
90 B5 Inversanda Highld
97 G4 Invershiel Highld
107 E5 Invershin Highld
110 C3 Invershore Highld
84 C6 Inversnaid Hotel Stirlg
103 F4 Inverugie Abers
84 C6 Inveruglas Ag & B
99 F3 Inveruglass Highld
102 D2 Inverurie Abers
15 E1 Inwardleigh Devon
34 C1 Inworth Essex
111 a3 Iochdar W Isls
88 D2 Iona Ag & B
10 B4 Iping W Susx
5 H3 Ipplepen Devon
19 H5 Ipsden Oxon
50 B2 Ipstones Staffs
35 E3 Ipswich Suffk
56 C1 Irby Wirral
53 F2 Irby in the Marsh Lincs
52 D5 Irby upon Humber NE Lin
32 B5 Irchester Nhants
71 E3 Ireby Cumb
63 F3 Ireby Lancs
32 D3 Ireland Beds
62 C4 Ireleth Cumb
72 C1 Ireshopeburn Dur
50 D2 Ireton Wood Derbys
57 G2 Irlam Salfd
42 C4 Irnham Lincs
29 E1 Iron Acton S Glos
39 F6 Iron Bridge Museum Wrekin
39 F6 Ironbridge Wrekin
63 G5 Ironmacannie D & G
51 E2 Ironville Derbys
45 F4 Irstead Norfk
71 G5 Irthington Cumb
32 B5 Irthlingborough Nhants
67 F2 Irton N York
76 C5 Irvine N Ayrs
110 A5 Isauld Highld
111 l4 Isbister Shet
11 G4 Isfield E Susx
32 B5 Isham Nhants
10 B6 Isington Hants
74 B5 Islay Airport Ag & B
17 E1 Isle Abbotts Somset
17 E1 Isle Brewers Somset
21 F3 Isle of Dogs Gt Lon
116 b2 Isle of Man Ronaldsway Airport IOM
8 C2 Isle of Purbeck Dorest
23 E2 Isle of Sheppey Kent
69 F2 Isle of Whithorn D & G
9 G2 Isle of Wight IOW
33 H6 Isleham Cambs
97 E3 Isleornsay Highld
2 b2 Isles of Scilly St Mary's Airport IOS
70 C6 Islesteps D & G
6 c2 Islet Village Guern
21 E3 Isleworth Gt Lon
41 E5 Isley Walton Leics
111 b6 Islibhig W Isls
21 F4 Islington Gt Lon
32 C6 Islip Nhants
31 F2 Islip Oxon
111 b6 Islivig W Isls
49 F1 Isombridge Wrekin
9 G6 Itchen Abbas Hants
9 G6 Itchen Stoke Hants
11 E5 Itchingfield W Susx
45 E5 Itteringham Norfk
15 F1 Itton Devon
28 C2 Itton Mons
71 G4 Ivegill Cumb
20 D3 Iver Bucks
20 D4 Iver Heath Bucks
73 E2 Iveston Dur
32 B1 Ivinghoe Bucks
32 B1 Ivinghoe Aston Bucks
39 E2 Ivington Herefs
39 E2 Ivington Green Herefs
22 B1 Ivy Hatch Kent
5 F3 Ivybridge Devon
13 E4 Ivychurch Kent
22 D2 Iwade Kent
8 B4 Iwerne Courtney or Shroton Dorset
8 B4 Iwerne Minster Dorset
34 C5 Ixworth Suffk
34 C5 Ixworth Thorpe Suffk

J

6 B5 Jack-in-the-Green Devon
85 E1 Jackton S Lans
4 C6 Jacobstow Cnwll
15 E2 Jacobstowe Devon
25 E3 Jameston Pembks
106 D2 Jamestown Highld
84 D4 Jamestown W Duns
110 D4 Janets-town Highld
110 C3 Janetstown Highld
78 D2 Jardine Hall D & G
73 G3 Jarrow S Tyne
34 B2 Jasper's Green Essex
85 G3 Jawcraig Falk
23 F6 Jaywick Essex
80 C2 Jedburgh Border
25 E3 Jeffreyston Pembks
107 F3 Jemimaville Highld
6 c1 Jerbourg Guern
7 a1 Jersey Airport Jersey
73 F3 Jesmond N u Ty
12 B2 Jevington E Susx
20 D6 Jockey End Herts
110 D6 John O' Groats Highld
71 G3 Johnby Cumb
95 G3 Johnshaven Abers
24 D4 Johnston Pembks
79 F3 Johnstone D & G
84 D2 Johnstone Rens
78 D2 Johnstonebridge D & G
25 G4 Johnstown Carmth
48 C4 Johnstown Wrexhm
86 D3 Joppa C Edin
37 E3 Joppa Cerdgn
76 D3 Joppa S Ayrs
24 D5 Jordanston Pembks
21 G3 Joyden's Wood Kent
72 D3 Juniper Nthumb
86 C3 Juniper Green C Edin
116 c5 Jurby IOM

K

64 C4 Kaber Cumb
86 A1 Kaimend S Lans
83 G3 Kames Ag & B
77 F4 Kames E Ayrs
3 E3 Kea Cnwll
60 C2 Keadby N Linc
53 E2 Keal Cotes Lincs
57 G3 Kearsley Bolton
72 D4 Kearsley Nthumb
13 G6 Kearsney Kent
63 F4 Kearstwick Cumb
34 A3 Kedington Suffk
50 D1 Kedleston Derbys
61 E1 Keelby Lincs
49 G4 Keele Staffs
58 C3 Keelham Brad
24 C4 Keeston Pembks
18 B3 Keevil Wilts
41 F5 Kegworth Leics
2 C3 Kehelland Cnwll
102 B2 Keig Abers
58 B4 Keighley Brad
85 G5 Keilarsbrae Clacks
92 C2 Keillour P & K
94 B5 Keiloch Abers
82 D3 Keils Ag & B
17 F2 Keinton Mandeville Somset
78 C2 Keir Mill D & G
64 B5 Keisley Cumb
110 D5 Keiss Highld
101 G4 Keith Moray
93 E3 Keithick P & K
95 E3 Keithock Angus
106 D2 Keithtown Highld
58 A4 Kelbrook Lancs
84 B2 Kelburn N Ayrs
42 C6 Kelby Lincs
64 C3 Keld N York
59 G4 Kelfield N York
51 H2 Kelham Notts
71 E6 Kelhead D & G
56 D5 Kellamergh Lancs
93 F3 Kellas Angus
101 E4 Kellas Moray
5 H1 Kellaton Devon
44 D6 Kelling Norfk
59 F3 Kellington N York
73 G1 Kelloe Dur
77 F3 Kelloholm D & G
5 E5 Kelly Devon
41 H2 Kelmarsh Nhants
19 E6 Kelmscot Oxon
35 G5 Kelsale Suffk
49 E6 Kelsall Ches
33 E2 Kelshall Herts
71 E6 Kelsick Cumb
80 D3 Kelso Border
51 E3 Kelstedge Derbys
53 E4 Kelstern Lincs
17 H5 Kelston BaNES
92 A4 Keltneyburn P & K
70 D6 Kelton D & G
86 B5 Kelty Fife
34 C1 Kelvedon Essex
22 B5 Kelvedon Hatch Essex
2 A2 Kelynack Cnwll
93 F1 Kemback Fife
39 G6 Kemberton Shrops
29 G3 Kemble Gloucs
29 G6 Kemerton Worcs
28 B3 Kemeys Commander Mons
102 C1 Kemnay Abers
11 F3 Kemp Town Br & H
29 E5 Kempley Gloucs
29 E5 Kempley Green Gloucs
39 H1 Kempsey Worcs
18 D6 Kempsford Gloucs
19 G2 Kempshott Hants
32 C3 Kempston Beds
38 D4 Kempton Shrops
22 A2 Kemsing Kent
13 E5 Kenardington Kent
38 D1 Kenchester Herefs
30 D1 Kencot Oxon
63 E5 Kendal Cumb
26 D1 Kenfig Brdgnd
40 D1 Kenilworth Warwks
21 F2 Kenley Gt Lon
39 E5 Kenley Shrops
105 F2 Kenmore Highld
92 A4 Kenmore P & K
6 B4 Kenn Devon
17 E5 Kenn N Som
83 F2 Kennacraig Ag & B
15 G2 Kennerleigh Devon
56 D3 Kennessee Green Sefton
85 H4 Kennet Clacks
102 B2 Kennethmont Abers
34 A5 Kennett Cambs
6 B4 Kennford Devon
44 D1 Kenninghall Norfk
13 E6 Kennington Kent
19 G6 Kennington Oxon
86 D6 Kennoway Fife
17 E1 Kenny Somset
33 H6 Kennyhill Suffk
60 B6 Kennythorpe N York
88 B3 Kenovay Ag & B
104 C1 Kensaleyre Highld
21 E3 Kensington Gt Lon
32 C1 Kensworth Beds
32 C1 Kensworth Common Beds
29 E5 Kent's Green Gloucs
9 E5 Kent's Oak Hants
90 B4 Kentallen Highld
28 C5 Kentchurch Herefs
34 A5 Kentford Suffk
6 C6 Kentisbeare Devon
15 F5 Kentisbury Devon
21 F4 Kentish Town Gt Lon
63 E6 Kentmere Cumb
6 B4 Kenton Devon
21 E4 Kenton Gt Lon
73 F3 Kenton N u Ty
35 E5 Kenton Suffk
89 G5 Kentra Highld
3 E4 Kenwyn Cnwll
108 D5 Keoldale Highld
97 F4 Keppoch Highld
66 B3 Kepwick N York
40 D2 Keresley Covtry
2 B2 Kerris Cnwll
38 B5 Kerry Powys
84 A2 Kerrycroy Ag & B
51 H3 Kersall Notts
6 C4 Kersbrook Devon
34 D3 Kersey Suffk
111 d6 Kershader W Isls
6 C6 Kerswell Devon
39 H1 Kerswell Green Worcs
35 E3 Kesgrave Suffk
45 H1 Kessingland Suffk
3 F4 Kestle Cnwll
3 E5 Kestle Mill Cnwll
21 G2 Keston Gt Lon
71 F2 Keswick Cumb
45 E3 Keswick Norfk
53 F3 Ketsby Lincs
32 B6 Kettering Nhants
45 E2 Ketteringham Norfk
93 E3 Kettins Angus
34 C4 Kettlebaston Suffk
86 D6 Kettlebridge Fife
35 F4 Kettleburgh Suffk
79 E1 Kettleholm D & G
50 B4 Kettleshulme Ches
58 D5 Kettlesing N York
58 D5 Kettlesing Bottom N York
44 C5 Kettlestone Norfk
52 B3 Kettlethorpe Lincs
111 j3 Kettletoft Ork
64 D1 Kettlewell N York
42 C3 Ketton Rutlnd
21 E3 Kew Gt Lon
21 E3 Kew Gardens Gt Lon
17 E5 Kewstoke N Som
52 B4 Kexby Lincs
60 B5 Kexby York
50 A3 Key Green Ches
41 G4 Keyham Leics
9 E3 Keyhaven Hants
61 F3 Keyingham E R Yk
11 F3 Keymer W Susx
17 G5 Keynsham BaNES
32 C5 Keysoe Beds
32 C4 Keysoe Row Beds
32 C6 Keyston Cambs
41 G6 Keyworth Notts
73 F2 Kibblesworth Gatesd
41 G3 Kibworth Beauchamp Leics
41 G3 Kibworth Harcourt Leics
21 G3 Kidbrooke Gt Lon
39 H4 Kidderminster Worcs
31 F2 Kidlington Oxon
20 A3 Kidmore End Oxon
69 F2 Kidsdale D & G
49 H4 Kidsgrove Staffs
25 G3 Kidwelly Carmth
90 B3 Kiel Crofts Ag & B
72 A5 Kielder Nthumb
82 C3 Kiells Ag & B
84 D2 Kilbarchan Rens
97 E3 Kilbeg Highld
83 E2 Kilberry Ag & B
84 C1 Kilbirnie N Ayrs
90 A2 Kilbride Ag & B
83 F3 Kilbride Ag & B
83 H2 Kilbride Ag & B
100 D5 Kilbuiack Moray
51 E2 Kilburn Derbys
21 E4 Kilburn Gt Lon
66 B2 Kilburn N York
41 G3 Kilby Leics
83 F2 Kilchamaig Ag & B
82 C5 Kilchattan Ag & B
84 A1 Kilchattan Ag & B
89 H3 Kilcheran Ag & B
89 E5 Kilchoan Highld
82 B2 Kilchoman Ag & B
90 C2 Kilchrenan Ag & B
87 E6 Kilconquhar Fife
29 E5 Kilcot Gloucs
107 E1 Kilcoy Highld
84 B4 Kilcreggan Ag & B
66 C4 Kildale N York
75 F3 Kildalloig Ag & B
107 F3 Kildary Highld
83 H2 Kildavaig Ag & B
83 H2 Kildavanan Ag & B
109 H2 Kildonan Highld
75 H3 Kildonan N Ayrs
109 H2 Kildonan Lodge Highld
96 C1 Kildonnan Highld
68 C3 Kildrochet House D & G
101 G2 Kildrummy Abers
58 B4 Kildwick N York
83 G3 Kilfinan Ag & B
98 B2 Kilfinnan Highld
25 E3 Kilgetty Pembks
76 C2 Kilgrammie S Ayrs
28 C3 Kilgwrrwg Common Mons
60 D6 Kilham E R Yk
88 A3 Kilkenneth Ag & B
75 E3 Kilkenzie Ag & B
14 C2 Kilkhampton Cnwll
51 F4 Killamarsh Derbys
26 C2 Killay Swans
85 E4 Killearn Stirlg
107 F2 Killen Highld
65 F5 Killerby Darltn
6 B5 Killerton Devon
91 F4 Killichonan P & K
89 F3 Killiechronan Ag & B
92 B5 Killiecrankie P & K
97 G5 Killilan Highld
91 G2 Killin Stirlg
58 D5 Killinghall N York
63 F4 Killington Cumb
73 F4 Killingworth N Tyne
87 E1 Killochyett Border
84 C3 Kilmacolm Inver
85 E6 Kilmahog Stirlg
83 F5 Kilmahumaig Ag & B
104 C3 Kilmaluag Highld
93 F2 Kilmany Fife
76 D5 Kilmarnock E Ayrs
83 F5 Kilmartin Ag & B
76 D5 Kilmaurs E Ayrs
83 F6 Kilmelford Ag & B
17 H4 Kilmersdon Somset
9 G5 Kilmeston Hants
75 E3 Kilmichael Ag & B
83 G5 Kilmichael Glassary Ag & B
83 F4 Kilmichael of Inverlussa Ag & B
6 D5 Kilmington Devon
18 A1 Kilmington Wilts
8 A6 Kilmington Common Wilts
8 A6 Kilmington Street Wilts
106 D1 Kilmorack Highld
90 A2 Kilmore Ag & B
97 E3 Kilmore Highld
83 E3 Kilmory Ag & B
89 F5 Kilmory Highld
75 G3 Kilmory N Ayrs
104 B1 Kilmuir Highld
104 C3 Kilmuir Highld
107 F1 Kilmuir Highld
107 F3 Kilmuir Highld
84 B4 Kilmun Ag & B
73 E2 Kiln Pit Hill Nthumb
82 B3 Kilnave Ag & B
77 G6 Kilncadzow S Lans
12 C5 Kilndown Kent
89 H1 Kilninver Ag & B
61 G2 Kilnsea E R Yk
58 B6 Kilnsey N York
60 D5 Kilnwick E R Yk
82 C5 Kiloran Ag & B
75 G3 Kilpatrick N Ayrs
28 C5 Kilpeck Herefs
60 B3 Kilpin E R Yk
87 F6 Kilrenny Fife
41 F1 Kilsby Nhants
93 E2 Kilspindie P & K
68 C2 Kilstay D & G
85 F3 Kilsyth N Lans
98 D6 Kiltarlity Highld
66 C5 Kilton R & Cl
66 C5 Kilton Thorpe R & Cl
104 C3 Kilvaxter Highld
16 C3 Kilve Somset
42 A6 Kilvington Notts
76 C5 Kilwinning N Ayrs
44 D3 Kimberley Norfk
51 F1 Kimberley Notts
51 E5 Kimberworth Rothm
73 F2 Kimblesworth Dur
32 C5 Kimbolton Cambs
39 E2 Kimbolton Herefs
41 G2 Kimcote Leics
8 B2 Kimmeridge Dorset
19 E2 Kimpton Hants
32 D1 Kimpton Herts
109 H3 Kinbrace Highld
85 G5 Kinbuck Stirlg
93 G1 Kincaple Fife
85 H4 Kincardine Fife
107 E4 Kincardine Highld
95 E5 Kincardine O'Neil Abers
92 D3 Kinclaven P & K
95 H6 Kincorth C Aber
100 C5 Kincorth House Moray
99 F3 Kincraig Highld
92 C4 Kincraigie P & K
92 C4 Kindallachan P & K
75 E6 Kinerarach Ag & B
30 C3 Kineton Gloucs
31 E5 Kineton Warwks
92 D2 Kinfauns P & K
76 C5 Kinfold S Ayrs
47 F2 King Arthur's Labyrinth Gwynd
40 C5 King's Bromley Staffs
42 C2 King's Cliffe Nhants
30 C5 King's Coughton Warwks
40 C2 King's Heath Birm
43 G4 King's Lynn Norfk
6 b1 King's Mills Guern
40 B2 King's Norton Birm
41 G3 King's Norton Leics

King's Nympton - Latteridge 177

15 F3 King's Nympton Devon
38 D1 King's Pyon Herefs
9 F6 King's Somborne Hants
7 H6 King's Stag Dorset
29 F3 King's Stanley Gloucs
31 F4 King's Sutton Oxon
32 D1 King's Walden Herts
84 A2 Kingarth Ag & B
95 G5 Kingcausie Abers
28 C3 Kingcoed Mons
52 C4 Kingerby Lincs
14 C2 Kingford Devon
30 D3 Kingham Oxon
70 C6 Kingholm Quay D & G
86 C4 Kinghorn Fife
86 C5 Kinglassie Fife
93 F4 Kingoldrum Angus
93 F2 Kingoodie P & K
28 D5 Kings Caple Herefs
22 B1 Kings Hill Kent
90 D4 Kings House Hotel Highld
20 D5 Kings Langley Herts
64 A5 Kings Meaburn Cumb
79 F6 Kings Muir Border
41 F1 Kings Newnham Warwks
33 E6 Kings Ripton Cambs
28 D1 Kings Weston Bristl
9 G6 Kings Worthy Hants
5 E2 Kingsand Cnwll
93 H1 Kingsbarns Fife
5 G2 Kingsbridge Devon
16 B3 Kingsbridge Somset
104 C2 Kingsburgh Highld
21 E4 Kingsbury Gt Lon
40 D3 Kingsbury Warwks
17 F1 Kingsbury Episcopi Somset
19 G3 Kingsclere Hants
29 F2 Kingscote Gloucs
15 E3 Kingscott Devon
75 H4 Kingscross N Ayrs
17 F2 Kingsdon Somset
13 H6 Kingsdown Kent
18 D5 Kingsdown Swindn
18 A3 Kingsdown Wilts
86 B5 Kingseat Fife
20 B5 Kingsey Bucks
11 E5 Kingsfold W Susx
95 G6 Kingsford C Aber
76 D6 Kingsford E Ayrs
23 H3 Kingsgate Kent
34 C5 Kingshall Street Suffk
15 E4 Kingsheanton Devon
91 G1 Kingshouse Hotel Stirlg
6 A3 Kingskerswell Devon
86 D6 Kingskettle Fife
39 E2 Kingsland Herefs
54 B4 Kingsland IOA
49 E6 Kingsley Ches
10 B5 Kingsley Hants
50 B2 Kingsley Staffs
10 C5 Kingsley Green W Susx
31 H6 Kingsley Park Nhants
93 G4 Kingsmuir Angus
87 E6 Kingsmuir Fife
13 E5 Kingsnorth Kent
6 A3 Kingsteignton Devon
28 C5 Kingsthorne Herefs
31 H6 Kingsthorpe Nhants
33 E4 Kingston Cambs
4 D4 Kingston Cnwll
5 F2 Kingston Devon
7 H6 Kingston Dorset
8 C2 Kingston Dorset
87 E4 Kingston E Loth
9 G2 Kingston IOW
23 F1 Kingston Kent
19 F6 Kingston Bagpuize Oxon
20 A5 Kingston Blount Oxon
18 B1 Kingston Deverill Wilts
19 E5 Kingston Lisle Oxon
11 G3 Kingston near Lewes E Susx
41 F6 Kingston on Soar Notts
101 F6 Kingston on Spey Moray
7 G4 Kingston Russell Dorset
17 E5 Kingston Seymour N Som
16 D2 Kingston St Mary Somset
61 E3 Kingston upon Hull C KuH
21 E2 Kingston upon Thames Gt Lon
28 C6 Kingstone Herefs
17 E1 Kingstone Somset
40 B6 Kingstone Staffs
6 A1 Kingswear Devon
95 G6 Kingswells C Aber
40 A2 Kingswinford Dudley
31 G2 Kingswood Bucks
29 E2 Kingswood Gloucs
17 G6 Kingswood S Glos
16 C3 Kingswood Somset
21 E1 Kingswood Surrey
40 C1 Kingswood Warwks
39 H6 Kingswood Common Staffs
52 D3 Kingthorpe Lincs
38 C2 Kington Herefs
29 D2 Kington S Glos
30 B5 Kington Worcs
18 B4 Kington Langley Wilts
8 A5 Kington Magna Dorset
18 B4 Kington St Michael Wilts
99 F3 Kingussie Highld
17 F2 Kingweston Somset
103 E3 Kinharrachie Abers
70 C5 Kinharvie D & G
92 B1 Kinkell Bridge P & K
103 F3 Kinknockie Abers
86 C3 Kinleith C Edin
39 G4 Kinlet Shrops
108 D3 Kinloch Highld
109 E4 Kinloch Highld
96 C2 Kinloch Highld
92 D4 Kinloch P & K
93 E4 Kinloch P & K
97 G3 Kinloch Hourn Highld
91 G4 Kinloch Rannoch P & K
84 D5 Kinlochard Stirlg
108 C5 Kinlochbervie Highld
90 B6 Kinlocheil Highld
105 H2 Kinlochewe Highld
98 D2 Kinlochlaggan Highld
90 D5 Kinlochleven Highld
89 G6 Kinlochmoidart Highld
97 E1 Kinlochnanuagh Highld
100 D5 Kinloss Moray
55 G4 Kinmel Bay Conwy
102 D2 Kinmuck Abers
103 E2 Kinmundy Abers
74 B5 Kinnabus Ag & B
103 E4 Kinnadie Abers
92 C5 Kinnaird P & K
93 H5 Kinnaird Castle Angus
101 E6 Kinneddar Moray
95 G4 Kinneff Abers
78 D3 Kinnelhead D & G
93 H4 Kinnell Angus
48 D2 Kinnerley Shrops
38 D1 Kinnersley Herefs
39 H1 Kinnersley Worcs
38 C2 Kinnerton Powys
86 C6 Kinnesswood P & K
65 E5 Kinninvie Dur
93 F4 Kinnordy Angus
41 G6 Kinoulton Notts
86 B6 Kinross P & K
92 D3 Kinrossie P & K
38 D3 Kinsham Herefs
29 G6 Kinsham Worcs
59 E2 Kinsley Wakefd
8 C3 Kinson Bmouth
19 F3 Kintbury W Berk
100 C5 Kintessack Moray
97 G4 Kintail Highld
92 D1 Kintillo P & K
38 D3 Kinton Herefs
48 D2 Kinton Shrops
102 D1 Kintore Abers
74 C5 Kintour Ag & B
88 D2 Kintra Ag & B
83 F5 Kintraw Ag & B
75 F4 Kintyre Ag & B
99 G4 Kinveachy Highld
39 H4 Kinver Staffs
59 E3 Kippax Leeds
85 F5 Kippen Stirlg
70 B4 Kippford or Scaur D & G
12 B5 Kipping's Cross Kent
111 h2 Kirbister Ork
86 B1 Kirburd Border
45 F3 Kirby Bedon Norfk
41 H5 Kirby Bellars Leics
45 G2 Kirby Cane Norfk
35 E1 Kirby Cross Essex
41 F4 Kirby Fields Leics
60 C6 Kirby Grindalythe N York
65 E4 Kirby Hill N York
59 E6 Kirby Hill N York
66 B2 Kirby Knowle N York
35 E1 Kirby le Soken Essex
66 D2 Kirby Misperton N York
41 F4 Kirby Muxloe Leics
45 G2 Kirby Row Norfk
65 G3 Kirby Sigston N York
60 B5 Kirby Underdale E R Yk
65 G2 Kirby Wiske N York
70 C6 Kirconnel D & G
10 D4 Kirdford W Susx
110 C5 Kirk Highld
59 G2 Kirk Bramwith Donc
59 E5 Kirk Deighton N York
60 D3 Kirk Ella E R Yk
51 F1 Kirk Hallam Derbys
59 F5 Kirk Hammerton N York
50 D2 Kirk Ireton Derbys
50 D1 Kirk Langley Derbys
65 F6 Kirk Merrington Dur
116 b4 Kirk Michael IOM
85 G2 Kirk of Shotts N Lans
59 G1 Kirk Sandall Donc
59 F2 Kirk Smeaton N York
80 D3 Kirk Yetholm Border
111 I2 Kirkabister Shet
69 G2 Kirkandrews D & G
71 F5 Kirkandrews upon Eden Cumb
71 F5 Kirkbampton Cumb
70 C5 Kirkbean D & G
71 E5 Kirkbride Cumb
93 G5 Kirkbuddo Angus
79 F6 Kirkburn Border
60 D5 Kirkburn E R Yk
58 D2 Kirkburton Kirk
56 D3 Kirkby Knows
52 C4 Kirkby Lincs
66 B4 Kirkby N York
65 F3 Kirkby Fleetham N York
52 C1 Kirkby Green Lincs
51 F2 Kirkby in Ashfield Notts
42 C6 Kirkby la Thorpe Lincs
63 F4 Kirkby Lonsdale Cumb
58 A5 Kirkby Malham N York
41 F3 Kirkby Mallory Leics
65 F1 Kirkby Malzeard N York
53 E2 Kirkby on Bain Lincs
59 E5 Kirkby Overblow N York
64 C4 Kirkby Stephen Cumb
64 A5 Kirkby Thore Cumb
42 C4 Kirkby Underwood Lincs
59 F4 Kirkby Wharf N York
62 C4 Kirkby-in-Furness Cumb
66 C2 Kirkbymoorside N York
86 C5 Kirkcaldy Fife
71 H6 Kirkcambeck Cumb
69 G3 Kirkchrist D & G
68 B4 Kirkcolm D & G
77 F3 Kirkconnel D & G
69 G3 Kirkconnell D & G
69 E3 Kirkcowan D & G
69 G3 Kirkcudbright D & G
56 D2 Kirkdale Lpool
77 G5 Kirkfieldbank S Lans
70 C5 Kirkgunzeon D & G
56 D5 Kirkham Lancs
60 B6 Kirkham N York
58 D2 Kirkhamgate Wakefd
72 D5 Kirkharle Nthumb
72 B2 Kirkhaugh Nthumb
58 C2 Kirkheaton Kirk
72 D4 Kirkheaton Nthumb
107 E1 Kirkhill Highld
78 C3 Kirkhope S Lans
96 D4 Kirkibost Highld
93 E4 Kirkinch P & K
69 E3 Kirkinner D & G
85 F3 Kirkintilloch E Duns
70 D1 Kirkland Cumb
77 F3 Kirkland D & G
78 B2 Kirkland D & G
78 D2 Kirkland D & G
66 C5 Kirkleatham R & Cl
66 A4 Kirklevington S on T
45 H2 Kirkley Suffk
65 G2 Kirklington N York
51 G3 Kirklington Notts
71 G5 Kirklinton Cumb
86 B3 Kirkliston C Edin
69 F3 Kirkmabreck D & G
68 C2 Kirkmaiden D & G
94 A2 Kirkmichael P & K
76 C2 Kirkmichael S Ayrs
77 G5 Kirkmuirhill S Lans
81 E3 Kirknewton Nthumb
86 B3 Kirknewton W Loth
101 G3 Kirkney Abers
71 H3 Kirkoswald Cumb
76 B2 Kirkoswald S Ayrs
78 C2 Kirkpatrick D & G
116 b3 Kirkpatrick IOM
70 B6 Kirkpatrick Durham D & G
71 F6 Kirkpatrick-Fleming D & G
62 B4 Kirksanton Cumb
58 D3 Kirkstall Leeds
52 D2 Kirkstead Lincs
102 B3 Kirkstile Abers
79 F2 Kirkstile D & G
110 D6 Kirkstyle Highld
59 E2 Kirkthorpe Wakefd
102 C2 Kirkton Abers
102 D4 Kirkton Abers
78 C1 Kirkton D & G
93 F2 Kirkton Fife
97 F5 Kirkton Highld
97 G6 Kirkton Highld
92 C1 Kirkton P & K
79 E6 Kirkton Manor Border
93 E4 Kirkton of Airlie Angus
93 F3 Kirkton of Auchterhouse Angus
107 G1 Kirkton of Barevan Highld
92 D3 Kirkton of Collace P & K
101 F1 Kirkton of Glenbuchat Abers
103 E3 Kirkton of Logie Buchan Abers
95 E3 Kirkton of Menmuir Angus
93 G3 Kirkton of Monikie Angus
102 C3 Kirkton of Rayne Abers
95 G6 Kirkton of Skene Abers
93 F3 Kirkton of Strathmartine Angus
93 F3 Kirkton of Tealing Angus
102 B1 Kirkton of Tough Abers
103 E5 Kirktown Abers
103 F4 Kirktown Abers
102 D2 Kirktown of Bourtie Abers
95 G4 Kirktown of Fetteresso Abers
101 F3 Kirktown of Mortlach Moray
103 F2 Kirktown of Slains Abers
111 h2 Kirkwall Ork
111 h2 Kirkwall Airport Ork
72 D5 Kirkwhelpington Nthumb
61 E1 Kirmington N Linc
52 D4 Kirmond le Mire Lincs
84 B3 Kirn Ag & B
93 F4 Kirriemuir Angus
45 F2 Kirstead Green Norfk
71 E6 Kirtlebridge D & G
34 A4 Kirtling Cambs
34 A4 Kirtling Green Suffk
31 F2 Kirtlington Oxon
109 G5 Kirtomy Highld
43 E5 Kirton Lincs
51 G3 Kirton Notts
35 F3 Kirton Suffk
52 B5 Kirton in Lindsey N Linc
84 D3 Kirtonhill W Duns
69 E3 Kirwaugh D & G
97 F6 Kishorn Highld
31 G5 Kislingbury Nhants
16 C2 Kittisford Somset
95 H6 Kittybrewster C Aber
28 C5 Kivernoll Herefs
52 A4 Knaith Lincs
8 A5 Knap Corner Dorset
20 C2 Knaphill Surrey
15 G4 Knaplock Somset
17 E2 Knapp Somset
67 E1 Knapton N York
45 F5 Knapton Norfk
59 F5 Knapton York
33 E5 Knapwell Cambs
59 E5 Knaresborough N York
72 B2 Knarsdale Nthumb
103 E4 Knaven Abers
66 A2 Knayton N York
33 E1 Knebworth Herts
60 B3 Knedlington E R Yk
51 G3 Kneesall Notts
33 E3 Kneesworth Cambs
51 G2 Kneeton Notts
26 B2 Knelston Swans
50 A1 Knenhall Staffs
31 E5 Knightcote Warwks
49 G2 Knightley Staffs
41 G3 Knighton C Leic
7 G6 Knighton Dorset
38 C3 Knighton Powys
16 D3 Knighton Somset
49 G3 Knighton Staffs
49 G2 Knighton Staffs
39 F3 Knighton on Teme Worcs
39 G2 Knightwick Worcs
38 C2 Knill Herefs
42 A5 Knipton Leics
50 D2 Kniveton Derbys
64 B5 Knock Cumb
97 E3 Knock Highld
102 B4 Knock Moray
111 d6 Knock W Isls
84 B2 Knock Castle N Ayrs
110 B2 Knockally Highld
106 B6 Knockan Highld
101 E3 Knockando Moray
98 D6 Knockbain Highld
107 E2 Knockbain Highld
110 B5 Knockdee Highld
18 B5 Knockdown Wilts
76 C1 Knockeen S Ayrs
75 H3 Knockenkelly N Ayrs
76 D5 Knockentiber E Ayrs
21 G2 Knockholt Kent
21 G2 Knockholt Pound Kent
48 D2 Knockin Shrops
76 D5 Knockinlaw E Ayrs
68 B4 Knocknain D & G
69 G5 Knocksheen D & G
70 B6 Knockvennie Smithy D & G
35 G5 Knodishall Suffk
17 F2 Knole Somset
57 G1 Knolls Green Ches
48 D3 Knolton Wrexhm
18 B1 Knook Wilts
42 A3 Knossington Leics
62 D1 Knott End-on-Sea Lancs
32 C5 Knotting Beds
32 C5 Knotting Green Beds
59 F2 Knottingley Wakefd
56 D2 Knotty Ash Lpool
39 F3 Knowbury Shrops
69 E4 Knowe D & G
69 G6 Knowehead D & G
76 C3 Knoweside S Ayrs
20 B3 Knowl Hill W & M
17 G5 Knowle Bristl
15 E4 Knowle Devon
15 G2 Knowle Devon
6 B6 Knowle Devon
6 C4 Knowle Devon
39 F3 Knowle Shrops
40 C1 Knowle Solhll
16 B3 Knowle Somset
57 F6 Knowle Green Lancs
7 E6 Knowle St Giles Somset
71 G5 Knowlefield Cumb
56 D2 Knowsley Knows
57 E2 Knowsley Safari Park Knows
15 G3 Knowstone Devon
12 C6 Knox Bridge Kent
38 C3 Knucklas Powys
32 B5 Knuston Nhants
57 G1 Knutsford Ches
58 B2 Krumlin Calder
2 D1 Kuggar Cnwll
97 E5 Kyle of Lochalsh Highld
97 E5 Kyleakin Highld
97 F4 Kylerhea Highld
111 c5 Kyles Scalpay W Isls
108 C3 Kylesku Highld
97 F2 Kylesmorar Highld
108 C3 Kylestrome Highld
49 F1 Kynnersley Wrekin
39 F3 Kyrewood Worcs

L

6 c2 L'Ancresse Guern
6 a1 L'Eree Guern
7 a2 L'Etacq Jersey
6 b1 La Bellieuse Guern
6 c2 La Fontenelle Guern
6 b1 La Fosse Guern
6 c2 La Greve Guern
7 a2 La Greve de Lecq Jersey
7 c1 La Hougue Bie Jersey
6 b1 La Houguette Guern
6 b2 La Passee Guern
7 a1 La Pulente Jersey
7 c1 La Rocque Jersey
6 b2 La Rousaillerie Guern
6 b1 La Villette Guern
111 d6 Lacadal W Isls
111 d6 Lacasaigh W Isls
52 D5 Laceby NE Lin
20 B5 Lacey Green Bucks
49 G6 Lach Dennis Ches
34 B5 Lackford Suffk
34 B5 Lackford Green Suffk
18 B3 Lacock Wilts
31 E5 Ladbroke Warwks
12 C6 Laddingford Kent
3 E4 Ladock Cnwll
62 C4 Lady Hall Cumb
111 j3 Lady Village Ork
86 D6 Ladybank Fife
78 C5 Ladygill S Lans
81 E4 Ladykirk Border
40 B2 Ladywood Birm
39 H2 Ladywood Worcs
78 C2 Lag D & G
89 G5 Laga Highld
74 C5 Lagavulin Ag & B
75 G3 Lagg N Ayrs
98 B2 Laggan Highld
99 E2 Laggan Highld
108 D5 Laid Highld
105 G5 Laide Highld
96 C1 Laig Highld
76 D6 Laigh Clunch E Ayrs
76 D5 Laigh Fenwick E Ayrs
77 E3 Laigh Glenmuir E Ayrs
85 F1 Laighstonehall S Lans
22 B4 Laindon Essex
107 E6 Lairg Highld
58 C3 Laisterdyke Brad
9 G2 Lake IOW
8 C3 Lake Poole
18 D1 Lake Wilts
62 C6 Lake District National Park Cumb
44 A1 Lakenheath Suffk
43 G2 Lakesend Norfk
27 E1 Laleston Brdgnd
86 C2 Lamancha Border
34 C2 Lamarsh Essex
45 F4 Lamas Norfk
80 D4 Lambden Border
12 B5 Lamberhurst Kent
12 B5 Lamberhurst Down Kent
81 E5 Lamberton Border
21 F3 Lambeth Gt Lon
34 A4 Lambfair Green Suffk
51 G2 Lambley Notts
72 B3 Lambley Nthumb
19 E4 Lambourn W Berk
21 G4 Lambourne End Essex
11 E5 Lambs Green W Susx
4 C3 Lamellion Cnwll
5 E4 Lamerton Devon
73 F3 Lamesley Gatesd
78 C5 Lamington S Lans
75 H4 Lamlash N Ayrs
71 G3 Lamonby Cumb
2 B2 Lamorna Cnwll
3 E3 Lamorran Cnwll
37 E2 Lampeter Cerdgn
25 E4 Lampeter Velfrey Pembks
24 D3 Lamphey Pembks
70 D2 Lamplugh Cumb
41 H1 Lamport Nhants
17 G3 Lamyatt Somset
77 G5 Lanark S Lans
63 E2 Lancaster Lancs
73 F2 Lanchester Dur
11 E3 Lancing W Susx
2 A2 Land's End Cnwll
2 A2 Land's End Airport Cnwll
110 C3 Land-hallow Highld
33 F5 Landbeach Cambs
14 D3 Landcross Devon
95 F6 Landerberry Abers
9 E5 Landford Wilts
26 B2 Landimore Swans
15 E4 Landkey Devon
15 E4 Landkey Town Devon
26 C2 Landore Swans
4 D3 Landrake Cnwll
5 H4 Landscove Devon
5 E3 Landulph Cnwll
3 E5 Lane Cnwll
20 B4 Lane End Bucks
18 A2 Lane End Wilts
62 B5 Lane End Waberthwaite Cumb
40 D6 Lane Ends Derbys
65 E4 Lane Head Dur
4 C5 Laneast Cnwll
52 A3 Laneham Notts
72 C1 Lanehead Dur
16 D2 Langaller Somset
41 H6 Langar Notts
84 C3 Langbank Rens
58 C5 Langbar N York
63 G3 Langcliffe N York
67 E3 Langdale End N York
9 F4 Langdown Hants
86 D6 Langdyke Fife
34 D1 Langenhoe Essex
32 D3 Langford Beds
6 B5 Langford Devon
22 D6 Langford Essex
52 A2 Langford Notts
30 D1 Langford Oxon
16 C2 Langford Budville Somset
32 D4 Langford End Beds
34 D2 Langham Essex
44 D6 Langham Norfk
42 A3 Langham Rutlnd
34 C5 Langham Suffk
57 G5 Langho Lancs
79 F1 Langholm D & G
80 B3 Langlee Border
9 F3 Langley Hants
32 D1 Langley Herts
22 C1 Langley Kent
72 C3 Langley Nthumb
20 D3 Langley Slough
16 C2 Langley Somset
10 B5 Langley W Susx
30 C6 Langley Warwks
18 B4 Langley Burrell Wilts
34 C1 Langley Green Essex
16 C2 Langley Marsh Somset
73 F1 Langley Park Dur
45 G2 Langley Street Norfk
33 F2 Langley Upper Green Essex
12 B2 Langney E Susx
51 G5 Langold Notts
4 D5 Langore Cnwll
17 E2 Langport Somset
43 E6 Langrick Lincs
17 H5 Langridge BaNES
71 E4 Langrigg Cumb
10 A4 Langrish Hants
50 D6 Langsett Barns
92 A1 Langside P & K
65 F3 Langthorne N York
59 E6 Langthorpe N York
64 D3 Langthwaite N York
60 D6 Langtoft E R Yk
42 D3 Langtoft Lincs
65 F5 Langton Dur
52 D2 Langton Lincs
53 F2 Langton Lincs
60 B6 Langton N York
52 D3 Langton by Wragby Lincs
12 A5 Langton Green Kent
7 G4 Langton Herring Dorset
8 C2 Langton Matravers Dorset
14 D3 Langtree Devon
71 H3 Langwathby Cumb
110 B2 Langwell House Highld
52 C3 Langworth Lincs
3 G5 Lanhydrock House & Gardens Cnwll
3 F5 Lanivet Cnwll
3 G6 Lank Cnwll
3 G5 Lanlivery Cnwll
2 D3 Lanner Cnwll
4 C3 Lanreath Cnwll
4 C2 Lansallos Cnwll
4 B5 Lanteglos Cnwll
4 C2 Lanteglos Highway Cnwll
80 C2 Lanton Border
81 E3 Lanton Nthumb
15 F2 Lapford Devon
74 C5 Laphroaig Ag & B
49 H1 Lapley Staffs
40 C1 Lapworth Warwks
89 G4 Larachbeg Highld
85 G4 Larbert Falk
102 B3 Largie Abers
83 G4 Largiemore Ag & B
87 E6 Largoward Fife
84 B2 Largs N Ayrs
75 H3 Largybeg N Ayrs
75 H3 Largymore N Ayrs
84 B3 Larkfield Inver
22 C2 Larkfield Kent
77 F6 Larkhall S Lans
18 D1 Larkhill Wilts
44 D1 Larling Norfk
64 D5 Lartington Dur
10 A6 Lasham Hants
50 A2 Lask Edge Staffs
86 B5 Lassodie Fife
86 D3 Lasswade Mdloth
66 D2 Lastingham N York
22 D5 Latchingdon Essex
5 E4 Latchley Cnwll
49 H4 Latebrook Staffs
32 B3 Lathbury M Keyn
110 C3 Latheron Highld
110 C3 Latheronwheel Highld
87 E6 Lathones Fife
20 D5 Latimer Bucks
29 E2 Latteridge S Glos

178 Lattiford - Llanbedr-y-Cennin

17 H2 Lattiford Somset
18 D6 Latton Wilts
80 B4 Lauder Border
25 F4 Laugharne Carmth
52 A3 Laughterton Lincs
11 G3 Laughton E Susx
41 G2 Laughton Leics
52 A5 Laughton Lincs
42 C5 Laughton Lincs
51 F5 Laughton-en-le-Morthen Rothm
14 C2 Launcells Cnwll
4 D5 Launceston Cnwll
31 G2 Launton Oxon
95 F3 Laurencekirk Abers
69 G4 Laurieston D & G
85 H3 Laurieston Falk
32 B4 Lavendon M Keyn
34 C3 Lavenham Suffk
16 D5 Lavernock V Glam
71 G5 Laversdale Cumb
8 D6 Laverstock Wilts
19 G2 Laverstoke Hants
30 C3 Laverton Gloucs
65 F1 Laverton N York
18 A2 Laverton Somset
48 D5 Lavister Wrexhm
85 G1 Law S Lans
85 G1 Law Hill S Lans
91 H3 Lawers P & K
34 D2 Lawford Essex
16 C3 Lawford Somset
92 D2 Lawgrove P & K
4 D5 Lawhitton Cnwll
63 G3 Lawkland N York
24 D3 Lawrenny Pembks
34 C4 Lawshall Suffk
111 d6 Laxay W Isls
111 d6 Laxdale W Isls
116 c4 Laxey IOM
35 F5 Laxfield Suffk
108 C4 Laxford Bridge Highld
111 I3 Laxo Shet
60 B3 Laxton E R Yk
42 B2 Laxton Nhants
51 H3 Laxton Notts
58 B4 Laycock Brad
34 C1 Layer Breton Essex
34 C1 Layer Marney Essex
34 C1 Layer-de-la-Haye Essex
34 D3 Layham Suffk
7 E6 Laymore Dorset
60 B4 Laytham E R Yk
71 E5 Laythes Cumb
71 H3 Lazonby Cumb
6 b1 Le Bigard Guern
6 b1 Le Bourg Guern
7 c1 Le Bourg Jersey
6 b1 Le Gron Guern
7 c1 Le Haguais Jersey
7 c1 Le Hocq Jersey
6 b2 Le Villocq Guern
51 E3 Lea Derbys
28 D5 Lea Herefs
52 A4 Lea Lincs
38 D5 Lea Shrops
18 C5 Lea Wilts
40 D3 Lea Marston Warwks
107 E1 Leachkin Highld
86 C2 Leadburn Mdloth
22 B6 Leaden Roding Essex
52 B1 Leadenham Lincs
73 E2 Leadgate Dur
78 C4 Leadhills S Lans
30 D2 Leafield Oxon
32 C1 Leagrave Luton
53 F1 Leake Common Side Lincs
66 D4 Lealholm N York
104 D2 Lealt Highld
31 E6 Leamington Hastings Warwks
30 D6 Leamington Spa Warwks
63 E4 Leasgill Cumb
42 C6 Leasingham Lincs
65 F6 Leasingthorne Dur
21 E1 Leatherhead Surrey
58 D4 Leathley N York
49 E2 Leaton Shrops
23 E1 Leaveland Kent
34 C3 Leavenheath Suffk
60 B6 Leavening N York
21 G2 Leaves Green Gt Lon
67 F2 Lebberston N York
18 D6 Lechlade Gloucs
82 B3 Lecht Gruinart Ag & B
63 F4 Leck Lancs
91 H3 Leckbuie P & K
19 F1 Leckford Hants
31 H4 Leckhampstead Bucks
19 F4 Leckhampstead W Berk
19 F4 Leckhampstead Thicket W Berk
29 G4 Leckhampton Gloucs
106 B5 Leckmelm Highld
60 D4 Leconfield E R Yk
90 B3 Ledaig Ag & B
32 B1 Ledburn Bucks
29 E6 Ledbury Herefs
38 D1 Ledgemoor Herefs
108 C1 Ledmore Junction Highld
59 F3 Ledsham Leeds
59 E3 Ledston Leeds
31 E3 Ledwell Oxon
14 D5 Lee Devon
21 F3 Lee Gt Lon
49 E2 Lee Brockhurst Shrops
22 C4 Lee Chapel Essex
20 C5 Lee Clump Bucks
5 F3 Lee Mill Devon
9 G3 Lee-on-the-Solent Hants
39 E5 Leebotwood Shrops
62 C3 Leece Cumb
22 D1 Leeds Kent
58 D3 Leeds Leeds
58 D4 Leeds Bradford Airport Leeds
22 D1 Leeds Castle Kent
2 C3 Leedstown Cnwll
50 B2 Leek Staffs
30 D6 Leek Wootton Warwks
62 C2 Leeming N York
65 F2 Leeming Bar N York
50 D1 Lees Derbys
58 B1 Lees Oldham
50 D1 Lees Green Derbys
42 A3 Leesthorpe Leics
48 C5 Leeswood Flints
93 E2 Leetown P & K
49 F6 Leftwich Ches
53 F4 Legbourne Lincs
80 B4 Legerwood Border
20 C3 Legoland W & M
52 D4 Legsby Lincs
41 G4 Leicester C Leic
41 F4 Leicester Forest East Leics
7 G6 Leigh Dorset
29 F5 Leigh Gloucs
12 A6 Leigh Kent
11 E6 Leigh Surrey
57 F3 Leigh Wigan
18 C5 Leigh Wilts
39 G2 Leigh Worcs
22 C4 Leigh Beck Essex
18 B4 Leigh Delamere Wilts
12 D5 Leigh Green Kent
77 E6 Leigh Knoweglass S Lans
8 C3 Leigh Park Dorset
39 G1 Leigh Sinton Worcs
17 H4 Leigh upon Mendip Somset
17 G6 Leigh Woods N Som
22 D4 Leigh-on-Sea Sthend
29 F2 Leighterton Gloucs
38 C6 Leighton Powys
39 F6 Leighton Shrops
32 D6 Leighton Bromswold Cambs
32 B2 Leighton Buzzard Beds
39 E3 Leinthall Earls Herefs
38 D3 Leinthall Starkes Herefs
38 D3 Leintwardine Herefs
41 F2 Leire Leics
35 G5 Leiston Suffk
93 E4 Leitfie P & K
86 C3 Leith C Edin
80 D4 Leitholm Border
2 C3 Lelant Cnwll
61 F3 Lelley E R Yk
39 G3 Lem Hill Worcs
80 D3 Lempitlaw Border
111 d5 Lemreway W Isls
21 E6 Lemsford Herts
30 B4 Lenchwick Worcs
68 C6 Lendalfoot S Ayrs
85 E6 Lendrick Stirlg
103 F3 Lendrum Terrace Abers
22 D1 Lenham Kent
22 D1 Lenham Heath Kent
98 D5 Lenie Highld
80 D4 Lennel Border
69 G3 Lennox Plunton D & G
85 E3 Lennoxtown E Duns
51 F1 Lenton C Nott
42 C5 Lenton Lincs
44 D4 Lenwade Norfk
85 F3 Lenzie E Duns
102 B1 Leochel-Cushnie Abers
39 E2 Leominster Herefs
29 F3 Leonard Stanley Gloucs
7 a2 Leoville Jersey
104 A1 Lephin Highld
60 B6 Leppington N York
58 D2 Lepton Kirk
4 C3 Lerryn Cnwll
111 I2 Lerwick Shet
6 b1 Les Arquets Guern
6 c1 Les Hubits Guern
6 b1 Les Lohiers Guern
6 b1 Les Murchez Guern
6 b1 Les Nicolles Guern
6 c2 Les Quartiers Guern
7 a1 Les Quennevais Jersey
6 b1 Les Sages Guern
6 b1 Les Villets Guern
81 G2 Lesbury Nthumb
102 B2 Leslie Abers
86 C6 Leslie Fife
78 B6 Lesmahagow S Lans
4 C5 Lesnewth Cnwll
45 G4 Lessingham Norfk
71 E4 Lessonhall Cumb
68 B4 Leswalt D & G
21 E5 Letchmore Heath Herts
32 D2 Letchworth Herts
19 F5 Letcombe Bassett Oxon
19 F5 Letcombe Regis Oxon
93 G4 Letham Angus
80 C1 Letham Border
85 G4 Letham Falk
93 E1 Letham Fife
93 H4 Letham Grange Angus
92 D3 Lethendy P & K
102 B2 Lethenty Abers
102 D3 Lethenty Abers
35 F4 Letheringham Suffk
44 D5 Letheringsett Norfk
105 G3 Letterewe Highld
97 F4 Letterfearn Highld
98 B2 Letterfinlay Lodge Hotel Highld
97 E2 Lettermorar Highld
106 B4 Letters Highld
78 C4 Lettershaw S Lans
24 D5 Letterston Pembks
99 H4 Lettoch Highld
100 D3 Lettoch Highld
38 D1 Letton Herefs
21 F6 Letty Green Herts
51 F5 Letwell Rothm
93 F2 Leuchars Fife
111 d5 Leumrabhagh W Isls
111 d6 Leurbost W Isls
40 A5 Levedale Staffs
33 F1 Level's Green Essex
61 E4 Leven E R Yk
86 D5 Leven Fife
63 E4 Levens Cumb
33 E1 Levens Green Herts
57 H2 Levenshulme Manch
111 I1 Levenwick Shet
111 c4 Leverburgh W Isls
43 F3 Leverington Cambs
20 D5 Leverstock Green Herts
43 F6 Leverton Lincs
35 F3 Levington Suffk
67 E3 Levisham N York
31 E1 Lew Oxon
4 D5 Lewannick Cnwll
5 E5 Lewdown Devon
11 G3 Lewes E Susx
24 D5 Leweston Pembks
21 F3 Lewisham Gt Lon
98 D5 Lewiston Highld
20 A5 Lewknor Oxon
23 E2 Lewson Street Kent
5 E5 Lewtrenchard Devon
34 C2 Lexden Essex
16 D3 Lexworthy Somset
20 C5 Ley Hill Bucks
22 B2 Leybourne Kent
65 E2 Leyburn N York
32 D2 Leygreen Herts
57 E5 Leyland Lancs
102 D1 Leylodge Abers
103 E4 Leys Abers
93 E3 Leys Angus
93 F4 Leys of Cossans Angus
23 E3 Leysdown-on-Sea Kent
93 H4 Leysmill Angus
39 E3 Leysters Herefs
21 F4 Leyton Gt Lon
21 G4 Leytonstone Gt Lon
4 D5 Lezant Cnwll
116 c4 Lezayre IOM
101 E5 Lhanbryde Moray
27 F5 Libanus Powys
78 D6 Libberton S Lans
86 C3 Liberton C Edin
40 C4 Lichfield Staffs
40 B1 Lickey Worcs
40 B1 Lickey End Worcs
10 C4 Lickfold W Susx
89 H5 Liddesdale Highld
18 D4 Liddington Swindn
34 B4 Lidgate Suffk
32 C3 Lidlington Beds
93 F3 Liff Angus
40 B2 Lifford Birm
5 E5 Lifton Devon
4 D5 Liftondown Devon
31 E5 Lighthorne Warwks
31 E5 Lighthorne Heath Warwks
20 C2 Lightwater Surrey
41 F1 Lilbourne Nhants
49 G1 Lilleshall Wrekin
32 D2 Lilley Herts
80 B3 Lilliesleaf Border
31 G4 Lillingstone Dayrell Bucks
31 G4 Lillingstone Lovell Bucks
7 G6 Lillington Dorset
8 C2 Lilliput Poole
16 C3 Lilstock Somset
32 C1 Limbury Luton
29 F5 Lime Street Worcs
77 F6 Limekilnburn S Lans
86 B4 Limekilns Fife
85 G3 Limerigg Falk
9 F2 Limerstone IOW
17 F2 Limington Somset
77 E4 Limmerhaugh E Ayrs
45 G3 Limpenhoe Norfk
18 A3 Limpley Stoke Wilts
21 G1 Limpsfield Surrey
21 G1 Limpsfield Chart Surrey
51 F2 Linby Notts
10 B5 Linchmere W Susx
78 C1 Lincluden D & G
52 B3 Lincoln Lincs
39 G3 Lincomb Worcs
62 C3 Lindal in Furness Cumb
62 D4 Lindale Cumb
11 F4 Lindfield W Susx
10 B5 Lindford Hants
58 C2 Lindley Kirk
58 D5 Lindley Green N York
39 F3 Lindridge Worcs
33 H2 Lindsell Essex
34 D3 Lindsey Suffk
34 D3 Lindsey Tye Suffk
66 C5 Lingdale R & Cl
38 D3 Lingen Herefs
11 F6 Lingfield Surrey
45 F3 Lingwood Norfk
104 C3 Linicro Highld
29 F5 Linkend Worcs
19 F3 Linkenholt Hants
4 D4 Linkinhorne Cnwll
86 C5 Linktown Fife
101 E5 Linkwood Moray
38 D5 Linley Shrops
39 F2 Linley Green Herefs
39 F5 Linleygreen Shrops
86 A4 Linlithgow W Loth
107 E5 Linsidemore Highld
32 B2 Linslade Beds
35 F6 Linstead Parva Suffk
71 G5 Linstock Cumb
40 B1 Linthurst Worcs
58 C2 Linthwaite Kirk
87 H2 Lintlaw Border
101 G5 Lintmill Moray
80 D3 Linton Border
33 G3 Linton Cambs
40 D5 Linton Derbys
28 D5 Linton Herefs
22 C1 Linton Kent
59 E4 Linton Leeds
58 B6 Linton N York
29 E5 Linton Hill Gloucs
59 F5 Linton-on-Ouse N York
52 D4 Linwood Lincs
84 D2 Linwood Rens
111 b3 Lionacleit W Isls
111 e7 Lional W Isls
10 B5 Liphook Hants
56 C2 Liscard Wirral
15 G4 Liscombe Somset
4 C3 Liskeard Cnwll
14 B4 Liss Hants
61 E5 Lissett E R Yk
52 D4 Lissington Lincs
27 G1 Lisvane Cardif
28 B2 Liswerry Newpt
44 C4 Litcham Norfk
31 G5 Litchborough Nhants
19 F2 Litchfield Hants
56 D3 Litherland Sefton
33 E3 Litlington Cambs
11 H2 Litlington E Susx
33 G3 Little Abington Cambs
32 B5 Little Addington Nhants
69 E2 Little Airies D & G
30 C6 Little Alne Warwks
56 C3 Little Altcar Sefton
21 F6 Little Amwell Herts
63 F6 Little Asby Cumb
40 C3 Little Aston Staffs
66 B4 Little Ayton N York
22 C6 Little Baddow Essex
18 A5 Little Badminton S Glos
71 F4 Little Bampton Cumb
33 H2 Little Bardfield Essex
32 D4 Little Barford Beds
45 E5 Little Barningham Norfk
30 D2 Little Barrington Gloucs
49 E6 Little Barrow Ches
72 D4 Little Bavington Nthumb
19 E3 Little Bedwyn Wilts
35 E2 Little Bentley Essex
21 F6 Little Berkhamsted Herts
32 A5 Little Billing Nhants
32 B1 Little Billington Beds
28 C5 Little Birch Herefs
34 D3 Little Blakenham Suffk
71 G3 Little Blencow Cumb
10 D4 Little Bognor W Susx
50 D2 Little Bolehill Derbys
57 G2 Little Bollington Ches
20 D1 Little Bookham Surrey
31 F4 Little Bourton Oxon
34 A4 Little Bradley Suffk
22 D6 Little Braxted Essex
95 E2 Little Brechin Angus
32 B2 Little Brickhill M Keyn
31 G6 Little Brington Nhants
34 D2 Little Bromley Essex
49 F5 Little Budworth Ches
22 B4 Little Burstead Essex
42 C4 Little Bytham Lincs
53 F4 Little Carlton Lincs
42 C3 Little Casterton Rutlnd
53 E4 Little Cawthorpe Lincs
20 C5 Little Chalfont Bucks
12 D6 Little Chart Kent
33 G3 Little Chesterford Essex
18 C2 Little Cheverell Wilts
33 F3 Little Chishill Cambs
35 E1 Little Clacton Essex
70 D2 Little Clifton Cumb
30 B4 Little Comberton Worcs
12 C3 Little Common E Susx
30 D3 Little Compton Warwks
34 C3 Little Cornard Suffk
39 F1 Little Cowarne Herefs
19 E5 Little Coxwell Oxon
65 F2 Little Crakehall N York
44 C2 Little Cressingham Norfk
56 D3 Little Crosby Sefton
50 C1 Little Cubley Derbys
41 H4 Little Dalby Leics
103 F4 Little Dens Abers
28 C5 Little Dewchurch Herefs
33 H4 Little Ditton Cambs
43 G1 Little Downham Cambs
60 D5 Little Driffield E R Yk
44 C3 Little Dunham Norfk
92 C3 Little Dunkeld P & K
33 H1 Little Dunmow Essex
8 D6 Little Durnford Wilts
33 G1 Little Easton Essex
51 E1 Little Eaton Derbys
44 D2 Little Ellingham Norfk
31 G5 Little Everdon Nhants
33 F4 Little Eversden Cambs
19 E6 Little Faringdon Oxon
65 F3 Little Fencote N York
59 F3 Little Fenton N York
44 C3 Little Fransham Norfk
20 C6 Little Gaddesden Herts
35 F4 Little Glemham Suffk
29 E5 Little Gorsley Herefs
33 E4 Little Gransden Cambs
17 H4 Little Green Somset
53 E4 Little Grimsby Lincs
33 F1 Little Hadham Herts
42 D6 Little Hale Lincs
51 F1 Little Hallam Derbys
33 G1 Little Hallingbury Essex
32 B5 Little Harrowden Nhants
19 H6 Little Haseley Oxon
61 E4 Little Hatfield E R Yk
24 C4 Little Haven Pembks
40 C3 Little Hay Staffs
40 B5 Little Haywood Staffs
41 E2 Little Heath Covtry
39 E3 Little Hereford Herefs
34 C2 Little Horkesley Essex
33 F2 Little Hormead Herts
11 G4 Little Horsted E Susx
58 C3 Little Horton Brad
32 A2 Little Horwood Bucks
59 E1 Little Houghton Barns
32 A4 Little Houghton Nhants
50 C4 Little Hucklow Derbys
66 B1 Little Hutton N York
32 B5 Little Irchester Nhants
18 A2 Little Keyford Somset
20 B5 Little Kimble Bucks
31 E5 Little Kineton Warwks
20 C5 Little Kingshill Bucks
70 B5 Little Knox D & G
62 D6 Little Langdale Cumb
18 C1 Little Langford Wilts
14 D2 Little Lashbrook Devon
49 F6 Little Leigh Ches
34 B1 Little Leighs Essex
57 G3 Little Lever Bolton
32 A3 Little Linford M Keyn
17 F2 Little Load Somset
12 B4 Little London E Susx
33 F2 Little London Essex
19 F2 Little London Hants
19 H3 Little London Hants
50 C4 Little Longstone Derbys
29 E6 Little Malvern Worcs
34 B2 Little Maplestead Essex
29 E6 Little Marcle Herefs
20 C4 Little Marlow Bucks
44 B4 Little Massingham Norfk
45 E3 Little Melton Norfk
28 B3 Little Mill Mons
19 H6 Little Milton Oxon
20 C5 Little Missenden Bucks
64 B4 Little Musgrave Cumb
48 D2 Little Ness Shrops
24 D5 Little Newcastle Pembks
65 E5 Little Newsham Dur
17 F1 Little Norton Somset
35 E2 Little Oakley Essex
42 B1 Little Oakley Nhants
49 H1 Little Onn Staffs
71 F4 Little Orton Cumb
40 D2 Little Packington Warwks
32 D5 Little Paxton Cambs
3 E6 Little Petherick Cnwll
45 F3 Little Plumstead Norfk
42 B5 Little Ponton Lincs
31 G5 Little Preston Nhants
33 E6 Little Raveley Cambs
60 B2 Little Reedness E R Yk
59 E5 Little Ribston N York
30 C2 Little Rissington Gloucs
30 D3 Little Rollright Oxon
44 C4 Little Ryburgh Norfk
71 H3 Little Salkeld Cumb
33 H2 Little Sampford Essex
48 D6 Little Saughall Ches
34 B5 Little Saxham Suffk
106 C2 Little Scatwell Highld
66 B1 Little Sessay N York
33 F4 Little Shelford Cambs
15 G1 Little Silver Devon
56 D6 Little Singleton Lancs
59 G4 Little Skipwith N York
59 F2 Little Smeaton N York
44 C5 Little Snoring Norfk
18 A5 Little Sodbury S Glos
9 F6 Little Somborne Hants
18 C5 Little Somerford Wilts
49 G2 Little Soudley Shrops
65 G5 Little Stainton Darltn
48 D6 Little Stanney Ches
32 C5 Little Staughton Beds
53 F2 Little Steeping Lincs
35 E4 Little Stonham Suffk
41 G3 Little Stretton Leics
39 E5 Little Stretton Shrops
71 H2 Little Strickland Cumb
32 D6 Little Stukeley Cambs
49 G3 Little Sugnall Staffs
72 D4 Little Swinburne Nthumb
70 A4 Little Sypland D & G
31 E3 Little Tew Oxon
34 C1 Little Tey Essex
33 G6 Little Thetford Cambs
73 H1 Little Thorpe Dur
34 A4 Little Thurlow Green Suffk
22 B3 Little Thurrock Thurr
15 E3 Little Torrington Devon
57 F6 Little Town Lancs
62 C3 Little Urswick Cumb
22 D4 Little Wakering Essex
33 G3 Little Walden Essex
34 C3 Little Waldingfield Suffk
44 C5 Little Walsingham Norfk
22 C6 Little Waltham Essex
29 G5 Little Washbourne Gloucs
60 D3 Little Weighton E R Yk
42 B1 Little Weldon Nhants
34 D3 Little Wenham Suffk
39 F6 Little Wenlock Wrekin
17 G2 Little Weston Somset
9 G2 Little Whitefield IOW
33 G4 Little Wilbraham Cambs
29 F4 Little Witcombe Gloucs
39 G3 Little Witley Worcs
19 G5 Little Wittenham Oxon
30 D3 Little Wolford Warwks
21 F2 Little Woodcote Surrey
34 A3 Little Wratting Suffk
32 B5 Little Wymington Beds
32 D2 Little Wymondley Herts
40 B4 Little Wyrley Staffs
34 B3 Little Yeldham Essex
52 A3 Littleborough Notts
58 B2 Littleborough Rochdl
23 G1 Littlebourne Kent
7 G4 Littlebredy Dorset
107 E2 Littleburn Highld
33 G3 Littlebury Essex
33 F3 Littlebury Green Essex
29 E4 Littledean Gloucs
14 D3 Littleham Devon
6 B4 Littleham Devon
10 D2 Littlehampton W Susx
11 E5 Littlehaven W Susx
5 H3 Littlehempston Devon
94 C5 Littlemill Abers
100 C4 Littlemill Highld
31 F1 Littlemore Oxon
41 E6 Littleover C Derb
43 G1 Littleport Cambs
13 F4 Littlestone-on-Sea Kent
41 F3 Littlethorpe Leics
59 E6 Littlethorpe N York
93 F4 Littleton Angus
48 D5 Littleton Ches
69 G3 Littleton D & G
9 F6 Littleton Hants
17 F2 Littleton Somset
20 D2 Littleton Surrey
18 B4 Littleton Drew Wilts
18 C2 Littleton Pannell Wilts
28 D2 Littleton-on-Severn S Glos
73 G1 Littletown Dur
20 B3 Littlewick Green W & M
19 E6 Littleworth Oxon
40 B5 Littleworth Staffs
30 A5 Littleworth Worcs
34 A1 Littley Green Essex
17 G4 Litton BaNES
50 C4 Litton Derbys
64 D1 Litton N York
7 F4 Litton Cheney Dorset
111 d6 Liurbost W Isls
56 D2 Liverpool Lpool
56 D1 Liverpool Airport Lpool
58 D2 Liversedge Kirk
5 H4 Liverton Devon
66 D5 Liverton R & Cl
86 B3 Livingston W Loth
86 B3 Livingston Village W Loth
5 G2 Lixton Devon
48 B6 Lixwm Flints
2 D1 Lizard Cnwll
46 C5 Llanaelhaearn Gwynd
37 F4 Llanafan Cerdgn
54 D4 Llanallgo IOA
48 B3 Llanarmon Dyffryn Ceiriog Wrexhm
48 C5 Llanarmon-yn-Ial Denbgs
36 D3 Llanarth Cerdgn
28 B4 Llanarth Mons
26 B4 Llanarthne Carmth
56 B1 Llanasa Flints
37 E5 Llanbadarn Fawr Cerdgn
38 B4 Llanbadarn Fynydd Powys
28 B3 Llanbadoc Mons
28 B2 Llanbeder Newpt
47 E4 Llanbedr Gwynd
27 G4 Llanbedr Powys
48 B5 Llanbedr-Dyffryn-Clwyd Denbgs
55 F3 Llanbedr-y-Cennin Conwy

Llanbedrgoch - Lower Shuckburgh 179

54 D4 Llanbedrgoch IOA
46 C4 Llanbedrog Gwynd
54 D2 Llanberis Gwynd
16 B5 Llanbethery V Glam
38 B3 Llanbister Powys
16 B6 Llanblethian V Glam
25 F5 Llanboidy Carmth
27 G2 Llanbradach Caerph
47 G2 Llanbrynmair Powys
16 B5 Llancadle V Glam
16 C5 Llancarfan V Glam
28 C4 Llancloudy Herefs
27 G1 Llandaff Cardif
47 E4 Llandanwg Gwynd
54 D3 Llanddanielfab IOA
26 B4 Llanddarog Carmth
37 E4 Llanddeiniol Cerdgn
54 D3 Llanddeiniolen Gwynd
47 H5 Llandderfel Gwynd
54 B4 Llanddeusant IOA
27 F5 Llanddew Powys
26 A2 Llanddewi Swans
37 F2 Llanddewi Brefi Cerdgn
28 B4 Llanddewi Rhydderch Mons
25 E4 Llanddewi Velfrey Pembks
38 B3 Llanddewi Ystradenni Powys
55 F3 Llanddoget Conwy
54 D4 Llanddona IOA
25 F4 Llanddowror Carmth
55 G4 Llanddulas Conwy
47 E4 Llanddwywe Gwynd
54 D4 Llanddyfnan IOA
27 G5 Llandefaelog-Trer-Graig Powys
27 F6 Llandefalle Powys
54 D4 Llandegfan IOA
48 C4 Llandegla Denbgs
38 B2 Llandegley Powys
28 B2 Llandegveth Mons
26 C5 Llandeilo Carmth
38 B1 Llandeilo Graban Powys
24 C5 Llandeloy Pembks
28 C3 Llandenny Mons
28 C2 Llandevaud Newpt
28 C2 Llandevenny Mons
38 A4 Llandinam Powys
25 E4 Llandissilio Pembks
28 C3 Llandogo Mons
16 B6 Llandough V Glam
16 C6 Llandough V Glam
26 D6 Llandovery Carmth
16 B6 Llandow V Glam
37 F1 Llandre Carmth
37 E5 Llandre Cerdgn
25 E5 Llandre Isaf Pembks
48 A3 Llandrillo Denbgs
55 F4 Llandrillo-yn-Rhos Conwy
38 B2 Llandrindod Wells Powys
48 C1 Llandrinio Powys
55 F4 Llandudno Conwy
55 F4 Llandudno Junction Conwy
46 C5 Llandudwen Gwynd
37 G1 Llandulas Powys
54 C2 Llandwrog Gwynd
26 C4 Llandybie Carmth
25 G4 Llandyfaelog Carmth
36 C1 Llandyfriog Cerdgn
54 D3 Llandygai Gwynd
36 B1 Llandygwydd Cerdgn
48 B5 Llandyrnog Denbgs
38 C5 Llandyssil Powys
36 D1 Llandysul Cerdgn
27 G1 Llanedeyrn Cardif
27 F6 Llaneglwys Powys
47 E2 Llanegryn Gwynd
26 B4 Llanegwad Carmth
54 C5 Llaneilian IOA
55 F4 Llanelian-yn-Rhos Conwy
48 B4 Llanelidan Denbgs
27 G5 Llanelieu Powys
28 B4 Llanellen Mons
26 B3 Llanelli Carmth
47 F3 Llanelltyd Gwynd
38 A2 Llanelwedd Powys
47 E4 Llanenddwyn Gwynd
46 C4 Llanengan Gwynd
54 C4 Llanerchymedd IOA
48 A1 Llanerfyl Powys
54 B4 Llanfachraeth IOA
47 F4 Llanfachreth Gwynd
54 B3 Llanfaelog IOA
46 B4 Llanfaelrhys Gwynd
54 B5 Llanfaethlu IOA
47 E4 Llanfair Gwynd
38 B6 Llanfair Caereinion Powys
37 E2 Llanfair Clydogau Cerdgn
48 B5 Llanfair Dyffryn Clwyd Denbgs
54 D3 Llanfair P G IOA
55 G3 Llanfair Talhaiarn Conwy
38 C4 Llanfair Waterdine Shrops
54 D3 Llanfair-is-gaer Gwynd
54 C3 Llanfair-y-Cwmwd IOA
54 B4 Llanfair-yn-Neubwll IOA
55 E4 Llanfairfechan Conwy
54 B5 Llanfairynghornwy IOA
25 E4 Llanfallteg Carmth
25 E4 Llanfallteg West Carmth
37 E4 Llanfarian Cerdgn
48 C2 Llanfechain Powys
54 C5 Llanfechell IOA
48 C5 Llanferres Denbgs
55 G2 Llanfihangel Glyn Myfyr Conwy
27 E6 Llanfihangel Nant Bran Powys
38 B3 Llanfihangel Rhydithon Powys
28 C2 Llanfihangel Rogiet Mons
54 B4 Llanfihangel yn Nhowyn IOA
36 D1 Llanfihangel-ar-Arth Carmth
37 F4 Llanfihangel-y-Creuddyn Cerdgn
47 E5 Llanfihangel-y-traethau Gwynd
48 B1 Llanfihangel-yng-Ngwynfa Powys
27 G5 Llanfilo Powys
28 B4 Llanfoist Mons
47 H5 Llanfor Gwynd
28 B2 Llanfrechfa Torfn
27 F5 Llanfrynach Powys
48 B5 Llanfwrog Denbgs
54 B4 Llanfwrog IOA
48 B2 Llanfyllin Powys
26 B5 Llanfynydd Carmth
48 C5 Llanfynydd Flints
25 F5 Llanfyrnach Pembks
48 A1 Llangadfan Powys
26 C5 Llangadog Carmth
54 C3 Llangadwaladr IOA
54 C3 Llangaffo IOA
37 H2 Llangammarch Wells Powys
27 E1 Llangan V Glam
28 C4 Llangarron Herefs
26 B5 Llangathen Carmth
27 G4 Llangattock Powys
28 B4 Llangattock Lingoed Mons
48 C2 Llangedwyn Powys
54 C4 Llangefni IOA
27 E2 Llangeinor Brdgnd
54 C3 Llangeinwen IOA
37 E3 Llangeitho Cerdgn
36 C1 Llangeler Carmth
47 E2 Llangelynin Gwynd
26 A4 Llangendeirne Carmth
26 B3 Llangennech Carmth
25 G2 Llangennith Swans
55 G3 Llangernyw Conwy
46 C4 Llangian Gwynd
24 C5 Llangloffan Pembks
25 F5 Llanglydwen Carmth
54 D4 Llangoed IOA
48 C3 Llangollen Denbgs
25 E5 Llangolman Pembks
27 G5 Llangors Powys
47 G4 Llangower Gwynd
36 C2 Llangranog Cerdgn
54 C4 Llangristiolus IOA
28 C4 Llangrove Herefs
38 C3 Llangunllo Powys
25 G4 Llangunnor Carmth
37 G4 Llangurig Powys
47 H5 Llangwm Conwy
28 C3 Llangwm Mons
24 D4 Llangwm Pembks
28 C3 Llangwm-isaf Mons
46 B4 Llangwnnadl Gwynd
37 E4 Llangwyryfon Cerdgn
37 E2 Llangybi Cerdgn
46 D5 Llangybi Gwynd
28 B2 Llangybi Mons
48 B5 Llangynhafal Denbgs
27 G4 Llangynidr Powys
25 F4 Llangynin Carmth
25 G4 Llangynog Carmth
48 A2 Llangynog Powys
27 E2 Llangynwyd Brdgnd
27 F5 Llanhamlach Powys
27 F1 Llanharan Rhondd
27 F1 Llanharry Rhondd
28 B2 Llanhennock Mons
27 G3 Llanhilleth Blae G
37 H5 Llanidloes Powys
46 C4 Llaniestyn Gwynd
27 G6 Llanigon Powys
37 E4 Llanilar Cerdgn
27 E1 Llanilid Rhondd
36 D3 Llanina Cerdgn
27 G1 Llanishen Cardif
28 C3 Llanishen Mons
55 E3 Llanllechid Gwynd
28 B3 Llanllowell Mons
38 B6 Llanllugan Powys
25 G4 Llanllwch Carmth
38 B5 Llanllwchaiarn Powys
36 D1 Llanllwni Carmth
54 C2 Llanllyfni Gwynd
25 H2 Llanmadoc Swans
16 B5 Llanmaes V Glam
28 B2 Llanmartin Newpt
25 F3 Llanmiloe Carmth
55 G3 Llannefydd Conwy
26 B3 Llannon Carmth
46 C5 Llannor Gwynd
36 D3 Llanon Cerdgn
28 B3 Llanover Mons
25 G5 Llanpumsaint Carmth
48 B2 Llanrhaeadr-ym-Mochnant Powys
24 C5 Llanrhian Pembks
26 B2 Llanrhidian Swans
55 F3 Llanrhychwyn Conwy
54 B5 Llanrhyddlad IOA
37 E4 Llanrhystud Cerdgn
28 C4 Llanrothal Herefs
54 D3 Llanrug Gwynd
27 G1 Llanrumney Cardif
55 F3 Llanrwst Conwy
25 F4 Llansadurnen Carmth
26 C5 Llansadwrn Carmth
54 D4 Llansadwrn IOA
25 G3 Llansaint Carmth
26 C3 Llansamlet Swans
55 F4 Llansanffraid Glan Conwy Conwy
55 G3 Llansannan Conwy
27 G5 Llansantffraed Powys
37 H3 Llansantffraed-Cwmdeuddwr Powys
38 B2 Llansantffraed-in-Elvel Powys
36 D3 Llansantffraid Cerdgn
48 C2 Llansantffraid-ym-Mechain Powys
26 C6 Llansawel Carmth
48 C2 Llansilin Powys
28 C3 Llansoy Mons
27 F5 Llanspyddid Powys
24 D3 Llanstadwell Pembks
25 G4 Llansteffan Carmth
28 B2 Llantarnam Torfn
25 F4 Llanteg Pembks
28 B4 Llanthewy Skirrid Mons
28 B5 Llanthony Mons
28 B4 Llantilio Pertholey Mons
28 B4 Llantilio-Crossenny Mons
28 B2 Llantrisant Mons
27 F1 Llantrisant Rhondd
16 C6 Llantrithyd V Glam
27 F2 Llantwit Fardre Rhondd
16 B5 Llantwit Major V Glam
47 G4 Llanuwchllyn Gwynd
28 C2 Llanvaches Newpt
28 C2 Llanvair Discoed Mons
28 B4 Llanvapley Mons
28 B4 Llanvetherine Mons
28 B4 Llanvihangel Crucorney Mons
48 A2 Llanwddyn Powys
36 D2 Llanwenog Cerdgn
28 B2 Llanwern Newpt
25 F5 Llanwinio Carmth
54 C2 Llanwnda Gwynd
24 D6 Llanwnda Pembks
37 E2 Llanwnnen Cerdgn
38 A5 Llanwnog Powys
26 C5 Llanwrda Carmth
47 F2 Llanwrin Powys
37 H3 Llanwrthwl Powys
37 G2 Llanwrtyd Wells Powys
38 B6 Llanwyddelan Powys
48 C2 Llanyblodwel Shrops
25 G4 Llanybri Carmth
36 D2 Llanybydder Carmth
25 E5 Llanycefn Pembks
24 D6 Llanychaer Bridge Pembks
47 G3 Llanymawddwy Gwynd
48 C2 Llanymynech Powys
54 B4 Llanynghenedl IOA
48 B5 Llanynys Denbgs
38 A2 Llanyre Powys
46 D5 Llanystumdwy Gwynd
27 F5 Llanywern Powys
25 E4 Llawhaden Pembks
37 H5 Llawryglyn Powys
48 D5 Llay Wrexhm
27 F3 Llechrhyd Caerph
36 B1 Llechryd Cerdgn
37 E4 Lledrod Cerdgn
46 C5 Lleyn Peninsula Gwynd
46 C5 Llithfaen Gwynd
56 B1 Lloc Flints
27 G6 Llowes Powys
27 F3 Llwydcoed Rhondd
48 A1 Llwydiarth Powys
36 D3 Llwyncelyn Cerdgn
36 C2 Llwyndafydd Cerdgn
47 E2 Llwyngwril Gwynd
48 C3 Llwynmawr Wrexhm
27 F2 Llwynypia Rhondd
48 C2 Llynclys Shrops
54 C4 Llynfaes IOA
24 D5 Llys-y-fran Pembks
55 G4 Llysfaen Conwy
27 G6 Llyswen Powys
16 B6 Llysworney V Glam
27 E5 Llywel Powys
85 H3 Loan Falk
86 C3 Loanhead Mdloth
70 C5 Loaningfoot D & G
76 C4 Loans S Ayrs
5 E5 Lobhillcross Devon
111 b2 Loch Baghasdail W Isls
111 b4 Loch Euphoirt W Isls
84 D6 Loch Katrine Pier Stirlg
84 C4 Loch Lomond
105 G3 Loch Maree Hotel Highld
111 b4 Loch nam Madadh W Isls
98 D5 Loch Ness Highld
97 E1 Lochailort Highld
89 G3 Lochaline Highld
68 C3 Lochans D & G
78 D1 Locharbriggs D & G
90 B1 Lochavich Ag & B
90 C2 Lochawe Ag & B
111 b2 Lochboisdale W Isls
89 F2 Lochbuie Ag & B
97 F6 Lochcarron Highld
89 G2 Lochdon Ag & B
89 G2 Lochdonhead Ag & B
83 F3 Lochead Ag & B
91 G2 Lochearnhead Stirlg
73 F3 Lochee C Dund
90 B6 Locheilside Station Highld
98 D6 Lochend Highld
111 b4 Locheport W Isls
70 C6 Lochfoot D & G
83 G4 Lochgair Ag & B
86 C5 Lochgelly Fife
83 G4 Lochgilphead Ag & B
84 B5 Lochgoilhead Ag & B
93 E1 Lochieheads Fife
101 E5 Lochill Moray
100 C3 Lochindorb Lodge Highld
108 B2 Lochinver Highld
106 C2 Lochluichart Highld
78 D1 Lochmaben D & G
111 b4 Lochmaddy W Isls
86 C5 Lochore Fife
75 G5 Lochranza N Ayrs
95 F3 Lochside Abers
78 C1 Lochside D & G
107 G1 Lochside Highld
68 D5 Lochton S Ayrs
95 E2 Lochty Angus
87 E6 Lochty Fife
89 H4 Lochuisge Highld
84 C2 Lochwinnoch Rens
78 D2 Lochwood D & G
3 F5 Lockengate Cnwll
79 E1 Lockerbie D & G
18 D3 Lockeridge Wilts
9 E5 Lockerley Hants
17 E5 Locking N Som
57 F2 Locking Stumps Warrtn
60 D4 Lockington E R Yk
49 F2 Lockleywood Shrops
9 G4 Locks Heath Hants
21 G2 Locksbottom Gt Lon
67 E2 Lockton N York
42 A2 Loddington Leics
32 A6 Loddington Nhants
5 G2 Loddiswell Devon
45 F2 Loddon Norfk
33 G5 Lode Cambs
40 C2 Lode Heath Solhll
7 F5 Loders Dorset
10 C4 Lodsworth W Susx
59 E3 Lofthouse Leeds
65 E1 Lofthouse N York
59 E3 Lofthouse Gate Wakefd
66 D5 Loftus R & Cl
77 E3 Logan E Ayrs
86 A2 Loganlea W Loth
49 G3 Loggerheads Staffs
95 F3 Logie Angus
93 F2 Logie Fife
100 C4 Logie Moray
94 D6 Logie Coldstone Abers
95 F3 Logie Pert Angus
92 C4 Logierait P & K
103 E2 Logierieve Abers
25 E5 Login Carmth
33 F5 Lolworth Cambs
105 E2 Lonbain Highld
60 C4 Londesborough E R Yk
21 F3 London Gt Lon
3 F4 London Apprentice Cnwll
21 E5 London Colney Herts
65 G2 Londonderry N York
42 B5 Londonthorpe Lincs
105 F4 Londubh Highld
105 F4 Lonemore Highld
17 F5 Long Ashton N Som
39 G3 Long Bank Worcs
42 A6 Long Bennington Lincs
7 G4 Long Bredy Dorset
31 G6 Long Buckby Nhants
41 H5 Long Clawson Leics
49 H2 Long Compton Staffs
30 D3 Long Compton Warwks
20 A6 Long Crendon Bucks
8 C4 Long Crichel Dorset
21 E2 Long Ditton Surrey
51 E4 Long Duckmanton Derbys
41 F6 Long Eaton Derbys
49 E6 Long Green Ches
29 F5 Long Green Worcs
31 E2 Long Hanborough Oxon
31 E6 Long Itchington Warwks
41 F1 Long Lawford Warwks
17 F2 Long Load Somset
20 C6 Long Marston Herts
59 F5 Long Marston N York
30 C5 Long Marston Warwks
64 B5 Long Marton Cumb
34 C3 Long Melford Suffk
29 F2 Long Newnton Gloucs
87 E3 Long Newton E Loth
63 H2 Long Preston N York
61 E4 Long Riston E R Yk
45 E2 Long Stratton Norfk
32 A3 Long Street M Keyn
10 A6 Long Sutton Hants
43 F4 Long Sutton Lincs
17 F2 Long Sutton Somset
34 D5 Long Thurlow Suffk
49 F1 Long Waste Wrekin
41 F5 Long Whatton Leics
19 G5 Long Wittenham Oxon
73 F3 Longbenton N Tyne
30 C3 Longborough Gloucs
40 B1 Longbridge Birm
18 B1 Longbridge Deverill Wilts
7 G6 Longburton Dorset
50 D2 Longcliffe Derbys
5 H3 Longcombe Devon
19 E5 Longcot Oxon
38 D6 Longden Shrops
40 C4 Longdon Staffs
29 F6 Longdon Worcs
40 C4 Longdon Green Staffs
49 F1 Longdon upon Tern Wrekin
6 A4 Longdown Devon
2 D3 Longdowns Cnwll
22 B2 Longfield Kent
50 D1 Longford Derbys
29 F4 Longford Gloucs
49 F3 Longford Shrops
49 G2 Longford Wrekin
93 E2 Longforgan P & K
87 G2 Longformacus Border
73 E6 Longframlington Nthumb
8 C3 Longham Dorset
44 C3 Longham Norfk
103 F3 Longhaven Abers
73 F5 Longhirst Nthumb
29 E4 Longhope Gloucs
111 g1 Longhope Ork
73 E5 Longhorsley Nthumb
81 G2 Longhoughton Nthumb
50 D1 Longlane Derbys
18 A1 Longleat Safari Park Wilts
29 F4 Longlevens Gloucs
58 B2 Longley Calder
93 E3 Longleys P & K
102 C5 Longmanhill Abers
10 B5 Longmoor Camp Hants
101 E5 Longmorn Moray
50 A4 Longmoss Ches
80 B3 Longnewton Border
65 G5 Longnewton S on T
29 E4 Longney Gloucs
87 E3 Longniddry E Loth
39 E5 Longnor Shrops
50 C3 Longnor Staffs
19 F2 Longparish Hants
57 F6 Longridge Lancs
85 H2 Longridge W Loth
85 G3 Longriggend N Lans
2 B2 Longrock Cnwll
50 B2 Longsdon Staffs
103 F4 Longside Abers
33 F5 Longstanton Cambs
19 F1 Longstock Hants
33 E4 Longstowe Cambs
18 D2 Longstreet Wilts
42 D2 Longthorpe C Pete
71 G2 Longthwaite Cumb
50 A1 Longton C Stke
57 E5 Longton Lancs
71 G6 Longtown Cumb
28 B5 Longtown Herefs
7 c1 Longueville Jersey
39 E5 Longville in the Dale Shrops
20 B5 Longwick Bucks
73 E5 Longwitton Nthumb
70 A5 Longwood D & G
19 F6 Longworth Oxon
87 E3 Longyester E Loth
103 F5 Lonmay Abers
104 B1 Lonmore Highld
4 C2 Looe Cnwll
22 C1 Loose Kent
20 B5 Loosley Row Bucks
102 B4 Lootcherbrae Abers
17 E1 Lopen Somset
49 E2 Loppington Shrops
22 C2 Lords Wood Medway
92 D4 Lornty P & K
51 E2 Loscoe Derbys
101 E6 Lossiemouth Moray
3 F4 Lost Gardens of Heligan Cnwll
49 F6 Lostock Gralam Ches
49 F6 Lostock Green Ches
57 E5 Lostock Hall Lancs
4 B3 Lostwithiel Cnwll
107 H6 Lothbeg Highld
58 B4 Lothersdale N York
110 A1 Lothmore Highld
41 F5 Loughborough Leics
26 B3 Loughor Swans
21 G5 Loughton Essex
32 A3 Loughton M Keyn
39 F4 Loughton Shrops
42 C4 Lound Lincs
51 G5 Lound Notts
45 H2 Lound Suffk
41 E5 Lount Leics
53 E4 Louth Lincs
57 G5 Love Clough Lancs
10 A3 Lovedean Hants
8 D5 Lover Wilts
51 F6 Loversall Donc
22 B5 Loves Green Essex
25 E3 Loveston Pembks
17 G2 Lovington Somset
59 E2 Low Ackworth Wakefd
68 B4 Low Barbeth D & G
63 F3 Low Bentham N York
63 F4 Low Biggins Cumb
63 F5 Low Borrowbridge Cumb
50 D5 Low Bradfield Sheff
58 B4 Low Bradley N York
52 A5 Low Burnham N Linc
60 B5 Low Catton E R Yk
71 G5 Low Crosby Cumb
65 G4 Low Dinsdale Darltn
59 F2 Low Eggborough N York
65 F2 Low Ellington N York
73 F3 Low Fell Gatesd
84 D4 Low Gartachorrans Stirlg
65 F1 Low Grantley N York
17 F2 Low Ham Somset
58 D5 Low Harrogate N York
71 G4 Low Hesket Cumb
60 B6 Low Hutton N York
71 E2 Low Lorton Cumb
52 A2 Low Marnham Notts
66 C3 Low Mill N York
73 G2 Low Moorsley Sundld
60 C6 Low Mowthorpe N York
62 D4 Low Newton Cumb
72 A3 Low Row Cumb
64 D3 Low Row N York
68 B4 Low Salchrie D & G
60 D2 Low Santon N Linc
45 E2 Low Tharston Norfk
86 A4 Low Torry Fife
65 G4 Low Worsall N York
62 D6 Low Wray Cumb
51 G2 Lowdham Notts
16 D3 Lower Aisholt Somset
8 A4 Lower Ansty Dorset
29 F5 Lower Apperley Gloucs
6 A4 Lower Ashton Devon
20 B4 Lower Assendon Oxon
57 E5 Lower Bartle Lancs
19 H4 Lower Basildon W Berk
11 E4 Lower Beeding W Susx
42 C1 Lower Benefield Nhants
30 B6 Lower Bentley Worcs
31 F5 Lower Boddington Nhants
10 B6 Lower Bourne Surrey
30 D4 Lower Brailes Warwks
97 E4 Lower Breakish Highld
39 G2 Lower Broadheath Worcs
39 F2 Lower Brockhampton Manor Herefs
28 C6 Lower Bullingham Herefs
8 D5 Lower Burgate Hants
32 D3 Lower Caldecote Beds
29 E3 Lower Cam Gloucs
27 F6 Lower Chapel Powys
8 C6 Lower Chicksgrove Wilts
19 E2 Lower Chute Wilts
21 F4 Lower Clapton Gt Lon
40 A2 Lower Clent Worcs
58 D1 Lower Cumberworth Kirk
32 C5 Lower Dean Beds
105 F2 Lower Diabaig Highld
12 A3 Lower Dicker E Susx
38 D4 Lower Down Shrops
59 E6 Lower Dunsforth N York
39 F1 Lower Egleton Herefs
32 B3 Lower End M Keyn
23 G1 Lower Eythorne Kent
17 F6 Lower Failand N Som
10 A5 Lower Farringdon Hants
20 D3 Lower Feltham Gt Lon
10 B6 Lower Froyle Hants
6 B3 Lower Gabwell Devon
107 E5 Lower Gledfield Highld
17 F3 Lower Godney Somset
32 D2 Lower Gravenhurst Beds
12 B5 Lower Green Kent
12 B6 Lower Green Kent
20 D2 Lower Halliford Surrey
22 D2 Lower Halstow Kent
8 C3 Lower Hamworthy Poole
23 F1 Lower Hardres Kent
20 B6 Lower Hartwell Bucks
38 C2 Lower Hergest Herefs
31 F3 Lower Heyford Oxon
57 G2 Lower Irlam Salfd
74 B5 Lower Killeyan Ag & B
48 D5 Lower Kinnerton Ches
17 F5 Lower Langford N Som
86 D6 Lower Largo Fife
40 B6 Lower Leigh Staffs
15 E4 Lower Loxhore Devon
28 D4 Lower Lydbrook Gloucs
38 D3 Lower Lye Herefs
27 G2 Lower Machen Newpt
16 D3 Lower Merridge Somset
31 F4 Lower Middleton Cheney Nhants
30 B4 Lower Moor Worcs
28 D2 Lower Morton S Glos
21 G5 Lower Nazeing Essex
16 D5 Lower Penarth V Glam
39 H5 Lower Penn Staffs
49 G6 Lower Peover Ches
30 C4 Lower Quinton Warwks
34 D3 Lower Raydon Suffk
16 B3 Lower Roadwater Somset
18 C4 Lower Seagry Wilts
32 C3 Lower Shelton Beds
20 B3 Lower Shiplake Oxon
31 F6 Lower Shuckburgh Warwks

180 Lower Slaughter - Merstham

30 C2 **Lower Slaughter** Gloucs
13 G5 **Lower Standen** Kent
18 B4 **Lower Stanton St Quintin** Wilts
22 D3 **Lower Stoke** Medway
29 E2 **Lower Stone** Gloucs
44 C2 **Lower Stow Bedon** Norfk
45 F5 **Lower Street** Norfk
35 E4 **Lower Street** Suffk
32 C2 **Lower Sundon** Beds
9 G4 **Lower Swanwick** Hants
30 D5 **Lower Swell** Gloucs
50 B1 **Lower Tean** Staffs
5 G4 **Lower Town** Devon
24 D6 **Lower Town** Pembks
31 E4 **Lower Tysoe** Warwks
6 A4 **Lower Upcott** Devon
9 G5 **Lower Upham** Hants
16 C3 **Lower Vexford** Somset
17 E4 **Lower Weare** Somset
29 G6 **Lower Westmancote** Worcs
17 H4 **Lower Whatley** Somset
57 F1 **Lower Whitley** Ches
19 H1 **Lower Wield** Hants
12 B2 **Lower Willingdon** E Susx
49 G6 **Lower Withington** Ches
8 D6 **Lower Woodford** Wilts
7 G5 **Lower Wraxhall** Dorset
41 H4 **Lowesby** Leics
45 H2 **Lowestoft** Suffk
71 E2 **Loweswater** Cumb
11 F5 **Lowfield Heath** W Susx
32 C6 **Lowick** Nhants
81 F4 **Lowick** Nthumb
62 C4 **Lowick Green** Cumb
30 C6 **Lowsonford** Warwks
71 H2 **Lowther** Cumb
61 E5 **Lowthorpe** E R Yk
16 D1 **Lowton** Somset
16 B1 **Loxbeare** Devon
10 D5 **Loxhill** Surrey
15 E5 **Loxhore** Devon
30 D5 **Loxley** Warwks
17 E4 **Loxton** N Som
10 D5 **Loxwood** W Susx
109 F4 **Loyal Lodge** Highld
41 G2 **Lubenham** Leics
16 B3 **Luccombe** Somset
9 G2 **Luccombe Village** IOW
81 G3 **Lucker** Nthumb
5 E4 **Luckett** Cnwll
34 B2 **Lucking Street** Essex
18 B5 **Luckington** Wilts
16 A3 **Luckwell Bridge** Somset
38 D3 **Lucton** Herefs
111 b2 **Ludag** W Isls
53 E5 **Ludborough** Lincs
5 G3 **Ludbrook** Devon
25 E4 **Ludchurch** Pembks
58 B3 **Luddenden** Calder
58 B3 **Luddenden Foot** Calder
22 B2 **Luddesdown** Kent
60 C2 **Luddington** N Linc
30 C5 **Luddington** Warwks
42 C1 **Luddington in the Brook** Nhants
52 D4 **Ludford** Lincs
39 E3 **Ludford** Shrops
31 G2 **Ludgershall** Bucks
19 E2 **Ludgershall** Wilts
2 B3 **Ludgvan** Cnwll
45 G4 **Ludham** Norfk
39 E3 **Ludlow** Shrops
7 E6 **Ludney** Somset
8 B5 **Ludwell** Wilts
73 G1 **Ludworth** Dur
4 D6 **Luffincott** Devon
87 E4 **Luffness** E Loth
77 E3 **Lugar** E Ayrs
87 F3 **Luggate Burn** E Loth
85 F3 **Luggiebank** N Lans
84 D1 **Lugton** E Ayrs
28 D6 **Lugwardine** Herefs
96 D5 **Luib** Highld
28 C6 **Lulham** Herefs
40 D4 **Lullington** Derbys
18 A2 **Lullington** Somset
17 F5 **Lulsgate Bottom** N Som
39 G2 **Lulsley** Worcs
58 B2 **Lumb** Calder
57 H5 **Lumb** Lancs
59 F3 **Lumby** N York
85 E3 **Lumloch** E Duns
95 E6 **Lumphanan** Abers
86 C5 **Lumphinnans** Fife
101 G2 **Lumsden** Abers
95 F2 **Lunan** Angus
93 G4 **Lunanhead** Angus
92 D2 **Luncarty** P & K
60 D4 **Lund** E R Yk
59 G3 **Lund** N York
93 E3 **Lundie** Angus
85 F5 **Lundie** Stirlg
86 D6 **Lundin Links** Fife
86 D6 **Lundin Mill** Fife
111 I3 **Lunna** Shet
22 C2 **Lunsford** Kent
12 C3 **Lunsford's Cross** E Susx
56 D3 **Lunt** Sefton
6 C6 **Luppitt** Devon
5 G2 **Lupridge** Devon
58 D2 **Lupset** Wakefd
63 E4 **Lupton** Cumb
10 C4 **Lurgashall** W Susx
16 B1 **Lurley** Devon
5 H3 **Luscombe** Devon
84 C5 **Luss** Ag & B
104 B2 **Lusta** Highld
5 H5 **Lustleigh** Devon
39 E2 **Luston** Herefs
95 F3 **Luthermuir** Abers
93 E2 **Luthrie** Fife
6 C5 **Luton** Devon
6 A3 **Luton** Devon
32 C1 **Luton** Luton
22 C2 **Luton** Medway
32 D1 **Luton Airport** Luton
41 F2 **Lutterworth** Leics
5 F3 **Lutton** Devon
5 G3 **Lutton** Devon
43 F4 **Lutton** Lincs
42 D1 **Lutton** Nhants
16 B3 **Luxborough** Somset
3 F5 **Luxulyan** Cnwll
110 C3 **Lybster** Highld
38 D4 **Lydbury North** Shrops
13 E4 **Lydd** Kent
13 E4 **Lydd Airport** Kent
13 G6 **Lydden** Kent
23 H2 **Lydden** Kent
42 B2 **Lyddington** Rutlnd
16 C2 **Lydeard St Lawrence** Somset
5 E5 **Lydford** Devon
17 G2 **Lydford on Fosse** Somset
58 A3 **Lydgate** Calder
38 D5 **Lydham** Shrops
18 D5 **Lydiard Millicent** Wilts
18 D5 **Lydiard Tregoze** Swindn
56 D3 **Lydiate** Sefton
40 B1 **Lydiate Ash** Worcs
17 H1 **Lydlinch** Dorset
28 D3 **Lydney** Gloucs
25 E3 **Lydstep** Pembks
40 A2 **Lye** Dudley
11 G5 **Lye Green** E Susx
30 D6 **Lye Green** Warwks
18 A2 **Lye's Green** Wilts
19 F6 **Lyford** Oxon
13 F6 **Lymbridge Green** Kent
7 E5 **Lyme Regis** Dorset
13 F6 **Lyminge** Kent
9 E3 **Lymington** Hants
10 D3 **Lyminster** W Susx
57 F1 **Lymm** Warrtn
13 F5 **Lympne** Kent
17 E4 **Lympsham** Somset
6 B4 **Lympstone** Devon
45 E3 **Lynch Green** Norfk
99 F3 **Lynchat** Highld
9 E4 **Lyndhurst** Hants
42 B3 **Lyndon** Rutlnd
79 E6 **Lyne** Border
20 D2 **Lyne** Surrey
102 D1 **Lyne of Skene** Abers
49 E3 **Lyneal** Shrops
30 D2 **Lyneham** Oxon
18 C4 **Lyneham** Wilts
18 C4 **Lyneham Airport** Wilts
111 g1 **Lyness** Ork
44 D4 **Lyng** Norfk
17 E2 **Lyng** Somset
15 F5 **Lynmouth** Devon
101 E3 **Lynn of Shenval** Moray
22 D2 **Lynsted** Kent
15 F5 **Lynton** Devon
7 G6 **Lyon's Gate** Dorset
38 D2 **Lyonshall** Herefs
8 B3 **Lytchett Matravers** Dorset
8 C3 **Lytchett Minster** Dorset
110 C5 **Lyth** Highld
56 D5 **Lytham** Lancs
56 D5 **Lytham St Anne's** Lancs
67 E4 **Lythe** N York
110 B5 **Lythmore** Highld

M

2 D3 **Mabe Burnthouse** Cnwll
70 C6 **Mabie** D & G
53 G4 **Mablethorpe** Lincs
50 A4 **Macclesfield** Ches
102 C5 **Macduff** Abers
75 F2 **Macharioch** Ag & B
27 G2 **Machen** Caerph
75 G4 **Machrie** N Ayrs
75 E3 **Machrihanish** Ag & B
82 C5 **Machrins** Ag & B
47 F2 **Machynlleth** Powys
26 B3 **Machynys** Carmth
50 D1 **Mackworth** Derbys
87 E3 **Macmerry** E Loth
5 F6 **Maddaford** Devon
92 C2 **Madderty** P & K
85 H3 **Maddiston** Falk
49 G4 **Madeley** Staffs
33 F4 **Madingley** Cambs
28 C6 **Madley** Herefs
39 G1 **Madresfield** Worcs
2 B2 **Madron** Cnwll
36 C3 **Maen-y-groes** Cerdgn
25 E5 **Maenclochog** Pembks
16 B6 **Maendy** V Glam
47 F5 **Maentwrog** Gwynd
49 G3 **Maer** Staffs
27 E3 **Maerdy** Rhondd
48 C2 **Maesbrook** Shrops
48 C2 **Maesbury** Shrops
48 D2 **Maesbury Marsh** Shrops
36 C2 **Maesllyn** Cerdgn
27 E2 **Maesteg** Brdgnd
26 B4 **Maesybont** Carmth
27 G2 **Maesycwmmer** Caerph
101 F4 **Maggieknockater** Moray
33 F2 **Maggots End** Essex
12 B3 **Magham Down** E Susx
56 D3 **Maghull** Sefton
28 C2 **Magor** Mons
18 A1 **Maiden Bradley** Wilts
17 G5 **Maiden Head** N Som
7 G5 **Maiden Newton** Dorset
24 D3 **Maiden Wells** Pembks
11 F5 **Maidenbower** W Susx
6 B3 **Maidencombe** Torbay
5 D5 **Maidenhayne** Devon
20 C3 **Maidenhead** W & M
76 B2 **Maidens** S Ayrs
53 E2 **Maidenwell** Lincs
31 C5 **Maidford** Nhants
31 G3 **Maids Moreton** Bucks
22 C1 **Maidstone** Kent
41 H1 **Maidwell** Nhants
28 B2 **Maindee** Newpt
94 D3 **Mains of Balhall** Angus
95 E3 **Mains of Balnakettle** Abers
100 D3 **Mains of Dalvey** Highld
95 F3 **Mains of Haulkerton** Abers
65 G6 **Mainsforth** Dur
70 C5 **Mainsriddle** D & G
38 C4 **Mainstone** Shrops
29 F4 **Maisemore** Gloucs
51 E1 **Makeney** Derbys
5 G1 **Malborough** Devon
21 E2 **Malden** Surrey
22 D5 **Maldon** Essex
58 A6 **Malham** N York
97 E2 **Mallaig** Highld
97 E2 **Mallaigvaig** Highld
86 C3 **Malleny Mills** C Edin
54 C3 **Malltraeth** IOA
47 G3 **Mallwyd** Gwynd
18 B5 **Malmesbury** Wilts
15 G5 **Malmsmead** Somset
49 E4 **Malpas** Ches
3 E3 **Malpas** Cnwll
28 B2 **Malpas** Newpt
51 F5 **Maltby** Rothm
66 B4 **Maltby** S on T
53 F3 **Maltby le Marsh** Lincs
34 C1 **Malting Green** Essex
12 D6 **Maltman's Hill** Kent
66 D1 **Malton** N York
39 G1 **Malvern Hills**
39 G1 **Malvern Link** Worcs
29 E6 **Malvern Wells** Worcs
69 E3 **Malzie** D & G
39 F3 **Mamble** Worcs
28 B3 **Mamhilad** Mons
2 D2 **Manaccan** Cnwll
38 B6 **Manafon** Powys
111 c5 **Manais** W Isls
5 G5 **Manaton** Devon
53 F4 **Manby** Lincs
40 D3 **Mancetter** Warwks
57 H3 **Manchester** Manch
57 G1 **Manchester Airport** Manch
48 D5 **Mancot** Flints
98 B3 **Mandally** Highld
80 D5 **Manderston House** Border
43 F1 **Manea** Cambs
40 C3 **Maney** Birm
65 F4 **Manfield** N York
17 G6 **Mangotsfield** S Glos
111 c5 **Manish** W Isls
49 E6 **Manley** Ches
27 G3 **Manmoel** Caerph
88 B3 **Mannel** Ag & B
11 E5 **Manning's Heath** W Susx
18 D3 **Manningford Bohune** Wilts
18 D3 **Manningford Bruce** Wilts
58 C3 **Manningham** Brad
8 C4 **Mannington** Dorset
34 D2 **Manningtree** Essex
95 H6 **Mannofield** C Aber
21 G4 **Manor Park** Gt Lon
25 E3 **Manorbier** Pembks
24 D3 **Manorbier Newton** Pembks
80 C3 **Manorhill** Border
24 D6 **Manorowen** Pembks
38 D1 **Mansell Gamage** Herefs
38 D1 **Mansell Lacy** Herefs
77 E3 **Mansfield** E Ayrs
51 F3 **Mansfield** Notts
51 F3 **Mansfield Woodhouse** Notts
8 A5 **Manston** Dorset
59 E3 **Manston** Leeds
23 G2 **Manston Airport** Kent
8 C4 **Manswood** Dorset
42 C3 **Manthorpe** Lincs
52 B5 **Manton** N Linc
42 B3 **Manton** Rutlnd
18 D3 **Manton** Wilts
33 F2 **Manuden** Essex
17 G2 **Maperton** Somset
51 G3 **Maplebeck** Notts
19 H4 **Mapledurham** Oxon
20 A1 **Mapledurwell** Hants
11 E4 **Maplehurst** W Susx
22 B2 **Maplescombe** Kent
50 C2 **Mapleton** Derbys
51 E1 **Mapperley** Derbys
51 F1 **Mapperley Park** C Nott
7 F5 **Mapperton** Dorset
30 C6 **Mappleborough Green** Warwks
61 F4 **Mappleton** E R Yk
59 E1 **Mapplewell** Barns
7 H6 **Mappowder** Dorset
2 D4 **Marazanvose** Cnwll
2 B2 **Marazion** Cnwll
49 E4 **Marbury** Ches
43 F2 **March** Cambs
78 D4 **March** S Lans
19 F6 **Marcham** Oxon
49 F2 **Marchamley** Shrops
40 C6 **Marchington** Staffs
48 D4 **Marchwiel** Wrexhm
9 F4 **Marchwood** Hants
16 B5 **Marcross** V Glam
39 E1 **Marden** Herefs
12 C6 **Marden** Kent
18 D3 **Marden** Wilts
12 C6 **Marden Thorn** Kent
28 B4 **Mardy** Mons
53 E2 **Mareham le Fen** Lincs
53 E2 **Mareham on the Hill** Lincs
10 D4 **Marehill** W Susx
11 G4 **Maresfield** E Susx
61 E3 **Marfleet** C KuH
48 D5 **Marford** Wrexhm
26 D2 **Margam** Neath
8 A5 **Margaret Marsh** Dorset
22 B5 **Margaretting** Essex
22 B5 **Margaretting Tye** Essex
23 H3 **Margate** Kent
75 H4 **Margnaheglish** N Ayrs
69 G3 **Margrie** D & G
66 C5 **Margrove Park** R & Cl
44 A3 **Marham** Norfk
14 B2 **Marhamchurch** Cnwll
42 D2 **Marholm** C Pete
15 F3 **Mariansleigh** Devon
22 D3 **Marine Town** Kent
95 F6 **Marionburgh** Abers
104 D2 **Marishader** Highld
5 E3 **Maristow** Devon
76 C5 **Maritime Centre** N Ayrs
78 D1 **Marjoriebanks** D & G
17 E4 **Mark** Somset
12 B5 **Mark Cross** E Susx
11 G6 **Markbeech** Kent
53 F3 **Markby** Lincs
41 E4 **Market Bosworth** Leics
42 D3 **Market Deeping** Lincs
49 F3 **Market Drayton** Shrops
41 H2 **Market Harborough** Leics
18 C2 **Market Lavington** Wilts
42 B4 **Market Overton** Rutlnd
52 D4 **Market Rasen** Lincs
52 D3 **Market Stainton** Lincs
60 C4 **Market Weighton** E R Yk
34 D6 **Market Weston** Suffk
41 F4 **Markfield** Leics
27 G3 **Markham** Caerph
51 H4 **Markham Moor** Notts
86 D6 **Markinch** Fife
58 D6 **Markington** N York
87 F4 **Markle** E Loth
34 C1 **Marks Tey** Essex
17 G5 **Marksbury** BaNES
32 C1 **Markyate** Herts
18 D3 **Marlborough** Wilts
30 C5 **Marlcliff** Warwks
6 A2 **Marldon** Devon
35 F4 **Marlesford** Suffk
45 E3 **Marlingford** Norfk
24 C3 **Marloes** Pembks
20 B4 **Marlow** Bucks
20 B4 **Marlow Bottom** Bucks
11 G6 **Marlpit Hill** Kent
8 A5 **Marnhull** Dorset
50 B5 **Marple** Stockp
59 F1 **Marr** Donc
65 E3 **Marrick** N York
58 B2 **Marsden** Kirk
73 G3 **Marsden** S Tyne
19 G6 **Marsh Baldon** Oxon
53 E5 **Marsh Chapel** Lincs
31 G2 **Marsh Gibbon** Bucks
6 C5 **Marsh Green** Devon
11 G6 **Marsh Green** Kent
51 E4 **Marsh Lane** Derbys
16 B3 **Marsh Street** Somset
21 E6 **Marshalswick** Herts
45 E4 **Marsham** Norfk
23 G1 **Marshborough** Kent
38 D5 **Marshbrook** Shrops
28 A1 **Marshfield** Newpt
18 A4 **Marshfield** S Glos
4 C6 **Marshgate** Cnwll
43 G3 **Marshland St James** Norfk
7 E5 **Marshwood** Dorset
65 E3 **Marske** N York
66 C5 **Marske-by-the-Sea** R & Cl
38 D2 **Marston** Herefs
42 B6 **Marston** Lincs
31 F1 **Marston** Oxon
40 A5 **Marston** Staffs
18 C2 **Marston** Wilts
40 C2 **Marston Green** Solhll
17 G2 **Marston Magna** Somset
18 D6 **Marston Meysey** Wilts
50 C1 **Marston Montgomery** Derbys
32 C3 **Marston Moretaine** Beds
40 D6 **Marston on Dove** Derbys
31 F4 **Marston St Lawrence** Nhants
41 G2 **Marston Trussell** Nhants
28 D4 **Marstow** Herefs
20 C6 **Marsworth** Bucks
19 E3 **Marten** Wilts
49 G6 **Marthall** Ches
45 G4 **Martham** Norfk
8 C5 **Martin** Hants
13 H6 **Martin** Kent
52 D2 **Martin** Lincs
53 E2 **Martin** Lincs
39 H2 **Martin Hussingtree** Worcs
15 F5 **Martinhoe** Devon
7 G4 **Martinstown** Dorset
35 F3 **Martlesham** Suffk
35 F3 **Martlesham Heath** Suffk
24 D4 **Martletwy** Pembks
39 G2 **Martley** Worcs
17 F1 **Martock** Somset
49 H6 **Marton** Ches
61 E4 **Marton** E R Yk
52 A3 **Marton** Lincs
66 B5 **Marton** Middsb
59 E6 **Marton** N York
66 D2 **Marton** N York
38 C6 **Marton** Shrops
31 E6 **Marton** Warwks
65 G1 **Marton-le-Moor** N York
9 G6 **Martyr Worthy** Hants
111 g2 **Marwick** Ork
15 E4 **Marwood** Devon
5 E5 **Mary Tavy** Devon
106 D2 **Marybank** Highld
107 E2 **Maryburgh** Highld
95 G5 **Maryculter** Abers
87 G2 **Marygold** Border
102 D4 **Maryhill** Abers
85 E3 **Maryhill** C Glas
95 F3 **Marykirk** Abers
21 F3 **Marylebone** Gt Lon
57 F3 **Marylebone** Wigan
101 E3 **Marypark** Moray
70 D3 **Maryport** Cumb
68 C1 **Maryport** D & G
5 E5 **Marystow** Devon
95 F2 **Maryton** Angus
95 E5 **Marywell** Abers
95 H5 **Marywell** Abers
93 H4 **Marywell** Angus
65 F2 **Masham** N York
63 F3 **Masongill** N York
51 F4 **Mastin Moor** Derbys
21 H6 **Matching Green** Essex
21 G6 **Matching Tye** Essex
73 E4 **Matfen** Nthumb
12 B6 **Matfield** Kent
28 C2 **Mathern** Mons
39 G1 **Mathon** Herefs
24 C5 **Mathry** Pembks
45 E5 **Matlask** Norfk
50 D3 **Matlock** Derbys
50 D3 **Matlock Bath** Derbys
29 F4 **Matson** Gloucs
51 G5 **Mattersey** Notts
20 A2 **Mattingley** Hants
44 D3 **Mattishall** Norfk
44 D3 **Mattishall Burgh** Norfk
76 D4 **Mauchline** E Ayrs
103 E4 **Maud** Abers
7 c2 **Maufant** Jersey
30 D3 **Maugersbury** Gloucs
116 d4 **Maughold** IOM
98 C6 **Mauld** Highld
32 C3 **Maulden** Beds
64 A5 **Maulds Meaburn** Cumb
65 G2 **Maunby** N York
39 E1 **Maund Bryan** Herefs
16 C2 **Maundown** Somset
45 G3 **Mautby** Norfk
40 C5 **Mavesyn Ridware** Staffs
53 E2 **Mavis Enderby** Lincs
70 D4 **Mawbray** Cumb
57 E4 **Mawdesley** Lancs
26 D1 **Mawdlam** Brdgnd
2 D2 **Mawgan** Cnwll
3 E5 **Mawgan Porth** Cnwll
2 D4 **Mawla** Cnwll
2 D2 **Mawnan** Cnwll
2 D2 **Mawnan Smith** Cnwll
42 D3 **Maxey** C Pete
40 D2 **Maxstoke** Warwks
13 F6 **Maxted Street** Kent
80 C3 **Maxton** Border
13 G6 **Maxton** Kent
70 C6 **Maxwell Town** D & G
4 D6 **Maxworthy** Cnwll
49 H4 **May Bank** Staffs
76 C3 **Maybole** S Ayrs
20 D2 **Maybury** Surrey
12 B4 **Mayfield** E Susx
86 D3 **Mayfield** Mdloth
50 C2 **Mayfield** Staffs
20 C1 **Mayford** Surrey
12 B4 **Maynard's Green** E Susx
45 G2 **Maypole Green** Norfk
34 C4 **Maypole Green** Suffk
17 G4 **Meadgate** BaNES
20 B5 **Meadle** Bucks
73 F1 **Meadowfield** Dur
5 E5 **Meadwell** Devon
71 E4 **Mealrigg** Cumb
58 D4 **Meanwood** Leeds
17 F3 **Meare** Somset
17 E2 **Meare Green** Somset
16 D2 **Meare Green** Somset
85 E1 **Mearns** E Rens
32 A5 **Mears Ashby** Nhants
41 E4 **Measham** Leics
62 D4 **Meathop** Cumb
5 F4 **Meavy** Devon
42 A2 **Medbourne** Leics
51 G4 **Meden Vale** Notts
20 B4 **Medmenham** Bucks
73 E2 **Medomsley** Dur
19 H1 **Medstead** Hants
50 B3 **Meerbrook** Staffs
33 F2 **Meesden** Herts
15 E2 **Meeth** Devon
45 F4 **Meeting House Hill** Norfk
25 F4 **Meidrim** Carmth
48 B1 **Meifod** Powys
93 E4 **Meigle** P & K
77 G3 **Meikle Carco** D & G
85 F1 **Meikle Earnock** S Lans
83 H2 **Meikle Kilmory** Ag & B
92 C3 **Meikle Obney** P & K
102 C3 **Meikle Wartle** Abers
92 D3 **Meikleour** P & K
26 A4 **Meinciau** Carmth
50 B1 **Meir** C Stke
33 F3 **Melbourn** Cambs
41 E5 **Melbourne** Derbys
60 B4 **Melbourne** E R Yk
8 B5 **Melbury Abbas** Dorset
7 G6 **Melbury Bubb** Dorset
7 G6 **Melbury Osmond** Dorset
32 C5 **Melchbourne** Beds
8 A4 **Melcombe Bingham** Dorset
5 F6 **Meldon** Devon
73 E5 **Meldon** Nthumb
33 F3 **Meldreth** Cambs
85 F5 **Meldrum** Stirlg
90 A1 **Melfort** Ag & B
93 G4 **Melgund Castle** Angus
56 B1 **Meliden** Denbgs
48 A4 **Melin-y-wig** Denbgs
71 H2 **Melkinthorpe** Cumb
72 B3 **Melkridge** Nthumb
18 B3 **Melksham** Wilts
63 F3 **Melling** Lancs
56 D3 **Melling** Sefton
34 D6 **Mellis** Suffk
105 F5 **Mellon Charles** Highld
105 G5 **Mellon Udrigle** Highld
57 F5 **Mellor** Lancs
50 B5 **Mellor** Stockp
57 F5 **Mellor Brook** Lancs
17 H4 **Mells** Somset
72 A1 **Melmerby** Cumb
65 E2 **Melmerby** N York
65 G1 **Melmerby** N York
109 E5 **Melness** Highld
7 F5 **Melplash** Dorset
80 B3 **Melrose** Border
111 g1 **Melsetter** Ork
65 F4 **Melsonby** N York
58 C1 **Meltham** Kirk
60 D3 **Melton** E R Yk
35 F4 **Melton** Suffk
44 D5 **Melton Constable** Norfk
41 H5 **Melton Mowbray** Leics
60 D1 **Melton Ross** N Linc
105 F4 **Melvaig** Highld
48 D1 **Melverley** Shrops
109 H5 **Melvich** Highld
6 D5 **Membury** Devon
103 E5 **Memsie** Abers
93 F5 **Memus** Angus
54 D3 **Menai Bridge** IOA
45 F1 **Mendham** Suffk
17 F4 **Mendip Hills**
34 D5 **Mendlesham** Suffk
34 D5 **Mendlesham Green** Suffk
4 D3 **Menheniot** Cnwll
77 G2 **Mennock** D & G
58 C4 **Menston** Brad
85 G5 **Menstrie** Clacks
32 B1 **Mentmore** Bucks
97 F1 **Meoble** Highld
49 E1 **Meole Brace** Shrops
9 H5 **Meonstoke** Hants
22 B2 **Meopham** Kent
33 F6 **Mepal** Cambs
32 D2 **Meppershall** Beds
57 G1 **Mere** Ches
8 A6 **Mere** Wilts
56 D4 **Mere Brow** Lancs
57 H5 **Mereclough** Lancs
22 B1 **Mereworth** Kent
40 D2 **Meriden** Solhll
96 B5 **Merkadale** Highld
24 D2 **Merrion** Pembks
7 F6 **Merriott** Somset
20 D1 **Merrow** Surrey
21 E4 **Merry Hill** Herts
40 A3 **Merryhill** Wolves
4 D3 **Merrymeet** Cnwll
13 E5 **Mersham** Kent
21 F1 **Merstham** Surrey

Merston - Myton-on-Swale 18

10 C2 Merston W Susx
9 G2 Merstone IOW
3 E4 Merther Cnwll
27 F6 Merthyr Cynog Powys
27 E1 Merthyr Mawr Brdgnd
27 F3 Merthyr Tydfil Myr Td
27 F3 Merthyr Vale Myr Td
15 E2 Merton Devon
21 E2 Merton Gt Lon
44 C2 Merton Norfk
31 F2 Merton Oxon
15 G3 Meshaw Devon
34 C1 Messing Essex
52 B5 Messingham N Linc
35 F6 Metfield Suffk
5 E4 Metherell Cnwll
52 C2 Metheringham Lincs
86 D5 Methil Fife
86 D5 Methilhill Fife
59 E3 Methley Leeds
102 D3 Methlick Abers
92 C2 Methven P & K
44 B2 Methwold Norfk
44 A2 Methwold Hythe Norfk
45 F1 Mettingham Suffk
45 E5 Metton Norfk
3 F4 Mevagissey Cnwll
51 F6 Mexborough Donc
110 C6 Mey Highld
46 B4 Meyllteyrn Gwynd
18 D6 Meysey Hampton Gloucs
111 c6 Miabhig W Isls
111 c6 Miavaig W Isls
28 C5 Michaelchurch Herefs
28 B5 Michaelchurch Escley Herefs
16 C6 Michaelston-le-Pit V Glam
27 G1 Michaelstone-y-Fedw Newpt
4 B5 Michaelstow Cnwll
19 G1 Micheldever Hants
19 G1 Micheldever Station Hants
9 F5 Michelmersh Hants
35 E5 Mickfield Suffk
49 E6 Mickle Trafford Ches
51 F6 Micklebring Donc
66 D4 Mickleby N York
59 E3 Micklefield Leeds
21 E1 Mickleham Surrey
40 D6 Mickleover C Derb
64 D5 Mickleton Dur
30 C4 Mickleton Gloucs
59 E3 Mickletown Leeds
65 F1 Mickley N York
34 B4 Mickley Green Suffk
73 E3 Mickley Square Nthumb
103 E5 Mid Ardlaw Abers
95 E6 Mid Beltie Abers
86 B3 Mid Calder W Loth
110 C3 Mid Clyth Highld
10 B3 Mid Lavant W Susx
98 C6 Mid Mains Highld
111 l4 Mid Yell Shet
111 h3 Midbea Ork
31 F3 Middle Aston Oxon
31 E3 Middle Barton Oxon
17 F1 Middle Chinnock Somset
31 H3 Middle Claydon Bucks
29 G3 Middle Duntisbourne Gloucs
51 E4 Middle Handley Derbys
83 G4 Middle Kames Ag & B
30 C4 Middle Littleton Worcs
50 C2 Middle Mayfield Staffs
52 C4 Middle Rasen Lincs
6 A3 Middle Rocombe Devon
22 D3 Middle Stoke Medway
2 a1 Middle Town IOS
31 E4 Middle Tysoe Warwks
19 E1 Middle Wallop Hants
9 E6 Middle Winterslow Wilts
18 D1 Middle Woodford Wilts
71 E6 Middlebie D & G
92 B5 Middlebridge P & K
65 E2 Middleham N York
18 A3 Middlehill Wilts
39 E5 Middlehope Shrops
7 G6 Middlemarsh Dorset
66 B5 Middlesbrough Middsb
63 E5 Middleshaw Cumb
65 E1 Middlesmoor N York
65 F6 Middlestone Dur
58 D2 Middlestown Wakefd
80 C4 Middlethird Border
88 A3 Middleton Ag & B
50 D3 Middleton Derbys
50 D2 Middleton Derbys
34 C3 Middleton Essex
19 F1 Middleton Hants
39 E3 Middleton Herefs
58 D3 Middleton Leeds
84 D1 Middleton N Ayrs
58 C5 Middleton N York
66 D2 Middleton N York
42 A1 Middleton Nhants
43 H4 Middleton Norfk
73 E5 Middleton Nthumb
86 B6 Middleton P & K
57 H3 Middleton Rochdl
39 E4 Middleton Shrops
35 G5 Middleton Suffk
25 G2 Middleton Swans
40 C3 Middleton Warwks
31 F4 Middleton Cheney Nhants
35 G5 Middleton Moor Suffk
39 E3 Middleton on the Hill Herefs
60 D5 Middleton on the Wolds E R Yk
65 G4 Middleton One Row Darltn
65 G2 Middleton Quernhow N York
39 F4 Middleton Scriven Shrops
65 G4 Middleton St George Darltn
31 F2 Middleton Stoney Oxon
65 F4 Middleton Tyas N York
64 D5 Middleton-in-Teesdale Dur
10 C2 Middleton-on-Sea W Susx
48 C1 Middletown Powys
49 G5 Middlewich Ches
4 D4 Middlewood Cnwll
34 D4 Middlewood Green Suffk
77 E4 Middleyard E Ayrs
17 E2 Middlezoy Somset
18 A3 Midford BaNES
19 G3 Midgham W Berk
58 B3 Midgley Calder
58 D2 Midgley Wakefd
50 D6 Midhopestones Sheff
10 C4 Midhurst W Susx
80 B3 Midlem Border
83 H2 Midpark Ag & B
17 G4 Midsomer Norton BaNES
109 E5 Midtown Highld
94 D6 Migvie Abers
17 G1 Milborne Port Somset
8 A3 Milborne St Andrew Dorset
17 G1 Milborne Wick Somset
73 E4 Milbourne Nthumb
18 B5 Milbourne Wilts
64 B6 Milburn Cumb
29 E2 Milbury Heath S Glos
59 E6 Milby N York
31 E3 Milcombe Oxon
34 C3 Milden Suffk
34 A6 Mildenhall Suffk
18 D4 Mildenhall Wilts
11 E3 Mile Oak Br & H
22 D3 Mile Town Kent
44 C4 Mileham Norfk
57 H3 Miles Platting Manch
86 B4 Milesmark Fife
81 E3 Milfield Nthumb
51 E2 Milford Derbys
40 B5 Milford Staffs
10 C6 Milford Surrey
24 C3 Milford Haven Pembks
9 E3 Milford on Sea Hants
28 D3 Milkwall Gloucs
82 B2 Mill Bank Calder
50 B5 Mill Brow Stockp
20 B4 Mill End Bucks
33 E2 Mill End Herts
33 G3 Mill Green Cambs
22 B5 Mill Green Essex
42 D4 Mill Green Lincs
34 C3 Mill Green Suffk
34 D4 Mill Green Suffk
35 E4 Mill Green Suffk
21 E4 Mill Hill Gt Lon
49 H3 Mill Meece Staffs
92 B1 Mill of Drummond P & K
84 D4 Mill of Haldane W Duns
34 D5 Mill Street Suffk
7 a2 Millais Jersey
10 B5 Milland W Susx
103 E4 Millbreck Abers
102 D4 Millbrex Abers
10 B6 Millbridge Surrey
32 C3 Millbrook Beds
9 F4 Millbrook C Sotn
5 E2 Millbrook Cnwll
7 b1 Millbrook Jersey
102 D1 Millbuie Abers
107 E1 Millbuie Highld
76 D4 Millburn S Ayrs
12 D4 Millcorner E Susx
107 F3 Millcraig Highld
50 C2 Milldale Staffs
50 C4 Miller's Dale Derbys
86 D3 Millerhill Mdloth
85 F2 Millerston N Lans
38 C1 Millhalf Herefs
77 F6 Millheugh S Lans
83 G3 Millhouse Ag & B
58 D1 Millhouse Green Barns
78 D2 Millhousebridge D & G
51 E5 Millhouses Sheff
84 D2 Milliken Park Rens
60 C5 Millington E R Yk
62 B4 Millom Cumb
84 B1 Millport N Ayrs
63 F5 Millthrop Cumb
95 G6 Milltimber C Aber
101 E1 Milltown Abers
101 G1 Milltown Abers
71 F6 Milltown D & G
15 E5 Milltown Devon
95 F6 Milltown of Campfield Abers
101 E3 Milltown of Edinvillie Moray
95 E6 Milltown of Learney Abers
86 B6 Milnathort P & K
85 E3 Milngavie W Duns
58 A2 Milnrow Rochdl
63 E4 Milnthorpe Cumb
104 A1 Milovaig Highld
39 F3 Milson Shrops
22 D2 Milstead Kent
18 D2 Milston Wilts
31 G4 Milthorpe Nhants
33 F5 Milton Cambs
71 H5 Milton Cumb
68 D3 Milton D & G
70 B6 Milton D & G
40 D5 Milton Derbys
110 D4 Milton Highld
97 E6 Milton Highld
98 D5 Milton Highld
107 E1 Milton Highld
107 F3 Milton Highld
84 C3 Milton Inver
22 B3 Milton Kent
101 G5 Milton Moray
17 E5 Milton N Som
51 G4 Milton Notts
31 F3 Milton Oxon
19 G5 Milton Oxon
92 D5 Milton P & K
24 D3 Milton Pembks
17 F2 Milton Somset
84 D5 Milton Stirlg
84 D3 Milton W Duns
8 A3 Milton Abbas Dorset
5 E5 Milton Abbot Devon
86 C2 Milton Bridge Mdloth
32 B2 Milton Bryan Beds
17 G3 Milton Clevedon Somset
5 E3 Milton Combe Devon
14 D2 Milton Damerel Devon
32 C4 Milton Ernest Beds
49 E5 Milton Green Ches
19 F5 Milton Hill Oxon
32 B3 Milton Keynes M Keyn
18 D3 Milton Lilbourne Wilts
31 H5 Milton Malsor Nhants
91 G3 Milton Morenish P & K
95 E6 Milton of Auchinhove Abers
86 D5 Milton of Balgonie Fife
84 D4 Milton of Buchanan Stirlg
85 F3 Milton of Campsie E Duns
99 E6 Milton of Leys Highld
94 C5 Milton of Tullich Abers
8 A6 Milton on Stour Dorset
22 D2 Milton Regis Kent
30 D2 Milton-under-Wychwood Oxon
16 C2 Milverton Somset
30 D6 Milverton Warwks
40 B6 Milwich Staffs
83 G5 Minard Ag & B
29 F3 Minchinhampton Gloucs
16 B4 Minehead Somset
48 C4 Minera Wrexhm
18 C5 Minety Wilts
47 E5 Minffordd Gwynd
89 G5 Mingarrypark Highld
53 E2 Miningsby Lincs
4 D4 Minions Cnwll
76 C3 Minishant S Ayrs
47 G3 Minllyn Gwynd
69 E4 Minnigaff D & G
102 D5 Minnonie Abers
59 E6 Minskip N York
9 E4 Minstead Hants
10 B4 Minsted W Susx
23 E3 Minster Kent
23 G2 Minster Kent
30 D2 Minster Lovell Oxon
38 D6 Minsterley Shrops
29 E4 Minsterworth Gloucs
7 G6 Minterne Magna Dorset
52 D3 Minting Lincs
103 E4 Mintlaw Abers
80 B2 Minto Border
38 D5 Minton Shrops
70 C1 Mirehouse Cumb
58 D2 Mirfield Kirk
29 G3 Miserden Gloucs
27 F1 Miskin Rhondd
51 G6 Misson Notts
41 F2 Misterton Leics
51 H6 Misterton Notts
7 F6 Misterton Somset
35 E2 Mistley Essex
21 F2 Mitcham Gt Lon
28 C4 Mitchel Troy Mons
29 E4 Mitcheldean Gloucs
3 E4 Mitchell Cnwll
78 C2 Mitchellslacks D & G
73 F5 Mitford Nthumb
2 D4 Mithian Cnwll
31 G3 Mixbury Oxon
57 G1 Mobberley Ches
50 B1 Mobberley Staffs
38 B5 Mochdre Powys
69 E2 Mochrum D & G
12 C6 Mockbeggar Kent
70 D2 Mockerkin Cumb
5 G2 Modbury Devon
50 A1 Moddershall Staffs
54 D5 Moelfre IOA
48 C2 Moelfre Powys
78 D3 Moffat D & G
32 D4 Mogerhanger Beds
40 D5 Moira Leics
96 C3 Mol-chlach Highld
23 E1 Molash Kent
48 C5 Mold Flints
58 C2 Moldgreen Kirk
33 G2 Molehill Green Essex
60 D4 Molescroft E R Yk
32 C6 Molesworth Cambs
15 G4 Molland Devon
48 D6 Mollington Ches
31 E4 Mollington Oxon
85 F3 Mollinsburn N Lans
95 F4 Mondynes Abers
35 F4 Monewden Suffk
92 C2 Moneydie P & K
78 B2 Moniaive D & G
93 G3 Monifieth Angus
93 G3 Monikie Angus
93 E1 Monimail Fife
59 F3 Monk Fryston N York
19 H2 Monk Sherborne Hants
35 E5 Monk Soham Suffk
33 G2 Monk Street Essex
11 E4 Monk's Gate W Susx
21 E5 Monken Hadley Gt Lon
39 F1 Monkhide Herefs
71 F5 Monkhill Cumb
39 F5 Monkhopton Shrops
39 E2 Monkland Herefs
14 D3 Monkleigh Devon
16 B5 Monknash V Glam
15 E2 Monkokehampton Devon
34 C3 Monks Eleigh Suffk
49 H6 Monks Heath Ches
13 F5 Monks Horton Kent
41 F2 Monks Kirby Warwks
73 G4 Monkseaton N Tyne
16 C3 Monksilver Somset
53 F2 Monksthorpe Lincs
28 B3 Monkswood Mons
6 D5 Monkton Devon
23 G2 Monkton Kent
76 C4 Monkton S Ayrs
73 G3 Monkton S Tyne
18 A3 Monkton Combe BaNES
18 B1 Monkton Deverill Wilts
18 A3 Monkton Farleigh Wilts
16 D2 Monkton Heathfield Somset
7 E5 Monkton Wyld Dorset
73 G3 Monkwearmouth Sundld
9 H6 Monkwood Hants
40 A3 Monmore Green Wolves
28 C4 Monmouth Mons
38 D1 Monnington on Wye Herefs
69 E2 Monreith D & G
6 b1 Mont Saint Guern
17 F1 Montacute Somset
48 D1 Montford Shrops
48 D1 Montford Bridge Shrops
102 B2 Montgarrie Abers
77 E4 Montgarswood E Ayrs
38 C5 Montgomery Powys
76 C5 Montgreenan N Ayrs
95 F2 Montrose Angus
9 E1 Monxton Hants
50 C3 Monyash Derbys
102 C1 Monymusk Abers
92 B2 Monzie P & K
85 F3 Moodiesburn N Lans
93 F1 Moonzie Fife
58 D4 Moor Allerton Leeds
8 C4 Moor Crichel Dorset
58 B3 Moor End Calder
59 F5 Moor Monkton N York
53 E2 Moorby Lincs
8 D3 Moordown Bmouth
57 F1 Moore Halton
59 G2 Moorends Donc
51 F2 Moorgreen Notts
58 C4 Moorhead Brad
71 F5 Moorhouse Cumb
51 H3 Moorhouse Notts
21 G1 Moorhouse Bank Surrey
17 E3 Moorlinch Somset
66 C4 Moorsholm R & Cl
8 A5 Moorside Dorset
4 C3 Moorswater Cnwll
59 F1 Moorthorpe Wakefd
58 D4 Moortown Leeds
52 C5 Moortown Lincs
107 F4 Morangie Highld
97 E2 Morar Highld
42 D2 Morborne Cambs
15 G2 Morchard Bishop Devon
7 E5 Morcombelake Dorset
42 B2 Morcott Rutlnd
48 C2 Morda Shrops
8 B3 Morden Dorset
21 E2 Morden Gt Lon
28 D6 Mordiford Herefs
65 G5 Mordon Dur
38 D5 More Shrops
16 B2 Morebath Devon
80 D3 Morebattle Border
62 D3 Morecambe Lancs
18 D5 Moredon Swindn
106 A5 Morefield Highld
13 G5 Morehall Kent
5 G2 Moreleigh Devon
91 G3 Morenish P & K
70 D2 Moresby Cumb
9 G5 Morestead Hants
8 A2 Moreton Dorset
21 H5 Moreton Essex
39 E3 Moreton Herefs
20 A5 Moreton Oxon
56 C2 Moreton Wirral
49 E2 Moreton Corbet Shrops
39 F1 Moreton Jeffries Herefs
30 D5 Moreton Morrell Warwks
39 E1 Moreton on Lugg Herefs
31 F5 Moreton Pinkney Nhants
49 F3 Moreton Say Shrops
29 E4 Moreton Valence Gloucs
30 D3 Moreton-in-Marsh Gloucs
5 G5 Moretonhampstead Devon
46 C5 Morfa Nefyn Gwynd
87 E3 Morham E Loth
64 A5 Morland Cumb
57 G1 Morley Ches
51 E1 Morley Derbys
58 D3 Morley Leeds
57 G1 Morley Green Ches
44 D2 Morley St Botolph Norfk
86 C3 Morningside C Edin
85 G1 Morningside N Lans
45 E2 Morningthorpe Norfk
73 F5 Morpeth Nthumb
95 F3 Morphie Abers
40 C5 Morrey Staffs
26 C3 Morriston Swans
44 D6 Morston Norfk
14 D5 Mortehoe Devon
51 F5 Morthen Rothm
19 H3 Mortimer W Berk
19 H3 Mortimer West End Hants
21 E3 Mortlake Gt Lon
71 G4 Morton Cumb
51 E3 Morton Derbys
52 A4 Morton Lincs
42 C4 Morton Lincs
51 H2 Morton Notts
48 C2 Morton Shrops
45 E4 Morton on the Hill Norfk
65 G3 Morton-on-Swale N York
2 A3 Morvah Cnwll
4 D3 Morval Cnwll
97 G4 Morvich Highld
39 F5 Morville Shrops
5 E4 Morwellham Quay Devon
14 B3 Morwenstow Cnwll
51 E4 Mosborough Sheff
76 D5 Moscow E Ayrs
40 C2 Moseley Birm
40 B3 Moseley Wolves
39 G2 Moseley Worcs
88 A3 Moss Ag & B
59 G2 Moss Donc
57 E3 Moss Bank St Hel
62 D1 Moss Edge Lancs
56 C3 Moss Side Sefton
100 B5 Moss-side Highld
101 G2 Mossat Abers
111 l3 Mossbank Shet
70 D2 Mossbay Cumb
76 D4 Mossblown S Ayrs
80 C2 Mossburnford Border
69 G4 Mossdale D & G
76 D2 Mossdale E Ayrs
85 F2 Mossend N Lans
50 B6 Mossley Tamesd
79 G3 Mosspaul Hotel Border
101 F5 Mosstodloch Moray
57 E4 Mossy Lea Lancs
69 F3 Mossyard D & G
7 F6 Mosterton Dorset
57 H3 Moston Manch
56 B1 Mostyn Flints
8 B5 Motcombe Dorset
5 F2 Mothecombe Devon
71 G2 Motherby Cumb
85 F2 Motherwell N Lans
21 E2 Motspur Park Gt Lon
21 G3 Mottingham Gt Lon
9 E5 Mottisfont Hants
9 F2 Mottistone IOW
50 B6 Mottram in Longdendale Tamesd
57 H1 Mottram St Andrew Ches
6 b1 Mouilpied Guern
49 E6 Mouldsworth Ches
92 C5 Moulin P & K
11 F3 Moulsecoomb Br & H
19 G5 Moulsford Oxon
32 B3 Moulsoe M Keyn
107 E3 Moultavie Highld
49 F6 Moulton Ches
43 E4 Moulton Lincs
65 F4 Moulton N York
32 A5 Moulton Nhants
34 A5 Moulton Suffk
16 C5 Moulton V Glam
43 E4 Moulton Chapel Lincs
43 E4 Moulton Seas End Lincs
45 G3 Moulton St Mary Norfk
4 C4 Mount Cnwll
2 D3 Mount Ambrose Cnwll
34 C2 Mount Bures Essex
2 D4 Mount Hawke Cnwll
86 C2 Mount Lothian Mdloth
51 E2 Mount Pleasant Derbys
34 B3 Mount Pleasant Suffk
58 B3 Mount Tabor Calder
58 C3 Mountain Brad
27 F3 Mountain Ash Rhondd
86 B1 Mountain Cross Border
12 C4 Mountfield E Susx
107 E2 Mountgerald House Highld
3 E5 Mountjoy Cnwll
22 B5 Mountnessing Essex
28 C2 Mounton Mons
41 F4 Mountsorrel Leics
10 C6 Mousehill Surrey
2 B2 Mousehole Cnwll
70 D6 Mouswald D & G
80 D2 Mowhaugh Border
41 G2 Mowsley Leics
95 G5 Mowtie Abers
99 F5 Moy Highld
98 C1 Moy Highld
97 F4 Moye Highld
36 A2 Moylgrove Pembks
75 E5 Muasdale Ag & B
28 C5 Much Birch Herefs
39 F1 Much Cowarne Herefs
28 C5 Much Dewchurch Herefs
33 F1 Much Hadham Herts
57 E5 Much Hoole Lancs
28 D5 Much Marcle Herefs
39 F5 Much Wenlock Shrops
95 G5 Muchalls Abers
17 E2 Muchelney Somset
17 F2 Muchelney Ham Somset
4 C3 Muchlarnick Cnwll
44 D6 Mucklebrugh Collection Norfk
49 G3 Mucklestone Staffs
53 F3 Muckton Lincs
15 E4 Muddiford Devon
12 A3 Muddles Green E Susx
8 D3 Mudeford Dorset
17 G1 Mudford Somset
17 F1 Mudford Sock Somset
85 E3 Mugdock Stirlg
96 C6 Mugeary Highld
50 D1 Mugginton Derbys
102 B1 Muir of Fowlis Abers
101 E5 Muir of Miltonduff Moray
107 E1 Muir of Ord Highld
92 C3 Muir of Thorn P & K
102 C4 Muirden Abers
93 G3 Muirdrum Angus
102 C4 Muiresk Abers
93 F3 Muirhead Angus
86 C6 Muirhead Fife
85 F3 Muirhead N Lans
77 F4 Muirkirk E Ayrs
85 F4 Muirmill Stirlg
98 A1 Muirshearlich Highld
103 E3 Muirtack Abers
85 H6 Muirton P & K
106 D2 Muirton Mains Highld
92 D3 Muirton of Ardblair P & K
64 D3 Muker N York
45 E2 Mulbarton Norfk
101 F4 Mulben Moray
89 F3 Mull Ag & B
2 D1 Mullion Cnwll
2 C1 Mullion Cove Cnwll
53 G3 Mumby Lincs
39 F2 Munderfield Row Herefs
39 F1 Munderfield Stocks Herefs
45 F5 Mundesley Norfk
44 B2 Mundford Norfk
45 F2 Mundham Norfk
22 D5 Mundon Hill Essex
71 F2 Mungrisdale Cumb
107 E2 Munlochy Highld
76 C6 Munnoch N Ayrs
29 E6 Munsley Herefs
39 E4 Munslow Shrops
5 G5 Murchington Devon
31 G2 Murcott Oxon
110 B5 Murkle Highld
97 G2 Murlaggan Highld
93 G3 Murroes Angus
43 F3 Murrow Cambs
32 A2 Mursley Bucks
93 G5 Murthill Angus
92 D3 Murthly P & K
64 B5 Murton Cumb
73 G2 Murton Dur
81 E4 Murton Nthumb
59 G5 Murton York
6 D5 Musbury Devon
86 D3 Musselburgh E Loth
42 A5 Muston Leics
67 G2 Muston N York
21 F4 Muswell Hill Gt Lon
69 G3 Mutehill D & G
45 G1 Mutford Suffk
92 B1 Muthill P & K
110 B4 Mybster Highld
26 D5 Myddfai Carmth
49 E2 Myddle Shrops
36 D2 Mydroilyn Cerdgn
3 E3 Mylor Cnwll
3 E3 Mylor Bridge Cnwll
25 E5 Mynachlog ddu Pembks
38 D5 Myndtown Shrops
28 C2 Mynydd-bach Mons
26 C3 Mynydd-Bach Swans
95 F5 Myrebird Abers
72 A6 Myredykes Border
20 C1 Mytchett Surrey
58 B3 Mytholm Calder
58 B3 Mytholmroyd Calder
59 E6 Myton-on-Swale N York

N

111 c5 Na Buirgh W Isls
105 F4 Naast Highld
59 G4 Naburn York
23 F1 Nackington Kent
35 E3 Nacton Suffk
60 D5 Nafferton E R Yk
16 D2 Nailsbourne Somset
17 F5 Nailsea N Som
41 E4 Nailstone Leics
29 F3 Nailsworth Gloucs
100 B5 Nairn Highld
48 B6 Nannerch Flints
41 F5 Nanpantan Leics
3 F4 Nanpean Cnwll
3 F5 Nanstallon Cnwll
54 D2 Nant Peris Gwynd
27 E2 Nant-y-moel Brdgnd
36 C3 Nanternis Cerdgn
26 B4 Nantgaredig Carmth
55 H3 Nantglyn Denbgs
38 A3 Nantmel Powys
47 E5 Nantmor Gwynd
49 F4 Nantwich Ches
27 G4 Nantyglo Blae G
20 B5 Naphill Bucks
31 F6 Napton on the Hill Warwks
25 E4 Narberth Pembks
41 F3 Narborough Leics
44 B3 Narborough Norfk
54 C2 Nasareth Gwynd
41 G2 Naseby Nhants
32 A2 Nash Bucks
28 B1 Nash Newpt
39 F3 Nash Shrops
19 H2 Nash's Green Hants
42 C2 Nassington Nhants
64 C4 Nateby Cumb
63 E1 Nateby Lancs
5 F2 National Shire Horse Centre Devon
41 G4 National Space Science Centre C Leic
63 E5 Natland Cumb
34 D3 Naughton Suffk
30 C2 Naunton Gloucs
29 F6 Naunton Worcs
30 B5 Naunton Beauchamp Worcs
52 C2 Navenby Lincs
21 H5 Navestock Essex
22 B5 Navestock Side Essex
110 A1 Navidale House Hotel Highld
107 G3 Navity Highld
66 C2 Nawton N York
34 C2 Nayland Suffk
21 G5 Nazeing Essex
111 I2 Neap Shet
50 C2 Near Cotton Staffs
62 D5 Near Sawrey Cumb
21 E4 Neasden Gt Lon
65 G4 Neasham Darltn
26 D3 Neath Neath
10 B5 Neatham Hants
45 F4 Neatishead Norfk
37 E3 Nebo Cerdgn
55 F2 Nebo Conwy
54 C2 Nebo Gwynd
54 C5 Nebo IOA
44 C3 Necton Norfk
108 B3 Nedd Highld
34 D3 Nedging Suffk
34 D4 Nedging Tye Suffk
35 E6 Needham Norfk
34 D4 Needham Market Suffk
33 E5 Needingworth Cambs
39 F4 Neen Savage Shrops
39 F3 Neen Sollars Shrops
39 F4 Neenton Shrops
46 C5 Nefyn Gwynd
84 D2 Neilston E Rens
27 F2 Nelson Caerph
57 H6 Nelson Lancs
77 G5 Nemphlar S Lans
17 F5 Nempnett Thrubwell BaNES
72 C1 Nenthead Cumb
80 C4 Nenthorn Border
48 C5 Nercwys Flints
82 B1 Nereabolls Ag & B
85 F2 Nerston S Lans
81 E3 Nesbit Nthumb
58 C5 Nesfield N York
48 C6 Ness Botanic Gardens Ches
48 D2 Nesscliffe Shrops
56 C1 Neston Ches
18 B3 Neston Wilts
39 F5 Netchwood Shrops
49 H6 Nether Alderley Ches
80 B4 Nether Blainslie Border
41 G5 Nether Broughton Notts
7 G5 Nether Cerne Dorset
17 G1 Nether Compton Dorset
102 D2 Nether Crimond Abers
101 F5 Nether Dallachy Moray
6 B5 Nether Exe Devon
78 C4 Nether Fingland S Lans
93 F3 Nether Handwick Angus
51 E6 Nether Haugh Rothm
51 H4 Nether Headon Notts
51 E2 Nether Heage Derbys
31 G5 Nether Heyford Nhants
78 D4 Nether Howcleugh S Lans
63 E3 Nether Kellet Lancs
103 F4 Nether Kinmundy Abers
51 F4 Nether Langwith Notts
51 E3 Nether Moor Derbys
50 D4 Nether Padley Derbys
59 F5 Nether Poppleton York
66 B3 Nether Silton N York
16 D3 Nether Stowey Somset
19 E1 Nether Wallop Hants
62 B6 Nether Wasdale Cumb
30 D2 Nether Westcote Gloucs
40 D3 Nether Whitacre Warwks
78 B4 Nether Whitecleuch S Lans
31 H2 Nether Winchendon Bucks
18 D2 Netheravon Wilts
102 D5 Netherbrae Abers
77 G6 Netherburn S Lans
7 F5 Netherbury Dorset
59 E4 Netherby N York
79 E2 Nethercleuch D & G
28 D3 Netherend Gloucs
12 C4 Netherfield E Susx
12 C4 Netherfield Road E Susx
8 D6 Netherhampton Wilts
7 E6 Netherhay Dorset
70 B4 Netherlaw D & G
95 G5 Netherley Abers
78 D2 Nethermill D & G
103 E4 Nethermuir Abers
85 E1 Netherplace E Rens
40 D4 Netherseal Derbys
58 C1 Netherthong Kirk
93 G5 Netherton Angus
6 A3 Netherton Devon
40 B2 Netherton Dudley
85 G1 Netherton N Lans
81 E1 Netherton Nthumb
92 D4 Netherton P & K
39 G4 Netherton Shrops
85 E3 Netherton Stirlg
58 D2 Netherton Wakefd
62 A6 Nethertown Cumb
110 D6 Nethertown Highld
40 C5 Nethertown Staffs
86 B1 Netherurd Border
73 E5 Netherwitton Nthumb
99 H4 Nethy Bridge Highld
9 F4 Netley Hants
9 E4 Netley Marsh Hants
20 A4 Nettlebed Oxon
17 G4 Nettlebridge Somset
7 F5 Nettlecombe Dorset
20 D6 Nettleden Herts
52 C3 Nettleham Lincs
22 B1 Nettlestead Kent
22 B1 Nettlestead Green Kent
9 H3 Nettlestone IOW
73 F2 Nettlesworth Dur
52 D5 Nettleton Lincs
18 A4 Nettleton Wilts
18 D1 Netton Wilts
36 A1 Nevern Pembks
42 A2 Nevill Holt Leics
70 C5 New Abbey D & G
103 E5 New Aberdour Abers
21 F2 New Addington Gt Lon
9 G6 New Alresford Hants
93 E4 New Alyth P & K
22 B2 New Ash Green Kent
52 A1 New Balderton Notts
22 B2 New Barn Kent
21 F5 New Barnet Gt Lon
81 F2 New Bewick Nthumb
41 F1 New Bilton Warwks
53 E1 New Bolingbroke Lincs
52 B3 New Boultham Lincs
32 A3 New Bradwell M Keyn
51 E4 New Brampton Derbys
73 F1 New Brancepeth Dur
56 C2 New Brighton Wirral
44 D1 New Buckenham Norfk
102 D4 New Byth Abers
45 E3 New Costessey Norfk
59 E2 New Crofton Wakefd
21 F3 New Cross Gt Lon
17 E1 New Cross Somset
77 E3 New Cumnock E Ayrs
103 E4 New Deer Abers
20 D4 New Denham Bucks
31 H6 New Duston Nhants
59 G5 New Earswick York
51 F6 New Edlington Donc
101 E5 New Elgin Moray
61 E4 New Ellerby E R Yk
21 G3 New Eltham Gt Lon
30 B5 New End Worcs
42 D2 New England C Pete
42 D2 New Fletton C Pete
9 E4 New Forest Hants
69 G5 New Galloway D & G
87 E6 New Gilston Fife
2 a2 New Grimsby IOS
73 G4 New Hartley Nthumb
20 D2 New Haw Surrey
44 C5 New Holkham Norfk
61 E2 New Holland N Linc
51 F3 New Houghton Derbys
44 B4 New Houghton Norfk
63 E5 New Hutton Cumb
26 B6 New Inn Carmth
28 B3 New Inn Torfn
38 C4 New Invention Shrops
78 C6 New Lanark S Lans
79 F1 New Langholm D & G
53 F1 New Leake Lincs
103 E5 New Leeds Abers
59 E1 New Lodge Barns
57 E5 New Longton Lancs
68 D4 New Luce D & G
21 E2 New Malden Gt Lon
66 C5 New Marske R & Cl
31 F1 New Marston Oxon
95 G4 New Mill Abers
2 B3 New Mill Cnwll
58 C1 New Mill Kirk
3 E4 New Mills Cnwll
50 B5 New Mills Derbys
38 B6 New Mills Powys
9 E3 New Milton Hants
35 E2 New Mistley Essex
25 E5 New Moat Pembks
51 G3 New Ollerton Notts
103 E5 New Pitsligo Abers
76 C4 New Prestwick S Ayrs
36 C3 New Quay Cerdgn
45 F3 New Rackheath Norfk
38 C2 New Radnor Powys
73 E3 New Ridley Nthumb
13 E4 New Romney Kent
51 G6 New Rossington Donc
85 G5 New Sauchie Clacks
59 E2 New Sharlston Wakefd
73 G2 New Silksworth Sundld
42 B5 New Somerby Lincs
85 F2 New Stevenston N Lans
32 D3 New Town Beds
8 B5 New Town Dorset
8 C5 New Town Dorset
87 E3 New Town E Loth
11 G4 New Town E Susx
27 G3 New Tredegar Caerph
77 G5 New Trows S Lans
43 F3 New Walsoken Cambs
53 E5 New Waltham NE Lin
87 E3 New Winton E Loth
53 E1 New York Lincs
58 D4 Newall Leeds
111 j3 Newark Ork
52 A1 Newark-on-Trent Notts
85 G2 Newarthill N Lans
86 D3 Newbattle Mdloth
71 E5 Newbie D & G
71 G2 Newbiggin Cumb
71 H4 Newbiggin Cumb
64 A6 Newbiggin Cumb
64 D5 Newbiggin Dur
64 D2 Newbiggin N York
73 G5 Newbiggin-by-the-Sea Nthumb
63 G6 Newbiggin-on-Lune Cumb
93 E3 Newbigging Angus
93 F3 Newbigging Angus
93 G3 Newbigging Angus
86 A1 Newbigging S Lans
51 E4 Newbold Derbys
41 F1 Newbold on Avon Warwks
30 D4 Newbold on Stour Warwks
30 D5 Newbold Pacey Warwks
41 E4 Newbold Verdon Leics
42 D3 Newborough C Pete
54 C3 Newborough IOA
40 C5 Newborough Staffs
35 F3 Newbourne Suffk
86 B3 Newbridge C Edin
27 G3 Newbridge Caerph
2 B2 Newbridge Cnwll
78 C1 Newbridge D & G
9 E5 Newbridge Hants
9 F2 Newbridge IOW
29 F6 Newbridge Green Worcs
38 A2 Newbridge on Wye Powys
72 C3 Newbrough Nthumb
15 G2 Newbuildings Devon
103 E5 Newburgh Abers
103 E2 Newburgh Abers
93 E1 Newburgh Fife
57 E4 Newburgh Lancs
66 B1 Newburgh Priory N York
73 F3 Newburn N u Ty
17 H4 Newbury Somset
19 F3 Newbury W Berk
21 G4 Newbury Park Gt Lon
64 A5 Newby Cumb
63 G1 Newby Lancs
66 B4 Newby N York
63 G3 Newby N York
62 D4 Newby Bridge Cumb
71 G5 Newby East Cumb
71 F4 Newby West Cumb
65 G2 Newby Wiske N York
28 C4 Newcastle Mons
38 C4 Newcastle Shrops
73 F4 Newcastle Airport Nthumb
36 C1 Newcastle Emlyn Carmth
73 F3 Newcastle upon Tyne N u Ty
49 H4 Newcastle-under-Lyme Staffs
79 G2 Newcastleton Border
36 B1 Newchapel Pembks
11 F6 Newchapel Surrey
9 G2 Newchurch IOW
13 E5 Newchurch Kent
28 C3 Newchurch Mons
38 C1 Newchurch Powys
40 C5 Newchurch Staffs
86 D3 Newcraighall C Edin
11 E6 Newdigate Surrey
20 C3 Newell Green Br For
12 D4 Newenden Kent
29 E5 Newent Gloucs
65 F6 Newfield Dur
107 G3 Newfield Highld
24 C5 Newgale Pembks
21 F5 Newgate Street Herts
49 F4 Newhall Ches
11 G2 Newhaven E Susx
67 E4 Newholm N York
85 G2 Newhouse N Lans
11 G4 Newick E Susx
22 D2 Newington Kent
13 F5 Newington Kent
19 H6 Newington Oxon
60 D3 Newland C KuH
28 D4 Newland Gloucs
59 G3 Newland N York
15 G4 Newland Somset
39 G1 Newland Worcs
86 D2 Newlandrig Mdloth
79 H2 Newlands Border
73 E2 Newlands Nthumb
101 F4 Newlands of Dundurcas Moray
2 B2 Newlyn Cnwll
3 E4 Newlyn East Cnwll
103 E2 Newmachar Abers
85 G2 Newmains N Lans
34 C3 Newman's Green Suffk
33 H5 Newmarket Suffk
111 d6 Newmarket W Isls
79 G4 Newmill Border
101 G4 Newmill Moray
94 D2 Newmill of Inshewan Angus
59 E2 Newmillerdam Wakefd
86 C3 Newmills C Edin
86 A4 Newmills Fife
28 C3 Newmills Mons
92 D2 Newmiln P & K
77 E5 Newmilns E Ayrs
22 B5 Newney Green Essex
29 E4 Newnham Gloucs
20 A1 Newnham Hants
33 E3 Newnham Herts
23 E1 Newnham Kent
31 F5 Newnham Nhants
39 F3 Newnham Worcs
4 D5 Newport Cnwll
15 E4 Newport Devon
60 C3 Newport E R Yk
33 G2 Newport Essex
29 E3 Newport Gloucs
110 B2 Newport Highld
9 G2 Newport IOW
28 B2 Newport Newpt
25 E6 Newport Pembks
49 G2 Newport Wrekin
32 B3 Newport Pagnell M Keyn
93 F2 Newport-on-Tay Fife
3 E5 Newquay Cnwll
3 E5 Newquay Airport Cnwll
102 C3 Newseat Abers
57 E6 Newsham Lancs
65 E4 Newsham N York
65 G2 Newsham N York
73 G4 Newsham Nthumb
60 B3 Newsholme E R Yk
80 B3 Newstead Border
51 F2 Newstead Notts
81 G3 Newstead Nthumb
101 G4 Newtack Moray
59 F3 Newthorpe N York
51 F2 Newthorpe Notts
83 H5 Newton Ag & B
32 D3 Newton Beds
80 C2 Newton Border
26 D1 Newton Brdgnd
43 F3 Newton Cambs
33 F4 Newton Cambs
48 D6 Newton Ches
49 E5 Newton Ches
62 C3 Newton Cumb
51 E3 Newton Derbys
28 B5 Newton Herefs
39 E2 Newton Herefs
107 E1 Newton Highld
107 F1 Newton Highld
107 G2 Newton Highld
107 F3 Newton Highld
63 F1 Newton Lancs
42 C5 Newton Lincs
86 D3 Newton Mdloth
100 D5 Newton Moray
101 F5 Newton Moray
42 B1 Newton Nhants
44 B3 Newton Norfk
51 G1 Newton Notts
73 E3 Newton Nthumb
85 F2 Newton S Lans
78 C5 Newton S Lans
16 C3 Newton Somset
40 B5 Newton Staffs
34 C3 Newton Suffk
86 B4 Newton W Loth
41 F2 Newton Warwks
6 A3 Newton Abbot Devon
71 E4 Newton Arlosh Cumb
65 F5 Newton Aycliffe Dur
66 B5 Newton Bewley Hartpl
32 B4 Newton Blossomville M Keyn
32 C5 Newton Bromswold Beds
41 E4 Newton Burgoland Leics
52 C4 Newton by Toft Lincs
4 D3 Newton Ferrers Cnwll
5 F2 Newton Ferrers Devon
111 b4 Newton Ferry W Isls
45 E2 Newton Flotman Norfk
41 G3 Newton Harcourt Leics
57 H3 Newton Heath Manch
59 F4 Newton Kyme N York
32 B2 Newton Longville Bucks
85 E1 Newton Mearns E Rens
65 F4 Newton Morrell N York
92 D1 Newton of Balcanquhal P & K
87 E6 Newton of Balcormo Fife
59 F5 Newton on Ouse N York
52 A3 Newton on Trent Lincs
6 C4 Newton Poppleford Devon
31 G3 Newton Purcell Oxon
40 D4 Newton Regis Warwks
71 G3 Newton Reigny Cumb
110 D4 Newton Row Highld
40 D5 Newton Solney Derbys
15 H1 Newton St Cyres Devon
45 E4 Newton St Faith Norfk
17 H5 Newton St Loe BaNES
14 D2 Newton St Petrock Devon
19 F1 Newton Stacey Hants
69 E4 Newton Stewart D & G
19 E1 Newton Toney Wilts
15 E4 Newton Tracey Devon
66 B4 Newton under Roseberry R & Cl
60 B5 Newton upon Derwent E R Yk
10 A5 Newton Valence Hants
78 D2 Newton Wamphray D & G
57 E5 Newton with Scales Lancs
81 G3 Newton-by-the-Sea Nthumb
65 F2 Newton-le-Willows N York
57 F2 Newton-le-Willows St Hel
66 D2 Newton-on-Rawcliffe N York
81 G1 Newton-on-the-Moor Nthumb
102 B3 Newtongarry Croft Abers
86 D3 Newtongrange Mdloth
95 G5 Newtonhill Abers
86 D2 Newtonloan Mdloth
95 E3 Newtonmill Angus
99 E3 Newtonmore Highld
49 F4 Newtown Ches
50 A3 Newtown Ches
70 D4 Newtown Cumb
71 G5 Newtown Cumb
77 G3 Newtown D & G
6 C5 Newtown Devon
15 G3 Newtown Devon
29 E3 Newtown Gloucs
9 H4 Newtown Hants
39 F1 Newtown Herefs
29 E6 Newtown Herefs
98 C3 Newtown Highld
9 F3 Newtown IOW
73 E6 Newtown Nthumb
81 F3 Newtown Nthumb
8 C3 Newtown Poole
38 B5 Newtown Powys
48 D2 Newtown Shrops
49 E3 Newtown Shrops
6 D6 Newtown Somset
57 E3 Newtown Wigan
39 H2 Newtown Worcs
41 F4 Newtown Linford Leics
84 C2 Newtown of Beltrees Rens
80 B3 Newtown St Boswells Border
93 E3 Newtyle Angus
83 G6 Newyork Ag & B
24 D3 Neyland Pembks
16 C1 Nicholashayne Devon
26 B2 Nicholaston Swans
58 D5 Nidd N York
95 H6 Nigg C Aber
107 G3 Nigg Highld
16 A2 Nightcott Somset
18 D5 Nine Elms Swindn
72 C2 Ninebanks Nthumb
39 F3 Nineveh Worcs
12 C3 Ninfield E Susx
9 F2 Ningwood IOW
80 C3 Nisbet Border
80 D5 Nisbet Hill Border
9 G1 Niton IOW
85 E2 Nitshill C Glas
49 E4 No Man's Heath Ches
40 D4 No Man's Heath Warwks
52 C2 Nocton Lincs
31 F2 Noke Oxon
24 C4 Nolton Pembks
24 C4 Nolton Haven Pembks
15 G2 Nomansland Devon
9 E5 Nomansland Wilts
49 E2 Noneley Shrops
23 G1 Nonington Kent
63 E4 Nook Cumb
21 E2 Norbiton Gt Lon
49 E4 Norbury Ches
50 C1 Norbury Derbys
21 F2 Norbury Gt Lon
38 D5 Norbury Shrops
49 G2 Norbury Staffs
39 H3 Norchard Worcs
43 G2 Nordelph Norfk
39 F5 Nordley Shrops
45 G3 Norfolk Broads Norfk
81 E4 Norham Nthumb
58 C2 Norland Town Calder
49 E6 Norley Ches
9 F3 Norleywood Hants
6 C5 Norman's Green Devon
52 C4 Normanby Lincs
60 C2 Normanby N Linc
66 D2 Normanby N York
66 B5 Normanby R & Cl
52 D4 Normanby le Wold Lincs
20 C1 Normandy Surrey
41 E6 Normanton C Derb
42 A6 Normanton Leics
42 B6 Normanton Lincs
51 G2 Normanton Notts
59 E2 Normanton Wakefd
41 E4 Normanton le Heath Leics
41 F5 Normanton on Soar Notts
41 G6 Normanton on the Wolds Notts
52 A2 Normanton on Trent Notts
10 C6 Norney Surrey
51 F5 North Anston Rothm
31 F3 North Aston Oxon
9 F5 North Baddesley Hants
90 C5 North Ballachulish Highld
17 G2 North Barrow Somset
44 C5 North Barsham Norfk
22 C4 North Benfleet Essex
10 C2 North Bersted W Susx
87 E4 North Berwick E Loth
9 G4 North Boarhunt Hants
5 G5 North Bovey Devon
18 B2 North Bradley Wilts
5 E5 North Brentor Devon
17 H3 North Brewham Somset
14 D5 North Buckland Devon
45 G3 North Burlingham Norfk
17 G2 North Cadbury Somset
52 B3 North Carlton Lincs
51 G5 North Carlton Notts
60 C3 North Cave E R Yk
30 B1 North Cerney Gloucs
11 G4 North Chailey E Susx
8 D5 North Charford Hants
81 G2 North Charlton Nthumb
21 E2 North Cheam Gt Lon
17 H2 North Cheriton Somset
7 E5 North Chideock Dorset
60 C4 North Cliffe E R Yk
52 A3 North Clifton Notts
53 F4 North Cockerington Lincs
90 B2 North Connel Ag & B
26 D1 North Cornelly Brdgnd
90 A4 North Corry Highld
53 E5 North Cotes Lincs
45 G1 North Cove Suffk
65 F4 North Cowton N York
32 B3 North Crawley M Keyn
44 C5 North Creake Norfk
17 E2 North Curry Somset
60 C5 North Dalton E R Yk
59 E5 North Deighton N York
22 D1 North Downs
59 G4 North Duffield N York
104 C3 North Duntulm Highld
13 F6 North Elham Kent
44 D4 North Elmham Norfk
59 F2 North Elmsall Wakefd
9 H3 North End C Port
33 H1 North End Essex
8 D5 North End Hants
32 B5 North End Nhants
10 C3 North End W Susx
105 F4 North Erradale Highld
41 G4 North Evington C Leic
22 D5 North Fambridge Essex
60 D3 North Ferriby E R Yk
61 E5 North Frodingham E R Yk
8 D4 North Gorley Hants
35 F5 North Green Suffk
60 C6 North Grimston N York
10 A2 North Hayling Hants
4 D4 North Hill Cnwll
20 D4 North Hillingdon Gt Lon
31 F1 North Hinksey Oxon
11 E6 North Holmwood Surrey
5 G3 North Huish Devon
52 B2 North Hykeham Lincs
52 C5 North Kelsey Lincs
107 F1 North Kessock Highld
61 E2 North Killingholme N Linc
65 H2 North Kilvington N York
41 G2 North Kilworth Leics
52 D1 North Kyme Lincs
67 H1 North Landing E R Yk
20 B6 North Lee Bucks
31 E2 North Leigh Oxon
52 A3 North Leverton with Habblesthorpe Notts
30 C4 North Littleton Worcs
44 D1 North Lopham Norfk
42 B2 North Luffenham Rutlnd

North Marden - Parham 183

10 B4 **North Marden** W Susx
31 H2 **North Marston** Bucks
86 D2 **North Middleton** Mdloth
68 C3 **North Milmain** D & G
15 F4 **North Molton** Devon
19 G5 **North Moreton** Oxon
10 C2 **North Mundham** W Susx
52 A2 **North Muskham** Notts
60 C4 **North Newbald** E R Yk
31 E4 **North Newington** Oxon
18 D3 **North Newnton** Wilts
17 E2 **North Newton** Somset
29 E2 **North Nibley** Gloucs
66 B5 **North Ormesby** Middsb
53 E4 **North Ormsby** Lincs
65 G2 **North Otterington** N York
52 C4 **North Owersby** Lincs
7 F6 **North Perrott** Somset
16 D2 **North Petherton** Somset
4 D5 **North Petherwin** Cnwll
44 C3 **North Pickenham** Norfk
30 B5 **North Piddle** Worcs
5 H1 **North Pool** Devon
7 F5 **North Poorton** Dorset
16 B3 **North Quarme** Somset
86 B4 **North Queensferry** C Edin
15 G4 **North Radworthy** Devon
42 C6 **North Rauceby** Lincs
53 F4 **North Reston** Lincs
58 D5 **North Rigton** N York
50 A3 **North Rode** Ches
111 j3 North Ronaldsay Airport Ork
43 H4 **North Runcton** Norfk
52 B2 **North Scarle** Lincs
90 B3 **North Shian** Ag & B
73 G3 **North Shields** N Tyne
22 D4 **North Shoebury** Sthend
56 C6 **North Shore** Bpool
43 E2 **North Side** C Pete
53 F5 **North Somercotes** Lincs
65 F1 **North Stainley** N York
22 B3 **North Stifford** Thurr
17 H5 **North Stoke** BaNES
19 H5 **North Stoke** Oxon
10 D3 **North Stoke** W Susx
23 E2 **North Street** Kent
19 H4 **North Street** W Berk
81 G3 **North Sunderland** Nthumb
14 C1 **North Tamerton** Cnwll
15 F2 **North Tawton** Devon
85 F4 **North Third** Stirlg
53 E5 **North Thoresby** Lincs
19 E2 **North Tidworth** Wilts
15 E2 **North Town** Devon
17 G3 **North Town** Somset
20 C3 **North Town** W & M
44 D3 **North Tuddenham** Norfk
45 F5 **North Walsham** Norfk
19 G2 **North Waltham** Hants
20 A1 **North Warnborough** Hants
21 G5 **North Weald Bassett** Essex
51 H5 **North Wheatley** Notts
17 G4 **North Widcombe** BaNES
52 D4 **North Willingham** Lincs
51 E3 **North Wingfield** Derbys
42 B4 **North Witham** Lincs
17 G1 **North Wootton** Dorset
43 H4 **North Wootton** Norfk
17 G3 **North Wootton** Somset
18 A4 **North Wraxall** Wilts
66 D3 **North York Moors National Park**
32 B1 **Northall** Bucks
65 G3 **Northallerton** N York
9 F4 **Northam** C Sotn
14 D4 **Northam** Devon
31 H6 **Northampton** Nhants
39 H3 **Northampton** Worcs
21 F5 **Northaw** Herts
6 D6 **Northay** Somset
42 D3 **Northborough** C Pete
23 G1 **Northbourne** Kent
19 G1 **Northbrook** Hants
10 C5 **Northchapel** W Susx
20 C6 **Northchurch** Herts
4 D6 **Northcott** Devon
19 G6 **Northcourt** Oxon
23 H3 **Northdown** Kent
31 E5 **Northend** Warwks
57 G2 **Northenden** Manch
40 B2 **Northfield** Birm
103 E1 **Northfield** C Aber
60 D3 **Northfield** E R Yk
42 C3 **Northfields** Lincs
23 B3 **Northfleet** Kent
12 D4 **Northiam** E Susx
32 D3 **Northill** Beds
19 G1 **Northington** Hants
53 E1 **Northlands** Lincs
30 C2 **Northleach** Gloucs
6 D5 **Northleigh** Devon
15 E1 **Northlew** Devon
31 E1 **Northmoor** Oxon
93 F4 **Northmuir** Angus
10 A3 **Northney** Hants
21 E4 **Northolt** Gt Lon
48 C6 **Northop** Flints
48 C6 **Northop Hall** Flints
52 B5 **Northorpe** Lincs
42 D5 **Northorpe** Lincs
58 C3 **Northowram** Calder
8 B2 **Northport** Dorset
45 F5 **Northrepps** Norfk
111 b5 **Northton** W Isls
72 C6 **Northumberland National Park** Nthumb
16 C2 **Northway** Somset
49 F6 **Northwich** Ches
39 H2 **Northwick** Worcs
44 B2 **Northwold** Norfk
20 D4 **Northwood** Gt Lon
9 G3 **Northwood** IOW
49 E3 **Northwood** Shrops
29 E4 **Northwood Green** Gloucs
59 F2 **Norton** Donc
11 G2 **Norton** E Susx
29 F5 **Norton** Gloucs
66 D1 **Norton** N York
31 G6 **Norton** Nhants
51 F4 **Norton** Notts
38 C3 **Norton** Powys
66 B5 **Norton** S on T
39 G5 **Norton** Shrops
34 C5 **Norton** Suffk
10 C3 **Norton** W Susx
18 B5 **Norton** Wilts
39 H1 **Norton** Worcs
30 B4 **Norton** Worcs
18 B1 **Norton Bavant** Wilts
49 H2 **Norton Bridge** Staffs
40 B4 **Norton Canes** Staffs
38 D1 **Norton Canon** Herefs
52 B2 **Norton Disney** Lincs
16 D2 **Norton Fitzwarren** Somset
9 E2 **Norton Green** IOW
17 G5 **Norton Hawkfield** BaNES
22 B5 **Norton Heath** Essex
49 G3 **Norton in Hales** Shrops
30 D6 **Norton Lindsey** Warwks
34 C5 **Norton Little Green** Suffk
17 G5 **Norton Malreward** BaNES
18 A2 **Norton St Philip** Somset
17 F1 **Norton sub Hamdon** Somset
45 G2 **Norton Subcourse** Norfk
38 D1 **Norton Wood** Herefs
41 E4 **Norton-Juxta-Twycross** Leics
65 G1 **Norton-le-Clay** N York
51 H3 **Norwell** Notts
51 H3 **Norwell Woodhouse** Notts
45 E3 **Norwich** Norfk
45 E3 Norwich Airport Norfk
45 E3 **Norwich Cathedral** Norfk
111 m4 **Norwick** Shet
85 G5 **Norwood** Clacks
21 E3 **Norwood Green** Gt Lon
11 E6 **Norwood Hill** Surrey
41 H3 **Noseley** Leics
5 F2 **Noss Mayo** Devon
65 F2 **Nosterfield** N York
97 F5 **Nostie** Highld
30 C2 **Notgrove** Gloucs
26 D1 **Nottage** Brdgnd
5 E3 **Notter** Cnwll
51 F1 **Nottingham** C Nott
59 E2 **Notton** Wakefd
18 B4 **Notton** Wilts
39 G3 **Noutard's Green** Worcs
48 D1 **Nox** Shrops
19 H5 **Nuffield** Oxon
59 F5 **Nun Monkton** N York
60 C4 **Nunburnholme** E R Yk
41 E3 **Nuneaton** Warwks
19 G6 **Nuneham Courtenay** Oxon
21 F3 **Nunhead** Gt Lon
61 E5 **Nunkeeling** E R Yk
17 H3 **Nunney** Somset
66 C2 **Nunnington** N York
53 E6 **Nunsthorpe** NE Lin
66 B4 **Nunthorpe** Middsb
59 G5 **Nunthorpe** York
66 B4 **Nunthorpe Village** Middsb
8 D5 **Nunton** Wilts
65 G1 **Nunwick** N York
9 F5 **Nursling** Hants
10 B3 **Nutbourne** W Susx
10 D4 **Nutbourne** W Susx
21 F1 **Nutfield** Surrey
51 F1 **Nuthall** Notts
33 F2 **Nuthampstead** Herts
11 E4 **Nuthurst** W Susx
11 G4 **Nutley** E Susx
110 D5 **Nybster** Highld
10 C2 **Nyetimber** W Susx
10 B4 **Nyewood** W Susx
15 F2 **Nymet Rowland** Devon
15 F1 **Nymet Tracey** Devon
29 F3 **Nympsfield** Gloucs
10 C3 **Nyton** W Susx

O

22 D2 **Oad Street** Kent
41 G3 **Oadby** Leics
15 E1 **Oak Cross** Devon
50 B1 **Oakamoor** Staffs
86 B3 **Oakbank** W Loth
27 G3 **Oakdale** Caerph
16 C2 **Oake** Somset
39 H6 **Oaken** Staffs
63 E1 **Oakenclough** Lancs
49 G1 **Oakengates** Wrekin
73 F1 **Oakenshaw** Dur
58 C3 **Oakenshaw** Kirk
50 D3 **Oaker Side** Derbys
36 D3 **Oakford** Cerdgn
16 B1 **Oakford** Devon
42 B3 **Oakham** Rutlnd
10 B5 **Oakhanger** Hants
17 G4 **Oakhill** Somset
33 F5 **Oakington** Cambs
29 E4 **Oakle Street** Gloucs
32 C4 **Oakley** Beds
31 G2 **Oakley** Bucks
86 A5 **Oakley** Fife
19 G2 **Oakley** Hants
35 E6 **Oakley** Suffk
29 F3 **Oakridge** Gloucs
29 G2 **Oaksey** Wilts
40 D4 **Oakthorpe** Leics
51 E1 **Oakwood** C Derb
11 E5 **Oakwoodhill** Surrey
58 B4 **Oakworth** Brad
23 E2 **Oare** Kent
15 G5 **Oare** Somset
18 D3 **Oare** Wilts
42 C5 **Oasby** Lincs
17 E2 **Oath** Somset
93 G5 **Oathlaw** Angus
20 D2 **Oatlands Park** Surrey
90 A2 **Oban** Ag & B
38 D4 **Obley** Shrops
92 C3 **Obney** P & K
17 G1 **Oborne** Dorset
35 E5 **Occold** Suffk
110 C3 **Occumster** Highld
76 D3 **Ochiltree** E Ayrs
41 E6 **Ockbrook** Derbys
20 D1 **Ockham** Surrey
89 F5 **Ockle** Highld
11 E5 **Ockley** Surrey
39 F1 **Ocle Pychard** Herefs
17 F1 **Odcombe** Somset
17 H5 **Odd Down** BaNES
30 A5 **Oddingley** Worcs
30 D3 **Oddington** Gloucs
31 F2 **Oddington** Oxon
32 B4 **Odell** Beds
20 B1 **Odiham** Hants
58 C3 **Odsal** Brad
33 E3 **Odsey** Herts
8 D5 **Odstock** Wilts
41 E4 **Odstone** Leics
31 E6 **Offchurch** Warwks
30 B4 **Offenham** Worcs
11 G3 **Offham** E Susx
22 B1 **Offham** Kent
10 D3 **Offham** W Susx
32 D5 **Offord Cluny** Cambs
32 D5 **Offord Darcy** Cambs
34 D4 **Offton** Suffk
6 D5 **Offwell** Devon
18 D4 **Ogbourne Maizey** Wilts
18 D4 **Ogbourne St Andrew** Wilts
18 D4 **Ogbourne St George** Wilts
73 E4 **Ogle** Nthumb
56 D1 **Oglet** Lpool
16 A6 **Ogmore** V Glam
27 E2 **Ogmore Vale** Brdgnd
16 A6 **Ogmore-by-Sea** V Glam
8 A4 **Okeford Fitzpaine** Dorset
5 F6 **Okehampton** Devon
32 A5 **Old** Nhants
95 H6 **Old Aberdeen** C Aber
9 G6 **Old Alresford** Hants
77 F1 **Old Auchenbrack** D & G
51 F1 **Old Basford** C Nott
19 H2 **Old Basing** Hants
81 F2 **Old Bewick** Nthumb
53 E2 **Old Bolingbroke** Lincs
58 D4 **Old Bramhope** Leeds
51 E4 **Old Brampton** Derbys
70 B5 **Old Bridge of Urr** D & G
44 D2 **Old Buckenham** Norfk
19 F3 **Old Burghclere** Hants
66 B2 **Old Byland** N York
51 G6 **Old Cantley** Donc
53 E6 **Old Clee** NE Lin
16 C3 **Old Cleeve** Somset
51 G3 **Old Clipstone** Notts
76 B2 **Old Dailly** S Ayrs
41 G5 **Old Dalby** Leics
103 E4 **Old Deer** Abers
51 F6 **Old Edlington** Donc
61 E4 **Old Ellerby** E R Yk
35 F2 **Old Felixstowe** Suffk
42 D2 **Old Fletton** C Pete
28 D4 **Old Forge** Herefs
2 a2 **Old Grimsby** IOS
33 F1 **Old Hall Green** Herts
21 G6 **Old Harlow** Essex
44 A6 **Old Hunstanton** Norfk
33 E6 **Old Hurst** Cambs
63 E4 **Old Hutton** Cumb
3 E3 **Old Kea** Cnwll
84 D3 **Old Kilpatrick** W Duns
32 D1 **Old Knebworth** Herts
57 F6 **Old Langho** Lancs
53 F1 **Old Leake** Lincs
66 D1 **Old Malton** N York
59 E3 **Old Micklefield** Leeds
30 D6 **Old Milverton** Warwks
34 D5 **Old Newton** Suffk
38 C2 **Old Radnor** Powys
102 C2 **Old Rayne** Abers
13 E4 **Old Romney** Kent
11 E3 **Old Shoreham** W Susx
29 E1 **Old Sodbury** S Glos
42 B5 **Old Somerby** Lincs
31 H4 **Old Stratford** Nhants
40 A2 **Old Swinford** Dudley
66 A2 **Old Thirsk** N York
63 F4 **Old Town** Cumb
12 B2 **Old Town** E Susx
2 b2 **Old Town** IOS
57 G2 **Old Trafford** Traffd
32 D3 **Old Warden** Beds
32 C6 **Old Weston** Cambs
110 D4 **Old Wick** Highld
20 C3 **Old Windsor** W & M
23 E1 **Old Wives Lees** Kent
20 D1 **Old Woking** Surrey
108 B3 **Oldany** Highld
30 C6 **Oldberrow** Warwks
40 B2 **Oldbury** Sandw
39 G5 **Oldbury** Shrops
40 D3 **Oldbury** Warwks
18 A5 **Oldbury on the Hill** Gloucs
28 D2 **Oldbury-on-Severn** S Glos
28 B5 **Oldcastle** Mons
51 G5 **Oldcotes** Notts
39 H3 **Oldfield** Worcs
18 A2 **Oldford** Somset
58 A1 **Oldham** Oldham
87 G3 **Oldhamstocks** E Loth
17 G6 **Oldland** S Glos
102 D2 **Oldmeldrum** Abers
4 D4 **Oldmill** Cnwll
17 E4 **Oldmixon** N Som
108 B5 **Oldshoremore** Highld
66 B2 **Oldstead** N York
71 G5 **Oldwall** Cumb
26 B2 **Oldwalls** Swans
40 C5 **Olive Green** Staffs
78 D5 **Oliver** Border
9 F6 **Oliver's Battery** Hants
111 l3 **Ollaberry** Shet
96 C5 **Ollach** Highld
57 G1 **Ollerton** Ches
51 G3 **Ollerton** Notts
49 F2 **Ollerton** Shrops
32 B4 **Olney** M Keyn
110 C5 **Olrig House** Highld
40 C2 **Olton** Solhll
28 D2 **Olveston** S Glos
39 H3 **Ombersley** Worcs
51 G3 **Ompton** Notts
116 c3 **Onchan** IOM
50 B2 **Onecote** Staffs
39 E4 **Onibury** Shrops
90 C5 **Onich** Highld
26 D4 **Onllwyn** Neath
49 G4 **Onneley** Staffs
20 C1 **Onslow Village** Surrey
49 F6 **Onston** Ches
105 F3 **Opinan** Highld
101 F5 **Orbliston** Moray
96 A6 **Orbost** Highld
53 F2 **Orby** Lincs
16 D2 **Orchard Portman** Somset
18 C2 **Orcheston** Wilts
28 C5 **Orcop** Herefs
28 C5 **Orcop Hill** Herefs
102 C5 **Ord** Abers
102 C1 **Ordhead** Abers
94 D6 **Ordie** Abers
101 F5 **Ordiequish** Moray
72 D3 **Ordley** Nthumb
51 G4 **Ordsall** Notts
12 D3 **Ore** E Susx
35 G4 **Orford** Suffk
57 F2 **Orford** Warrtn
8 B3 **Organford** Dorset
13 E5 **Orlestone** Kent
39 E3 **Orleton** Herefs
39 F3 **Orleton** Worcs
32 B5 **Orlingbury** Nhants
66 B5 **Ormesby** R & Cl
45 G3 **Ormesby St Margaret** Norfk
45 G3 **Ormesby St Michael** Norfk
105 F5 **Ormiscaig** Highld
86 D3 **Ormiston** E Loth
89 E5 **Ormsaigmore** Highld
83 F3 **Ormsary** Ag & B
56 D3 **Ormskirk** Lancs
82 C4 **Oronsay** Ag & B
111 g2 **Orphir** Ork
21 G2 **Orpington** Gt Lon
56 D2 **Orrell** Sefton
57 E3 **Orrell** Wigan
70 B4 **Orroland** D & G
22 B3 **Orsett** Thurr
49 G1 **Orslow** Staffs
51 H1 **Orston** Notts
63 F6 **Orton** Cumb
32 A6 **Orton** Nhants
39 H5 **Orton** Staffs
42 D2 **Orton Longueville** C Pete
42 D2 **Orton Waterville** C Pete
40 D4 **Orton-on-the-Hill** Leics
33 E4 **Orwell** Cambs
57 F5 **Osbaldeston** Lancs
59 G5 **Osbaldwick** York
41 E4 **Osbaston** Leics
48 D2 **Osbaston** Shrops
9 G3 Osborne House IOW
42 C5 **Osbournby** Lincs
49 E5 **Oscroft** Ches
96 B6 **Ose** Highld
41 E5 **Osgathorpe** Leics
52 C4 **Osgodby** Lincs
59 G3 **Osgodby** N York
67 F2 **Osgodby** N York
96 D5 **Oskaig** Highld
89 E3 **Oskamull** Ag & B
50 D1 **Osmaston** Derbys
7 H4 **Osmington** Dorset
7 H4 **Osmington Mills** Dorset
59 E3 **Osmondthorpe** Leeds
66 B3 **Osmotherley** N York
31 F1 **Osney** Oxon
23 E2 **Ospringe** Kent
58 D2 **Ossett** Wakefd
51 H3 **Ossington** Notts
21 E3 **Osterley** Gt Lon
66 C2 **Oswaldkirk** N York
57 G5 **Oswaldtwistle** Lancs
48 C2 **Oswestry** Shrops
21 H2 **Otford** Kent
22 C1 **Otham** Kent
17 E2 **Othery** Somset
58 D4 **Otley** Leeds
35 E4 **Otley** Suffk
83 G4 **Otter Ferry** Ag & B
9 F5 **Otterbourne** Hants
63 H2 **Otterburn** N York
72 C5 **Otterburn** Nthumb
4 C5 **Otterham** Cnwll
16 D3 **Otterhampton** Somset
111 b4 **Otternish** W Isls
20 D2 **Ottershaw** Surrey
111 l3 **Otterswick** Shet
6 C4 **Otterton** Devon
5 E4 **Ottery** Devon
6 C5 **Ottery St Mary** Devon
13 F6 **Ottinge** Kent
61 F3 **Ottringham** E R Yk
71 E3 **Oughterside** Cumb
50 D5 **Oughtibridge** Sheff
57 F2 **Oughtrington** Warrtn
66 B1 **Oulston** N York
71 E4 **Oulton** Cumb
45 E5 **Oulton** Norfk
40 A6 **Oulton** Staffs
45 H2 **Oulton** Suffk
45 H2 **Oulton Broad** Suffk
45 E4 **Oulton Street** Norfk
42 C1 **Oundle** Nhants
39 H5 **Ounsdale** Staffs
64 A6 **Ousby** Cumb
34 B4 **Ousden** Suffk
60 C2 **Ousefleet** E R Yk
73 F2 **Ouston** Dur
56 D6 **Out Rawcliffe** Lancs
62 D5 **Outgate** Cumb
64 C3 **Outhgill** Cumb
30 C6 **Outhill** Warwks
58 C2 **Outlane** Kirk
43 G3 **Outwell** Norfk
11 F6 **Outwood** Surrey
49 G1 **Outwoods** Staffs
59 E3 **Ouzlewell Green** Leeds
33 F5 **Over** Cambs
17 G1 **Over Compton** Dorset
40 C3 **Over Green** Warwks
50 D3 **Over Haddon** Derbys
63 E3 **Over Kellet** Lancs
31 E2 **Over Kiddington** Oxon
30 D3 **Over Norton** Oxon
49 G6 **Over Peover** Ches
66 B3 **Over Silton** N York
16 D3 **Over Stowey** Somset
17 F1 **Over Stratton** Somset
19 E1 **Over Wallop** Hants
40 D3 **Over Whitacre** Warwks
31 E3 **Over Worton** Oxon
29 G6 **Overbury** Worcs
7 H4 **Overcombe** Dorset
17 F3 **Overleigh** Somset
56 D1 **Overpool** Ches
108 D2 **Overscaig Hotel** Highld
40 D5 **Overseal** Derbys
23 E1 **Oversland** Kent
32 A5 **Overstone** Nhants
45 F5 **Overstrand** Norfk
31 F4 **Overthorpe** Nhants
102 D1 **Overton** C Aber
19 G2 **Overton** Hants
62 D2 **Overton** Lancs
59 F5 **Overton** N York
39 E3 **Overton** Shrops
26 A2 **Overton** Swans
58 D2 **Overton** Wakefd
48 D3 **Overton** Wrexhm
63 F3 **Overtown** Lancs
85 G1 **Overtown** N Lans
32 A1 **Oving** Bucks
10 C3 **Oving** W Susx
11 F3 **Ovingdean** Br & H
73 E3 **Ovingham** Nthumb
65 E4 **Ovington** Dur
34 B3 **Ovington** Essex
9 G6 **Ovington** Hants
44 C2 **Ovington** Norfk
73 E3 **Ovington** Nthumb
9 E5 **Ower** Hants
8 A2 **Owermoigne** Dorset
51 E5 **Owlerton** Sheff
20 B2 **Owlsmoor** Br For
20 B5 **Owlswick** Bucks
52 C5 **Owmby** Lincs
52 C4 **Owmby** Lincs
9 G5 **Owslebury** Hants
59 F1 **Owston** Donc
41 H4 **Owston** Leics
52 A5 **Owston Ferry** N Linc
61 F3 **Owstwick** E R Yk
61 G3 **Owthorne** E R Yk
41 G6 **Owthorpe** Notts
44 B2 **Oxborough** Norfk
7 F5 **Oxbridge** Dorset
53 E3 **Oxcombe** Lincs
33 H2 **Oxen End** Essex
62 D4 **Oxen Park** Cumb
63 E5 **Oxenholme** Cumb
58 B3 **Oxenhope** Brad
17 F3 **Oxenpill** Somset
29 G5 **Oxenton** Gloucs
19 E3 **Oxenwood** Wilts
31 F1 **Oxford** Oxon
20 D5 **Oxhey** Herts
30 D4 **Oxhill** Warwks
40 A3 **Oxley** Wolves
22 D6 **Oxley Green** Essex
43 F1 **Oxlode** Cambs
80 C2 **Oxnam** Border
45 E4 **Oxnead** Norfk
21 E2 **Oxshott** Surrey
50 D6 **Oxspring** Barns
21 F1 **Oxted** Surrey
80 B5 **Oxton** Border
59 F4 **Oxton** N York
51 G2 **Oxton** Notts
26 B2 **Oxwich** Swans
26 B2 **Oxwich Green** Swans
106 C5 **Oykel Bridge Hotel** Highld
102 C2 **Oyne** Abers
26 C2 **Oystermouth** Swans

P

111 e6 **Pabail** W Isls
41 E4 **Packington** Leics
93 F4 **Padanaram** Angus
31 H3 **Padbury** Bucks
21 F3 **Paddington** Gt Lon
22 B2 **Paddlesworth** Kent
13 F5 **Paddlesworth** Kent
12 B6 **Paddock Wood** Kent
57 G5 **Padiham** Lancs
58 C5 **Padside** N York
3 E6 **Padstow** Cnwll
19 H3 **Padworth** W Berk
10 C2 **Pagham** W Susx
22 D4 **Paglesham** Essex
6 A2 **Paignton** Torbay
41 F2 **Pailton** Warwks
38 B1 **Painscastle** Powys
73 E3 **Painshawfield** Nthumb
60 C5 **Painsthorpe** E R Yk
29 F4 **Painswick** Gloucs
23 E2 **Painter's Forstal** Kent
84 D2 **Paisley** Rens
45 H1 **Pakefield** Suffk
34 C5 **Pakenham** Suffk
20 C3 **Paley Street** W & M
35 E6 **Palgrave** Suffk
8 A3 **Pallington** Dorset
76 D3 **Palmerston** E Ayrs
70 B5 **Palnackie** D & G
69 F4 **Palnure** D & G
51 F3 **Palterton** Derbys
19 H3 **Pamber End** Hants
19 H3 **Pamber Green** Hants
19 H3 **Pamber Heath** Hants
29 G5 **Pamington** Gloucs
8 C3 **Pamphill** Dorset
33 G3 **Pampisford** Cambs
93 G3 **Panbride** Angus
14 C2 **Pancrasweek** Devon
28 B5 **Pandy** Mons
55 F3 **Pandy Tudur** Conwy
34 B2 **Panfield** Essex
19 H4 **Pangbourne** W Berk
11 F3 **Pangdean** W Susx
58 D5 **Pannal** N York
58 D5 **Pannal Ash** N York
94 D5 **Pannanich Wells Hotel** Abers
48 C2 **Pant** Shrops
46 D6 **Pant Glas** Gwynd
27 E1 **Pant-ffrwyth** Brdgnd
37 H4 **Pant-y-dwr** Powys
48 C5 **Pant-y-mwyn** Flints
48 B6 **Pantasaph** Flints
47 F2 **Pantglas** Powys
52 D3 **Panton** Lincs
45 F3 **Panxworth** Norfk
111 h3 Papa Westray Airport Ork
70 D3 **Papcastle** Cumb
110 D4 **Papigoe** Highld
87 F3 **Papple** E Loth
51 F2 **Papplewick** Notts
33 E5 **Papworth Everard** Cambs
33 E5 **Papworth St Agnes** Cambs
3 G4 **Par** Cnwll
57 E4 **Parbold** Lancs
17 G3 **Parbrook** Somset
47 G4 **Parc** Gwynd
28 C2 **Parc Seymour** Newpt
70 D2 **Pardshaw** Cumb
35 F4 **Parham** Suffk

95 G5 Park Abers
78 C2 Park D & G
83 B3 Park Nthumb
20 A4 Park Corner Oxon
13 E5 Park Farm Kent
9 G4 Park Gate Hants
58 C4 Park Gate Leeds
21 E3 Park Royal Gt Lon
21 E5 Park Street Herts
28 D3 Parkend Gloucs
12 B6 Parkers Green Kent
56 C1 Parkgate Ches
78 D2 Parkgate D & G
11 E6 Parkgate Surrey
84 D3 Parkhall W Duns
14 D3 Parkham Devon
103 E1 Parkhill House Abers
26 B2 Parkmill Swans
73 H2 Parkside Dur
85 G2 Parkside N Lans
8 C3 Parkstone Poole
21 G6 Parndon Essex
15 F5 Parracombe Devon
43 F3 Parson Drove Cambs
34 D2 Parson's Heath Essex
85 E2 Partick C Glas
57 G2 Partington Traffd
53 F2 Partney Lincs
70 C2 Parton Cumb
11 E4 Partridge Green W Susx
50 C2 Parwich Derbys
32 A3 Passenham Nhants
10 B5 Passfield Hants
45 F5 Paston Norfk
11 F3 Patcham Br & H
10 D3 Patching W Susx
28 D1 Patchway S Glos
58 C6 Pateley Bridge N York
92 D1 Path of Condie P & K
86 C5 Pathhead Fife
86 D2 Pathhead Mdloth
76 D3 Patna E Ayrs
18 C3 Patney Wilts
65 F3 Patrick Brompton N York
57 G3 Patricroft Salfd
61 F2 Patrington E R Yk
23 F1 Patrixbourne Kent
71 G1 Patterdale Cumb
39 G5 Pattingham Staffs
31 G5 Pattishall Nhants
34 B2 Pattiswick Green Essex
2 B2 Paul Cnwll
8 D6 Paul's Dene Wilts
31 H4 Paulerspury Bucks
61 E3 Paull E R Yk
17 G4 Paulton BaNES
73 E6 Pauperhaugh Nthumb
32 C4 Pavenham Beds
16 D3 Pawlett Somset
30 C4 Paxford Gloucs
81 E5 Paxton Border
6 C5 Payhembury Devon
63 G2 Paythorne Lancs
11 G2 Peacehaven E Susx
50 C5 Peak District National Park
50 C4 Peak Forest Derbys
42 D3 Peakirk C Pete
89 G6 Peanmeanach Highld
11 F5 Pease Pottage W Susx
17 H4 Peasedown St John BaNES
44 D4 Peaseland Green Norfk
19 F4 Peasemore W Berk
35 F5 Peasenhall Suffk
10 D6 Peaslake Surrey
57 E2 Peasley Cross St Hel
12 D4 Peasmarsh E Susx
87 E6 Peat Inn Fife
103 E5 Peathill Abers
41 G3 Peatling Magna Leics
41 G2 Peatling Parva Leics
34 C2 Pebmarsh Essex
30 C4 Pebworth Worcs
58 B3 Pecket Well Calder
49 E5 Peckforton Ches
21 F3 Peckham Gt Lon
41 F3 Peckleton Leics
13 F5 Pedlinge Kent
40 A2 Pedmore Dudley
17 E3 Pedwell Somset
79 F6 Peebles Border
116 b3 Peel IOM
13 F5 Peene Kent
32 D2 Pegsdon Beds
73 F5 Pegswood Nthumb
23 H2 Pegwell Kent
96 D5 Peinchorran Highld
104 C2 Peinlich Highld
34 D1 Peldon Essex
40 B4 Pelsall Wsall
73 F2 Pelton Dur
4 C3 Pelynt Cnwll
26 B3 Pemberton Carmth
57 E3 Pemberton Wigan
25 G3 Pembrey Carmth
38 D2 Pembridge Herefs
24 D3 Pembroke Pembks
24 D3 Pembroke Dock Pembks
24 C4 Pembrokeshire Coast National Park Pembks
12 B6 Pembury Kent
26 D4 Pen Rhiwfawr Neath
37 F5 Pen-bont Rhydybeddau Cerdgn
25 E5 Pen-ffordd Pembks
36 B1 Pen-rhiw Pembks
28 C3 Pen-twyn Mons
48 C2 Pen-y-bont Powys
48 B2 Pen-y-bont-fawr Powys
36 B1 Pen-y-bryn Pembks
28 C3 Pen-y-clawdd Mons
27 F2 Pen-y-coedcae Rhondd
24 C5 Pen-y-cwn Pembks
48 B6 Pen-y-felin Flints
48 B2 Pen-y-Garnedd Powys
46 B4 Pen-y-graig Gwynd
48 C4 Pen-y-stryt Denbgs
28 C4 Penallt Mons
25 E3 Penally Pembks
28 D5 Penalt Herefs
16 D6 Penarth V Glam
36 C2 Penbryn Cerdgn
25 H6 Pencader Carmth
87 E3 Pencaitland E Loth
54 B4 Pencarnisiog IOA
37 E2 Pencarreg Carmth
27 F5 Pencelli Powys
26 B2 Penclawdd Swans
27 E1 Pencoed Brdgnd
39 F2 Pencombe Herefs
28 D4 Pencraig Herefs
48 A2 Pencraig Powys
2 A3 Pendeen Cnwll
27 E3 Penderyn Rhondd
25 F3 Pendine Carmth
57 G3 Pendlebury Salfd
57 G6 Pendleton Lancs
29 E5 Pendock Worcs
4 B5 Pendoggett Cnwll
7 F6 Pendomer Somset
16 C6 Pendoylan V Glam
47 F2 Penegoes Powys
27 G3 Pengam Caerph
27 G1 Pengam Cardif
21 F3 Penge Gt Lon
4 B5 Pengelly Cnwll
3 F4 Pengrugla Cnwll
2 D4 Penhallow Cnwll
2 D3 Penhalvean Cnwll
18 D5 Penhill Swindn
28 C2 Penhow Newpt
86 C2 Penicuik Mdloth
96 C6 Penifiler Highld
75 F3 Peninver Ag & B
58 D1 Penistone Barns
76 B2 Penkill S Ayrs
40 A4 Penkridge Staffs
14 B1 Penlean Cnwll
48 D3 Penley Wrexhm
16 B6 Penllyn V Glam
55 F2 Penmachno Conwy
27 G3 Penmaen Caerph
26 B2 Penmaen Swans
55 E4 Penmaenmawr Conwy
47 F3 Penmaenpool Gwynd
16 C5 Penmark V Glam
47 E5 Penmorfa Gwynd
54 D4 Penmynydd IOA
20 C4 Penn Bucks
20 C5 Penn Street Bucks
47 F2 Pennal Gwynd
102 D5 Pennan Abers
47 G2 Pennant Powys
38 D5 Pennerley Shrops
58 B3 Pennines
62 C4 Pennington Cumb
27 F5 Pennorth Powys
62 C4 Penny Bridge Cumb
43 E4 Penny Hill Lincs
89 F2 Pennycross Ag & B
89 F2 Pennyghael Ag & B
76 C3 Pennyglen S Ayrs
15 G2 Pennymoor Devon
36 B2 Penparc Cerdgn
28 B3 Penperlleni Mons
4 C3 Penpoll Cnwll
2 C3 Penponds Cnwll
78 B2 Penpont D & G
36 C2 Penrhiw-pal Cerdgn
27 F3 Penrhiwceiber Rhondd
36 C1 Penrhiwllan Cerdgn
46 C4 Penrhos Gwynd
28 C4 Penrhos Mons
55 F4 Penrhyn Bay Conwy
54 D3 Penrhyn Castle Gwynd
47 E5 Penrhyndeudraeth Gwynd
26 B2 Penrice Swans
75 G5 Penrioch N Ayrs
71 H2 Penrith Cumb
3 E6 Penrose Cnwll
71 G2 Penruddock Cumb
2 D3 Penryn Cnwll
25 G4 Pensarn Carmth
55 G4 Pensarn Conwy
39 G3 Pensax Worcs
17 H2 Penselwood Somset
17 G5 Pensford BaNES
30 B4 Pensham Worcs
73 G2 Penshaw Sundld
11 H6 Penshurst Kent
4 D4 Pensilva Cnwll
3 F4 Pentewan Cnwll
54 D3 Pentir Gwynd
2 D5 Pentire Cnwll
34 B3 Pentlow Essex
44 B3 Pentney Norfk
19 E2 Penton Mewsey Hants
79 G1 Pentonbridge Cumb
54 D4 Pentraeth IOA
27 E2 Pentre Rhondd
48 D1 Pentre Shrops
54 C3 Pentre Berw IOA
38 D4 Pentre Hodrey Shrops
48 B5 Pentre Llanrhaeadr Denbgs
16 B6 Pentre Meyrick V Glam
27 E5 Pentre-bach Powys
48 B4 Pentre-celyn Denbgs
47 G2 Pentre-celyn Powys
26 C2 Pentre-chwyth Swans
25 G6 Pentre-cwrt Carmth
26 C4 Pentre-Gwenlais Carmth
55 F3 Pentre-tafarn-y-fedw Conwy
27 F3 Pentrebach Myr Td
48 C4 Pentredwr Denbgs
47 E5 Pentrefelin Gwynd
55 F2 Pentrefoelas Conwy
36 C2 Pentregat Cerdgn
51 E2 Pentrich Derbys
8 C5 Pentridge Hill Dorset
27 G2 Pentwynmaur Caerph
27 F1 Pentyrch Cardif
3 F4 Penwithick Cnwll
26 C5 Penybanc Carmth
38 B3 Penybont Powys
48 C4 Penycae Wrexhm
48 C5 Penyffordd Flints
27 F2 Penygraig Rhondd
26 B4 Penygroes Carmth
54 C2 Penygroes Gwynd
54 C5 Penysarn IOA
27 E3 Penywaun Rhondd
2 B2 Penzance Cnwll
2 B2 Penzance Heliport Cnwll
30 B5 Peopleton Worcs
49 F2 Peplow Shrops
76 C5 Perceton N Ayrs
95 E5 Percie Abers
103 E5 Percyhorner Abers
6 b1 Perelle Guern
16 B3 Periton Somset
21 E4 Perivale Gt Lon
6 B4 Perkins Village Devon
51 G4 Perlethorpe Notts
2 D3 Perranarworthal Cnwll
2 D4 Perranporth Cnwll
2 B2 Perranuthnoe Cnwll
2 D3 Perranwell Cnwll
2 D4 Perranzabuloe Cnwll
40 C3 Perry Barr Birm
18 C5 Perry Green Wilts
49 G2 Pershall Staffs
30 B4 Pershore Worcs
32 C5 Pertenhall Beds
92 D2 Perth P & K
48 D3 Perthy Shrops
28 D6 Perton Herefs
39 H5 Perton Staffs
5 E4 Peter Tavy Devon
32 D1 Peter's Green Herts
42 D2 Peterborough C Pete
28 B6 Peterchurch Herefs
95 G6 Peterculter C Aber
103 F4 Peterhead Abers
73 H1 Peterlee Dur
14 D2 Peters Marland Devon
10 B4 Petersfield Hants
21 E3 Petersham Gt Lon
16 C6 Peterston-super-Ely V Glam
28 A1 Peterstone Wentlooge Newpt
28 D5 Peterstow Herefs
23 F1 Petham Kent
4 D5 Petherwin Gate Cnwll
15 E2 Petrockstow Devon
12 D3 Pett E Susx
35 E4 Pettaugh Suffk
93 F3 Petterden Angus
78 C6 Pettinain S Lans
35 F4 Pettistree Suffk
16 B2 Petton Devon
21 G2 Petts Wood Gt Lon
86 C4 Pettycur Fife
103 E2 Pettymuk Abers
10 C4 Petworth W Susx
12 B3 Pevensey E Susx
18 D3 Pewsey Wilts
30 B5 Phepson Worcs
14 C3 Philham Devon
79 G5 Philiphaugh Border
2 C3 Phillack Cnwll
3 E3 Philleigh Cnwll
86 B4 Philpstoun W Loth
20 B1 Phoenix Green Hants
99 E2 Phoines Highld
17 F2 Pibsbury Somset
70 D2 Pica Cumb
59 F1 Pickburn Donc
66 D2 Pickering N York
40 D2 Pickford Covtry
65 G2 Pickhill N York
38 D5 Picklescott Shrops
57 F1 Pickmere Ches
16 D2 Pickney Somset
57 G5 Pickup Bank Bl w D
42 A3 Pickwell Leics
42 C3 Pickworth Lincs
42 C5 Pickworth Lincs
102 C1 Pictillum Abers
48 D6 Picton Ches
65 G4 Picton N York
11 G2 Piddinghoe E Susx
32 A4 Piddington M Keyn
31 G2 Piddington Oxon
7 H5 Piddlehinton Dorset
7 H5 Piddletrenthide Dorset
33 E6 Pidley Cambs
65 F5 Piercebridge Darltn
111 h3 Pierowall Ork
22 B5 Pilgrims Hatch Essex
52 B4 Pilham Lincs
4 D3 Pillaton Cnwll
30 D5 Pillerton Hersey Warwks
30 D4 Pillerton Priors Warwks
51 E6 Pilley Barns
9 E3 Pilley Hants
62 D1 Pilling Lancs
28 D2 Pilning S Glos
50 C3 Pilsbury Derbys
7 E5 Pilsdon Dorset
50 D4 Pilsley Derbys
51 E3 Pilsley Derbys
45 G3 Pilson Green Norfk
11 G4 Piltdown E Susx
15 E4 Pilton Devon
42 C1 Pilton Nhants
42 B2 Pilton Rutlnd
17 G3 Pilton Somset
8 B4 Pimperne Dorset
33 E2 Pin Green Herts
43 E4 Pinchbeck Lincs
6 B5 Pinhoe Devon
30 D6 Pinley Green Warwks
76 B1 Pinminnoch S Ayrs
76 B1 Pinmore S Ayrs
6 C4 Pinn Devon
20 D4 Pinner Gt Lon
20 D4 Pinner Green Gt Lon
30 B5 Pinvin Worcs
68 D6 Pinwherry S Ayrs
51 F2 Pinxton Derbys
39 E1 Pipe and Lyde Herefs
49 G3 Pipe Gate Shrops
100 B4 Piperhill Highld
42 A1 Pipewell Nhants
20 C1 Pirbright Surrey
80 C3 Pirnie Border
75 G5 Pirnmill N Ayrs
32 D2 Pirton Herts
30 A4 Pirton Worcs
20 A4 Pishill Oxon
46 C5 Pistyll Gwynd
92 B5 Pitagowan P & K
103 E5 Pitblae Abers
92 C2 Pitcairngreen P & K
107 G3 Pitcalnie Highld
102 C2 Pitcaple Abers
94 C3 Pitcarity Angus
20 B5 Pitch Green Bucks
10 C5 Pitch Place Surrey
29 F3 Pitchcombe Gloucs
31 H2 Pitchcott Bucks
39 E6 Pitchford Shrops
101 E3 Pitchroy Moray
17 G2 Pitcombe Somset
87 F3 Pitcox E Loth
102 C1 Pitfichie Abers
102 C4 Pitglassie Abers
107 G5 Pitgrudy Highld
93 G4 Pitkennedy Angus
86 D6 Pitlessie Fife
92 B5 Pitlochry P & K
102 C2 Pitmachie Abers
99 F3 Pitmain Highld
103 E2 Pitmedden Abers
103 E2 Pitmedden Garden Abers
93 G4 Pitmuies Angus
102 C1 Pitmunie Abers
17 F2 Pitney Somset
93 E2 Pitroddie P & K
93 F1 Pitscottie Fife
22 C4 Pitsea Essex
31 H6 Pitsford Nhants
20 C6 Pitstone Bucks
16 B1 Pitt Devon
95 F3 Pittarrow Abers
87 E6 Pittenweem Fife
86 C5 Pitteuchar Fife
73 G1 Pittington Dur
102 C2 Pittodrie House Hotel Abers
8 D6 Pitton Wilts
103 E3 Pittulie Abers
73 F2 Pity Me Dur
21 E1 Pixham Surrey
85 G2 Plains N Lans
39 E5 Plaish Shrops
51 E2 Plaistow Derbys
21 G4 Plaistow Gt Lon
10 D5 Plaistow W Susx
9 E5 Plaitford Hants
54 B4 Plas Cymyran IOA
19 G3 Plastow Green Hants
22 B1 Platt Kent
73 F2 Plawsworth Dur
22 B1 Plaxtol Kent
20 A3 Play Hatch Oxon
12 D4 Playden E Susx
35 E3 Playford Suffk
29 E5 Playley Green Gloucs
38 D6 Plealey Shrops
85 G4 Plean Stirlg
93 E1 Pleasance Fife
57 F5 Pleasington Bl w D
51 F3 Pleasley Derbys
6 b2 Pleinheaume Guern
7 a2 Plemont Jersey
49 E6 Plemstall Ches
22 B6 Pleshey Essex
97 F5 Plockton Highld
38 D4 Plowden Shrops
38 D6 Plox Green Shrops
12 D6 Pluckley Kent
12 D6 Pluckley Thorne Kent
71 E3 Plumbland Cumb
49 G6 Plumley Ches
71 G3 Plumpton Cumb
11 F3 Plumpton E Susx
31 G4 Plumpton Nhants
31 H4 Plumpton End Nhants
11 F4 Plumpton Green E Susx
21 G3 Plumstead Gt Lon
45 E5 Plumstead Norfk
41 G6 Plumtree Notts
41 H6 Plungar Leics
12 D5 Plurenden Kent
7 H5 Plush Dorset
36 C2 Plwmp Cerdgn
5 E3 Plymouth C Plym
5 E3 Plymouth Airport C Plym
5 F3 Plympton C Plym
5 F2 Plymstock C Plym
6 C5 Plymtree Devon
66 C2 Pockley N York
60 B5 Pocklington E R Yk
17 F2 Podimore Somset
32 B5 Podington Beds
49 G3 Podmore Staffs
42 D5 Pointon Lincs
8 D3 Pokesdown Bmouth
105 H6 Polbain Highld
4 D3 Polbathic Cnwll
86 A2 Polbeth W Loth
2 D2 Poldark Mine Cnwll
42 C1 Polebrook Nhants
12 B3 Polegate E Susx
40 D3 Polesworth Warwks
105 H6 Polglass Highld
3 F4 Polgooth Cnwll
77 F2 Polgown D & G
10 D3 Poling W Susx
10 D3 Poling Corner W Susx
4 B2 Polkerris Cnwll
59 G2 Pollington E R Yk
89 H5 Polloch Highld
85 E2 Pollokshaws C Glas
85 E2 Pollokshields C Glas
3 F4 Polmassick Cnwll
85 H3 Polmont Falk
97 E1 Polnish Highld
4 C2 Polperro Cnwll
4 C2 Polruan Cnwll
34 D3 Polstead Suffk
83 F5 Poltalloch Ag & B
6 B5 Poltimore Devon
86 C3 Polton Mdloth
80 D5 Polwarth Border
4 D5 Polyphant Cnwll
4 A5 Polzeath Cnwll
86 C2 Pomathorn Mdloth
21 F5 Ponders End Gt Lon
43 E2 Pondersbridge Cambs
2 D3 Ponsanooth Cnwll
5 G4 Ponsworthy Devon
48 B1 Pont Robert Powys
26 B4 Pont-ar-gothi Carmth
27 F5 Pont-faen Powys
27 E3 Pont-Nedd-Fechan Neath
26 D2 Pont-rhyd-y-fen Neath
55 F2 Pont-y-pant Conwy
7 c1 Pontac Jersey
25 H4 Pontantwn Carmth
26 C3 Pontardawe Neath
26 B3 Pontarddulais Swans
25 H5 Pontarsais Carmth
48 C5 Pontblyddyn Flints
59 F2 Pontefract Wakefd
73 F4 Ponteland Nthumb
37 F5 Ponterwyd Cerdgn
38 D6 Pontesbury Shrops
38 D6 Pontesford Shrops
48 C3 Pontfadog Wrexhm
24 D5 Pontfaen Pembks
36 C2 Pontgarreg Cerdgn
26 B3 Ponthenry Carmth
28 B2 Ponthir Torfn
36 B2 Ponthirwaun Cerdgn
27 G2 Pontllanfraith Caerph
26 C3 Pontlliw Swans
54 C2 Pontlyfni Gwynd
28 B2 Pontnewydd Torfn
73 E2 Pontop Dur
37 F3 Pontrhydfendigaid Cerdgn
37 F4 Pontrhydygroes Cerdgn
28 B5 Pontrilas Herefs
12 B4 Ponts Green E Susx
36 D2 Pontshaen Cerdgn
28 D4 Pontshill Herefs
27 F4 Pontsticill Powys
36 D1 Pontwelly Carmth
26 B3 Pontyates Carmth
26 B4 Pontyberem Carmth
48 C5 Pontybodkin Flints
27 F1 Pontyclun Rhondd
27 E2 Pontycymer Brdgnd
28 B3 Pontypool Torfn
27 F2 Pontypridd Rhondd
27 G2 Pontywaun Caerph
2 D3 Pool Cnwll
58 D4 Pool Leeds
86 A5 Pool of Muckhart Clacks
34 B3 Pool Street Essex
8 C3 Poole Poole
18 C6 Poole Keynes Gloucs
105 F4 Poolewe Highld
71 G2 Pooley Bridge Cumb
50 A3 Poolfold Staffs
29 E5 Poolhill Gloucs
21 F3 Poplar Gt Lon
9 F3 Porchfield IOW
45 F2 Poringland Norfk
2 D3 Porkellis Cnwll
15 H5 Porlock Somset
15 G5 Porlock Weir Somset
90 B3 Port Appin Ag & B
82 C3 Port Askaig Ag & B
84 A2 Port Bannatyne Ag & B
71 E5 Port Carlisle Cumb
82 B2 Port Charlotte Ag & B
83 H3 Port Driseach Ag & B
26 B2 Port Einon Swans
74 C5 Port Ellen Ag & B
102 D2 Port Elphinstone Abers
116 a2 Port Erin IOM
4 B5 Port Gaverne Cnwll
84 C3 Port Glasgow Inver
105 F3 Port Henderson Highld
4 B5 Port Isaac Cnwll
68 C2 Port Logan D & G
89 E6 Port Mor Highld
111 e6 Port nan Giuran W Isls
111 b4 Port nan Long W Isls
111 e7 Port Nis W Isls
85 E5 Port of Menteith Stirlg
111 e7 Port of Ness W Isls
4 A5 Port Quin Cnwll
90 A3 Port Ramsay Ag & B
116 c2 Port Soderick IOM
116 a2 Port St Mary IOM
26 D2 Port Talbot Neath
74 A5 Port Wemyss Ag & B
69 E2 Port William D & G
97 E5 Port-an-Eorna Highld
83 F5 Portachoillan Ag & B
83 G3 Portavadie Ag & B
17 F6 Portbury N Som
9 H4 Portchester Hants
68 B4 Portencalzie D & G
76 B6 Portencross N Ayrs
7 G4 Portesham Dorset
101 G5 Portessie Moray
24 D4 Portfield Gate Pembks
5 E5 Portgate Devon
101 F5 Portgordon Moray
110 A1 Portgower Highld
3 E5 Porth Cnwll
27 F2 Porth Rhondd
2 D2 Porth Navas Cnwll
2 D2 Porthallow Cnwll
4 C2 Porthallow Cnwll
26 D1 Porthcawl Brdgnd
3 E6 Porthcothan Cnwll
2 A2 Porthcurno Cnwll
24 C5 Porthgain Pembks
2 A2 Porthgwarra Cnwll
16 C5 Porthkerry V Glam
2 C2 Porthleven Cnwll
47 E5 Porthmadog Gwynd
3 E2 Porthoustock Cnwll
3 F4 Porthpean Cnwll
2 D4 Porthtowan Cnwll
26 B4 Porthyrhyd Carmth
84 B5 Portincaple Ag & B
7 a2 Portinfer Jersey
60 B3 Portington E R Yk
83 G6 Portinnisherrich Ag & B
71 F2 Portinscale Cumb
17 F6 Portishead N Som
101 G6 Portknockie Moray
95 H5 Portlethen Abers
70 C4 Portling D & G
3 F3 Portloe Cnwll
107 H4 Portmahomack Highld
47 E5 Portmeirion Gwynd
3 F3 Portmellon Cnwll
90 B4 Portnacroish Ag & B
111 e6 Portnaguran W Isls
74 A6 Portnahaven Ag & B
96 B5 Portnalong Highld
86 D3 Portobello C Edin
40 B3 Portobello Wolves
18 D1 Porton Wilts
68 B3 Portpatrick D & G
2 C4 Portreath Cnwll
96 C6 Portree Highld
3 E3 Portscatho Cnwll
9 H3 Portsea C Port
109 H5 Portskerra Highld
28 C2 Portskewett Mons
11 E3 Portslade Br & H
11 F3 Portslade-by-Sea Br & H
68 B3 Portslogan D & G
9 H3 Portsmouth C Port
58 A3 Portsmouth Calder
90 C1 Portsonachan Hotel Ag & B
102 B5 Portsoy Abers
9 F4 Portswood C Sotn
89 E5 Portuairk Highld
40 C1 Portway Worcs

Portwrinkle - Rochdale 185

4 D2 Portwrinkle Cnwll
69 F2 Portyerrock D & G
34 B3 Poslingford Suffk
79 E5 Posso Border
5 G5 Postbridge Devon
20 A5 Postcombe Oxon
13 F5 Postling Kent
45 F3 Postwick Norfk
95 E5 Potarch Abers
32 B2 Potsgrove Beds
50 B4 Pott Shrigley Ches
20 D6 Potten End Herts
67 F1 Potter Brompton N York
45 G4 Potter Heigham Norfk
52 C2 Potterhanworth Lincs
52 C2 Potterhanworth Booths Lincs
18 C3 Potterne Wilts
18 C3 Potterne Wick Wilts
21 E5 Potters Bar Herts
20 D5 Potters Crouch Herts
41 F3 Potters Marston Leics
31 H4 Potterspury Nhants
103 E1 Potterton Abers
66 B4 Potto N York
32 D4 Potton Beds
14 B2 Poughill Cnwll
15 G2 Poughill Devon
8 D4 Poulner Hants
18 C3 Poulshot Wilts
18 D6 Poulton Gloucs
56 D6 Poulton-le-Fylde Lancs
11 G4 Pound Green E Susx
34 B4 Pound Green Suffk
11 F5 Pound Hill W Susx
26 B2 Poundffald Swans
31 G3 Poundon Bucks
5 G4 Poundsgate Devon
14 B1 Poundstock Cnwll
69 F2 Pouton D & G
11 F6 Povey Cross Surrey
81 F2 Powburn Nthumb
6 B4 Powderham Devon
7 F5 Powerstock Dorset
71 E5 Powfoot D & G
71 E4 Powhill Cumb
39 H2 Powick Worcs
86 A5 Powmill P & K
7 H4 Poxwell Dorset
20 D3 Poyle Slough
11 F3 Poynings W Susx
17 G1 Poyntington Dorset
50 A5 Poynton Ches
49 E2 Poynton Green Wrekin
2 C2 Praa Sands Cnwll
21 G2 Pratt's Bottom Gt Lon
2 C3 Praze-an-Beeble Cnwll
49 E3 Prees Shrops
49 E3 Prees Green Shrops
62 D1 Preesall Lancs
36 D2 Pren-gwyn Cerdgn
81 F2 Prendwick Nthumb
47 E5 Prenteg Gwynd
57 E2 Prescot Knows
16 C1 Prescott Devon
94 B3 Presnerb Angus
56 B1 Prestatyn Denbgs
50 A4 Prestbury Ches
29 G5 Prestbury Gloucs
38 D3 Presteigne Powys
17 G3 Prestleigh Somset
87 G2 Preston Border
11 F3 Preston Br & H
6 A3 Preston Devon
7 H4 Preston Dorset
87 F4 Preston E Loth
61 E3 Preston E R Yk
18 C6 Preston Gloucs
32 D2 Preston Herts
23 E2 Preston Kent
23 G2 Preston Kent
57 E5 Preston Lancs
81 G3 Preston Nthumb
42 B2 Preston Rutlnd
16 C3 Preston Somset
34 C4 Preston Suffk
6 A2 Preston Torbay
19 E4 Preston Wilts
30 C6 Preston Bagot Warwks
31 G3 Preston Bissett Bucks
16 C2 Preston Bowyer Somset
49 E2 Preston Brockhurst Shrops
57 E1 Preston Brook Halton
19 H1 Preston Candover Hants
31 F5 Preston Capes Nhants
30 C6 Preston Green Warwks
49 E2 Preston Gubbals Shrops
30 D5 Preston on Stour Warwks
57 E1 Preston on the Hill Halton
28 B6 Preston on Wye Herefs
63 E4 Preston Patrick Cumb
17 F1 Preston Plucknett Somset
49 F1 Preston upon the Weald Moors Wrekin
39 E1 Preston Wynne Herefs
65 E3 Preston-under-Scar N York
86 D3 Prestonpans E Loth
57 G3 Prestwich Bury
76 C4 Prestwick S Ayrs
76 C4 Prestwick Airport S Ayrs
20 C5 Prestwood Bucks
33 G6 Prickwillow Cambs
17 F4 Priddy Somset
63 E3 Priest Hutton Lancs
77 E5 Priestland E Ayrs
38 C5 Priestweston Shrops
87 G2 Primrosehill Border
80 D3 Primsidemill Border
20 B5 Princes Risborough Bucks
41 E1 Princethorpe Warwks
5 F4 Princetown Devon
31 F5 Priors Hardwick Warwks
31 F5 Priors Marston Warwks
29 F5 Priors Norton Gloucs
17 H5 Priston BaNES
22 D4 Prittlewell Sthend
10 A4 Privett Hants
3 E4 Probus Cnwll
87 E4 Prora E Loth
71 E3 Prospect Cumb
12 C2 Prospidnick Cnwll
102 D5 Protstonhill Abers
73 E3 Prudhoe Nthumb
17 G5 Publow BaNES
33 F1 Puckeridge Herts
17 E1 Puckington Somset
17 H6 Pucklechurch S Glos
48 D6 Puddington Ches
15 G2 Puddington Devon
7 H5 Puddletown Dorset
58 D3 Pudsey Leeds
10 D4 Pulborough W Susx
48 D5 Pulford Ches
7 H6 Pulham Dorset
45 E1 Pulham Market Norfk
45 E1 Pulham St Mary Norfk
32 C2 Pulloxhill Beds
86 B3 Pumpherston W Loth
37 E1 Pumsaint Carmth
24 D5 Puncheston Pembks
7 F4 Puncknowle Dorset
12 B4 Punnett's Town E Susx
10 A3 Purbrook Hants
22 A3 Purfleet Thurr
17 E3 Puriton Somset
22 D5 Purleigh Essex
21 F2 Purley Gt Lon
19 H4 Purley W Berk
17 H1 Purse Caundle Dorset
7 E6 Purtington Somset
29 E3 Purton Gloucs
29 E3 Purton Gloucs
18 D5 Purton Wilts
18 D5 Purton Stoke Wilts
31 G4 Pury End Nhants
19 F6 Pusey Oxon
28 D6 Putley Herefs
28 D6 Putley Green Herefs
29 E4 Putloe Gloucs
21 E3 Putney Gt Lon
6 C1 Putron Village Guern
10 C6 Puttenham Surrey
31 H4 Puxley Nhants
17 E5 Puxton N Som
26 B3 Pwll Carmth
25 F4 Pwll Trap Carmth
48 B4 Pwll-glas Denbgs
26 D2 Pwll-y-glaw Neath
27 F5 Pwllgloyw Powys
46 C5 Pwllheli Gwynd
28 C2 Pwllmeyric Mons
51 E2 Pye Bridge Derbys
21 G6 Pye Corner Herts
11 F3 Pyecombe W Susx
26 D1 Pyle Brdgnd
16 C2 Pyleigh Somset
17 G3 Pylle Somset
43 F1 Pymoor Cambs
7 F5 Pymore Dorset
20 D2 Pyrford Surrey
20 A5 Pyrton Oxon
32 B6 Pytchley Nhants
14 C2 Pyworthy Devon

Q

42 D5 Quadring Lincs
31 H2 Quainton Bucks
16 D3 Quantock Hills Somset
19 E1 Quarley Hants
51 E1 Quarndon Derbys
84 C2 Quarrier's Village Inver
42 C6 Quarrington Lincs
73 G1 Quarrington Hill Dur
40 A2 Quarry Bank Dudley
101 E5 Quarrywood Moray
84 B2 Quarter N Ayrs
85 F1 Quarter S Lans
39 G5 Quatford Shrops
39 G4 Quatt Shrops
73 F1 Quebec Dur
29 F4 Quedgeley Gloucs
33 G6 Queen Adelaide Cambs
17 G2 Queen Camel Somset
17 G5 Queen Charlton BaNES
84 D5 Queen Elizabeth Forest Park Stirlg
8 A6 Queen Oak Dorset
12 B6 Queen Street Kent
9 G2 Queen's Bower IOW
22 D3 Queenborough Kent
29 F6 Queenhill Worcs
58 C3 Queensbury Brad
48 D6 Queensferry Flints
85 F2 Queenslie C Glas
85 F3 Queenzieburn N Lans
33 G2 Quendon Essex
41 G4 Queniborough Leics
30 C1 Quenington Gloucs
4 D3 Quethiock Cnwll
44 D1 Quidenham Norfk
8 D6 Quidhampton Wilts
31 H5 Quinton Nhants
3 E5 Quintrell Downs Cnwll
5 E5 Quither Devon
87 G2 Quixwood Border
14 D1 Quoditch Devon
41 F5 Quorn Leics
78 D6 Quothquan S Lans
111 h2 Quoyburray Ork
111 g2 Quoyloo Ork

R

79 E5 Rachan Mill Border
55 E3 Rachub Gwynd
15 G3 Rackenford Devon
10 D3 Rackham W Susx
45 F3 Rackheath Norfk
70 D6 Racks D & G
111 g1 Rackwick Ork
40 D6 Radbourne Derbys
57 G3 Radcliffe Bury
73 F6 Radcliffe Nthumb
51 G1 Radcliffe on Trent Notts
31 G3 Radclive Bucks
107 F2 Raddery Highld
87 E6 Radernie Fife
31 E6 Radford Semele Warwks
21 E5 Radlett Herts
19 G6 Radley Oxon
22 B5 Radley Green Essex
20 B5 Radnage Bucks
17 G4 Radstock BaNES
31 G4 Radstone Nhants
31 E4 Radway Warwks
32 C4 Radwell Beds
32 D2 Radwell Herts
33 G3 Radwinter Essex
27 G1 Radyr Cardif
100 D5 Rafford Moray
41 G5 Ragdale Leics
28 C3 Raglan Mons
52 A3 Ragnall Notts
99 F5 Raigbeg Highld
39 H2 Rainbow Hill Worcs
57 E3 Rainford St Hel
21 H3 Rainham Gt Lon
22 C2 Rainham Medway
57 E2 Rainhill St Hel
57 E2 Rainhill Stoops St Hel
50 B4 Rainow Ches
65 G1 Rainton N York
51 G3 Rainworth Notts
60 C6 Raisthorpe N York
93 E2 Rait P & K
53 E4 Raithby Lincs
53 F2 Raithby Lincs
10 B4 Rake W Susx
99 E2 Ralia Highld
96 A6 Ramasaig Highld
2 D3 Rame Cnwll
5 E2 Rame Cnwll
7 G5 Rampisham Dorset
62 C3 Rampside Cumb
33 F5 Rampton Cambs
52 A3 Rampton Notts
57 G4 Ramsbottom Bury
19 E4 Ramsbury Wilts
110 B2 Ramscraigs Highld
10 A4 Ramsdean Hants
19 G3 Ramsdell Hants
31 E2 Ramsden Oxon
22 C4 Ramsden Bellhouse Essex
43 E1 Ramsey Cambs
35 E2 Ramsey Essex
116 d4 Ramsey IOM
43 E1 Ramsey Forty Foot Cambs
43 E1 Ramsey Heights Cambs
23 E5 Ramsey Island Essex
43 E1 Ramsey Mereside Cambs
43 E1 Ramsey St Mary's Cambs
23 H2 Ramsgate Kent
65 E1 Ramsgill N York
80 D1 Ramshope Nthumb
50 C2 Ramshorn Staffs
10 C5 Ramsnest Common Surrey
52 D3 Ranby Lincs
51 G4 Ranby Notts
52 D3 Rand Lincs
29 F3 Randwick Gloucs
84 D2 Ranfurly Rens
40 C5 Rangemore Staffs
29 E2 Rangeworthy S Glos
76 D3 Rankinston E Ayrs
57 G5 Rann Bl w D
91 F4 Rannoch Station P & K
16 B3 Ranscombe Somset
51 G5 Ranskill Notts
49 H2 Ranton Staffs
49 H2 Ranton Green Staffs
45 F3 Ranworth Norfk
85 G5 Raploch Stirlg
111 h3 Rapness Ork
70 B4 Rascarrel D & G
84 B4 Rashfield Ag & B
30 A6 Rashwood Worcs
66 B1 Raskelf N York
58 C2 Rastrick Calder
97 G4 Ratagan Highld
41 F4 Ratby Leics
41 E3 Ratcliffe Culey Leics
41 F6 Ratcliffe on Soar Notts
41 G4 Ratcliffe on the Wreake Leics
103 E5 Rathen Abers
93 F2 Rathillet Fife
63 G2 Rathmell N York
86 B3 Ratho C Edin
101 G5 Rathven Moray
31 E4 Ratley Warwks
23 G1 Ratling Kent
38 D5 Ratlinghope Shrops
110 C6 Rattar Highld
5 G3 Rattery Devon
34 C4 Rattlesden Suffk
12 B2 Ratton Village E Susx
92 D4 Rattray P & K
32 C5 Raunds Nhants
51 F6 Ravenfield Rothm
62 B5 Ravenglass Cumb
45 G2 Raveningham Norfk
67 F3 Ravenscar N York
49 H4 Ravenscliffe C Stke
32 C4 Ravensden Beds
51 F2 Ravenshead Notts
58 D2 Ravensthorpe Kirk
41 G1 Ravensthorpe Nhants
41 E4 Ravenstone Leics
32 B4 Ravenstone M Keyn
63 G6 Ravenstonedale Cumb
77 H5 Ravenstruther S Lans
65 E4 Ravensworth N York
59 G2 Rawcliffe E R Yk
59 F5 Rawcliffe York
58 D4 Rawdon Leeds
22 D2 Rawling Street Kent
51 E6 Rawmarsh Rothm
22 C4 Rawreth Essex
6 D6 Rawridge Devon
57 G5 Rawtenstall Lancs
34 D3 Raydon Suffk
22 C4 Rayleigh Essex
34 B1 Rayne Essex
21 E2 Raynes Park Gt Lon
33 G5 Reach Cambs
57 G6 Read Lancs
20 A3 Reading Readg
12 D5 Reading Street Kent
23 H2 Reading Street Kent
64 A5 Reagill Cumb
107 F5 Rearquhar Highld
41 G4 Rearsby Leics
110 A5 Reay Highld
23 G2 Reculver Kent
16 C1 Red Ball Somset
8 D3 Red Hill Bmouth
30 C5 Red Hill Warwks
34 A5 Red Lodge Suffk
25 F4 Red Roses Carmth
73 F6 Red Row Nthumb
54 D4 Red Wharf Bay IOA
25 E3 Redberth Pembks
20 D6 Redbourn Herts
52 B5 Redbourne N Linc
28 D4 Redbrook Gloucs
49 E3 Redbrook Wrexhm
12 D5 Redbrook Street Kent
100 C4 Redburn Highld
66 C5 Redcar R & Cl
70 B5 Redcastle D & G
107 E1 Redcastle Highld
85 H3 Redding Falk
85 H3 Reddingmuirhead Falk
30 B6 Redditch Worcs
34 B4 Rede Suffk
45 F1 Redenhall Norfk
72 C4 Redesmouth Nthumb
95 F3 Redford Abers
93 G4 Redford Angus
10 B4 Redford W Susx
79 F4 Redfordgreen Border
92 D2 Redgorton P & K
34 D6 Redgrave Suffk
95 F6 Redhill Abers
33 E2 Redhill Herts
17 F5 Redhill N Som
21 F1 Redhill Surrey
45 G1 Redisham Suffk
17 G6 Redland Bristl
111 h2 Redland Ork
35 E5 Redlingfield Suffk
35 E5 Redlingfield Green Suffk
17 H2 Redlynch Somset
8 D5 Redlynch Wilts
39 G3 Redmarley Worcs
29 E5 Redmarley D'Abitot Gloucs
65 G5 Redmarshall S on T
42 A5 Redmile Leics
65 E3 Redmire N York
95 F4 Redmyre Abers
48 D2 Rednal Shrops
80 B3 Redpath Border
105 E3 Redpoint Highld
2 D3 Redruth Cnwll
92 D3 Redstone P & K
28 C1 Redwick Newpt
28 D2 Redwick S Glos
65 F5 Redworth Darltn
33 E2 Reed Herts
45 G2 Reedham Norfk
60 B2 Reedness E R Yk
52 C3 Reepham Lincs
44 D4 Reepham Norfk
65 E3 Reeth N York
40 D1 Reeves Green Solhll
108 A1 Reiff Highld
21 E1 Reigate Surrey
67 G1 Reighton N York
103 E2 Reisque Abers
110 D4 Reiss Highld
2 C3 Relubbus Cnwll
100 C4 Relugas Moray
20 B4 Remenham Wokham
20 B4 Remenham Hill Wokham
41 F5 Rempstone Notts
30 B1 Rendcomb Gloucs
35 F5 Rendham Suffk
84 D2 Renfrew Rens
32 C4 Renhold Beds
51 E4 Renishaw Derbys
81 G2 Rennington Nthumb
84 D3 Renton W Duns
72 A1 Renwick Cumb
45 G4 Repps Norfk
40 D5 Repton Derbys
107 F1 Resaurie Highld
3 F3 Rescassa Cnwll
89 G5 Resipole Highld
2 C3 Reskadinnick Cnwll
107 F3 Resolis Highld
26 D3 Resolven Neath
84 B6 Rest and be thankful Ag & B
87 H2 Reston Border
93 G4 Reswallie Angus
51 G4 Retford Notts
22 C5 Rettendon Essex
53 E2 Revesby Lincs
9 F3 Rew Street IOW
6 B5 Rewe Devon
35 G6 Reydon Suffk
44 D3 Reymerston Norfk
25 E3 Reynalton Pembks
26 B2 Reynoldston Swans
4 D4 Rezare Cnwll
37 F1 Rhandirmwyn Carmth
37 H3 Rhayader Powys
106 D1 Rheindown Highld
48 C6 Rhes-y-cae Flints
48 B5 Rhewl Denbgs
48 B4 Rhewl Denbgs
108 B2 Rhicarn Highld
108 C4 Rhiconich Highld
107 F3 Rhicullen Highld
27 E3 Rhigos Rhondd
105 H5 Rhireavach Highld
107 G5 Rhives Highld
27 G1 Rhiwbina Cardif
28 A2 Rhiwderyn Newpt
54 D3 Rhiwlas Gwynd
12 B6 Rhoden Green Kent
13 F6 Rhodes Minnis Kent
24 B5 Rhodiad-y-brenin Pembks
70 B5 Rhonehouse D & G
16 C5 Rhoose V Glam
25 G6 Rhos Carmth
26 D3 Rhos Neath
55 F4 Rhos-on-Sea Conwy
47 H5 Rhos-y-gwaliau Gwynd
54 C5 Rhosbeirio IOA
54 B4 Rhoscolyn IOA
24 C3 Rhoscrowther Pembks
48 C6 Rhosesmor Flints
38 C1 Rhosgoch Powys
36 B1 Rhoshill Pembks
46 B4 Rhoshirwaun Gwynd
47 E2 Rhoslefain Gwynd
48 C4 Rhosllanerchrugog Wrexhm
54 C4 Rhosmeirch IOA
54 B3 Rhosneigr IOA
25 G2 Rhossili Swans
54 D2 Rhostryfan Gwynd
48 C4 Rhostyllen Wrexhm
54 C5 Rhosybol IOA
48 C3 Rhosymedre Wrexhm
84 C4 Rhu Ag & B
48 B6 Rhuallt Denbgs
83 H3 Rhubodach Ag & B
55 H4 Rhuddlan Denbgs
75 E5 Rhunahaorine Ag & B
47 E5 Rhyd Gwynd
54 D2 Rhyd-Ddu Gwynd
47 G5 Rhyd-uchaf Gwynd
37 E5 Rhyd-y pennau Cerdgn
46 C5 Rhyd-y-clafdy Gwynd
55 G4 Rhyd-y-foel Conwy
54 D3 Rhyd-y-groes Gwynd
25 H5 Rhydargaeau Carmth
26 B6 Rhydcymerau Carmth
36 C2 Rhydlewis Cerdgn
36 D2 Rhydowen Cerdgn
26 C3 Rhydyfro Neath
55 H4 Rhyl Denbgs
27 G3 Rhymney Caerph
92 D2 Rhynd P & K
101 G2 Rhynie Abers
107 G4 Rhynie Highld
39 G3 Ribbesford Worcs
57 E5 Ribbleton Lancs
57 F6 Ribchester Lancs
52 D5 Riby Lincs
59 G4 Riccall N York
79 H2 Riccarton Border
76 D5 Riccarton E Ayrs
39 E3 Richards Castle Herefs
21 E3 Richmond Gt Lon
65 F3 Richmond N York
51 E5 Richmond Sheff
6 b1 Richmond Fort Guern
40 A5 Rickerscote Staffs
17 F5 Rickford N Som
5 G1 Rickham Devon
34 D6 Rickinghall Suffk
33 F2 Rickling Essex
33 G2 Rickling Green Essex
20 D4 Rickmansworth Herts
80 B3 Riddell Border
15 E3 Riddlecombe Devon
58 C4 Riddlesden Brad
8 B2 Ridge Dorset
21 E5 Ridge Herts
8 B6 Ridge Wilts
40 D3 Ridge Lane Warwks
17 F5 Ridgehill N Som
51 E4 Ridgeway Derbys
34 B3 Ridgewell Essex
11 G4 Ridgewood E Susx
32 B2 Ridgmont Beds
72 D3 Riding Mill Nthumb
45 F5 Ridlington Norfk
42 B2 Ridlington Rutlnd
72 D5 Ridsdale Nthumb
66 C2 Rievaulx N York
66 C2 Rievaulx Abbey N York
71 F5 Rigg D & G
85 F3 Riggend N Lans
100 B4 Righoul Highld
53 F3 Rigsby Lincs
78 C6 Rigside S Lans
57 F5 Riley Green Lancs
4 D4 Rilla Mill Cnwll
67 E1 Rillington N York
63 G1 Rimington Lancs
17 G2 Rimpton Somset
61 F3 Rimswell E R Yk
24 D5 Rinaston Pembks
39 G5 Rindleford Shrops
69 H3 Ringford D & G
45 E3 Ringland Norfk
11 G3 Ringmer E Susx
5 G2 Ringmore Devon
6 B3 Ringmore Devon
101 E4 Ringorm Moray
45 G1 Ringsfield Suffk
45 G1 Ringsfield Corner Suffk
20 C6 Ringshall Bucks
34 D4 Ringshall Suffk
34 D4 Ringshall Stocks Suffk
32 C6 Ringstead Nhants
44 A5 Ringstead Norfk
8 D4 Ringwood Hants
13 H6 Ringwould Kent
11 G3 Ripe E Susx
51 E2 Ripley Derbys
8 D3 Ripley Hants
58 D5 Ripley N York
20 D1 Ripley Surrey
9 H5 Riplington Hants
65 G1 Ripon N York
42 C4 Rippingale Lincs
23 H1 Ripple Kent
29 F6 Ripple Worcs
58 B2 Ripponden Calder
74 B5 Risabus Ag & B
39 E2 Risbury Herefs
34 B5 Risby Suffk
27 G2 Risca Caerph
61 E4 Rise E R Yk
42 D5 Risegate Lincs
32 C5 Riseley Beds
20 A2 Riseley Wokham
35 E5 Rishangles Suffk
57 G5 Rishton Lancs
58 B2 Rishworth Calder
41 F6 Risley Derbys
57 F2 Risley Warrtn
58 D6 Risplith N York
13 G6 River Kent
10 C4 River W Susx
107 E2 Riverford Highld
21 G1 Riverhead Kent
57 F4 Rivington Lancs
31 H5 Roade Nhants
77 G6 Roadmeetings S Lans
77 E3 Roadside E Ayrs
110 B5 Roadside Highld
16 B3 Roadwater Somset
96 B6 Roag Highld
76 C2 Roan of Craigoch S Ayrs
33 F2 Roast Green Essex
27 G1 Roath Cardif
79 G4 Roberton Border
78 C5 Roberton S Lans
12 C4 Robertsbridge E Susx
58 D2 Roberttown Kirk
25 E4 Robeston Wathen Pembks
71 F6 Robgill Tower D & G
67 E4 Robin Hood's Bay N York
15 E3 Roborough Devon
5 E3 Roborough Devon
56 D2 Roby Knows
50 C1 Rocester Staffs
24 C4 Roch Pembks
58 A2 Rochdale Rochdl

3 F5 **Roche** Cnwll
22 C2 **Rochester** Medway
72 C6 **Rochester** Nthumb
22 D4 **Rochford** Essex
39 F3 **Rochford** Worcs
3 F6 **Rock** Cnwll
81 G2 **Rock** Nthumb
39 G3 **Rock** Worcs
56 D2 **Rock Ferry** Wirral
6 B5 **Rockbeare** Devon
8 D5 **Rockbourne** Hants
71 F5 **Rockcliffe** Cumb
70 B4 **Rockcliffe** D & G
6 B2 **Rockend** Torbay
107 H4 **Rockfield** Highld
28 C4 **Rockfield** Mons
15 G5 **Rockford** Devon
28 D2 **Rockhampton** S Glos
38 C4 **Rockhill** Shrops
42 B2 **Rockingham** Nhants
44 D2 **Rockland All Saints** Norfk
45 F3 **Rockland St Mary** Norfk
44 D2 **Rockland St Peter** Norfk
51 H4 **Rockley** Notts
18 D4 **Rockley** Wilts
84 B4 **Rockville** Ag & B
20 B4 **Rockwell End** Bucks
29 F3 **Rodborough** Gloucs
18 D5 **Rodbourne** Swindn
18 B5 **Rodbourne** Wilts
7 G4 **Rodden** Dorset
18 A2 **Rode** Somset
49 G5 **Rode Heath** Ches
111 c4 **Rodel** W Isls
49 F1 **Roden** Wrekin
16 B3 **Rodhuish** Somset
49 F1 **Rodington** Wrekin
49 F1 **Rodington Heath** Wrekin
29 E4 **Rodley** Gloucs
29 G3 **Rodmarton** Gloucs
11 G3 **Rodmell** E Susx
22 D2 **Rodmersham** Kent
22 D2 **Rodmersham Green** Kent
17 F4 **Rodney Stoke** Somset
50 D1 **Rodsley** Derbys
21 E6 **Roe Green** Herts
33 E2 **Roe Green** Herts
59 E6 **Roecliffe** N York
21 E3 **Roehampton** Gt Lon
11 E5 **Roffey** W Susx
107 F6 **Rogart** Highld
10 B4 **Rogate** W Susx
28 B2 **Rogerstone** Newpt
111 c4 **Roghadal** W Isls
28 C2 **Rogiet** Mons
19 H5 **Roke** Oxon
73 G3 **Roker** Sundld
45 G3 **Rollesby** Norfk
41 H3 **Rolleston** Leics
51 H2 **Rolleston** Notts
40 D5 **Rolleston** Staffs
61 F4 **Rolston** E R Yk
12 D5 **Rolvenden** Kent
12 D5 **Rolvenden Layne** Kent
64 B5 **Romaldkirk** Dur
28 B2 **Roman Amphitheatre Caerleon** Newpt
17 H5 **Roman Baths & Pump Room** BaNES
65 G3 **Romanby** N York
86 B1 **Romanno Bridge** Border
15 F3 **Romansleigh** Devon
104 C2 **Romesdal** Highld
8 C4 **Romford** Dorset
21 G4 **Romford** Gt Lon
50 B5 **Romiley** Stockp
9 F5 **Romsey** Hants
39 G4 **Romsley** Shrops
40 B2 **Romsley** Worcs
83 F1 **Ronachan** Ag & B
72 D1 **Rookhope** Dur
9 G2 **Rookley** IOW
17 E4 **Rooks Bridge** Somset
16 C2 **Rooks Nest** Somset
65 F2 **Rookwith** N York
61 F3 **Roos** E R Yk
32 C4 **Roothams Green** Beds
9 H6 **Ropley** Hants
9 H6 **Ropley Dean** Hants
42 C5 **Ropsley** Lincs
103 F4 **Rora** Abers
38 C5 **Rorrington** Shrops
101 F4 **Rosarie** Moray
2 D4 **Rose** Cnwll
15 G3 **Rose Ash** Devon
34 C2 **Rose Green** Essex
34 C3 **Rose Green** Suffk
34 C3 **Rose Green** Suffk
10 C2 **Rose Green** W Susx
57 G5 **Rose Hill** Lancs
77 G6 **Rosebank** S Lans
25 E5 **Rosebush** Pembks
66 D3 **Rosedale Abbey** N York
106 D6 **Rosehall** Highld
103 E6 **Rosehearty** Abers
100 D6 **Roseisle** Moray
12 B2 **Roselands** E Susx
24 D3 **Rosemarket** Pembks
107 F2 **Rosemarkie** Highld
16 C1 **Rosemary Lane** Devon
92 D3 **Rosemount** P & K
3 F5 **Rosenannon** Cnwll
86 C2 **Rosewell** Mdloth
65 H5 **Roseworth** S on T
71 H1 **Rosgill** Cumb
96 B6 **Roskhill** Highld
71 F4 **Rosley** Cumb
86 C2 **Roslin** Mdloth
40 D5 **Rosliston** Derbys
84 C4 **Rosneath** Ag & B
69 G2 **Ross** D & G
28 D5 **Ross-on-Wye** Herefs
48 D5 **Rossett** Wrexhm
58 D5 **Rossett Green** N York
51 G6 **Rossington** Donc
84 D3 **Rossland** Rens
110 C3 **Roster** Highld
57 G1 **Rostherne** Ches
71 F1 **Rosthwaite** Cumb
50 C1 **Roston** Derbys
86 B4 **Rosyth** Fife
73 E6 **Rothbury** Nthumb
41 G5 **Rotherby** Leics
12 A5 **Rotherfield** E Susx
20 A3 **Rotherfield Greys** Oxon
20 A3 **Rotherfield Peppard** Oxon
51 E5 **Rotherham** Rothm
31 H5 **Rothersthorpe** Nhants
20 A1 **Rotherwick** Hants
101 E4 **Rothes** Moray
84 A2 **Rothesay** Ag & B
102 D3 **Rothiebrisbane** Abers
102 B4 **Rothiemay** Moray
99 G3 **Rothiemurchus Lodge** Highld
102 C3 **Rothienorman** Abers
41 G4 **Rothley** Leics
102 C3 **Rothmaise** Abers
59 E3 **Rothwell** Leeds
52 D5 **Rothwell** Lincs
32 A6 **Rothwell** Nhants
94 C3 **Rottal Lodge** Angus
11 F2 **Rottingdean** Br & H
70 C1 **Rottington** Cumb
78 D1 **Roucan** D & G
23 F2 **Rough Common** Kent
44 B4 **Rougham** Norfk
34 C5 **Rougham Green** Suffk
101 F1 **Roughpark** Abers
53 E2 **Roughton** Lincs
45 E5 **Roughton** Norfk
39 G5 **Roughton** Shrops
22 B6 **Roundbush Green** Essex
7 E6 **Roundham** Somset
59 E4 **Roundhay** Leeds
18 C3 **Roundway** Wilts
93 F4 **Roundyhill** Angus
30 B5 **Rous Lench** Worcs
6 D4 **Rousdon** Devon
31 F3 **Rousham** Oxon
84 B2 **Routenburn** N Ayrs
61 E4 **Routh** E R Yk
4 B4 **Row** Cnwll
63 E5 **Row** Cumb
34 B1 **Row Green** Essex
79 G1 **Rowanburn** D & G
84 C5 **Rowardennan Hotel** Stirlg
84 C5 **Rowardennan Lodge** Stirlg
50 B5 **Rowarth** Derbys
17 F4 **Rowberrow** Somset
18 C3 **Rowde** Wilts
55 F3 **Rowen** Conwy
72 B3 **Rowfoot** Nthumb
34 D1 **Rowhedge** Essex
40 D1 **Rowington** Warwks
50 D4 **Rowland** Derbys
10 A3 **Rowland's Castle** Hants
73 F3 **Rowland's Gill** Gatesd
10 B6 **Rowledge** Surrey
73 E2 **Rowley** Dur
60 D3 **Rowley** E R Yk
41 E2 **Rowley Green** Covtry
40 B2 **Rowley Regis** Sandw
28 B5 **Rowlstone** Herefs
10 D6 **Rowly** Surrey
9 G3 **Rowner** Hants
40 B1 **Rowney Green** Worcs
9 F5 **Rownhams** Hants
70 D2 **Rowrah** Cumb
32 B1 **Rowsham** Bucks
50 D3 **Rowsley** Derbys
52 C1 **Rowston** Lincs
49 E5 **Rowton** Ches
49 F2 **Rowton** Wrekin
80 C3 **Roxburgh** Border
60 C2 **Roxby** N Linc
32 D4 **Roxton** Beds
22 B6 **Roxwell** Essex
98 B1 **Roy Bridge** Highld
86 C3 **Royal Botanic Gardens** C Edin
21 G6 **Roydon** Essex
44 A4 **Roydon** Norfk
34 D6 **Roydon** Norfk
21 G6 **Roydon Hamlet** Essex
59 E1 **Royston** Barns
33 E3 **Royston** Herts
58 A1 **Royton** Oldham
7 c2 **Rozel** Jersey
48 C4 **Ruabon** Wrexhm
88 B4 **Ruaig** Ag & B
3 E3 **Ruan Lanihorne** Cnwll
2 D1 **Ruan Major** Cnwll
2 D1 **Ruan Minor** Cnwll
28 D4 **Ruardean** Gloucs
28 D4 **Ruardean Hill** Gloucs
28 D4 **Ruardean Woodside** Gloucs
40 B1 **Rubery** Birm
111 b2 **Rubha Ban** W Isls
28 C6 **Ruckhall** Herefs
13 E5 **Ruckinge** Kent
39 E5 **Ruckley** Shrops
66 B4 **Rudby** N York
73 E3 **Rudchester** Nthumb
41 F6 **Ruddington** Notts
18 B2 **Rudge** Somset
28 D2 **Rudgeway** S Glos
10 D5 **Rudgwick** W Susx
22 D5 **Rudley Green** Essex
18 B4 **Rudloe** Wilts
27 G2 **Rudry** Caerph
61 E6 **Rudston** E R Yk
50 B3 **Rudyard** Staffs
80 C2 **Ruecastle** Border
57 E4 **Rufford** Lancs
59 F5 **Rufforth** York
41 F1 **Rugby** Warwks
40 B5 **Rugeley** Staffs
16 D2 **Ruishton** Somset
20 D4 **Ruislip** Gt Lon
101 F4 **Rumbach** Moray
86 A5 **Rumbling Bridge** P & K
35 F6 **Rumburgh** Suffk
3 E6 **Rumford** Cnwll
85 H3 **Rumford** Falk
27 G1 **Rumney** Cardif
57 E1 **Runcorn** Halton
10 C2 **Runcton** W Susx
43 G3 **Runcton Holme** Norfk
10 B6 **Runfold** Surrey
44 D3 **Runhall** Norfk
45 G3 **Runham** Norfk
16 C2 **Runnington** Somset
66 D5 **Runswick** N York
94 C3 **Runtaleave** Angus
22 C4 **Runwell** Essex
20 B3 **Ruscombe** Wokham
23 F6 **Rush Green** Essex
21 G4 **Rush Green** Gt Lon
28 D6 **Rushall** Herefs
45 E1 **Rushall** Norfk
18 D2 **Rushall** Wilts
34 C4 **Rushbrooke** Suffk
39 E5 **Rushbury** Shrops
33 E2 **Rushden** Herts
32 B5 **Rushden** Nhants
34 C6 **Rushford** Norfk
12 B4 **Rushlake Green** E Susx
45 G1 **Rushmere** Suffk
10 C5 **Rushmoor** Surrey
40 A1 **Rushock** Worcs
57 H2 **Rusholme** Manch
49 F5 **Rushton** Ches
42 A1 **Rushton** Nhants
50 B3 **Rushton Spencer** Staffs
39 G2 **Rushwick** Worcs
65 F6 **Rushyford** Dur
85 E5 **Ruskie** Stirlg
52 C1 **Ruskington** Lincs
62 D4 **Rusland** Cumb
11 E5 **Rusper** W Susx
29 E4 **Ruspidge** Gloucs
11 E5 **Russ Hill** Surrey
20 A4 **Russell's Water** Oxon
12 B5 **Rusthall** Kent
10 D2 **Rustington** W Susx
67 E2 **Ruston** N York
60 D6 **Ruston Parva** E R Yk
67 E4 **Ruswarp** N York
80 C3 **Rutherford** Border
85 E2 **Rutherglen** S Lans
3 F5 **Ruthernbridge** Cnwll
48 B5 **Ruthin** Denbgs
95 H6 **Ruthrieston** C Aber
101 G4 **Ruthven** Abers
93 E4 **Ruthven** Angus
99 F3 **Ruthven** Highld
93 E4 **Ruthven House** Angus
3 E5 **Ruthvoes** Cnwll
70 D5 **Ruthwell** D & G
48 D2 **Ruyton-XI-Towns** Shrops
72 D4 **Ryal** Nthumb
7 E5 **Ryall** Dorset
29 F6 **Ryall** Worcs
22 B2 **Ryarsh** Kent
62 D6 **Rydal** Cumb
9 G3 **Ryde** IOW
12 D4 **Rye** E Susx
12 D4 **Rye Foreign** E Susx
29 E6 **Rye Street** Worcs
42 C3 **Ryhall** Rutlnd
59 E2 **Ryhill** Wakefd
73 G2 **Ryhope** Sundld
52 C3 **Ryland** Lincs
41 F6 **Rylands** Notts
58 B5 **Rylstone** N York
7 G6 **Ryme Intrinseca** Dorset
59 F4 **Ryther** N York
73 E3 **Ryton** Gatesd
39 G6 **Ryton** Shrops
41 E1 **Ryton-on-Dunsmore** Warwks

S

57 G6 **Sabden** Lancs
33 E1 **Sacombe** Herts
73 F2 **Sacriston** Dur
65 G5 **Sadberge** Darltn
75 F4 **Saddell** Ag & B
41 G3 **Saddington** Leics
43 G3 **Saddle Bow** Norfk
11 F3 **Saddlescombe** W Susx
33 G3 **Saffron Walden** Essex
25 E3 **Sageston** Pembks
44 C2 **Saham Hills** Norfk
44 C2 **Saham Toney** Norfk
49 E5 **Saighton** Ches
81 E6 **St Abbs** Border
87 F2 **St Agnes** Border
2 D4 **St Agnes** Cnwll
21 E6 **St Albans** Herts
3 E4 **St Allen** Cnwll
6 b1 **St Andrew** Guern
16 C6 **St Andrew's Major** V Glam
93 G1 **St Andrews** Fife
7 F5 **St Andrews Well** Dorset
78 D2 **St Ann's** D & G
5 G2 **St Ann's Chapel** Devon
56 D5 **St Anne's** Lancs
2 D2 **St Anthony** Cnwll
12 B2 **St Anthony's Hill** E Susx
28 C2 **St Arvans** Mons
48 A6 **St Asaph** Denbgs
16 B5 **St Athan** V Glam
7 b1 **St Aubin** Jersey
3 F4 **St Austell** Cnwll
70 C1 **St Bees** Cumb
3 G4 **St Blazey** Cnwll
80 B3 **St Boswells** Border
7 a1 **St Brelade** Jersey
7 a1 **St Brelade's Bay** Jersey
3 F6 **St Breock** Cnwll
4 B4 **St Breward** Cnwll
28 D3 **St Briavels** Gloucs
16 A6 **St Bride's Major** V Glam
27 F1 **St Brides super-Ely** V Glam
28 B1 **St Brides Wentlooge** Newpt
5 E3 **St Budeaux** C Plym
2 B2 **St Buryan** Cnwll
84 B6 **St Catherines** Ag & B
29 F3 **St Chloe** Gloucs
25 F4 **St Clears** Carmth
4 C4 **St Cleer** Cnwll
3 E3 **St Clement** Cnwll
7 c1 **St Clement** Jersey
4 C5 **St Clether** Cnwll
83 H2 **St Colmac** Ag & B
3 E5 **St Columb Major** Cnwll
3 E5 **St Columb Minor** Cnwll
3 E5 **St Columb Road** Cnwll
103 F5 **St Combs** Abers
45 F1 **St Cross South Elmham** Suffk
95 F3 **St Cyrus** Abers
92 C2 **St David's** P & K
24 B5 **St David's** Pembks
2 D3 **St Day** Cnwll
3 F5 **St Dennis** Cnwll
36 B2 **St Dogmaels** Cerdgn
5 E4 **St Dominick** Cnwll
16 B5 **St Donats** V Glam
4 B4 **St Endellion** Cnwll
3 E5 **St Enoder** Cnwll
3 E4 **St Erme** Cnwll
4 D3 **St Erney** Cnwll
2 C3 **St Erth** Cnwll
2 C3 **St Erth Praze** Cnwll
3 E6 **St Ervan** Cnwll
3 F4 **St Ewe** Cnwll
27 G1 **St Fagans** Cardif
27 G1 **St Fagans Welsh Life Museum** Cardif
103 F4 **St Fergus** Abers
91 H2 **St Fillans** P & K
25 E3 **St Florence** Pembks
14 B1 **St Gennys** Cnwll
55 G4 **St George** Conwy
16 C6 **St George's** V Glam
17 E5 **St Georges** N Som
4 D3 **St Germans** Cnwll
15 E3 **St Giles in the Wood** Devon
4 D5 **St Giles-on-the-Heath** Cnwll
38 A3 **St Harmon** Powys
65 F5 **St Helen Auckland** Dur
45 E4 **St Helena** Norfk
9 H2 **St Helens** IOW
57 E2 **St Helens** St Hel
21 F2 **St Helier** Gt Lon
7 b1 **St Helier** Jersey
2 C2 **St Hilary** Cnwll
16 B6 **St Hilary** V Glam
32 D2 **St Ippollitts** Herts
24 C3 **St Ishmael's** Pembks
3 F6 **St Issey** Cnwll
4 D4 **St Ive** Cnwll
33 E5 **St Ives** Cambs
2 B3 **St Ives** Cnwll
35 F6 **St James South Elmham** Suffk
31 H5 **St James's End** Nhants
5 E2 **St John** Cnwll
7 b2 **St John** Jersey
116 b3 **St John's** IOM
15 E4 **St John's Chapel** Devon
72 C1 **St John's Chapel** Dur
43 G3 **St John's Fen End** Norfk
78 C6 **St John's Kirk** S Lans
69 G5 **St John's Town of Dalry** D & G
21 F4 **St John's Wood** Gt Lon
21 H1 **St Johns** Kent
20 C2 **St Johns** Surrey
39 H2 **St Johns** Worcs
116 c5 **St Jude's** IOM
2 A2 **St Just** Cnwll
3 E3 **St Just-in-Roseland** Cnwll
102 D3 **St Katherines** Abers
2 D2 **St Keverne** Cnwll
3 F6 **St Kew** Cnwll
3 F6 **St Kew Highway** Cnwll
4 C3 **St Keyne** Cnwll
23 E5 **St Lawrence** Essex
9 G1 **St Lawrence** IOW
7 b2 **St Lawrence** Jersey
23 H2 **St Lawrence** Kent
20 C5 **St Leonards** Bucks
8 D4 **St Leonards** Dorset
12 C3 **St Leonards** E Susx
2 A2 **St Levan** Cnwll
16 C6 **St Lythans** V Glam
3 F6 **St Mabyn** Cnwll
92 D2 **St Madoes** P & K
45 F1 **St Margaret South Elmham** Suffk
13 H6 **St Margaret's at Cliffe** Kent
111 h1 **St Margaret's Hope** Ork
28 B5 **St Margarets** Herefs
21 F6 **St Margarets** Herts
116 b3 **St Marks** IOM
4 D3 **St Martin** Cnwll
6 b1 **St Martin** Guern
7 c2 **St Martin** Jersey
92 D2 **St Martin's** P & K
48 D3 **St Martins** Shrops
7 a2 **St Mary** Jersey
19 F2 **St Mary Bourne** Hants
16 B6 **St Mary Church** V Glam
21 G2 **St Mary Cray** Gt Lon
13 E4 **St Mary in the Marsh** Kent
111 h2 **St Mary's** Ork
13 F4 **St Mary's Bay** Kent
22 C3 **St Mary's Hoo** Medway
6 B2 **St Marychurch** Torbay
28 C4 **St Maughans Green** Mons
3 E3 **St Mawes** Cnwll
3 E5 **St Mawgan** Cnwll
5 E3 **St Mellion** Cnwll
27 G1 **St Mellons** Cardif
3 E6 **St Merryn** Cnwll
3 F4 **St Mewan** Cnwll
3 F3 **St Michael Caerhays** Cnwll
17 E2 **St Michael Church** Somset
3 E3 **St Michael Penkevil** Cnwll
45 F1 **St Michael South Elmham** Suffk
57 E6 **St Michael's on Wyre** Lancs
12 D5 **St Michaels** Kent
39 F3 **St Michaels** Worcs
3 F6 **St Minver** Cnwll
87 E6 **St Monans** Fife
4 C4 **St Neot** Cnwll
32 D4 **St Neots** Cambs
24 C6 **St Nicholas** Pembks
16 C6 **St Nicholas** V Glam
23 G2 **St Nicholas at Wade** Kent
85 G4 **St Ninians** Stirlg
45 G2 **St Olaves** Norfk
23 F6 **St Osyth** Essex
7 a2 **St Ouen** Jersey
28 D5 **St Owens Cross** Herefs
32 D1 **St Paul's Walden** Herts
21 G2 **St Pauls Cray** Gt Lon
7 a2 **St Peter** Jersey
6 c1 **St Peter Port** Guern
6 b1 **St Peter's** Guern
23 H2 **St Peter's** Kent
4 C3 **St Pinnock** Cnwll
76 C4 **St Quivox** S Ayrs
6 c2 **St Sampson** Guern
6 b1 **St Saviour** Guern
7 b1 **St Saviour** Jersey
3 F4 **St Stephen** Cnwll
3 F4 **St Stephen's Coombe** Cnwll
4 D5 **St Stephens** Cnwll
5 E3 **St Stephens** Cnwll
4 B5 **St Teath** Cnwll
3 G6 **St Tudy** Cnwll
24 D3 **St Twynnells** Pembks
4 C3 **St Veep** Cnwll
93 H3 **St Vigeans** Angus
3 F5 **St Wenn** Cnwll
28 C5 **St Weonards** Herefs
30 C4 **Saintbury** Gloucs
90 C4 **Salachail** Ag & B
5 G1 **Salcombe** Devon
6 C4 **Salcombe Regis** Devon
23 E6 **Salcott** Essex
57 G2 **Sale** Traffd
30 A5 **Sale Green** Worcs
53 F3 **Saleby** Lincs
12 C4 **Salehurst** E Susx
37 F5 **Salem** Cerdgn
54 D2 **Salem** Gwynd
89 F3 **Salen** Ag & B
89 G5 **Salen** Highld
32 B3 **Salford** Beds
30 D3 **Salford** Oxon
57 G3 **Salford** Salfd
30 C5 **Salford Priors** Warwks
11 F6 **Salfords** Surrey
45 F3 **Salhouse** Norfk
86 A5 **Saline** Fife
8 D6 **Salisbury** Wilts
8 D6 **Salisbury Cathedral** Wilts
18 C2 **Salisbury Plain** Wilts
71 H3 **Salkeld Dykes** Cumb
45 E4 **Salle** Norfk
53 E3 **Salmonby** Lincs
30 C2 **Salperton** Gloucs
85 G2 **Salsburgh** N Lans
40 B6 **Salt** Staffs
58 C4 **Saltaire** Brad
5 E3 **Saltash** Cnwll
107 F3 **Saltburn** Highld
66 C5 **Saltburn-by-the-Sea** R & Cl
42 B4 **Saltby** Leics
76 B5 **Saltcoats** N Ayrs
11 F2 **Saltdean** Br & H
70 D2 **Salterbeck** Cumb
58 A4 **Salterforth** Lancs
18 D1 **Salterton** Wilts
53 F4 **Saltfleet** Lincs
53 F4 **Saltfleetby All Saints** Lincs
53 F4 **Saltfleetby St Clement** Lincs
53 F4 **Saltfleetby St Peter** Lincs
17 G5 **Saltford** BaNES
44 D6 **Salthouse** Norfk
60 B3 **Saltmarshe** E R Yk
48 D5 **Saltney** Flints
66 D2 **Salton** N York
14 D3 **Saltrens** Devon
13 F5 **Saltwood** Kent
10 D3 **Salvington** W Susx
39 H2 **Salwarpe** Worcs
7 F5 **Salwayash** Dorset
30 B6 **Sambourne** Warwks
49 G2 **Sambrook** Wrekin
57 F5 **Samlesbury** Lancs
16 C1 **Sampford Arundel** Somset
16 C3 **Sampford Brett** Somset
15 F1 **Sampford Courtenay** Devon
16 C1 **Sampford Moor** Somset
16 B1 **Sampford Peverell** Devon
5 F4 **Sampford Spiney** Devon
111 j2 **Samsonlane** Ork
87 E3 **Samuelston** E Loth
82 B3 **Sanaigmore** Ag & B
2 B2 **Sancreed** Cnwll
60 C4 **Sancton** E R Yk
59 E4 **Sand Hills** Leeds
60 C4 **Sand Hole** E R Yk
59 G5 **Sand Hutton** N York
97 E3 **Sandaig** Highld
59 E2 **Sandal Magna** Wakefd
96 C1 **Sandavore** Highld
111 j3 **Sanday Airport** Ork
49 G5 **Sandbach** Ches
84 B4 **Sandbank** Ag & B
8 C2 **Sandbanks** Poole
102 B5 **Sandend** Abers
21 F2 **Sanderstead** Gt Lon
64 B5 **Sandford** Cumb
15 G2 **Sandford** Devon
8 B2 **Sandford** Dorset
8 D3 **Sandford** Hants
9 G2 **Sandford** IOW
17 E5 **Sandford** N Som
77 F5 **Sandford** S Lans
17 G1 **Sandford Orcas** Dorset
31 E3 **Sandford St Martin** Oxon
19 G6 **Sandford-on-Thames** Oxon
13 F5 **Sandgate** Kent
103 E6 **Sandhaven** Abers
68 C3 **Sandhead** D & G
31 F1 **Sandhills** Oxon
10 C5 **Sandhills** Surrey
72 D3 **Sandhoe** Nthumb
83 H5 **Sandhole** Ag & B
60 C3 **Sandholme** E R Yk
20 B2 **Sandhurst** Br For
29 F5 **Sandhurst** Gloucs
12 C5 **Sandhurst** Kent
65 G2 **Sandhutton** N York
51 F1 **Sandiacre** Derbys
53 G3 **Sandilands** Lincs
8 D5 **Sandleheath** Hants
19 F6 **Sandleigh** Oxon
8 A5 **Sandley** Dorset
111 k2 **Sandness** Shet
22 C5 **Sandon** Essex
33 E2 **Sandon** Herts
40 B6 **Sandon** Staffs
40 B6 **Sandon Bank** Staffs
9 G2 **Sandown** IOW
4 C3 **Sandplace** Cnwll
21 E6 **Sandridge** Herts
44 A5 **Sandringham** Norfk
67 E4 **Sandsend** N York
60 B1 **Sandtoft** N Linc
22 D1 **Sandway** Kent
23 G2 **Sandwich** Kent
111 l1 **Sandwick** Shet
111 d6 **Sandwick** W Isls
70 C1 **Sandwith** Cumb
32 D3 **Sandy** Beds
18 C3 **Sandy Lane** Wilts
5 G5 **Sandy Park** Devon
79 E2 **Sandyford** D & G

6 A3 Sandygate Devon
116 C5 Sandygate IOM
70 C4 Sandyhills D & G
62 D2 Sandylands Lancs
108 D5 Sangobeg Highld
108 D5 Sangomore Highld
39 G3 Sankyn's Green Worcs
89 E5 Sanna Bay Highld
111 d6 Sanndabhaig W Isls
75 H5 Sannox N Ayrs
77 G3 Sanquhar D & G
62 B6 Santon Bridge Cumb
44 B1 Santon Downham Suffk
41 F3 Sapcote Leics
39 G3 Sapey Common Herefs
34 C6 Sapiston Suffk
29 G3 Sapperton Gloucs
42 C5 Sapperton Lincs
43 E4 Saracen's Head Lincs
110 D3 Sarclet Highld
9 G4 Sarisbury Hants
46 B4 Sarn Gwynd
47 H2 Sarn Powys
38 C5 Sarn Powys
36 C2 Sarnau Cerdgn
48 C1 Sarnau Powys
38 D1 Sarnesfield Herefs
26 C4 Saron Carmth
54 D3 Saron Gwynd
20 D5 Sarratt Herts
23 G2 Sarre Kent
30 D2 Sarsden Oxon
73 E1 Satley Dur
15 F3 Satterleigh Devon
62 D5 Satterthwaite Cumb
102 C1 Sauchen Abers
92 D3 Saucher P & K
95 F3 Sauchieburn Abers
29 E3 Saul Gloucs
52 A4 Saundby Notts
25 E3 Saundersfoot Pembks
20 B5 Saunderton Bucks
14 D4 Saunton Devon
53 F2 Sausthorpe Lincs
58 D2 Savile Town Kirk
31 F6 Sawbridge Warwks
21 G6 Sawbridgeworth Herts
67 E2 Sawdon N York
63 G1 Sawley Lancs
58 B6 Sawley N York
33 F3 Sawston Cambs
42 D1 Sawtry Cambs
42 A4 Saxby Leics
52 C4 Saxby Lincs
60 D2 Saxby All Saints N Linc
41 G5 Saxelbye Leics
34 D4 Saxham Street Suffk
52 B3 Saxilby Lincs
44 D5 Saxlingham Norfk
45 E2 Saxlingham Green Norfk
45 E2 Saxlingham Nethergate Norfk
45 E2 Saxlingham Thorpe Norfk
35 G5 Saxmundham Suffk
34 A4 Saxon Street Cambs
51 G1 Saxondale Notts
35 F5 Saxtead Suffk
35 F5 Saxtead Green Suffk
35 F5 Saxtead Little Green Suffk
45 E5 Saxthorpe Norfk
59 F4 Saxton N York
11 H4 Sayers Common W Susx
66 C1 Scackleton N York
62 C6 Scafell Pike Cumb
51 G5 Scaftworth Notts
67 E1 Scagglethorpe N York
82 C5 Scalasaig Ag & B
60 C3 Scalby E R Yk
67 F2 Scalby N York
41 H1 Scaldwell Nhants
71 G5 Scaleby Cumb
71 G5 Scalebyhill Cumb
71 F2 Scales Cumb
62 C3 Scales Cumb
41 H5 Scalford Leics
66 D4 Scaling N York
111 I2 Scalloway Shet
53 E3 Scamblesby Lincs
90 A6 Scamodale Highld
67 E1 Scampston N York
52 B3 Scampton Lincs
99 E6 Scaniport Highld
58 C2 Scapegoat Hill Kirk
67 F2 Scarborough N York
3 E4 Scarcewater Cnwll
51 F3 Scarcliffe Derbys
59 E4 Scarcroft Leeds
110 C6 Scarfskerry Highld
65 E4 Scargill Dur
88 B3 Scarinish Ag & B
56 D4 Scarisbrick Lancs
44 C3 Scarning Norfk
51 H1 Scarrington Notts
53 E5 Scartho Lincs
111 I3 Scatsta Airport Shet
52 B5 Scawby N Linc
59 F1 Scawsby Donc
59 F1 Scawthorpe Donc
66 B2 Scawton N York
11 F4 Scayne's Hill W Susx
27 F5 Scethrog Powys
58 C1 Scholes Kirk
59 E4 Scholes Leeds
51 E6 Scholes Rothm
57 F3 Scholes Wigan
58 D1 Scissett Kirk
24 D6 Scleddau Pembks
51 G4 Scofton Notts
35 E6 Scole Norfk
92 D2 Scone P & K
96 C5 Sconser Highld
86 D6 Scoonie Fife
52 C1 Scopwick Lincs
105 H5 Scoraig Highld
60 D4 Scorborough E R Yk
2 D3 Scorrier Cnwll
63 E1 Scorton Lancs
65 F3 Scorton N York
73 E5 Scot's Gap Nthumb
71 G4 Scotby Cumb
65 F4 Scotch Corner N York
63 E2 Scotforth Lancs
52 C3 Scothern Lincs
86 C6 Scotlandwell P & K
110 B4 Scotscalder Station Highld
102 B2 Scotsmill Abers

85 E2 Scotstoun C Glas
73 F3 Scotswood N u Ty
52 B5 Scotter Lincs
52 B5 Scotterthorpe Lincs
52 B5 Scotton Lincs
65 F3 Scotton N York
59 E5 Scotton N York
44 D2 Scoulton Norfk
108 B4 Scourie Highld
108 B3 Scourie More Highld
111 I1 Scousburgh Shet
110 B6 Scrabster Highld
80 C2 Scraesburgh Border
43 F6 Scrane End Lincs
41 G4 Scraptoft Leics
45 H3 Scratby Norfk
60 B5 Scrayingham N York
42 C5 Scredington Lincs
53 F2 Scremby Lincs
81 F5 Scremerston Nthumb
51 H1 Screveton Notts
59 E5 Scriven N York
51 G5 Scrooby Notts
40 D6 Scropton Derbys
52 D1 Scrub Hill Lincs
93 G3 Scruschloch Angus
65 G3 Scruton N York
109 F5 Scullomie Highld
44 C5 Sculthorpe Norfk
60 C1 Scunthorpe N Linc
45 G4 Sea Palling Norfk
7 E6 Seaborough Dorset
13 F5 Seabrook Kent
73 G3 Seaburn Sundld
59 E3 Seacroft Leeds
96 C5 Seafield Highld
86 A3 Seafield W Loth
11 G2 Seaford E Susx
56 D2 Seaforth Sefton
41 G5 Seagrave Leics
73 G2 Seaham Dur
81 G3 Seahouses Nthumb
22 A1 Seal Kent
10 C6 Seale Surrey
66 B4 Seamer N York
67 F2 Seamer N York
76 B6 Seamill N Ayrs
52 C5 Searby Lincs
23 F2 Seasalter Kent
62 A5 Seascale Cumb
62 C5 Seathwaite Cumb
71 F1 Seatoller Cumb
4 D3 Seaton Cnwll
70 D3 Seaton Dur
6 D4 Seaton Devon
61 E4 Seaton E R Yk
23 G2 Seaton Kent
73 G4 Seaton Nthumb
42 B2 Seaton Rutlnd
66 B6 Seaton Carew Hartpl
73 G4 Seaton Delaval Nthumb
60 B4 Seaton Ross E R Yk
73 G4 Seaton Sluice Nthumb
7 E5 Seatown Dorset
66 B3 Seave Green N York
9 H3 Seaview IOW
71 E4 Seaville Cumb
17 E1 Seavington St Mary Somset
17 E1 Seavington St Michael Somset
71 F3 Sebergham Cumb
40 D4 Seckington Warwks
63 F5 Sedbergh Cumb
28 D2 Sedbury Gloucs
64 C3 Sedbusk N York
30 B4 Sedgeberrow Worcs
42 B5 Sedgebrook Lincs
65 G6 Sedgefield Dur
44 A5 Sedgeford Norfk
8 B6 Sedgehill Wilts
40 A3 Sedgley Dudley
63 E4 Sedgwick Cumb
12 C4 Sedlescombe E Susx
20 B6 Sedrup Bucks
18 B3 Seend Wilts
18 B3 Seend Cleeve Wilts
20 C4 Seer Green Bucks
45 F2 Seething Norfk
56 D3 Sefton Sefton
49 H2 Seighford Staffs
54 D3 Seion Gwynd
39 H5 Seisdon Staffs
48 C3 Selattyn Shrops
10 B5 Selborne Hants
59 G3 Selby N York
10 C4 Selham W Susx
21 F2 Selhurst Gt Lon
79 G2 Selkirk Border
28 D5 Sellack Herefs
111 I4 Sellafirth Shet
16 D1 Sellick's Green Somset
13 F5 Sellindge Kent
23 E1 Selling Kent
18 B3 Sells Green Wilts
40 B2 Selly Oak Birm
11 G3 Selmeston E Susx
21 F2 Selsdon Gt Lon
10 B2 Selsey W Susx
64 C1 Selside N York
29 F3 Selsley Gloucs
13 G6 Selsted Kent
51 F2 Selston Notts
16 B4 Selworthy Somset
34 D3 Semer Suffk
18 B3 Semington Wilts
8 B5 Semley Wilts
20 D1 Send Surrey
27 G2 Senghenydd Caerph
2 A2 Sennen Cnwll
2 A2 Sennen Cove Cnwll
27 E5 Sennybridge Powys
66 B1 Sessay N York
43 H3 Setchey Norfk
87 E3 Seton Mains E Loth
63 G2 Settle N York
67 E1 Settrington N York
16 C2 Seven Ash Somset
21 G4 Seven Kings Gt Lon
26 D3 Seven Sisters Neath
34 C2 Seven Star Green Essex
30 C3 Seven Wells Gloucs
30 B2 Sevenhampton Gloucs
18 D5 Sevenhampton Swindn
21 H1 Sevenoaks Kent
21 H1 Sevenoaks Weald Kent
28 D3 Severn Beach S Glos

39 H1 Severn Stoke Worcs
13 E6 Sevington Kent
33 G3 Sewards End Essex
32 C1 Sewell Beds
61 F6 Sewerby E R Yk
2 D2 Seworgan Cnwll
42 B4 Sewstern Leics
111 e7 Sgiogarstaigh W Isls
31 G1 Shabbington Bucks
41 E4 Shackerstone Leics
10 C6 Shackleford Surrey
111 d7 Shader W Isls
73 G1 Shadforth Dur
45 G1 Shadingfield Suffk
13 E5 Shadoxhurst Kent
44 C1 Shadwell Norfk
33 G4 Shaftenhoe End Herts
8 B5 Shaftesbury Dorset
59 E1 Shafton Barns
19 E3 Shalbourne Wilts
10 A6 Shalden Hants
6 B3 Shaldon Devon
9 F2 Shalfleet IOW
34 B2 Shalford Essex
10 D6 Shalford Surrey
34 A2 Shalford Green Essex
23 F1 Shalmsford Street Kent
31 G4 Shalstone Bucks
10 D6 Shamley Green Surrey
94 D2 Shandford Angus
84 C4 Shandon Ag & B
107 G3 Shandwick Highld
41 H3 Shangton Leics
9 G2 Shanklin IOW
71 H1 Shap Cumb
8 B3 Shapwick Dorset
17 E3 Shapwick Somset
41 E6 Shardlow Derbys
40 B4 Shareshill Staffs
59 E2 Sharlston Wakefd
32 C4 Sharnbrook Beds
41 F3 Sharnford Leics
57 E5 Sharoe Green Lancs
65 G1 Sharow N York
32 C2 Sharpenhoe Beds
81 E1 Sharperton Nthumb
29 E3 Sharpness Gloucs
44 D5 Sharrington Norfk
39 G4 Shatterford Worcs
5 F3 Shaugh Prior Devon
49 F4 Shavington Ches
58 B1 Shaw Oldham
19 E3 Shaw W Berk
18 B3 Shaw Wilts
58 D6 Shaw Mills N York
111 d7 Shawbost W Isls
49 E2 Shawbury Shrops
41 F2 Shawell Leics
9 F5 Shawford Hants
70 C6 Shawhead D & G
77 G6 Shawsburn S Lans
70 D5 Shearington D & G
41 G3 Shearsby Leics
16 D2 Shearston Somset
14 D2 Shebbear Devon
49 G2 Shebdon Staffs
110 A5 Shebster Highld
85 E2 Sheddens E Rens
9 G4 Shedfield Hants
50 C3 Sheen Derbys
58 D3 Sheepscar Leeds
29 F4 Sheepscombe Gloucs
5 F4 Sheepstor Devon
14 D2 Sheepwash Devon
41 E3 Sheepy Magna Leics
41 E3 Sheepy Parva Leics
21 G6 Sheering Essex
22 D3 Sheerness Kent
20 D2 Sheerwater Surrey
10 B4 Sheet Hants
51 E5 Sheffield Sheff
51 E5 Sheffield City Airport Sheff
32 D3 Shefford Beds
108 B5 Sheigra Highld
39 F6 Sheinton Shrops
38 D4 Shelderton Shrops
40 C2 Sheldon Birm
50 C3 Sheldon Derbys
6 C6 Sheldon Devon
23 E1 Sheldwich Kent
45 E1 Shelfanger Norfk
51 G1 Shelford Notts
81 E4 Shellacres Border
58 D1 Shelley Kirk
34 D3 Shelley Suffk
19 E5 Shellingford Oxon
22 B6 Shellow Bowells Essex
39 G2 Shelsley Beauchamp Worcs
39 G2 Shelsley Walsh Worcs
32 C5 Shelton Beds
45 E1 Shelton Norfk
42 A6 Shelton Notts
49 G3 Shelton Under Harley Staffs
38 D5 Shelve Shrops
39 E1 Shelwick Herefs
22 B5 Shenfield Essex
31 E4 Shenington Oxon
21 E5 Shenley Herts
32 A2 Shenley Brook End M Keyn
32 A2 Shenley Church End M Keyn
28 B6 Shenmore Herefs
69 E4 Shennanton D & G
40 C4 Shenstone Staffs
39 H3 Shenstone Worcs
41 E3 Shenton Leics
33 E1 Shephall Herts
21 E3 Shepherd's Bush Gt Lon
13 G6 Shepherdswell Kent
58 D1 Shepley Kirk
20 D2 Shepperton Surrey
33 F3 Shepreth Cambs
41 F5 Shepshed Leics
17 E1 Shepton Beauchamp Somset
17 G3 Shepton Mallet Somset
17 G2 Shepton Montague Somset
22 C1 Shepway Kent
66 B6 Sheraton Dur
17 G1 Sherborne Dorset
30 D2 Sherborne Gloucs
17 G4 Sherborne Somset

19 H2 Sherborne St John Hants
30 D6 Sherbourne Warwks
73 G1 Sherburn Dur
67 E1 Sherburn N York
73 G1 Sherburn Hill Dur
59 F3 Sherburn in Elmet N York
10 D6 Shere Surrey
44 C5 Shereford Norfk
9 E5 Sherfield English Hants
20 A2 Sherfield on Loddon Hants
5 H2 Sherford Devon
59 G6 Sheriff Hutton N York
49 G1 Sheriffhales Shrops
45 E6 Sheringham Norfk
32 B3 Sherington M Keyn
44 A5 Shernborne Norfk
18 C1 Sherrington Wilts
18 B5 Sherston Wilts
51 F1 Sherwood C Nott
51 G2 Sherwood Forest Notts
85 F2 Shettleston C Glas
57 E3 Shevington Wigan
4 D3 Sheviock Cnwll
58 C3 Shibden Head Brad
9 G2 Shide IOW
80 D4 Shidlaw Nthumb
97 G4 Shiel Bridge Highld
105 F2 Shieldaig Highld
78 D1 Shieldhill D & G
85 G3 Shieldhill Falk
78 D6 Shieldhill House Hotel S Lans
85 G1 Shields N Lans
89 G5 Shielfoot Highld
93 F5 Shielhill Angus
84 B3 Shielhill Inver
39 G6 Shifnal Shrops
81 G1 Shilbottle Nthumb
65 F5 Shildon Dur
84 D2 Shillford E Rens
16 B2 Shillingford Devon
19 G5 Shillingford Oxon
6 A4 Shillingford Abbot Devon
6 A4 Shillingford St George Devon
8 B4 Shillingstone Dorset
32 D2 Shillington Beds
30 D1 Shilton Oxon
41 E2 Shilton Warwks
45 E1 Shimpling Norfk
34 C4 Shimpling Suffk
34 C4 Shimpling Street Suffk
73 G1 Shincliffe Dur
73 G2 Shiney Row Sundld
20 A2 Shinfield Wokham
109 E1 Shinness Highld
22 B1 Shipbourne Kent
44 C3 Shipdham Norfk
17 H4 Shipham Somset
6 A2 Shiphay Torbay
20 B3 Shiplake Oxon
58 C4 Shipley Brad
11 E4 Shipley W Susx
11 F5 Shipley Bridge Surrey
45 G1 Shipmeadow Suffk
19 G6 Shippon Oxon
30 D4 Shipston on Stour Warwks
30 B2 Shipton Gloucs
59 F5 Shipton N York
39 E5 Shipton Shrops
19 E2 Shipton Bellinger Hants
7 F4 Shipton Gorge Dorset
10 B2 Shipton Green W Susx
29 F2 Shipton Moyne Gloucs
31 F2 Shipton-on-Cherwell Oxon
30 D2 Shipton-under-Wychwood Oxon
60 C4 Shiptonthorpe E R Yk
20 A5 Shirburn Oxon
56 D4 Shirdley Hill Lancs
51 F3 Shirebrook Derbys
51 E5 Shiregreen Sheff
28 D1 Shirehampton Bristl
73 G4 Shiremoor N Tyne
28 C2 Shirenewton Mons
51 F4 Shireoaks Notts
51 E3 Shirland Derbys
9 F4 Shirley C Sotn
50 D1 Shirley Derbys
21 F2 Shirley Gt Lon
40 C2 Shirley Solhll
9 G4 Shirrell Heath Hants
83 G4 Shirvan Ag & B
15 E4 Shirwell Devon
75 G4 Shiskine N Ayrs
38 D2 Shobdon Herefs
15 G1 Shobrooke Devon
41 G5 Shoby Leics
48 D4 Shocklach Ches
22 D4 Shoeburyness Sthend
23 H1 Sholden Kent
9 F4 Sholing C Sotn
14 C3 Shop Cnwll
3 E6 Shop Cnwll
35 E5 Shop Street Suffk
21 F4 Shoreditch Gt Lon
16 D2 Shoreditch Somset
21 G2 Shoreham Kent
11 E3 Shoreham Airport W Susx
11 E3 Shoreham-by-Sea W Susx
9 G5 Shorley Hants
22 C3 Shorne Kent
11 G3 Shortgate E Susx
3 E4 Shortlanesend Cnwll
32 C3 Shortstown Beds
9 F2 Shorwell IOW
17 H4 Shoscombe BaNES
45 F2 Shotesham Norfk
22 C5 Shotgate Essex
35 E2 Shotley Suffk
73 F2 Shotley Bridge Dur
35 F2 Shotley Gate Suffk
35 E2 Shotley Street Suffk
23 E1 Shottenden Kent
30 C5 Shottery Warwks
31 E4 Shotteswell Warwks
35 F3 Shottisham Suffk
50 D2 Shottle Derbys
50 D2 Shottlegate Derbys
73 G1 Shotton Dur
48 C6 Shotton Flints
85 G1 Shotts N Lans
48 D6 Shotwick Ches
101 E5 Shougle Moray
44 A3 Shouldham Norfk

43 H3 Shouldham Thorpe Norfk
39 G2 Shoulton Worcs
48 D1 Shrawardine Shrops
39 G3 Shrawley Worcs
30 D6 Shrewley Warwks
49 E1 Shrewsbury Shrops
18 C1 Shrewton Wilts
10 C2 Shripney W Susx
19 E5 Shrivenham Oxon
44 D2 Shropham Norfk
28 D6 Shucknall Herefs
33 G3 Shudy Camps Cambs
29 G4 Shurdington Gloucs
20 B3 Shurlock Row W & M
110 A5 Shurrery Highld
110 A5 Shurrery Lodge Highld
16 D3 Shurton Somset
40 D3 Shustoke Warwks
49 H2 Shut Heath Staffs
6 D5 Shute Devon
31 E4 Shutford Oxon
29 F6 Shuthonger Gloucs
31 H5 Shutlanger Nhants
40 D4 Shuttington Warwks
51 F4 Shuttlewood Derbys
57 G4 Shuttleworth Bury
111 d7 Siabost W Isls
111 d7 Siadar W Isls
41 G2 Sibbertoft Nhants
31 E4 Sibford Ferris Oxon
31 E4 Sibford Gower Oxon
34 B2 Sible Hedingham Essex
33 G2 Sibley's Green Essex
53 E1 Sibsey Lincs
42 C3 Sibson Cambs
41 E3 Sibson Leics
110 D4 Sibster Highld
51 H4 Sibthorpe Notts
51 H2 Sibthorpe Notts
35 F5 Sibton Suffk
34 C4 Sicklesmere Suffk
59 E4 Sicklinghall N York
6 C5 Sidbury Devon
39 F4 Sidbury Shrops
17 E4 Sidcot N Som
21 G3 Sidcup Gt Lon
49 H6 Siddington Ches
18 C6 Siddington Gloucs
45 F5 Sidestrand Norfk
6 C4 Sidford Devon
10 B2 Sidlesham W Susx
12 C3 Sidley E Susx
6 C4 Sidmouth Devon
61 E4 Sigglesthorne E R Yk
16 B6 Sigingstone V Glam
19 H3 Silchester Hants
41 G4 Sileby Leics
62 B4 Silecroft Cumb
45 E2 Silfield Norfk
42 C6 Silk Willoughby Lincs
58 D1 Silkstone Barns
58 D1 Silkstone Common Barns
73 G2 Silksworth Sundld
70 D4 Silloth Cumb
67 F3 Silpho N York
58 B4 Silsden Brad
32 C2 Silsoe Beds
8 A6 Silton Dorset
34 B1 Silver End Essex
86 C2 Silverburn Mdloth
63 E3 Silverdale Lancs
49 G4 Silverdale Staffs
102 D5 Silverford Abers
31 G4 Silverstone Nhants
6 B5 Silverton Devon
39 F4 Silvington Shrops
72 C4 Simonburn Nthumb
16 C1 Simons Burrow Devon
15 G5 Simonsbath Somset
57 G5 Simonstone Lancs
80 D4 Simprim Border
32 B2 Simpson M Keyn
24 C4 Simpson Cross Pembks
80 D5 Sinclair's Hill Border
76 D3 Sinclairston E Ayrs
65 G2 Sinderby N York
57 G2 Sinderland Green Traffd
20 B2 Sindlesham Wokham
41 E6 Sinfin C Derb
35 G4 Singleton Lancs
10 C3 Singleton W Susx
22 B3 Singlewell Kent
101 G1 Sinnarhard Abers
66 D2 Sinnington N York
39 G2 Sinton Worcs
39 G2 Sinton Green Worcs
12 C5 Sissinghurst Kent
17 G6 Siston S Glos
2 C2 Sithney Cnwll
22 D2 Sittingbourne Kent
39 G5 Six Ashes Staffs
33 G4 Six Mile Bottom Cambs
7 b2 Six Rues Jersey
52 D4 Sixhills Lincs
13 F6 Sixmile Cottages Kent
8 C5 Sixpenny Handley Dorset
63 E4 Sizergh Castle Cumb
111 h2 Skaill Ork
77 E3 Skares E Ayrs
95 G5 Skateraw Abers
87 G3 Skateraw E Loth
104 C1 Skeabost Highld
65 F3 Skeeby N York
41 H3 Skeffington Leics
61 G2 Skeffling E R Yk
51 F3 Skegby Notts
52 A2 Skegby Notts
53 F2 Skegness Lincs
107 G5 Skelbo Highld
107 G5 Skelbo Street Highld
59 F2 Skelbrooke Donc
43 E5 Skeldyke Lincs
52 B3 Skellingthorpe Lincs
59 F1 Skellow Donc
58 D1 Skelmanthorpe Kirk
57 E2 Skelmersdale Lancs
84 A5 Skelmorlie N Ayrs
109 F4 Skelpick Highld
78 B3 Skelston D & G
71 G1 Skelton Cumb
60 B3 Skelton E R Yk
66 C5 Skelton R & Cl
59 F5 Skelton N York
62 D6 Skelwith Bridge Cumb
53 F2 Skendleby Lincs
102 D1 Skene House Abers

28 C4 **Skenfrith** Mons
60 D5 **Skerne** E R Yk
109 F5 **Skerray** Highld
108 C4 **Skerricha** Highld
63 E2 **Skerton** Lancs
41 E3 **Sketchley** Leics
26 C2 **Sketty** Swans
26 D2 **Skewen** Neath
66 C1 **Skewsby** N York
110 A5 **Skiall** Highld
60 D3 **Skidby** E R Yk
111 e7 **Skigersta** W Isls
16 B2 **Skilgate** Somset
42 B4 **Skillington** Lincs
71 E5 **Skinburness** Cumb
85 H4 **Skinflats** Falk
104 B1 **Skinidin** Highld
83 G2 **Skipness** Ag & B
61 E5 **Skipsea** E R Yk
58 B5 **Skipton** N York
65 G2 **Skipton-on-Swale** N York
59 G4 **Skipwith** N York
61 E4 **Skirlaugh** E R Yk
78 D6 **Skirling** Border
20 B4 **Skirmett** Bucks
60 B5 **Skirpenbeck** E R Yk
64 A6 **Skirwith** Cumb
110 D5 **Skirza** Highld
97 E4 **Skulamus** Highld
96 C5 **Skye** Highld
34 C1 **Skye Green** Essex
99 G5 **Skye of Curr** Highld
58 B3 **Slack** Calder
102 D4 **Slacks of Cairnbanno** Abers
29 F3 **Slad** Gloucs
15 E5 **Slade** Devon
15 G4 **Slade** Somset
21 H3 **Slade Green** Kent
51 F5 **Slade Hooton** Rothm
72 B2 **Slaggyford** Nthumb
63 G2 **Slaidburn** Lancs
58 C2 **Slaithwaite** Kirk
72 D3 **Slaley** Nthumb
85 G3 **Slamannan** Falk
32 B1 **Slapton** Bucks
5 H2 **Slapton** Devon
31 G4 **Slapton** Nhants
11 E4 **Slaugham** W Susx
18 B4 **Slaughterford** Wilts
41 H3 **Slawston** Leics
10 B5 **Sleaford** Hants
42 C6 **Sleaford** Lincs
64 A5 **Sleagill** Cumb
49 F1 **Sleapford** Wrekin
107 E5 **Sleasdairidh** Highld
60 C6 **Sledmere** E R Yk
64 D4 **Sleightholme** Dur
67 E4 **Sleights** N York
110 C5 **Slickly** Highld
75 G3 **Sliddery** N Ayrs
96 C5 **Sligachan** Highld
84 B4 **Sligrachan** Ag & B
29 G3 **Slimbridge** Gloucs
49 G3 **Slindon** Staffs
10 C3 **Slindon** W Susx
10 D5 **Slinfold** W Susx
66 C1 **Slingsby** N York
32 C1 **Slip End** Beds
33 E3 **Slip End** Herts
32 B6 **Slipton** Nhants
40 B5 **Slitting Mill** Staffs
83 F5 **Slockavullin** Ag & B
69 G4 **Slogarie** D & G
5 G5 **Sloncombe** Devon
53 F5 **Sloothby** Lincs
20 C3 **Slough** Slough
16 D1 **Slough Green** Somset
97 F6 **Slumbay** Highld
63 E3 **Slyne** Lancs
80 C3 **Smailholm** Border
11 E3 **Small Dole** W Susx
40 C2 **Small Heath** Birm
12 D5 **Small Hythe** Kent
45 F4 **Smallburgh** Norfk
51 E1 **Smalley** Derbys
11 F6 **Smallfield** Surrey
7 E5 **Smallridge** Devon
34 D6 **Smallworth** Norfk
19 F2 **Smannell** Hants
12 D6 **Smarden** Kent
12 D6 **Smarden Bell** Kent
11 H6 **Smart's Hill** Kent
89 G6 **Smearisary** Highld
6 D6 **Smeatharpe** Devon
13 E5 **Smeeth** Kent
41 G3 **Smeeton Westerby** Leics
110 B3 **Smerral** Highld
39 H5 **Smestow** Staffs
40 B2 **Smethwick** Sandw
41 E5 **Smisby** Derbys
33 H3 **Smith's Green** Essex
71 G5 **Smithfield** Cumb
105 F4 **Smithstown** Highld
107 F1 **Smithton** Highld
108 D5 **Smoo** Highld
34 C1 **Smythe's Green** Essex
78 B2 **Snade** D & G
38 D6 **Snailbeach** Shrops
33 H5 **Snailwell** Cambs
67 E2 **Snainton** N York
59 G2 **Snaith** E R Yk
65 F2 **Snape** N York
35 G4 **Snape** Suffk
35 G4 **Snape Street** Suffk
21 G4 **Snaresbrook** Gt Lon
41 E4 **Snarestone** Leics
52 C3 **Snarford** Lincs
13 E5 **Snargate** Kent
13 E5 **Snave** Kent
67 E4 **Sneaton** N York
52 C3 **Snelland** Lincs
50 C1 **Snelston** Derbys
44 D1 **Snetterton** Norfk
44 A5 **Snettisham** Norfk
29 E5 **Snig's End** Gloucs
81 F1 **Snitter** Nthumb
52 C4 **Snitterby** Lincs
30 D5 **Snitterfield** Warwks
39 E3 **Snitton** Shrops
22 C2 **Snodland** Kent
33 F2 **Snow End** Herts
54 D2 **Snowdon** Gwynd
47 G4 **Snowdonia National Park**
30 C3 **Snowshill** Gloucs
9 H4 **Soake** Hants
9 H5 **Soberton** Hants

9 G4 **Soberton Heath** Hants
65 G4 **Sockburn** Darltn
33 G5 **Soham** Cambs
111 b4 **Solas** W Isls
9 H6 **Soldridge** Hants
22 B2 **Sole Street** Kent
23 F1 **Sole Street** Kent
40 C2 **Solihull** Solhll
38 D2 **Sollers Dilwyn** Herefs
28 D5 **Sollers Hope** Herefs
24 C5 **Solva** Pembks
79 F1 **Solwaybank** D & G
41 H4 **Somerby** Leics
52 C5 **Somerby** Lincs
51 E2 **Somercotes** Derbys
8 D3 **Somerford** Dorset
18 C6 **Somerford Keynes** Gloucs
10 B2 **Somerley** W Susx
45 G2 **Somerleyton** Suffk
40 C6 **Somersal Herbert** Derbys
53 E3 **Somersby** Lincs
33 G6 **Somersham** Cambs
34 D3 **Somersham** Suffk
31 F3 **Somerton** Oxon
17 F2 **Somerton** Somset
34 B4 **Somerton** Suffk
11 E3 **Sompting** W Susx
20 B3 **Sonning** Wokham
20 A3 **Sonning Common** Oxon
8 D3 **Sopley** Hants
18 B5 **Sopworth** Wilts
69 F2 **Sorbie** D & G
110 B5 **Sordale** Highld
88 D5 **Sorisdale** Ag & B
77 E4 **Sorn** E Ayrs
110 C5 **Sortat** Highld
70 D2 **Sosgill** Cumb
52 D3 **Sotby** Lincs
52 D2 **Sots Hole** Lincs
45 G1 **Sotterley** Suffk
48 C5 **Soughton** Flints
32 B2 **Soulbury** Bucks
64 B4 **Soulby** Cumb
31 F3 **Souldern** Oxon
32 C5 **Souldrop** Beds
101 H4 **Sound Muir** Moray
17 G6 **Soundwell** S Glos
5 F5 **Sourton** Devon
62 C4 **Soutergate** Cumb
44 B3 **South Acre** Norfk
13 G6 **South Alkham** Kent
5 H1 **South Allington** Devon
85 G4 **South Alloa** Falk
10 C4 **South Ambersham** W Susx
51 F5 **South Anston** Rothm
13 E6 **South Ashford** Kent
9 F3 **South Baddesley** Hants
59 G5 **South Bank** York
17 G2 **South Barrow** Somset
21 F2 **South Beddington** Gt Lon
22 C4 **South Benfleet** Essex
10 C2 **South Bersted** W Susx
59 G1 **South Bramwith** Donc
5 G3 **South Brent** Devon
17 H3 **South Brewham** Somset
73 F6 **South Broomhill** Nthumb
45 G3 **South Burlingham** Norfk
17 G2 **South Cadbury** Somset
52 B3 **South Carlton** Lincs
51 G5 **South Carlton** Notts
60 C3 **South Cave** E R Yk
18 C6 **South Cerney** Gloucs
11 G4 **South Chailey** E Susx
81 G2 **South Charlton** Nthumb
17 H2 **South Cheriton** Somset
65 F6 **South Church** Dur
60 C3 **South Cliffe** E R Yk
52 A2 **South Clifton** Notts
53 F4 **South Cockerington** Lincs
26 D1 **South Cornelly** Brdgnd
35 G6 **South Cove** Suffk
44 C5 **South Creake** Norfk
41 G4 **South Croxton** Leics
60 D4 **South Dalton** E R Yk
11 F3 **South Downs**
59 G3 **South Duffield** N York
53 E4 **South Elkington** Lincs
59 F1 **South Elmsall** Wakefd
105 F3 **South Erradale** Highld
22 D4 **South Fambridge** Essex
60 D2 **South Ferriby** N Linc
60 D3 **South Field** E R Yk
8 D4 **South Gorley** Hants
73 F3 **South Gosforth** N u Ty
22 B4 **South Green** Essex
22 D2 **South Green** Kent
44 D3 **South Green** Norfk
86 C3 **South Gyle** C Edin
22 C5 **South Hanningfield** Essex
10 B4 **South Harting** W Susx
10 A2 **South Hayling** Hants
20 C5 **South Heath** Bucks
73 G2 **South Hetton** Dur
59 E2 **South Hiendley** Wakefd
4 D4 **South Hill** Cnwll
31 F1 **South Hinksey** Oxon
11 E6 **South Holmwood** Surrey
21 H2 **South Hornchurch** Gt Lon
5 G1 **South Huish** Devon
52 B2 **South Hykeham** Lincs
73 G2 **South Hylton** Sundld
52 C5 **South Kelsey** Lincs
107 F1 **South Kessock** Highld
61 E2 **South Killingholme** N Linc
65 H2 **South Kilvington** N York
41 G3 **South Kilworth** Nhants
59 E1 **South Kirkby** Wakefd
52 D1 **South Kyme** Lincs
30 D2 **South Lawn** Oxon
31 E1 **South Leigh** Oxon
52 A3 **South Leverton** Notts
30 C4 **South Littleton** Worcs
42 B2 **South Luffenham** Rutlnd
11 G3 **South Malling** E Susx
18 D5 **South Marston** Swindn
21 F1 **South Merstham** Surrey
59 F3 **South Milford** N York
31 H5 **South Milton** Devon
21 E5 **South Mimms** Herts
15 F3 **South Molton** Devon
73 F2 **South Moor** Dur
19 G5 **South Moreton** Oxon
10 C2 **South Mundham** W Susx
60 C3 **South Newbald** E R Yk
31 F6 **South Newington** Oxon
8 D6 **South Newton** Wilts

51 E2 **South Normanton** Derbys
21 F2 **South Norwood** Gt Lon
22 B4 **South Ockendon** Thurr
53 F3 **South Ormsby** Lincs
65 G2 **South Otterington** N York
52 C4 **South Owersby** Lincs
11 E6 **South Park** Surrey
7 F6 **South Perrott** Dorset
17 F1 **South Petherton** Somset
4 D5 **South Petherwin** Cnwll
44 C3 **South Pickenham** Norfk
5 E3 **South Pill** Cnwll
5 H1 **South Pool** Devon
7 F5 **South Poorton** Dorset
86 B4 **South Queensferry** C Edin
15 G4 **South Radworthy** Devon
42 C6 **South Rauceby** Lincs
44 C4 **South Raynham** Norfk
53 F4 **South Reston** Lincs
43 H3 **South Runcton** Norfk
52 A2 **South Scarle** Notts
90 B3 **South Shian** Ag & B
73 G3 **South Shields** S Tyne
56 C5 **South Shore** Bpool
58 D6 **South Stainley** N York
17 H5 **South Stoke** BaNES
42 B4 **South Stoke** Lincs
19 G5 **South Stoke** Oxon
10 D3 **South Stoke** W Susx
23 E2 **South Street** Kent
23 F2 **South Street** Kent
86 A2 **South Tarbrax** S Lans
5 G6 **South Tawton** Devon
53 F3 **South Thoresby** Lincs
45 F3 **South Walsham** Norfk
10 A6 **South Warnborough** Hants
22 B4 **South Weald** Essex
20 A5 **South Weston** Oxon
4 C6 **South Wheatley** Cnwll
17 G4 **South Widcombe** BaNES
41 G3 **South Wigston** Leics
13 E6 **South Willesborough** Kent
52 D4 **South Willingham** Lincs
65 G6 **South Wingate** Dur
51 E2 **South Wingfield** Derbys
42 B4 **South Witham** Lincs
22 C5 **South Woodham Ferrers** Essex
43 H4 **South Wootton** Norfk
18 B3 **South Wraxall** Wilts
5 G6 **South Zeal** Devon
20 D3 **Southall** Gt Lon
29 G5 **Southam** Gloucs
31 E6 **Southam** Warwks
9 F4 **Southampton** C Sotn
9 F5 **Southampton Airport** Hants
21 G2 **Southborough** Gt Lon
12 B6 **Southborough** Kent
8 D3 **Southbourne** Bmouth
10 B3 **Southbourne** W Susx
44 D3 **Southburgh** Norfk
60 D5 **Southburn** E R Yk
22 D4 **Southchurch** Sthend
4 C6 **Southcott** Cnwll
5 F6 **Southcott** Devon
5 G5 **Southcott** Devon
20 B6 **Southcourt** Bucks
11 G3 **Southease** E Susx
75 E2 **Southend** Ag & B
22 D4 **Southend Airport** Essex
22 D4 **Southend-on-Sea** Sthend
16 A6 **Southerndown** V Glam
70 C4 **Southerness** D & G
6 C4 **Southerton** Devon
43 G2 **Southery** Norfk
85 G3 **Southfield** Falk
22 B3 **Southfleet** Kent
21 H4 **Southgate** Gt Lon
26 B2 **Southgate** Swans
32 D3 **Southill** Beds
19 G2 **Southington** Hants
6 D5 **Southleigh** Devon
23 E3 **Southminster** Essex
19 F6 **Southmoor** Oxon
93 F4 **Southmuir** Angus
32 D5 **Southoe** Cambs
35 E5 **Southolt** Suffk
42 C2 **Southorpe** C Pete
7 G5 **Southover** Dorset
58 C2 **Southowram** Calder
56 D4 **Southport** Sefton
45 F5 **Southrepps** Norfk
52 D2 **Southrey** Lincs
30 D1 **Southrop** Gloucs
19 H2 **Southrope** Hants
9 H3 **Southsea** C Port
65 E5 **Southside** Dur
45 H3 **Southtown** Norfk
71 G4 **Southwaite** Cumb
21 F3 **Southwark** Gt Lon
11 E4 **Southwater** W Susx
51 G2 **Southwell** Notts
9 H4 **Southwick** Hants
42 C2 **Southwick** Nhants
73 G3 **Southwick** Sundld
11 E3 **Southwick** W Susx
18 B2 **Southwick** Wilts
35 H6 **Southwold** Suffk
58 B2 **Sowerby** Kirk
66 A2 **Sowerby** N York
58 B2 **Sowerby Bridge** Calder
58 C2 **Sowood** Calder
5 E3 **Sowton** Devon
6 B5 **Sowton** Devon
58 B2 **Soyland Town** Calder
33 H3 **Spain's End** Essex
43 E4 **Spalding** Lincs
60 B3 **Spaldington** E R Yk
32 D5 **Spaldwick** Cambs
52 A2 **Spalford** Notts
52 D2 **Spanby** Lincs
44 D4 **Sparham** Norfk
62 C4 **Spark Bridge** Cumb
17 G2 **Sparkford** Somset
40 C2 **Sparkhill** Birm
5 F3 **Sparkwell** Devon
50 C4 **Sparrowpit** Derbys
12 B5 **Sparrows Green** E Susx
19 F6 **Sparsholt** Hants
19 F5 **Sparsholt** Oxon
66 D2 **Spaunton** N York
16 D3 **Spaxton** Somset
98 B1 **Spean Bridge** Highld
9 E6 **Spearywell** Hants
8 D6 **Speen** Bucks

19 F3 **Speen** W Berk
67 G1 **Speeton** N York
56 D1 **Speke** Lpool
12 A6 **Speldhurst** Kent
33 F1 **Spellbrook** Herts
49 G5 **Spen Green** Ches
20 A2 **Spencers Wood** Wokham
65 E2 **Spennithorne** N York
65 F6 **Spennymoor** Dur
30 A5 **Spetchley** Worcs
8 B3 **Spetisbury** Dorset
35 G6 **Spexhall** Suffk
101 F5 **Spey Bay** Moray
100 D2 **Speybridge** Highld
101 E3 **Speyview** Moray
53 F2 **Spilsby** Lincs
51 F4 **Spinkhill** Derbys
107 F5 **Spinningdale** Highld
51 G5 **Spital Hill** Donc
87 E4 **Spittal** E Loth
110 B4 **Spittal** Highld
81 F5 **Spittal** Nthumb
24 D5 **Spittal** Pembks
94 C4 **Spittal of Glenmuick** Abers
94 C4 **Spittal of Glenshee** P & K
80 B2 **Spittal-on-Rule** Border
92 D3 **Spittalfield** P & K
45 F3 **Spixworth** Norfk
15 E2 **Splatt** Cnwll
11 G4 **Splayne's Green** E Susx
27 G1 **Splottlands** Cardif
59 E5 **Spofforth** N York
41 E6 **Spondon** C Derb
44 D2 **Spooner Row** Norfk
44 C3 **Sporle** Norfk
87 F3 **Spott** E Loth
80 C5 **Spottiswoode** Border
41 H1 **Spratton** Nhants
10 B6 **Spreakley** Surrey
15 F1 **Spreyton** Devon
5 F2 **Spriddlestone** Devon
52 C4 **Spridlington** Lincs
85 E3 **Springburn** C Glas
71 F6 **Springfield** D & G
22 C6 **Springfield** Essex
93 F1 **Springfield** Fife
70 B6 **Springholm** D & G
76 C5 **Springside** N Ayrs
52 B4 **Springthorpe** Lincs
73 F3 **Springwell** Sundld
61 E3 **Sproatley** E R Yk
49 G5 **Sproston Green** Ches
51 F6 **Sprotbrough** Donc
35 E3 **Sproughton** Suffk
80 D3 **Sprouston** Border
45 F3 **Sprowston** Norfk
42 B3 **Sproxton** Leics
66 C2 **Sproxton** N York
49 E5 **Spurstow** Ches
7 F5 **Spyway** Dorset
50 D5 **Stableford** Shrops
50 D5 **Stacey Bank** Sheff
63 G3 **Stackhouse** N York
24 D2 **Stackpole** Pembks
5 E2 **Staddiscombe** C Plym
19 H6 **Stadhampton** Oxon
111 a3 **Stadhlaigearraidh** W Isls
71 H3 **Staffield** Cumb
104 D3 **Staffin** Highld
40 A5 **Stafford** Staffs
32 C3 **Stagsden** Beds
70 D2 **Stainburn** Cumb
58 D5 **Stainburn** N York
42 B4 **Stainby** Lincs
59 E1 **Staincross** Barns
65 E3 **Staindrop** Dur
20 D3 **Staines** Surrey
59 G2 **Stainforth** Donc
63 G3 **Stainforth** N York
56 D6 **Staining** Lancs
58 C2 **Stainland** Calder
67 E4 **Stainsacre** N York
71 G2 **Stainton** Cumb
63 E4 **Stainton** Cumb
51 F5 **Stainton** Donc
65 E5 **Stainton** Dur
66 B4 **Stainton** Middsb
52 C3 **Stainton by Langworth** Lincs
52 D4 **Stainton le Vale** Lincs
62 C3 **Stainton with Adgarley** Cumb
67 F3 **Staintondale** N York
76 D4 **Stair** E Ayrs
68 D3 **Stair Haven** D & G
66 D5 **Staithes** N York
73 F5 **Stakeford** Nthumb
10 A3 **Stakes** Hants
17 H1 **Stalbridge** Dorset
17 H1 **Stalbridge Weston** Dorset
45 G4 **Stalham** Norfk
23 E1 **Stalisfield Green** Kent
17 G1 **Stallen** Dorset
61 E1 **Stallingborough** NE Lin
62 D1 **Stalmine** Lancs
50 B6 **Stalybridge** Tamesd
34 B3 **Stambourne** Essex
34 A3 **Stambourne Green** Essex
42 C3 **Stamford** Lincs
81 G2 **Stamford** Nthumb
49 E5 **Stamford Bridge** Ches
58 B2 **Stamford Bridge** Calder
21 F4 **Stamford Hill** Gt Lon
73 E4 **Stamfordham** Nthumb
32 B1 **Stanbridge** Beds
58 B4 **Stanbury** Brad
85 H3 **Stand** N Lans
85 H3 **Standburn** Falk
40 A4 **Standeford** Staffs
23 E1 **Standen** Kent
18 A2 **Standerwick** Somset
10 B5 **Standford** Hants
70 D2 **Standingstone** Cumb
57 F2 **Standish** Wigan
31 E1 **Standlake** Oxon
9 G2 **Standon** Hants
33 F1 **Standon** Herts
49 G5 **Standon** Staffs
85 G2 **Stane** N Lans
44 C4 **Stanfield** Norfk
32 D3 **Stanford** Beds
13 F5 **Stanford** Kent
39 F2 **Stanford Bishop** Herefs
39 G2 **Stanford Bridge** Worcs
19 G4 **Stanford Dingley** W Berk
19 E5 **Stanford in the Vale** Oxon

22 B3 **Stanford le Hope** Thurr
41 G2 **Stanford on Avon** Nhants
41 F5 **Stanford on Soar** Notts
39 G2 **Stanford on Teme** Worcs
51 F4 **Stanfree** Derbys
66 C5 **Stanghow** R & Cl
42 D2 **Stanground** C Pete
44 B5 **Stanhoe** Norfk
79 E5 **Stanhope** Border
72 D1 **Stanhope** Dur
38 D3 **Stanion** Nhants
51 E1 **Stanley** Derbys
73 F2 **Stanley** Dur
92 D3 **Stanley** P & K
50 A2 **Stanley** Staffs
73 F1 **Stanley Crook** Dur
30 B3 **Stanley Pontlarge** Gloucs
11 F3 **Stanmer** Br & H
21 E4 **Stanmore** Gt Lon
9 F6 **Stanmore** Hants
72 B5 **Stannersburn** Nthumb
34 C4 **Stanningfield** Suffk
73 F4 **Stannington** Nthumb
50 D5 **Stannington** Sheff
73 F4 **Stannington Station** Nthumb
38 D2 **Stansbatch** Herefs
34 A4 **Stansfield** Suffk
34 B4 **Stanstead** Suffk
21 F6 **Stanstead Abbotts** Herts
34 B4 **Stanstead Street** Suffk
22 B2 **Stansted** Kent
33 G1 **Stansted Airport** Essex
33 G2 **Stansted Mountfitchet** Essex
30 C3 **Stanton** Gloucs
73 E3 **Stanton** Nthumb
50 C2 **Stanton** Staffs
34 C5 **Stanton** Suffk
41 E5 **Stanton by Bridge** Derbys
51 F1 **Stanton by Dale** Derbys
17 G5 **Stanton Drew** BaNES
18 D5 **Stanton Fitzwarren** Swindn
31 E1 **Stanton Harcourt** Oxon
50 D3 **Stanton in Peak** Derbys
39 E4 **Stanton Lacy** Shrops
50 D3 **Stanton Lees** Derbys
39 F5 **Stanton Long** Shrops
41 G6 **Stanton on the Wolds** Notts
17 G5 **Stanton Prior** BaNES
18 B3 **Stanton St Bernard** Wilts
31 F1 **Stanton St John** Oxon
18 B4 **Stanton St Quintin** Wilts
34 C5 **Stanton Street** Suffk
41 F4 **Stanton under Bardon** Leics
49 E2 **Stanton upon Hine Heath** Shrops
17 G5 **Stanton Wick** BaNES
34 C1 **Stanway** Essex
30 B3 **Stanway** Gloucs
20 D3 **Stanwell** Surrey
32 C5 **Stanwick** Nhants
71 G5 **Stanwix** Cumb
111 a3 **Staoinebrig** W Isls
66 D3 **Stape** N York
49 F4 **Stapeley** Ches
40 D5 **Stapenhill** Staffs
23 E1 **Staple** Kent
16 C3 **Staple** Somset
16 B1 **Staple Cross** Devon
12 C4 **Staple Cross** E Susx
16 C1 **Staple Fitzpaine** Somset
11 F4 **Staplefield** W Susx
33 F4 **Stapleford** Cambs
33 E1 **Stapleford** Herts
42 A4 **Stapleford** Leics
52 B1 **Stapleford** Lincs
51 F1 **Stapleford** Notts
8 C1 **Stapleford** Wilts
21 G4 **Stapleford Abbotts** Essex
16 D2 **Staplegrove** Somset
16 D2 **Staplehay** Somset
12 C6 **Staplehurst** Kent
23 E2 **Staplestreet** Kent
38 D3 **Stapleton** Herefs
41 E3 **Stapleton** Leics
65 F4 **Stapleton** N York
39 E6 **Stapleton** Shrops
17 F1 **Stapleton** Somset
16 D1 **Stapley** Somset
32 D4 **Staploe** Beds
29 E6 **Staplow** Herefs
86 D6 **Star** Fife
25 F6 **Star** Pembks
17 F4 **Star** Somset
59 E5 **Starbeck** N York
64 D1 **Starbotton** N York
6 B4 **Starcross** Devon
41 E4 **Stareton** Warwks
33 F2 **Starlings Green** Essex
45 E1 **Starston** Norfk
65 E5 **Startforth** Dur
18 B5 **Startley** Wilts
23 G1 **Statenborough** Kent
17 E2 **Stathe** Somset
41 H6 **Stathern** Leics
32 D5 **Staughton Green** Cambs
28 D4 **Staunton** Gloucs
29 E5 **Staunton** Gloucs
28 D2 **Staunton Green** Herefs
38 D2 **Staunton on Arrow** Herefs
38 D2 **Staunton on Wye** Herefs
62 D4 **Staveley** Cumb
63 E4 **Staveley** Cumb
51 E4 **Staveley** Derbys
59 E6 **Staveley** N York
5 H3 **Staverton** Devon
29 F5 **Staverton** Gloucs
31 F6 **Staverton** Nhants
18 B3 **Staverton** Wilts
17 E3 **Stawell** Somset
16 C2 **Stawley** Somset
110 D4 **Staxigoe** Highld
67 F2 **Staxton** N York
91 D1 **Staynall** Lancs
65 F1 **Stean** N York
31 F4 **Steane** Nhants
66 C1 **Stearsby** N York
16 D3 **Steart** Somset
33 H1 **Stebbing** Essex
34 A1 **Stebbing Green** Essex
33 H2 **Stebbing Park** Essex
10 B4 **Stedham** W Susx

Steele Road - Tal-y-Cafn 189

79 H2 Steele Road Border
86 A5 Steelend Fife
39 E2 Steen's Bridge Herefs
10 B4 Steep Hants
58 B2 Steep Lane Calder
22 D5 Steeple Essex
18 B2 Steeple Ashton Wilts
31 F3 Steeple Aston Oxon
34 A3 Steeple Bumpstead Essex
31 G3 Steeple Claydon Bucks
32 D6 Steeple Gidding Cambs
18 C1 Steeple Langford Wilts
33 E3 Steeple Morden Cambs
58 B4 Steeton Brad
104 B2 Stein Highld
13 F6 Stelling Minnis Kent
17 E1 Stembridge Somset
3 F5 Stenalees Cnwll
77 G1 Stenhouse D & G
85 G4 Stenhousemuir Falk
104 C3 Stenscholl Highld
87 F3 Stenton E Loth
111 d6 Steornabhagh W Isls
25 E3 Stepaside Pembks
21 F3 Stepney Gt Lon
32 C2 Steppingley Beds
85 F3 Stepps N Lans
35 G4 Sternfield Suffk
18 C3 Stert Wilts
33 H4 Stetchworth Cambs
32 D2 Stevenage Herts
76 C5 Stevenston N Ayrs
19 G2 Steventon Hants
19 F5 Steventon Oxon
33 G3 Steventon End Essex
32 C4 Stevington Beds
32 C3 Stewartby Beds
85 E1 Stewartfield S Lans
76 D5 Stewarton E Ayrs
32 B2 Stewkley Bucks
17 E1 Stewley Somset
11 E3 Steyning W Susx
24 D3 Steynton Pembks
14 B2 Stibb Cnwll
14 D3 Stibb Cross Devon
19 E3 Stibb Green Wilts
44 D5 Stibbard Norfk
42 C2 Stibbington Cambs
80 C4 Stichill Border
3 F4 Sticker Cnwll
53 E2 Stickford Lincs
5 F6 Sticklepath Devon
33 F2 Stickling Green Essex
53 E1 Stickney Lincs
44 C6 Stiffkey Norfk
111 a3 Stilligarry W Isls
59 G4 Stillingfleet N York
59 G6 Stillington N York
65 G5 Stillington S on T
42 D1 Stilton Cambs
29 E3 Stinchcombe Gloucs
7 H4 Stinsford Dorset
38 D5 Stiperstones Shrops
103 F4 Stirling Abers
85 G5 Stirling Stirlg
32 D5 Stirtloe Cambs
58 B5 Stirton N York
34 B2 Stisted Essex
2 D3 Stithians Cnwll
41 E1 Stivichall Covtry
52 D2 Stixwould Lincs
48 D6 Stoak Ches
79 E6 Stobo Border
8 B2 Stoborough Dorset
80 B1 Stobs Castle Border
73 F6 Stobswood Nthumb
22 C5 Stock Essex
17 F5 Stock N Som
30 B5 Stock Green Worcs
30 B5 Stock Wood Worcs
9 F6 Stockbridge Hants
77 G5 Stockbriggs S Lans
22 D2 Stockbury Kent
19 F3 Stockcross W Berk
42 A2 Stockerston Leics
28 D5 Stocking Herefs
33 F2 Stocking Pelham Herts
41 E3 Stockingford Warwks
6 D6 Stockland Devon
16 D3 Stockland Bristol Somset
15 G2 Stockleigh English Devon
15 G2 Stockleigh Pomeroy Devon
18 C3 Stockley Wilts
17 E1 Stocklinch Somset
50 A5 Stockport Stockp
50 D6 Stocksbridge Sheff
73 E3 Stocksfield Nthumb
39 E2 Stockton Herefs
45 G2 Stockton Norfk
39 G5 Stockton Shrops
31 E6 Stockton Warwks
18 C1 Stockton Wilts
49 G1 Stockton Wrekin
57 F2 Stockton Heath Warrtn
39 G3 Stockton on Teme Worcs
59 G5 Stockton on the Forest York
66 B5 Stockton-on-Tees S on T
17 G5 Stockwood Bristl
7 G6 Stockwood Dorset
23 G2 Stodmarsh Kent
44 D5 Stody Norfk
108 A2 Stoer Highld
17 G1 Stoford Somset
8 C6 Stoford Wilts
16 C3 Stogumber Somset
16 D3 Stogursey Somset
41 E2 Stoke Covtry
14 C3 Stoke Devon
19 F2 Stoke Hants
10 A2 Stoke Hants
22 D3 Stoke Medway
7 F5 Stoke Abbott Dorset
42 A1 Stoke Albany Nhants
35 E5 Stoke Ash Suffk
51 G1 Stoke Bardolph Notts
39 F2 Stoke Bliss Worcs
31 H5 Stoke Bruerne Nhants
34 B3 Stoke by Clare Suffk
6 B5 Stoke Canon Devon
19 G1 Stoke Charity Hants
4 D4 Stoke Climsland Cnwll
39 F1 Stoke Cross Herefs
20 D2 Stoke D'Abernon Surrey
42 C1 Stoke Doyle Nhants
42 B2 Stoke Dry Rutlnd
28 D6 Stoke Edith Herefs
8 C5 Stoke Farthing Wilts
44 A2 Stoke Ferry Norfk
6 A1 Stoke Fleming Devon
6 A2 Stoke Gabriel Devon
28 D1 Stoke Gifford S Glos
41 E3 Stoke Golding Leics
32 A3 Stoke Goldington M Keyn
32 B2 Stoke Hammond Bucks
45 E2 Stoke Holy Cross Norfk
39 F1 Stoke Lacy Herefs
31 F3 Stoke Lyne Oxon
20 B6 Stoke Mandeville Bucks
21 F4 Stoke Newington Gt Lon
29 F5 Stoke Orchard Gloucs
20 C4 Stoke Poges Bucks
39 E2 Stoke Prior Herefs
30 B6 Stoke Prior Worcs
15 F4 Stoke Rivers Devon
20 A4 Stoke Row Oxon
17 E2 Stoke St Gregory Somset
16 D2 Stoke St Mary Somset
17 G4 Stoke St Michael Somset
39 E4 Stoke St Milborough Shrops
17 F1 Stoke sub Hamdon Somset
20 A5 Stoke Talmage Oxon
17 H2 Stoke Trister Somset
49 F2 Stoke upon Tern Shrops
8 A4 Stoke Wake Dorset
34 D2 Stoke-by-Nayland Suffk
49 A2 Stoke-on-Trent C Stke
49 H4 Stoke-upon-Trent C Stke
8 B2 Stokeford Dorset
52 A3 Stokeham Notts
6 B3 Stokeinteignhead Devon
20 B5 Stokenchurch Bucks
5 H2 Stokenham Devon
38 D4 Stokesay Castle Shrops
45 G3 Stokesby Norfk
66 B4 Stokesley N York
16 D3 Stolford Somset
17 G4 Ston Easton Somset
22 B5 Stondon Massey Essex
20 B6 Stone Bucks
29 E2 Stone Gloucs
12 D4 Stone Kent
51 F5 Stone Rothm
40 A6 Stone Staffs
39 H3 Stone Worcs
17 E4 Stone Allerton Somset
23 G1 Stone Cross Kent
22 B1 Stone Street Kent
35 G6 Stone Street Suffk
17 E5 Stonebridge N Som
40 D2 Stonebridge Solhll
51 E3 Stonebroom Derbys
12 C5 Stonecrouch Kent
61 E3 Stoneferry C KuH
83 G3 Stonefield Castle Hotel Ag & B
12 B5 Stonegate E Susx
66 C1 Stonegrave N York
95 G4 Stonehaven Abers
18 D1 Stonehenge Wilts
5 E2 Stonehouse C Plym
49 E6 Stonehouse Ches
79 B6 Stonehouse D & G
29 F3 Stonehouse Gloucs
77 F5 Stonehouse S Lans
41 E1 Stoneleigh Warwks
35 E2 Stones Green Essex
42 A4 Stonesby Leics
31 E2 Stonesfield Oxon
101 E5 Stonewells Moray
50 D4 Stoney Middleton Derbys
41 F3 Stoney Stanton Leics
17 H2 Stoney Stoke Somset
17 G3 Stoney Stratton Somset
48 D1 Stoney Stretton Shrops
111 a3 Stoneybridge W Isls
86 A2 Stoneyburn W Loth
41 G3 Stoneygate C Leic
68 C3 Stoneykirk D & G
103 E1 Stoneywood C Aber
85 G4 Stoneywood Falk
35 E4 Stonham Aspal Suffk
40 C4 Stonnall Staffs
20 A4 Stonor Oxon
41 H3 Stonton Wyville Leics
51 F3 Stony Houghton Derbys
32 A3 Stony Stratford M Keyn
15 F4 Stoodleigh Devon
16 B1 Stoodleigh Devon
10 D4 Stopham W Susx
32 C1 Stopsley Luton
111 d6 Stornoway W Isls
111 d6 Stornoway Airport W Isls
10 D3 Storrington W Susx
60 B4 Storwood E R Yk
101 E6 Stotfield Moray
32 D2 Stotfold Beds
39 F4 Stottesdon Shrops
41 G3 Stoughton Leics
20 C1 Stoughton Surrey
10 B3 Stoughton W Susx
97 E2 Stoul Highld
30 A5 Stoulton Worcs
8 A5 Stour Provost Dorset
8 A5 Stour Row Dorset
40 A2 Stourbridge Dudley
8 B4 Stourpaine Dorset
39 G3 Stourport-on-Severn Worcs
39 H4 Stourton Staffs
30 D4 Stourton Warwks
8 A6 Stourton Wilts
17 H1 Stourton Caundle Dorset
111 l1 Stove Shet
35 G6 Stoven Suffk
87 E1 Stow Border
52 B3 Stow Lincs
43 G3 Stow Bardolph Norfk
44 C2 Stow Bedon Norfk
32 D5 Stow Longa Cambs
22 D5 Stow Maries Essex
33 G4 Stow-cum-Quy Cambs
30 C3 Stow-on-the-Wold Gloucs
43 G3 Stowbridge Norfk
38 C3 Stowe Shrops
40 B5 Stowe by Chartley Staffs
17 G2 Stowell Somset
17 G5 Stowey BaNES
14 D1 Stowford Devon
15 F5 Stowford Devon
5 E5 Stowford Devon
34 C5 Stowlangtoft Suffk
34 D4 Stowmarket Suffk
13 F6 Stowting Kent
13 F6 Stowting Common Kent
34 D4 Stowupland Suffk
99 G4 Straanruie Moray
95 F5 Strachan Abers
84 A5 Strachur Ag & B
95 E3 Stracthro Hospital Angus
35 E5 Stradbroke Suffk
34 B4 Stradishall Suffk
43 H3 Stradsett Norfk
52 B1 Stragglethorpe Lincs
86 C3 Straiton Mdloth
76 D2 Straiton S Ayrs
102 D2 Straloch Abers
92 C5 Straloch P & K
40 C6 Stramshall Staffs
116 c3 Strang IOM
28 D5 Strangford Herefs
68 C3 Stranraer D & G
19 H3 Stratfield Mortimer W Berk
20 A2 Stratfield Saye Hants
20 A2 Stratfield Turgis Hants
21 F4 Stratford Gt Lon
35 F4 Stratford St Andrew Suffk
34 D2 Stratford St Mary Suffk
8 D5 Stratford Tony Wilts
30 D5 Stratford-upon-Avon Warwks
105 F4 Strath Highld
108 B2 Strathan Highld
109 E5 Strathan Highld
77 F5 Strathaven S Lans
85 E3 Strathblane Stirlg
106 B5 Strathcanaird Highld
97 G6 Strathcarron Station Highld
89 G2 Strathcoil Ag & B
101 F1 Strathdon Abers
93 F1 Strathkinness Fife
85 H3 Strathloanhead W Loth
98 D2 Strathmashie House Highld
86 C6 Strathmiglo Fife
106 D2 Strathpeffer Highld
92 B4 Strathtay P & K
75 H4 Strathwhillan N Ayrs
109 G5 Strathy Highld
109 G5 Strathy Inn Highld
91 G1 Strathyre Stirlg
14 C2 Stratton Cnwll
7 G5 Stratton Dorset
30 B1 Stratton Gloucs
31 G3 Stratton Audley Oxon
18 D5 Stratton St Margaret Swindn
45 E2 Stratton St Michael Norfk
45 E4 Stratton Strawless Norfk
17 G4 Stratton-on-the-Fosse Somset
93 G1 Stravithie Fife
11 F3 Streat E Susx
21 F3 Streatham Gt Lon
32 C2 Streatley Beds
19 G4 Streatley W Berk
6 D4 Street Devon
17 F3 Street Somset
41 F2 Street Ashton Warwks
48 D3 Street Dinas Shrops
23 F1 Street End Kent
10 B2 Street End W Susx
17 G3 Street on the Fosse Somset
40 C4 Streethay Staffs
65 G3 Streetlam N York
33 G3 Streetly End Cambs
92 D3 Strelitz P & K
51 F1 Strelley Notts
59 G5 Strensall York
16 D3 Stretcholt Somset
5 H2 Strete Devon
57 G2 Stretford Traffd
33 F3 Strethall Essex
33 G6 Stretham Cambs
10 C3 Strettington W Susx
51 E3 Stretton Derbys
42 B3 Stretton Rutlnd
40 A4 Stretton Staffs
40 D5 Stretton Staffs
57 F1 Stretton Warrtn
39 F1 Stretton Grandison Herefs
30 D4 Stretton on Fosse Warwks
28 C6 Stretton Sugwas Herefs
41 F2 Stretton under Fosse Warwks
39 F5 Stretton Westwood Shrops
41 E1 Stretton-on-Dunsmore Warwks
103 E5 Strichen Abers
16 D3 Stringston Somset
32 B5 Strixton Nhants
28 D3 Stroat Gloucs
97 F5 Stromeferry Highld
111 g2 Stromness Ork
84 D6 Stronachlachar Stirlg
83 H4 Stronafian Ag & B
108 C1 Stronchrubie Highld
84 B4 Strone Ag & B
98 A1 Strone Highld
98 A1 Stronenaba Highld
90 C2 Stronmilchan Ag & B
111 j2 Stronsay Airport Ork
89 H5 Strontian Highld
22 C2 Strood Medway
29 F3 Stroud Gloucs
10 A4 Stroud Hants
22 D4 Stroud Green Essex
29 F3 Stroud Green Gloucs
42 B5 Stroxton Lincs
96 B5 Struan Highld
92 A5 Struan P & K
45 F3 Strumpshaw Norfk
77 F6 Strutherhill S Lans
86 D6 Struthers Fife
98 C6 Struy Highld
103 E4 Stuartfield Abers
9 G4 Stubbington Hants
57 G4 Stubbins N York
42 B6 Stubton Lincs
8 D4 Stuckton Hants
32 C1 Studham Beds
71 F5 Studholme Cumb
8 C2 Studland Dorset
30 C6 Studley Warwks
18 C4 Studley Wilts
65 G1 Studley Roger N York
65 F1 Studley Royal N York
33 G6 Stuntney Cambs
34 A3 Sturmer Essex
8 A4 Sturminster Common Dorset
8 B3 Sturminster Marshall Dorset
8 A4 Sturminster Newton Dorset
23 F2 Sturry Kent
52 B5 Sturton N Linc
52 B3 Sturton by Stow Lincs
52 A4 Sturton le Steeple Notts
35 E6 Stuston Suffk
59 F4 Stutton N York
35 E2 Stutton Suffk
57 H1 Styal Ches
101 F5 Stynie Moray
51 G5 Styrrup Notts
84 C6 Succoth Ag & B
39 G2 Suckley Worcs
32 B6 Sudborough Nhants
35 G4 Sudbourne Suffk
42 B6 Sudbrook Lincs
28 C2 Sudbrook Mons
52 C3 Sudbrooke Lincs
40 C6 Sudbury Derbys
21 E4 Sudbury Gt Lon
34 C3 Sudbury Suffk
39 H2 Suddington Worcs
67 F3 Suffield N York
45 E5 Suffield Norfk
49 G3 Sugnall Staffs
28 C6 Sugwas Pool Herefs
96 D4 Suisnish Highld
116 c4 Sulby IOM
31 F4 Sulgrave Nhants
31 F4 Sulgrave Manor Nhants
19 H4 Sulham W Berk
19 H3 Sulhamstead W Berk
111 l3 Sullom Shet
111 l3 Sullom Voe Shet
16 C5 Sully V Glam
111 l1 Sumburgh Airport Shet
58 D6 Summerbridge N York
3 E4 Summercourt Cnwll
44 B5 Summerfield Norfk
65 F5 Summerhouse Darltn
10 B3 Summersdale W Susx
57 G4 Summerseat Bury
31 F1 Summertown Oxon
20 D2 Sunbury Surrey
78 B1 Sundaywell D & G
82 B2 Sunderland Ag & B
71 E3 Sunderland Cumb
62 D2 Sunderland Lancs
73 G2 Sunderland Sundld
73 F1 Sunderland Bridge Dur
79 F5 Sundhope Border
21 G1 Sundridge Kent
20 C2 Sunningdale W & M
20 C2 Sunninghill W & M
19 G6 Sunningwell Oxon
73 E1 Sunniside Dur
73 F3 Sunniside Gatesd
41 E6 Sunnyhill C Derb
57 F5 Sunnyhurst Bl w D
85 G5 Sunnylaw Stirlg
31 F1 Sunnymead Oxon
21 E2 Surbiton Gt Lon
43 E4 Surfleet Lincs
45 F3 Surlingham Norfk
34 C1 Surrex Essex
45 E5 Sustead Norfk
52 A5 Susworth Lincs
14 C2 Sutcombe Devon
14 C2 Sutcombemill Devon
53 F3 Sutterby Lincs
43 E5 Sutterton Lincs
32 D3 Sutton Beds
42 C2 Sutton C Pete
33 F6 Sutton Cambs
5 G2 Sutton Devon
11 G2 Sutton E Susx
21 E2 Sutton Gt Lon
23 G1 Sutton Kent
59 F3 Sutton N York
45 G4 Sutton Norfk
51 H1 Sutton Notts
39 G4 Sutton Shrops
49 G2 Sutton Staffs
35 F3 Sutton Suffk
10 C3 Sutton W Susx
22 A2 Sutton at Hone Kent
41 H2 Sutton Bassett Nhants
18 B4 Sutton Benger Wilts
41 F5 Sutton Bonington Notts
43 F4 Sutton Bridge Lincs
41 E3 Sutton Cheney Leics
40 C3 Sutton Coldfield Birm
19 G6 Sutton Courtenay Oxon
51 G5 Sutton cum Lound Notts
65 F1 Sutton Grange N York
20 D1 Sutton Green Surrey
65 G2 Sutton Howgrave N York
51 F3 Sutton in Ashfield Notts
39 G6 Sutton Maddock Shrops
17 E3 Sutton Mallet Somset
8 C6 Sutton Mandeville Wilts
17 G2 Sutton Montis Somset
53 G3 Sutton on Sea Lincs
40 D6 Sutton on the Hill Derbys
52 A2 Sutton on Trent Notts
19 F1 Sutton Scotney Hants
43 F3 Sutton St Edmund Lincs
43 F4 Sutton St James Lincs
39 E1 Sutton St Nicholas Herefs
60 B4 Sutton upon Derwent E R Yk
12 C6 Sutton Valence Kent
18 B1 Sutton Veny Wilts
8 B5 Sutton Waldron Dorset
57 E1 Sutton Weaver Ches
17 G5 Sutton Wick BaNES
19 G6 Sutton Wick Oxon
58 B4 Sutton-in-Craven N York
61 E3 Sutton-on-Hull C KuH
59 F6 Sutton-on-the-Forest N York
30 D4 Sutton-under-Brailes Warwks
66 B2 Sutton-under-Whitestonecliffe N York
53 F3 Swaby Lincs
40 D5 Swadlincote Derbys
44 B3 Swaffham Norfk
33 G5 Swaffham Bulbeck Cambs
33 G5 Swaffham Prior Cambs
45 F5 Swafield Norfk
66 B3 Swainby N York
45 E2 Swainsthorpe Norfk
18 A3 Swainswick BaNES
31 E4 Swalcliffe Oxon
23 F2 Swalecliffe Kent
52 D5 Swallow Lincs
52 B2 Swallow Beck Lincs
8 C5 Swallowcliffe Wilts
20 A2 Swallowfield Wokham
49 G6 Swan Green Ches
8 C2 Swanage Dorset
32 A2 Swanbourne Bucks
60 D3 Swanland E R Yk
21 G2 Swanley Kent
21 H2 Swanley Village Kent
9 G5 Swanmore Hants
41 E5 Swannington Leics
45 E4 Swannington Norfk
52 B2 Swanpool Garden Suburb Lincs
22 B3 Swanscombe Kent
26 C2 Swansea Swans
26 B2 Swansea Airport Swans
45 F4 Swanton Abbot Norfk
44 D4 Swanton Morley Norfk
44 D5 Swanton Novers Norfk
51 E2 Swanwick Derbys
9 G4 Swanwick Hants
42 C5 Swarby Lincs
45 E2 Swardeston Norfk
41 E6 Swarkestone Derbys
73 F6 Swarland Nthumb
19 G1 Swarraton Hants
62 C4 Swarthmoor Cumb
42 D5 Swaton Lincs
33 E5 Swavesey Cambs
9 E3 Sway Hants
42 C4 Swayfield Lincs
9 F5 Swaythling C Sotn
15 H1 Sweetham Devon
11 G5 Sweethaws E Susx
4 C6 Sweets Cnwll
3 G5 Sweetshouse Cnwll
35 F5 Swefling Suffk
41 E4 Swepstone Leics
31 E3 Swerford Oxon
49 G5 Swettenham Ches
35 E4 Swilland Suffk
59 E3 Swillington Leeds
15 F4 Swimbridge Devon
15 E4 Swimbridge Newland Devon
30 D2 Swinbrook Oxon
58 D5 Swincliffe N York
52 B2 Swinderby Lincs
29 G5 Swindon Gloucs
39 H5 Swindon Staffs
18 D5 Swindon Swindn
61 E3 Swine E R Yk
60 B2 Swinefleet E R Yk
32 C5 Swineshead Beds
43 E5 Swineshead Lincs
110 C3 Swiney Highld
41 F2 Swinford Leics
13 G6 Swingfield Minnis Kent
13 G6 Swingfield Street Kent
34 C3 Swingleton Green Suffk
81 G3 Swinhoe Nthumb
65 E2 Swinithwaite N York
50 C2 Swinscoe Staffs
71 E2 Swinside Cumb
42 C4 Swinstead Lincs
80 D4 Swinton Border
65 F2 Swinton N York
66 D1 Swinton N York
51 E6 Swinton Rothm
57 G3 Swinton Salfd
41 F4 Swithland Leics
107 E3 Swordale Highld
97 F2 Swordland Highld
109 G5 Swordly Highld
49 H3 Swynnerton Staffs
7 F4 Swyre Dorset
38 A6 Sychtyn Powys
29 G4 Syde Gloucs
21 F3 Sydenham Gt Lon
20 A5 Sydenham Oxon
5 E4 Sydenham Damerel Devon
44 B5 Syderstone Norfk
7 G5 Sydling St Nicholas Dorset
19 G3 Sydmonton Hants
51 H2 Syerston Notts
54 D2 Sygun Copper Mine Gwynd
59 G2 Sykehouse Donc
111 l3 Symbister Shet
76 D4 Symington S Ayrs
78 D6 Symington S Lans
28 D4 Symonds Yat Herefs
7 F5 Symondsbury Dorset
109 F3 Syre Highld
30 B2 Syreford Gloucs
31 G4 Syresham Nhants
41 G4 Syston Leics
42 B6 Syston Lincs
39 H3 Sytchampton Worcs
32 A5 Sywell Nhants

T

31 F2 Tackley Oxon
45 E2 Tacolneston Norfk
59 F4 Tadcaster N York
50 C4 Taddington Derbys
30 C3 Taddington Gloucs
19 G3 Tadley Hants
33 E3 Tadlow Cambs
31 E4 Tadmarton Oxon
21 E1 Tadworth Surrey
27 G1 Taff's Well Cardif
26 D2 Taibach Neath
110 C5 Tain Highld
107 F4 Tain Highld
111 c5 Tairbeart W Isls
33 G1 Takeley Essex
33 G1 Takeley Street Essex
37 E5 Tal-y-bont Cerdgn
55 F3 Tal-y-Bont Conwy
47 E3 Tal-y-bont Gwynd
54 D3 Tal-y-bont Gwynd
55 F3 Tal-y-Cafn Conwy

28 C4 **Tal-y-coed** Mons
6 C5 **Talaton** Devon
24 C4 **Talbenny** Pembks
6 C5 **Taleford** Devon
47 H2 **Talerddig** Powys
36 D2 **Talgarreg** Cerdgn
27 G5 **Talgarth** Powys
96 B5 **Talisker** Highld
49 G4 **Talke** Staffs
71 H5 **Talkin** Cumb
79 E4 **Talla Linnfoots** Border
105 G3 **Talladale** Highld
76 D2 **Tallaminnock** S Ayrs
49 E4 **Tallarn Green** Wrexhm
70 D3 **Tallentire** Cumb
26 C5 **Talley** Carmth
42 C3 **Tallington** Lincs
109 E5 **Talmine** Highld
25 G5 **Talog** Carmth
37 E2 **Talsarn** Cerdgn
47 E5 **Talsarnau** Gwynd
3 C5 **Talskiddy** Cnwll
54 D4 **Talwrn** IOA
27 G5 **Talybont-on-Usk** Powys
54 C4 **Talysarn** Gwynd
5 E3 **Tamerton Foliot** C Plym
40 D4 **Tamworth** Staffs
36 C2 **Tan-y-groes** Cerdgn
21 F1 **Tandridge** Surrey
73 F2 **Tanfield** Dur
73 F2 **Tanfield Lea** Dur
19 E2 **Tangley** Hants
10 C3 **Tangmere** W Susx
111 a1 **Tangusdale** W Isls
111 h2 **Tankerness** Ork
51 E6 **Tankersley** Barns
23 F2 **Tankerton** Kent
110 D4 **Tannach** Highld
95 F4 **Tannachie** Abers
93 G5 **Tannadice** Angus
40 C1 **Tanner's Green** Worcs
35 F5 **Tannington** Suffk
85 E7 **Tannochside** N Lans
51 E3 **Tansley** Derbys
42 C1 **Tansor** Nhants
73 F2 **Tantobie** Dur
66 B4 **Tanton** N York
40 C1 **Tanworth in Arden** Warwks
111 b5 **Taobh Tuath** W Isls
20 C3 **Taplow** Bucks
75 E5 **Tarbert** Ag & B
83 E5 **Tarbert** Ag & B
111 c5 **Tarbert** W Isls
84 C5 **Tarbet** Ag & B
108 B4 **Tarbet** Highld
97 F2 **Tarbet** Highld
76 D4 **Tarbolton** S Ayrs
86 A2 **Tarbrax** S Lans
30 B6 **Tardebigge** Worcs
94 D4 **Tarfside** Angus
94 D6 **Tarland** Abers
57 E4 **Tarleton** Lancs
29 G3 **Tarlton** Gloucs
17 E4 **Tarnock** Somset
49 E5 **Tarporley** Ches
15 G4 **Tarr** Somset
16 C2 **Tarr** Somset
8 B4 **Tarrant Crawford** Dorset
8 B4 **Tarrant Gunville** Dorset
8 B4 **Tarrant Hinton** Dorset
8 B4 **Tarrant Keyneston** Dorset
8 B4 **Tarrant Launceston** Dorset
8 B4 **Tarrant Monkton** Dorset
8 B4 **Tarrant Rawston** Dorset
8 B4 **Tarrant Rushton** Dorset
11 G3 **Tarring Neville** E Susx
28 D6 **Tarrington** Herefs
96 D3 **Tarskavaig** Highld
102 D3 **Tarves** Abers
92 C5 **Tarvie** P & K
49 E5 **Tarvin** Ches
45 E2 **Tasburgh** Norfk
40 D5 **Tatenhill** Staffs
53 E4 **Tathwell** Lincs
21 G1 **Tatsfield** Surrey
49 E5 **Tattenhall** Ches
44 C4 **Tatterford** Norfk
44 C5 **Tattersett** Norfk
52 D1 **Tattershall** Lincs
52 D2 **Tattershall Thorpe** Lincs
35 E3 **Tattingstone** Suffk
35 E3 **Tattingstone White Horse** Suffk
7 E6 **Tatworth** Somset
101 F4 **Tauchers** Moray
16 D2 **Taunton** Somset
45 E3 **Taverham** Norfk
25 F4 **Taverspite** Pembks
5 E4 **Tavistock** Devon
15 F1 **Taw Green** Devon
15 G4 **Tawstock** Devon
50 B4 **Taxal** Derbys
92 A5 **Tay Forest Park** P & K
90 D2 **Taychreggan Hotel** Ag & B
75 E5 **Tayinloan** Ag & B
29 E5 **Taynton** Gloucs
30 D2 **Taynton** Oxon
90 B2 **Taynuilt** Ag & B
93 F2 **Tayport** Fife
83 F4 **Tayvallich** Ag & B
52 D4 **Tealby** Lincs
73 F3 **Team Valley** Gatesd
97 E3 **Teangue** Highld
107 E2 **Teanord** Highld
63 F6 **Tebay** Cumb
32 C2 **Tebworth** Beds
5 H6 **Tedburn St Mary** Devon
29 G5 **Teddington** Gloucs
21 E3 **Teddington** Gt Lon
39 F2 **Tedstone Delamere** Herefs
39 F2 **Tedstone Wafer** Herefs
65 G4 **Teesside Airport** S on T
41 G1 **Teeton** Nhants
8 C6 **Teffont Evias** Wilts
8 C6 **Teffont Magna** Wilts
25 F5 **Tegryn** Pembks
42 B3 **Teigh** Rutlnd
6 A3 **Teigngrace** Devon
6 A3 **Teignmouth** Devon
79 G3 **Teindside** Border
39 F6 **Telford** Wrekin
18 A2 **Tellisford** Somset
11 G3 **Telscombe** E Susx
91 H4 **Tempar** P & K

78 D2 **Templand** D & G
4 C4 **Temple** Cnwll
86 D2 **Temple** Mdloth
37 E2 **Temple Bar** Cerdgn
17 G4 **Temple Cloud** BaNES
13 G6 **Temple Ewell** Kent
30 C3 **Temple Grafton** Warwks
30 C3 **Temple Guiting** Gloucs
59 G3 **Temple Hirst** N York
51 E3 **Temple Normanton** Derbys
95 G4 **Temple of Fiddes** Abers
98 D5 **Temple Pier** Highld
64 A5 **Temple Sowerby** Cumb
17 H2 **Templecombe** Somset
15 H2 **Templeton** Devon
25 E4 **Templeton** Pembks
73 E2 **Templetown** Dur
32 D4 **Tempsford** Beds
43 G2 **Ten Mile Bank** Norfk
39 F3 **Tenbury Wells** Worcs
25 E3 **Tenby** Pembks
35 E1 **Tendring** Essex
35 E2 **Tendring Green** Essex
35 E2 **Tendring Heath** Essex
12 D5 **Tenterden** Kent
22 C6 **Terling** Essex
49 F3 **Ternhill** Shrops
78 C1 **Terregles** D & G
66 C1 **Terrington** N York
43 G4 **Terrington St Clement** Norfk
43 G3 **Terrington St John** Norfk
22 C1 **Teston** Kent
9 F4 **Testwood** Hants
29 F2 **Tetbury** Gloucs
48 D3 **Tetchill** Shrops
14 C1 **Tetcott** Devon
53 E4 **Tetford** Lincs
53 E5 **Tetney** Lincs
20 A5 **Tetsworth** Oxon
40 A3 **Tettenhall** Wolves
51 E4 **Teversal** Notts
33 F4 **Teversham** Cambs
79 G3 **Teviothead** Border
21 F6 **Tewin** Herts
29 F3 **Tewkesbury** Gloucs
23 E2 **Teynham** Kent
58 C4 **Thackley** Brad
10 D4 **Thakeham** W Susx
20 A5 **Thame** Oxon
21 E2 **Thames Ditton** Surrey
21 E3 **Thamesmead** Gt Lon
23 F1 **Thanington** Kent
78 C6 **Thankerton** S Lans
45 E2 **Tharston** Norfk
19 G3 **Thatcham** W Berk
33 G2 **Thaxted** Essex
18 C6 **The Beeches** Gloucs
96 D5 **The Braes** Highld
87 F3 **The Brunt** E Loth
116 c4 **The Bungalow** IOM
29 F4 **The Butts** Gloucs
20 B5 **The City** Bucks
9 E6 **The Common** Wilts
38 D4 **The Corner** Shrops
76 C6 **The Den** N Ayrs
3 F4 **The Eden Project** Cnwll
12 D6 **The Forstal** Kent
13 E5 **The Forstal** Kent
62 B4 **The Green** Cumb
34 B1 **The Green** Essex
66 D4 **The Green** N York
62 B4 **The Hill** Cumb
20 C5 **The Lee** Bucks
116 c5 **The Lhen** IOM
101 F5 **The Lochs** Moray
12 C5 **The Moor** Kent
26 C2 **The Mumbles** Swans
85 E1 **The Murray** S Lans
95 F5 **The Neuk** Abers
29 F4 **The Reddings** Gloucs
92 A2 **The Ross** P & K
12 D4 **The Stocks** Kent
18 B3 **The Strand** Wilts
65 G2 **Theakston** N York
60 C2 **Thealby** N Linc
17 F3 **Theale** Somset
19 H4 **Theale** W Berk
61 E4 **Thearne** E R Yk
35 G5 **Theberton** Suffk
41 G2 **Theddingworth** Leics
53 F4 **Theddlethorpe All Saints** Lincs
53 F4 **Theddlethorpe St Helen** Lincs
34 D6 **Thelnetham** Suffk
35 E6 **Thelveton** Norfk
57 F2 **Thelwall** Warrtn
44 D4 **Themelthorpe** Norfk
31 H4 **Thenford** Nhants
33 F4 **Therfield** Herts
44 C1 **Thetford** Norfk
44 B1 **Thetford Forest Park**
21 G5 **Theydon Bois** Essex
18 B4 **Thickwood** Wilts
53 E2 **Thimbleby** Lincs
66 B3 **Thimbleby** N York
56 C1 **Thingwall** Wirral
66 B2 **Thirkleby** N York
66 B2 **Thirlby** N York
80 B4 **Thirlestane** Border
71 F1 **Thirlspot** Cumb
65 F2 **Thirn** N York
65 H2 **Thirsk** N York
56 D6 **Thistleton** Lancs
42 B4 **Thistleton** Rutlnd
33 H6 **Thistley Green** Suffk
60 C5 **Thixendale** N York
72 D2 **Thockrington** Nthumb
43 F3 **Tholomas Drove** Cambs
59 F6 **Tholthorpe** N York
102 B3 **Thomastown** Abers
44 C2 **Thompson** Norfk
22 B3 **Thong** Kent
64 D2 **Thoralby** N York
52 D5 **Thoresway** Lincs
52 D5 **Thorganby** Lincs
59 G4 **Thorganby** N York
66 D3 **Thorgill** N York
35 G6 **Thorington** Suffk
35 E2 **Thorington Street** Suffk
58 B5 **Thorlby** N York
21 H6 **Thorley** Herts
9 F7 **Thorley Street** IOW
66 B2 **Thormanby** N York
66 B5 **Thornaby-on-Tees** S on T

44 D5 **Thornage** Norfk
31 H3 **Thornborough** Bucks
65 G2 **Thornborough** N York
58 D3 **Thornbury** Brad
14 D2 **Thornbury** Devon
39 F2 **Thornbury** Herefs
28 D2 **Thornbury** S Glos
41 G1 **Thornby** Nhants
50 B3 **Thorncliff** Staffs
7 E5 **Thorncombe** Dorset
35 E5 **Thorndon** Suffk
5 F6 **Thorndon Cross** Devon
59 G2 **Thorne** Donc
91 F1 **Thorne** Stirlg
16 C1 **Thorne St Margaret** Somset
59 E4 **Thorner** Leeds
40 C4 **Thornes** Staffs
43 E3 **Thorney** C Pete
52 B3 **Thorney** Notts
17 E2 **Thorney** Somset
9 D3 **Thorney Hill** Hants
16 D2 **Thornfalcon** Somset
17 G1 **Thornford** Dorset
72 C3 **Thorngrafton** Nthumb
61 F3 **Thorngumbald** E R Yk
44 B6 **Thornham** Norfk
34 D5 **Thornham Magna** Suffk
35 E5 **Thornham Parva** Suffk
42 C2 **Thornhaugh** C Pete
9 F4 **Thornhill** C Sotn
78 C2 **Thornhill** D & G
50 D5 **Thornhill** Derbys
58 D2 **Thornhill** Kirk
85 F5 **Thornhill** Stirlg
61 E6 **Thornholme** E R Yk
8 B4 **Thornicombe** Dorset
81 E3 **Thornington** Nthumb
73 E1 **Thornley** Dur
73 G1 **Thornley** Dur
85 E2 **Thornliebank** E Rens
84 B4 **Thorns** Suffk
50 B5 **Thornsett** Derbys
71 E2 **Thornthwaite** Cumb
58 C5 **Thornthwaite** N York
93 F4 **Thornton** Angus
58 C3 **Thornton** Brad
31 H3 **Thornton** Bucks
60 D4 **Thornton** E R Yk
86 C5 **Thornton** Fife
56 D6 **Thornton** Lancs
41 F4 **Thornton** Leics
53 E2 **Thornton** Lincs
66 B4 **Thornton** Middsb
81 E4 **Thornton** Nthumb
61 G2 **Thornton Curtis** N Linc
21 F2 **Thornton Heath** Gt Lon
56 C1 **Thornton Hough** Wirral
63 F3 **Thornton in Lonsdale** N York
67 E2 **Thornton le Dale** N York
52 C5 **Thornton le Moor** Lincs
64 D2 **Thornton Rust** N York
65 F2 **Thornton Steward** N York
65 F2 **Thornton Watlass** N York
58 A4 **Thornton-in-Craven** N York
65 G2 **Thornton-le-Beans** N York
59 G6 **Thornton-le-Clay** N York
65 G2 **Thornton-le-Moor** N York
48 D6 **Thornton-le-Moors** Ches
65 G2 **Thornton-le-Street** N York
85 E1 **Thorntonhall** S Lans
87 G3 **Thorntonloch** E Loth
80 C4 **Thornydykes** Border
71 G2 **Thornythwaite** Cumb
51 H1 **Thoroton** Notts
59 E4 **Thorp Arch** Leeds
50 C2 **Thorpe** Derbys
60 D4 **Thorpe** E R Yk
58 B6 **Thorpe** N York
51 H2 **Thorpe** Notts
20 D2 **Thorpe** Surrey
35 E6 **Thorpe Abbotts** Norfk
41 H5 **Thorpe Arnold** Leics
59 F2 **Thorpe Audlin** Donc
67 E1 **Thorpe Bassett** N York
22 D4 **Thorpe Bay** Sthend
42 B2 **Thorpe by Water** Rutlnd
40 D4 **Thorpe Constantine** Staffs
45 F3 **Thorpe End** Norfk
35 E1 **Thorpe Green** Essex
34 C4 **Thorpe Green** Suffk
51 E6 **Thorpe Hesley** Rothm
59 G1 **Thorpe in Balne** Donc
52 B3 **Thorpe in the Fallows** Lincs
41 H3 **Thorpe Langton** Leics
60 C4 **Thorpe le Street** E R Yk
20 D3 **Thorpe Lea** Surrey
32 A6 **Thorpe Malsor** Nhants
31 F4 **Thorpe Mandeville** Nhants
45 F5 **Thorpe Market** Norfk
34 C4 **Thorpe Morieux** Suffk
52 B2 **Thorpe on the Hill** Lincs
20 D2 **Thorpe Park** Surrey
51 F4 **Thorpe Salvin** Rothm
41 H4 **Thorpe Satchville** Leics
45 F3 **Thorpe St Andrew** Norfk
52 F2 **Thorpe St Peter** Lincs
65 G5 **Thorpe Thewles** S on T
52 D1 **Thorpe Tilney** Lincs
59 F5 **Thorpe Underwood** N York
32 C6 **Thorpe Waterville** Nhants
59 F3 **Thorpe Willoughby** N York
35 E1 **Thorpe-le-Soken** Essex
35 G4 **Thorpeness** Suffk
34 D1 **Thorrington** Essex
6 B5 **Thorverton** Devon
34 B3 **Thrandeston** Suffk
32 C6 **Thrapston** Nhants
48 D4 **Threapwood** Ches
50 B1 **Threapwood** Staffs
76 C2 **Threave** S Ayrs
70 B5 **Threave Castle** D & G
11 F5 **Three Bridges** W Susx
12 D5 **Three Chimneys** Kent
27 G6 **Three Cocks** Powys
26 B2 **Three Crosses** Swans
12 B4 **Three Cups Corner** E Susx
11 B5 **Three Leg Cross** E Susx
8 C4 **Three Legged Cross** Dorset
20 A2 **Three Mile Cross** Wokham
86 B3 **Three Miletown** W Loth
12 D3 **Three Oaks** E Susx

42 C5 **Threekingham** Lincs
80 B4 **Threepwood** Border
71 F2 **Threlkeld** Cumb
58 B6 **Threshfield** N York
45 G3 **Thrigby** Norfk
41 E5 **Thringstone** Leics
65 G3 **Thrintoft** N York
33 F2 **Thriplow** Cambs
33 E2 **Throcking** Herts
73 E2 **Throckley** N u Ty
30 B5 **Throckmorton** Worcs
8 D3 **Throop** Bmouth
72 D6 **Thropton** Nthumb
85 G4 **Throsk** Stirlg
78 C1 **Throughgate** D & G
23 E1 **Throwley Forstal** Kent
41 F6 **Thrumpton** Notts
110 D4 **Thrumster** Highld
53 E6 **Thrunscoe** NE Lin
29 F3 **Thrupp** Gloucs
21 G5 **Thrushesbush** Essex
41 G5 **Thrussington** Leics
19 E2 **Thruxton** Hants
28 C6 **Thruxton** Herefs
51 F6 **Thrybergh** Rothm
41 E6 **Thulston** Derbys
22 C4 **Thundersley** Essex
41 F4 **Thurcaston** Leics
51 F5 **Thurcroft** Rothm
51 G2 **Thurgarton** Norfk
51 G2 **Thurgarton** Notts
50 D6 **Thurgoland** Barns
41 F3 **Thurlaston** Leics
41 F1 **Thurlaston** Warwks
16 D1 **Thurlbear** Somset
52 B2 **Thurlby** Lincs
42 C4 **Thurlby** Lincs
53 F3 **Thurlby** Lincs
32 C4 **Thurleigh** Beds
5 G2 **Thurlestone** Devon
34 A4 **Thurlow** Suffk
17 G1 **Thurloxton** Somset
58 D1 **Thurlstone** Barns
45 G2 **Thurlton** Norfk
41 G4 **Thurnby** Leics
45 G3 **Thurne** Norfk
22 C1 **Thurnham** Kent
42 C1 **Thurning** Nhants
44 D5 **Thurning** Norfk
59 F1 **Thurnscoe** Barns
71 F4 **Thursby** Cumb
44 D5 **Thursford** Norfk
10 C4 **Thursley** Surrey
110 B5 **Thurso** Highld
56 C1 **Thurstaston** Wirral
34 C5 **Thurston** Suffk
71 F5 **Thurstonfield** Cumb
58 C1 **Thurstonland** Kirk
45 F2 **Thurton** Norfk
50 D1 **Thurvaston** Derbys
44 D3 **Thuxton** Norfk
64 C3 **Thwaite** N York
35 E5 **Thwaite** Suffk
62 D5 **Thwaite Head** Cumb
45 E2 **Thwaite St Mary** Norfk
67 F1 **Thwing** E R Yk
92 C2 **Tibbermore** P & K
78 C2 **Tibbers** D & G
29 E5 **Tibberton** Gloucs
30 A5 **Tibberton** Worcs
49 F2 **Tibberton** Wrekin
79 E4 **Tibbie Shiels Inn** Border
45 E1 **Tibenham** Norfk
51 E3 **Tibshelf** Derbys
60 D5 **Tibthorpe** E R Yk
12 C5 **Ticehurst** E Susx
9 G3 **Tichborne** Hants
42 C3 **Tickencote** Rutlnd
17 F6 **Tickenham** N Som
51 G5 **Tickhill** Donc
39 E5 **Ticklerton** Shrops
41 E5 **Ticknall** Derbys
60 D4 **Tickton** E R Yk
19 E3 **Tidcombe** Wilts
31 G1 **Tiddington** Oxon
30 D5 **Tiddington** Warwks
12 B5 **Tidebrook** E Susx
4 D3 **Tideford** Cnwll
28 D2 **Tidenham** Gloucs
50 C4 **Tideswell** Derbys
19 H4 **Tidmarsh** W Berk
30 D4 **Tidmington** Warwks
31 G5 **Tiers Cross** Pembks
31 G5 **Tiffield** Nhants
95 E3 **Tigerton** Angus
111 a4 **Tigh a Ghearraidh** W Isls
111 a1 **Tigharry** W Isls
83 G3 **Tighnabruaich** Ag & B
5 G3 **Tigley** Devon
32 C5 **Tilbrook** Cambs
22 B3 **Tilbury** Thurr
34 B3 **Tilbury Green** Essex
40 D1 **Tile Hill** Covtry
19 H4 **Tilehurst** Readg
10 C6 **Tilford** Surrey
11 F5 **Tilgate** W Susx
17 F3 **Tilham Street** Somset
85 H5 **Tillicoultry** Clacks
77 G5 **Tillietudlem** S Lans
23 E3 **Tillingham** Essex
39 E1 **Tillington** Herefs
10 C4 **Tillington** W Susx
39 E1 **Tillington Common** Herefs
95 F6 **Tillybirloch** Abers
94 D5 **Tillycairn** Abers
102 C3 **Tillyfourie** Abers
103 E2 **Tillygreig** Abers
86 B6 **Tillyrie** P & K
23 G1 **Tilmanstone** Kent
43 G4 **Tilney All Saints** Norfk
43 G4 **Tilney High End** Norfk
43 G3 **Tilney St Lawrence** Norfk
18 C2 **Tilshead** Wilts
49 E3 **Tilstock** Shrops
49 E4 **Tilston** Ches
49 F5 **Tilstone Fearnall** Ches
32 C1 **Tilsworth** Beds
41 H4 **Tilton on the Hill** Leics
29 F3 **Tiltups End** Gloucs
52 D2 **Timberland** Lincs
50 A3 **Timbersbrook** Ches
16 B3 **Timberscombe** Somset
58 C5 **Timble** N York
71 G4 **Timpanheck** D & G
57 G2 **Timperley** Traffd

17 G5 **Timsbury** BaNES
9 F5 **Timsbury** Hants
111 c6 **Timsgarry** W Isls
111 c6 **Timsgearraidh** W Isls
34 C5 **Timworth** Suffk
34 C5 **Timworth Green** Suffk
8 A3 **Tincleton** Dorset
72 A3 **Tindale** Cumb
65 F5 **Tindale Crescent** Dur
31 G3 **Tingewick** Bucks
58 D3 **Tingley** Leeds
32 C2 **Tingrith** Beds
111 I2 **Tingwall Airport** Shet
5 E5 **Tinhay** Devon
51 E5 **Tinsley** Sheff
11 F5 **Tinsley Green** W Susx
4 B5 **Tintagel** Cnwll
4 B5 **Tintagel Castle** Cnwll
28 D3 **Tintern Abbey** Mons
28 C3 **Tintern Parva** Mons
17 F1 **Tintinhull** Somset
50 B6 **Tintwistle** Derbys
78 D1 **Tinwald** D & G
42 C3 **Tinwell** Rutlnd
40 B3 **Tipton** Sandw
6 C4 **Tipton St John** Devon
34 C1 **Tiptree** Essex
22 D6 **Tiptree Heath** Essex
37 F2 **Tirabad** Powys
88 B3 **Tiree Airport** Ag & B
83 E2 **Tiretigan** Ag & B
29 F5 **Tirley** Gloucs
27 G3 **Tirphil** Caerph
71 G2 **Tirril** Cumb
8 B6 **Tisbury** Wilts
50 C2 **Tissington** Derbys
14 C4 **Titchberry** Devon
9 G4 **Titchfield** Hants
32 C6 **Titchmarsh** Nhants
44 B6 **Titchwell** Norfk
51 G1 **Tithby** Notts
38 D2 **Titley** Herefs
21 G1 **Titsey** Surrey
49 H3 **Tittensor** Staffs
44 C4 **Tittleshall** Norfk
39 G3 **Titton** Worcs
49 E5 **Tiverton** Ches
6 B6 **Tiverton** Devon
45 E1 **Tivetshall St Margaret** Norfk
45 E1 **Tivetshall St Mary** Norfk
16 B3 **Tivington** Somset
40 B5 **Tixall** Staffs
42 B2 **Tixover** Rutlnd
89 F4 **Tobermory** Ag & B
83 F6 **Toberonochy** Ag & B
111 a3 **Tobha Mor** W Isls
102 C3 **Tocher** Abers
101 F4 **Tochieneal** Moray
18 C4 **Tockenham** Wilts
57 F5 **Tockholes** Bl w D
28 D2 **Tockington** S Glos
59 F5 **Tockwith** N York
8 A5 **Todber** Dorset
73 E6 **Todburn** Nthumb
32 C2 **Toddington** Beds
30 B3 **Toddington** Gloucs
30 D3 **Todenham** Gloucs
93 F3 **Todhills** Angus
71 F5 **Todhills** Cumb
58 B3 **Todmorden** Calder
51 F5 **Todwick** Rothm
33 E4 **Toft** Cambs
42 C4 **Toft** Lincs
111 I3 **Toft** Shet
65 H6 **Toft Hill** Dur
45 G2 **Toft Monks** Norfk
52 C4 **Toft next Newton** Lincs
44 C4 **Toftrees** Norfk
73 F6 **Togston** Nthumb
96 D3 **Tokavaig** Highld
20 A3 **Tokers Green** Oxon
111 e7 **Tolastadh** W Isls
59 F1 **Toll Bar** Donc
16 C2 **Tolland** Somset
8 B5 **Tollard Royal** Wilts
7 G5 **Toller Fratrum** Dorset
7 G5 **Toller Porcorum** Dorset
7 G5 **Toller Whelme** Dorset
59 F6 **Tollerton** N York
41 G6 **Tollerton** Notts
23 E6 **Tollesbury** Essex
22 D6 **Tolleshunt D'Arcy** Essex
22 D6 **Tolleshunt Knights** Essex
22 D6 **Tolleshunt Major** Essex
111 I1 **Tolob** Shet
8 A3 **Tolpuddle** Dorset
111 e7 **Tolsta** W Isls
21 E2 **Tolworth** Gt Lon
99 G5 **Tomatin** Highld
98 B4 **Tomchrasky** Highld
98 A3 **Tomdoun** Highld
107 E6 **Tomich** Highld
98 B5 **Tomich** Highld
107 E1 **Tomich** Highld
107 F3 **Tomich** Highld
101 G2 **Tomintoul** Moray
98 D6 **Tomnacross** Highld
101 G2 **Tomnavoulin** Moray
12 B6 **Tonbridge** Kent
27 E1 **Tondu** Brdgnd
16 C1 **Tonedale** Somset
58 D3 **Tong** Brad
23 E1 **Tong** Kent
39 G6 **Tong** Shrops
39 G6 **Tong Norton** Shrops
58 C3 **Tong Street** Brad
41 E5 **Tonge** Leics
10 C6 **Tongham** Surrey
69 H3 **Tongland** D & G
109 E5 **Tongue** Highld
27 F2 **Tongwynlais** Cardif
26 D3 **Tonna** Neath
33 E1 **Tonwell** Herts
27 F2 **Tonypandy** Rhondd
27 F2 **Tonyrefail** Rhondd
19 G6 **Toot Baldon** Oxon
21 G5 **Toot Hill** Essex
18 D5 **Toothill** Swindn
21 E3 **Tooting** Gt Lon
21 E3 **Tooting Bec** Gt Lon
65 F6 **Topcliffe** N York
45 F2 **Topcroft** Norfk
45 F2 **Topcroft Street** Norfk
34 B3 **Toppesfield** Essex
45 E2 **Toprow** Norfk
6 B4 **Topsham** Devon

75 G4 Torbeg N Ayrs
107 F5 Torboll Highld
99 E6 Torbreck Highld
5 H4 Torbryan Devon
90 C6 Torcastle Highld
5 H2 Torcross Devon
107 E2 Tore Highld
83 F2 Torinturk Ag & B
52 A3 Torksey Lincs
18 A4 Tormarton S Glos
75 G4 Tormore N Ayrs
107 F1 Tornagrain Highld
95 E6 Tornaveen Abers
98 D5 Torness Highld
65 F6 Toronto Dur
89 G3 Torosay Castle Ag & B
71 E3 Torpenhow Cumb
86 A3 Torphichen W Loth
95 E6 Torphins Abers
5 E3 Torpoint Cnwll
6 B2 Torquay Torbay
87 E1 Torquhan Border
104 D1 Torran Highld
87 E3 Torrance E Duns
76 C5 Torranyard N Ayrs
105 G2 Torridon Highld
105 F2 Torridon House Highld
96 D4 Torrin Highld
75 F4 Torrisdale Ag & B
109 F5 Torrisdale Highld
110 A4 Torrish Highld
63 E2 Torrisholme Lancs
107 E6 Torrobull Highld
95 H6 Torry C Aber
86 A4 Torryburn Fife
39 H3 Tortan Worcs
6 a1 Torteval Guern
78 D1 Torthorwald D & G
29 E2 Tortworth S Glos
96 C6 Torvaig Highld
62 C5 Torver Cumb
85 G4 Torwood Falk
79 G6 Torwoodlee Border
51 G5 Torworth Notts
97 E5 Toscaig Highld
33 E5 Toseland Cambs
63 G2 Tosside N York
34 C5 Tostock Suffk
104 A1 Totaig Highld
104 C1 Tote Highld
104 D2 Tote Highld
9 E2 Totland IOW
50 D4 Totley Sheff
5 H3 Totnes Devon
41 F6 Toton Notts
88 C4 Totronald Ag & B
104 C3 Totscore Highld
21 F4 Tottenham Gt Lon
43 H3 Tottenhill Norfk
21 E4 Totteridge Gt Lon
32 C1 Totternhoe Beds
57 G4 Tottington Bury
9 F4 Totton Hants
16 D2 Toulton Somset
107 G4 Toulvaddie Highld
22 C1 Tovil Kent
73 E1 Tow Law Dur
84 B3 Toward Ag & B
84 A2 Toward Quay Ag & B
31 G5 Towcester Nhants
2 B3 Towednack Cnwll
20 A5 Towersey Oxon
101 G1 Towie Abers
43 F2 Town End Cambs
62 C5 Town End Cumb
11 G4 Town Littleworth E Susx
44 B1 Town Street Suffk
80 D3 Town Yetholm Border
84 D3 Townend W Duns
50 C6 Townhead Barns
78 D2 Townhead D & G
70 B5 Townhead of Greenlaw D & G
86 B5 Townhill Fife
19 G3 Towns End Hants
2 C3 Townshend Cnwll
59 G5 Towthorpe York
59 F4 Towton N York
55 G4 Towyn Conwy
56 D2 Toxteth Lpool
21 G1 Toy's Hill Kent
53 F2 Toynton All Saints Lincs
76 D3 Trabboch E Ayrs
76 D3 Trabbochburn E Ayrs
100 B5 Tradespark Highld
36 C2 Traethsaith Cerdgn
27 E5 Trallong Powys
51 E2 Tramway Museum Derbys
86 D3 Tranent E Loth
56 D2 Tranmere Wirral
109 H4 Trantelbeg Highld
109 H4 Trantlemore Highld
26 C4 Trapp Carmth
87 F3 Traprain E Loth
79 F5 Traquair Border
15 E4 Traveller's Rest Devon
58 A4 Trawden Lancs
47 F5 Trawsfynydd Gwynd
37 F5 Tre Taliesin Cerdgn
36 D2 Tre-groes Cerdgn
27 F2 Trealaw Rhondd
56 D5 Treales Lancs
54 B4 Trearddur Bay IOA
104 C2 Treaslane Highld
4 B5 Trebarwith Cnwll
4 A4 Trebetherick Cnwll
16 B3 Treborough Somset
4 D4 Trebullett Cnwll
4 D4 Treburley Cnwll
27 E5 Trecastle Powys
24 D5 Trecwn Pembks
27 F3 Trecynon Rhondd
4 C5 Tredaule Cnwll
27 G3 Tredegar Blae G
29 F5 Tredington Gloucs
30 D4 Tredington Warwks
28 B2 Tredunhock Mons
2 A2 Treen Cnwll
51 E5 Treeton Rothm
24 C6 Trefasser Pembks
27 G5 Trefecca Powys
37 H5 Trefeglwys Powys
24 D5 Treffgarne Pembks
24 C5 Treffgarne Owen Pembks
27 F2 Trefforest Rhondd
37 E3 Trefilan Cerdgn
24 C5 Trefin Pembks
48 A6 Trefnant Denbgs
48 C2 Trefonen Shrops
46 C5 Trefor Gwynd
4 B5 Trefrew Cnwll
55 F3 Trefriw Conwy
4 D5 Tregadillett Cnwll
28 C4 Tregare Mons
37 F3 Tregaron Cerdgn
54 D3 Tregarth Gwynd
4 C5 Tregeare Cnwll
48 B3 Tregeiriog Wrexhm
54 C5 Tregele IOA
2 D2 Tregidden Cnwll
24 C5 Treglemais Pembks
14 B1 Tregole Cnwll
3 F5 Tregonetha Cnwll
3 E4 Tregony Cnwll
27 G6 Tregoyd Powys
38 B5 Tregynon Powys
27 F2 Trehafod Rhondd
5 E3 Trehan Cnwll
27 F2 Treharris Myr Td
27 E3 Treherbert Rhondd
4 D4 Trekenner Cnwll
4 B5 Treknow Cnwll
56 B1 Trelawnyd Flints
25 F5 Trelech Carmth
24 B5 Treleddyd-fawr Pembks
27 F2 Trelewis Myr Td
4 A5 Trelights Cnwll
4 B4 Trelill Cnwll
3 E3 Trelissick Garden Cnwll
28 C3 Trelleck Mons
56 B1 Trelogan Flints
3 E6 Trelow Cnwll
47 E5 Tremadog Gwynd
4 C5 Tremail Cnwll
36 B2 Tremain Cerdgn
4 C5 Tremaine Cnwll
4 D4 Tremar Cnwll
5 E3 Trematon Cnwll
48 B6 Tremeirchion Denbgs
3 E5 Trenance Cnwll
3 F6 Trenance Cnwll
14 B1 Trencreek Cnwll
2 D2 Trenear Cnwll
4 C5 Treneglos Cnwll
17 G1 Trent Dorset
15 F5 Trentishoe Devon
27 E1 Treoes V Glam
27 E3 Treorchy Rhondd
3 F6 Trequite Cnwll
27 F1 Trerhyngyll V Glam
4 D3 Trerulefoot Cnwll
2 a2 Tresco Heliport IOS
2 C2 Trescowe Cnwll
2 D5 Tresean Cnwll
29 F2 Tresham Gloucs
3 E4 Tresillian Cnwll
14 B1 Treskinnick Cross Cnwll
4 C5 Tresmeer Cnwll
4 C6 Tresparrett Cnwll
92 B5 Tressait P & K
111 l2 Tresta Shet
111 m4 Tresta Shet
52 A3 Treswell Notts
4 B5 Trethevey Cnwll
2 A2 Trethewey Cnwll
3 F4 Trethurgy Cnwll
28 C5 Tretire Herefs
27 G4 Tretower Powys
48 C5 Treuddyn Flints
4 C5 Trevague Cnwll
4 B5 Trevalga Cnwll
48 D5 Trevalyn Wrexhm
3 E5 Trevarrian Cnwll
2 D5 Treveal Cnwll
4 B5 Treveighan Cnwll
2 D4 Trevellas Downs Cnwll
4 C3 Trevelmond Cnwll
2 D2 Treverva Cnwll
2 A2 Trevescan Cnwll
3 F4 Treviscoe Cnwll
3 E6 Trevone Cnwll
48 C3 Trevor Denbgs
4 B5 Trewalder Cnwll
4 D5 Trewarlett Cnwll
4 B5 Trewarmett Cnwll
4 C5 Trewen Cnwll
3 F6 Trewen Cnwll
4 C5 Trewint Cnwll
3 E3 Trewithian Cnwll
3 F4 Trewoon Cnwll
10 B4 Treyford W Susx
58 B2 Triangle Calder
65 G6 Trimdon Dur
65 G6 Trimdon Colliery Dur
65 G6 Trimdon Grange Dur
45 F5 Trimingham Norfk
35 F3 Trimley Suffk
26 A3 Trimsaran Carmth
15 E5 Trimstone Devon
91 H5 Trinafour P & K
20 C6 Tring Herts
95 E2 Trinity Angus
7 b2 Trinity Jersey
92 C1 Trinity Gask P & K
16 B3 Triscombe Somset
16 C3 Triscombe Somset
90 C6 Trislaig Highld
3 E4 Trispen Cnwll
73 F5 Tritlington Nthumb
92 C3 Trochry P & K
36 C2 Troedyraur Cerdgn
27 F3 Troedyrhiw Myr Td
7 b2 Trois Bois Jersey
2 C3 Troon Cnwll
76 C4 Troon S Ayrs
59 E4 Tropical World Roundhay Park Leeds
84 D6 Trossachs Stirlg
34 C5 Troston Suffk
30 A5 Trotshill Worcs
22 B2 Trottiscliffe Kent
10 B4 Trotton W Susx
72 C5 Troughend Nthumb
62 D6 Troutbeck Cumb
62 D5 Troutbeck Bridge Cumb
51 E4 Troway Derbys
18 B3 Trowbridge Wilts
51 F1 Trowell Notts
45 F3 Trowse Newton Norfk
17 H3 Trudoxhill Somset
16 D2 Trull Somset
104 B2 Trumpan Highld
28 D6 Trumpet Herefs
33 F4 Trumpington Cambs
45 F5 Trunch Norfk
3 E4 Truro Cnwll
3 E4 Truro Cathedral Cnwll
6 A4 Trusham Devon
40 D6 Trusley Derbys
53 G4 Trusthorpe Lincs
39 H5 Trysull Staffs
19 F6 Tubney Oxon
5 H3 Tuckenhay Devon
39 G4 Tuckhill Shrops
2 C3 Tuckingmill Cnwll
8 B6 Tuckingmill Wilts
8 D3 Tuckton Bmouth
34 B5 Tuddenham Suffk
35 E3 Tuddenham Suffk
12 B6 Tudeley Kent
65 F6 Tudhoe Dur
46 B5 Tudweiloig Gwynd
29 F4 Tuffley Gloucs
19 F2 Tufton Hants
24 D5 Tufton Pembks
41 H3 Tugby Leics
39 E4 Tugford Shrops
81 G3 Tughall Nthumb
85 G5 Tullibody Clacks
99 E5 Tullich Highld
107 G3 Tullich Highld
92 C4 Tulliemet P & K
102 D3 Tulloch Abers
91 F1 Tulloch Stirlg
98 C1 Tulloch Station Highld
83 G5 Tullochgorm Ag & B
92 C3 Tullybeagles Lodge P & K
102 B2 Tullynessle Abers
21 F3 Tulse Hill Gt Lon
26 B4 Tumble Carmth
53 E2 Tumby Lincs
53 E1 Tumby Woodside Lincs
92 A5 Tummel Bridge P & K
12 B5 Tunbridge Wells Kent
79 E1 Tundergarth D & G
49 H4 Tunstall C Stke
61 F3 Tunstall E R Yk
22 D2 Tunstall Kent
63 F3 Tunstall Lancs
65 F3 Tunstall N York
45 G3 Tunstall Norfk
49 G2 Tunstall Staffs
35 F4 Tunstall Suffk
73 G2 Tunstall Sundld
50 C4 Tunstead Derbys
45 F4 Tunstead Norfk
50 B4 Tunstead Milton Derbys
10 A6 Tunworth Hants
41 H3 Tur Langton Leics
20 A2 Turgis Green Hants
30 C2 Turkdean Gloucs
18 A3 Turleigh Wilts
28 B6 Turnastone Herefs
76 B2 Turnberry S Ayrs
50 D2 Turnditch Derbys
11 F5 Turner's Hill W Susx
8 B3 Turners Puddle Dorset
86 B3 Turnhouse C Edin
8 A4 Turnworth Dorset
102 C4 Turriff Abers
57 G4 Turton Bottoms Bl w D
43 E2 Turves Cambs
32 B4 Turvey Beds
20 B4 Turville Bucks
31 G4 Turweston Bucks
79 F4 Tushielaw Inn Border
49 E4 Tushingham cum Grindley Ches
40 D6 Tutbury Staffs
28 D2 Tutshill Gloucs
45 E4 Tuttington Norfk
51 H4 Tuxford Notts
111 g2 Twatt Ork
111 l2 Twatt Shet
85 F3 Twechar E Duns
81 F5 Tweedmouth Nthumb
78 D5 Tweedsmuir Border
2 D3 Twelveheads Cnwll
49 G6 Twemlow Green Ches
42 D4 Twenty Lincs
17 H5 Twerton BaNES
21 E3 Twickenham Gt Lon
29 F5 Twigworth Gloucs
11 E4 Twineham W Susx
34 C2 Twinstead Essex
15 G4 Twitchen Devon
50 D3 Two Dales Derbys
41 E4 Twycross Leics
40 D4 Twycross Zoo Leics
31 G3 Twyford Bucks
9 G5 Twyford Hants
41 H4 Twyford Leics
44 D4 Twyford Norfk
20 B3 Twyford Wokham
69 G3 Twynholm D & G
29 F6 Twyning Gloucs
29 F6 Twyning Green Gloucs
26 D5 Twynllanan Carmth
32 B6 Twywell Nhants
48 C3 Ty'n-dwr Denbgs
55 F3 Ty'n-y-Groes Conwy
48 A4 Ty-nant Conwy
28 B6 Tyberton Herefs
26 C4 Tycroes Carmth
48 B2 Tycrwyn Powys
43 F4 Tydd Gote Lincs
43 F4 Tydd St Giles Cambs
43 F4 Tydd St Mary Lincs
33 G2 Tye Green Essex
57 F3 Tyldesley Wigan
23 F2 Tyler Hill Kent
27 F2 Tylorstown Rhondd
27 F2 Tyn-y-nant Rhondd
91 E2 Tyndrum Stirlg
73 G3 Tynemouth N Tyne
87 F4 Tyninghame E Loth
77 G1 Tynron D & G
37 F4 Tynygraig Cerdgn
32 B3 Tyringham M Keyn
27 E1 Tythegston Brdgnd
50 A4 Tytherington Ches
29 E2 Tytherington S Glos
18 B1 Tytherington Wilts
7 E5 Tytherleigh Devon
18 B4 Tytherton Lucas Wilts
3 G4 Tywardreath Cnwll
47 E2 Tywyn Gwynd

U

35 F5 Ubbeston Green Suffk
17 F4 Ubley BaNES
65 F3 Uckerby N York
11 G4 Uckfield E Susx
29 F6 Uckinghall Worcs
29 F5 Uckington Gloucs
49 F1 Uckington Shrops
85 F2 Uddingston S Lans
78 C5 Uddington S Lans
12 D4 Udimore E Susx
103 E2 Udny Green Abers
103 E2 Udny Station Abers
16 C1 Uffculme Devon
42 C3 Uffington Lincs
19 E5 Uffington Oxon
49 E1 Uffington Shrops
42 C3 Ufford C Pete
35 F4 Ufford Suffk
31 E6 Ufton Warwks
19 H3 Ufton Nervet W Berk
75 F4 Ugadale Ag & B
5 G3 Ugborough Devon
35 G6 Uggeshall Suffk
67 E4 Ugglebarnby N York
50 D5 Ughill Sheff
33 G2 Ugley Essex
33 G2 Ugley Green Essex
66 D4 Ugthorpe N York
88 C4 Uig Ag & B
104 A2 Uig Highld
104 C2 Uig Highld
111 c6 Uig W Isls
104 C1 Uigshader Highld
89 E1 Uisken Ag & B
110 D3 Ulbster Highld
71 G2 Ulcat Row Cumb
53 F3 Ulceby Lincs
61 E2 Ulceby N Linc
61 E2 Ulceby Skitter N Linc
12 D6 Ulcombe Kent
71 F3 Uldale Cumb
29 E3 Uley Gloucs
73 F5 Ulgham Nthumb
106 A5 Ullapool Highld
30 C6 Ullenhall Warwks
59 F4 Ulleskelf N York
41 F2 Ullesthorpe Leics
51 F5 Ulley Rothm
39 F1 Ullingswick Herefs
96 B5 Ullinish Lodge Hotel Highld
70 D2 Ullock Cumb
71 G2 Ullswater Cumb
62 C5 Ulpha Cumb
61 E5 Ulrome E R Yk
111 l3 Ulsta Shet
62 C4 Ulverston Cumb
8 C2 Ulwell Dorset
105 E1 Umachan Highld
15 E3 Umberleigh Devon
108 C3 Unapool Highld
79 G1 Under Burnmouth Border
22 A1 Under River Kent
63 E5 Underbarrow Cumb
58 C3 Undercliffe Brad
49 E1 Underdale Shrops
51 F2 Underwood Notts
28 C2 Undy Mons
116 c3 Union Mills IOM
51 E4 Unstone Derbys
7 G5 Up Cerne Dorset
6 B5 Up Exe Devon
57 E3 Up Holland Lancs
10 B3 Up Marden W Susx
17 G1 Up Mudford Somset
20 A1 Up Nately Hants
9 F6 Up Somborne Hants
7 G5 Up Sydling Dorset
18 D2 Upavon Wilts
22 D2 Upchurch Kent
15 G4 Upcott Devon
16 A2 Upcott Somset
45 E4 Upgate Norfk
7 F5 Uphall Dorset
86 B3 Uphall W Loth
15 H2 Upham Devon
9 G5 Upham Hants
38 D2 Uphampton Herefs
39 H3 Uphampton Worcs
17 E4 Uphill N Som
84 D1 Uplawmoor E Rens
29 E5 Upleadon Gloucs
66 C5 Upleatham R & Cl
7 F5 Uploders Dorset
16 B1 Uplowman Devon
7 E5 Uplyme Devon
22 B4 Upminster Gt Lon
6 D6 Upottery Devon
32 D2 Upper & Lower Stondon Beds
39 E4 Upper Affcot Shrops
107 E4 Upper Ardchronie Highld
39 G4 Upper Arley Worcs
19 G4 Upper Basildon W Berk
11 E3 Upper Beeding W Susx
42 C1 Upper Benefield Nhants
30 B6 Upper Bentley Worcs
109 H5 Upper Bighouse Highld
31 F5 Upper Boddington Nhants
30 D4 Upper Brailes Warwks
97 E4 Upper Breakish Highld
39 G2 Upper Broadheath Worcs
41 G5 Upper Broughton Notts
19 G3 Upper Bucklebury W Berk
8 D5 Upper Burgate Hants
32 D3 Upper Caldecote Beds
31 F5 Upper Catesby Nhants
27 F6 Upper Chapel Powys
8 C6 Upper Chicksgrove Wilts
19 E2 Upper Chute Wilts
21 F4 Upper Clapton Gt Lon
19 F1 Upper Clatford Hants
29 G4 Upper Coberley Gloucs
39 E6 Upper Cound Shrops
58 D1 Upper Cumberworth Kirk
101 F5 Upper Dallachy Moray
23 H1 Upper Deal Kent
32 C5 Upper Dean Beds
58 D1 Upper Denby Kirk
12 A3 Upper Dicker E Susx
110 A5 Upper Dounreay Highld
35 E2 Upper Dovercourt Essex
85 F6 Upper Drumbane Stirlg
59 E6 Upper Dunsforth N York
10 C6 Upper Eashing Surrey
107 F2 Upper Eathie Highld
39 F1 Upper Egleton Herefs
50 B3 Upper Elkstone Staffs
50 C1 Upper Ellastone Staffs
10 A5 Upper Farringdon Hants
29 E4 Upper Framilode Gloucs
10 B6 Upper Froyle Hants
17 F3 Upper Godney Somset
32 D2 Upper Gravenhurst Beds
33 G2 Upper Green Essex
19 F3 Upper Green W Berk
10 B6 Upper Hale Surrey
20 D2 Upper Halliford Surrey
42 B3 Upper Hambleton Rutlnd
23 F2 Upper Harbledown Kent
11 G5 Upper Hartfield E Susx
29 F4 Upper Hatherley Gloucs
58 C2 Upper Heaton Kirk
59 G5 Upper Helmsley N York
38 C2 Upper Hergest Herefs
31 G5 Upper Heyford Nhants
31 F3 Upper Heyford Oxon
39 E2 Upper Hill Herefs
58 D2 Upper Hopton Kirk
50 B3 Upper Hulme Staffs
18 D6 Upper Inglesham Swindn
26 B2 Upper Killay Swans
90 D2 Upper Kinchrackine Ag & B
19 E4 Upper Lambourn W Berk
40 B4 Upper Landywood Staffs
17 F5 Upper Langford N Som
51 F3 Upper Langwith Derbys
87 E6 Upper Largo Fife
50 B1 Upper Leigh Staffs
40 B4 Upper Longdon Staffs
110 C3 Upper Lybster Highld
28 D4 Upper Lydbrook Gloucs
38 D3 Upper Lye Herefs
39 G3 Upper Milton Worcs
18 C5 Upper Minety Wilts
101 F4 Upper Mulben Moray
39 F5 Upper Netchwood Shrops
40 B6 Upper Nobut Staffs
10 C4 Upper Norwood W Susx
59 F5 Upper Poppleton York
30 C4 Upper Quinton Warwks
9 E5 Upper Ratley Hants
39 F3 Upper Rochford Worcs
69 G4 Upper Ruscoe D & G
39 F3 Upper Sapey Herefs
18 B4 Upper Seagry Wilts
32 C3 Upper Shelton Beds
45 E6 Upper Sheringham Norfk
84 B2 Upper Skelmorlie N Ayrs
30 C2 Upper Slaughter Gloucs
28 D4 Upper Soudley Gloucs
13 G5 Upper Standen Kent
78 C1 Upper Stepford D & G
45 F2 Upper Stoke Norfk
31 G5 Upper Stowe Nhants
8 D5 Upper Street Hants
45 F4 Upper Street Norfk
45 F4 Upper Street Norfk
34 B4 Upper Street Suffk
34 D4 Upper Street Suffk
32 C2 Upper Sundon Beds
30 C3 Upper Swell Gloucs
45 E2 Upper Tasburgh Norfk
50 B1 Upper Tean Staffs
50 D3 Upper Town Derbys
39 F1 Upper Town Herefs
17 F5 Upper Town N Som
34 C5 Upper Town Suffk
26 B4 Upper Tumble Carmth
31 E4 Upper Tysoe Warwks
93 G3 Upper Victoria Angus
31 F4 Upper Wardington Oxon
11 G3 Upper Wellingham E Susx
35 E6 Upper Weybread Suffk
19 H1 Upper Wield Hants
31 H2 Upper Winchendon Bucks
18 D1 Upper Woodford Wilts
18 A4 Upper Wraxall Wilts
71 G4 Upperby Cumb
104 B1 Upperglen Highld
58 B1 Uppermill Oldham
58 C1 Upperthong Kirk
10 C4 Upperton W Susx
110 D6 Uppertown Highld
42 B2 Uppingham Rutlnd
49 F1 Uppington Shrops
66 B2 Upsall N York
81 E4 Upsettlington Border
21 G5 Upshire Essex
23 G2 Upstreet Kent
31 H2 Upton Bucks
42 D2 Upton C Pete
32 D6 Upton Cambs
48 D6 Upton Ches
4 D4 Upton Cnwll
6 C5 Upton Devon
5 G2 Upton Devon
7 H4 Upton Dorset
8 C3 Upton Dorset
19 F2 Upton Hants
9 F5 Upton Hants
41 E3 Upton Leics
52 B4 Upton Lincs
45 G3 Upton Norfk
51 H2 Upton Notts
51 H4 Upton Notts
19 G5 Upton Oxon
20 C3 Upton Slough
16 B2 Upton Somset
17 F2 Upton Somset
59 F2 Upton Wakefd
8 B6 Upton Wilts
56 C2 Upton Wirral
28 D5 Upton Bishop Herefs
17 H5 Upton Cheyney S Glos
39 F5 Upton Cressett Shrops
4 D4 Upton Cross Cnwll
10 A6 Upton Grey Hants
15 G2 Upton Hellions Devon
18 B1 Upton Lovell Wilts
49 E1 Upton Magna Shrops
17 H3 Upton Noble Somset
6 B5 Upton Pyne Devon
18 B2 Upton Scudamore Wilts
30 B5 Upton Snodsbury Worcs
29 F4 Upton St Leonards Gloucs
29 F6 Upton upon Severn Worcs
30 A6 Upton Warren Worcs
10 C3 Upwaltham W Susx
43 G2 Upwell Norfk

33 F1 **Upwick Green** Herts
43 E1 **Upwood** Cambs
18 C3 **Urchfont** Wilts
57 G2 **Urmston** Traffd
101 E5 **Urquhart** Moray
66 B3 **Urra** N York
106 D2 **Urray** Highld
95 F2 **Usan** Angus
73 F1 **Ushaw Moor** Dur
28 B3 **Usk** Mons
52 C4 **Usselby** Lincs
73 G3 **Usworth** Sundld
49 E5 **Utkinton** Ches
58 B4 **Utley** Brad
15 G1 **Uton** Devon
53 E4 **Utterby** Lincs
40 C6 **Uttoxeter** Staffs
20 D4 **Uxbridge** Gt Lon
111 m4 **Uyeasound** Shet
24 D4 **Uzmaston** Pembks

V
6 c2 **Vale** Guern
37 F4 **Vale of Rheidol Railway** Cerdgn
54 B4 **Valley** IOA
104 D2 **Valtos** Highld
111 c6 **Valtos** W Isls
22 C4 **Vange** Essex
111 I4 **Vatsetter** Shet
96 B6 **Vatten** Highld
27 F4 **Vaynor** Myr Td
6 b1 **Vazon Bay** Guern
27 G6 **Velindre** Powys
6 C4 **Venn Ottery** Devon
14 D2 **Venngreen** Devon
9 G1 **Ventnor** IOW
5 F3 **Venton** Devon
19 E2 **Vernham Dean** Hants
19 F3 **Vernham Street** Hants
8 D4 **Verwood** Dorset
3 E3 **Veryan** Cnwll
62 C3 **Vickerstown** Cumb
3 F5 **Victoria** Cnwll
111 I3 **Vidlin** Shet
101 E5 **Viewfield** Moray
85 F2 **Viewpark** N Lans
22 B2 **Vigo** Kent
7 a2 **Ville la Bas** Jersey
6 b1 **Villiaze** Guern
12 B4 **Vines Cross** E Susx
20 D2 **Virginia Water** Surrey
4 D6 **Virginstow** Devon
17 H4 **Vobster** Somset
111 I3 **Voe** Shet
28 B6 **Vowchurch** Herefs

W
65 E5 **Wackerfield** Dur
45 E2 **Wacton** Norfk
30 A4 **Wadborough** Worcs
31 H2 **Waddesdon** Bucks
6 A2 **Waddeton** Devon
52 C5 **Waddingham** Lincs
63 G1 **Waddington** Lancs
52 B2 **Waddington** Lincs
3 F6 **Wadebridge** Cnwll
7 E6 **Wadeford** Somset
42 C1 **Wadenhoe** Nhants
33 E1 **Wadesmill** Herts
12 B5 **Wadhurst** E Susx
50 D4 **Wadshelf** Derbys
51 F6 **Wadworth** Donc
53 G2 **Wainfleet All Saints** Lincs
4 C6 **Wainhouse Corner** Cnwll
22 C3 **Wainscott** Medway
58 B3 **Wainstalls** Calder
64 B4 **Waitby** Cumb
53 E5 **Waithe** Lincs
59 E2 **Wakefield** Wakefd
42 B2 **Wakerley** Nhants
34 C2 **Wakes Colne** Essex
35 G6 **Walberswick** Suffk
10 C3 **Walberton** W Susx
70 B6 **Walbutt** D & G
17 H4 **Walcombe** Somset
42 C5 **Walcot** Lincs
49 F1 **Walcot** Shrops
18 D5 **Walcot** Swindn
35 E6 **Walcot Green** Norfk
41 F2 **Walcote** Leics
52 D1 **Walcott** Lincs
45 F5 **Walcott** Norfk
59 F2 **Walden Stubbs** N York
22 C2 **Walderslade** Medway
10 B3 **Walderton** W Susx
7 F5 **Walditch** Dorset
73 F2 **Waldridge** Dur
35 F3 **Waldringfield** Suffk
12 A4 **Waldron** E Susx
51 F5 **Wales** Rothm
17 G2 **Wales** Somset
52 D4 **Walesby** Lincs
51 G4 **Walesby** Notts
38 D3 **Walford** Herefs
28 D4 **Walford** Herefs
49 E2 **Walford Heath** Shrops
49 F4 **Walgherton** Ches
32 A5 **Walgrave** Nhants
57 H5 **Walk Mill** Lancs
57 G3 **Walkden** Salfd
73 H3 **Walker** N u Ty
39 E1 **Walker's Green** Herefs
79 F6 **Walkerburn** Border
51 H5 **Walkeringham** Notts
52 A4 **Walkerith** Lincs
33 E2 **Walkern** Herts
86 C5 **Walkerton** Fife
8 D3 **Walkford** Dorset
5 F4 **Walkhampton** Devon
60 D4 **Walkington** E R Yk
51 E5 **Walkley** Sheff
30 B6 **Walkwood** Worcs
72 D3 **Wall** Nthumb
40 C4 **Wall** Staffs
76 C2 **Wallacetown** S Ayrs
76 C3 **Wallacetown** S Ayrs
11 G3 **Wallands Park** E Susx
56 C2 **Wallasey** Wirral
19 G5 **Wallingford** Oxon
21 F2 **Wallington** Gt Lon

9 G4 **Wallington** Hants
33 E2 **Wallington** Herts
8 C3 **Wallisdown** Poole
111 k2 **Walls** Shet
73 G3 **Wallsend** N Tyne
86 D3 **Wallyford** E Loth
23 H1 **Walmer** Kent
57 E5 **Walmer Bridge** Lancs
35 F6 **Walpole** Suffk
43 G4 **Walpole Cross Keys** Norfk
43 G3 **Walpole Highway** Norfk
43 G4 **Walpole St Andrew** Norfk
43 G4 **Walpole St Peter** Norfk
40 B3 **Walsall** Wsall
58 B2 **Walsden** Calder
34 D5 **Walsham le Willows** Suffk
59 E5 **Walshford** N York
43 F3 **Walsoken** Norfk
86 B1 **Walston** S Lans
32 D2 **Walsworth** Herts
13 F6 **Waltham** Kent
53 E5 **Waltham** NE Lin
21 F5 **Waltham Abbey** Essex
9 G5 **Waltham Chase** Hants
21 F5 **Waltham Cross** Herts
42 A4 **Waltham on the Wolds** Leics
20 B3 **Waltham St Lawrence** W & M
71 H5 **Walton** Cumb
51 E3 **Walton** Derbys
59 E4 **Walton** Leeds
41 G2 **Walton** Leics
32 B2 **Walton** M Keyn
38 C2 **Walton** Powys
17 F3 **Walton** Somset
35 F2 **Walton** Suffk
10 B3 **Walton** W Susx
59 E2 **Walton** Wakefd
49 F2 **Walton** Wrekin
29 F5 **Walton Cardiff** Gloucs
24 D5 **Walton East** Pembks
21 E1 **Walton on the Hill** Surrey
35 F1 **Walton on the Naze** Essex
41 G5 **Walton on the Wolds** Leics
17 E6 **Walton Park** N Som
24 C4 **Walton West** Pembks
17 E6 **Walton-in-Gordano** N Som
57 E5 **Walton-le-Dale** Lancs
20 D2 **Walton-on-Thames** Surrey
40 B5 **Walton-on-the-Hill** Staffs
40 D5 **Walton-on-Trent** Derbys
65 F5 **Walworth** Darltn
21 F3 **Walworth** Gt Lon
24 C4 **Walwyn's Castle** Pembks
6 D6 **Wambrook** Somset
10 C6 **Wanborough** Surrey
18 D5 **Wanborough** Swindn
21 E3 **Wandsworth** Gt Lon
35 G6 **Wangford** Suffk
41 G4 **Wanlip** Leics
78 C4 **Wanlockhead** D & G
12 B3 **Wannock** E Susx
42 C2 **Wansford** C Pete
60 D5 **Wansford** E R Yk
12 C6 **Wanshurst Green** Kent
21 G4 **Wanstead** Gt Lon
17 H3 **Wanstrow** Somset
29 E3 **Wanswell** Gloucs
19 F5 **Wantage** Oxon
29 E1 **Wapley** S Glos
41 E1 **Wappenbury** Warwks
31 G4 **Wappenham** Nhants
12 B4 **Warbleton** E Susx
19 G5 **Warborough** Oxon
33 E6 **Warboys** Cambs
56 D6 **Warbreck** Bpool
4 C5 **Warbstow** Cnwll
57 F2 **Warburton** Traffd
64 B4 **Warcop** Cumb
72 D3 **Warden** Nthumb
31 H4 **Wardington** Oxon
49 F5 **Wardle** Ches
58 A2 **Wardle** Rochdl
73 G3 **Wardley** Gatesd
42 A2 **Wardley** Rutlnd
50 C4 **Wardlow** Derbys
33 F6 **Wardy Hill** Cambs
21 F6 **Ware** Herts
8 B2 **Wareham** Dorset
13 E5 **Warehorne** Kent
81 G3 **Warenford** Nthumb
21 G6 **Wareside** Herts
33 E4 **Waresley** Cambs
20 C3 **Warfield** Br For
6 A1 **Warfleet** Devon
20 B3 **Wargrave** Wokham
44 C6 **Warham All Saints** Norfk
44 C6 **Warham St Mary** Norfk
80 D4 **Wark** Nthumb
72 C4 **Wark** Nthumb
15 F3 **Warkleigh** Devon
32 B6 **Warkton** Nhants
31 F4 **Warkworth** Nhants
81 G1 **Warkworth** Nthumb
65 G3 **Warlaby** N York
4 C4 **Warleggan** Cnwll
58 B3 **Warley Town** Calder
21 F2 **Warlingham** Surrey
71 E6 **Warmanbie** D & G
59 E2 **Warmfield** Wakefd
49 G5 **Warmingham** Ches
42 C1 **Warmington** Nhants
31 E4 **Warmington** Warwks
18 B2 **Warminster** Wilts
17 G6 **Warmley** S Glos
51 F6 **Warmsworth** Donc
7 H4 **Warmwell** Dorset
9 H5 **Warnham** Hants
11 E5 **Warnham** W Susx
10 D3 **Warningcamp** W Susx
11 E4 **Warninglid** W Susx
50 A4 **Warren** Ches
24 D3 **Warren** Pembks
20 B3 **Warren Row** W & M
22 D1 **Warren Street** Kent
78 C6 **Warrenhill** S Lans
32 B4 **Warrington** M Keyn
57 F2 **Warrington** Warrtn
86 C3 **Warriston** C Edin
9 G4 **Warsash** Hants
50 C3 **Warslow** Staffs
51 F3 **Warsop** Notts
60 C5 **Warter** E R Yk
65 F2 **Warthermaske** N York
59 G5 **Warthill** N York

12 B3 **Wartling** E Susx
41 C5 **Wartnaby** Leics
56 D5 **Warton** Lancs
63 E3 **Warton** Lancs
40 D4 **Warton** Warwks
71 E4 **Warwick** Cumb
30 D6 **Warwick** Warwks
30 D6 **Warwick Castle** Warwks
111 h3 **Wasbister** Ork
62 C3 **Wasdale Head** Cumb
3 F6 **Washaway** Cnwll
5 H3 **Washbourne** Devon
35 E3 **Washbrook** Suffk
16 B1 **Washfield** Devon
65 E3 **Washfold** N York
16 C3 **Washford** Somset
15 G2 **Washford Pyne** Devon
52 C3 **Washingborough** Lincs
73 G2 **Washington** Sundld
10 D3 **Washington** W Susx
30 D5 **Wasperton** Warwks
66 B2 **Wass** N York
16 C3 **Watchet** Somset
19 E5 **Watchfield** Oxon
63 E5 **Watchgate** Cumb
5 G5 **Water** Devon
60 B4 **Water End** E R Yk
33 G3 **Water End** Essex
42 D2 **Water Newton** Cambs
40 C3 **Water Orton** Warwks
31 G3 **Water Stratford** Bucks
33 F5 **Waterbeach** Cambs
10 C3 **Waterbeach** W Susx
79 F1 **Waterbeck** D & G
7 H4 **Watercombe** Dorset
50 C2 **Waterfall** Staffs
85 E1 **Waterfoot** S Lans
21 F6 **Waterford** Herts
4 B5 **Watergate** Cnwll
77 E3 **Waterhead** E Ayrs
86 C1 **Waterheads** Border
50 C2 **Waterhouses** Staffs
22 C1 **Wateringbury** Kent
97 E4 **Waterloo** Highld
85 G1 **Waterloo** N Lans
92 C3 **Waterloo** P & K
24 D3 **Waterloo** Pembks
56 D3 **Waterloo** Sefton
10 A3 **Waterlooville** Hants
71 G2 **Watermillock** Cumb
31 G1 **Waterperry** Oxon
16 C2 **Waterrow** Somset
49 F2 **Waters Upton** Wrekin
10 D4 **Watersfield** W Susx
57 G5 **Waterside** Bl w D
76 D2 **Waterside** E Ayrs
76 D5 **Waterside** E Ayrs
85 F3 **Waterside** E Duns
104 A1 **Waterstein** Highld
31 G1 **Waterstock** Oxon
24 D3 **Waterston** Pembks
20 D5 **Watford** Herts
31 G6 **Watford** Nhants
58 C6 **Wath** N York
65 G1 **Wath** N York
51 E6 **Wath upon Dearne** Rothm
43 G3 **Watlington** Norfk
20 A4 **Watlington** Oxon
110 C4 **Watten** Highld
34 D6 **Wattisfield** Suffk
34 D4 **Wattisham** Suffk
7 F5 **Watton** Dorset
60 D5 **Watton** E R Yk
44 C2 **Watton** Norfk
33 E1 **Watton-at-Stone** Herts
85 G3 **Wattston** N Lans
27 G2 **Wattsville** Caerph
95 E5 **Waulkmill** Abers
26 C2 **Waunarlwydd** Swans
37 E5 **Waunfawr** Cerdgn
54 D2 **Waunfawr** Gwynd
32 B3 **Wavendon** M Keyn
71 E4 **Waverbridge** Cumb
49 E5 **Waverton** Ches
71 E4 **Waverton** Cumb
61 E4 **Wawne** E R Yk
45 G4 **Waxham** Norfk
15 H2 **Way Village** Devon
7 E6 **Wayford** Somset
7 F5 **Waytown** Dorset
16 C3 **Weacombe** Somset
19 E6 **Weald** Oxon
21 E4 **Wealdstone** Gt Lon
58 D4 **Weardley** Leeds
17 E4 **Weare** Somset
14 D3 **Weare Giffard** Devon
72 C1 **Wearhead** Dur
17 E2 **Wearne** Somset
44 C4 **Weasenham All Saints** Norfk
44 C4 **Weasenham St Peter** Norfk
57 G3 **Weaste** Salfd
49 F6 **Weaverham** Ches
67 F1 **Weaverthorpe** N York
30 B6 **Webheath** Worcs
102 D3 **Wedderlairs** Abers
41 E3 **Weddington** Warwks
18 C3 **Wedhampton** Wilts
17 H4 **Wedmore** Somset
40 B3 **Wednesbury** Sandw
40 B3 **Wednesfield** Wolves
32 A1 **Weedon** Bucks
31 G5 **Weedon** Nhants
31 G4 **Weedon Lois** Nhants
40 C4 **Weeford** Staffs
16 B2 **Week** Somset
14 C1 **Week St Mary** Cnwll
9 F6 **Weeke** Hants
32 D4 **Weekley** Nhants
60 D4 **Weel** E R Yk
35 E1 **Weeley** Essex
35 E1 **Weeley Heath** Essex
92 B4 **Weem** P & K
30 B5 **Weethley** Warwks
44 B1 **Weeting** Norfk
61 G2 **Weeton** E R Yk
56 D6 **Weeton** Lancs
58 D4 **Weeton** N York
58 D4 **Weetwood** Leeds
57 H5 **Weir** Lancs
5 E3 **Weir Quay** Devon
44 D3 **Welborne** Norfk
52 B1 **Welbourn** Lincs
60 B6 **Welburn** N York
65 G1 **Welbury** N York
42 B5 **Welby** Lincs

14 C3 **Welcombe** Devon
41 G2 **Welford** Nhants
19 F4 **Welford** W Berk
30 C5 **Welford-on-Avon** Warwks
41 H3 **Welham** Leics
51 H4 **Welham** Notts
21 E5 **Welham Green** Herts
10 B6 **Well** Hants
53 F3 **Well** Lincs
65 F2 **Well** N York
32 D2 **Well Head** Herts
29 F6 **Welland** Worcs
93 G3 **Wellbank** Angus
30 D5 **Wellesbourne** Warwks
32 B5 **Welling** Gt Lon
32 B5 **Wellingborough** Nhants
44 C4 **Wellingham** Norfk
52 C1 **Wellingore** Lincs
62 B6 **Wellington** Cumb
39 E1 **Wellington** Herefs
16 C1 **Wellington** Somset
49 F1 **Wellington** Wrekin
29 E6 **Wellington Heath** Herefs
17 H4 **Wellow** BaNES
9 F2 **Wellow** IOW
51 G3 **Wellow** Notts
17 F3 **Wells** Somset
44 C6 **Wells-next-the-sea** Norfk
33 H1 **Wellstye Green** Essex
92 C2 **Welltree** P & K
86 B4 **Wellwood** Fife
43 G2 **Welney** Norfk
48 D3 **Welsh Frankton** Shrops
28 C4 **Welsh Newton** Herefs
16 B6 **Welsh St Donats** V Glam
48 D3 **Welshampton** Shrops
38 C6 **Welshpool** Powys
71 F4 **Welton** Cumb
60 D3 **Welton** E R Yk
52 C3 **Welton** Lincs
31 G6 **Welton** Nhants
53 F3 **Welton le Marsh** Lincs
53 E4 **Welton le Wold** Lincs
61 G2 **Welwick** E R Yk
32 D1 **Welwyn** Herts
21 E6 **Welwyn Garden City** Herts
49 E2 **Wem** Shrops
16 D3 **Wembdon** Somset
21 E4 **Wembley** Gt Lon
5 F5 **Wembury** Devon
15 F2 **Wembworthy** Devon
84 B3 **Wemyss Bay** Inver
33 G2 **Wendens Ambo** Essex
31 F2 **Wendlebury** Oxon
44 C3 **Wendling** Norfk
20 B6 **Wendover** Bucks
2 D2 **Wendron** Cnwll
33 E3 **Wendy** Cambs
35 E6 **Wenhaston** Suffk
33 E6 **Wennington** Cambs
21 G3 **Wennington** Gt Lon
63 F3 **Wennington** Lancs
50 D2 **Wensley** Derbys
65 E2 **Wensley** N York
59 F2 **Wentbridge** Wakefd
38 D5 **Wentnor** Shrops
33 F6 **Wentworth** Cambs
51 E6 **Wentworth** Rothm
16 C6 **Wenvoe** V Glam
38 D2 **Weobley** Herefs
38 D1 **Weobley Marsh** Herefs
10 D3 **Wepham** W Susx
44 A2 **Wereham** Norfk
42 D2 **Werrington** C Pete
4 D5 **Werrington** Cnwll
48 D6 **Wervin** Ches
56 D5 **Wesham** Lancs
51 E3 **Wessington** Derbys
44 B3 **West Acre** Norfk
5 G2 **West Alvington** Devon
15 G4 **West Anstey** Devon
53 E3 **West Ashby** Lincs
10 B3 **West Ashling** W Susx
18 B2 **West Ashton** Wilts
65 F5 **West Auckland** Dur
67 F2 **West Ayton** N York
16 D2 **West Bagborough** Somset
57 E1 **West Bank** Halton
52 D3 **West Barkwith** Lincs
66 D4 **West Barnby** N York
87 F4 **West Barns** E Loth
44 C5 **West Barsham** Norfk
7 F4 **West Bay** Dorset
45 E5 **West Beckham** Norfk
20 D3 **West Bedfont** Surrey
34 C2 **West Bergholt** Essex
7 F4 **West Bexington** Dorset
44 A3 **West Bilney** Norfk
11 F3 **West Blatchington** Br & H
73 G3 **West Boldon** S Tyne
58 C3 **West Bowling** Brad
13 F6 **West Brabourne** Kent
44 C3 **West Bradenham** Norfk
63 G1 **West Bradford** Lancs
17 F3 **West Bradley** Somset
58 D2 **West Bretton** Wakefd
51 G1 **West Bridgford** Notts
40 B3 **West Bromwich** Sandw
79 F4 **West Buccleuch Hotel** Border
15 F4 **West Buckland** Devon
64 D2 **West Burton** N York
52 A5 **West Butterwick** N Linc
20 D2 **West Byfleet** Surrey
68 C1 **West Cairngaan** D & G
45 H3 **West Caister** Norfk
86 A2 **West Calder** W Loth
17 G2 **West Camel** Somset
8 A2 **West Chaldon** Dorset
19 F5 **West Challow** Oxon
5 G2 **West Charleton** Devon
73 F6 **West Chevington** Nthumb
10 D4 **West Chiltington** W Susx
17 F1 **West Chinnock** Somset
20 D1 **West Clandon** Surrey
13 H6 **West Cliffe** Kent
17 G3 **West Coker** Somset
17 G3 **West Compton** Somset
7 G5 **West Compton Abbas** Dorset
59 G4 **West Cottingwith** N York
59 G2 **West Cowick** E R Yk
26 C2 **West Cross** Swans
71 F4 **West Curthwaite** Cumb
10 B3 **West Dean** W Susx
9 E5 **West Dean** Wilts
42 D3 **West Deeping** Lincs

56 D2 **West Derby** Lpool
43 H2 **West Dereham** Norfk
15 E5 **West Down** Devon
20 D3 **West Drayton** Gt Lon
51 G4 **West Drayton** Notts
110 C6 **West Dunnet** Highld
60 D3 **West Ella** E R Yk
32 C4 **West End** Beds
9 F4 **West End** Hants
17 F5 **West End** N Som
45 H3 **West End** Norfk
20 C2 **West End** Surrey
6 C5 **West End** Wilts
19 H3 **West End Green** Hants
22 C1 **West Farleigh** Kent
31 F5 **West Farndon** Nhants
48 D2 **West Felton** Shrops
11 G3 **West Firle** E Susx
19 E3 **West Grafton** Wilts
8 B1 **West Green** Hants
8 D5 **West Grimstead** Wilts
11 E4 **West Grinstead** W Susx
59 F3 **West Haddlesey** N York
31 G1 **West Haddon** Nhants
19 G5 **West Hagbourne** Oxon
40 A2 **West Hagley** Worcs
51 E1 **West Hallam** Derbys
60 C2 **West Halton** N Linc
21 G4 **West Ham** Gt Lon
51 E4 **West Handley** Derbys
19 F5 **West Hanney** Oxon
22 C5 **West Hanningfield** Essex
8 D6 **West Harnham** Wilts
17 F3 **West Harptree** BaNES
10 B4 **West Harting** W Susx
16 D1 **West Hatch** Somset
8 B6 **West Hatch** Wilts
93 G3 **West Haven** Angus
40 B1 **West Heath** Birm
110 A1 **West Helmsdale** Highld
19 F5 **West Hendred** Oxon
67 E1 **West Heslerton** N York
17 E5 **West Hewish** N Som
6 C5 **West Hill** Devon
11 F5 **West Hoathly** W Susx
8 B2 **West Holme** Dorset
24 B4 **West Horndon** Essex
17 G4 **West Horrington** Somset
20 D1 **West Horsley** Surrey
13 G5 **West Hougham** Kent
6 C3 **West Howe** Bmouth
92 D2 **West Huntingtower** P & K
17 E3 **West Huntspill** Somset
13 F5 **West Hythe** Kent
19 F5 **West Ilsley** W Berk
10 B2 **West Itchenor** W Susx
18 D3 **West Kennett** Wilts
76 B6 **West Kilbride** N Ayrs
22 B2 **West Kingsdown** Kent
18 A4 **West Kington** Wilts
56 C2 **West Kirby** Wirral
67 E1 **West Knapton** N York
7 H4 **West Knighton** Dorset
8 B6 **West Knoyle** Wilts
17 E1 **West Lambrook** Somset
13 G6 **West Langdon** Kent
90 C4 **West Laroch** Highld
10 C4 **West Lavington** W Susx
18 C2 **West Lavington** Wilts
65 E4 **West Layton** N York
41 F5 **West Leake** Notts
15 F2 **West Leigh** Devon
5 G3 **West Leigh** Devon
16 C2 **West Leigh** Somset
44 B4 **West Lexham** Norfk
59 G6 **West Lilling** N York
86 B2 **West Linton** Border
18 A4 **West Littleton** S Glos
19 F5 **West Lockinge** Oxon
8 A2 **West Lulworth** Dorset
60 C6 **West Lutton** N York
17 G2 **West Lydford** Somset
17 E2 **West Lyng** Somset
43 G4 **West Lynn** Norfk
22 B2 **West Malling** Kent
39 G1 **West Malvern** Worcs
10 B3 **West Marden** W Susx
51 H4 **West Markham** Notts
61 F1 **West Marsh** NE Lin
58 A5 **West Marton** N York
8 B5 **West Melbury** Dorset
9 H5 **West Meon** Hants
23 E6 **West Mersea** Essex
39 G3 **West Midlands Safari Park** Worcs
7 F5 **West Milton** Dorset
22 D3 **West Minster** Kent
21 E2 **West Molesey** Surrey
16 D2 **West Monkton** Somset
8 C4 **West Moors** Dorset
8 B3 **West Morden** Dorset
80 C4 **West Morriston** Border
17 G1 **West Mudford** Somset
66 C2 **West Ness** N York
61 F4 **West Newton** E R Yk
44 A4 **West Newton** Norfk
16 D2 **West Newton** Somset
21 F3 **West Norwood** Gt Lon
5 H4 **West Ogwell** Devon
8 A5 **West Orchard** Dorset
18 D3 **West Overton** Wilts
8 D3 **West Parley** Dorset
22 B1 **West Peckham** Kent
73 F2 **West Pelton** Dur
17 F3 **West Pennard** Somset
2 D5 **West Pentire** Cnwll
32 D5 **West Perry** Cambs
15 G5 **West Porlock** Somset
7 H6 **West Pulham** Dorset
14 D3 **West Putford** Devon
16 C3 **West Quantoxhead** Somset
15 H2 **West Raddon** Devon
73 G2 **West Rainton** Dur
52 C4 **West Rasen** Lincs
44 C4 **West Raynham** Norfk
65 G4 **West Rounton** N York
34 A6 **West Row** Suffk
44 B4 **West Rudham** Norfk
45 E6 **West Runton** Norfk
87 E3 **West Saltoun** E Loth
15 G2 **West Sandford** Devon
111 I3 **West Sandwick** Shet
65 E2 **West Scrafton** N York
7 H4 **West Stafford** Dorset
52 A4 **West Stockwith** Notts
10 B3 **West Stoke** W Susx

8 A5 **West Stour** Dorset
23 G2 **West Stourmouth** Kent
34 B5 **West Stow** Suffk
18 D3 **West Stowell** Wilts
34 D5 **West Street** Suffk
65 F2 **West Tanfield** N York
4 **West Taphouse** Cnwll
83 F2 **West Tarbert** Ag & B
10 D3 **West Tarring** W Susx
73 F6 **West Thirston** Nthumb
10 B2 **West Thorney** W Susx
41 G5 **West Thorpe** Notts
22 B3 **West Thurrock** Thurr
22 B3 **West Tilbury** Thurr
9 H6 **West Tisted** Hants
52 D3 **West Torrington** Lincs
10 A2 **West Town** Hants
17 F5 **West Town** N Som
9 E6 **West Tytherley** Hants
43 F3 **West Walton** Norfk
43 F3 **West Walton Highway** Norfk
9 E5 **West Wellow** Hants
5 F2 **West Wembury** Devon
86 D5 **West Wemyss** Fife
33 G4 **West Wickham** Cambs
21 F2 **West Wickham** Gt Lon
24 D3 **West Williamston** Pembks
43 H4 **West Winch** Norfk
9 E6 **West Winterslow** Wilts
10 B2 **West Wittering** W Susx
65 E2 **West Witton** N York
72 C5 **West Woodburn** Nthumb
19 F3 **West Woodhay** W Berk
10 B5 **West Worldham** Hants
11 E2 **West Worthing** W Susx
33 G4 **West Wratting** Essex
14 C3 **West Youlstone** Cnwll
23 F2 **Westbere** Kent
42 B6 **Westborough** Lincs
8 C3 **Westbourne** Bmouth
10 B3 **Westbourne** W Susx
23 H3 **Westbrook** Kent
19 F4 **Westbrook** W Berk
31 G3 **Westbury** Bucks
38 D6 **Westbury** Shrops
18 B2 **Westbury** Wilts
18 B2 **Westbury Leigh** Wilts
29 E4 **Westbury on Severn** Gloucs
28 D1 **Westbury-on-Trym** Bristl
17 F4 **Westbury-sub-Mendip** Somset
56 D5 **Westby** Lancs
22 D4 **Westcliff-on-Sea** Sthend
17 F5 **Westcombe** Somset
30 D2 **Westcote** Gloucs
31 H2 **Westcott** Bucks
6 B6 **Westcott** Devon
11 E6 **Westcott** Surrey
19 E3 **Westcourt** Wilts
11 H2 **Westdean** E Susx
4 B5 **Westdowns** Cnwll
99 E5 **Wester Drumashie** Highld
86 A3 **Wester Ochiltree** W Loth
87 E6 **Wester Pitkierie** Fife
105 G4 **Wester Ross** Highld
110 B4 **Westerdale** Highld
66 C4 **Westerdale** N York
35 E4 **Westerfield** Suffk
10 C3 **Westergate** W Susx
21 G1 **Westerham** Kent
73 F3 **Westerhope** N u Ty
6 A2 **Westerland** Devon
29 E1 **Westerleigh** S Glos
93 H4 **Westerton** Angus
17 G4 **Westfield** BaNES
70 D2 **Westfield** Cumb
12 C3 **Westfield** E Susx
110 B5 **Westfield** Highld
85 F3 **Westfield** N Lans
44 D3 **Westfield** Norfk
85 H3 **Westfield** W Loth
92 D4 **Westfields of Rattray** P & K
72 D1 **Westgate** Dur
60 B1 **Westgate** N Linc
23 G3 **Westgate on Sea** Kent
35 G6 **Westhall** Suffk
7 G3 **Westham** Dorset
12 B3 **Westham** E Susx
17 E4 **Westham** Somset
10 C3 **Westhampnett** W Susx
17 F3 **Westhay** Somset
39 F1 **Westhide** Herefs
95 G6 **Westhill** Abers
39 E1 **Westhope** Herefs
39 E4 **Westhope** Shrops
42 D5 **Westhorpe** Lincs
34 D5 **Westhorpe** Suffk
57 F3 **Westhoughton** Bolton
63 F3 **Westhouse** N York
51 E3 **Westhouses** Derbys
21 E1 **Westhumble** Surrey
5 F2 **Westlake** Devon
14 D4 **Westleigh** Devon
16 C1 **Westleigh** Devon
35 G5 **Westleton** Suffk
34 B5 **Westley** Suffk
33 G4 **Westley Waterless** Cambs
31 H1 **Westlington** Bucks
71 G5 **Westlinton** Cumb
23 G2 **Westmarsh** Kent
11 F3 **Westmeston** E Susx
33 E2 **Westmill** Herts
21 F3 **Westminster** Gt Lon
93 F4 **Westmuir** Angus
71 E4 **Westnewton** Cumb
73 G3 **Westoe** S Tyne
17 H5 **Weston** BaNES
49 G4 **Weston** Ches
6 C5 **Weston** Devon
6 C4 **Weston** Devon
10 A4 **Weston** Hants
33 E2 **Weston** Herts
43 E4 **Weston** Lincs
58 C4 **Weston** N York
31 G4 **Weston** Nhants
51 H3 **Weston** Notts
39 F5 **Weston** Shrops
48 C2 **Weston** Shrops
40 B5 **Weston** Staffs
19 E4 **Weston** W Berk
28 D6 **Weston Beggard** Herefs
41 H3 **Weston by Welland** Nhants
19 G1 **Weston Colley** Hants

33 G4 **Weston Colville** Cambs
10 A6 **Weston Corbett** Hants
50 B1 **Weston Coyney** C Stke
32 A5 **Weston Favell** Nhants
33 G4 **Weston Green** Cambs
49 G1 **Weston Heath** Shrops
49 G2 **Weston Jones** Staffs
45 E3 **Weston Longville** Norfk
48 D2 **Weston Lullingfields** Shrops
10 A6 **Weston Patrick** Hants
48 C3 **Weston Rhyn** Shrops
30 C4 **Weston Subedge** Gloucs
20 B6 **Weston Turville** Bucks
28 D5 **Weston under Penyard** Herefs
41 E1 **Weston under Wetherley** Warwks
50 D1 **Weston Underwood** Derbys
32 B4 **Weston Underwood** M Keyn
17 F6 **Weston-in-Gordano** N Som
31 F2 **Weston-on-the-Green** Oxon
17 E5 **Weston-Super-Mare** N Som
49 G1 **Weston-under-Lizard** Staffs
49 E2 **Weston-under-Redcastle** Shrops
41 E6 **Weston-upon-Trent** Derbys
18 B5 **Westonbirt** Gloucs
32 C2 **Westoning** Beds
17 E3 **Westonzoyland** Somset
60 B6 **Westow** N York
17 E1 **Westport** Somset
85 H3 **Westquarter** Falk
111 h3 **Westray Airport** Ork
19 G4 **Westridge Green** W Berk
85 H2 **Westrigg** W Loth
18 D5 **Westrop** Swindn
80 C5 **Westruther** Border
43 F2 **Westry** Cambs
71 F4 **Westward** Cumb
14 D4 **Westward Ho!** Devon
30 D1 **Westwell** Oxon
13 E6 **Westwell Leacon** Kent
33 F5 **Westwick** Cambs
6 B5 **Westwood** Devon
23 H2 **Westwood** Kent
18 A3 **Westwood** Wilts
51 H6 **Westwoodside** N Linc
71 G4 **Wetheral** Cumb
59 E4 **Wetherby** Leeds
34 D5 **Wetherden** Suffk
35 E5 **Wetheringsett** Suffk
34 A2 **Wethersfield** Essex
35 E5 **Wetherup Street** Suffk
50 B2 **Wetley Rocks** Staffs
49 F5 **Wettenhall** Ches
50 C2 **Wetton** Staffs
60 C5 **Wetwang** E R Yk
49 G3 **Wetwood** Staffs
19 E3 **Wexcombe** Wilts
45 E6 **Weybourne** Norfk
35 F6 **Weybread** Suffk
35 F6 **Weybread Street** Suffk
20 D2 **Weybridge** Surrey
7 E5 **Weycroft** Devon
110 B5 **Weydale** Highld
19 E2 **Weyhill** Hants
7 G3 **Weymouth** Dorset
32 A2 **Whaddon** Bucks
33 E3 **Whaddon** Cambs
29 F4 **Whaddon** Gloucs
18 B3 **Whaddon** Wilts
8 D5 **Whaddon** Wilts
51 F4 **Whaley** Derbys
50 B4 **Whaley Bridge** Derbys
51 F4 **Whaley Thorns** Derbys
110 D3 **Whaligoe** Highld
57 G6 **Whalley** Lancs
73 E4 **Whalton** Nthumb
43 E3 **Whaplode** Lincs
43 E3 **Whaplode Drove** Lincs
31 E3 **Wharf** Warwks
63 G3 **Wharfe** N York
57 E6 **Wharles** Lancs
50 D6 **Wharncliffe Side** Sheff
60 C6 **Wharram-le-Street** N York
39 E2 **Wharton** Herefs
65 E4 **Whashton** N York
63 E4 **Whasset** Cumb
30 D4 **Whatcote** Warwks
40 D3 **Whateley** Warwks
34 D3 **Whatfield** Suffk
7 E6 **Whatley** Somset
17 H4 **Whatley** Somset
12 C4 **Whatlington** E Susx
13 F6 **Whatsole Street** Kent
51 E2 **Whatstandwell** Derbys
51 H1 **Whatton** Notts
69 E3 **Whauphill** D & G
45 G2 **Wheatacre** Norfk
21 E6 **Wheathampstead** Herts
39 F4 **Wheathill** Shrops
10 B5 **Wheatley** Hants
31 G1 **Wheatley** Oxon
73 G1 **Wheatley Hill** Dur
59 G1 **Wheatley Hills** Donc
49 H1 **Wheaton Aston** Staffs
16 B3 **Wheddon Cross** Somset
49 G5 **Wheelock** Ches
57 F4 **Wheelton** Lancs
59 G4 **Wheldrake** York
18 D6 **Whelford** Gloucs
20 C5 **Whelpley Hill** Bucks
33 E1 **Whempstead** Herts
66 C1 **Whenby** N York
34 B4 **Whepstead** Suffk
35 E3 **Wherstead** Suffk
19 F1 **Wherwell** Hants
50 C4 **Wheston** Derbys
12 B6 **Whetsted** Kent
41 F3 **Whetstone** Leics
62 B4 **Whicham** Cumb
30 D3 **Whichford** Warwks
73 F3 **Whickham** Gatesd
5 G6 **Whiddon Down** Devon
93 G4 **Whigstreet** Angus
31 G6 **Whilton** Nhants
6 C5 **Whimple** Devon
45 G5 **Whimpwell Green** Norfk

44 D3 **Whinburgh** Norfk
70 A4 **Whinnie Liggate** D & G
103 F3 **Whinnyfold** Abers
9 G3 **Whippingham** IOW
32 C1 **Whipsnade** Beds
32 C1 **Whipsnade Wild Animal Park** Beds
6 B5 **Whipton** Devon
52 B2 **Whisby** Lincs
42 A3 **Whissendine** Rutlnd
44 C4 **Whissonsett** Norfk
84 B5 **Whistlefield** Ag & B
84 B5 **Whistlefield Inn** Ag & B
20 B3 **Whistley Green** Wokham
57 E2 **Whiston** Knows
32 A4 **Whiston** Nhants
51 E5 **Whiston** Rothm
40 A4 **Whiston** Staffs
50 B2 **Whiston** Staffs
62 B4 **Whitbeck** Cumb
39 G2 **Whitbourne** Herefs
73 G3 **Whitburn** S Tyne
85 H2 **Whitburn** W Loth
67 E4 **Whitby** N York
87 G2 **Whitchester** Border
17 G5 **Whitchurch** BaNES
32 A1 **Whitchurch** Bucks
27 G1 **Whitchurch** Cardif
5 E4 **Whitchurch** Devon
19 F2 **Whitchurch** Hants
28 D4 **Whitchurch** Herefs
31 H4 **Whitchurch** Oxon
24 C5 **Whitchurch** Pembks
49 E3 **Whitchurch** Shrops
7 E5 **Whitchurch Canonicorum** Dorset
19 H4 **Whitchurch Hill** Oxon
7 H4 **Whitcombe** Dorset
38 D5 **Whitcot** Shrops
38 C4 **Whitcott Keysett** Shrops
16 C1 **White Ball** Somset
57 E6 **White Chapel** Lancs
34 C2 **White Colne** Essex
2 D2 **White Cross** Cnwll
29 E6 **White End** Worcs
7 H5 **White Lackington** Dorset
30 A5 **White Ladies Aston** Worcs
34 B1 **White Notley** Essex
53 F3 **White Pit** Lincs
22 B6 **White Roding** Essex
28 D6 **White Stone** Herefs
20 B3 **White Waltham** W & M
40 D3 **Whiteacre Heath** Warwks
98 D4 **Whitebridge** Highld
28 D3 **Whitebrook** Mons
103 E2 **Whitecairns** Abers
21 F3 **Whitechapel** Gt Lon
28 D4 **Whitecliffe** Gloucs
86 D3 **Whitecraig** E Loth
68 C3 **Whitecrook** D & G
85 H3 **Whitecross** Falk
107 F4 **Whiteface** Highld
75 G5 **Whitefarland** N Ayrs
76 C3 **Whitefaulds** S Ayrs
57 G3 **Whitefield** Bury
16 C2 **Whitefield** Somset
102 C2 **Whiteford** Abers
49 F6 **Whitegate** Ches
111 j2 **Whitehall** Ork
70 C1 **Whitehaven** Cumb
10 B5 **Whitehill** Hants
102 C5 **Whitehills** Abers
102 C1 **Whitehouse** Abers
83 F2 **Whitehouse** Ag & B
87 F4 **Whitekirk** E Loth
17 E1 **Whitelackington** Somset
9 G2 **Whiteley Bank** IOW
100 C4 **Whitemire** Moray
51 F1 **Whitemoor** C Nott
2 F5 **Whitemoor** Cnwll
111 j2 **Whiteness** Shet
9 E5 **Whiteparish** Wilts
102 D2 **Whiterashes** Abers
110 D4 **Whiterow** Highld
100 C5 **Whiterow** Moray
29 F3 **Whiteshill** Gloucs
11 H3 **Whitesmith** E Susx
6 D6 **Whitestaunton** Somset
6 A5 **Whitestone Cross** Devon
63 F1 **Whitewell** Lancs
13 G6 **Whitfield** Kent
31 G4 **Whitfield** Nhants
72 C3 **Whitfield** Nthumb
29 E2 **Whitfield** S Glos
56 B1 **Whitford** Devon
60 C2 **Whitgift** E R Yk
40 A6 **Whitgreave** Staffs
69 F7 **Whithorn** D & G
75 H3 **Whiting Bay** N Ayrs
59 E3 **Whitkirk** Leeds
25 F4 **Whitland** Carmth
80 B2 **Whitlaw** Border
76 C4 **Whitletts** S Ayrs
59 F2 **Whitley** N York
20 A3 **Whitley** Readg
51 E6 **Whitley** Sheff
18 B3 **Whitley** Wilts
73 G4 **Whitley Bay** N Tyne
72 D3 **Whitley Chapel** Nthumb
58 D2 **Whitley Lower** Kirk
29 E3 **Whitminster** Gloucs
49 G3 **Whitmore** Staffs
16 B1 **Whitnage** Devon
31 E6 **Whitnash** Warwks
38 C1 **Whitney-on-Wye** Herefs
71 H3 **Whitrigglees** Cumb
8 D5 **Whitsbury** Hants
81 E5 **Whitsome** Border
28 B1 **Whitson** Newpt
23 F2 **Whitstable** Kent
14 C1 **Whitstone** Cnwll
81 F2 **Whittingham** Nthumb
38 D5 **Whittingslow** Shrops
51 E4 **Whittington** Derbys
30 B2 **Whittington** Gloucs
63 F3 **Whittington** Lancs
44 A2 **Whittington** Norfk
48 D3 **Whittington** Shrops
40 C4 **Whittington** Staffs
39 H4 **Whittington** Warwks
39 H4 **Whittington** Worcs
57 F4 **Whittle-le-Woods** Lancs
31 G4 **Whittlebury** Nhants
43 E2 **Whittlesey** Cambs
33 F3 **Whittlesford** Cambs

60 C3 **Whitton** N Linc
73 E6 **Whitton** Nthumb
38 C2 **Whitton** Powys
65 G5 **Whitton** S on T
39 F3 **Whitton** Shrops
73 E2 **Whittonstall** Nthumb
19 F3 **Whitway** Hants
51 F4 **Whitwell** Derbys
32 D1 **Whitwell** Herts
9 G2 **Whitwell** IOW
65 F3 **Whitwell** N York
42 B3 **Whitwell** Rutlnd
44 D4 **Whitwell Street** Norfk
60 B6 **Whitwell-on-the-Hill** N York
41 E5 **Whitwick** Leics
58 A2 **Whitworth** Lancs
49 E3 **Whixall** Shrops
59 E5 **Whixley** N York
51 E5 **Whorlton** Dur
66 B3 **Whorlton** N York
39 E2 **Whyle** Herefs
21 F2 **Whyteleafe** Surrey
58 C3 **Wibsey** Brad
41 F2 **Wibtoft** Warwks
39 G2 **Wichenford** Worcs
22 D1 **Wichling** Kent
8 D3 **Wick** Bmouth
110 D4 **Wick** Highld
17 H6 **Wick** S Glos
16 B6 **Wick** V Glam
10 D3 **Wick** W Susx
30 B3 **Wick** Worcs
110 D4 **Wick Airport** Highld
17 E5 **Wick St Lawrence** N Som
33 G5 **Wicken** Cambs
31 H4 **Wicken** Nhants
33 G2 **Wicken Bonhunt** Essex
52 C3 **Wickenby** Lincs
34 C3 **Wicker Street Green** Suffk
51 F5 **Wickersley** Rothm
22 C4 **Wickford** Essex
9 G4 **Wickham** Hants
19 F4 **Wickham** W Berk
22 B6 **Wickham Bishops** Essex
34 D5 **Wickham Green** Suffk
35 F4 **Wickham Market** Suffk
34 B2 **Wickham Skeith** Suffk
34 B2 **Wickham St Paul** Essex
34 D5 **Wickham Street** Suffk
23 G2 **Wickhambreaux** Kent
34 B4 **Wickhambrook** Suffk
30 C4 **Wickhamford** Worcs
45 G3 **Wickhampton** Norfk
44 D2 **Wicklewood** Norfk
45 E5 **Wickmere** Norfk
29 E2 **Wickwar** S Glos
33 G2 **Widdington** Essex
73 F6 **Widdrington** Nthumb
73 F5 **Widdrington Station** Nthumb
73 F4 **Wide Open** N Tyne
5 G4 **Widecombe in the Moor** Devon
4 D3 **Widegates** Cnwll
14 B2 **Widemouth Bay** Cnwll
22 C5 **Widford** Essex
33 F1 **Widford** Herts
20 C5 **Widmer End** Bucks
41 G6 **Widmerpool** Notts
21 G2 **Widmore** Gt Lon
57 E1 **Widnes** Halton
6 D5 **Widworthy** Devon
57 F3 **Wigan** Wigan
17 F1 **Wigborough** Somset
6 C5 **Wiggaton** Devon
43 G3 **Wiggenhall St Germans** Norfk
43 G3 **Wiggenhall St Mary Magdalen** Norfk
43 G3 **Wiggenhall St Mary the Virgin** Norfk
33 H3 **Wiggens Green** Essex
33 E1 **Wigginton** Herts
31 E3 **Wigginton** Oxon
40 D4 **Wigginton** Staffs
59 G5 **Wigginton** York
63 G2 **Wigglesworth** N York
71 F4 **Wiggonby** Cumb
59 F4 **Wighill** N York
44 C5 **Wighton** Norfk
39 H5 **Wightwick** Wolves
38 D3 **Wigmore** Herefs
22 C2 **Wigmore** Medway
52 B2 **Wigsley** Notts
32 C6 **Wigsthorpe** Nhants
41 G3 **Wigston** Leics
41 F3 **Wigston Parva** Leics
51 G5 **Wigthorpe** Notts
43 E5 **Wigtoft** Lincs
71 F4 **Wigton** Cumb
69 F3 **Wigtown** D & G
59 E4 **Wike** Leeds
42 A1 **Wilbarston** Nhants
60 B5 **Wilberfoss** E R Yk
33 F6 **Wilburton** Cambs
32 B5 **Wilby** Nhants
44 D1 **Wilby** Norfk
35 F5 **Wilby** Suffk
18 D3 **Wilcot** Wilts
48 D2 **Wilcott** Shrops
50 B3 **Wildboarclough** Ches
32 C4 **Wilden** Beds
39 G3 **Wilden** Worcs
85 G1 **Wildmanbridge** S Lans
40 B1 **Wildmoor** Worcs
42 A5 **Wildsworth** Lincs
49 F3 **Wilkesley** Ches
107 H4 **Wilkhaven** Highld
86 B3 **Wilkieston** W Loth
6 B6 **Willand** Devon
56 D1 **Willaston** Ches
49 F4 **Willaston** Ches
32 B3 **Willen** M Keyn
41 E1 **Willenhall** Covtry
40 B3 **Willenhall** Wsall
60 D3 **Willerby** E R Yk
67 F2 **Willerby** N York
30 C4 **Willersey** Gloucs
38 C1 **Willersley** Herefs
13 E6 **Willesborough** Kent
13 E6 **Willesborough Lees** Kent
21 E4 **Willesden** Gt Lon
17 H5 **Willett** Somset
39 F5 **Willey** Shrops
41 F2 **Willey** Warwks

20 C1 **Willey Green** Surrey
31 F4 **Williamscot** Oxon
32 D2 **Willian** Herts
22 B6 **Willingale** Essex
12 B2 **Willingdon** E Susx
33 F5 **Willingham** Cambs
52 B4 **Willingham by Stow** Lincs
33 H4 **Willingham Green** Cambs
32 A5 **Willington** Beds
40 D6 **Willington** Derbys
65 F6 **Willington** Dur
22 C1 **Willington** Kent
30 D4 **Willington** Warwks
73 G3 **Willington Quay** N Tyne
60 B3 **Willitoft** E R Yk
16 C3 **Williton** Somset
53 F3 **Willoughby** Lincs
31 F6 **Willoughby** Warwks
41 F3 **Willoughby Waterleys** Leics
41 G5 **Willoughby-on-the-Wolds** Notts
52 B4 **Willoughton** Lincs
34 B1 **Willows Green** Essex
17 E2 **Willtown** Somset
30 C5 **Wilmcote** Warwks
6 D5 **Wilmington** Devon
12 A3 **Wilmington** E Susx
21 H3 **Wilmington** Kent
57 H1 **Wilmslow** Ches
57 F5 **Wilpshire** Lancs
58 C4 **Wilsden** Brad
42 C6 **Wilsford** Lincs
18 D3 **Wilsford** Wilts
18 D1 **Wilsford** Wilts
58 C1 **Wilshaw** Kirk
58 C6 **Wilsill** N York
41 E5 **Wilson** Leics
85 H1 **Wilsontown** S Lans
32 C3 **Wilstead** Beds
42 C3 **Wilsthorpe** Lincs
20 C6 **Wilstone** Herts
28 D5 **Wilton** Herefs
67 E2 **Wilton** N York
66 C5 **Wilton** R & Cl
8 D6 **Wilton** Wilts
19 E3 **Wilton** Wilts
80 B2 **Wilton Dean** Border
33 G2 **Wimbish** Essex
33 G2 **Wimbish Green** Essex
21 E3 **Wimbledon** Gt Lon
43 F2 **Wimblington** Cambs
49 F5 **Wimboldsley** Ches
8 C3 **Wimborne Minster** Dorset
8 C4 **Wimborne St Giles** Dorset
43 G3 **Wimbotsham** Norfk
33 H4 **Wimpole** Cambs
30 D5 **Wimpstone** Warwks
17 H2 **Wincanton** Somset
86 B3 **Winchburgh** W Loth
30 B3 **Winchcombe** Gloucs
12 D4 **Winchelsea** E Susx
9 G6 **Winchester** Hants
12 C6 **Winchet Hill** Kent
20 B1 **Winchfield** Hants
20 C5 **Winchmore Hill** Bucks
21 F4 **Winchmore Hill** Gt Lon
50 B3 **Wincle** Ches
51 E6 **Wincobank** Sheff
62 D5 **Windermere** Cumb
31 E4 **Winderton** Warwks
107 E1 **Windhill** Highld
20 C2 **Windlesham** Surrey
3 E6 **Windmill** Cnwll
12 B3 **Windmill Hill** E Susx
17 E1 **Windmill Hill** Somset
30 C2 **Windrush** Gloucs
102 B5 **Windsole** Abers
20 C3 **Windsor** W & M
20 C3 **Windsor Castle** W & M
34 C4 **Windsor Green** Suffk
29 F3 **Windsoredge** Gloucs
40 D1 **Windy Arbour** Warwks
86 D5 **Windygates** Fife
11 E4 **Wineham** W Susx
61 F3 **Winestead** E R Yk
45 E1 **Winfarthing** Norfk
9 G2 **Winford** IOW
17 F5 **Winford** N Som
38 C1 **Winforton** Herefs
8 A2 **Winfrith Newburgh** Dorset
32 B1 **Wing** Bucks
42 B2 **Wing** Rutlnd
73 G1 **Wingate** Dur
51 E3 **Wingerworth** Derbys
32 C2 **Wingfield** Beds
35 E6 **Wingfield** Suffk
18 A2 **Wingfield** Wilts
23 G1 **Wingham** Kent
13 F6 **Wingmore** Kent
32 B1 **Wingrave** Bucks
51 G3 **Winkburn** Notts
20 C3 **Winkfield** Br For
20 C3 **Winkfield Row** Br For
50 B2 **Winkhill** Staffs
15 F2 **Winkleigh** Devon
65 F1 **Winksley** N York
73 F3 **Winlaton** Gatesd
110 D4 **Winless** Highld
63 E1 **Winmarleigh** Lancs
9 G6 **Winnall** Hants
20 B3 **Winnersh** Wokham
49 F6 **Winnington** Ches
17 E4 **Winscombe** N Som
49 F5 **Winsford** Ches
16 A3 **Winsford** Somset
15 E5 **Winsham** Devon
7 E6 **Winsham** Somset
40 D5 **Winshill** Staffs
26 C2 **Winshwen** Swans
64 A6 **Winskill** Cumb
19 H2 **Winslade** Hants
18 A3 **Winsley** Wilts
31 H3 **Winslow** Bucks
30 C1 **Winson** Gloucs
9 E4 **Winsor** Hants
62 D5 **Winster** Cumb
50 D3 **Winster** Derbys
65 E5 **Winston** Dur
34 E4 **Winston** Suffk
29 G4 **Winstone** Gloucs
15 E2 **Winswell** Devon
7 H4 **Winterborne Came** Dorset
8 B4 **Winterborne Clenston** Dorset

8 A4 Winterborne Houghton Dorset
8 B3 Winterborne Kingston Dorset
7 G4 Winterborne Monkton Dorset
8 B4 Winterborne Stickland Dorset
8 B3 Winterborne Whitechurch Dorset
8 B3 Winterborne Zelston Dorset
28 D1 Winterbourne S Glos
19 F4 Winterbourne W Berk
7 G4 Winterbourne Abbas Dorset
18 D4 Winterbourne Bassett Wilts
8 D6 Winterbourne Dauntsey Wilts
8 D6 Winterbourne Earls Wilts
8 D6 Winterbourne Gunner Wilts
18 D4 Winterbourne Monkton Wilts
7 G4 Winterbourne Steepleton Dorset
18 C1 Winterbourne Stoke Wilts
58 B5 Winterburn N York
60 C2 Winteringham N Linc
49 G5 Winterley Ches
9 E6 Winterslow Wilts
60 C2 Winterton N Linc
45 G4 Winterton-on-Sea Norfk
52 A1 Winthorpe Notts
8 D3 Winton Bmouth
64 C4 Winton Cumb
67 E1 Wintringham N York
32 C6 Winwick Cambs
41 G1 Winwick Nhants
57 F2 Winwick Warrtn
50 D2 Wirksworth Derbys
56 C2 Wirral
49 E4 Wirswall Ches
43 F3 Wisbech Cambs
43 F3 Wisbech St Mary Cambs
10 D4 Wisborough Green W Susx
25 E3 Wiseman's Bridge Pembks
51 H5 Wiseton Notts
85 G1 Wishaw N Lans
40 C3 Wishaw Warwks
20 D2 Wisley Gardens Surrey
52 D3 Wispington Lincs
35 F6 Wissett Suffk
34 C2 Wissington Suffk
38 D4 Wistanstow Shrops
49 F2 Wistanswick Shrops
49 F4 Wistaston Ches
24 D4 Wiston Pembks
78 C5 Wiston S Lans
11 E3 Wiston W Susx
33 E6 Wistow Cambs
59 G3 Wistow N York
57 G6 Wiswell Lancs
33 F6 Witcham Cambs
8 C4 Witchampton Dorset
33 G6 Witchford Cambs
17 F2 Witcombe Somset
22 D6 Witham Essex
17 H3 Witham Friary Somset
42 C4 Witham on the Hill Lincs
53 E4 Withcall Lincs
11 F3 Withdean Br & H
12 B4 Witherenden Hill E Susx
15 G3 Witheridge Devon
41 E3 Witherley Leics
53 F3 Withern Lincs
61 G3 Withernsea E R Yk
61 E4 Withernwick E R Yk
35 F6 Withersdale Street Suffk
33 H3 Withersfield Essex
62 D4 Witherslack Cumb
62 D4 Witherslack Hall Cumb
3 F5 Withiel Cnwll
16 B2 Withiel Florey Somset
30 B2 Withington Gloucs
39 E1 Withington Herefs
57 H2 Withington Manch
49 F1 Withington Shrops
40 B6 Withington Staffs
6 A6 Withleigh Devon
40 B1 Withybed Green Worcs
41 E2 Withybrook Warwks
16 B3 Withycombe Somset
11 G5 Withyham E Susx
15 G4 Withypool Somset
17 G5 Withywood Bristl
10 C5 Witley Surrey
35 E4 Witnesham Suffk
31 E1 Witney Oxon
42 C2 Wittering C Pete
12 D4 Wittersham Kent
40 C3 Witton Birm
45 F3 Witton Norfk
45 F5 Witton Norfk
73 F2 Witton Gilbert Dur
65 E6 Witton le Wear Dur
65 F6 Witton Park Dur
16 C2 Wiveliscombe Somset
19 H1 Wivelrod Hants
11 F4 Wivelsfield E Susx
11 F4 Wivelsfield Green E Susx
34 D1 Wivenhoe Essex
44 D6 Wiveton Norfk
35 E2 Wix Essex
30 C5 Wixford Warwks
34 B3 Wixoe Essex
32 B2 Woburn Beds
32 B2 Woburn Abbey Beds
32 B2 Woburn Sands M Keyn
20 D2 Woking Surrey
20 B2 Wokingham Wokham
67 F1 Wold Newton E R Yk
53 E5 Wold Newton NE Lin
21 F1 Woldingham Surrey
24 D5 Wolf's Castle Pembks
78 D6 Wolfclyde S Lans
43 H5 Wolferton Norfk
92 D3 Wolfhill P & K
24 D4 Wolfsdale Pembks
40 A2 Wollaston Dudley
32 B5 Wollaston Nhants
48 D1 Wollaston Shrops
51 F1 Wollaton C Nott
49 F2 Wollerton Shrops
40 A2 Wollescote Dudley
40 B5 Wolseley Bridge Staffs
73 E1 Wolsingham Dur
49 H4 Wolstanton Staffs
41 E1 Wolston Warwks
31 F1 Wolvercote Oxon
40 A3 Wolverhampton Wolves
39 G4 Wolverley Worcs
19 G3 Wolverton Hants
32 A3 Wolverton M Keyn
30 D6 Wolverton Warwks
8 A6 Wolverton Wilts
28 C3 Wolvesnewton Mons
41 E2 Wolvey Warwks
41 E2 Wolvey Heath Warwks
81 F3 Wolviston S on T
66 B5 Wombleton N York
66 C2 Wombleton N York
39 H5 Wombourne Staffs
51 E6 Wombwell Barns
23 G1 Womenswold Kent
59 F2 Womersley N York
10 D6 Wonersh Surrey
6 B5 Wonford Devon
19 F1 Wonston Hants
20 C4 Wooburn Bucks
20 C4 Wooburn Green Bucks
30 B5 Wood Bevington Warwks
44 D4 Wood Dalling Norfk
20 D3 Wood End Gt Lon
33 E2 Wood End Herts
40 C1 Wood End Warwks
53 E2 Wood Enderby Lincs
21 F4 Wood Green Gt Lon
40 B3 Wood Hayes Wolves
44 D4 Wood Norton Norfk
45 G4 Wood Street Norfk
20 C1 Wood Street Surrey
32 D6 Wood Walton Cambs
12 B4 Wood's Corner E Susx
12 B5 Wood's Green E Susx
51 F4 Woodall Rothm
45 F3 Woodbastwick Norfk
51 G2 Woodborough Notts
18 D3 Woodborough Wilts
6 D5 Woodbridge Devon
35 F3 Woodbridge Suffk
6 B4 Woodbury Devon
6 B4 Woodbury Salterton Devon
29 F3 Woodchester Gloucs
12 D5 Woodchurch Kent
16 B4 Woodcombe Somset
21 F2 Woodcote Gt Lon
19 H5 Woodcote Oxon
49 G1 Woodcote Wrekin
28 D2 Woodcroft Gloucs
33 H4 Woodditton Cambs
31 F2 Woodeaton Oxon
89 H5 Woodend Highld
31 G5 Woodend Nhants
85 H3 Woodend W Loth
10 B3 Woodend W Susx
33 G2 Woodend Green Essex
8 D5 Woodfalls Wilts
29 E2 Woodford Gloucs
21 G4 Woodford Gt Lon
32 B6 Woodford Nhants
50 A5 Woodford Stockp
21 G4 Woodford Bridge Gt Lon
31 F5 Woodford Halse Nhants
21 G4 Woodford Wells Gt Lon
40 B2 Woodgate Birm
16 C1 Woodgate Devon
10 C3 Woodgate W Susx
30 B6 Woodgate Worcs
8 D5 Woodgreen Hants
64 D2 Woodhall N York
52 D2 Woodhall Spa Lincs
31 G2 Woodham Bucks
20 D2 Woodham Surrey
22 C5 Woodham Ferrers Essex
22 C5 Woodham Mortimer Essex
22 C5 Woodham Walter Essex
102 D3 Woodhead Abers
17 E2 Woodhill Somset
73 G5 Woodhorn Nthumb
58 D3 Woodhouse Leeds
41 F4 Woodhouse Leics
51 E5 Woodhouse Sheff
59 E2 Woodhouse Wakefd
41 F4 Woodhouse Eaves Leics
86 C3 Woodhouselee Mdloth
71 G6 Woodhouselees D & G
40 C5 Woodhouses Staffs
33 E6 Woodhurst Cambs
11 F3 Woodingdean Br & H
58 D3 Woodkirk Leeds
103 E2 Woodland Abers
5 H4 Woodland Devon
5 F3 Woodland Devon
65 E5 Woodland Dur
13 F6 Woodland Kent
76 B1 Woodland S Ayrs
95 G5 Woodlands Abers
59 F1 Woodlands Donc
8 C4 Woodlands Dorset
9 E4 Woodlands Hants
59 E5 Woodlands N York
16 C3 Woodlands Somset
20 B3 Woodlands Park W & M
5 G2 Woodleigh Devon
20 B3 Woodley Wokham
29 G5 Woodmancote Gloucs
30 B1 Woodmancote Gloucs
29 E3 Woodmancote Gloucs
10 B3 Woodmancote W Susx
11 E3 Woodmancote W Susx
19 G1 Woodmancott Hants
60 D4 Woodmansey E R Yk
10 B4 Woodmansgreen W Susx
21 F2 Woodmansterne Surrey
6 B4 Woodmanton Devon
23 G1 Woodnesborough Kent
42 C2 Woodnewton Nhants
57 E6 Woodplumpton Lancs
44 D2 Woodrising Norfk
49 G2 Woodseaves Staffs
51 F5 Woodsetts Rothm
8 A3 Woodsford Dorset
20 C3 Woodside Br For
86 D6 Woodside Fife
21 F2 Woodside Gt Lon
93 E3 Woodside P & K
31 E2 Woodstock Oxon
42 D2 Woodston C Pete
45 F2 Woodton Norfk
14 D3 Woodtown Devon
39 E3 Woofferton Shrops
17 F3 Wookey Somset
17 F4 Wookey Hole Somset
8 B2 Wool Dorset
14 D5 Woolacombe Devon
23 G1 Woolage Green Kent
28 D3 Woolaston Gloucs
28 D3 Woolaston Common Gloucs
17 E3 Woolavington Somset
10 C4 Woolbeding W Susx
6 C4 Woolbrook Devon
16 B2 Woolcotts Somset
81 F3 Wooler Nthumb
14 C3 Woolfardisworthy Devon
15 G2 Woolfardisworthy Devon
86 A2 Woolfords S Lans
19 G3 Woolhampton W Berk
28 D6 Woolhope Herefs
8 A4 Woolland Dorset
17 H5 Woolley BaNES
32 D6 Woolley Cambs
58 D2 Woolley Wakefd
33 E1 Woolmer Green Herts
30 B6 Woolmere Green Worcs
7 E6 Woolminstone Somset
34 C5 Woolpit Suffk
39 E5 Woolstaston Shrops
42 A5 Woolsthorpe Lincs
42 B4 Woolsthorpe-by-Colsterworth Lincs
9 F4 Woolston C Sotn
48 D2 Woolston Shrops
38 D4 Woolston Shrops
16 C3 Woolston Somset
17 G2 Woolston Somset
57 F2 Woolston Warrtn
5 H3 Woolston Green Devon
29 G5 Woolstone Gloucs
32 B3 Woolstone M Keyn
19 E5 Woolstone Oxon
56 D2 Woolton Lpool
19 F3 Woolton Hill Hants
35 E3 Woolverstone Suffk
18 A2 Woolverton Somset
21 G3 Woolwich Gt Lon
38 D2 Woonton Herefs
49 G3 Woore Shrops
35 E5 Wootten Green Suffk
32 C3 Wootton Beds
13 G6 Wootton Kent
61 E2 Wootton N Linc
31 H5 Wootton Nhants
31 E2 Wootton Oxon
19 G6 Wootton Oxon
50 C2 Wootton Staffs
18 C5 Wootton Bassett Wilts
9 G3 Wootton Bridge IOW
16 B3 Wootton Courtenay Somset
7 E5 Wootton Fitzpaine Dorset
18 D3 Wootton Rivers Wilts
19 G2 Wootton St Lawrence Hants
30 C6 Wootton Wawen Warwks
39 H2 Worcester Worcs
21 E2 Worcester Park Gt Lon
40 A2 Wordsley Dudley
39 G5 Worfield Shrops
70 D2 Workington Cumb
51 G4 Worksop Notts
60 D2 Worlaby N Linc
19 G4 World's End W Berk
9 H4 Worlds End Hants
11 F4 Worlds End W Susx
17 E5 Worle N Som
49 F5 Worleston Ches
45 G1 Worlingham Suffk
15 G2 Worlington Devon
34 A5 Worlington Suffk
35 E5 Worlingworth Suffk
58 D6 Wormald Green N York
28 C5 Wormbridge Herefs
43 H3 Wormegay Norfk
28 C5 Wormelow Tump Herefs
50 C4 Wormhill Derbys
34 C2 Wormingford Essex
31 G1 Worminghall Bucks
30 B4 Wormington Gloucs
93 F2 Wormit Fife
31 E5 Wormleighton Warwks
21 F5 Wormley Herts
10 C5 Wormley Surrey
22 D1 Wormshill Kent
38 D1 Wormsley Herefs
20 C1 Worplesdon Surrey
50 D5 Worrall Sheff
51 E6 Worsbrough Barns
59 E1 Worsbrough Bridge Barns
59 E1 Worsbrough Dale Barns
57 G3 Worsley Salfd
45 F4 Worstead Norfk
57 H5 Worsthorne Lancs
5 F2 Worston Devon
57 G6 Worston Lancs
23 G1 Worth Kent
8 C1 Worth Matravers Dorset
34 D6 Wortham Suffk
38 D6 Worthen Shrops
48 D4 Worthenbury Wrexhm
44 D4 Worthing Norfk
11 E2 Worthing W Susx
41 E5 Worthington Leics
50 D6 Wortley Barns
58 D3 Wortley Leeds
64 D2 Worton N York
18 C3 Worton Wilts
45 F1 Wortwell Norfk
31 G2 Wotton Underwood Bucks
29 E2 Wotton-under-Edge Gloucs
32 B3 Woughton on the Green M Keyn
22 C2 Wouldham Kent
39 G5 Woundale Shrops
35 E2 Wrabness Essex
15 E4 Wrafton Devon
52 D3 Wragby Lincs
59 E2 Wragby Wakefd
5 G3 Wrangaton Devon
53 F1 Wrangle Lincs
16 C1 Wrangway Somset
17 E2 Wrantage Somset
52 C6 Wrawby N Linc
17 F6 Wraxall N Som
17 G3 Wraxall Somset
63 F3 Wray Lancs
20 D3 Wraysbury W & M
63 F3 Wrayton Lancs
56 D5 Wrea Green Lancs
71 G4 Wreay Cumb
10 B6 Wrecclesham Surrey
73 F3 Wrekenton Gatesd
66 D2 Wrelton N York
49 F4 Wrenbury Ches
45 E2 Wreningham Norfk
35 H6 Wrentham Suffk
38 D6 Wrentnall Shrops
60 B3 Wressle E R Yk
52 B6 Wressle N Linc
33 E3 Wrestlingworth Beds
44 A2 Wretton Norfk
48 D4 Wrexham Wrexhm
39 G3 Wribbenhall Worcs
49 G4 Wrinehill Staffs
17 F5 Wrington N Som
17 H4 Writhlington BaNES
22 B5 Writtle Essex
49 F1 Wrockwardine Wrekin
60 B1 Wroot N Linc
58 C4 Wrose Brad
22 B2 Wrotham Kent
18 D4 Wroughton Swindn
9 G2 Wroxall IOW
40 D1 Wroxall Warwks
39 E6 Wroxeter Shrops
45 F4 Wroxham Norfk
31 E4 Wroxton Oxon
50 C1 Wyaston Derbys
43 E5 Wyberton East Lincs
32 D4 Wyboston Beds
49 F4 Wybunbury Ches
30 A6 Wychbold Worcs
40 C5 Wychnor Staffs
10 B5 Wyck Hants
30 C2 Wyck Rissington Gloucs
65 E4 Wycliffe Dur
58 B4 Wycoller Lancs
41 H5 Wycomb Leics
20 C4 Wycombe Marsh Bucks
33 F2 Wyddial Herts
13 E6 Wye Kent
58 C3 Wyke Brad
8 A5 Wyke Dorset
17 G3 Wyke Champflower Somset
7 G3 Wyke Regis Dorset
67 F2 Wykeham N York
41 E2 Wyken Covtry
39 G5 Wyken Shrops
48 D2 Wykey Shrops
73 E3 Wylam Nthumb
40 C3 Wylde Green Birm
18 C1 Wylye Wilts
41 G5 Wymeswold Leics
32 B5 Wymington Beds
42 B4 Wymondham Leics
45 E2 Wymondham Norfk
7 G5 Wynford Eagle Dorset
30 B4 Wyre Piddle Worcs
41 G5 Wysall Notts
40 C1 Wythall Worcs
31 F1 Wytham Oxon
57 G2 Wythenshawe Manch
33 E5 Wyton Cambs
61 E3 Wyton E R Yk
34 D5 Wyverstone Suffk
34 D5 Wyverstone Street Suffk

Y

54 D3 Y Felinheli Gwynd
36 B2 Y Ferwig Cerdgn
46 D5 Y Ffor Gwynd
48 B5 Y Gyffylliog Denbgs
48 A4 Y Maerdy Conwy
46 B4 Y Rhiw Gwynd
52 B5 Yaddlethorpe N Linc
65 G3 Yafforth N York
6 A2 Yalberton Torbay
22 C1 Yalding Kent
71 H2 Yanwath Cumb
30 C2 Yanworth Gloucs
60 B5 Yapham E R Yk
10 C2 Yapton W Susx
17 E4 Yarborough N Som
53 E4 Yarburgh Lincs
6 D6 Yarcombe Devon
15 G3 Yard Devon
40 C2 Yardley Birm
31 H4 Yardley Gobion Nhants
32 B4 Yardley Hastings Nhants
40 C2 Yardley Wood Birm
28 D6 Yarkhill Herefs
17 F3 Yarley Somset
17 G2 Yarlington Somset
65 G4 Yarm S on T
9 F2 Yarmouth IOW
18 B2 Yarnbrook Wilts
49 H3 Yarnfield Staffs
15 E3 Yarnscombe Devon
31 F2 Yarnton Oxon
39 E3 Yarpole Herefs
79 F5 Yarrow Border
79 F5 Yarrow Feus Border
79 G5 Yarrowford Border
42 C2 Yarwell Nhants
29 E1 Yate S Glos
20 B2 Yateley Hants
18 C4 Yatesbury Wilts
19 G4 Yattendon W Berk
38 D3 Yatton Herefs
28 D5 Yatton Herefs
17 F5 Yatton N Som
18 B4 Yatton Keynell Wilts
9 H2 Yaverland IOW
44 D3 Yaxham Norfk
42 D2 Yaxley Cambs
35 E5 Yaxley Suffk
38 D1 Yazor Herefs
20 D3 Yeading Gt Lon
58 D4 Yeadon Leeds
63 E3 Yealand Conyers Lancs
63 E3 Yealand Redmayne Lancs
5 F2 Yealmpton Devon
66 C1 Yearsley N York
48 D2 Yeaton Shrops
50 C1 Yeaveley Derbys
81 E3 Yeavering Nthumb
67 E2 Yedingham N York
31 E1 Yelford Oxon
33 E5 Yelling Cambs
41 G1 Yelvertoft Nhants
5 F4 Yelverton Devon
45 F2 Yelverton Norfk
17 H1 Yenston Somset
15 G1 Yeoford Devon
4 D5 Yeolmbridge Cnwll
17 F1 Yeovil Somset
17 F1 Yeovil Marsh Somset
17 F2 Yeovilton Somset
17 F2 Yeovilton Fleet Air Arm Museum Somset
111 g2 Yesnaby Ork
7 G6 Yetminster Dorset
6 C4 Yettington Devon
86 A6 Yetts o' Muckhart Clacks
32 C5 Yielden Beds
77 G6 Yieldshields S Lans
20 D3 Yiewsley Gt Lon
27 F2 Ynysboeth Rhondd
27 G2 Ynysddu Caerph
27 F2 Ynyshir Rhondd
26 C3 Ynystawe Swans
27 F2 Ynysybwl Rhondd
48 D1 Yockleton Shrops
60 C3 Yokefleet E R Yk
84 D3 Yoker C Glas
59 G5 York York
59 G5 York Minster York
20 B2 York Town Surrey
23 F2 Yorkletts Kent
28 D3 Yorkley Gloucs
64 C1 Yorkshire Dales National Park
50 D3 Youlgreave Derbys
60 B5 Youlthorpe E R Yk
59 F6 Youlton N York
34 B1 Young's End Essex
40 C5 Yoxall Staffs
35 G5 Yoxford Suffk
55 F2 Ysbyty Ifan Conwy
37 F4 Ysbyty Ystwyth Cerdgn
48 B6 Ysceifiog Flints
26 D3 Ystalyfera Powys
27 F2 Ystrad Rhondd
36 D2 Ystrad Aeron Cerdgn
37 F3 Ystrad Meurig Cerdgn
27 G2 Ystrad Mynach Caerph
27 E4 Ystradfellte Powys
26 D4 Ystradgynlais Powys
27 F1 Ystradowen V Glam
103 E3 Ythanbank Abers
102 C3 Ythanwells Abers
103 E3 Ythsie Abers

Z

15 F2 Zeal Monachorum Devon
8 A6 Zeals Wilts
2 B3 Zennor Cnwll
41 F5 Zouch Notts